The Russian Civil War of 1917–1921 was
overlapping conflicts. It was a pivotal event in modern history, and left a deep imprint on the participants and their descendents for decades after its end. It was the Bolshevik victory in this bloody struggle, not in the skirmishes on the streets of Petrograd and Moscow in October 1917, which secured the victory of Soviet Communism and provided the legitimacy for seventy years of rule. The narrowness of Lenin's victory and the principles for which his opponents fought, have been largely neglected. This book traces the clash between the 'Reds' of the Moscow-based Soviet régime and the 'Whites', the militaristic, counter-revolutionary governments which were established around the periphery of Russia and aided by Allied interventionists. In particular, it details the history of the White movement in Siberia, and the fortunes of its leader, Admiral Alexandr Kolchak, the 'Supreme Ruler' of Russia. Using a wide range of contemporary sources, Jonathan Smele examines Kolchak's political and military record, and concludes that the White defeat resulted as much from the harsh facts of Siberian economy and geography as from the failures of White policy and leadership.

Civil war in Siberia

Civil war in Siberia

The anti-Bolshevik government of
Admiral Kolchak, 1918–1920

Jonathan D. Smele

Queen Mary and Westfield College
University of London

CAMBRIDGE
UNIVERSITY PRESS

CAMBRIDGE UNIVERSITY PRESS
Cambridge, New York, Melbourne, Madrid, Cape Town, Singapore, São Paulo

Cambridge University Press
The Edinburgh Building, Cambridge CB2 2RU, UK

Published in the United States of America by Cambridge University Press, New York

www.cambridge.org
Information on this title: www.cambridge.org/9780521573351

First published 1996
This digitally printed first paperback version 2006

A catalogue record for this publication is available from the British Library

Library of Congress Cataloguing in Publication data

Smele, Jon.
Civil war in Siberia: the anti-Bolshevik government of Admiral
Kolchak, 1918–1920 / by Jonathan D. Smele.
p. cm.
Includes bibliographical references
ISBN 0 521 57335 1 (hbk)
1. Siberia (Russia)–History–Revolution, 1917–1921. 2. Kolchak,
Alexsandr Vasiliyevich, 1873–1920. I. Title.
DK265.8.S5S59 1997
957.08–dc20 96–14039 CIP

ISBN-13 978-0-521-57335-1 hardback
ISBN-10 0-521-57335-1 hardback

ISBN-13 978-0-521-02907-0 paperback
ISBN-10 0-521-02907-4 paperback

To Robina

'Learn how to utilize the environment. Be patient in military matters. Do not succumb to temporary passions. And never underestimate your enemy, regardless of who he may be.'

(From a letter of A.V. Suvorov to his godson, A. Karachai, 1796)

Contents

Maps

Preface

The complexity of the history of anti-Bolshevism in Siberia and the fact that it has hitherto occupied only a minor place in western historiography of the Russian Revolution and Civil War has had two unavoidable impacts upon the study of it which is before you. In the first place it has clearly added to the length of the book, as events, organizations and persons unfamiliar even to those with some specialist knowledge of the period have had to be introduced in some detail. In this regard I would beg my readers' indulgence, whilst referring those requiring additional biographical detail on persons mentioned herein (and additional information regarding the acts and institutions of the White régime and its opponents and allies in Siberia) to the annotations I supplied for the two-volume collection of documentary and memoir materials, Collins, D. and Smele, J.D. (eds.) *Kolchak i Sibir': dokumenty i issledovaniia, 1919–1926* (White Plains NY, 1988). In the second place, the complexity and novelty of its subject has forcibly limited the scope of the present study. Although, whenever necessary, an effort has been made to set the history of the Kolchak government into the context of developments in the wider world – in particular, of course, into the history of the White movement and the civil war as a whole – no apology needs to be made for *Civil War in Siberia*'s concentration upon events in the east. The aim of the work is to contribute but one more piece to the jigsaw and to bring us but one more step towards a general and thoroughly comprehensible tableau of the Russian Revolution and Civil War.

The bulk of the research upon which *Civil War in Siberia* was based was undertaken in the years before access to archival holdings on the civil war period which are held in the former Soviet Union was made available for western scholars. It has always been the author's judgement, however, that the Soviet/Russian archives can yield little significant information additional to that to be found in the copious materials sent or carried out of Siberia by members and observers of the Kolchak government at Omsk – materials which are now housed in western archival collections. Apart from the materials included in British War Office and Foreign Office files at the Public Record Office, of particular value to the author have been the papers of Sir

Bernard Pares at the School of Slavonic and East European Studies, University of London. Pares, the founder of the School, served as an unofficial Foreign Office envoy to the Kolchak government in 1919, returning with several boxes of official documents and publications of the Omsk government, private correspondence with Kolchak and his ministers, newspapers, pamphlets, press releases, etc. Also of great value were the unpublished memoirs of Kolchak's close friend and foreign minister, I.I. Sukin, housed at the Leeds Russian Archive, University of Leeds.

Post-Soviet publications on Kolchak and the Whites have tended only to confirm my impression that western archival holdings relating to the Whites are at least as rich as those in Russia. In recent years the Whites have attracted what might be termed a 'cult' following in Russia (no doubt a reflection of the 'forbidden' nature of the subject in the years of Communist rule). This has naturally led to the appearance of some interesting, but essentially ephemeral, new works: for example, A. Kuznetsov's *O Beloi armii i ee nagradakh, 1917–1922gg.* (Moscow, 1991), a work which strays dangerously close to the territory occupied in the west (and nowadays, indeed, the east) by the fashion for Nazi memorabilia. The newfound freedoms of post-Communist Russia have also generated the publication of numerous White memoirs and documentary collections – but, regretably, for the most part only those, such as Kolchak's own testimony and the memoirs of Denikin and Wrangel, which have long been available in the west. There have even appeared in Russia some new, quite serious, historical studies of the Kolchak régime, written by authors who have utilized the holdings of the archives in Moscow – for example, K.A. Bogdanov's *Admiral Kolchak: biograficheskii povest'-khronika* (Moscow, 1993). But, to date, these authors have been unable to unearth anything which substantially challenges the facts and opinions presented in *Civil War in Siberia*.

A few points of form and style. The word 'Siberia' has been employed throughout this work as the equivalent of '*Sibir'*' in the pre-revolutionary official terminology of Russia – i.e. to describe that part of the empire's territory on the Eurasian landmass lying between the Ural Mountains and the Pacific Ocean and the Arctic Ocean and the borders of China and Mongolia, or what in modern Soviet/Russian usage is denoted by 'West Siberia, East Siberia and the Far East'. Occasionally the terms 'western Siberia' and 'eastern Siberia' have been employed to describe the subdivisions of that area, lying west of the River Ob and from the Ob to Lake Baikal respectively. Furthermore, when appropriate, a term originally coined by

Lenin, 'Kolchakia', has been resorted to as the best means of describing the eastern White zone at that time when it encompassed not only Siberia but the Urals and parts of the Volga-Kama basin, i.e. regions of what is generally termed 'European Russia'. Conversely, 'Sovdepia' ('the land of the Soviets of [workers' and peasants'] deputies'), a term coined by the Whites, has sometimes been used to describe the amoebic Red-held region of European Russia. By 'Whites' are connoted the conservative and militarist elements of the counter-revolution which, in Siberia, came to the fore during the autumn of 1918. Throughout the work, for the sake of continuity and in order to achieve a sense of contemporaneousness with what remained common practice on both sides throughout the civil war, Lenin's followers have been referred to as 'Bolsheviks' rather than as 'Communists', even though the Russian Social Democratic and Labour Party (Bolsheviks) officially changed its name to the Russian Communist Party at the beginning of March 1918.

Dates follow the practice of the central Russian authorities of the time. This means, as the bulk of the work deals with the period from the summer of 1918 to February 1920, that they are predominantly 'new style' – i.e. they match the calendar employed in the west, rather than the 'old style' Julian calendar (thirteen days behind our Gregorian calendar), which was abolished by the Soviet Government on February 14th 1918. Readers should be aware, however, that as a matter of political principle some Whites continued to use the 'old style' calendar (as, indeed, they adhered to the old Russian orthography) well into the 1920s, which has almost certainly led to some confusion of dates (both on the part of this and other writers on the period). The Library of Congress system, with the customary simplifications, has been used to transliterate the cyrillic alphabet in the text: soft and hard signs have not been rendered at the end of most proper names and exceptions have been made for aberrant forms of names which have become standardized over time (e.g. 'Trotsky' rather than 'Trotskii'). A fuller version has been employed in the footnotes and bibliography.

In the many years it has taken to complete this project, no little part of which was spent in collecting materials, I have had cause to be grateful for the services of a number of institutions and their staffs. In particular I would like to express my thanks to the following: the Bancroft Library (Regional Oral History Office), University of California, Berkeley; the British Library; the Brotherton Library (History and Modern Languages Section), University of Leeds; Edinburgh

University Library (Inter-Library Loans Department); the Hoover Institution on War, Revolution and Peace, Stanford; the Institute of Soviet and East European Studies Library, University of Glasgow; the Leeds Russian Archive, University of Leeds; the Library of Congress (European Law Division); Killam Library (Russian Micro Project), Dalhousie University; the National Library of Scotland; Queen Mary and Westfield College Library (Inter-Library Loans Department), University of London; the School of Slavonic and East European Studies Library, University of London; University College of Swansea Library (Inter-Library Loans Department); University of Illinois at Urbana-Champaign Library (Slavic Reference Service).

My sincere thanks are also due to a number of colleagues, friends and correspondents for their invaluable advice, support and assistance: Olga Bakich, David Collins, Paul Dukes, Peter Kenez, Alexander R. Kolchak, John Long, Pat Polansky, Evan Mawdsley, Serge Petroff, Alan Wood (and all members of his British Universities' Siberian Studies Seminar). I am especially indebted to Jimmy White of Glasgow University, who – although he may long since have forgotten this – in 1982 prompted and encouraged my initial interest in Kolchak; and to Professor Norman Pereira of Dalhousie University, who supplied some of the materials from American collections which have enriched my work. Finally, I pay glad tribute to Professor Roger Pethybridge, for his encouragement, his patience and for his wise supervision of the research I undertook for my PhD thesis at University College Swansea (University of Wales) – a work, entitled 'White Siberia', which forms the backbone of this study. Without Roger Pethybridge's patient readings and critiques of the drafts of that thesis, *Civil War in Siberia* would have been a far less complete piece of work. Any shortcomings which remain, however, are my own responsibility.

Glossary and abbreviations

In the text

AFSR	Armed Forces of South Russia (Denikin's army)
arshin	Russian unit of length = 71 cm
ataman	A Cossack chieftain
atamanshchina	The régime of an ataman or atamans
Britmis	The British Military Mission to Siberia
CBMO	Central Bureau of Military Organizations (part of the anti-Kolchak, SR underground)
CER	Chinese Eastern Railway
desiatina	Russian land measure = 10,800 square metres
duma	An elected municipal council
essaul	A Cossack captain
guberniia	An administrative division, a province
gubkom	Bolshevik *guberniia* committee
IARC	The Inter-Allied Railway Committee
Kadets	The Constitutional Democratic Party
kapel'evtsy	Followers of General V.O. Kappel
kerenki	20- and 40-rouble bank notes, originally issued in 1917
Komuch	The Committee of Members of the Constituent Assembly, at Samara
krasnoarmeets	A Red Army soldier
KssZs	*Komitet sodeistviia sozyvu Zemskogo sobora* (Committee for the Co-ordination of the Convocation of a *Zemskii sobor'*[q.v.]), part of the anti-Kolchak, SR underground
MRC	Military Revolutionary Committee, a group of commanders and commissars in charge of a Red Army or a Red Army group
National Centre	The underground anti-Bolshevik organization, founded in Moscow in early 1918 and dominated by the Kadets, which advocated military dictatorship
obkom	Bolshevik *oblast'* committee

oblast'	An administrative division, larger than a *guberniia*, a region
oblastnichestvo	The Siberian regionalist/autonomist movement and its ideology
oblastnik	An advocate of *oblastnichestvo*
okrug	An administrative division, an urban district
pood	Russian unit of weight = 16.38 kg
PGAS	The Provisional Government of Autonomous Siberia (the Derber Government)
PSG	The Provisional Siberian Government
PSR	The Party of Socialists-Revolutionaries
revkom	Bolshevik revolutionary committee
RTA	Russian Telegraph Agency
SEC	The State Economic Conference
semenovtsy	Followers of Ataman Semenov
SLA	The State Land Assembly
sibirki	Siberian roubles, issued at Omsk in 1918–1919
Sibobduma	The Siberian *oblast'* Duma
Sibzemgor	The All-Siberian Union of Zemstvos and Municipal Authorities
SR	Socialist-Revolutionary, a member of the PSR
sotnia	A Cossack squadron
stanitsa	A Cossack settlement
stavka	Army staff headquarters
Tsentrosibir'	The Central Executive Committee of Siberian Soviets
uezd	An administrative division, a county
UIC	The Urals Industrial Committee, part of the White administration
VOTsK	*Vostochnyi Otdel Tsentral'nogo Komiteta* (Eastern Section of the Central Committee) of the Kadets
uchredil'ovtsy	Members of the Constituent Assembly (the *Uchreditel'noe sobranie*)
URR	The Union for the Regeneration of Russia, a joint SR-Kadet anti-Bolshevik underground organization which supported the Directory
vedro	Russian unit of liquid volume = 12 litres
versta	Russian unit of distance = 1.06 km

voisko	A Cossack host
volost'	An administrative division, a rural district
Vsekosovet	Standing Committee of the All-Siberian Co-operative Congress
WSC	Western Siberian Commissariat
Zakupsbyt	'Buy and Sell', the All-Siberian Union of Co-operative Associations
Zemskii sobor'	The Congregation of the Lands, a proto-democratic institution of early modern Russia which some parties hoped to revive in Siberia during 1919
zemstvo	An elected rural council
zolotnik	Russian unit of weight = 3.5 grams

In the footnotes

DBFP	Woodward, E.L. and Butler, R. (eds.) *Documents on British Foreign Policy* (First Series). London (1948–1949)
FO	Foreign Office
FRUS	United States (Department of State) *Foreign Relations of the United States...* Washington (1931–)
NAM	National Army Museum
PSS	Lenin, V.I. *Polnoe sobranie sochinenii* (5th Edition). Moscow (1962–1965)
USMI	*United States Military Intelligence: Weekly Summaries.* New York (1978)
WO	War Office

SWEDEN
FINLAND
Berlin
Baltic Sea
Murmansk
Barents Sea
Petrograd
White Sea
Warsaw
Arkhangel'sk
POLAND
Vologda
Kotlas
MOSCOW
Kiev
Nakhodka
Ukraine
RUSSIA
Viatka
Black Sea
Kharkov
Urals
Penza
Kazan
Perm
Don
Simbirsk
Saratov
Kuban
Tsaritsyn
Samara
Ekaterinburg
Novorossiisk
Zlatoust
Tobol'sk
Ural'sk
Ufa
Cheliabinsk
Tiumen
TURKEY
Orenburg
Astrakhan
Omsk
Kustanai
Caspian Sea
Baku
Aral Sea
Semipalatinsk
Khiva
Tehran
Ashkabad
Bukhara
Tashkent
Merv
PERSIA
AFGHANISTAN
Sinkia

1 Red and White Russia, November 1918

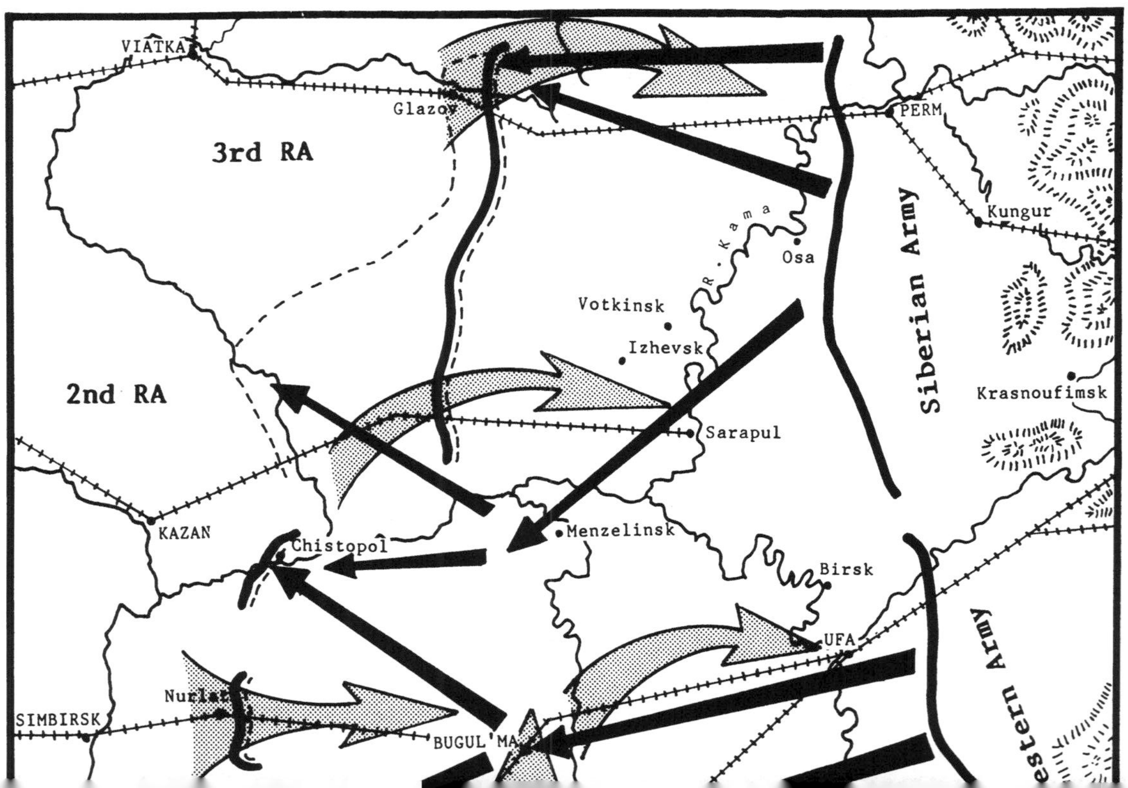
VIATKA
Glazov
3rd RA
2nd RA
KAZAN
Chistopol
SIMBIRSK
Nurlat
BUGUL'MA
PERM
Kungur
R. Kama
Osa
Votkinsk
Izhevsk
Sarapul
Menzelinsk
Birsk
UFA
Siberian Army
Krasnoufimsk
Western Army

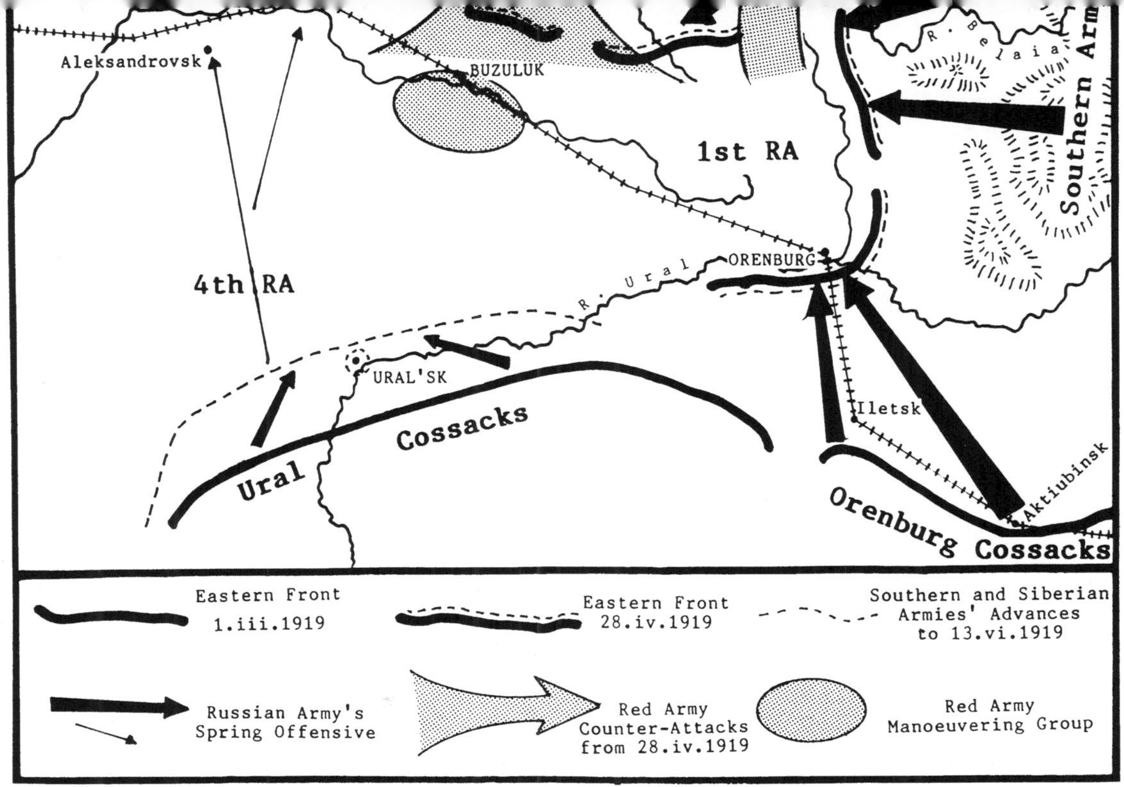

2 Eastern front, March to June 1919

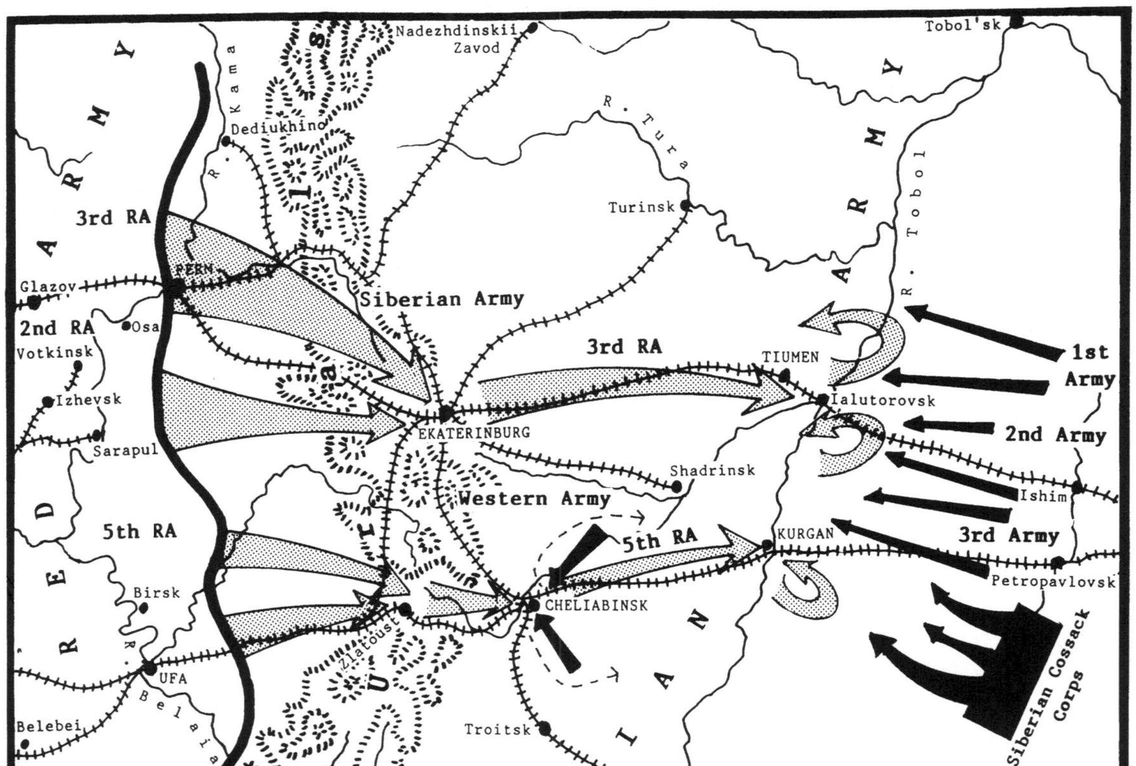
Tobol'sk
Nadezhdinskii Zavod
R. Kama
Dediukhino
R. Tura
Turinsk
R. Tobol
3rd RA
PERM
Glazov
Siberian Army
2nd RA
Osa
Votkinsk
Izhevsk
Sarapul
3rd RA
TIUMEN
1st Army
Ialutorovsk
2nd Army
EKATERINBURG
Shadrinsk
Western Army
Ishim
5th RA
5th RA
KURGAN
3rd Army
Petropavlovsk
Birsk
CHELIABINSK
Zlatoust
UFA
R. Belaia
Belebei
Troitsk
Siberian Cossack Corps
RED ARMY
ARMY

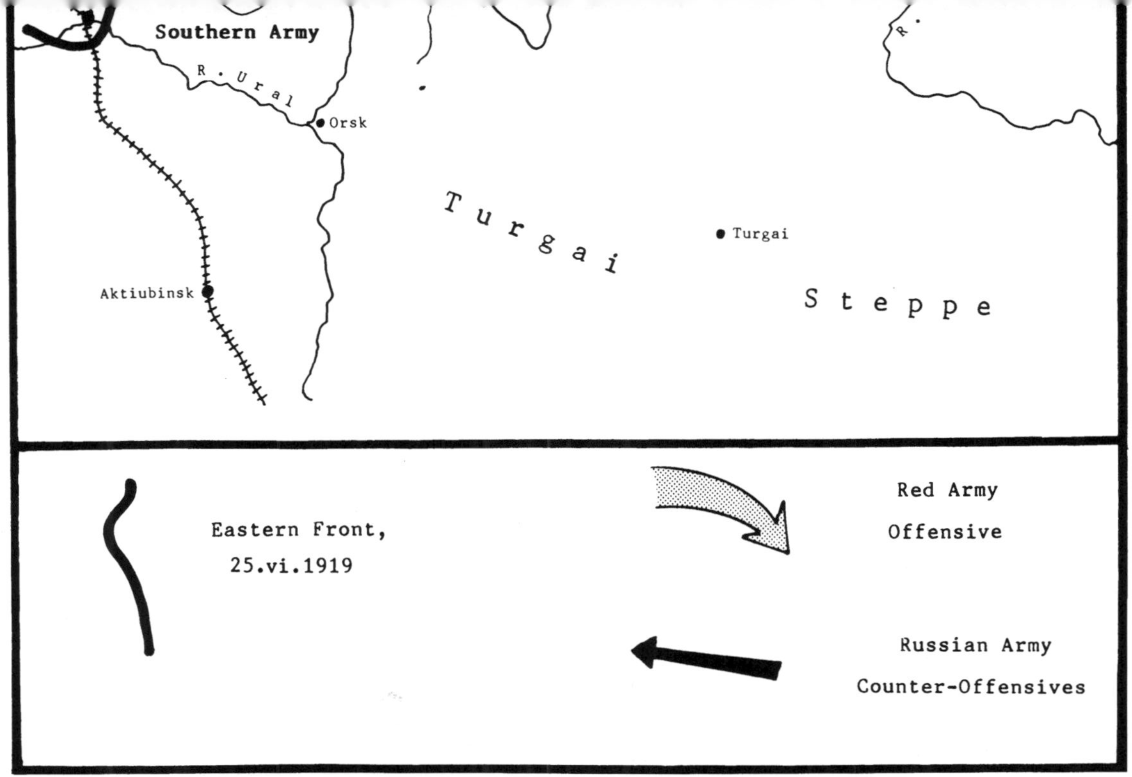

3 Eastern front, June to October 1919

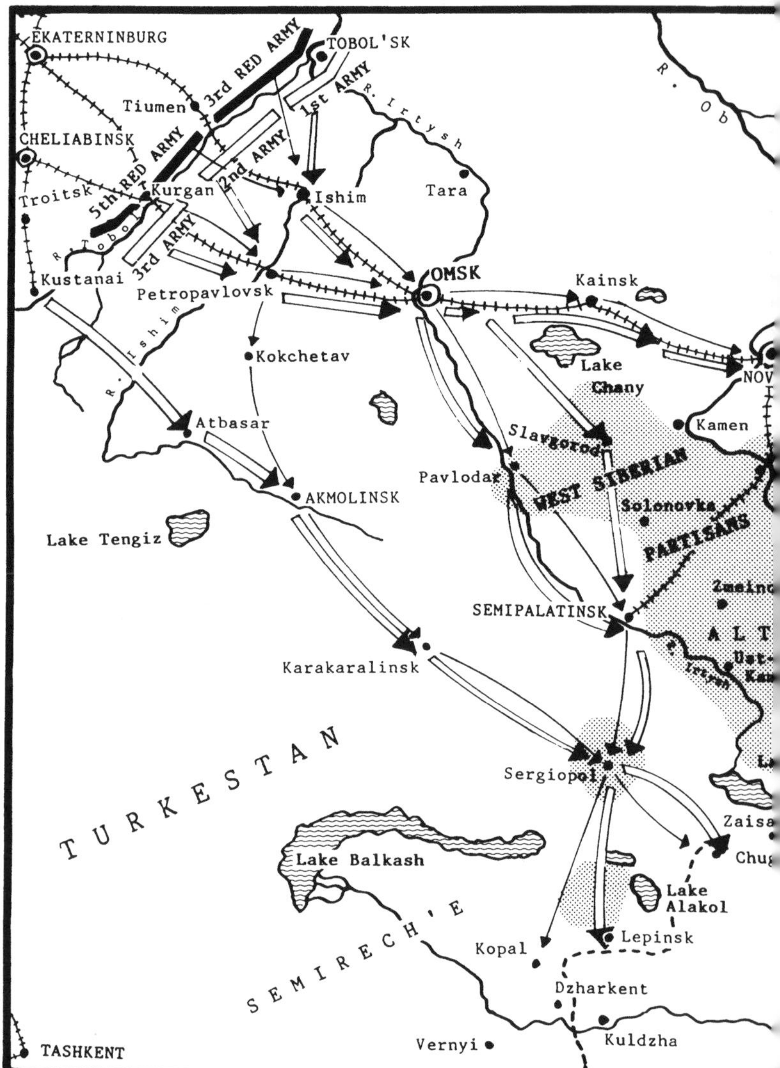

EKATERNINBURG
3rd RED ARMY
TOBOL'SK
1st ARMY
R. Irtysh
R. Ob
Tiumen
CHELIABINSK
5th RED ARMY
2nd ARMY
Troitsk
Kurgan
Ishim
Tara
R. Tobol
3rd ARMY
Kustanai
Petropavlovsk
OMSK
Kainsk
R. Ishim
Kokchetav
Lake Chany
NOV
Atbasar
Kamen
Slavgorod
Pavlodar
WEST SIBERIAN
AKMOLINSK
Solonovka
PARTISANS
Lake Tengiz
SEMIPALATINSK
R. Irtysh
Karakaralinsk
TURKESTAN
Sergiopol
Zaisa
Lake Balkash
Chug
Lake Alakol
SEMIRECH'E
Kopal
Lepinsk
Dzharkent
TASHKENT
Vernyi
Kuldzha

4 The retreat of the Russian Army, October to March 1920

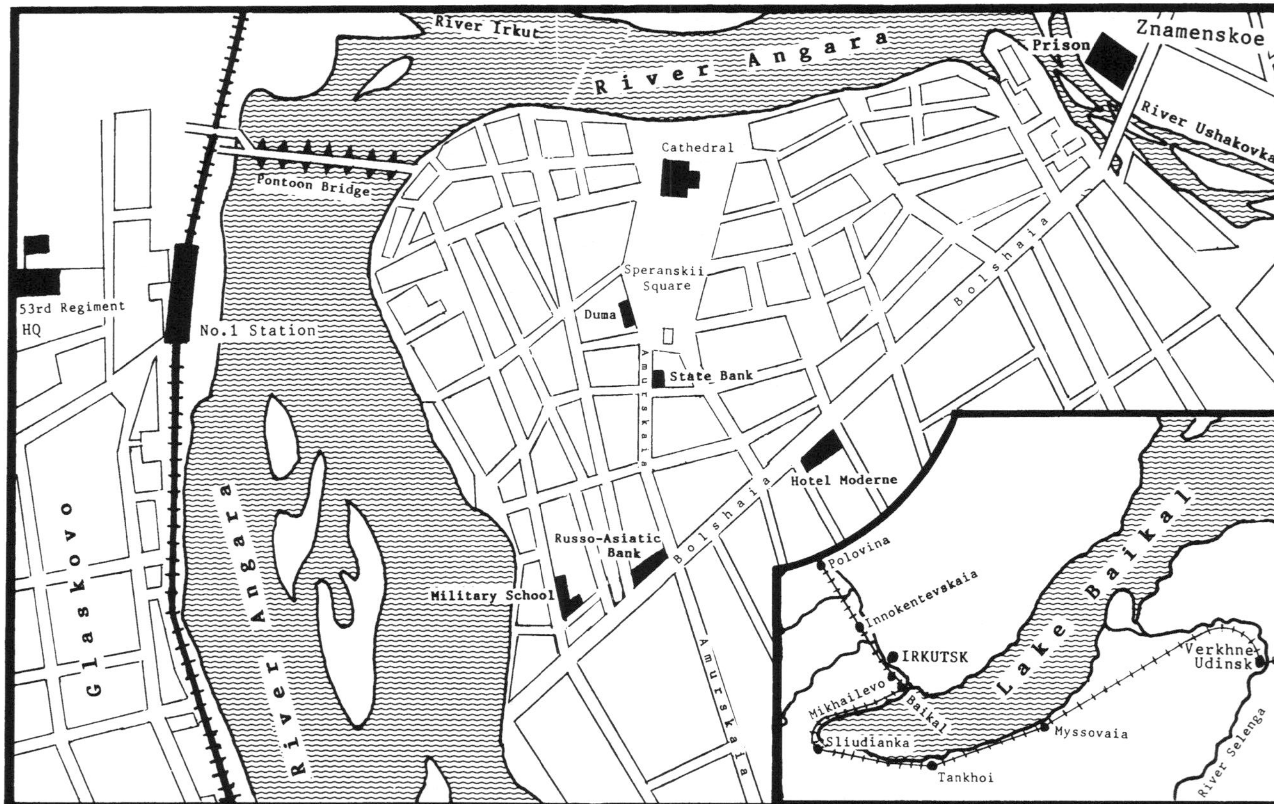
River Irkut
River Angara
Prison
Znamenskoe
River Ushakovka
Cathedral
Pontoon Bridge
Speranskii Square
Duma
53rd Regiment HQ
No.1 Station
Amurskaia
State Bank
Bolshaia
Hotel Moderne
Glaskovo
River Angara
Russo-Asiatic Bank
Military School
Bolshaia
Amurskaia
Polovina
Innokentevskaia
IRKUTSK
Lake Baikal
Verkhne-Udinsk
Mikhailevo
Baikal
Sliudianka
Tankhoi
Myssovaia
River Selenga

5 Irkutsk

Introduction

The Russian Civil War of 1917 to 1921 was a cataclysmic conflict – or, rather, it was a cataclysmic series of overlapping conflicts. A pivotal event in modern history, the war grew directly out of the social, political and economic turmoil in Russia which had been unleashed by the revolutions of 1917 and by the country's defeat in the Great War. Like all civil wars, it, on the one hand, made bloodily manifest the tensions underlying prior decades of political and socio-economic development; on the other, it left a deep imprint upon its participants and their descendants for decades after the guns had fallen silent. In so far as the outcome of the Russian Civil War witnessed the triumph of Communism and its principles in the largest country on earth, the conflict also exerted a profound influence upon the history of the twentieth century. The sheer viciousness, deep tragedy, geographical scope, and complexity of the battles waged made the impact of the Russian Civil War especially great: following the Bolsheviks' seizure of power in Petrograd, across the length and breadth of a former empire which had covered fully one-sixth of the land surface of the globe, from the borders of Poland to the shores of the Pacific Ocean, for four tumultuous and agonizing years army fought army, party fought party, nation fought nation, town fought country, and family fought family. It was a truly Hobbesian struggle of 'all against all'. Often forgotten is the fact that the Russian Civil War was also a struggle of man against nature, as of the ten million who had fallen fatally victim to it by the end of 1921, only some 800,000 had been lost in battle; the overwhelming majority of the dead had succumbed to the pandemic waves of typhus, cholera, Spanish flu and famine which were attendant upon this new 'Time of Troubles'.[1]

1 The reference is to the anarchic period of Russian history at the beginning of the seventeenth century – an era of famine, economic collapse, crises of succession and foreign invasion which in many ways is comparable to the civil war period. Significantly, one of the leading actors of the civil war, General Anton Denikin, entitled his memoirs *Ocherki russkoi smuty* ('Sketches of the Russian Time of Troubles'). The best modern surveys of the civil war are Lincoln, W. Bruce *Red Victory: A History of the Russian Civil War*. New York (1989); and Mawdsley, E. *The Russian Civil War*. Boston (1987). A recent monograph expertly traces the genesis of the struggle: Swain, G. *The Origins of the Russian Civil War*. London (1995).

Central to the military and political contest, however, was the clash of the Moscow-based Soviet régime, 'the Reds', with their most dangerous and implacable enemies 'the Whites' – the militaristic, counter-revolutionary governments which established themselves around the periphery of Russia throughout the course of 1918, and which, in 1919, with the aid of Allied interventionists, launched a series of offensives against the Red-held heartland of Russia. From Siberia, from North Russia, from the Baltic, from South Russia and from Poland were successive White attacks repulsed by Trotsky's Red Army.[2] On several occasions the White armies were stopped on the direct road to Moscow; on others they had to be dislodged from the very suburbs of Petrograd; at one point or another virtually all the other major cities situated in those parts of the former empire lying beyond the marches of fifteenth-century Musvovy came under the occupation of the Whites and their allies – Kiev, Kharkov, Voronezh, Odessa, Rostov, Baku, Tsaritsyn, Orenburg, Ufa, Samara, Kazan, Simbirsk, Arkhangel′sk, Irkutsk, Vladivostok. But, ultimately, the Reds emerged from the war victorious, the principles for which they had fought being elevated in the process to the Procrustean laws which would shape the destiny of Soviet Russia for generations. The vanquished Whites, meanwhile, fell into despair, destitution and diaspora. The principles for which *they* had fought were largely forgotten.

It would be impossible to determine precisely at which point the Reds could be said to have been unshakeably victorious, or to determine at which juncture the war could be said to have irrevocably ended – the civil war was to rumble on, in the form of peasant and national uprisings, and foreign or foreign-backed incursions, for a number of years, while Japanese interventionist forces did not relinquish southern Sakhalin until 1925. Nevertheless, it is safe to say, with regard to the struggle of White against Red, that the *beginning* of the end of this crucial element of the civil war in Russia was marked on January 15th 1920, when Admiral Aleksandr Vasil′evich Kolchak, erstwhile leader of the White movement in Siberia – a man marked out by Lenin in 1919 as 'enemy number one' of the Soviet Republic and one recognized as 'Supreme Ruler' of Russia by White foes of Lenin from the Baltic and Black Seas to Vladivostok – was captured and incarcerated by

2 Precisely how and when the militarist anti-Bolsheviks came to call themselves 'Whites' remains a mystery. One credible version has it, however, that the name was chosen to invoke the spirit of the formidable and ruthless General Mikhail Skobelev, the hero of Russia's Central Asian campaigns of the 1880s. Skobelev was nicknamed 'the White General' by his men because he invariably went into battle wearing a dazzling white uniform and riding a white charger.

revolutionary forces at Irkutsk as he fled eastwards from his abandoned capital, Omsk. Crouched in the dark, damp cells of Irkutsk's grim prison building, comforted only by his mistress and those few of his ministers and generals who had not already abandoned or betrayed him, the toppled Supreme Ruler had ample opportunity to dwell upon the history of his own attempt to oust Lenin from the Kremlin, and upon the failure of the White movement in general. Of course, other White leaders remained at liberty and would continue to struggle on against the Reds for some time to come – notably General Wrangel, who was to launch an offensive from the Crimea during the summer of 1920 – but never again would the possibility of victory seem anything other than hopelessly remote.

Over the three weeks following Kolchak's imprisonment the captive admiral was interrogated – if that is not too strong a word, for the proceedings were surprisingly leisurely – by an Extraordinary Investigating Commission consisting of three members of the Menshevik-Socialist Revolutionary régime (the Political Centre) which had succeeded the Whites at Irkutsk, and two representatives of the local Bolshevik Revolutionary Committee which, before the end of January 1920, seized power in the town. The manner in which the sessions of the interrogation developed and were then unexpectedly and unfortunately curtailed, was later described by one of the Bolsheviks present, the lawyer K.A. Popov (Vice-Chairman of the Extraordinary Investigating Commission), in his introduction to Gosizdat's publication of the stenographic record of the proceedings:

> The Commission conducted the examination according to a previously determined plan. It wanted to construct, by means of this examination, not only the history of the Kolchak régime as described by its supreme head, but also the autobiography [*sic.*] of Kolchak, in order to have a more complete picture of this 'leader' of the counter-revolutionary offensive against the young Soviet Republic. This plan was correct, but was not carried to its completion. The events on the still active front of the civil war and the threat, which for several days hung over Irkutsk, of a temporary seizure of the town by the last survivors of the Kolchak bands, compelled the Revolutionary Committee to have Kolchak shot during the night of February 6th–7th, instead of having him sent, after the questioning, to Moscow for trial, as had been intended. The questioning, therefore, was discontinued at the beginning of its most essential part – that dealing with the Kolchak régime proper, the period of Kolchak's dictatorship as 'Supreme Ruler'. In this manner the historical-biographical character of the examination, by force of events and owing to unforeseen circumstances, led to negative results. The examination no doubt yielded not a bad self-portrait of Kolchak, and gave his own version of the emergence of the Kolchak dictatorship and a number of the

most characteristic features of the Kolchak régime, but failed to yield a complete and exhaustive history and portrait of the Kolchak régime itself.[3]

Although a full biography remains to be written of a man who was an eminent scholar in his own right and one of the leading military and public figures of his generation, since the publication of Kolchak's remarkably candid testimony there have, at regular intervals, appeared works by western and émigré historians which (in manners ranging from the banal to the engrossing) have expanded upon Gosizdat's text in order to recount what was in many ways a tragic and heroic end to the life of Admiral Kolchak.[4] A brilliant (but, regrettably, unpublished) doctoral thesis delved somewhat deeper in 1970 and presented a detailed account of post-revolutionary political events in Siberia down to the moment of Kolchak's seizure of power at Omsk on November 18th 1918.[5] Otherwise, one can only note the appearance in 1991 of a brief synthesis of more recent western writings on aspects of the revolution and civil war in Siberia.[6] Both in the West and in the Soviet Union, in contrast, the Allied intervention in Siberia was the subject of a considerable body of scholarly research – the extent of which, it must be said, was on both sides more a factor of the significance which the intervention assumed in Cold War rhetoric than it was a true reflection of the military or political importance of Allied contingents on the ground during the struggle, particularly in Siberia.[7]

3 Popov, K.A. (ed.) *Dopros Kolchaka*. Leningrad (1925), pp. iii–iv. This work later appeared in a famous translation as the main element of Varneck, E. and Fisher, H.H. *The Testimony of Kolchak and Other Siberian Materials*. Stanford (1935).

4 Notably Mel′gunov, S.P. *Tragediia admirala Kolchaka: iz istorii grazhdanskoi voiny na Volge, Urale i v Sibiri* (3 Vols.). Belgrade (1930–1931); Footman, D. 'Kolchak: the Last Phase', in his *Civil War in Russia*. London (1961); and Fleming, P. *The Fate of Admiral Kolchak*. London (1963). Connaughton, R. *The Republic of the Ushakovka: Admiral Kolchak and the Allied Intervention in Siberia*. London (1990) is a disappointingly unambitious heir to this tradition.

5 Berk, S.M. 'The *Coup d'État* of Admiral Kolchak: Counter-Revolution in Siberia and Eastern Russia, 1917–1918'. Columbia University PhD Thesis (1971).

6 Channon, J. 'Siberia in Revolution and Civil War', in Wood, A. (ed.) *The History of Siberia: From Russian Conquest to Revolution*. London (1991), pp. 158–80.

7 Notably, for our purpose, on the western side: White, J.A. *The Siberian Intervention*. New York (1950), and the relevant sections of the general works on the intervention by G. Kennan, R.H. Ullman, J.F.N. Bradley and M. Kettle. Two relatively recent works by Soviet authors, although weighted, are very informative and less polemical than most of what had appeared before: Livshits, S.G. *Imperialisticheskaia interventsiia v Sibiri*. Barnaul (1979); and Svetachev, M.I. *Imperialisticheskaia interventsiia v Sibiri i na Dal′nem Vostoke*. Novosibirsk (1983).

Meanwhile, as might be expected, an extensive Soviet historiography developed regarding the civil war proper in Siberia. It, however, quite naturally concentrated on the opponents of White power in the east – the Bolshevik underground and the partisan movement – and on the military victory of the Red Army.[8] Even studies which emerged in the Soviet Union in the 1980s purporting to deal with the period of Kolchak's government at Omsk fought shy of the crucial year 1919, and dwelt, rather, upon the genesis of the White dictatorship during the summer of 1918 and its dénouement at Irkutsk in 1920.[9] What is lacking, in other words, is that which has been lacking ever since the admiral's precipitate execution: that which his Bolshevik interrogator, Popov, described as 'a complete and exhaustive history and portrait of the Kolchak régime itself'.[10] It is hoped, however, that, in having drawn upon the holdings of a number of western archives, and, in particular, in having collated what gradually emerged to be a huge but scattered fund of published primary and secondary materials dealing with diverse aspects of the Omsk government and the civil war in Siberia, the present study comes close to providing such a history.

But why should one study the Whites at all? After all, there is surely greater utility in investigating the histories of movements which 'succeed' – in order to laud, to understand, or to challenge the principles of 'victors' in political and military struggles such as the Russian Revolution and Civil War. As Michael Karpovich, writing in 1955, noted with regard to the general attitude of historians towards one specific element of the White movement, the Russian liberals, the Kadets: 'Why should one pay much attention to a political trend which could not achieve any

8 Among the best publications of the late Soviet period were Zhurov, Iu.V. *Grazhdanskaia voina v sibirskoi derevne*. Krasnoiarsk (1986) and a collection of articles dealing with an unusually diverse array of subjects: Korablev, Iu.V. and Shishkin, B.I. (eds.) *Iz istorii interventsii i grazhdanskoi voiny v Sibiri i na Dal'nem Vostoke, 1917–1922gg*. Novosibirsk (1985). On military affairs Spirin, L.M. *Razgrom armii Kolchaka*. Moscow (1957) and Eikhe, G.Kh. *Oprokinutyi tyl*. Moscow (1966) remain unsurpassed for the breadth and detail of their coverage.

9 Ioffe, G.Z. *Kolchakovskaia avantiura i ee krakh*. Moscow (1983), although a fine work in its own right, offers only one short chapter (22 pages, from a total of 269) by way of an analysis of the Kolchak government at Omsk.

10 Korablev and Shishkin (*Iz istorii interventsii*, pp. 3–4) chose to introduce their work by admitting that in Soviet historiography 'the camp of the counter-revolution has been very weakly studied in comparison to the history of the Red Army, the Bolshevik underground, the partisans, etc.'.

lasting results, and which suffered such a crushing defeat?'[11] Karpovich's answer, that the historical process recognizes no final defeats or victories and that the significance of historical phenomena can only be assessed in relation to the time in which they occured, seems doubly insightful from the point of view of post-Soviet 1995. Perhaps, in the light of the collapse of Communism in the late 1980s, the 'long view' of future historians will be that the Reds never really did win the civil war. Moreover, it seems to me to be beyond doubt that a full historical understanding of the Russian Revolution can only be approached with a comprehension of the motives and behaviour of Lenin's most puissant opponents: what the Whites did (or attempted to do) influenced Bolshevik thought and tactics on a day-to-day basis during the civil war; while the party's post-civil war behaviour was indelibly stamped with its leaders' and members' experience and memory of the struggle against the Whites.[12] Equally, the experience of the civil war largely determined the attitudes of the millions who constituted the first wave of the emigration from the Soviet Russia. The émigrés tended to belong to the educated élite of Russian society. Their spokesmen and their descendants would exert no insignificant influence upon western political, cultural and (especially) academic communities for decades to come.[13]

11 Karpovich, M. 'Two Types of Russian Liberalism: Maklakov and Miliukov', in Simmons, E.J. (ed.) *Continuity and Change in Russian and Soviet Thought*. Cambridge, MA (1955), p. 130. With regard to the civil war, the practitioner *par excellence* of the approach Karpovich referred to was E.H. Carr: in his monumental, three-volume study of the period – *The Bolshevik Revolution*. London (1950–1953) – Carr made a conscious choice to grant barely a passing mention to Denikin, Kolchak and other anti-Bolshevik leaders. Even today, the balance has hardly begun to shift: as Peter Kenez has recently noted, two major collections of articles dealing with the civil war which were published in the 1980s, containing contributions by the leading western scholars of the period, 'paid not the slightest attention to the Whites. Not a single article was devoted to the White cause.' See: Kenez, P. 'Western Historiography of the Russian Civil War', in Schelbert, L. and Ceh, N. (eds.) *Essays in Russian and East European History: Festschrift in Honor of Edward C. Thaden*. Boulder (1995), p. 203. Kenez was referring to Gleason, A. et al. (eds.) *Bolshevik Culture*. Bloomington (1985); and Koenker, D. et al. (eds.) *Party, State and Society in the Russian Civil War*. Bloomington (1989).

12 In this regard, see: Fitzpatrick, S. 'The Legacy of the Civil War', in Koenker, D. et al., pp. 385–98; and Lewin, M. 'The Civil War: Dynamics and Legacy' in *ibid.*, pp. 399–423. See also: Fitzpatrick, S. 'Origins of Stalinism: How Important was the Civil War?', *Acta Slavica Iaponica* Vol. 2 (1984), pp. 105–16; and Fitzpatrick, S. 'The Civil War as Formative Experience', in Gleason et al.

13 The history of the Russian emigration may be traced from the following sources: Dawatz, W. *Fünf Sturmjahre mit General Wrangel* (transl. by G.H. von Leuchtenberg). Berlin (1927); Delage, J. *La Russie en exil*. Paris (1930); Essad Bey *Das weisse Russland. Menschen ohne Heimat*. Berlin

At the risk of stating the obvious, it is also indisputable that a full historical understanding of the Russian Revolution will only be approached when historians are in a position to know precisely what happened during the turbulent years in which the Soviet state was born. For decades after the revolution western scholarship on the subject tended towards grand, but ultimately hollow, statements regarding the 'inner meaning' of the events, shying away from the spadework involved in uncovering what exactly had happened, when it had happened, where it had happened, and how.[14] Although some valuable groundwork was done by Soviet scholars during the 1920s, the onset of Stalinism and the vagaries of post-Stalin Soviet (and, indeed, post-Soviet) developments lent a tendentious quality to most of the publications emanating from the Communist east.[15] Émigré writings,

(1932); Johnston, R.H. *New Mecca, New Babylon: Paris and the Russian Exiles, 1920–1945*. Montreal (1988); Ledre, C. *Les émigrés russes en France*. Paris (1930); Macartney, C.A. *Refugees: The Work of the League*. London (1931); Mierau, F. (ed.) *Russen in Berlin 1918–1933: Eine Kulturelle Begegnung*. Weiheim/Berlin (1988); Oberländer, E. 'Nationalbolschewistische Tendenzen in der russischen Intelligenz: Die "Smena Vekh" Diskussion, 1921–1922', *Jahrbücher für Geschichte Osteuropas* Vol. 16 (1968), No. 2, pp. 194–211; Raeff, M. *Russia Abroad: A Cultural History of the Russian Emigration*. Oxford (1990); von Rimscha, H. *Der russische Bürgerkrieg und die russische Emigration, 1917–1921*. Jena (1924); von Rimscha, H. *Russlands jenseits der Grenzen, 1921–1926*. Jena (1927); Stephan, J.J *The Russian Fascists: Tragedy and Farce in Exile*. New York (1978); Volkmann, H.-E. *Die Russische Emigration in Deutschland 1919–1929*. Würzburg (1966); Williams, R.C. *Culture in Exile: Russian Émigrés in Germany, 1881–1941*. Ithaca (1972); Williams, R.C. '"Changing Landmarks" in Russian Berlin, 1922–1924', *Slavic Review* Vol. 27 (1968), No. 4, pp. 581–93.

14 One notable and still widely admired exception to this rule was W.H. Chamberlin's two-volume *The Russian Revolution*. New York (1935). Another was Stewart, G. *The White Armies of Russia: A Chronicle of Counter-Revolution and Allied Intervention*. New York (1933). For some useful reviews and conceptualizations of the first half-century of western historiography on the period, see: Karpovich, M. 'The Russian Revolution of 1917', *Journal of Modern History* Vol. 2 (1930), No. 2, pp. 258–80; von Mohrenschildt, D. 'The Early American Observers of the Russian Revolution', *Russian Review* Vol. 5 (1945–1946), No. 1, pp. 31–41; Philips Price, M. 'Witnesses of the Revolution', *Survey* No. 41 (1962), pp. 14–26; Billington, J.H. 'Six Views of the Russian Revolution', *World Politics* Vol. 18 (1965–1966), No. 3, pp. 452–73; Warth, R.D. 'On the Historiography of the Russian Revolution', *Slavic Review* Vol. 26 (1967), No. 2, pp. 247–64.

15 The Stalinist years are thoroughly surveyed in McNeal, R.H. 'Soviet Historiography on the October Revolution: A Review of Forty Years', *American Slavic and East European Review*, Vol. 17 (1958), No. 3; and Thompson, J.M. 'Allied-American Intervention in Russia, 1918–1921', in Black, C.E. (ed.) *Rewriting Russian History: Soviet Interpretations of Russia's Past*. New York (1957), pp. 334–400. For two 'insiders'' views of post-Soviet writing see: Buldakov, V.P 'The October Revolution: Seventy-Five Years On' (transl. by A. Wood), *European History Quarterly* Vol. 22 (1992), No. 4, pp. 497–516; and Shishkin, V.I. 'The October Revolution and *Perestroika*: A Critical Review of Recent Soviet Historiography' (transl. by A. Wood), *European History Quarterly* Vol. 22 (1992), No. 4, pp. 517–40. See also: 'The Civil War in Russia: A Roundtable Discussion' (Summary prepared by A.I. Stepanov), *Russian Studies in History* Vol. 32 (1993-94),

whilst often valuable for their commentary upon developments in diverse regions of the former Empire, were generally more concerned with recrimination against the Allies, with the exposure of alleged conspiracies and with apocalyptic diatribes against the evils of Communism.[16] The situation has improved greatly over recent decades, however, with the development in the west of two inter-connected, new schools of historical writing on the revolutionary period. The first, largely as a reaction against earlier scholars' perceived over-emphasis of the role of political élites, has delved deeply into the minutae of the everyday experiences during the period of peasants and workers (especially the latter).[17] The second has served to divert our attention away from the streets of the Petrograd of 1917 towards the diversity of the events and contrasts of chronology which characterized the revolution in the outlying regions of the former Russian Empire.[18] It is towards this

No. 4, pp. 73-95. On the subtle problems involved in utilizing Soviet sources from the 1920s, see: Holmes, A.G. 'Soviet Rewriting of 1917: The Case of A.G. Shliapnikov', *Slavic Review* Vol. 38 (1979), No. 2, pp. 224–42; and, especially, White, J.D. 'Early Soviet Historical Interpretations of the Russian Revolution, 1918–1924', *Soviet Studies* Vol. 37 (1985), No. 3, pp. 330–52; also White, J.D. 'Historiography of the Russian Revolution', *Critique* Vol. 1 (1973), No. 1, pp. 42-54.

16 To date, no comprehensive, dedicated historiographical study of the émigré literature has been published. But see: Arans, D. (ed.) *'How We Lost the Civil War': A Bibliography of Russian Émigré Memoirs of the Russian Revolution, 1917–1920.* Newtonville, MA (1988); and Foster, L.A. 'The Revolution and Civil War in Russian Emigre Novels', *Russian Review* Vol. 31 (1972), No. 2, pp. 153–62.

17 For an influential review of developments in this field see: Suny, R.G. 'Towards a Social History of the October Revolution', *American Historical Review* Vol. 88 (1983), pp. 31–52. For a thoughtful critique of this approach, see: Marot, J.E. 'Class Conflict, Political Competition and Social Transformation: Critical Perspectives on the Social History of the Russian Revolution', *Revolutionary Russia* Vol. 7 (1994), No. 2, pp. 111–63. See also: Keep, J. 'Social Aspects of the Russian Revolutionary Era (1917–1923) in Recent English Language Historiography', *East European Quarterly* Vol. 34 (1990), No. 2. A recent survey, although commendably venturing beyond the traditional concentration upon the political and military leaderships of the civil war's belligerents, is harshly critical of the assumptions of the social historians: Brovkin, V.N. *Behind the Front Lines of the Civil War: Political Parties and Social Movements in Russia, 1918–1922.* Princeton (1994).

18 Among the works which might be said to have established and developed this tradition the following are perhaps the most noteworthy: Kirimal, E. *Der nationale Kampf der Krimtürken, mit besonderer Berücksichtigung der Jahre 1917–1918.* Emsdetten (1952); Smith, C.F. *Vladivostok under Red and White Rule: Revolution and Counter-Revolution in the Russian Far East, 1920–1922.* Seattle (1975); Raleigh, D.J. *Revolution on the Volga: 1917 in Saratov.* Ithaca (1986); Radkey, O.H. *The Unknown Civil War in Russia: A Study of the Green Movement in the Tambov Region, 1920–1921.* Stanford (1976); Getzler, I. *Kronstadt 1917–1921: The Fate of a Soviet Democracy.* Cambridge (1983); Figes, O. *Peasant Russia, Civil War: The Volga Countryside in Revolution, 1917–1921.* Oxford (1989); Reshetar, J.S. *The Ukrainian Revolution, 1917–1920: A Study in Nationalism.* Princeton, NJ (1952); Hunczak, T. (ed.) *The Ukraine, 1917–1921: A Study*

latter tendency that *Civil War in Siberia* gravitates, investigating the growth and failure of the White movement east of the Urals.

in Revolution. Cambridge, MA (1977); Adams, A.E. *The Bolsheviks in the Ukraine: The Second Campaign, 1918–19*. New Haven (1963); Fiddick, T.C. *Russia's Retreat from Poland, 1920: From Permanent Revolution to Peaceful Coexistence*. London (1990); Davies, N. *White Eagle, Red Star: The Polish–Soviet War, 1919–20*. London (1972); Park, A.G. *Bolshevism in Turkestan, 1917–1927*. New York (1957); Zürrer, W. *Kaukasien, 1918–1921: Der Kampf der Grossmächte um die Landbrücke zwischen Schwarzem und Kaspischem Meer*. Düsseldorf (1978); Swietochowski, T. *Russian Azerbaidjan, 1905–1920: The Shaping of National Identity in a Muslim Community*. Cambridge (1985); Suny, R.G. *The Baku Commune, 1917–1918*. Princeton (1972); Kazemzadeh, F. *The Struggle for Transcaucasia, 1917–1921*. New York (1951); Hovannisian, R.G. *Armenia on the Road to Independence: 1918*. Berkeley/Los Angeles (1967); Hovannisian, R.G. *The Republic of Armenia, Vol. 1: The First Year, 1918–1919*. Berkeley (1971); Hovannisian, R.G. *The Republic of Armenia, Vol. 2: From Versailles to London, 1919–1920*. Berkeley (1982); Afanasyan, S. *L'Arménie, l'Azerbaidjan et la Géorgie: de l'independence à l'instauration du pouvoir soviétique, 1917–1923*. Paris (1981); Ezergailis, A. *The 1917 Revolution in Latvia*. Boulder, CO (1974); Ezergailis, A. *The Latvian Impact on the Bolshevik Revolution: The First Phase (September 1917 – April 1918)*. New York (1983); Upton, A.F. *The Finnish Revolution, 1917–1918*. Minneapolis (1980). The works most directly comparable in their scope to the present study are: Kenez, P. *Civil War in South Russia, 1918: The First Year of the Volunteer Army*. Berkeley (1971), and *idem.*, *Civil War in South Russia, 1918–1919: The Defeat of the Whites*. Berkeley (1977); and Brinkley, G.A. *The Volunteer Army and Allied Intervention in South Russia, 1917–1921: A Study in the Politics and Diplomacy in the Russian Civil War*. Notre Dame (1966).

Chapter 1

The triumphal march of reaction

> The counter-revolution in Siberia, which has hitherto developed under the banner of the petite-bourgeoisie, must now evolve into military dictatorship – counter-revolution in its most severe form.[1]

Such was the verdict of the first underground conference of Siberian Bolsheviks at Tomsk on August 23rd 1918. This clandestine party meeting was held almost three months after what Lenin termed the 'Triumphal March of Soviet Power' had been rudely reversed east of the Volga by the famous revolt of the Czechoslovak Legion – those armed ex-POWs, en route for evacuation via Vladivostok in order to join the Allied cause in France, who had despaired under their maltreatment at the hands of the Soviet authorities and had then seized control of the Trans-Siberian Railway and its environs. Three months later, with the establishment of an avowedly militaristic government at Omsk in November 1918, the fugitive Bolsheviks' prediction would be fulfilled, as the triumphal march of reaction reached its zenith in a White Siberia.

Between times, in September 1918, representatives of the myriad anti-Bolshevik governments which established themselves, under the aegis of the Czechoslovaks, to claim authority over territories from the Volga to the Pacific, would yet gather to parley at a grand State Conference, at Ufa. And there, indeed, contending parties would merge uneasily in the guise of a Provisional All-Russian Government, the Directory, which was committed to democracy. This, however, proved to be an unworkable and toothless compromise of a coalition, respected by neither of the chief pretenders to power in the east during the summer of 1918 – the Socialist-Revolutionary (SR) dominated Committee of Members of the Constituent Assembly (Komuch), at Samara; and the more right-wing Provisional Siberian Government (PSG), based at Omsk. Indeed, the latter was quite definitely determined that the Directory should not be afforded a lengthy existence: hardly had that rickety flagship of coalition and compromise left its harbour at Ufa than it was swamped by the

1 Shpilev, G. (ed.) 'Iz istorii partiinoi raboty v Sibiri pri Kolchake', *Proletarskaia revoliutsiia*, No. 1 (1928), p. 71.

rising tide of Siberian reaction; and then, in the course of a *coup d'état* at Omsk on November 18th, it was swept away altogether, its socialist members arrested by Cossacks and exiled at the behest of their own ministers, to be supplanted by the putative dictatorship of Admiral Kolchak.

The story of how the leadership of the anti-Bolshevik movement in Siberia thereby passed from the proponents of various forms of democracy and into the hands of a dictatorship in the space of only six months is a complicated and a tortuous one, interlarded with obscuration, obfuscation and malice in the accounts of witnesses on both sides of the Omsk-Samara divide. It is, however, a story which is deserving of the telling: from it the converging lines of political ideas and military activity which made a dictatorship possible become conspicuous. When crossed with the contemporaneously converging paths of the key figures involved in the Omsk coup and mixed with a healthy dose of pressure for strong government from influential agents of Russia's wartime Allies (who were attracted to the region in the hope of resurrecting an eastern front against Germany), it becomes apparent that an attempt to establish a military dictatorship in Siberia in 1918 could probably not have been averted.

That the attempt to impose a dictatorship of the type favoured by right-wing elements both within Russia and abroad was, moreover, likely to be successful in the east a year after the thwarting in Petrograd of their first candidate, General Kornilov, becomes clear as an examination of the events of the summer of 1918 further reveals the political paralysis of the democratic parties, led by the SRs. Hoping against hope that the generals, atamans and increasingly authoritarian Kadets with whom they were consorting were *bona fide* democrats, in the face of successive steps to the right in government and virulent anti-socialist belligerency among the military groups massing in Siberia, the SRs, a survey of the period shows, steadfastly refused to create a rift in the anti-Bolshevik camp until, at the Ufa State Conference, they committed the fatal mistake of sanctioning the transfer of legitimate authority to the powerless Directory. This defenceless, infant All-Russian Government – 'a premature child with not long to live', as one source has it[2] – they then duly delivered into the care of the rapacious military and political groups milling around Omsk, where its fate was a foregone conclusion.

2 Gan [Gutman], A. *Rossiia i Bol'shevizm: materialy po istorii revoliutsii i bor'by s bol'shevizmom (chast' pervaia, 1914–1920)*. Shanghai (1921), p. 285.

The SRs' failure to halt the slide towards reaction, as one of their members later admitted, was partly a failure of judgement and partly a failure of will.[3] More than that, however, it was an illustration of the regrettable inability of that party to mould impressive levels of electoral support into effective political and military organizations. Without an armed force to counter the machinations of Omsk it is difficult to see what the SRs could have done to forestall the triumphal march of reaction. On the Volga, of course, Komuch had an army, the People's Army, but its strength was waning rapidly and the loyalty of its officer corps was always open to question. Moreover, it was engaged in holding off the Reds throughout the summer of 1918. Meanwhile, in the rear of the eastern anti-Bolshevik front, it emerged that Omsk would only tolerate the proponents of democracy for as long as it was convenient to do so. Throughout the summer the proponents of dictatorship used the SRs' immature democracy – physically in the case of the People's Army and morally in the case of the Directory – as an expedient cloak, a screen behind which to consolidate their own military organization, political power and diplomatic support in the comparatively peaceful haven of Western Siberia. Once the Volga front began to collapse during October 1918, however, and the Red Army began to advance through Ufa *guberniia* towards the Ural passes, Omsk no longer had a compelling reason to preserve its partnership with Komuch and the SRs. Thereafter, the Directory, the symbol of that partnership, was harried and harassed as reaction bent the feeble government to its will, seemingly enjoying the death throes of the so-called 'democratic counter-revolution' – like a rather vicious cat toying with a particularly timid mouse.

In this period, of October–November 1918 – the agony of democracy and the advent of military dictatorship – certain SRs, the elected representatives of Russia's most popular party, even seemed, to their shame, to be doing much to ease the path of the would-be dictator to office: the socialists of the Directory connived in doing away with some of the better and most popular achievements and institutions of the revolution even *before* the establishment of military rule. They dug their own graves – or, at least, they helped to dig them. Only slowly did the PSR begin to learn the harsh lesson of the first year of the struggle for power in Russia – that political ideals would only be victorious in civil war if harnessed to a vigorous and controllable military organization. Meanwhile, as one leading SR later confessed, in

3 Sviatitskii, N.V. *Reaktsiia i narodovlastie*. Moscow (1920), p. 14.

a contrite letter to a Soviet journal: 'In the years of the great revolution our party committed a huge and unforgivable error... We left the door wide open to military dictatorship.'[4]

The democratic counter-revolution in Siberia

The Bolshevik revolution had come quickly to Siberia, primarily through the proclamations and gun barrels of the supporters of Lenin who were shipped into the region along the Trans-Siberian Railway. As the early Red chroniclers of the events delighted in recording, Soviet power was established in all major cities and towns from the Urals to the Pacific as early as February 1918, with serious resistance being encountered only at Irkutsk.[5] Some western accounts have since argued that this was more than a superficial seizure of power and that the Soviet régime, centred on the Central Executive Committee of Siberian Soviets (*Tsentrosibir'*) at Irkutsk, was actually on the way to consolidating itself during the spring before being unexpectedly interrupted in its work by the revolt of the Czechoslovak Legion.[6] Whatever its potential, however, Soviet power in Siberia during early 1918 did not really progress beyond the rudimentary. In the vast, primitive expanses east of the Urals it was difficult for the writ of any régime to run far beyond city limits and the narrow, developed ribbon of the railway – let alone a régime dominated by a party which had gained, as had the Bolsheviks in the elections of November 1917 to the Constituent Assembly, only 10% of the regional vote. There were, after all, relatively few workers in Siberia to form a natural constituency for Lenin's party and only a small intelligentsia. The overwhelming majority (some 90%) of the population were peasants, but of a relatively prosperous and independent kind, not in thrall to large landowners and, consequently, not attracted to the land

4 Krakovetskii, A. in *Sibirskii ogni* (Novonikolaevsk), No. 1 (1922), p. 189.

5 Maksakov, V.V. and Turunov, A.N. (eds.) *Khronika grazhdanskoi voiny v Sibiri*. Moscow–Leningrad (1926), pp. 49–60. The 2nd All-Siberian Congress of Soviets, at Irkutsk, proclaimed the triumph of Soviet power throughout Siberia on February 23rd 1918.

6 Snow, R.E. *The Bolsheviks in Siberia, 1917–1918*. London (1977), p. 222; Berk, S.M. 'The *Coup d'État* of Admiral Kolchak and the Counter-Revolution in Siberia and East Russia, 1917–1918'. Columbia University PhD Thesis (1971), pp. 122–3, 479. On *Tsentrosibir'* see Riabikov, V.V. (ed.) *Tsentrosibir'*. Moscow (1949); and Agalakov, V.T. 'Tsentrosibir'', *Voprosy istorii Sibiri* (Tomsk), No. 4 (1969), pp. 133–47. See also below, Chapter 4, note 43.

redistribution policy which had served the Bolshevik party so well in land-hungry European Russia. They did, however, display a marked inclination for socialist politics, and in the Constituent Assembly poll this progressive yeoman class had formed the basis of an overwhelming victory for the SRs in Siberia, with the party securing no less than 85% of the votes cast in Tomsk *guberniia* and in the Altai, 65% in Enisei *guberniia* and 55% in Irkutsk *guberniia* (compared to a 37.3% SR share of the national vote).[7]

Stoical village indifference to the distant and predominantly urban political contests of the time might yet have been a factor enabling the Bolsheviks to maintain a grip on, for them, such barren soil. For, as one observer put it, from the point of view of the isolated settlements of rural Siberia, 'the replacement of one kind of socialism by another was a kind of parlour game, incomprehensible to the sturdy peasant mind.'[8] Any hope of such quiescence was dashed, however, when the food crisis of urban Russia during the spring of 1918 demanded a solution which only the countryside could provide – and of the 500,000 tons of grain requisitioned nationally by Sovnarkom to feed its hungry towns no less than 80% was collected, much of it by force, in Western Siberia.[9] Although little of what was collected was actually removed from Siberia, resentment of this remorseless grain gathering campaign was to cost the Bolsheviks dear in the east. When the Czechoslovak Legion struck in late May, seizing every Siberian and mid-Volga town in a matter of weeks, few indeed were those of the local population who sprang to the party's aid. The only real resistance Soviet power could muster came, firstly, in the form of some 'Internationalist' detachments of predominantly Magyar POWs (fired as much, one suspects, by a taste of freedom and a longstanding national animosity towards the Czechoslovaks as by Marxist ideology) and, secondly, along some weak fronts at Irkutsk and in Transbaikalia where (at the expense of security in Western Siberia) *Tsentrosibir'* had been concentrating the meagre Red Guard forces at its disposal against an earlier Cossack rising. Even these efforts, however, were

7 Radkey, O.H. *Russia Goes to the Polls: The Election to the All-Russian Constituent Assembly, 1917*. Ithaca (1989), pp. 150–1.

8 Guins [Gins], G.K. *Sibir', soiuzniki i Kolchak: povorotnyi moment russkoi istorii, 1918–1920gg.* Peking (1921), Vol. 1, p. 48.

9 Berk, p. 111.

subdued by the Legion in July. Meanwhile, the forces of what is generally termed the 'democratic counter-revolution' began to establish themselves.[10]

In the wake of the Czechoslovaks' action, from a diverse underground network of counter-revolutionary and SR organizations, which the hard-pressed Soviet authorities had had neither the strength nor the time to neutralize, there quickly emerged to claim suzerainty over this or that patch of territory between the Volga and the Pacific, a bewildering array of rival anti-Bolshevik 'governments' in Siberia – nineteen of them according to one count.[11] However, to understand the nature of these variform authorities – and, in particular, to appreciate their susceptibility to the right-wing pressure which was to be exerted on them during the summer of 1918 – it is necessary to trace their genesis back to a period before Soviet power had gained even its first foothold in the region.

The kindling of the democratic counter-revolution east of the Urals was complicated by its stirring of the dying embers of the Siberian autonomous movement (*oblastnichestvo*). Since the third quarter of the nineteenth century Siberian regionalists (*oblastniki*), led by M.N. Iadrintsev and, more latterly, by the eminent ethnographer and folklorist G.N. Potanin, had been labouring to have the central Russian authorities grant a limited degree of self-government to their region. Initially concerned with having the 'Great Reforms' of the 1860s extended to the east, with the establishment of a university at Tomsk and with putting an end to Russia's crude exploitation of Siberia as a colony (both economically and as a dumping ground for political and social undesirables), after 1905 the programme of the *oblastniki* had been broadened to encompass calls for the local control of important regional concerns (including justice, land rights, education, immigration and trade) through a representative assembly, the Siberian Regional (*oblast'*) Duma (*Sibobduma*).

10 Maksakov and Turunov (1926), pp. 66–87; Vegman, V. 'Kak i pochemu pala v 1918 godu Sovetskaia vlast' v Tomske', *Sibirskie ogni* (Novonikolaevsk), Nos. 1–2 (1923), pp. 132–6. On the Transbaikal fronts of 1918 see Kutskii, G.S. 'Grodekovskie i Zabaikal'skie fronty vesnoi i letom 1918g.', in *Trudy Dal'nevostochnogo filiala Sib. otdel. AN SSSR (seriia ist.)*, Vol. 5 (1963), pp. 11–22. On the Internationalist detachments in Siberia see: Girchenko, V. *Revoliutsionnaia deiatel'nost' innostrannykh internatsionalistov voennoplennykh v vostochnoi Sibirii*. Verkhneudinsk (1933); Okladnikov, A.P. (ed.) *Vengerskie internatsionalisty v Sibiri i na Dal'nem Vostoke, 1917–1922*. Moscow (1980), pp. 11–90; Manusevich, A. Ia. (ed.) *Internatsionalisty*. Moscow (1987), pp. 256–76; *Vengerskie internatsionalisty v Oktiabr'skoi revoliutsii i grazhdanskom voine v SSSR: sbornik dokumentov*. Moscow (1980), Vol. 1, pp. 139–50.

11 White, J.A. *The Siberian Intervention*. New York (1950), p. 95.

Unlike Russia's liberals, however, the experience of the 1905 revolution did not convince the *oblastniki* of the merits of party-political organization. Although regionalists elected to the 2nd and 3rd State Dumas tended to associate themselves with the right wing of the PSR and the left wing of the liberal Constitutional Democratic Party (Kadets), as a whole the movement attempted to distance itself from the class-based divisions of Russian politics and would accept only the loosest of discipline and association as the Siberian Regionalist Union.

Potanin thereby avoided (*pace* the claims of doctrinaire Soviet authors) becoming slave to bourgeois class interests – certainly to a greater extent than did the Kadets, who, like the *oblastniki*, aspired to 'being above class issues' (*nadklassnost'*). His movement was genuinely populistic in its approach. That, however, did not prevent *oblastnichestvo*'s appeal being limited from the very beginning: firstly, predicated as it was on territorial-economic interests alone, rather than on any truly separate cultural and ethnic bonds distinguishing the people who occupied the territory, it obviously lacked the élan and the sentimental appeal of a national movement; secondly, unlike other groups of comparable colonial malcontents (in eighteenth-century British North America, for example), the movement was susceptible to constant pressure from the mother country along a contiguous land border; thirdly, the very size and diversity of Siberia, together with its underdeveloped communications, made it difficult to fashion a homogeneous regionalism east of the Urals. Moreover, after the turn of the century, as millions of Russian peasant and working class immigrants, knowing nothing and caring less about the *oblastniki*, poured into Siberia along the newly completed Trans-Siberian Railway, regionalist idealism seemed increasingly anachronistic: 'Its aims were understood only by small groups of the Siberian intelligentsia. It had no active propagation among the masses of the population', recalled one *oblastnik*, the geographer I.I. Serebrennikov. It was, rather, the standard Social Democratic and (in particular) Socialist Revolutionary politics of Russia which came to dominate the Siberian opposition to tsarism before the war – the former antagonistic to regionalism as a diversion from the class struggle; the latter theoretically committed to federalism, but fully absorbed by more urgent, all-Russian affairs. Consequently, recalled Serebrennikov, 'the Russian revolution of [February] 1917 found the Siberian regionalists unprepared'.[12]

12 Serebrennikov, I.I. 'The Siberian Autonomous Movement and its Future', *Pacific Historical Review* Vol. 3 (1934), Pt.3, pp. 400–6. The basic text of Siberian regionalism is Iadrintsev, N.M. *Sibir' kak koloniia v geograficheskom, etnograficheskom i istoricheskom otnoshenii*. St Petersburg

In 1917, however, the loose grip of Kerensky's Provisional Government on the Russian periphery did permit the *oblastniki* a window of opportunity and, from August 2nd to 9th at Tomsk, under the chairmanship of the by then aged and ailing Potanin, there was convened a 1st Siberian Regional Conference. This, for the first time, ran up the green and white Siberian flag (symbolic of forests and snow), proclaimed the slogan 'Long Live an Autonomous Siberia!' and summoned delegates to a full congress to prepare for the convocation of the long awaited *Sibobduma*. Straight away, however, the *oblastniki*'s narrow base of support was apparent – the overwhelming majority of the sixty-seven delegates to the August conference were of the professional classes (most were academics) and only three were peasants; there were no representatives of Siberia's small but highly concentrated working class.[13] Very little had changed in this respect by the time that the 1st All-Siberian Regional Congress duly met at Tomsk on October 8th to 15th to draft a constitution for an autonomous Siberia (placing legislative power in the *Sibobduma* and executive power in a Council of Ministers responsible to it, subject to the verification of the anticipated All-Russian Constituent Assembly). In fact, when a subsequent Extraordinary Regional Congress met from December 6th to 15th, again at Tomsk, it became apparent that *oblastnichestvo* was having difficulty in retaining its identity in the revolutionary turmoil. The Extraordinary Congress was convened, in the wake of the Bolshevik seizure of power in Petrograd, in order to elect a Provisional Regional Council to guide Siberia through the current crisis (by insisting on the observance only of laws passed prior to October 24th to 25th) and to prepare for the emergency convocation of *Sibobduma* – not now

(1882). On the development of regionalism in Siberia down to and including 1917 see: Watrous, S.D. 'Russia's "Land of the Future": Regionalism and the Awakening of Siberia, 1819–1894'. University of Washington PhD Thesis (1970); Watrous, S. 'The Regionalist Conception of Siberia, 1860–1920', in Diment, G. and Slezkine, Y. (eds.) *Between Heaven and Hell: The Myth of Siberia in Russian Culture*. London (1993), pp. 134–51; Faust, W. *Russlands goldener Boden: Der sibirische Regionalismus in der zweiten Halfte des 19. Jahrhunderts*. Cologne (1980); Mohrenschildt, D. von *Towards a United States of Russia: Plans and Projects of Federal Reconstruction of Russia in the Nineteenth Century*. London (1982), pp. 85–130; Krusser, G.V. *Sibirskie oblastniki (ot 1864g. do epokhi Kolchaka)*. Novosibirsk (1931); Sesiunina, M.G. *G.N. Potanin i N.M. Iadrintsev – ideologi sibirskogo oblastnichestva*. Tomsk (1974); Razgon, I.M. and Plotnikova, M.E. 'G.N. Potanin v gody sotsialisticheskoi revoliutsii i grazhdanskoi voiny v Sibiri', *Voprosy istorii Sibiri (Trudy TGU, seriia istoricheskaia)* (Tomsk), Vol. 158 (1965), pp. 138–53.

13 Pereira, N.G.O. 'Regional Consciousness in Siberia Before and After October 1917', *Canadian Slavonic Papers*, No. 1 (1988), pp. 6–7; Vegman, V. 'Oblastnicheskie illiuzii rasseianie revoliutsii (k istorii vozniknovenii Sibirskoi Oblastnoi Dumy)', *Sibirskie ogni* (Novonikolaevsk), No. 3 (1923), pp. 92–6.

through popular elections but from delegates selected by local zemstvos, municipal dumas and other democratic organizations. However, to Potanin and his circle's consternation, an absolute majority of delegates to both the October and December congresses were Socialists-Revolutionaries – that party accounting for 87 of the 169 present at the former meeting and 92 of the 155 at the latter – many of them not even having been born in Siberia.[14] This was a deliberate tactic of the SRs, who, as Serebrennikov recalled with chagrin:

> having lost their former great influence upon the masses in European Russia, where Bolshevism was now predominant, hoped to use their influential position in the Siberian autonomous movement in the interests of their own party.[15]

The true, non-party *oblastniki*, who aspired to a movement above class interests, found themselves swamped by the SRs' superior organizational skills and political acumen. Consequently, only eight of Potanin's disciples found their way into the October congress and two into that of December (according to archival sources cited by a Soviet account).[16] Potanin was still to be elected Chairman of the Provisional Siberian Regional Council (which, incidentally, being subdivided in several departments, might properly be regarded as the first Siberian government of the civil war). However, it was clear that the SRs were using him as a figurehead; and when the other six members of the Regional Council insisted that the *Sibobduma* would welcome representatives only of socialist parties ('from the Popular Socialists to the Bolsheviks inclusive', as the rubric ran) and would exclude those of the 'propertied' (*tsenzovyi*) classes, the doyen of regionalism resigned the chairmanship. In an open letter of January 12th 1918, Potanin announced that he was depriving the embryonic Siberian régime of his prestigious services, protested at the SRs' 'Bolshevik inclinations', and accused them of 'playing with Soviets'.[17]

14 *ibid.*, p. 100; Serebrennikov (1934), pp. 407–9; Razgon and Plotnikova, pp. 142–3; Razgon, I.M. and Goriushchkin, L.M. (eds.) *Oktiabr' v Sibiri: khronika sobytii.* Novosibirsk (1987), p. 208; Berk, pp. 135–48.

15 Serebrennikov, p. 408.

16 Shidlovskii, M.V. 'Sibirskoe oblastnichestvo i kontrrevoliutsiia: k probleme vziamootnosheniia', in Korablev, Iu.V. and Shishkin, B.I. *Iz istorii interventsii i grazhdanskoi voiny v Sibiri i na Dal'nem Vostoke, 1917–1922gg.* Novosibirsk (1985), pp. 170–1.

17 *Sibirskaia zhizn'* (Tomsk) No. 8, 12.i.1918; Guins (1921), Vol. 1, pp. 73–4.

As *Sibobduma* delegates duly gathered at Tomsk during January 1918, it was to become apparent that, to an extent, Potanin's fears of a PSR usurpation of Siberian regionalism, complete with that party's commitment to radical land reform, were exaggerated – many who called themselves 'SRs' did so merely as a hangover from the confused days of 1917 (when the name had come to connote little more than a general support of the Provisional Government). In fact, many of these 'SRs' anathematized Chernov and held views rather more conservative than did Potanin himself.[18] Among them were men later to become stalwarts of the Kolchak régime – Ivan Mikhailov, Vologodskii, Gattenberger and the afore-mentioned Serebrennikov, for example. Nevertheless, at the very moment of the realization of its long-cherished dream, the convocation of the *Sibobduma*, *oblastnichestvo* as an alternative focus of political activity lost its coherence and was deprived of its organizational apex, as a resentful Potanin drifted rapidly towards the right over the following year. In the *oblastnik* newspaper *Sibirskaia zhizn'* (later to serve as a mouthpiece of Kolchak's Ministry of the Interior) he was constantly castigating the PSR, which he regarded as having abducted his movement for use as a device of merely 'agitational significance' and whose 'rural Bolshevism' he contemned as having nothing to offer landlordless Siberia; he derided Siberian democracy and its intelligentsia as 'too immature' even for autonomy; and by the summer of 1918 was to come out in favour of a 'firm authority' (*tverdaia vlast'*) to 'restore order' as a counter to Bolshevism.[19] Thus, the *oblastnik* elder was to provide the new wave of political refugees soon to arrive in the region – intent (in the wake of the Bolsheviks' signing of the Brest-Litovsk Treaty) upon the establishment of a centralist, Great-Russianist dictatorship – with a ready (and still influential) conduit for disseminating the view that the *Sibobduma* was illegal, illegitimate, ill-conceived and not truly representative of Siberian society.

The *Sibobduma*'s convocation was postponed from January 6th 1918 until the 26th, by which time ninety-three delegates had arrived at Tomsk. Although no details are available, one contemporary report has it that the assemblage was 'almost

18 *Soiuznicheskaia interventsiia na Dal'nem Vostoke i v Sibiri. Doklad Pichona*. Moscow–Leningrad (1925), p. 44.

19 Razgon and Plotnikova, pp. 145–50; *Sibirskii vestnik* (Omsk) No. 53, 26.ix.1918. Having continued, his waning health permitting, to urge the Siberian peasantry to join the White armies throughout 1919 – see, for example, his contributions to *Sibirskaia zhizn'* (Tomsk) No. 176, 22.viii.1919 and No. 187, 5.ix.1919 – Potanin died at Tomsk on June 6th 1920.

exclusively SR'.[20] The duma did not formally convene, however, for during the night of January 25th–26th local Red Guard units, emboldened by Lenin's dispersal of the Constituent Assembly at Petrograd of January 6th, somewhat belatedly stirred themselves to oust this regionalist cuckoo in the nest of Soviet power (which had been proclaimed at Tomsk as early as December 8th). Many delegates fled from the armed Bolshevik patrols sent to hunt them out, but some eighteen were arrested.[21] Another forty or so, meanwhile, managed to secrete themselves at the offices of the Tomsk *uezd* Supply Board where, during the night of January 27th–28th, 'in an atmosphere of tense nervousness', recalled one who was present, they elected what was to become known as the Provisional Government of Autonomous Siberia (PGAS) under the premiership of a veteran SR, Petr Iakovlevich Derber. Some fourteen 'ministers' and six other officials were selected, but, according to our witness, Serebrennikov, 'they were not carefully chosen and about half of them were elected in their absence and without their previous knowledge'. Care was taken, however, in an attempt to heal the rift with Potanin, to include not only PSR loyalists but also figures of a more moderate and authentically regionalist hue.[22] This was a gesture which, as will become clear, was to have profound repercussions in Siberia during the summer of 1918 – not least because, pausing only to draw up inaugural proclamations (declaring war on the Soviet government and vowing to work for a 'free, Autonomous Siberian Republic'), on January 29th Derber and those ministers who were both closest to him politically and at liberty from the Bolsheviks, fled to the Far East (from where it was hoped that the Allies might soon launch an intervention against the Soviet régime). There the Derber government was to drag out, on the railway sidings of first Harbin and then Vladivostok, a desultory, semi-official existence which, as a result of the prolonged Red Guard grip on Irkutsk and Transbaikalia, was to leave it totally isolated from the Siberian anti-Bolshevik

20 Piontkovskii, S. (ed.) 'Kontrrevoliutsiia v Sibiri: doklad podpolkovnika Glukhareva', *Krasnaia letopis'* (Petrograd) No. 5, 1923, p. 359.

21 Vegman 'Kak i pochemu pala', pp. 129–30; *Bor'ba za vlast' sovetov v Tomskoi gubernii*. Tomsk (1959), p. 218; *Sovety Tomskoi gubernii (mart 1917–mai 1918gg.): sbornik dokumentov i materialov*. Tomsk (1976), pp. 122–3.

22 Serebrennikov, p. 410; Vegman, V. 'Sibirskie kontrrevoliutsionnye organizatsii 1918g.', *Sibirskie ogni* (Novosibirsk), No. 1 (1928), p. 135.

rising of the spring.[23] Meanwhile the less radical members of the PGAS remained behind in Western Siberia to organize and greet that rising.

The Provisional Siberian Regional Council of December 1917 had recognized, *ab initio*, the desirability of founding a volunteer force to defend the *Sibobduma*. The Soviet authorities' temporary predominance in Western Siberia, however, had precluded local recruitment, so a *Siboduma* envoy (the SR-*oblastnik*, Colonel A.A. Krakovetskii) had been sent to far-off Kiev to negotiate with the Ukrainian nationalist Rada, and then to Jassy to meet the Commander-in-Chief of the South West Front, General Shcherbachev. From both Krakovetskii received a favourable response to his petitions for the return east of the Siberian regiments who were at that point still serving at the front. When the Bolsheviks' December push into the Ukraine foiled that plan, however, Krakovetskii returned to Tomsk. There he was made Minister of War in the PGAS, and was left behind by Derber to organize a secret force from SR soldiers and sympathetic fugitive officers known to be resident in the Siberian garrison towns. Also left behind, with instructions from Derber to co-ordinate the political and military preparations for a rising against the Bolsheviks, was a clandestine rump of the PGAS, dubbed the Western Siberian Commissariat (WSC). It consisted of four SRs (P.Ia. Mikhailov, B.D. Markov, M.E. Lindberg and V.O. Sidorov) and was formally convened at Novonikolaevsk on February 14th.[24]

Initially results were disappointing. Too few *bona fide* SR or regionalist sympathizers were forthcoming to create a meaningful force, while officers fleeing east from the October revolution were chary of serving the representatives of the very party whose lassitude they held to be responsible for the Bolsheviks' October success. As one officer put it: 'The SRs were singing that very same tune which in

23 Maksakov and Turunov, pp. 57–8, 143–4, 149–53; Maksakov, V.V. (ed.) 'Vremennoe pravitel'stvo avtomnoi Sibiri', *Krasnyi arkhiv* (Moscow), No. 4 (1928), pp. 86–138; No. 4 (1929), pp. 37–106; and No. 5 (1929), pp. 31–60; Nazimok, V.N. 'K istorii kak nazyvaemogo "Vremennogo pravitel'stva avtomnoi Sibiri"', *Voprosy istorii Sibiri* (Tomsk), Vol. 205 (1969); Livshits, S.G. 'Krakh Vremennogo pravitel'stva avtomnoi Sibiri', *Voprosy istorii*, No. 8 (1974); Livshits, S.G. 'Vneshnepoliticheskii kurs pravitel'stva avtomnoi Sibiri', in *Voprosy novoi i noveishei istorii*. Barnaul (1974), pp. 3–38.

24 On the first efforts at military organization in the anti-Bolshevik underground in Siberia see: Iakushev, I.A. 'Ocherki oblastnicheskogo dvizheniia v Sibiri', *Vol'naia Sibir'* (Prague), No. 4 (1928), pp. 100–3; Razgon and Goriushchkin, p. 208; Maksakov and Turunov, pp. 60–1; Belousov, G.M. 'Eserovskoe vooruzhennoe podpol'e v Sibiri (1918g.)', in *Sibirskii istoricheskii sbornik*. Irkutsk (1974), Vol. 2, pp. 129–30. On the WSC in general see Livshits, S.G. 'K istorii Zapadno-sibirskogo komissariata', *Uchennye zapiski Barnaulskogo gos. ped. inst.*. Barnaul (1974).

1917 had unavoidably dragged down Kerensky; they were pursuing an out-and-out party-political programme above the interests of the state.'[25] As the weeks went by, however, shared indignation at news of the Brest-Litovsk negotiations seems to have defined some common ground and engendered a degree of readiness to compromise on both sides: thus, as Trotsky and Ludendorff parleyed on the Polish border, into the WSC orbit was drawn a nucleus of officer recruits willing to don green and white cockades and accept the minimum SR-*oblastnik* programme of loyalty to the Constituent Assembly, the provisional authority of the *Sibobduma* and the introduction of some democratic principles into the army to replace the strict tsarist disciplinary code. Noteworthy among them was one Colonel G.N. Grishin-Almazov, who was made Chief of Staff to the WSC.[26] Meanwhile Krakovetskii departed in March on a tour of Siberia and the Far East, establishing a subordinate Eastern Siberian Commissariat and outposts of supporters throughout the region on the basis of the 'group of five' (*piaterok*) beloved of Russian conspirators. He also encouraged SR sympathizers to enter the Soviet institutions and the Red Guard as fifth-columnists, which they did with a degree of success at Tomsk, Irkutsk and elsewhere.[27]

This burgeoning underground network was largely financed by contributions from Siberia's influential co-operative movement, which had been as thoroughly permeated by the SRs as had Siberian regionalism. Indeed, the WSC had chosen to base itself at Novonikolaevsk precisely because it was the headquarters of the giant 'Zakupsbyt' co-operative, two directors of which (N.V. Fomin and A.V. Sazonov) were soon seconded to Grishin-Almazov's staff.[28] Rather less generous with funds were Siberia's Trade and Industry groups, who remained suspicious of the WSC's

25 Filat'ev, D.B. *Katastrofa belogo dvizheniia v Sibiri, 1918–1922 (vpechatleniia ochevidtsa).* Paris (1985), p. 35.

26 Dotsenko, P. *The Struggle for a Democracy in Siberia: An Eye-witness Account of a Contemporary.* Stanford (1983), p. 36; Belousov, pp. 136–7.

27 Belousov (*ibid.*, p. 147) calculates that over thirty Siberian towns housed anti-Bolshevik underground cells by May 1918; Vegman ('Sibirskie kontrrevoliutsionnye organizatsii', pp. 136–7) lists the key organizers as Colonel A.N. Pepeliaev at Tomsk, Colonel Elerts-Usov at Irkutsk and Colonel Rakitin at Barnaul. Notable infiltrators of the Soviet authorities included V.A. Shchepachev (Head of Militia at Irkutsk), and Merkulov (Head of Militia at Tomsk) – see Belousov, p. 148; Vegman 'Kak i pochemu pala', p. 132.

28 Vladimirova, V.F. *God sluzhby 'sotsialistov' kapitalistami.* Moscow–Leningrad (1927), p. 347; Gukhovskii, A. (ed.) 'K istorii iaskogo soveshchaniia', *Krasnyi arkhiv* (Moscow), No. 5 (1926), p. 111; Morozov, K. 'How Siberia was Liberated from the Bolsheviks', *Struggling Russia* (New York), Vol. 1, No. 22 (August 1919), pp. 355–6.

socialist and regionalist leanings. Rather, in so far as business circles were funding nascent anti-Bolshevik organizations, they tended to be those of a more authoritarian persuasion, who had resisted SR attempts to corral them. For example, in the Cossack *stanitsy* (settlements) of Atamansk, Pavlodar and Sherapovsk around Omsk, there was active the so-called 'Group of Thirteen', an avowedly monarchistic organization, which united figures who were later to emerge as among the most bloodthirsty satraps of the White movement in Siberia: Ataman B. Annenkov, Major (later Ataman) P.P. Ivanov-Rinov and Colonel V.I. Volkov.[29] Although they were willing to pay lip-service to the WSC, it transpired that such groups, existing on such funds as business could channel to them, were merely awaiting strong political leadership from the right before displaying their true reactionary colours.

The focus of the 'Group of Thirteen' on Omsk was no more accidental than was the SR-*oblastnik* blossoming around Tomsk University and the major co-operative headquarters at Novonikolaevsk. Omsk was a town of markedly conservative repute. It was the capital of the Siberian Cossack *voisko* (host) and a stronghold of Siberian business and trading circles. Yet, belying such local affiliation and in distinct contrast to the regionalist traditions of Tomsk, as the administrative centre of Akmolinsk *oblast'* and the headquarters of the Trans-Siberian Railway, Omsk was also a recognizable outpost of the centralist Petersburg system. With its predominance of one-storey wooden buildings clustered on the banks of the Irtysh, this rather dismal settlement struck pre-war visitors as somewhat 'artificial'. It was a 'dull and depressing place', they found, still betraying its heritage as the 'overgrown village' so vividly depicted more than half a century earlier by the exiled Dostoevsky (in *House of the Dead*), despite the addition of some imposing stone structures in its centre. Even the official guide to the Trans-Siberian Railway of 1900 had found little to recommend the town, warning the unwary traveller of 'the monstrous architecture, the unpaved streets and the wooden side walks, the absence of vegetation which perishes on the saline soil'; while Ivan Maiskii, who was raised there as a child, recalled Omsk as 'tedious and boring...covered in snow in winter, choking with dust in summer, and shrouded in an impenetrable mist in both autumn and winter.' Yet newcomers found it more comfortingly Russian and less Siberian

29 Dotsenko, P. *The Struggle for the Liberation of Siberia, 1918–1921* (An Interview Conducted by R.A. Pierce). Berkeley (1960), p. 33; *Belaia Rossiia* (Al'bom No. 1). New York (1937), pp. 54–5; Vegman 'Sibirskie kontrrevoliutsionnye organizatsii', p. 137.

than the towns further east. After the revolution such an impression of Omsk's foreignness within Siberia was strongly reinforced as, being (unlike Tomsk) sited on the Trans-Siberian mainline, it attracted the first waves of bourgeois refugees from central Russia; or perhaps it was precisely because Omsk was, welcomely, not too different to home, that the refugees broke their journey there, in the hope of an early return to their bases west of the Urals.[30]

The WSC underground, therefore, was divided from the very beginning – both geographically and politically – between its predominantly SR political leadership, which retained a degree of regionalist sympathy, and its unaffiliated but distinctly more rightist military wing, in which but few cared for the principles of *oblastnichestvo* (particularly as new cohorts of refugee officers arrived from European Russia in the spring). As one SR-*oblastnik* organizer recognized: 'It was urgently necessary to carry on educational work among the soldiers who came to us to join...for we knew that if we could not control and direct them they would engulf us.'[31] Nevertheless, when General Flug and Colonel Glukharev, emissaries of Kornilov's Volunteer Army (then based in the Kuban), arrived in Western Siberia during March to survey the prospects east of the Urals for an anti-Bolshevik rising akin to their own, they emerged relatively optimistic from meetings with the WSC and its rivals. General Flug reported to his commander that some 7,000 to 8,000 anti-Bolshevik officers were in contact with each other across Siberia (including 3,000 at Omsk, 1,500 at Tomsk and 1,000 at Irkutsk). He recognized that many were not socialists and had fallen under nominal WSC command 'by accident', but predicted that fruitful co-operation was possible. And indeed, in the wake of General Flug's tour of the region, in a spirit of compromise which was not reciprocated, the WSC accepted the replacement of their SR commissars in some areas by more experienced, but less politically reliable, officers.[32]

30 Dmitriev-Mamontov, A.J. and Zdziarskii, A.F. *Guide to the Great Siberian Railway (1900)*. Newton Abbot (1971), p. 193; Maiskii, pp. 294–5; Yurlova, M. *Cossack Girl*. London (1934), p. 128; Fraser, J.F. *The Real Siberia*. London (1902), p. 34; Wright, R.L. and Digby, B. *Through Siberia*. New York (1913), p. 9. Bernard Pares found Omsk to have 'nothing in common with the rest of Siberia' because of its refugee population and 'the dominance of a military atmosphere'. 'Report on Political Conditions in Siberia, 20.vi.1919' (*Pares Papers*, Box 41).

31 Dotsenko, *The Struggle for the Liberation*, p. 30.

32 Flug, V.S. 'Otchet o komandirovke iz Dobrovol′cheskoi armii v Sibiri', *Arkhiv russkoi revoliutsii* (Berlin), Vol. 9 (1923), pp. 253–64; Iakushev, pp. 103–4; Dotsenko *The Struggle for the Liberation*, p. 34.

Finances, however, remained critically short in the anti-Bolshevik underground and unity remained superficial. Grishin-Almazov later spoke of constant squabbling between SRs and officers over funds, over precisely what form of government should replace the Soviets should a rising be successful and of 'the absolute impossibility of finding a political banner on which all could agree'.[33] Consequently, attempts at risings against the Bolsheviks in the period down to May 1918 were an unmitigated failure. In Blagoveshchensk, for example, workers and peasants organized to thwart the attempt of Ataman Gamov to arrest their soviet in February; similar attempts were foiled at Barnaul and Semipalatinsk in the Altai. Meanwhile the Red Guard drove Ataman Dutov's rebellious Orenburg Cossacks from the town of Orenburg in January and pushed them back into the desert steppe (achieving a notable victory over Dutov at Verkhne-Ural'sk on April 28th); and attacks launched upon Omsk by Annenkov's Cossacks were twice beaten off in February. Finally, at Tomsk in May, a planned rising was detected in advance by Red Guards and was liquidated.[34] As officers themselves had informed Flug in March, and as a WSC staff conference had concluded in May, what the anti-Bolshevik underground in Siberia clearly lacked was the injection of financial and military support from the Allies.[35]

The revolt of the Czechoslovak Legion and the Provisional Siberian Government

At the end of May 1918 this crucial external stimulus to anti-Bolshevism in Siberia was provided by the revolt of the Czechoslovak Legion. Under the military command of General Jan Syrovy and the political leadership of Boris Pavlu, this migrant force – created at Masaryk's behest in 1917 of Czech and Slovak deserters from the Austro-Hungarian Army (who had refused to fight their brother Slavs), and

33 Gukhovskii, pp. 111–12.

34 On Dutov's revolt see *Belaia Rossiia (Al'bom No. 1)*, pp. 36–8 and Podshivalov, I. *Grazhdanskaia bor'ba na Urale, 1917–1918gg.* Moscow (1925), pp. 111–22. On events at Tomsk see Vegman 'Kak i pochemu pala', p. 136; and Vegman 'Sibirskie kontrrevoliutsionnye organizatsi', p. 141. On events at Omsk see Razgon and Goriushchkin, p. 248.

35 Flug, pp. 251, 253; Iakushev, p. 104.

of their compatriots who had been living in Russia since before the Great War – had in early 1918 obtained the permission of the Soviet government to leave Russia, via Vladivostok, to join the Allied armies on the Western Front. By the spring of that year, bolstered by new recruits either anxious to quit revolutionary Russia or keen to avail themselves of a chance to fight for a national homeland, the Legion was some 38,000 strong and was strung out along the Trans-Siberian Railway in three army groups.

Throughout May, however, there developed among the Czechoslovaks a dangerous mixture of frustration at the western powers' delays in providing for their evacuation and fear that repeated Bolshevik attempts to disarm them in the weeks after the signing of the Brest-Litovsk treaty might evince a secret commitment to betray the Legion to the Germans its members had deserted. Into this combustible cocktail of emotions was tossed a match at Cheliabinsk on May 25th when eastbound Czechs clashed, with mortal issue, with the westbound repatriation of soldiers of their former Austrian and Magyar oppressors (being released by the Bolsheviks, post-Brest, from Siberian concentration camps). A minor skirmish at the station flared-up into a full scale revolt when the local Soviet attempted to intercede; the angry Legionnaires seized the town on the 26th, urged their compatriots along the line to do likewise, and within a couple of weeks had toppled the Soviet authorities throughout western Siberia. Irkutsk and eastern Siberia soon followed suit and on June 29th Czechoslovak units captured the port of Vladivostok. Finding no means there for their evacuation from the Far East and encouraged by intimations from Europe that they were soon to be joined in Russia by Allied contingents for the establishment of a new front against the Germans (who were, post-Brest, advancing through the Ukraine), the Legionnaires were then to concentrate their efforts anew in the west, building a front on the Volga – initially against their embittered Bolshevik pursuers and, potentially, against the Kaiser.[36]

The extent to which the revolt of the Czechoslovak Legion was a spontaneous rebellion of mistreated, frightened evacuees, the extent to which it was a result of

[36] On the Czechoslovak rising and its historiography see Fic, V.M. *The Bolsheviks and the Czechoslovak Legion: the Origin of their Armed Conflict (March–May 1919)*. New Delhi (1978); Bradley, J.F.N. 'The Czechoslovak Revolt against the Bolsheviks', *Soviet Studies* (Glasgow), Vol. 15 (1963–1964), pp. 124–51; Bradley, J.F.N. *The Czechoslovak Legion in Russia, 1914–1920*. New York (1991); Kettle, M. *The Road to Intervention (March–November 1918)*. London (1988), pp. 49–182; Medek, R. *The Czechoslovak Anabasis Across Russia and Siberia*. London (1929); Golochek, V. *Chekhoslovatskoe voisko v Rossii*. Irkutsk (1919).

official and unofficial machinations on the part of the western Allies and their agents seeking a *casus belli* for intervention in Russia against Germany (and her perceived Bolshevik partners), and the extent to which it signified the duping of the Czechoslovak soldiery, which was generally sympathetic to socialist politics, by its more right-wing and committedly anti-Bolshevik officers (notably the commander of the 2nd Division around Omsk and Novonikolaevsk, one Rudolf Gajda, of whom more later), is a matter which has occasioned no little conjecture and historical controversy among students of the Russian civil war.[37] Probably it was all of these things at once. The origins of the revolt, however, are a matter which need not overly distract us here. It will suffice merely to note that members of the disparate anti-Bolshevik underground organizations being fashioned in Siberia during the early spring of 1918 later admitted that they were in contact with Czechoslovak leaders (both locally, in Siberia, and in Moscow), that they were informed well in advance of the Cheliabinsk incident that the Legion might be encouraged by its officers to resort to force in order to gain control of the railway and, in the words of an SR activist, 'made their plans accordingly'.[38]

In tandem with the Czechoslovak rising the SR-officer-Cossack underground began to emerge into the open. At Tomsk, Omsk, Novonikolaevsk and Krasnoiarsk, all of which were captured by the end of the first week of June, they worked hand in hand with the Legion to disperse the Soviets; further west (at Penza, Syzran, Ufa and Zlatoust), although the evidence is contradictory, Russians seemed to have been less involved.[39] As early as June 1st, however, the WSC at Novonikolaevsk felt

37 A recent account (Kettle, pp. 75–6 and Chapter 3 *passim*), argues that the Allies were seeking to co-ordinate the Czechoslovak rising in Siberia with Boris Savinkov's action north of Moscow.

38 Dotsenko *The Struggle for a Democracy*, pp. 25–6. See also Belousov, pp. 140–2 and Gukhovskii, pp. 111–12. Syrovy's Head of Chancery confirmed that 'contacts with anti-Bolshevik groups' were made via co-operatives who were supplying food to the Legion. See Klevanskii, A.Kh. *Chekhoslovatskie internatsionalisty i prodanyi korpus*. Moscow (1965), p. 175.

39 Golovin, N.N. *Rossiiskaia kontr-revoliutsiia v 1917–1918gg. (Chast' IV: Osvobozhdenie Sibiri i obrazovanie 'Belago' voennago fronta Grazhdanskoi voiny)*. Paris–Tallinn (1937), Vol. 8, pp. 7–8 stresses the Russian participation, as does Dotsenko (*The Struggle for the Liberation*, p. 40). Soviet accounts emphasize the Czechoslovak involvement – see Vegman 'Kak i pochemu pala', pp. 140–4; Eikhe, G.Kh. *Oprokinutyi tyl*. Moscow (1966), pp. 14–23. It is of note that Ataman Dutov concluded that 'for our liberation we are wholly beholden to the Czechoslovaks' – see Ermolin, A.P. *Revoliutsiia i kazachestvo*. Moscow (1982), p. 113. The *oblastnik* leader Iakushev concurred: 'It is hard to say how soon the coup would have been made had our glorious friends the Czechoslovaks not come to our aid.' See *Istoriia Sibiri* Leningrad (1968), Vol. 4, p. 91. For a detailed account of the operations of the first White military formations at this time see Filimonov,

confident enough to proclaim its provisional regional authority in lieu of the convocation of the *Sibobduma* and to postulate the urgent convocation of a Siberian Constituent Assembly. A week later, following the capture of Omsk on June 7th, the WSC made the fateful decision to transfer its headquarters to that town.[40]

Almost immediately this new government at Omsk ran into problems in its attempt to establish an administration in Siberia – problems which were a legacy of the tsars' colonial governance of the region and which were to bedevil the anti-Bolsheviks' every attempt to establish a state apparatus in the east over the next eighteen months. At the heart of the SRs' dilemma was the dearth of reliable, educated men able to staff their administration. This was particularly the case outside of the main centres of population. But even at Omsk, recalled one SR:

> In building an administrative staff a major obstacle was met: the absence of personnel suitable for such assignments; as a consequence the positions became staffed with people who not only could not share our democratic philosophy, but, worse yet, were intolerant of the new government.[41]

In particular, the leftist WSC came quickly to rely for its personnel upon the members of the Omsk Military Industrial Committee, who were of a notably conservative-*oblastnik* inclination. Led by the educationalist V.V. Sapozhnikov, this was the seed from which later Siberian administrations were to grow. Within days it had fashioned itself into a Business Cabinet to 'assist' the WSC, but was soon to emerge as a rival source of authority, drawing its strength from the support of local officer groups who were themselves emboldened by the Czechoslovak revolt and less inclined than ever to kowtow to the SRs now that the Bolsheviks had been disposed of. In its published programme, for example, the WSC expressed a desire to keep some of the decrees of the Soviet government on the statute book, to maintain public control of industry where that would safeguard jobs and to tolerate the existence of workers' councils alongside resuscitated zemstvos and municipal dumas. The opposition of the Business Cabinet, however, made it impossible to

B.B. *Na putiakh k Urala; pokhod stepnykh polkov letom 1918g.* Shanghai (1934), pp. 25–150.

40 Guins, Vol. 1, pp. 86–7. For the WSC's declaration see Vegman, V. 'Sibobduma', *Sibirskie ogni* (Novonikolaevsk), No. 4 (1923), p. 92. On the capture of Omsk see Filimonov, *Na putiakh k Urala*.

41 Dotsenko, *The Struggle for the Liberation*, p. 103.

realize these aims. Meanwhile Grishin-Almazov turned on his erstwhile SR partners and insisted that, contrary to the wishes of the WSC (which had its own candidate), he should remain as commander-in-chief of the army then being organized. This force, the nascent Western Siberian Army (founded on June 13th), attracted officers who had never sworn loyalty to the WSC or *Sibobduma* – which was all the more dangerous because much of the WSC's original corps of supporters had been despatched to clear *Tsentrosibir'* from Irkutsk – and was soon engaged in the forcible dispersal of soviets, the return of all industrial enterprises to their former owners and the arrest and imprisonment of anyone who had served, however unwillingly, in the Soviet administration.[42] And where Omsk led the rest of Siberia soon followed. At Krasnoiarsk, for example, the WSC's accredited Commissar for Eniseisk *guberniia*, Paul (Pavel) Dotsenko, found himself completely ostracized by the emerging military, who, ominously, preferred to deal with the town's minuscule Kadet organization.[43]

Within a month the Business Cabinet had seized upon a chance to rid itself of the WSC and establish an executive authority less directly associated with the PSR. The opportunity arose because, while Derber's PGAS remained isolated and trapped in the Far East, as a result of the continued Red Guard hold on Transbaikalia, other members of the government elected at Tomsk in January, with weaker or non-existent socialist affinities, began to converge on Omsk: 'How convenient it was that there remained in the liberated territory those members of the Siberian Government who were most acceptable to broad circles', commented one close to the cabinet.[44]

Pre-eminent among these 'acceptables' was the liberal lawyer Peter Vasil'evich Vologodskii, President of the Omsk District Court, editor of the co-operative newspaper *Trudovaia Sibir'*, and one of Siberia's leading public men. The Business Cabinet began to entreat him to establish a new provisional government, one less parochial and, they claimed, less partisan, which could win the respect of the Allies as the intervention got underway (Japanese and British marines having disembarked at Vladivostok on April 5th–6th). Particularly active in the behind the scenes moves

42 Guins, Vol. 1, pp. 87–96. For the programme of the WSC see Piontkovskii, S. (ed.) *Grazhdanskaia voina v Rossii, 1919–1921gg.: khrestomatiia*. Moscow (1925), pp. 260–2. The Western Siberian Army consisted of 4,236 men and 219 officers by June 18th; by August (by which time it was known as the Siberian Army) it had grown to a total of 35,000, including 6,872 officers and 26,075 volunteers. See Eikhe, pp. 21–2, 139.

43 Dotsenko, *The Struggle for the Liberation*, pp. 46–52.

44 Guins, Vol. 1, pp. 102–3.

to oust the WSC was a young Siberian economist, Ivan Adrianovich Mikhailov. Although all were impressed by his energy, nobody seemed to know much about Mikhailov, apart from the fact that he was the prison-born son of a famous exiled populist (A.F. Mikhailova), had proclaimed himself an SR in 1917 (and served in various ministries of the Provisional Government as an assistant to A.I. Shingarev), had entered the Siberian Government at Tomsk in January touting himself as a moderate, non-party socialist and had served in the anti-Bolshevik underground at Novonikolaevsk. Soon, however, his conspiratorial activities, often directed against those with whom he had worked in the past, were to gain him notoriety across Russia as the 'Siberian Caesar Borgia' or '*Van'ka Kain*' (the Irrepressible Cain).[45] Upon his arrival at Omsk, Mikhailov managed to attract to himself an informal cabal of ministers and heads of departments – 'my group', he called it – to exert pressure on the government. This 'Mikhailov Group' remained in existence for the next year, until its eponym's political disgrace. It fought off any socialist involvement in the Omsk government and, for Soviet commentators on the period, was 'the embryo of the bourgeois-landowner counter-revolution' which, according to their historiography, was to culminate in the Omsk coup.[46]

At first Vologodskii resisted the petitions. He was not a healthy man and, at the age of fifty-five, felt himself to be too old to be forming governments. However, when (in a move he was very soon to regret) the SR Chairman of the *Sibobduma*, I.A. Iakushev, joined the call, Vologodskii succumbed. On June 30th a declaration was duly issued announcing the creation of a Provisional Siberian Government (PSG) with Vologodskii as its premier. At the head of the government was a Council of Ministers, initially numbering five: Vologodskii, Mikhailov, M.B. Shatilov (who had made his way from Derber's train in the Far East), V.M Krutovskii and G.B. Patushinskii. Later it was supplemented by the inclusion of Serebrennikov.[47] The party-political profile of this group is difficult to define – Soviet authors ventured labels ranging from 'Kadet-monarchist' to 'petit-bourgeois'

45 *ibid.*, Vol. 1, pp. 97, 111–12; Soloveichik, A. *Bor'ba za vozrozhdenie Rossii na Vostoke*. Rostov-on-Don (1919), p. 22.

46 Ioffe, G.Z. *Krakh rossiiskogo monarkhicheskoi kontrrevoliutsii*. Moscow (1977), p. 170.

47 *Sobranie uzakonenii i rasporiazhenii Vremennogo sibirskogo pravitel'stva* (Omsk), No. 1, 5.vii.1919, pp. 1–2; Vegman 'Oblastnicheskie illiuzii', p. 94.

(i.e. SR).[48] All (except Mikhailov) were sympathetic to Siberian regionalism and all had professed themselves to be socialists in 1917. By the summer of 1918, however, perhaps only Shatilov could still be characterized as retaining socialist sympathies, while Vologodskii and Serebrennikov, disillusioned by the experience of 1917, were clearly on the same track as their *oblastnik* mentor, Potanin, towards a tactical subordination of regionalism to an authoritarian and centralist counter to Bolshevism.

In this rightward process Mikhailov was far ahead of the field. In collaboration with leaders of the Siberian Army then being fashioned, on the basis of traditional military discipline, into a powerful and conservative force of nearly 40,000 around Omsk by the end of July (including almost 10,000 officers and many Siberian Cossacks), the anti-socialist and anti-regionalist machinations of *Van′ka Kain* and his group had soon provoked Shatilov, Krutovskii and Patushinskii into abandoning Omsk, thereby leaving the capital of anti-Bolshevik Siberia in the hands of the military. Subsequent to the SR-*oblastniki*'s retreat, in July and August Vologodskii and Mikhailov would decree the complete denationalization of industry in Siberia, end the government bread monopoly, raise taxes on necessities (spirits, matches, yeast, etc.) and demand the immediate payment of tax arrears. Moreover, the extent to which the government was coming to apply itself to matters of extra-regional concern was signalled when the PSG went so far as to order the return to landowners of all property seized by peasants during the revolution. In landlordless Siberia this was largely meaningless; but it was of huge symbolic importance for the officers and landowners from European Russia who were beginning to dominate political affairs at Omsk. Finally, when the government's policies gave rise to strikes among railway workers and the first ripples of what was to become a wave of peasant unrest in the Siberian countryside, the death penalty was re-introduced, reinforced by a system of so-called extraordinary 'field-courts' which pre-dated the February Revolution.[49]

48 See Plotnikova, M.E. 'Rol′ Vremennogo sibirskogo pravitel′stva v podgotovke kolchakovskogo perevorota', *Voprosy istorii Sibiri* (Tomsk), Vol. 167 (1964), p. 66; Garmiza, V.V. *Krushenie eserovskykh pravitel′stv*. Moscow (1970), p. 105; Shukletsov, V.T. *Sibiriaki v bor′be za vlast′ sovetov*. Novosibirsk (1981), p. 90. The pre-Omsk careers of the leading members of the PSG are described in Guins, Vol. 1, pp. 104–19.

49 Aspects of the PSG's activities are summarized in Livshits, S.G. 'Vremennoe sibirskoe pravitel′stvo', *Voprosy istorii* (Moscow), No. 12 (1979), pp. 98–108; Kadeikin, V.A. 'Antirabotnaia politika Vremennogo sibirskogo pravitel′stva', *Voprosy istorii Sibiri* (Tomsk), Vol. 214 (1969); Sokolov, N.G. 'Antinarodnaia sushchnost′ nalogovoi politiki v derevne esero-men′shevistskikh

Such activities naturally raised the hackles of the scattered, socialistic membership of the *Sibobduma*. So too did speeches made by Vologodskii in early July in which the premier opined that, although the PSG had 'sprung from the heart of the duma', by virtue of the *Sibobduma*'s restricted franchise, only the government and not the duma could claim 'the support of all classes'.[50] At least, initially, the PSG did appear willing to permit the duma to convene as a provisional legislature, albeit not as early as July 20th, as delegates wished, and only on the condition that its first act would be to admit the representatives of the *tsenzovye* classes excluded in its original constitution.[51] When the duma was finally convened at Tomsk University Library on August 15th–16th, however, it became clear that a struggle for power was underway between the ascendant Vologodskii, who strove to have the PSG's Council of Six recognized as an autonomous, sovereign directory, and the SR duma majority (fifty of the ninety-two delegates), who insisted that Vologodskii was merely the head of a council of ministers responsible to the *Sibobduma*. With the bristling Siberian Army at his back and with the encouragement of the published declaration of a newfound social organization, the Omsk Bloc (a coalition of conservative co-operators, trades and industry circles and Siberian Cossacks), the premier maintained in his uncompromising and vaguely minatory address to the duma that the Provisional Siberian Government derived its authority not from the duma but by virtue of the 'general recognition' it enjoyed among all classes and social groups. The notion that there could be a legitimate governmental authority without even the pretence of a popular mandate to test such claims was thereby re-introduced to Siberia for the first time since 1905 (although the descent of Prince L'vov's Provisional Government from the Committee of the State Duma was cited by Vologodskii's supporters as a precedent, it was hardly apposite in the post-revolutionary circumstances) much to the consternation of the SRs.[52] However, the

pravitel'stv i kolchakovskogo rezhima v Sibiri, 1918–1919gg.', in *Neproletarskie partii i organizatsii natsional'nykh raionov Rossii v Oktiabr'skoi revoliutsii i grazhdanskoi voiny*. Moscow (1980), pp. 265–70. For the texts of the PSG's key decrees on political and economic affairs see Piontkovskii, *Grazhdanskaia voina*, pp. 270–4. On the reintroduction of the death penalty see *Zaria* (Omsk) No. 79, 18.ix.1919.

50 *Zaria* (Omsk) No. 24, 11.vii.1918.

51 *Sobranie uzakonenii i rasporiazhenii Vremennogo sibirskogo pravitel'stva* (Omsk) No. 2, 15.vii.1919, p. 2.

52 *Sibirskii Vestnik* (Omsk) No. 53, 26.x.1918; Krol', M. 'Sibirskoe pravitel'stvo i avgustovskaia sessiia Sibirskoi oblastnoi dumy', *Vol'naia Sibir'* (Prague), Vol. 4 (1928), pp. 69–82; Guins, Vol. 1, pp. 121–7; Vegman 'Sibobduma', pp. 93–106.

socialists' protests and their obviously begrudging agreement to disperse and meet again only in September with a broader franchise, could have but little disquieted Vologodskii – he had already been informed that, with or without permission, Grishin-Almazov had vowed to disperse the duma by force if any attempt was made to interfere in the composition of the government. The colonel, moreover, in his own speech to the duma, did not shrink from asserting that less and not more democracy was what Russia needed and that the sole means of national salvation was the establishment of a military dictatorship.[53]

The Omsk–Samara rivalry

Apart from a general distaste for its SR majority, Vologodskii and Grishin-Almazov's decision to challenge the authority of the *Sibobduma* sprang from a fear that it might choose to subordinate itself and Siberia to Komuch – the Committee of Members of the Constituent Assembly, which, in the wake of the Czechoslovak revolt, had established itself in the Volga town of Samara on June 8th and, with Czechoslovak assistance for its fledgling People's Army of volunteers and peasant conscripts, was soon to capture Simbirsk, Kazan and much of the Volga-Kama region. Originally consisting of just five members of the Constituent Assembly which had been dispersed by Lenin in January, eventually attracting more than ninety members to Samara by September 1918, and always predominantly SR in orientation, Komuch claimed to be the legitimate caretaker of all-Russian authority until such a time as the original Constituent Assembly could be reconvened.[54] As such it was anathema to the immobilistes of Omsk, and was even more reviled than

53 Vologodskii, P.V. 'Dnevnik' (*Hoover Archives*), cited in Dotsenko *The Struggle for a Democracy*, p. 40. Many on the right feared that elements in the duma were considering coming to terms with the Bolsheviks. See Krol', L. *Za tri goda: vospominaniia, vpechatleniia i vstrechi*. Vladivostok (1921), pp. 72–3.

54 The history of Komuch is ably and concisely told in Berk, S.M. 'The Democratic Counter-Revolution: Komuch and the Civil War on the Volga', *Canadian-American Slavic Studies*, Vol. 7 (1973), pp. 443–59. The memoirs of leading participants include Klimushkin, P.D. 'Bor'ba za demokratiiu na Volge', in *Grazhdanskaia Voina na Volge*. Prague (1930), pp. 38–102; and the accounts of Brushvit, Chechek, Lebedev and Nikolaev collected in *Volia Rossii* (Prague), Vols. 8–9, 10 (1928–1929). See also Il'in, I.S. 'Komuch', *Novyi zhurnal* (New York), Vol. 65 (1961), pp. 221–42; and Nikolaev, S.N. 'Konets Komucha', *Sovremennaia zapiski* (Paris), No. 45 (1931), pp. 333–361.

the *Sibobduma* (which could be dismissed as a local aberration): in fact, the very mention of the Constituent Assembly of 1917 was as a red rag waved in the face of the reactionary bulls of the Siberian Army and their PSG supporters, for with its socialist majority the Assembly which had met so briefly in the Tauride Palace rendered meaningless their faith in the essential conservatism and goodness of the Russian people and, in the one piece of legislation it had passed, sanctioning radical land reform, had attacked the property rights sacred to those coming to dominate anti-Bolshevism in Siberia. In fact, such was the contempt in which the original Constituent Assembly (and, in particular, its chairman, the SR leader Viktor Chernov) were held by those coming to the fore in Omsk that one soon to be pre-eminent among them was to opine that the Bolsheviks, for all their faults, had done Russia a great service when they had dispersed it.[55]

It was no surprise, therefore, that by July 1918 a war of words had flared up between the two chief rivals for the leadership of anti-Bolshevism in the east, Komuch and the PSG: when Samara demanded that Omsk recognize its supremacy, Grishin-Almazov raged that 'a dozen SRs do not constitute an all-Russian government' and Vologodskii countered by declaring the provisional autonomy of Siberia on July 4th.[56] Mutual insults then matured into a trade war, with the PSG refusing to permit grain stockpiled at Cheliabinsk to be sent west unless a surcharge was paid (a remarkable variation on the Cheliabinsk Grain Tariff with which pre-revolutionary Russian régimes had artificially inflated the price of Siberian grain to protect less productive Russian farmers), while Komuch withheld oil and manufactured goods demanded in Siberia. Moreover, even though Komuch was engaged in decisive battles against the Red Army, Omsk refused to send military assistance to the Volga front: 'Not one soldier, not one cartridge, not one gun did Samara receive from or through Siberia', recalled one Komuch member, I.N. Rakitnikov. Indeed, the People's Army was obliged to divert troops from the front to Zlatoust in order to prevent Omsk from laying claim to the Ural passes![57] And all this at the time

55 Varneck, E. and Fisher, H.H. (eds.) *The Testimony of Kolchak and Other Siberian Materials*. Stanford (1935), pp. 106–7.

56 *Sobranie uzakonenii i rasporiazhenii Vremennogo sibirskogo pravitel'stva* (Omsk) No. 2, 18.vii.1919, p. 2. The choice of July 4th for the promulgation of Siberian independence was no coincidence – the *oblastniki* had long been admirers of the American constitution.

57 Rakitnikov, N.I. *Sibirskaia reaktsiia i Kolchak*. Moscow (1920), p. 14; Boldyrev, V.S. *Direktoriia, Kolchak, Interventsii*. Novosibirsk (1925), pp. 31–2; Vishniak, M. *Vserossiiskoe uchreditel'noe sobranie*. Paris (1932), pp. 175–7. This contest is described in Golovin, Vol. 8, pp. 60–64 and in

which Trotsky himself later posited as the turning point of the entire civil war: having been able to establish only the loosest grip on Kazan, which was soon to be retaken by the Red Army, noted Lenin's Commissar for War, anti-Bolshevik forces would never again place a foot on the vulnerable eastern approach road to Moscow.[58]

Yet, despite their ingrained mutual antagonism and mistrust, Komuch and the PSG were eventually obliged to begin a series of negotiations which would eventually lead to the creation of a single (though barely united) anti-Bolshevik government in the east. The compelling force behind the movement for coalition and compromise, however, came neither from Omsk nor Samara, but from the Czechoslovaks, whose units were bearing the brunt of the fighting on the Volga and who were, unsurprisingly, wearying somewhat of their well-doing. Throughout July the Legion's National Council (the local branch of the emergent government of the Czechoslovak Republic) articulated its soldiers' disgust that their Russian allies were bickering amongst themselves while their fellow Slavs were fighting themselves to exhaustion for Russia's sake, and, in a memorandum of early August, bluntly demanded that the Omsk–Samara rivals either come to terms or face the consequences of the Legionnaires' disillusionment.[59] The National Council (and the Czechoslovak soldiery as a whole) was more sympathetic to the SRs of Samara than to Omsk, but their strong military presence all along the Trans-Siberian Railway put them in a favourable position to exert pressure on both sides and they persistently did so.

The Legion was seconded in its call for unity by certain politically moderate figures newly arrived in the east who were united under the loose banner of the Union for the Regeneration of Russia (URR). Founded at secret gatherings at Moscow during the spring of 1918, the URR was comprised of Popular Socialists (such as the veteran revolutionist N.V. Chaikovskii), right-SRs (for example, the former Chairman of the All-Russian Soviet of Peasant Deputies, N.D. Avksent′ev) and a number of Kadets (including the liberals' leader, N.I. Astrov) who were averse

Mel′gunov, S.P. *Tragediia admirala Kolchaka*. Belgrade (1930–1931), Vol. 1, pp. 168–70. On the Cheliabinsk Grain Tariff see Mote, V.L. 'The Cheliabinsk Grain Tariff and the Rise of the Siberian Butter Industry', *Slavonic Review*, Vol. 35, No. 2 (1976), pp. 304–18.

58 Trotsky, L. *Stalin*. London (1947), p. 310. Lenin too felt that 'the entire destiny of the revolution' was decided on the Volga front during the summer of 1918. See Lenin, V.I. *Polnoe sobranie sochinenii* (5th ed.). Moscow (1964–1970), Vol. 50, p. 133 (hereafter cited as *PSS*).

59 Maksakov and Turunov, pp. 230–1.

to their comrade Miliukov's collaboration with the Germans at Kiev. Its programme called for the establishment of an all-Russian representative Directory of three national figures, who, until the convocation of a new Constituent Assembly, would co-ordinate the struggle against Bolshevism and Germany in collaboration with the Allies. This was a fragile partnership – the *quid pro quo* of Kadet involvement was that the SRs drop their recognition of the old Constituent Assembly (wherein, of course, the Kadets had won a mere handful of seats), the election of which they regarded as flawed and whose membership they denigrated as an unrepresentative SR caucus. Moreover, the Kadets also made it very clear from the outset that they would prefer the establishment of a provisional military dictatorship and would only support a Directory if on it, *primus inter pares*, would serve a Russian military figure of international repute such as General M.V. Alekseev (the former Supreme Commander-in-Chief of 1917 who had fled to South Russia with Kornilov to found the Volunteer Army).[60] Nevertheless, despite such weak foundations, when URR representatives began to arrive in the east in the early summer of 1918, they were to gain considerable support and respect for their principled standing aloof from the Omsk and Samara governments. In the charged atmosphere of the east their calls for compromise won an audience.[61]

Finally, the changing circumstances of the war also spoke eloquently for an Omsk–Samara rapprochement and for a more consolidated approach to the anti-Bolshevik campaign. Komuch's hastily organized People's Army was not attracting many volunteers – despite the SRs' record of electoral success in the Volga region – and even a July mobilization of the 1897–1898 age group barely raised the complement to more than 20,000. Komuch, in fact, was fearful by August that, with the Czechoslovaks clearly loath to hold the line against the increasingly effective strikes of Trotsky's mushrooming Red Army, it might soon be driven from its

60 The genesis of the Union is charted in Rosenberg, W.H. *Liberals in the Russian Revolution: The Constitutional Democratic Party, 1917–1921*. Princeton (1974), pp. 289–300; Ioffe, G.Z. *Kolchakovskaia avantiura i ee krakh*. Moscow (1983), pp. 39–54; Ignat'ev, V.I. *Nekotorye fakty i itogi chetyrikh let grazhdanskoi voiny*. Moscow (1922). For personal accounts see 'Pis'mo moskovskikh politicheskikh deiatelei', *Zaria* (Omsk) No. 79, 18.ix.1918; and Miakotin, V. 'Iz nedalekogo proshlogo', *Na chuzhdoi storone* (Berlin), No. 2 (1923), pp. 178–200.

61 Guins, Vol. 1, pp. 181–2; Mel'gunov, Vol. 1, p. 197; Argunov, A.A. 'Omskie dni v 1918g.', *Sibirskii arkhiv* (Prague), Vol. 5 (1935), pp. 191–2.

capital. This in turn caused the Siberian government to ponder upon the fact that the front would then approach its own undefended borders in the Urals.[62]

Mutual suspicion remained such that an initial, exploratory meeting of Omsk and Samara delegates at Cheliabinsk of July 15th–18th broke up in acrimony. However, the increasingly parlous state of the Volga front, the pleadings of the URR and the veiled threats of Czechoslovak and other Allied agents that only a united anti-Bolshevik government could count upon the moral and material support of the Allies elicited agreement to parley once again at Cheliabinsk on August 23rd–25th. Subsequently, at this second preparatory conference (chaired by the URR plenipotentiary N.D. Avksent′ev), Omsk and Samara committed themselves to organizing a full State Conference at Ufa in September to determine the composition of a Provisional All-Russian Government.[63] Clearly arms, not principles, were to be the prime mover in Siberia – politics were already at a discount in the anti-Bolshevik camp, but guns and ammunition were hard to come by.

It was expected that the crucial negotiations at Ufa would last several weeks. However, the respect in which any government they produced was likely to be held by Omsk may be deduced from the fact that Vologodskii and his leading ministers not only did not care to attend the State Conference but were to be found on the very day that it convened (September 8th) heading eastwards from Omsk on a mission to buttress the authority of the PSG by securing the subordination to it of the major anti-Bolshevik authorities in the Far East and, it was hoped, the recognition of the Omsk régime by the Allied representatives who now controlled Vladivostok.[64]

62 Berk 'The *Coup d'État*', pp. 350–64 examines in more detail the forces compelling a coalition. Most significant for Komuch was that it had been able to raise a force of only 20,000 men on the Volga – see Lebedev, V.I. *The Russian Democracy and its Struggle Against the Bolsheviks*. New York (1919), pp. 12–17. Moreover, the loyalty of its officer corps was in serious doubt. Some officers were secretly preparing to overthrow the SR government – see Popov, F. *Chekhoslovatskii miatezh i samarskaia uchredil′ka*. Moscow (1932), p. 191; Nikolaev, S. 'Narodnaia Armiia na Simbirske', *Volia Rossii* (Prague), Nos. 10–11 (1928), pp. 126–7. Others simply deserted in a steady stream towards the quieter life and more conservative politics to be found at Omsk – see Boldyrev, p. 30; N.N. 'Zapiski belogvardeitsa', *Arkhiv russkoi revoliutsii* (Berlin), Vol. 10 (1923), pp. 84, 88; and Dotsenko, *The Struggle for the Liberation*, p. 104.

63 Vladimirova, *God sluzhby*, pp. 356–7; Guins, Vol. 1, pp. 183–4; Gan, p. 275; Argunov, pp. 192–3.

64 For the Allied declaration of their protectorate in Vladivostok see *Deistviia Iaponii v Priamurskom krae: sbornik offitsial′nykh dokumentov, otnosiashchikhsia k interventsii derzhav v predelakh Priamur′ia*. Vladivostok (1921), pp. 12–19.

On September 17th the Vologodskii mission reached the Manchurian capital of Harbin, where negotiations were immediately entered into with a Japanese diplomat, Count Matsudara, and, rather more fruitfully, with the newly arrived British High Commissioner to Siberia, Sir Charles Eliot (the Vice-Chancellor of Hong Kong University). Driven by regional self-interest, the Japanese, as we shall see, were wary of all unifying tendencies in the anti-Bolshevik camp and preferred to sponsor their own disruptive puppet régimes on the east Asian mainland. Eliot, in contrast, was carrying instructions from the British Foreign Secretary (the Conservative statesman, Arthur Balfour) to the effect that everything possible should be done to encourage a move towards a strong and united régime in Siberia and that, in particular, any moves towards the establishment of a military government should be supported.[65]

One who encountered Vologodskii on this mission later recalled that the Omsk premier was given to opining that 'the time may be approaching when a dictatorship is necessary'.[66] And clearly Eliot descried the germ of such a government in the PSG, for, although (unfortunately) no record of their meeting exists, some informal agreement seems to have been arrived at: it could only really have been by brandishing the favour of the British Government that Vologodskii was able, over the following week, to subdue the two chief rivals for power in the Russian Far East, Derber's PGAS and General D.L. Horvath, the Governor of the Chinese Eastern Railway. The socialist Derber and the arch-conservative Horvath had been at each others' throats for months – the former's proclamation of the authority of his government in the wake of the Czechoslovak capture of Vladivostok on June 29th had been swiftly echoed by the latter's assumption of the title 'Supreme Ruler' in the east on July 9th – but the prospect of Allied assistance to a united government, the talisman which all Siberian parties sought and which, apparently, Vologodskii was able to flaunt, was sufficient for both to swear loyalty to the PSG.[67] Indeed,

65 FO 371/3365/154852 'Curzon to Eliot (Vladivostok)', 15.ix.1918. On these talks see also Ullman, R.H. *Anglo-Soviet Relations, 1917–1921*. London (1961), Vol. 1, pp. 273–4; and Livshits, S.G. *Imperialisticheskaia interventsiia v Sibiri*. Barnaul (1979), pp. 39–42.

66 Menshikov, A. 'Praktika Priamurskogo zemstva', *Sibirskii arkhiv* (Prague), Vol. 4 (1928), p. 170.

67 Livshits, pp. 40–42; Svetachev, M.I. 'Interventsiia i sibirskaia kontrrevoliutsiia, noiabr′ 1917–noiabr′ 1918', *Voprosy istorii Dal′nego Vostoka* (Khabarovsk), No. 3 (1973), pp. 58–60. To be fair, it has to be said that it was unlikely that Derber would have recognized Vologodskii had he been properly apprised of the plight of the *Sibobduma* under the PSG – see Guins, Vol. 1, p. 229. On the Derber–Horvath rivalry see sources listed above in n. 23 and the eye-witness account of Budberg, A.P. 'Dnevnik', *Arkhiv russkoi revoliutsii* (Berlin), Vol. 13 (1923), pp. 150–205.

following their lead, even the SR- and Menshevik-dominated zemstvo board of the Maritime Provinces was to recognize Vologodskii.[68]

Vologodskii's confidence in the PSG's future in the wake of his meeting with Eliot may be judged by the fact that the very next day (that is on September 18th, in advance of coming to terms with Derber and Horvath) he sent secret telegraphic instructions to Omsk to the effect that his plenipotentiaries at Ufa should make no concessions to Komuch because the situation in the Far East seemed to indicate that the Allies might be disposed to recognize the PSG and accept *it* as the basis for an all-Russian authority.[69] The premier might, however, have saved the telegraphist the trouble, for from Omsk (where he had been left in charge), Mikhailov had already sent word to Serebrennikov (head of the PSG delegation to the State Conference) that he should prevaricate – even at the risk of a breakdown in the negotiations – but on no account should any concessions be made to the SRs. Least of all, he warned, should Komuch be allowed, as it would surely try, to insist that any new government be responsible to the old Constituent Assembly.[70] Time, Mikhailov knew, was on the side of whoever could boast the support of a powerful army: and with each day that passed the forces of Komuch were crumbling while the Siberian Army matured. Meanwhile, moreover, he – 'the Siberian Borgia' – was making the best of the breathing space offered by the negotiations at Ufa to attempt to subdue the recalcitrant *Sibobduma*, to rid the PSG of its vestigial socialist and regionalist elements, to cleave the Siberian Army to the 'Mikhailov Group' and thereby to guarantee the pre-eminence of his own clique in Siberia (and, indeed, in Russia as a whole) if events proceeded satisfactorily. One more step on the road to dictatorship.

68 Iakushev, I.A. 'Dal'ne-vostochnoe samoupravlenie v gody bor'ba za vlast', 1917–1919gg.', in *Mestnoe samoupravlenie*. Prague (1926), pp. 196–201.

69 Guins, Vol. 1, p. 212; Livshits 'Vremennoe sibirskoe pravitel'stvo', p. 104.

70 Maksakov and Turunov, p. 240; Serebrennikov, I.I. 'Iz istorii Sibirskogo Pravitel'stva', *Sibirskii arkhiv* (Prague), Vol. 1 (1929), p. 11.

The Novoselov affair: dress rehearsal for the coup

Since the inception of the PSG, business circles at Omsk and the Mikhailov Group had been concerned that the lack of clarity in the government's constitution might permit *Sibobduma* delegates and 'ministers' of the PGAS to claim seats in it. They had, therefore, prevailed upon Vologodskii not only to regard the Council of Six as an inviolate executive directory, but also to elevate its informal 'Business Cabinet' of advisers into a formally constituted council of heads of government departments, responsible exclusively to the Council of Six and equally impervious to any attempts to change its composition by SR authorities at Tomsk and Vladivostok. This was duly legislated for and, on August 24th, the Administrative Council came into being, consisting of the heads of the emergent Siberian ministries and their deputies – most of them loyal to Mikhailov – and being empowered to discuss all projected laws before their submission to the Council of Six and to nominate candidates for all government offices. On September 7th, the eve of Vologodskii's departure for the east, these already very broad powers for a largely unelected body were again augmented: thenceforth, in the absence of a majority of the Council of Six, the Administrative Council was to assume full executive and legislative responsibility, including the right (insisted upon by Mikhailov) to prorogue the *Sibobduma*, which was scheduled to re-assemble on September 10th.[71]

Being the sole minister at Omsk after September 8th (Vologodskii was in the east, Serebrennikov was at Ufa and the three absentee SR-*oblastniki* were at Tomsk), Mikhailov and his group very soon had the opportunity to exercise this newly won authority. Even before then, however, their first target had been lined up and eliminated – not the duma but the Commander-in-Chief of the Siberian Army, Grishin-Almazov. The colonel's credentials as a military leader were respected by neither right nor left (he was reputedly a very heavy drinker) and many officers in the army were unhappy with his penchant for 'revolutionary' rather than traditional discipline. Moreover, Mikhailov personally hoped to find a means of removing this ambitious officer from Omsk in order to secure his own political hegemony and, according to Paul Dotsenko, to pursue an affair with Grishin-Almazov's wife – reputedly a beautiful and imposing woman, the brightest star in Omsk's murky

71 Golovin, Vol. 8, pp. 27–30; Guins, Vol. 1, pp. 185–92, 198, 202; Vladimirova, 357–9; Maksakov and Turunov, p. 86.

social firmament, among whose many talents was the ability to drink any man (including her crapulent spouse) under the table. When the commander was unwise enough to involve himself during August in an unseemly public slanging match with Czech and other Allied representatives at Cheliabinsk, Mikhailov and Golovachev (Deputy Minister of Foreign Affairs) – even though they certainly sympathized with what the general had said (namely that Allied matériel assistance was, at this stage, mean) – seized their chance: they insisted that Grishin be removed and, on September 5th, Vologodskii's Council complied.[72] The new commander-in-chief, nominated on September 5th by the Administrative Council – to the delight of Cossack officers at Omsk – was Major Pavel Pavlovich Ivanov-Rinov, recently elected as Ataman of the Siberian Cossack Host, already infamous for his part (as a tsarist police officer) in the bloody suppression of the Kirghiz rebellion of 1916 and regarded – even by members of the government according to Guins – as 'a man without doubt of the old régime and displaying the worst type of "police" habits'.[73] Ivanov-Rinov's first act was to install as Omsk Commandant his friend Colonel V.I. Volkov, later characterized by N.N. Golovin as 'a typical example of that spirit of arbitrariness and illegality which became known in Siberia as "*atamanshchina*".'[74] It was such developments, and the general impression that Mikhailov and his army and business cronies were greedy cuckoos in the nest of the government, which caused one of the SR-*oblastniki* on the Council of Six, Patushinskii, to proffer his resignation.[75]

Patushinskii's regionalist partners, Shatilov and Krutovskii, meanwhile, newly incensed by the army's waylaying at Irkutsk of a duma delegation which had attempted to shadow Vologodskii to the Far East, were themselves hoping to utilize the absence from Omsk of Vologodskii and Serebrennikov. On September 19th the two SR-*oblastnik* ministers arrived, unannounced, back at Omsk accompanied by the *Sibobduma* Chairman, Iakushev, and another PGAS member, a popular Siberian author, the SR Aleksandr Novoselov. At a meeting of the Administrative Council

72 Guins, Vol. 1, pp. 193–6; Golovin, Vol. 8, pp. 32–3; Dotsenko, *The Struggle for the Liberation*, pp. 55–8. One eye-witness account of the scandal at Cheliabinsk has an American officer bowling apples 'baseball-style' at Grishin-Almazov in response to his criticisms of Allied policy. See Preston, T. *Before the Curtain*. London (1950), p. 117.

73 Guins, Vol. 1, p. 197; Eikhe, pp. 34–5.

74 Golovin, Vol. 8, p. 33. The Russian suffix '*-shchina*' denotes 'the rule of', but has condemnatory overtones. '*Atamanshchina*', therefore, translates as 'the misrule of the Cossack chieftains'.

75 Guins, Vol. 1, pp. 201–2.

they then signalled their intention to grant Novoselov a seat on the Council of Ministers, thereby creating a quorum and (since Patushinskii had now thought better of his resignation) an inbuilt majority for the SR-*oblastnik* ministers desirous of repealing PSG laws, of sending a more moderate delegation to Ufa and of diminishing the powers of the unelected heads of ministries in the pocket of Mikhailov on the Administrative Council. Moreover, if successful, such a move would have once and for all established that Vologodskii's Council was not a directory, wielding supreme authority (as conservatives desired), but merely an executive body responsible to the leftist duma.

In fact, however, all that was to be proven was that, having failed to establish an armed force of its own, the *Sibobduma* would remain for ever impotent. On September 21st, Commandant Volkov's troops arrested Shatilov, Krutovskii and Novoselov on the charge of plotting an illegal coup against the government. 'The circumstances under which the arrests were made were apparently not in accordance with the usual procedure', reported the British vice-consul at Omsk matter-of-factly.[76] In fact, what transpired was to become *all too* usual a procedure in the White capital over the coming months: with guns at their brows, on September 22nd Shatilov and Krutovskii were forced to resign their seats on the PSG and were given twenty-four hours to leave town; the unfortunate Novoselov, entrusted to the tender care of an escort led by two inveterate monarchists (Lieutenant Semchenko and Cossack Cornet Mefod'ev), was marched that night to the Zagorodnaia Roshcha (literally, 'the out of town copse'). This had once been the favourite site for picnics and promenades among Omsk society, but was now a lonely spot, soon to become notorious as the chosen killing fields of such officers. There Novoselov was 'shot whilst trying to escape', a phrase soon to become clichéd amid a welter of such political killings at Omsk.[77]

A subsequent investigation of this affair conducted by the URR supporter and veteran SR, Andrei Argunov, found grounds for suspicion that responsibility for the arrests and the murder could be traced at least to Volkov and possibly to Mikhailov himself. However, as their enquiries were impeded by stonewalling on Mikhailov's

76 FO 538/3 'Vice Consul (Omsk) to FO, 30.ix.1919 ('Memorandum on the Political Crisis in Omsk')'.

77 For the accounts of Shatilov and Krutovskii see Boldyrev, pp. 517–8. On Novoselov see Berezovskii, F. 'Aleksandr Efremovich Novoselov', *Sibirskie ogni* (Novonikolaevsk) No. 1 (1922), pp. 157–8. See also Guins, Vol. 1, pp. 219–22, 233–5; Golovin, Vol. 8, pp. 35–9; Vegman 'Oblastnicheskie illiuzii', pp. 106–7.

part and by Ivanov-Rinov's despatch of Volkov on a conveniently urgent mission to the Far East, and as Argunov's documents were later destroyed by the army, no firm conclusions can be arrived at on that score.[78] What was indubitably clear to elements of the Siberian Army, however, both from Mikhailov's apparent intention to launch no investigation of his own into the murder and from Ivanov-Rinov's bald declaration that he would not permit the questioning of Volkov on the grounds that even if the latter's action were 'legally a crime' he was 'fulfilling his state duty',[79] was that in the eyes of the most senior political and military figures of the PSG the cause of order demanded that the army be imprescriptible. Cossacks and right-wing officers were to make full and bloody use of this freedom over the coming months.

If the almost blasé manner in which the murder of Novoselov was committed and all judicial consequences avoided was indicative both of the reactionaries' growing confidence and of the final erasure of the qualification 'democratic' from the eastern counter-revolution's lexicon,[80] for the moment the right did not have a totally free rein. That lesson was learned when, with his SR-*oblastnik* rival ministers disposed of, on September 23rd, invoking the special powers of the Administrative Council, Mikhailov ordered the immediate and indefinite proroguing of the *Sibobduma*. Had this long-cherished desire of right-wing circles at Omsk been achieved in the wake of the Novoselov affair it would clearly have signified the victory of reaction in Siberia: it would have signified a coup from the right. However, *Sibobduma*'s chairman, Iakushev, ignored the demand and countered it with a decree of his own, dismissing the Administrative Council and indicting Mikhailov and his assistants Gratsianov and Butov for preparing a coup against the legitimate authority of the duma. Of itself, of course, such a measure would have been as pointless as every other resolution adopted by the duma throughout the

78 Argunov 'Omskie dni', pp. 201–5; Argunov, A.A. *Mezhdu dvumia bol'shevizami*. Paris (1919), pp. 25–7; Golovin, Vol. 9, 17–18. Another source has it that the murder was actually committed by Volkov's Chief of Staff, A.S. Stepanov, who was then transferred to the Far East with a 2,000 roubles stipend and a new name. See Dotsenko *The Struggle for the Liberation*, p. 46.

79 Boldyrev, p. 71.

80 There is some historiographical debate on the question of whether, because of the ascendancy of Mikhailov and the Administrative Council at Omsk, the chronological limit of the term democratic counter-revolution' in Siberia might not be appropriately placed at some point in September 1918, rather than, as has traditionally been the case, the point of Kolchak's seizure of power on November 18th. See my introduction to Collins, D. and Smele, J.D. *Kolchak i Sibir': dokumenty i issledovaniia, 1919–1926*. New York (1988), Vol. 1, pp. xii–xiii; and Shikanov, L.A. 'K voprosu o khronologicheskikh ramkakh "demokraticheskoi" kontrrevoliutsii v Sibiri', in Korablev and Shishkin, pp. 65–7.

summer of 1918. The SRs, however, still had one card to play: Iakushev appealed to local Czechoslovak forces for assistance.[81] There were some 3,000 well-armed Legionnaires in the vicinity of Omsk and although, as time was to tell, certain of their leaders were in sympathy with the most right-wing elements in Siberia, most of the soldiers preferred the socialistic politics of the duma. In a move which was to earn them the lasting resentment of the succeeding régimes at Omsk and which was to be invoked time and again over the following year as evidence of the Legion's disloyalty, the Czechoslovaks (under the command of General Jan Syrovy) proceeded to liberate duma members already detained by the Tomsk *guberniia* commissar A.N. Gattenberger, and sent a unit into Omsk to arrest Gratsianov and Mikhailov.[82]

Although the latter managed to avoid capture, whilst in hiding 'the Siberian Borgia' perhaps had time to ponder upon the fact that by virtue of their military strength and a discipline which, for the time being, remained the envy of both sides in the civil war, the Czechoslovaks would be the determining factor in Siberian politics for as long as they cared to be so. Perhaps too *Van'ka Kain* reflected that a coup would only succeed when the Legion had lost interest in the Siberian imbroglio or when the attempt was linked to the name of a man sufficiently respected by the Legion's officers that they would counter the socialist leanings of the rank and file. Perhaps it was even at this juncture that Mikhailov first began to consider the name of a man whom he had not met, but a name already to be heard on the lips of those seeking to establish a military dictatorship in Siberia – the name Admiral Aleksandr Vasil'evich Kolchak.[83]

The Ufa State Conference

Whatever their longer term aims, however, for the time being Mikhailov and his allies at Omsk were committed to respecting the outcome of the State Conference

81 Vegman 'Oblastnicheskie illiuzii', pp. 107–8. For an English language version see Bunyan. J. (ed.) *Intervention, Communism and Civil War in Russia*. Baltimore (1936), p. 338. For a description of the events at Tomsk see Nikolaevsky Collection (*Hoover Institution Archives*), Box 1, File 1.

82 *Zaria* (Omsk) No. 85, 26.ix.1918; Mel'gunov, Vol. 1, pp. 160–2; Guins, Vol. 1, pp. 235–41.

83 See below, n. 165.

then drawing to a close at Ufa. Around 170 delegates had gathered at Ufa, a small, prettily situated fortress town on the Belaia River, which had been founded by the Russians in the sixteenth century as a centre from which to subdue the warlike natives of the district, the Bashkirs. The delegates represented a total of twenty-three regional governments, party central committees, congresses of trade and industry, Cossack hosts and other organizations. Many laid claim to mandates from groups in central, southern or western Russia, but the most influential, of course, were the plenipotentiaries of Komuch (which accounted for 73 delegates) and the PSG (comprising a smaller delegation under Serebrennikov and Sapozhnikov), whose mutual acrimony and reluctance to compromise were all too apparent – the Siberians even arrived four days late.[84] Also influential, however, were those delegates accrediting themselves to the URR – including the former commander of the Riga front, General Vasilii Georgevich Boldyrev, and the so-called 'Grandmother of the Russian Revolution', the venerable populist Ekaterina Brezhko-Brezhkovskaia, as well as the afore-mentioned Avksent′ev. And the Union of Regeneration's calls for coalition and unity, forcefully articulated by Avksent′ev (as Chairman of the State Conference) in an inaugural address which exhorted delegates 'to take a solemn oath not to leave this place...without establishing a unified Russian state', had to be taken all the more seriously as the mounting crisis at the front painted an alarming backdrop to the negotiations: as symbolic Kazan was lost to the Red Army on September 10th and the important Volga crossing at Simbirsk was surrendered four days later, both Bolshevik and Czech witnesses concluded that the People's Army was on the point of disintegration, while its officers were forced to admit to organizational inefficiencies and accept that the open road to Moscow they had expected had been firmly barricaded by Trotsky.[85]

The State Conference held four plenary sessions from September 8th to 16th at which all the delegations had a chance to express their conflicting viewpoints. At a fifth and final session, however, delegates accepted a constitution drawn up by a Committee of Elders they had previously elected, and endorsed the nominations,

84 Serebrennikov, 'K istorii', p. 6.

85 Kakurin, N. *Kak srazhalas′ revoliutsiia*. Moscow–Leningrad (1925–1926) Vol. 1, p. 157; Golochek, p. 77; Lebedev, V.I. 'Ot Petrograda do Kazani' *Volia Rossiia* (Prague) Vols. 8–9 (1928), pp. 125–9; Petrov, P.P. *Ot Volgi do Tikhago okeana v riadakh belykh, 1918–1922gg*. Riga (1931), p. 42.

which that committee proposed, for a five-man Directory to serve as a Provisional All-Russian Government.[86] Avksent′ev later reflected upon the debates which took place at Ufa: 'The basic question which divided left from right,' he noted, 'was not the programme of the Government, nor even the form or composition of the Directory, but the question of the Constituent Assembly.'[87] That was confirmed by the head of the PSG delegation: debate centred not on the principle of a directory, said Serebrennikov, but on the question of 'before whom was the Directory to be responsible'.[88] For Komuch (which was supported by the *Sibobduma*, the Union of Zemstvos and Town Councils and the various delegations of Central Asian and Muslim peoples who enjoyed good relations with the SRs), V.K. Vol′skii demanded that the new provisional government should be answerable to the Constituent Assembly of 1917 or, pending its reconvention, a committee of its members (i.e. Komuch itself). In reply, Serebrennikov (supported by the Cossack delegations) insisted that the Directory must be responsible before nothing but its own conscience until a new national assembly could be elected, that of 1917 being invalid as it had been elected under conditions of civil disorder.[89] Debate on this point, in fact, was to dominate relations between the left and right wings of anti-Bolshevism throughout the civil war period. In the end, as time was to prove, the question of whose view was to prevail could only be decided by brute force. For the time being, however, with the Red Army approaching the gates of Komuch's Samara capital and with Czechoslovak and French observers at Ufa urging moderation on both sides and, behind the scenes, threatening that if no agreement was reached the Legion would leave the front, a compromise resolution was adopted along the lines proposed by the URR delegates: the Directory was to be a sovereign power, responsible before

86 Vishniak, M. 'Grazhdanskaia voina', *Sovremennye zapiski* (Paris), No. 45 (1935), pp. 317ff and Utgov, V.L. 'Ufimskoe gosudarstvennoe soveshchanie', *Byloe* (Petrograd), No. 6 (1921), pp. 15–42, are two interesting eye-witness accounts of the proceedings. The stenographic record of the conference, together with related documents, was published in Iziumov, A.F. (ed.) *Russkii istoricheskii arkhiv* (Prague), Vol. 1 (1929), pp. 57–280. Further documents appear in Piontkovskii, S. (ed.) 'Ufimskoe soveshchanie i Vremennoe sibir′skoe pravitel′stvo', *Krasnyi arkhiv* (Moscow), Vol. 6 (1933), pp. 58–81. A Soviet summary is provided by Garmiza, V.V. 'Bankrotstvo politiki "Tret′ogo puti" v revoliutsii (Ufimskoe gosudarstvennoe soveshchanie 1918g.) *Istoriia SSSR* (Moscow), No. 6 (1965), pp. 3–25.

87 Piontkovskii, S. (ed.) 'Materialy po istorii kontrrevoliutsiia: pis′mo Avksent′eva k SR-ami iuga Rossii, 31.x.1918', *Proletarskaia revoliutsiia* (Moscow) No. 1 (1921), p. 116.

88 Serebrennikov, 'K istorii', p. 9.

89 Iziumov, pp. 68, 105–24, 227, 247–51. The view of Guins (Vol. 1, pp. 132, 209) was that the revolution had debased the Constituent Assembly of 1917 just as surely as it had the monarchy.

no other authority, until January 1st 1919, when it would transfer power to a 250 member quorum of the Constituent Assembly of 1917, or until February 1st 1919, when it might transfer power to a 170 member quorum of that same body if the larger quorum could not be assembled.[90]

Once the expediency of compromise had been grudgingly accepted by the major protagonists there was little argument over the actual membership of the Directory. Vologodskii was named as its Chairman, although until his return from the Far East that role would be filled by the PSG's Sapozhnikov. Also from the right was elected the Kadet leader N.I. Astrov, although until he could be summoned from South Russia his place was to be filled by a deputy, V.A. Vinogradov (a Kadet lawyer from Siberia who had served in the Third and Fourth State Dumas). The representatives of 'the Russian democracy', as they liked to be known, were two right-SRs of URR affiliation: Vladimir Mikhailovich Zenzinov (the renowned SR publicist and former terrorist), who was to deputize for the Popular Socialist leader N.V. Chaikovskii until the latter's arrival from North Russia; and the ubiquitous Avksent′ev. The fifth seat was filled by General Boldyrev, a relatively little-known but politically moderate soldier of humble origin (his father had been a blacksmith at Syzran) and a founder member of the URR. Having invested this Directory with provisional supreme power, on September 24th the State Conference adjourned.

On the face of things the Ufa settlement was a victory for the Union of Regeneration: a coalition government had been established and three of its five members belonged to the URR. This, indeed, is the conclusion of the fullest western account of the proceedings.[91] It is, however, a rather superficial view, for it is clear that the compromise was forced upon both Komuch and the PSG and that the Directory would not be tolerated by either of the real forces behind those rivals (the SR Central Committee and the Siberian Army) for a moment longer than each felt it was expedient to do so. It may be argued – as, for example, did N.N. Golovin – that in proposing subordination to a quorum of the old Constituent Assembly so as to appease the SRs, Boldyrev and other URR delegates were gambling that, in the current disturbed conditions, the targets would not be met and a new assembly would have to be elected in any case.[92] That, however, was a very dangerous game

90 Iziumov, p. 227.

91 Berk, 'The *Coup d'État*', pp. 397–8.

92 Golovin, Vol. 8, pp. 83–4.

to play: after Ufa, as we shall see, it became a prime aim of the right to ensure, by fair means or foul, that a quorum could not be gathered. Moreover, the right were extremely unhappy that the ex-terrorist Zenzinov was to serve, albeit as a deputy, on the Directory. The PSG regarded him as 'a man of little probity' and, despite his professions of independence, as one too closely tied to SR party policy. His candidature was only accepted, said Serebrennikov, because following the Novoselov affair, the PSG delegation felt themselves to be on the defensive and lacking 'moral authority' and because they were deceived into believing that Chaikovskii's arrival in the east was imminent.[93] For their part, the Komuch delegation were unhappy that the quorum targets, however apparently modest (even the 250 sought by January was only about one-third of the assembly's full complement), were so high. They rightly perceived that it would be all but impossible to gather such numbers, but were obliged to accept the compromise because of the increasingly voluble impatience of officers in their People's Army – exemplified when it became known that even members of the Komuch garrison at Ufa were swapping their red and white cockades for green and white Siberian insignia.[94] Consequently, there was little euphoria evident on either side as the delegates departed Ufa: 'The agreement was not born into an atmosphere of enthusiasm', recalled Serebrennikov; 'I don't remember one person being truly happy with the result of the conference', confirmed Komuch's P.D. Klimushkin.[95]

Outwith the delegations themselves, the auguries for the success of the Directory were even less propitious. At least one SR had walked out of the State Conference in disgust at his colleagues' kowtowing to the right, while others repudiated the whole affair as an execrable 'Walpurgis Night' of witches and sorcerers. The SR leader Viktor Chernov, who arrived at Ufa from Soviet territory only after the State Conference had concluded its work, was certainly less than satisfied. At a banquet held to celebrate the creation of the new government he pointedly declined to stand when his erstwhile party colleague, Avksent′ev, entered the room. Soon afterwards Chernov was to propose to SR caucuses, albeit initially without success, that the party should not recognize the Directory. Perspicaciously he charged that, whilst

93 Serebrennikov, 'K istoriii', pp. 13–14; Guins, Vol. 1, p. 261.

94 Vishniak, *Vserossiskoe*, pp. 182–3; Boldyrev, p. 45.

95 Serebrennikov, 'K istorii', p. 13.; Klimushkin, P.D. *Chekhoslovatskoe vstuplenie (Tom 1: Volzhskoe dvizhenie i obrazovanie Direktorii*. Prague (1925), p. 229. See also Garmiza, V.V. 'Direktoriia i Kolchak', *Voprosy istorii* (Moscow), No. 10 (1976), p. 21.

jettisoning Komuch's claim of an exclusive right to form a new government on the basis of the 1917 Constituent Assembly, the Directory would be incapable of rallying the support of democratic forces to whom it would be clear that, for all the new government's vaunted supreme authority, it would be powerless to stave off encroachments from the right. Reaction, Chernov correctly foretold, would not regard the Directory as the saviour of democracy in Russia, but merely as a temporary diversion on the road to dictatorship. The new government would only last as long as those in control of the Siberian Army felt obliged to tolerate it, he predicted.[96]

Perhaps even more ominous for the Directory was that it did not even secure the support of the Kadet members of the URR, who might just conceivably have exerted a restraining influence on the irascible Siberian military. On several counts, in fact, the Kadets held that the Ufa settlement was in breach of the contract they had entered into with the right-SRs when joining the Union of Regeneration back in the spring of 1918 at Moscow. For one thing, the original agreement had envisaged that General Alekseev would be the military leader of the provisional government with Boldyrev as his second, but Ufa – for reasons which are not apparent either from the conference record or from the surviving accounts of participants – had reversed their roles.[97] In addition, charged Astrov in a letter refusing to accept his election to the new government, the State Conference had established a Directory of five rather than the three originally agreed to at Moscow, and was therefore, in his opinion, too prone to debate when what was required was action. Finally, and most damningly, charged the Kadet leader, Ufa had admitted the possibility, however remote, of a reconvention of the Constituent Assembly of 1917: 'I shall not enter into a debate as to whether that assembly was good or bad,' he remonstrated, 'I shall

96 Utgov, p. 41; Sviatitskii, N. *K istorii Vserossiiskogo uchreditel′nogo Sobraniia: S″ezd chlenov uchreditel′nogo sobraniia, sentiabr′–dekabr′ 1918g.* Moscow (1921), p. 68; Chernov, V.M. *Pered burei: vospominaniia.* New York (1953), pp. 377–82. Chernov was incensed that his colleagues had sanctioned a provisional government including only one SR, Avksent′ev (Zenzinov being only the deputy for Chaikovskii), and one who was self-confessedly more committed to the URR than the PSR.

97 Although it is debatable whether General Alekseev would have accepted a seat on a government subordinate (however remotely) to the Constituent Assembly of 1917, Boldyrev's elevation was unfortunate for the advocates of compromise – he was less well known than Alekseev (whose status would have provided a much needed boost to the prestige of the Directory) and the very fact that he had apparently usurped the place reserved for the right's favourite general led to rumours that he was an SR nominee. See Golovin, Vol. 8, p. 96.

only point out that it simply does not exist and to build an all-Russian government on the basis of it is the grandest illusion.'[98]

If the Ufa settlement was a victory for the URR, therefore, it was, at best, a Cadmean victory. In fact, as we shall see, whilst providing one last extension of the democratic curtain behind which reaction was garnering its forces in Siberia, the creation of the Directory acted as a call to arms to those for whom such a government raised the spectre of a dread return to intolerable Kerenskyism, to the indecisiveness they viewed as being the hamartia of the Provisional Government of 1917. In fact, the creation of the Directory – even its name reeked of the Provisional Government's final, desperate manifestation – spurred a conspiracy into action. The Kadet organizations of Siberia, following Astrov's lead, immediately turned on the new government, chastising their party colleagues who, by attending the State Conference at Ufa, had trodden the path to this 'socialist Canossa'.[99] Soon the eastern leadership of the 'Party of the People's Freedom' would take their place alongside the tsarist officers, Cossack atamans and the politicians and businessmen of the Mikhailov clique as the organizers and promoters, the leadership corps, of the final manifestation of the counter-revolution in Siberia – military dictatorship.

Siberian Kadets and the counter-revolution

The Kadets of Siberia were far from being numerically strong. But in the civil war years they were at the centre stage of anti-Bolshevik politics, and were able to exert influence beyond anything their organization ever had or would experience, by virtue of being the only non-socialist party to retain its cohesion in the aftermath of the 1917 upheavals in a region destined to become the focus of the White movement.

For a brief period during July–August 1918, Lev Krol, the most moderate of a number of emissaries sent to the east from Moscow by the Kadet Central Committee charged with propagandizing the cause of the URR, had succeeded in winning his

98 Iziumov, pp. 274–5. Mel'gunov (Vol. 1, pp. 214, 226–7) makes the same point from the point of view of his party, the Popular Socialists, who were angered that an SR (Zenzinov) was chosen to deputize for their leader, Chaikovskii.

99 Dumova, N.G. *Kadetskaia kontrrevoliutsiia i ee razgrom*. Moscow (1982), pp. 172–6.

Siberian colleagues over to the cause of a *union sacrée* with moderate socialists. Subsequently, they had at first gone along with Krol's participation in the preparations for the Ufa State Conference; and URR branches, with Kadet affiliates, were opened in a number of Siberian towns and cities.[100] This, however, was only the very briefest interregnum in a longstanding and enduring tradition of outspoken conservatism which had placed the Siberian Kadets on the extreme right wing of their party since its foundation in the early years of the century. Of course, almost the entire party had lurched to the right in 1917 when it had found itself isolated as the only political grouping of significance which was in favour of the defence of property rights. But it was a whole decade earlier that one of the Siberian Kadets' notables had coined the political maxim which was to guide the eastern branch of Russia's 'liberals' through the revolutionary period: 'Better to do away with a reformist government than to submit to the dictates of extremist parties', warned V.A. Karulov.[101] So it had been that, in 1917, the Siberian Kadets had come out staunchly in favour of General Kornilov – even going so far as to withdraw their recognition of the Provisional Government in the aftermath of the Commander-in-Chief's arrest – while their local party organ, *Sibirskaia rech'*, had thundered that, for allegedly having undermined the fighting ability of the army, SRs were 'more deserving of contempt than the most odious of tsarist officials'.[102]

At Omsk the leader of the largest and most influential Kadet city committee in Siberia was the lawyer and editor of *Sibirskaia rech'*, V.A. Zhardetskii, an unpleasant character who struck even party colleagues as 'a fanatic' and 'an egotistical, cunning and hateful man'.[103] He had been briefly imprisoned by the Bolsheviks in early 1918, and had then spent several months in hospital recovering from the nervous disorder his internment had induced. Upon discharge he remained subject to intermittent bouts of depression and hysterical anger – symptoms which his supporters seemed to interpret as indicative of strong character, to the surprise of newcomers to Omsk. Like many on the right, Zhardetskii held the PSR to blame

100 Krol' *Za tri goda*, pp. 63–9. The URR programme appeared in *Zaria* (Omsk) No. 47, 8.viii.1919. For examples of wall posters announcing the opening of URR branches at Barnaul and Omsk see *Pares Papers*, Box 28.

101 Mosina, I.G. *Formirovanie burzhuazii v politicheskuiu silu v Sibiri*. Tomsk (1978), pp. 75–9.

102 Rosenberg *Liberals*, p. 199; Ioffe *Kolchakovsaia avantiura*, p. 107.

103 Ustrialov, N. 'Iz proshlago', *Russkaia zhizn'. Al'manakh* (Harbin), No. 3 (1922), p. 54; Borodin, N.A. *Idealy i deiatel'nost': sorok let zhizny i raboty riadovogo russkogo intelligenta*. Berlin– Paris (1930), p. 203.

for the Bolshevik success of October 1917, and such was his detestation of Chernov's party that he could not even pronounce its name without literally choking upon it. The revolution, he was apt to proclaim, was nothing but 'a mutiny', planned and executed by 'international criminals' who had goaded the benighted Russian people into revolt. His conclusion was that only a strong military government might restore order and grant salvation to Russia.[104]

Nor was Zhardetskii alone in making this analysis. The crumbling of the Russian Empire which was a major feature of the revolution and civil war touched the Kadets' Great Russian-nationalist consciousness to the very quick. At the same time the class forces released in the conflagration flew in the face of the liberals' assumption that there was an essential oneness, a unity, to the Russian people – a force stronger than fissiparous class loyalties and one which a party claiming to be national and 'above politics' could nurture. With both of these cornerstones of their national-liberal credo being attacked so vigorously and effectively, it is not to be wondered at that the Kadets as a whole fell back upon obeisance to what was traditionally seen as the repository and custodian of Russia's truest and purest spirit, the self-sacrificing defender of the national interest: the army. They were neither the first nor last political party whose insecurity would lead them to flirt with the allure of martial strength in an attempt to resolve social problems beyond their own comprehension. As we shall see, however, rarely has there been an army less worthy of the faith invested in it than much of the profligate mass of incompetents and semi-bandits who went under that name in Siberia during the civil war.

That the Siberian Kadets in particular were to fall so easily under the spell of the military was perhaps a result of the party's almost total political isolation east of the Urals in 1918. They had never had strong roots in the region, with committees in only a few of the larger towns. Even at Omsk their best organized group had managed only to snatch a handful of seats in the municipal duma elections of 1917, while in the elections to the Constituent Assembly the party had done very badly in Siberia, falling well below their already meagre national average of 8% of the vote.[105]

104 Spirin, L.M. *Klassy i partii v grazhdanskom voine v Rossii*. Moscow (1968), p. 282; Il'in, I.S. 'Omsk, Direktoriia, i Kolchak', *Novyi zhurnal* (New York), Vol. 72 (1963), p. 202; Krol', L., p. 144.

105 Rosenberg, W.G. 'Russian Municipal Elections of 1917: a Preliminary Computation of the Results', *Soviet Studies* (Glasgow), Vol. 21 (1969), p. 158; Radkey, *Russia Goes to the Polls*, pp. 150–1.

The Kadets, of course, faced a unique problem in Siberia in that they were in direct competition with the influential *oblastniki*. Potanin's regionalists cut deeply into the liberals' natural constituencies among the Russian professional classes and the intelligentsia (of which there were already few enough in the underdeveloped east of the empire), and although there had been some collaboration between the two groups even as late as 1917, Kadets and *oblastniki* parted company immediately after the October Revolution as the latter attempted to utilize the confused circumstances of the time to establish the regional authority of the Extraordinary Siberian Conference and the planned *Sibobduma*. Unwilling, as they saw it, to contribute to the disintegration of Russia through such activities, and clinging to the Great Russian nationalism which in the civil war years was to be by far the most enduring strand of the Kadets' duplex liberal-nationalist shibboleth, Zhardetskii and his colleagues could take no part in the activities of the Western Siberian Commissariat and consequently found themselves excluded from the PSG apparatus which was to become the germ of all anti-Bolshevik administrations in Siberia. Not that the Kadets were altogether perturbed by this isolation. In fact, to some observers the local Kadets actually seemed to have preferred the Bolsheviks to the SR-*oblastnik* authorities which emerged in the wake of the Czechoslovak revolt. Recalled Paul Dotsenko:

> Many of them believed that it would be easier to deal with the Bolsheviks than with the democratic elements which had seized power, in as much as they knew that the Bolsheviks did not have popular support and we did.[106]

The Kadets were, however, sympathetic to the activities of the right wing of the PSG and, following Vologodskii's successful mission to the Far East, were to urge the premier to disown the Omsk government's regionalist genesis and proclaim the PSG to be an all-Russian authority.[107] Zhardetskii and his associates were particularly attracted to the activities of Mikhailov – 'a very useful man for the time', a Kadet informed the British vice-consul at Omsk[108] – and developed contacts with his increasingly centralist and anti-regionalist group as it began to work for the establishment of a military dictatorship. Having never recognized the

106 Dotsenko, *The Struggle for a Democracy*, p. 48.

107 Pepeliaev, V.N. 'Dnevnik', *Krasnye zori* (Irkutsk), No. 4 (1923), p. 85.

108 FO 538/3 'Translation of a Report on the PSG (n.d.)'.

authority of the *Sibobduma* and having found themselves alienated from the emergent authorities at Omsk which were – however unhappily – associated with the duma, 'believing themselves threatened by this situation', observed Dotsenko, the Siberian Kadets 'began to work on the army officers' and had called for the establishment of military rule since the first days of the overthrow of Soviet power in the east.[109] Military dictatorship, they no doubt saw, might be not only the harbinger of law and order but a useful means by which they, the self-appointed guardians of Russia's true interests, could obtain a position of power through association – a position which they could not hope to win through a popular mandate in Siberia.

Many Siberian Kadets' original choice for the role of dictator was General Horvath, Governor of the Chinese Eastern Railway, whose ribbon of Russian power through Manchuria had remained free of Bolshevik encroachment in 1918. It had been Kadets among the entourage of this long-serving administrator who, as early as July 9th, had persuaded him, in the words of his own proclamation, 'as the sole remaining representative of the Provisional Government, to do something to save the country from disaster and to assume the prerogatives of supreme state authority'.[110] At that time, however, with the Czechoslovaks having only recently captured Vladivostok and with Soviet power in Transbaikalia isolating him from events to the west, Horvath had no influence beyond the Manchurian railway enclave and his assumption of supreme power over all of anti-Bolshevik Russia was a fiction. Moreover, Kadet emissaries who were gradually arriving in the east from central and southern Russia had men of greater national reputations in mind for the role of dictator.

But for the moment the identity of the dictator was not a question of prime importance. Rather, what mattered to the Kadets was to establish the *principle* of the necessity of a dictatorship in Russia as the only viable alternative to Bolshevism or SR 'semi-Bolshevism'. To achieve this the party needed allies. They found them in the emergent Siberian Army, among the powerful trading and industrial classes of the Urals and Siberia (a group swelled daily by the arrival of capitalists and financiers fleeing from the Soviet zone) and among the Allied military agents arriving in the east as the intervention got underway. With their party organization

109 Dotsenko, *The Struggle for a Democracy*, p. 49.

110 *Dalekaia okraina* (Vladivostok) No. 3,587, 11.vii.1918.

and contacts the Kadets were to provide such disparate advocates of dictatorship with a leadership corps. The price which they had to pay for such influence, however, was to largely abandon any commitment to liberal and democratic principles, to ditch the Russian liberals' longstanding pretension to *nadklassnost'* and to throw in their lot with the particular class interests of the bourgeoisie and officer-landowners. In the course of the summer of 1918 they did precisely that. When the afore-mentioned URR Kadet Lev Krol returned to Omsk from the Ufa State Conference he was shocked to find his party colleagues, 'driven crazy by hatred and bloodshed' it seemed, having abandoned all cultivated and European values in favour of a fetishism for the army which struck him as 'Asiatic'. Krol found himself ostracized and almost faced a duel with the unbalanced Zhardetskii, who publicly excoriated all those who had been party to the establishment of the Directory as 'criminals and traitors'.[111] Krol attempted to win back the party for the URR, but it was too late. At a regional conference of Kadet committees in late August, the Omsk party leader had already put the seal on the tripartite alliance of the Kadets, the Siberian Army and the bourgeoisie in declaring that in the circumstances of the civil war every sacrifice had to be made – even if that meant that the Kadets 'must build the entire Party of the People's Freedom into a bonfire'.[112]

Zhardetskii knew that in the promotion of dictatorship his Kadets could count upon the support of the strongest of the bourgeoisie's own class organizations. On July 16th at a meeting of the Trades and Industry Congress at Omsk, for example, he had led an impassioned call for the PSG to transfer its authority to a military ruler. He and other delegates would have no truck with the government – not simply because of its (increasingly cosmetic) regionalism, but because of what Zhardetskii termed its 'pandering' to the SRs in the duma. That such 'pandering' was to kill Aleksandr Novoselov did not seem to concern the Kadet leader. Nor was he alone in his detestation of the duma. In fact, the very mention of the possibility of a convocation of the *Sibobduma* was sufficient to bring forth such a general paroxysm of anger from the floor of the congress that the PSG's Minister of Justice, Grigorii Patushinskii, was barely able to continue his address to the assembled businessmen. Zhardetskii's reply, on the other hand, elicited a standing ovation: 'The introduction

111 Krol', L., pp. 152, 163.

112 *Sibirskaia rech'* (Omsk), 25.viii.1918. This was essentially only a restatement of the thesis advanced by P.I. Novgorodov at the Kadets' Moscow Conference of May 1918. See Rosenberg *Liberals*, pp. 283–4.

of a strong, unipersonal rule cannot be avoided,' he stormed: 'No soviets! No peasants' congresses! There must be no Siberian *oblast'* Duma!'[113]

By September, with Komuch increasingly hard-pressed by the Red Army whilst, in the rear, the Siberian Army was growing daily in strength and audacity, business organizations were becoming even more outspoken in their pronouncements. The timbre of their attitude to the nascent Directory, for example, was set at a meeting of the All-Russian Trades and Industry Congress at Ufa in the days immediately preceding the State Conference. 'With gnashing teeth', reported one observer, congress delegates accused the democratic parties of 'the destruction of the Russian state', while the congress's chairman, A.A. Kropotkin, insisted that, if the new government expected to receive the moral and material support of the business class, then all Socialist Revolutionaries should be excluded from it: 'They must be removed – now it is time for other hands to guide the army', he added darkly.[114] Precisely what hands Kropotkin had in mind became clear when, at its final plenary session, this All-Russian Congress of Trades and Industry adopted a political programme which demanded that supreme military and civil authority should be transferred to an all-powerful commander-in-chief.[115]

Enter Pepeliaev

By the early autumn of 1918, therefore, as the Directory was launched at Ufa, the idea of a unipersonal military dictatorship was looming ominously and ineluctably on the Siberian horizon. It was discussed at meetings of Kadets and bourgeois organizations, debated in officers' clubs and political salons and featured in the

113 Rakitnikov, p. 8; Maksakov and Turunov, pp. 207–8.

114 *Golos rabochego* (Ufa) No. 1, 10.ix.1918.

115 Kornatovskii, N.A. (ed.) *Kolchakovshchina: iz belykh memuarov*. Leningrad (1930), p. 8. This document bears a rather striking resemblance to the later Statute on the Structure of Provisional State Power in Russia of November 18th 1918 (the so-called 'Kolchak constitution') – see below, pp. 123–4. Meanwhile, a call for the establishment of a unipersonal dictatorship met with 'stormy applause throughout the hall' at the 1st Urals Congress of Trades and Industry at Ekaterinburg in October – see Taniaev, A. (ed.) *Kolchakovshchina na Urale*. Moscow (1930), pp. 49–50. And, on August 29th, the Vladivostok Chamber of Commerce also resolved that only a dictatorship was 'capable of completing the regeneration of the Russian Army and the entire country' – see *Golos Primor'ia* (Vladivostok) No. 277, 31.viii.1918, cited in Krushanov, A.I. *Grazhdanskaia voina v Sibiri i na Dal'nem Vostoke, 1918–1920*. Vladivostok (1972), Vol. 1, p. 102.

instructions of Allied diplomats. Susurrations regarding it could even be heard on the street corners of Omsk. All that remained was for someone to take the notion of dictatorship and mould it into a tangible programme of political action. And at this juncture there duly arrived on the stage of anti-Bolshevism in the east just such a king-maker: Viktor Nikolaevich Pepeliaev, a forty-four year old ex-schoolmaster from Biisk in the Altai who, after a brief spell in the Fourth State Duma on the Kadet ticket, had entered the Central Committee of the self-proclaimed Party of the People's Freedom in 1917.

A rather robust figure with a stentorian voice, Viktor Pepeliaev's inborn distaste for all things socialist had been galvanized during the disturbances of Russia's year of revolution by his humiliation (and near imprisonment) at the hands of the unruly pro-Bolshevik sailors of Kronstadt during his short service as commissar to the naval base for the Provisional Government.[116] Immediately after the October Revolution Pepeliaev got his first taste of conspiratorial work, organizing a network of officer groups in Petrograd as a prelude to the abortive Kadet-sponsored rising in the capital. Later, in July 1918, he was sent east by his Central Committee, as an emissary to anti-Bolshevik Siberia.

Ostensibly Viktor Pepeliaev was entrusted with precisely the same mission in the east as was his Kadet colleague Lev Krol: that is, he had undertaken to propagandize in the Urals and in Siberia for the coalition policies of the Union of Regeneration. However, Pepeliaev was evidently far from being happy with the task, remaining unconvinced of the utility of a rapprochement with even the mildest of the SRs. In fact, in retrospect it can be seen that Pepeliaev was acting not as an emissary of the URR, but as an advocate of a quite different and far more extreme anti-Bolshevik group, the National Centre. In this underground network of opponents of soviet rule, although numerically predominant, the Kadets (by their own admission) served only as 'the left flank' in alliance with a variegated group of disillusioned politicians of the former Provisional Government and the State Duma, united by a desire for the establishment of an unalloyed and unrestrained dictatorship under the former Commander-in-Chief of the Russian Army, General M.V. Alekseev (who, in the spring of 1918, was engaged in the rallying of a Volunteer Army in south Russia in collaboration with General Kornilov and Ataman Kaledin of the Don

116 Mawdsley, E. *The Russian Revolution and the Baltic Fleet*. London (1978), pp. 52–4.

Cossacks).[117] At some point during the spring of 1918 the National Centre did accept the URR programme for a Directory. However, as a Soviet historian of the party has convincingly demonstrated, the Kadets in the National Centre only went along with their Central Committee's support of the URR in order (in the wake of Miliukov's flirtation with the Germans at Kiev, which had tarnished the party's reputation) to preserve a semblance of party unity.[118] Certainly Pepeliaev never took his mission to the east on behalf of the URR very seriously, for even by the time that he reached Ufa (in late July) he was openly calling for anti-Bolshevism's adoption of the National Centre's minimum programme of a government based on a military ruler (Alekseev) with two non-party assistants.[119] He then continued eastwards, pausing only at Omsk to congratulate Zhardetskii for having had a programme of pure dictatorship adopted at the Siberian Kadets' regional conference in August and to express, at public and party meetings, his pessimism with regard to the likely outcome of the Ufa Conference – he held that the creation of a strong government in collaboration with the SRs would be 'nothing short of a miracle' – before beginning a six-week mission to spread the word of the National Centre in the Far East.[120]

The salient features of Pepeliaev's trip can be reconstructed from the published extracts from his diary.[121] He held talks with local Kadet leaders along his route – they would come to his carriage to discuss and to routinely damn the *Sibobduma*

117 Dolgorukov, P.D. *Natsional'naia politika i partiia narodnoi svobody*. Rostov-on-Don (1919), pp. 9–11.

118 Dumova, p. 126. On the development of the National Centre see Rosenberg *Liberals*, pp. 395–9 and Ioffe *Krakh rossiiskoi*, pp. 100–15. Golinkov, D.L. *Krushenie antisovetskogo podpol'ia v SSSR*. Moscow (1978), pp. 106–8 provides lists of members of the URR, the National Centre and the even more right-wing, pro-German, Rightist Centre.

119 Ioffe *Kolchakovskaiia avantiura*, p. 107. Rosenberg (*Liberals*, p. 390) is certainly mistaken in asserting that Viktor Pepeliaev only abandoned the policies of the URR after consulting with his younger brother Anatoli, a White commander, at Ekaterinburg. If anything, his sibling tended to exert a moderating influence on V.N. Pepeliaev. According to one source, the National Centre desired that Astrov and Avksent'ev should assist the dictator, Alekseev (see Borodin, p. 199). Presumably both would have been required to resign their party cards.

120 *Sibirskaia rech'* (Omsk) 30.viii.1918, cited in Ioffe *Kolchakovskaiia avantiura*, p. 112. On the Kadet conference see Maksakov and Turunov, pp. 207-8.

121 Pepeliaev's diary for the period September 1918 – October 1919 has appeared in print. The early sections were published in the Irkutsk journal *Krasnye zori* in 1923; the later, better known sections appeared in *Krasnyi arkhiv* in 1928.

and the Ufa State Conference. But of such meetings the diarist recorded very little. On September 28th, however, he set down a detailed transcript of a conversation he had held that day with Rudolf (Radola) Gajda, the young Czech general who had so aggressively and effectively organized the Legion's revolt against Soviet rule and had then so ruthlessly cleared eastern Siberia of Red Guard forces. The care with which Pepeliaev recorded their talks perhaps reveals the importance he attached to this exchange. Gajda was an ambitious, fiery character, who had begun the world war as a lowly *Feldscher* (hospital orderly) in the Austro-Hungarian Army before deserting to Serbia and making his way to Russia, where he achieved a rapid promotion through the ranks of the Czechoslovak Legion. He met Pepeliaev at Manchuria (the border station between Russia and China) on his return from the Far East, where reports of his dazzling capture from the Bolsheviks (who were intent on sabotage) of the important railway tunnels around the southern shore of Lake Baikal had, according to one witness, earned him the reputation of 'a national hero – his photograph was displayed on stations, his name resounded across the country'.[122] So impressed was Vologodskii that the touring Siberian premier had first promoted the Czech to Main Commander-in-Chief of Army and Naval Forces in the Far East and then (on September 21st) to Main Commander-in-Chief of the Siberian Army itself.[123] This chance meeting of Pepeliaev and Gajda, men whose fates and careers were to be so inextricably bound up with the subsequent development of anti-Bolshevism in the east, was of such key importance to the steady drift towards dictatorship in Siberia that it is worth dwelling upon in some detail.

After an exchange of mutual disillusionment with the Allies (who were not as yet committing the anticipated resources to the anti-Bolshevik struggle) the conversation, recorded Pepeliaev, 'turned to the question of the government':

> I said that I had not gone to the Ufa Conference because I did not believe that a proper government could be formed in such a manner – salvation lies in the person of a military dictator who must create an army.

122 Sukin, I.I. 'Zapiski I.I. Sukina' (*Leeds Russian Archive*), p. 9. On Gajda's capture of Irkutsk and the Baikal tunnels see Eikhe, pp. 25-7.

123 FO 371/3365/21389 'Alston (Vladivostok) to FO, 5.xi.1919'; Guins (1921), Vol. 1, p. 231; Livshits (1979), p. 104. The opposition of Russian officers to becoming subordinate to a Czech was to prevent Gajda assuming supreme command (although he was to be given the command of the Siberian Army Group of the Directory's and later Kolchak's armies). See Piontkovskii, S. 'Ufimskoe gosudarstvennoe soveshchanie', p. 73; Guins, Vol. 2, p. 60.

Gajda agreed with this prognosis wholeheartedly, but dismissed the candidatures of both Horvath and the unruly Ataman of the Transbaikal Cossacks, Grigorii Semenov, both of whom he regarded as being in the pockets of the Japanese. Both General Alekseev and his assistant, General Denikin, were stronger possibilities, he conceded, but both were far away (and, in Gajda's view, the former was too old).

'I am very glad to learn your views,' responded Pepeliaev. 'In your own interest, I trust that you have kept them hidden in the past?'

'Yes, so long as things were not prepared and the military force was not organized', said Gajda, clearly implying that he felt they now were.[124] Mutual trust and shared confidence having been established, the general, in a most innocent manner, made a definite proposal: 'Kolchak,' he mused, 'is coming here.'

'To this,' recorded Pepeliaev, 'I said that in Moscow General Alekseev had been favoured, but there are no communications with him. Meanwhile time presses on. Kolchak was considered, but as a secondary candidate. It is possible to support him. But when might this be?' he asked Gajda. Thus the conversation, which had started on the level of a political discussion, took a decisive turn towards conspiracy. It continued:

> Gajda: 'In about twenty days. I can keep the Czechs quiet.'
> Pepeliaev: 'But does he think the same?'
> Gajda: 'We think alike. He will support me.'

Thus was the agreement on a coup to establish the military dictatorship of Kolchak sealed. To finalize the plans Gajda then promised to telegraph the candidate dictator, who was in Vladivostok, and to have him meet Pepeliaev at the port. In the event, however, Pepeliaev and Kolchak were unable to rendezvous in the Far East and Gajda's twenty-day timetable proved too restrictive for the Kadet to make all the necessary arrangements. Consequently, when on October 7th he received a telegram from the Omsk Kadets suggesting that an All-Siberian Kadet Congress should be convened at Ekaterinburg a fortnight thereafter, Pepeliaev was immediately to send word that November 15th at Omsk would be a more appropriate time and place for such a gathering.[125] On that date, Pepeliaev was

124 In fact, at a Vladivostok press conference on September 16th, Gajda had already made public his belief that only a dictatorship could save Russia. See *Dokumenty i materialy po istorii sovetsko–chekhoslovatskikh otnoshenii*. Moscow (1973), Vol. 1, p. 164.

125 Pepeliaev, V.N. 'Dnevnik', *Krasnye zori* (Irkutsk), No. 4 (1923), pp. 77–9.

clearly hoping, the Kadets' congress would be perfectly placed to applaud, honour and preconize the investiture of supreme military and civil authority in the person of a dictator.

The candidate dictator, Kolchak, a vice-admiral of the Russian fleet, was to duly arrive at Omsk on October 13th. Later, to an investigatory committee established by his Bolshevik captors at Irkutsk in 1920, he was to claim that he had been journeying to south Russia, with the intention of joining his wife and son in the Crimea.[126] Yet, with remarkably little effort, General Boldyrev was able to persuade Kolchak to remain in Siberia and to accept the post of Minister of War and Marine in the Directory's nascent Council of Ministers.[127] As we shall see, negotiations surrounding the formation of that body were to be prolonged and dogged by arguments as to who was to be included between the SR members of the Directory on the one hand and the PSG on the other. The nomination of Kolchak, however, met no resistance from either side. According to a colleague who was accompanying him, Kolchak was welcomed by SR and conservative politicians alike at Omsk, as a man 'of irreproachable honour and high patriotism'.[128] A rather slight figure, but elegant and well-groomed, with a poised, aristocratic bearing, dark and serious of countenance, and graced with an aquiline nose and a pair of intense black eyes, the admiral certainly looked the very figure of severity, authority and martiality that the times seemed to demand of anti-Bolshevism. Outside of governing circles, however, the average Siberian – and even some of the less informed members of the local Kadet committee – were entitled to be asking: '*Kto takoi Kolchak*'? ('Who is this Kolchak?').[129] How, they wondered, had this mysterious sailor suddenly come to appear and be lauded at a spot more distant from the sea than virtually any other on the face of the earth? And why, they pondered, in this land-locked city teeming with generals, had an admiral been named as

126 Varneck and Fisher, pp. 144–5.

127 Varneck and Fisher, p. 145; Boldyrev, p. 72.

128 Smirnov, M.I. *Admiral Kolchak: kratkii biograficheskii ocherk.* Paris (1930), p. 43. Various observers record that Avksent'ev was keener than anyone that Kolchak should enter the Council of Ministers. See Serebrennikov 'K istorii', p. 19; Sukin (*Leeds Russian Archive*), p. 21.

129 Krol', L., p. 151; [Ovchinnikov, A.Z.] 'Memoirs of the Red Partisan Movement in the Russian Far East, 1918–1920', in Varneck and Fisher, p. 273. Later was published in South Russia a pamphlet by N. Morskoi, *Vozhd' i geroi Rossii – kto takoi Kolchak* (Narodnaia Biblioteka, No. 3). Rostov-on-Don (1919).

Minister of War? Fortunately history allows us to build up a more complete biography of Admiral Kolchak than that to which his Siberian contemporaries would have been privy. It enables us, moreover, to establish that he was not such an 'accidental' choice for the role of dictator as has sometimes been claimed and to confirm that his arrival at Omsk at such an auspicious moment for the anti-Bolshevik movement was not simply the coincidence that has sometimes been assumed.[130]

Kto takoi Kolchak?

At the time of his arrival at Omsk, Aleksandr Vasil'evich Kolchak was approaching his forty-fourth birthday, having been born at the Obukhov armaments works near St Petersburg on November 17th 1874.[131] His father, a long-serving naval engineer who was employed as an inspector at the works, was of Russified Turkish stock (a distant ancestor from Bosnia having settled in Russia after being captured during the Empress Anne's war against Turkey in 1739). His mother, although more immediately descended from the nobility of Kherson province in south Russia, was of Don Cossack heritage. Such a mix of blood no doubt accounted for the future dictator's rather Asiatic countenance, while his warrior-like ancestry certainly influenced his own martial leanings.[132]

130 See, for example, Rosenberg *Liberals*, p. 397; Berk 'The *Coup d'État*', pp. 445ff; Kettle, *The Road to Intervention*, p. 354; Fleming, P. *The Fate of Admiral Kolchak*. London (1963), pp. 95–6; Connaughton, R. *The Republic of the Ushakovka: Admiral Kolchak and the Allied Intervention in Siberia, 1918–1920*. London (1990), p. 92.

131 Curiously, Kolchak's date of birth is sometimes cited as 1873 and sometimes as 1874. His son Rostislav, surely the most reliable source, gives the latter in his published genealogy of the Kolchak family: see Kolchak, R. 'Admiral Kolchak: ego rod i sem'ia', *Voenno-istoricheskii vestnik* (Paris), No. 16 (1960), p. 15. The following summary of Kolchak's career down to the end of 1917 (except where footnoted as being otherwise) is drawn from the following sources: Smirnov *Admiral Kolchak*, pp. 7–42; Smirnov, M.I. 'Admiral Kolchak', *Slavonic and East European Review* (London), Vol. 11, No. 32 (1930), pp. 373–80; Auslander, S. *Verkhovnyi pravitel Admiral Kolchak*. Omsk (1919), pp. 16–33; Kniazev, V.V. *Zhizn' dlia vsekh i smert' za vsekh: zapiski lichnogo ad"iutanta Verkhovnogo pravitelia admirala A.V. Kolchaka, rotmistra V.V. Kniazeva*. Jordanville, NY (1971); and, chiefly, from Kolchak's own account, in Varneck and Fisher, pp. 1–107.

132 The name 'Kolchak' is derived from the Turkish (Osmarli) word '*Qolcaq*', meaning an iron or wooden gauntlet – not an inappropriate name for a future dictator.

Kolchak was raised, by his own admission, 'in a purely military atmosphere and milieu'. After attending the 6th Classical Gymnasium at St Petersburg he entered the capital's Naval Academy in 1888. The possibility of the young Aleksandr pursuing any career other than that of the sea, which had been his father's life, was never even raised. A successful and popular scholar, in 1894 he graduated as second in his class and with the prestigious Admiral Rikord Prize. From the 7th St Petersburg Naval Battalion, the following year he was posted to his first ship (the cruiser 'Riurik') and over the next five years (latterly on the 'Kreiser') served tours of duty in the Pacific and Indian Oceans which saw him rise steadily to the rank of naval lieutenant. Most of Kolchak's duties during this period were concerned with academic research into hydrology and other marine sciences. It was, however, to reading matter on polar exploration that he turned during his spare time. By the turn of the century the maturing Kolchak had developed a passionate and informed interest in the contemporary race to uncover the secrets of the earth's icy extremities and it was his cherished ambition to lead an expedition to plant the Russian flag at the South Pole. Clearly, a strong sense of national pride was a feature of his developing character.

In December 1899, whilst on duty in the Mediterranean and bound for the Far East, Kolchak learned that he had been invited to join the esteemed geologist, Baron E.V. von Toll, on a voyage of exploration along the northern coast of Siberia. He leapt at the chance and, having completed the necessary formalities for secondment from the navy to the Imperial Academy of Sciences and undertaken a period of preparatory study under Fridtjof Nansen at Christiania, he was to spend the next two years on board the 'Zaria' helping Toll to chart the New Siberian Islands and the Nordenskjold Archipelago whilst conducting his own experiments into the physics of ice and the earth's magnetics. After a brief return to St Petersburg in late 1902, Kolchak set off northwards once again in February 1903 to lead an heroic (but ultimately fruitless) eighteen-month-long attempt to locate and rescue Baron Toll, who had disappeared during the previous summer on a rather reckless voyage to far-off Bennet Island. Spending the six weeks of the final 400 km of his own trip to Bennet Island in an open whaleboat, Kolchak displayed characteristic bravery and loyalty to his mentor and achieved a voyage which has rarely been equalled in the history of polar exploration. It would not be until 1908 that he would find the time to write up his hydrological researches – but upon their publication he was to be rewarded with the Imperial Russian Geographical Association's most prestigious scientific award, the Great Konstantin Gold Medal, for his significant contribution to man's knowledge of the Arctic. Moreover, his exploits gained him a certain reputation in society for his attractive mix of patriotism and courageousness, while his scholarship would accord him a mention in the list of 'authorities' on Siberia appended to the Tsarist government's official survey of the empire's eastern reaches, *Aziatskaia Rossiia.*[133]

The delay in finishing his reports on the Arctic was occasioned by the fact that whilst at Iakutsk, en route back to St Petersburg, in February 1904, Kolchak heard of the outbreak of Russia's war against Japan in the Far East. He paused only briefly at Irkutsk in March to rendezvous with and to marry his fiancée from the capital, Sofia Fedorovna Omireva, before rejoining the navy and heading east to the Pacific. During that war, so ignominious for his country, Kolchak personally was to accrue yet more honours – he received, for example, the coveted Gold St George's Sword of Honour for distinguished mine-laying work and for the sinking of an enemy cruiser by the first ship at his command, the destroyer 'Serdityi'. Subsequently, however, ill-health in the form of pneumonia and rheumatism – Kolchak was never

133 Toll's notes on the 1900–1902 voyage, in which (p. 289) he generously and presciently praised Kolchak as 'a clever, multifaceted young man, who may go a long way', were published posthumously as *Die Russische Polarfahrt der 'Sarja', 1900–1902*. Berlin (1909). Kolchak's researches (ackowledged in *Aziatskaia Rossiia*, Vol. 2, p. 631) were published as 'Led Karskogo i Sibirskogo morei', *Imperatorskaia Akademiia nauk. Zapiski* (St Petersburg), Series 8, Vol. 26, No. 1 (1909); later translated as 'The Arctic Pack and Polynia' in Joerg, W.L. (ed.) *Problems of Polar Research*. New York (1928). For an interesting memoir by another participant in Toll's expedition, including the author's impressions of the young Kolchak, see Kolomeitsev, N.N. 'Russkaia poliarnaia ekspeditsiia, 1900–1903gg.', *Russian Émigré Archives*. (Fresno, CA), Vol. 5 (1974), pp. 1–50. A concise account of Kolchak's arctic experiences is presented in Barr, W. 'A.V. Kolchak: Arctic Scientist and Explorer', *Polar Record* (Cambridge), Vol. 20, No. 129 (1981), pp. 507–24. Barr notes that Kolchak's interest in the Arctic did not end in 1904, although he was never to return to the far north. In 1910 he was among the chief inspirers and planners of the 'Russian Hydrographic Expedition' which charted the northern coast of Siberia for the next five years and which in 1913 made the last great discovery of Arctic exploration – the Severnaia Zemlia archipelago. Already in 1900, Baron Toll, as a tribute to Kolchak's work, had named a 'Kolchak Island' in Tamyr Bay (*Tamyrskii zaliv*). However, when this speck of land appeared on Soviet charts of the region (and occasionally it did not appear!) it bore the name 'Rastorgiev Island' (in memory of a Yakut participant in the 1900 expedition). See 'Unperson Becomes Unisland', *Polar Record* (Cambridge), Vol. 19, No.118 (1978), pp. 73–4. Because of his later role in the civil war, Soviet accounts of the period generally either avoided mentioning Kolchak's name, so as to conceal his contribution to Arctic exploration – see, for example, Vittenburg, P.V. *Zhizn' i nauchnaia deiatel'nost' E.V. Tollia*. Moscow (1960) and Starokadomskii, L.M. *Piat' plavanii v Severnom ledovitom okeane, 1910–1915*. Moscow (1959) – or deliberately denigrated Kolchak's role and gave undue emphasis to the part played by more ideologically acceptable participants. For example, from Bolotnokov, N. *Nikifor Begichev*. Moscow (1949), it would appear that the leader of the expedition to Bennet Island to rescue Toll was not Kolchak but his bosun, Begichev.

fully to recover from the strains of the years which he had spent in the arctic – obliged him to enter hospital for some weeks and then to seek a commission on land. Finally, during the prolonged Japanese siege of the Russian garrison at Port Arthur, he would command a naval battery on the north-west perimeter. With the capitulation of the port's defences in January 1905, Kolchak fell, exhausted and racked with such rheumatic pains that he was barely able to walk, into enemy hands and spent some time in a Japanese hospital at Nagasaki before being repatriated via Canada.

After a four-month recuperative furlough, from 1906 to 1914 Kolchak worked diligently at the Admiralty in St Petersburg. As a founder member of the capital's Naval Circle, he gained the reputation of a modernizer, struggling against the graven conservatism of the naval hierarchy in order to rebuild the shattered Russian fleet on a modern, scientific basis and to drag the administration and training methods of the service into the twentieth century. He was soon appointed as Chief of the Organization Section for the Baltic Fleet attached to the new Naval General Staff (an innovation which he and his circle had strongly advocated), and as such was noted as one of the so-called 'Young Turks' among the Russian military of the period who were not averse to bargaining and negotiating with the State Duma for increased defence credits. By 1914, therefore, Kolchak had established a progressive reputation amongst both the military and scientific communities and could even count some members of the Duma among his admirers.[134] This brilliant young officer made an agreeable impression on almost everyone with whom he came into contact. One of his admirers, the wife of Kolchak's colleague (later Admiral) S.N. Timirev, a woman of whom we will hear more later, recalled meeting him for the first time in 1911 and falling instantly in love: 'Not to notice Aleksandr Vasil′evich was impossible – he was always the centre of things', she remembered.[135]

With the outbreak of war in 1914, Kolchak again volunteered for active service. He began work in the Baltic Fleet and gained the Cross of St George and a certain

134 For additional information on this period of Kolchak's life see Adams, C.E. 'Der Wiederaufstieg der russischen Kriegsmarine in den Jahren 1910–1915', *Marine Rundschau*, Vol. 61 (1964), pp. 14–16; Perrins, M. 'The Russian Military 1904–1917, and its Role in Russian Political Affairs', University of London PhD Thesis (1983), pp. 171–4; Savich, N. 'Tri vstrechi', *Arkhiv russkoi revoliutsii* (Berlin), Vol. 10 (1923), pp. 168–74.

135 Timireva, A.V. 'Vospominaniia', *Novyi zhurnal* (New York), Vol. 159 (1985), p. 210.

amount of public acclaim for a daring mine-laying raid to the mouth of the Kiel Canal (an operation which, characteristically, he not only planned but executed personally) and for his part in the defence of Riga. His reward on this occasion was promotion to the rank of vice-admiral by 1916 and, on July 16th of that year, an appointment as Commander-in-Chief of the Black Sea Fleet. Considering that it was only twenty-two years since his graduation from the Naval Academy and that many of his contemporaries at the school were currently serving only as captains 1st class, this was a remarkable rise indeed. Nor did Kolchak disappoint his sponsors – in fact, so thorough were his mine-laying operations around the Bosphorus and so vigilant was his patrolling, that from November 1916 until his retirement in June 1917 not one new enemy vessel was able to enter the Black Sea while all Bulgarian and Turkish vessels remained confined to port, as did the two German warships at Istanbul, and enemy submarine activity in Kolchak's sector was virtually nil. This, plus the fact that only one Russian steamer was lost in the Black Sea under Kolchak (compared to thirty in the six months preceding his appointment), is sufficient testimony to his remarkable naval skills, while the fact that the bloody massacre of officers by sailors which accompanied the February revolution at Kronstadt and Reval (culminating in the murder of Admiral Nepenin, Kolchak's counterpart as Commander of the Baltic Fleet) was not in any way repeated at Odessa or Sevastopol informs us of the respect in which Kolchak was held by his men and the fairness with which he dealt with their complaints in a most difficult situation. All in all, according to the leading western authority on the Russian navy of that era, Kolchak was 'the most successful Admiral of the Fleet'; under his command the Black Sea Fleet enjoyed 'total superiority' over the enemy.[136]

In a country generally starved of military success and heroes in the German war, Kolchak and his achievements were something of an exception. Of course, the

136 Greger, R. *The Russian Fleet, 1914–1917.* London (1972), pp. 56–65. Kolchak himself modestly ascribed the relative quietude of the Black Sea Fleet to its distance from the front. That, as well as the fact that there were far fewer sailors of working class origin in his fleet than Nepenin's, must have been a factor; but the admiral's personal authority must have had some effect. On Kolchak's service in the Black Sea see also Smirnov, M.I. 'Admiral Kolchak vo vremia revoliutsii v Chernomorskom flote', *Istoriia i sovremennaia* (Berlin), No. 4 (1923), pp. 3–28; and Nekrasov, G. *North of Gallipoli: The Black Sea Fleet at War, 1914–1917.* Boulder, CO (1992). Rather more critical Soviet accounts of his command include Platonov, A.V. *Chernomorskii flot v revoliutsii 1917g. i admiral Kolchak.* Leningrad (1925); and Zhukov, V.A. *Chernomorskii flot v revoliutsii, 1917–1918gg.* Moscow (1932).

imperial defence establishments were never very adept at publicizing their rare successes, and Kolchak was far from being a household name in Russia by 1917. Nevertheless, among the military and certain nationalist and liberal circles, his exploits at sea, his conspicuous patriotism and his leadership qualities had not gone unnoticed. It is not surprising, then, that from the very first days of the February Revolution until his sudden arrival at Omsk in November 1918, we find Kolchak's name being constantly raised as the potential rallying point for a government of national salvation among various liberal and right-wing groups who saw the revolution not as a mechanism for urgently required social change but as the best hope for military victory and conquest for Russia. We find, in fact, that Kolchak received repeated invitations to involve himself in politics, particularly as reactionary, conservative and even liberal forces became convinced that the revolution would have to be halted and a dictatorship installed as a prerequisite of survival in the war against Germany.

Believing that the Protopopov ministry was hopelessly corrupt and beyond redemption by the Tsar, Kolchak was among the first of Russia's senior officers to greet the February Revolution. Even though he had theretofore considered himself to be a monarchist, he was later to claim, he felt that as a military man his first duty was to his country rather than to any particular government or form of government. Besides, he had friends in the Duma whom he trusted to create a patriotic administration capable of winning the war. On March 2nd, therefore, he informed the men of the Black Sea Fleet of the events in the capital and urged them to assist the new central authorities at Petrograd in pursuing the war 'to a victorious conclusion'.[137] And at first Kolchak found himself able to work with the elected committees of sailors in Sevastopol – even to the extent of issuing joint communiqués with them on the necessity of maintaining discipline and recognizing the 'legitimate authority' of officers.[138] By April, however, as the flames of anti-war sentiment were fanned into life across Russia by the Bolsheviks, and as agitators from the north began to arrive on the Black Sea coast armed with all sorts of demoralizing propaganda, Kolchak had become convinced that the burgeoning committee system in the armed services would inevitably undermine the war effort.

137 For the text of Kolchak's order of March 2nd 1917 see Iakushkin, E. *Kolchakovshchina*. Moscow–Leningrad (1928), pp. 21–2.

138 Browder, R.P. and Kerensky, A.F. (eds.) *The Russian Provisional Government, 1917*. Stanford (1961), Vol. 2, pp. 870–1.

Subsequently, in May, on his first trip to revolutionary Petrograd he heard and supported General Kornilov's demand that the Provisional Government should permit the dispersal of demonstrations in the capital by force. And upon returning to his headquarters, increasingly frustrated by the disruption caused by the Sevastopol Soviet, in late May Kolchak was moved to tender his resignation. A visit from Kerensky persuaded him to soldier on for two more weeks, but when on June 9th the Sevastopol Soviet, believing that a counter-revolutionary organization existed in the port, took the step of ordering the disarming of all officers, Kolchak could contain himself no longer: summoning the crew of his flagship 'Georgii Pobedonosets' up on deck, the admiral declared that even as a POW in Japan he had not been so humiliated and then tossed his cherished Sword of Honour overboard into the harbour.[139] Although this dramatic gesture was undoubtedly an expression of wounded pride and the first public instance of an inability to control his temper which was later to embarrass Kolchak, and although it was far from being motivated by political passion, it nevertheless brought forth an immediate response from the budding counter-revolutionary cells of the Officers' Union and the Military League which (together with other such organizations) sent Kolchak telegrams of salutation and sympathy – the former even presented the admiral with a replacement sword, replete with, according to his diary, 'an extremely flattering inscription'.[140] Moreover, Kolchak's impulsive sword pitching was later to become embellished as an inspirational symbol for the anti-Bolshevik movement and was to figure prominently in the hagiographical mythologizing of the dictatorship and the incipient personality cult which was to surround the admiral in 1919.[141]

In 1917, however, Kolchak had no need for symbols or mythologies: he was already quite heavily embroiled in the *business* of conspiracy. At his interrogation in 1920, the admiral recounted that he had attended meetings of the 'National Centre' on returning to Petrograd in June, following his resignation. This may have

139 On Kolchak's resignation see also Kerensky, A.F. *Russia and History's Turning Point*. New York (1965), pp. 278–81; Fedotoff-White, D. *Survival Through War and Revolution in Russia*. Philadelphia (1939), pp. 149–54.

140 Khessin, S.S. *Oktiabr'skaia revoliutsiia i flot*. Moscow (1971), p. 182; Iordanskii, N. 'Admiral Kolchak', *Put'* (Helsingfors), 11.ii.1921; Ioffe, G.Z. *Beloe delo. General Kornilov*. Moscow (1989), pp. 59–60.

141 Auslander, pp. 33–4 and 'Admiral Kolchak', *Sbornik 'Ruskogo biuro pechati'* (Tokyo), No. 1 (1919), p. 19, are prime examples of this. The incident also featured prominently in White propaganda leaflets distributed among troops at the front – for example, the fly sheet 'Admiral Kolchak' of the Siberian Army's Mobile Printshop, 'Vpered' (*Pares Papers*, Box 47).

been a slip of the tongue. It may equally, however, have been an attempt to mislead his captors, for as we have seen the National Centre (the Kadet-dominated organization promoting the dictatorship of Alekseev) was not formed until May 1918.[142] In fact, the secret meetings which Kolchak attended on the capital's Vasilevskii Island were those of the *Republican* Centre – a shadowy, underground group with links to right-wing terrorists and staff officers which was the *primum mobile* of the Kornilov affair of August. One member of this organization, the banker P.N. Finisov, recalled that Kolchak not only attended their meetings but agreed to lead their military organization; another, General G.I. Klerzhe, asserted that in the wake of the sword-throwing incident, Kolchak's popularity among right-wing circles in Petrograd was such that moves were afoot to have *him* named dictator rather than Kornilov once the Provisional Government had been removed.[143] Certainly such a move would have attracted a level of support, for during the summer of 1917 right-wing newspapers such as *Malenkaia gazeta* and *Zhivoe slovo* were demanding exactly that: 'All power to Kolchak!', they proclaimed.[144]

Kolchak's friend and Chief of Staff in the Black Sea, Admiral M.I. Smirnov, has also recorded that Kolchak formed an agreement at this time with certain unnamed 'patriotic organizations' that he should head their movement to establish a military dictatorship. Hearing of this upon his return to the capital in July, asserts Smirnov,

142 Varneck and Fisher, p. 87. Kolchak managed to confuse not only his captors but the editors of the English-language version of his testimony: Varneck and Fisher (*ibid.*, n. 93) not only failed to spot Kolchak's mistake but embellished it with one of their own.

143 Browder and Kerensky, Vol. 3, p. 1,535; Klerzhe, G.I. *Revoliutsiia i grazhdanskaia voina*. Mukden (1932), pp. 21–4; Swain, G. *The Origins of the Russian Civil War*. London (1995), pp. 20–3. On the Republican Centre see Ivanov, N.Ia. *Kontrrevoliutsiia v Rossii v 1917g.*. Moscow (1977), pp. 41–2; Ioffe, G.Z. 'K voprosu o mezhpartiinykh ob″edineniiakh rossiiskoi kontrrevoliutsii', in *Velikii Oktiabr′ i neproletarskie partii*. Moscow (1982), pp. 11–21; and the letter of Colonel V. Sidorin to *Poslednye novosti* (Paris), 26.ii.1937. Kolchak failed altogether to mention the fact that he had been approached as early as his April visit to Petrograd (that is, while he was still Commander-in-Chief of the Black Sea Fleet) by militarist groups wishing to know of his views on the feasibility of dictatorship. See Vladimirova, V.G. *Kontrrevoliutsiia v 1917g.* Moscow (1924), pp. 43–6; Gurevich, V. Ia. 'Kornilov', *Poslednye novosti* (Paris) No. 4,118, 1.viii.1932; Mints, I.I. (ed.) *Istoriia Velikogo Oktiabria*. Moscow (1968) Vol. 2, pp. 308–10.

144 'Kolchak v proshlom', *Nash put′* (Ufa) No. 21, 5.ii.1919; Ioffe, G.Z. 'Iz istorii kadetsko-monarkhicheskoi kontrrevoliutsii v Rossii', in Korablev and Shishkin (1985), pp. 161–6. It is of interest that, at the behest of Trades and Industry circles in Moscow, some Kadets (notably Astrov, Tret′iakov and Kishkin) tried to have Kolchak's promotion to Minister of Marine made a condition of their rejoining the Provisional Government in July 1917. See Rosenberg *Liberals*, pp. 181–2.

Kerensky ordered Kolchak to leave the country and packed him off on a naval mission to the United States. More recent analysis, however, is inclined to accept Kolchak's own version of events (proffered at his interrogation), according to which he eagerly volunteered to participate in a mission which, being concerned with the possibility of an American attack on the Dardanelles, he found to be of considerable professional interest.[145] What remains obscure, however, is why, having entered the right-wing underground, he chose to leave Russia at such a crucial juncture for the movement. Perhaps he recognized that Kornilov was a more suitable candidate for the dictatorship, that with the failure of the June offensive and the dissemination of the Commander-in-Chief's programme of national salvation, in the words of a well-informed Soviet commentator, 'an unemployed admiral could not compete with Kornilov'.[146] Or perhaps the admiral welcomed participation in the mission as a means of avoiding the consequences of a coup whose success was far from guaranteed. Certainly the Kadet leader Paul Miliukov said that in July 1917 Kolchak 'followed the advice of some political friends to save himself for the future and left for America'.[147]

But perhaps an even more significant factor in Kolchak's decision to leave Russia in the summer of 1917, as Miliukov went on to suggest, was that although his soldierly sense of duty to his country might have impelled him to listen to the

145 Smirnov, M.I. 'Pamiati Admirala Kolchaka', *Morskoi sbornik* (Paris) Vol. 9, p. 23; Weeks, C. and Bayen, J. 'Admiral Kolchak's Mission to the United States', *Military Affairs*, Vol. 40, No. 2 (1976), pp. 40–2; and Weeks, C.J. *An American Naval Diplomat in Revolutionary Russia: The Life and Times of Vice Admiral Newton A. McCully*. Annapolis (1993). Weeks and Bayen doubt whether the US Navy ever seriously intended to launch the attack on the Bosphorus which Kolchak had gone to Washington to discuss.

146 Ioffe 'Iz istorii kadetsko-monarkhicheskoi kontrrevoliutsii', p. 166. That there was no rivalry between Kornilov and Kolchak may be surmised from the fact that the Commander-in-Chief included the admiral's name on the list of members of a 'Council of National Defence' he had planned to establish to rule Russia had his August coup been successful. See Katkov, G. *The Kornilov Affair*. London (1980), pp. 79, 180.

147 Miliukov, P.N. *Russia Today and Tomorrow*. New York (1922), p. 154. Miliukov was in a position to know – since first meeting Kolchak in 1908 the Kadet leader was among the admiral's closest contacts in the State Duma. General Denikin recalled that the two met early in 1917 (presumably during Kolchak's April visit to the capital) and discussed the prospects for a dictatorship. See Denikin, A.I. *Ocherki Russkoi smuty*. Paris–Berlin (1921–1926), Vol. 2, p. 29. Interestingly, a British Foreign Office memorandum of December 1919, which reviewed Kolchak's career, also states that he left Russia in 1917 on Miliukov's advice to 'be in readiness' for when the time came to restore order. See Woodward, E.L. and Butler, R. (eds.) *Documents on British Foreign Policy, 1919–1939* (First Series, Vol. 3). London (1948–1949), p. 703. (Hereafter cited as *DBFP*.)

plans of those he respected to make him dictator in 1917, there was 'something in him' that would not permit him to go along with such a scheme.[148] For although by then Kolchak might have been committed to the principle of the necessity of dictatorship to save Russia, both at this time and later, in 1918, Kolchak evinced a marked reluctance to take upon himself the leadership of any movement for its imposition. In short, he was a fierce patriot rather than a natural counter-revolutionary conspirator. Consequently, it is not surprising that we find him, having heard of the Bolsheviks' October success and of their armistice approaches to Germany upon his arrival in Japan (whilst en route back to Russia from the USA), not hastening on to join the incipient anti-Bolshevik underground in the Russian Far East but presenting himself at the British Embassy in Tokyo as available for service, in any capacity, in the British armed forces.[149] Kolchak's heightened sense of nationalism demanded that, for the sake of his country's honour, he help fulfil Russia's obligations to its allies before all else.

Enter Kolchak

Admiral Kolchak's activities of 1917 to 1918, in first the British and then the Russian service in the Far East prior to his arrival at Omsk in October 1918, were quite candidly chronicled by the admiral himself before his interrogators at Irkutsk in 1920 and have since been elaborated upon in a number of works.[150] All that is necessary here, therefore, is to adumbrate the major features of his career in this year, to stress the importance of certain facts underplayed or omitted in previous accounts and to emphasize the significance which the admiral's known association with the British Government was to have for those who were later to select him for the role of dictator in Siberia.

148 Miliukov, p. 154.

149 Varneck and Fisher, pp. 101–2. Smirnov claims that Kolchak told him as early as June 1917 that this was his intention now that he had resigned his post in the Black Sea. See Smirnov, *Admiral Kolchak*, p. 39.

150 Varneck and Fisher, pp. 105–40 has Kolchak's own account which, for the most part, is quite frank. It also forms the basis of the accounts of Fleming, pp. 34–6, 47–56, 68–76; Ioffe, *Kolchakovskaia avantiura*, pp. 22–38; Connaughton, pp. 44–52, 70–1; and Kolz, A.W.F. 'British Foreign Policy and the Kolchak Government', Boston University PhD Thesis (1965), pp. 85–92.

The War Office took some weeks to consult with figures in the Admiralty who had become acquainted with Kolchak during the latter's passage through London en route to the USA in the summer of 1917 (among them Admiral Jellicoe and Admiral Hall), before it officially accepted Kolchak's request to enter the British Army in December. Consequently, it was to be early in the new year before Kolchak was to set off for his first posting in Mesopotamia (possibly as a preliminary to a role in Dunsterforce's operations on the Caspian). With no source of income, however, he had made his way only as far as Singapore by March 1918, when his orders were suddenly rescinded. He was told instead, in view of changed circumstances, to report to the Russian Ambassador at Peking, Prince Kudyshev, who had been petitioning the British to involve the admiral in plans afoot to mount armed opposition to the Bolsheviks in the Far East. In fact, Kudyshev's was not the only invitation – Kolchak's services seem to have been demanded by every budding anti-Bolshevik government in the east at this time. An emissary was to meet him in Peking, for example, with an offer of the post of Minister of Marine in the Derber Government. Before that, at Shanghai, an adjutant of Ataman Semenov, the freebooting Cossack marauder in the Japanese pay, had interviewed the admiral at Shanghai and asked him to join a planned Cossack government to be based in Manchuria.[151] This courting of Kolchak can be explained both by the great store set by an individual's foreign contacts among those Russians contemplating the attraction of Allied military assistance to the anti-Bolshevik cause and by the enduring impression the admiral must have made during his political liaisons of 1917.

Despite the number of offers, however, Kolchak's choice of with whom to serve was quite limited. He clearly detested Derber – reserving for the SR and his government a rare outburst of anti-semitism in the Tokyo daily *Asahi*, for example[152] – while Semenov, apart from being a bandit in the classic *Hung hu tze* tradition of Asia's wild east, was patently a Japanese stooge. Thus, although

151 Fleming, pp. 33–6; Varneck and Fisher p. 109. Grigorii Mikhailovich Semenov was born of mixed Cossack and Buriat parentage at Kurzhana, Transbaikalia, in 1890. A graduate of the Orenburg Military Academy, he served on various fronts in the Great War, including a period under General Wrangel in Galicia. In 1917 he had volunteered to recruit a Mongol-Buriat regiment in his homeland. After the October Revolution he immediately redirected this activity against the Bolsheviks, initially winning financial support from Britain and France. As his campaigns quickly degenerated into banditry, however, subsidies from the west were curtailed and Semenov came to rely upon the support of Japan. See Smith, C.F. 'Atamanshchina in the Russian Far East', *Russian History*, Vol. 6 (1979), pp. 57–67; and below, pp. 188–95, 456–8.

152 Reprinted in *The Times* (London) 16.vii.1918.

annoyed at having pointlessly and expensively embarked on his journey to the Middle East, Kolchak accepted Kudyshev's invitation. On April 27th at Peking he duly joined, as member with military responsibility, what Kudyshev and General Horvath had conceived as nothing less than the organizational centre for the overthrow of the Soviet government – a newly reconstructed board of the Chinese Eastern Railway.[153]

The very next day Kolchak left Peking to join General Horvath at Harbin, whence for the next two months he was to traverse and re-traverse the length of the Chinese Eastern Railway, attempting to instil some order and centralized authority into the various small and jealously independent units of officers, Cossacks and Chinese and Mongol mercenaries which had sprouted in the Bolshevik-free zone of the railway. However, in what proved to be a microcosm of the squabbling rivalry and insubordination which was to afflict anti-Bolshevik Siberia on a grander scale in the following year, Kolchak's task was a thankless, not to say hopeless, one. The only lever the admiral could apply to influence the armed groups was his hold over the purse-strings of a one-million-rouble monthly subsidy provided for his endeavours by the Harbin branch of the Russo-Asiatic Bank. However, although this might occasionally impress the smaller forces at Harbin (for example the Orlov and Makovkin detachments), the three groups which commanded real military power in the railway zone had no great need for Kolchak's money: the Japanese Military Mission of General Nakajima; Semenov's motley collection of Buriats, Mongols, Koreans and Cossacks on the border with Transbaikalia, which boasted the title of the 'Special Manchurian Detachment'; and the equally unruly Ussuri Cossack band of Semenov's associate, Captain Ivan Kalmykov, which were massing at Pogranichnaia Station (on the border of Manchuria and the Bolshevik-held Maritime Provinces). Although funding which had for some months arrived from Britain and

153 United States Department of State, *Papers Relating to the Foreign Relations of the United States: 1918*. Washington (1931–1932), Vol. 2, pp. 155–6 (hereafter cited as *FRUS*); Fleming, p. 55. The board's other members were subsequently to play important roles in the anti-Bolshevik movement in the east: D.L. Horvath (former Imperial Governor of the CER and Kolchak's High Plenipotentiary to the Far East of 1918 to 1919); A.I. Putilov (Chairman since 1906 of the Russo-Asiatic Bank, which held a majority of the shares in the CER and was to administer the fiscal policy of the Kolchak Government in the Far East); and Engineer L.A. Ustrugov (Minister of Ways and Communications for the Provisional Government of 1917, PGAS, PSG and Kolchak and Chairman of the Inter-Allied Railway Commission in 1917). Note also that banking associates of Putilov had been active in the Republican Centre which had approached Kolchak in 1917 – see Laverychev, V.Ia. 'Russkie monopolisty i zagovor Kornilova', *Voprosy istorii* (Moscow), No. 4 (1964), p. 36.

France had since been curtailed, Kalmykov, like Semenov, was still quite adequately subsidized and provisioned by the Japanese Mission (which, in turn, was patiently pursuing its government's policy of sponsoring disorder and disunity in eastern Russia in order to facilitate and excuse Japan's planned military and economic domination of the region). Kolchak's aims being quite contrary to this, the admiral naturally found himself in the greatest of difficulties.

During May Kolchak had bitter and humiliating arguments with both Nakajima and Semenov – the latter, a mere captain of the Imperial Russian Army, at first rudely declining to receive Kolchak when the admiral lowered himself to visiting the ataman at his Manchuria Station headquarters.[154] This and other insulting incidents 'made me boil', recalled the admiral. By early July, despairing of the possibility of launching a successful attack on Soviet power from Manchuria (Semenov had already been beaten back twice from inglorious advances into Red Transbaikalia), having also broken with Horvath (whom he perhaps unjustly suspected of having also succumbed to Japanese lucre) and once again in ill health, Kolchak resigned his post and, after almost two decades of uninterrupted and enervating service, departed for a much needed period of recuperation at a resort in Japan.[155] In that country he was to renew his special relationship with the British War Office and begin the task of creating what he now saw as the only salvation of anti-Bolshevism – the creation of an all-powerful and united Russian Army.

Kolchak was to remain convalescing in Japan until September 1918. It was during this period that he developed a close friendship with a British officer whom he had first met in 1917 – Major General (later Sir) Alfred Knox, the former military attaché in St Petersburg and generally acknowledged at the time as the best informed and shrewdest British observer of the Russian scene, who was currently on his way into Siberia as the Head of the British Military Mission. Knox, who in 1917 had openly sided with Kornilov and lambasted the SRs and Order No. 1 for allegedly destroying the Russian Army, was found by at least one other who knew him to be a 'naturally autocratic' man – one who was not averse, for example, to classifying the entire Russian peasantry as 'swine'. The Bolsheviks he regarded as subhuman; anti-Bolshevism to him was a crusade: 'Civilization demands that we

154 Varneck and Fisher, pp. 113–28; Semenov, G.M. *O sebe: vospominaniia, mysli i vyvody*. Harbin (1936), pp. 111–12; Morely, J.W. *Japan's Thrust into Siberia*. New York (1950), pp. 199–205. On the Orlov band see Budberg, Vol. 13, pp. 214–20. On Kalmykov see *ibid.*, pp. 261–304.

155 Varneck and Fisher, p. 124; Budberg, Vol. 13, pp. 219–20.

intervene in Russia', he once reported to London. In short, Knox was in many ways to prove himself during the civil war to be more White than the Whites.[156]

The meeting of Kolchak and Knox during the summer of 1918 was the beginning of a partnership which, although it did not always run smoothly, was to last for the next year. In the course of lengthy conversations in Japan they came to the mutual conclusion that the only form of government that could save Russia was one that 'leans upon the armed force at its disposal' (that is, a military government). Knox then went on to share with Kolchak the 'far reaching plans' that he entertained for the anti-Bolshevik movement in Siberia.[157] Time was to tell that these plans by no means excluded active and vociferous support for those intent upon the establishment of a dictatorship in the region. Clearly the general was impressed with Kolchak and descried in the admiral the makings of a candidate for the dictatorship. He admired Kolchak's purposefulness and was probably flattered that this Russian believed that only the supply of British arms might secure the overthrow of Bolshevism. Moreover, by August, with Vladivostok declared to be an Allied protectorate, with the Trans-Siberian Railway completely in the hands of Russian and Czechoslovak forces and with a new All-Russian Government about to be born at Ufa, Knox probably realized that there was little time for the British to lose, if they wished – as they certainly did – to obtain an influence in the intervention in Siberia which, if the anti-Bolshevik movement was successful, could be translated into postwar economic and political prizes. Consequently, Knox put his 'plans' into operation. From Tokyo he eulogized Kolchak in messages to the War Office, informing his superiors that 'there is no doubt that he is the best Russian for our purposes in the Far East'.[158] Then, in negotiations with the Japanese staff (who formally held the supreme command of the Allied intervention in the east), Knox insistently cleared the way for his protegé – one whom the Japanese undoubtedly

156 FO 371/3365/18857 'Knox to WO, 4.x.1918'; Graves, W.S. *America's Siberia Adventure*. New York (1931), pp. 19, 87, 337. See also *FRUS: 1919 (Russia)*, pp. 540–1 for Graves's views on Knox. Knox's contribution to anti-Bolshevism is summarized in Long, J. 'General Sir Alfred Knox and the Russian Civil War', *Sbornik of the Study Group on the Russian Revolution* Vol. 9 (1983), pp. 54–64.

157 Varneck and Fisher, pp. 144–5. WO 158/741/2 contains a letter on 'A Scheme to Restore the Russian Army' from Kolchak to Knox (in the admiral's own handwriting), dated 29.iv.1918, Tokyo. In it the admiral proposes that a dictatorship in Russia should rely heavily on the French and, especially, the British commands, he being convinced that 'the Japanese will directly or indirectly do all in their power in order that nothing takes place'.

158 WO 33 962/186 'Knox to DMI, 31.viii.1918'.

were reluctant to see returning to service after their clashes with him of the spring – to return to Russia. So it was that on September 8th 1918, after more than a year's absence, Admiral Kolchak made landfall on Russian soil at Vladivostok.

It is at this point, with his arrival back in Russia, that Kolchak's own version of his activities, presented to his interlocutors at Irkutsk in 1920, becomes somewhat less than frank. In particular, he claimed that it had been a mixture of misgivings over the intervention (which at Vladivostok was at its most intrusive, not to say humiliating for a Russian nationalist such as the admiral) and concern for the fate of his wife and young son (Rostislav Aleksandrovich) whom he had left at Sevastopol in the summer of 1917, which had induced him to set off along the Trans-Siberian Railway, intent on finding a way through to South Russia.[159] This version has generally been accepted by western and émigré commentators. Only the admiral's highly developed sense of duty, his apologists suggest, allowed this loyal husband and father to abandon his familial quest at Omsk (where he arrived on October 13th), and instead to join the Council of Ministers then being formed by the Directory.[160] Something about all of this, however, has never really rung true: why should Kolchak choose to make his way *overland* from Japan to the Crimea, a journey which would necessitate running the gauntlet of the Red Army's control of the Volga and the Caspian Sea, when there existed the alternative of the perfectly safe (and for a sailor so much more natural) sea route around Asia which was likely to take less time into the bargain? Moreover, evidence exists which casts serious doubt upon Kolchak's assertions and which must lead us to believe that he went to Omsk with at least a quite different and possibly a quite definite purpose in mind – one not unconnected with the 'plans' of his friend, General Knox.

Writing to his wife a year later, in October 1919, Kolchak was to present to her the same version as he was to present at Irkutsk, musing melancholically that a full twelve months had passed since he had arrived at Omsk intending to fight his way through to the south to rejoin her.[161] Whether such a profession of regret could

159 Varneck and Fisher, pp. 144–5.

160 See, for example: Fleming, pp. 95–6; Connaughton, p. 70; Guins, Vol. 1, p. 307; Melgun′ov, Vol. 1, p. 130. Kolchak's chief propagandist, Sergei Auslander, asserted that the admiral only decided to remain at Omsk after hearing of the death in South Russia of the cancer-stricken General Alekseev. That, however, was unlikely, for Kolchak agreed to join the Council of Ministers on October 13th, before news of Alekseev's death on October 8th could have reached central Siberia.

161 Kolchak, R., p. 18.

have comforted his spouse, Sophia Fedorovna, however, is doubtful, as for some time she had been aware that her husband had a mistress. The existence and identity of Kolchak's escort as Supreme Ruler at Omsk in 1918 and 1919 has long been known to historians and commentators: she was that same Anna Vasil′evna Timireva (her husband since 1918 being the senior Russian naval officer at Vladivostok) who back in 1911 had first fallen in love with the glittering admiralty officer who had been 'always at the centre of things'. What has not previously been appreciated, however, is that the pair's relationship did not assume a consummate form only after Kolchak's investiture at Omsk, but long before that. In her memoirs (which were published only in the 1980s) Madame Timireva, who had no apparent reason to lie, informs us that the couple had first revealed their affections for one another as early as 1915 (when the war had thrown their families together at Helsingfors) and had maintained a copious and impassioned correspondence during the whole of Kolchak's tenure as Commander-in-Chief of the Black Sea Fleet. His mission to the United States and the disruption wrought by the revolution – which saw the Timirevs flee to the Far East – might have separated them, as so many others, for ever. But by chance, in March 1918, Anna Vasil′evna heard that Kolchak was in Harbin. Immediately, she abandoned her husband at Vladivostok and joined her inamorato in Manchuria. From this time forth they were lovers. Timireva accompanied Kolchak to Japan in July 1918 and subsequently followed him to Omsk.[162]

In the light of Timireva's contribution to our knowledge, therefore, it seems at least unlikely that Kolchak truly entertained thoughts only of travelling to South Russia to rejoin his wife when, having crossed the Sea of Japan with General Knox, he set off along the Chinese Eastern Railway towards Siberia on September 20th. Moreover, in his unpublished memoirs one who subsequently became the very closest confidant of the admiral, Ivan Sukin, claims with certainty that 'it was only having heard of the rapid developments in Siberia…that Kolchak decided to go to Omsk'.[163] And even an Allied officer with only a passing acquaintance with the admiral during his short stay at Vladivostok asserted that he could not help but feel that Kolchak left the Far East with some definite purpose in mind and that this was

162 Timireva, pp. 209–28. In a letter to the author of 13.i.1987, the admiral's grandson, Alexander Kolchak, affirmed that Timireva was 'an exceptionally fine woman' and a reliable source: 'I know enough about the lady to think that whatever she wrote was true', he affirmed.

163 Sukin (*Leeds Russian Archive*), p. 20.

'not unconnected' with a long-standing plot to put him in power.[164] It is not altogether unfeasible to assert, therefore, that Kolchak was on his way to the Siberian hinterland to assume a pre-arranged role. Back in May 1918, Alekseev's plenipotentiaries to Siberia, the afore-cited General Flug and Colonel Glukharev, had concluded their reports on the region with the assertion that what was needed to unite and galvanize anti-Bolshevik forces in the east was for a figure of 'great national reputation' to come and take charge.[165] Had not such a figure – a brave explorer, a laurelled scholar of the Siberian Arctic, a naval modernizer, a war hero, a darling of the political right, an associate of British and American generals and ministers – now duly arrived?

Although Kolchak told his inquisitors at Irkutsk very little of his activities during his stay at Vladivostok, he did admit the occurrence of two important meetings. The first was with Vologodskii, the visiting Siberian premier, whose mission had just arrived at the port. Nothing definite came out of this meeting according to Kolchak.[166] Yet, three weeks later, the admiral was to enter Vologodskii's government. This was surely no coincidence. The second of Kolchak's meetings was with General Gajda. He concurred with the Czech hero's assertion that a dictatorship was essential for Russia, Kolchak later admitted at Irkutsk. However, he claimed, the Czech made no mention of any concrete plans being laid for the imposition of such a rule.[167] Yet, as we have seen, just a few days later, at Manchuria Station,

164 Bell, J.M. *Sidelights on the Siberian Campaign*. Toronto (1920), pp. 94–5.

165 Piontkovskii 'Kontr-revoliutsiia v Sibiri', pp. 367–70. There are a number of curious references to Kolchak in relation to an impending dictatorship, which date to the period of June–July 1918 which the admiral spent in Harbin and Tokyo. Dotsenko ('The Struggle for the Liberation', p. 52) recalled hearing in June that Kadets from central Siberia had contacted Kolchak at Harbin and concluding that 'the next step, the seizure of power, was being prepared'. His memory, of course, might have been betraying him, at forty years' distance from the events of that summer. However, in his researches into the Czechoslovak revolt Bradley ('The Czechoslovak Revolt', p. 139) uncovered German intelligence reports from Siberia dated June 25th which also spoke of Kolchak's readiness to assume supreme command in Siberia. Finally, in Vologodskii's diary for July 30th – cited in Berk, 'The *Coup d'État*, pp. 238–9 – there is recorded a note that Mikhailov had that day informed the Siberian premier of the intention of the Commander-in-Chief of the Siberian Army, Grishin-Almazov, to establish a dictatorship under Admiral Kolchak.

166 Varneck and Fisher, p. 140. See also Ioffe *Kolchakovskaia avantiura*, p. 88; Livshits, *Imperialisticheskaia interventsiia*, p. 43.

167 Varneck and Fisher, pp. 151–2. It has been suggested that at this meeting Kolchak agreed to enter Czechoslovak service, the better to work with Gajda and achieve their aims. Dr. Girsa, the Czechoslovak plenipotentiary at Vladivostok, with whom Kolchak was billeted at the port, told

Gajda was to inform Viktor Pepeliaev that Admiral Kolchak was on his way to Siberia as a willing candidate for the role of military ruler. Again, this could surely have been no coincidence.

The martyrs of compromise

At the same time as the dictator elect was travelling westwards from Vladivostok, 5,000 km away at Ufa the newly created Directory was on the point of making a fateful, inexiably impolitic decision to move eastwards to Omsk to establish its capital. SRs in Siberia sternly warned the new government against such a move: 'Knowing the political situation in Omsk, we insisted that the Directory should not go to Omsk... In no circumstances should they go to Omsk', recalled Paul Dotsenko. Likewise, at Ufa, Komuch members painted a dim portrait of Omsk as 'the hornets' nest of Siberian *atamanshchina*'.[168] And, at least initially, the SR members of the Directory were indeed loath to place themselves in such close proximity to the killers of Novoselov. Thus, when Vologodskii's deputy Sapozhnikov suggested such a move he was rebuffed: 'Repression and the general political situation in Siberia frighten me greatly', shivered Zenzinov. 'We would be nothing but a plaything in the hands of the Black Hundred generals.'[169] Sapozhnikov and Vinogradov, however, were insistent: the advancing Red Army might soon arrive at Ufa, they said, making it impossible for the Directory to remain there; Ekaterinburg too was not secure; a move to Cheliabinsk, on the eastern foothills of the Urals, might be considered, were the town not one giant Czecho-slovak hutment; that only left Omsk, as the nearest large settlement in Siberia, as a potential capital for the All-Rusian Government. Moreover, added Boldyrev, he at least would have to base himself at Omsk in order to marshal the forces of the Siberian Army for the new régime. Finally, Sapozhnikov tipped the scales in favour of such a move by pointing out that the Directory was a government without an

a British officer that the admiral had confirmed this – see Baerlin, H. *The March of the Seventy Thousand*. London (1926), p. 209. If, indeed, this plan was considered, it was probably dropped when Gajda was promoted to a command in the Russian service by Vologodskii (see above, pp. 41–2).

168 Dotsenko, 'The Struggle for the Liberation', pp. 63–4; Vishniak, *Vserossiiskoe*, p. 195.

169 Maiskii, p. 282; Guins, Vol. 1, p. 266.

administrative apparatus of any description – it would simply have to utilize that which was already in existence in Siberia.[170]

With such logic the SRs of the Directory could not argue. The government they had joined had neither an army nor a civil service of its own and would have to attempt to annex those which the PSG had already established in Siberia. The Mikhailov clique, however, would not be easily tamed. Avksent′ev at least was aware of that. He anticipated that there would be a struggle for power once he and his colleagues arrived at Omsk and that only the victors of that struggle would stand any chance of spreading their authority across Siberia or of attracting the support of the Allies. The sole weapon in the Directory's armoury, however, was its doubtful claim to legal and moral authority on an all-Russian scale. Its SR members had to hope that this alone would be enough to smother their Siberian rivals – although, to their credit, they took cognizance of the possibility that they themselves might come off worst. 'We must put our heads in the lion's mouth', Avksent′ev informed critics of the decision to move to Omsk. 'Either it will eat us or we will choke it.'[171]

Arriving at Omsk on October 9th, the most cursory sampling of its foetid political atmosphere and the briefest of tours of its muddy, unpaved streets (so recently stained with the blood of other socialists) should have relieved Avksent′ev and Zenzinov of any illusions as to who was about to swallow whom and who was going to choke whom. There had been 'no special pomp and circumstance' in the welcome arranged by their PSG hosts, recalled Serebrennikov; in fact, the station was conspicuously deserted as the All-Russian Government's train drew in.[172] And within three days Zenzinov formed the impression, imparted to the Menshevik Ivan Maiskii, that the Directory was regarded by the local authorities 'as an uninvited guest, which – as the proverb says – is about as welcome as the Tatars!': the PSG did not even offer the All-Russian Government any accommodation (they had initially to eke out a meagre and uncomfortable existence in their railway carriages)

170 Boldyrev, pp. 52, 63; Zenzinov, V.M. *Iz zhizni revoliutsionera*. Paris (1919), pp. 112–13. For the Directory's official announcement of the move to Omsk see Gan, pp. 291–2.

171 Krol′, L., p. 140. Avksent′ev and Zenzinov may also have been influenced by the presence at Ufa of SR-URR members, such as Argunov, who were so disillusioned with their party central committee's negative attitude to the coalition that they deemed it best to place physical distance between the Directory and Chernov. See Argunov 'Omskie dni', pp. 191–2.

172 Serebrennikov, 'K istorii', p. 16.

and the Directors could not even obtain access to telegraph facilities without a rescript from the PSG's Ministry of Communications.[173]

Ominously, moreover, the Directors soon came to realize that the Siberian Government was no longer truly the master in its own house and was not the enemy of whom they had the most to fear: 'Practically all power in Omsk, and consequently in Siberia, is in the hands of the reactionarily inclined military party', Avksent′ev reported to party colleagues in the Urals on November 1st.[174] The Commander of the Siberian Army, the former policeman Ivanov-Rinov, lived like a lord in the Governor's Palace at Omsk, while his nominal Commander-in-Chief, Boldyrev, shivered with his Directory colleagues in the goods-yards. From his lavish headquarters Ivanov-Rinov, with the blessing of Mikhailov, sent forth orders to re-introduce the disciplinary code of the Imperial Russian Army into the Siberian Army (including the right of officers to administer corporal punishment in the form of a beating). He also indulged the pre-revolutionary officers' peculiar fondness for ostentatious epaulettes – in fact, officers of the Siberian Army could be arrested on sight for failing to display their insignia of rank.[175] That the SRs in the Directory were known to oppose such actions only reinforced the belief of officers and the Mikhailov Group that Avksent′ev and Zenzinov were 'soft on the left', and hardened their lack of respect for the coalition, recalled an anonymous 'White Guard'.[176]

However, as Cossack bands paraded the town, terrorizing the populace and harassing workers' social clubs, even the most Machiavellian schemers of the PSG began to feel a little unsure of their ability to maintain control over events. At one point Mikhailov had a special guard surround Vologodskii's house because he was convinced that a plot had been hatched in the army to abduct the premier. His caution, however, served only to terrorize Vologodskii, who believed that it was Mikhailov's guard which had come to arrest him. Both Boldyrev and Serebrennikov also heard tell of their own imminent arrests.[177] Plots and counter-plots,

173 Maiskii, p. 303.

174 Rakitnikov, p. 15.

175 *Zaria* (Omsk) No. 72, 8.ix.1918 and No. 91, 4.x.1918; Guins, Vol. 1, pp. 119–21; Il′in, 'Omsk, Direktoriia', Vol. 72, p. 198.

176 N.N., p. 92.

177 Guins, G.C[K]. *Professor and Government Official: Russia, China and California* (An Interview Conducted by B. Raymond [Romanov]). Berkeley (1966), p. 210; Serebrennikov, 'K istorii', p. 18.

conspiracies and counter-conspiracies abounded. 'It is a farce', the Director Boldyrev confided to his diary: 'Like Mexico with snow and frosts!'[178]

Monarchistic sympathies were openly displayed by Cossack leaders and others who, incensed by recent confirmation of the murder of Nicholas II and his immediate family at Ekaterinburg, organized martial demonstrations in favour of a restoration. At the political salons and drinking clubs which blossomed in what was once a cultural backwater but was now a capital, the health of the Grand Duke Michael Romanov was toasted and reassurances exchanged that he would soon arrive at Omsk to claim the Russian throne as his own.[179] The government's inability to restrain the military's reactionary fervour was revealed at two particularly notorious public incidents when a local Cossack leader, Ataman I.N. Krasil′nikov, and his henchmen had forced orchestras at gunpoint to play 'God Save the Tsar' during the official receptions at Krasnoiarsk and Omsk of the British and French military missions. On the first occasion British officers made a diplomatic withdrawal from the banquet as it degenerated into a drunken brawl. On the second, Krasil′nikov personally threatened to shoot a representative of the Directory when the latter refused to stand for the tsarist anthem. The terrified ambassador of the All-Russian Government managed to make his escape from the hall, but only to a barrage of spirited and inebriated cries of 'Get lost, you lousy SR!', from the assembled Cossacks.[180]

The monarchists, however, were not content with merely hurling insults. Evidence exists to suggest that in Omsk at this time there existed an officer-terrorist organization, thinly and with black irony posing as 'The Mikhailovskii Hunting and Fishing Society', which, as the first step to a restoration, had set themselves the task of exterminating as many Socialist-Revolutionary members of the Constituent Assembly of 1917 as they could ensnare. Both conservative and SR observers have attested to the existence of such an underground organization.[181] That said, however, it is certainly wise to cast doubt (as did the Soviet historian G.Z. Ioffe) on

178 Boldyrev, p. 72.

179 Krol′, L., pp. 149–50; Boldyrev, p. 83; Il′in, 'Omsk, Direktoriia', Vol. 72, p. 206; Kolosov, E.E. *Sibir′ pri Kolchake*. Petrograd (1923), p. 73; Quénet, C., 'L'Arrière Sibérien', *Le Monde Slave* (Paris), Vol. 8 (1926), p. 180.

180 Dotsenko 'The Struggle for the Liberation', pp. 60–3; Il′in, 'Omsk, Direktoriia', Vol. 72, pp. 204–5; Maiskii, pp. 305–6.

181 Rakov, D.F. *V zastenkakh Kolchaka: golos′ iz Sibiri*. Paris (1920), pp. 19–20; Sviatitskii, *K istorii*, p. 66; Gopper, G. *Chetyrye katastrofy*. Riga (1933), p. 167.

the accuracy of estimates as to the group's strength and international influence offered by the most fulsome of these accusers, the SR D.K. Rakov (who was jailed by Kolchak): Rakov simply seems to have lumped together the names of every right-wing figure in Siberia and dubbed them an 'organization'.[182] Equally, it would be absurd to suggest that the group was trying to eliminate the entire 715 members of the old Constituent Assembly. The point is, however, that they did not need to hunt down or fish out the entire assembly. They needed only to prevent the gathering before January and February 1919 of the modest quorums allowed for at the Ufa Conference. After that the Directory would lose its authority, there would be no legitimate government to replace it, and, in the volatile political climate of Siberia, who knew what might then transpire.

It is known that by August 1918, of the elected members of the 1917 assembly (known, collectively, as '*uchredil'ovtsy*'), there were about one hundred in the vicinity of the Volga, the Urals and Siberia.[183] Given that of the total membership (of 715) some 26% were Bolshevik (or Left-SR) and 2% Kadet, neither of whose parties any longer recognized the Constituent Assembly of 1917, and that at least another 25% of the elected members were representatives of minority nationalist organizations who, being opposed to the Russifying tendencies of the eastern anti-Bolsheviks, were hardly more likely or willing than the Bolsheviks to accept invitations to a reconvention in Siberia, it was always going to be very difficult to tempt any more *uchredil'ovtsy* to the east: simple arithmetic, therefore, revealed that there was only a pool of rather less than 300 members (most of them SRs), scattered or in hiding in the Soviet zone, or in exile or already dead, from which the 75 to 125 men needed to meet the Ufa quorums would have to be garnered. On arriving in the east Viktor Pepeliaev met few who believed that such numbers could be achieved; and, in fact, according to one historian of the Constituent Assembly, the body which had been formally adjured by the Ufa State Conference with the task of finding the necessary quorums to take over from the Directory in the new year (the so-called Congress of Members of the Constituent Assembly, which was based at Ekaterinburg) had brought only one more elected member into Siberia before the Omsk coup was to make such efforts redundant. The 'Mikhailovskii Hunting and Fishing Club', in other words, had set themselves a reasonable aim in attempting to

182 Rakov, p. 20; Ioffe, G.Z. *Krakh rossiiskoi monarkhicheskoi kontrrevoliutsii*. Moscow (1977), p. 177.

183 Gan, p. 274; Golovin, Vol. 8, p. 106.

block a reconvention. And by October 1918 they had set very rigorously about achieving it: 'There is murder on the streets', Boldyrev recorded in his diary that month.[184]

The URR emissary, Lev Krol, noted how during October 1918 Omsk was teeming with men dressed as officers, but who were not registered as members of the regular forces. Late in the month one of these types arrived at the Directory's quarters and asked if the new government would be so kind as to furnish him with details of the names and addresses of all members of the Constituent Assembly who were resident at Omsk. He was stalled and persuaded to return the next day, by which time he had been identified as an impostor and a member of the monarchist organization.[185] Although the persecution of SRs was not to reach its bloodiest depths until the end of the year, it is unlikely that this bogus officer required the members' addresses in order to pay house calls. In fact, the very day after the unmasking of that 'officer', the veteran SR organizer, V.N. Moiseenko, was surrounded by a group of similarly uniformed men outside the popular Omsk Commercial Club and, in broad daylight, was bundled into a car. A few days later his corpse was found, mutilated by torture, on the banks of Omsk's river: in what was to become common parlance in the murderous and miasmatic Siberian capital, he had been 'despatched to the Kingdom of the Irtysh'. A member of the PSG's Ministry of Justice was later to propagate the myth that Moiseenko was killed by common criminals, in an attempt to relieve him of the millions of roubles in his charge as Treasurer of Komuch.[186] But Omsk was overflowing at this time with Russian millionaires who had escaped, with all the jewellery and money they could carry, from Soviet Russia. Why should the unfortunate Moiseenko have been singled out, if it was not for the fact that he was a member of the Constituent Assembly of 1917? And his was only the first death in a bloody wave of enormity which was to break upon any member of the Assembly unlucky enough to find himself trapped in Siberia over the coming months.

184 Pepeliaev, 'Dnevnik', Vol. 4, p. 86; Vishniak, *Vserossiiskoe*, p. 195; Boldyrev, p. 85.

185 Krol', L., pp. 149–50; Boldyrev, p. 82. The officer in question was duly arrested along with several of his cohorts. However, the Siberian Army authorities in charge of the Omsk prison allowed them to go free. See Argunov *Mezhdu dvumia*, p. 32.

186 Rudnev, S.P. *Pri vechernykh ogniakh: vospominaniia*. Harbin (1928), p. 259.

If the Directory had few friends in Omsk when it arrived in the town in October, it was to become even more isolated and imperilled when it became known in the town that the SRs in the government had been compromised by the activities of their party central committee. After the departure of Avksent′ev and Zenzinov for Omsk, Chernov and other leftist members of the committee had won a vote censuring those SRs party to the Ufa settlement.[187] Chernov's solution to his fissiparous and impuissant party's problems, however, was almost as hopeless as the SR Directors' attempt to 'choke' the Siberian lions: huddling in Chernov's flat at his chosen base of Ekaterinburg, this small group of increasingly marginalized SR mandarins not only condemned the Directory for pandering to reaction and for permitting the re-introduction of pre-revolutionary discipline into the army, but grandiloquently called for the SRs to adopt a 'Third Path', simultaneously rejecting and struggling against both Bolshevism to the west and reaction to the east.

Albeit with the promise of somewhat sterner opposition to the right than they had exhibited before, this was essentially little more than a restatement of the policy of Komuch prior to the Ufa settlement. However, as the hard pressed People's Army was already fully occupied with fighting the Reds on the Volga and as many of its traditionalist officers were only too pleased to see the swing to the right in Siberia, there was really little hope of forces being diverted from the front to march against Ivanov-Rinov. Furthermore, in the SR Central Committee document which enshrined this new policy – the so-called 'Chernov Manifesto' – which was circulated in late October, the party leadership called upon all SRs to enlist in new volunteer detachments to defend the Congress of Members of the Constituent Assembly.[188] But in the circumstances this provocative call to arms was also nothing other than a pointless exercise in verbosity which the right had long since identified as typical of the SRs. Certainly very little, apart from the creation of one Russo-Czechoslovak Battalion, seems actually to have been done to organize such units.[189] Yet, in calling for their establishment, the SR leadership had provided right-wing forces in Siberia with the perfect excuse for attacking the Directory,

187 Berk, 'The *Coup d'État*, pp. 425–6.

188 Gusev, K.V. *Partiia eserov: ot melko-burzhuaznogo revoliutsionerizma k kontrrevoliutsii*. Moscow (1975), p. 128. The manifesto appears in full in Golovin, Vol. 9, pp. 46–50.

189 For an account, by one of its reluctant 'volunteers', of how the Russo-Czech Battalion was allowed to languish, unused by the Siberian Army, see the memoirs of Anton Ovchinnikov in Varneck and Fisher, pp. 273–7.

which, it was now to be claimed, was a 'Red' herring, a screen behind which (with the complicity of Zenzinov and Avksent'ev) the reviled Chernov was preparing to seize power. Finally, whilst propagating this canard, the Siberian right were also now reassured that, when they came to choose their moment to overthrow the Directory, the SR Central Committee was not going to leap to the defence of the All-Russian Government. For Mikhailov and his fellow conspirators it was really too good to be true. 'Reaction could not have wished for a better gift', lamented Avksent'ev, recalling how copies of the Chernov Manifesto were being mimeographed and distributed around Omsk not by the SRs but by officers of the Siberian Army![190]

Once it was obvious that the Directory did not even have the support of the majority of the PSR, Avksent'ev and Zenzinov became little more than the prisoners of the Siberian Army at Omsk. They went to extreme lengths to prove that they were not party to any projected SR coup and to dissociate themselves from Chernov: for example, they encouraged Boldyrev to go to the front to disband the few SR detachments that had come into being; and they sanctioned the opening of an official investigation into the activities of the SR Central Committee.[191] But it was all to no avail: the SR Directors' enemies, after all, did not want to be convinced of their innocence. In fact, the Siberian right were only too happy to sit back and enjoy the undignified spectacle of Avksent'ev and Zenzinov falling into a trap of their own making, as, in the words of one of their disillusioned party colleagues, 'they not only did nothing to promote the cause of the Constituent Assembly, but carried out measures to undermine and even to do away with the very forces which supported and represented that body'.[192]

190 Piontkovskii, 'Materialy po istorii kontrrevoliutsii', p. 118; Zenzinov, *Gosudarstvennyi perevorot*, pp. 190–1.

191 Vladimirova, *God sluzhby 'sotsialistov'*, p. 374; Boldyrev, pp. 93–4; Zenzinov, *Gosudarstvennyi perevorot*, p. 199.

192 The charge is made in Burevoi, K.S. *Kolchakovshchina*. Moscow (1919), p. 13. Burevoi was one of the Vol'skii ('Narod') group of SRs who crossed into Soviet Russia in late 1918 in disgust at their party's pandering to reaction (see below, Chapter 2, n. 206). For an equally bitter condemnation of SR 'conciliationism' in 1918 see Tumarkin, D. 'Kontrrevoliutsiia v Sibiri', *Sibirskie ogni* (Novonikolaevsk), No. 1 (1922), pp. 87–90.

In fact, even before news of the 'Chernov Manifesto' reached Omsk, the SR ministers had been playing into the hands of the Siberian right. Isolated and defenceless, they were not so much choking the reactionary lion as feeding it.

Upon their arrival at Omsk, the Directory had found that the PSG, despite the rap over the knuckles which had been administered to it by the Czechoslovaks during the Novoselov affair, being still more or less in control of its own army, remained strong and audacious enough to lay before what was supposed to be an authoritative All-Russian Government a list of conditions without the acceptance of which it would refuse to renounce its own regional independence. It was made very clear at Omsk from the beginning, for example, that there could be no thought of reversing the policies of the PSG – thus, private ownership of land and industry were to be strengthened by the Directory, the state trading monopoly further dismantled, the eight-hour working day renounced, Ivanov-Rinov's preference for pre-revolutionary discipline in the army maintained, and so on.[193] Moreover, in a series of debates of October 12th–29th, the SR Directors had to sit feebly and quiescently by as the PSG insisted that only *their* candidates should be admitted to the envisaged Council of Ministers of the All-Russian Government, which was intended to advise the Directory and implement its decisions. Avksent'ev and Zenzinov clearly baulked at the inclusion on the PSG list of Ivan Mikhailov – they were more inclined to indict him as an accessory to the murder of Novoselov than offer him power – and whispered of resigning. However, when General Knox and the British Military Mission (Britmis), which had arrived at Omsk on October 21st, let it be publicly and none too subtly known that no British aid would be forthcoming for the Directory unless a speedy agreement was reached, the SRs caved in. The 'Siberian Borgia' was duly installed as Minister of Finance, while the SR Directors' own preferred candidate for the key post of Minister of the Interior, their party colleague Evgenii Rogovskii (formerly of Komuch and, in February 1917, the Provisional Government's Governor of Petrograd), was rejected by the PSG and had to settle for a non-ministerial post as Chief of Militia. This was hardly a fair trade – especially when it is noted that before the PSG, on November 3rd, would agree to issue notification of its own dissolution, in addition to Mikhailov, another seven members of the fourteen-strong Council of Ministers which now came into being had been members of the PSG (Vologodskii was again made Chairman of the

193 Garmiza, 'Direktoriia', pp. 25–6; Garmiza, 'Bankrotstvo politiki', *passim*.

Council), while each of the other seven (including Admiral Kolchak and, as Acting Minister of Foreign Affairs, the Kadet Professor Iu.V. Kliuchnikov) was clearly more sympathetic to the PSG than to the Directory. The same goes for the new State Comptroller, Grigorii Adrianovich Krasnov (who had worked in various ministries of the tsarist régime which had repeatedly imprisoned and exiled both Avksent′ev and Zenzinov) and the new Administrative Secretary, the Kadet-sympathizing lawyer, Georgii (George) Konstantinovich Guins (a scion of Nicholas II's Ministry of Agriculture), who had been associated with the PSG since its inception.[194]

Thus, when the Directory first met with its Council of Ministers on November 5th 1918, not a single representative of their own 'Russian democracy' was before them. Then, over the following days, with this putatively All-Russian but patently 'Siberian' cabinet in place, the socialist Directors proceeded to saw away what remained of the precarious branch on which the All-Russian Directory was sitting: on November 6th they acceded to the cabinet's demand that, as the PSG had now 'dissolved' itself, all other regional authorities east of the Volga – the very bodies which had founded the Directory – should be commanded to do likewise. Subsequently, orders to that effect went out.[195] So-called 'responsible' (*delovyie*) groups, such as the Kadet-dominated Urals *oblast′* Government, were trusted to disband themselves. However, a special commission was despatched to Ufa to oversee the disbanding of the Council of Heads of Departments (the rump of Komuch, which had been charged at the State Conference with the local administration of Ufa *guberniia*). Finally, Avksent′ev himself went to Tomsk to secure what the attacks of Mikhailov and the Siberian Army had failed to achieve, the right's long-cherished dissolution of the *Sibobduma*.[196] It is really hard to imagine a more ineffably foolish move than the Socialist-Revolutionary Directors' sanctioning of the dispersal of these local governments, for governmental authority now being so concentrated in one town (not to say one railway carriage), governmental authority was now all the easier to seize.[197]

194 Guins, *Sibir′*, Vol. 1, pp. 269–75; Krol′, L., pp. 147–8; Boldyrev, pp. 69–79; Kliuchnikov Iu.V. 'Vospominaniia', *Nakanune* (Berlin) 1922, No. 7.

195 *Vestnik Vremennogo vserossiiskogo pravitel′stva* (Omsk) No. 1, 6.xi.1918; Maiskii, p. 322; Livshits, S.G. 'Kolchakovskaia perevorot', *Voprosy istorii* (Moscow) 1982, No. 3, p. 22.

196 Guins, *Sibir′*, Vol. 1, pp. 291–2; Vegman, 'Oblastnicheskie illiuzii, pp. 110–11.

197 As Lev Krol′ pointed out (*Za tri goda*, p. 164), the legality of the Directory's dissolution of local authorities was open to question, for the Ufa constitution had empowered the provisional government only to delegate responsibility to local governments, not to disband them. See also

Suffering from an almost Hamlet-like paralysis of the will, the SR Directors even refused to grab at a last straw of hope offered to them as the crisis of authority mounted. Their chance came when the local division of the Czechoslovak Legion let it be known that they were willing to defend the Directory: that Avksent′ev 'had only to give the word' and they would 'clean out the Omsk mire in two days flat', in the words of a message passed to the SRs. But Avksent′ev would not give the word, choosing instead to agree with Boldyrev that such an interference in Russian affairs could not be countenanced and consoling himself with the thought that, if the worst came to the worst, at least he would not have it on his conscience that he had initiated a new civil war within the anti-Bolshevik camp.[198] These, however, were rather obtuse views, given that without Czechoslovak 'interference', in the form of their spring revolt, there was likely to have been no significant anti-Bolshevik movement in the east, and that even if the SRs were able to avoid initiating internecine strife in the anti-Bolshevik east (in itself, a moot point), they were equally doing nothing to prevent a right-wing take-over of the movement. Yet, hoping against hope that Boldyrev could somehow tether the rampant Siberian Army to the cause of coalition and compromise, gambling that the Allies would offer recognition to the Directory so as to boost its prestige, and ignoring the lingering influence of the PSG, Avksent′ev chose to play this impossibly dangerous game: 'We are the martyrs of compromise', he explained to Ivan Maiskii during the afternoon of November 15th: 'It is like sitting on the edge of a volcano which is due to erupt at any moment. Every night we await arrest.' They did not have long to wait, for that very evening Rogovskii reported to the SR Directors that there was a definite plot afoot to arrest them.[199] They had put their heads into the lion's mouth, as Avksent′ev had suggested: all that remained was the question of the precise hour at which its Siberian jaws would snap shut.

Iziumov, pp. 247–51.

198 Sviatitskii, *K istorii*, p. 66; Maiskii, pp. 309–11; Piontkovskii, 'Materialy po istorii kontr-revoliutsii', pp. 117–18.

199 Maiskii, p. 306.

The conspiratorial staff

Rogovskii's report came as no surprise. Everyone in Omsk knew that the officer and Cossack bands roaming the streets of the town on 'hunting and fishing' expeditions and raising the roofs of restaurants with intoxicated battle hymns and sentimental renditions of 'God Save the Tsar' would not long tolerate the timorous Directory, cowering in its miserable quarters. Indeed, it was clear that they had it in mind to stage a coup and install the *tverdyi* (firm) régime which the right and many erstwhile liberals had been hankering after since Kornilov. 'This was gossiped about on every street corner', recalled Ivan Maiskii, who arrived at Omsk in October: 'News of it passed from ear to ear. People even indicated where the plotters' staff was housed and named the leaders.'[200] Moreover, at least two of the non-socialist *members* of the Directory were aware not only that a plot to remove the government was in motion but of precisely by whom the Directory was going to be replaced. On October 28th Boldyrev confided to his diary that 'the idea of dictatorship is gaining ground... I hear hints of it on many sides. This time the idea will most probably be connected with Kolchak.' Two days later the general was visited by Vologodskii, who confirmed that 'military circles [have] designated to Kolchak the role of dictator'.[201] Even at far-away Ekaterinburg, in the Urals, Kolchak's name, as that of the future dictator, was at this time being toasted at officers' banquets and parties.[202]

Before Pepeliaev had left Omsk on his trip to the Far East, he had commissioned Zhardetskii with the task of propagandizing among the Siberian capital's Kadet and bourgeois circles, with the aim of popularizing the notion of a dictatorship. Zhardetskii duly had Union of Regeneration policies condemned at Kadet caucuses and had their proponent, Lev Krol, ostracized by his Omsk party colleagues, who at a meeting of October 29th backed Zhardetskii's motion that they should commit

200 *ibid.*, p. 326. At least one rumour came out of Siberia in October to the effect that the Directory had already been overthrown and a military dictatorship established. See *Manchester Guardian* (Manchester) 3.xi.1918.

201 Boldyrev, pp. 80, 82.

202 Grondijs, L.H. *Le Cas Koltchak*. Leiden (1939), p. 32.

themselves to 'doing away with the Directory'.[203] Having thus secured the support of his own party, the Kadet leader began to look further afield. For instance, he was spotted almost daily doing the rounds of the foreign missions now established at Omsk, informing the representatives of the Allies that Siberian society would not tolerate this noxious 'cocktail' government, the Directory, poisoned as it was by its SR members' ties to the treacherous Chernov.[204] Moreover, whilst generally undermining the authority of the Directory and attempting to demonstrate the demand for a dictatorship, Zhardetskii, as an anonymous eye-witness has recalled, after the arrival at Omsk of Pepeliaev and Gajda's chosen candidate for the role, was also *specifically* attempting to determine that none other than Admiral Kolchak should be offered the post. His first opportunity to introduce this new face to the Omsk scene came on October 19th when he had Kolchak invited to address a special Trades and Industry Conference on the subject of the political and military situation in the Far East. The admiral was quite an accomplished public speaker, and proved a great success.[205] All in all the news of Kolchak's arrival was broadcast far and wide. And to great effect. At the front, recalled one officer, 'to all the military it now seemed that the long desired establishment of a strong authority, mindful of the disruptive course of the Chernov party, was coming into its time'.[206]

On November 1st Pepeliaev arrived back at Omsk and, now that Zhardetskii had set the dictatorial ball in motion, began to apply himself to the final details of the impending coup. He seems to have offered one last warning to the Kadet member of the Directory, Vladimir Aleksandrovich Vinogradov, being overheard to warn the latter that unless Avksent′ev and Zenzinov were removed from the government 'an accident being prepared by the military cannot be avoided'.[207] From a recently published letter of the Siberian Army's Quartermaster General, Colonel A.D. Syromiatnikov, it is clear that Pepeliaev could warn of this 'prepared accident' because the mechanism of the coup and its triumvirate of leaders was by now

203 Krol′, L., p. 152.

204 Il′in, 'Omsk, Direktoriia', Vol. 72, p. 204.

205 N.N., p. 91; M.K. '*Tragediia Admirala Kolchaka*, S.P. Mel′gunov', *Morskii zhurnal* (Paris), No. 4 (1930), pp. 7–10. Varneck and Fisher (n. 176) suggest that the author of this review was Admiral M.A. Kedrov.

206 N.N., p. 88.

207 Borodin, p. 203.

established: Pepeliaev had allotted to himself the task of currying the support of political circles at Omsk; Syromiatnikov was to take in hand the military side; and Mikhailov was to 'win over' the Council of Ministers.[208] In fact, on the very day of his arrival back at Omsk, Pepeliaev had spent some time with Mikhailov (with whom he had first become acquainted at the 2nd Cheliabinsk Conference in August). Their relationship now cemented in cabalry, the Kadet recorded in his diary: 'I talked with Mikhailov. Agreement reached. I consulted with him personally. It is ready.'[209]

Pepeliaev's next move was to approach Kolchak himself. It will be recalled that they had been unable to meet a month earlier in the Far East. At Omsk, however, on November 5th, Pepeliaev set down in his diary the record of 'a long and interesting discussion' with the admiral. The Kadet informed Kolchak that the National Centre at Moscow had originally favoured the candidacy of General Alekseev for the dictatorship. They had 'not forgotten' Kolchak, he stressed, but were simply trying to avoid a damaging rivalry. In reply Kolchak said that he would be more than happy to recognize Alekseev as the supreme commander.[210] As for the question of a dictatorship, Kolchak had already let it be known around Omsk that he was in favour of a unipersonal rule.[211] However, he told Pepeliaev on this occasion that, for the moment, he did not feel it was necessary to 'force events'. The Directory, he opined, might yet be supported: 'But in the future all will depend on whether Avksent'ev and Zenzinov are still linked to their party. If they are, they cannot be dealt with.' Nevertheless, concluding their talk, Pepeliaev extracted from the admiral the firm commitment that, if the crisis reached a point where he felt it was indispensable that the Directory should be disposed of, he, Kolchak, would be 'prepared to make the sacrifice' and assume the mantle of dictatorship.[212]

208 Shishkin, V.I. (ed.) 'K istorii kolchakovskogo perevorota', *Izvestiia sibirskogo otdeleniia Ak. nauk SSSR (seriia istorii, filologii i filosofii)* (Novosibirsk), Vol. 1 (1989), pp. 60–1. Guins later confirmed that he was among the members of the cabinet approached by Mikhailov, who posed the question 'what about Kolchak' as a solution to the country's problems. See Guins, 'Professor and Government Official', p. 178.

209 Pepeliaev, 'Dnevnik', No. 4, p. 84.

210 *ibid.*, No. 4, p. 85.

211 Boldyrev, pp. 22, 29.

212 Pepeliaev, p. 84. There could be perhaps no better testimony to the significance of this encounter and promise than the fact that Kolchak failed to mention them before his investigatory commission at Irkutsk. In fact, he specifically stated that 'of the non-military persons, the politicians, no one approached me on the question of unipersonal power'. See Varneck and

In the course of the next few days news reached Omsk of two events which had a vital bearing upon the agreement thus reached between Kolchak and Pepeliaev. Firstly, it became known that recently, at Ekaterinodar, General Alekseev had died of a heart attack, leaving Kolchak as the unchallenged candidate for the national dictatorship among right-wing and Kadet circles associated with the National Centre. Secondly, it became known that at Ekaterinburg the SR Central Committee had published the 'Chernov Manifesto', thereby, in the eyes of the military, irrevocably damning by association both Avksent′ev and Zenzinov and the government of which they were a part, no matter how fervent was the SR Directors' disowning of Chernov. With its call for overtly party-political armed units, recalled Kolchak, the document was 'profoundly insulting to the whole officer corps'.[213]

Throughout the summer of 1918 a military take-over had never really been much more than a gunshot away in anti-Bolshevik Siberia. Now, with Pepeliaev's conspiratorial staff complete and with both of the conditions which Kolchak had set for his acceptance of the mantle of dictatorship having been met, the gun was cocked and fingers itching for the trigger. Pepeliaev stepped up his preparations accordingly. On November 9th, so as to sever once and for all any links with the URR-conciliationist line being toed by some Kadet national leaders who were still in hiding in Moscow, he founded the Eastern Section of the Kadet Central Committee (known by its Russian acronym, *VOTsK*) to independently run the affairs of the right-wing Siberian Kadets. As Chairman, Pepeliaev was actually the lone Central Committee member on *VOTsK*, but he was ably seconded by Zhardetskii and other National Centre supporters at Omsk. Lev Krol, who was predictably excluded from *VOTsK*, dubbed Pepeliaev's new organization 'the most fervent conductor of reaction in Siberia', as indeed it was to be.[214] A week later, on November 15th, the Kadets' first full Siberian Conference was convened at Omsk, just as Pepeliaev had planned (see above, pp. 60–1). He must have been more than confident that his own resolution demanding the overthrow of the Directory would be supported, for on his eastern tour he had encountered little difficulty in persuading local party gatherings that the All-Russian Government was an SR front. Now, 'the party must declare that it is not afraid of dictatorship – but, rather, that

Fisher, p. 169.

213 *ibid.*, pp. 160–1.

214 Krol′, L., p. 150. For the 'Charter' of *VOTsK* (the acronym of *Vostochnyi otdel tsentral′nogo komiteta*) see *Pares Papers*, Box 28.

it concludes that dictatorship is unavoidable', he urged at the conference's opening session. He held that this was especially so in Siberia, where the peasantry (who had never really known Bolshevism) and the bourgeoisie (who were tainted with regionalism) would have to be *compelled* to fight for a Great Russia. Thus, the Kadets' self-appointed role as the conscience of Russian nationalism had reached its logical conclusion – knowing what was best for them, the Party of the People's Freedom would compel the people to fight – as they threw themselves wholeheartedly behind the military: Viktor Pepeliaev's resolution was carried by a resounding forty-four votes to one.[215]

If Pepeliaev had been successful in his work with Kolchak and the Kadets, Zhardetskii's attempts to curry support for the proposed dictatorship among the Allied missions had not been inefficacious. He found particular sympathy for the plans among the staff of Britmis and a true ally in its chief, General Knox (who was present at Omsk from October 21st to November 5th). In reports to Paris at the time and in the memoirs several of them were subsequently to publish, French officers who were serving in Siberia accused Knox of nothing less than having laid the entire groundwork for the coup during his two weeks' sojourn in the capital: Kolchak they characterized as 'Knox's man'; the admiral was 'in the Briton's pocket'.[216] Much of their carping, however, could be dismissed as sour grapes, for Britmis – for reasons which might be quite unconnected to any complicity in the coup – was to fare much better in Siberia than were the French. Certainly the French provide no firm evidence for their accusations. Knox himself, naturally, in his only published statement on the matter, flatly denied any connection with a plot to put Kolchak in power.[217] Years later, in a private conversation with the émigré

215 Maksakov and Turunov, p. 98; Dumova, p. 120.

216 Lasies, J. *La Tragédie sibérienne*. Paris (1920), pp. 59–60, 135; Pichon, A. 'Le Coup d'État de l'amiral Koltchak', *Le Monde Slave* (Paris), No. 2 (1925), p. 259; Janin, M. 'Otryvki iz moego sibirskogo dnevnika', in Kornatovskii, p. 122. The Dutch war correspondent, Grondijs, was of similar opinions. See Grondijs, L.H. *La Guerre en Russie et en Sibérie*. Paris (1926), p. 122.

217 Knox, A. '*Fragments of My Siberian Diary*, by M. Janin', *Slavonic Review* (London), Vol. 3, No. 9 (1925), p. 724. This was a letter to the editor of the *Slavonic Review*, published as a review and rebuttal of Janin's recently published account – 'Fragments de mon journal sibérien', *Le Monde Slave* (Paris) 1924, No. 2, pp. 221–40 and 1925, No. 3, pp. 339–55. The Frenchman replied, reaffirming the veracity of his views, in 'Le journal sibérien du général Janin', *Le Monde Slave* (Paris), Vol. 4 (1925), pp. 19–24. He later went on to use his diaries as the basis of the fuller records of his mission: *Moje ucast na ceskoslovenskem boji za svobodu*. Prague (1928); *Ma mission en Sibérie, 1918–1920*. Paris (1933).

historian S.P. Mel′gunov, he was to repeat that blanket denial – although, significantly, he *did* admit that he had been aware that such a move was imminent.[218] Had he chosen to continue his published memoirs of his service in Russia past the end of 1917, so as to cover his role in the civil war which was at least as influential as that which had gone before, Knox could perhaps have enlightened us further and may have laid to rest the speculation which has surrounded his name ever since. But, regrettably, he chose not to do so. And even in his lengthy and otherwise comprehensive report to the War Office on the role of Britmis, he spared not so much as a full sentence to the fall of the Directory, despite the accusations of British involvement flying back and forth at the time.[219] Such dogged taciturnity from such a loquacious general has to be marked down as curious to say the least.

In the absence of sufficient evidence to the contrary, however, we are obliged to concur with those western scholars who have previously speculated on the matter of Knox's collaboration with the conspirators, and to conclude that the French accusations were probably based on hearsay. It is, after all, unlikely that such a senior officer as Knox would have involved himself directly in the execution of the coup.[220] Over and above this, though, it is necessary to bear in mind that by his activities and pronouncements of the time, Knox did more to encourage those who desired to make Kolchak a dictator than he might have been able to do even if he had involved himself *directly* in the plot. We have already seen how, having agreed with Kolchak in Japan that only a military government backed by British arms could save Russia, Knox had escorted Kolchak to Vladivostok. The pair had then travelled west together into Siberia. Knox made a point en route of presenting himself only to military authorities along the way and rudely ignored the SR-*oblastnik* commissars still in power in some towns. Moreover, in widely reported

218 Mel′gunov, Vol. 1, pp. 113–15. General Sakharov, who left Omsk with Knox on November 5th, confirmed that the impending coup was being openly discussed by the time they departed. See Sakharov, K.V. *Belaia Sibir′*. Munich (1923), p. 19.

219 WO 32/5707 'Report of the Military Mission in Siberia, 10.xii.1919'. The title of Knox's memoirs provides adequate testimony to their limitations: *With the Russian Army, 1914–1917*. London (1921).

220 Ullman, Vol. 1, p. 282; Berk, 'The *Coup d'État*', p. 460; Kolz, 'British Foreign Policy', p. 117; Connaughton, pp. 99–100; Lincoln, W.B. *Red Victory: A History of the Russian Civil War*. London (1989), pp. 242–3.

conversations and in public speeches made during his journey, the general had let it be known that, in his opinion:

> Siberia is not ready for democracy. What is needed is a dictator. The only question is that of who is most suitable for the role – General Gajda or Admiral Kolchak.[221]

This, of course, was precisely the sort of talk which Pepeliaev and his partners wanted to hear from the head of the most important military mission in Siberia. And it got better…

On arrival at Omsk Knox made no secret of where his sympathies lay in the ongoing dispute between the Directory and the PSG on the question of the composition of the Council of Ministers. He announced that no British aid would be forthcoming unless an agreement was reached, virtually insisted that Kolchak be accepted as a member of the cabinet, and proceeded further to undermine the Directory's authority by refusing to meet it as a body. He could 'admit no point of contact between a general and a socialist', he announced over tea with a group of Siberian Army officers on one occasion. On another, in what Boldyrev hoped was a joke, he talked of gathering his own 'gang' to arrest the Directory. On yet another he opined that, for his alleged undermining of discipline in the army, Viktor Chernov should be shot.[222]

Such outspoken statements as these, however lightheartedly delivered, were unlikely to calm the turbulent political waters of the Siberian capital. At best they might be dismissed as betraying political ingenuousness. At worst they could not really have been better fashioned to jolt any latent conspiracy into gear. Moreover, such reports of Knox's behaviour must surely cast doubt upon the acceptance by Peter Fleming and other commentators that, just because Knox reported to the War Office on November 4th that he had tried to dissuade Kolchak from being party to a coup, the general was not actively encouraging the conspirators.[223] If Knox had

221 Boldyrev, p. 84; Sakharov, pp. 26–7; Dotsenko, 'The Struggle for the Liberation', p. 60. Knox was not the only Briton in Siberia to hold such views. Mr Nash, HM Consul at Irkutsk, concluded in August: 'What is needed is a MILITARY DICTATOR, as the people are not fit to govern themselves.' FO 538/3 'Situation in Siberia, August 1918'.

222 Guins, *Sibir'*, Vol. 1, p. 307; Boldyrev, pp. 79, 84.

223 Fleming, p. 113; Lincoln, *Red Victory*, pp. 242–3. Although valuable and insightful in many respects (he saw many private archives of Britmis members), Peter Fleming's conjectures on the level of British involvement in the coup cannot be regarded as wholly objective, for his chief adviser in the writing of his book was none other than Captain Leo Steveni (see above, p. 73).

been deliberately inspiriting Mikhailov and Pepeliaev with his barbed after-dinner asides, that was *precisely* what he would have to report to his superiors. Those who observed Knox's activity at the time were certainly in no doubt as to his responsibility for what happened: he was 'the primary inspiration behind the coup', said Boldyrev; 'the moving spirit behind the change of government', confirmed General Graves of the American Expeditionary Force.[224] Another who came upon Knox in the autumn of 1918 felt that he was regarded (and regarded himself) as 'the leading figure of the whole White movement'[225] – as chief of Britmis, he was in a unique position to determine which of the competing Siberian factions would receive Allied aid; his every less than Delphic hint and intimation that he would look favourably upon a dictatorship and that he respected Kolchak, had to be interpreted as an exhortation by the right-wing officers with whom he socialized.

Nor was Knox the only British officer in Omsk that the conspiratorial triumvirate of Pepeliaev, Mikhailov and Syromiatnikov could trust to go along with their plans. When he left the capital, bound for Vladivostok, on November 5th, the general placed Britmis in the hands of two of his staff, Colonel J. Neilson and Captain L. Steveni, who were more than willing to continue their chief's encouragement of the plotters. Both men spoke fluent Russian and had had longstanding associations with the anti-Bolshevik right as intelligence and liaison officers in the region since before the Czechoslovak revolt. Steveni (the son of a Russian noblewoman), in the words of one historian of Britmis was 'a thorough going reactionary who desired a complete restoration of the Tsarist régime'.[226] Neilson was later to fall out with what he termed the 'gang of adventurers' surrounding Kolchak (as, indeed, was Knox), but he was clearly quite enamoured of the admiral himself during the autumn of 1918: the morning after the coup the British colonel was to be found chauffeuring the newly inaugurated Supreme Ruler on a round of the foreign missions.[227] Once

For Knox's claim that he warned Kolchak against involving himself in any plot to unseat the Directory, see WO 33/962/573 'Knox to WO, 7.xi.1918'.

224 Boldyrev, p. 523 (n. 77); Graves, p. 99.

225 Alioshin, D. *Asian Odyssey*. London (1941), p. 58.

226 Ullman, Vol. 1, p. 282.

227 Fleming, p. 114. In a later report to the War Office, whilst pointedly denying any complicity in the actual planning of the coup, Neilson nevertheless admitted that he 'knew the coup was coming and [felt] it was necessary... I did not commit the [British] Government to the support of Admiral Kolchak, but if [the conspirators] gambled on the future support of the British Government it was logical.' FO 371/4108/40831 'Report on the Action Taken by Britmis (Omsk)

again it is in the accounts of French officers that we find the most strident criticism of the pair. General Janin and his aide, Colonel Rouquérol, both claimed that Neilson and Steveni were in attendance at a crucial meeting of November 17th (see below, pp. 103–4) at which plans for the coup were finalized.[228] On this occasion, however, their charges are substantiated by other accounts: one Lieutenant Il'in, a staff officer at Omsk, noticed the prominence of Neilson and Steveni at political soirées at which Pepeliaev and others would voice their determination to depose the Directory, while Syromiatnikov later asserted nothing less than that:

> Colonel Neilson and Captain Steveni assured me, on my informing them of the forthcoming coup, that they could guarantee the neutrality of the British (and consequently also the French).

Their one caveat was that there should be no blood spilled.[229]

It was, however, the third tier of British involvement in the Kolchak coup which was the most tangible. This was the activity of the 23rd Middlesex Battalion (one of two British units in Siberia), led by Colonel John Ward, which had arrived at Omsk together with Kolchak and was assigned to be his personal bodyguard when the admiral entered the Council of Ministers. No other minister received such protection. Moreover, on the morning following the coup, Ward would take the extraordinary action of surrounding the government buildings in the centre of Omsk and of guarding their approaches with British machine-gun detachments. He later claimed to have acted merely to preserve order.[230] But clearly, to preserve the status quo by armed force *after* a coup is rather different to preserving the status quo *before* one. Ward's move was obviously intended to deter any Czechoslovak units in the area from attempting to restore the Directory.

Even before the coup, however, Ward had shown a devotion to Kolchak which was beyond the normal call of duty. His Middlesex 'Die-Hards' had accompanied the admiral on a week-long tour of the front immediately prior to the coup. During

During the Coup d'État of 17–18th November 1918, by J.F. Neilson, 22.iii.1919'.

228 Janin *Ma mission*, pp. 30–1; Rouquérol, J.G.M. *La Guerre des Rouges et des Blancs*. Paris (1929), p. 44.

229 Il'in, 'Omsk, Direktoriia', Vol. 72, p. 202; Shishkin, 'K istorii', p. 60.

230 Ward, J. *With the 'Die-Hards' in Siberia*. London (1920), pp. 129–31. General Graves was informed that British troops were patrolling the streets of Omsk 'all night' as the coup took place. Graves, p. 73.

the return journey, at Petropavlovsk on November 16th, it became known that General Boldyrev had arrived from Omsk and wished to board Kolchak's train for consultations. Ward, claiming that he suspected 'trouble', ordered his men to load their guns and prepare for action.[231] That when the Russian Commander-in-Chief asked to speak with his Minister of War a British colonel felt it necessary to order battle stations was curious to say the least. We can only speculate as to what lengths Ward might have gone to had Boldyrev (by then convinced that Kolchak was party to a plot to remove the Directory) actually attempted to arrest the admiral rather than simply talk to him.

Kolchak's tour of the front is also worthy of note for the light it throws upon the preparations being made for the coup by officers of the Staff (*stavka*) of the Siberian Army and for determining the extent of the admiral's foreknowledge of the planned overturn. This is of significance because before his inquisitors at Irkutsk in 1920, Kolchak was to claim that he had no prior knowledge whatsoever of the plans being made by the conspirators at Omsk and only became aware *post facto* that 'most of the *stavka* were involved'.[232]

On this, his first visit to the front, Kolchak went first to the northern Urals capital of Ekaterinburg, the sector in which the Siberian Army was by then being deployed (what was left of the People's Army was still fighting to the south, before Ufa). There he met General Anatoli Pepeliaev (younger brother of Viktor) and the ultra-conservative General V.V. Golitsyn (a former aide of Kornilov) who had been mobilizing support for the PSG in the area. Kolchak also took up with Gajda the thread of the conversations they had had in the Far East. Later Kolchak would admit that he had at this meeting once again agreed with the Czech that only a dictatorship could provide the direction and unity necessary for anti-Bolshevism to triumph. Gajda himself, however, recalled that Kolchak had gone on to state that he was now fully resolved to take the burden of dictatorship upon his own shoulders and requested a guarantee of Czechoslovak neutrality, which was duly given.[233]

231 Ward, p. 160.

232 Varneck and Fisher, pp. 162, 166–7.

233 Gajda, R. *Moje pameti*. Prague (1924), p. 114. See also Ioffe, G.Z. 'Ot kontrrevoliutsii "demokraticheskoi" k burzhuazno-pomeshchich'ei diktature', *Istoriia SSSR* (Moscow), No. 1 (1982), pp. 112–14.

When answering questions at Irkutsk about this tour, Kolchak was clearly nervous, at one point saying that he did not get as far as the town of Cheliabinsk, at another that he did. Was this perhaps because his sojourn at the front was not merely the 'tour of inspection' he claimed, but an opportunity taken to introduce the candidate dictator to the officers at the front? Certainly Kolchak's trusted confidant, Ivan Sukin, was to make no secret in his memoirs of his impression that the sole purpose of Kolchak's visit had been to gain the assurance that officers at the front were in favour of the establishment of a military government. If at Ekaterinburg, however, he had been reassured, at Cheliabinsk (which, in fact, he did visit), the headquarters of the Czechoslovak Legion, his reception was rather less uniformly perfervid. The Commander-in-Chief of the Legion, General Syrovy, was absent from the town, but Kolchak reportedly held prolonged and cordial talks with General M.K. Dieterichs, a Russian officer of pronounced monarchistic sympathies then serving as Syrovy's Chief of Staff (but subsequently to be one of the foremost generals in Kolchak's service). From members of the Czechoslovak National Council, messieurs Girsa and Pavlu, however, Kolchak received the warning that if the Directory fell from power their soldiers would certainly leave the front.[234] Then, before he could proceed any further on his tour, Kolchak suddenly left Cheliabinsk on November 15th and headed back east, telling Ward that 'urgent reasons' compelled him to return to Omsk.[235]

At his interrogation Kolchak was careful to deny that he had had any contact whatsoever with the capital during his tour of the front.[236] If so, one wonders, what 'urgent reasons' could have compelled him to return there so peremptorily? And was it a mere coincidence that he arrived at Omsk at 5.30 p.m. on November 16th, a mere thirty hours before the coup was to take place? Or was his sudden return connected with the fact that on his train was an agent of the *stavka*, commissioned by Syromiatnikov with the task of keeping the admiral informed of how the plot was progressing at Omsk and with instructions to have the candidate dictator appear there on cue? S.P. Mel′gunov later interviewed a Captain Shchepin who claimed to have detailed an officer to perform precisely such a mission on Kolchak's train, but the émigré historian was reluctant to accept as valid this

234 Varneck and Fisher, pp. 166–7, 182; *Dumy* (Biisk) 20.xi.1918, cited in Livshits, *Imperialisticheskaia interventsiia*, p. 56.

235 Ward, p. 122.

236 Varneck and Fisher, pp. 166–7.

officer's claims of such a detailed preparation of the coup.[237] However, in the afore-cited letter of Syromiatnikov to Mikhailov of April 1919, the Quartermaster General records that in the weeks before the coup he had, in fact, detailed a number of officers to perform a variety of tasks around Omsk: one was to ascertain the strength of Rogovskii's militia; another to test the loyalty to the Directory of some elements of the Omsk garrison and ascertain how to confine them to barracks should they attempt to prevent the coup; another was to keep a constant tail on Avksent′ev and Zenzinov; another was to prepare convoys to escort the arrested Directors to the pre-arranged place of confinement (at the Agricultural School); another was to plan the seizure of all telegraphic communications with the front, so as to forestall any attempt by supporters of the government to summon reinforcement. Shchepin is also mentioned in the letter, as having been assigned the task of placing officers on the train of General Boldyrev, to prevent him or other units at the front taking action.[238] It is at least possible, therefore, that this captain also detailed agents to the train of Kolchak.

A contention as to the careful planning of the Omsk overturn may be further substantiated by an examination of the afore-cited memoirs of Lieutenant Il′in. Il′in tells an interesting tale of how the Quartermaster General, Syromiatnikov, had informed him some time in advance of the event that Pepeliaev was preparing a coup, but went on to warn him that he should on no account inform Boldyrev's newly appointed Chief of Staff, General S.N. Rozanov (who had recently arrived at Omsk from the Red zone), for it was feared that he might put forward candidates other than Kolchak for the role of dictator.[239] Then, on November 17th, the eve of the coup, Syromiatnikov ordered Il′in to report to the *stavka* headquarters at 9.00

237 Mel′gunov, Vol. 2, p. 139.

238 Shishkin, 'K istorii', p. 61. It has to be born in mind that Syromiatnikov's letter was a diplomatically framed complaint that those in the *stavka* who had done most to secure the success of the coup had received scant reward, while those who had done little or nothing (by which he certainly implied Kolchak's favourite and Chief of Staff, D.A. Lebedev) had prospered by it. He may, therefore, have exaggerated the role of his men. Nevertheless, this letter does seem to cast doubt on the generally accepted view of western and émigré histories of the coup as having involved no planning (a view exemplified by Mel′gunov's assertion that the events were a 'semi-spontaneous movement' of uncontrollable Cossacks – see Mel′gunov, Vol. 2, pp. 104, 141).

239 Il′in, 'Omsk, Direktoriia', Vol. 72, p. 206. Il′in fails to cite the precise date of this encounter, but it must have been prior to Kolchak's departure for the front on November 9th because the lieutenant was on his daily trip from the *stavka* to see the admiral and enquire as to his needs when he was buttonholed by Syromiatnikov. This confirms that the plot was well under way before Kolchak's sojourn in the Urals.

p.m. Puzzled, Il′in complied with this order. Arriving punctually at the *stavka*, which was housed in the largest building in Omsk, the former offices of the Trans-Siberian Railway Administration, he found it almost deserted. He was then told to sit at the telephone in Syromiatnikov's office and, if Rozanov called, to report only that everything was in order. While Il′in waited, Syromiatnikov departed to make his particular contribution to the coup at the direct wire office, explaining to Il′in that:

> It must be smashed. Soon it will begin. Colonel Volkov and Krasil′nikov will arrest the SR members of the Directory. Everything will be done without a single shot being fired. Pepeliaev and the young Cossacks have planned this business well![240]

Colonel V.I. Volkov, it will be recalled, was the former Commander of the Omsk Garrison implicated in the Novoselov affair; Ataman I.N. Krasil′nikov was the Siberian Cossack leader responsible for the outrages at the receptions of the British and French missions. These incidents were currently the subject of a legal investigation launched by the Directory, and Boldyrev was threatening to send the guilty parties to the front. The Siberian Cossacks at their *voisko* centre, Omsk, had been railing against the Directory since its inception – and as early as July 1918 their congress had demanded the installation of a dictatorship. Now the Cossack leaders had an added incentive to topple the government, before any unpleasant facts could be uncovered about their activities of the past months which might force them to swap the rather comfortable life they enjoyed at Omsk for the constraints of life at the front.[241]

Kolchak was still on his train at Omsk station, some four kilometres from the town centre, during the evening of November 17th (coincidentally his birthday), when he was visited by a delegation of Cossacks and *stavka* officers. They told him 'quite definitely that the Directory had little longer to live', he recalled, 'and that the creation of a unipersonal authority was necessary'. When he asked them whom they proposed to name as dictator, they replied unhesitatingly: 'You must do this.' To his

240 *ibid.*, Vol. 72, pp. 211–12.

241 Zenzinov, *Gosudarstvennyi perevorot*, pp. 114–15; Argunov, *Mezhdu dvumia*, pp. 22, 35–6; Argunov, 'Omskie dni', pp. 203–4.

investigators at Irkutsk, Kolchak later claimed to have declined the invitation.[242] Moreover, his friend Sukin recalled that when he had talked with Kolchak during the afternoon of the 17th, although the admiral said that from his visit to the front he was convinced that 'all the officers without exception were dissatisfied with the Directory', he remained unsure that a coup was the best step (mentioning a fear of damaging repercussions abroad).[243] On the other hand, we have already seen how on November 5th the admiral had given Pepeliaev his word that he would 'make the sacrifice' and assume the mantle of dictatorship if required. Moreover, I.I. Serebrennikov (who had been made Minister of Supply to the Directory) states quite categorically that, according to what he heard, Kolchak 'gave the conspirators his agreement to assume the mantle of dictator', before they acted. Venturing forth from his hotel on the night of November 17th–18th Serebrennikov was to run into a patrol. The officer in charge, *Essaul* (Cossack Captain) Porotnikov, informed him that the SR members of the Directory were at that very moment being arrested:

'Who will it be?' asked the minister.

'It will be Kolchak', came the unequivocal reply.[244] If a lowly *essaul* could make such a definite prediction, it can only be concluded that, whether or not Kolchak had expressed doubts to the men who approached him during the evening of the 17th, they had in any case decided to proceed in his name.

The group that visited Kolchak's train on the 17th, were delegates from a meeting which was taking place that day at the offices of the Omsk Military Industrial Committee, at which the plans for the coup were being finalized. According to the Soviet historian, P.S. Parfenov (Altaiskii), present were members of the Kadet *VOTsK* and the Omsk URR, Cossack officers, representatives of the the foreign missions and, in person, Ivan Mikhailov.[245] Although Parfenov,

242 Varneck and Fisher, pp. 168–9. Kolchak said that he could not recall whether Krasil'nikov was part of this delegation, although he did add that Colonel Volkov (who was also implicated in the scandals) was among his visitors, as were Captain Katanaev (son of a prominent general of the Siberian Cossacks) and Colonel Lebedev (who was to become Kolchak's Chief of Staff). The Soviet historian, P.S. Parfenov, claims that Krasil'nikov was indeed present. He also asserts that Kolchak did not decline the offer of supreme power, but merely requested twenty-four hours to consider it. Unfortunately he cites no source for this information. See Parfenov, P.S. *Uroki proshlogo*. Harbin (1921), p. 81.

243 Sukin (*Leeds Russian Archive*), pp. 33–4.

244 Serebrennikov, I.I. *Moi vospominaniia*. Tientsin (1937), pp. 216–19.

245 Parfenov, *Uroki*, p. 82. Sukin (*Leeds Russian Archive*), p. 39 also mentions the occurrence of this meeting to settle the final details of the coup, and adds that also present was Colonel Lebedev.

unfortunately, provides no source for these details, the fact that such a cabal met is confirmed by the diary of Pepeliaev, who in his entry for that day recorded:

> I went from the [Kadet] conference to the meeting. All participated. It is decided... Arrangements are complete.[246]

The precise timing of the coup was now set. The Directory was dying on borrowed time.

Coup d'état at Omsk, November 18th 1918

At around 1.15 a.m. on November 18th, two battalions of the First Siberian Cossack Regiment and a squadron of mounted Cossack partisans commanded by Krasil'nikov turned down the happily named Ataman Street in the centre of Omsk and proceeded to surround the apartment building which contained the rooms of the Directory's Chief of Militia, Rogovskii. (The guards at the door, men of Rogovskii's force, reportedly fell for the unlikely story that the Cossacks had heard of a plot to depose the government and had taken it upon themselves to offer protection to the vulnerable SRs.) Krasil'nikov knew that inside the apartment were not only Rogovskii, Avksent'ev and Zenzinov, but also two members of the SR Central Committee (M.Ia. Gendel'man and D.F. Rakov) and three SR representatives of the anti-Bolshevik Northern Government (M.A. Laibach, S.S. Maslov and Ia.D. Dedusenko). Ironically, the gathering was very probably discussing the officers' coup which had recently overthrown the moderate socialist régime headed by N.V. Chaikovskii at Arkhangel'sk, when a dozen or so Cossack officers, clearly the worse for drink, burst through the door brandishing pistols to announce that everyone in the room was under arrest.

The SRs were placed under guard and marched off into the frozen night, shortly to find themselves, as previously arranged by Syromiatnikov, incarcerated in makeshift cells at the headquarters of Krasil'nikov's Cossack squadron, the Agricultural Institute, on the outskirts of the city. There they were soon joined by their party colleague, A.A. Argunov, the investigator of the Novoselov affair, who

246 Pepeliaev, 'Dnevnik', No. 4, p. 87.

had been waylaid outside his hotel in a co-ordinated action that night. The prisoners fully expected to follow their late friends Novoselov and Moiseenko into the 'Kingdom of the Irtysh'. But one of their guards assured them that as long as they co-operated their lives would be spared – foreign representatives at Omsk had demanded it, he said.[247]

The political bankruptcy of the path which the SRs of the Directory had decided to follow was made clear by the fact that no attempt was made from *any* quarter to reverse the Cossacks' arrest of their Provisional All-Russian Government or to rescue any of its arrested members. As the coup was being executed, the 150-strong Battalion of State Defence, the meagre force which Rogovskii had been able to assemble at Omsk to protect the government, was surrounded in its barracks near the station by a Cossack detachment and meekly laid down its arms at the threat of force. One of its members was slightly injured in the confusion, but as far as can be ascertained this was the only blood spilt in the defence of the Directory.[248] There were some noises of protest over the next few days from Czechoslovak units on the Urals front who were dismayed at the summary dispersal of the coalition they had sponsored. But, as we have seen, Kolchak had established close relations with some of their most influential leaders, including Gajda and Dieterichs, who were able to keep their men in check. Moreover, Allied representatives in the Urals, at Omsk and in the Far East were making it plain that they were far from displeased with what had occurred and would not appreciate any interference from the Legion.[249] Thus were the conspirators given a free hand to proceed with the enthronement of Admiral Kolchak.

At 6.00 a.m. on the morning of November 18th a number of bleary-eyed ministers and rather more alert staff officers gathered at the former Governor's

247 Most of the eight men arrested that night left accounts of the coup, on which the following is based: Argunov, *Mezhdu dvumia* (1919), pp. 36–8; Rakov, pp. 2–8; Zenzinov, *Gosudarstvennyi perevorot*, pp. 115–18; Avksent′ev, in *Japan Advertiser* (Tokyo) 28.xii.1918 and in Alekseev, S.A (ed.) *Grazhdanskaia voina v Sibiri i na Severnoi oblastei: memuary*. Moscow (1927), pp. 2–5. See also the joint statements of Avksent′ev, Zenzinov, Argunov and Rogovskii published in *Russkoe slovo* (New York) 27.ii.1919 and 2.iii.1919.

248 A Lieutenant Malyshev left the only eye-witness account of this incident I have been able to discover, in *Narod* (Ufa) 26.xi.1918.

249 Krol′, L., p. 160; Boldyrev, p. 165; Pepeliaev, 'Dnevnik', No. 4, p. 89; Maksakov and Turunov, p. 98. Equally significant in forestalling any Czechoslovak movement on Omsk was the Legion's rapidly declining morale and sheer exasperation at yet another political battle being waged at Omsk while they held the front against the Reds. See below, pp. 195–9.

Palace, which was now the headquarters of the Council of Ministers. Vologodskii and Vinogradov, the only remaining Directors who were both at liberty and in Omsk, were also in attendance. It was an extraordinary meeting in every sense of the word: no minutes were taken, apparently; while, although it was subsequently described as a meeting of the Council of Ministers, staff officers seem to have played a leading role in the proceedings. The various extant eye-witness accounts of what took place differ slightly in detail, but agree on the main course of the discussions.[250]

The first question posed was that of what was to be done in the light of the arrest of the two SR members of the Directory. Even though at least two of those present were fully aware of where the prisoners were being held – Syromiatnikov and Minister of Justice S.S. Starynkevich (who, according to Avksent′ev, visited the Agricultural Institute immediately after the SRs' incarceration) – this circumstance was treated as an unalterable, irreversible *fait accompli*. It was suggested that the three Directors still at liberty might continue to function as a governing body. That idea, however, was given short shrift. The general opinion was that a government which could not prevent the arrest of its own members 'ceased to be the government'. The legal niceties of such an argument might have discomforted the liberal sprinkling of lawyers among the assembled ministers, but the question soon resolved itself when Vinogradov offered to resign his post and then left the meeting. With only two of its members now remaining, and only one of them present at Omsk, the Directory was clearly no more.

Predictably, immediately upon Vinogradov's announcement of his resignation, it was suggested that all civil and military power be united in the hands of one man, as a dictator. Kolchak recalled that it was 'a member of the military' who first broached the subject.[251] Referring to the unpublished memoirs of one present, Colonel Baftolovskii, a Soviet historian has been able to confirm that this was indeed the case, and that the proposer of a dictatorship was none other than Colonel Syromiatnikov.[252] His suggestion was seconded by the Chief of Staff, Rozanov, who despite the best efforts of Il′in and others at the *stavka* had somehow come to

250 The following is based on the eye-witness accounts of Kolchak (in Varneck and Fisher, pp. 170–5); Guins, *Sibir′*, Vol. 1, pp. 306–10; Serebrennikov, *Moi vospominaniia*, pp. 219–20; Sukin (*Leeds Russian Archive*), pp. 36–8.

251 Varneck and Fisher, p. 173.

252 Ioffe, *Kolchakovskaia avantiura*, p. 144.

hear of the coup and had made his way to the meeting. Exactly as the conspirators had feared, however, Rozanov tried to thwart those who had already fitted-out Kolchak for the role of dictator by promoting the candidature of his own superior, the politically moderate General Boldyrev. Rozanov, however, was shouted down. It appears that Kolchak, citing the need to preserve a continuity in the command of the army, then also began to speak in favour of Boldyrev: again he was having second thoughts and tried to dodge the crown being thrust upon him. But his modesty little perturbed the assembly. They were set on Kolchak. To avoid embarrassment, the admiral left the room while his own candidature was discussed. After minimal debate it was the arch-conspirator Mikhailov who proposed a ballot. It may have been that more than one vote was taken, for some accounts mention that General Horvath was also proposed by a former member of his cabinet (now Minister of Ways and Communications at Omsk), the engineer L.A. Ustrugov. But in the poll that mattered Kolchak received ten votes and Boldyrev only one.

At this point Kolchak was summoned back into the meeting from Vologodskii's office, where he had been awaiting the outcome of the ministers' deliberations. He was informed of the meeting's decision and accepted it. At his request official documents were drawn up announcing the transfer of power and by the time that the inhabitants of Omsk ventured out of their houses later that morning to brave one of the first blizzards of what was to be one of the harshest winters in living memory, Kolchak's inaugural proclamation adorned the walls and hoardings of the town:

> On November 18th 1918 the All-Russian Government collapsed. The Council of Ministers took all power into its own hands and then bestowed it upon me – Admiral of the Russian Fleet, A.V. KOLCHAK. Having taken up the heavy cross of power in the exceptionally difficult circumstances of civil war and the complete disruption of the life of the state, I declare: I will follow neither the path of reaction nor the fatal path of party politics. I set as my chief aims the creation of a battleworthy army, victory over Bolshevism and the establishment of law and order, so that the people may freely choose for themselves the form of government that they desire and realize the great ideas of freedom which are currently being advanced the entire world around. I summon you, citizens, to victory, to the struggle with Bolshevism, to labour and sacrifice.
>
> SUPREME RULER, A.V. KOLCHAK, Omsk, 18th November 1918[253]

253 *Pravitel'stvennyi vestnik* (Omsk) No. 1, 19.xi.1919, cited in Zenzinov *Gosudarstvennyi perevorot*, p. 11. Kolchak had been hastily promoted from vice-admiral to full admiral by the Council of Ministers before he assumed supreme power – see *ibid.*, p. 9

Chapter 2

The establishment of the Kolchak Government

In the days following the Omsk coup a series of communications, explanations and generalized promises were issued by the press agencies which had been founded by the new government:

> The events which have occurred are absolutely not a consequence of the weakening of authority in eastern Russia. On the contrary – they are a consequence of the ever-increasing strengthening of our principle of state-minded responsibility.
> (Iu.V. Kliuchnikov, Director of the Ministry of Foreign Affairs, 23.xi.1918)[1]

> With deep sincerity, I declare to you now...that I am strongly and more firmly than ever convinced that in this day and age the State may live and be revived only upon a solid, democratic foundation. I have always been a supporter of order and *gosudarstvennost'* ('state-minded responsibility') and now in particular I will demand of everybody not only respect for the law but also that which is most important of all in the process of re-establishing the State – the support of order.
> (A.V. Kolchak, Supreme Ruler, 28.xi.1918)[2]

In the short term, these declarations by the new government at Omsk were moderate enough to allay the fears of some of the most sceptical of observers. 'State-mindedness', 'support for the law', 'freedom', 'a democratic foundation' – what could be more encouraging? Even General Graves, Commander of the American Expeditionary Force, who was to prove himself no friend of reaction, had to admit that he was impressed.[3] And that, of course, was precisely what had been intended. In drawing up his inaugural declarations, noted Pepeliaev, the Supreme Ruler had instructed his advisers that they should take full account of the fact that

1 Rakitnikov, N.I. *Sibirskaia reaktsiia i Kolchak*. Moscow (1920), p. 25.

2 *Pravitel'stvennyi vestnik* (Omsk) No. 12, 30.xi.1919. Kolchak's statement to the press of 28th November appears in full in Pinegin, M.N. (ed.) *Nastol'nyi kalandar' na 1919 god*. Tomsk (1918), pp. 79–80.

3 Graves, W.S. *America's Siberian Adventure*. New York (1931), p. 117.

'the Allies want something said about democracy and the absence of reactionary intentions'. And 'thus it was done', the king-maker confided to his diary.[4] The declarations were for foreign consumption only, for it was feared that, with the war against Germany now over, the Allies (and, in particular, the still puissant Americans) would have to be goaded – or, if necessary, duped – into maintaining a commitment to the struggle against Bolshevism in Russia. Consequently, blandiloquent paeans to democracy issued forth from Omsk on a daily basis, to be faithfully reproduced in the foreign press. 'No reasonable person can doubt the intentions of the new ruler', affirmed the London *Times* on November 28th; 'Admiral Kolchak's declarations are unimpeachable', it added a few days later.[5] There had been a coup, but there was a new constitution and there remained the Council of Ministers, whose lineage might – however tortuously – be traced back to the popular mandate of the *Sibobduma*; there was a dictatorship, but only a provisional one; there was military rule, but if it could rally the army, perhaps it should be supported. Such were the thoughts successfully inculcated in the minds of potential doubters by the new government's propaganda offensive.[6] Others, on hearing of the events at Omsk, hoped that a military leader of Kolchak's standing could '*administrer le knout salutaire*' to the Russian people. Moreover, and this was of special allure to the war-ravaged Europeans, one of the very first acts of the new government had been to assume complete responsibility for the massive Russian foreign debt repudiated by the Bolsheviks.[7]

In Siberia itself, however, there were to be few indeed who entertained any illusions as to the desire or ability of the Kolchak régime to fulfil its inaugural promises. Even a loyal servant of the régime had to admit that, at least in the area under his jurisdiction, 'neither the Left nor, in general, perhaps anybody at all believed the truth of the new government's declarations'.[8] And indeed, as this and succeeding chapters will demonstrate, the constitution was to be contradicted, democracy derided and freedom forgotten, for the Kolchak government was not

4 Pepeliaev, V.N. 'Dnevnik', *Krasnye zori* (1923), No. 4, p. 88.

5 *The Times* (London) 28.xi.1918 and 17.xii.1918.

6 Sukin noted that the title 'Supreme Ruler' was itself chosen in preference to the more blunt 'dictator' to soften the blow, while the Council of Ministers' prominence in the constitution was intended 'to maintain the decorum of the civic spirit'. Sukin (*Leeds Russian Archive*), pp. 37–8.

7 *Pravitel'stvennyi vestnik* (Omsk) No. 6, 24.xi.1919; *FRUS: 1918*, Vol. 3, p. 447.

8 Andrushkevich, N.A. 'Posledniaia Rossiia', *Beloe delo* (Berlin) No. 4, (1928), p. 115.

what it pretended to be: the Council of Ministers was not a check on arbitrary military authority and the dictator was not a dictator; neither would enjoy much influence beyond the confines of their ostentatious offices at Omsk. Moreover, their impotence was largely of their own making, for, as a result of Kolchak and his ministers' firm faith in the honesty and apoliticism of a mythically glorious Russian Army and their unshakeable optimism in its imminent and complete victory over Bolshevism, the leading lights of the Omsk Government came to entrust all power to the military. Unfortunately for them, however, the army of White Siberia, redubbed the Russian Army soon after Kolchak's assumption of power, proved itself to be one of the most dishonest, inglorious and overtly politicized groupings ever to bear that name. Eventually some members of the government would realize their mistake – and even the Supreme Ruler himself would suffer doubt – but by then it would be too late. Meanwhile, all across Siberia military chiefs seized the opportunity handed to them by the weakness of the government to establish their own personal fiefdoms. Harking back to the privileges and institutions of the tsarist past, the officers and atamans of Kolchak's army would exhibit an unquenchable thirst not so much for victory as for revenge upon those who, through revolution, had denied the military caste its cherished place in that dead empire. So it was that even before the year 1918 was over, on the streets of Omsk itself, a frightening massacre committed by members of the armed forces would reveal the black heart of the White régime in Siberia.

Cui bono?

What precisely the new régime at Omsk meant by its oft-expressed principles of 'law and order' and 'state-minded responsibility' was very soon made clear by the contrasting manner in which it dealt with the Cossacks who had executed the coup through their summary arrest of the SR members of the Directory, on the one hand, and the Directors who had been thus abducted, on the other. In fact, it is useful to examine this and other incidents and developments in the immediate aftermath of the coup from the point of view of the legal test, *cui bono*? – to ask what the facts reveal as to for whose benefit the coup was made and for whose benefit the Kolchak régime was likely to operate.

On November 19th the Minister of Justice, Starynkevich, informed the Council of Ministers that at noon on that day the Cossack officers Krasil′nikov and Volkov, together with their associate Katanaev, had called at his office. There they had freely admitted to having instigated the coup: 'by mutual agreement between themselves', the Cossacks confessed, 'having no other accomplices and guided by the love of their Motherland, they had decided to put an end to the activities of the All-Russian Government' by arresting certain of its members, now being held at the Agricultural Institute. After receiving Starynkevich's report, the cabinet decided that the confessedly guilty trio should be placed under arrest and that, charged with 'an attack on supreme state authority' (i.e. treason), they should be brought to trial before a special military court to be convened on November 21st under the presidency of the Commander of Omsk Military District, General A.F. Matkovskii.[9]

It was, of course, very convenient for all those others who had participated in the plot against the Directory that the three Cossacks had accepted sole responsibility for what had happened. So convenient, in fact, that the suspicion arises that they must have been put up to their confession. Certainly the three knew that there was little danger of their being cashiered for their actions by a tribunal of an army which had never accepted the Directory's authority. And soon everybody else knew as much too – on the evening of November 19th, blatantly prejudicing the forthcoming trial, Kolchak chose to issue orders promoting the three indicted Cossacks for their 'excellent military service'.[10] Later he admitted that he had 'never countenanced punishment for these persons', for he had 'already accepted responsibility for what they had done', in accepting the post of Supreme Ruler.[11]

On the morning of November 21st the sham trial duly opened. The Cossacks were defended by two Kadet lawyers close to Kolchak – Zhardetskii and

9 FO 371/4095/55981 'Memorandum on the Establishment of a Regency, by Mr Jordan (HM Vice Consul, Omsk), 30.xi.1918'; Zenzinov, V. (ed.) *Gosudarstvennyi perevrot admirala Kolchaka v Omske 18 noiabria 1918 goda*. Paris (1919), pp. 13, 19; Golovin, N.N. *Rossiiskaia kontrrevoliutsiia v 1917–1918gg. (Chast′ 4: Osvobozhdenie Sibiri i obrazovanie 'belogo' voennogo fronta grazhdanskoi voiny)*. Paris–Tallinn (1937), Vol. 9, pp. 54–5.

10 Subbotovskii, I. *Soiuzniki i russkie reaktsionery: kratkii obzor (iskliuchitel′no po ofitsial′nym arkhivnym dokumentam Kolchakovskogo pravitel′stva)*. Leningrad (1926), p. 65. Lieutenant Colonels Krasil′nikov and Katanaev were made full colonels; Colonel Volkov was promoted to the rank of major general and made Commander-in-Chief of the 4th and 5th Amur Corps (see below, pp. 190ff).

11 Varneck, E. and Fisher, H.H. (eds.) *The Testimony of Admiral Kolchak and Other Siberian Materials*. Stanford (1935), p. 177.

Soloveichik (Secretary of *VOTsK*), who claimed that their clients' actions had been inspired solely by 'a sense of duty' and 'love of their Motherland'. As evidence of this the court was shown documents purporting to substantiate claims of treasonous activities by the SR Directors – 'conspiratorial' conversations over the direct wire with their party colleagues in the Urals, and connivance in both the defalcation of central government funds by SRs at Ufa and the formation of SR military units at Ekaterinburg. In fact, the proceedings soon turned from an examination of the Cossacks' demerits into a trial *in absentia* of the SR Directors and their colleagues. That Krasil'nikov, Volkov and Katanaev, as a result of their confessions, *had* to be found guilty as charged went almost unnoticed, as, despite that, Matkovskii did not hesitate to set them free to assume their new promotions, while the official press dwelt exclusively on the allegations against Avksent'ev, Zenzinov and Rogovskii and lauded the Cossacks for thwarting an alleged SR coup.[12]

If the Kolchak government had proceeded to publish the evidence it claimed to hold against the SR Directors – as at one stage it promised to do[13] – perhaps some credence could be given to the régime's professed commitment to 'law'. As, however, there was no such official publication, but only an eloquent official silence on the matter, whatever were the activities which SR groups at Ufa and Ekaterinburg might have been contemplating, the charge of the complicity of Avksent'ev and Zenzinov in them was at best specious and at worst fabricated (as Zenzinov claimed in his publication on the coup).[14] After all, as we have seen, the SR Directors had gone out of their way throughout their eight weeks in office to distance themselves from Chernov and PSR policy and had endeavoured to appease the Siberian military on every issue. They were guilty of political naivety, not treason. Moreover, had the government found the slightest shred of hard evidence that any of the arrested men (who, since the 19th, had been held under house arrest) had been involved in some plot, then the logical step would surely have been to rush

12 Zenzinov, pp. 20, 69–76; Guins, G.K. *Sibir' soiuzniki i Kolchak: povorotnyi moment russkoi istorii, 1918–1920gg*. Peking (1921), Vol. 2, pp. 15–16; Golovin, Vol. 9, pp. 101–5; Gan, A. *Rossiia i bol'shevizmom: materialy po istorii revoliutsii i bor'by s bol'shevizm (chast' pervaia, 1914–1920)*. Shanghai (1921), pp. 296–8. For foreign consumption the Omsk government's agents in Europe went so far as to claim that the SR Central Committee had organized 'execution squads' to massacre officers and that, whilst in power at Omsk, Avksent'ev 'was in direct communication with Trotsky'! See FO 371/3365/203796 'Nabokov [Russian Chargé d'Affairs, London] Report to FO, 9.xii.1918'.

13 *Pravitel'stvennyi vestnik* (Omsk) No. 26, 26.i.1919.

14 Zenzinov, pp. 69–70.

them to court to face charges. But that was not done – for, as Kolchak was later to concede, scotching all the stories filling official newspapers of the time, 'there were no grounds for trying them'.[15] Instead, on the very day that the calumnies against them were being voiced at the Cossacks' trial, Avksent′ev, Zenzinov and the other arrested SRs were quietly put on board a special train bound for the Far East and, on condition that they refrain from political activity, were provided with government subsidies amounting to 50,000 to 75,000 roubles per man to finance their exile.[16]

On November 27th the group of miserable exiles was shunted across the Chinese border at Chang Chung. And at that, Kolchak would presumably have preferred to have forgotten about the matter and to have got on with the business of winning the war. That, however, was a vain hope. The stigma of this deceitful trial, the government's grubby nativity, was forever to mark the régime and would vitiate its claims to legitimacy throughout its existence. Even Pepeliaev noted at the time that, in promoting those very Cossacks whom the Council of Ministers and a court martial had pronounced guilty of crimes against legitimate authorities of the state, whilst at the same time financing the exile of SRs who were being lambasted as traitors in the official press, the government had tried to be 'too clever by half'.[17] A régime which had proclaimed itself to be the guardian of law and order, which demanded state-mindedness from its citizens, had been seen to relish the perversion of the legal process. Moreover, and even more ominously for Kolchak, a clear precedent had been established by the events of November 18th–21st: an example whereby patriotism was whatever Cossack atamans deemed it to be, one whereby the arbitrary and unlawful activities of military commanders went not only unpunished but rewarded if committed 'in the name of the Motherland'. As Pepeliaev again acknowledged of the trial, becoming gradually aware of the storm

15 Varneck and Fisher, p. 178. Guins too later admitted that the charges made against the SR Directors had been somewhat 'distorted through malice' – Guins, Vol. 1, p. 315 – but he never dropped the accusation that Zenzinov and Avksent′ev had remained tied to their party and its treasonous activities. See Guins, G. [K.] 'The Siberian Intervention', *Russian Review*, Vol. 28, No. 4 (1969), p. 439.

16 Alekseev, S.A. (ed.) *Grazhdanskaia voina v Sibiri i v severnoi oblasti*. Moscow (1927), pp. 6–7; Guins, *Sibir′*, Vol. 2, pp. 70–1; Guins, 'The Siberian Intervention', pp. 179–80; Varneck and Fisher, pp. 178–80. The charges were further undermined by the fact that in 1919 reports reaching Omsk from Paris of the 'patriotic and statesmanlike attitude' adopted by Avksent′ev, who was in exile there, persuaded Kolchak to offer him a post in the diplomatic service. (See Subbotovskii, pp. 70–1). Would such an offer have been made to a proven (or even suspected) traitor?

17 Pepeliaev, 'Dnevnik', No.4, p. 88.

which his conspiracy might have unleashed: 'It would have been better if it had not taken place at all.'[18]

With the Cossacks promoted for their part in the events of November 18th, next in line for reward was the second military wing of the conspiracy, the officers of the Omsk *stavka*. Lieutenant Il'in, for example, found himself suddenly promoted to the rank of colonel, and was informed by Syromiatnikov that 'this is for your participation in the coup'.[19] Meanwhile, General Rozanov was thanked for his coolness towards Kolchak's candidature by being removed from his post as Chief of Staff. He was replaced by Colonel Dmitri Antonovich Lebedev, who was soon promoted to the rank of major-general and who was to be one of the Supreme Ruler's closest confidants and advisers in the coming year, as we shall see.

We shall see also how, under Lebedev's tutelage, the *stavka* was gradually to extend its jurisdiction over ever-increasing swathes of Siberian territory and branches of the administration. What immediately astonished and scandalized visitors to Omsk, however, was the sheer number of officers seconded to the Omsk *stavka* under Kolchak – men who would surely have been better deployed at the front. General Knox was to conclude that most of the bedizened and epauletted officers of the old army who found themselves in Siberia had deliberately chosen the east in preference to the rugged and perilous existence described in reports of the Volunteer Army in South Russia in early 1918. By the end of 1918 he estimated that 2,000 of these *embusqués* had secured comfortable sinecures for themselves at Omsk, but was unable to ascertain precisely what any of them were supposed to be doing there. Visitors to Harbin, Vladivostok and other towns found identical situations and were equally disillusioned by the White military's precocious talent for spending a lot of time and money achieving little that was detectable. One of them, Captain Francis McCullagh of the British Military Mission, noting the existence in the rear of 'committees for underclothing' and 'committees for furniture', was to estimate the one function of the entire military establishment in White Siberia to be:

18 Pepeliaev, p. 88.

19 Il'in, I.S. 'Omsk, Direktoriia i Kolchak', *Novyi zhurnal* Vol. 73 (1963), p. 217.

> to create posts for a crowd of lusty officers who are afraid to fight at the front. The stories I could tell in that regard would fill a volume. It is to the last degree disgraceful and shameful.[20]

Other reports revealed that most of the officers at the front were NCOs.[21] Meanwhile, in the capital, their commissioned colleagues fell into two categories. Some spent their time shifting files or constructing elaborate plans which were never to see the light of day. But the majority struck observers as the epitomes of Oblomovism: firmly believing that serene inactivity was a symbol of social superiority, 'these officers preferred to be boozing in Omsk, where wine was freely available', noted N.A. Borodin.[22] 'The only martial ardour they showed,' added the correspondent of the *Manchester Guardian*, 'was exhibited in those restaurants where, late at night, they sometimes covered the orchestra with their revolvers and demanded that they play "God Save the Tsar".'[23] British and American observers were particularly dismayed that many 'swaggering' officers seemed completely and coldly indifferent to the sufferings of the refugees and underfed troops who were becoming all too conspicuous on the streets of the capital. In short, they concluded, Kolchak's officers were quite out of touch with their men, had little contact with the front and even less insight into the state of affairs in that part of Siberia which extended beyond the confines of Omsk's fashionable Aquarian Cafe and its ornamental gardens where they chose to disport themselves.[24]

20 WO 32/5707 'Report of the Military Mission in Siberia, 10.xii.1919 (App. F, p. 1)'; 'McCullagh (Omsk) to Pares, 1.xi.1919' (*Pares Papers*, Box 43). An observer in the Russian capitals during 1918 confirms that the officers most emotionally or ideologically committed to anti-Bolshevism gravitated towards south Russia in early 1918, before the Czechoslovak rising had made Siberia an alternative. See Borman, A. 'My Meetings with White Generals', *Russian Review* Vol. 27, No. 2 (1968), pp. 215–19. A critic of the Omsk régime noted that, in contrast to Kolchak's teeming *stavka*, even Marshal Foch had only required a staff of 180. See Krol', L. *Za tri goda: vospominaniia, vpechatleniia i vstrechi*. Vladivostok (1921), p. 185.

21 *The Times* (London) 22.xi.1918.

22 Borodin, N.A. *Idealy i deiatel'nost': sorok let zhizni i raboty riadovago russkago intelligenta (1879–1919)*. Berlin–Paris (1930), p. 202.

23 Cited in Coates, W.P. and Coates, Z.K. (eds.) *Armed Intervention in Russia*. London (1935), p. 204.

24 Pares, 'Siberian Diary' (*Pares Papers*, Box 43), p. 117; Brown, W.A. *The Groping Giant: Revolutionary Russia as seen by an American Democrat*. New Haven (1920), p. 172; Vining, L.E. *Held by the Bolsheviks: The Diary of a British Officer in Russia, 1919–1920*. London (1924), pp. 47–8.

One of the first sections of society to greet the Kolchak government, in a series of telegrams of felicitations, were the Trades and Industry Congresses of Siberia (and of refugee industrialists) who had been agitating for the establishment of a dictatorship throughout the summer.[25] 'In the dictatorship of political adventurers', sneered an SR, such groups 'recognized a safe harbour from the storms of revolution'.[26] It will be recalled that the PSG had already gone some way towards the construction of such a haven, having dismantled most of the Soviet Government's state monopolies in Siberia. Within days of assuming power Kolchak rewarded businessmen for their support by completing the task: on November 27th all trade in meat, bread and butter was freed from governmental control (leaving only the lucrative vodka monopoly in state hands) – just as congresses of trades and industry had been demanding.[27] Thus, the gates were opened to what was to become an epidemic of speculation and manufactured shortages. In times of such economic dislocation as civil war in Russia, as Lenin had predicted, freedom of trade meant little more than 'freedom to prosper for the rich; freedom to die for the poor'.[28]

That private enterprise was so very rapidly and handsomely repaid for its support of the coup comes as little surprise when it is considered that Kolchak selected his closest advisers on economic affairs from the Trades and Industry network. Particularly influential was the Petrograd financier, S.G. Feodos′ev – the erstwhile State Comptroller of the Stürmer cabinet, who was currently serving as the manager of the giant Kyshtim, Irtysh and Tanalyk Mining Companies. Feodos′ev was received by Kolchak on a regular, daily basis – but in a purely private capacity, having refused to join the government. He claimed to 'prefer to exert influence from the side'.[29] It may well have been, however, that *had* Feodos′ev entered the cabinet

25 *Pravitel′stvennyi vestnik* (Omsk) No. 4, 22.xi.1918; Zenzinov, pp. 80–1; Shemelev, V. (ed.) *Profsoiuzy Sibiri v bor′be za vlast′ sovetov, 1917–1927gg.* Novosibirsk (1927), pp. 157–8; Taniaev, A. 'Perevorot 18 no. 1918g. i burzhuaziia', *Ural-kommunist* (Sverdlovsk), No. 3 (1929), pp. 33–43.

26 Rakitnikov, N.I. *Sibirskaia reaktsiia i Kolchak.* Moscow (1920), p. 8.

27 Maksakov, V.V. and Turunov, A. *Khronika grazhdanskoi voiny v Sibiri.* Moscow–Leningrad (1926), p. 102; Taniaev, A. (ed.) *Kolchakovshchina na Urale (1918–1919gg.).* Sverdlovsk (1929), p. 49. Until the end of the year the central government retained a degree of control over some prices and over the movement of freight, but abandoned even that in January 1919.

28 Lenin, *PSS*, Vol. 37, p. 481.

29 Guins, *Sibir′*, Vol. 2, p. 22.

his conflicting loyalties would have proved embarrassing: for the chairman of the Kyshtim-Irtysh-Tanalyk group to whom he was subordinate was the Scottish entrepreneur, Leslie Urquhart. Responsible through his extensive mining concessions in the Urals and the Altai for much of the old empire's gold production, for no less than half of its copper production and for its entire output of lead and zinc, after the revolution Urquhart had become a staunch advocate of Allied intervention in Russia – both as a general principle and as a means of recovering his mines, which had been nationalized by the Soviet government. In the summer of 1918, moreover, Urquhart had been recruited by the British Foreign Office to run the Siberian Supply Company – a Whitehall-funded agency which was intended in the short term to relieve shortages in Siberia through trade, but which had clearly been designed with the longer-term aim in mind of securing for Britain as much of a monopoly of Siberian trade as possible.[30] A public acknowledgment of dependency on the agents and agencies of foreign powers and foreign business would obviously not have been becoming to a Russian dictator. Consequently, Feodos′ev and Urquhart remained behind the scenes: 'and from the very first days the Council of Ministers ran up against the influence of chancers and irresponsible men', rued Guins.[31]

The first casualty of the introduction of freedom of trade, which was overseen by Feodos′ev, was Omsk's Ministry of Supply. This establishment, under the direction of I.I. Serebrennikov, had long been regarded with distaste by the merchants and capitalists of Siberia, as well as by the political right, because it had retained a distinctly regionalist orientation – both in its personnel and in its enduring relationship with Siberia's powerful co-operative organizations, which for years had been denuding the power of private capital in the east. With Kolchak in office from November 18th, however, Serebrennikov's ministry was dismantled by the beginning of December, its functions being assumed by the Ministry of Food under N.S. Zefirov and two deputies selected from the Omsk Trades and Industry Congress (I.G. Znamenskii and N.A. Mel′nikov).[32] Although Zefirov had long served as an accountant for various Siberian co-operatives, under his guidance, as we shall see, the supply policies of the régime would be firmly wedded to private

30 On the history of the Siberian Supply Company see Kolz, A.W.F. 'British Economic Interests in Siberia during the Russian Civil War', *Journal of Modern History*, Vol. 47 (1976), pp. 883–91.

31 Guins, *Sibir′*, Vol. 2, p. 22. On Urquhart see Kennedy, K.H. *Mining Tsar: The Life and Times of Leslie Urquhart*. London (1986), pp. 33–40 and *passim*.

32 Serebrennikov, I.I. *Moi vospominaniia*. Tientsin (1937), p. 233.

interests – not to say to the private interest of Zefirov, who was to be suspended from office in 1919 for gross malfeasance and was, in general, to do little to dispel the widespread impression that the government was 'a front for a syndicate of speculators and financiers'.[33]

Next in line for the grateful Kolchak's requitals were General Knox and Britmis. Before the coup the British mission, alongside all others, had suffered a certain privation, being housed in cramped railway cars at Omsk station, which was situated an awkward (and inordinately expensive) three-and-a-half-kilometre ride by *izvozchik* (horse-drawn cab) from the town centre. Accommodation at Omsk was in terribly short supply. Some 6,000 wartime refugees from Poland and the Baltic had already stretched the housing stock to its limits by 1917, even before the town became transformed from a minor administrative centre into a White capital and before, in a matter of months during 1918, an inundation of refugees caused its population to rocket from around 134,000 to over half a million (excluding the military) by most estimates.[34] Every type of Russian dignitary was drawn to the White capital: admirals, generals, businessmen and the high nobility promenaded along its main thoroughfares, Liubinskii Prospekt and Nikolskaia Square; in its crowded cafes famous poets and novelists conversed with professors of St Petersburg, Moscow and Kazan universities. For some the social whirl stirred fond memories of the pre-war Nevskii Prospekt.[35] But while princes and generals might secure relatively commodious billets in the few hotels (in 1914 Baedeker had listed only three of them) or in private homes, many thousands of the less fortunate refugees thronged the miserable streets of a shanty town which had grown up on the outskirts of Omsk. There even noble families were to be found huddled in holes dug in the frozen ground. To some observers the rows of improvised huts, sheltered from

33 Janin, [P.T.C.]M. 'Otryvki iz moego sibirskogo dnevnika', in Kornatovskii, N.A. (ed.) *Kolchakov-shchina: iz belikh memuarov*. Leningrad (1930), p. 128.

34 Maiskii, I.M. *Demokraticheskaia kontrrevoliutsiia*. Moscow (1923), pp. 299–301; *The Times* (London) 19.xii.1918; Rouquérol, p. 15. On general population movements at this time see Koenker, D. 'Urbanization and Deurbanization in the Russian Revolution and Civil War', *Journal of Modern History*, Vol. 57 (1985), No. 3, pp. 424–50.

35 For lists of the most prominent social figures at Omsk see: Arnol'dov, V. *Zhizn' i revoliutsiia. Groza piatogo goda. Belyi Omsk*. Shanghai (1935), pp. 179–80; Rudnev, S.P. *Pri vechernykh ogniakh: vospominaniia*. Harbin (1928), pp. 272–3 and Gidney, J.B. (ed.) *Witness to a Revolution: Letters from Russia (1916–1919) by Edward T. Heald*. Kent State (1972), pp. 259–60.

the elements only by flimsy wooden roofs, were reminiscent of the traditonal military *zemlianki*.[36]

Britmis, however, was not long to share such indignity once Kolchak was in power. In late November Knox's contacts at the *stavka* were able to secure for his mission a dwelling in the town centre more befitting the most trusted sponsor of the régime. The fact that it was already occupied by the reviled Ministry of Supply was no great obstacle: Serebrennikov returned to his offices one day to find Britmis *in situ* and his own departmental furniture and records being piled on the street by Russian staff officers.[37]

In their new abode the British officers dwelt, according to one observer, 'in complete comfort – in the manner to which they had grown accustomed to living in the colonies'.[38] But the British were far from being idle. In fact, having been so active in the machinations which had brought Kolchak to Omsk and elevated him to supreme power, Britmis was to become one of the pillars of the White establishment. Ward's battalion continued to provide Kolchak with a ceremonial guard of honour; while, at Kolchak's behest, Ward himself – 'the navvies' MP' – undertook propaganda missions among Siberian railwaymen.[39] Another British officer, Captain F. McCullagh, was secretly detailed to serve in Kolchak's intelligence and information services.[40]

Knox himself was rewarded for his service to Kolchak with a particularly influential role. The Allied Supreme Command in Paris had determined on November 26th that one General Maurice Janin, France's leading expert on the

36 Maiskii, pp. 299–301.; Becvar, G. *The Lost Legion: A Czechoslovak Epic*. London (1939), pp. 214–5. Many scores of these unfortunates were to perish in the blizzards which hit Omsk on February 14th–15th 1919, making it 'practically impossible to remain alive outside shelter' – see Gidney, pp. 297–9; *The Times* (London) 24.ii.1919; Rudnev, pp. 265–6. The housing crisis was so acute that, as Minister of War to the Directory, Kolchak himself could obtain only a room in the house of a Siberian businessman. See Varneck and Fisher, p. 165.

37 Serebrennikov, pp. 227–9. It was at this point that Serebrennikov resigned.

38 Il'in, Vol. 72, p. 202.

39 See below, p. 340. Ward, the Labour (and, in his last parliaments, Liberal) MP for Stoke-on-Trent from 1906 to 1929, had originally been a navvy and had helped found the British Navvies' Union in 1886.

40 Unfortunately, in his published memoirs McCullagh was as silent as was Knox concerning Britmis and the Kolchak period, beginning his account only in November 1919, when he was captured by the Bolsheviks during the White retreat. See McCullagh, F. *A Prisoner of the Reds*. London (1921). However, he did summarize and describe the nature of his service under Kolchak in a letter to Bernard Pares. See 'McCullagh to Pares, 13.vi.1919' (*Pares Papers*, Box 28).

Russian Army, would command all Allied troops in Siberia – including the Russians themselves. And in December Janin duly arrived at Omsk, expecting to assume such a command. Kolchak, however, would have none of it, insisting that the command of Russian troops should remain in Russian hands. After a month of acrimonious debate the Frenchman was obliged to accept the limitation of his purview to non-Russian troops west of Lake Baikal – i.e. chiefly to the increasingly inactive Czechoslovak Legion. There was an understanding that Kolchak would always consult Janin on 'general operational directives', so as to satisfy the latter's considerable reserves of *amour-propre*. But this agreement was not to be observed by Kolchak, consigning Janin to an operationally limited and frustrating commission. General Knox, in contrast, as a result of the same series of negotiations, was made *Directeur d'Arrière* – a post nominally inferior to Janin's, but in practice one of far greater significance, in that it granted Britmis control over the supply of Allied aid to Kolchak's forces as well as the direction of officer training schools established at Vladivostok, Irkutsk and Tomsk.[41] As a result, in the event of a White victory in the civil war, there can be little doubt that British influence would have supplanted the pre-war French sway over the Russian Army.

Moreover, apart from his considerable official tasks, by virtue of his self-confessed 'outspokenness' and his close personal ties to Kolchak, Knox was to admit that he was able to have more influence over military operations than was Janin.[42] His influence was, however, far from decisive – and, as we shall see (below, pp. 228ff), those who thought they could detect Knox's hands at work in determining Kolchak's strategy were undoubtedly mistaken – but when it is considered that the Supreme Ruler wore a British greatcoat, was habitually escorted by the Middlesex battalion and was flanked by Knox and Ward at state banquets where 'God Save the King' would inevitably follow the Russian anthem, it is not surprising that such suspicions were aroused.

On the evening of November 18th, Pepeliaev presented news of the coup to the Kadets' 1st Siberian Conference, then drawing to a close at Omsk. Unsurprisingly, his address was 'greeted enthusiastically' by the party which had provided the chief

41 Guins, *Sibir'*, Vol. 2, pp. 80–1; FO 371/3365/212459 'Knox (Vladivostok) to WO, 21.xii.1918'; FO 371/4094/9794 'Knox (Omsk) to WO, 17.i.1919'. For the full text of the agreements see WO 158/738.

42 FO 371/4096 'Knox (Vladivostok) to WO, 7.vii.1919'.

political sponsorship of the overturn.[43] With Kolchak in office and a national government proclaimed, the Kadets would feel able to accept the sort of posts which their anti-regionalism had denied them in previous Siberian régimes. 'From that time,' the Chairman of *VOTsK*, A.K. Klafton, was to remind a later gathering of Kadets, referring to the November days:

> we became the party of the *coup d'état*. We took upon ourselves complete responsibility for the declared formula. We became the best friends of the government.[44]

This was no exaggeration. Despite their anomalous and weak position in Siberia, by virtue of the part they had played in bringing Kolchak to power, Siberian Kadets (and Kadets drawn to Siberia) were able to become, in the words of a western historian of the party, 'the leadership corps' of the Omsk régime.[45] At the very highest ministerial levels *VOTsK* provided the Supreme Ruler with his first Minister of the Interior (A.N. Gattenberger) and Director of the Ministry of Foreign Affairs (Iu.V. Kliuchnikov) as well as his initial Administrative Secretary (G.G. Tel'berg). Meanwhile, for his pre-eminent role in the planning of the coup, Pepeliaev was offered the portfolio of his choice. Initially, not wanting to oust any incumbent, the king-maker was to content himself with the post of Director of the Department of Militia (recently vacated by Rogovskii). Soon, however, he began to climb the governmental ladder of promotion. Indeed, the hold of Kadets in general over ministerial positions expanded inexorably throughout the Kolchak period.[46]

43 Pepeliaev, No. 4, p. 87.

44 *Sibirskaia rech'* (Omsk), No. 128, 28.v.1919; *Pravitel'stvennyi vestnik* (Omsk) No. 112, 22.v.1919. The fact that transcripts of the proceedings of the Kadet conference were carried in the official government newspaper speaks volumes.

45 Rosenberg, W.G. *Liberals in the Russian Revolution: The Constitutional Democratic Party, 1917–1921*. Princeton (1974), p. 397.

46 Pepeliaev was promoted firstly to Assistant Minister of the Interior (February 1919), then to Minister of the Interior (April 1919) and, finally, to Prime Minister (November 1919). Tel'berg went on to become Procurator General and Minister of Justice (May 1919) and Acting Prime Minister (August 1919). K.N. Nekliutin of *VOTsK* became Assistant Minister of Food and Supply (December 1918) and then full minister (April 1919). The arrival in Siberia during 1919 of Kadets from South Russia further strengthened the party's grip on the administration: N.K. Volkov became one of Kolchak's economic advisers as Acting Chairman of the State Economic Conference (August 1919); S.N. Tret'iakov became Minister of Trade (September 1919) and, subsequently, Deputy Prime Minister and Acting Head of the Ministry of Foreign Affairs (November 1919); A.A. Cherven-Vodali became Director of the Ministry of the Interior

Quite apart from the seats it gained in cabinet, moreover, the party was able to exert influence over policy by means which were neither less direct nor less effective in the rather Byzantine system of administration which developed in Kolchak's capital. Firstly, as Supreme Ruler, the admiral was to retain his trust in Vladimir Zhardetskii. The doyen of the local Kadet group, like his friend Feodos′ev, was to refuse a cabinet portfolio, preferring to exert an unofficial (and unaccountable) influence over Kolchak, who granted him interviews on a regular, daily basis.[47] Secondly, key appointments in the régime's burgeoning information, propaganda and press establishments were filled by Kadet writers and academics, enabling them to assume the role of ideological pillars of the White régime in Siberia. The Kadet publicists A.K. Klafton (a Samara doctor of Scottish ancestry) and N.V. Ustrialov (a professor of law who had taught at Moscow and Perm, and who in the early 1920s was to achieve prominence as a founder of the *Smena vekh* movement) became, respectively, Director and Assistant Director of the government's official publishers at Omsk, the Russian Press Bureau. Meanwhile, their colleagues from *VOTsK* assumed control of the dissemination of news for domestic and foreign consumption as Director of the Russian Telegraph Agency (S.B. Sverzhanskii) and the successive editors of the daily government bulletin, *Pravitel′stvennyi vestnik* (V.A. Kudriatsev and G.G. Tel′berg). The Director of the Chief Information Department of the Ministry of Foreign Affairs at Omsk was another influential party member, E.A. Elachich. And these names are only the foremost – such, in fact, was the Kadet presence in Omsk's official press and information bureaux that a rare non-party journalist recruited to them felt that he had stumbled into a 'a Kadet party cell'.[48]

This same observer, having spent some months at work in the White capital, went on to conclude that the Kadets' virtual monopoly of the gathering and dissemination of news in Siberia under Kolchak actually gave their party more influence than they could have exercised via ministerial channels.[49] This, indeed, may well have been the case. For, as we shall see, the constitutional role of the

(November 1919) and Acting Prime Minister (December 1919); P.A. Buryshkin became Head of the Foreign Section of the Department of State Procurement (August 1919) and Minister of Finance (November 1919).

47 Krol′, L., p. 181.

48 Arnol′dov, pp. 216–17.

49 *ibid.*, p. 217.

Council of Ministers was vague to the point of meaninglessness – a weakness of the White government in Siberia which was only compounded by the fact that Kolchak chose to govern on a personal basis, relying on the advice of *ad hoc* political groupings and whichever of his ambitious favourites was able to catch his ear from day to day.

A 'real dictator' and the demise of the Council of Ministers

On the day following the coup the *Pravitel'stvennyi vestnik* reported that, having placed Kolchak in power, the emergency session of the Council of Ministers 'proceeded to consider a draft statute'. Apparently one of the ministers, although officially ignorant of the arrest of the Directory, had been sufficiently perspicacious to bring with him a draft of what was to become the constitution of the Kolchak régime – 'The Statute on the Provisional Structure of State Power in Russia'. This was hurriedly worked up into a finished form and was then published.[50] Sources indicate that the constitution was a combination of the efforts of Tel'berg, Guins and Starynkevich.[51] That being the case, it is somewhat surprising to find Guins himself later criticizing the constitution as 'rather vague'.[52] But vague it certainly was. And for others it was more than that: 'For me,' asserted Lev Krol, 'the Statute...of November 18th was so much word-mongering.'[53] The major fault lay in the glaring contradiction in the document whereby, on the one hand, the Council of Ministers (which had, after all, proclaimed the dictatorship) was portrayed as the font of the Supreme Ruler's authority and legitimacy, able to review all projected laws and decrees before passing them on to Kolchak for ratification; yet, on the other hand, the Supreme Ruler was empowered to adopt undefined 'extraordinary measures' without having to consult his ministers, let alone obtain their unanimous or even

50 *Pravitel'stvennyi vestnik* (Omsk) No. 1, 19.xi.1918, published in Zenzinov, pp. 11–12.

51 Rudnev, p. 258; Sukin (*Leeds Russian Archive*), p. 39.

52 Guins, *Sibir'*, Vol. 1, p. 310. In his defence, it has to be said that Guins assumed the November statute was only a stop-gap and expected that Tel'berg would draw up a better constitution in due course.

53 Krol', L., p. 162.

majority agreement. It was through this rift in the logic of the régime's very foundation that irresponsible and reactionary elements were able to seep.

At a press conference a few days after the coup Vologodskii was to assert that:

> the powers of the Supreme Ruler are set about by limitations. Not one order, not one proclamation can be put into effect before it has gone through the Council of Ministers, with which he confers every day.[54]

The casual Siberian reader of these words – and the foreign audiences to which they were subsequently relayed – might be forgiven for picturing Kolchak as a figurehead. That, however, was not even definitely the case in law; and it was certainly not the case in practice – whatever the hopes of Vologodskii and other ministers. By sanctioning and legitimizing the coup they were to find that they had unleashed some of the blackest forces of reaction in Siberia. Right-wing and military groups rallied to the dictator, cutting him off from his régime's tenuous Siberian roots, surrounding him, in the words of a British observer, like 'a magic circle through which nothing penetrated save that which seemed good to the leaders of this band'.[55] A gang of political adventurers, confirmed Guins, began to creep into the government 'through the back door'.[56]

Within days of the coup, a fawning camarilla – some clearly hypnotized by the notion of a military dictatorship as a panacea for Russia's political and social ills, others clearly keen to exploit the arbitrary system of government for personal advancement – had bedecked the Supreme Ruler with such ostentatious regulations, ritual and quasi-oriental ceremony as would have befitted a new tsar: hymns and anthems were written in Admiral Kolchak's honour; the small, rather dingy and reportedly 'far from spotless' residence of the Governor of the Steppe Region at Omsk was rechristened the 'Palace of the Supreme Ruler'. Even the Allied High Commissioners had to obtain official dispensation before they might even drive along the road leading to Kolchak's residence; and once there, they, like everyone else, had to address the admiral by the sonorous, pre-revolutionary title of '*Vashe*

54 *Man'zhuriia* (Harbin) No. 78, 21.xii.1918.

55 Nielson, J.F. 'Extracts from my Diary' (*Pares Papers*, Box 43), p. 1.

56 Guins, *Sibir'*, Vol. 2, p. 18.

Vysokoprevoskhoditel'stvo' (Your Most High Excellency).[57] Finally, on December 3rd 1918, the accoutrements of Kolchak's regentship were made complete when the Russian criminal code was amended so that 'any person found guilty of an attempt on the life, health, liberty and general well-being of the Supreme Ruler...should suffer the punishment of execution'. By the same order, slander against this virtual demigod was to be punishable by an unlimited term of imprisonment.[58]

However, those not out to flatter in the hope of personal advantage, those who honestly to the very end (and beyond) lauded Kolchak as an inspired choice for the role of dictator – 'the symbol, the personification, the standard bearer of the Russian national cause... the Russian Washington'[59] – were either to be sadly disappointed or become masters in self-deception. According to General Klerzhe:

> From the very first month of the supreme rule, those who put the admiral in power could not have helped but realize that he would not pass muster as a politician, economist or diplomat.[60]

As we have seen, the admiral had originally attracted attention as a candidate for the dictatorship for his bravery and patriotism as well as for his foreign contacts and the talisman of British support which he bore. And indeed, as dictator, neither his personal courage nor his devotion to Russia would ever be impugned. Also, at least initially, *pace* Klerzhe's assertion, Kolchak was rather successful in cultivating the support of the Allied missions and their governments. A compact, dapper figure of a man, clean-shaven and with concentrated, penetrating eyes, it probably helped that, as was often remarked, Kolchak looked more like an English gentleman than the archetypically (and rather alarmingly) robust and bearded Russian officer. With his manner noble and unaffected, taciturn and apparently frugal in his habits, an aesthete, to foreigners who came across him at the sink of iniquity and folly which

57 Fedotoff-White, D. *Survival Through War and Revolution in Russia*. Philadelphia (1939), p. 214; Baerlin, H. *The March of the Seventy Thousand*. London (1926), p. 222. A hymn to the Supreme Ruler, 'Glorious Admiral (*Slavnyi admiral*)' is included in the eulogistic pamphlet *Admiral A.V. Kolchak*. Omsk (1919).

58 El'tsin, B. (ed.) *Po tu storonu Urala*. Ufa (1919), p. 13; FO 371/4096/108311 'Order of the Council of Ministers (Omsk), 30.xi.1918'.

59 The words are those of K.D. Nabokov. See *The New Russia* (London) No. 4, 26.ii.1920.

60 Klerzhe, G.I. *Revoliutsiia i grazhdanskaia voina: lichnye vospominaniia (chast' pervaia)*. Mukden (1932), p. 119.

was Omsk, Kolchak seemed attractively apart from the feckless society over which he ruled; the admiral certainly assorted oddly with the tyros, incompetents and crooks of his administration and army. Americans found him to be 'a good man' and 'a courageous man';[61] to the British and Canadians he was 'remarkable', 'intensely patriotic', 'the best man in Siberia', 'one of the few Russians who think more of their country than they think of themselves'.[62] In the ultimate tribute of Bernard Pares, Kolchak had 'something kingly about him'.[63]

Even such enviable and rare personal attributes, however, were not sufficient to meet the tasks ahead. From a base in underdeveloped and isolated Siberia, in order to drive the Bolsheviks from their stronghold in the Russian heartland, the White movement would in addition require Kolchak to be a military chief of almost Napoleonic genius, which he was not. It would require also a charismatic leader, able to rally popular support and harness undisciplined and selfish Cossack and officer groups to the higher cause. But that might only be achieved through the sort of persuasive and intelligent political leadership which the admiral's past life as a naval officer, accustomed to giving orders and having them instantly obeyed, had been in no way designed to inculcate.

The unfortunate truth was that Kolchak was without political guile. He was not quite a political illiterate; but he was a political naif. 'He did not inspire people politically – he did not have the common touch', concluded General Klerzhe.[64] And how could he, having spent most of his adult life not merely in the distinctly uncommon society of the navy, but in action, in the service's scientific cloisters or in the Arctic? 'He did not,' realized Guins, 'understand the complexity of the political system, the role of political parties, or the part of self-interest as a factor of

61 *FRUS: 1918*, Vol. 2, pp. 443–4; *FRUS: 1919 (Russia)*, pp. 200–1, 403; Gidney, p. 302.

62 WO 32/5707 'Report of the Military Mission in Siberia, 10.xii.1919', p. 7; Ward, J. *With the 'Die-Hards' in Siberia*. London (1920), p. 112; Pares, B. '*Dopros Kolchaka* [review]', *Slavonic and East European Review* (London), Vol. 8, No. 22 (1929), p. 226; Bell, J.M. *Sidelights on the Siberian Campaign*. Toronto (1920) pp. 102–3. Knox for one did not temper his personal regard for Kolchak, even in the light of the Supreme Ruler's political and military defeat. See, for example, his letter to the American historian George Stewart of 1924, reproduced in Long, J. 'General Sir Alfred Knox and the Russian Civil War', *Sbornik of the Study Group on the Russian Revolution*, Vol. 9 (1983), pp. 58–9; and his eulogy at a memorial service for the admiral, organized by the Russian Colony in London, of February 20th 1920, in *The New Russia* (London) No. 4, 26.ii.1920, p. 122.

63 Pares, B. *My Russian Memoirs*. London (1931), p. 524.

64 Klerzhe, p. 117.

government life.'[65] Another who knew him well noted that, eventually, Kolchak would develop a political programme (and, later, we shall examine it): 'but it was only one which was simple and inconclusive for, by its nature, it was founded not for the attraction of support, but as a symbol of the faith which he had'.[66]

Nor could he deal tactfully with political subordinates. Local officials prone to question the dictates of the central authorities soon found that 'Kolchak did not negotiate, he ordered – and always in the sharpest of manners', as if dealing with an insubordinate naval rating. Yet some senior politicians he seemed apt to trust for no better reason than that they were senior.[67] His entire life as a man of the ship's cabin, wrapped in a narrow, specialized career and in scientific researches, had ill-prepared him for the task he was called upon to perform after November 18th 1918. A well run ship, after all, is one thing – perhaps no other human institution runs more smoothly, more automatically, more impersonally – but the ship of state, especially when battered by the storms of a civil war, is quite another. To one of Kolchak's severest critics (the Acting Minister of War of the summer of 1919), Baron Budberg, it was almost painful to witness this 'confirmed slave of duty' struggling to understand and master a system where dutiful service was but rarely to be encountered: 'A narrow sailor...absolutely ignorant of administration...he did not know life in its severe, practical application', was Budberg's verdict.[68] Others, who had met Kolchak in 1917, came to the same conclusion on seeing him again in 1919, albeit with words more sympathetic to the admiral's plight: 'He did not look to me to be a "man of destiny", but rather one thoroughly tired of groping and struggling in an unfamiliar environment', recalled a naval officer; 'a man out of his proper place', echoed General Klerzhe.[69]

Little wonder that Kolchak looked 'all at sea', for by his own admission his family

> ...was of an entirely military character and of military tendencies. I grew up under the influence of an entirely military atmosphere and milieu... I hardly interested myself

65 Guins, *Sibir'*, Vol. 2, pp. 368–9.

66 Sukin (*Leeds Russian Archive*), pp. 206–7.

67 Andrushkevich, p. 117.

68 Budberg, A.P. von 'Dnevnik', *Arkhiv russkoi revoliutsii*, Vol. 13 (1924), p. 263; Vol. 15 (1924), pp. 331–2.

69 Fedotoff-White, p. 216; Klerzhe, pp. 116–7.

with any political problems. So far as I can tell, I remember nothing at all concerning questions of a political or social nature.[70]

Of course, it is only natural to avoid entanglement in the unfamiliar, to keep to known ground; and in this Kolchak was no exception. 'Thus,' lamented Guins, 'in the first and still confused days of the dictatorship, there was established an unfortunate trait: the admiral as Commander-in-Chief swallowed the admiral as Supreme Ruler, together with his Council of Ministers.'[71] Avoiding the *terra incognita* of politics, Kolchak concentrated almost exclusively on military affairs. In fact, *pace* Vologodskii's afore-mentioned assurances to the press, it is clear from the records of Guins, Budberg, Sukin, Pepeliaev and others that the admiral would only very rarely attend sittings of the Council of Ministers (even though they took place in his own official residence by the Irtysh) and would see his premier only to discuss the most important business – although, in contrast, as he himself admitted, Kolchak would receive his chief of staff two or three times a day.[72]

Not that military experts were, for their part, happy with the admiral's involvement in their affairs. As General Knox later noted, had Kolchak been content to limit himself to the regular tours of Omsk's barracks, 'making the fiery little speeches he was so adept at', no soldier could have objected.[73] But with such a symbolic role Kolchak was not content. Despite the fact, as Budberg noted, that as a specialist in the laying of mines at sea, Admiral Kolchak was 'absolutely ignorant of land warfare',[74] he deliberately chose to spend all of his time worrying about and attempting to direct affairs at the front. To facilitate this he often abandoned his office at Omsk to depart for the Urals, where he would undertake lengthy train and automobile excursions along the lines. In fact, by tracing Kolchak's movements during the fifty-one weeks (360 days) for which he held office at Omsk, from the coup to the evacuation of the capital, it is possible to establish that he was either at the front (or ill), and consequently not in command of the government, for over nineteen weeks (136 days). That is to say, for two-fifths of his period in office in

70 Varneck and Fisher, pp. 38–9.

71 Guins, *Sibir'*, Vol. 2, p. 42.

72 *ibid.*, Vol. 2, p. 68; Varneck and Fisher, p. 197; Sukin (*Leeds Russian Archive*), p. 221.

73 Long, p. 59.

74 Budberg, Vol. 15, p. 332; WO 5707 'Report of the Military Mission', p. 8.

White Siberia, the desk of the Supreme Ruler remained unoccupied – usually because the Commander-in-Chief was busy touring the front.

In these facts is revealed an aspect of Admiral Kolchak's character which is little discussed: his vanity. He may very well have seen the office of Supreme Ruler as a burden; but, as a professional soldier, he clearly relished the honour of being Russia's Commander-in-Chief. In a letter to his wife of mid-October 1919, for example, Kolchak would somewhat vaingloriously compare his own efforts to Suvorov's legendary Italian campaign of 1799, whilst rejoicing that even if – as, in an all too rare moment of foresight, he feared – he himself would not survive to see the war through to a victorious conclusion, at least 'the beginning of the end of Bolshevism was all mine... Trotsky understands and openly admits,' the admiral glowed, 'that I am the major enemy of the Soviet Republic.'[75]

A man with such reserves of hubris would clearly not be content to rubber-stamp the decrees of the Council of Ministers, as Vologodskii had implied. On the contrary: 'Listen!' the admiral would chide Pepeliaev, when approaching the end of his tether in 1919, 'Don't you think that a dictator must be a *real* dictator!'[76] But the ambition to rule authoritatively was there from the very beginning for those who cared to take note: 'They call me a dictator', Kolchak told a press conference at Omsk on November 28th 1918. 'Well, so be it – I am not afraid of the word.'[77] However, no matter what hopes had been placed in Kolchak and no matter what hopes he had for himself, to discerning observers it was very soon apparent that 'the long-awaited dictator was no dictator at all'.[78] He was just not of the stuff from which the fabled 'man on horseback' could be fashioned. In fact, he had every attribute of the dictator except the strength of will to dictate – for, as Knox came to see, the admiral's hamartia was that 'he fell easily under the influence of anyone who happened to be in his company.'[79] Having no critical mind of his own – in either political or military strategy – he was naively trusting of others' judgements, no matter how paltry were their authors' qualifications. Mourned Budberg:

[75] Kolchak, R.A. 'Admiral Kolchak: ego rod i sem′ia', *Voenno-istoricheskii vestnik*, No. 16 (1960), p. 18.

[76] Pepeliaev, No. 5, p. 49.

[77] *Pravitel′stvennyi vestnik* (Omsk), 30.xi.1918; *Zaria* (Omsk) 30.xi.1918.

[78] Serebrennikov, *Moi vospominaniia*, p. 242.

[79] WO 32/5707 'Report of the Military Mission', p. 8.

> His own plans, his own system, his own will, he has not. And in this he was like soft wax from which his advisers and entourage could fashion whatsoever they pleased... He was like a helpless toy in the hands of anyone who could win his trust and take possession of his will.[80]

In particular, all too aware of his limited experience of land warfare, he tended to defer to the judgements of military men, 'before whom', recalled Sukin, 'he was afraid – scared to say anything which from the military point of view might be considered ignorant or foolish.'[81]

Had Kolchak enjoyed the company at Omsk of men of the requisite energy, sincerity and devotion, had the admiral been blessed with advisers whose sagacity could bolster his symbolic supreme power as a rallying point for the White movement and counter his political inexperience and ignorance of land warfare, none of this would have mattered. That, however – with one or two exceptions – was not the case. Kolchak was surrounded instead by a gang of political adventurers and unscrupulous social climbers who were all too well aware, noted Budberg, that it was sufficient simply to portray any hair-brained scheme or corrupt plan 'in the guise of a necessity for Russia and for the good of the cause to obtain the guaranteed assent of the admiral'.[82] Such catchwords as 'Russia' and 'the cause' were enough to trigger an almost instinctive reaction in this straightforward sailor's mind. The debilitating effects on that cause of his lieutenants' political and personal squabbles will become clear in succeeding chapters. At the time it was very apparent to outsiders. 'I have every confidence in the admiral himself,' opined Colonel Ward, who was well acquainted with the Omsk scene, 'but the pigmies by whom he is surrounded are so many dregs on the wheels of state. I would not trust one of them to manage a whelk stall.'[83] Bernard Pares spent less time in Kolchak's capital, but was similarly unimpressed with the dim luminaries of the Omsk régime: he shuddered at the prospect for Russia if 'this mob of adventurers and incompetents' should ever reach Moscow.[84]

80 Budberg, Vol. 15, p. 332.

81 Sukin (*Leeds Russian Archive*), pp. 44–5.

82 Budberg, Vol. 15, p. 331.

83 Ward, pp. 198–9.

84 Pares *My Russian Memoirs*, p. 526.

Of course, to a certain extent 'one gets the advisers one deserves', as a stern French critic of the White government observed.[85] And for having allowed himself to be steered from the Far East to Omsk and for giving his blessing to the coup which put him in power, Kolchak must bear ultimate responsibility for the nature of the régime to which he lent his name. But there were mitigating circumstances. Firstly, there were few politicians of a truly national standing at Omsk on whom the admiral might have relied – only local, rather parochial figures. 'In the Omsk ministries the level of statesmanship was no greater than on the average *uezd* [zemstvo] board', according to one source (who might have added that even such boards had not existed in Siberia until 1917 for budding statesmen to perfect their art).[86]

Secondly, the strains of war and revolution and the depressing vista of what he saw as the degeneration of Russia did not only inspire in Kolchak a moral response in the form of his injured nationalism and heightened sense of personal honour. More than that, the political maelstrom inflicted both psychological and physiological damage on his person. His four years in the Arctic, a decade of unstinting labour at the Admiralty and four years of war service had, by the autumn of 1918, left Kolchak in no state to withstand the unique strains of high office: it can have been no coincidence that on December 12th, just three weeks after having assumed the heavy mantle of dictatorship, he was laid low with a serious bout of influenza, complicated by pneumonia, which brought him very close to death in the new year.[87] He recovered, but was not seen again in public until early February. It was, however, the admiral's mental health which most concerned those in close contact with him. Even in October 1918, Viktor Pepeliaev had described him as 'a man with completely shattered nerves' (and, incidentally, it speaks volumes of the Kadet's political acumen that he proceeded to steer the invalid admiral into power).[88] Once he had been proclaimed Supreme Ruler, the stress became unbearable. He was quite plainly 'a sick man', concluded a British diplomat;

85 Nachbaur, A. *Le Dossier Koltchak: Sibérie, 1918–1920*. Peking (1920), p. 15.

86 Filat'ev, D.B. *Katastrofa belogo dvizheniia v Sibiri, 1918–1922gg. (vpechatleniia ochevidtsa)*. Paris (1985), p. 30.

87 Sukin (*Leeds Russian Archive*), pp. 42–3.

88 Pepeliaev, No. 4, p. 79. One of Pepeliaev's more astute party colleagues was not at all impressed upon meeting Kolchak for the first time in October 1918 – far from looking as though he had just enjoyed three months' rest in Japan, thought Lev Krol, the admiral looked precisely as though he was in dire *need* of a three months' holiday. See Krol', L., p. 151.

'certainly a neurasthenic,' concurred Budberg.[89] As we shall see, sunk in a world of political chicanery totally alien to his own patriotic devotion, in 1919 Kolchak's frustration at his own inability to control events would ever more frequently become manifested in outbursts of raging, ungovernable temper. At such times he would strike Budberg as 'a big, sickly child'.[90]

Kolchak was, in other words, quite simply unfit – in terms both of his physical and mental health and of his education and experience – to perform the Herculean tasks placed before him as Supreme Ruler. He was in no fit state to differentiate between good and bad counsel. As such, he succumbed all too easily to the self-serving blandishments of certain members of the government who soon realized that the best way to win the admiral's ear was to tell him precisely what he wanted to hear.

Pre-eminent among Kolchak's coterie was the young Minister of Finance, Ivan Mikhailov. He alone, it was said, felt able to converse with the Supreme Ruler 'as an equal to an equal'.[91] As during the 'democratic counter-revolution' he had been implicated in everything from the demise of the Western Siberian Commissariat and the arrest of the SR Directors to the deaths of Novoselov and Moiseenko, so under Kolchak, opined a journalist who was acquainted with the 'Siberian Borgia', Mikhailov was at the centre of a web of subterfuge, the focal point at which all the political tendencies, interests and intrigues in Omsk met: 'he was involved in every successive conspiracy involving the promotion of one person or the fall of another', reported L.V. Arnol′dov. 'Politics,' confirmed Guins, 'were entirely in his hands.'[92] And woe betide anyone who failed to pay due respect to Mikhailov. A master of the art of patronage, he managed to insinuate his own men into the upper echelons of every ministry and government commission. 'It was no lie to say that Mikhailov's eyes followed you everywhere', noted one who had offended against him.[93]

The key to Mikhailov's character was that, despite being a small fish in a rather parochial and isolated political pond, he nevertheless felt himself to be within 'the

89 FO 371/4094/2408 'Eliot (Omsk) to FO, 4.i.1920'; Budberg, Vol. 15, p. 331.

90 *ibid.*, Vol. 15, p. 255.

91 Arnol′dov, pp. 187–90.

92 Arnol′dov, pp. 187–90; Guins, *Sibir′*, Vol. 1, p. 264.

93 Arnol′dov, pp. 187–90.

whirlpool of great events'. Anxious that he should look the part, the lavish fixtures and fittings acquired for his departmental offices, in that most down-market of capitals, gave his Omsk department the impression of being 'truly ministerial' and would reportedly have put some of the old St Petersburg establishments to shame (although even it was inferior in majesty to the *stavka*).[94] In fact, Mikhailov's expenditure on maintaining the Ministry of Finance rather embarrassed the government – a special commission chaired by the State Comptroller, Krasnov, was to find in 1919 that it could shed several hundred posts without any loss of efficiency.[95] Yet, despite the grandeur and ostentation of the accoutrements of his office, as a minister Mikhailov failed to make a good impression on visiting experts. A Canadian financier, for example, was far from impressed with his rudimentary grasp of the principles of economics.[96] And, as we shall see, the catastrophic financial and economic policies pursued by Mikhailov's bloated staff were to play no inconsiderable part in the collapse of the White movement in Siberia in 1919.

The second of Kolchak's most trusted and powerful political lieutenants was the twenty-seven year old diplomat, Ivan Ivanovich Sukin, with whom the admiral had become acquainted in Washington in 1917. Formerly a quite junior functionary of Bakhmet′ev's Embassy in the American capital, Sukin arrived in Siberia in October 1918, soon ingratiated himself with Mikhailov, and, after the coup, was installed as Head of the Diplomatic Section of the *stavka* on Kolchak's recommendation and as Assistant Minister of Foreign Affairs. He took to conspiratorial Omsk 'like a fish to water', it was said. And although his qualifications for his post were scanty and although it was soon obvious (to Guins at least) that he was 'inept', his pre-eminance had to be accepted, for, admitted Guins, Sukin was 'the only one amongst us who had any diplomatic experience at all'.[97] A rather superficially cultured socialite and a blatant poseur – his wardrobe was entirely American and he had perfected a Yankee pronunciation of Russian words – the most that anyone could subsequently find to say of Sukin's diplomacy was that it displayed 'a cleverness

94 Arnol′dov, pp. 187–90.

95 Krol′, L., p. 185.

96 Rodney, W. 'Siberia in 1919: A Canadian Banker's Impressions', *Queens' Quarterly* (Kingston, Ontario), Vol. 79, No. 3 (1972), p. 332.

97 Guins, G.K. 'Professor and Government Official: Russia, China and California', University of California Russian Émigré Series (1966), pp. 180–2; Guins, *Sibir′*, Vol. 2, pp. 21–2, 71–2.

which bordered very closely to cunning'.[98] Probably thanks to his access to Mikhailov's system of spies, however, Sukin was invariably better informed than his rivals in the Foreign Ministry proper. Consequently, even before he was able to replace Kliuchnikov as Director of the Ministry of Foreign Affairs (in January 1919), Kolchak was content to allow Sukin to conduct practically all official negotiations with the foreign missions at Omsk (thereby vitiating the authority of the Council of Ministers).[99] Once having entered the cabinet, Sukin proceeded to vie with Mikhailov for the prize of who could appear most like a 'real minister' – with excruciatingly embarrassing consequences for those so unfortunate as to witness this quondam clerk's insistence that senior foreign dignitaries treat him 'like a real Russian Minister of Foreign Affairs'.[100] He was unable to attract the same numbers of staff as the Ministry of Finance, and had, in fact, to be content with a rather small establishment – but his vanity was satisfied by dividing it into more than twenty departments and sections, each precisely modelled on the pre-1917 Ministry of Foreign Affairs at St Petersburg.[101]

The pernicious influence of unofficial advisers to Kolchak and the favouritism he displayed towards the Mikhailov–Sukin axis, however, merely supplemented other splits and rifts within the Council of Ministers, which in their own right would probably have been sufficient to have crushed any hope that the Omsk Government might exert a steadying influence on the army as it plunged headlong and vengeful into the struggle against Bolshevism. There remained extant, for example, the 'Mikhailov Group', which now united not only departmental heads and adminstrative high-flyers but several ministers. Prominent in it were Sukin and the Kadet Administrative Secretary, Tel'berg; Kolchak's old friend, Omsk's rather superfluous Minister of Marine, Rear Admiral Smirnov; and the most ambitious, but professionally torpid, of the other ministers – N.I. Petrov (Minister of Agriculture) and N.S. Zefirov (Minister of Food and Supply). Between the hours of four and five

98 Ward, p. 226.

99 Guins, *Sibir'*, Vol. 2, p. 72; Arnol'dov, pp. 197–8.

100 Guins, 'Professor and Government Official', p. 184.

101 Lipkina, A.G. *1919 god v Sibiri: bor'ba s kolchakovshchinoi*. Moscow (1962), p. 50. Sukin, from January 1919, was the Director of the Ministry of Foreign Affairs at Omsk. Kolchak's Foreign Minister (and, indeed, Denikin's) was the former Imperial Minister of Foreign Affairs, S.D. Sazonov, who, for the sake of comfort and convenience, operated out of the Russian Embassy at Paris.

in the afternoon, on as many as three afternoons a week throughout the period of White government at Omsk, these men would gather at a private apartment to discuss the questions of the day before taking their cars or carriages to the evening sessions of the Council of Ministers. Often the group would then vote as a bloc in cabinet. But that was not always the case, for the common characteristic of the members of the Mikhailov Group, said Guins, was that 'they struggled not for this or that principle but for personal influence'.[102] The eternal quest for kudos and reflected glory, it was noted, could lead many of Kolchak's parvenu ministers to oppose any scheme which they had not been personally associated with initiating – and, if another's scheme did slip through, a minister might use his own retainers in his rival's department to delay its implemenation.[103]

Perhaps the most important schism in the Council of Ministers correlated closely (although not exactly) with the division between the remaining Siberian elements of the government and the increasing numbers of those from west of the Urals, whose all-Russian ambitions led them to denigrate or even ignore local issues in obeisance to the one prevailing all-national White concern, the war. The distinction is a hazy one – blurred by the fact that personal ambitions orientated some native Siberians (such as Mikhailov and Zefirov) towards centralist positions, while Siberian Kadets in the cabinet (such as Tel′berg and, later, Pepeliaev) were imbrued with the Russian nationalist sentiments of their party – but it is, nevertheless, a useful one.[104] Moreover, although information on this is scanty, it is a differentiation which may have been even more distinct at the intermediate level of the governmental pyramid of power, in Omsk's ministerial departments and press offices. These, we know, came increasingly to be staffed by Kadets and refugee bureaucrats from Russia, swamping the indigenous intelligentsia and middle classes of Siberia (who were, in many cases, already tainted in the eyes of Kolchak's military advisers for their former associations with their region's dominant social institutions, the co-operatives). One of the latter – the afore-cited journalist, Arnol′dov – recalled that by the middle of 1919 the offices of Omsk were 'sharply divided' between those who were 'of Siberia' and those latterly arrived from Moscow or from St Petersburg

102 Sukin (*Leeds Russian Archive*), pp. 209–10; Guins, *Sibir′*, Vol. 2, p. 141.

103 Krol′, L., p. 170.

104 Interestingly, this division corresponds also with a generation gap: Mikhailov was aged only 23 in 1918, Sukin was only 27 and Lebedev was 35; Vologodskii, on the other hand, was 56, as was Sapozhnikov, and Starynkevich was 43 years of age.

'who were obtaining more and more influence over the government'.[105] Even Siberian Kadets such as the Minister of the Interior, Gattenberger, could be hounded from office by the incomers if they seemed overly concerned with local issues and disinclined to admit complete subservience to the nationalistically inclined army.[106]

Under the influence of Mikhailov, Sukin and Lebedev, from the very first days of his rule Kolchak showed a marked discrimination, declining to grant audiences to ministers of Siberian loyalties. Such a sifting of appointments was facilitated by the fact that between the cabinet and the office of the Supreme Ruler sat the Administrative Secretary, the rightist Kadet Tel′berg, who was hostile to even the faint aura of regionalism which still distinguished the likes of Vologodskii and Professor V.V. Sapozhnikov (the Minister of Education). Tel′berg was only too willing and able to vet the admiral's visitors, according to Guins, and rarely found appointments for those who did not firmly toe the centralist, Great-Russianist line.[107] The consequence was that some very sharply conflicting points of view on the political questions affecting Kolchak's Siberian domain in the years of the civil war only rarely reached the ears of the Supreme Ruler. And rather than actively seek second opinions on questions of which he himself was ignorant, Kolchak would spare himself the agony of having to choose between a variety of solutions. Instead he would content himself with the sort of eschewing and repeated deprecation of political discourse and social uncertainties which are the natural refuge of the type of military mind which prefers decisiveness to considered debate. This, at least, was a clearly defined aspect of the type of 'real dictator' which the admiral aspired to be. Earlier in 1918 he had revealingly reflected:

> Every practical politician knows, if he is not either a theorist or a scoundrel, that the decision of two people is invariably worse than that of one; three is worse than two, and so forth... Finally, it is not possible for twenty or thirty people to come to any reasonable decisions – only stupidity.[108]

105 Guins, *Sibir′*, Vol. 2, pp. 168–9; Arnol′dov, p. 147. Changes in the Omsk government in early 1919, noted the British High Commissioner, were 'partly due to the desire to make the Ministry more representative of European Russia, but are complicated by the struggle of revolutionary and anti- revolutionary factions.' FO 371/4095/84128 'Eliot (Vladivostok) to FO, 5.vi.1919'.

106 Guins, *Sibir′*, Vol. 2, pp. 168–9.

107 Guins, *Sibir′*, Vol. 2, pp. 98–9, 167.

108 The admiral's comment was recorded in his so-called 'diaries' – two books of notes on diverse personal and philosophical topics entrusted by Kolchak to a General Apushkin during the government's eastward flight at the end of 1919. Apushkin was able to convey the diaries out of

A further opportunity to avoid more contact with the mobocracy he clearly believed cabinet government to be, was provided for Kolchak in mid-December when he fell ill. For a six-week period thereafter he saw hardly anyone. To all intents and purposes, noted a British diplomat, the admiral ceased to stand at the head of the government – although, in contrast, he kept in contact (when physically able) with his military advisers and was active as Commander-in-Chief.[109] It was, in fact, during this period that the Council of Ministers came to be all but divorced from the decision-making process. The already indefinite constitutional role mapped out for the cabinet on November 18th was usurped in a new, administrative coup which was executed by a nebulous grouping of Kolchak's closest and most trusted advisers, known as the Council of the Supreme Ruler. In this so-called 'Star Chamber', the military authorities – represented primarily by Lebedev, General A.A. Mart′ianov (Chief of the Supreme Ruler's Private Chancellery) and Captain Udintsov (Commander of Kolchak's Personal Guard) – were always predominant. Also invited to it were Mikhailov, Sukin and the governmental representatives most subservient to the army (the Kadets Tel′berg, Kliuchnikov and Pepeliaev). The institution had actually been founded soon after the coup, with a quite definite and quite limited brief: it was supposed to assist Kolchak in establishing a consistent line in foreign policy and to act as an intermediary between the Supreme Ruler and his Council of Ministers.[110] However, from the day that Kolchak fell ill, noted Guins, in the thrice-weekly meetings of the Council of the Supreme Ruler 'was concentrated the entire business of the government'. The Council of Ministers continued to draft legislation and its rather grand ceremonial meetings were still convened (albeit ever more rarely in the first half of 1919), but it was the Council of the Supreme Ruler which was responsible for the policy of the White government in Siberia. 'There was decided the entire fate of the country', said Guins. Yet it remained a purely *ad hoc* grouping: none of the members of the Council of the

Russia and later deposited them with the Russian Émigré Archive at Prague. From there, along with all other of the archive's holdings, they were taken to Moscow after World War II and incorporated into the Central State Archive of the October Revolution (*TsGAOR*), now renamed the State Archive of the Russian Federation (*GARF*). See Fedotov, B.F. 'O maloizvestnykh istochnikakh perioda grazhdanskoi voiny i inostrannoi voennoi interventsii v SSSR', *Voprosy istorii* (Moscow), Vol. 8 (1968), pp. 24–7.

109 FO 371/4094/1704 'Eliot (Omsk) to FO, 30.xii.1918'; FO 371/4094/14281 'Eliot (Omsk) to FO, 23.1.1919'.

110 Varneck and Fisher, p. 177.

Supreme Ruler ever knew for sure when, where or if it would meet on a given day, or for how long it would meet; there was never a formal agenda – only Mikhailov and Sukin seemed to know in advance what was likely to be discussed (and were, therefore, able to prepare themselves accordingly); and, apparently, no minutes were ever taken. Those who sought to establish an orderly, regular and responsible governmental system in Siberia were dismayed as this ill-defined body, one not even alluded to in the régime's constitution, 'turned out decisions like hot cakes made from poor quality flour', according to Guins. For those not party to its secret deliberations, its decisions were frequently 'astounding in their ill-advisedness and unexpectedness', he added.[111]

As the authority of the Council of the Supreme Ruler expanded to cover every sphere of political activity – and it continued to meet three times a week from 1.00 p.m. to 2.00 p.m. even when Kolchak was at the front – the Council of Ministers languished in ignorance of events. Often the cabinet would only come to hear by accident (or even through the press) of important political and military decisions made by Kolchak.[112] In fact, by the summer of 1919, recalled Sukin, the Council of Ministers had 'lost all influence'; a study of the appointments listed in Pepeliaev's diary confirms that it met ever more infrequently during the first half of 1919, and would only occasionally summon up the energy to complain about the 'superficial and tendentious' reports with which it was furnished by Kolchak's camarilla.[113] Quite simply, the ministers were 'amateurs' at political manoeuvring, noted one officer – they lacked the cunning and gall to compete with Mikhailov and the military clique within which the Supreme Ruler preferred to immure himself.[114]

It was notable that many of those ministers content to accept the demise of cabinet government hailed from Siberia's single grove of academe, the University of Tomsk, or from other educational institutions whose ivory towers were a world away from the conspiratorial quagmire of Omsk. These professors had no taste for political power and were strongly averse to indulging in the political manoeuvering

111 Guins, *Sibir'*, Vol. 2, pp. 36–7, 168, 265. See also Arnol'dov, pp. 176–7; Budberg, Vol. 15, pp. 331–2.

112 Guins, *Sibir'*, Vol. 2, pp. 47–8.

113 Sukin (*Leeds Russian Archive*), p. 286; [Pepeliaev, V.N.] 'Razval kolchakovshchiny (iz dnevnika V.N. Pepeliaeva)', *Krasnyi arkhiv* (Moscow) No. 6 (31), (1928), p. 54 – hereafter cited as Pepeliaev 'Razval'.

114 Filat'ev, pp. 30, 43.

which the Mikhailov wing had mastered. Guins, for example, who had been a professor of law, admitted that throughout his tenure in office at Omsk he 'longed for the pleasure of tranquil and interesting work... Suffering from the sin common to Omsk politicians, I did not possess the gift of foresight or the strength of perseverance', he confessed.[115] Perhaps, however, Guins was being a little unfair to himself here, for he was at least to remain in government, fighting for his point of view, until the very – and very bitter – end of the White movement in Siberia. Aged thirty-one in 1918, he was, of course, relatively young. In contrast, his more venerable (although far from pensionable) academic colleagues in the cabinet fell very quickly by the wayside, frustrated at their inability to cope with government or to counter the all-pervading influence of the military. Ivan Serebrennikov (Professor of Economics at Tomsk), as we have seen, was goaded into resignation as early as December 1918. And in January 1919, as we know, the Director of the Ministry of Foreign Affairs, Iu.V. Kliuchnikov (Professor of History at Moscow University), was ousted by Sukin. In May 1919 they were to be followed into retirement by the Minister of Justice, S.S. Starynkevich (Professor of Law at Tomsk), and the Minister of Education, V.V. Sapozhnikov (Rector of Tomsk University), who gladly returned to their desks at the Siberian university, even though in the eyes of at least one visitor they were 'the most distinguished members of the government'.[116] Whereas the likes of Sukin and Mikhailov revelled in the wheeling and dealing of Omsk politics, these cloistered dons could not stand the pressure of government service. As Serebrennikov recalled, for him and his kind, governmental work under the White régime was 'a source of much grief and little happiness'.[117] They were only too glad to relinquish their wearisome burden and depart for Tomsk: 'They have taken all responsibility upon themselves,' said Sapozhnikov of the 'Star Chamber' with barely concealed satisfaction, 'well, let them get on with it!'[118]

115 Guins, *Sibir'*, Vol. 2, pp. 141, 264.

116 Pares, 'Siberian Diary' (*Pares Papers*, Box 43), pp. 77–8. See also Pepeliaev 'Dnevnik', No. 5, p. 39. Later in the year Professor M.P. Golovachev and Professor N.Ia. Novombergskii followed Sapozhnikov and Starynkevich back to Tomsk 'to give lectures in peace', they said. See Arnol'dov, p. 182.

117 Serebrennikov, p. 232.

118 Guins, *Sibir'*, Vol. 2, pp. 71–2, 265.

If, given their lack of political experience, the academics of the Council of Ministers might be forgiven for their inability to stem the legislative confusion engendered by the self-seeking tactics of the Mikhailov Group and the irresponsible ascendancy of the Council of the Supreme Ruler, rather less exoneration can be afforded to the premier, Chairman of the Council of Ministers, Petr Vologodskii. Almost alone among Kolchak's ministers, he had had a quite substantial political career, having served on the 2nd State Duma for Tomsk and having been a long-standing member of that town's municipal council. He was also an accomplished lawyer – who, incidentally, had gained a radical reputation for his defence of socialist offenders against the tsar around the turn of the century and who had been expelled from St Petersburg University as a youth for narodnik activities. By 1918, of course, Vologodskii's youthful, liberal radicalism had evolved into the conservatism which the shock of the revolution had made characteristic of many former moderates. As head of the Provisional Siberian Government, for example, he had consistently sided with the political right and the army in their efforts to drive the SRs and radical *oblastniki* from office. Nevertheless, as a lawyer, he might have been expected at least to have attempted to counter the arbitrary, careless and unaccountable rule of Kolchak's sycophantic entourage and to protest at the excesses of the Supreme Ruler's military satraps. That, however, was not to be, for Premier Vologodskii's health and vigour seemed to have waned along with his liberal sympathies.

Aged fifty-six, Vologodskii was relatively old (although, again, not yet pensionable) by the time that Kolchak took power; and ill-health was to bar him from participation in governmental affairs for significant parts of the following year. He was on leave for most of July and August 1919, for example. But even on those occasions upon which he was able to attend cabinet meetings, he appeared very frail, said Budberg, 'like some sort of precious relic'.[119] Others found Vologodskii unwilling to express an opinion on policy matters, reluctant to meet with Kolchak and all too apt to be 'not at home' when petitioners called on him.[120] For Pepeliaev, in fact, it was entirely possible to forget that the premier even existed.[121] Unable or unwilling to aspire to even those hazy powers which the

119 Budberg, Vol. 14, p. 300.

120 FO 371/4094/6505 'Eliot (Omsk) to FO, 10.i.1919'; Guins, *Sibir'*, Vol. 2, pp. 139–40, 148; Guins, 'Professor and Government Official', p. 176.

121 Pepeliaev (1923), Vol. 5, p. 44.

constitution had granted the ministry, Vologodskii, the passive premier, seemed quite incapable of halting the slide into the chaos characteristic of governmental affairs by the middle of 1919. Only then, on the very eve of the disintegration of the White movement in Siberia, was he to act, participating in a tardy effort to reform the administration.[122]

With neither Kolchak nor Vologodskii willing or able to offer leadership, the rudderless Omsk government was apt to flounder. Instead of initiating policy, the political novices of the cabinet gave the Council of the Supreme Ruler free rein, whilst themselves becoming absorbed in the day-to-day running of their departments – even writing all of their own speeches, reports and orders, in some cases.[123] This, however, was not only the result of an inability to delegate or of inexperience of high office. It was also a question of personnel: there was a chronic shortage of trained manpower in Siberia, which the panicked and transient flood of refugees was unable to make good. The degree to which different ministries were affected naturally tended to reflect the priorities of the government. Thus, the Ministry of War was a grandiose and stately affair, its myriad staff occupying an imposing commercial school in the town centre, where visitors were awed by its 'spacious, bright corridors...and even more spacious and more bright reception rooms, impressive lobbies etc.' and where one was 'received' by 'a real minister'.[124] The Ministry of Labour, on the other hand, under the honest but ineffectual former Menshevik L.I. Shumilovskii, was accommodated in one room of a house in a far-flung Omsk suburb and was provided with an annual vote so mean as to allow the hiring of only a handful of staff.[125]

Nor was such ministerial imbalance the only consequence of the absence of leadership. Equally debilitative was the duplication of responsibilities which was allowed to develop. At one point, for example, Guins was astonished to discover that no less than three separate departments (his own Administrative Secretariat, the

122 See below, pp. 498ff. Vologodskii was well aware of his own lethargy, admitting in 1919 that 'I have not in the past been distinguished for my initiative or my activity. Now, after ten months of difficult and responsible work, I am more worn out and weaker than ever.' See Vologodskii, P.V. 'Dnevnik' (*Hoover Archives*), p. 319, cited in Dotsenko, *The Struggle for a Democracy*, p. 67.

123 Guins, *Sibir'*, Vol. 2, p. 140; Sukin (*Leeds Russian Archive*), pp. 219–20.

124 Arnol'dov, pp. 146–7.

125 Kozlova, S.A. 'Trud i okhrana truda v Sibiri pri Kolchake', in *Iz proshlogo Sibiri*. Omsk (1927), pp. 69–70.

Foreign Ministry and Sukin's Diplomatic Section at the *stavka*) had all been commissioned by Kolchak to supervise Omsk's communications with the White forces in southern Russia.[126] The *stavka* and the Ministry of War, as we shall see, were also in competition for much of 1919, with consequences damaging to the war effort. And, finally, a plethora of counter-intelligence units was developed – by the *stavka*, by Kolchak's personal staff, by the Ministry of the Interior, by individual army units and so on – which, according to General Klerzhe, were in a state of 'semi-war' and wasted much time and effort in surveillance of each other![127] This was precisely the sort of thing which should not have happened had the premier energetically fulfilled his constitutional role as the chief intermediary between the Supreme Ruler and the Council of Ministers and had not Kolchak neglected his political office in favour of that of commander-in-chief.

It would be unjust not to admit, however, that the Whites' poor leadership was not the sole factor contributing to the administrative morass at Omsk. Perhaps equally significant was the parvenu capital's dire overcrowding and crisis of accommodation. Various departments of a single ministry might be scattered all across the town – there being so few buildings of substantial proportions in that 'overgrown village' – operating in ignorance of the work being done by their colleagues or even of their very existence. (A sparse and wholly unreliable telephone network was to compound this confusion.) When, on arriving at Omsk, for example, Bernard Pares attempted to track down an old friend whom he knew to be working at the Ministry of Supply, it took him some time to find anyone who could direct him to any section of that establishment. And when eventually the British historian did track down one of its branches – typically located in a backstreet stable – nobody there could tell him the address of the other department, at which his friend worked.[128] This experience clearly confirms the point of a rather lame joke then doing the rounds of the Siberian capital:

Question: 'What is the difference between St Petersburg and Omsk?'

126 Guins, *Sibir'*, Vol. 2, p. 368.

127 Klerzhe, p. 132.

128 Pares, 'Siberian Diary' (*Pares Papers*, Box 43), pp. 98–9.

> *Answer*: 'In Petersburg everybody knew where to find the ministries, but it was hard work to find a minister. In Omsk you find ministers everywhere, but it is impossible to locate their ministries!'[129]

That Vologodskii was patently inept and that most ministers were inexperienced did not, however, overly concern either Kolchak or his gaggle of close advisers – and not simply because they themselves could lay claim to no better qualifications to govern, but because they had never really *intended* that the Council of Ministers should govern. They wanted the cabinet, rather, to provide a façcade of regular, constitutional government. When asked by a guileless general, for example, why a bumbling old liberal like Vologodskii was tolerated as premier, Kolchak chuckled and replied:

> Yes, he is such an SR! He is old and he avoids all work... But remember, he is needed here as *le vieux drapeau*.[130]

However tenuously, Kolchak was aware, Vologodskii's political lineage could be traced back to the Siberian Government elected at Tomsk in January 1918 and to the (indirect) popular mandate of the *Sibobduma*. That the right had always opposed those bodies as unrepresentative was conveniently passed over now that they were no longer in existence and no longer a threat to the White government. His loose connections with Siberian democracy made Vologodskii a useful propaganda tool – the prime symbol of the commitment to democracy which Kolchak knew he would have to display in order to secure the assistance of the Allies.[131] Thus, immediately after the coup of November 18th, Sukin was hard at work drawing Washington's attention to the 'continuity of the administrative bodies of the country'.[132] Meanwhile, Kolchak's agents in Europe, using more than a little artistic licence, were endeavouring to allay the qualms of governments there with regard to the installation of a military régime in Siberia: Nabokov in London and Sazonov in Paris were trumpeting the predominance in the government of '*les*

129 Arnol'dov, pp. 146–7. 'There was no apparatus of government, but ministers were two-a-penny', confirmed General Filat'ev. See Filat'ev, p. 24.

130 Sakharov, K.V. *Belaia Sibir'*. Munich (1923), p. 89.

131 Budberg, Vol. 14, p. 300, noted this. See also *The Times* (London) 23.iv.1919, which praises 'the constitutional thread' linking Kolchak to previous régimes in Siberia.

132 *FRUS: 1918*, Vol. 2, pp. 439, 453.

socialistes à Omsk'. Shumilovskii and Petrov (both long since disowned by their former parties) were still Social Democrats, it was claimed; even Mikhailov was portrayed as 'a socialist'.[133]

Even more useful for establishing the moderate credentials and quasi-legitimacy of the Kolchak régime in the minds of foreign statesmen and of the Allied representatives in Siberia (who rarely ventured outside the capital) were the activities of a government front posing as a popular front – the 'Omsk National Bloc of 14 Political and Social Organizations' (or, more commonly, the Omsk Bloc). This group purported to represent a cross-section of Siberian society and a broad spectrum of political opinions. It included delegates of Cossack hosts, the All-Russian Congress of Trades and Industry, the Central Military-Industrial Committee, the Omsk Kadets and their party's *VOTsK*, all of whom were naturally supportive of the régime their organizations had helped establish. But in addition – and this, noted Guins, was 'most advantageous' to the dictator[134] – the Omsk Bloc also contained conciliationist elements from the region's co-operatives (the nominal chairman of the Bloc was the founder of Siberian co-operation, A. Balakshin), from the Popular Socialists and even from the PSR branch at Omsk.

That everyone in Siberia, from the extreme left to the extreme right, knew very well that the Bloc was completely dominated by its right-wing majority, that its socialist members had been disowned by their parties and that it was the Kadet grandee Zhardetskii rather than the aged Balakshin who was the driving force behind the Bloc, was no disincentive; neither did the fact that, in common parlance, the organization's leaders were dismissed as 'the fourteen blockheads', or that even Pepeliaev himself might, in moments of candour, refer to it as 'the Bloc of the Right,' arouse the scruples of the White régime's publicists.[135] Rather, by them the Bloc was portrayed as a symbol of Kolchak's legitimacy and of the popular consensus on which his régime was established. For example, citing the formation of the Bloc, Sukin was letting it be known abroad that even 'rank-and-file SRs' in

133 *Bulletin Russe* (Lausanne) No. 3, 15.iii.1919 and No. 8, 1.vi.1919. Starynkevich and Petrov had long since allowed their Menshevik affiliations to lapse and had drifted to the right in politics. Mikhailov had been among the most uncommitted of 'March SRs' and had worked against Chernov's party ever since. Vologodskii too had flirted with the SRs in the past – and these 'radical' associations were played up for all they were worth in official biographies, such as that presented in the official Desk Diary of the régime – see Pinegin, pp. 79–80.

134 Guins, *Sibir'*, Vol. 2, p. 36.

135 Krol', L., p. 144; Rudnev, p. 258; Maiskii, pp. 335–6; Pepeliaev, 'Dnevnik', No. 4, p. 90.

Siberia were supportive of Kolchak.[136] Then, on December 19th, there occurred a ceremonial meeting between the Supreme Ruler and representatives of the Bloc, at which Kolchak was handed a resolution pledging support. As at this time the admiral was very ill and was not generally receiving visitors, he must have felt that this was an occasion necessitating the leaving of his sickbed. And certainly the propagandists of his régime were able to make the most of the Bloc's declaration over the coming months, repeatedly citing it as evidence that the government's constituency extended to the 'patriots of the left'.[137] In fact, at times in 1919 it appeared that the régime was falling for its own propaganda, as it sponsored the establishment of branches of the Omsk Bloc in other Siberian towns – towns distant from Allied eyes and therefore quite superfluous.[138] Only the military disasters of the late spring and summer of that year would persuade the Siberian Whites that something broader and more substantial than the Bloc's chimerical impression of a popular mandate should be sought.

The veneration of the military

With Vologodskii's premiership moribund, the responsibility for reporting the Council of Ministers' deliberations to Kolchak fell to his Administrative Secretary, Georgii Gustavovich Tel'berg. It was widely felt, however, that he and other members of the Council of the Supreme Ruler combined to ensure that the admiral 'was not always told the truth about the real state of affairs in the government', or, at least, was fed information 'in such a manner as was likely to confuse him'.[139] Certainly the Supreme Ruler only rarely came to learn of the minority view in any debate in his cabinet – even, as we shall see in relation to the land question, when resolutions were passed by the narrowest of majorities on matters of vital national

136 Kim, P.M. (ed.) 'Iz arkhiva organizatorov grazhdanskoi voiny i interventsii v Sovetskoi Rossii', *Istoricheskii arkhiv* (Moscow), No. 6 (1961), pp. 76–7.

137 *Pravitel'stvennyi vestnik* (Omsk) No. 46, 26.i.1919; FO 371/4094/52933 'Telegram of the Russian Telegraph Agency (Omsk) to its London office, 29.iii.1919'.

138 FO 371/4095/77016 'Pares (Irkutsk) to FO, 14.v.1919'.

139 FO 371/4096/117980 'Eliot (Omsk) to FO, 15.viii.1919'; FO 538/3 'Memorandum on the Recent Political Crisis in Omsk (by HM Vice Consul, Omsk), 30.xi.1918'; Guins, *Sibir'*, Vol. 2, pp. 167–8.

importance. Of course, Tel′berg was a Kadet. And he and the increasing number of his party colleagues who entered the government, at least until the military defeats of 1919 revealed the weakness of the régime, saw nothing wrong with such procedures.[140]

The Soviet historian G.Z. Ioffe once alleged that the Kadets saw, in Kolchak, liberal democracy's 'guarantee against the autocratic-restorationist strivings of the Siberian White Guards'.[141] However, he used a press statement of Vologodskii's to substantiate this. Vologodskii was not a Kadet and was not even very close to the party (which had its own candidates for the premiership). Moreover, his aspirations were not those of the party. In fact, the Siberian Kadets seem to have believed, at least until the middle of 1919, that no safeguard or 'guarantee' against autocracy was necessary. Rather, they offered the dictatorship their unconditional support. On the other hand, another Soviet writer, M.A. Gudoshnikov, did not hit quite the right note in claiming that for Kolchak and the White Siberian military 'even the Kadets were too left wing'.[142] Certainly party moderates such as Lev Krol were denied access to power. But Krol, as we have seen, was disowned by *VOTsK*. In fact, for as long as the party as a whole did not attempt to interfere with the army and confined itself to ritual declarations of support for the military dictatorship, it was permitted an aura of power and influence which in any régime relying upon a popular mandate it could not have hoped to have won.

Initially at least the Kadets were content with this unspoken agreement. During the summer of 1919, as we shall see, things were to change quite significantly. But until then the party positively worshipped the dictatorship and lionized Kolchak. Arriving in Siberia in April 1919, for example, the British historian Bernard Pares was quite shaken to discover that the moderate and liberal constitutionalists and democrats that he had known and sympathized with both before and during the Great War, had now somehow 'quite forgotten that they had formerly stood for representative government' and had, lock, stock and barrel, 'thrown in their lot with

140 According to Pepeliaev ('Dnevnik', No. 4, p. 89), the Kadets who entered government office were formally obliged to renounce their party allegiance. However, the fact that as Minister of the Interior he made reports to *VOTsK* and addressed the Kadets' 3rd Regional Conference in Siberia confirms that, far from severing their links with the party, the Kadets in and close to government office were able to form party cells within the régime, as Arnol′dov suggested (see above, pp. 122–3).

141 Ioffe, G.Z. *Krakh rossiiskoi monarkhicheskoi kontrrevoliutsii*. Moscow (1977), p. 190.

142 Gudoshnikov, M.A. *Ocherki po istorii grazhdanskoi voiny v Sibiri*. Irkutsk (1959), p. 87.

the military'. In fact Pares found the party members he met in Siberia to have evolved into something 'hopelessly narrow and unintelligently reactionary'.[143]

The foundations of the Kadets' idolatry of the army had been firmly established in the party's relatively brief history. This was particularly true in the case of the Siberian Kadets who, as we have seen, were typical of the right wing of the Party of the People's Freedom. Often of a background and training in the law – almost to a man in the case of those close to Kolchak[144] – they instinctively venerated legal principles. However, as much as the pre-revolutionary careers of Zhardetskii, Tel′berg, Pepeliaev and others provide examples of their respect for the rule of law and instances of their condemnation of abuses of political power, like the rest of their party, their first and foremost characteristic was a fear of the undermining of recognized authority. Moreover, as fervent nationalists above all else, the *primum mobile* of their political thought and action was the quest for the expansion of Russia's state power. In times of national crisis this imperative clearly demanded that their reformism should be subordinated to respect and support for established authority of whatever political hue. Such a policy the party held to be the essence and the cornerstone of social order.[145] This had not only ensured that their occasionally less than loyal opposition to Tsarism of the period 1905 to 1914 was transformed into a patriotic (if qualified) support for the régime on the outbreak of war, but also that, in turn, the party should welcome the February Revolution which toppled the Tsar – for they saw the revolution not so much as an opportunity to improve the social and political well-being of the long-suffering Russian people (to say nothing of the minority nationalities), but as a chance to snatch the victory against Germany which Nicholas II had seemed incapable of delivering to his country.

It has already been intimated that the lesson the Kadets had drawn from the subsequent developments of 1917 itself was not that to flirt with military coups was to court disaster, but that the moderate socialist parties were inept at government and

143 FO 371/4095/64204 'Pares (Chita) to FO, 22.iv.1919'; Pares, 'Siberian Diary' (*Pares Papers*, Box 43), p. 45.

144 Zhardetskii was a lawyer at Omsk; Tel′berg had been Professor of Jurisprudence at Tomsk and Samara Universities; even Pepeliaev had studied law (graduating in 1908 from Tomsk University) and had taught it at the Gymnasium at Biisk in the Altai.

145 See Rosenberg, *Liberals*, pp. 5–35, 466–7 and *passim*.

too inclined to pander to the transient and selfish interests of the masses at the expense of Russia's enduring national interests. This interpretation had determined the Siberian Kadets' anti-conciliationist policy of 1918. In contrast, however, what remained unshaken and undinted by their experience of war and revolution was the party's conservative faith in the Russian Army as the glorious, self-sacrificing defender of the nation, immaculately standing above the self-seeking vagaries of political struggle, the unsullied custodian and guarantor of Russia's truest and purest values. Suggestions that the army's conduct during the Great War had been rather inglorious and that its leaders (particularly in relation to Kornilov's adventure) had revealed themselves to be in no way disinclined to sully themselves with political conspiracy, were readily countered by resort to that convenient and familiar excuse of outraged nationalism – the 'stab in the back'. Extraordinary measures, the Kadets claimed, were justified to counter the treachery of the left and, in particular, the Bolshevik subservience to Germany. Thus, in a 1918 appeal to the Allies for anti-Bolshevik intervention, for example, ignoring every socio-political and economic foundation of the October Revolution, the Kadets of Harbin accounted for Russia's turmoil solely in terms of Lenin's alleged loyalty to the Kaiser:

> The heroic effort to restore the front and renew the offensive [in June 1917], which was begun so successfully, proved a failure and the great, powerful Russian Army, coming daily more under the influence of the German agents of Bolshevism, turned the front facing Germany towards Russia for a Civil War. The Russian front completely vanished in October, when Germanophile Bolshevism usurped authority with the help of deceived troops. Shamefully and dishonestly the treaties with our Allies, which had been cemented in blood, were broken...and an ignominious and treacherous peace, which the Russian people cannot and will never recognize, was bought [at Brest-Litovsk] from our inveterate foe at the price of a terrible and endless slavery of the State and of huge territorial losses... The approach of Russia's political and economic death must now be evident to everyone in whom a Russian heart beats.[146]

It was in the alleged forcefulness and honour of a military dictatorship that the Siberian Kadets envisaged the first and most important step on the road to the renewal of the national strength and pride of which they held the Bolsheviks to have robbed Russia: 'Society believes and hopes to see, in the near future, our Motherland re-invigorated and returned to its proper place in the world', they hailed

146 FO 371/3365/164029 'Text of an Appeal by a Group of Russian Political Parties and the Horvath Government (Harbin), 18.vi.1918'.

Kolchak as he assumed power in November 1918.[147] As to what the Allies might contribute to achieve this aim, they implied that neither economic assistance for Siberia nor political advice and guidance for their floundering government at Omsk were what was required: if the Bolsheviks were to be defeated, an American diplomat was told by one close to the Kadets, then the Allies must send 'in the first place soldiers, in the second place soldiers and in the third place soldiers'.[148] Later, during the early months of 1919 when Kolchak's forces were achieving success on the battlefield, the party's wholesale prostration before the military ikon was to reach its nadir. At the Kadets' 3rd Regional Conference, of May 1919, for example, Klafton, the then Chairman of *VOTsK*, was to declare: 'Our basic task is, above all else, the elimination of the military forces of Bolshevism. Therefore, everything else must be subordinated to this chief, military objective.' The 'temporary, exceptional means of state power', he insisted, referring to Kolchak's irregular government, were without exception to be endorsed.[149] Further, the conference decided, in defiance of the Kadets' reformist traditions, even the *discussion* of political and social reform could not be tolerated – in society or in the party – for it would only distract from the war effort. Finally, a resolution was passed calling for the unification of all social and political groups behind the military cause, as personified by its supreme *vozhd'*, Admiral Kolchak.[150]

One of their number would later insist that, although *VOTsK* did contain men who were 'reactionary in the real meaning of the word', the majority of Kadets at Omsk were still democrats, were still committed (in the long term) to 'a broad transformation of Russia on democratic lines', and regarded the dictatorship as being 'of a definitely temporary nature and of a purely tactical significance'.[151] Be that as it may, however, their party's so forceful and fulsome veneration of the military and the military way in 1918 to 1919 had a damaging influence upon Kolchak: for not only was the Kadets' policy an endorsement of the admiral's own aversion to

147 *Russkaia armiia* (Omsk) No. 6, 24.xi.1918; Maksakov and Turunov, p. 267.

148 FO 371/3365/168244 'Alston (Vladivostok) to FO, 6.x.1918'.

149 *Pravitel'stvennyi vestnik* (Omsk) No. 142, 24.v.1919.

150 *Sibirskaia rech'* (Omsk) 24.v.1919; *Report of the Russian Telegraph Agency* (Omsk) 20.v.1919. The rather archaic term '*vozhd'*' (chieftain) was evidently favoured for its militaristic, romantic and historical overtones, rather than the more neutral '*pravitel'*' (ruler).

151 Ustrialov, N. 'Iz proshlogo', *Russkaia zhizn': al'manakh* (Harbin), No. 3 (December 1922), pp. 53, 55.

politics, it was a bastion to a little known and definitely militaristic aspect of Kolchak's personal philosophy: for Kolchak, it seems (at least in part), divined qualities born of war and military rule as not merely of tactical import either for himself or for his country.

For the admiral, the Supreme Ruler *manqué*, war and militarism were regarded as a baptism of fire for a people, a strengthening process. Such ideas had been planted in the mind of Kolchak by a rather mysterious Japanese general called Khizakhida, a self-styled 'military Buddhist', with whom he become acquainted at Shanghai in February 1918. Always apt to fall under the sway of stronger characters than himself, Kolchak had recorded in his diary of this time that he had become convinced by Khizakhida that 'the natural form of government, which corresponds to the very meaning of of the word "government" is that which goes under the name of "militarism".' He was also instructed by the general that 'a statesman in time of war must be militaristic in spirit and intention'. In reply Kolchak expressed himself to be 'profoundly impressed' with these thoughts and delighted to converse with someone whose ideas so closely corresponded to his own. During his brief sojourn at Shanghai, therefore, it is clear that Kolchak soon came to regard the war as something of a cleansing, purifying agent – a sacred visitation which might rid his beloved Russia of the filth of 'anarchy and revolution'. He agreed with Khizakhida that 'war is to be esteemed to a far higher degree than justice or personal happiness; it is higher than life itself'. Indeed, Kolchak wrote in February 1918, the point at which he was swapping direct participation in the war against Germany for the (in his mind related) struggle against Bolshevism:

> War is beautiful...the natural condition of man. Nothing can revitalize the nation other than war, and revival is only conceivable through war. We must await a new war as the one and only radiant future.

As we know, like the majority of Kadets, Kolchak had evolved during the course of 1917 from regarding the overthrow of the Tsar as a necessary precondition of a successful prosecution of the war against Germany to a reviling of the new republic as 'a nightmare', the nadir of 'bedlam' and 'political chaos'. Later, under the influence of Khizakhida, he began to envisage a solution: 'Revolutionary democracy', he wrote in February 1918, 'must choke on its own dirt or drown in its own blood... There is no other way', he enthused, only military rule and a purifying, liberating, war.[152]

Consequently, once enthroned as dictator, as the leader of the declared war of national regeneration, Kolchak would guarantee that the military and the military way were to predominate in every sphere of his government's life. He would admit no criticism of the Russian Army of the past, which he held to have 'staggered the world with its selfless heroism, infusing the history of Russia with glory'.[153] As for the Russian Army of the future, which he himself was committed to founding, he informed the press on November 28th 1918:

> The current situation forces my advisers and myself to concentrate all of our attentions upon the establishment of a powerful, battleworthy Army. This is our prime task. Without an Army it is impossible to defend the dignity and honour of our Motherland... so crudely and impertinently violated at the criminal hands of the Bolsheviks.[154]

Of course, the power of civilian authorities had been seriously eroded even before Kolchak came to power. Even under the Directory, for example, the Commander-in-Chief, General Boldyrev, had held supreme authority over all territory west of the River Irtysh. In that region all civil administrations and establishments, including the entire legal system, were already subordinate to the army. Under Kolchak they remained so and a system of military courts was imposed.[155] The same circumstances prevailed in the Far East – and, once again, had done so before the establishment of the dictatorship – for on October 24th 1918 General Ivanov-Rinov (who had been made Military Governor of Vladivostok by Kolchak, as Minister of War to the Directory), was empowered to place the Amur, Maritime, Sakhalin and Kamchatka regions under direct military rule.[156] Consequently, as Transbaikalia and Semipalatinsk–Semirech'e were also under

152 Kolchak's thoughts were again recorded in his 'diaries'. See above, n. 108, and Ioffe, G.Z. *Kolchakovskaia avantiura i ee krakh*. Moscow (1983), pp. 13, 23–4; Fedotov, p. 26; Spirin, L.M. (ed.) *Razgrom Kolchaka: vospominaniia*. Moscow (1969), p. 3.

153 Kolchak's speech is partially reproduced in Bonch-Osmolovskii, A. *Komu zemlia dostanetsia?* Ekaterinburg (1919), p. 16.

154 *Pravitel'stvennyi vestnik* (Omsk) No. 12, 30.xi.1918; Pinegin, pp. 78–9.

155 *Priishim'e* (Petropavlovsk) No. 133 (1,655), 25.vi.1919; Guins, *Sibir'*, Vol. 2, pp. 137–8; Sukin (*Leeds Russian Archive*), pp. 152–3.

156 Graves, p. 143.

'military' control (albeit the less formal kind enforced by the Cossack atamans Semenov and Annenkov), while even as early as the autumn of 1918 much of the hinterland of Enisei and Irkutsk *guberniias* were in the hands of rebel partisan forces, it can be said that even from day one of the dictatorship the 'All-Russian Government' at Omsk could only realistically have claimed jurisdiction over western Siberia (essentially Tomsk *guberniia*) and the narrow strip of territory adjacent to the Trans-Siberian Railway between Omsk and Lake Baikal. Even in this ribbon-like zone of White civilian authority, however, governmental control was to be eroded at the Supreme Ruler's behest. On November 30th, for example, the Military Censor's Department of Lebedev's *stavka* was empowered to close down, without even informing the civilian authorities, any newspaper it deemed offensive.[157] By this means all legal opposition to the dictatorship was stifled. Then, on February 1st 1919, military courts were empowered to impose the death penalty in any district under their jurisdiction 'for the guaranteeing of general order' or (after February 18th) 'for avoidance of, or assistance to avoid, military service'.[158] Finally, during March 1919, Kolchak was to extend the territory under direct military rule to encompass not only areas adjacent to the front but also every major town in Siberia, thereby completing the edifice of military rule in White Siberia from the Urals to the Pacific.[159]

What was really to damn the White movement, however, was that Kolchak and the Kadets' veneration of the military ideal had apparently blinded them, had seemingly deprived them of any rational perception of the true nature of that army to which they were handing over such boundless power. They expected the Siberian Army – redubbed the Russian Army in the first days of Kolchak's governance – to act decisively and apolitically, as, they held, the Russian Army had always done. And when, on November 23rd, Kolchak appealed to 'officers and soldiers at the front and

157 By January 1st 1919 the censor had banned virtually every moderate and left-wing newspaper in Siberia, including those which had applauded or even assisted in the overthrow of Soviet power in Siberia the previous spring. Among the casualties were *Altaiskii put'*, *Nash put'*, *Ural*, *Sibir'*, *Delo*, *Zheleznodorozhnik*, *Delo naroda*, *Golos rabochego*, etc. See Parfenov, *Uroki proshlogo*, p. 100.

158 Krushanov, A.I. *Grazhdanskaia voina v Sibiri i na Dal'nem Vostoke (1918–1920gg.)*, Vol.1. Vladivostok (1972), p. 112.

159 Guins, *Sibir'*, Vol. 2, pp. 137–8. The towns and cities affected were Omsk, Tatarsk, Slavgorod, Kansk, Novonikolaevsk, Barnaul, Mariinsk, Achinsk, Minusinsk, Eniseisk, Krasnoiarsk, Kainsk, Nizhneudinsk, Irkutsk, Biisk and Tomsk.

in the rear to divest themselves of all politics and all types of party-political work', he clearly expected to be obeyed.[160] However, modern sociological studies of the military as a professional organization generally agree that even the best trained and most professional army does not act apolitically because of an 'unblinkered' view of the national interest such as that which Kolchak and the Kadets were apt to attribute to their forces in 1918 to 1919. Rather, such researches concur, professional armies act compulsively, because as a closed organization in which repetitious training, inculcated obedience and a devout trust of hierarchy are endowed with semi-mystical qualities, and as a closed organization in which order and predictability are at all times to be revered, the professional army can do nothing else. It must in addition be noted, however, that even when professional armies do reject politics – as Kolchak and his like desired – it is only politics in its narrowest sense: the business of politicking, the wheeler-dealing, deceitfulness and compromise which are the stuff of day-to-day political activity. And even at best such a rejection may be a covertly political act, for – as one of Kolchak's most esteemed contemporaries had to admit – such a rejection invariably implies an acceptance of the political status quo.[161] In fact, it might well be that in the majority of cases officers who decry politics in its narrow, day-to-day form as totally alien to their professional nature, do so only because they have most definite ideas about that which informs politics in its broader and more general sense – the consideration of what is best for their community or nation and the means by which it is to be achieved.[162]

An examination of the nature of officer corps of the Russian Army will reveal not only that this could be the case among the revered military of White Siberia in 1918 to 1919, but also that the process of the development of those forces might have tended to ensure that they proceed a step further and actively intervened in routine politics so as to further their own group interests.

160 *Pravitel'stvennyi vestnik* (Omsk) No. 4, 23.xi.1918; Maksakov and Turunov, p. 269. This informal appeal was transformed into a statutory law in March 1919. Thereafter it was illegal for anybody in military service (and those associated with the army, such as doctors) as well as those in the civil service to join a political party, attend a meeting or demonstration or even to make a public statement on political affairs.

161 Denikin, A.I. *Staraia armiia*. Paris (1929–1931), Vol. 2, pp. 89–90.

162 Perlmutter, A. *The Military and Politics in Modern Times*. London (1977), p. 285; Tromp, H.W. 'The Assessment of the Military Mind', in van Gils, M.R. (ed.) *The Perceived Role of the Military*. Rotterdam (1971), p. 361.

The politicization of the Russian Army in Siberia

With the exception of the Decembrist revolt of 1825, there was no precedent for the military's political activity in the Russian Civil War. Eighteenth-century Russia had witnessed several palace coups involving officers of guards regiments. But the coup-makers had espoused no political aims beyond self-interest, had remained loyal to the principle of autocracy, and were content with the replacing of one pretender to the throne with another.[163] Throughout the nineteenth and early twentieth centuries politics remained something which the Russian Army – while vaguely regarding the very notion of it as being subversive and possibly treasonous – made no attempt to understand, let alone participate in. In fact, noted General Sukhomlinov, 'it was considered rude to talk about politics in society'.[164] Kolchak concurred: 'Generally speaking it was difficult in former times to say what the political convictions of an officer were,' he told his inquisitors at Irkutsk, 'as this question simply did not exist before the war.'[165] If anything, in fact, in the immediate pre-war years, the army became even more closeted and isolated, even more estranged from Russia's rudimentary political society in the aftermath of the revolution of 1905, as it withdrew into itself, resentful of accusations that military incompetence had lost the war against Japan and contributed to social unrest.[166]

It was the war of 1914, of course, which changed everything. By the time that the Bolsheviks seized power in Petrograd in October 1917, the changes wrought by the European struggle had occasioned in Russia at least three transformations which can be identified as enhancing the military's propensity to intervene in politics. Firstly, the officer corps in Russia had become markedly unprofessional; secondly,

163 Seton-Watson, G.H.N. 'Russia: Army and Autocracy', in Howard, M. (ed.) *Soldiers and Governments*. London (1957), pp. 103–4. In so far as many White officers were avowed monarchists, it might be said that this tradition had endured.

164 Sukhomlinov, V.A. *Vospominaniia*. Moscow (1926). On this point see also Kenez, P. 'The Russian Officer Corps Before the Revolution: the Military Mind', *Russian Review* Vol. 31, No. 3 (1972), pp. 233–4; and Ray, O.A. 'The Imperial Russian Army Officer', *Political Science Quarterly* Vol. 76, No. 4 (1961), pp. 584–5.

165 Varneck and Fisher, p. 103.

166 Bushnell, J. 'The Tsarist Officer Corps: Customs, Duties, Efficiency', *American Historical Review* Vol. 86, No. 4 (1981), pp. 766–9; and Perrins, M. 'The Russian Military 1904–1917 and its Role in Russian Political Affairs', London University PhD Thesis (1980), pp. 42–4.

there had developed an officer corps of great social heterogeneity; and thirdly, a political vacuum had developed in the country.

It might seem paradoxical to talk of a burgeoning unprofessionalism in the Russian officer corps during the Great War. Had it not, after all, been the case that already on the eve of the war there had been no other major power in Europe whose officers received so poor a military and general education as did those of the Russian Army? Was there another state whose officers might so barbedly (but so accurately) be lampooned in popular novels, such as Aleksander Kuprin's *The Duel*, as a mob of illiterate drunkards, thieves, cheats and rapists? Surely, it might be held, the experience of the war could only have improved matters, bolstering the army's professionalism, for in the course of the struggle against Germany had not the Russian officer corps at least developed a practical knowledge of warfare, whatever their failings on the battlefield? And that, of course, was the case: although by 1916 excessively high casualty rates had necessitated the commissioning of cohorts of men with the bare minimum of an education and only four months of basic training,[167] the recruits had acquired in a few weeks at the front a knowledge of their art which far outshone their pre-war counterparts (among whom it had been common practice to take furlough during the period of the army's annual manoeuvres, who had held it to be the height of bad taste to express an interest in anything so base as military science and who had spent most of their 'active service' behind desks or at their clubs).[168]

The point is, however, that, whatever their battlefield skills, that which the cohorts of new officers who were commissioned during the world war and the civil war could not acquire was a second and equally important fundament of military professionalism – one that has little to do with guns or strategy – that is, a sense of corporatism. This attribute of the professional army (and, indeed, of all professional groups) has been usefully defined as 'the development of a sense of unity and a

167 Mayzel, M. *Generals and Revolutionaries (The Russian General Staff during the Revolution): a Study in the Transformation of a Military Élite*. Osnabruck (1979), pp. 44–5. Observers attributed the high casualty rate of Russian officers at the front during the Great War (a feature repeated on the White side in the civil war – see below, pp. 187, 324ff.) to their foolhardy heroism and romantic view of war. See Pares, B. *Day by Day with the Russian Army, 1914–1915*. London (1915), p. 222.

168 Bushnell, pp. 166-9; Williams, A.K. *The End of the Russian Imperial Army*. Princeton (1980), p. 8.

collective recognition of the differentiation of the body from other organizations'.[169] It is a quality which cannot be acquired from a few months' training and one which should not be confused with the comradeship engendered by the shared horrors of life in the trenches. Rather, it is something inculcated only by years of shared experience of barracks life and the slow absorption of military mores: a process which precipitates the internalization and socialization by the army of non-political values. In brief, it is the development of a specific code of conduct. It was precisely such a quality which was lacking in the Siberian Army and in Kolchak's Russian Army in 1918 and 1919. In fact, as early as 1917 General Wrangel had remarked upon the absence of such a quality among the newly commissioned officers in his charge and had correctly attributed it to the fact that, because of the lack of time, the young captains and lieutenants had not been sufficiently distanced from their civilian lives: they had been suddenly 'uprooted from their normal and anything but military work', Wrangel noted.[170] How much more, then, must this have been the case in Kolchak's White Siberia where, as the head of the Officer Training School at Vladivostok (General Sakharov) informed General Knox, 'engineers, agriculturalists, students, clerks, peasants etc.' were rushed through their classes in a matter of weeks and sent directly onto active service.[171]

The absence of this sense of corporatism in Kolchak's forces was to prove extremely debilitating, for it is perhaps the key element of professionalism. Whatever the conservative or even reactionary nature of the military mind, corporatism can ensure that the army puts the knowledge, violent skills and lethal resources at its disposal to responsible social uses. Indeed, it may even guarantee the political neutrality of an army at times of extreme change in the composition of governments – the relative passivity of the German Army in 1933 and of the Czechoslovak Army in 1948 have been cited as cases in point.[172] Moreover, in an example more directly relevant to this study, it was a fact that of the pre-war Russian Army's 1,000 or so general staff officers (its most long-serving and professional elite), no less than 559 of those who had not been killed by 1917 were to serve in the Red Army in the civil war. There were, of course, many other

169 McKinlay, R.D. 'Professionalism, Politicization and Civil-Military Relations', in van Gils, p. 251.

170 Wrangel [Vrangel], P.N. *Memoirs*. London (1929), p. 3.

171 'General Sakharov (Vladivostok) to General Knox, 4.iii.1919', (*Pares Papers*, Box 41).

172 Doorn, J. van *The Soldier and Social Change*. London (1975), pp. 81–2.

reasons why such men chose to remain at their posts after October. A rare study of the phenomenon (by David Jones) has listed such factors as a fear of inadvertently allowing Kerensky and the SRs back into power by attacking the Bolsheviks; the isolation of officer groups one from another as communications and command structures broke down; and their common belief that the Bolshevik government would collapse of its own accord – and, when it did not, of course, there was added to these factors Trotsky's infamous system of hostage-taking among officers' families. Also of significance, however, as Jones acknowledges, was a desire among professional officers not to undermine the moral state of the armed forces through interference in political events.[173] By the end of 1918 such men were few on the ground in Kolchakia.

One authority on civil-military relations has argued, on the basis of an analysis of coup-prone, underdeveloped states of post-imperial Africa and Asia (whose circumstances are not altogether dissimilar to early twentieth-century Russia), that whatever the level of corporatism and professionalism among the armed forces, they might still be inclined to intervene in politics, for the spur to action is not a factor internal to the army.[174] Rather, in such societies, the key factor triggering the politicization of the military seems to be what S.E. Finer, in his classic analysis of 'the men on horseback', termed the prevailing 'low level of political culture' – i.e. the absence of functioning and regular governmental and party-political structures at all but the centre of society and the mass acceptance of extraordinary and *ad hoc* means of administration as the norm. In such circumstances, it has been postulated, the army's sense of duty and national pride and its commitment to order will determine that it is irresistibly drawn into politics to fill what it would regard as an unstable and dangerous political vacuum.[175]

This factor was indubitably present in the White Siberia of 1918 to 1919. The political culture of the region was very low – a joint legacy of the sparse communications network east of the Urals and the tsarist tradition of regarding the

173 Jones, D. 'The Officers and the October Revolution', *Soviet Studies* (Glasgow) Vol. 28 (1976), No. 2, pp. 217–19 and *passim*. For details of general staff officers' service in the Red Army see *Spisok ofitserov General'nogo shtaba, nakhodiashchikhsia za rubezhami Sovetskoi Rossii, po dannykh k 1-omu avg. 1922g.* Belgrade (1922), cited in Mayzel, M. p. 220.

174 Janowitz, M. *The Military in the Political Development of New Nations*. Chicago (1964), *passim*.

175 Finer, S.E. *The Men on Horseback: The Role of the Military in Politics*. London (1976), pp. 86ff.

region as little more than a mine of cheap raw materials and foodstuffs and a convenient dump for criminals and social malcontents. Siberia had always relied on Moscow for the little government it had, but ties to the centre had, of course, been severed in 1918; local government, in the form of zemstvos, had only been introduced to the region in 1917. In the following years the political vacuum was not filled by the successive administrations at Omsk, whose authority outwith that one town remained negligible. Indeed, the very fact that such political authority as existed was concentrated within the capital – the fact that there were few complicating factors of local or regional governments – may well have further encouraged military involvement in politics, for in such simplified circumstances the belief may be fostered in elements of an officer corps that the army would be capable of running such an uncomplicated political system, one resembling the army itself in its direct hierarchies and centralized authority.[176]

There can also be little doubt that the third factor generally identified as enhancing the military's propensity to intervene in politics was particularly prevalent in Kolchak's Siberia – a marked heterogeneity in the social origins of the officer corps. This feature of the army in Russia had, in fact, been increasingly evident even before World War I. By 1912, for example, although the Guards and the General Staff had preserved their aristocratic intake, of the officer cadets in a typical higher military school in Moscow only 9% were scions of the hereditary nobility – the remainder being 28% personal nobles, 28% bourgeoisie and 19% of peasant origin.[177] Well in advance of the February Revolution, moreover, the mix must have become yet more diverse, for the 50,000 regular officers and 35,000 officer reserves of the pre-war line which the Tsar had been able to mobilize in 1914 actually totalled less than the 92,500 officers either killed or captured by the enemy by 1916. To take their place and to run the increasingly large army, no fewer than 170,000 men were commissioned in the course of the fighting – many of them of

176 Hopkins, K. 'Civil-Military Relations in Developing Countries', *British Journal of Sociology* Vol. 17 (1976), discusses this phenomenon. An analogy might be drawn with the view of modern capitalist states drawn by Lenin in *The State and Revolution*, wherein he argued that most workers would be capable of grasping the basic accounting techniques which were all that were required to run a centralized, state economy.

177 Garthoff, R.L. 'The Military as a Social Force', in Black, C.E. (ed.) *The Transformation of Russian Society*. Cambridge, MA (1960), p. 326.

peasant stock or from the urban middle and even working classes.[178] Such was the rate of attrition that by the end of the war, noted General Sakharov in his afore-cited letter to Knox of March 1919, some 85–90% of Russian officers had received their commission after August 1914: 'And at the present time the correlation is yet sharper', he added,[179] passing in silence over the fact that many of the officers of Kolchak's army had not even attended the makeshift courses run at training schools such as his own on Russian Island, but, rather, had been commissioned by one or other of the myriad Siberian 'governments' of 1918, which, according to one observer, manufactured generals at will.[180]

In the absence of the dual controls of an ideologically motivated cause and without a commissar system of the type favoured in the Red Army by the Bolsheviks, such a democratization of social origins has been observed in no way to strengthen the army's willingness to submit to civilian direction: 'In fact, there are clear-cut cases where the reverse may be the case', commented one leading authority on the sociology of armies.[181] Unlike, for example, officers recruited from the landed gentry, those drawn from less privileged social strata may expect a marked decline in personal prestige and lifestyle, and a loss of income and material possessions, if they are forced to leave the army in mid-career as a result of political upheavals having established a government opposed to the army as it stands. They consequently have a vested interest in the support and maintenance of régimes, like that of Kolchak, which promise to maintain or even enhance the army's place in society and to safeguard its budget. Moreover, if, as was the case in White Siberia, the régime relies for its very existence on the military, there will naturally arise ample opportunity for officers of few inherited material means to secure personal enrichment as a guarantee against the possibility of future losses. Thus, the British consul at Ekaterinburg was to observe that elements of the officer

178 Kenez, P. 'Changes in the Social Composition of the Officer Corps in World War I', *Russian Review* Vol. 31, No. 4 (1972), pp. 369–72. Perrins, p. 223 suggests that the numbers of new officers may have been even higher.

179 'General Sakharov (Vladivostok) to General Knox, 4.iii.1919' (*Pares Papers*, Box 41). The researches of a Soviet military historian confirmed this figure. See Eikhe, G. Kh. *Oprokinutyi tyl.* Moscow (1966), p. 148.

180 Bell, p. 96. According to one British officer, some of the officers graduating from Sakharov's schools were 'perfectly disreputable'. See Vining, p. 38.

181 Janowitz, M. 'Armed Forces and Society', in van Doorn, J. (ed.) *Armed Forces and Society: Sociological Essays.* The Hague (1968), pp. 27–8.

corps of Kolchak's Russian Army were 'prepared to go to any extreme to gain their ends – i.e. the privileges and prestige the old régime gave to them' – prizes of which the Bolsheviks threatened to deprive them. Russia's national interests, *pace* the faith which Kolchak and the Kadets had invested in the army's patriotism, was 'a matter of secondary interest' to the officers with whom he had contact at the front, continued the consul. General Pepeliaev agreed: from first-hand observation of the workings of the Omsk *stavka* he concluded that the parvenus and sycophants of Lebedev's ilk were 'selling Russia with the object of personal gain'.[182] An American who had the opportunity to dine with the Chief of Staff, confirmed that the young General Lebedev was:

> ...the type of military man who looks backwards not forwards. For himself and his own people he wanted every privilege, every power, every advantage they had enjoyed before [the war]...yet not a word about the great needs, economic, political and spiritual of the Russian people.[183]

Finally, of the representatives of the Russian Army in the Far East, the American commander at Vladivostok wrote:

> Their backs were against the wall and their main object was to establish in Russia some government that would restore [the officer class] to the position they had before the war, which they had no hope of reaching if the Soviets remained in power.[184]

Apart from the fading hope of material gain, moreover, the White officers of Kolchak had made an enormous emotional investment in the army and in the Russian Empire it served. Many of the young captains, lieutenants, colonels and even the generals who fought for Kolchak had spent almost their entire adult life in the war against Germany. As Wrangel noted, they had been 'uprooted' from civilian life and, little more than boys, thrown into the trenches. Yet they had hardly learned to identify with the strange new life that they found there, as an SR observer continued, than once again 'they were thrown off track by the revolution' and told

182 FO 538/4 'Memorandum on the Political and Military Situation in Siberia (by HM Consul, Ekaterinburg), 7.viii.1919'.

183 Brown, W.A. *The Groping Giant: Revolutionary Russia as Seen by an American Diplomat*. New Haven (1920), pp. 176–7.

184 Graves, p. 152.

by revolutionary orators that all their struggles and privations at the front, all the love and faith they had bestowed upon their Motherland had been misguided, wrong and even shameful. Continued the SR:

> Half-educated and unable to adapt to anything, they had not found a place for themselves in the new society. It was back there, in the past, in Tsarism, in the old barrack room army, with its epaulettes and galloons, its disciplinary slaps in the mouth, its blind discipline – only there could they see salvation.[185]

Of course, only a fraction of the officer corps had ever actually experienced life in the army of the past, the peacetime army. But in the uncertain and frightening days of 1918 and 1919, that could only have made their perception of such a life even more alluring – the pre-war army must have beckoned as a vision of order, normality, privilege and comfort.

Intellectually impoverished and politically illiterate as they were, the revolution of 1917 had taught the majority of Kolchak's officers nothing, lamented a more sagacious general, Baron Budberg: 'They have learned nothing new and forgotten nothing which is old', he opined.[186] In fact, impervious to all reasoned argument with regard to the liberation and potential for development of the social, political and economic rights of the Russian people in 1917, the White officers seemed to care only that they themselves had been deprived of the opportunity to rise above the mass. They had no political credo, observed one refusing to join their cause, merely a shared 'indignation'.[187] Incensed by this alleged injustice, they exhibited a blind and emotional rage, an unquenchable thirst for revenge – and one that was extracted all the more bloodily against the traditionally violent background of Siberia for the fact that many of Kolchak's young officers had never known a state in their adult life other than war. They had become imbruted in the almost medieval conditions which had prevailed on the Eastern Front of the Great War and had lost any lingering respect for the sanctity of human life during the fierce struggle on the Volga in the summer of 1918: having themselves paid the price for their military superiors' incompetence and for the administrative shortcomings of succeeding governments, they had developed no new moral code of their own. Budberg, for

185 Rakitnikov, *Sibirskaia reaktsiia*, p. 9.

186 Budberg, Vol. 14, p. 298.

187 Alioshin, *Asian Odyssey*, p. 83.

example, was certain that very few indeed were the officers at Omsk who would have exchanged the chance of the catharsis of extracting revenge on the left for the possibility of rebuilding Russia in a spirit of forgiveness and conciliation, for they were generally incapable of looking beyond the satisfaction of their immediate desires.[188] Another witness confirmed, after a depressing conversation during the autumn of 1918 with an anonymous White colonel who had bemoaned the end of the empire and the 'chaos' of revolution:

> Suddenly I realized that only in blood, rivers of blood, could men like this seek relief... certainly they would make someone pay dearly for the bitterness of their disappointments.[189]

Initially the officers' hatred was directed against the servants of the deposed Soviet régime in the east. There was a spate of killings in which the Bolshevik leadership in Siberia, including almost the entire establishment of *Tsentrosibir'*, was exterminated and which was marked by the hunting down of individual Bolsheviks by officers who had personal scores to settle with them.[190] Those gruesome tasks completed, however, the spiral of White violence and terror expanded apace with the Siberian Army's developing self-confidence and political successes during the autumn of 1918 – and with a military dictator installed at Omsk on November 18th their bloodlust would know no bounds. Betraying the trust which the Supreme Ruler placed in it, his Russian Army was, in fact, to resort to the most extreme form of party politics conceivable. In short, it served a swift death sentence upon every member of the Bolshevik Party and of the Left-SRs unfortunate enough to fall into its hands. Moreover, because this insecure and politically ignorant military were apt to associate *any* form of socialism, no matter how asinine, with Bolshevism – because, said General Graves, the White officers had broadened the very definition of the word 'Bolshevik' to mean 'a human being who did not by act and word give

188 Budberg, Vol. 13, p. 312.

189 Alioshin, p. 20.

190 On these events see Snow, R.E. *The Bolsheviks in Siberia, 1917–1918*. London (1977), p. 228; Novgorodov, A.I. *Oktiabr'skaia revoliutsiia i grazhdanskaia voina v Iakutii*. Novosibirsk (1969), pp. 179–81; Dvorianov, N.V. and Dvorianov, V.N. *V tylu Kolchaka*. Moscow (1966), pp. 26–8; and Varneck and Fisher, p. 138. For an extensive list and obituaries of Bolsheviks and Bolshevik supporters who were killed by the Whites (concentrating, primarily on Transbaikalia and the Far East) see Zhukovskii, I. and Mokin, Z. (eds.) *Krasnaia golgofa – sbornik posviashchennyi pamiati tovarishchei pogibshchikh za raboche-krest'ianskoe delo*. Blagoveshchensk (1920), pp. 4–134.

encouragement to the restoration to power of the representatives of Autocracy in Russia'[191] – anyone who was not an enthusiastic advocate of the military régime was qualified to become a target of the officers' and Cossacks' revanchism.

The Omsk massacre and the demise of SR opposition in Siberia

Although the restraint placed on the White military at Omsk by the need to respect the sensibilities of Allied representatives in the immediate aftermath of the coup had necessitated the mere exile of the SR Directors, the vengeful officer corps of the Siberian Army were unlikely to exhibit such temperance in their dealings with the remaining centres of SR activity in the east once the Kolchak régime was firmly established. In fact, away from the prying eyes of the capital, the first attempt at mopping up vestigial Constituent Assembly authorities in which many of the reviled Chernovites still gathered was made within days of the coup.

In the northern Urals capital of Ekaterinburg a Congress of Members of the Constituent Assembly – the body formally charged at the Ufa State Conference with responsibility for gathering a quorum of members of the Constituent Assembly before the new year – had combined with members of the Socialist-Revolutionary Central Committee to issue protests against Kolchak's seizure of power in the name of a hastily organized Extraordinary Committee of Opposition (led by Chernov).[192] Among its acts was the despatch of a telegram to Omsk, optimistically demanding that the Supreme Ruler relinquish power or face the possibility of a combined 'Allied-Russian' (i.e. Czechoslovak-Russian) force being sent against him.[193] However, the threat was an obvious bluff, for although two local representatives of

191 Graves, pp. 101–2. Bernard Pares made an almost identical claim. See FO 371/4095/65215 'Note on the Coup d'Etat of Admiral Kolchak, November 22nd [sic] 1918 (with reference to the recent arrests at Vladivostok, ?.iv.1919)'.

192 Sviatitskii, N. *K istorii Vserossiiskogo uchreditel'nogo sobraniia: S"ezd chlenov uchreditel'nogo sobraniia (sentiabr'–dekabr' 1918g.)*. Moscow (1921), gives an insider's history of the Congress. For its statute see also Gan, pp. 279–80, 284. The Committee of Opposition consisted of V. Chernov, V.K. Vol'skii and I. Alkin of the Congress, plus the SRs N. Fomin, S. Fedorovich and I. Brushvit.

193 Chernov, V.N. *Pered burei: vospominaniia*. New York (1953), p. 390; Zenzinov, pp. 47–8; Golovin, Vol. 9, pp. 68–9, 108.

the Russian Section of the Czechoslovak National Council (P.N. Medek and K. Svoboda) pledged their support to Chernov, they had no influence over the Siberian Army and Legion's military chiefs in the Urals, who would never have contemplated withdrawing troops from the front to serve the SRs. On the other hand, one Siberian Army unit – the 25th Rifle Corps – did find time independently to arrest this troublesome SR committee. Thus, on the night of November 19th, justifying their unauthorised action with the claim to be 'saving our brothers at the front from treachery in the rear' – the 25th Riflemen and a number of officers from other units surrounded Chernov's apartment at the Ekaterinburg Hotel Palais Royale. Panic ensued, shots were fired, a grenade was thrown and one man (I.N. Maksukov, a member of the Constituent Assembly) was fatally injured. Chernov, Vol′skii, Rakitnikov and sixteen other SR leaders were then arrested and led away, expecting only one, bloody fate. At this crucial moment, however, a Czechoslovak unit came across the column of prisoners and insisted on replacing the trigger-happy Russian escort with a guard of its own, thereby almost certainly preventing a massacre.[194]

The following day, November 20th, the detainees and about seventy other SRs left Ekaterinburg, bound for Cheliabinsk, in the goods wagons of a specially chartered train. They were still guarded by their Czechoslovak saviours. One of their number, Sviatitskii, later left a sorry and ironic account of the luminaries of Russia's first parliament ignobly fleeing from Russian troops under the protection of foreign mercenaries.[195]

On arrival at Cheliabinsk, however, the forsaken SR fugitives found that their troubles were far from being over. General Dieterichs, who now commanded that sector, having entered the Russian service, and who was a staunch supporter of the coup, was endeavouring to have their train sent on to its ultimate destination, Shadrinsk, by a somewhat circuitous route... via Omsk![196] The SRs would almost certainly not have escaped the Whites' clutches as easily there as they had at Ekaterinburg, as time was to tell. For the moment, however, wisely refraining from following his erstwhile party comrades Zenzinov and Avksent′ev quite so meekly

194 Chernov, pp. 392–3; Sviatitskii, *K istorii*, pp. 110–11.

195 *ibid.*, pp. 111–12. See also the account of a French officer who was at Ekaterinburg: Pichon, Colonel 'Le Coup d'État de L'amiral Koltchak', *Le Monde Slave* (Paris), No. 2 (1925), pp. 259–61.

196 According to Sukin (*Leeds Russian Archive*), p. 70, Kolchak had ordered Dieterichs to arrest the group of SRs.

into the 'lion's mouth' which was the Siberian capital, Chernov was at the last minute able (again with the help of the Czechoslovak National Council) to thwart Dieterichs's scheme and have his train diverted instead to the more friendly territory of Ufa.[197]

At Ufa resided the second residual body of Komuch, the Council of Heads of Departments, which (in the absence of the arrival from Omsk of any central commissioners to take over its business in accordance with the Directory's instruction of November 4th) still regarded itself as the regional government of Ufa *guberniia* and the Volga-Kama territories.[198] Like their Ekaterinburg colleagues, this Ufa group of SRs had protested strongly against the Kolchak coup, initially issuing an 'Appeal to the Population' in which they formally re-assumed their regional authority and promised to consult with the Czechoslovak National Council and other Russian bodies on measures which could be taken to restore the Directory to power.[199] Later that same day, November 18th, they too had despatched a telegram to Omsk, castigating Kolchak and Vologodskii, declaring them to be 'enemies of the Motherland', and vaingloriously threatening to unite with other regional governments to send their 'volunteer units' against the Siberian capital if the Directory was not restored to power forthwith.[200] Mere vituperation, however, could not disguise the SRs' impotence. Their volunteers existed only on paper – and only 2,000 men (and women) of them, under the nominal command of B.K. Fortunatov, at that – whilst, as at Ekaterinburg, whatever were the sympathies of Czechoslovak moderates in the area, there was no chance of their tired men being sent against Omsk.[201] Moreover, Allied (especially British) representatives across the region were letting it be known that they and their governments were far from displeased with what had transpired at Omsk – the inference being that if the Legionnaires still wanted their passage home they had better not interfere. Thus, as one member of the doomed party was later to repent, with the fall of the Directory

197 Chernov, pp. 394–5.

198 The Committee was headed by V. Filipovskii, P. Klimushkin, I. Nesterov and Vedemiapin.

199 FO 371/4094/36137 'Preston (Ekaterinburg) to Eliot (Omsk), 30.xi.1919'.

200 Maksakov and Turunov, pp. 270–1.

201 Ioffe, *Kolchakovskaia avantiura*, p. 154. General Syrovy, Chief of Staff of the Legion, had recently received direct orders to this effect from his commander, General Janin. See Vesely, I. *Chekhi i Slovaki v revoliutsionnoi Rossii*. Moscow (1965), p. 149; Boldyrev, V.G. *Direktoriia, Kolchak, interventy: vospominaniia*. Novosibirsk (1925), p. 165.

the SRs returned to what had always been their forte – drawing up resolutions and holding meetings, while their opponents organized and acted.[202]

No sooner had Chernov and the Ekaterinburg group arrived at Ufa to join the Council of Heads of Departments in yet another ritual condemnation of the military and the coup, than on November 30th Kolchak acted, issuing his infamous Order No. 56. In his testimony at Irkutsk the Supreme Ruler was to assert that this was a direct response to the Ufa Council's combative telegram of November 18th, which he regarded as treasonous, and that in instructing (in Order No. 56) 'all Russian military leaders to cut short the criminal work of these people by the most decisive means, not excluding the use of armed force', he was referring only to the signatories of that telegram.[203] However, although it is indeed the case that the preamble of Order No. 56 cites the activities of the Council of Heads of Department, in referring in its main clauses merely to 'these people' and vaguely to 'such people', Kolchak made a great mistake: in handing over police powers to the army in such a manner, granting them the right to arrest the political opponents of the government whilst laying down only the most indefinite of guidelines, both the Supreme Ruler's political naivety and his slavish faith in military rectitude were apparent. Certainly the wolfish officer bands converging on Ufa – some of them having trailed Chernov all the way from Ekaterinburg in the hope of just such an opportunity – were only too pleased to interpret Order No. 56 not just as a licence to arrest the Council of Heads of Departments, but as a *carte blanche* to round up *all* members of the Constituent Assembly, or even all SRs. And that, with the assistance of the 41st Urals Regiment, they proceeded to do.[204] Viktor Chernov, V.K. Vol′skii, P.D. Klimushkin and Vedemiapin managed to escape, but on December 2nd at Ufa twenty-seven other leading SRs were captured – including Speranskii, V.N. Filippovskii, I.P. Nesterov, Fedorovich and I.I. Deviatov.

202 Rakitnikov, p. 30.

203 *Russkaia armiia* (Omsk) 3.xii.1918, published in Piontkovskii, S.A. (ed.) *Grazhdanskaia voina v Rossii (1919–1921gg.): krestomatiia*. Moscow (1925), pp. 300–1; Varneck and Fisher, p. 191.

204 Sviatitskii, p. 127; Petrov, *Ot Volgi do Tikhago okean*. Riga (1930), pp. 62–3. Kolchak should not have been too surprised that the officers instigated a general round-up of SRs, when he himself was evidently not at all clear about which of them had been responsible for what. He complained to his interrogators at Irkutsk that of those arrested only Deviatov had actually signed the offending telegram from Ufa, while Fomin, he thought, was not a member of the Constituent Assembly. He was wrong on both counts : Deviatov had *not* signed the telegram (as, indeed, had neither Nesterov nor Filipovskii, who were also arrested) and Fomin *was* a member of the Constituent Assembly.

Meanwhile at Cheliabinsk other officers picked up the esteemed SR and co-operator Nils Fomin and his assistant, M.V. Lokt′ev. That pair, like virtually every other arrested man, had nothing whatsoever to do with the Council of Heads of Departments' telegram of November 18th.

The officer groups then gleefully despatched their prisoners to the Siberian capital, where it was hoped that they would be put before the 'special military courts' which Kolchak had mentioned in his order. So it was that, after a miserable three-day journey, on December 5th the failed conciliationists and fallen members of the Constituent Assembly of 1917 found themselves in Dostoevsky's 'House of the Dead', the Omsk prison. Ironically, their cellmates turned out to be those very Bolshevik leaders of the Siberian soviet régime which the SRs had been instrumental in destroying during the spring of 1918.[205] Now, in deepest winter, the SRs too were to languish in a White prison, with time to meditate upon the sorry end to which their search for a 'third path', neither Bolshevik nor reactionary, had led not only their party but all Siberia.

Meanwhile, those of the SR Central Committee still at liberty in the east gathered for a secret meeting at Ufa. It declared, too late, that the PSR and Komuch could no longer permit reaction to conceal its true face behind the banner of the Constituent Assembly. There was, in addition, some typically fanciful talk of pulling imaginary SR units out of the front line to seize Ufa and then to join 'on an equal footing' with the Red Army to defeat Kolchak. But, as such units simply did not exist, the final resolution merely and meekly accepted that the party which had for so long nurtured the counter-revolutionary cuckoos in its democratic nest, the party which had won the trust of the majority of the Russian people according to the elections of 1917, was now powerless to do anything but 'withdraw from the struggle'.[206]

205 FO 371/3365/201998 'Eliot (Omsk) to FO, 5.xii.1918'. Rumour had it that the SRs would be used as hostages in case of an attempt on Kolchak's life.

206 *Sovremennyi moment v otsenke Partii sotsialistov-revoliutsionerov*. Paris (1919), p. 4; Gusev, K.V. and Eritsian, Kh.A. *Ot soglashatel′stva k kontrrevoliutsii: ocherki istorii politicheskogo bankrotstva i gibeli Partii sotsialistov-revoliutsionerov*. Moscow (1968), p. 340; Sviatitskii, pp. 138–9. Chernov and the majority of the participants in this conference, however, had not yet finally abandoned the hope of waging a war on two fronts. Rather, they decided to lie low until a more propitious moment. They subsequently led an 'illegal' existence in Soviet- and White-held territory and spent their time defining rather arcane notions of the 'hostile neutrality' they claimed to observe in relation to Kolchak and the 'benevolent neutrality' they would offer Lenin. Neither Kolchak nor Lenin was much interested, however, and soon the Chernovites slipped away into exile or obscurity. The minority left wing of the SR Central Committee, meanwhile, apparently more embittered at the treatment of their colleagues by Kolchak, followed Vol′skii, Klimushkin

As the SRs were acting out the final chapter of their political collapse at Ufa and Cheliabinsk, the first steps towards a practical opposition to the Kolchak régime were being taken quite separately in western Siberia. Just five days after the coup, the 2nd Underground Conference of Siberian Bolsheviks (also known as the 1st All-Siberian Conference in recognition of the broader geographic representation than had been present at the previous gathering, in August) was assembling in a worker's house at Tomsk. This conference roundly denounced the 'democratic illusions' of the SRs, placed what was left of the Siberian Bolshevik organization on 'a war footing' and ordered the rapid preparation of an all-Siberian rising against the White dictatorship. At the same time, however, it sanctioned planning for smallscale, localized revolts as diversionary tactics and as preliminaries to the general rising.[207] A newly elected Bolshevik *oblast'* committee (*obkom*) then moved to Omsk and, in co-operation with the capital's Bolshevik committee, initiated preparations for an armed revolt, establishing party cells among the Omsk railwaymen, the garrison and the 10,000 or so POWs held at the Omsk military *gorodok* (cantonment).[208] What subsequently transpired is of interest not simply as an example of the ferocity with which the forces of White Siberia were to crush one of what became a series of Bolshevik revolts at urban centres during the winter of 1918 to 1919, but also as a startling illumination of the fact that neither the Council of Ministers nor Kolchak himself could enjoy any real authority on the streets of their own capital.

The Bolshevik *obkom* had scheduled the Omsk rising for the early hours of December 22nd, little knowing that spies in their midst had revealed everything to Kolchak's intelligence services and the local militia. Shortly before midnight on

and Sviatitskii to Moscow for an ill-fated attempt to co-operate with the Soviet government. See *K prekrashcheniiu voiny vnutri demokratii (Ufimskie peregovory i nasha positsiia).* Moscow (1919), p. 48; and, for a Soviet analysis, Chemeriskii, I.A. 'Eserovskaia gruppa "Narod" i ee raspad', in *Bankrotstvo melkoburzhuaznykh partii Rossii, 1917–1922gg.* Moscow (1977), pp. 77–86.

207 Molotov, K. *Kontrrevoliutsiia v Sibiri.* Saratov (1921), pp. 18–24; Vegman, V. 'Sibirskaia oblastnaia organizatsiia RKP(b) pri Kolchake', *Sibir'* No. 4 (1925), pp. 22–5.

208 For details of the preparation of the Omsk rising, which was admitted by Soviet historians to have been woefully inadequate, see Kolmogorov, N.S. *Vosstanie omskikh rabochykh protiv Kolchaka, 22 dekabria 1918g.* Omsk (1957), pp. 10–21; Naumov, N.V. *Omskie bol'sheviki.* Omsk (1960), pp. 65–8; and Cheremnov, S.G. 'Omskoe vosstanie: vospominaniia', in Spirin, L.M. (ed.) *Razgrom Kolchaka: vospominaniia.* Moscow (1969), pp. 239–48.

December 21st, therefore, when a series of raids were conducted against party headquarters at 105, Krasnoiarsk Street and other addresses around Omsk, the Bolsheviks were caught unawares. Eighty-eight members of the party were captured. Thirty-three of the prisoners, including the entire Military Revolutionary Committee of the *obkom*, were executed on the spot. Those party leaders still at large, finally realizing that their plans had been betrayed, then voted to call off the rising. However, probably as Kolchak's police had hoped in delaying their raid until the last possible moment, many messengers could not get through to deliver the cancellation order or, in the confusion, were not believed. Consequently, at the appointed hour of 2.00 a.m. on December 22nd, Bolsheviks, workers and mutineer soldiers of the 20th Siberian Infantry set about their previously appointed tasks at locations around the city. The rebels secured a tenuous hold on some of their objectives (being particularly successful in the industrial suburb of Kulomzino Station and the workers' district of Novo-Omsk); but, at first light, two battalions of Ivanov-Rinov's Siberian Cossacks and a Czechoslovak machine gun detachment commanded by Colonel Zaichek tore into the poorly armed and isolated rebel redoubts with, regretted Guins, 'exceptional severity'.[209] The Cossacks had only arrived in Omsk the previous day, clearly in anticipation of a turkey shoot – and they were not to be disappointed. The razzia continued throughout the day of December 22nd. According to official figures 247 rebels were killed during the fighting.[210] But that was certainly an underestimate of the blood-letting: an Omsk Bolshevik estimated that at least 900 were killed; the British colonel, John Ward, reckoned it must have been at least 1,000; SR estimates were even higher, ranging from 1,500 to 2,500 deaths.[211]

This butchery, however, did not sate Ivanov-Rinov's bloodlust. As the rising was being suppressed during December 22nd he posted an emergency order (No. 160)

209 Guins, *Sibir'*, Vol. 2, p. 96. On the course of the rising see, from the SR point of view, Kolosov, E.E. 'Kak eto bylo? Massovye ubiistva pri Kolchake v dekabre 1918g. i gibel' N.V. Fomina', *Byloe* (Petrograd) Vol. 21 (1923), pp. 270–3; and, from the Bolshevik side, Zubov, A.I. 'Vosstanie 22 dekabria 1918g.', in *V ogne revoliutsii i grazhdanskoi voiny; vospominaniia uchastnikov*. Omsk (1959), pp. 124–8.

210 *Sibirskaia rech'* (Omsk) No. 113, 28.xii.1918.

211 *Iz istorii grazhdanskoi voiny*. Moscow (1960–1961), Vol. 1, pp. 454–5; Ward, p. 102; Rakov, D.F. *V zastenkakh Kolchaka: golos iz Sibiri*. Paris (1920), pp. 16–17; Burevoi, K.S. *Kolchakovshchina*. Moscow (1919), p. 29.

to the Siberian Army, demanding that all 'provocateurs' be brought before especially established field courts at the Omsk barracks.[212] Kolchak himself was to issue a similar order on December 22nd (Order No. 81 of the Supreme Ruler),[213] but this must have been some time later in the day, for it was not until the *afternoon* of the 22nd that the dictator learned from Chief of Staff Lebedev that Ivanov-Rinov had placed the capital under martial law. In other words, Kolchak's order was clearly designed to foster the illusion that, although bed-ridden, the Supreme Ruler was in control of events. That in reality, however, sheer panic reigned in the government throughout December 22nd, as Cossack bands roamed the town kicking down doors, setting homes ablaze, rounding up suspected workers and beating, whipping and killing at will, may be judged from Guins' candid response to a contemporary interviewer at Omsk: 'To interfere in the direction of the military's suppression of the rising was impossible', he admitted. All that the ministers could do was maintain a facade of calmness. As for Ivanov-Rinov's Order No. 160, 'on what grounds he gave such an order, who gave him the right, I don't know', Guins was obliged to confess, adding only that 'Minister of Justice Starynkevich was unable to issue a protest.'[214]

There is no record of any person brought before the military courts over the following days having been found not guilty. All that has been preserved are official figures, once again undoubtedly deflated, which record that 166 were executed on the banks of the Irtysh and that 37 were sentenced to hard labour.[215]

But the horror did not end there. During the rising the Bolshevik-led rebels had briefly managed to capture the Omsk prison, from where they released over two hundred internees. Of these 134 were political prisoners, including the batches of SRs and members of the Constituent Assembly only recently arrested in the Urals on Kolchak's orders.[216] On December 22nd the new Commander of the Omsk Garrison, General Brzhezovskii, duly ordered that the escapees should return at once

212 *Russkaia armiia* (Omsk) No. 27, 23.xii.1918.

213 *Pravitel'stvennyi vestnik* (Omsk) 24.xii.1918; Varneck and Fisher, p. 199.

214 Guins, *Sibir'*, Vol. 2, p. 96. The Minister of Justice and the Omsk Legal Chambers did not even know that the military court was in session until the Public Prosecutor, Korshunov, went personally to enquire of the Commander of the Omsk Garrison on December 23rd. See Konstantinov, M (ed.) 'Omskie sobytiia pri Kolchake (21–23 dekabria 1918g.)', *Krasnyi arkhiv* (Moscow) Vol. 7 (1924), p. 212.

215 *Sibirskaia rech'* (Omsk) No. 113, 28.xii.1918.

216 Konstantinov, Vol. 7, pp. 209, 212.

to the prison or risk being shot on sight, together with anyone harbouring them.[217] Although the safety of those families and friends with whom the escaped SRs were by now hiding was clearly put at risk by this order, in retrospect it seems incredible that, somehow still trusting in the democratic and law-abiding façade of the Kolchak government, nineteen of the Ufa contingent did not take the opportunity to make good their escape from Omsk, but complied with Brzhezovskii's order and voluntarily returned to the prison during the 22nd to attempt to negotiate a pardon.[218] Fomin, Deviatov and Bruderer, it is true, felt sufficiently unsure of their captors to phone Starynkevich to obtain a guarantee of their safety before they surrendered. But surely the experience of the previous months should have informed them that members of the Omsk government had little influence over its renegade military. Moreover, already on December 17th the SR prisoners at Omsk had learned that a group of intoxicated officers had arrived at the jail and demanded that Fomin, Deviatov and Speranskii should be handed over to them. They had, of course, no written orders, and on that occasion the prison governor, one Veretennikov, had been able to persuade the officers to desist and go away.[219] But the military were clearly growing impatient. And precisely because it had since come to the barracks' ears that (far from being tried at a court martial) the SRs were actually likely to be freed, precisely because the Omsk Public Prosecutor had since dismissed the charges against the SRs for lack of evidence, and precisely because the Supreme Ruler was said to have lost interest in the case and had sanctioned a general pardon,[220] precisely because of all this it was unlikely that the army would again deny themselves the pleasure of having these 'semi-Bolsheviks' lynched. Yet the SRs obediently returned to prison.

When Natalia Fomina arrived at the Omsk prison gates at 9.00 a.m. on the following morning (December 23rd) bearing food and clothing for her husband and his colleagues, she was to find that the army had, indeed, not denied itself its bloody revenge: she found that the prison was now under new management – the too

217 *Russkaia armiia* (Omsk) No. 28, 24.xii.1918.

218 Konstantinov, Vol. 7, pp. 212–13.

219 *ibid.*, Vol. 8, pp. 180–1.

220 Varneck and Fisher, pp. 191–2; Guins, *Sibir'*, Vol. 2, p. 75. 'I personally do not want these prisoners', Kolchak had told the Minister of Justice, on eventually being informed that men unconnected with the telegram of November 19th were being held. See Kolosov, 'Kak eto bylo', p. 268.

scrupulous Veretennikov had been replaced by an appointee of Lebedev – and, despite all their guarantees from the government, Fomin and many other political prisoners had disappeared during the night. Fomin's distraught wife, together with Sofia Deviatova, then rushed to the Ministry of Justice to find out what had happened. All that Starynkevich – the man who had guaranteed the returnees' safety – could tell the women, however, was that he knew absolutely 'nothing definite' of their husbands' whereabouts, and could say 'only that it appears some people have been executed'.[221] The women then petitioned Guins, who could be of no more assistance and who was even more pessimistic: 'We, the civilian authorities, are in such a state of confusion', he confessed. 'The military run everything now… I am afraid it is too late to do anything.'[222]

For the next few hours the two women combed the town, trying to ignore the rumours reaching their ears of what had befallen their husbands and the others who had returned to prison – rumours increasingly horrendous, but which could not have prepared them for the shambles they were eventually to uncover on the banks of the Irtysh. Sifting through the snow there at around 2.00 p.m., within sight of Kolchak's official residence, the searchers came across a grisly pile of disfigured corpses. First was revealed the body and severed head of Markovetskii and the grim remains of Bruderer, whose face was so smashed that his own wife could only identify him by the pattern on those few parts of his shirt not soaked in blood. Next was found the corpse of Lissau, his head cut cleanly in half. Deviatov's remains were not among those uncovered, but more and more corpses were pulled from the snow or found simply lying near the water until, eventually, Natalia Fomina guessed that one body with a red beard on the remains of its smashed face had to be that of her husband (although she could not be sure until a closer inspection revealed the initials 'N.F.' she had herself once embroidered upon his now torn and filthy clothes).[223]

Later that day an autopsy performed on Fomin's corpse by a sympathetic doctor revealed the full horror of the attack: Dr N. Kabalkin certified that of the thirteen serious wounds on the body only five had been directly responsible for Fomin's death – two sabre strokes which had cut through each shoulder and diagonally into the torso (a mounted Cossack's trademark method of despatch) and three bullet

221 Konstantinov, Vol. 8, p. 176.

222 Kolosov, 'Kak eto bylo', p. 277.

223 *ibid.*, pp. 278–9; Rakov, p. 17; Konstantinov, Vol. 8, pp. 176–7.

wounds to the body and head; eight more wounds, of a purely mutilating character, the doctor judged to have been inflicted after death.[224] Clearly, whoever had killed Fomin had been infused by a hatred so intense that they had not even followed the 'normal' course of such brutalities – torture, then slow, agonizing execution. Rather, the killers had been so anxious to see Fomin safely on his way to 'the Kingdom of the Irtysh' that only after swiftly murdering him had they allowed themselves the macabre pleasure of disfiguring his body.

What was the meaning of this unnatural massacre? Kolchak was later to tell his inquisitors at Irkutsk that, far from being an example of his officers' vicious and blind revanchism against the representatives of democracy in Russia, 'this was an act directed personally against me, in order to discredit me in the eyes of the foreigners'.[225] There certainly were rumours in Omsk at the time that Ivanov-Rinov and other monarchistic officers, who had not understood the purely symbolic nature of Kolchak's reception of the Omsk Bloc and the other democratic trappings of the régime, had 'thrown the corpses of the members of the Constituent Assembly in Kolchak's face as a challenge': angered by what they saw as his pandering to society and by his close relations with the British (the monarchists favoured co-operation with Japan), it was said, Ivanov-Rinov and his cronies intended to remove the 'upstart' Kolchak and replace him with Michael Romanov, who was still rumoured to be in hiding somewhere in Siberia.[226] And certainly Vologodskii was concerned enough, as the Cossacks roamed the streets on December 22nd–23rd, to request (and receive) a contingent of British troops of the Middlesex Battalion to guard Kolchak's palace and the Council of Ministers which was in session there.[227] However, although there may well have been monarchists at the very highest level of Kolchak's army (and, indeed, in his personal entourage), as one

224 Parfenov, *Uroki proshlogo*, pp. 85–6. Dotsenko, who attended the autopsy and once owned a photograph of Fomin's corpse, recalled that the body had seventeen wounds. See Dotsenko, 'The Struggle for the Liberation', p. 76.

225 Varneck and Fisher, p. 201.

226 Kolosov, 'Kak eto bylo', p. 266; Zenzinov, p. 145. Ivanov-Rinov's animosity towards Kolchak dated back to October 1918 when the admiral, whom (as a sailor) the general and his clique at Omsk regarded as 'not suited to such a role', had replaced Ivanov-Rinov as Minister of War to the Directory – see Eikhe *Oprokinutyi tyl*, pp. 96–102. Rumours of the presence of Mikhail Romanov continued throughout 1919 – see, for example, *Sibirskaia rech'* (Omsk) No. 116, 3.vi.1919, which reports a sighting of him at Irkutsk.

227 W0 95/5433 'Monthly War Diary of the 23rd Middlesex, No. F413 (22.xii.1918)'.

British officer attested,[228] the ludicrous nature of the assertions of another, Colonel Ward, rather give the lie to any definite plot to unseat Kolchak. Ward states in his memoirs that the events of December 22nd–23rd were indicative of a joint 'monarchist-Bolshevik' plot against democracy, as personified by Kolchak.[229] The wrongheadedness of such a charge is typical of the confusion and fear which reigned in this 'Mexico with snow and frosts'. Faint hearts could conjure up a conspiracy behind every door – and quite often there was one. In this case, however, what the elements of the army behind the Omsk events probably had in mind was not to remove Kolchak, but simply to make it clear once and for all who held the reins of the White movement. And they made that very clear. That, perhaps, was why Kolchak turned down requests from the Council of Ministers on December 25th to authorize an official investigation into the massacre and to rule that the army should 'confine itself to military activities':[230] perhaps the death of Fomin and the others had convinced him that the army was a law unto itself.

Eventually, on January 14th 1919, the Supreme Ruler was persuaded by the representations of the Omsk legal establishment to authorize an inquiry, chaired by Senator A.K. Viskovatov. Having entrusted the case to Viskovatov, however, Kolchak recalled that he then 'forgot all about it'.[231] Certainly from his ill-informed and confused replies to his inquisitors at Irkutsk with regard to this affair, it has to be doubted whether he ever read any of the reports sent to him from Viskovatov over the coming months. Of course the admiral was busy with the conduct of the war, but perhaps he was only too glad to be so – for the reports would not have made pleasant reading for the 'real dictator'. Perhaps, in fact, Kolchak feared that a thorough investigation of the Omsk massacre would reveal, in the stark black and white of corpses silhouetted against the Omsk snow, the rotten heart of his régime. Was it for this reason that he was reported to have broken down in tears upon hearing of the murder of Fomin and his colleagues? It could surely not have been grief for the dead or bereaved, for Kolchak was no friend of the SRs.

228 Nielson, 'Extracts from my Diary' (*Pares Papers*, Box 43), p. 1.

229 Ward, p. 155.

230 Vologodskii, 'Dnevnik' (*Hoover Archives*), p. 273, cited in Dotsenko, *The Struggle for a Democracy*, pp. 72–3. The Omsk Bloc too was urgently demanding an official inquiry into the affair and 'exemplary legal retribution'. See 'A Declaration of the Omsk Bloc Regarding the Events of 21st–23rd December' (*Pares Papers*, Box 28).

231 Varneck and Fisher, p. 207.

Was it at that moment that this sick, enervated sailor realized the depth of the hypocrisy in which he allowed himself to become involved? In the name of law and order he had allowed himself to be sucked into the criminal and conspiratorial mire of Omsk politics; he had allowed a gang of drunken Cossacks to arrest the Directory and place him in power; he had sanctioned their indiscipline and wilfulness by the very act of accepting the title of Supreme Ruler. He had chosen to ride the tiger and now he dared not dismount.

Certainly, for their part, the leaders of the White Army now knew that they had Kolchak and his government precisely where they wanted them, that they were free to pursue their vicious, vengeful counter-revolution to the bloody conclusion they desired, behind a façade of constitutionalism and legality. For to the very face of the Supreme Ruler, without fear of punishment, Ivanov-Rinov could now sneer: 'Remember, it remains only for me to pull the trigger and not a trace of you, admiral, would remain.'[232]

Although Viskovatov's inquiry was not given the chance to reach any definite conclusions, from the various materials it gathered and from the supplementary findings of a Soviet enquiry in 1920, it is nevertheless possible to draw a fairly clear picture of what befell Nils Fomin and those other members of the Constituent Assembly who had been unwise enough to return themselves to the hands of the White military, forsaking the chance to escape offered to them by the rising of Bolshevik workers during the night of December 21st–22nd 1918. The conclusions to be drawn match what we have surmised to have been Kolchak's fears about the affair; and they directly contradict the public statements of the Minister of Justice, Starynkevich, who claimed that the killings were a cut and dried case of a 'spontaneous lynching' (*samosud*) instituted by ungovernable (and, by implication, junior) officers in the heat of the suppression of the Omsk rising.[233] In fact, the conclusions to be drawn reveal the existence of a cold-blooded, premeditated plot to murder the representatives of a party which elements of the military held to have been responsible for engineering the downfall of Russia and for their own personal losses – a plot, moreover, which was sanctioned at the highest levels of the White

232 Budberg, Vol. 13, p. 280. Similarly, when Ataman Krasil'nikov was reprimanded for having hanged the SR mayor of Kansk (I.P. Stepanov) as retribution for his alleged connivance in a rising there on December 27th, the Cossack chief shrugged it off, saying of Kolchak: 'I set him up and I can remove him!' See Guins, *Sibir'*, Vol. 2, p. 398.

233 Kolosov, 'Kak eto bylo', p. 291.

military establishment in Siberia. If the motive for the crime was illogical, however – Fomin, for example, had been among the chief instigators of the rising against Bolshevism in 1918, and had personally plotted to assassinate Lenin – it is nevertheless understandable: reason did not come into it; it was a killing for catharsis, a purgative massacre, calculated to dissipate the frustrations of a dislocated officer class which the revolution was threatening to swallow.[234]

It appears that around 3.00 a.m. on December 23rd, one Captain F. Bartashevskii of Krasil′nikov's Cossack *sotnia* had arrived at Omsk prison with a heavily armed escort and had demanded that six of the recaptured prisoners – most of them Bolsheviks – should be handed over to him for transfer to a court martial.[235] As authorization he showed the new governor of the prison, Khlybov, an order signed by the Chairman of Ivanov-Rinov's newly instituted Military Field Court, and was duly allowed to march the six men off to the garrison headquarters, where the court was sitting in a special night-time session. Just outside the prison gates one prisoner, the *krasnoarmeets* (Red Army soldier) Rudenko, was shot by a Cossack 'whilst trying to escape'. The column then waited whilst another prisoner (a Bolshevik called Makov) was extracted from the jail to take the dead man's place, before continuing on to the court, where sentences were handed out in a matter of minutes: Maevskii got ten years' hard labour; Makov and Vintner were not charged but were ordered to be returned to prison pending further investigations; Bachurin, Zherov and Fateev were sentenced to death. Viskovatov's enquiry was to find that the court did not have the authority to try these men. Nevertheless, it was done. Strangely, moreover, none of the sentenced or remanded men were taken back to prison or to a place of execution. Instead they remained at the garrison, whilst Bartashevskii was sent off to fetch another batch of prisoners for trial.

Meanwhile, however, a Captain Rubtsov, Head of the Omsk Officer Training School, had appeared at the prison. He was acting, he later admitted, on the direct orders of General V.V. Brzhezovskii, the Commander of the Omsk Garrison, and of Brzhezovskii's assistant, Colonel Sabel′nikov. Rubtsov demanded of governor Khlybov that a further five of the political prisoners who had been freed and had

234 For a full obituary of Fomin see *Sibirskaia kooperatsiia* (Novonikolaevsk) 1919, No. 1, pp. 1–13. The following account of the events of 22nd–23rd December 1918 is drawn from the documents published by Konstantinov, Vol. 7, pp. 201–46 and Vol. 8, pp. 176–92; and Subbotovskii, *Soiuzniki i russkie reaktsionery*, pp. 288–300.

235 The six were Bachurin, E. Maevskii (V.A. Gutovskii), Vintner, Rudenko, Fateev and Zherov – all Bolshevik commissars or *krasnoarmeetsy*.

then surrendered themselves should be handed over to him for trial on the basis of Kolchak's Order No. 81. The fact that the Supreme Ruler's order applied only to those who had 'participated in the disorder' was apparently forgotten, for all of the men named by Rubtsov had actually been in prison at the time of the rising and had played no part in its planning or execution. On further inspection, however, it was revealed that only two of those indicted by Rubtsov had returned to prison the previous day; and these – the SR I.I. Deviatov and the Menshevik E.I. Kirienko (both members of the Constituent Assembly) – Rubtsov took away. Outside the prison, in accordance with Brzhezovskii's orders, they were placed among a group of forty-four of the soldiers who had abandoned their posts at the prison during the rising (and who had therefore been judged to be Bolsheviks and had already been condemned to death – not so much for their crimes as the fact that there were not enough cells at the prison to accommodate them). Faced with the taxing problem of forty-four troublesome mutineers who were going to be shot anyway and a pair of Constituent Assembly members who had not yet been to court, Rubtsov (or, according to him, his assistant Iadrishenko) decided to cut through the red tape and had Kirienko and Deviatov shot on Tobol′sk Street for 'inciting revolt amongst the guard' and for 'slandering the Supreme Ruler'. The mutineer soldiers, according to plan, were then taken to a mass grave already prepared in the Zagorodnaia Roshcha and put to death – the bodies of the two SRs were tossed in with them – although it was only at 6.00 a.m. that morning, at least three hours after the event, that the Chairman of the Military Court signed the order for the soldiers' execution.

It was precisely as Rubtsov was leading his group of prisoners out of the jail that Bartashevskii arrived for his second contingent. This time he too cited Kolchak's Order No. 81 (suggesting, perhaps, that he too was now operating under orders from Brzhezovskii). However, the four men he demanded from the governor were all unavailable: Kudriatsev and Deviatov had already been taken care of, Mikel′son had been wise enough not to return to prison and the Bolshevik K.A. Popov (later to be the chief of Kolchak's inquisitors at Irkutsk) was in quarantine at the prison hospital with typhus. Not to be deterred, Bartashevskii then requested a list of the names of all members of the Constituent Assembly currently held in the prison. When this was presented to him he checked off the names over the telephone with a Lieutenant Chuchin of Kolchak's staff (a man who was well acquainted with those arrested at Ufa), before returning the list to Khlybov as a list of men to be tried by the court martial. Moments later he left the prison, taking with him under guard the SRs N.V.

Fomin, A.A. Bruderer, G.N. Sarov and M.V. Lokt′ev and the Mensheviks N.Ia. Barsov, V.A. Markovetskii and A.I. Lissau, together with a certain von Mek who was not a member of the Constituent Assembly.

If Bartashevskii had ever intended that the eight should stand trial, by the time that he reached the garrison headquarters with them he found that the court had concluded its business for the night and gone home. Once again, however, the enterprising captain was not to be deterred: he simply herded his new group together with the five of the first group who still remained at the court building (Vintner, for reasons unaccounted for by the enquiries, was no longer present by this point) and marched all thirteen off to one of the Cossacks' favourite killing fields on the banks of the Irtysh. Sarov and Lokt′ev were reportedly shot en route – 'whilst trying to escape', of course – and their bodies were never found. The remaining eleven reached their destination around dawn and were cold-bloodedly hacked to death or shot, before their corpses were cruelly mutilated. Only three of those killed had actually been both tried and sentenced to death by the military court.

This was clearly not a spontaneous *samosud*: it was a premeditated political murder, born of pent-up frustration married with blind prejudice. And in private, contrary to his public statements, Minister Starynkevich had to admit as much.[236] Bartashevskii, Rubtsov and their assistants were following the instructions of the Commander of the Garrison, Brzhezovkii, who in turn may well have been acting on the authority of Ivanov-Rinov or of their own immediate superior, one of the most important figures in the White Army, the Commander of Omsk Military District, General A.F. Matkovskii. Certainly some very senior and very influential hand was at work in this affair, for it frustrated every attempt of Senator Viskovatov to reach a final conclusion in his investigation. Although it could not offer final proof, his commission of inquiry was adamant that 'certain officers, especially agitated against the Bolsheviks and anyone who, in their opinion, was associated with them', had been 'unable to bear' the fact that only three of the first group of Bartashevskii's prisoners had been sentenced to death by the field court and, before any semblance of calm or order might return to the town in the wake of the rising, had determined to extract their own justice. Consequently, they had killed all fifteen

236 Kolosov, 'Kak eto bylo', p. 293.

political prisoners 'as Bolsheviks', including the nine members of the Constituent Assembly.[237]

However, Viskovatov was unable to act and bring the culprits to justice because the chief of these 'certain officers', Bartashevskii, together with a number of his Cossack henchmen, were provided with false passports and (early in the new year) were sent away to the sanctuary of Semipalatinsk – the remote fastness of the renegade Ataman Annenkov – beyond the reach of a mere Omsk senator.[238] Likewise, the Chief of the Military Court, Ivanov, and his two assistants, returned to their base at Tomsk and refused to come back to Omsk to face questioning. Finally, Brzhezovskii too was sent by his superiors on a long reconnaissance trip to the distant Altai.[239]

Even had this deliberate and blatant wrecking of Senator Viskovatov's efforts not transpired, however, it is doubtful whether any charges would have been pressed against the 'certain officers'. With the military in such a hawkish mood and with all Omsk simply frozen with terror in the wake of the massacre, the Minister of Justice himself admitted to one of Fomin's friends that no public investigation which valued the life of its prosecutors and witnesses would dare to indict any officer – presuming, he added, that prosecutors would be willing to work or witnesses willing to testify against the army in open court.[240]

The pattern of political violence on the part of the military, which had begun in the summer of 1918 with the murder of Novoselov and Moiseenko, had thus reached its bloody consummation. Omsk, the White capital, had been christened in blood. For some time its populace was stunned, fearful of condemning the rampaging White army, but eventually a moderate newspaper gave its apocalyptic verdict:

237 Konstantinov, Vol. 7, pp. 216–7.

238 *ibid.*, Vol. 7, pp. 205–6. Bartashevskii did eventually return to Omsk, and both he and Chuchin were brought in for questioning by the commission. However, they were foolishly released on bail, whence they slipped away into the closed mass of the army and obscurity. See *ibid.*, Vol. 8, pp. 185, 190.

239 *ibid.*, Vol. 7, pp. 220, 217; Subbotovskii, p. 295.

240 Kolosov, p. 293. In a contemporaneous case, noted Kolosov, even the Public Prosecutor commissioned to try the Deputy Chief of Militia at Omsk, who was charged with masterminding a huge diamond robbery, refused to appear in court after having received a death threat from one of Krasil'nikov's Cossacks.

> We are returning to the prehistoric period of human history. We are verging on the death of human civilization and the culture for which so many generations of our more worthy ancestors laboured.[241]

Never again would the flag of the Constituent Assembly of 1917 fly above the Siberian counter-revolution – rather, as people said at the time, that banner had been torn up to be used as foot-rags by the Whites – and, for at least the next six months, Kolchak's government would be unable to pretend, even to itself, that it was anything other than a mere appendage to the imprescriptible and revanchist army. Of course, some of the Supreme Ruler's less intelligent ministers and the Kadets who fawned upon him were not immediately alive to the true meaning of what had occurred – some were even pleased to praise the 'forcefulness' of the army's suppression of the Omsk rebellion.[242] Moreover, noted a British observer, even some of the more intelligent members of the Council of Ministers – those who could see that the army was making a mockery of their attempts to establish a legitimate government on a 'law and order' platform – were loath to criticize, let alone chastise, the army in public.[243] They knew – and Kolchak himself said much the same thing – that an equally essential key to legitimacy in wartime was not the law but success on the battlefield. No matter what the failings of the government, it could still see hope and a future for itself among the fruits of military victory – particularly if that victory could be quickly won. For that, they knew, material support from abroad would be necessary. What was significant, therefore, was not what the régime really *was*, but what it *appeared* to be from the distance of London, Paris and Washington. Consequently, we find Guins, who must certainly have known better in his heart, instructing Kolchak's ambassadors abroad to inform the publics of their hosts that the events of December 21st–23rd at Omsk had been 'insignificant'; whilst others, with some success, did their best to keep Allied diplomatic representatives and pressmen in Siberia in ignorance of the massacre.[244]

241 Cited in Mel'gunov, S.P. *Tragediia admiral Kolchaka (iz istorii grazhdanskoi voiny na Volge, Urale i v Sibiri).* Belgrade (1930–1931), Vol. 3, Part 1, p. 57.

242 *Sibirskaia rech'* (Omsk) No. 112, 26.xii.1918.

243 FO 371/4096/128846 'Memorandum by Mr Peacock (HM Vice Consul at Krasnoiarsk) on the Political Situation in Krasnoiarsk, 25.v.1919.'

244 M. Girs File (*Hoover Archives*) cited in Dotsenko, *The Struggle for a Democracy*, p. 73. The London *Times* was furnished with only a very brief and inaccurate account of the events by its correspondent at Omsk (see *The Times*, 30.xii.1918). And even the generally well-informed and

Any embarrassment officials might have felt at having to engage in such duplicity, however, was soon happily deflected by news from the front. Since November, in an operation which had been initiated by General Boldyrev and confirmed by Kolchak, the Siberian Army under General Gajda had been steadily advancing through the northern Urals from Ekaterinburg. There, in what the Bolsheviks came to call, from their point of view, 'the Perm catastrophe', with fresh troops drawn from the Siberian conscriptions of the summer and autumn, Gajda was able to brave the winter frosts approaching –35 degrees to throw the 3rd Red Army back some 200 km in a month. Ultimately, on December 24th–25th his men entered the city of Perm (a *guberniia* centre and the focus of an important industrial-metallurgical district), where they captured no less than 31,000 prisoners, 120 field guns, 9 armoured trains, 260 locomotives, 5,000 railway carriages and the veritable arsenal which was the Motovilovka armaments factory.[245] 'The Soviet 3rd Army Corps has been ANNIHILATED!' Britmis was informed.[246] What the Omsk *stavka*'s information had (mistakenly, as we shall see) led them to believe was by far the largest and most dangerous of the Red Armies had been routed and the news of the Perm victory was fanfared around the world. The timing, of course, could not have been more perfect or fortunate for Kolchak. As Lev Krol sighed: 'And so here was repeated the same old story – external victory diverts attention from the internal disease.'[247] The coup, the massacre and all the other illegalities surrounding the establishment of the White régime at Omsk had been vindicated overnight, as it gloried in victory in the field.

There was especial rejoicing in the army itself, recalled one who was at Perm: 'People believed, or wanted to believe, that the future was now clear, bright and of unlimited happiness', said General Klerzhe.[248] Others in the Urals noticed how the victory of the Siberian Army at Perm led immediately to a tendency among White officers to belittle the contribution of the Czechoslovak Legion and to a hubristic

inquisitive American consul, Mr Harris, was only able to report that 'a small rising in a village near Omsk was suppressed'. See *FRUS: 1918*, Vol. 2, p. 463.

245 *FRUS: 1918*, Vol. 2, p. 467 and *FRUS: 1919 (Russia)*, pp. 196–7; *The Times* (London) 11.i.1919. On the history of the Perm operation see Eikhe, *Oprokinutyi tyl*, pp. 197–202; and Pazdnikov, N.F. *Bor'ba za Perm': Permskie sobytiia v grazhdanskoi voine*. Perm' (1988), pp. 32–40.

246 WO 106/1284 'Blair (Vladivostok) to WO, 3.i.1919'.

247 Krol', L., p. 160. Serebrennikov was to make almost precisely the same point in his memoirs. See Serebrennikov, *Moi vospominaniia*, p. 237.

248 Klerzhe, pp. 113–14.

boasting by them that Russia could be won without significant Allied aid.[249] At the Omsk *stavka*, meanwhile, a feverish optimism spawned plans for the rapid commencement of a general spring offensive against Soviet Russia.[250] In fact, hope sprang so unbridled that some would no longer even content themselves merely with the capture of Moscow. Chief of Staff Lebedev, for example, was henceforth barely able to contain himself in his boundless ambition: looking beyond the defeat of the Bolsheviks, in all seriousness he informed an American visitor to Omsk that with an army the like of which had now been fashioned in White Siberia, he could envisage not only the recapture of the Ukraine, the Baltic coast, Finland and Poland, but 'the realization of the old dream of a Russian Constantinople'.[251]

249 Preston, T. *Before the Curtain*. London (1930), p. 130.

250 Budberg, Vol. 15, p. 340; Janin 'Otryvki', p. 112.

251 Brown, p. 176

Chapter 3

'What Kolchak Wants!': military versus polity in White Siberia

As news of the Siberian Army's victory at Perm began to filter through to western Europe in early 1919, the question of the precise aims of the Kolchak government came to occupy no insignificant place in the minds of the peacemakers then gathering at Paris (to say nothing of observers within Russia). After all, if – as many optimists in the anti-Bolshevik camp believed – the demise of the Soviet government at Moscow was now only a matter of weeks away, then the political programme of the 'Supreme Ruler of All Russia' would obviously have a serious bearing upon any efforts to establish a stable post-war order. However, on the basis of information supplied by the Omsk government since the coup of November 18th 1918, the question of Kolchak's aims was one which nobody either inside or outside Siberia was qualified to answer. As we have seen, in the first days subsequent to the overthrow of the Directory there had been some rather vague promises made of Omsk's commitment to the causes of 'democracy' and 'law and order' so as to assuage any Allied qualms regarding the establishment of the dictatorship. But since that time even a member of the Kolchak coterie would have been hard pressed to cite a single official statement or enactment which gave a more precise indication of the All-Russian Government's political commitments and desires; for, in truth, no such acts had been passed or statements issued during the final weeks of 1918, while the new régime had been preoccupied with disposing of the vestiges of the SR cause in Siberia.

This silence caused some concern among pro-White groups in Europe. As early as January 1919 Russian patriots in Paris, under the leadership of the Kadet, V.A. Maklakov, were warning the Omsk Foreign Ministry that following the Allied victory over Germany 'the spirit of democracy' was in the ascendant; therefore, they urged, it was necessary for Kolchak 'not only to refrain from any steps which might give the impression of preparations for the restoration of privileges, but also to give positive and solemn declarations which might indicate the true face of the Russia of the future'.[1] Subsequently, in the first months of 1919, there ensued a flurry of activity as the Omsk government began to issue declarations of intent in such specific fields as labour relations, industrial organization, finance, land reform and local government, as well as drafting proposals on the future of Russia's national minorities, notification of official attitudes towards the would-be successor states of the Baltic and the Caucasus and plans for the convocation of a new Constituent Assembly. In Siberia itself Kolchak and his ministers began broaching such topics at public meetings and in the press; meanwhile, for the edification of the Allies, groups of White supporters in London and Paris (the Russian Liberation Committee and the Russian Political Conference respectively) reprinted and elaborated upon communications from Omsk's newfound government mouthpiece, the Russian Press Bureau, in pamphlets with such bald titles as 'What Kolchak Wants'.[2]

Even then, however, during the first months of 1919, no substantial details were released of work being done in any sphere of the 'progressive legislation' said to be in the pipeline. This, as will be demonstrated, was partly because little was actually being done and partly because open discussion of political issues would have both highlighted the paucity of White ideas and exacerbated rivalries within the supposedly united anti-Bolshevik camp. Instead it was once again emphasised in early 1919 that 'for the moment the principal duty of the government is to crush the Bolshevist military forces. All other matters are merely subordinate.' In addition it was repeatedly stressed that the government was of a purely provisional nature and, as such, it could and should not make any settlement in political or economic life which might predetermine matters which were the sole prerogative of the future Constituent Assembly.[3]

In fact, it was not to be until the period of the Russian Army's spring offensive of March–April 1919, that any legislation concerning political and economic affairs was actually enacted at Omsk; and even then the new laws remained variously incomplete, contradictory or disappointingly provisional (when not blatantly evasive). Thus, even by the end of May 1919, half a year after having assumed

1 Kim, P.D. (ed.) 'Iz arkhiva organizatorov grazhdanskoi voiny i interventsii v sovetskoi Rossii', *Istoricheskii arkhiv* (Moscow), No. 6 (1961), pp. 69–70.

2 'What Kolchak Wants' [Russian Liberation Committee, London, 1919] in Collins, D.N. and Smele, J.D. (eds.) *Kolchak i Sibir': dokumenty i issledovaniia, 1919–1926*. New York (1988), Vol. 1, pp. 3–4.

3 *ibid.*, p. 4.

supreme power, what Kolchak wanted away from the battlefield was still so unclear in the minds of the Allied leaders (then debating the possibility of recognizing the Omsk régime) that they would request that the Supreme Ruler once more define his programme and commit himself to a set of democratic principles which they enumerated. In due course, in early June, Kolchak would answer to the Allies' satisfaction; but, as ever, he did so in terms hedged about with the White lexicon of non-predetermination and avoided any concrete promises or immediate undertakings.

Nevertheless, it is because of, rather than despite, its incompleteness, that the legislation and elucidation of government policy in White Siberia during the first half of 1919 is worthy of study: its obfuscatory and frequently contradictory nature may provide many insights into the real aims of the various competing groups and personalities at or near the commanding heights of the Omsk régime and may even reveal some clues as to the type of order which the Siberian Whites might have established in Russia proper had they succeeded in defeating the Bolsheviks and capturing Moscow.

The inspiration behind these tentative and, in some cases, disingenuous moves towards the definition of what might be termed a 'Kolchak manifesto' in 1919 had a tripartite character. Firstly, as the Russian Army began to advance across the Urals towards the agricultural and industrial heartlands of Russia – with all the attendant economic and social problems which had not been encountered to the same degree in underdeveloped, landlordless Siberia – it came to be realized at Omsk that, for all the Whites' decrying of politicking, for all their devotion to the military way and for all their reluctance to compete for popularity with a Bolshevik government which they generally regarded as no better than a criminal conspiracy, something would have to be said (if nothing else, with regard to the land question) in order to convince the population that Kolchak was not intent upon the restoration of the old order. Secondly, although 'non-predetermination' remained, publicly, the watchword of the régime, there were those (particularly in the army) for whom that concept had never been more than a convenient excuse for procrastination until such time as they felt strong enough to impose their own will upon Russia; with the Red Army believed to be crumbling after Gajda's victory at Perm, some now held that this time was at hand. (Similarly, among less bullish circles in the government, the new legislation was thought to be timely, for, although they would admit that ultimately supreme authority might have to be transferred to a new Constituent Assembly, it was clear that those responsible for establishing the blueprint of the future régime could expect a privileged position within it – particularly, of course, if they were responsible for defining the rules according to which this proto-parliament was to be summoned.)

Finally, and possibly most significantly from the point of view of Kolchak himself, even before the afore-mentioned Allied note of May 1919, it was becoming apparent that although, above all else, the Russian Army would have to be militarily successful in order to gain the attention and the respect of the outside world, only a régime which committed itself publicly to democratic principles would enjoy the active support and *de jure* recognition of the Allies. And the Supreme Ruler knew that the support and recognition of the powers was essential to his cause on several counts: only recognition would guarantee Russia a place at the Peace Conference and the right to an influence upon the shape of the post-war world which her military efforts of 1914 to 1917 were claimed, by the Whites, to have merited; only Allied support could provide the weapons and matériel necessary for an army based in underdeveloped Siberia to wage a victorious campaign against the Red stronghold in central Russia; only Allied pressure might dissuade Japan from fostering disorder in the Far East by her support of renegade Cossack elements hostile and dangerous to the Omsk régime; and only Allied influence might persuade the still powerful Czechoslovak Legion to desist from anti-government activity, to muzzle its antipathy to Kolchak and even, perhaps, to return to the front.

PART ONE: HOPES AND DISAPPOINTMENTS

As the year 1919 dawned, the rewards to be reaped from Allied goodwill had to be uppermost in the minds of Kolchak and his government, for a number of infelicitous omens for the future of White Siberia could now be descried: in the wake of the European armistice there was serious confusion among the Allied leaders gathering at Paris with regard to the policy to be pursued in Russia; meanwhile, both the disillusioned Czechoslovaks (who were absenting themselves from the Urals front) and the freebooting antics of Ataman Semenov in the Far East were becoming painful and embarrassing thorns in the side of the Supreme Ruler.

These factors were all the more worrying because at least the more sentient members of the Omsk régime were coming to realize that they would be unable to defeat the Bolsheviks without substantial foreign aid.[4] As the rodomontade and euphoria surrounding December's victory at Perm subsided and a more realistic assessment of its significance was made, it was concluded that although the victory might boost morale amongst the troops and although the capture of the important mining district of Kizel and the Motovilovka armaments factory at Perm would certainly ease supply problems to a degree, all was not as bright as had at first been hoped. Investigations had revealed, for example, that of the 5,000 casualties suffered by the Siberian Army during the December operation no less than 494 had been officers whom Kolchak could ill afford to lose.[5] Moreover, many of the widely publicized 31,000 prisoners captured at Perm turned out not to be Red Army soldiers at all. In fact, the 3rd Red Army had retreated in comparatively good order: the majority of the captured men were POWs returning from Germany via Perm to their homes in Siberia.[6] Then, on December 31st 1919, only a few days after the White victory in the north, the central Urals city of Ufa fell to the Bolsheviks. Already in November the Reds had regained control of the factory towns of Izhevsk and Votkinsk. The latter losses, quite apart from denying Kolchak access to arms-producing facilities, were an unpleasant moral blow to the Whites, who had made much in their propaganda of the anti-Bolshevik workers' risings at Izhevsk and Votkinsk of August 1918; but the former, the loss of Ufa, totally negated the success of the Perm offensive which had originally been conceived as the first stage of a flanking operation to *prevent* the 5th Red Army from capturing what was regarded as the gateway to the Urals passes.

At the very best General Dieterichs was now inclined to dismiss both victory at Perm and defeat at Ufa as being 'of merely local significance, without far-reaching results'.[7] However, even Dieterichs would be unable to treat with like indifference the surrender to Red Army forces in late January of Ural'sk and the strategically

4 Without Allied military aid an advance would be 'impossible', said Vologodskii in February 1919. See Mints, I.I. (ed.) 'Vneshnaia politika kontr-revoliutsionnykh pravitel'stv v nachale 1919g. (iz dokumentov Parizhskogo posol'stva)', *Krasnyi arkhiv* (Moscow), Vol. 37 (1929), p. 72.

5 Bradley, J.F.N. *Civil War in Russia*. London (1975), p. 100.

6 Janin, [P.T.C.]M. 'Otryvki iz moego sibirskogo dnevnika', in Kornatovskii, N.A. (ed.) *Kolchakovschina: iz belykh memuarov*. Leningrad (1930), p. 112; WO 106/1251 'Janin (Omsk) to Paris, 11.ii.1919'; FO 371/4095/55982 'Preston (Ekaterinburg) to Eliot (Omsk), 4.i.1919'.

7 WO 33/962/858 'General Bowes (Cheliabinsk) to WO, 4.i.1919'.

important centre of Orenburg astride the Samara–Tashkent railway – particularly as these defeats were to a significant degree the result of the inaction or, worse, the desertion of the very Cossack units which were supposed to be the backbone of the White armies.[8] These were major setbacks for Kolchak; despite the optimistic mood of the *stavka*, the war was clearly going to demand considerable effort and resourcefulness from the Whites.

Kolchak's problems at the front, with the Japanese and their puppets in the Far East, with the Czechoslovaks and with the vacillating policies of the Allies would all be patched up in the first months of 1919. Subsequently, fevered optimism at Omsk and expectations of an imminent Bolshevik collapse would reach a new crescendo at the height of the Russian Army's spring offensive. However, no matter how superficially promising things appeared, none of these issues was completely and satisfactorily resolved; the seeds of the terminal failure to come remained firmly embedded in the fabric of the régime and the only briefly suppressed cacophony of crises which surrounded it. In his memoirs a senior member of Omsk's Ministry of Justice perfectly encapsulated the spirit of the first half of 1919, when he recalled: 'Ah! What joy, what hope...and what disappointment we lived through then!'[9]

The Semenov incident

In the wake of the collapse of Soviet rule in Transbaikalia during the summer of 1918, Ataman Grigorii Semenov (Kolchak's old adversary of the spring at Harbin) had managed, at the third attempt, to lead a motley band of Mongol and Cossack followers with the inflated title of 'The South Manchurian Special Detachment', out of the Chinese Eastern Railway zone and on to Chita, which he captured in September.[10] There, with the financial support of the Japanese Expeditionary Force, Semenov established a personal fiefdom – one which was to surpass Kolchak's government at Omsk in terms both of longevity and brutality. For almost two years,

8 Kakurin, N. *Strategicheskii ocherk grazhdanskoi voiny*. Moscow–Leningrad (1926), pp. 85–96; *Inostrannaia voennaia interventsiia i grazhdanskaia voina v Srednei Azii i Kazakhstane (Tom 1: mai 1919g.–sentiabr' 1919g.)*. Alma-ata (1963), pp. 192ff; *FRUS: 1919 (Russia)*, pp. 196–8.

9 Rudnev, S.P. *Pri vechernykh ogniakh: vospominaniia*. Harbin (1928), p. 260.

10 Detailed accounts of Semenov's operations in early 1918 can be found in two lengthy intelligence reports at FO 371/4094/3298.

while his murderous satraps Ataman Kalmykov and Ungern von Sternberg (the infamous 'Bloody Baron') cast a reign of terror across the Amur and Ussurii regions and the Manchurian marches, Semenov himself held court in his armoured train, 'The Terrible', and acted out his fantasies of power. In June 1918 he had had himself proclaimed *pokhodnii* (battle) ataman of the Transbaikal Cossacks – and reluctant visitors to his court he regaled with plans of leading a mighty Mongol army against Bolshevik Russia and decadent Europe in general in imitation of Ghengis Khan; or he sought to impress them with comparisons between himself and Napoleon.[11] Semenov, however, did not act like a battle ataman or a man of destiny; rather, he restricted himself to mimicking the coiffure of Napoleon and the manners of Ghengis. After seizing Chita, he never again led his men in open battle against the Reds, refused to send troops to the anti-Bolshevik front and lived a life of feasting, wenching and razzia from his eastern enclave.

It has frequently been conjectured that Semenov was insane. But, mad or not, having seized control of territories astride both the Amur and the Chinese Eastern Railways, the ataman was of great moment to Kolchak. Most immediately, it could not be treated lightly that of all the reactions within the anti-Bolshevik camp to news of the Omsk coup his was the most negative. The presence of Czechoslovak forces east of Baikal had induced Semenov to proffer recognition to the earlier régimes at Omsk; but by November the Czechs were no longer a threat, and the toppling of the Directory seemed to offer the perfect opportunity to enhance his own power. Thus, on November 23rd 1918, the ataman despatched an ultimatum to Omsk: having commanded the most active anti-Bolshevik forces in the Far East during 1918, he said, it was only proper that he, Semenov, should have some say in the selection of a new leader for the movement. He adamantly refused to recognize Kolchak even as a candidate for such a post and demanded that supreme power should be immediately transferred to General Denikin, General Horvath or to Ataman Dutov of the Orenburg Cossacks.[12] To show that he meant business, and in a move which threatened to leave the Omsk régime entirely cut off from the outside world,

11 *The Times* (London) 24.iii.1919; Alioshin, pp. 15–16.

12 Maksakov, V.V. and Turunov, A. *Khronika grazhdanskoi voiny v Sibiri*. Moscow–Leningrad (1926), p. 271. In August 1918 Ataman Semenov had refused to recognize the Provisional Siberian Government, but had relented and formally (if not in practice) subordinated himself to Vologodskii's régime when the Czechoslovaks threatened to use force against him. See Golovin, N.N. *Rossiiskoe kontrrevoliutsiia v 1917–1918gg. (Chast' 4: Osvobozhdenie Sibiri i obrazovanie 'belogo' voennogo fronta grazhdanskoi voiny)*. Paris–Tallinn (1937), Vol. 8, p. 48.

Semenov then proceeded to waylay military supply trains at Chita and to sever Kolchak's telegraphic links with Vladivostok.[13] In response the Supreme Ruler hastily issued two orders (Nos. 60 and 61) which denounced Semenov as a traitor and replaced him as Commander of the 5th Amur Corps (a post to which he had been raised by the Provisional Siberian Government) with the newly promoted Colonel Volkov.[14]

The White movement as a whole was deeply riven by personal animosities; and certainly Semenov made no secret at the time that his actions were directed against Kolchak 'personally'.[15] Consequently, inspired by the stern admiral's clashes of earlier in the year with the unruly ataman, there was no shortage of invective in the missives issuing from Chita during the last weeks of 1918: in one statement to the press Semenov made the not altogether unreasonable charge that, theretofore, Kolchak had done nothing for the anti-Bolshevik cause beyond tossing his sword into Sevastopol harbour and had allowed 'self-seeking' political groups at Omsk to use him for their own ends.[16] Another article, belligerently entitled 'What to do with Admiral Kolchak' (part of the Chita brochure *Admiral Kolchak i Ataman Semenov*), was even more abusive: 'Citizens!', it railed, 'Now is a grave political moment and such a mediocre invalid as Kolchak cannot be permitted to be our leader. Away with him! Kolchak himself is ambition personified and if he will not go away of his own accord it will be necessary to remove him.'[17]

Such hostility from Semenov was potentially dangerous; but it was not something which should have been beyond the means of Kolchak to suppress. The ataman boasted that there were some 15,000 warriors in what he now termed his 'Eastern Siberian Army'; but American observers doubted that he controlled more than 3,000, while Volkov, who was sent east to suppress this rebellion against Kolchak, was

13 *FRUS: 1918* Vol. 2, p. 442. Semenov claimed that only messages in codes for which he had not been provided with a key were interrupted. See Zenzinov, V (ed.) *Gosudarstvennyi perevorot admirala Kolchaka v Omske 18 noiabria 1918 goda*. Paris (1919), p. 90.

14 Guins, G.K. *Sibir', soiuzniki i Kolchak: povorotnyi moment russkoi istorii, 1918–1920gg. (Vpechatleniia i mysli chlena Omskogo pravitel'stva*. Peking (1921), Vol. 2, p. 38; Livshits, S.G. '"Verkhovnyi pravitel'" Kolchak i Ataman Semenov (K istorii "semenovskogo intsidenta")', in Korablev, Iu.V. and Shishkin, V.I. (eds.) *Iz istorii interventsii i grazhdanskoi voiny v Sibiri i na Dal'nem Vostoke, 1917–1922gg*. Novosibirsk (1985), pp. 177–8. Volkov was also named Governor General of Transbaikalia, directly subordinate to Kolchak.

15 *FRUS: 1918*, Vol. 2, p. 450.

16 Zenzinov, pp. 94–5.

17 See Alekseev, S.A. (ed.) *Nachalo grazhdanskoi voiny*. Moscow–Leningrad (1926), p. 371.

certain that his loyal troops could dispose of Semenov's band in three or four days.[18] Semenov, however, was only part of the problem. Of the gravest danger to the very viability of the Omsk régime was that the ataman's disruptive activities and accusations were encouraged by elements which Omsk was powerless to quell – namely the Japanese Government and, in particular, the command of the Japanese Expeditionary Force. The latter was still smarting from Kolchak's opposition to its heavy-handed activities in Manchuria earlier in the year and was now further incensed by the fact that, in the very first days of his rule, Kolchak had despatched a most undiplomatic note to Tokyo refusing permission for Japanese troops to be garrisoned in eastern Siberian towns and ruling out the possibility of granting concessions to Japanese businessmen in the Far East.[19] Consequently, in November 1918, the Japanese Foreign Minister sent a message to Semenov saying that 'Japanese public opinion does not approve of Kolchak. You must protest against him'; and, when the required protests resulted in the despatch of Volkov against Chita, General Iuki, the Commander of the Japanese 3rd Division stationed in Transbaikalia, proclaimed that 'Japan will not permit any kind of measures against Semenov and will not stop at armed force to prevent such.'[20] With the 3rd and other Japanese divisions ranged against him in the Far East, Volkov could not proceed beyond Irkutsk and, in fact, was never able to take up his command of the Amur Corps.

As one of the officials at Kolchak's Foreign Ministry surmised, because of Japanese involvement the Semenov incident 'could only be liquidated by diplomatic as opposed to military force'.[21] However, with the Omsk government as yet unrecognized and its ambassadors as yet not admitted by the powers, even this would not be an easy task. Nevertheless, from December 8th–14th 1918, Kolchak attempted to muster the requisite diplomatic arsenal by writing personal notes to the

18 *FRUS: 1918*, Vol. 2, p. 458.

19 Sukin (*Leeds Russian Archive*), pp. 49–56, 106–7.

20 Livshits, pp. 176–7; Rouquerol, J.G.M. *La Guerre des Rouges et des Blancs: l'aventure de l'amiral Koltchak*. Paris (1929), pp. 46–7. On November 12th 1918, the Commander-in-Chief of the Japanese Expeditionary Force, General Oi, had already informed the Directory that his troops alone were responsible for maintaining order in the Far East and in Transbaikalia and that no Russian troops would be allowed to enter the region without his permission. See *United States Military Intelligence. Weekly Summaries*. New York (1978), Vol. 5 (No. 74), p. 70. (Hereafter cited as *USMI*.)

21 Guins, Vol. 2, p. 15.

governments of Britain, France and the USA, bringing Japan's 'interference in Russia's internal affairs' to their attention and requesting advice and assistance in dealing with the matter.[22]

Kolchak was only informing the powers of something of which they were already all too well aware. It was an open secret in 1918 that Japanese policy in the Russian Far East and in Manchuria was based upon the fostering of all types of mischief-makers and miscreants (Semenov was only the most prominent) in order to prevent the establishment of a single, united Russian authority in the region. The aim was to induce the Allies eventually to accept any authority east of Baikal which could stop the chaos – even one which relied upon Japanese troops, one which offered territorial and economic concessions to Japan, and one which would firmly slam shut the 'Open Door' which President Wilson had been attempting to promote in the Far East.[23] Above all Tokyo was determined that the end of the World War would not signal the resurgence of British and American domination of a free market in a region which was now of vital importance to the overheated Japanese economy.[24] By November 1918, therefore, Japan had moved 72,000 troops to the mainland and had established various puppet régimes to ensure that this was not the case; meanwhile Japanese businessmen had seized Russian fishing, forestry and trading companies along the Amur and coal mines on Northern Sakhalin (they had, of course, controlled the southern part of the island since the Treaty of Portsmouth of 1905), whilst military agents took over customs houses on the Russo-Chinese and Russo-Korean borders, regulated the movement of traffic on the railways and despatched teams of geologists to survey the coastline 'for future possibilities'. Quite simply, as a puzzled Bernard Pares noticed on arriving at Vladivostok, 'the Japanese went everywhere tapping the rocks'.[25]

22 *FRUS: 1918*, Vol. 2, p. 461; Livshits, p. 178.

23 As early as the beginning of June 1918, American military intelligence sources had concluded that 'the Japanese do not desire to have order restored by the Russians in Siberia, as in such a case they would have no excuse for their own intervention'. See *USMI*, Vol. 5 (week ending 8.vi.1918), pp. 20–1.

24 Without the markets and raw materials available in the Russian Far East and in Manchuria it was feared that Japan's economic boom of the war years would turn to depression and social conflict (as was apparently presaged by the 'rice riots' of the summer of 1918). On Japanese policy see White, J.A. *The Siberian Intervention*. New York (1950), pp. 161–201 and Morely, J.W. *Japan's Thrust into Siberia*. New York (1950), *passim*.

25 FO 371/3365/181806 'Alston (Vladivostok) to FO, 8.x.1918'; Pares, B. *My Russian Memoirs*. London (1931), p. 509.

Whether the joint *démarche* at Tokyo by the western powers which Kolchak desired would have brought Japan into line cannot be known for sure. In 1918 perhaps it would have done, for Tokyo was not then prepared for the imperial adventures and confrontations Japan would undertake in the 1930s. However, it is unlikely that her long-term aims could have been blocked at this point by an Anglo-American protest on behalf of Admiral Kolchak. For, unfortunately for the Omsk government, Japan was enmeshed in the international web of alliances and post-war rivalries; and although Britain generally thought that Kolchak should be supported, Whitehall was nevertheless reluctant to bring too much pressure to bear upon its Pacific ally and was, unwisely in retrospect, not altogether displeased to witness US–Japanese rivalry in the Far East presenting opportunities for the putative expansion of British interests in the region.[26] Eventually Britain was prevailed upon to join with the USA in requesting that Japan cut her subsidies to Semenov. But the protest was not a strong one – and anyway, there was little that either power could do or say when, on January 6th 1919, Japan replied quite persuasively that until all the powers recognized one authority as the legitimate Russian government she had every right to support Semenov who, unlike Kolchak, at least had a lengthy record of anti-Bolshevik military activity.[27]

The only key to the solution of the Semenov problem, therefore, was the recognition of the Kolchak government; for this, if for no other reason, the achievement of international recognition had to be among Omsk's prime aims in 1919. Over the next few months, to Kolchak's relief, Britain and the USA might persuade Japan to modify her attitude somewhat (in withdrawing half of her troops and in reaching agreement on the international control of Siberian railways, for example) and Japan herself, having realized that Kolchak was not going to disappear overnight, might at least begin to attempt to prize concessions from Russia through negotiations rather than main force. Nevertheless, until recognition was achieved – and, as we shall see, it never was – Tokyo would covertly continue to encourage Semenov in his rape of Transbaikalia and his frustration of the White military effort in Siberia. In February 1919, for example, even whilst making increasingly friendly

26 See Ullman, R.V. *Anglo-Soviet Relations, 1917–1921*. London (1961–1972), Vol. 2, pp. 37–8; and Svetachev, M.I. *Imperialisticheskaia interventsiia v Sibiri i na Dal'nem Vostoke, 1918–1920*. Leningrad (1983), p. 118. There were even those in the British Foreign Office who were of the opinion that if Japan had to have territorial expansion somewhere then the Russian Far East was not a bad place for her to have it. See *DBFP* Vol. 3, pp. 730–1.

27 Ullman, Vol. 2, p. 38.

noises in Kolchak's direction, Japan sponsored a Pan-Mongol Conference at Chita at which Semenov (who paraded himself as a half-Buriat) announced his intention to establish an independent Mongol-Buriat kingdom.[28] This would have effectively cut Russia off from the Pacific and was a direct insult to Kolchak and to all Russian nationalists. However, it was by then obvious that there was really nothing that Omsk could do; Kolchak had, he told Guins, become resigned to the fact that 'it is impossible to subject these atamans to central authority' and, rather than make the attempt, he declared his intention to 'cut loose' from events in the Far East and to deal with the situation there only after matters had been settled in European Russia.[29] Whether this was a realistic policy option, given the complete dependence of the Russian Army on imports through Vladivostok and via Chita, is debatable; and, as his régime disintegrated during the winter of 1919 to 1920, Kolchak would have bitter cause to regret that he could not summon a loyal lieutenant from Transbaikalia to his assistance. However, in late January 1919 it might at least be construed as hopeful that Semenov (in deference to his paymasters' more tactful approach) had ceased to interrupt the telegraph, had informed General Janin that he would recognize Kolchak's leadership (as long as the latter undertook to transfer supreme power to Denikin at the first opportunity) and was even promising to send troops to the front.[30] In return – making the best of what was a hopeless situation and in the forlorn hope of inducing Japan to provide a division or two for the Urals front – Kolchak would eventually return the command of the 5th Amur Corps to Semenov in May 1919.[31]

28 Demidov, V.A. *Oktiabr' i natsional'nyi vopros v Sibiri, 1917–1922gg.* Novosibirsk (1983), pp. 174–5; Speranskii, A.F. 'Rol' Iaponii v "Panmongol'skom dvizhenii"', *Novyi vostok* (Vladivostok), No. 2 (1922), pp. 591–603; Phillips, C.D.R. *Dawn in Siberia – the Mongols of Lake Baikal.* London (1942), pp. 119–24.

29 *FRUS: 1918*, Vol. 2, p. 445; *FRUS: 1919 (Russia)*, pp. 484–5; Guins, Vol.,2, p. 253. In February 1919 an Investigatory Commission sent by Kolchak to Chita reported that in spite of the innumerable 'anti-state' crimes of which he was guilty and in spite of all the well-documented atrocities being committed in his prisons, forcible opposition to Semenov could not be recommended. See Elagin, V.I. (ed.) 'Iz istorii semenovshchiny v 1919g.', *Krasnyi arkhiv*, Vol. 6 (1934), pp. 131–46.

30 Livshits, p. 179; FO 371/4094/13960 'Eliot (Omsk) to FO, 24.i.1919'.

31 *Russkaia armiia* (Omsk) No. 115, 4.vi.1919, *Nasha zaria* (Omsk) No. 117, 4.vi.1919. According to one source, Kolchak's decision to reinstate Semenov was also influenced by pressure brought to bear in the ataman's favour by other Cossack leaders at Omsk. See Sukin (*Leeds Russian Archive*), pp. 242–3.

The Semenov incident was thought, thereby, to be resolved. But it was only superficially so. In reality little had actually changed since November 1918. Japan's ambition in north Asia continued to ferment while, more immediately, her aid to Kolchak was to prove meagre and unreliable; Semenov maintained his potential stranglehold over Kolchak's supply route and would exercise his grip from time to time; and neither Japan nor Semenov would ever send any troops to the front.[32] Moreover, by failing in 1919 publicly and unequivocally to oppose the brutal régime which was established in the Far East by Japan and her Cossack puppets, in the popular mind Kolchak was to become identified and equated with that régime. This fact would not only wreck untold damage upon the White cause by besmirching their nationalist banner with the suspicion of having sold Russian interests and territory to a foreign power, but would also play a part in the personal tragedy which was to befall Kolchak at Irkutsk in 1920.

The pacification of the Czechoslovak Legion

Hardly less abusive than Semenov's defamations of Kolchak, and equally inauspicious for the future prospects of the Omsk régime, was the response of the Czechoslovak Legion to the overthrow of the Directory – a government which, after all, the Legionnaires had done so much to promote during the summer of 1918. Following the Kolchak coup, 'filled with indignation and bitter disappointment, the Legionnaires lost the last of their enthusiasm for the anti-Bolshevik cause', recalled one Czech officer.[33] The soldiery's mute resentment was made articulate on November 21st 1918 when their political leadership, the Czechoslovak National Council at Cheliabinsk, published an open letter to Kolchak, demanding the reinstatement of the Directory and declaring that 'the Czechoslovak Army, fighting for the ideals of freedom and democracy, cannot and will not either unite or co-operate with the makers of *coups d'état* which run contrary to these principles'. The letter, signed by Svoboda and Poteidl, inveighed scathingly against the Russian

[32] In fact, some reports indicated that Semenov was forcibly preventing those who wished to join Kolchak from leaving Chita. See Serebrennikov, I.I. *Moi vospominaniia*. Tientsin (1937), pp. 258–9.

[33] Becvar, G. *The Lost Legion*. London (1939), p. 195.

military which, they alleged, preferred the luxury of political in-fighting in the rear to the sort of privations which the Legion had been enduring on their behalf at the front for the past six months. 'This cannot be allowed to continue', it warned ominously.[34]

Discipline in the Legion and commitment to the anti-Bolshevik cause had been on the wane ever since the Czechoslovaks had achieved, during the summer of 1918, the one aim upon which all sections of their forces were united – the clearing of hostile forces along the railway from the Volga to the Pacific in order to facilitate evacuation. There had, in fact, been instances of mutiny in both August and September and from October Czechoslovak forces had been leaving the front. Now, following the Omsk coup, the disgruntled Bohemians were openly refusing to obey the orders of their pro-Kolchak officers, such as Gajda and Dieterichs (who then chose to join the Russian Army) and looked instead to the socialistic political leadership of their National Council. In December, during the Perm offensive, there ensued a renewed spate of mutinies, as soldiers' committees of the 2nd Battalion of the 5th Czechoslovak Regiment, parts of the 6th Regiment and the entire 7th Regiment refused to go to the front.[35]

It is only possible to feel sympathy for the men of this 'lost legion', for their grievances were many. Over a third of the men whom they had put into this ineffably foreign field in June 1918 had been killed, wounded, were missing presumed dead or were seriously ill by November.[36] Moreover, not only had the Siberian military left them to bear the brunt of the fighting whilst overthrowing a government with which they were in sympathy, but the Allies too seemed to have abandoned them. They had hoped that the armistice would stimulate some definitive statement of Allied policy in Russia and that British, French, American and Japanese forces might be moved to the Urals from their snug billets in the Far East. All that the Legion got in the harsh Siberian winter of 1918 to 1919, however, was a new commander in the shape of General Janin – 'a fat general without troops', as one

34 *Vlast' naroda* (Cheliabinsk) 22.xi.1919, cited in Zenzinov, p. 74.

35 Becvar, p. 203; FO 371/4095/55982 'Preston (Ekaterinburg) to Eliot (Omsk), 4.1.1919'; Golovin, Vol. 8, p. 76.

36 *FRUS: 1918*, Vol. 2, p. 459.

disgusted Czech remarked.[37] The Russian Whites did not even appear to be at all grateful for the service rendered to their cause by their brother Slavs in 1918. Kolchak, for example, would constantly abuse the Legionnaires for trying to 'interfere' in Russian affairs, which he held to be 'absolutely none of their concern'; he would opine that they were 'no good' and maintain that 'the sooner they cleared out the better'.[38] Eliot was properly disappointed at the admiral's 'harsh and ungrateful manner', while Janin reflected: 'These people evidently forget that without the Czechs...they would long ago have ceased to exist.'[39] Such ingratitude in so inhospitable a country must have been hard for the Legionnaires to bear – particularly at a time when their own nations' centuries-long struggle for independence had at last born fruit in the formation of the Czechoslovak Republic on October 28th 1918. Thenceforth they would need little persuasion to leave the White Siberian ingrates to their fate.

The situation was calmed, fleetingly, with the arrival in western Siberia on December 10th 1918 of the new Czechoslovak Minister of War, General Stefanik. This 'soldier's general' was able to convince some Legionnaires that the future of their new state was still dependent upon the goodwill of the Allies, who would not be impressed by mutinies in the Urals. Subsequently, at least one rebel unit returned to the front and it was hoped that the victories at Perm might inspire more to do so.[40] Stefanik, however, was forced to return home because of ill-health; and anyway, he could do nothing to soften the final, shattering blow to the Legion's morale of the news of the massacres at Omsk of December 22nd–23rd. The Czechoslovak soldiery were incensed by the murder of their SR friends; and their protests at the massacre were, in fact, so violent that in the first days of January

37 Becvar, p. 205. On one splendidly embarrassing occasion during November 1918, some British soldiers did actually get as far west as the Czechoslovak-held trenches at the front near Kungur. However, they were only the Hampshires' regimental band, whose spirited renditions of 'God Save the King' and 'It's a Long Way to Tipperary' served only to enrage the nearby Red troops who sent a barrage of artillery fire down upon the unfortunate Legionnaires' positions. The musicians hurriedly reboarded their train and hightailed it back to Omsk. 'All it had done was to supply our pessimists with ample material for their many and not too complimentary remarks', recalled Becvar, (p. 195). See also Ward, J. *With the 'Die-Hards' in Siberia*. London (1920), pp. 118–19.

38 Varneck, E. and Fisher, H.H. *The Testimony of Admiral Kolchak and Other Siberian Materials*. Stanford (1935), p. 163; Guins, Vol. 2, p. 7; *DBFP*, p. 446.

39 Janin, p. 126; *DBFP*, Vol. 3, pp. 730–1.

40 *The Times* (London) 31.xi.1918; Becvar, p. 200; *USMI*, Vol. 6 (No. 85), p. 401; Sukin (*Leeds Russian Archive*), pp. 72–4.

1919, Kolchak had to demand that all of their units be removed from the Urals, lest their discontent spread to Russian troops in the region. On January 13th General Janin duly gave the order for the withdrawal and, thereafter, the Legion ceased to be a factor on the anti-Bolshevik front.[41]

As a damage limitation exercise, it seemed that Omsk could count the Czechoslovak withdrawal as something of a success. True, the Whites had lost the use of the Legion at the front; but at least the Czechoslovaks – who, for all their disillusionment, were still stronger and more concordant than any Russian forces in Siberia – had not followed up their protests against the coup with any physical effort to remove Kolchak in order to reinstate the Directory.[42] On the contrary, negotiations with Stefanik, Janin and the Allied governments in late January procured the invaluable bonus for Kolchak that the Legion would not yet be withdrawn altogether from Siberia, but would instead take up policing duties along the Trans-Siberian Railway between Novonikolaevsk and Irkutsk.[43] This was a vital function, for although the railway – the 4,000-mile-long lifeline of Kolchak's army – was extremely vulnerable to attacks from the growing bands of partisans haunting the east Siberian taiga, Omsk could not have hoped to spare sufficient of its own hard-pressed troops to guard it effectively. Moreover, as long as the Czechoslovaks remained in Siberia, there remained the hope that, after a period of recuperation in the rear, at least part of the Legion might be induced to return to the front.

But again Kolchak's success was more apparent than real. For the moment the Czechoslovaks readily agreed to guard the line – after all, they had a strong vested interest in maintaining their escape route to the east – but they would carry no torch for the Supreme Ruler. It is true that during the spring and summer of 1919 partisan attacks upon the line were beaten off by the Czechoslovaks, but it was only very

41 Bradley, J.F.N. *Allied Intervention in Russia, 1917–1920*. London (1968), p. 115; WO 106/1251 'Janin (Omsk) to Paris, 7.i.1919'; WO 106/1251 'Janin (Omsk) to Paris, 17.ii.1919'.

42 The Czechoslovaks had already been made well aware by the Allied agents in Siberia that any attempt at a counter-coup would be frowned upon in London and Paris. See Krol', L. *Za tri goda: vospominaniia, vpechatleniia i vstrechi*. Vladivostok (1921), p. 160; Boldyrev, V.G. *Direktoriia, Kolchak, interventy*. Novosibirsk (1925), p. 165; Maksakov and Turunov, p. 98; and Pepeliaev, V.N. 'Dnevnik', *Krasnye zori* (1923), No. 4, p. 89. But the truth was that the Legion was by now so thoroughly disillusioned with the Russian political morass that any further intervention was unlikely on their part.

43 Mints, 'Vneshnaia politika', pp. 72, 83; Mazler, V.S. 'Chekhoslovatskii korpus i Kolchak', in *K 50-letiiu osvobozhdenie Sibiri ot kolchakovshchiny*. Tomsk (1970), p. 39.

rarely that they could be persuaded to form punitive detachments and pursue the insurgents into the taiga in order to eradicate them. As early as May 1919, moreover, reports were reaching Omsk of armed mutinies in the 5th Czechoslovak Regiment, while in July an illegal Legion Soviet near Irkutsk had to be broken up by force and its leaders deported. In general, noted one traveller on the Trans-Siberian Railway at this time, in the zone patrolled by the Czechs 'the danger was less, but the disorder was greater'.[44] Moreover, with the exception of a handful of volunteers, no Legionnaires would be persuaded to return to the front, despite the grandiose plans being hatched in Europe (notably by Winston Churchill) to have them fight their way through Russia for evacuation from Odessa or Arkhangel'sk. Instead, anticipating a Pacific evacuation, the Legionnaires tended increasingly to occupy themselves with the commandeering of rolling stock sorely needed by the Russian Army and the government, or with utilizing their dominant position on the railway to line their pockets (some through honest endeavour, others through speculation and black marketeering). The sometimes ostentatious comfort of their brightly painted and comparatively well-furnished carriage domiciles contrasted starkly with the poverty of Russian soldiers, refugees and Siberian workers, who resentfully nicknamed these 'affluent' foreigners '*Chekho-sobaki*' (Czech-dogs) or '*Chekho-svoloch'*' (Czech-scum).[45] And once again Kolchak's own popular reputation was tarnished by association, for the Legionnaires were, however reluctantly, his plenipotentiaries in eastern Siberia.

Like the Semenov problem therefore, the Czechoslovak problem had only been superficially resolved. Resentment was allowed to fester among the Legionnaires throughout 1919 as Kolchak and the Russians continued to contemn them as cowards or robbers, while the Allies, unable to settle upon a definite Russian policy and incapable of providing sufficient tonnage to repatriate the Legion, repeatedly postponed the date of their evacuation. Thus, another element of the fate awaiting Kolchak at Irkutsk in 1920 was firmly in place from the dawn of his dictatorship.

44 *ibid.*, p. 40; Mazler, V.S. 'Chekhoslovatskii korpus, soiuznaia interventsiia i Kolchak', *Baikal* (Ulan-Ude) 1970, No. 5, p. 147; Arnol'dov, V. *Zhizn' i revoliutsiia. Groza piatogo goda. Belyi Omsk*. Shanghai (1935), p. 253.

45 Fleming, P. *The Fate of Admial Kolchak*. London (1963), pp. 77–8; Krusser, G.V. *Kolchakovshchina*. Novosibirsk (1928), p. 29; Gan, A. *Rossiia i bol'shevizmom: materialy po istorii revoliutsii i bor'by s bol'shevizm (chast' pervaia, 1914–1920)*. Shanghai (1921), pp. 285–6.

The spectre of recognition

In the White camp the palladium which would guarantee success in the civil war and the key to the favourable resolution of many problems was widely held to be the attainment of the recognition of the Omsk régime by the Allies as the *de jure* Provisional Russian Government. 'Every branch of our government work to one degree or another came up against the necessity of obtaining the support of the powers – we needed foreign help for the railway, for the army, in the question of trade, of finance and even education', recalled Foreign Minister Sukin. Such assistance could not be relied upon without recognition.[46] Recognition was 'the "spectre" which guided every government act', confirmed a leading general.[47] However, undoubtedly the most serious of the problems facing Kolchak upon his assumption of power was the increasingly indefinite and vacillating policy of the Allies towards the anti-Bolshevik governments in Russia in the wake of the armistice of November 11th 1918.

By November 1918 there had been Allied troops on Russian territory for the best part of a year. Soviet historians, of course, consistently construed this intervention and the concomitant sponsorship of counter-revolution in Siberia and European Russia as being purely anti-Bolshevik in origin and inspiration.[48] Unfortunately for Kolchak and the Whites, however, this was far from being the whole story. Some western statesmen and military leaders may well have welcomed or even planned intervention during early 1918 as the first step in the crushing of the revolution, but its major inspiration had been the creation of a new Eastern Front to keep German troops tied down in Russia, to deny the Central Powers easy access to the natural resources of the Ukraine, the Caucasus, Central Asia and Siberia and to safeguard the massive stockpiles of war materials at Vladivostok, Murmansk and Arkhang-el′sk. Any Russian group which opposed the Treaty of Brest-Litovsk and held out

46 Sukin (*Leeds Russian Archive*), p. 214.

47 Sakharov, K.V. *Belaia Sibir′*. Munich (1923), p. 39.

48 See, for example, Krusser, *Kolchakovshchina*, p. 8 who claimed that 'the Allied intervention in Siberia followed one aim: to encircle Moscow...in an iron ring of counter-revolutionary fronts, thereby to crush the revolution'. The first four decades of Soviet historiography of the intervention are comprehensively surveyed in Thompson, J.M. 'Allied-American Intervention in Russia, 1918–1921', in Black, C.E. (ed.) *Rewriting Russian History: Soviet Interpretations of Russia's Past*. London (1957), pp. 334–400.

against surrender to the Kaiser would, therefore, be supported by the Allies in 1918. These groups, by implication, tended to be anti-Bolshevik in orientation – although it should not be forgotten that Allied agents in Petrograd made an abortive effort in February–March of that year to co-operate with Trotsky and to buttress his opposition to the impending treaty with Germany – but the fact remains that no decision had been taken in any individual Allied capital, let alone by the Allies in concert, which defined the intervention as being primarily or even partly anti-Bolshevik in intention; nor had it even been admitted by November 1918 (at least not by Lloyd George or President Wilson) that intervention had evolved from being anti-German to being anti-Bolshevik in effect, although objectively this was the case by that time. That, for Kolchak, was the whole problem.

Although after November 1918 the intervention was obviously something different to what it had been prior to the German surrender, throughout the following year the Allies would never define what the intervention in Russia had become and what its aims were meant to be. They would not do so because the only conceivable aim of the action could be the overthrow of the Bolsheviks, but, in order to assist the Whites to do that, Paris, London and Washington would have had to commit men and resources on a scale unacceptably massive for the war-weary European countries or the increasingly isolationist Americans. On the other hand, as Lloyd George recalled, the logical alternative – to call a halt to intervention and to sue for peace with the Bolsheviks – was equally unpalatable: that would have entailed the dishonourable abandonment of the White governments which the Allies had called into existence in 1918.[49] No wonder, then, that even by February 1920 Kolchak could complain that 'the meaning and essence of this intervention remains quite obscure to me'.[50]

Had the intervention been unequivocally directed against Lenin and not the Kaiser, as Soviet historians argued, then one might expect the November armistice to have been welcomed rapturously in White Siberia, for it would have freed Allied troops, war materials and finance for a vigorous campaign against Lenin. In fact,

49 Lloyd George, D. *Memoirs of the Peace Conference*. New Haven (1939), Vol. 1, p. 247. Winston Churchill and other conservative MPs regaled Lloyd George in the House of Commons with the need to meet this 'debt of honour' to the anti-Bolsheviks. See *Parliamentary Debates*. London, Vol. 114 (1919), column 374 for a typical intervention by Churchill and *ibid.*, columns 367–8, 374, 756–7, 1327–30, 1333–4, 1648, 2142–82, 2939 and 2944 for speeches by Guinness, Hoare etc. in the same vein.

50 Varneck and Fisher, p. 144.

however, the very opposite was the case. 'The more serious that talk of peace becomes', noted one officer in October 1918, 'the more distressed I become'; another Kolchak supporter found the sight of Tommies celebrating the armistice to elicit feelings which were 'not particularly joyous'; and, in retrospect, George Guins and General Filat′ev would even go as far as to assert (respectively) that the collapse of Germany was 'fatal to the anti-Bolshevik struggle' and that 'from the 11th of November onwards Kolchak had no Allies'.[51]

The root of such pessimism lay in the fact that, by the end of 1918, all those at Omsk were becoming aware that it would be their unenviable task not only to keep the war-weary Allies interested and involved in Russia and to persuade them that until Lenin too had been defeated their victory would not be secure, but also to induce them to step up the flow of material support to the White armies to a level sufficient to guarantee the demise of Bolshevism. It would clearly demand considerable effort to convince the jubilant victors that their laurels had not yet been earned and to divert their attention from the myriad other domestic and international questions demanding settlement in 1919. Of course, propaganda and indications of the democratic intentions of the Omsk régime might play a part in this; but, as principles buckled before Realpolitik in the post-war climate, it was becoming increasingly obvious that only the definite possibility of the Whites capturing central Russia would be of sufficient weight to convince the powers of the need to deal with Kolchak on an equal footing and to recognize him as the legitimate ruler of Russia. In turn, only recognition would give Kolchak and other Russian nationalists that which they desired above all else – a seat at the Paris Peace Conference and the chance to ensure that Russia was rewarded for her part in the war and restored to her proper place among the family of nations. Thus, when in one of his inaugural proclamations Kolchak defined the tasks ahead for his régime, his emphasis was not on the elaboration of any sophisticated political programme. Instead he stressed that:

> The day is dawning when the inexorable course of events will demand victory of us: upon this victory or defeat will depend our life or death, our success or failure, our freedom or ignoble slavery. The hour of the great international peace conference is now

51 Budberg, A.P. 'Dnevnik', *Arkhiv russkoi revoliutsii* Vol. 13 (1924), p. 260; Andrushkevich, N.A. 'Posledniaia Rossiia', *Beloe delo* No. 4 (1928), p. 109; Guins, Vol. 2, pp. 61–2; Filat′ev, D.B. *Katastrofa belogo dvizheniia v Sibiri, 1918–1922gg. (Vpechatleniia ochevidsta).* Paris (1985), p. 116.

> near and if by that hour we are not victorious then we will lose our right to a vote at the conference of victor nations and our freedom will be decided upon without us.[52]

Thus, it was anticipated that recognition would be won by some initial success upon the battlefield. It was evidently this (rather than final victory) which Kolchak was referring to here, for he clearly could not have hoped to have achieved final victory before the Paris conference was to convene in January 1919. Once recognition was achieved, however, it was widely anticipated that it, of itself, would make a major contribution towards the ultimate goal of destroying Bolshevism. It would, as we have seen, have eased Kolchak's problems with Semenov and the Czechoslovaks. In addition, noted Omsk's representative in London, recognition would considerably ease the task of negotiating loans in Europe and America which were needed to purchase arms for the Russian Army.[53] Moreover, added a government propagandist at Omsk, recognition would have great psychological consequences for the régime: 'The forces of the state will rally', predicted A.S. Belorussov:

> ...and this must have an effect upon the front. Recognition will strengthen...the prestige of the Supreme Ruler and of his political programme, both at home and abroad. It will be another decisive blow at the Soviet authorities and will give the population strength to rise against them.[54]

In other words, the hint of military victory would bring the possibility of recognition; recognition would then hasten the achievement of final victory.[55] Or so it was believed.

In reality, however, in the immediate aftermath of the coup, the prospects for the Kolchak government of redoubling Allied support for their cause were by no means particularly bright. Of course, there were those vehemently anti-Bolshevik Allied representatives in Siberia who returned glowing reports of the Omsk régime to their superiors and who championed recognition of the Supreme Ruler – notably General

52 Burevoi, K.S. *Kolchakovshchina*. Moscow (1919), pp. 20–1. See also Varneck and Fisher, p. 188.

53 Mints, pp. 86–7.

54 *Bulletins of the Russian Liberation Committee* (London), No. 17, 16.vi.1919.

55 This was the ideal of the most staunchly pro-Kolchak members of the British Foreign Office. See, for, example, Curzon's statement of April 1919 in Bourne, K. and Watt, D.C. (eds.) *British Documents on Foreign Affairs: Reports and Papers from the Foreign Office Confidential Print*. Frederick, MD (1984–). Part 2 (Series A), Vol. 1, pp. 80–1.

Knox and Colonel Nielson of Britmis, who had smoothed Kolchak's path to power, and the American Consul at Irkutsk, Mr Harris.[56] And there were also influential figures in Paris, London and Washington whose innate antipathy to Bolshevism made them more than willing to countenance exaggerated reports of Kolchak's success and popularity – notably the Allied Commander-in-Chief, Marshal Foch, the British Minister of War, Winston Churchill, and the American Acting Secretary of State, Mr Polk. By December 31st 1918, supporters of this tendency in London, for example, had succeeded in having the British High Commissioner to Siberia, Sir Charles Eliot, instructed to present Kolchak with a warmly supportive official greeting : 'As Your Excellency has assumed control at Omsk,' it read, 'His Majesty's Government desire to express their warm sympathy with every effort to establish a free Russian government on the basis of public confidence.'[57] Never mind the public, Kolchak's *own* confidence was now boosted to new heights. Assured, apparently, of Allied sympathy and support, he replied: 'We have firmly decided to overcome all obstacles and our faith in the triumph of arms taken up against the enemies of civilization is unshaken.'[58] Subsequently, in a private interview, the admiral would permit no talk of the dangers of war-weariness or indecisiveness in Europe and asserted that he had cast-iron 'assurances' from Allied diplomatists that the *de jure* recognition of the Omsk government 'was within the realms of possibility'.[59]

However, Knox, Churchill, Harris and their ilk were not having it all their own way. Sir Charles Eliot himself, for example, was far from being happy with his initial impressions of the Kolchak government, informing the Foreign Office on December 29th 1918 that the new régime was predominantly monarchistic and reactionary, that it was thoroughly compromised by the violent activities of renegade officers and that it would always be regarded with distrust by moderate groups and

56 On January 19th 1919, for example, Knox informed the War Office that Kolchak had 'more grit, pluck and honest patriotism than any man in Siberia'. See Ullman, Vol. 2, pp. 43–4. For US Consul Harris's statements see *FRUS: 1918*, Vol. 2, pp. 455, 459 and *FRUS: 1919 (Russia)*, pp. 200–1.

57 FO 371/4094/1189 'FO to Eliot (Omsk), 31.xii.1918'. Perhaps because of Kolchak's serious illness of early 1919, Eliot did not present this note to the Supreme Ruler until late January. Two days later his French counterpart, M Reno, presented a similar note from his own government. See Guins, Vol. 2, pp. 103–4.

58 FO 371/4095/61330 'Eliot (Omsk) to FO, 22.i.1919'.

59 Fedotoff-White, D. *Survival Through War and Revolution in Russia*. Philadelphia (1939), p. 215.

by the population as a whole. 'I cannot consider it as a strong government or recommend that we should back it unreservedly', he declared.[60] The reports to Washington of the Commander of the American Expeditionary Force, General Graves – who, being based at Vladivostok, had first-hand experience only of Semenov's and other warlords' banditry – were even more condemnatory of the White régime. Graves was convinced that Kolchak had no popular support whatsoever and that the Omsk government would collapse within a month if Allied aid was withdrawn.[61]

What was most damaging for Kolchak, however, was that the tenor of such reports from local agents only confirmed the suspicions of the dominant Allied leaders soon to gather at Paris. President Wilson had always been extremely sceptical as to the utility of the intervention in Russia – he regarded other questions as being far more important – and had only been drawn into the action most reluctantly in the first place.[62] And by the winter of 1918 to 1919 Lloyd George was hardly more convinced of the policy's chances of success. At a War Cabinet meeting on December 31st he informed Churchill that 'the only thing to spread Bolshevism is the attempt to suppress it'; over the following weeks, for the benefit of the first gatherings of the peacemakers at Paris, he reiterated that no government could be imposed upon the Russian people by the Allies, that the Bolsheviks were clearly the dominant force in the country, that they had a considerable degree of popular support, that they were not going to be defeated by any force of arms which there was any hope of deploying against them at the end of a four-year-long world war, and that, sooner or later, everybody was going to have to come to terms with this. Even Clemenceau was at one point to concede that the Bolsheviks were going to have to be dealt with 'as if they were our equals'.[63]

60 Ullman, Vol. 2, pp. 42–3.

61 Graves, W.S. *America's Siberian Adventure*. New York (1931), pp. 108, 157 and *passim*.

62 On Wilson's policy in 1918 see Kennan, G. *The Decision to Intervene*. London (1958), *passim*; Trani, E.P. 'President Wilson and the Decision to Intervene in Russia', *Journal of Modern History*, Vol. 49 (1976), pp. 440–61; Gardener, L.C. *Safe for Democracy: The Anglo-American Response to Revolution, 1913–1923*. Oxford (1984), pp. 177–92; Fic, V.M. *The Collapse of American Policy in Russia and Siberia, 1918: Wilson's Decision not to Intervene (March–October, 1918)*. Boulder, CO (1995); and Schild, G.M. *Between Ideology and Realpolitik: Woodrow Wilson and the Russian Revolution, 1917–1921*. London (1995).

63 Gilbert, M. *Winston S. Churchill*. London (1975), Vol. 4, pp. 228–9; *FRUS: Paris Peace Conference* (hereafter *PPC*), Vol. 3, pp. 643–6 and Vol. 4, pp. 15–16.

The practical consequences of the Allies' ambivalence towards the question of Bolshevism versus anti-Bolshevism were soon felt at Omsk. It was to no avail, for example, that on December 31st 1918, Kolchak appealed to the Allied governments to postpone any discussion of the Russian question at the Peace Conference for as long as possible; for, at this stage, with the untested Russian Army still ensconced in Siberia, the Supreme Ruler's threat that 'should Russia fail to gain a seat at the Peace Conference the political consequences may prove extremely serious', rang hollow. Nor would his warning that 'Russia could never forgive because of merely transitory reasons [sic] the settlement of her destiny without her voice being heard', have any effect for as long as at least a part of Russia proper had not been conquered by the Whites.[64] Consequently, despite such representations, the Russian question *was* raised during the very first weeks of the Paris Conference and in terms most distasteful to Kolchak: at meetings of January 12th–19th 1919, the Council of Ten determined that although the Bolsheviks might have no right to represent their nation at the conference, neither would any of the myriad Russians swarming about Paris (including those loyal to Omsk) until the powers had defined their policy on Russia. Such a definition was never to be arrived at, and, consequently, no Russian representative would be admitted to the official deliberations which were shaping the destiny of the post-war world (although certain individuals, notably the venerable populist N.V. Chaikovskii, were sometimes interviewed on a personal basis).[65]

The Allies were, of course, in a cleft stick with regard to the Russian question. One possible solution was full-scale military intervention to crush the Bolsheviks. But even if sufficient armed forces could have been mustered for such a campaign (which was unlikely, given the precedent that the German army was known to have been obliged to keep a million men in the Ukraine alone even when at peace with

64 FO 371/4094/592 'Russian Chargé d'Affairs (London) to FO, 31.xii.1918'.

65 *FRUS: PPC*, Vol. 3, pp. 540–6, 581–4, 589–93 and Vol. 4 pp. 472–91. For fuller accounts than can be given here of the powers' deliberations on Russia during the Peace Conference see Thomson, J.M. *Russia, Bolshevism and the Versailles Peace.* Princeton (1966); Mayer, A.J. *The Politics and Diplomacy of Peacemaking: Containment and Counter-Revolution at Versailles.* London (1968); Silverlight, J. *The Victors' Dilemma.* London (1970); Hovi, K. *'Cordon Sanitaire' or 'Barrière de l'Est'? The Emergence of the New French Eastern European Alliance Policy, 1917–1919.* Turku (1975); Epstein, F.T. 'Studien zur Geschichte der "Russischen Frage" auf der Pariser Friedenskonferenz von 1919', *Jahrbücher für Geschichte Osteuropas* Vol. 7 (1959), pp. 431–78; Hölzle, E. 'Versailles und der russische Osten', *Ostdeutsche Wissenschaft* (Munich), Vol. 5 (1958), pp. 486–503; Kennan, G. 'Russia and the Versailles Conference', *American Scholar* Vol. 30 (1960–1), pp. 13–42; and, from the orthodox Soviet point of view, Skaba, A.D. *Parizhskaia mirnaia konferentsiia i inostrannaia interventsiia v strane Sovetov.* Kiev (1971).

the Soviet Government), it was doubtful whether the necessary political support for renewed warfare could have been mobilized among the peoples of Europe. Moreover, it was equally doubtful whether the Russians could ever be induced to accept a government even partly imposed from abroad. Yet the only logical alternative, the erection in eastern Europe of a *cordon sanitaire* against revolution, behind which the Russians would be left to determine their own fate, however bloodily, was inhumane and would inevitably punish the very Russian people that the Allies were theoretically pledged to protect.

Lloyd George had broached these thorny questions at meetings of the Imperial War Cabinet and with the Canadian Prime Minister, Robert Borden, before leaving for Paris.[66] And, on arrival at the conference in January, he immediately set about winning the support of President Wilson and Clemenceau for what he adjudged to be a more realistic and moral solution. Days later, in an ominous demonstration of how little the Allies understood the White cause and of the lengths to which the powers were prepared to go in order to extricate themselves from the dilemma posed by the Russian question, this new blow, Lloyd George's 'solution', was dealt to Kolchak. On January 22nd an invitation was broadcast from Paris (from a radio station atop the Eiffel Tower) to all contending parties and armies in Russia, suggesting that they meet on the Island of Prinkipo, off Constantinople, for their own peace conference at which 'some understanding or agreement' could be reached between them.[67]

The reaction of the Whites was universally and unequivocally hostile to any such suggestion. Admiral Kolchak's flabbergasted response was not untypical: 'Good God!', he exclaimed to Guins, 'Can you believe it! An invitation to peace with the Bolsheviks!'[68] It was not simply that the idea of a conference was felt to be a bad tactic at that particular juncture – indeed, there were those who contended that the opportunity for Kolchak, Denikin and the other White paladins to meet and confer was one which should not be missed.[69] Nor was it that the Allies' suggestion of coming to terms with Lenin was in fundamental contradiction to the Whites' one clearly expressed aim of fighting for a Great Russia (not one divided and certainly

66 Maclaren, R. *Canadians in Russia*. Toronto (1976), pp. 245–7.

67 *Dokumenty vneshnei politiki SSSR*. Moscow (1959), Vol. 2, pp. 45–6.

68 Guins, Vol. 2, p. 88. It may have particularly rankled with Kolchak that it was on Prinkipo that his father had been interned by the British in 1855 (after he had been captured at Sevastopol).

69 *ibid.*, Vol. 2, p. 90; Mints, pp. 75–6.

not one with a Red Muscovy) and that even to be seen to consider such a scheme would undermine the leadership's prestige in the army.[70] All of that was almost by the way. What was most alarming for Kolchak was that the Allies had failed to appreciate how horribly offensive their suggestion was to the inflamed nationalistic sentiments prevalent in Siberia and that they did not understand that the Omsk government could only consider it 'beneath its dignity' to read, let alone reply to, an invitation to sit down at the same table as the Bolsheviks.[71] Consequently, no official reply to the Prinkipo proposal was forthcoming from Omsk. On February 19th Sazonov eventually submitted a note to the Peace Conference on behalf of all the White governments, informing the powers that there could be 'no question' of their accepting a Bolshevik presence at any conference; but, in the main, it was left to the Omsk government's front, the Omsk Bloc, to spell out the White reaction to the Allies in the following statement of February 9th, which was subsequently distributed in Paris:

> The Bloc considers that the Bolsheviks do not constitute a political party in Russia, but – as the product of a disease in the state – are representative in the national and international spheres of a criminal group trying to overthrow the apparatus of government exclusively for the planned and total destruction of the political and economic well-being of the Russian people.[72]

From the White point of view, therefore, Kolchak could hardly agree to negotiate with a gang of international criminals.

Nor was Prinkipo an isolated case of what some in Siberia were already referring to as Allied duplicity as opposed to mere insensitivity. In early February 1919, for example, Borden announced in Paris that Canada (which had many more troops in Siberia than either Britain or France and fewer only than the USA and Japan) was pulling out of the intervention, leading to fears being voiced at Omsk that the British

70 Such were the terms in which Kolchak denounced the Prinkipo proposal in interviews with the British and French High Commissioners in Siberia and in a telegram of protest to Paris. See *FRUS: PPC*, Vol. 4, pp. 18–19. Sukin (*Leeds Russian Archive*), p. 216 confirms that the general opinion in Omsk was that the proposals were a sign of the Allies' intention to dismember Russia.

71 FO 371/4096/215 'Speech by Kolchak at the Joint Conference of Zemstvos and Public Organizations, 14.11.1919'; General Sakharov expressed the army's disgust in a personal letter to Knox ('Sakharov to Knox, 4.iii.1919', *Pares Papers*, Box 41).

72 Cumming, C.K. and Pettit, W.W. (eds.) *Russian–American Relations (March 1917–March 1920)*. New York (1920), pp. 305–6; 'Resolution of the Omsk Bloc, 9.ii.1919' (*Pares Papers*, Box 28); Mints, p. 85.

forces would soon follow them.[73] Then, during March, rumours reached Kolchak's capital of a semi-official American peace delegation to Moscow (the so-called Bullitt mission) which had conducted direct negotiations with Lenin.[74] Finally, during April, news arrived of an inter-Allied scheme to supply food to the hungry peoples of central Russia – that is, to provide comfort for those whose very dissatisfaction with the economic failings of Bolshevism could only be of benefit to the White cause.[75] Kolchak was clearly entitled to wonder if these were the same Allies who had wished his government well in their notes of January – there had been no changes in government, but policy had apparently been reversed. Was the White cause to be abandoned? Why, even Trotsky was being heard to chuckle 'We have before us the betrayal of the minor brigands by the major ones!'[76]

In fact, this was far from being the case. Clemenceau for one, mindful of the millions of French francs invested in Russia which were unlikely to be recouped if the Bolsheviks remained in power, was not at all sorry to see the Prinkipo proposals sink without trace.[77] Lloyd George and Wilson, it is true, were initially dismayed by the Whites' blanket condemnation of their peace conference scheme – the former told his War Cabinet on February 13th that perhaps the Russians might actually desire 'something like Bolshevism' and should be left to it, while the latter suggested on the following day that all Allied troops should now be withdrawn.[78] But at this stage nothing at all was done to halt the shipments of arms with which the Allies had been sustaining Kolchak's war effort since the previous autumn; indeed, new tranches of aid were soon to be despatched.[79]

73 Maclaren, pp. 245–7; Eayers, J. (ed.) *In Defence of Canada*. Toronto (1964), p. 63; Mints, p. 72.

74 On this incident see [Bullitt, W.C.] *The Bullitt Mission to Russia*. New York (1919).

75 On this plan, drawn up by Fridtjof Nansen and Herbert Hoover, see Hoover, H. *The Memoirs of Herbert Hoover*. London (1952), Vol. 1, pp. 411–20; and Kennan, G.F. *Russia and the West Under Lenin and Stalin*. London (1961), pp. 136–40. Kolchak issued an official denunciation of this relief effort – see *Russkaia zhizn'* (Helsingfors) No. 50, 5.v.1919.

76 Trotsky, L. *How the Revolution Armed*. London (1979), Vol. 2 (1919), p. 494.

77 It was, in fact, in the knowledge of the French premier's dissatisfaction with the policy of Lloyd George and Wilson that Kolchak felt safe to despatch his blunt rejection of the Prinkipo proposal. See Subbotovskii, I. *Soiuzniki i russkie reaktsionery: kratkii ozbor (iskliuchitel'no po ofitsialnym arkhivnym dokumentam Kolchakovskogo pravitel'stva)*. Leningrad (1926), pp. 67, 229–30.

78 Ullman, Vol. 2, pp. 118–19; *FRUS: PPC*, Vol. 3, pp. 1042–3.

79 By March 1919 British shipments of uniforms and equipment to outfit 200,000 men had reached Vladivostok (or were in transit there) together with 142 field guns, 52 Howitzers, 550 machine guns and 1,000,000 grenades (See Bourne and Watt, p. 132). Britmis, meanwhile, was in the

There were several reasons why this was so. In part it was, as Lloyd George informed the House of Commons on April 16th, that the Allies had encouraged and nurtured the anti-Bolshevik governments in 1918 because they were the only organizations in Russia opposing the Germans and, however much the stubbornness of their leaders might be regretted, they could not simply be left in the lurch now that they had served their purpose. To renege on such a debt of honour would involve substantiating the charge of double standards being levelled against the victor nations and would undermine the moral high ground which they were so anxious to claim at Paris. Also, European leaders could not be immune to constant White pleading that it was their duty to assist patriotic Russians because of their contribution to the Allied cause from 1914 to 1917.[80] A major factor, however, was the increasingly intense and quite proficient propaganda campaign being waged in both Europe and Siberia by the agents of the Kolchak government – a campaign which drew attention to the horrors of the Red Terror of late 1918, when the Bolsheviks had ruthlessly exterminated many of their captured political opponents. In London, for example, General Golovin was addressing meetings of both Houses of Parliament on this topic and was holding illustrated talks at which he enlisted the support of many MPs and prominent members of the British establishment.[81] Meanwhile, in Paris, the Russian Political Conference began distributing materials supplied by Omsk attesting to the increased stability and popularity of the Kolchak government and outlining for the first time the progressive legislation said to be in preparation. 'The Russian National Movement has no hidden aims for a restoration',

process of training a total of 3,067 officers and 2,307 NCOs at schools it ran at Russian Island (Vladivostok), Irkutsk and Tomsk (WO 32/5707 'Report of the Military Mission in Siberia, 10.xii.1919'). A Soviet historian of the intervention adds that the French Government supplied to Kolchak a further 900 machine guns, 126 aircraft, 70 automobiles and 442 artillery pieces – see Svetachev, M.I. *Imperialisticheskaia interventsiia v Sibiri i na Dal'nem Vostoke (1918–1920gg.)*. Leningrad (1983), p. 123. Finally, R.J. Maddox has established that in early 1919 President Wilson and the US State Department were doing everything possible to assist the Russian Embassy in Washington in its ongoing task of purchasing weaponry (including 200,000 Remington rifles) and forwarding it to Kolchak – even though the contracts for these purchases (as well as the chartering of the tonnage for their shipment to Vladivostok) had been originally negotiated with the Provisional Government of 1917, of which Kolchak had not been recognized as the legitimate successor. See Maddox, R.J. 'Woodrow Wilson, the Russian Embassy and the Siberian Intervention', *Pacific Historical Review*, Vol. 36 (1967), No. 4, pp. 435–48.

80 *DBFP*, Vol. 3, pp. 310–11; Guins, Vol. 2, pp. 62–6.

81 Ioffe, G.Z. *Kolchakovskaia avantiura i ee krakh*. Moscow (1983), p. 206.

it informed the Allies in April.[82] Simultaneously, in Siberia itself, western newspaper correspondents were being supplied with interviews and ingenious official statements which stressed the 'constitutional thread' which was claimed to link the Kolchak régime with the *Sibobduma*.[83] Moreover, information routed to Europe by the powers' diplomatic representatives in Siberia now seemed to substantiate these claims. By April 5th, for example, Sir Charles Eliot was filing reports which portrayed the popularity of the Kolchak régime in a very favourable light compared to his correspondence of a few months earlier. The basis of Eliot's change of heart, however, could not have been first-hand observation, for he rarely ventured out of Omsk and never went into the Siberian countryside; it must, rather, be attributed to his having succumbed to the increasingly sophisticated wiles of government propaganda (or, perhaps, to the dubious information supplied to the High Commissioner by the strongly pro-Kolchak Britmis).[84]

Whatever its probity, such was the effectiveness of this multi-channelled campaign (when harnessed to other factors) that on April 29th 1919 the British War Cabinet decided that not only should Kolchak receive continued support but that he should be offered *de jure* recognition as the head of the Provisional Government of Siberia. At meetings of the Council of Five on May 7th and 9th Lloyd George was able to place these recommendations before the Allies.[85] At first the talk in Paris was only of continued 'support' of Kolchak; by the end of the month, however, the British Prime Minister would secure the Council's agreement to what looked very much like the first step towards the recognition of Kolchak – and not merely as the ruler of Siberia and the Far East, but of all Russia.[86]

This was all a very long way indeed from the days of Prinkipo. However, although, as has been suggested, pro-Kolchak and anti-Bolshevik propaganda undoubtedly played an important part in assuaging any lingering western qualms about promoting reaction in Russia through the support of the Whites, what was

82 Subbotovskii, pp. 72–3.

83 *The Times* (London), 23.iv.1919.

84 Ullman, Vol. 2, p. 161. The favourable reports on Kolchak's standing being sent to Wilson by Consul Harris were even less likely to have been true reflections of the situation in Siberia, having been written at Irkutsk and in the Far East, far beyond the scope of Kolchak's effective authority.

85 Ullman, Vol. 2, pp. 162–3; *FRUS: PPC*, Vol. 5, pp. 497–8, 528–30.

86 Correspondingly, both the returning Bullitt mission and the Hoover-Nansen relief plan were treated very coolly in Allied deliberations of mid-May. See *FRUS: PPC*, Vol. 5, pp. 734–5.

clearly more decisive in swinging Lloyd George and the Allies behind Kolchak at this particular juncture, in April–May 1919, was the news then arriving in Europe of the Russian Army's recent, glittering military successes. Since the commencement of a general spring offensive in early March, it was becoming known in Paris, Kolchak's army (now rumoured to be a million strong) had made significant advances in the north, had recaptured all of the territory lost since the previous summer in the central Urals and was approaching the very banks of the Volga.[87] The news created great excitement throughout Europe. 'The entire press of Paris was screaming on the subject', noted one observer; while in London *The Times* trumpeted 'The Tide of Victory in Russia' on April 30th and, a few days later, forecast the imminent collapse of the Soviet Government.[88]

Lloyd George for one seemed to be convinced that the tide had turned irrevocably in the Whites' favour in Russia. Of particular significance for him may have been that in early May a small contingent of Russian troops (together with one British officer), having marched from Arkhangel'sk, had established contact with Kolchak's advancing Siberian Army west of Perm. This was heartening news because throughout April the War Office had been working on a plan of Churchill's to send a volunteer force to north Russia in order to stage an advance, achieve a union between the North Russian and Siberian anti-Bolshevik centres, and thereby facilitate the withdrawal of all British forces from Arkhangel'sk and Murmansk.[89] Originally Lloyd George had only very reluctantly agreed to this operation – he did not like the idea of committing more troops in Russia, but probably concluded that this plan would at least satisfy the belligerent Churchill's demands to commit more resources to the anti-Bolshevik campaign. By May 9th, however, heartened by Kolchak's victories, the British Prime Minister was moved to suggest sending additional contingents of regular troops to North Russia to enable the volunteer force and the Russians to hasten the union of Omsk and Arkhangel'sk. This, he hoped,

87 Also encouraging to the Allies was the news that on May 10th 1919, cavalry of the Volunteer Army of the AFSR had defeated the 10th Red Army and were beginning to close on Tsaritsyn from the south, raising the possibility of a union of Denikin's forces with those of Kolchak. See Denikin, A.I. *Ocherki russkoi smuty*. Paris–Berlin (1921–1926), Vol. 5, pp. 81–4; *FRUS: PPC*, Vol. 5, p. 687.

88 Bullitt, p. 90; *The Times* (London) 30.iv.1919, 5.v.1919.

89 Gilbert, Vol. 4, pp. 273–7, 280–7; Ullman, Vol. 2, pp. 183–5.

would ease Kolchak's supply problems and, he contended, to all intents and purposes 'would be the end of Bolshevism'.[90]

What was uppermost in the Allies' minds by May 1919, therefore, was not that Kolchak's government had now satisfied them (by hook or by crook) that it was morally deserving of further support and recognition. Indeed the Council of Five's lengthy interview with N.V. Chaikovskii in Paris on May 11th sowed *new* doubts as to Kolchak's immunity from reactionary influences; and as late as May 24th President Wilson was *still* expressing concern that Kolchak was incapable of guaranteeing order and democracy.[91] What counted, rather, was that Kolchak was now victorious: that, with or without Allied aid, he might be on the brink of toppling Lenin – and if it was to be without Allied aid, or even if Kolchak felt himself to have been slighted by the Allies, there would ensue a host of difficulties, embarrassments and dangers in dealing with a resentful White government in Moscow.[92] To avoid such unpleasant consequences was the primary intention of the Allied note despatched to Kolchak on May 26th 1919, following prolonged discussion of the Russian question by the Council of Five throughout the previous week. Despite frequent assertions to the contrary in historical literature, there was still no *overt* offer of recognition to be found in this celebrated communication. Nevertheless, the *promise* of recognition in the near future was implicit in the fact that the Allies pledged therein further assistance to the Omsk régime, in order to enable Kolchak to establish a government representing 'all Russia'.[93]

There was, of course, attached to the Allied note a well-known list of conditions with which Kolchak was requested to comply before the promised aid (and, by inference, recognition) would be delivered. Kolchak's acceptance of these 'democratic principles', it was held, would demonstrate that his policy had 'the same objects in view as that of the Allied and Associated powers'. Included here were requests for guarantees that upon reaching Moscow the Supreme Ruler would summon a Constituent Assembly; that he would permit free local elections in the

90 *ibid.*, Vol. 2, p. 163; Thompson, p. 295; *FRUS: PPC*, Vol. 5, pp. 528–9.

91 *ibid.*, Vol. 5, pp. 545, 560, 901–4 and Vol. 6, p. 15.

92 Not the least of the Allies' fears was that a resentful White government might turn to Germany for support upon victory. For an analysis of such thinking upon British policy see Kolz, A.W.F. 'British Foreign Policy and the Kolchak Government', Boston University PhD Thesis, 1965, pp. 20–6, 58.

93 *FRUS: PPC*, Vol. 6, pp. 73–5.

areas already liberated; that he would revive no special privileges in land ownership for any social class in Russia; that he would recognize the independence of Poland and Finland and the autonomy of national groups in the Baltic, the Caucasus and Transcaucasus; that he would permit the League of Nations to determine the future of Bessarabia; and that a future Russian government would join the League and would honour all Russia's foreign debts.[94] Ostensibly, the thinly veiled threat was that if Kolchak failed to agree to these principles then the military aid from the Allies which he would probably need to be sure of reaching Moscow would be curtailed. But was Kolchak seriously expected to believe that, at what seemed to be the very hour of the victory of a cause in which they had already invested so much moral, military and financial support, the Allies were suddenly going to abandon him? Moreover, did the Allies really believe that, if there was a chance he might require their aid and recognition to reach Moscow, Kolchak was going to do anything other than agree to any conditions, within reason, that were laid before him – especially as no mechanism had been established to monitor Omsk's observance of those conditions?

Unsurprisingly, therefore, the Allied note was greeted with joy and anticipation in the Siberian capital.[95] There were some regrets that recognition had not been proffered unequivocally and a little distaste aroused by what seemed to be an unprecedented attempt to interfere in the internal affairs of the Russian state; but such cavils were not an obstacle to acceptance of the note. For, as a last minute attempt to tether Kolchak to the cause of democracy, the note was clearly and woefully insufficient. Even the most affronted Russian nationalist could hold fire when there were pointed out to him the unmistakable advantages of a knock-down bargain whereby aid was guaranteed and recognition promised in return for no concrete concessions on Kolchak's part. After all, as reactionary groups in Omsk were openly stating, the government could agree to anything now, but would be able to 'speak in a different tone' once the Russian Army was in Moscow.[96] Few eyebrows could have been raised, therefore, when on June 4th 1919 Kolchak replied to the Allied note and all its conditions in a most moderate tone.[97] As one Soviet

94 *ibid.*, Vol. 6, pp. 74–5.

95 See, for example, *Nasha zaria* (Omsk) No. 117, 4.vi.1919.

96 Arnol′dov, p. 158; Janin, 'Otryvki', p. 119.

97 *FRUS: PPC*, Vol. 6, pp. 321–3.

historian accurately noted: 'The Allies and Kolchak were playing a game with a predetermined result. Kolchak knew what he would be asked and the Allies knew what he would reply.'[98]

What was of significance, however, was the message which the Kolchak régime could read between the lines of the Allies' note. The unspoken implications of that otherwise asinine communication were that it scarcely mattered whether or not Omsk was committed to the convocation of a new Constituent Assembly, whether it held local elections, satisfied peasant demands for land reform or recognized the rights of national minorities – or even, perhaps, whether it promised eventually to do so. Rather, the clear lesson to be drawn was that the Allies had sat up and taken notice of Kolchak because the Russian Army had been successful on the battlefield. Certainly the Supreme Ruler was under no illusions as to the source of his sudden good fortune. 'All foreign policy relations have been founded upon our success', he later admitted in a letter to his wife. 'When I had victories everything went well.'[99] But, just in case either Kolchak or his advisers should be entertaining any false notions as to what was demanded of the Siberian régime, his Foreign Minister drove the message home in communications from his office in Paris: 'Further steps towards [our] recognition as the All-Russian Government', reported Sazonov on June 17th, 'will undoubtedly depend directly upon the military success of the army.'[100]

PART TWO: *NA MOSKVU*

All of these direct and indirect signals from Europe in early 1919 highlighting the need for military victory caused but few ripples of concern among the leadership of the Russian Army and their supporters in the government. From the outset and by

98 Ioffe, *Kolchakovskaia avantiura*, p. 210.

99 Kolchak, R.A. 'Admiral Kolchak: ego rod i sem'ia', *Voenno-istoricheskii vestnik* No. 16 (1960), p. 18.

100 Konstantinov, M.M. (ed.) *Poslednie dni kolchakovshchiny*. Moscow (1926), p. 99.

its very nature the régime had been geared towards conquest – for many, indeed, that was the whole point of the dictatorship – and for the first eight months of its existence few protests were heard inside the government camp against the adopting of the slogan and the policy of 'Everything for the Army'. Certainly, as we have seen, Kolchak himself was contemptuous of all politics, was devoted to the military way, and was surrounded by a carapace of military advisers who likewise dreamed of the achievement of national destinies and personal glory through war. So it was that, when in one of his very first published proclamations Kolchak established the agenda for his rule, he declared that, in giving supreme power to a member of the military, 'government and society' had recognized that:

> Only in the Army, only in armed force is there salvation. Everything else must be subordinated to its interests, to its tasks. And I appeal to you now with a request to assist me in achieving the sole aim to which each of us must apply all of his powers, all of his strength and, when it is necessary, his life: the formation of a disciplined, battleworthy Russian Army, capable of granting victory to our Motherland.[101]

Moreover, the Siberian Whites' confidence that the Russian Army was capable not merely of achieving victory but of achieving it in the earliest possible march *na Moskvu* (on Moscow) was supreme and immutable. In part this was a feeling inspired and nurtured by a superficial reading of the developments of early 1919 – the victory at Perm, the understanding with Semenov, the pacification of the Czechoslovaks and the encouraging signals from Europe – which have already been dwelt upon. In part it was also a result of the intellectual failure to appreciate the logistical and economic problems inherent in launching a campaign from Siberia (even with Allied assistance); this aspect of White thought will be dealt with in the succeeding chapter. But for the moment we will concern ourselves with another facet of the movement's psychology: this was a confidence born of a fatal misunderstanding of the appeal and the strength of Bolshevism married to the firm belief that not only the best soldiers and not only the heart and soul of the Russian people, but justice and even the Supreme Being were on the side of the Supreme Ruler. Apparently it was all very simple: 'God wishes, and I therefore believe, that we shall win', pronounced Kolchak.[102]

101 Burevoi, *Kolchakovshchina*, pp. 21–2.

102 *Biulleten'* (Omsk) No. 117, 26.x.1919.

Although Allied forces had not been committed to Siberia in the numbers that had been hoped for in 1918, and while the Czechoslovaks were clearly reluctant to fight at the front, military leaders in Omsk were sure that so long as they were granted a steady flow of material assistance from abroad they would be able to establish their 'new, young Russian Army' east of the Urals. Hoping to build upon the recruitment drives carried out in western Siberia by the Provisional Siberian Government during August and September 1918 and the nucleus of thousands of officers who had fled into Siberia, by the end of 1918 Kolchak's *stavka* had drawn up plans for a mass mobilization. The aim was to create a force no less than 700,000 strong, consisting of twenty army corps and thirty-four cavalry regiments.[103] And, as the general mobilization began to take effect, spirits rose among the Siberian military; for, no matter how notorious was the cruelty with which the Russian officer treated his men (both in the Great War and in the Civil War) and no matter how disillusioning had been the experience of 1917, it was, paradoxically, still true that the mere sight of a Russian peasant in uniform was an emotive ikon for the White officers, a symbol of the old order to which that dislocated class still clung. Officer nationalism was incurably romantic and the spectacle of peasant soldiers drilling, however reluctantly, in Siberian towns is recorded as having brought a lump to the throat of the most battle-hardened colonel; it was sufficient too to convince a formerly sceptical colonel that victory, after all, would be theirs.[104] The very fact of the existence of the new army, in other words, was sufficient to fuel optimism.

Moreover, despite some reassessment of its strategic significance, the December victory at Perm was still being cited in some military circles in early 1919 as proof – as if any were needed – of the fact that the Russian Army's leadership, the former colonels and generals of the Tsar, had a monopoly of experience and knowledge in the conduct of warfare which the political agitators at the head of the Red Army could not match.[105] 'On that question,' recalled one observer, 'there existed no difference of opinion in the Kolchak camp.'[106]

103 FO 371/3365/19133 'Russian Liaison Service (Vladivostok) to the Russian Mission (Washington), ?.xi.1919'.

104 Fedotoff-White, p. 216.

105 Sukin (*Leeds Russian Archive*), p. 144.

106 Eikhe, G. Kh. *Oprokinutyi tyl*. Moscow (1966), p. 143.

If the outcome of the war was certain, the only real bone of contention which arose during the debates on future military policy during January and February 1919 concerned the timing and direction of the advance necessary to achieve it. Some of Kolchak's abler field commanders (including General Dieterichs, Major-General Voitsekhovskii and Colonel Kappel), supported by General Knox, argued that it would be wise to delay any further operations for a few months until the Russian Army was fully trained and equipped, until a strategic reserve could be forged from the three new divisions the Supreme Ruler ordered to be mobilized in February, until a strategic plan was agreed upon, and until Denikin and Iudenich were ready to move in support of an advance from the east from their own bridgeheads in the North Caucasus and the Baltic. Attempts were made to enlist the support of the Minister of War, General N.A. Stepanov, for such a scheme, but that notorious martinet was found to be too busy drawing up a new drill manual and attempting to expand his establishment so as to make it more imposing than the *stavka* to be concerned with anything so mundane.[107] The all-powerful Chief of Staff, Colonel Lebedev, meanwhile, advised Kolchak that the *stavka* considered delay to be unnecessary and that an immediate advance would take advantage of the Red Army's indiscipline and unpreparedness.[108] Lebedev's personal hold over the admiral was becoming ever stronger in early 1919, despite this young colonel's almost complete lack of command and operational experience; and, consequently, it was his argument which won the day. By this time, in fact, Lebedev felt himself to be on such sure ground that he would not even feel obliged to inform opponents of the spring offensive (such as the *Chef d'Arrière*, General Knox) of the commencement of operations on March 3rd; in breach of the agreement of January 16th, he did not even deign to inform General Janin.[109] And, following the subsequent military victories of March–April, Lebedev's star was to reach its zenith as, in late May, he ousted Stepanov and combined the post of Minister of War with that of Chief of Staff which he already held. For the next two months, to ultimately

107 Klerzhe, G.I. *Revoliutsiia i grazhdanskaia voina: lichnye vospominaniia*. Mukden (1932), pp. 150–1.

108 Eikhe, p. 143; WO 32/5707 'Report of the Military Mission in Siberia, 10.xii.1919', pp. 11–15.

109 *ibid.*, p. 16. General Janin had heard indirectly of Lebedev's intention to launch a major offensive at the beginning of March, but he dismissed the order as 'of no importance', believing that no such operation could be initiated, given the state of the Russian Army, even if the White leadership seriously intended to attempt it. See WO 106/1251 'Janin (Omsk) to Paris, 20.ii.1919'.

disastrous effect, this tyro would exercise complete control over all military affairs – both at the front and in the rear.

There were, of course, pressing political reasons why Kolchak should favour an early advance: above all else he wanted to make a good impression in Paris. But even had this not been the case, it is doubtful whether the outcome of the debate on the timing of the offensive would have been very different. From the beginning, commented a senior member of the military establishment, there were few officers in Siberia – and certainly none among the rash and inexperienced embusqués who populated the *stavka* of 'that young chancer' Lebedev – who could be persuaded to take the Bolsheviks at all seriously as military opponents.[110] When fleeing into Siberia during the summer of 1918, as the Red Army captured their original base at Samara, for example, many White officers had refrained from taking any winter clothing with them, being certain that they would be home again before their furs were required.[111] Although this was not the case, the optimism prevalent at Omsk was heightened by the capture of Perm in December. Thereafter, recalled a stern critic of the *stavka*, 'the young, fervent and wet-behind-the-ears colonels, in their ignorance and confidence, were certain that the Red Army would offer no serious opposition'.[112] Thus, the retreat of the 3rd Red Army, unbeknownst to its leaders, had served to substantiate everything which the White officers had always said about Lenin's party.

In all wars a combatant's perception of his enemy is at least of some academic interest; in the Russian Civil War it was a factor of very great military and political significance. In describing the Bolsheviks and their Red Army in everything from propaganda and press releases to official orders, the Siberian Whites habitually referred to the Soviet Government as 'the agonizing yoke of Latvians, Jews, Magyars and Chinamen', 'brigands', 'the dregs of society', 'ex-vagabonds and scoundrels, scum the lot of them'.[113] Red propaganda, of course, was barely less vituperative and caricatured in its portrayal of the Whites. But at least in depicting Kolchak and Denikin as the dupes and puppets of world imperialism the implication

110 Budberg, Vol. 14, pp. 240–3 and Vol. 15, p. 340–1.

111 N.N. 'Zapiski belogvardeitsa', *Arkhiv russkoi revoliutsii* Vol. 10 (1923), p. 87.

112 Filat'ev, p. 76.

113 See, for example, the propaganda leaflets headed 'Krasnoarmeetsy!', 'Tovarishchi!' and 'Khleb idet' (*Pares Papers*, Box 50) and FO 538/4 'Orders of General Rozanov (Krasnoiarsk), 26.iii.1919'.

was that they were enemies to be taken seriously. Quite the opposite was the conclusion to be drawn from White publications. And not just from propaganda – that such allegations evince sincerely held convictions in the White camp is clear from the fact that even in official diplomatic communications the Russian ambassador in Paris would refer to the Soviet Government as 'a riot' and that even in his private correspondence, when he had no compulsion to maintain any official line, one of Kolchak's most trusted generals, Konstantin Sakharov, would portray his Red Army opponents as 'bands of the refuse of Russia, criminals, Magyars – in a word, all that is the support of Bolshevism', even as this alleged mob drove his own army back through the Urals.[114]

Perhaps even more common (and more sincerely held) was the view expressed by the Whites and their supporters of all complexions that the Bolsheviks were nothing more than the agents of Germany. Kolchak himself, for example, would routinely refer to his opponents as 'the German-Bolsheviks'. In fact, this was an appellation used in White Siberia as frequently as plain 'Bolsheviks'. It was also commonly held in Omsk that the Red Army was 'led by German officers'.[115] Rumours of the Bolsheviks' alleged allegiance to the Kaiser had, of course, been prevalent ever since Lenin's journey through Germany in March 1917 and P.N. Pereverzev's leak during the July Days of documents pertaining to the party's finances; and such charges had been redoubled following the 'treachery' of Brest-Litovsk. With regard to the Whites' perceptions of their opponents, the problem was that this line of reasoning logically led to the conclusion that (notwithstanding concern that the armistice might cause the Allies to lose interest in the White cause) the collapse of Imperial Germany in November 1918 would presage the collapse of Bolshevism: 'We know that their days are numbered,' proclaimed an Irkutsk newspaper in November 1918: 'Since they no longer have Magyar-German support, they will soon be driven from Russia.'[116]

Even when the fall of the Kaiser did not immediately occasion the demise of Lenin, perhaps indicating that their fates had not been linked in the manner supposed in the White camp, no more sophisticated attempt was made to account for the durability of the Bolshevik régime. Thus, even by the middle of 1919, the

114 Kim, 'Iz arkhiva', p. 61; 'Sakharov to Knox, 4.iii.1919' (*Pares Papers*, Box 41).

115 See, for example, Kolchak's 'Declaration to the Russian Army, 23.xi.1918', in Burevoi, p. 20.

116 *Delo* (Irkutsk) 23.xi.1918.

official line was as follows: 'The Bolsheviks would have had none of the material means to do what they did without the enormous and systematic help which they got from Germany.'[117] That is, in the face of all the evidence that German occupation had actually *denied* the Soviet Government access to resources which they would have otherwise controlled in the Ukraine in 1918, the Whites chose to believe that Lenin only managed to survive into 1919 because of some stockpile of aid delivered by the Kaiser. In fact, the only new element injected into the Whites' analysis of Bolshevism in 1919 was a none too subtle variation of that longstanding vice of the Russian right, anti-Semitism. 'The Bolsheviks are still entirely a German organization being run in Russia by Jews', claimed one of Kolchak's most senior generals in July 1919, while the Russian Army's intelligence service's unlikely excuse for their poor results was that surveillance was complicated by the fact that Red Army communications were made 'exclusively in Yiddish which, as is known, is a jargon of German'.[118]

For the Whites and their supporters, then, Bolshevism constituted merely a riot, a mobocracy, a conspiracy of Magyars, Jews or Germans. Whatever it was, it was clearly inconceivable to them that it was something born of the Russian soil with any real basis of popular support. 'To regard Bolshevism as Russian or anything to do with Russia,' opined a White sympathizer, 'is like quoting against him the words of a man's delirium.'[119] If, to date, the Bolsheviks had enjoyed some success, then that could be passed off, as Nabokov assured Omsk, as 'the fruit of military defeat' in the Great War or as a 'temporary phenomenon of war sickness' in the civil

117 Pares, B. 'Siberian Diary' (*Pares Papers*, Box 43), p. 103.

118 FO 538/4 'Memorandum on the Evacuation of Ekaterinburg by HM Consul, Mr. Preston, 13–21.vii.1919'; Pares, B. 'Siberian Diary' (*Pares Papers*, Box 43), p. 112. 'Our enemy is not a Russian worker or a Russian peasant, he is THE JEW', proclaimed General Dieterichs in *Bei zhidov!* ['Kill the Yids!']. Omsk (1919). For extensive examinations of White anti-Semitism see Szajkowskii, Z. *Kolchak, Jews and the American Intervention in Northern Russia and Siberia, 1918–1920*. New York (1977); Dacy, D.A. 'The White Russian Movement: A Study of the Failure of the Counter-Revolution, 1917–1921', University of Texas at Austin PhD Thesis (1972), pp. 278–88; Kenez, P. 'The Ideology of the White Movement', *Soviet Studies* (Glasgow), Vol. 32 (1980), pp. 75–80; Heifetz, E. *The Slaughter of the Jews in the Ukraine in 1919*. New York (1921); Klier, J.D. and Lambroza, S. (eds.) *Pogroms: Anti-Jewish Violence in Modern Russian History*. London (1989); Schulman, E. 'Pogroms in the Ukraine in 1919', *The Jewish Quarterly*, Vol. 17 (1966), pp. 159–66.

119 Pares, B. 'Siberian Diary' (*Pares Papers*, Box 43), p. 10.

war.[120] Incredibly, from the point of view which saw Bolshevism almost literally as a disease, even Kolchak's isolation in Siberia could be construed as a cause for optimism – for, claimed the Omsk Kadets' *Nasha zaria*, 'the unification and re-establishment of a new and united Russian state...will be all the easier precisely because of the enforced quarantine of this healthy part of the body of the Russian state from the nidus of infection'![121]

The common belief was, then, that although the Germans might have utilized Bolshevism to defeat Russia through 'sullying and perverting the mind of the average Russian', this was a situation which could not endure – not least because the average Russian was held to be 'a decent and right-thinking fellow in the normal course of things'.[122] Consequently there could be little debate in the White camp on the means to be deployed to bring about the rapid defeat of Lenin. Those, like the moderate Kadet Lev Krol, who would argue for the institution of an attractive and popular government programme of political reform were castigated as unbelievers (or even as 'Bolsheviks'). All politics, as we have seen, was regarded with suspicion by the military. Advocacy of the use of propaganda was treated with equal scepticism by the army: if it was to be used at all, decreed a *stavka* conference on the matter, then its function would be not to goad the population into supporting programmes opposed to Bolshevism, but simply 'to open the eyes of the benighted masses to the fact that all the leaders of Bolshevism are not Russians'.[123] Most White leaders, however, doubted if even that would be necessary for, as Denikin contested, the Russian people would naturally rally to the side which promised 'regeneration' and 'rebirth'.[124] General Sakharov, for example, was certain that as long as the Russian Army was properly supplied by the rear it would quickly smash the Red Army on the Urals front and then 'speed' on an open road to Moscow, for 'the entire people would come over to our side and stand openly beneath the

120 Kim, p. 68; Pares, B. 'Memorandum on the Position in Russia, 22.iii.1919' (*Pares Papers*, Box 42).

121 *Nasha zaria* (Omsk) No. 12, 10.iii.1919.

122 Becvar, p. 96.

123 Miroshchenko, P. (ed.) 'Iz istorii kolchakovshchiny', *Krasnyi arkhiv* 1928, No. 3 (28), p. 226.

124 Denikin, *Ocherkii*, Vol. 2, p. 237.

admiral's banner – the Bolsheviks and the rest of the socialist filth would be destroyed from the roots up by the burning rage of the popular masses'.[125]

And this was not only the view of blustering and politically ignorant generals. Rather, it was an opinion shared by a wide range of the civilian supporters of the Kolchak régime – from the former populist, the journalist A.S. Belorussov (Belitskii), who declared that 'a single counter-blow by nationalism against internationalism will be sufficient to arouse the spirits of the population against the Bolsheviks', to the right-wing luminaries of the Kadet *VOTsK* whose calculations, said its Chairman, L.A. Ustrialov, 'were founded in the main upon the belief that the appearance of the rapidly organized Siberian Army within the boundaries of European Russia would be met by powerful support from the population...and the soviets would then fall'.[126] And once that this had occurred, and the capitals had been liberated, there could be no question of Bolshevism lingering on in the hearts of the Russian people or in any Russian province to threaten the stability of a new nationalist government, for the Whites were convinced – in defiance of the long history of socialism in Russia – that the creed had no basis of support in the country: 'I am convinced,' avowed Kolchak, 'that as soon as the Cossacks appear in Moscow the Bolsheviks will disappear.'[127]

Given the distrust with which elitist Kadet politicians, let alone those further to the right, had always regarded the 'wild beast' of the masses – they had, after all, sponsored the dictatorship in the belief that the people were not to be trusted to choose their own leaders – not to mention the cruelty and open contempt with which their Cossack and officer allies treated peasants and peasant conscripts, such blind faith in a spontaneous wave of popular support for the White cause might seem rather paradoxical. After all, could not even one of the most sober and intelligent of the Siberian military, the one-time Acting Minister of War, Baron Budberg, declare that the Russian peasantry consisted of 'a mixture of slugs, slaves, self-seekers and hooligans' and rue the necessity of having to admit them to his precious 'noble' army?[128] Nevertheless, this faith in the Russian people as the saviour of the White

[125] Sakharov, p. 177.

[126] Krol', L., p. 165; Ustrialov, p. 49.

[127] *The Times* (London) 11.iv.1919.

[128] Budberg, Vol. 13, p. 258.

cause was all-pervading – perhaps not least because this faith in the Russian people was an essential article of *the* Faith, Russian Orthodoxy.

It seems that for the most devout of Kolchak's generals, the corollary of their denial of earthly politics and their refusal to acknowledge the existence of a class system based on material interests was an emphasis on the spiritual union (and uniqueness) of the Russian nation. 'Our party is Holy Russia, our class the entire Russian people', proclaimed General Sakharov; while, from the extreme evangelical point of view of General Popov, 'the whole revolution represented the apocalyptic advent of the Beast'. Most influentially of all, for General Dieterichs (who became increasingly powerful as 1919 wore on and who was for some months both Chief of Staff and Main Commander-in-Chief) the civil war was 'undeniably a Holy War' which was 'not about political differences...but about the overthrow at the hands of ungodly aliens of the faith of the [Russian] fore-fathers'.[129] Such a belief necessarily had to to assume that the Russian peasantry which, outwardly at least, was slave to every sublimity of religious devotion, would side with God against 'the Beast'. Even a general such as A.N. Pepeliaev, more moderate in his politics and less given to mysticism than Sakharov, Popov or Dieterichs, evidently believed for most of 1919 that the best hope for the White cause was not to satisfy the peasants' demands for land, but to induce them to rise against Bolshevism in the name of 'truth and Holy Russia'.[130]

This unwavering optimism and belief in the inherent superiority of their cause was the prime fundament, the mainspring, of both the military and political philosophies of the Siberian Whites. As such, although it was not the only factor at play, it naturally determined their conduct of the civil war both at the front and in the rear.

129 Sakharov, p. 112; Fedotoff-White, p. 339; FO 371/4096/[p. 28] 'Eliot (Omsk) to FO, 29.vi.1919'; *The Times* (London) 9.viii.1919.

130 Parfenov, P.S. *Uroki proshlogo: grazhdanskaia voina v Sibiri (1918, 1919, 1920gg.)*. Harbin (1921), p. 119.

Planning the spring offensive

Since the summer of 1918, the command of the anti-Bolshevik forces in Siberia had instituted a series of mobilizations designed to produce a massive army, which they believed would simply swamp the Bolshevik forces in an advance to be organized and commenced at the earliest possible moment. This process was to culminate in April 1919, when Kolchak ordered the levy of the entire male population in Siberia of the 1897 to 1900 age groups (i.e. all 19–22-year-olds) – a move which, in theory, would have placed almost a million Siberians under arms.[131] To precisely what extent these mobilizations were successful it is not possible to determine. One White officer, for example, later maintained that there were 800,000 men in the Russian Army by the summer of 1919; another that there were 200,000.[132] Perhaps the truth was that in Kolchak's vast domain nobody really knew the precise dimensions of the army – not least because the *stavka* permitted individual army group commanders to institute mobilizations in the areas under their control with virtually no central, co-ordinated superintendence. The local commands would then proceed to exaggerate the size of their muster-rolls in reports to the centre in an attempt to procure sufficient of the scarce supplies of food at Omsk's disposition to feed the number of men they actually had. The State Comptroller, Krasnov, for example, believed that he could count on all reports of the number of troops to be fed at the front being inflated by 500%;[133] less certainly, the Minister of Supply, Serebrennikov, who was (at least in part) responsible for victualling the army, could only hazard a guess in late 1918 that there might be 'some tens of thousands of soldiers, if not more' stationed in the Urals.[134]

On the other hand, although we may never know the total size of Kolchak's army throughout Siberia, Soviet historians (on the basis of archival materials unavailable in the west) quite consistently cited figures which indicate the presence of around 130,000 to 145,000 men on and in the immediate rear of the eastern front by the

131 'Report of the Russian Telegraph Agency, 18.iv.1919', *Struggling Russia*, Vol. 1, No. 6, 26.iv.1919.

132 cf. Filat′ev, p. 62 and Denikin, Vol. 3, p. 104.

133 Budberg, Vol. 14, p. 274.

134 Serebrennikov, p. 226.

time that the Russian Army's spring offensive commenced in March 1919.[135] And this is the force with which we will be chiefly concerned in our analysis of Kolchak's offensive. From January 3rd 1919 it had been divided into three army groups: General Gajda's Siberian Army (occasionally referred to as the Northern Army), which was based at Perm; the Western Army (incorporating General Belov's Cossack Group) under General M.V. Khanzhin (an artillery officer of Orenburg Cossack origin and a former military leader of Komuch's People's Army), which was operating in the vicinity of Ufa; and the Southern Army (occasionally referred to as the Orenburg Army), comprising the Ural Cossacks of Lieutenant-General Ataman V.S. Tolstov and the Orenburg Cossacks of Ataman Dutov.

On paper this was a mighty force. However, Kolchak's Russian Army was far from being an 'army' in the proper sense of the word. For one thing, the Southern Army Group was only nominally under Kolchak's control – the immense difficulties of communication between Omsk and Dutov's headquarters in the Turgai Steppe east of Orenburg after the loss to the Bolsheviks in October 1918 of the Kinel′ railway junction (east of Samara) meant that, according to local observers, Dutov's forces were 'almost entirely self-supporting', with only a few cartloads of supplies and the occasional message by courier getting through.[136]

But at least Dutov was able to draw his recruits from among the Whites' natural constituency, the Cossacks (of the Orenburg and Ural hosts). In the absence of any sizable hosts in Siberia proper and with the Cossacks east of Baikal in thrall to Semenov and Kalmykov,[137] in order to create the mass army they desired, Kolchak's other commanders had to rely upon the services of untried peasant conscripts, who – despite the hopes of the *stavka* and the idealization of the Russian peasantry indulged in by the likes of Dieterichs – it was usually necessary to mobilize by force. Moreover, the peasants who were mobilized were almost invariably very young, for it was feared that to take any man over the age of twenty

135 See, for example, *Istoriia grazhdanskoi voiny*. Moscow, 1959, Vol. 4, pp. 50–2 ('130,000–145,000 men'); Ogorodnikov, T.E. *Udar po Kolchak vesnoi 1919g.* Moscow (1938), p. 73 ('300,000 men, of whom 130,000 were at the front'); Spirin, L.M. *Razgrom armii Kolchaka*. Moscow (1957), p. 93 ('130,000 men at the front'); Svetachev, *Imperialisticheskaia interventsiia*, p. 122 ('140,000 at the front').

136 N.N., p. 98; Borodin, N.A. *Idealy i deiatel′nost′: sorok let zhizni i raboty riadovago russkago intelligenta (1879–1919)*. Berlin–Paris (1930), p. 204.

137 On the relative contributions to the White war effort of Cossacks in South Russia and Siberia, see below pp. 529–33.

or twenty-one was to run the risk of infecting the White army with elements who might have been Bolshevized during service in the Great War – of the six hundred recruits from Orenburg who arrived at Omsk in March, for example, only one hundred were old enough to smoke, according to an American observer (who had already expressed himself shocked at the fact that every seventeen-year-old he had met in Siberia smoked regularly).[138] The mobilization of workers, of course, was out of the question for the Whites – not only were they politically unreliable, but they were sorely needed in Urals and Siberian factories – while repeated attempts to raise units from the Siberian and refugee intelligentsia proved unworkable, given their too critical view of the excesses of the army.[139] Consequently, the Russian Army was deprived of the services of anybody of military experience, technical ability or education. Instead, noted a Red commander, the forces of his opponents consisted almost entirely of 'green youths' driven unwillingly from the Siberian villages.[140]

This qualitative weakness of Kolchak's forces was compounded by the fact that the perceived shortage of time (the Whites' desire to achieve military success at the earliest possible moment) together with the army command's immutable confidence and their tendency to underestimate politics – in other words, all the elements of what might be termed the 'White psychology' – determined that little effort was made either to train these raw recruits or to instil in them any understanding of or sympathy for the White cause beyond that which it was blithely assumed would be innate in them. The assumption was totally false. 'If you asked a soldier what he was fighting for, he always told you that he did not know', reported a British intelligence officer;[141] if the recruits had any inkling of the Whites' aims, added the correspondent of the *Manchester Guardian*, it was only sufficient to make them 'very doubtful of the uses to which their victory, if they were finally victorious,

[138] Filat'ev, p. 47; Gidney, J.B. (ed.) *Witness to a Revolution: Letters from Russia (1916–1919) by Edward T. Heald.* Kent State University (1972), pp. 306, 331. The Whites feared *frontoviki* 'like they feared the devil', said Budberg, (Vol. 14, p. 274).

[139] See below pp. 526–7.

[140] Eikhe, pp. 149–50.

[141] FO 371/4096/113468 'Report of a British Intelligence Officer, 31.vii.1919'.

would be put'. In general, gloated the afore-mentioned Red commander, his opponents' forces were 'political infants'.[142]

But even the debilitating effects of the conscripts' ignorance of 'their' cause paled in comparison to the damage done to Kolchak's war effort by the Whites' overweening optimism and the *stavka*'s blind insistence that every available soldier should be rushed to the front in the first months of 1919. One of the sternest critics of this 'mad rush' was General Knox of Britmis. Again and again he protested to Kolchak and to Lebedev that it was utterly pointless, if not downright dangerous, to call men to arms whom he (as *Chef d'Arrière*) well knew that the government could neither clothe nor equip, let alone feed for any length of time. As early as October 8th 1918 Knox had predicted that, unless the size of the army was reduced by 40–50%, the deficiencies of supplies would lead to disaster.[143] Of course, the British general may not have been fully cognizant of – or, at least, he may not have fully appreciated – the political imperatives driving Kolchak into launching an early attempt to advance into European Russia: such a straightforward soldier as Knox may not have been best equipped to view the Russian Army as the 'premier diplomat' of a political cause. Nevertheless, Knox was undoubtedly correct in his assessment that this khaki-clad diplomat, if diplomat it was to be, was nothing like properly prepared for the task ahead. However, completely under the spell of Lebedev (who dismissed the Briton's criticisms as 'trifles'), Kolchak chose to ignore Knox and, over the winter of 1918 to 1919, untrained and unreliable peasant conscripts continued to be rushed to the Urals front as fast as Siberia's railways could carry them. Once there, they would be left to fend for themselves in the daily scavenge for food and shelter – a demoralizing process which, as Sukin noted, not only led to resentment from the local peasantry (from whom the abandoned troops requisitioned 'everything that came to hand') but also bred disrespect for the central authorities among the ranks and the lower levels of command and contributed to the development of an independent, 'partisan' spirit in these elements of the army.[144]

142 Coates, W.P and Coates, Z.K. (eds.) *Armed Intervention in Russia, 1918–1922*. London (1935), p. 204; Eikhe, p. 150.

143 FO 371/3365/170485 'Knox to WO, 8.x.1918'; WO 32/5707 'Report of the Military Mission in Siberia, 10.xii.1919', pp. 11–12; WO 33/966/1087 'Knox (Omsk) to WO, 2.ii.1919'. At a memorial service for Kolchak Knox later said that he had advised the admiral to 'go slow' as early as August 1918. See *New Russia* (London) Vol. 1, No. 4 (April 1920), p. 122.

144 Sukin (*Leeds Russian Archive*), p. 142.

Knox also attempted to convince Kolchak that an army is only ever as strong as its reserve. As of the date of the commencement of the Russian Army's spring offensive, however, it had no reserve: every available man had been sent to the front or was in the process of being sent there. In February, at a conference at the *stavka*, Knox had at last prevailed upon the Russians to muster the necessary troops for the establishment and training of five reserve divisions in the rear (the Siberian 11th, 12th, 13th and 14th Divisions and one more to be added to the Kappel Corps), four of which would be fitted out by Britmis with the equipment arriving from the British Army. But, due to the otiose pace at which the Omsk military establishment preferred to work – the Minister of War, Stepanov, had 'a congenital reluctance to decide anything', according to Knox – the necessary orders were not even issued until March 18th; and it was not until May (after Knox had fired off a couple of missives to the lethargic Minister of War and to Kolchak) that the conscripts for the reserve divisions actually began to be levied.[145] Thus, if the unthinkable should happen and Kolchak's great offensive of March did not occasion the immediate demise of the Bolsheviks but signalled instead only the beginning of a lengthy campaign – and worse still if the Red Army should counter-attack and manage to break through into Siberia – Kolchak would have no means of replenishing the Russian Army, for the new reserve could not possibly have been ready to step into the line before the summer of 1919.

Apart from to a large extent determining the form of their army, the Siberian Whites' inflated self-confidence and self-esteem would also affect the manner in which it was planned to have the Russian Army operate at the front; i.e. it would to a significant degree determine strategic planning.

With the Eastern Front stretching for almost 1,500 km from the Kama to the Ural rivers by the spring of 1919, choices were clearly going to have to be made in the White camp with regard to where to concentrate the bulk of their forces. The most obvious course of action would have been for Kolchak's army to concentrate upon a move south-westwards in order to end the isolation of the Southern Army in the Orenburg steppe and, eventually, to establish contact with Denikin's army, the

145 WO 32/5707 'Report of the Military Mission', App. B; WO 33/966/1530 'Knox (Omsk) to WO, 31.iii.1919'; WO 33/977A 'Narrative of Events in Siberia, 1918–1920', p. 11, App. E and App. F. See also Knox's letter to the American historian of the civil war, G. Stewart, included in Long, J. 'General Sir Alfred Knox and the Russian Civil War', *Sbornik of the Study Group on the Russian Revolution* Vol. 9 (1983), pp. 58–9.

Armed Forces of South Russia (AFSR), somewhere in the vicinity of Tsaritsyn. Even the distinctly unmartial predecessors of the Omsk dictator, the Directory, had recognized the sagacity of such a strategy and, on October 2nd 1918, one of their first actions had been to despatch a message to the then commander of White forces in the South, General Alekseev, suggesting a union at Tsaritsyn.[146] The strategic advantages to be gained from such a campaign would have included the opportunity, thereafter, to create a joint command in order to plan and co-ordinate congruent advances from the south and the east upon the Bolshevik stronghold in central Russia; this would have denied Trotsky the chance to move units from one front to another to meet different threats at different times. Moreover, the way would then have been clear for Kolchak to receive supplies from Europe via the Black Sea rather than along the greatly over-burdened Trans-Siberian Railway. The political prize of union with Denikin would have been the opportunity to harmonize the relations with the Allies of the two senior White leaders as well as to concur upon policy declarations for the future of Russia, avoiding any embarrassing contradictions. In South Russia the most able of Denikin's generals (and arguably the most successful of all White leaders), Baron P.N. Wrangel, saw the arguments in favour of such a union as being incontrovertible: it was, he said, 'a crying need [which] simply stared us in the face'.[147]

Until January 1919, less senior members of the Omsk régime, such as Guins, could only assume that efforts were being made to achieve a union with Denikin even if he (a lowly Assistant Minister of Education at that time) was not hearing of them. When he returned to high office in February, however, Guins was astounded to discover that no attempt had been made to co-ordinate military activities between Siberia and the south.[148] In fact, Kolchak's Order No. 779 of January 6th 1919 (which had formally established the Western Army), and battle orders published following strategic planning conferences at the front of February 1919, which had been attended by Kolchak, Lebedev and army commanders, envisaged only that operations in March–April would concentrate *initially* upon the recapture of territory in Ufa *guberniia* up to the River Ik in order to establish 'a favourable point of departure for decisive operations against the Bolsheviks'. No mention at all was

146 Grey, M. and Bourdier, J. *Les Armées Blanches*. Paris (1968), p. 160.

147 Wrangel, P.N. *Always with Honour*. New York (1957), p. 76.

148 Guins, G.C. 'Professor and Government Official: Russia, China and California', University of California, Berkeley: Russian Émigré Series (1966), p. 198.

made of any *strategic* plan to unite with Denikin at Tsaritsyn. Moreover, time (and the fact that it was to be the Siberian Army, rather than forces in the central and southern Urals, which was supposed to receive the bulk of men and equipment) was to reveal that the strategic weight of the 'decisive operations' Kolchak planned to succeed the local operation against Ufa, would take place far to the north, in the hope of a combination with an advance of Allied and White forces from their base at Arkhangel′sk.[149]

Arriving at Omsk in May 1919 to take up a post in the Ministry of War, Baron Budberg, a military specialist of the old school, could only gasp in incomprehension at how Kolchak and Lebedev's *stavka* could have ignored the patently obvious advantages of a concentration to the south in favour of 'shallow estimations' of what could be achieved in the north 'which only fools could believe in'.[150] Of course there was the factor, which Budberg did not consider, of military inertia: the autumn and winter campaign of 1918 to 1919 had been directed against Perm and thereafter motivation, resources and manpower kept flowing in the same direction (particularly because the campaign had been successful).[151] Also, the northern Urals were rather better supplied with railways and industrial resources than was the case to the south. This, however, was a factor only of local and temporary significance and would have ceased to apply once that the Russian Army had moved across the Urals into European Russia, where the south was rather more developed than the north. And as for the problem of inertia, this was not something which it should have been beyond the power of the Supreme Ruler and his high command to stem if they had deemed it propitious to do so. The problem was that they did not.

Initially, however, it has to be said that Admiral Kolchak himself appears to have been very much in favour of establishing closer links with Denikin. He constantly badgered the British High Commissioner at Omsk, Sir Charles Eliot, to obtain from London more information about developments in the south of Russia and, moreover, requested in December 1919 that the following very cordial message should be forwarded via London to Denikin:

149 *Iz istorii grazhdanskoi voiny v SSSR (Tom pervyi: mai 1918–mart 1919)*. Moscow (1960), pp. 66–8.

150 Budberg, Vol. 14, pp. 240–1. The *stavka* had adopted 'the plan of a simpleton', agreed General Filat′ev, (*Katastrofa*, p. 53).

151 Ultimately the concentration of forces on the northern sector can be traced back to commands issued by Czechoslovak leaders in August 1918 to capture Perm in anticipation of Allied landings in North Russia. See Golovin, Vol. 8, pp. 115; Eikhe, p. 198.

> I consider it indispensable to co-ordinate our actions. For this purpose it is necessary to know the direction of your main operations. I sincerely believe in our common friendship which will not be broken in any circumstances. I look forward to joining you and meeting with you as soon as possible. May God be with you.[152]

A few days later, in January 1919, Omsk received a telegram of greeting from Denikin's representative in Paris (Sazonov) which offered recognition of the Supreme Ruler's authority and briefly outlined the programme of the AFSR (namely the re-establishment of a Great Russia, struggle with Bolshevism until complete victory and the co-ordination of a plan of campaign between the Siberian and South Russian White centres). Kolchak replied to this on January 10th, expressing his entire agreement with these aims and once again asserting that 'our common purpose to attain internal union guarantees the success of our mutual action'.[153]

That this 'internal union' of the White movements in South Russia and in Siberia was never forged and such 'mutual action' never taken was not the fault of General Denikin. Although he was initially rather embarrassed by Sazonov's telegram to Kolchak of December (for, at that early stage, he had actually intended only to recognize the admiral's authority in Siberia and the Far East, rather than in Russia as a whole), Denikin took cognizance of advice from his representatives in Paris to the effect that a politically and militarily united front between Siberia and South Russia was essential to maximize Allied respect for the anti-Bolshevik cause. Consequently, on May 30th 1919, the Commander-in-Chief of the AFSR issued his Order No. 145, recognizing Kolchak both as Supreme Ruler and Supreme Commander.[154]

Of course, this order might be dismissed as an empty gesture, which meant little in terms of real subordination for as long as Kolchak and Denikin remained isolated from each other – and, indeed, Denikin's subsequent tactics have been cited as evidence that the general was actually driven solely by a personal ambition to beat Kolchak in a race to capture Moscow. General Wrangel, for example, was later to

152 FO 371/4094/1753 'Eliot (Omsk) to FO, 1.i.1919'.

153 *The Times* (London) 17.1.1919; Denikin, Vol. 5, pp. 86–8.

154 *ibid.*, Vol. 5, pp. 97–8. On the evolution of Denikin's decision to recognize Kolchak see Astrov, N.I. 'Priznanie gen. Denikinym adm. Kolchaka: prikaz 30 maia 1919g – No. 145', *Golos minuvshago na chuzhoi storone* (Paris), Vol. 14, No. 1 (1926), pp. 201–21. For Kolchak's reply of July 1st, which named Denikin as Deputy Supreme Commander, see Grey and Bourdier, p. 213; and Denikin, Vol. 5, p. 103.

criticize Denikin for spending too much time in early 1919 in consolidating his hold over the North Caucasus rather than making a move to unite with Kolchak at Tsaritsyn.[155] But this is surely unfair. Before he could safely move north, Denikin really had to subdue the two Red Armies in his rear. Once that had been achieved, he would almost certainly, given the choice, have attempted to have forged a physical union with the Russian Army. He was well aware, he said in a letter to Kolchak of February 14th, of 'the huge advantage' to be gained by 'the possibility of direct and uninterupted links between the East and the South' and expressed regret that news reaching him at the time from Omsk seemed to indicate that 'the thrust of the Siberian forces is evidently directed to the north'.[156] Also, in early May, Denikin was moved to despatch another message to Omsk, yet again suggesting a joint advance (this time on Saratov) and yet again anticipating a meeting with Kolchak on the Volga for the establishment of a joint command. This last message from the south was never to reach Siberia for its courier, Grishin-Almazov, was captured by the Reds whilst crossing the Caspian.[157] But even had it reached Omsk, Denikin's plea would have been to no avail. For what had actually damned the possibility of 'internal union' was that since January all thoughts of an advance on Tsaritsyn or Saratov had been ditched in Omsk. Kolchak had simply not waited for Denikin to be ready before beginning his own advance; by May the Siberian troops were, in fact, approaching the very height of their spring offensive (which had been planned in February to commence in the first days of March); and, as Denikin had feared, they were not concentrating on either Saratov or Tsaritsyn.

Thus, although Denikin appears to have been keen to develop the initial contacts which had been made with Kolchak in January 1919 into real co-ordination, the feeling was not reciprocated at Omsk. As a result, there was no 'general agreement' on strategy, as one history of Denikin's campaigns has suggested.[158] In a telegram which Denikin received in April Kolchak might still be suggesting that 'as soon as connections are made between your army and mine, we must meet personally to decide the questions of a single government and command', but he now seemed to be referring to some indefinite time and place in the future. Gone was the sense of

155 Wrangel, pp. 76–9; Denikin, Vol. 5, p. 114.

156 *Sbornik Istparta*, No. 1 (1923), p. 138.

157 Denikin, Vol. 5, pp. 85, 88–89; Grey and Bourdier, p. 196.

158 Brinkley, G.A. *The Volunteer Army and the Allied Intervention in South Russia, 1917–1921*. Notre Dame, IN (1960), p. 190.

urgency which had permeated the admiral's telegrams to the south of January 2nd and 10th.[159] Now Kolchak not only proposed no concrete measures to ensure that the Russian Army and the AFSR did meet (and soon), but by this time had actually put his name to a strategic plan which seemed precisely framed to guarantee that they did not. This was perhaps the single most disastrous consequence of the hectoring arrogance which had gripped the Siberian Whites and, in particular, the *stavka* of General Dmitri Antonovich Lebedev.

Most historians of the Russian civil war have, to one degree or another, concerned themselves with the phenomenon of the failure of Kolchak and Denikin to co-ordinate their military activity in 1919. Hitherto the influence of the Siberian camp's overweening self-confidence has not been fully appreciated. In fact, several other factors have generally been accepted as being responsible for that strategic failure – factors which further investigation seems to suggest were, at best, of secondary significance.

Often cited as militating against the co-ordination of the various anti-Bolshevik fronts are the tortuous and unreliable communication links between South Russia and Siberia.[160] White couriers, it is pointed out, had either to run the gauntlet of Bolshevik-held sectors along the lower Volga and on the northern Caspian – the fate of Grishin-Almazov is invariably referred to here – or face an around-the-world voyage by sea to Vladivostok and thence along the Trans-Siberian Railway to Omsk (a total of some 15,000 miles). In the turbulent days of 1919, the latter journey was to take another of Denikin's envoys, Major-General Sychev, no less than four months to complete.[161] Telegraphic exchanges were possible – though only via the roundabout route of the old Russian embassies in Paris or Athens and, for the most part, Kolchak tended to rely on Bolshevik radio broadcasts for information as to what was going on in the rest of Russia. The consequence of these impediments was that even by January 1919, little more than rumours were known in Siberia of developments in South Russia. 'Neither Kolchak, nor the French High Commissioner nor myself knows more than that Denikin's HQ is near Ekaterinodar', reported Sir Charles Eliot to London at that time. 'We do not know what extent of

159 Denikin, Vol. 5, p. 87.

160 See, for example, Brinkley, p. 193; Kenez, P. *Civil War in South Russia, 1919–1920*. London (1977), p. 51.

161 *Russkaia armiia* (Omsk) No. 114, 3.vi.1919.

territory he controls, nor where he is advancing nor in what direction.' Kolchak himself was sufficiently in the dark as to enquire of Eliot as to whether it was true that the Grand Duke Nicholas was playing an active political role in the South.[162]

Clearly, therefore, there was room for misunderstanding and delay in any attempt to establish military co-ordination between the anti-Bolshevik fronts. However, communications problems alone cannot explain the complete absence of co-ordination. True, as Denikin complained, telegrams could take as much as a month to get through.[163] But, on the other hand, examination of the messages passed between Omsk and Ekaterinodar via Paris in January–February 1919 reveals that the medium of the Russian Political Conference could keep Kolchak and Denikin fully informed of each other's opinions in far less time than that. Moreover, when a crisis raised its head, in the shape of the Prinkipo proposal, which within the White camps was universally deemed to be a threat to their cause, the two leaders were able to arrange a *perfectly* co-ordinated and orderly political response.[164] Why should this not also have been the case in military affairs?

Crucially, moreover, the existence of difficulties in communication with Denikin and the south can in no way explain why Kolchak's spring offensive was aimed, contrarily, at facilitating union with the White régime at Arkhangel'sk (after an initial tactical move to secure Ufa). General Miller's Provisional Government of North Russia *was* in intermittent radio communication with Omsk and, on April 30th 1919, *had* recognized Kolchak as Supreme Ruler, a month before Denikin did so.[165] Both of these factors might be construed as favouring a concentration on the north. If anything, however, Omsk was even less aware of the prevailing situation in the territory occupied by Miller than it was with regard to the south. At least a trickle of emissaries from Kornilov, Alekseev and Denikin had got through to Siberia from March 1918 onwards, whereas the first physical contact with the north was not established until late April 1919, when eighteen Russians and a British officer had unexpectedly appeared near Perm after a seven-week trek from the

162 FO 371/4094/6350 'Eliot (Omsk) to FO, 11.i.1919'; FO 371/4094/1752 'Eliot (Omsk) to FO, 2.i.1919'. On Kolchak's reliance on Bolshevik radio broadcasts, see Pepeliaev, 'Dnevnik', Vol. 4, p. 49.

163 Denikin, Vol. 5, pp. 89–90.

164 See Mints, 'Vneshnaia politika', pp. 72–5 and *passim*.

165 FO 538/4/[p. 4] 'Declaration of the Provisional Government at Archangel, 30.iv.1919'; *Union (Bureau de Presse Russe)* (Paris), No. 9, 5.viii.1919.

White Sea.[166] Such arrivals were eagerly debriefed by the *stavka* and by Kolchak personally – as, indeed, was anybody who had been anywhere near North Russia in the past two years. Nevertheless, noted Guins, 'It was plain to see that the admiral had no more information about the operations and conditions on the potential northern front than did anyone else.'[167]

A surprising variety of commentators have concurred that another of the major factors in persuading Kolchak to opt for a union with Arkhangel'sk rather than with South Russia was advice alleged to have been given to him by the head of Britmis, General Alfred Knox.[168] Such assertions are primarily based on an unquestioning acceptance of a rumour reported by Baron Budberg. On May 11th 1919, the latter inscribed in his diary that:

> The humble folk of the *stavka* are saying that the northern advance was chosen under the influence of the insistent advice of General Knox, who dreams of the most rapid acquisition of British aid and supplies via Kotlas, from where there are direct river communications with Arkhangel'sk which houses significant amounts of British stores.[169]

To this alleged evidence of British involvement is sometimes appended the claim of the Director of the Ministry of Foreign Affairs at Omsk, I.I. Sukin, that Knox had special instructions from London to press for an advance on Kotlas in order that, once the union of Arkhangel'sk and Omsk had been forged, Britain would be free to withdraw its own weary and disaffected troops from North Russia.[170]

166 *The Times* (London), 9.v.1919. For an account of the journey from North Russia to Omsk, see Kislitsin, V.A. *V ogne grazhdanskoi voiny: memuary.* Harbin (1936).

167 Fedotoff-White, pp. 216–7; Guins, 'Professor and Government Official', p. 199.

168 See, for example, Dacy (p. 78) and the otherwise strikingly conflicting and partisan accounts given by Mel'gunov, S.P. *Tragediia admirala Kolchaka (iz istorii grazhdanskoi voiny na Volge, Ural i v Sibiri* (1930–1931), Part 3, Vol. 1, pp. 126–7, on the one hand, and, on the other, the Soviet editors of *Istoriia grazhdanskoi voiny* (Vol. 4, p. 52), Kuz'min, G.V. *Razgrom interventov i belogvardeitsev v 1917–1922gg.* Moscow (1977), p. 210, and Anishev, A. *Ocherki istorii grazhdanskoi voiny.* Moscow (1925), p. 231.

169 Budberg, Vol. 14, p. 241.

170 See the references to Sukin's memoirs (pp. 247–8 of the t.s. at *Leeds Russian Archive*) in Denikin, Vol. 5, p. 91; and Mel'gunov, Part 3, Vol. 1, p. 129.

Now it may well have been that Knox was generally in favour of a northern advance; certainly no evidence has come to light to refute such an assertion.[171] It is also true that the Englishman had enjoyed the confidence of Kolchak to a greater extent than most foreign representatives at Omsk. However, it is surely to be doubted whether Knox's preferences could have been of overriding significance in determining Kolchak's strategy. Firstly, due account must be taken of the Supreme Ruler's aversion to accepting in good grace the advice of *any* foreigners, habitually denigrating it as 'interference'.[172] Secondly, account must be taken of chronology. It has already been noted that Knox was one of the most vociferous critics of the decision to undertake any aggressive military operations in early 1919. In so far as he was offering any advice to Kolchak in January–February, therefore, it was that there should be *no* advance in *any* direction until the summer. As for the oft-cited British plan to encourage the union of Omsk and Arkhangel′sk in order to facilitate the withdrawal of their own troops from the north, there was indeed such a scheme. However, it was not even formulated by Churchill's War Office until mid-April 1919 (and was subsequently transmitted to Knox, in very cautious terms, on April 30th), was not approved by Lloyd George until May 4th and operations from the north were not planned to commence until after July 1st.[173] In fact, the Churchill plan's very inspiration may well have been the reports of March–April from Siberia indicating that Kolchak's armies were making advances in the northern sector; and this was certainly the motivation, when it was was eventually elicited, behind Lloyd George's approval of the scheme.[174]

To claim that the British plan played any part in determining the strategy of Kolchak's spring offensive, which was settled upon at conferences of early February, is, therefore, to put the cart before the horse. At the most it can perhaps be assumed that Knox did not object to the northerly bias of the advance – if

171 Knox's second in command, Ward, was also in favour of a northern advance, believing that, if union with the forces from Arkhangel′sk could be achieved, 'the slightest movement would result in a combination which could move straight to Petrograd' (Ward, pp. 147–9). Ward was, however, under the illusion that the Siberian Army's objective, Glazov, was only 300 miles from Petrograd; in fact the distance is over 700 miles.

172 See, for example, Varneck and Fisher, p. 187.

173 WO 33/966/1735 'WO to Knox. 30.iv.1919'; WO 33/967/2158 'WO to Knox (Omsk), 10.vi.1919'; Churchill, W.S. *The World Crisis: The Aftermath.* London (1929), pp. 249–50.; Ullman, Vol. 2, pp. 183–5.

174 Gilbert, Vol. 4, p. 283.

advance, against his own better judgement, there had to be – once operations were in progress. When, however, on May 6th 1919, Knox read to Kolchak the text of a message from the War Office indicating that more support could be expected from the British Government 'if he finds it possible to reconcile a northern movement' rather than one on Tsaritsyn 'with his main plan' of capturing Moscow, then it could only at best have served to confirm that which Kolchak had decided upon some three months earlier.[175]

The exigencies of those who from a variety of motives have sought to criticize Kolchak personally for the Whites' strategic mistakes have occasioned some strange bedfellows in the historiography of the Russian Army's spring offensive of 1919. Thus, the editors of one standard Soviet history of the civil war choose to accept the claim of the Czech adventurer (whom they otherwise invariably vilify), Radola Gajda, that at the conference of White military commanders at Cheliabinsk in February 1919, it was the Supreme Ruler himself who specifically insisted that union with Denikin should be avoided and that the main thrust of the advance should be on the northern flank. According to Gajda, Kolchak's motive for this was not only distrust of Denikin personally and the desire to avoid the thorny problem of 'superiority' (i.e. seniority) should their forces combine, but also the ambition to hang on to his supreme authority beyond the defeat of the Bolsheviks: Kolchak was concerned, alleged Gajda, that 'he who first reaches Moscow will be in a dominant position'.[176]

In this instance, however, we must surely concur with the émigré historian, S.P. Mel′gunov, who guessed that Gajda's version of events was specious.[177] Not least the claim contradicts what we know of Gajda's own nature. The young Czech was of a notoriously perfidious character – in 1918 he had been Kolchak's right-hand

175 WO 33/966/1735 'WO to Blair (Vladivostok), 30.iv.1919'; WO 33/966/1879 'Knox (Omsk) to WO, 6.v.1919'.

176 Gajda, R. *Moje pameti: Ceskolovenska anabase zret na Ural proti Bolshevikum*. Prague (1924), p. 134; *Istoriia grazhdanskoi voiny v SSSR* Vol. 4, p. 52. Even more surprising is that the Kadet leader, Paul Miliukov, who had much personal regard for Kolchak, goes along with Gajda's account. See Miliukov, P.N. *Rossiia na perelome*. Paris (1927), pp. 128–9. To this day even otherwise balanced and considered accounts of the civil war accept this version. Thus, Bruce Lincoln writes that Kolchak was 'too envious of Denikin's growing success in the South to consider forcing his advance in that direction', but offers no evidence to support the contention. See Lincoln, W.B. *Red Victory: A History of the Russian Civil War*. London (1989), p. 250.

177 Mel′gunov, Part 3, Vol. 1, p. 126.

man; in late 1919 he was to associate himself with an SR rising against the dictatorship; in the 1920s he was to lead a Czech fascist party; later still he collaborated with the Nazi occupation of his homeland. Such a man would certainly not have been above libelling the deceased Kolchak in his memoirs, having broken acrimoniously with him during the summer of 1919. Personal improbity aside, however, Gajda undermines his allegations against the Supreme Ruler by insisting that, at the afore-mentioned Cheliabinsk conference at which the northerly bias to the offensive was determined, he himself had argued in favour of concentrating on the southern flank.[178] Common sense tells us that this adventurous and fiercely ambitious young commander would have been unlikely to have argued for a strategy which would condemn his own Siberian Army to playing second fiddle to Dutov's Cossacks in any forthcoming operations – it had not been selflessness on that scale which had propelled Gajda from the job of a *Feldscher* in the Austrian Army in 1914 to his current exalted position, or had won him the popularity and reputation he so enjoyed. Moreover, those who had the chance to converse with Gajda at the time confirm that he was, in fact, strongly and vociferously *in favour* of training the spring offensive on Kotlas so that the forces under his own command would play the leading role.[179] It can only be concluded, therefore, that in making his oft-cited allegations, the Czech was motivated by the retrospective desire to traduce Kolchak and the Omsk *stavka* with which he was to clash, for quite different reasons, later in 1919.

Gajda's account also contradicts what we know of Kolchak's character. The admiral was undoubtedly ambitious and, as we have seen, was intensely proud of his role as Supreme Commander; he, no less than any other White leader, would undoubtedly have relished the prospect of leading a column of troops into Moscow. It is also true that he was inexperienced in land warfare and, as a consequence, may not have fully appreciated the advantages of co-ordinating his operations with Denikin. But equally, Kolchak was not stupid. On the contrary, he was an accomplished scholar, a naval commander of great repute and in 1917 had been one of the five most senior military men in Russia. And he knew his weaknesses: he invariably requested advice on strategy from those he trusted. Surely, therefore, had he been presented with evidence by his trusted advisers – and in February 1919 they

178 Gajda, p. 134.

179 Guins, *Sibir'*, Vol. 2, p. 195; Budberg, Vol. 14, pp. 235ff; Sukin (*Leeds Russian Archive*), pp. 144, 248.

still included Gajda – that failure to combine with Denikin might lead to the collapse of the whole White movement, Kolchak would have done everything in his power to achieve such a combination. As for wanting to guarantee for himself a 'dominant position' upon reaching Moscow, Kolchak never once expressed a desire to remain in power beyond the achievement of military victory over the Bolsheviks; and, he being one to whom soldiering was everything and peacetime politics and civilian government such an impenetrable mystery, we must accept that this was probably not a case of false modesty.

Those who subscribe to the theory of a mutually destructive race to Moscow between Kolchak and Denikin sometimes bolster the allegations of Gajda by reference to an entry in the diary of Omsk's Minister of the Interior, V.N. Pepeliaev, for July 6th 1919. There Kolchak is reported as voicing a suspicion that there were those around Denikin in favour of an independent march on the capital; and the implication often drawn is that the Supreme Ruler consequently decided to respond in kind.[180] But to utilize this reference in such a manner is also misleading. By July there were, indeed, influential soldiers and politicians in Ekaterinodar who favoured a separate advance on Moscow; and on July 3rd Denikin had, in fact, issued his famous 'Moscow Directive' ordering precisely that.[181] The point is, however, that Denikin's separate advance was only settled upon four months *after* Kolchak's offensive had begun (and at least five months after its northerly bias had been determined). Moreover, by July Kolchak's forces were no longer advancing in *any* direction and, for the most part, had actually been retreating for several weeks. Denikin could not realistically have been expected, therefore, to push east at this time in the hope of joining the Supreme Ruler somewhere in Siberia. To make the best of the undesirable situation which prevailed during the summer of 1919, and, in particular, to take advantage of the fact that four Red Armies were tied down in the Urals in pursuit of the Russian Army, an independent advance against central Russia was the logical choice for Denikin and his AFSR. And, as time was to tell, it was very nearly a choice which paid dividends, for the Bolsheviks' failure during the summer to withdraw surplus forces from the pursuit of Kolchak in order to meet the threat from the south would enable the AFSR to advance to a position less than

180 [Pepeliaev, V.N.] 'Razval kolchakovshchiny (iz dnevnika V.N. Pepeliaeva)', *Krasnyi arkhiv* No. 6 (1928), p. 55. An example of such a utilization of this reference is to be found in Ioffe, *Kolchakovskaia avantiura*, p. 218.

181 Denikin, Vol. 5, pp. 97–8.

300 km from Moscow by mid-October. And had Denikin actually succeeded in reaching the capital there would have ensued no political problems or embarrassments for Kolchak. Irrespective of his failure to co-ordinate his strategy with the southern commander, in so far as Kolchak had exchanged opinions with him on political questions, there is no evidence other than that they were in complete accord: most significantly, despite his disappointment at the bias of Kolchak's offensive, Denikin had expressed his unconditional acceptance of Kolchak's avowed plans for the future of Russia as represented in the Supreme Ruler's note to the Allies of June 4th; while, despite initial doubts, both Union of Regeneration and National Centre leaders in South Russia had accepted the subordination of their general to Kolchak.[182]

To cast doubt upon the existence of any personal or political rivalry between Kolchak and Denikin is not to say, however, that a spirit of jealousy and competition did not exist between Siberia and South Russia. But the eastern nexus of these destructive forces was not the Supreme Ruler's office but his *stavka* and, in particular, the person of his Chief of Staff, Lebedev. The latter consistently argued in favour of a northerly bias to the spring offensive and the avoidance of union with Denikin. It was Kolchak's misfortune that, as has been demonstrated, circumstances had combined to produce a community of interests between Lebedev and other key figures in the military hierarchy – notably Knox and Gajda – who, although they were generally critical of the Chief of Staff, were for reasons of their own in favour of the strategy he proposed. It was perhaps this chance consensus which ultimately convinced Kolchak of the sagacity of the attempted move via Kotlas which has puzzled commentators ever since.[183]

Since 1919 universal and unqualified reprobation has rained down upon the memory of Major-General Dmitri Antonovich Lebedev, the formerly quite

182 *ibid.*, Vol. 5, pp. 85ff; Lukomskii, A.S. *Vospominaniia.* Berlin (1922), Vol. 2, pp. 152–4; Sokolov, K.N. *Pravlenie generala Denikina (iz vospominanii).* Sofia (1921), pp. 128–9.

183 Another powerful pressure group within the Siberian White camp, whose own priorities led them to favour a northern advance, was the commanding staff of Kolchak's Siberian 'navy', the Kama River Fleet. (See Budberg, Vol. 14, p. 241.) Their leader, Minister of Marine Admiral M.I. Smirnov, had Kolchak's ear as an old friend and colleague (he had been Kolchak's Chief of Staff in the Black Sea from 1916 to 1917 and had accompanied him on his mission to the USA) and he would no doubt have prevailed upon the Supreme Ruler to sanction an advance on Moscow via Viatka, for that would have provided an opportunity for his fleet to shine in operations along the Kama, Volga and Oka rivers.

insignificant colonel of the tsar's *stavka*, who was only thirty-five at the time he was promoted to his lofty position under Kolchak. At least two observers (partisans of quite different wings of Siberian politics during the civil war) have deemed Kolchak's Chief of Staff and (from June to August) Minister of War to have been nothing less than 'an evil genius'.[184] That, however, may well be to overestimate Lebedev's political prowess. More convincing is the estimation of Budberg, who knew him well, that Lebedev was a 'fortuitous parvenu' who just happened to be in the right place at the right time to take advantage of Kolchak's notorious inability to select sagacious advisers.[185]

In the admiral's defence, it has to be said that, in comparison to the relative superfluity of officers in the southern White zone, his choice of military councillors in Siberia was quite limited. In particular, most of the *genshtabisty* (officers of the Imperial General Staff) who were to fight the Bolsheviks had gravitated to South Russia to support Alekseev in early 1918.[186] However, it is clear that Kolchak did not even make the best use of the resources of military experience and knowledge which were available to him. Of the former tsarist generals in Siberia, for example, General V.E. Flug and Baron Budberg were both of considerable experience in military-organizational work and had lengthy records of active service; yet Flug was allowed to languish ineffectively in the Far East, while Budberg was only employed (and only from May 1919 onwards) in mainly bureaucratic work at the Ministry of War, where he was blocked in his every attempt to influence strategic planning. General Golovin was not employed at all on active service, despite the widespread hopes among the army and society that his arrival in Siberia presaged an assumption of the role of commander-in-chief. Meanwhile General A.I. Andogskii, the Chief of the Imperial General Staff Academy, for several months was virtually exiled to

184 Dotsenko, P. *The Struggle for a Democracy in Siberia: An Eye-Witness Account of a Contemporary*. Stanford (1983), p. 68; Arnol'dov, p. 177.

185 Budberg, Vol. 14, p. 241.

186 Some witnesses speak of colonels serving as privates in the early days of the Volunteer Army, such was their abundance in the south. See Shebeko, B. *Russian Civil War (1918–1922) and Emigration*. (University of California, Berkeley: Russian Émigré Series, Oral History Collection No. 9) Berkeley (1961), pp. 14–15. The stimulus for officers committed to opposing the Bolsheviks had, of course, arisen some months earlier in the south (with Kornilov's flight to the Don of November 1917) than it had in Siberia (with the Czechoslovak revolt of May 1918), which may explain the disparity in the numbers of officers serving in the two White regions. See Burman, A. 'My Meetings with White Generals', *Russian Review* Vol. 27, No. 2 (April 1965), p. 215 on this point.

Tomsk along with his pupils, being regarded, despite his anti-socialist credentials, as a collaborator with the Bolsheviks because he had not led his charges across the lines to the White side until the autumn of 1918. Even more scandalous was that General Dieterichs, who had one of the most distinguished war records of 1914 to 1917, and who had positively shone during the Czechoslovak campaigns against the Bolsheviks in 1918, was employed for much of the first half of 1919 in chairing an investigation into the execution of the Romanovs and was not given an important command at the front until the summer. One officer in the Ministry of War was later to charge that this waste of talent occurred because 'certain people, already having reserved senior posts, did not wish to give them up to more suitable, knowledgeable generals'.[187]

The Supreme Ruler, of course, had the power to put an end to such abuses; but instead he encouraged them. Shunning the obvious talents and experience of Flug, Andogskii, Golovin et al., in November 1918, as we have seen, Kolchak had promoted Lebedev to Major-General and made him Chief of Staff. As such, given the admiral's own ignorance of land warfare and the civil responsibilities constantly demanding his attention as Supreme Ruler, Lebedev was to become 'practically Commander-in-Chief of the Russian Army' from the very beginning, as one source has it.[188] In this capacity, acting in Kolchak's name, he had always to be obeyed; he was able, in fact, noted Budberg, 'to manage everything but be accountable to nobody'.[189]

How Kolchak came to select Lebedev to be his most senior military adviser remains 'an unsolved mystery', as another officer noted.[190] Rumours abounded in the wake of the coup that Lebedev's ascendancy was a reward for the part he had played in bringing Kolchak to power.[191] Such blatant favouritism, however, was not Kolchak's style (and anyway Syromiatnikov would have been the more logical recipient of such a reward). More convincing is the suggestion made by some observers that the impressionable and idealistic admiral was swayed by 'the spirit of Kornilov' which Lebedev had brought to Omsk with his arrival from the south

187 Klerzhe, pp. 125–7; Sukin (*Leeds Russian Archive*), pp. 45–7.

188 Guins, *Sibir'*, Vol. 2, p. 21.

189 Budberg, Vol. 13, p. 267.

190 Filat'ev, p. 59.

191 See, for example, Budberg, Vol. 14, p. 227.

in October 1918. The verve and the élan of the Volunteer Army, epitomized by Kornilov's legendary 'Ice March' through the Kuban, was much admired by the Siberian Whites (who had no such myth-making material to draw upon in their own experiences as unfaithful servants of Komuch or the Directory).[192] At his interrogation at Irkutsk in 1920 Kolchak was to assert that it was precisely because he regarded Lebedev as an 'official representative' of the southern Whites that he had promoted him.[193] Of course, we do not know what Lebedev told the admiral of his standing in the south (which had actually been nothing of significance); but whether he could properly have been regarded as the 'official representative' of Denikin at the court of Kolchak, having been originally sent east by Alekseev on a simple reconnaissance mission, is at least debatable. What is undoubtedly true, however, is that whether he was really an 'official representative' of the south or just a symbol, Lebedev should have been disqualified from holding the highest office in the Russian Army because, having spent his entire career in administrative posts he had, as Denikin bore witness, 'practically no command experience'. In fact, opined Budberg, 'he was ignorant of military affairs'.[194] Once in office his scheming and empire-building preoccupations, together with the organizational and operational disasters which were to befall the Russian Army in 1919, did little to convince anybody that he had a natural talent for high command or strategy which Kolchak alone had been able to spot. British officers were particularly scathing about Lebedev's abilities: for Knox he was 'sadly wanting in common sense'; for Colonel Ward he was 'the centre of a group of desperadoes who were only in want of a cool brain to make them formidable'.

And Lebedev was, indeed, only the tip of the iceberg. Around himself at the *stavka* this *Wunderkind*, as Budberg dubbed him with heavy sarcasm, attracted legions of young officers equally lacking in experience and ability. Together they then issued orders and proclamations which to Budberg and other soldiers of the old school (who tended to be attached to the Ministry of War) were 'incomprehensible in military terms, the work of fantasists and dilettantes with no knowledge of the

192 This was suggested by both Guins (*Sibir'*, Vol. 2, p. 21) and Sukin (*Leeds Russian Archive*, pp. 31, 47). For an example of Siberian propaganda mythologizing the exploits of the Volunteer Army in 1918 see 'Dobrovol'cheskoe dvizhenie', *Sbornik 'Russkago Biuro Pechati'* (Tokyo), No. 1 (1919), pp. 31–60.

193 Varneck and Fisher, pp. 155–6.

194 Denikin, Vol. 3, p. 259; Budberg, Vol. 15, p. 241.

real situation or of the physical and moral state of the troops, and all done without planning, without consideration, on the spur of the moment'.[195]

Despite his obvious shortcomings, for the first half of 1919 the power of Lebedev and his *stavka* was to remain undiminished. This was at least partly because Lebedev was able to cultivate the friendship of Omsk's most influential civilian ministers – and in particular his kindred spirits Mikhailov and Sukin – in order to create a mutually supportive combination which the British High Commissioner and others regarded as the real centre of power in Siberia. Together they were 'ruling the country from both the military and the civilian point of view', reported Eliot, adding that this all-powerful troika did not always tell Kolchak the truth about developments at the front and in the rear, let alone proffer sound advice on how to surmount the wave of crises which beset the régime as 1919 wore on.[196] Nevertheless, it seems that amidst all the plots, counter-plots and vendettas which bedevilled the White administration in Siberia – and in which, if the truth be told, Lebedev was usually to be found playing a supporting role to Mikhailov's lead – Kolchak had somehow convinced himself that in his Chief of Staff he had found a trustworthy lieutenant: 'At least he will not stab me in the back', wrote the admiral of his Chief of Staff.[197]

In fact it seems that Lebedev was gilding his reputation in the eyes of the easily depressed Kolchak simply by refusing to be the harbinger of bad news. Like so many others in White Siberia, the Chief of Staff had made a profoundly optimistic assessment of the military situation. According to Knox, he was convinced that the Bolsheviks would be defeated within 'ten minutes' of the Russian Army appearing west of the Urals.[198] Kolchak swallowed this sweet prognosis whole. Those like Budberg or Stepanov at the Ministry of War, who were aware of the immense logistical and organizational problems to be surmounted in 1919, were deeply suspicious of the 'wholeheartedly optimistic' predictions of the *stavka*; but they did not have the ear of the Supreme Ruler who, according to Budberg, was 'bewitched

195 *ibid.*, Vol. 14, p. 228. Lebedev's *stavka* 'did not include a single talented worker' in Sukin's view. See Sukin (*Leeds Russian Archive*), p. 149.

196 FO 371/4096/117980 'Eliot (Omsk) to FO, 15.viii.1918'.

197 Cited in Fleming *The Fate of Admiral Kolchak*, p. 136. Sukin alleges that Kolchak would defer to Lebedev's judgement because he was fearful of revealing the extent of his own ignorance of land warfare. See Sukin (*Leeds Russian Archive*), pp. 44–7.

198 WO 32/5707 'Report of the Military Mission in Siberia, 10.xii.1919', p. 11.

by those who spoke to him in a hopeful and optimistic tone' and had no time for 'pessimists'. Even by the end of May 1919, with his Western Army on the point of collapse, Kolchak was still to be found 'smiling contentedly' as Lebedev and others informed him in mellifluous tones that, in spite of this local setback, the Siberian Army would 'enter Moscow to the accompaniment of pealing bells' within a matter of weeks.[199]

As chief military adviser to Kolchak in the first half of 1919, therefore, it is Lebedev who must bear the greatest responsibility for presenting to Kolchak the case that an early advance, in the spring, was a military possibility and that victory was certain. Moreover, during a tour of the front in May of 1919 Budberg came to learn that it had been Lebedev and the *stavka* who had been the foremost advocates of the northerly bias in strategic planning. Budberg was shown the transcript of a conference of senior staff officers at which, in the presence of Kolchak, Lebedev had stated that he did not believe in the 'strength or resilience' of Denikin's forces in the south and considered them to be 'unreliable'. The Chief of Staff had then proceeded to portray the populations of the southern *guberniias* of Russia as likewise 'unreliable', the region being infected, he claimed, with 'many workers, runaways and bandits'. Moreover, Lebedev had asserted, the railway network of the south was in a 'poor state', chronically short of rolling stock and in no way suitable as a bridgehead for 'a general advance on Moscow'. Conversely, the northern *guberniias*, their populace and their communications systems he had consistantly portrayed in a very favourable light. All of this, of course, was the most arrant nonsense. It was, said Budberg, 'a one-sided analysis which only idiots could believe in'.[200] After all, if general Denikin's armies, with their abundance of officers and their battle-hardened Cossack contingents were 'unreliable', what hope was there for Kolchak's own rudderless and unmotivated peasant conscript force? And by no reasonable stretch of the imagination could the sparsely populated, densely forested and alternately frozen and swamp-infested regions of the north be perceived as a more favourable base for an offensive than the populous and rich agricultural regions of the south. True, there were workers in the south who might be sympathetic to Bolshevism. But at least the presence of workers implied the presence of industry in that region and at least the hope of re-establishing industrial

199 Budberg, Vol. 14, pp. 225, 235–8.

200 *ibid.*, Vol. 14, p. 242

production of the type of goods for the want of which the Russian Army was marching into battle unclothed, unshod and unarmed. As for disparaging the communications network of the south, with its numerous railways sprouting from the ice-free and accessible ports of the Black and Azov Seas to converge on Moscow, whilst praising ice-bound Arkhangel'sk and the almost railwayless northern territories, Lebedev's logic does not bear examination. Suffice to note that a single bridge destroyed by retreating Bolsheviks on the line from Viatka to Vologda would have created insurmountable transportation problems for an advancing Siberian Army.

So ludicrous, in fact, were Lebedev's assertions that it must be concluded that the true motivation for the *stavka*'s promotion of the northern route to Moscow lay outwith the arguments he offered. Budberg contended that:

> ...the main reason for choosing the northern direction was the possibility of avoiding union with Denikin, because infants who occupy the senior posts [in the *stavka*] are terrified that they would be replaced by more senior and experienced specialists,

who might be recruited from the AFSR in the event of such a union.[201] Given what we know of the *Wunderkind* and the petty scheming of Kolchak's young and vain staff officers, it would be very difficult indeed to argue that this was not a factor. However, to uncover the root cause of the Siberian Whites' apparently insane military strategy we must dig a little deeper. After all, no matter how vain, how inexperienced and how self-seeking were Lebedev and his cohorts, they were not consciously traitors to the cause of anti-Bolshevism and would not *deliberately* have selected a strategic option which they believed might be ruinous to the Whites. No, the fundamental cause of their failure to appreciate that the strategy chosen was indeed suicidal was the picture which they had drawn for themselves of their foes, the 'German-Bolsheviks' and of the prospects for that 'scum' in a clash with the Russian Army. Their fatal underestimation of the Red Army had led them to conclude not simply that union with Denikin was undesirable or that it might prove problematic, but that it was *simply not necessary* to guarantee victory. Ultimately, then, as one officer concluded, Kolchak opted for an early and independent advance on Moscow because his 'young, fervent and wet-behind-the-ears colonels, in their

201 *ibid.*, Vol. 14, pp. 242–3.

ignorance and confidence, were certain that the Reds would offer no serious opposition'.[202]

PART THREE: 'DICTATORSHIP FOR THE SAKE OF DEMOCRACY' – WHITE POLITICS IN EARLY 1919

The Kolchak government, despite its Kadet ministers, its juradicial and constitutional trappings, its Senate and other apings of the imperial system which it presented to the outside world, was a military government in spirit; to the extent that most of Siberia was governed either directly or indirectly by the army, it was also a military government in fact. We have seen that its objectives were defined in military terms, that its very *raison d'être* was the military defeat of Bolshevism, and that this predilection was bolstered by the Whites' firm belief in the imminence of victory in 1919. Moreover, although his underground activities of 1917 to 1918 evince a strong authoritarian streak, Kolchak himself had no palpable interest in or talent for day-to-day politics; it had been his renown as a rare national hero, his war record and his contacts abroad which had primarily commended him to those various Siberian groups thirsting for dictatorship in 1918. And, once in power, the Supreme Ruler displayed no doubts as to what was to be his function. 'My chief aim is to eliminate Bolshevism', he declared. 'After that it is up to God.'[203] To his inquisitors at Irkutsk in 1920, he elaborated a little upon this dictum, saying:

> My task was very plain: to supply the army, to increase it, to continue the struggle which was going on. I did not intend to make any sweeping, complicated reforms. I should do only what necessity demanded, having one task in view – the continuation of the struggle on our Urals front. This defined my whole policy... I had absolutely no political objectives.[204]

202 Filat'ev, p. 76.

203 Kolchak, R., p. 18.

204 Varneck and Fisher, p. 187,

In this avowed anti-politicism, the Supreme Ruler was seconded by his major allies, the Kadet party and its *VOTsK*. Having come to the conclusion that dictatorship was necessary for the successful prosecution of the war, recalled *VOTsK* Chairman N.V. Ustrialov, the Kadets 'naturally could not support formal-democratic policies, but had to subscribe to the slogan "Dictatorship for the Sake of Democracy".' Consequently, when asked what the Party of the People's Freedom was doing to safeguard democracy in Russia, continued Ustrialov, it could only logically reply that, during the course of the war, it was not promoting liberalism or political reform but, on the contrary, was doing everything within its power to strengthen the Kolchak dictatorship and to stifle all opposition (even loyal opposition) to the admiral.[205]

Anti-politicism itself, of course, may be a covertly political path; that was demonstrated by the suppression of SRs in 1918 by the Kadets and their 'apolitical' military partners. However, by 1919 there were a number of factors genuinely militating against the Kolchak régime cleaving itself to any definite set of political policies. Some of these have been examined earlier in this chapter – namely the signals emanating from Europe that the Allies were primarily interested in military success, not political reform, and the Siberian Whites' unshakeable optimism. In such circumstances political debate and reform could be regarded, by Kadets and generals alike, not simply as potentially debilitative or divisive but as unnecessary: politics could wait for a few weeks or months until the Bolsheviks were eradicated.[206]

Also militating against political initiatives was the fact that the Kolchak government was only a provisional government. Like its ill-fated predecessor of 1917, even on its own terms it could not legally pass laws or take decisions on foreign and domestic policy which would be binding upon any future government. 'I am only a temporary administrator', Kolchak informed Bernard Pares. 'My task is to bring the country to a National Constituent Assembly.'[207] And, in this, he was once again seconded by the Kadets: 'Only the All-Russian Constituent Assembly, to be convoked upon the ending of the civil war, will have the right to

205 Ustrialov, N. 'Iz proshlogo', *Russkaia zhizn': al'manakh* No. 3 (December 1922), pp. 46–7, 53.

206 *ibid.*, pp. 46–7, 53.

207 Pares, B. 'Notes on an interview with Admiral Kolchak, Omsk 21.v.1919' (*Pares Papers*, Box 28).

finally settle the major social and political problems of Russia', decreed *VOTsK*.[208] Subsequently, on May 15th 1919, at the Kadets' 3rd Siberian Conference, the most dogmatic delegates would demand that even the discussion of political reform could not be tolerated.[209] And three weeks later, whilst waxing moderate in his reply to the Allied note, Kolchak would commit himself to no political reforms and in response to each point raised by the Allies would add the rider that 'the final solution' to it had to be the prerogative of the future Constituent Assembly.[210] Such were the extreme expressions of the Whites' doctrine of non-predetermination, a notion which permeated all Siberian politics under Kolchak.

It does not follow, however, that White Siberia was barren of politics. Both the Kadet conference and Kolchak's reply to the Allied note came shortly before the high-water mark of the spring offensive of 1919, when it was still widely accepted that Moscow would be captured in a matter of weeks. But both prior and subsequent to this heady period of most fevered optimism it was recognized that provisional or preparatory measures could be taken by the Omsk government. It was part of his function, conceded Kolchak, 'to create such conditions that we may be free to proceed to the election of the Constituent Assembly'.[211] And, once more, his Kadet lieutenants expanded upon and formularized this political brief, as *VOTsK* decreed:

> The dictator whom the Party of the People's Freedom recognizes is not only the dictator-liberator (*diktator-osvoboditel'*) but is at the same time the dictator-organizer (*diktator-ustroitel'*); his tasks include not only the liberation [of Russia] from the Bolsheviks, but also the establishment of order so as to curtail the growth of Bolshevism.[212]

Clearly, however, any measures taken during the course of the struggle against the Bolsheviks – even those designated as 'provisional' or contributing to 'the

208 'Report of the Russian Telegraph Agency, 15.vii.1919', *Struggling Russia* Vol. 1, No. 21, 2.viii.1919, p. 298.

209 Rosenberg, W.G. *Liberals in the Russian Revolution: The Constitutional Democratic Party, 1917–1921*. Princeton (1974), p. 410.

210 *FRUS: PPC*, Vol. 6, pp. 321–3.

211 'Iz prizyva V[erkhovnogo] P[ravitelia]', (an undated legend to a poster featuring a likeness of Kolchak in *A Collection of Poster Portraits of Anti-Bolshevik Generals* at the British Library (Catalogue No. 1856.g.9), London.

212 Ustrialov, p. 52.

establishment of order' – could not do other than have some influence over the nature of the régime the Whites hoped to establish in Russia upon victory. After all, means may or may not justify ends, but there is no denying that they have some effect upon them. Kolchak himself recognized this fact – and implicitly admitted that, 'temporary administrator' or not, he had to take cognizance of his régime's conditioning effect upon the postwar government – when discussing the command of the anti-Bolshevik armies with General Janin in December 1918. In response to Janin's demand that all forces in Siberia, including the Russian Army, be placed under his own personal control, the admiral argued that such a move could not be contemplated: 'In order to guarantee the stability of the government after victory', he maintained, 'the command must remain Russian throughout the course of the struggle.'[213] It could hardly be denied that a similar relationship existed between the present and the future in political life. This was as true for the innumerable schemes drawn up during the lifetime of the Kolchak régime in which various Omsk ministries anticipated the nature of post-war economic and social reconstruction,[214] as it was for a question so fundamental as the elaboration of the statute for a new Constituent Assembly. In fact the very act of deciding to summon a Constituent Assembly (as opposed, for example, to a workers' and peasants' soviet or a monarchy), to say nothing of determining the extent of the franchise, was an overtly political act which would have a great influence over the nature of any future government.

In his heart Kolchak must surely have realized all this. But at least he, who was almost certainly sincere in his promise to relinquish supreme power upon victory, can be exonerated from any suspicion of seeking personal advancement through abuse of the doctrine of non-predetermination. The same cannot be said, however, of his Kadet supporters. Local and national magnates of the party who were present in Siberia during 1919 were active in every government ministry, department and commission – including that responsible for drawing up the statute of the planned assembly – and were all too well aware that their influential position as the

213 Janin, 'Otryvki', p. 109; WO 106/1251 'Kolchak to the French Government, 21.xii.1919'.

214 Immensely detailed reports drawn up by Kolchak's ministries were presented to Bernard Pares in May 1919 in anticipation of British assistance in postwar reconstruction (*Pares Papers*, Box 42). They would have committed any future Russian government to the expenditure of many billions of roubles on materials for education, land amelioration etc., as well as to a definitely pro-British orientation in foreign policy (which was exactly what the British Foreign Office, Pares's sponsors, desired).

leadership corps of Kolchak's Provisional All-Russian Government at Omsk would stand them in very good stead when it came to claiming an analogous position in any future régime. 'Victory over Bolshevism,' Ustrialov informed the party's triumphant May conference with no mean degree of understatement, 'will raise the prestige of that government under whose leadership the struggle was conducted.'[215] And of one thing we can be certain – if a new Constituent Assembly had been elected in the wake of a Kolchak victory, it would have been chosen in a political climate and in such a manner as to guarantee that the Kadets did not repeat their disastrous showing in the elections of November 1917.

Whatever their party and personal ambitions, however, it can at least be said with a fair degree of certainty, of both the Kadets and Kolchak, that they were committed to the convocation of a new Constituent Assembly. As will be demonstrated, the form of that which they envisaged might have been severely restricted, even undemocratic, but a Constituent Assembly it was to be. Time and time again the Supreme Ruler affirmed that 'the old forms of political and social life have been done away with'; often he opined that 'to go back to the old way of things is impossible – the new state will demand new forms of public life'; repeatedly he averred that 'the future government must, of course, be grounded on the people'. And, once again, he was echoed by the Kadets, as the Chairman of *VOTsK* informed their May conference that, 'We must strongly and quite definitely declare that neither in the field of politics nor in society...can there be any return to the past.'[216] And all of this was not merely propaganda; nor was it cant. The Kadets were experienced enough politicians to know that, given the volatile state of the Russian masses, to attempt, following victory, to completely renege upon their promises of 1919 would be to court certain disaster and renewed civil strife. A transformation of Russian society would have to be considered; it was a matter of degree and direction.

The question was, however, whether either Kolchak or the Kadets in his government would have been strong or politically astute enough to have harnessed

215 '3-ia vostochnaia konferentsiia Partii narodnoi svobody' [unsigned ms.] (*Pares Papers*, Box 28); *A Collection of Poster Portraits*. The Kadets in South Russia disagreed, claiming that, although Denikin had personally subordinated himself to Kolchak, the arrangements did not apply to his government which had equal status with the government at Omsk until victory. See Trubetskoi, G.N. *Gody smuty i nadezhdy, 1917–1919. Vospominaniia*. Montreal (1981), pp. 251–2.

216 Pares, B. 'Notes on an interview with Admiral Kolchak, Omsk 21.v.1919' (*Pares Papers*, Box 28); Ustrialov (1922), p. 53.

to their envisaged form of democracy all the mob of political and military adventurers, the atamans and the *essauls*, who constituted such an important stratum of the Siberian régime in 1918 and 1919. Even leaving aside the Semenovs and Kalmykovs on the Siberian scene, it surely has to be doubted whether, upon victory, the likes of Mikhailov, Sukin and Lebedev, the youthful luminaries of the All-Russian Government itself, would have been willing to bow meekly to the electoral will of the people, step from their newfound celebrity in the political spotlight and dismantle the grandiose ministerial establishments which they had spent much of their time at Omsk in promoting. Sukin, for example, was in the habit of dispensing promises of future work to his friends, telling one, 'Just think of the career that will be before you when we reach Moscow. You could have whichever ambassadorship you wanted – even Washington.'[217] Certainly their pious espousals of non-predetermination cannot be accepted at face value. For the truth was that those members of the régime who were most closely associated with the search for self-aggrandizement (epitomized by the afore-mentioned triumvirate) tended to be those who occupied the most senior and influential posts in the Council of Ministers and, in particular, the Council of the Supreme Ruler; i.e., those who had ridden to power in the train of the military's striving for dictatorship in 1918; i.e., those most closely associated with the reactionary and not infrequently monarchistic politics favoured by the army. Superficially, therefore, the tactics they adopted – namely the staunch defence of the status quo and the blocking of all attempts at political reform – were in many ways closest to the ideal form of Kolchak and the Kadets' doctrine of non-predetermination (which accounts, perhaps, for the political success of Mikhailov et al. and the favour with which they were regarded by the Supreme Ruler in 1919). In reality, however, in proposing to do absolutely nothing until military victory was complete, these tactics were designed to protect their proponents' currently elevated status and their hold over local and national government from the threats posed by political reform, to protect the newfound status of the army (and to guarantee it a special role in determining the post-war order) and to protect the interests of landowners.

Non-predetermination, in other words, could mean all things to all men. For example, even the most reactionary advocate of the dictatorship could find nothing to argue with in the Supreme Ruler's reply to the Allies' May note, for it committed

[217] Arnol'dov, *Zhizn' i revoliutsiia*, p. 253.

the régime to no concrete reforms during its provisional governance. In Paris the Allies might find the reply reassuringly moderate, but 'in Omsk itself', according to a Siberian journalist, 'could be seen a political grouping who were prepared to promise anything that the Allies wanted whilst saying that "When we reach Moscow we can talk to them in a different tone".'[218]

However, in opposition to those who (for reasons whether of principle or convenience) would adhere to a strict observance of non-predetermination, stood a loosely defined and vaguely reformist political grouping which also had representatives within and close to the government. Epitomized, if not actually led, by Kolchak's Administrative Secretary, George Guins, this tendency still recognized the primacy of military dictatorship during the course of the civil war, anathematized party politics, claimed to support only 'national slogans' and accepted that the prime function of the Omsk régime was to do everything possible to support the army at the front. At the same time, however, Guins and others sought to penetrate the military-reactionary carapace of the Council of the Supreme Ruler which Mikhailov, Lebedev and the most right-wing of the Kadets, G.G. Tel′berg, had fashioned around Kolchak; they sought to regularize the *ad hoc* nature of the administration; and, above all, said Guins, they sought to communicate to Kolchak their belief that 'a single, negative slogan of "Down with Bolshevism!"' would not unite all Russia, and to warn him against repeating the mistakes of the Provisional Government of 1917, which they perceived as having failed because of its unwillingness to counter Lenin's promises with a sufficiently 'progressive programme' of its own.

Only broad domestic and international support, Guins counselled the admiral, would enable the government at Omsk to surmount the economic obstacles to supplying the army; and, consequently, although it was he who admitted that the Russian Army might be Kolchak's 'premier diplomat', Guins also argued that 'the second most significant diplomat is social solidarity'. To this end Guins proposed that the government should provide not evasive or preparatory half-measures, which only bred distrust at home and abroad, but 'real solutions' to such pressing problems as local government reform, the land question and the desire of national minority groups to secede from Russia.[219]

218 *ibid.*, p. 158.

219 Guins, *Sibir′*, Vol. 2, pp. 26, 25; Guins, 'Professor and Government Official', p. 198; see also Guins's speech before the State Economic Conference in *Priishim'e* (Petropavlovsk) No. 133 (1655), 25.vi.1919.

Such relatively progressive views as these, of course, were certain to raise the hackles of the immobilistes who were Kolchak's closest political and military advisers at Omsk. Nevertheless, such voices were making themselves heard above the reactionary hubbub of the capital in early 1919 – and at the most senior government levels. Although its formal meetings were rare, the Council of Ministers debated political questions, while Guins (who had direct access to Kolchak both as Administrative Secretary and as Chairman of the State Economic Conference) could take matters even higher. Both overtly and covertly, therefore, politics in a sense not merely as tawdry as scrambling for influence within Kolchak's entourage did exist in White Siberia. Under the influence of external and internal pressures during the months of the preparation for and the execution of the spring offensive, debates, differences and consensuses arose over a range of issues. A closer examination of a selection of these may reveal which, if any, could have betokened 'What Kolchak Wanted' beyond victory on the battlefield. Some clues may even be discerned as to what might have been in store for Russia had the Whites won the civil war and had Kolchak and what even sympathizers to his cause termed 'the mob of adventurers and incompetents which surrounded him'[220] found themselves in possession of Moscow.

A new Constituent Assembly?

'Only blockheads could believe that Kolchak is fighting for popular rule', charged one of the group of SRs who had escaped from Siberia at the end of 1918 with Vladimir Vol'skii.[221] And, indeed, the establishment of the dictatorship hardly augured well for Russian democracy. As we have seen, Kolchak had taken power in November 1918 at the behest of those who believed that it was precisely too much democracy in 1917 which had been responsible for the Bolshevik seizure of power; then, over the following weeks, those same forces had combined to eliminate the SR-dominated vestiges of the old Constituent Assembly in Siberia. Moreover, there were extremists among Kolchak's supporters – and not only in the army –

220 Pares, *My Russian Memoirs*, p. 526.

221 Burevoi, *Kolchakovshchina*, p. 32.

who, in their rejoicing at the establishment of unipersonal rule, could no longer conceal their conviction that, far from being a temporary or emergency measure, dictatorship was the form of government which 'corresponded to the spirit and historic make-up of the Russian people' and should be made permanent.[222]

Even more ominously, the Council of Ministers itself had not seen fit to include in the Statute on the Provisional Structure of State Power in Russia any provision for the termination of the dictatorship. It was not actually written into the constitution of the Omsk régime, in other words, that the Supreme Ruler should relinquish his office upon the defeat of the Bolsheviks.

In innumerable public and private declarations, on the other hand, Admiral Kolchak put on record a solemn pledge not to retain power 'for a single day longer than the interests of the country demand' and asserted that 'in the future the only admissible form of government in Russia will be a democratic one'. And, 'once the normal conditions of life have been established, once law and order rule in the country', he promised, 'then it will be possible to set about the convocation of a National Assembly'. His government, the admiral said, would then transfer all power to that Assembly:

> ...where the people, through their fully empowered representatives, will lay down the principle of state rule corresponding to the interests of Russia [and] according to their own will.

Elections to the new Assembly, Kolchak avowed on more than one occasion, would be 'based on the principle of universal suffrage'.[223]

To what extent all this was merely propaganda and to what extent it represented the true convictions of Kolchak is a question which perhaps can never be finally resolved. We do know, however, that even if the admiral did really desire, in the event of a White victory, to summon some form of popular assembly to succeed his own rule, his experiences in Petrograd and Sevastopol during the disturbed days of the spring of 1917 had engendered within him a significant degree of mistrust of the

222 *Amurskoe ekho* (Blagoveshchensk) 21.xi.1918, cited in Ioffe, *Kolchakovskaia avantiura*, p. 10.

223 FO 371/4096/116715 'Speech by Kolchak at the Joint Conference of Members of Ekaterinburg City Duma, the Representatives of Zemstvos and Public Organizations, 14.ii.1919'; FO 371/4095/82400 'Declaration of the Supreme Ruler, May 1919'; 'What Kolchak Wants' in Collins and Smele, Vol. 1, pp. 3–4; Pinegin, M.N. (ed.) *Nastol'nyi kalendar na 1919g.* Tomsk (1918), pp. 79–80.

Russian masses and had re-affirmed the authoritarian side of his nature which had been temporarily subdued during the February Revolution. Of course, his apologists might retort that the course of events during 1917 had actually only alerted Kolchak (and others) to the dangers of a benighted, undereducated people becoming slaves to revolutionary demagogues and German agents. And it could certainly be argued that in time of war any wise head of state must give precedence to order and to military considerations. Nevertheless, it is a somewhat unsavoury impression of Kolchak's political credo which is to be gleaned from one senior White officer's reported conversation with Kolchak shortly after the despatch of the conciliatory reply to the Allied note of May 1919.

General M.A. Inostrantsev, a man who was no enemy of the Omsk government and who had no apparent reason to defame the admiral, recalled that Kolchak had chuckled with regard to the principles laid down by the Allies, 'Well, they want me to confess that I am a democrat!'; and had then proceeded to indicate that he would indeed summon a Constituent Assembly, as the Allies desired, but that he would permit only 'state-minded' and 'healthy' elements to participate in it. On no account would 'idle talkers' be admitted, Kolchak had said, employing the preferred White euphemism for socialists. 'Then the admiral began to smile', recalled Inostrantsev. 'He looked around at us and said, "That is the sort of democrat I am."'[224]

If Kolchak had retained any abstract regard for democracy after 1917, therefore, it was probably only in a quite limited sense of the word. He was, moreover, in full accord with those among the Kadets and the military who were insistent in 1919 that the dictatorship should remain completely unencumbered by any pre-parliaments or advisory organs and that there should be no of question putting theory into practice and holding elections to a new Constituent Assembly until military victory was complete. 'Until then,' he told Inostrantsev, 'there can be no question of speechifying.'[225] Even when others began to have doubts and contemplate the use of elections as a gesture of goodwill to moderate parties and a sign of the government's beneficent intentions, Kolchak would not be swayed. Mindful as ever of the 'nightmare' of 1917 to 1918, the Supreme Ruler told one interlocutor that 'political contests will only bring a new struggle to the rear, which may disrupt the

224 Inostrantsev, M.A. 'Pervoe poruchenie admirala Kolchaka', *Beloe delo*, Vol. 1 (1926), p. 107.

225 '3-ia vostochnaia konferentsiia partii narodnoi svobody' (*Pares Papers*, Box 28); Inostrantsev, p. 107.

army and, disturbing the entire country, may once again return us to anarchy for an indefinite period'.[226]

Kolchak was even more adamant that there could be no thought of a reconvention of the Constituent Assembly of 1917 – not even (as the Allies suggested somewhat ingenuously in their note of May 1919) as a temporary measure, pending new elections. There were valid practical obstacles to the reconvention of the old assembly: the elections of 1917 had been neither complete nor faultlessly scrutineered and many of the old constituencies (in the army and western border areas) had ceased to exist. Moreover, many of the former delegates were either dead or in exile. Consequently, as government spokesmen pointed out with only slight exaggeration, 'convening the Constituent Assembly of 1917 would mean the gathering of an indefinite number of persons who in most cases would not only be unable to prove the legality of their election but would not be able to produce any verification at all that their election had actually taken place'.[227] It might also have entailed the embarrassing prospect of Lenin, Trotsky and other members of the Soviet Government attempting to claim their seats in the assembly. That was, perhaps, unlikely, but for Kolchak and the other White leaders there were already sufficient ideological and political reasons why the old assembly should never be permitted to meet again: its absolute SR majority, strong Bolshevik and minority nationalist contingents, the paltry showing of the Kadets and the complete absence of any representatives of parties to their right made it anathema to the Omsk régime. It contradicted their own deeply held nationalist convictions about the nature of the Russian people and, through the single piece of legislation its one sitting had framed (the SR-sponsored land reform) had undermined the principles of private property which were so close to their hearts. Typically, the Whites found explanations for the old assembly's make-up and for the poor showing in it of the Kadets and the right not in the policies upon which they had fought the elections, but in the charge that the elections themselves had taken place under 'abnormal conditions of illegal external war and bitter class struggle' which were said to have 'affected the will of the people'.[228] The result, claimed Kolchak, was that 'instead of a Constituent Assembly it was a party meeting which took place' and – as if this fact alone was

226 Kim, 'Iz arkhiva', p. 77; N.N., 'Zapiski', p. 102.

227 *Bulletin of the Russian Liberation Committee* (London) No. 17, 16.iv.1919.

228 Legend on a poster headed 'Altaiskoe ob[shchestvo]. Vozrozhdenie Rossii' (*Pares Papers*, Box 48).

sufficient grounds for condemning it – 'it sang "The Internationale"'. The upshot was that, although he may not have been in sympathy with such enormities as the execution of Constituent Assembly members indulged in by officers in 1918, the admiral was not afraid to admit that to his mind the Bolsheviks had 'done Russia a service' in dispersing the old assembly, and threatened to hang anybody who attempted a reconvention.[229]

We cannot know for sure whether, granted the Whites' stipulated conditions of internal and external peace ere the holding of new elections (which is granting quite a lot) the results could have improved the standing of the Kadets and the right in a new assembly. It must surely be assumed, however, that any significant improvement was unlikely. The Kadet party, let alone any of the weak groupings to its right, had no mass constituency in Russia. At best they could only hope to appeal to the middle classes and to the intelligentsia and these, as one observer commented, were only 'the thinnest film on the surface of the Russian peasant ocean'.[230] Moreover, the Kadets lacked the political will and the ability to sell their own limited programmes of social reform (in particular on the land question) to a population hungry for and newly practised in maximalist solutions. Finally, as has already been suggested, it is doubtful whether some of the more extreme of Kolchak's supporters would have permitted the Kadets to summon an assembly of any description once the army had reached Moscow and felt itself free to 'talk in a different tone'. When, for example, during his address of February 1919 to the Ekaterinburg Municipal Duma, Kolchak promised to transfer power to a 'freely elected assembly' upon victory, officers from among his own entourage in the audience were overheard to mutter darkly, 'Just let us get to Moscow – then we will show him a Constituent Assembly!'[231] And in the provinces, away from the comparative glare of publicity in the major towns and cities of Siberia and the Urals, White officers were even less reticent about displaying their true sympathies: at Barnaul in the Altai several soldiers were executed on December 30th 1918 for discussing the need for a Constituent Assembly; elsewhere even books on the

229 Varneck and Fisher, pp. 106–7; Inostrantsev, p. 107.

230 Gorn, V. *Grazhdanskaia voina na severo-zapade Rossii*. Berlin (1923), p. 363, quoted in Mawdsley, M. *The Russian Civil War*. London (1987), p. 278.

231 Krol', L., p. 167.

subject were being burned by the military, as though once and for all to eviscerate the very concept from the Russian body politic.[232]

Nevertheless, from the very beginning of the dictatorship, Kolchak and the civilian wing of his régime made much of their intentions to begin the preparations for the convocation of a new assembly even while the war was still in progress. It boded ill, however, that their primary concern appeared for some time to be not the implementation of any practical steps towards the elaboration of regulations for such elections, but word games designed to distance their promised assembly from its distasteful predecessor of 1917. The word 'constituent' had in itself become odious to the Supreme Ruler and his Kadet ministers and was pointedly avoided; it was 'too much compromised', said Kolchak in an early press statement. 'I prefer to talk of a National Assembly.'[233] Thereafter these words (or occasionally a hybrid form, 'National Constituent Assembly') cropped up in every private or official declaration of Kolchak or his ministers. But, as the months went by and the year changed with still no news of progress towards even a draft electoral law, sceptics began to comment that these promises of a National Assembly were being made only for decorum's sake: 'The appellation has taken on the character of some fashionable new cravat, without which it is unthinkable to appear in public', jibed one feuilletonist.[234] There seemed to be no urgency at all in the government's approach to the problem; and when in late April 1919 the Supreme Ruler finally ratified the ordinance which established an electoral commission, doubts as to the sincerity of his promises were hardly quelled: to the legion of governmental institutions at Omsk was now appended 'The Preparatory Commission for the Elaboration of Questions Pertaining to the Election of an All-Russian Representative Assembly of a Constituent Character.'[235] Would a régime which was prepared to go to such lengths to avoid even using words associated with democracy ever permit truly democratic elections, it was wondered. Even members of the commission itself had

232 Parfenov, *Uroki*, pp. 99, 111.

233 Pinegin, p. 80.

234 V.K. 'Oblastnoe obozrenie', *Sibirskie zapiski* (Krasnoiarsk), No. 4 (1919), pp. 90–1.

235 *Sobranie uzakonenii i rasporiazhenii pravitel'stva, izdavaemoe pri pravitel'stvuiushchem senate* (Omsk) No. 6, 22.v.1919, p. 12.

to point out to the Council of Ministers that behind this tortuously verbose nomenclature people detected 'an ulterior motive'.[236]

It was not until May 8th 1919, nearly six months after Kolchak had come to power, that the electoral commission finally got down to work under its chairman, A.S. Belorussov. He and all other members of the commission were nominated by Kolchak; they were charged with defining 'the limits of competence and the structure' of the future National Assembly and of *oblast'* organs, the elaboration of 'general principles of the organization' for these bodies and, of most immediate import, 'the collection, examination and evaluation of materials relating to the Constituent Assembly of 1917 to assist in the preparation of a new electoral law'.[237] Word was soon abroad in Omsk that, working within this framework, Zhardetskii and other Kadets on the commission were going to fix matters 'in order not to repeat the mistakes of the past and so as to ensure that the SRs do not grab power'.[238]

Such chicanery, however, was not immediately apparent from the public declarations of Belorussov. He announced that his commission would operate under the assumption that 'the suffrage on which the elections are to be based must be a universal and equal one, as only such a suffrage in which the entire nation participates can ensure the moral and political authority of the Assembly'.[239] And the scheme which he eventually submitted to the Council of Ministers (ratified by them on August 22nd 1919), while not being quite 'universal and equal', was nevertheless very broad and, given its provenance at a White military citadel, rather progressive. True, only large towns were to have direct elections to the National Assembly, with one representative for each of forty-three towns or city *okruga*

236 Ioffe, *Kolchakovskaia avantiura*, p. 172.

237 *Pravitel'stvennyi vestnik* (Omsk) No. 112, 22.v.1919. The reference to *oblast'* organs was a sop to those Siberian *oblastniki* who continued to support Kolchak in 1919. N.P. Koz'min (in the stead of the ailing and aged Potanin) was subsequently chosen to head a sub-committee of Belorussov's commission which would establish a statute for a 'Siberian Representative Organ'. Like the main commission, however, the Siberian committee was made up of government nominees and had no contact with Siberian society. Even the region's dumas and zemstvos were not invited to participate in its work. More enlightened regionalists were certain that a régime which was loath to recognize Finnish independence would never grant meaningful autonomy to Siberia and lambasted Koz'min's tame committee as 'representative of three Siberians, not of Siberia'. See V.K., pp. 90–1.

238 Il'in, I.S. 'Omsk, Direktoriia, Kolchak', *Novyi zhurnal* Vol. 73 (1963), p. 220.

239 *Bulletins of the Russian Liberation Committee* (London) No. 18, 21.vi.1919.

(districts) with populations of 250,000 to 300,000 people. Russia's overwhelming rural majority, meanwhile, were to have two-stage elections, whereby a further 567 representatives were to be chosen for the National Assembly by colleges of *uezd* electors who had themselves been selected at *volost'* level (in a ratio of one elector for every 2,000 voters). On the other hand, all elections were to be by secret ballot and suffrage was to be granted to all citizens (except criminals and soldiers) aged twenty-five and over.[240]

Whatever the apparent liberalism of the project, however, it does not take much imagination to envisage that in the post-civil war atmosphere of political retribution and intimidation in which the elections would have been held, with the army at their backs the Kadets and other parties of the right would have been well placed to press home a certain practical advantage. Moreover, we must assume that certainly the Bolsheviks, at least the Left and Chernovite factions of the SRs, and also probably the Mensheviks and minority nationality parties would have had their political organizations proscribed in any post-war situation of which the Omsk régime was the master.

Such a proscription was never officially announced, but it was the clear implication not only of the brutal attacks launched against any group critical of the government in 1918 and 1919, but also of certain specific statements made by Belorussov. The assembly to be summoned would be 'a truly national one', he said. Therefore, 'first of all it had to be free of all internationalist tendencies'. How, one wonders, given near universal suffrage, was this to be achieved without banning the Bolsheviks and other parties of the left? Secondly, declared the chairman of the electoral commission, 'in its composition and organization [the National Assembly] must represent the entire nation as a result of its historical progress and the process of civilization'. This phrase was the Russian nationalists' code for a Great Russia within the borders of the old empire. But, given the national minorities' impressive showing in the elections of 1917 (when they had won some 11 % of the seats – 22% if the Ukrainian SRs are included – despite there having been no elections in Muslim Central Asia), Russian dominance in the new assembly could only have been guaranteed by the banning of the national organizations of the Ukrainians, Transcaucasians, Kazakhs, Baltic peoples etc. Finally, said Belorussov, the National Assembly 'must represent the entire nation...without giving preponderance to any

240 FO 538/4 'Memorandum by H.M. Consul at Ekaterinburg, Mr. Preston, 1.viii.1919'; *Sbornik 'Russkago Biuro Pechati'* (Tokyo), No. 1 (1919), pp. 106–8.

one class or any one social group'.[241] But demographically, of course, Russia itself was inescapably dominated by one class – the peasantry. The peasants' party, the SRs, had won an absolute majority in the Constituent Assembly elected in 1917, despite Bolshevik harassment during the post-October polls. All the evidence was that, by and large, they were still the peasants' natural choice and that, given universal suffrage, the SRs or something quite like them would win a similarly commanding position in any new assembly. To meet Belorussov's condition, therefore, it follows that either the SRs too would have had to be banned or some gerrymandering mechanism built into the organization of the National Assembly to neutralize their otherwise certain electoral success.

At best, then, the Whites' projected post-civil war national assembly would only have been democratic in a strictly limited sense, granting power to the Kadets and the parties of the right unjustified by their likely level of popular support. At worst, given the attitude of the army, Kolchak's promised parliament would not have been democratic at all and might not even have been permitted to meet. Of course, these conclusions are by necessity speculatory for, being on the losing side in the civil war, Kolchak had neither the opportunity of putting into practice the promises he made in early 1919 nor the chance of reneging upon them. As will become clear, however, their gloomy message is only confirmed by the nature of the measures which the Siberian Whites did take in other areas of political concern – areas in which solutions and actions were demanded of the régime even while the war was still in progress.

Local government in White Siberia

Judging solely by the public references to the question of local self-government in the declarations of the Supreme Ruler during the first months of 1919, the uninitiated observer might be forgiven for concluding that the relations between Omsk and the zemstvo and duma authorities of Siberia were the height of cordiality. In his June 4th reply to the Allied note of May 26th, for example, Kolchak assured the powers that his government 'would not obstruct' the useful work being done by

241 *Bulletins of the Russian Liberation Committee* (London) No. 18, 21.vi.1919; *Union (Bureau de Presse Russe)* (Paris) No. 13, 24.ix.1919, pp. 12–13.

local representative bodies and that, in fact, it regarded 'the principle of [local] self-government as the necessary condition for the reconstruction of the country'.[242] Two months earlier, in March 1919, he had drawn the powers' attention to 'the existence across the entire length of Siberia of zemstvos and municipal dumas which, despite their socialist make-up, are not only completely loyal to the government but are a real support for it'.[243] And, in widely publicized declarations intended for internal consumption, Kolchak had promised that this 'loyalty' would be properly rewarded: 'Vast assistance to the zemstvos occupies a prominent place in the programme of the government', he said. Finally, as his armies moved into the Volga region during the spring offensive of 1919, the Supreme Ruler pledged that local administrations and legal rights which had been destroyed by the Bolsheviks would be 're-established'.[244]

All of this was, however, very far from the the truth. It was, in fact, little more than the most mendacious propaganda designed to boost the White government's image at home and abroad. In reality the relations between Omsk and the local authorities of Siberia were not at all cordial. Not least was this because the Kolchak régime was steeped in the traditional attitudes of the Russian right which, quite apart from its general prejudice against democratic institutions and its particular loathing for those elected in 1917, had always displayed great apprehension with regard to the consequences of the election of zemstvos in Siberia. This frontier region, with its individualistic, enterprising and free peasantry, virtually non-existent nobility and variegated smattering of political and social malcontents, was traditionally deemed to be unsuitable for democracy. Consequently, as recently as 1908, Nicholas II's State Council had rejected a State Duma proposal for the introduction of zemstvos east of the Urals.[245] It was only in June 1917 that, by decree of the Kerensky government, local self-government had finally been established in Siberia. The result had been exactly what conservatives had always feared: with the Kadets and other

242 *FRUS: PPC*, Vol. 6, pp. 321–3.

243 Kim, 'Iz arkhiva', pp. 76–7. For the decree of June 17th 1917 introducing the zemstvo to Siberia see Browder, R.P. and Kerensky, A.F. (eds.) *The Russian Provisional Government*. Stanford (1961), Vol. 1, pp. 303–4.

244 FO 371/4096/116715 'Speech by Kolchak at a Joint Conference, 14.ii.1919'; FO 371/4095/82400 'Declaration of the Supreme Ruler, May 1919'.

245 Seton-Watson, H. *The Russian Empire*. London (1967), p. 657.

parties of the right so poorly organized away from the Russian centre, uniformly socialist councils sprang up from the Urals to the Pacific.[246]

These new institutions would have no truck with the increasingly reactionary central authorities which developed in Siberia in the wake of the Czechoslovak revolt. Especially damaging to the Kadets and the right (often united under a collective 'Householders' ticket for electoral purposes) was that with no residential qualification to the franchise of 1917, soldiers garrisoned in Siberia (or returning there, disillusioned, from the front) could play a decisive role in elections. This frequently resulted in strong Bolshevik showings in some localities of what was, by nature, an SR-dominated region. As late as July 27th–28th 1918, for example, elections at Vladivostok gave the Bolsheviks an absolute majority (of 53 seats out of 101) on the municipal duma of a town which housed at least one would-be all-Siberian government of Socialists-Revolutionaries (Derber's Provisional Government of Autonomous Siberia), a town which was teeming with Allied troops, a town which was on the very eve of being made an Allied protectorate.[247] This result was soon to be declared invalid by the SR-dominated regional zemstvo of Primorskii *krai*; and, over the following weeks, Bolsheviks throughout Siberia were to be forced out of legal institutions and into the underground by the terroristic activities of the Siberian Army.[248] That, however, was of little comfort to the authorities at Omsk, whose increasingly right-wing character and centralizing tendencies were bringing the Siberian capital into conflict with the moderate SR local authorities which then remained.[249] Unsurprisingly, when the military dictatorship was finally installed in November, every major SR-led zemstvo and municipal duma from Primor′e through Irkutsk to Ekaterinburg, Cheliabinsk and Ufa published protests against the coup and demanded the immediate reinstatement of the Directory.[250]

246 Iurtovskii, N.S. *Sibirskoe zemstvo v pervyi god ego sushchestvovanii*. Omsk (1919); Butenii, N.A. 'Krushenie esero-men′shevistskogo kontrrevoliutsii na Dal′nem Vostoke v 1918g.' in *Voprosy istorii obshchestvenno-politicheskoi zhizni Sibiri perioda Oktiabria i grazhdanskoi voiny*. Tomsk (1982), pp. 103–13.

247 *USMI*, Vol. 5, p. 23; Budberg, Vol. 13, p. 237.

248 Butenii, p. 118.

249 Whenever possible the Whites would rely on the village elders or representative of the former central authorities (the *upravliaiushchii*) and would by-pass the zemstvos. See Zhurov, Iu.V. *Grazhdanskaia voina v Sibirskoi derevne*. Krasnoiarsk (1986), p. 43.

250 Zenzinov, *Gosudarstvennyi perevorot*, pp. 103–11.

Of course, compared to the active work being engaged in at this time by the Bolshevik groups preparing armed risings against Kolchak, the wordy resolutions of the SR zemstvos would inflict little material damage on the White government and would contribute little towards the unseating of the dictator. Nevertheless, intolerant as it was of any manifestation of internal opposition, in the weeks following the coup Kolchak's Military Censor's Department at the *stavka* would proceed to close down virtually every moderate and zemstvo-produced newspaper in Siberia – not sparing even those which had campaigned against Soviet rule in 1917 and 1918.[251] Even more ominously for the region's zemstvos and dumas, on November 28th Viktor Pepeliaev, as Director of Militia, issued an official condemnation of 'the criminal activities of the organs of local self-government' (i.e. their protests against the coup) and warned that the Ministry of the Interior was drawing up plans for a 'new system' of local administration.[252]

Thenceforward, in a transparent attempt to undermine the power of potential political rivals, the Kolchak government undertook a systematic erosion of the rights and obligations of local authorities. Formerly charged with broad supervision of local administration and economy, the zemstvos were to see many of their functions transferred to Omsk's Ministry of the Interior – including the formation and control of militia and police forces, public alimentation, supervision of medical and veterinary institutions and control of labour exchanges. Meanwhile the supervision of land transfers was assumed by the Ministry of Agriculture and control of higher education was placed within the jurisdiction of the Ministry of Public Education, which was based at Tomsk.[253] But perhaps most damaging of all for local government was Omsk's suspension of the budgets of all local authorities at the end of 1918. Eventually, in April 1919, a law was promulgated which detailed the budgetary and taxation rights of the municipal dumas, putting an end to their four-month-long financial limbo. The zemstvos, however, were not so lucky – under the Kolchak régime no subsequent law was to be passed laying down how the rural

251 Parfenov, *Uroki*, p. 100.

252 *ibid.*, p. 89.

253 FO 371/4097/150869 'Admiral Kolchak's Government and the Zemstvos', by Capt. O.T. Rayner (Vladivostok, 28.v.1919). In what was a return to pre-revolutionary mores, the Ministry of Education was charged with 'overseeing the morals of colleges and college students' through the re-introduction of centrally nominated school boards and directors and the exclusion of dubious topics (such as modern history) from the syllabus. See Parfenov, *Uroki*, pp. 110-11.

authorities were entitled to raise funds to defray the costs of the few functions which remained to them.[254]

The next step in the undermining of local democracy in White Siberia involved the introduction of reforms to the electoral laws. In this process, Kolchak insisted in a communication to the Allies of February 1919, the principle to be followed would 'at all times be the principle of universal suffrage, with only a few reservations due to their inappropriateness at this juncture'.[255] And, indeed, on paper the reforms were not to be quite as proscriptive as might have been expected. In reality, however, their general effect, in the atmosphere of intimidation and repression which gripped Siberia under military rule, spelled death to local democracy.

The new electoral law for municipal dumas was ratified by the Supreme Ruler on February 2nd 1919, in accordance with a project which had been presented by the Council of Ministers on December 27th 1918. (In fact, the scheme was essentially the same as that which the Kadet Minister of the Interior, A.N. Gattenberger, had placed before the Provisional Siberian Government during the summer of 1918.) Thenceforth candidates for elections to the dumas had to be aged twenty-five years or over; the voting age was raised to twenty-one; and, finally, a residential qualification of one year was introduced. These measures were clearly designed to disenfranchise the often young and always troublesome Bolshevized elements among the town garrisons and labour forces.[256] At the same time the system of proportional representation was abolished in favour of a 'first past the post' system of direct elections. This provision reflected Gattenberger's avowed intention to maximize the role of individual candidates and to lessen the influence of political parties.[257] It was a measure intended to hamstring the more organized parties of the left – which had invariably bested Siberia's fledgling Kadet organizations at the hustings – whilst maximizing the advantages of political scions of the Omsk régime. Yet, it must be said, things could have been very much worse:

254 Guins, *Sibir'*, Vol. 2, p. 112; *Sobranie uzakonenii i rasporiazhenii pravitel'stva, izdavaemoe pri pravitel'stvuiushchem senate* (Omsk), No. 8, 7.v.1919, pp. 15–16.

255 Kim, 'Iz arkhiva', p. 76.

256 Mel'gunov, Part 3, Vol. 1, pp. 253–4. The Omsk régime was well aware that during the revolution in Siberia 'the most active role was played by the young – and, in particular, the young of the military', noted a leading White journalist. See Arnol'dov, p. 118.

257 Guins, *Sibir'*, Vol. 2, p. 112.

at least Gattenberger (with an eye, no doubt, to the impression his reform might make in Paris) had remained immune to calls from the extreme right, the army command and even hard-line elements of his own *VOTsK* to limit the franchise to citizens with a private income or to property owners.[258]

Probably in deference to a growing recognition of the government's inability to effectively impose central authority outside the Siberian towns, in the field of electoral reform the rural zemstvos were again to fare less well than the municipal dumas. The tenure of the region's zemstvo boards, which had been elected in 1917, was due to expire on January 1st 1919. However, on December 20th 1918, the Council of Ministers adopted Gattenberger's recommendation to suspend the election of new boards (except in special cases to be determined by the Ministry of the Interior) and to permit the sitting zemstvo boards (which, courtesy of the army, had long been purged of most of the elements more offensive to Omsk) to continue to function until the promulgation of a new electoral law.[259] Such a law was never to be promulgated by the Kolchak government. Thus, bereft of legitimacy and any meaningful functions, the rural boards had to confine their activities to such tasks as the collection of tax arrears, noted a British intelligence officer. 'The zemstvo system as a whole,' he continued, 'cannot carry out its functions... As local government organs their work is practically at a halt.'[260]

Manpower shortages at the Ministry of the Interior and the inability of Omsk's *chinovniki* to deal with the complex legal questions involved were, it was claimed, to blame for the failure to issue the promised electoral law for the zemstvos. If so, this would be rather ironic, given that the Ministry had so vastly increased its own workload by annexing the functions of the local authorities. But it seems likely that, in reality, other factors were of primacy. Not least among these was the time-consuming and debilitating struggle for dominance within the Ministry of the Interior, which was only to cease once Viktor Pepeliaev, reaping the rewards of his direction of the November coup, had replaced Gattenberger as Minister on April 28th 1919. Also of import, however, was the successive ministers' common effort to avoid a clash with the military on the related question of the election of zemstvos

258 Krol', L., p. 163; Guins, *Sibir'*, Vol. 2, p. 112.

259 Mel'gunov, Part 3, Vol. 1, p. 255.

260 FO 371/4097/150869 'Admiral Kolchak's Government and the Zemstvos'.

in the newly liberated areas of the Urals and the Volga-Kama basin.[261] Contrary to opinion within the Ministry of the Interior and to Kolchak's assurances to the Allies, military leaders were actually demanding that there should be no elections at all in the liberated areas and that the local administration of all frontal districts should be left entirely to the army (or, failing that, to centrally appointed civilian governors) 'until the stormy sea of the country has become calm'. In such demands the army was seconded by a resolution of the Kadets' regional conference.[262] Evidently the influence of these two powerful pressure groups over government affairs was sufficient to ensure that even if no law was passed prohibiting elections in the newly occupied areas no law was ever passed to sanction them. And, as long as that question remained unresolved, so too would the question of the elections to the zemstvos in general. All the indications were, however, that had such a law been promulgated it would, once again, have been considerably more restrictive than that relating to the municipal dumas. In April 1919, for example, Pepeliaev informed zemstvo representatives that he desired to raise the voting age to twenty-five years for *volost'* zemstvos and to exclude from the franchise anyone deemed guilty of the catch-all charge of 'anti-government activities'. He was also known to favour the abandonment of direct elections to the higher *uezd* zemstvos in favour of a more easily monitored (and influenced) two-stage contest.[263]

Apart from such electoral gerrymandering, the distrust and even hostility which characterized the Kolchak régime's attitude to the organs of local self-government in Siberia was evinced by a number of other circumstances. Firstly, despite official promises to the contrary, the zemstvos and dumas were woefully underfunded. In the six months before January 10th 1919, for example, of the total of 351,113,219 roubles distributed by the government in the form of loans and grants, only 10,916,600 roubles (or 3.1%) was destined for local government, compared to 110,000,000 roubles (31.4%) for private banks, 109,052,697 roubles (31%) for

261 Pepeliaev, 'Dnevnik', No. 5, pp. 77–9; Guins, *Sibir'*, Vol. 2, p. 112.

262 Shendrikov, I. 'K voprosu o mestnom upravlenii', *Irtysh: golos Sibirskogo kazach'iago voiska* (Omsk) No. 2, 1.vi.1919; '3-ia vostochnaia konferentsiia Partii narodnoi svobody' (*Pares Papers*, Box 28).

263 [Pares, B.] 'An Account of Two Meetings. Part 1: With the Minister of Internal Affairs and Zemstvo Representatives on the question of provisional laws on elections (early April 1919)' (*Pares Papers*, Box 28); Guins, *Sibir'*, Vol. 2, p. 112.

private enterprises and 114,093,922 roubles (32.5%) for railway companies.[264] Admittedly, in the first six months of 1919 the proportion of government subsidies destined for local government was more than doubled (to 7.1% of total expenditure); by that time, however, the value of the 47,000,000 roubles this represented had fallen so dramatically as a result of inflation and other monetary factors that the zemstvos and dumas were actually receiving less subsidy in real terms than they had in 1918.[265] Desperate appeals for extra funds invariably went unanswered – even when supported by the government's own district governors and even when emanating from areas of the most obvious hardship (such as the Urals).[266] Moreover, quite apart from the provision of emergency relief, Omsk was frequently tardy in meeting its regular and statutory obligations to recompense local authorities for the services they rendered to central government. In April 1919, for example, the Irkutsk *guberniia* zemstvo board, which was virtually bankrupt, complained that the government owed it 346,000 roubles for the maintenance of the post roads.[267] All of this was far from the 'vast assistance' which Kolchak had publicly pledged to the zemstvos and dumas in February; it can hardly even be said to square with the Ministry of Finance's less public and more restricted commitment to provide local authorities in 1919 with funds to cover 'only the most unavoidable necessities'.[268]

In a manner which recalled the last tsars' persistent refusal to countenance the creation of an All-Russian Zemstvo Congress and, no doubt, as a direct result of the fact that many on the right still regarded Nicholas II's breach of that tradition (in permitting such a body to convene in 1904) as the first step towards a decade of unrest and three revolutions in Russia, the Kolchak government strove further to undermine the potential sources of opposition within its domain by refusing to grant official sanction to the already existing regional corporation of local authorities, the

264 Maslov, P.P. 'Economic Problems in Siberia', *Struggling Russia* (New York) Vol. 1, No. 20, 1.vii.1919, p. 294.

265 *Bulletins of the Russian Liberation Committee* (London) No. 36, 25.x.1919. It is not known what proportion of the central funds supplied to local authorities were designated as loans (said to be repayable over a seven-to-nine-month period at a rather generous interest rate of 7% per annum – see *Sibirskaia rech'* (Omsk) No. 116, 3.vi.1919) as opposed to grants.

266 Guins, *Sibir'*, Vol. 2, pp. 183–6. Guins quotes in full a letter of resignation from the Kolchak government's own Head of the Urals Industrial region, S.P. Postnikov, who registered his protest at Omsk's indifference to the plight of the localities.

267 *Svobodnyi krai* (Irkutsk) No. 213, 26.iv.1919.

268 FO/371/4096/116715 'Kolchak's Speech to a Joint Conference, 14.ii.1919'; *Obozrenie deiatel'nosti Ministerstva finansov – vtoroi poloviny 1918g.* Omsk, 1919, pp. 43–4.

All-Siberian Union of Zemstvos and Municipal Authorities (*Sibzemgor*). This body had been first convened in September 1918; but in 1919, under the Kolchak régime's blend of official prescription and military repression, *Sibzemgor* could lead only a desultory, semi-legal existence as an appendage of the Tomsk *guberniia* zemstvo. This was despite the fact that many of its members were not opposed to the principle of a provisional dictatorship and that the organization as a whole had pledged to do everything possible to assist Kolchak and the Russian Army in defeating Bolshevism.[269] In the spring of 1919 there were hints of an improvement in relations, as Guins petitioned for the legalization of *Sibzemgor* – on the grounds that it was safer to draw critics of the government out of the underground. At one point the premier, Vologodskii, intimated that recognition of the assembly was imminent.[270] On the advice of Pepeliaev, however, Kolchak himself cancelled a scheduled meeting with *Sibzemgor* representatives in April and, when the Council of Ministers came to debate the merits of recognition of the body in June, speeches made were 'violently opposed to it and to social organizations in general' according to one witness; and, at that, the matter was dropped.[271] This was perhaps as clear a presentiment as any of the likely fate of organized groups even mildly opposed to the dictates of the military régime at national level had the Whites been victorious.

Finally, when neither electoral conjuring tricks and financial strangulation nor political and administrative emasculation served to bring the most stubbornly independent of Siberia's local authorities into line, the Omsk régime could always rely upon the brute force of the military to do the job for them. For example, when in January and February of 1919 the Far Eastern Congress of Zemstvos and Municipal Dumas at Vladivostok refused to obey the order of the Minister of the Interior to restrict itself to the discussion of only social and economic questions, to avoid politics and to refrain in its deliberations from any reference whatsoever to the constitution, the coup or the dictatorship, Kolchak's military governor of the port was swift to act. Major-General Ivanov-Rinov arrested every member and supporter of the Congress he could lay his hands on (including its President, A.S. Medvedev, and the editor of the popular moderate daily, *Dalekaia okhrana*) and began to deport

269 Pares, B. 'Siberian Diary' (*Pares Papers*, Box 43), pp. 77–8; Parfenov. *Uroki*, p. 104.

270 Sukin (*Leeds Russian Archive*), pp. 175–6; Pares, B. 'Notes on an Interview with P. Vologodskii (Omsk, 22.v.1919)', (*Pares Papers*, Box 28).

271 Budberg, Vol. 14, p. 300; Sukin, (*Leeds Russian Archive*), pp. 175–6.

his prisoners to Mongolia and Japan.[272] Of course, the central authorities could always deny all responsibility for such excesses: Ivanov-Rinov was duly reprimanded, most of those arrested were released and a judicial inquiry into the affair was ordered.[273] Needless to say, however, the inquiry never reported its findings, Ivanov-Rinov's murderous career was but briefly interrupted, and for many months thereafter the zemstvos of the Far East became noticeably less vocal in their criticism of government policy in the knowledge that their members' lives might be the price to be paid to the army for any further outbursts against Kolchak. This atmosphere of terror prevailed, in fact, across the whole of White Siberia. By February 1919, said *Narodnaia Sibir'*, it had become 'a general phenomenon – socialists, even those who are state-minded, and the socialist press, even the most moderate, though officially tolerated by the government have in reality been outlawed; their position today is even worse than that which prevailed under tsarism'.[274]

The cumulative effect of the Kolchak régime's multifaceted political, financial, administrative and physical repression of Siberia's elected organs of local government can be discerned in the results of the elections to municipal dumas which took place, under the new laws, in parts of the region in 1919. The major feature of these contests was a high level of absenteeism. Even the most conservative sections of the Siberian press, anxious to extol the popular legitimacy of the the White régime, could find no more favourable figures to report than a 40% turn-out at Tara. Closer to the average, however, were the 28% turn-out at Shadrinsk, the 30% turn-out at Irkutsk, the 22% turn-out at Novonikolaevsk, and the 20% turn-out at Kurgan. Other areas exhibited an even greater degree of indifference

272 *FRUS: 1919 (Russia)*, pp. 471, 476, 479; Pares, B. 'Siberian Diary' (*Pares Papers*, Box 43), p. 5. A variety of more subtle means of repression were also employed against the zemstvos of the Far East by the local White military, aided by the Japanese – for example, their cars, hotels and conference rooms were continually being requisitioned. See Menshikov, A. 'Praktika primorskogo zemstva', *Sibirskii arkhiv* (Prague), Vol. 4 (1932), p. 174.

273 FO 371/4097/150869 'Admiral Kolchak's Government and the Zemstvos'.

274 *Narodnaia Sibir'* (Irkutsk) 2.ii.1919.

among the electorate – only 6% of those eligible to do so voted at Biisk and only 7% at the town of Verkhneudinsk.[275]

Supporters of the Kolchak government, both at the time and in subsequent histories, attributed this phenomenon to 'a general disillusionment with elections and a general disappointment with political life', the desire of the populace for 'peace and quiet', a respite from the ceaseless political contests of the past two years.[276] A closer examination of some of the figures, however, suggests that far from being 'general' this 'disillusionment' was almost exclusively a feature of the former supporters of the parties of the left, as votes cast for all parties did not decline proportionally. At Vladivostok, for example, the elections under Kolchak, on an 11% turn-out, gave the non-socialists 55 out of the 101 seats on the city duma and the Socialist Bloc (chiefly SR) only 31. When this is compared with the freer elections of July 1918, which, on a 77% turn-out, had granted the Bolsheviks 53 seats out of the 101, the SRs 22 and the non-socialists only a handful of seats,[277] the implication is clear: those Bolshevik and SR supporters who remained enfranchised following electoral reforms aimed at maximizing the support of the right, were refusing to participate in elections for bodies which they well knew to have been emasculated by the various means of governmental and military repression described above. Much of the Siberian working class could see no future in local democracy as defined by Kolchak and were, in fact, turning to direct action in the form of the wave of political strikes which were to spread across all Siberia as 1919 wore on. What, after all, was the point of supporting those socialist candidates who put themselves forward when, as happened at Iman in May 1919, if even a single SR was returned to a municipal duma he was liable to be physically hounded from office by Kalmykov's Cossacks to the publicly expressed delight of the central government's local representative? What was the point of returning socialists to office when, as happened at Kansk, the mayor himself (the moderate

275 *Sibirskaia rech'* (Omsk) No. 137, 2.vi.1919; *Russkaia armiia* (Omsk) 2.vii.1919; *Nasha zaria* (Omsk) No. 114, 31.v.1919. Even when votes were cast they might often take the form of spoilt papers – the Governor of Eniseisk *guberniia*, for example, reported to the Ministry of the Interior in March 1919 that very often 'on the ballot papers was written "Who needs the zemstvos?" or "Lenin"'. See Zhurov, Iu.V. *Eniseiskoe krest'ianstvo v gody grazhdanskoi voiny*. Krasnoiarsk (1972), pp. 56–7.

276 *Russkaia armiia* (Omsk) 2.vii.1919.

277 *FRUS: 1918*, Vol. 2, pp. 467, 320, 327.

SR, I.P. Stepanov) could be lynched with impunity by the Cossacks of Krasil′nikov's band?[278]

Komu zemlia? Kolchak and the land question

Within the borders of Siberia itself, Kolchak was fortunate that Russia's all-consuming land question – the major political, social and economic conundrum of the entire revolution – was not of immediate concern. Although there were areas of actual and potential rural tension over land-holding (between peasants and Cossacks, Russians and natives, old and new settlers), at least landlordism, with all its attendant crises, was virtually unknown east of the Urals.[279] In Siberia the dominant form of land-holding was that of state lands invested in village communities in the form of individual peasant allotments; these the peasant households could utilize exclusively and privately. However, as leading members of the government were aware, as Kolchak planned and then executed his spring offensive of 1919, which was to take the Russian Army to the marches of European Russia, 'the activities of the government which was termed "All-Russian" began to assume an all-Russian significance'.[280] And there was no more urgent all-Russian concern than the land. Indeed, this was the only political question which really concerned the vast majority of Russia's peasants – ergo, the majority of the population of the country as a whole. As Supreme Ruler, Kolchak was, therefore, obliged to offer guidance to his White partners elsewhere in Russia and reassurance to the Allies.[281] He had, moreover, to explain his government's desires to the millions of Russian peasants who had carried out the revolution in the countryside in 1917 to 1918 through land seizures. These were the peasants upon whom the

278 Andrushkevich, N.A. 'Posledniaia Rossiia', *Beloe delo* No. 4 (1928), p. 120; Guins, *Sibir′*, Vol. 2, p. 398.

279 Zhurov (*Grazhdanskaia voina*, p. 43) calculates that there were only 1,188 private estates in all Siberia.

280 Guins, *Sibir′*, Vol. 2, p. 151.

281 The land question (together with the nationalities question) was among the policy issues which Kolchak reserved for himself the exclusive right to resolve in a communication to Denikin of June 1919, whilst delegating to the latter operational control of lesser matters within his own domain. See Trubetskoi, G.N. *Gody smuty i nadezhdy: 1917–1919gg.* Montreal (1981), pp. 250–2.

Russian Army and all other White forces would have to depend for food, forage and manpower in their advance on Moscow. But they were also, at least in the eyes of Kolchak's Ministry of Agriculture, 'the guarantors of the economic power and political health' of the Russia of the future without the satisfaction of whose desires there could be 'no satisfaction in the state and no commencement of any successful work in the question of [the resurrection of Russia's] statehood'.[282] Consequently, whilst as vigorously as ever insisting that 'it is not within our competence to definitely establish the principles' upon which future land relations in Russia would be based – that, as ever, was 'a matter for the Constituent Assembly' – Kolchak promised in early 1919 that his government would offer 'practical solutions' to the land question 'as the occasion arises'.[283]

In elaborating such solutions, however, Kolchak and every other White leader was faced with an exacting political dilemma – one which was later cogently defined by the editors of the major Soviet encyclopedia of Siberia:

> On the one hand it was necessary to consolidate the land rights of the peasantry in order to guarantee the upper strata of the peasants in the struggle against Bolshevism; but on the other hand it was also necessary to satisfy the demands of the refugee landlords and generals who had been deprived of their estates but who were in the process of securing their return.[284]

The alternatives were mutually exclusive. Which would be Kolchak's choice?

We know that the antecedent of Kolchak's All-Russian Government, the Provisional Siberian Government, had wasted little time in showing its colours with regard to the land question. On July 6th 1918, within days of assuming power, it had published a decree 'On the Return of Estates to their Former Owners', which had ordered precisely that (together with the return of all livestock and farm equipment seized by the peasants), pending a final resolution of the land question by the

282 Aver'ev, V. 'Agrarnaia politika kolchakovshchiny', *Na agrarnom fronte* (Moscow) 1929, No. 6, p. 25; Shafir, Ia. *Belogvardeitsy i krest'ianstvo*. Moscow (1928), p. 11.

283 'Kolchak's Speech to Zemstvo Representatives at Omsk, 10.iv.1919', *Bulletins of the Russian Liberation Committee* (London) No. 10, 26.iv.1919.

284 *Sovetskaia sibirskaia entsiklopediia*. Novosibirsk (1929), Vol. 2, p. 838.

Constituent Assembly.[285] Thus, although the landlords would have no absolute guarantee that their lands might not eventually be taken from them, they were at least to be granted the opportunity to extract profit from their estates until that yet to be determined time when the Constituent Assembly might meet; and, given the likely nature of any assembly gathered by the Whites, they would be in a far more favourable position to extract compensation for any expropriation which might take place. Of course, as there were so very few landlords within the empery of the Provisional Siberian Government, this ordinance was practically meaningless at the time it was issued. In fact, only 3–4% of Siberian peasants were likely to lose anything by its terms according to one calculation.[286] But, as the Minister of Agriculture, N.I. Petrov, intended, the PSG's land law had a great symbolic importance: it was designed 'to demonstrate to the population', he said, 'that the newly formed government would follow the road of strong legality...and would introduce order into agricultural affairs'. He also felt that the measure had the advantage of offering a 'clear' formula to resolve disputes – one which was necessary, said Petrov, in the emergency situation of the war.[287] Later, as the Siberian Army advanced through the northern Urals during the winter of 1918 to 1919, the decree of July 6th would assume some potential practical significance, as there were some estate lands in that region. At the same time, however, the naivety of its approach was made apparent: Soviet researchers found that, despite the reactionary nature of this official policy, the opposition of the peasants and local zemstvos (in Shadrinsk *uezd*, for example) was sufficient to counter the far from authoritative hold which the Omsk régime was able to exert over the newly occupied areas of the Urals and to prevent the return of any significant amounts of land to their former owners at that time.[288]

285 *Sobranie uzakonenii i rasporiazhenii Vremennogo sibirskogo pravitel'stva* (Omsk) No. 1, 6.vii.1918, pp. 15–16.

286 Zhurov, *Grazhdanskaia voina*, p. 43.

287 Aver'ev, pp. 27–8.

288 Redakova, E.P. 'Provedenie v zhizn' pervykh agrarnykh zakonov sovetskoi vlasti v Shadrinskom uezde (1918–1920gg.)', *Uchenye zapiski Kurganskogo pedagogicheskogo instituta* (Kurgan), No. 4 (1962), pp. 182–3; Kaputsgovich, I. 'Krest'ianskoe dvizhenie v 1917 godu i osushchestvlenie leninskogo dekreta o zemle v Permskoi gubernii', *kandidat* dissertation, Perm' (1962), cited in Channon, J. '"White" Agrarian Policy', *Sbornik of the Study Group on the Russian Revolution*, No. 12 (1986), pp. 109–114; Zhurov, *Eniseiskoe krest'ianstvo*, p. 49.

Later still, during the execution of the spring offensive of March–April 1919, there were some sporadic attempts to re-settle upon their former estates in Ufa *guberniia* landlords who returned in the wake of the Russian Army. Several reports indicate, for example, that in at least two *volosts* near Belebei restorations occurred and that the resultant peasant opposition was quelled by the razing of villages; another source details the order of the White Governor-General of Buguruslan that all land should be returned to its former owners within three days upon pain of death; yet another talks of restorations in Semipalatinsk.[289] It was later alleged by a Siberian SR that such acts occurred as a matter of policy wherever the army went.[290] However, more plausible is the conclusion of a Soviet historian that the restoration to landlords of their property was usually instigated by renegade, reactionary White officers 'on the spot', without reference to government policy.[291] For a survey of political debates surrounding the land question at Omsk reveals that such incidents cannot be regarded as truly representative of government policy as it had developed over the preceding months.

In fact, during the early months of 1919, the signals emanating from Omsk seemed to indicate that the government had definitely decided *against* resolving the land question in favour of the former landlords – that, on the contrary, it intended to satisfy the demands of the peasantry and perhaps even to confirm their rights to lands seized during the revolution. In a memorandum which formed the ideological basis for much of Kolchak's land policy (entitled 'Notes on the Aims of the Agrarian Policy of the Government') the Land Department of the Ministry of Agriculture had advised the Supreme Ruler that 'the nobility, which the old régime considered to be the foundation of state order, must give up its place to the peasantry'.[292] And, subsequently, in a message to the Allies, Kolchak averred that a solution to the land question would be found which 'reflects the interests of the

289 Aminev, Z.A. *Oktiabr'skaia sotsialisticheskaia revoliutsiia i grazhdanskaia voina v Bashkiri, 1917–1919gg.* Ufa (1966), pp. 420–1; Spirin, L.M. *Razgrom armii Kolchaka.* Moscow (1957), pp. 102–3; Parfenov, *Uroki*, pp. 95, 104.

290 Kolosov, E.E. *Sibir' pri Kolchake.* Leningrad (1923), p. 120.

291 Parfenov, pp. 95, 104. The same probably goes for allegations in some of the more doctrinaire Soviet accounts that 'the Kolchakites planted *pomeshchik* landownership in Siberia and the Far East' in areas where it had previously not existed, 'dividing up [peasant] land for officers and *chinovniki*'. See *Istoriia grazhdanskoi voiny v SSSR* Vol. 4, p. 61; and Krusser, *Kolchakovshchina*, p. 28.

292 Aver'ev, p. 30.

broad mass of the population'; to this his Minister of the Interior added that 'the welfare of the peasants – moral, mental and material – overshadows all other considerations'.[293] Most comprehensively of all, in a public declaration made during his tour of the front prior to the launching of the spring offensive of 1919, Kolchak made the following major commitments with regard to impending land legislation:

> In any country, and especially in Russia, there is no more difficult problem than the land problem. But the revolution made one thing absolutely clear – there must be a change in land-owning relations in the countryside. The previously dominant forms must be removed and replaced with new ones. There can be no return to the old order... The establishment of the right of ownership of the land is considered by the government to be fundamental to the sound development of the state.[294]

Finally, on April 5th 1919, precisely as Kolchak's Western Army began to advance through Ufa *guberniia* towards the formerly estate-dominated lands of the Volga, the Council of Ministers repealed the Provisional Siberian Government's land law of July 6th 1918 and disbanded the commission which had, theoretically, been responsible for putting the restoration of estates into practice.[295] Over the following week, however, as in expectation of a rapid and successful march on Moscow the government hurriedly published its own pieces of land legislation, it was to become apparent that, due to the opposing views and conflicting interests of various competing groups within the régime, the Kolchak government was actually far from reaching the final agreement on the exact aims of its own land policy which all these statements seemed to imply.

On only one matter, in fact, was there some degree of consensus: that peasants who had seized and cultivated lands in 1917 and 1918 were not to be denied the fruits of their labour. A resolution to that effect had been adopted by the Council of Ministers on April 3rd and, subsequently, the following statement formed the keynote of Kolchak's renowned 'Decree (*gramota*) on Land' of April 8th: 'Everyone who now possesses the land, everyone who has sown and worked upon

293 Kim, 'Iz arkhiva', pp. 76–7; *The Times* (London) 19.vi.1919.

294 Bonch-Osmolovskii, A. *Komu zemlia dostanetsia*. Ekaterinburg (1919), p. 14. The author was a member of the Kadet *VOTsK*.

295 Ioffe, *Kolchakovskaia avantiura*, p. 181.

it, will have the right to gather in the harvest.'[296] Later this clause was widely broadcast, 'above all and for all to hear' it was said, in government propaganda.[297] Indeed, the *gramota* was the government's most widely publicized piece of land policy – perhaps of any policy – both at home and abroad. It was not, however, a solution to Russia's land problem. Rather, it was an attempt at a solution of the production problem in White-held areas. It offered peasant occupiers security only for the year of 1919 and was merely designed to facilitate the supply of food and forage to Kolchak's armies as they waged war against the Bolsheviks. An identical motive inspired the Ministry of Agriculture's subsequent 'Rules on the Manner of Production and Harvesting of Crops in 1919 on Lands Not Owned by Those Who Cultivate Them' of April 8th, published as the 'Law on Crops' (*Zakon o posevakh*) on April 13th. This confirmed the sower's right to the harvest in 1919 and, in order to maximize the sown area, offered for rent to peasants all state lands, open fields and woods.[298]

What was not settled by any of these pieces of legislation or rhetoric was the major point of contention on the land question within the anti-Bolshevik camp: what was to become of lands occupied by the peasants (and lands they desired to occupy) in the future? For some time Kolchak had been receiving advice and reports on land policy from the more moderate, Kadet-minded members of Omsk's Central Commission on the Land Question (which included both government and non-government figures) and of the Land Department of the Ministry of Agriculture. They warned that the Kerensky government had fallen precisely because 'it did not take sufficient measures to unite the peasants with the land seized by them, being of the general tendency to support the noble landowners'; now, these sources demanded, 'with the population roused', the nobility 'must give up their place to the peasantry, without the support of whom any kind of future existence for a Russian government is unthinkable'.[299] It was probably in response to such arguments that,

296 *Pravitel'stvennyi vestnik* (Omsk) No. 112, 10.iv.1919, in Piontkovskii, S.A. (ed.) *Grazhdanskaia voina v Rossii: khrestomatiia*. Moscow (1925), pp. 301–2; *Sbornik 'Russkago Biuro Pechati'* (Tokyo), No. 1 (1919), pp. 89–92.

297 *Komu zemlia*. Omsk (1919).

298 Lipkina, A.G. *1919 god v Sibiri*. Moscow (1962), p. 112; Aver'ev, p. 29.

299 Rudnev, S.P. *Pri vechernykh ogniakh: vospominaniia*. Harbin (1928), pp. 261–3; Ioffe, *Kolchakovskaia avantiura*, p. 183. The vestigial Kadet Central Committee in Moscow had been urging its colleagues in the east to impress upon Kolchak the foolishness of any attempt to restore occupied land to its former owners – see Spirin, L.M. *Krushenie pomeshchichikh i burzhuaznykh*

in his *gramota* of April 8th, Kolchak promised that although 'the ancient land problem' could only be finally resolved by a future National Assembly, 'in order to facilitate the passing of the land into the possession of working peasant households, the government will make available to them wide opportunities for acquiring full property rights in these lands'.[300] Notably, however, the decree did not say when or upon what terms this would be done. Moreover, despite the pleadings of George Guins in the Council of Ministers, the Kolchak government could not bring itself to issue a final, unequivocal and binding promise that in the future no land would be returned to the landowners. Nor, even as a provisional measure, would it sanction any further division of state lands or estates where the landlord was absent, as the more liberal-minded reformers desired. To have done so would have been to repudiate the sanctity of private property, a principle which was at the heart of the conservative philosophy of many of the pillars of the Kolchak régime: 'Such a measure,' shuddered one member of the *stavka*, for example, 'would amount to the legalization of robbery!'[301] In deference to such views (and probably in line with his own most heartfelt convictions), the Supreme Ruler chose also to include in the *gramota* of April 8th the emphatic warning that 'in the future no arbitrary seizures of land – be it state, public or private – will be permitted'; he also cautioned that 'all those who violate the land rights of others will be brought before a court of law'.[302]

In this minatory codicil to an otherwise quite moderate document can be detected the influence of conservative and reactionary elements in the Council of Ministers and the Council of the Supreme Ruler. Lebedev and Mikhailov, in fact, had moved that the *gramota* of April 8th should not be issued at all, arguing that even the temporary sanctioning of the land appropriations already accomplished by the peasantry which it enshrined would be offensive to many landowners among the officers at the front and would sap the morale of the army. Given the fact that Kolchak's officer corps was not actually very aristocratic (see above pp. 156ff.), that argument could be discounted. More significant, perhaps, was that Lebedev (as well

partii v Rossii (nachalo XXv–1920g.). Moscow (1977), p. 275.

300 Piontkovskii, *Grazhdanskaia voina*, pp. 301–2.

301 *Biulleten' otdela informatsii pri vedomstve pressa etat-maiora Glavnokommanduiushchago* (Omsk) 17.vii.1919.

302 Piontkovskii, *Grazhdanskaia voina*, pp. 301–2.

as other leading members of the *stavka*'s own Agricultural Affairs Department) was known to have close contacts among the droves of refugee landlords from European Russia then resident at Omsk. The latter exercised considerable economic, financial and political influence over the government through a newly established Eastern Section of the Union of Russian Landowners.[303] The Union, not unsurprisingly, was vehemently opposed to the expropriation of *any* land from the estates and – through Lebedev, Minister of War Stepanov and other placemen on the Ministry of Agriculture's Legal Department – they propounded the legalistic and apparently selfless view that as a temporary ruler Kolchak's sole legal duty was to restore order in the countryside pending the decision of the future Constituent Assembly.[304] In reality, however, as one minister noted, the landowners 'hoped that the Constituent Assembly might decide things differently – or, better still, that it might never meet'.[305]

When the future of the manorial lands came to be debated by the Council of Ministers, however, neither the most moderate nor the reactionary factions were strong enough to win an absolute majority. The result was that a compromise proposal tabled by the Minister of Agriculture, N.I. Petrov, was adopted by a margin of seven votes to six as the expression of government policy; and, on April 13th 1919, there was duly issued the self-explanatory 'Statute (*polozhenie*) on the Entrusting to the Temporary Charge of the Government Organs of Lands which have gone from the Practical Possession of their Legal Owners and Passed into the Practical Utilization of the Rural Population'.[306] The essence of the *polozhenie* was that all estate lands thereto seized and divided by the peasantry would immediately pass into the temporary stewardship of the government, which would then lease the land back to the peasants until such time as a National Assembly should determine a permanent solution to the land question. It remained unsaid, but was implicit in the terms of the *polozhenie*, that the intention was for the land to be sold to the

303 Guins, *Sibir'*, Vol. 2, pp. 153–4; Arnol'dov, p. 177. The only member of the Main Committee of the Union of Russian Landowners resident at Omsk was N.S. Lopukhin, who became chairman of the Eastern Section. All other members were nominated by Kolchak and, as one of them conceded, 'in general the Siberian countryside looked askance at this committee of refugees'. Rudnev, pp. 268–71.

304 Lipkina, p. 114; Aver'ev, p. 42; Ioffe, *Kolchakovskaia avantiura*, p. 186.

305 Sukin (*Leeds Russian Archive*), p. 194.

306 Aver'ev ('Agrarnaia politika', p. 32) cites this as being published in *Russkaia armiia* (Omsk) No. 218, 9.x.1919.

peasant occupiers at a later date (once the assembly had sanctioned the scheme) in order to raise funds with which to compensate the former legal owners of the land.[307] The researches of an early Soviet historian suggest that this compromise solution was possible because it had the support of a faction of refugee landowners in Omsk who, unlike their rivals on the Union of Russian Landowners, were not opposed to divesting themselves of their estates. This group hailed mostly from the Urals region, where they had long since been voluntarily parcelling out their land into lots for rental to peasants. Given the currently disturbed situation, they were only too glad to have the government take over the thankless job of landlord in 1919, if they were to receive suitable compensation at a later date.[308]

Far from settling matters, however, such a compromise could only have led to adverse consequences for Kolchak. Not least, as Guins and Starynkevich warned, the government already had enough on its plate without becoming the landlord of half of Russia and could not have handled the administrative nightmare involved in implementing the terms of the *polozhenie* even had the peasantry agreed to co-operate.[309] And their co-operation was most unlikely – as the moderate daily *Ekho* of Vladivostok noted, the peasants 'who already see the government as one set upon the re-establishment of the old order in the countryside' were concerned, in the absence of a categorical government pledge to the contrary, that the lands might be taken away from them once that the war was over. 'The peasants do not understand the juridical niceties of the government's acts,' said the *Ekho*, 'and all the vagaries and indefiniteness they regard as an attempt to hoodwink them and to take advantage of their peasant trustfulness.'[310] The fear was, in other words, that non-predetermination was yet again to be utilized not simply as an excuse for inaction but as a means to establish a form of temporary regimen which, at a later date, would be more conducive to restorationism than it would be to a revolutionary change to land relations in the countryside. All in all, said E.E. Iashonov, a leading Omsk critic of the measures, Kolchak's land legislation was 'the best propaganda weapon the Bolsheviks could have'; he expected to see the Soviet Government

307 See Guins, *Sibir'*, Vol. 2, pp. 154–5; and Lipkina, p. 186.

308 Aver'ev, pp. 40–1.

309 Guins, *Sibir'*, Vol. 2, pp. 153–4; Zhurov, *Grazhdanskaia voina*, p. 49.

310 *Ekho* (Vladivostok) No. 38, 16.iv.1919.

reprint and redistribute it themselves, for it was certain to rouse against the Whites all those millions of peasants who had taken land or who desired to do so.[311]

But no matter how valid were Guins's and other reformers' criticisms of the potential effect of the government's half-hearted land legislation, it has to be emphasized that it was really the *anti*-reform lobby which had the most to fear from the true intentions of Kolchak and many of his most senior advisers with regard to a final settlement of the land question. Landowners who wished to maintain possession of their estates were quick to object that, by taking the seized lands into its provisional stewardship rather than returning them to their legal proprietors, the government were impinging upon property rights and seemed to be predetermining that the lands would eventually be granted, in perpetuity, to the peasant occupiers. And they indeed had cause for concern, for there can be little or no doubt that this was Kolchak's desire.[312] In the concluding paragraphs of his *gramota* of April 8th the Supreme Ruler had averred that 'the general objective' of his land legislation was 'the transfer of the use of land from the non-workers to the workers'; he had earlier promised, moreover, as we know, that 'in order to facilitate the passing of the land into the possession of working peasant households, the government will make available to them wide opportunities for acquiring full property rights'.[313] And, in contemporaneous public declarations, he had expressed the unshakeable belief that 'Russia will only be prosperous when the many millions of Russian peasants are provided with land' and had proceeded to speak of his plans for 'future enactments to transfer to the peasantry, by due legal process, the lands of the large landowners, who will in their turn be paid a suitable compensation'.[314] The strength of this remarkable reformist feeling may be further adjudged from the fact that some of Kolchak's supporters in the Ministry of Agriculture were not only planning to introduce measures such as the levying of punitively heavy taxes on large landholdings in order to induce reluctant landlords to sell up as quickly as possible, but were even suggesting that, if some still refused to divest themselves of their estates, they should be coerced into doing so by compulsory purchases. This was clearly not

311 Guins, *Sibir'*, Vol. 2, p. 156.

312 Guins, *Sibir'*, Vol. 2, pp. 153–4.

313 Piontkovskii, *Grazhdanskaia voina*, pp. 301–2.

314 FO 371/4095/82400 'Declaration of the Supreme Ruler, May 1919'.

the voice of the homogeneously reactionary goverment Omsk is usually painted as.[315]

However, although these intended measures were discussed in the Siberian press and in the ministries, by the summer of 1919 government legislation, as one critic noted, had not progressed much beyond 'the level of newspaper articles'.[316] No measures had actually been adopted either to induce or to coerce landowners to sell land to the peasantry and no guidelines had been established for the level of compensation to be paid to those whose lands had already been seized. The sole exception was a law of June 1919 on the 'Settlement of Exchanges in Land' which determined that, in order to prevent new large-scale land-holdings from coming into being (through land transactions which were to be legalized in July), the maximum amount of land which could be acquired by an individual should not exceed the levels laid down by the Statute of the State Land Bank (Paragraph 1, Article 6) of 1882.[317]

Apart from the continued opposition of the Union of Russian Landowners (which would remain influential for as long as Lebedev was retained as Kolchak's confidant), the major problem for the advocates of land reform was the difficulties inherent in their own vision of the future of rural Russia. Their vision, in the words of the Minister of Agriculture, was one of a Russia dominated 'by the institution of small-scale, private landownership', which, he argued, 'may best of all create that

315 Aver′ev, pp. 34–5. Clearly such policies are at variance with the too simplistic interpretations of Kolchak's land policy by many later, more doctrinaire Soviet historians. They also contradict the contentions of the only previous western study of White land policy in Siberia – Channon '"White" Agrarian Policy' – which concludes (p. 114) that Kolchak 'resolved the dilemma by establishing a land policy biased towards *pomeshchik* landownership'. Perhaps a more accurate characterization was that of A.L. Litvin, who concluded that 'Kolchak was a supporter of the capitalistic path of development in agriculture, with some consideration for the interests of landowners.' See Litvin, A.L. *Krest′ianstvo Srednego Povolzh′ia v gody grazhdanskoi voiny*. Kazan′ (1972), p. 261.

316 *Irtysh* (Omsk) No. 20, 1.vi.1919; Guins, *Sibir′*, Vol. 2, p. 184.

317 *Nasha zaria* (Omsk) No. 127, 17.vi.1919; *Biulleten′ otdela informatsii pri vedomstve pressa etat-maiora Glavnokommanduiushchago* (Omsk), 15.vi.1919; Zhurov, *Grazhdanskaia voina*, p. 50. It should be added that in April–May 1919 the Omsk government approved new charters for branches of the Peasant Land Bank at Samara, Simbirsk and Kazan (none of which were actually to fall to the Russian Army) to finance rental and purchase of land by peasants. See Litvin, A.L. 'Krakh agrarnoi politiki kontrrevoliutsii (1918–1919gg.)', *Uchenye zapiski Kazanskogo gosudarstvennogo pedagogicheskogo instituta – Voprosy istoriografii i istochnikovedeniia (sbornik 4)* (Kazan), Vol. 71 (1969), p. 222.

strong, many-numbered mass [of individual peasant farmers] the presence of which in a state guarantees stability'.[318] The old system of communal farming was attacked by the reformers as vehemently as were the evils of landlordism. The commune might have brought equality, they said, 'but it was equality in destitution and in hunger'. Instead they held up as an ideal the individual peasant land holdings (*otruba*) and, in particular, the consolidated farmsteads (*khutora*) which had broken away from the peasant communes following the reforms of the Stolypin era a decade earlier. 'Only in the *otruba* and especially in the *khutora*,' trumpeted reformist propaganda, 'is there the possibility of the development of agriculture – only in the land user who is the complete master of his land.'[319] This argument, familiar to all students of pre-revolutionary Russian history, ran that only individual farmers, who were assured of their families' ownership of their land in perpetuity, free from the periodic redistributions and ancient farming practices characteristic of the commune, would invest in fertilization, mechanization and the other land improvements which would lead to the greater productivity of Russian agriculture. Kolchak himself was convinced of this and was a firm advocate of a Stolypinite system of individual peasant farming as the solution to Russia's ills. In his 'Decree on Land' of April 8th and elsewhere, therefore, the Supreme Ruler gave prominence to an order that (in contrast to occupied estate lands) all *otrub* and *khutor* farmsteads which had been seized by other peasants during the revolution were to be immediately restored to their former owners.[320] Furthermore, he subsequently promised that, having taken the temporary stewardship of estate lands under the *polozhenie* of April 13th, 'the entire task of the state apparatus will quite honestly lie in the strengthening of individual land holdings' in their stead; meanwhile, Petrov's ministry was engaged in the drafting of further legislation to reactivate the Stolypin law of June 14th 1910, which had facilitated peasants' withdrawal from the commune.[321]

But this was easier said than done. In the first place, the scale on which Kolchak and the Ministry of Agriculture seemed intent upon foisting small-scale landownership upon Russia seemed to threaten the virtual eradication of larger

318 *Istoriia grazhdanskoi voiny v SSSR*, Vol. 4, pp. 60–1.

319 Bonch-Osmolovskii, pp. 11–12.

320 Piontkovskii, *Grazhdanskaia voina*, pp. 301–2; *Komu zemlia*.

321 *Irtysh* (Omsk) No. 20, 1.vi.1919; Litvin, pp. 220–1.

holdings – even those which had successfully developed on capitalistic lines in the latter half of the last century for the farming of grain and industrial crops such as sugar beet. Consequently, even some of those who favoured giving as much as possible to the peasants in order to transform them into a class of conservative proprietors, a bastion against revolution, were to argue that the unbounded Stolypinism which the Supreme Ruler seemed to envisage might be an economically disastrous step. The Kazan landowner, Prince A.A. Kropotkin, for example, warned Kolchak in a private letter that if his policies were taken to the extreme 'there will be no really productive agriculture in Russia, and no exports, and it will come to the point where we cannot pay our debts'.[322] Before the reforms which the Supreme Ruler and the Ministry of Agriculture desired could be implemented, therefore, a lengthy and complicated process of defining and protecting lands of national and industrial importance and of developing large-scale, efficient farming of certain categories of produce would have to be gone through.

Moreover, whatever the intrinsic merits and demerits of the Stolypin system and no matter to precisely what degree it was desirable to introduce it in the long run, even its staunchest supporters had to admit that the system as a whole was not the best material for constructing a viable and popular land policy during a civil war. Not least was this the case because such a system would necessarily involve a new, massive and to many peasants unwelcome upheaval in the countryside. Some efforts were made to play down this fact: thus, in the *gramota* of April 8th, Kolchak would promise that the envisaged system would 'provide for the landless and for those who have little land'; whilst in a simply worded propaganda leaflet intended for peasant consumption it would be repeated that 'the Government of Russia is applying all possible measures to endow those with little or no land with some land'.[323] However, such reassuring public commitments were incompatible with advice offered to Kolchak by his Ministry of Agriculture in the afore-mentioned memorandum 'On the Basic Agricultural Policy of the Government'. This had warned that under no circumstances should the government permit small, uneconomic plots to be established – as would, perforce, be the case if every land-hungry peasant in land-hungry European Russia was to be provided for.[324] To do

322 Aver'ev, p. 43.

323 Piontkovskii, *Grazhdanskaia voina*, pp. 301–2; *Komu zemlia*.

324 Ioffe, *Kolchakovskaia avantiura*, p. 185.

that, admitted a former aide of Stolypin then working at Omsk, 'would only defer the acuteness of the land question for another thirty years' and do nothing to boost Russia's agricultural productivity.[325]

In other words, it was inherent in the calculations of the advocates of small-scale farming units that, if their preferred system was to be successfully introduced into Russia, very many peasants would have to be cleared from the land in order that those who remained might be guaranteed plots of sufficient dimensions to make their efforts viable. Naturally, under such a scheme it would be the richer and more powerful of the peasants who would receive land and the poorer of them who would be uprooted, as Bolshevik commentators were quick to point out.[326] This could not really have been concealed from the rural population, although it was only in more sophisticated and less widely disseminated propaganda leaflets than the one quoted above that the Stolypinite case was developed to its logical conclusion: 'The deprived section of the population must leave the countryside for the towns', explained one such, *Komu zemlia dostanetsia*: 'The *khutora*, which have subsequently grown rich, thus become the reliable customers for such new goods as the factories and workshops produce.'[327]

In the context of a civil war this plan could only have been a liability, which may explain why no efforts were actually made to implement it under Kolchak. On the one hand, the prospect of the further development of an urban proletariat and the further development of Russia on capitalist lines had been the nightmare of the traditionalists on the right for the past century and their fears had hardly been allayed by the experience of the revolution. On the other hand, in many areas of European Russia acute land shortages and ever-worsening inequalities in land-holding had occurred in districts notable for the paucity or complete lack of estate lands – with the consequence that it had been precisely those more prosperous, consolidated farms which dissatisfied peasants had attacked during the revolution.[328] Peasants of such districts, foremost exponents of the return to the commune which had been such a feature of the very last years of Tsarism, would obviously take no more kindly to any efforts to re-establish and spread the

325 Pares, B. 'Siberian Diary' (*Pares Papers*, Box 43), pp. 94–5.

326 Shafir, p. 18.

327 Bonch-Osmolovskii, p. 11.

328 Channon, J. '"Peasant Revolution" and "Land Reform": Land Redistribution in European Russia, October 1917–1920', Birmingham University PhD thesis (1983), Chapter 1.

individual-consolidated system than those of other districts would take to the re-establishment of landlordism.

It may be such considerations as these which provide the answer to the riddle of why it was that, whatever the inconclusive land legislation which Kolchak passed in April 1919 did (never mind what it was intended to do), the one thing it most notably did not do was to take any practical step towards the spreading of the *otrub* and *khutor* farming systems which the Supreme Ruler and many of his closest advisers held up as the ideal.

Another factor which determined that the land legislation was so ineffectual, however, has to be a lack of political will and sustained interest on the part of the admiral. Privately Kolchak may well have been convinced of the virtues of the Stolypin system; and he was occasionally willing to advocate it in public. But from Guins we learn that when the Supreme Ruler was presented for ratification with the *polozhenie* of April 13th – a measure which did nothing to promote individual-consolidated farming and which raised so much suspicion as to the true intentions of the government – he initialled it without even pausing to enquire as to the view of the minority of the Council of Ministers (led by Guins). Kolchak did so despite the fact that the proposals of the minority more closely reflected his own opinions on the land question (in so far as Guins would have made a definite promise to the peasantry that there would be no restoration of land to landlords and would generally have hurried along the process of setting up individual-consolidated farmers in business rather than settle for the stop-gap, non-predeterminational compromise of Petrov); and he did so despite the fact that the minority view had been defeated by a single vote.[329] Perhaps it was the very non-predeterminational nature of the *polozhenie* which recommended it to Kolchak, the provisional Supreme Ruler, over and above his own personal convictions. More probable, however, is that Kolchak the Supreme Commander-in-Chief was so preoccupied with the battles then being fought on the western slopes of the Urals that he was unwilling to spare the time for the intricacies of political and economic debate at Omsk. In fact, within days Kolchak had put the week's work on the land question behind him and had

329 Guins, *Sibir'*, Vol. 2, pp. 157–8. Guins's scheme seems to have envisaged the establishment of a state land fund to reimburse the landlords, rather than risk attempting to extract compensation directly from the peasantry.

returned to the more familiar concerns and more soldierly company which were to be found at the front.

The national minorities and the question of secession

In hindsight it is clear that ranking high among the victors in the Russian civil war were some of those groups who fought not in favour of White or Red but in the name of national autonomy – the Finns, Poles, Balts and (albeit briefly) the Georgians. To some extent it can also be said the Bolsheviks too were victorious because in the conflict of 1917 to 1921 their pragmatic political ideology was such that it allowed them variously to neutralize, ally with or exploit the nationalistic aspirations of certain of the crumbling Russian Empire's minority peoples. That was a path never open to the Whites, whose very resistance to Soviet power in 1918 was to a large part inspired by their outraged Russian nationalist sentiments in the wake of the alleged 'German-Jewish' conspiracy of the October Revolution and the 'criminal peace' of Brest-Litovsk. This sense of outrage, together with a yearning both sentimental and materialistic for the re-establishment of a Great Russia, blinded Kolchak and other Whites to the fact that, as much as they themselves desired to be rid of the Bolsheviks, many of the old Empire's minority peoples wanted to be rid of the Russians.

On paper there were degrees of White opposition to the aspirations of the national minorities. Consequently, Kolchak received different advice from different quarters. The Russian Political Conference at Paris, for example, mindful of the Allies' fashion for self-determination, would announce in March 1919 that:

> The New Russia cannot conceive of her reconstruction except by the free association of the peoples who make up her entity on the principles of autonomy and federalism, or even – in certain cases and conditions mutually agreed upon between Russia and these peoples – on the basis of their complete independence.[330]

330 Subbotovskii, *Soiuzniki*, pp. 245–6.

A prominent Siberian general, on the other hand, would have no qualms about including in an appeal of July 1919 the assertion that 'One Motherland, a great indivisible Russia – that is the slogan which must unite everybody.'[331]

These different perspectives within the White camp should not, however, be exaggerated. They were not sufficient to engender any real political debate comparable to that engaged in at Omsk over the land question, let alone a political crisis, for the Whites were all Great-Russianists at heart. Even those apparently willing to countenance the secession of minority peoples saw this as being applicable only in the case of the most dire necessity – i.e. where it would most benefit the White war effort (in Finland, for example) – and spent much of their time fighting (sometimes literally) equally valid national movements elsewhere (in Transcaucasia, for example). In other words, in no way was the doctrine of national self-determination a notion which Kolchak's supporters in the Russian Political Conference would have been inclined to support given the choice; their acceptance of it was a tactic designed to meet the needs of the moment as they saw them. It is not even clear that, had the Whites agreed to the secession of minority nationalities and then proceeded to crush the Bolsheviks, they would not immediately have turned their attentions to the recovery of any territories lost in the struggle. As Kolchak's Foreign Minister, S.D. Sazonov (one of the signatories of the mellifluous public declaration of the Russian Political Conference cited above), put it in a secret telegram to Omsk: military victory would enable the anti-Bolsheviks 'to bolster before the powers...our interpretation of questions of nationalism in the form of an Allied recognition of the principle of a Great Russia'.[332]

However, the opportunity for the Whites to engage in such duplicitous schemes – or even the chance to form honest and mutually beneficial agreements with the minority nationalities – never arose, because either through an 'uncompromising honesty' which would not permit him to depart from his heartfelt patriotic convictions (as his apologists would have it), or through political 'cretinism' (as his detractors would prefer), Kolchak would make no concessions whatsoever to

331 Parfenov, *Uroki*, p. 119.

332 Piontkovskii, S. (ed.) 'Materialy po istorii kontrrevoliutsii: pis′ma Sazonova Predsetateliu sov. min. prav. Kolchaka Vologodskomu i Nabokova Kolchaku', *Krasnyi arkhiv* (Moscow), No. 1, 1921, p. 131.

Russia's unhappy minority peoples during the period of his rule.[333] On no other question was the Supreme Ruler's opinion so unequivocal, on no other question was he so voluble and on no other question would he insist upon (and get) his own way so completely. This was, no doubt, because like so many others among the Whites, Kolchak viewed this issue in terms of national honour and duty rather than of the politics which even so insistently apolitical a man as the admiral would have to admit might enter calculations on such questions as the summoning of a new Constituent Assembly, local government and the land question. He had been placed in power as the provisional Supreme Ruler of the Russian state as it was constituted in 1917 (i.e. that 'Russia One and Indivisible' enshrined in the Empire's Fundamental Laws of 1906) and as a fervent Russian nationalist he was determined that he should return that state to 'the people' with its unity and greatness undiminished. Certainly he would not even consider the tactical acceptance of any secessions; he would not 'sell Russia', he disdainfully informed the advocates of compromise, for any mere 'transitory advantage'.[334]

The omniscient diarist of Kolchak's Omsk, Baron Budberg, suspected that Lebedev and Sukin were behind Kolchak's unyielding stance on the nationalities question. Evidence supplied by Guins confirms that Sukin was indeed opposed to any deals with the minority peoples.[335] Everything we know of Kolchak's nationalistic devotions, however, must lead us to conclude that he needed little prompting to toe the Great Russian line. He was acutely aware of the symbolic importance of his role as Supreme Ruler of the White movement: 'History will never forgive me', he told General Sakharov, 'if I surrender what Peter the Great won'; and, to the British High Commissioner, he repeated, bluntly, that 'Russia must remain united'.[336] Moreover, so ingrained were these convictions that they would not permit Kolchak to stand idly by while the Empire disintegrated of its own accord. Rather, he intended to pursue an active policy to maintain its unity. 'My government's most vital task,' he told a meeting at Kurgan in February 1919, 'lies

333 cf. Mel′gunov, *Tragediia*, Part 3, Vol. 1, p. 328 and Spirin, L.M. *Klassy i partii v grazhdanskom voine v Rossii, 1917–1921*. Moscow (1968), p. 354.

334 Nelidov, N. (ed.) 'Kolchak i Finlandiia', *Krasnyi arkhiv* (Moscow), No. 2 (33), 1929, pp. 95–6.

335 Budberg, Vol. 15, p. 273; Guins, *Sibir′*, Vol. 2, p. 318.

336 Filat′ev, *Katastrofa*, p. 139; *DBFP*, Vol. 3, p. 496.

in strengthening the work of every layer of the population towards the re-establishment of Russia within her former borders.'[337]

The force and the frequency with which Kolchak gave vent to his unashamedly restorationist convictions anent Russia's borders rather tended to give the lie to the Omsk régime's ritual espousal of non-predetermination in this field. Nevertheless, as on every other major political question, this was the official line. Russia was to be delivered to the new National or Constituent Assembly with her old borders intact. After that, the Supreme Ruler informed the Allies in his note of June 4th, the solution of questions concerning the fate of national groups would be settled through bilateral negotiations with, if necessary, the mediation of the League of Nations. The sole exception made was in the case of Poland which, having been granted its independence by the Provisional Government in April 1917, was duly recognized by Kolchak.[338] Similar recognition was not, however, accorded to Finland by Omsk, for she had only been restored to the status of an autonomous province of Russia by the Provisional Government (although, of course, the Soviet Government had recognized Finnish independence in December 1917, when it had seemed that a pro-Bolshevik government would win control of the country).

This legalistic formula was dutifully intoned by Kolchak's Kadet supporters in Siberia. During the inaugural days of the dictatorship, for example, his first Director of the Ministry of Foreign Affairs, the Kadet historian Iu.V. Kliuchnikov, told the Omsk press that although the new government did not reject 'self-determination of nations...as the ideal' basis for peace and as the 'highest achievement of natural justice', it would currently oppose any attempts to take such notions to 'the extreme conclusion' (i.e. the creation of nation states along Russia's western and southern borders) and would continue to do so at least until the Bolsheviks had been

337 *Narodnaia gazeta* (Kurgan) 20.ii.1919; Naumov, N.I. 'Natsional'nyi vopros vo vneshnei politike kolchakovskogo pravitel'stva', in *Voprosy istorii obshchestvenno-politicheskoi zhizni Sibiri perioda Oktiabria i grazhdanskoi voiny*. Tomsk (1982), p. 123.

338 *FRUS: PPC*, Vol. 6, pp. 321–3. Kolchak was even prepared in 1919 to attend a banquet at Omsk in celebration of Polish independence – see *Svobodnyi krai* (Irkutsk) No. 93 (499), 4.v.1919. There was, however, some dissent among the more extreme of his officers with regard to Poland's territorial claims. On the hazy ethnic line of Poland's eastern border this may well have been justified; General Dieterichs, however, was even distressed that the Allies had recognized Poland's right to Austrian Galicia because the region had a small Russian/Ukrainian population. Just one Russian under Polish rule, it seems, would have been too much for Dieterichs to bear. See Mel'gunov, S.P. (ed.) 'Dva generala (k psikologii grazhdanskoi voiny): razgovor gen. Diderikhsa i Riabikova', *Golos minuvshago na chuzhoi storone* (Paris), Vol. 14 (1926), p. 193.

defeated.[339] It is hardly even necessary to read between the lines of Kliuchnikov's statement, however, to appreciate the real motivation behind it. It was not respect for non-predetermination; he was simply afraid that, if the border peoples were allowed to secede, Russia would never be able to return to the powerful international position she had enjoyed before the war.

Kliuchnikov and his party were passionately committed to the veneration of Russia as a state and to the expansion of her state power. And they were all too well aware of the critical economic and strategic importance to Russia of her western provinces. Without them and with, instead, a string of potentially hostile states along her exposed western flank, Russia would be open to all sorts of international pressures and susceptible to invasion. And even in peacetime, 'How could the Urals survive without sugar from the Ukraine?' asked a Kadet delegate to a Congress of Trades and Industry at Ekaterinburg in 1918; and how could Russia herself survive without her ports on the Baltic, pondered a group of Kadet-led supporters of Kolchak in London in 1919, noting that 44.9% of her pre-war exports and 69.2% of her imports had passed through that region.[340] If self-determination were allowed to blossom, it seemed that Russia would be doomed to an uncertain future as a poor, eastern-facing and landlocked Muscovy. Consequently, when in December 1918 Kolchak came to establish a Special Preparatory Conference on the Peace Negotiations which was charged with furthering Russia's interests at Paris, it was hardly surprising that its debates, even more so than those of similar commissions in the European capitals, were dominated by the question of 'international and inter-state autonomy'. Equally predictable was that with Georgian, Azerbaijani, Ukrainian, Estonian, Latvian, Lithuanian, Finnish and diverse other national delegates converging on Paris to put their cases to the not unsympathetic ear of the Allies, it was not self-determination as Kliuchnikov's 'ideal' or 'highest achievement of national justice' with which this Special Preparatory Conference concerned itself, let alone the niceties of non-predetermination. Rather, in the words

339 *Russkaia armiia* (Omsk) 21.xi.1919, in Zenzinov, *Gosudarstvennyi perevorot*, p. 27.

340 Taniaev, A. (ed.) *Kolchakovshchina na Urale*. Moscow (1930), p. 50; *Memorandum on the Baltic Provinces Question* (Publication of the Russian Liberation Committee, No. 10). London (1919), p. 4. The main author of the latter publication was almost certainly P.N. Miliukov.

of one conference member, it was 'the means of defence against the demands' of the minorities which fuelled their discussions.[341]

Of course, as Kolchak was not invited to send a delegation to Paris, any diplomatic and other 'means of defence' which his Special Preparatory Conference may have envisaged were redundant. In their own minds, however, the Kadets and other Russian nationalists of Omsk had already won a significant victory in the synchronous ideological battle to justify and further the likelihood of a restoration of the Empire's old borders. Their tactic was deliberately to depreciate the ethnic and cultural differences between Russia's constituent peoples and to stress their historical and political unity (even when union had been imposed by force). Thus, even though the last census of 1897 had found that only 44.32% of the population of the Empire were ethnically Russian,[342] the Kadets maintained, in the rapturously received words of a delegate to their Siberian Regional Conference of May 1919, that 'We are all Russians – from the Carpathians to the Pacific.'[343] From that obtuse point of view the Kadets found that the Supreme Ruler could with a clear conscience defend his struggle against separatism – which, by the same token, could be denigrated as a form of 'Bolshevism' rather than praised as an ideal. As ever, the party had arrogated to itself the right to speak for all nationalities and all classes; indeed, in July 1919 *VOTsK* would declare that 'the majority of public opinion [in Russia] repudiates the idea that the struggle against Bolshevism should be made at the expense of national unity'.[344]

The question of how, given their rejection of self-determination, the Kadets at Omsk envisaged the future regulation of relations between the Russians and the other nationalities of a Great Russian state was addressed in two key party declarations of 1919. A New Year statement entitled 'Our Manifesto' spoke of a

341 Nelidov, pp. 87–8. On the establishment of the preparatory conference see also Skaba, *Parizhnaia mirnaia konferentsiia*, pp. 44ff.

342 Pipes, R. *The Formation of the Soviet Union*. Cambridge, MA (1964), p. 2. The true figures may have been closer to 40% for the territory of the extensive 'Great Russia' the Whites coveted at the end of the Great War. Estimates by Soviet demographers, for example, indicate that, even with the loss of much of the Empire's western marches to Germany, the proportion of Russians within the *unoccupied* areas was still less than 50%. See Poliakov, Iu.V and Kiselev, I.N. 'Chislennost′ i natsional′nyi sostav naseleniia Rossii v 1917 godu', *Voprosy istorii* (Moscow), No. 6 (1980), pp. 39–49.

343 '3-ia vostochnaia konferentsiia Partii narodnoi svobody, Omsk 1919' (*Pares Papers*, Box 28).

344 Zenzinov, *Gosudarstvennyi perevorot*, p. 27; 'Declaration of the Kadets', *Struggling Russia* (New York) Vol. 1, No. 21, 2.viii.1919.

'single, undivided Russia' which would permit only 'cultural autonomy' (i.e. the right to use their own language in their own schools, for example) for even the most distinct of the national minorities – and even then only with the proviso that the Russian Orthodox Church would maintain a universally dominant position throughout the state. Secondly, the final declaration of the party's May conference at Omsk went yet further; an adminicle to the Kadets' commitment to active Russification of minority regions, it read: 'Confirming the principle of the spiritual and political unity of the Russian nation within its multifarious national constituents, the party will fight for the supremacy of Russian culture as the greatest historical and state-building leader.'[345]

This persistent refusal of the Whites to jettison their one-Russia notions – a refusal maintained even when their cause looked lost – meant that they could offer little to the minority nationalities; there were not even any vague promises of 'jam tomorrow' as had been the case for the peasantry on the land question and for the population in general on electoral reform. In other words, the unashamed Great Russian chauvinism of Kolchak, the Kadets and the White generals precluded satisfying the fundamental desire of over half of the old Empire's population – the desire to be free, to one degree or another, of the very Russians who were so anxious to save them from Bolshevism.

For Kolchak, based as he was in the predominantly Russian province of Siberia, as opposed to the virulently separatist *okrainy* (marches) from which Denikin and Iudenich had to operate in south and north-west Russia, the nationalities problem was not obviously of the most immediate concern. After all, only about a quarter of the population of his own domains east of the Urals were non-Russians – and many of those that were tended to be in the nature of more or less primitive and scattered tribal peoples, with no organized national movements that could be compared to the sophisticated and long-established efforts of the Finns, Balts, Georgians or Ukrainians.[346] Nevertheless, there were cases of friction between Omsk and its

345 *Sibirskaia rech'* (Omsk) 1.i.1919; *Pravitel'stvennyi vestnik* (Omsk) 27.v.1919 – cited in Demidov, V.A. *Oktiabr' i natsional'nyi vopros v Sibiri, 1917–1923gg.* Novosibirsk (1983), p. 168.

346 Of a total population for Siberia and the Urals in 1920 of 21,122,000 some 5,845,000 (27.5%) were non-Russians. The largest of the non-Russian groups were the Kirghiz (961,000), the Bashkirs (1,015,000) and the Tatars (1,795,000). The only other native Siberian people numbering over 150,000 were the Chuvash, although there were also some 850,000 Ukrainians scattered around the region. Eikhe *Oprokinutyi tyl*, p. 368. On the little-studied subject of the native peoples

territories' national minorities – and these problems proved to be a significant thorn in the side of both the government and the Russian Army. Moreover, Kolchak was, at least putatively, the head of an all-Russian régime; he had, therefore, to deal with the nationalities question on a corresponding scale, as it impacted upon and bedevilled his own government's external affairs as well as the affairs of the other anti-Bolshevik régimes in Russia who were subordinate to him. Kolchak and the Siberian Whites' chauvinistic attitude to the nationalities question was, therefore, of very great significance during the civil war. In fact, as the following examples will reveal, it can ultimately be seen more clearly than any other single political factor to have made a direct contribution to the demise of the White movement.

Omsk and the peoples of the east

For as long as the pre-Kolchak anti-Bolshevik régimes in the east had been dominated by SRs and *oblastniki*, they faced few problems with the native peoples of the region and, in some cases, established warm relations with them. The *Sibobduma*, for example, was sympathetic to the needs of the native peoples of Siberia and actively championed their causes. It even planned to have indigenous representatives staff a Ministry of Native Affairs.[347] A ministry of that name, headed by M.B. Shatilov, was duly established in the first days of the Provisional Siberian Government and, in July 1918, mutually satisfactory agreements for joint struggle against the Bolsheviks were reached between Omsk and two of the most important native groups of the east – the Alash Orda Government at Semipalatinsk (the régime of the New National Party of the Kirghiz) and the Bashkir National Committee, headed by Z. Validov, which was based at Ufa. Kirghiz and Bashkir leaders subsequently commenced mobilizations of their peoples and formed military units which, although officially subordinate only to their own national authorities,

of the north during the revolution and civil war see Kriuk, V.A. 'Malye narody Severo-Vostoka v periode grazhdanskoi voiny i interventsii (1917–1922gg.)', in *Tret'ia nauchnaia konferentsiia po istorii, arkheologii i etnografii Dal'nego Vostoka*. Vladivostok (1962), Vol. 1, pp. 53–5; and Mukachev, B.I. *Stanovlenie sovetskogo vlasti i bor'ba s inostrannoi ekspansiei na Severo-Vostoke SSSR (1917–1920gg.)*. Novosibirsk (1975). See also: Forsyth, J. *A History of the Peoples of Siberia: Russia's North Asian Colony, 1581–1990*. Cambridge (1992), Chapter 11 (pp. 229–40).

347 Varneck, E. 'Siberian Native Peoples after the February Revolution', *Slavonic and East European Review* (London), Vol. 21 (1943), p. 71.

were to be constituent parts of the planned Siberian Army and might be deployed in areas of the front away from their home territories.[348]

However, early signs of promise in the relations between Russians and natives in the anti-Bolshevik camp were not fulfilled; concord gave way to discord and rivalry, as throughout the summer of 1918 reaction steadily gained the upper hand at Omsk. The Ministry of Native Affairs, hemmed in between the Russian-nationalist Charybdis of the Mikhailov Group and the reactionary Scylla of the Siberian Army, was moribund. Its activities ceased completely when Shatilov was toppled from power during the Novoselov affair of September; and by the time that Kolchak came to power in November the planned ministerial showcase of Russian-native co-operation had become a mere Department of Native Affairs within the strongly Russian and centralizing Ministry of the Interior.[349]

The first act of Kolchak's All-Russian Government with regard to the nationalities question was to abolish the Soviet government's 'Declaration on the Rights of the Peoples of Russia', announcing that all such legislation had to be the prerogative of a new National Assembly. In the meantime Kolchak despatched governors general of the imperial stamp to rule over the Kirghiz, Bashkirs, Tuvans, Buriats, Iakuts and other peoples. Then, again within days of Kolchak coming to power, at Omsk it was announced that autonomous national units would no longer be tolerated within the Siberian Army. Those which already existed were ordered to merge forthwith with Russian formations. Even more galling to the natives was that contrary to accepted practice elsewhere in Siberia – where Russian peasants were being called up no matter how insufficient were Omsk's means to feed and support them – the Kirghiz and Bashkir governments were ordered to cease mobilizations 'in view of the insufficiency of financial means' to maintain their conscripts. This was widely seen as little more than an excuse for the suppression of the armed units of the native

348 *Inostrannaia voennaia interventsiia...v Srednei Azii*, Vol. 1, pp. 60–1; Tipeev, Sh. *Osnovye etapy v istorii natsional'nogo dvizheniia v sovetskoi Bashkiri*. Ufa (1929), pp. 30–4. Similar agreements were also reached between Komuch and representatives of the Bashkirs and Kirghiz.

349 Lipkina, *1919 god v Sibiri*, p. 116. By December 1918, when an official desk calendar was published by the Ministry of Education, even the Department of Native Affairs had evidently ceased to exist, for it was not included in the detailed list of government departments and personnel included in the calendar. See Pinegin, *Nastol'nyi kalendar*, pp. 67–75.

peoples and, indeed, it was this measure which first sparked off clashes between the minority peoples and Omsk.[350]

Nevertheless, Kolchak's suppression of signs of self-assertion made by the native peoples was not completed – if only, at least in part, because of the inefficiency which characterized the White administration in this as in every other field. National units, in reality, remained intact at the front. Moreover, Kolchak and his advisers seem to have experimented with tentative efforts towards a more subtle means of controlling minority groups – namely the sponsoring of splinter groups within certain of their national movements; a policy of divide and rule. Some Bashkir and Kirghiz delegations to Omsk, for example, were offered vague hints that the government might be prepared to consider limited autonomy for their homelands (on the lines of that enjoyed by Cossack hosts) if they would disown the leaders of their radical, mainstream movements.[351]

The régime's general aura of Russian chauvinism was sufficient, however, to lead the national minorities within Kolchakia to perceive that the Omsk government had no real intention of satisfying their aspirations towards autonomy, nor even of summoning a National Assembly of the type that would – the very words 'National Assembly' appeared, in fact, to be a calculated insult to those peoples anxious to stress their differences not their oneness with the Russians – while those peoples of Turkic origin (which included the Kirghiz) remained wary of co-operation with parties (including the Kadets) who were still committed to winning the Straits for Russia. All the representatives of autochthonous native groups, having had their

350 *18 Fevral' 1919g.: materialy i dokumenty po istorii perekhoda Bashkirii na storonu Sovetskoi vlasti*. Ufa (1923), p. 19; Murtazin, M.L. *Bashkiria i Bashkirskie voiska v grazhdanskoi voine*. Moscow (1927), pp. 202–3; Tipeev, pp. 39. Kolchak also forbade General Janin to train national units of Estonian and Latvian settlers in eastern Siberia, even though the regiments were already in existence. See Janin, 'Otryvki', pp. 115–8; also Svetachev, *Imperialisticheskaia interventsiia*, pp. 125–8.

351 Demidov, pp. 170–1; Ioffe, *Kolchakovskaia avantiura*, p. 197. For a rather over-stated account of Kolchak's 'flexible' nationalities policy see Golisheva, L.A. 'Natsional'naia politika pravitel'stva Kolchaka' in *K 50-letiiu osvobozhdeniia Sibiri ot kolchakovshchiny*. Tomsk (1970), pp. 63–7. Golisheva states (without supplying sources) that the Kolchak government, as a matter of policy, used Siberian natives to form punitive detachments against rebellious Russian peasants, inspiring the former with the promise of expelling Russians from their lands. Such a sophisticated tactic, however, would have been highly uncharacteristic of the régime and would have been incompatible with its generally Russian chauvinist attitudes. More credible, perhaps, is the report of a British intelligence officer in Siberia, who noted that local Russian military commanders deliberately exacerbated tensions between native groups by using one to suppress another (e.g. Chinese against Kirghiz in southern Semipalatinsk). FO 371/4096/113468 'Intelligence Report'.

petitions to the Ministry of the Interior ignored or their approaches to the Supreme Ruler met with kind words but no action, grew increasingly cool if not hostile towards the Whites as 1919 wore on. This was particularly the case if their people's territory had to play host to one of the marauding Cossack bandits nominally subordinate to Kolchak. Semipalatinsk, for example, the seat of the Kirghiz's Alash Orda, had the dubious honour of entertaining Ataman Annenkov. His band of Cossack supporters inflicted widespread repressions across the region, but tended to concentrate upon the wrecking of Kirghiz villages.[352]

Of course, despite the resentment such activities engendered, neither the Kirghiz nor any of the other native peoples of Kolchakia actually rose in a united, national revolt against the Whites. There were occasional, localized and sporadic outbursts of discontent which had to be crushed by force; but these presented the régime with nothing like the scale of the military problems posed for Denikin by the warlike Caucasian and Transcaucasian peoples or for Iudenich by the more politically sophisticated Finns and Estonians. Nevertheless, if viewed from the point of view of the stock of men and resources denied to the White movement in Siberia, the impact of the eastern natives' sullen resistance to the dictatorship was not inconsiderable.[353]

Of even greater moment to the Siberian Whites, however, was the manifest discontent of the Bashkirs. More than a million of these Mongoloid peasant farmers inhabited the vital strategic area of Ufa *guberniia* between the Urals and the Volga. In early 1918 the local Bolshevik organizations, which consisted almost exclusively

352 On the Alash Orda Government see: Bochagov, A.K. *Alash Orda*. Kyzl-Orda (1927); Hayit, B. *Die Nationalen Regierungen von Kokand (Choqand) und der Alash Orda*. Münster (1950); Martianko, N.I. *Alash Orda*. Kyzl-Orda (1929); Zenkovsky, S.A. *Pan-Turkism and Islam in Russia*. Cambridge (1960), pp. 179–217; Mints, I.I. et al. (eds.) *Pobeda sovetskoi vlasti v Srednei Azii i Kazakhstane*. Tashkent (1967); Castagné, J. 'Le Turkestan depuis la révolution russe (1917–1921)', *Revue du monde musulman* Vol. 50 (1922), pp. 28–73; Castagné, L. 'Le Bolchévisme et l'Islam', *Revue du monde musulman*, Vol. 51 (1922), pp. 169–91; Allworth, E. 'The Search for Group Identity in Turkestan, March 1917–September 1922', *Canadian–American Slavic Studies* Vol. 17, pp. 487–502; ; Oraltay, H. 'The Alash Movement in Turkestan' *Central Asian Survey* Vol. 4 (1985), No. 2, pp. 41–58.

353 The same goes for the almost a million Ukrainians in Siberia, of whom only a couple of thousand could be induced to fight for the Whites – see Eikhe, *Oprokinutyi tyl*, p. 146 – and the many Letts in the region whose awareness of Kolchak's hostility to their own national aspirations led them to refuse to join the Russian Army and in many cases to participate in the partisan movement against the Omsk régime. The latter was particularly the case around Krasnoiarsk, where there dwelt many Letts who had been exiled to Siberia following disturbances in the Baltic region during 1905 to 1906. See Pares, B. 'Siberian Diary' (*Pares Papers*, Box 43), p. 50.

of Russian settlers, had suppressed and arrested the Bashkir National Council which subsequently (on being released from prison by the revolt of Dutov's Orenburg Cossacks) was only too pleased to co-operate with the anti-Bolsheviks (and particularly with Komuch) during the summer. But the Bashkirs' separatist demands were very extreme. Having suffered greatly at the hands of both land-hungry Russian peasant colonists during the past century and, since time immemorial, their ancient rivals, the more numerous and economically sophisticated Volga Tatars, the Bashkirs (uniquely among Muslim groups at this time) had come to the conclusion that nothing short of complete territorial autonomy would enable them to sustain and protect their nationhood.[354] That was clearly in excess of anything which Kolchak would be inclined to tolerate; and consequently, as the Red Army drove eastward into Ufa *guberniia* during the winter of 1918 to 1919, a stream of Bashkir desertions from Kolchak's forces to the Reds threatened to swell into a flood. Sensing the mood of his countrymen, Validov, the head of the Bashkir National Council, despatched plenipotentiaries to negotiate with the Bolsheviks at Ufa as early as February 1919. An agreement was quickly arrived at, as Lenin, in a crucial compromise of the kind which Kolchak was never able to make, abandoned his original plans for a so-called 'Greater Bashkiria' (in which Bashkirs would actually have been swamped by Russians and Tatars) and, at least for the time being, accepted Validov's demands for a broadly autonomous and ethnically homogeneous 'Little Bashkiria'. An amnesty for all Bashkir soldiers who had fought against the Red Army was also granted and, in return, the Bashkirs agreed to eliminate all 'counter-revolutionary elements' within their villages and military organizations.[355]

Within days of the agreement being reached, on February 18th, all but one of the eight Bashkir regiments of Kolchak's Western Army had deserted en masse to the 5th Red Army, leaving an 150 km breach in the front south of Verkhneuralsk. This was perhaps the most notable among many such events in the history of the civil war. According to Soviet historians 6,556 Bashkir troops were involved.[356]

354 Pipes, R. 'The Bashkir Republic, 1917–1920', *Russian Review*, Vol. 9, No. 4 (1950), p. 306.

355 Raimov, R.M. *Obrazovanie Bashkirskoi ASSR*. Moscow (1952), pp. 239–40; *Obrazovanie Bashkirskoi ASSR: sbornik dokumentov i materialov*. Ufa (1959), p. 211; *18 fevral' 1919g*., pp. 36–8.

356 Siraev, Z.I. 'Bashkirskie natsional'nye chasti Krasnoi armii v grazhdanskoi voine', in Kuzeev, R.G. and Iuldashbaev, B.Kh. (eds.) *Oktiabr'skaia sotsialisticheskaia revoliutsiia i rozhdenie sovetskoi Bashkirii*. Ufa (1959), p. 225; Iuldashbaev, B. Kh. 'Natsional'nyi vopros v Bashkirii na pervom etape sovetskogo natsional'no-gosudarstvennogo stroitel'stva', *Istoricheskie zapiski*, Vol.

Moreover, a further 6,600 of their brethren were recruited into the Red Army over the next nine months, whereas there had previously been virtually no native representation in the Red forces in the east. And these Bashkirs' military importance was far in excess of what mere numbers can convey, for they had excellent knowledge of the countryside and close ties to the local population. Until then they had posed a threat as skier partisans behind the Bolshevik lines; now the tables were turned.[357] Thus, Kolchak's obdurate and uncompromising Great Russianist policy on the nationalities question had denied his hard-pressed army a resource of skilled local troops on the major battlefield of the forthcoming spring offensive.

Kolchak and the Finns

The Supreme Ruler's intransigence was to prove an even more crippling handicap when it came to his role in having to deal with the non-Russian peoples along the old Empire's western border, many of whom had taken advantage of the confusion of 1917 and 1918 to carve themselves out an existence as separate states. In the case of the Poles, whose massive territorial ambitions in the Ukraine and Belorussia were little short of imperialistic in their own right, it has to be said that there was really little chance of an amicable relationship and peaceful settlement being arrived at involving a Russian of any political hue, let alone Kolchak and the other White leaders. The newly emerging Baltic states, on the other hand, were open to approaches from either side in the civil war. Of the three, Estonia seemed particularly promising from the anti-Bolshevik point of view. The newly created national government at Reval (soon rechristened Tallinn) had permitted the White Russian North-Western Army of General Iudenich to withdraw into Estonian territory in late 1918, as his former German sponsors collapsed and the Red Army moved west; and, in May 1919, Estonia was even to contribute troops to Iudenich's campaign to capture Pskov and other territory to the north of Lake Chud, thereby posing a threat to Petrograd itself. Even more hopeful from the White point of view, however, was Finland, whose own White Guard forces had recently routed the Finnish Reds in a bloody civil war. Here the Russian Whites had a potential ally of

115 (1989), pp. 63–6; WO 33/966/1213 'Nielson (Omsk) to Knox (Vladivostok), 26.ii.1919'.

357 Eikhe, G. Kh. *Ufimskaia avantiura Kolchaka*. Moscow (1960), p. 281; Turakaev, I. *Bashkirskie chasti v grazhdanskoi voine*. Ufa (1929). For further details on this and related topics see Stetten, N. 'The National Question and the Russian Civil War, 1917–1921', Chicago University PhD thesis (1977).

real worth – at least for as long as General C.G. Mannerheim, formerly an officer of the Imperial Russian Army, could retain his position as Regent of the nascent Finnish state. For several months Mannerheim permitted Iudenich to direct the North-Western Army's affairs from Helsingfors. Then, in May 1919, the Finnish leader gave a demonstration of what the 100,000 troops at his command (a quarter of them facing Petrograd across a border just twenty miles from Nevskii Prospekt) might contribute to the anti-Bolshevik cause: partisan units of the Finnish Army stole into Russian Karelia, briefly captured the town of Olonets and threatened to cut the Petrograd–Murmansk railway (the Red Army's sole supply line to the northern front).[358]

Iudenich's own North-Western Army was quite small – it numbered less than 15,000 men even at the zenith of its fortunes – but with guaranteed Estonian and Finnish assistance he could certainly have captured Petrograd, with all the economic, strategic and psychological perquisites this would have secured for the White movement as a whole. Kolchak was well aware of this, and, in a personal letter to Mannerheim of June 23rd 1919, he literally begged the Finnish leader to 'adopt decisive measures for the liberation of the northern capital of Russia'.[359] Since 1919 doubts have sometimes been expressed as to whether the Finns, still smarting after the three decades of Russification inflicted upon them by Alexander III and Nicholas II, could ever have been persuaded to fight for their former oppressors, the Russians; and there was certainly a significant strain of anti-Kolchak feeling in Finnish society.[360] At the time, however, Mannerheim for one was certain that his army would fight for the Russian Whites. He replied to Kolchak on July 10th, saying that although the recently established Finnish Diet was somewhat hesitant, the Army would certainly follow him in an attack on the Russian Bolsheviks (who were blamed for the sponsorship of residual revolutionary activity both within

358 The only substantial western history of Iudenich and the White effort in the Baltic was never published: Drujina, G. 'The History of the North West Army of General Iudenich', Stanford University PhD thesis (1950). See also: Footman, D. *Civil War in the Baltic Area, Part II: The Northwestern Army*. Oxford: St. Antony's Papers on Soviet Affairs (1959) [unbound]. For a first-hand account see: Kukk, H. 'The Failure of Iudenich's Northwestern Army in 1919: A Dissenting White Russian View', *Journal of Baltic Studies* Vol. 12 (1981), No. 4, pp. 362–83.

359 'Proposal of the Russian Political Conference in Paris to the Peace Conference on the Question of the Nationalities in Russia, 6.iii.1919' (Publication of the Russian Liberation Committee, London 1919); *DBFP*, p. 446.

360 See, for example, Mel'gunov, *Tragediia*, Part 3, Vol. 1, p. 336. On the Finnish public's attitude to Kolchak see *Russkaia zhizn'* (Helsingfors) No. 100, 5.vii 1919.

Finland and along her eastern frontier). However, Mannerheim continued, neither the Finnish government nor army would be willing to bear the financial and human costs of an advance on Bolshevik Petrograd 'unless we receive a guarantee that the New Russia for which we are fighting agrees to certain conditions, the fulfilment of which we consider not only as necessary for our participation but also as a vital guarantee of our future national and governmental survival'.[361] For several months Kolchak had been receiving advice from almost every quarter that he should grant Mannerheim any guarantees he might request, so vital was the capture of Petrograd to the anti-Bolshevik cause: 'Satisfy the Finns', urged Sazonov from Paris and Nabokov from London; while in Siberia even such arch-conservatives as General Andogskii of the Imperial General Staff Academy would follow this line in the Council of the Supreme Ruler. And, most urgently of all, 'pay any price', pleaded Iudenich from Helsingfors; after all, he added slyly, 'in the future a powerful Russia can redress any political losses'.[362] But Kolchak refused to pay.

It has to be said that the 'guarantees' which Mannerheim was demanding of the Whites were by no means inconsiderable. In fact, when in June 1919 the Finnish regent had attempted to come to a local agreement with Iudenich (already sensing that Kolchak would not agree to his terms) the small print was found to contain the following extensive demands: the transfer of all Russian military installations in Finland to the Finnish Government; access to the Arctic Ocean to be granted to Finland by the cession to her of Pechenga; self-determination by plebiscite for the Karel peoples of Olonets and Arkhangel′sk *guberniias*, so as to determine the line of the Russo-Finnish border; wide-ranging cultural autonomy for Finns in Russia; the right to be granted to Finland to transfer goods, duty-free, to and from the Finnish hinterland and her Baltic ports via Lake Ladoga and the River Neva; and the demilitarisation of Lake Ladoga.[363] Predictably (and with some justification, for the Finns were clearly attempting to exact their pound of flesh from the turmoil in Russia), Kolchak reacted angrily to these demands: the Finns were acting 'as if

361 Kostomarov, G.D. (ed.) 'Belofinny na sluzhbe anglo-frantsuzskikh interventov v 1919g.', *Krasnyi arkhiv* (Moscow), No. 1 (1940), pp. 59–65.

362 Mints, 'Vneshnaia politika', p. 97; Kim, 'Iz arkhiva', pp. 85, 91; Guins, *Sibir′*, Vol. 2, p. 317.

363 Kostomarov, pp. 59–65; Subbotovskii, *Soiuzniki*, pp. 249–51. On the Mannerheim–Iudenich negotiations see: Smith, C.J. *Finland and the Russian Revolution*. Athens, GA (1958), pp. 135–57; Paasivirta, J. *The Victors in World War I and Finland: Finland's Relations with the British, French and United States Governments in 1918–1919*. Helsinki (1965); Rintala, M. 'The Politics of Gustav Mannerheim', *Journal of Central European Affairs* Vol. 21 (1961–2), No. 1, pp. 67–83.

they had conquered Russia', he stormed to the British High Commissioner. Of course, any provisional government would have found it difficult to justify making economic and territorial concessions on such a scale; but for one so chauvinistic and bound to the principle of non-predetermination as Kolchak it was out of the question. Consequently, on July 21st 1919, citing the extreme demands of the Finns, the admiral ordered Iudenich not to sign the proposed agreement with General Mannerheim.[364]

But, in reality, consideration of the detail of Finnish demands was only of secondary import to Kolchak. The admiral's prime objection to the prospective Iudenich–Mannerheim agreement was that it entailed the 'unconditional recognition of Finnish independence'. He steadfastly refused to consider such recognition of the Helsingfors régime, even though, as Sazonov pointed out, Finnish independence was already an accomplished fact, it had been recognized by the Allies, it was not necessarily a threat to Russian security and anyway, by virtue of her geographical position, tiny Finland would always have to be dependent upon a regenerated Russia. Kolchak would not yield on this point even when informed that, irrespective of any other concessions or guarantees, Finland would not move against Petrograd unless she was recognized by the Whites and that this had to be the bottom line of any agreement.[365] Throughout the summer and autumn of 1919 Kolchak would instead adhere rigidly to the line he had adopted in his reply to the Allied note of May 27th, saying that neither he and his provisional government nor anybody else had the right to recognize Finnish independence: only the future National Assembly could do that. Once again, therefore, non-predetermination was raised as a barrier to political compromise and political progress. And once again such a policy raised the widespread (and, in this case, well-founded) suspicion that Kolchak was only too glad to evoke non-predetermination in order to avoid an action which he and his followers found politically unpalatable. It seemed to follow that any postwar régime established in Russia by the Supreme Ruler would be of like sentiment.

364 *DBFP*, Vol. 3, pp. 435–6. Kolchak's reluctance to deal with Helsingfors may have been compounded by lingering resentment of the White Finns' collaboration with Berlin of 1917 to 1918 and the suspicion that, as the admiral later informed his interrogators at Irkutsk, Mannerheim himself was 'a German appointee'. See Varneck and Fisher, p. 101. There were also fears in the White camp that if the Finns were invited down the Karelian Isthmus to Petrograd, they might not readily go home – see Mints, 'Vneshnaia politika', pp. 97–8; Mel′gunov, *Tragediia*, Part 3, Vol. 1, pp. 335–6.

365 Kim, 'Iz arkhiva', p. 95.

There can be no doubt that, however sincere his espousal of non-predetermination in general, the notion of Finnish independence was anathema to Kolchak. When Sazonov suggested that, as an alternative to the immediate recognition of Helsingfors, the Supreme Ruler might promise to speak in favour of Finnish independence at a gathering of the future National Assembly, the admiral sternly forbade his Foreign Minister to make any such declaration in his name.[366] Even by October 1919, when Sazonov and Iudenich (whose army's advance on Petrograd, without Finnish aid, was about to founder in the outskirts of the capital) renewed their appeals, urging Kolchak to think again and to pay any price to secure the Finns' military support, the Supreme Ruler would reluctantly assent only to the broadcast of a negative formula to the effect that he was 'prepared to do nothing to infringe upon [Finland's] practical independence'.[367] No positive step would be taken even to hint that the guarantees Mannerheim had demanded might be met or were even negotiable, still less to promise that the Whites would not attempt, if victorious, to re-impose Russian hegemony over the nations on her western marches.

By the autumn of 1919, however, Kolchak's hostile attitude was but one of several factors undermining White Russian–Finnish relations. During the summer Mannerheim's regency had been superseded by a republic and a less interventionist Diet had begun to append to the price of Finnish action against the Bolsheviks the condition that the Allies fund all military operations.[368] Such a scheme would have been given short shrift even in 1918, given the financial straits of postwar Britain and France; by the autumn of 1919, when both were coming to re-assess the value of intervention in Russia and were beginning to move towards disengagement, there was really no hope at all of such support (particularly for an ex-ally of Germany with territorial ambitions towards Russia).

Meanwhile, to the south of the Gulf of Finland, the Whites' hopes were also fading fast, as the limitrophe states of the Baltic were coming rapidly to the conclusion that if they did not obtain recognition from at least one of the embattled Russian factions while the civil war was still alive, they would not get it when either was victorious. Lenin, they were aware, was at least offering full recognition in 1919 (albeit in terms peppered with threats). Moreover, he merely required that the Baltic

366 Nelidov, 'Kolchak i Finlandiia', pp. 96–8.

367 Kholodkovskii, V.M. *Finlandiia i Sovetskaia Rossiia*. Moscow (1975), pp. 65–7; Piontkovskii, 'Materialy po istorii kontrrevoliutsii: pis′ma Sazonova', p. 141.

368 *DBFP*, Vol. 3, p. 407.

states stay out of the Russian civil war. Kolchak, on the other hand, was not offering recognition and yet was seeking active military assistance. Despite their political antipathy to the Bolsheviks, therefore, one by one the fledgling border states succumbed to the Soviet Government's offers of settlement. The Estonians, having negotiated an armistice with the Red Army (signed on December 31st 1919), disarmed and interned Iudenich's forces as they were pushed back across the border after the North-Western Army's failed autumn offensive; on February 2nd 1920 Tallinn was to sign a full peace treaty with Moscow. Lithuania signed a similar treaty on July 12th; Latvia followed suit on August 1st; and, finally, in October 1920, the Finns too agreed to terms.

Thus, on the nationalities question (as on the other major political question of the civil war, the land question) Bolshevik realism had outflanked and defeated White 'principles'. Lenin's willingness to review policy and his readiness to accept the necessary evil of minor defeats and compromises for the sake of greater goals, his readiness to adapt policy to accommodate what was popular, had demonstrably triumphed over Kolchak's determination to accept nothing short of the ideal. Despite all his statements to the contrary, his pledges that the military defeat of Bolshevism was all that concerned him, the deeply ingrained, knee-jerk nationalism which was so dominant a feature of the Supreme Ruler's character would not permit him to accept the logic of those who urged that 'the prime aim must be the defeat of the Bolsheviks and only second the putting back together of Russia'.[369] The problem was that for Kolchak the two things were not really separable: for him Russia could not be saved from the Bolsheviks if she was in pieces because Russia in pieces would not be his Russia.

In the end, then, 'What Kolchak wanted' may have been far less reactionary than the desires of some of the more extreme elements in the White camp. For example, the Supreme Ruler held, as we have seen, quite progressive views on the land question in comparison to others in the army and in his government. However, each of the policy areas studied above reveals that through an unholy alliance of the weak political leadership of the Supreme Ruler, the half-baked legalistic principles of the Kadets and the unscrupulous reactionaries' attraction to the expediency of offering only the vaguest of assurances about the future, the White régime in Siberia was

369 Guins, *Sibir'*, Vol. 2, p. 375.

never able to shake off the stench of restorationism which surrounded it. At the very most Omsk would only hint that the reforms for which all Russia was waiting were dependent upon such unknown factors as the political profile of a future National Assembly – even on a matter so pressing as the land question. 'We not only did not give the *muzhik* the bird in the hand,' was one officer's retrospective lament for White politics, 'we were even afraid to promise him the bird in the bush.'[370]

PART FOUR: RUSSIAN ARMY'S SPRING OFFENSIVE

The uncertainty and unattractiveness of their political programme would in the long run have posed serious problems for the Whites and might well have debarred the legitimization of the postwar régime they planned to establish. Of more immediate concern for Kolchak, however, was that widespread suspicion of Omsk's policies made it difficult to elicit a truly enthusiastic response among the population of the Volga-Kama basin through which his Russian Army would have to move during the first stages of the spring offensive which had been decided upon in the first weeks of 1919; it would also complicate the task of inspiring the troops gathered to make that advance with any belief in the cause for which they had been summoned to arms. This was all the more debilitating because it was during the very first weeks of Kolchak's offensive, at their 8th Party Congress of March 1919, that Bolshevik policies were undergoing something of a sea change. The former, divisively extremist stress upon collective farming and the sponsorship of class war in the countryside through the organization of *kombedy* (Committees of the Village Poor) for attacks upon all relatively prosperous peasants (not just the rich kulaks) was being replaced by a new emphasis on positive measures to attract to the Soviet Government the support of the rural majority, the so-called *seredniaki* (middle peasants).[371]

370 Filat'ev, *Katastrofa*, p. 139.

371 Lenin, V.I. *Collected Works*. London (1964–1970), Vol. 29, pp. 217–20.

But it would be unwise to place too great an emphasis on the effect of political competition between White and Red Russia at this precise juncture of the civil war. Partly because of the inadequacies of his propaganda effort and partly because of their inherent vagueness, Kolchak's policies remained quite unknown to the vast majority of Russian peasants in early 1919 and could not have decisively influenced their thinking; the original Bolshevik policies, on the other hand, involving food requisitioning and the Extraordinary Tax, were all too painfuly familiar in the villages, while the change of emphasis presaged by the decisions of the 8th Party Congress would take time to filter through. Consequently, as even one senior Soviet historian has admitted, when Kolchak's Siberian Army began its initial move westwards into Viatka *guberniia* in March 1919, its units were not infrequently greeted in the villages through which they passed by delegations of peasant elders bearing the traditional welcoming offerings of bread and salt. Further south, moreover, the advance of the Western Army through Ufa *guberniia* was rendered considerable assistance by disruption caused in the immediate rear of the opposing Eastern Army Group of the Red Army by a series of spontaneous revolts by the disgruntled peasants of Simbirsk and Kazan *guberniias* (particularly around Sengilei, Syzran *uezd*) throughout the spring of 1919.[372]

Kolchak rampant, March–April 1919

In accordance with the plans laid down over the previous months, Kolchak's major strategic force, General Gajda's Siberian Army, commenced its offensive on March 4th 1919.[373] Some units, overcoming initially stiff resistance from the 3rd Red Army, advanced 150 km westwards along the Perm–Viatka railway; the remainder drove the 2nd Red Army back down the Kama River, capturing Okhansk (March 7th), Osa (March 8th) and eventually entering Sarapul, site of an important river

372 Spirin, *Razgrom armii Kolchaka*, pp. 99, 124–5; Anishev, A. *Ocherki istorii grazhdanskoi voiny, 1917–1920gg.* Leningrad (1925), p. 228. For a recent western account of these revolts (which took place under the slogan of 'For Soviet Power but Against the Bolsheviks!'), see Figes, O. *Peasant Russia, Civil War. The Volga Countryside in Revolution (1917–1921).* Oxford (1989), pp. 205, 324–34.

373 The best summary of military operations on the Eastern Front in 1919 is to be found in Kakurin, N. *Strategicheskii ocherk grazhdanskoi voiny.* Moscow–Leningrad (1926), pp. 86–127.

crossing, on April 10th. The latter operation was designed to cover the right flank of Kolchak's other major force, General Khanzhin's Western Army, which had initiated its own offensive shortly after Gajda. Western Army's main thrust was being directed against the left flank of the 5th Red Army (which had until then been slowly continuing its own advance along the Ufa–Zlatoust line); as the 5th Red Army reeled under Khanzhin's unexpected blow, Western Army captured both Birsk (March 10th) and Ufa (March 14th). Steady pressure on this front brought more success and by early April, having in the process captured Belebei (April 7th) and Bugul′ma (April 10th), the Western Army had already surpassed its original tactical objective, the River Ik.

It had been thought that by the time the Ik had been gained by the Western Army the floods occasioned by the spring thaw (the uniquely disruptive Russian *rasputitsa*) would make further progress difficult for some weeks; consequently, it had originally been intended that the Western Army should dig in at that point, should institute mobilizations in the newly occupied territories and should await the arrival of reserves from the Kappel Corps (which, it was hoped, would be ready by May), pending the commencement of the strategic move on Moscow in which Gajda's Siberian Army would play the leading role. Such was the overwhelming scale and speed of Khanzhin's victories, however, that, in a crucial change of plan, Kolchak and the Russian Army's High Command now determined that the Western Army should no longer content itself with the river Ik, but should continue to move west in order to secure, before the thaw, a far superior river barrier from behind which might be launched the final move on the Red capital. Corps and divisional commanders at the front were warning that their men were tired and needed a ten- to twelve-day rest on the Ik. But in the euphoria at Omsk such appeals for caution were discounted as, in a directive of April 12th, the Supreme Ruler ordered: 'The armies in the field must eliminate the Red Armies operating to the east of the Volga and Kama rivers, cutting them off from the bridges over those rivers.'[374] At the same time plans were laid for a conference of all army commanders to be held before the end of April at Sarapul, where the details of what was expected to be the

374 WO 33/966/1645 'Knox (Omsk) to WO, 16.iv.1919'; WO 33/977A 'Narrative of Events in Siberia, 1918–1920', App. P (Knox to Britmis, 10.iv.1919); WO 106/1287/89 'Blair (Vladivostok) to WO, 22.iv.1919'; *Iz istorii grazhdanskoi voiny v SSSR*, Vol. 2, p. 77; Eikhe, *Oprokinutyi tyl*, p. 207. 'I do not recall a single voice at Omsk which spoke out in favour of halting the advance [at the Ik]', said Sukin (Sukin, *Leeds Russian Archive*, p. 244).

final campaign of the civil war, Russian Army's move on Moscow, would be settled upon.

In accordance with the new battle plan, Khanzhin continued to urge his forces westwards along the Ufa–Samara and Ufa–Simbirsk railways, capturing Buguruslan on April 15th. Meanwhile, to the north, other units of the Western Army drove through the Menzelinsk district; by the end of April they had captured Chistopol on the River Kama, thereby opening the road to Kazan and the northern reaches of the Volga itself.

The headlong retreat of the 5th Red Army from Ufa posed a serious threat to the security of the 1st Red Army, which was operating further south. In order to forestall an attack on its now dangerously exposed left flank, the latter was forced to withdraw from Sterlitamak in early April, relinquishing the town without serious resistance to Cossack units of Kolchak's Belov Army Group (which, although it was the northernmost section of Southern Army, was operationally subordinate to Western Army). At the same time the Cossacks of Ataman Dutov's Orenburg Army Group were advancing from Orsk to Aktiubinsk, which they captured on April 11th, thereby severing the Orenburg–Tashkent railway (isolating Red forces in Turkestan) and inspiring a renewed outbreak of anti-Soviet risings in the Cossack *stanitsy* of the Orenburg steppe.

Taking stock of all this activity at the end of April, Kolchak would apparently have had every right to feel satisfied with his forces' progress and to conclude that the optimistic projections of his *stavka* had been fully justified. In this brief, opening phase of the spring offensive the Russian Army had already annexed territory totalling some 300,000 square kilometres, containing much rich agricultural land, a population of five million and several large towns; in the process it had captured from the Reds over ten thousand prisoners, thirty-six field guns, nine thousand rifles, two armoured trains, six hundred railway wagons and one hundred river steamers. In rather less than two months, moreover, the van of Kolchak's forces had advanced almost 300 km westward. Most promisingly of all, his Western Army was only 80 km from Kazan, 80 km from Samara and 100 km from Simbirsk; and by the capture of Chistopol it had driven an 150 km wide wedge between the northern (2nd and 3rd Red Armies) and southern (5th, 4th and 1st Red Armies) components of his enemy's Eastern Army Group – an achievement which threatened disaster to the Bolsheviks' defence efforts on the Eastern Front.

And Kolchak was not alone in being impressed. Four thousand miles away in Paris the Allies too were coming to the conclusion that the Supreme Ruler's forces might well be capable of driving the Reds from Moscow. It was, in fact, on the basis of reports from Siberia at this juncture that the powers came to decide in May upon the first step towards the recognition of the Omsk government, the Allied note of May 26th. Meanwhile, news of the military successes of the Russian Army, and speculation as to their potential political repercussions, had raised to fever pitch the already endemic mood of optimism at Omsk. Even those who had not previously been convinced of the inevitability of military victory began to have second thoughts. Thus, the generally sceptical and cautious George Guins was to declare: 'We now have an army which is covered in martial glory... The knowledge that right is on its side has created the belief in victory.'[375] Other former critics of the régime fell silent, as plans were mooted of moving the *stavka* and the government apparatus west to Ekaterinburg, in anticipation of the imminent transfer to Moscow.[376] And in the *stavka* the general opinion was that 'within weeks' the new objectives would be achieved, Samara and Kazan would be captured and the Volga would be crossed. Even when, towards the very end of April, the Western Army seemed to be faltering a little in its hitherto steamrollering approach to the great river, the staff of Gajda's Siberian Army would reassure the Supreme Ruler that this was of no importance because their own units would be in Moscow 'in no more than six weeks'.[377] It was apparently inconceivable to the young officers who dominated Kolchak's military institutions that, after such a rout, the Bolsheviks would be able to muster any significant defence of the Russian heartland, let alone organize a counter attack – and no wonder they felt that way when even General Khanzhin, one of Kolchak's most respected and experienced senior officers, could opine that any Red counter-attack could only be a death spasm, 'could only be a last act of despair', while the Supreme Ruler himself began to talk of the possibility of

375 *Priishim'e* (Petropavlovsk) No. 133 (655), 25.vi.1919.

376 *FRUS: 1919 (Russia)*, pp. 201–2; Arnol'dov, *Zhizn' i revoliutsiia*, p. 160; *The Times* (London) 3.v.1919.

377 Fedotoff-White, *Survival Through War and Revolution*, p. 216; Budberg, Vol. 14, p. 235.

an advance direct on Moscow, quite independent of the planned strategic union with the forces from Arkhangel′sk.[378]

Despite all of this success and the attendant euphoria, however, the untrained and unmotivated peasant conscripts who formed the bulk of the troops at Kolchak's disposal remained of as poor quality as before; likewise, the army command remained as weak in its strategic thinking and as wrong-headed in its estimations of Bolshevik strength as it always had been. How, then, had the Russian Army achieved so much in March–April of 1919? An anonymous officer, apparently one of the few in the White camp given to reason, came at least half way to revealing the truth when, in conversation with the Kadet Lev Krol at Ekaterinburg, he counselled against drawing overly optimistic conclusions for the anti-Bolshevik cause from the recent triumphs on the Urals front: 'Don't think that our successful advances are a result of military prowess,' he warned, 'for it is all much simpler than that – when they run away we advance; when we run away they will advance.'[379]

There were, in fact, a number of factors, identified in contemporary Bolshevik postmortems on their retreat from the Urals, which had enabled the Russian Army to prompt the Red Army into 'running away'. Firstly, in comparison to Kolchak's troops (which were at least fresh) the men of the Red Eastern Army Group were physically and mentally exhausted, having been in the field for many months by the spring of 1919. Most of them had fought in the Volga campaigns of the summer and autumn of 1918 and had then participated in the pursuit of anti-Bolshevik forces to the Urals, where they had subsequently overwintered in terribly cold conditions without even the comfort of regular rations. Consequently, by the spring of 1919, the best fighting elements of the group had already been killed or injured in battle or were dead or dying of disease, as the Commander-in-Chief of the 3rd Red Army reported. Moreover, far from having these losses made good, Eastern Army Group had actually to suffer the depletion of its manpower from November 1918 to March 1919, as troops were transferred from the east to meet the threats on the southern and western fronts (particularly painfully felt was the withdrawal from the Urals of

378 Novitskii, F.F. 'Vse na vostok' in Spirin, L.M. (ed.) *Razgrom Kolchaka: vospominaniia*. Moscow (1969), p. 75; WO 33/977A 'Narrative of Events in Siberia, 1918–1920', App. S (Knox to WO, 14.v.1919).

379 Krol′, L. *Za tri goda*, p. 172.

Lettish and Estonian rifle units, the backbone of the Red Army).[380] The resources left to Eastern Army Group were then spread too thinly, as the very success of the group in 1918 led the Red high command, in early 1919, to order the eastern armies not only to advance to (and, indeed, beyond) the Ural Mountains, but also to despatch forces south-east, through the Orenburg Cossack region and on into Turkestan.

On top of all this, the very ad hoc nature, when it came, of the Kolchak advance, throwing as many troops against the centre of the front as it did in the north, caused no little confusion on the Red side. Colonel S.S. Kamenev, Commander-in-Chief of Eastern Army Group, had expected Kolchak's main thrust to continue to be in the northern Urals, as it had been during the autumn and winter, and deraigned his troops accordingly. The Western Army's Ufa offensive, therefore, caught him by surprise.[381] Another factor in the Whites' favour was that at the lower levels of command Red military leadership was deficient at this time: in the 3rd Red Army, for example, commanders were found to be lazy and unreliable and their commissars both inexperienced and undisciplined. Also, in the rout of the 5th Red Army at Ufa was revealed the disruptive effects of a local dominance of supporters of the so-called Military Opposition to Trotsky's efforts to increase the discipline, centralization and regularization of the Red Army. The most debilitating result of the commissars' shortcomings was found to be the neglect of food supply to the active units.[382]

Whatever the debilitative effects of the qualitative failings on the Red side, however, undoubtedly the most important factor in determining the early success of the Russian Army (and particularly of the Western Army Group) was the significant numerical superiority in troops which it enjoyed during the first weeks of the spring offensive. Of course, whether or not Kolchak's peasant conscripts would endure a lengthy campaign remained to be seen. But, in the short term, Omsk's policy of throwing every available man into the front line had produced a definite quantitative advantage for the Whites. This was very clear from calculations of the configuration

380 *Iz istorii grazhdanskoi voiny v SSSR*, Vol. 1, pp. 391–3 and Vol. 2, pp. 82–3; Meijer, J. (ed.) *The Trotsky Papers*. London–The Hague (1964–1973), Vol. 1, pp. 474, 478–9. Stalinist historians delighted in castigating Trotsky for these strategic errors – see, for example, Fedorov, A. *Permskaia katastrofa i kontrnastuplenie Vostochnogo fronta*. Moscow (1940), p. 83.

381 Mawdsley, *The Russian Civil War*, p. 140.

382 *Iz istorii grazhdanskoi voiny v SSSR*, Vol. 1, pp. 393–5; Meijer, Vol. 1, p. 322.

Table 3.1: Opposing forces on the Eastern Front, March 15th 1919

Sector	Soldiery	Artillery
Perm:		
Whites (Siberian Army)	32,000	84
Reds (3rd Army)	30,000	78
Sarapul:		
Whites (Siberian Army)	21,000	67
Reds (2nd Army)	19,500	76
Ufa:		
Whites (Western Army)	40,000	197
Reds (5th Army)	11,000	50
Orenburg–Ural'sk:		
Whites (Southern Army)	19,000	110
Reds (1st and 4th Armies)	36,000	173
Eastern Front (total):		
Whites (Russian Army)	112,000	440
Reds (Eastern Army Group)	96,500	377

of troops along the various sectors of the Eastern Front (as of March 15th 1919) drawn up by the Main Commander-in-Chief of the Red Army, Colonel I.I. Vatsetis. His figures, cited in Table 3.1 (above), have not been significantly challenged by subsequent military histories.

Vatsetis's statistics indicate that to the elements of surprise and the Red Army's temporary disorganization already in Kolchak's favour was added not only an overall numerical and matériel superiority along the Eastern Front but, in the key sector of Ufa, the crux of the early stages of the Russian Army's planned offensive, a local superiority of nearly 4:1 in both manpower and artillery.[383]

383 *Iz istorii grazhdanskoi voiny v SSSR*, Vol. 2, pp. 78–80.

Kolchak refluent, May–July 1919

By late April 1919, however, the factors which had been operating in Kolchak's favour no longer existed. The Military Opposition in the Red camp had been attenuated by decisions of the 8th Party Congress of March; subsequently discipline was significantly improved at the front and central control was restored. Meanwhile Vatsetis rapidly and successfully redeployed the available forces in the east. In particular he pulled troops north from the 1st Red Army to reinforce the 5th, thereby going some way towards nullifying the formerly overwhelming superiority of Khanzhin's Western Army in the Ufa salient; there were 24,000 Red troops on the Ufa front by April 17th.[384] As these emergency redeployments were being effected, the Red command made time to reflect upon both the disasters in the east and the comparatively favourable situation then developing on the other major fronts: by April the worst of the Don Cossack rising seemed to be over and the French and Greek interventionists had withdrawn from the Black Sea ports. In the light of this, in early April, the Bolshevik Central Committee issued a series of 'Special Theses' which, for the first time, identified Kolchak as the chief threat to the Soviet Republic and ordered the greatest efforts to be made to defeat him.[385]

In the following weeks the massive supply of human and industrial resources at Lenin's disposal in central Russia, compared to Kolchak's underdeveloped Siberian base, made itself felt. Bolshevik organizations and unions of industrial workers in Moscow, Petrograd and other major cities mobilized 10–20% of their members and sent them east to make up the numbers and to stiffen morale at the front. The conscription of ordinary workers and peasants was also stepped up. Some were lured by promises of better food supply to servicemen and their families; others were ideologically committed to the struggle against the 'evil band of landlords and capitalists', the simple colours in which Red propaganda had painted the tentative and contradictory politics of the Whites. Either way, the Bolsheviks having no qualms about the use of veterans of World War 1, many of these recruits were already trained and experienced in the art of war and could often be sent straight into the field. Through these massive efforts the manpower strength of the Eastern

384 Spirin, *Razgrom armii Kolchaka*, p. 116, 130.

385 *Kommunisticheskaia partiia Sovetskogo soiuza v rezoliutsiiakh i resheniakh s"ezdov, konferentsii i plenumov TsK*. Moscow (1970), Vol. 2, p. 88.

Army Group was more than trebled in two months: it had reached a total of 341,424 infantrymen (including reserves) by May 31st. The supply of military hardware was also focused on the east: in April 16,000 rifles, 325 machine-guns and 17,000,000 cartridges were despatched to Eastern Army Group; in May were sent a further 25,800 rifles, 390 machine-guns and 28,000,000 cartridges.[386]

The input of men and materials from the rich store of central Russia soon told on the eastern battlefronts. On April 28th a Manoeuvering Group of Red forces, which had been built up around Buzuluk under the command of the veteran Bolshevik millworker M.V. Frunze, drove northwards against the over-extended left flank of Khanzhin's advance. Although Frunze had ample experience of fighting on the barricades of Moscow during the revolution, this was the first front-line command of the man who was destined to become a Red legend. Within two days his forces had reached and recaptured Buguruslan; and only the desertion to the Whites at this time of the Commander of the 25th Division of the 5th Red Army, Colonel Avalov, prevented Frunze from continuing to drive northwards to completely cut off the spearhead of the Western Army (which was as far west as Sergievsk and Lazovka at the end of April). As it was, however, acting on Avalov's information, Khanzhin's army was able to retreat hurriedly, but fairly safely, through Bugul′ma; by May 15th the Western Army was back behind the River Ik. Meanwhile, to the north, Chistopol was relinquished to Red marines on May 4th, thereby closing the dangerous gap which the Western Army had opened between the two halves of the Reds' Eastern Army Group.

With the Manoeuvering Group now merged into the 5th Red Army, Frunze continued his eastern progress throughout May. Belebei was recaptured on May 15th and by the end of the month the now rapidly disintegrating Western Army had fled beyond the River Belaia. On June 7th, in a brilliant surprise attack, the charismatic V.I. Chapaev and his 26th Rifle division of the 5th Red Army crossed the Belaia; panic broke out in Ufa and the town fell to Chapaev on June 9th, together with the vast stores of food and military equipment abandoned by the Whites.[387]

386 Mikhailova, E. 'Profsoiuzy i razgrom Kolchaka', *Profsoiuzy SSSR* (Moscow) 1940, No. 10, pp. 63–5; Spirin, *Razgrom armii Kolchaka*, pp. 111, 121–2; *Iz istorii grazhdanskoi voiny v SSSR*, Vol. 2, pp. 94–6, 200–1.

387 On these operations see Shishkin, S.N. 'Kontrnastuplenie Krasnoi armii na Vostochnom fronte protiv Kolchaka (aprel′–iiun′ 1919g.)', in Naida, S.F. and Kovalenko (eds.) *Reshaiushchie pobedy sovetskogo naroda nad interventsii i belogvardeitsam v 1919g. (sbornik statei)*. Moscow (1960), pp. 69–120; Bol′tin, E.A. *Kontrnastuplenie Iuzhnoi gruppy Vostochnogo fronta i razgrom*

In the northern Urals at this point Gajda's Siberian Army was still advancing. In the first days of June it had even succeeded in capturing its original objective, the town of Glazov. The collapse of the Western Army, however, had rendered Gajda woefully exposed to an attack from the south – as was realized when the 28th Division of the 2nd Red Army recaptured Sarapul on June 2nd (almost trapping Kolchak's prized Kama River Fleet downriver in the process). In the light of this Gajda was obliged to relinquish Glazov on June 13th; a fortnight later his Siberian Army was back at Perm, whence it had initiated its advance almost four months earlier.

A similar pattern of activity was emerging on the southernmost reaches of the Eastern Front (albeit on a less grand scale). This sparse, steppe sector had remained fairly static from March to May. In June, however, expeditions of Urals Cossacks broke through the thinly spread lines of the 4th Red Army and drove north-west to capture Nikolaevsk – a move which seemed to presage a union with Wrangel's forces then besieging Tsaritsyn. By the end of the month other White cavalry units were just 40 km from Samara and Kratovka and seemed likely to succeed in cutting rail links from the Volga to the 5th Red Army. The Cossack raiders, however, were few in number and were soon forced to withdraw from such untenable, isolated positions.

By the end of June, therefore, Kolchak's forces along the entire Eastern Front had been driven back to roughly the line from which they had commenced their spring offensive. And the rout did not stop there. Sensing that the Western Army would entirely disintegrate under a sustained onslaught and that the Urals were within their grasp, the Military Revolutionary Committee of the Eastern Army Group were at this time seeking permission from Moscow to continue their eastward pursuit of Kolchak. Their plan was initially opposed by Trotsky and Vatsetis (who, mistakenly fearing that Kolchak had serried ranks of reserves in Siberia, wanted to hold firm on the Belaia and transfer units to meet the renewed threat from Denikin on the Southern Front) but plenums of the party Central Committee of June 15th and July 3rd backed the local commanders and the eastern advance was continued.

In the southern salient the Reds' progress was at first slow, although a newly formed army group commanded by Chapaev did break through Tolstov's Urals Cossack stranglehold on Ural′sk to relieve that town's long-isolated Red garrison on

Kolchaka. Moscow (1949); and Eikhe, G. Kh. *Forsirovanie reki Beloi chastiami 5-i Armii Vostochnogo fronta v iiune 1919g*. Moscow (1928).

July 11th. But meanwhile, with the White forces scattering before them, the remainder of Eastern Army Group moved swiftly on from the Kama–Belaia line. Having out-manoeuvred the remnants of the Western Army, on July 13th the 26th and 27th Rifle Divisions of the 5th Red Army entered the railway town of Zlatoust, key to the major pass through the Urals; there they captured several armoured trains abandoned in the Whites' panicky withdrawal, together with thirty locomotives, six hundred wagons, two million poods of grain, two million poods of coal, three million poods of steel, twenty thousand poods of copper and other valuable stocks, before pressing on in the direction of Cheliabinsk. Further north the 2nd Red Army continued in hot pursuit of Gajda, recapturing Perm on July 1st – once again with a vast array of trophies, including six hundred railway wagons.[388] A fortnight later Ekaterinburg, the Urals capital, was also in their hands.

Thus, in the space of ten weeks the Red Army's counter-offensive had pushed the Siberian Army back 500 km and the Western Army almost 600 km. The Urals, with their mines and factories and railway network, the only significant industrial base in Kolchak's possession, was now lost to the anti-Bolshevik cause. Moreover, although this rolling, hilly juncture between Europe and the Siberian plain was not the physical barrier of popular repute, the Urals were the best defendable line available to the Whites between the Volga and Lake Baikal; their loss placed the entire eastern branch of the anti-Bolshevik movement in peril. And this was not all that the Whites had to concern them. Just as the initial success of the Ufa offensive had brought instant rewards to Kolchak in the form of the Allied note of May 26th hinting at future recognition of the Omsk régime, so too were the political repercussions of the ultimate failure of the Russian Army's offensive made most rapidly clear. Having gambled all on military success in order to impress the Allies, having painstakingly balanced the juggling act of White politics and having obscured his aims with such deft politesse in his note to Paris of June 4th, Kolchak was to find that when the powers acknowledged his reply as 'satisfactory' on June 12th, recognition was no longer on the table. Already on June 3rd, even before Kolchak's reply had been despatched, the Council of Five had taken cognizance of incoming reports of 'serious reverses' having been suffered by Kolchak's troops;

388 Kolchak's pride and joy, the Kama River Fleet (which had only been involved in one engagement with Red forces) was, however, denied to the Reds at Perm when, apparently by accident, its 38 ships caught fire whilst dumping fuel. Fedotoff-White, pp. 227–31; *FRUS: 1919 (Russia)*, pp. 206–7. On the recapture of Perm by the 3rd Red Army see Pazdnikov, N.F. *Bor'ba za Perm': Permskie sobytiia v grazhdanskoi voine*. Perm' (1988), pp. 165–7.

and soon the Allied leaders would come to hear that the tide of the Russian Army's advance had been decisively turned on the approaches to the Volga, indicating that Moscow was not going to be captured quite so easily as had been expected. Consequently, in their note of June 12th, the powers limited themselves to a re-affirmation of their commitment to supply aid to the Omsk régime. The greater prize, the official recognition so desired by Kolchak, was no longer even hinted at: in the words of an American observer, it had 'fled like Eurydice's shade'.[389]

The organizational and strategic shortcomings of the Russian Army – the results of the military and political prejudices of the White leadership, their haste to achieve a lightning victory and their unwavering underestimation of their enemy – were starkly revealed in the circumstances of its brief success of March–April 1919 turning rapidly into the beginnings of anomic retreat in May–July. As General Knox and other advocates of a more cautious military policy had predicted, Kolchak's untrained and unmotivated peasant troops had proven to be poor stuff at the front. Things went well so long as his armies were advancing, but as soon as the Red Army had rallied and their counter-attack took effect the young and unwilling conscripts from Siberia deserted in their droves. And it was of no minor significance that the Red counter-attack coincided with the onset of warmer weather; Kolchak's conscripts saw more logic (and profit) in the work to be done at home in the fields. Some left their units even whilst en route to the front; others mutinied on the battlefront and went directly over to the Reds – as in the case of the 1,100 strong Taras Shevchenko Regiment (of Ukrainian settlers in Siberia) which deserted en bloc to the 5th Red Army on May 2nd.[390] Casualties among Kolchak's troops were also very high – hardly surprising when nineteen-year-old boys who had never before borne arms were thrown into the front-line immediately after a 60 km forced march, only six weeks after their mobilization (and having spent most of the intervening period on trains rather than in training).[391] The consequences of these desertions and casualties were enormous. By the time that the Western Army had

389 *FRUS: PPC*, Vol. 6, pp. 319, 348; *USMI*, Vol. 9, No. 117 (week ending 23.viii.1919), p. 1,580.

390 *Iz istorii grazhdanskoi voiny v SSSR*, Vol. 2, p. 223; *Istoriia grazhdanskoi voiny v SSSR*, Vol. 2, pp. 94–6, 200–1.

391 WO 32/5707 'Report of the Military Mission to Siberia, 10.xii.1919', pp. 14–15; WO 33/977A 'Narrative of Events in Siberia, 1918–1920', App. T (Knox to Kolchak, 7.vi.1919); *DBFP*, Vol. 3, p. 339.

been driven back to the River Belaia in May, for example, its strength had waned from a peak of 60,000 in March to less than half that number.[392]

Attempts to fill the gaps in the front line by a round of mobilizations in the areas of the immediate rear probably did more harm than good – for, as soon as the Red advance approached the home districts of the newly mobilized men, they would desert. General Knox put this down to the fact that '90% of the population' perceived little difference between the two sides or were fed up with the struggle and desired only 'to be on the side that was winning'.[393] And war-weariness must indeed have played a part – the prospects of a retreat into Siberia could not have been welcome to even the staunchest White fighter. An additional factor, however, as another member of Britmis realized, was that the conscripts were simply attempting to ensure that their home villages would not be pillaged by the approaching Bolsheviks.[394]

No more successful was the last-ditch effort in June to save the Western Army by throwing the only reserve at Kolchak's immediate disposal (the Volga Corps of Colonel V.O. Kappel and the 11th, 12th and 13th Siberian Divisions, being prepared by Knox) into the line before Belebei. By the time that any number of these units (chiefly those under Kappel) had been able to force their way through the Urals' congested railway network and into the theatre of operations, Belebei had already been lost. The Corps was hurriedly reformed and redeployed on the Belaia but, being no better trained than the men it had come to replace, it was to little effect. Knox had always opposed the reserves' deployment before (at the very earliest) August, telling Kolchak that it would be 'the equivalent of handing over their rifles and uniforms to the enemy'. Lebedev, however, insisted on their immediate deployment as the first step to a renewed offensive and would not hear of a strategic withdrawal. Within a month, reported Knox, at least 10,000 of Kappel's men had gone over to the Reds (together with their brand new British kit), while the new Siberian divisions were en route to the front and a similar fate at Cheliabinsk.[395]

392 *Iz istorii grazhdanskoi voiny v SSSR*, Vol. 2, p. 202.

393 WO 32/5707 'Report of the Military Mission', p. 9.

394 Vining, L.Ė. *Held by the Bolsheviks: The Diary of a British Officer in Russia, 1919–1920*. London (1924), p. 69.

395 WO 32/5707 'Report of the Military Mission to Siberia, 10.xii.1919', p. 12 and App. B, p. 2; WO 33/967/2240 'Knox (Omsk) to WO, 17.vi.1919'; WO 33/967/2277 'Narrative of Events in Siberia, 1918–1920 (Britmis to WO, 20.vi.1919)'. Knox even received a telegraphed message of thanks from the Red Army command for this unexpected British contribution to the Bolshevik war effort

A factor which undoubtedly added to the scale of the desertions from the White armies was the cruelty and summary justice meted out to their men by Kolchak's officers. For example, when a newly mobilized regiment at Tomsk sent a delegation to their commanding officer to complain that they were about to be sent to the front without food, clothing and boots, twenty of the delegates were immediately executed and several more were brutally flogged. When the remains of the regiment reached the front a week later it duly deserted en bloc to the Reds.[396] Of course, justice was severe on the Red side too – and there are well-documented accounts of desertions from the Red Army to the Whites – but at least Red justice seemed to follow some system and make sense; and at least on the Red side soldiers, officers and commissars alike were subject to it.

A marked contrast can also be identified between the manner in which the Red and Siberian White armies utilized a prime resource of the civil war – deserters from their enemy's units. Trotsky had ordered that all deserters from Kolchak's forces were to be treated 'in a friendly way, as comrades'; while even those forced to surrender in battle were 'in no case to be shot' unless they were proven class enemies. 'We will turn repentant enemies into friends', decreed Lenin's Commissar for War.[397] Officially this was also the policy of the Russian Army. Kolchak had declared in April 1919 that, although all those who had been volunteers in the Red Army should be sent to concentration camps, the mobilized *krasnoarmeetsy* deserved clemency and, after retraining, would be incorporated into White units if they so desired.[398] This message of forgiveness was dutifully re-iterated by the Supreme Ruler's army staffs at the front and was a prominent feature in emollient White propaganda calling upon the Red Army men to desert.[399] However, it was far from being the norm in practice. Even officers who had served the Bolsheviks

– see Grondijs, L.H. *La Guerre en Russie et en Sibérie*. Paris (1922), p. 528. These 'Tommies from Tomsk', as they became known, later turned up in Central Asia to puzzle a British witness – see Bailey, F.M. *Mission to Tashkent*. London (1946), p. 202.

396 Baerlin, H. *The March of the Seventy Thousand*. London (1926), p. 219; McCullagh, F. *A Prisoner of the Reds: The Story of a British Officer Captured in Siberia*. London (1921), p. 324.

397 Trotsky, L. *How the Revolution Armed*, Vol. 2, pp. 522–3.

398 *Bulletins of the Russian Liberation Committee* (London) No. 8, 12.iv.1918; *Union (Bureau de Presse Russe)* (Paris) No. 5, 8.v.1919.

399 *Velikaia Rossiia* (Ufa) No. 12, 3.iv.1919. White propaganda leaflets dropped by aircraft behind the Red lines even indicated that the *krasnoarmeets* would be paid if he surrendered with his rifle in working order. See the leaflet headed '*Tovarishchi!*' (*Pares Papers*, Box 50).

under duress, with their families held hostage for their loyalty, were regarded with deep suspicion, if not as criminals and traitors, by their White counterparts in Siberia. Even so illustrious an officer as General Andogskii, head of the Imperial General Staff Academy, for example, was abused in the Siberian press for having served the Bolsheviks, however unwillingly, for a few months in 1918 before leading dozens of his students across to the Whites at Kazan in September; and he was long deprived of a post in the Russian Army commensurate with his experience and seniority.[400]

Equally, very few Red soldiers were ever incorporated into the ranks of Kolchak's Russian Army. Rather, to the horror and blank incomprehension of British observers, the starving and demoralised prisoners from the 3rd Red Army who had been captured at Perm in December 1918 – ideal material for re-education and deployment against the Bolsheviks, who had so neglected them – were not delivered to Kappel for training and incorporation into the reserve, as had initially been promised; instead, entire Red regiments were summarily executed as 'Bolsheviks' by their captors while others were stripped of their clothing and left naked to die of cold or typhus in concentration camps.[401] Such actions may perhaps be partly explained by the Whites' confidence at that time. However, later reports indicate that even during the retreat to the Urals of May–June 1919, when the need for new recruits was so dire, officers' prejudice and vengeful bloodlust continued to dictate the wholesale slaughter of captured Red units and deserters.[402]

400 Guins, *Sibir'*, Vol. 1, p. 201 and Vol. 2, pp. 302, 305. General Andogskii was only to attain high office (as Quartermaster General) under Kolchak in the summer of 1919, because in 1918 the former head of the Imperial General Staff Academy had reluctantly co-operated with the Bolsheviks. He even found it necessary to publish a self-justificatory pamphlet (*Akademiia general'nago shtaba v 1917–1918gg.* Omsk, 1919) in response to a campaign of vilification against him in the Siberian press.

401 WO 32/5707 'Report of the Military Mission', p. 12; Ward, pp. 214–5. When a British diplomat asked a Russian colonel of the Siberian Army on what basis he decided to shoot, as 'Bolsheviks', a good proportion of the soldiers he captured, the colonel replied that he was 'largely guided by their physical appearance, being well-acquainted with the criminal types of the Bolsheviki' – see FO 371/4095/5592 'Preston (Ekaterinburg) to FO, 4.i.1919'.

402 *The Times* (London) 9.vii.1919. The *krasnoarmeetsy* who were executed or were left to die at the front were often the lucky ones. Thousands more Red prisoners were to spend many tortured, freezing and starving months traversing and retraversing the Trans-Siberian Railway aboard the infamous 'Trains of Death' – prison transports for which nobody in Siberia wished to accept responsibility and to which Kolchak's military seemed perversely and cruelly unwilling to allocate a final destination. The trains' population was rapidly diminished by typhus, hunger and the Siberian climate during their tortured peregrinations, but some prisoners survived until the winter of 1919 to 1920 – only then to be finally killed, as the White military commandeered all trains

In the long run Kolchak's officer corps were also incapable of fulfilling the promises they had made about their own fighting ability. During the early, successful stages of the spring offensive this may not have been the case – the Reds' Main Commander-in-Chief, for one, said that initially his opponents were better led than his own troops.[403] Like all the other factors in Kolchak's favour at that time, however, this was a transitory phenomenon. Red officership improved qualitatively and quantitatively as the spring wore on, while the Whites' got worse. Perhaps this was a result of a lack of imagination on the White officers' part. Having served their apprenticeships during the years of largely static trench warfare in Galicia, Poland and the Carpathians during the Great War, they may have been unable to adapt to the new battle conditions which confronted them in 1919, to operations in which areas half the size of Europe could be won or lost in a matter of weeks. Of course, the men leading the Red Army had no broader experience than their White opponents. The Bolsheviks, however, seemed better able to nurture young officers of verve, skill and imagination such as V.K. Bliukher and M.N. Tukhachevskii; and they were not afraid to promote and trust the instincts of inspirational born leaders, such as Frunze or the unorthodox Chapaev. There were few such stars in Kolchak's army – and those that existed, such as Kappel, were all too often, or too long, overlooked. Respect for tradition and deference to seniority were what counted on the White side; individuals who showed outstanding flair tended to be regarded with suspicion in Siberia. A case in point is that of Georgii Mayer, a junior naval officer. He had graduated only in 1917, but during 1918 had almost single-handedly built up the Kama River Fleet for Komuch, having numerous officers under his command who were, in rank, his seniors. By 1919, however, with the founding of the Kolchak dictatorship, more and more of the old naval establishment began to arrive at the

in their attempts to escape from the advancing Red Army. See Vilenskii, Vl. *Chernaia godina sibirskoi reaktsii*. Moscow (1919), pp. 40–4; Baturin, V. 'Eshelon smerti. Vospominaniia rabochego', *Sibirskie ogni* (Novosibirsk), No. 6 (1929), pp. 129–39; Bimba, A. 'Eshelon smerti', *Bor'ba klassov* (Moscow), Nos. 11–12 (1932); Popov, F.G. (ed.) *Poezd smerti*. Kuibyshev (1959); Gendlin, A.S. 'V kolchakovskom zastenke', in Nikitin, I.I. (ed.) *Nezabyvaemye gody: sbornik vospominanii starykh chlenov KPSS*. Yaroslavl' (1963), pp. 95–101; and, for the eye-witness accounts of American Red Cross workers: Williams, A.R. *Through the Russian Revolution*. New York (1921), pp. 288–92; Gidney, *Witness to a Revolution*, pp. 248–52. The latter remarked that, even by November 1918, the inhabitants of the trains 'looked more like animals than any group of human beings I ever saw'.

403 'Doklady I.I. Vatsetisa V.I. Leninu (fevral'–mai 1919g.)', *Istoricheskii arkhiv* (Moscow), No. 1 (1958), p. 43.

front and the talented Mayer found himself reduced to a mere flag-lieutenant in command of just one division of the fleet he himself had created.[404]

But the most distinguishing and most debilitating feature of the White officer corps – in battle as it was in the rear – was its all-pervading spirit of wilfulness, indiscipline and insubordination. There were exceptions, of course, and there was real heroism (albeit all too often of a romantically futile nature) on the White side, as some Red commanders readily conceded: an adjutant of Frunze, for example, recalled with admiration how, at Ufa, in a last-ditch attempt to prevent the town from falling, a shock battalion of White officers, consisting exclusively of Knights of St George, had emerged out of the dawn and advanced towards the Red machine-guns 'with fixed bayonets, silent, holding their fire'. With 'the skull and crossbones insignia mounted on their caps, sleeves and epaulettes,' he added, 'they made a terrifying impression.'[405] But all too often the young officers succumbed to the allure of quests for glory and military honour in what was expected to be an easy war and undertook cavalier raids against the Red lines. On at least three occasions, for example, unauthorised, devil-may-care advances along the Kama and the Irtysh undertaken by junior officers all but resulted in the loss of the bulk of Kolchak's river fleets.[406] Insubordination, however, was not confined to the junior ranks during the spring offensive. In late May, for example, Gajda was to refuse to acknowledge the orders of Chief of Staff Lebedev and demand that he, Gajda, be made commander-in-chief at the front (see below, pp. 474ff). Moreover, as Khanzhin's force collapsed in the central sector of the front, the Czech general single-mindedly pursued his own objectives and would not divert forces to the south so as to assist the Western Army (whose leadership he publicly and immoderately defamed).[407]

This atmosphere of rivalry and selfishness which had arisen among the Siberian military helped to damn the Kolchak offensive of 1919. 'Patriotism and public spirit do not exist to any extent', lamented a British observer of the White camp. 'Every man looks at every order from the personal point of view.'[408] In part this was

404 Fedotoff-White, pp. 219–20.

405 Bubnov, A.S. et al. (eds.) *Grazhdanskaia voina, 1918–1921gg.* Moscow (1928), Vol. 3, pp. 328–9.

406 Fedotoff-White, pp. 227–31, 236–43, 247–55.

407 Budberg, Vol. 14, pp. 274–6.

408 Ward, *With the 'Die-Hards'*, p. 175.

probably a consequence of the youth and ambition of the White commanders in question – General Gajda was only twenty-seven years old in 1919 and Lebedev was just thirty-six. The *Wunderkind* and his like were keen to make the maximum impression before the expected Bolshevik collapse, in order to stake their claims for senior positions in the postwar order. However, politics (or, rather, political prejudice) seems also to have played a part in this rivalry. Baron Budberg, for example, was horrified to discover that the news of Khanzhin's misfortune induced not consternation but barely concealed glee and *Schadenfreude* among officers of the Siberian Army's staff, for the defeated Western Army contained the remnants of what in 1918 had been the People's Àrmy of the still reviled SR Komuch on the Volga.[409]

A final factor which both contributed to this indifference and was a root cause of the failure of each individual army group's offensive during the spring of 1919, was the fierce daily competition between the various sectors of the front for the increasingly scarce resources of food and equipment.[410] The unavailability of items of even the most basic necessity had served to ensure that the advances of both the Western Army and the Siberian Army – alike unable to clothe, feed or re-arm their men – had been grinding to a halt in April–May even before the Red Army had launched its counter-attack. Moreover, being left more or less to their own devices, the armies had been forced to requisition the supplies they needed from the local peasants: 'At present we are taking everything from the countryside', reported Ataman Dutov in a letter to Kolchak of April 1919, urging the Supreme Ruler to improve the supply of the front.[411] Dutov's fear was not only that such widespread requisitioning of the peasants' property was making the Russian Army to appear more than ever to be an army of occupation rather than one of liberation in the eyes of people of the Volga-Kama basin, but that the activity was engendering a spirit of independent partisanship among White units which was beginning to border on insubordination and sheer banditry. As Kolchak himself had found, during

409 Emissaries sent by Colonel Kappel to the capital reported that precisely the same attitude was prevalent there with regard to the alleged 'Constituent Assemblyites' of the Western Army. See Dotsenko, *The Struggle for a Democracy*, p. 80.

410 The rift between the *stavka* and the Ministry of War also caused competition for resources between the front and the rear, as Minister of War Stepanov stockpiled food in the rear for the reserves he intended to mobilize. See Sukin (*Leeds Russian Archive*), p. 157.

411 Luchebnikov, P.S. et al. (eds.) *Grazhdanskaia voina na iuzhnom Urale, 1918–1919gg.: sbornik dokumentov*. Cheliabinsk (1962), p. 198.

his attempts to control officer detachments in Manchuria during the first stirrings of the civil war in the east, forces which are not supplied by the centre will not obey the centre. And with the chaotic retreat which the Red blow of May 1919 engendered, the supply situation became critical; no effective support was or could be offered to the contracting fronts by the disorganized, over-manned *stavka* and the inefficient government departments at Omsk, thereby hastening the Russian Army's collapse and swelling the tide of deserters to the Reds.[412] By the time that those deprived troops who remained with their units had retreated to the Urals their appearance struck witnesses as more befitting some ragged band of brigands from the Thirty Years' War than a twentieth-century army. In one case a report tells that a regiment was in such an impoverished state that it had to be marched through Perm at night, for fear that the soldiers' nakedness might cause offence to local women.[413]

The supply crisis was partly the result of yet more administrative and organizational confusion on the part of the military and governmental establishments of Omsk. More than that, however, the inanition and indigence of the Russian Army by the middle of 1919 was a reflection of the fact that, quite apart from the military contests being fought out on the Eastern Front, the Supreme Ruler was failing to win the perhaps unwinnable war against geography on the economic, financial and transportation fronts within his domain. Thus, as there drew to a close the first half of 1919 and the Kolchak offensive – a time and an event of which so much had been expected by the entire anti-Bolshevik movement – a British official at Omsk sounded the alarm for an equally anxious audience in Europe: 'The bad military situation would be only of momentary import so long as the position in the rear were sound,' he said. 'It is not.'[414]

412 Petrov, P.P. *Ot Volgi do Tikhago okeana*. Riga (1930), pp. 108–10.

413 *The Times* (London) 26.vii.1919. Yet some months later a captured British officer, who enquired as to how it was that so may Red Army soldiers were wearing British khaki, was informed by a Red commander that 'at Perm they had captured enough uniforms to clothe a division. They had found them unpacked in a storehouse, where they had probably been forgotten by the Whites.' See McCullagh, pp. 67–8. Similarly, when the Red Army entered Omsk they discovered 200 Colt machine-guns and 1,000 French mitrailleuses, all unassembled in storehouses. See Eikhe, *Oprokinutyi tyl*, pp. 126–7.

414 *DBFP*, Vol. 3, p. 340.

Chapter 4

Inside Kolchakia: from 'a land of milk and honey' to 'the dictatorship of the whip'

Travelling westwards along the Trans-Siberian Railway on a Foreign Office intelligence-gathering mission in April 1919, the British historian Bernard Pares perceptively remarked that, in the absence of the sort of patriotic fervour which a national war might engender, in the Russian Civil War 'to the average citizen politics is becoming more economics than anything else'.[1] It might, in fact, be argued that the average Russian citizen – a peasant, at best semi-literate – had never been attracted to abstract notions of democracy and political reform: the State Duma, the zemstvos and the Constituent Assembly were the totems only of the intelligentsia and of liberal elements of the bureaucracy. But certainly by 1919, as Pares implied, popular support was likely to be won or lost as a result of what the contending régimes in Russia could offer not tomorrow, in some socialist, monarchist or liberal-democratic utopia, but today, in terms of hard goods, hard cash and economic stability.

This was particularly true in Siberia. It was, after all, a region with a population which was not renowned for political activism, compared even with the rest of what had until recently been termed 'slumbering Russia'. Of course, White elements had been attracted to the east by the fact that Siberia was far from being a natural seed-bed of Bolshevism in terms of demography, consisting as it did of only a smattering of unorganized and disunited workers dissolved in the mass of a prosperous free peasantry. And, at least initially, their hopes had been realized. It was true, as Pares would have known, that the establishment of the Kolchak régime at Omsk in November 1918 had occasioned a spate of political strikes and armed risings in Siberian towns over the following winter. But (with a few exceptions) these involved only workers, no more than a fraction of the region's populace, and were easily contained by the army. The peasant masses meanwhile remained politically dormant: being already long confirmed in the possession of the land which they

[1] Pares, B. 'Report on Political Conditions in Eastern Siberia, 30.v.1919' (*Pares Papers*, Box 44), p. 3.

farmed, the peasants of landlordless Siberia had gained very little from the first months of Bolshevik rule and the Soviet Government's attendant sponsorship of land redistribution. Consequently, the peasantry had acquiesced in the overthrow of Soviet power in Siberia during the spring of 1918 with almost complete equanimity.

If there was some cause for concern in the rural scene, to an observer such as Pares, it might be only that since the demise of the Soviet régime east of the Urals the region's peasants had shown little *more* inclination to render active support to the various anti-Bolshevik governments which had succeeded each other at Omsk. This reticence, however, could be (and was) ascribed to a desire among the industrious Siberian farmers for a return, after three years of war and two of revolution, to some semblance of economic normality – normal wages, normal trade, even normal taxes. And, to this end, it was surely hopeful from the point of view of Kolchak's supporters that, whatever the political shortcomings of his régime, senior members of the Omsk Government were publicly and unequivocally declaring that 'a twofold victory must be achieved – over Bolshevism and over economic disorder'.[2]

Moreover, if Kolchak could introduce to his domains the 'order' he had promised, what great prospects could be anticipated by the anti-Bolshevik movement for the launching of the regeneration of Russia from the Supreme Ruler's base east of the Urals. For, contrary to the (still) dominant western perceptions of that region as being some vast and uniformly desolate arctic wasteland, in the black earth belts of Western Siberia (between 54° and 57° latitude) and in the foothills of the Altai, Siberia south of the taiga and tundra was actually a land containing sizable agricultural zones of almost unrivalled fecundity. A wartime survey of the region had estimated that these areas had the potential to feed the population of European Russia no less than six times over. Indeed, as Bernard Pares noted, with regard to the abundance of farm produce which he saw stockpiled at the stations along his route to Kolchak's capital, Siberia in many respects was 'literally a land overflowing with milk and honey'; he added that 'one's mouth waters at the inestimable material wealth'.[3] Pares, then, found good reason to be optimistic for the White cause on his journey towards Omsk.

2 *Priishim'e* (Petropavlovsk) No. 133 (1655), 25.vi.1919.

3 Beable, W.H. *Commercial Russia*. London (1918), p. 152; Pares, B. 'Siberian Diary' (*Pares Papers*, Box 43), pp. 43, 68.

However, at almost precisely the same time as our British agent was (for the enlightenment of Whitehall) recording such sanguine impressions of his passage into Siberia, a leading Canadian financier, A.D. Braithwaite, was returning from Kolchak's capital to report to his own government that thorough investigation of the situation in White Siberia had forced him to the conclusion that the prospects of placing the region's economy on the firm and stable footing necessary to pursue the war to a successful conclusion were 'quite hopeless'. The root of this pessimism, which further study reveals to have been quite justified, lay in Braithwaite's assessment of two factors militating against the possibility of the Siberian anti-Bolshevik régime winning popular support through the renewal of economic order and prosperity: firstly, the unlikelihood that the insensitive and revanchist army leadership, so immutably confident in the imminence of all-national victory, would be either willing or able to apply itself to the complexities of running a regional economy; and secondly, the inherent weaknesses of the Siberian economy, which (despite its spectacular successes of the recent past in some fields) was far from transcending its colonial heritage to the extent that it could function independently of the Russian centre – particularly under the sort of strains being placed upon it by the White war effort.[4]

PART ONE: THE URBAN SCENE

The industrial base

Clearly, Siberia itself did not possess a manufacturing and industrial base of a scale which might supply the needs of the massive army which Kolchak had placed in the field by 1919. Although the development of the Trans-Siberian Railway in the late 19th century had created an economic stimulus which, over the period 1900 to 1912,

[4] *Supplement to the Weekly Bulletin of the Department of Trade and Commerce: Report of the Canadian Economic Commission (Siberia)*. Ottawa (1919), pp. 56–7. (Hereafter cited as *Report of the CEC*.) For a concise account of the colonial legacy of Siberia see Gibson, J.R. 'The Significance of Siberia to Tsarist Russia', *Canadian Slavonic Papers*, No. 14 (1972), pp. 442–53.

occasioned a 15.4% increase in the number of factories in Siberia, a 22.9% increase in the number of industrial workers and a 22.2% increase in the value of industrial production, even by the eve of the Great War this massive region could boast of only 10.5% of Russia's factories, only 4.3% of her workforce and, most significantly, a mere 2.2% of the value of the Empire's industrial production.[5] Apart from a quantitative weakness, these figures reveal that, in terms of industrial quality, Siberia's factories were both smaller and less productive than the national average. Furthermore, it was significant that by far the largest employer east of the Urals was the Trans-Siberian Railway itself. Its 82,000 workers (constituting approximately one-third of the region's entire industrial labour force) were engaged in facilitating the prime economic task that Russia had traditionally assigned to her eastern colony – the export of raw materials and food to supply the heavy and manufacturing industries of the populous centre. Barely having considered Siberia economically as anything more than a cheap source of wood, grain, coal, furs, gold etc., the tsarist government had conceived of no reason to sponsor or protect such nascent industries as had developed east of the Urals – in fact, as the completion of the Trans-Siberian line had presented Siberia's infant, local manufactories with direct outside competition for the first time, there was a spate of factory closures in the region before World War I. Consequently, by 1914 even such a fundamental sector as metalworking could account for only 8% of Siberia's meagre industrial output, while arms-manufacturing, machine-tooling, chemical and textile industries were virtually non-existent. Not much had really changed since a prewar visitor had noted:

> The feeble industrial development of Siberia is abundantly evident in the fact that the houses, even in the largest cities, are built from planks sawn by hand, and the primitive river craft are innocent of a single nail in their construction.[6]

Siberia's colonial heritage had important implications for Kolchak. Firstly it meant that the only substantial means of communication and supply in the east, the Trans-Siberian Railway, was almost entirely reliant upon plants in European Russia for the manufacture and maintenance of its rolling-stock, rails and other needs; with those

[5] Mosina, I.G. 'Razvitie promyshlennosti i tovaro-denezhnykh otnoshenii v Sibiri v nachale xx v.', *Voprosy istorii Sibiri* (Tomsk), Vol. 3 (1967), pp. 102–3.

[6] Mosina, I.G. *Formirovanie burzhuazii v politicheskuiu silu v Sibiri*. Tomsk (1978), pp. 24–5; Stadling, J. *Through Siberia*. London (1901), p. 291.

plants in Bolshevik hands from 1918 to 1920, the railway's continued operation would, at best, be precarious. Secondly, Kolchak would be forced to rely upon his far from entirely enthusiastic Allies to meet the Russian Army's ordnance and other requirements – supplies which would have to be shipped halfway around the world to Vladivostok and then along that very vulnerable railway link into Siberia. The consequences of the weakness of domestic supply and the tenuous links to the outside world were soon felt. It is sufficient to note, with regard to a sector so essential to the war effort as textile manufacture, for example, that in early 1919 Omsk's Minister of Supply was forced to report that dire shortages of winter clothing at the front were a result of the fact that the Russian Army was dependent upon imported British uniforms (whose arrival had been delayed), for in the past Siberia had been almost entirely reliant for cloth upon the Alafusov Mills of Belebei, which was then in Bolshevik hands.[7]

Of course, the Whites did hold the far stronger industrial region of the Urals for a significant period of time. Cheliabinsk and Zlatoust had been amongst the first areas to fall to the Czechoslovaks in May–June 1918, Ekaterinburg was seized by the Legion in July and the north Urals capital of Perm was captured by the Siberian Army in December. However, the Urals – which was anyway a rather undiversified economy of mining and basic metallurgy – had been one of the battleground regions most scarred by the first wave of the civil war in 1918. Moreover, as the war settled down into a struggle between the established White and Red zones, the Ural region's traditional economic ties to European Russia had been severed by the Volga front. Thus, even by August 1918, the anti-Bolshevik Urals *oblast'* Government was reporting that 'the entire economic life of the region is disrupted: factories find themselves in complete disorder'.[8]

7 Guins, G.K. *Sibir', soiuzniki i Kolchak: povorotnyi moment russkoi istorii, 1918–1920gg. (Vpechatleniia i mysli chlena Omskogo pravitel'stva).* Peking (1921), Vol. 2, p. 220. In October 1918 the Ministry of Supply had already established that 300,000 greatcoats (required that winter by the Russian Army) could only be obtained from local sources if every Siberian textile factory and mill were committed to the task for the next three years. See Serebrennikov, I.I. *Moi vospominaniia.* Tientsin (1937), p. 230.

8 Taniaev, A. (ed.) *Kolchakovshchina na Urale.* Moscow (1930), p. 13. Of particular military significance were the munitions works at Izhevsk which produced 60,000 rifles whilst in anti-Bolshevik hands from August to November 1918. Although this was only equivalent to 22–25% of the average output of 2,000–2,200 rifles per day produced during 1914 to 1916, it was a boon to the Whites – see Eikhe, G. Kh. *Oprokinutyi tyl.* Moscow (1966), pp. 125, 370. On November 8th, however, the works were recaptured by the Red Army. For a concise account of the events at

Table 4.1: Output (in poods) of the Kizel Mines, Perm *gub.* (1916:1919)

	1916	1919
January	5,000,000	500,000
February	6,500,000	700,000
March	5,000,000	1,200,000

The insurmountable problem for Urals industry was, as a committee of leading industrialists informed the British consul at Ekaterinburg, that despite its enduring reputation as Russia's foremost mining centre, the Urals did not even produce sufficient amounts of the types of coal which its own railways and heavy industries demanded. In particular, the only significant source of steam coal in the region was the Kizel Mining District near the city of Perm – a locality which had experienced some of the fiercest fighting of 1918, one which had been severely damaged by Bolshevik sabotage, and one which was only finally conquered by Kolchak's forces in December of that year. Subsequent to this disrupted period, the industrialists reported (see Table 4.1, above), the Kizel mines' output for the first quarter of 1919 totalled only 2,400,000 poods – that is just 14.1% of the output achieved during the same quarter of 1916 and far short of the 3,000,000 poods of steam coal required by the Perm branch railway alone for each and every month of the year.

The second of the Urals major coal needs was in fuel for metallurgical purposes. This old and relatively backward industrial region, still recognizable two centuries later as the legacy of Peter the Great's innovation, had, in fact, traditionally utilized charcoal in the smelting process. Since the late nineteenth century, however, as indiscriminate felling of forests near the Urals factories had exhausted wood supplies and as the development of railways in Russia had begun to knit the empire's far-flung regional economies together, Urals metallurgists had finally converted their factories to the use of coking coal. The major source of that coal, the Don Basin of the eastern Ukraine, was completely inaccessible to the Siberian anti-Bolsheviks in

Izhevsk see Berk, S.M. 'The Class Tragedy of Izhevsk: Working Class Opposition to Bolshevism in 1918', *Russian History*, Vol. 2, No. 2 (1975), pp. 176–90.

1918 and 1919.[9] There were, of course, limited resources of steam and coking coal in other areas of Siberia and the Far East. However, the option of utilizing them to relieve the industries of the Urals was never open to the Kolchak Government. Quite apart from the logistical problems which would have been involved in the bulk transportation of coal along the already congested Trans-Siberian Railway, coal production in Siberia and the Far East by 1918 was insufficient even to meet local needs, let alone to provide 'exports' to the Urals. Figures released by the government made an effort to disguise the level of the production crisis in Siberia itself by making comparisons only with 1918 (hardly a normal year) – thus, the Cheremkhovo Basin of Irkutsk *guberniia* was admitted to be operating in 1919 at only 70% of the production level of the previous year, but it was claimed that the Anzhersk-Sudzhensk and the Kuznetsk Basins were achieving respectable outputs of 82% and 92% respectively in relation to 1918 figures. However, when comparisons are made with the years *before* 1918, as later Soviet studies pointed out, a significantly worse picture is revealed: as Tables 4.2 and 4.3 (below) illustrate, taking western Siberia as a whole, one Soviet economist found that the production of coal in the region in 1919 amounted to only 70% of the 1915 to 1917 average; while in the major mining basins of eastern Siberia, others' researches reveal that in 1919 Cheremkhovo was producing only 62% of its 1916 to 1917 average and Kuznetsk only 66%.[10]

9 FO 371/4114/105833 'Preston (Ekaterinburg) to Eliot (Omsk), 14.iv.1919'; Finkel'shtein, N. 'Obzor deiatel'nosti kamennougol'nykh kopei Urala za god (iiul' 1919–iiun' 1920g.)', *Gornoe delo* (Moscow) Vol. 1, No. 4 (1920), pp. 112–16. All stockpiles of wood at the factories had been commandeered by the army to fuel the railway in 1918 – see *USMI*, Vol. 7, No. 93 (week ending 8.iii.1919), p. 660.

10 *Gorniaki Sibiri – Revoliutsiia i grazhdanskaia voina. Profsoiuznoe stroitel'stvo, 1917–1927gg. (Sbornik statei i vospominaniia).* Novosibirsk (1927), p. 136; Shlain, V.I. 'Zapadno-sibirskii uglepromyshlennyi raion v 1914–1920gg.', *Gornoe delo* (Moscow), Vol. 1: Supplement No. 1 (1920), p. 25; 'Polozhenie sibirskoi promyshlennosti, 1917–1920 (doklad Sibbiuro VSNKh)', *Narodno khoziaistvo* (Moscow), No. 3 (1921), p. 58. When the depth of the production crisis in the Siberian mines could no longer be concealed government ministers were moved to dismiss it as insignificant and to imply that the shortfall could easily be offset by increasing production in the Far East – see the speech of the Minister of Trade and Industry in *Union (Agence Télégraphique Russe)* (Paris) No. 175, 27.ix.1919. Yet at that time, according to the researches of a Soviet scholar, the major mines of the Far East were producing only 44% of their normal output and coal had to be imported into the region from Japan – see Krushanov, A.I. *Grazhdanskaia voina v Sibiri i na Dal'nem Vostoke (1918–1920gg.).* Vladivostok (1972), Vol. 1, p. 127.

Table 4.2: Coal production (thousands of poods) in Western Siberia, 1915–1919

	Jan.–June	July–Dec.
1915	36.330	37.575
1916	36.616	42.032
1917	45.739	39.497
1918	29.406	30.943
1919	28.735	–

Table 4.3: Coal production (thousands of poods) in Eastern Siberia, 1916–1920

	Cheremkhovo Basin	Kuznetsk Basin
1916	44.616	58.209
1917	76.670	66.321
1918	52.322	47.104
1919	37.482	44.049
1920	28.519	50.285

Without relating output to demand, of course, even these figures cannot tell us the whole story. In discussing demand, however, we are hampered by the fact that figures for the whole of the Kolchak period are not available. Nevertheless, we may guess at the considerable gap between the supply of and demand for fuel in Kolchakia by considering that even by February of 1919, according to the Minister of Trade and Industry, N.N. Shchukin, mines in the Cheliabinsk district were producing only 37% of the coal required locally.[11] It is also known that leading Urals industrialists were predicting early in 1919 that unless 300,000 tons of coal, 8,000 tons of coke and 5,000 tons of lubricating oil were brought into their region

[11] Taniaev, pp. 82–3.

immediately, factories would be 'firmly set on the path which leads not only to their temporary suspension of activity but to the complete discontinuance of all work'.[12] The fuels did not arrive and many Urals factories were indeed to close down over the following months. Many more were smashed by the Whites during their retreat in the summer of 1919, so that they would not fall into Bolshevik hands.

Such physical factors as the fuel shortage and the severance of established supply routes for industry must lead us to conclude, therefore, that whatever the apparent agricultural abundance of parts of his domain, Kolchak would always have found it impossible to supply from domestic sources an army capable of dislodging the Bolsheviks from the relatively industrialized and populous centre of Russia. Alone, however, these factors are insufficient to explain the depth of the economic crisis which hit Siberia in 1918 to 1919. Certainly factories closed down for these reasons, but not a great many – an estimate by a Soviet scholar, based on archival research, places factory closures in the Urals under Kolchak at only 12% of all factories,[13] thereby discrediting earlier hyperbolic estimates of 70–80% closures.[14] The closure of 12% of Urals factories because of fuel shortages and the physical isolation of Kolchakia (given the equal distribution of closures) does not square with other well-documented claims that, for example, the output of cast iron in the region in 1919 was only 6% of what it had been in 1913 (and, indeed, only 45% of what it had been in 1918).[15] Still less can relatively insignificant numbers of factory closures in the Far East in 1919 explain 65% drops in production of cast iron reported in that area.[16] And although there may have been some feedback between factory closures on the one hand and the afore-mentioned low levels of production in Siberian coalmines on the other, the former was primarily a consequence rather than a cause of the latter. How, then, can be explained the dramatic decline in coal production under Kolchak?

12 FO 371/4114/105833 'Preston (Ekaterinburg) to Eliot (Omsk), 14.iv.1919'; Taniaev, p. 87.

13 Feldman, B.B. 'Sostoianie ural'skoi promyshlennosti v 1920g.', in Lisovoi, N.K. and Grigor'ev, B.V. (eds.) *Grazhdanskaia voina na Urale*. Cheliabinsk (1983), pp. 84–6.

14 *Istoriia grazhdanskoi voiny*, Vol. 4, p. 59; *Grazhdanskaia voina i inostrannaia interventsiia na Urale*. Sverdlovsk (1969), p. 381.

15 Spirin, L.M. *Klassy i partii v grazhdanskoi voiny v Rossii, 1917–1920gg.* Moscow (1968), p. 349.

16 Krushanov, Vol. 2, p. 126.

There were clearly additional factors at work within Kolchakia which were exacerbating the fundamental problem of the imbalance between supply of and demand for fuel; and the purpose of this chapter is to analyse the chief among their number. The first problem was connected to the shortcomings of the military régime. The excesses of the Russian Army contributed to a complete breakdown in industrial relations in Siberia and the Urals and their ignorance of the industrial management they took on contributed significantly to the scale of the economic collapse, while the purported strengths of their martial code proved incapable of bringing any of the promised logic or order to a private enterprise system which the government permitted to exist untrammelled by civil law. These evils, of course, might not necessarily have been beyond the powers of the right government or dictator to abate. Kolchak's second dilemma, however, was the collapse – both within Siberia and between Siberia and the outside world – of the trade in agricultural goods, upon which much of the wealth of the region he governed had traditionally been founded. This situation may well have been beyond the powers of any government, god or man to set right.

Deteriorating working conditions and the suppression of Siberian trade unions under Kolchak

Judging solely by the policy statements of the Omsk Government which were being broadcast worldwide via pro-White groups in Europe and the USA in 1919, Siberia under Kolchak should have been a form of paradise for industrial workers. In May of that year, for example, the Minister of Labour, L.I. Shumilovskii, issued the following statement:

> The state is interested in establishing working conditions under which the generations shall grow up strong – physically, morally and intellectually. We have decided upon an 8-hour working day in the industries. We have introduced sickness and unemployment insurance. With the help of the government, employment bureaux will be established everywhere in the territory liberated from the Bolsheviks. The Minister of Labour welcomes the tendency of the working men to organize themselves into unions,

considering it to be in the interests of the state that the working men should form themselves into an organized, disciplined body.[17]

In fact, however, far from being encouraged to organize, the Siberian unions had long since been suffering under the heel of severe military repression. Even by December 1918 union leaders were reporting that across the region as a whole union work was 'pale and insignificant'; deprived of the right to organize and even of the right to rent property, it was said, what were left of Siberia's unions 'huddle together wherever they can'.[18] Of course, the withering away of the unions might have been justified if, as Shumilovskii's statement implied, the workers' every desire had already been fulfilled as a result of beneficent government legislation. But this was hardly the case. In fact, as a direct result of repressive and/or ineffective government policies combined with arbitrary abuses of authority on the part of the military, industrial relations were in a state of crisis in Kolchak's Siberia. Between January 1st and November 1st 1919, for example, the Ministry of Labour's own Factory Inspectors for the Transbaikal, Amur, Irkutsk, Altai, Enisei, Novonikolaevsk, Tobol′sk and Akmolinsk districts registered no less than 1,130 separate conflicts involving 82,000 strikers.[19] This survey did not cover all of Kolchakia and not all strikes may have been registered; but, nevertheless, the figures would seem to indicate that at least one-third of the known total of Siberia's pre-revolutionary workforce took industrial action during these ten months – despite the danger of punishment at the hands of the military for so doing.[20]

At least until the late summer of 1919, when the rapid approach of the Red Army was to make conspicuous anti-White political activity more propitious for workers, strikes in Kolchakia almost invariably sprang from the economic rather than the political grievances of the labour force. Kolchak's military governors might routinely detect 'the work of Bolsheviks and Germans' at the root of every stoppage and

[17] *Struggling Russia* (New York) Vol. 1, Nos. 13–14 (14.vi.1919), p. 196; *The Russian/Russkii Zhurnal* (London) Vol. 1, No. 43 (7.viii.1919), p. 11.

[18] Taniaev, p. 104.

[19] Kal′nin, Ia. 'Trud pri belykh (po arkhivam Ministerstva truda)', *Sibirskie ogni* (Novosibirsk), No. 3 (1929), p. 136.

[20] In fact the 82,000 strikers must have constituted an even greater proportion of the Siberian labour force in 1919, for, as we shall see, throughout that year workers had been fleeing the factories in large numbers in order to escape from military rule.

protest,[21] but in the 1920s even a Soviet historian admitted that 'every strike had an economic cause'.[22] Another was more specific: 'The basic causes of the conflicts,' concluded Ia. Kal′nin in his researches of 1929, 'were i) low wages, ii) improper calculation of wages, iii) sackings and iv) lengthening of the working day.'[23] A decade earlier, in May 1919, a special commission of Allied representatives (which was inquiring into the frequent and prolonged strikes which had paralyzed the vital Suchan Mines of Primorskii *krai*) had reached exactly the same conclusion. Labour unrest, the commission found, was not indicative of 'Bolshevism', but was the direct result of low and improperly calculated wages; only after the strikes were underway were 'political agitators' able to take advantage of the situation to deflect workers' hostility away from the mines' management and towards the Kolchak Government.[24]

Certainly it was by no means unavoidable that Siberia's workers should become such a thorn in the side of the Omsk régime. It may have been the case, as one of the more doctrinaire Soviet historians of the 1960s emphasized, that within days of the establishment of the Provisional Siberian Government in July 1918 some workers on the Trans-Siberian Railway were striking in defence of the soviets and against the curtailment of press freedoms.[25] But this was an isolated outburst. For the most part, eye-witnesses attest that the railwaymen – who were the most numerous and radical of the region's workers – had actually *assisted* the Czechoslovak Legion in dispersing the Soviet authorities. At Omsk, for example, they had sabotaged the railway line, forcing Bolshevik leaders to make an undignified retreat to Tiumen by river.[26] Thereafter, Mensheviks had begun to resume their previously dominant positions within the trades union hierarchy of Siberia and the Urals and, at a series of union congresses during July and August of 1918 (representing groups as diverse as railwaymen and architects, building

21 *Iz istorii grazhdanskoi voiny*, Vol. 1, p. 441.

22 Espe *God v tsarstve Kolchaka (materialy po istorii rabochego dvizheniia v Sibiri s iiunia 1918 do iiunia 1919g.).* Kazan (1920), p. 23.

23 Kal′nin, p. 136.

24 WO 95/5433/F413 'Monthly Diary of Britmis (Vladivostok), 25.v.1919'.

25 Kadeikin, V.A. *Sibir′ nepokorennaia*. Kemerovo (1968), pp. 192–4.

26 Becvar, G. *The Lost Legion: A Czechoslovak Epic*. London (1939), pp. 98–102; Karmashev, V. *Poslednie dni sovetskoi vlasti v Zapadnoi Sibiri*. Moscow (1921), pp. 8–10.

labourers and civil servants) an archetypal Menshevik line was adopted by the regions' labour movement: the Bolsheviks were openly criticized for a 'criminal' and premature attempt to 'introduce socialism at the point of a gun'; the PSG was recognized as the legitimate governmental authority for the current stage of the Russian revolution, which was 'not socialist but bourgeois'; and individual unions were instructed to co-operate with the new authorities at Omsk and 'offer them full support, supply them with workers etc.' as long as 'the achievements of the working class' wrought by the February Revolution of 1917 were maintained. Until that point in the future was reached when capitalism in Russia had run its course and socialism could be established, the new union leadership dictated, the prime task of the labour movement was not to overthrow the existing order but to struggle for 'the economic and legal rights of workers'.[27]

Yet far from the unions being able to work in harmony with the successive manifestations of the 'democratic counter-revolution' at Omsk during the summer and autumn of 1918, instances of industrial unrest multiplied daily under both the PSG and the Directory. Some of the strikes which occurred at this time were not of great consequence – although that did not deter Soviet historians from eulogizing the struggle of the striking waiters of Tomsk! Other stoppages, however, such as that at the Anzhersk-Sudzhensk mines in July, were very damaging to the war effort.[28] Most serious of all, however, was that by October 1918 a dispute involving railwaymen at Omsk had spread east and west to paralyze sections of the Trans-Siberian and Chinese Eastern Railways from Kurgan to Harbin; meanwhile a correlative go-slow in the railway workshops had reduced productivity by up to 70%.[29]

Thus, the region's workers' acceptance of the initial anti-Bolshevik uprising in Siberia had evolved into hostility in the space of only four months: even before the

27 Taniaev, pp. 93–8; Semenova, N.M. 'Periodicheskaia pechat′ Sibiri kak istochnik po istorii professional′nogo dvizheniia Tomskoi gubernii v periode "demokraticheskoi kontrrevoliutsii"', in Bozhenko, P.M. (ed.) *Nekotorye voprosy istorii Sibiri: sbornik statei.* Tomsk (1973), Vol. 2, pp. 81–91. Semenova asserts, however, that conferences of union branches of the period were far more critical of the government than was the central union leadership. *ibid.*, pp. 91–3.

28 Semenova, N.M. 'Sibirskaia periodicheskaia pechat′ o rabochem dvizhenie v periode "demokraticheskoi kontrrevoliutsii"', in Bozhenko, pp. 71–2; *Bor′ba za vlast′ sovetov v Tomskoi gubernii (1917–1921gg.).* Tomsk (1957), pp. 330–6; Kadeikin, *Sibir′ nepokorennaia*, pp. 204–8.

29 Kadeikin, B.A. 'Zabastovochnoe dvizhenie sibirskykh rabochykh vo vtoroi polovine 1918g.', in Flerov, V.S. (ed.) *Bor′ba za vlast′ sovetov v Sibiri i na Dal′nem Vostoke.* Tomsk (1968), pp. 114–44.

establishment of the Kolchak dictatorship workers were willing to take action – albeit for economic reasons – which would unavoidably damage the anti-Bolshevik war effort. And with Kolchak in power the strike movement in 1919 was to reach massive proportions with, as we have already seen, one in three workers taking action. The causes of this dramatic transformation are not difficult to appreciate.

Both Kolchak and the Provisional Siberian Government formally undertook to guarantee workers' rights to unionize in accordance with the decree of the Provisional Government of April 12th 1917. Accordingly, in its own decree of July 6th 1918, the PSG sanctioned the formation of unions which had renounced political aims.[30] Kolchak would add nothing to the statute book during his year in office; but, concerned as ever with his image in Europe, the Supreme Ruler publicly professed himself to be aware of workers' grievances and promised that they would be afforded the opportunity 'to secure their self-organization on lines similar to those in the West'.[31] However, when in January 1919 the British colonel and Labour MP, John Ward, was recruited by the admiral to undertake a mission along the Trans-Siberian Railway to pacify striking railwaymen, he found that, despite Kolchak's word to the contrary, he was never able to offer workers 'anything definite' in return for their agreement to work for the White government and assist the Russian Army. On February 4th Ward wrote a personal letter to Kolchak, requesting clarification of the government's attitude to the unions and to the labour question in general. Kolchak's reply contained no details, but avouched that laws guaranteeing workers' rights were at that very moment being elaborated in his Ministry of Labour and would be put into effect 'as soon as the military situation allows'.[32] Yet, despite the military successes of the following months (and in contrast to the flood of legislation on other issues examined in the previous chapter), no law defining union rights was passed. Even by July 1919, when Kolchak received a delegation of printers in a much publicized propaganda exercise, the men's enquiries as to when a law defining their union rights might be expected elicited only circumlocution from the Supreme Ruler and pat reassurances that his

30 *Sobranie uzakonenii i rasporiazhenii Vremennogo sibirskogo pravitel'stva* (Omsk), No. 2, 18.vii.1918, p. 22; Kal'nin, p. 134.

31 FO 371/4095/8240 'Declaration of the Supreme Ruler, May 1919'.

32 *Angliia–Rossiia.* Omsk (1919), pp. 2, 5–9; Ward, J. *With the 'Die-Hards' in Siberia*. London (1920), p. 171.

government was 'entertaining thoughts' of such a measure. Then, a mere three minutes after their audience had begun, the printers were hurriedly ushered from Kolchak's presence – presumably before the silence became too embarrassing.[33]

If Kolchak was equivocal on the question of what unions might be permitted to do in the future, he was quite definite with regard to what they could not do in the present. Before the printers' hasty exit he had warned them that in times of war no form of strike action was permissible.[34] Accordingly, on March 14th 1919 he had already issued an emergency decree granting local militias of the Ministry of the Interior the rights:

> (a) to close those societies and unions whose activities mark them out as a threat to state security and social order.
> (b) to prohibit every type of stoppage and strike and all activity aimed at preparing for such.

In either case suspects were to be put before a military tribunal.[35]

Although the fundamental right to strike was therefore denied to Siberian labour, workers were told to 'rest assured that the workers' legal interests will always be defended'. Government communiqués stressed that there existed a Ministry of Labour at Omsk, led by the 'Social-Democrat' Leonid Ivanovich Shumilovskii, which could defend workers' interests at the highest level.[36] What was not publicized, however, was the fact that although on paper Shumilovskii's establishment consisted of eleven departments and innumerable sub-departments, it was actually a standing joke in Kolchak's capital that the Ministry of Labour was so starved of funds as to be able to afford only a skeleton staff housed in a single rented room in a not particularly salubrious Omsk suburb.[37] Certainly, if Shumilovskii's ministry was ever in a position to do any useful work, its endeavours escaped most people's attention. Even the Menshevik leadership of the Siberian

33 Although the meeting had no practical issue it made the front pages of the pro-government press. See *Sibirskaia rech'* (Omsk) No. 153, 18.vii.1919; *Biulleten'* (Omsk) No. 25, 19.vii.1919.

34 *Sibirskaia rech'* (Omsk) No. 153, 18.vii.1919.

35 Shemelev, V. (ed.) *Profsoizy Sibiri v bor'be za vlast' sovetov, 1917–1919gg.* Novosibirsk (1927), p. 183.

36 *Biulleten'* (Omsk) No. 25, 19.vii.1919.

37 Kozlova, S.A. 'Trud i okhrana truda v Sibiri pri Kolchake (po neizdannym materialam omskago arkhivnogo biuro)', in *Iz proshlogo Sibiri*. Omsk (1927), pp. 69–70.

Trades Union Council, for example, soon abandoned any faith they might have retained in their erstwhile party colleague, Shumilovskii, when his Ministry of Labour's replies to the unions' flood of complaints simply petered out early in 1919. As for the ministry's local agents, its Labour Inspectors, their rulings were so blatantly ignored by factory owners and military governors alike that the Siberian TUC voted to terminate all relations with them.[38]

In Shumilovskii's defence it must be said that his department was singled out by the military for particularly rough treatment – in some districts his Labour Inspectors were hounded from office by the army to be replaced with stooges from the local Chamber of Commerce; others, less fortunate, were arrested or even shot if they attempted to interfere with military rule. Also, Shumilovskii did have the mettle, having resigned his post in protest at military interference in his ministry's affairs in March 1919, to return to work and make some effort to ameliorate the worst excesses of military misrule when it became clear that the resignation of other 'moderates' in the government was simply playing into the hands of reaction.[39] Ultimately, however, Shumilovskii was powerless to alter the course plotted for the Kolchak régime by the Russian Army and by pro-army factions within and around the government: the All-Russian Congress of Trades and Industry at Omsk vetted projected laws on labour affairs even before they reached the Ministry of Labour, while certain other ministries would not reply to Shumilovskii's communications or even acknowledge his ministry's existence. By October 1919 he had come to realize the hopelessness of his position: 'I must admit to the complete defeat of my greatest hope', he wrote to Vologodskii. 'The Ministry of Labour has found itself in the position of a foreign body with which our social organization cannot coexist.'[40]

The 'social organization' of Siberia in 1919 was, of course, one in which the military was increasingly dominant. There were those in the anti-Bolshevik administration – Shumilovskii among them – who preached of co-operation with the unions, so as to deflect the workers from political struggle, to maintain calm in the factories and guarantee production. In the summer of 1918, for example, government

38 Shemelev, pp. 161–3; Kozlova, p. 76.

39 Guins, Vol. 2, p. 150.

40 Ioffe, G.Z. *Kolchakovskaia avantiura i ee krakh*. Moscow (1983), p. 194.

ministers could be seen in attendance at union conferences.[41] From the very beginning, however, the officers of the Siberian Army would not tolerate such a policy of reconciliation. At first they confined themselves to the arrest and persecution of those workers known to have been members or active supporters of the Bolshevik Party and of those who had worked in the Soviet administration. By October 1918 many hundreds of alleged Bolsheviks had been imprisoned.[42] Meanwhile, even before the official re-introduction of the death penalty on September 14th, many leading Bolsheviks who fell into the Siberian Army's clutches were summarily executed.[43] Very soon, however, this Siberian brand of White Terror began to be applied indiscriminately to ever broader circles of the urban working class population. As the Central *oblast'* Bureau of the Siberian Trades Union Council complained in a letter to Shumilovskii of April 1919:

> If formerly the victimization ended with the struggle against Bolshevism, then nowadays it must be said that this is no longer the case...[b]ecause the struggle is not now with Bolshevism but with the unions as workers' organizations in general, irrespective of what work they do.[44]

The Minister was apologetic. He publicly admitted that there was a problem with the military's prejudice against workers and he regretted that the officer class 'having lived through the terrors of Bolshevism', seemed to hold the working class in general responsible for Russia's woes. Officers were all too readily inclined, Shumilovskii said, 'to consider the working class to be the enemy of all state-mindedness...and to attempt to exact revenge upon them'.[45] But there was really very little he could do, particularly in the frontal zone (which extended as far east as Omsk), along the railway and in the major Siberian towns where martial law had been established. In these areas the army had a free hand and claimed to be fighting Bolshevism in the factories. However, it would be as well here to repeat what

41 Semenova, 'Periodicheskaia pechat'', p. 89.

42 Rakov, D.F. *V zastenkakh Kolchaka: golos iz Sibiri*. Paris (1920), pp. 28–9.

43 Notably N.N. Iakovlev and eight other members of the Central Executive Committee of Siberian Soviets (*Tsentrosibir'*). See Novgorodov, A.I. *Oktiabr'skaia revoliutsiia i grazhdanskaia voina v Iakutii*. Novosibirsk (1969), pp. 179–81; and Petrov, P. 'Novoe o gibeli tsentrosibirtsev', *Sibirskie ogni* (Novosibirsk), No. 7 (1964), pp. 163–5.

44 Shemelev, p. 164.

45 'Vserossiiskoe pravitel'stvo', *Sbornik 'Russkago Biuro pechati'* (Tokyo) No. 1 (1919), p. 93.

General Graves, the US commander, had observed with regard to the situation at Vladivostok, namely that Kolchak's officers had developed a rather crude definition of who was 'a Bolshevik' – to the Russian officer, said Graves, a Bolshevik was 'a human being who did not by act and word give encouragement to the restoration of the old order in Russia'.[46]

The army would have preferred to see the official proscription of all union activity. But, mindful of Allied sensibilities, Kolchak shrank from meeting that demand and had his Minister of Justice, Professor S.S. Starynkevich, reiterate that 'on the basis of the law of April 12th 1917 concerning trade unions...every Russian citizen, without exceptions, has the right to form societies and unions'.[47] However, officials of Siberia's unions later recalled how members of Starynkevich's own department and profession were responsible for making it virtually impossible for workers to exercise that 'right'. The problem was that in 1918 to 1919 all unions had to re-register with the White authorities, through the courts, to legitimize their activities. But such an application could take many months to be processed, as White judges rigorously examined unions' records for the slightest trace of what they might define as 'Bolshevism' or 'political activity'. There was no set procedure for such reviews and each court tended to interpret government policy differently. Consequently, the majority of Siberian unions existed in a legal limbo throughout the Kolchak period; in fact, only the printers and miners managed to register their *oblast'* organizations.[48]

The Siberian unions were, therefore, defenceless in the face of constant and multiform repression meted out by the army – repression which, by the spring of 1919, was to drive the majority of workers' organizations out of existence. Military harassment could be quite subtle – local commanders at Ekaterinburg and Biisk, for example, simply denied unions the right to publicize their activities and slashed their income by revoking the licences of union-run shops, cinemas etc.[49] Sometimes the tactics were more provocative – at Cheliabinsk, in December 1918, unions were

46 Graves, W.S. *America's Siberian Adventure*. New York (1931), pp. 101–2.

47 Espe, *God v tsarstve Kolchaka*, p. 11. The law stipulated that unions could only be closed by order of the courts, that workers elected by their peers to union posts were protected against losing their jobs, that factory owners had to provide premises for union meetings etc.

48 *ibid.*, pp. 11–12, 19; Kozlova, p. 78; Shemelev, p. 169.

49 *ibid.*, p. 161; Taniaev, pp. 102, 104.

ordered to apply in advance to the military authorities for permission to meet with either factory owners or Labour Inspectors (an act which induced the local Labour Inspector to resign in protest, leaving no intermediary between workers and the economic pressures applied by factory owners).[50] More often than not, however, military harassment of the unions took the form of naked violence. Thus, even as early as June 1918, the Omsk headquarters of the builders' and carpenters' unions were raided and boarded-up by the Siberian Army and their leaders arrested. On August 29th the Omsk Central Town Council of Trade Unions was raided by army officers, its property was impounded and its steering committee imprisoned. Then, on October 14th, the All-Siberian Trades Union Congress meeting at Tomsk was summarily disbanded when a group of militiamen burst into the hall and presented its chairman, Rabinovich, with an order of foreclosure signed by General Pepeliaev of the Siberian Army.[51] Further arrests and harassment awaited union leaders who subsequently returned to Omsk, culminating in the eviction of the capital's Central Town Council from its headquarters on October 28th – an event which prompted Shumilovskii to request that the army should be 'more tactful' in their handling of labour relations![52]

The foregoing catalogue of repression illustrates how complete was the army's smashing of Siberia's unions even before the Kolchak dictatorship had been established. Once the dictatorship of their own candidate had been initiated, the Siberian Army would know no bounds in dealing with workers' organizations. On November 19th, the day after the coup, General Gajda banned all open-air meetings in the Ekaterinburg district and ruled that indoor meetings could be held only after obtaining a licence from the army.[53] This draconian ordinance was followed by a wave of arrests of union personnel and requisitions of union property at Omsk

50 *ibid.*, p. 103.

51 *Narodnaia Sibir'* (Tomsk) No. 88, 19.x.1918; Kal'nin, p. 134; *Bor'ba za vlast' sovetov v Tomskoi gubernii*, pp. 359–60.

52 Naumov, N.B. *Omskie bol'sheviki v avangarde bor'by protiv belogvardeitsev i interventov*. Omsk (1960), p. 32.

53 Luchebnikov, P.S. (ed.) *Grazhdanskaia voina na iuzhnom Urala, 1918–1919gg.: dokumenty i materialy*. Cheliabinsk (1962), p. 168.

during the first weeks of December. As in earlier cases, the laying of formal charges against internees, let alone public trials, was the exception.[54]

Predictably, a third and decisive clampdown took place early in the New Year, as a reprisal against workers' participation in the Omsk rising of December 21st–22nd. Between January 1st and 20th 1919, every major union in Kolchak's capital was raided; union organizers lost their jobs, and were arrested and even exiled, while the last of their organizations' property was commandeered by the army.[55] And what was done at Omsk soon set the pattern for the rest of Kolchakia. From Ekaterinburg, in April, the government-appointed Governor of the Urals *krai* reported that, without any reference whatsoever to the civilian authorities, junior and senior army officers alike had initiated a reign of terror against the working population: 'Illegal actions, executions without trial, the whipping even of women, unexplained deaths in custody...investigations on the basis of intrigue and plots; all of this is being inflicted upon the civilian population', wrote S.S. Postnikov (and promptly resigned in protest).[56] In a letter of complaint to Shumilovskii of the same month, the Central *oblast′* Bureau of the Siberian Trades Union Congress confirmed that such events were not even confined to major centres such as Omsk and Ekaterinburg: 'Cases of persecution of union organizations, of arrests and executions of workers have become an everyday event in all Siberia, from Vladivostok to the Urals', they claimed, adding that 'in the mining towns of Cheremkhovo, Anzhersk-Sudzhensk and elsewhere the unions have been totally wiped out'.[57]

Under this sort of concerted attack it is hardly surprising that workers took to dissociating themselves from the labour organizations. To burn one's union card was a positive safeguard against a potential loss of livelihood (and even loss of life), while it was clear that neither the army nor the government would take any account of union opinion in the all too common event of disputes over the deteriorating conditions in the factories. Workers, consequently, deserted the unions in droves: by

54 Taniaev, pp. 142–7. An exception was the case of the members of the Siberian unions' Central *oblast′* Bureau arrested on December 17th 1918 (S.R. Kliachko, V.A. Luppov and V.M. Kortikov) who were formally charged with signing an 'anti-government' petition in protest at the Kolchak coup – even though the leaflet in question was not issued until December 29th when the trio were already in prison! By the time that the order was given for their release one of their number had died of typhus.

55 Shemelev, p. 159.

56 Guins, Vol. 2, pp. 183–4.

57 Kal′nin, p. 135.

December 1918 a meeting of the once powerful metalworkers' union at Cheliabinsk could attract an attendance of only 18 from the 1,000 or more members it boasted on paper.[58] And as membership declined, so too did the unions' income. Not untypical was the miners' union at Kemerovo which had enjoyed an average monthly income of 1,136 roubles during the period July–October 1918; by the spring of 1919 its average income was only 657 roubles per month. Bearing in mind the plummeting value of the currency in Siberia during 1919, the union admitted that this amounted to 'a complete drying-up of receipts'.[59]

With so little money and so few members the union organizations of Siberia could not continue to operate. Even by December 1918 the workers' newspaper of Cheliabinsk, *Gornyi krai*, was reporting that union work in the Urals was 'pale and insignificant', while by mid-1919 Shumilovskii was forced to concede that, despite his best efforts to preserve a relationship with them, across all Kolchakia 'the activity of the unions has practically ceased'.[60] With their funds depleted by sequestration and by the defection of terrorized members, and with their leadership, as one secretary put it, 'scared for their very skins' in the face of military rule, even those unions not forcibly smashed by the army began to conclude that legal work was impossible in the current atmosphere and opted for voluntary liquidation.[61] This was the case at Kamen in the Altai, at the mines of Cheremkhovo and Kulchugunsk and among the building workers' unions at Omsk, Krasnoiarsk and Achinsk.[62] Characteristic was the demise of the Union of Construction Workers at Omsk which, at its final meeting on February 2nd 1919, declared:

> Bearing in mind that the present administration is set upon the crushing of workers' organizations and the enslavement of workers to the capitalists, we find that the defence of the workers may only be obtained by the establishment of a soviet government... Until the establishment of a soviet government we decree: the union is liquidated and all of its property and funds, amounting to the sum of 3,652 roubles, is given into the safekeeping of the Chairman, Comrade Prokhurov.

58 *Gorniaki Sibiri*, pp. 202–3; Espe, pp. 16–17; Taniaev, p. 104.

59 Shemelev, p. 216.

60 Taniaev, pp. 103–4; Kal′nin, p. 135.

61 Shemelev, p. 160.

62 *ibid.*, pp. 160, 170; *Gorniaki Sibiri*, pp. 117, 154–5.

But even such a submissive declaration as this was no guarantee against military repression for the Siberian union leaders: Comrade Prokhurov was arrested within days and the paltry savings of his self-liquidated union were confiscated by the army.[63]

'Open war against labour'

We have already seen how, during July 1918, one of the very first acts of the Provisional Siberian Government had been to undertake the dismantlement of the Soviet Government's state trading monopoly and to decree the complete denationalization of industry.[64] Part of the corollary of this act was the military-capitalist campaign against Siberia's unions. At the same time it was emphasized by the Omsk government that factory owners – or, where owners were still absent, the army – were to 'manage the factories alone'. What this meant was that although factory committees of workers which had sprung up during 1917 could still exist (in accordance with the Provisional Government's decree of April 23rd 1917), workers' control of production, which had been a major aim of the committees, was not to be a legitimate aspiration under the anti-Bolshevik authorities of Siberia. Any resistance to this policy by workers, the factory owners were assured on August 30th 1918, would be subdued 'by force'.[65]

So, with both the factories and the trade apparatus now back in their own hands and with the unions and factory committees emasculated, factory owners proceeded to claw back everything that had been gained by workers in terms of wage levels and conditions of labour. Trade and Industry Congresses held over the summer and autumn of 1918 set the employers' agenda. They voiced demands for further restrictions on union and factory committee rights, for strict limits to be imposed on the power of labour exchanges and arbitration commissions, for fewer national holidays and longer working days, for lower contributions by employers to social

63 Shemelev, p. 170.

64 See above pp. 31, 116ff.

65 *Istoriia Sibiri*, Vol. 4, p. 96.

security provisions and for the setting of lower wage norms.[66] And, over the following months, many of these demands were to be met – either through government legislation or simply as a result of local White military and civilian authorities turning a blind eye as factory owners imposed illegal conditions upon their workforce. Throughout Kolchakia, announced the beleaguered Central *oblast'* Bureau of the Siberian Trades Union Congress, capital had declared 'open war against labour'.[67]

One of the first attacks was made upon the principle of collective wage bargaining. Siberian and Urals industrialists professed to be convinced that this was the 'most perfect' form of industrial relations, but claimed that it was 'inappropriate' for the conditions of 1918 to 1919 because 'authoritative' workers' organizations no longer existed.[68] The fact was, of course, that unions and their authority had been systematically and savagely eradicated by the Siberian Army during the second half of 1918. But the factory owners stuck to their guns – they insisted on their right to impose wage settlements and new conditions of service without negotiations; and if unions should object to the new terms, as happened at Turinsk in January 1919, for example, the local Chief of Militia would simply rule that unions no longer had the right to represent workers' collective interests and would insist that 'each worker must speak for himself'.[69]

By a decree of the Council of Ministers dated November 14th 1918, employers were also freed from the obligation to hire only registered labour from the union-run labour exchanges which had been established by the Soviet Government. The labour exchanges were left in existence, but fell quickly into disuse. In part their demise was a result of the fact that the White authorities refused to supply them with adequate premises and sufficient funds to maintain a service to the unemployed. Equally, however, they withered because workers did not trust the reconstituted boards imposed on the labour exchanges by Omsk, wherein two trade union representatives were consistently out-voted by the five representatives from Trades and Industry congresses and from the government. Mostly, however, the labour

66 Taniaev, pp. 52–4.

67 *ibid.*, p. 146.

68 *Velikaia Rossiia* (Ufa) No. 13, 4.iv.1919.

69 Shemelev, pp. 185–6; Taniaev, pp. 104–5.

exchanges declined simply because employers were free to ignore them and to turn to cheaper sources of non-union labour.[70] This was particularly the case in the Far East, where cheap, immigrant labour was plentiful. Thus, in October 1919, the Chief Factory Inspector of Primorskii *krai* reported to the Ministry of Labour that while Russian workers were reduced to unemployment and poverty, 'In Vladivostok almost every manufacturing enterprise is operated by Korean, Chinese and Japanese labour...and in the food-processing plants on the Kamchatka Peninsula are employed 5,000 Russians, 10,000 Chinese, 7,000 Koreans and 20,000 Japanese.' The Inspector also found that 70% of building labourers and 75% of miners within his region were Chinese.[71]

Where oriental workers were less abundant, unscrupulous capitalists could turn to another source of cheap labour – the hordes of German, Austrian and Magyar POWs who were still being held in Siberian camps (161,000 of them according to Red Cross figures).[72] POW labour was both popular and profitable. This was partly because many of the prisoners were skilled workmen from the factories of Central Europe, but the chief attraction was that a government decree of May 15th 1919 had laid down that POWs could be paid 'at a rate equivalent to two-thirds of the current wage for domestic labour in a corresponding speciality'. Moreover, much of the meagre wage paid to the prisoners could be clawed back by the employer as payment for food, clothing and tools (of which he was left free to determine the value). Of course, there was a rider to the decree stipulating that POWs could only be employed if local labour was making 'excessively high wage demands'; but, once

70 Shemelev, p. 180; Espe, p. 39. A similar fate befell the Arbitration and Reconciliation Chambers established for settling industrial disputes. These institutions had an inbuilt bias in favour of the employers, were consequently ignored by workers and fell into disuse. See Ioffe, *Kolchakovskaia avantiura*, p. 191.

71 Kal'nin, pp. 141–2. Before the war the tsar's Governor General of the Maritime Provinces, N.L. Gondatti, had strictly enforced an imperial order banning Chinese and Korean labour in the area (except for those few who had Russian citizenship) – see Nansen, F. *Through Siberia: The Land of the Future*. London (1914), pp. 339–40, 381–2. In 1919 Gondatti would criticize the Kolchak government specifically because 'it relies on individuals and parties and should rely on the economic interests of the mass of the population'. FO 371/4095/70076 'Robertson (Vladivostok) to FO, 1.v.1919'.

72 FO 371/4103/100327 'Memorandum by Captain Fuglede of the Danish Red Cross, [n.d.]'.

again, it was left entirely to the discretion of the employers and their military cohorts to determine when a wage claim was 'excessive'.[73]

Employers found a similarly convenient loophole in a decree passed by the PSG on June 28th 1918, which had obliged them to pay a full month's wages to workers who were made redundant. In this instance the employers' racket consisted of requesting local military authorities to invoke another decree of the PSG (of August 1st 1918) which determined that any 'active supporter of the Soviet power' could be dismissed from his job without compensation 'even if at the present time they do not exhibit any anti-government activity'. As, in the words of a Tomsk union executive, 'absolutely every artisan and worker fell "under suspicion" of Bolshevism in the eyes of the military', job security had obviously become a thing of the past in White Siberia.[74] In fact, Siberian employers seemed keen to take the opportunity to resurrect all the worst and most arbitrary aspects of the pre-revolutionary era in the field of labour relations: at the Berezovskii iron works in the Urals the factory owner made workers responsible for the cost of their own tools; in the Serginsk district a system of truck operated, with workers obliged to use factory shops, which were selling flour and other essentials at prices far in excess of market rates; and at the Solov′ev Tannery at Irkutsk arbitrary fines were imposed on workers by the factory owners (five roubles for 'intoxication', ten for 'laziness', ten for whatever was determined to be a 'breach of the peace' and one hour's wages for each minute a worker was late in the morning).[75]

Although these and other abuses were becoming commonplace in Siberia, it was not until May 9th 1919 that Kolchak's government passed its first and only measure aimed specifically at the defence of workers' interests. This was the 'Law on the Laying-Off of Workers and Officials'. According to its provisions, employees of from six- to twelve-months' standing were entitled to two weeks' pay as compensation if sacked, while those with more than a year's service should receive a full month's pay for the loss of their job.[76] However, there is no evidence that

[73] Kal′nin, pp. 141–2. The government itself made extensive use of POW labour – in, for example, the abortive construction of a railway line from Barnaul to Sergiopol'. See FO 371/4094/9751 'Eliot (Omsk) to FO, 15.i.1919'.

[74] Kal′nin, pp. 139, 134; Kozlova, p. 77.

[75] Taniaev, pp. 135–7; Dvorianov, N.V. and Dvorianov, V.N. *V tylu Kolchaka*. Moscow (1966), p. 30.

[76] Kal′nin, p. 139.

local White authorities enforced this measure any more strictly than any other edict of the simulacrum of power which was the Omsk government; furthermore, while by the spring of 1919 it was a little late to try and label workers as former supporters of the Soviet Government so as to avoid the payment of compensation as had been done in the summer of 1918, there was always the loophole that workers who had been employed for less than six months were entitled to no compensation if sacked. From Cheliabinsk there predictably came the news that mine-owners were freely sacking their long-standing employees by insisting that they were only 'temporary labour'.[77]

In 1919 the Minister of Labour, Shumilovskii, claimed that social security provision in Siberia 'goes further than the most progressive currently in operation anywhere in the world'.[78] In reality, however, the Omsk Government was doing nothing to temper Siberian employers' hostility to the very notion of social welfare or to safeguard the fundament of that provision in Russia, the institution of the workers' Sickness Fund (*bol′nichnaia kassa*) which had become established in Siberia during 1917 and was further nurtured by the Soviet authorities. The first conference of workers' representatives on the Sickness Fund boards to take place after the fall of Soviet power occurred at Tomsk in October 1918, and it revealed that the social security system was in a very dilapidated state indeed. The Omsk delegate reported that 'on June 7th [the day on which Omsk had fallen to the Whites]...there occurred a complete turnabout in the life of the Fund. The Sickness Fund began to be talked of as a "Bolshevik institution" – especially by the employers, who entirely ceased to contribute to it'. A government statement of June 19th in support of the principle of the Fund, added the Omsk delegate, had never been more than 'words on paper' which the employers knew would not be followed up by action to make them restore contributions. As a result, the Sickness Fund of Siberia had a deficit of some 40,000 roubles by September 1918 and many branches had gone out of existence. The October conference appealed to Shumilovskii for assistance, but the Ministry of Labour could only confirm that, as the old regulations on the Sickness Fund were

77 Taniaev, pp. 136–7.

78 'Vserossiiskoe pravitel′stvo', *Sbornik 'Russkago Biuro pechati'* (Tokyo) No. 1 (1919), p. 93.

no longer operative and no new ones had been set by the government, the employers were within their rights to withhold contributions.[79]

It was only on January 8th 1919, a full six months after the fall of Soviet power and the concurrent termination of the old Sickness Fund regulations, that a new law on the Fund was ratified by the Council of Ministers. However, it provided little comfort for the Siberian workers. Whereas under the old system the employers had contributed a sum equal to 10% of their wage bill to the Sickness Fund and workers a sum equal to 2% of the wage bill, thenceforth the Fund was to consist of contributions equivalent to 6% of the wage bill from the employers and 1.5% of the wage bill from workers. Thus, the total of contributions for social security provision was to fall (by 4.5% of the wage bill) and a greater proportion of the fund (20% rather than 16.66%) was to be provided by the workers themselves. Also, much to the consternation of the Sickness Fund administration, the employers were not to be required to make good the contributions they had avoided during the second half of 1918 – even though the government had required the Sickness Fund to provide for sick workers during that period.

Another blow to the region's workers was that from January 8th they were to lose their previously dominant position on the Sickness Fund boards. Under the old regulations 50% of the boards' seats had been offered to workers' representatives, 33% to employers and 17% to the representatives of local and national government; under the new arrangements, however, workers were granted only two seats on the reconstituted boards of sixteen members, with eight places going to the employers and six to government representatives. Finally, and perhaps most damagingly to the welfare of Siberia's workers, the law of January 8th did not apply to state-controlled industries, to the railways, to agricultural workers, to domestic workers or to local government employees.[80] Thus, all social security provision was to be denied to the vast majority of the industrial labour force in Kolchakia and to all agricultural labourers, and was to be severely curtailed in those sectors where it did operate.

79 Espe, pp. 29–31.

80 *ibid.*, pp. 33–9; Kozlova, p. 78; Shemelev, p. 180.

Also high on the employers' agenda was the abolition of the statutory eight-hour day in the factories which had become standard since the revolution.[81] However, the popularity of the eight-hour day amongst workers was such that neither the PSG nor the Kolchak administration could bring themselves to face the consequences of an official revocation of it, despite constant pressure in favour of such an act from the Siberian and Urals Congresses of Trade and Industry. On the other hand, neither did the successive anti-Bolshevik régimes at Omsk make any significant effort to ensure that the regulation was observed by employers (despite the fact that the PSG had committed itself to support the eight-hour day in its July 31st 'Decree on Measures for the Establishment of Normal Working in Industrial Enterprises'). Shifts of ten and even twelve hours were commonplace in the Urals, while the fact that the eight-hour day was being ignored across Kolchakia was apparent from the prominence of demands for its observance by striking workers from Ekaterinburg to Vladivostok. In many enterprises, however, as was noted by a Congress of Skilled and Unskilled Workers of the Trans-Siberian Railway, 'the introduction of piecework...rendered meaningless the regulations guaranteeing an eight-hour day', because longer hours had to be worked in order to earn anything approaching a living wage under the prevailing conditions of inadequate rates of payment and rampant inflation.[82]

As the working day lengthened, statutory holidays became ever rarer. Many Siberian factories refused to recognize Sunday as a holiday and would pay no bonus for shifts worked on that day. Meanwhile, in the Urals, the Siberian Army was called in by the mine owners to prevent workers from taking their traditional half-day holiday on the eve of religious festivals. Troops were also utilized, with varying degrees of effectiveness, to prevent workers from celebrating May Day in 1919.[83]

The employers' position was that, until a law was passed by the authorities at Omsk defining the standard working day and listing holidays, they would feel themselves at liberty to impose whatever hours they themselves felt to be appropriate in their factories. Kolchak did, in fact, let it be known time and again in 1919 that he had instructed the Ministry of Labour to draft a law enshrining the

81 The employers' aim was, of course, to maximize profits, but they preferred to couch their demands in terms of the need to guarantee the 'competitiveness' of Russian industry. See Espe, p. 20; Taniaev, p. 54.

82 *ibid.*, p. 148; Kal′nin, pp. 140–1.

83 Piontkovskii, S.A. (ed.) *Grazhdanskaia voina v Rossii (1919–1921gg.): khrestomatiia*. Moscow (1925), p. 304; Taniaev, p. 150.

principle of the eight-hour day. As in so many other instances, however, the Supreme Ruler's statements were made with an eye to impressing the Allies rather than actually improving social and economic conditions in Siberia. The businessmen and industrialists who surrounded Kolchak made sure that no law ever reached the statute book – and, indeed, it was not until the final panic-stricken days of the régime, in December 1919, that even a project law was to be debated by the Council of Ministers.[84]

This rapid erosion of workers' rights was the prime cause of the wave of strikes and stoppages which spread across Siberia in 1918 and 1919, despite the virtual eradication of the region's union organizations. It was rare indeed, however, that workers' demands were met – for, irrespective of the rights and wrongs of individual actions, employers could invariably count on the support of the army and the local militia of the Ministry of the Interior to force men back to work and to prevent any unwelcome interference in the settlement of disputes by the Ministry of Labour's Labour Inspectorate. 'Applications by the military authorities for permission to use force to end labour unrest were the norm across all Siberia', concluded one pioneering Soviet account.[85] And this, indeed, does seem to have been the case. It was not simply that the notorious renegade atamans of the Far East such as Semenov and Gamov were inclined to turn their guns on striking workers and to outlaw all industrial action within their domains, although that certainly was the case: for example, in September 1918 at Harbin Semenov broke up a dispute in the railway yards and had its ringleaders arrested and shot; while in September 1919 at Blagoveshchensk Ataman Gamov outlawed strikes and made any stoppage of work punishable by a 3,000-rouble fine or three months' imprisonment.[86] Even in districts governed by military authorities directly subordinate and loyal to Kolchak, force was routinely applied against strikers. And this was true even in the case of the most insignificant trades dispute. At Tomsk in November 1918, for example, General Pepeliaev used Siberian Army units to break up a strike of restaurant workers and at Vladivostok in January 1919 the Commander of Vladivostok

84 *ibid.*, p. 152; Kal'nin, p. 140; Shemelev, p. 181.

85 Kozlova, p. 88.

86 Tsiupkhin, S. et al. (eds.) *Oktiabr'skaia revoliutsiia i grazhdanskaia voina na Dal'nem Vostoke. Khronika sobitii, 1917–1922gg*. Moscow–Khabarovsk (1933), pp. 90, 97–8.

Fortress, General Butenko, sent in troops to put an end to a stoppage by the town's Union of Music Hall Workers, Cinema Usherettes and Stagehands![87]

It was, however, the workers on Siberia's major river and rail communications networks, so vital to the White war effort, who had the most to fear from the army. Throughout the summer and autumn of 1918, local military authorities – with or, if necessary, without the permission of the Minister of the Interior – had been placing stretches of the Trans-Siberian Railway on either a military footing (*voennoe polozhenie*) or the hardly less stringent emergency footing (*osadnoe polozhenie*).[88] The process culminated on October 21st 1918 when, in response to strike actions spreading east and west along the railway from a nexus at Omsk, the Commander-in-Chief of the Siberian Army, General Boldyrev, placed the entire Siberian railway network on an *osadnoe polozhenie*.[89] This meant that legal norms were suspended for the third of Siberia's workforce who worked on the Trans-Siberian line: thereafter unions could be banned at any time, their newspapers closed and their leaders held without trial at the army's behest; strikes were made totally illegal and agitators for strike action could be shot on sight. Essentially, as the Head of the Garrison at Bodaibo reminded workers, the army regarded railwaymen as being 'mobilized men' and therefore felt free to impose military discipline upon them.[90]

The enhanced military authority in the railway zone under the *osadnoe polozhenie* also meant that the 82,000 workers on the Trans-Siberian lines were deprived of even the limited protection offered by the Ministry of Labour's Labour Inspectorate in their dealings with the railway administration and with station commandants. When, for example, the Labour Inspector for Akmolinsk *oblast'* requested information from a station manager with regard to the sacking of a group of workers for the catch-all crime of 'Bolshevism', he received the following curt retort from the manager: 'Before I give an answer to your question, may I have the honour to ask by what authority does an Inspector of Labour petition me, an employee of the Ministry of Ways and Communication?' Emboldened by the army's backing, the Head of the Taishet Railway felt at liberty to insult Shumilovskii himself: 'Please

87 Semenova, 'Sibirskaia periodicheskaia pechat'', pp. 71–4; Shemelev, p. 184.

88 See, for example, Colonel Gajda's order regarding the Barabinsk–Krasnoiarsk line issued at Irkutsk on July 27th 1918 (in *Bor'ba za vlast' sovetov v Tomskoi gubernii*, pp. 338–9) and Colonel Pepeliaev's order regarding the Tomsk–Kolchuginsk line of October 14th 1918 (*ibid.*, p. 442).

89 *Volia Sibiri* (Tomsk) 22.x.1918, cited in Semenova, 'Sibirskaia periodicheskaia pechat'', p. 77.

90 *Gorniaki Sibiri*, p. 143.

do not interfere in my affairs', he told the Minister of Labour in 1919, when the latter attempted to investigate unrest on that sector of the line.[91]

The Trans-Siberian Railway was, of course, being run by the state to meet the needs of the all-important war effort and, in the circumstances of the civil war, it is not surprising that a degree of coercion was employed against the workforce. Little better off, however, were workers of the region's major privately owned operations. Characteristic was the case of the Ob-Enisei Merchant Fleet, with its headquarters at Tiumen, which was denationalized in January 1919 as the culmination of the White authorities' privatization drive. A special commission was set up by the Kolchak Government to oversee the transfer of ownership and to establish service regulations for the fleet. However, the commission contained no representatives from the unions nor even from the Ministry of Labour. Numerous protests from Shumilovskii's office eventually secured the admittance of a Labour Inspector to the commission's proceedings, but he could only take up his seat a matter of days before the commission was due to complete its work and could do nothing to influence its conclusions or to obtain any concessions for the labour force.[92] Immediately the fleet was back in private hands the erosion of workers' rights was begun and increasingly onerous terms of service dictated by the management. River pilots were forced (if necessary at gunpoint) to work three rather than two watches a day, while dockers – who had received no pay rise at all in 1918 – were offered such a nuggatory rise in such an insulting manner that it can only be interpreted as a provocation to strike. Strike the stevedores duly did, downing tools on March 3rd 1919. With hardly a pause for thought, the shipyard owners appealed to the army for assistance and, just two days later on March 5th, they were rewarded with the posting of the following order by the Commander-in-Chief of the Siberian Army, General Gajda:

> All strikers must return to work within three days of the publication of this order. Those failing to comply are to be arrested and placed before military courts organized for this purpose. Of the guilty one in ten will be executed and the remainder sentenced to hard labour in a place of exile [*katorga*].

91 Kozlova, pp. 74–6.

92 *ibid.*, pp. 77–8.

Realizing that resistance to Gajda was impossible, the workers' strike committee at the Tiumen docks disbanded after recommending an immediate return to work. However, despite reassurances from the Czech general that there would be no reprisals and despite his promises to examine workers' grievances, within the week repressions began: dozens of Tiumen dockers were rounded up and sent to the front and three members of the disbanded strike committee were arrested (of whom one was later executed). A few days later, so as to prevent a recurrence of such troubles, the entire water transport system joined the Trans-Siberian Railway on *osadnoe polozhenie*, whereby all industrial action was proscribed.[93]

Of all the attacks launched by Siberia's employers on the rights and conditions of labour, it was the treatment of wage settlements which caused the greatest hardship for workers. The single most frequently cited cause of industrial discontent was the question of wages. The government did establish a minimum wage level (*prozhitochnyi minimum*). This was periodically revised upwards to take account of inflation and it varied from place to place to take account of local conditions – in particular the fact that the closer one got to the front the higher was the cost of living.[94] If the government wage norms ever approached the true cost of living, however, then it was probably an accident. For one thing they were based on the assumption that the proportion of his wages which a worker spent on food, housing, fuel etc. would be the same in the disturbed days of 1919 as it had been in 1914, the year in which the system employed to set the norms had been devised; for another, the *prozhitochnyi minimum* was not statutory but purely advisory.[95] Moreover, even if the norm was fair at the time it was set and even if it was adhered to by factory owners, by the time that figures for each month had been established and broadcast,

93 Shemelev, pp. 189–90.

94 At Omsk the official monthly *prozhitochnyi minimum* rose as follows over time: 150 roubles (August 1918), 260 roubles (October 1918), 492 roubles (March 1919), 520 roubles (June 1919), 678 roubles (August 1919) – Naumov, M.B. *Omskie bol'sheviki v avangarde bor'by protiv belogvardeitsev i interventov*. Omsk (1960), pp. 32, 60–1; *Union (Agence Télégraphique Russe)* (Paris) No. 165, 15.ix.1919; *Zaria* (Omsk) No. 101, 15.v.1919. The increase in the cost of living as one travelled westwards from the Pacific to the front was reflected in the regional *prozhitochnyi minimum* figures published for June 1919, which ran as follows: Vladivostok 366 roubles; Krasnoiarsk 340 roubles; Omsk 520 roubles; Tiumen 517 roubles; Cheliabinsk 717 roubles. See *Biulleten' otdela informatsii pri vedomstve pressa etat-maiora Glavnokommanduiushchago* (Omsk) 19.vii.1919.

95 *Nasha zaria* (Omsk) No. 114, 17.vi.1919.

Siberia's spiralling rate of inflation would have rendered them obsolete. Mostly, however, the *prozhitochnoe minimum* was simply ignored by the factory owners. We therefore find that at a time in early 1919 when government officers were setting wage norms in the Urals which they recognized would demand wage rises of 100–200%, workers were being offered 2% rises on the rare occasion that they could persuade their managements to discuss the matter at all.[96]

The root cause of workers' wage problems was the widespread re-introduction of piecework during the summer of 1918, particularly on the Trans-Siberian Railway. A government commission reviewing wage levels on the Tomsk branch of the line reported (on January 13th 1919) that the system had caused 'a clear drop in workers' wages to an extremely low level' and that, in response to this, demoralized men were fleeing the factories at a growing rate (despite a ban on resignations under the terms of the region's *osadnoe polozhenie*). In addition the commission found that even among those who remained, 'this method [of payment] has not led to an increase in productivity'.[97] Yet despite this warning – a warning based on careful inspection of conditions in the workshops – the Minister of Trade and Industry at Omsk continued throughout 1919 to make fantastical assertions as to the capacity of piecework to increase productivity 'by 900 to 1,000%'.[98] Consequently, piecework remained the norm and workers' wages continued to decline both in nominal and absolute terms.

The problem was not that piecework was necessarily impractical or cruel in principle – indeed, some unions had welcomed its re-introduction in 1918 – but that the economic disruption of Siberia's industry and communications under military mismanagement and the strains of the war effort had deprived factories and workshops of supplies for long periods of time. With raw materials unavailable and with broken tools and machinery not repaired, workers were unable to work and, therefore, unable to earn.[99] Thus, as Table 4.(below) indicates, during the second half of 1918, a period in which the government-determined *prozhitochnyi minimum*

[96] Taniaev, pp. 150–2, 158–60; Kal'nin, p. 136.

[97] Shemelev, p. 193; Espe, p. 20.

[98] *Doklad 'Rossiiskago Biuro pechati'* (Omsk) 31.vii.1919.

[99] Masslenikov, A. 'Ekonomicheskoe polozhenie Sibiri s tekh por kak bylo svergnuta sovetskaia vlast'' in Smirnov, I.N. et al. (eds.) *Bor'ba za Ural i Sibir'*. Moscow–Leningrad (1926), p. 214; Gromov, I.V. et al. (eds.) *Partizanskoe dvizhenie v Zapadnoi Sibiri, 1918–1920gg*. Novosibirsk (1959), p. 103.

Table 4.4: Average monthly wage (in roubles) for miners on piecework, 1918

1918	*Prozhitochnyi minimum*	Mining District	
		Kemerovo	Kolchuginsk
July	375.00	298.00	254.00
August	–	391.00	253.00
September	533.25	314.60	281.00
October	694.05	300.80	269.60
November	794.95	278.60	260.00
December	780.60	–	–

Table 4.5: Average monthly wages (in roubles) for railwaymen on piecework, April 1919

Section	*Prozhitochnyi minimum*	Skilled	Unskilled
Zima	921.37	534.31	311.48
Novonikolaevsk	1037.20	482.50	364.50
Bogotol	1778.68	299.00	208.00
Nizhneudinsk	1003.81	312.50	250.00

was rising in the mining districts of Kemerovo and Kolchuginsk by well over 200%, wages were at best frozen and at worst falling even in nominal terms. Meanwhile, as a perusal of Table 4.5 will indicate, the wages of an unskilled railway worker at Novonikolaevsk would support his family for just ten days each month according to the government estimates, while a skilled railway man at Bogotol would bring home wages sufficient to survive for only five days a month.[100]

And of course these conclusions would only apply *if* the buying power of wages had remained stable. It did not. As we shall see, inflation was to reach proportions in Siberia in 1919 that would not have been out of place in Weimar Germany of the 1920s. Consequently, even by November 1918 observers of the factory scene were

100 Kal′nin, p. 137.

concluding that 'piecework has significantly lowered wages and, with the mad, galloping rise in prices of all goods of prime necessity, has left a yawning gap in the workers' budget'.[101]

Nor does consideration of the effect of inflation on each month's wages tell the final story, for even the inadequate wages workers did earn in each month could actually be paid to them as much as three months in arrears, by which time their value would have been all but nullified. Investigations by Allied agents in the Far East found delays in the wage payments to be the principal cause of unrest and stoppages at the vital Suchan mines of Primorskii *krai*, while the Chief Factory Inspector of Irkutsk *guberniia* attributed fourteen of the sixteen strikes at the no less important Cheremkhovo mines in the second half of 1918 to the tardy payment of wages.[102] Meanwhile in the Zlatoust mining district of the Urals, workers lost any hope of recovering the wages owed to them and, to the horror of the district Mining Chief (the local representative of the Ministry of Trade and Industry), were leaving the mines to rejoin their families in the countryside, thereby causing a massive fall in production.[103] Most serious of all for the fate of the Siberian economy in 1919, however, and indeed for the fate of the Kolchak régime itself, was that even the 82,000 workers on the vital Trans-Siberian Railway were not being paid on time by the railway administration. Inquiries by Colonel John Ward in January 1919 found that workers were owed 'several months' wages', while another foreign observer was reliably informed that the railway administration owed its employees over 60,000,000 roubles.[104]

The hungry towns

Even had every Siberian and Urals worker received fair wages and received them on time, however, it is unlikely that peace would have reigned in the factories, improbable that levels of production and productivity could have been maintained

101 *Golos naroda* (Tomsk) 3.xi.1918, cited in Semenova, 'Sibirskaia periodicheskaia pechat'', p. 76.

102 Kal'nin, p. 138.

103 Luchebnikov, *Grazhdanskaia voina na iuzhnom Urala*, p. 192.

104 Ward, pp. 171–3; *Angliia–Rossiia*. Omsk (1919), pp. 5–6; Bullard, A. *The Russian Pendulum – Autocracy, Democracy, Bolshevism*. New York (1919), p. 187.

and doubtful that workers could have been induced to remain at their benches. As the Urals Industrial Committee of the Ministry of Trade and Industry informed the Council of Ministers in April 1919, a single wage increase, no matter how generous, would not placate workers.[105]

The difficulty was that the prevailing conditions of the civil war in the east had created a situation in which money was worth very little – not only because of inflation and a variety of other currency problems (although they too were causing hardship, as we shall see) but also because there were very few items available for purchase. The overwhelming majority of the type of manufactured items which had been imported into Siberia before the war were virtually unobtainable by 1919 – and only at a prohibitively high price if they were obtainable – because the only realistic means of transporting goods into the region, the Trans-Siberian Railway, was almost exclusively given over to the movement of troops and military equipment. The few items that were brought in to the region through Vladivostok usually fell into the hands of speculators, who would convey them to the interior for resale at a huge profit. Consequently, foreigners who visited Omsk in 1919 found that items which they had formerly taken for granted were now unheard of luxuries: a YMCA secretary, for example, scoured the shops of Kolchak's capital in vain for a pen or a pencil, while John Ward found himself wondering whether he could possibly justify the expenditure of his entire week's wages (as a colonel in the British Army) on a box of safety pins.[106]

Of course, Siberia's workers could probably have survived without writing materials and safety pins, but even items which might be regarded as necessary for the lowliest type of existence carried prices beyond a worker's means by the end of 1918. The correspondent of the London *Times* found that in White Siberia 'cloth is worth its weight in gold', that the price of needles was 10,000% up over 1914 and that candles, when they could be found, cost eight roubles each. Fuel for heating, he added, was impossible to come by: 'There is enough forest quite close to the railway in the wooded parts of Siberia to keep the whole of the world warm for a century', he noted with only mild hyperbole, 'yet in cities like Omsk fuel stands at fabulous prices, thanks to the virtual breakdown of railway communications for non-

105 Taniaev, p. 164.

106 Gidney, J.B. (ed.) *Witness to a Revolution: Letters from Russia (1916–1919) by Edward T. Heald.* Kent State (1972), pp. 180–1; Ward, p. 198.

Table 4.5: Prices (in roubles) of basic consumer goods at Vladivostok and Omsk, 1918:1914

	Vladivostok December 1918	Omsk December 1918	Omsk 1914
High boots (per pair)	30.0	120.0	8.0
Men's boots (per pair)	50.0	150.0	12.0
Printed cotton (per *arshin*)	2.0	13.0	0.2
Soap (per pood)	50.0	100.0	7.0
Tea (per pood)	8.0	18.0	1.3
Coffee (per pood)	46.0	230.0	20.0
Matches (per box)	125.0	450.0	9.0
Table knives (each)	–	9.0	0.5

military purposes'.[107] Table 4.5 (above), the fruit of one of the earliest examinations of the Siberian economy under Kolchak (undertaken by local co-operatives) confirms these impressions and reveals how much worse was the supply situation at Omsk compared to Vladivostok.[108]

In the Siberian winter of 1918 to 1919 – which, as luck would have it, was a winter of particular severity – to want for clothes, shoes, lighting and fuel was bad enough. Yet in addition to this it must be considered that basic items of food were also in chronically short supply and that Siberia's workers were literally battling against starvation. Moreover, the price of the little food which was available increased from day to day at rates far in excess of wage rises. Consequently, even Foreign Minister Sukin had to concede of the workers of Omsk that 'their living conditions were simply pitiful' – an impression confirmed by the researches of Soviet historians of the 1920s, presented below as Table 4.6 and Table 4.7.[109]

107 *The Times* (London) 2.xi.1918 and 30.xii.1918.

108 Morozov, K.I. 'The Rouble Exchange and Trade with Siberia', *The Russian Co-operator* (London) Vol. 3, No. 4 (April 1919), p. 54.

109 Sukin (*Leeds Russian Archive*), p. 137; Masslenikov, 'Ekonomicheskoe polozhnie', p. 214; El'tsin, B. (ed.) *Po tu storona Urala*. Ufa (1919), p. 30.

Table 4.6: Inflation of food prices at Omsk (1913 = 100)	
Meat	1,199
Butter	662
Eggs	1,880
Wheat	1,060
Oats	838
Flour	1,240
Potatoes	1,049

Table 4.7: Comparative increase (in roubles) of wages and prices at Omsk, 1918–1919

Average Wages			Average Prices		
Factory	May 1918	January 1919	Product (1 pood)	May 1918	January 1919
Textiles	156.50	349.50	Bread	9.50	50.00
Printing	208.40	394.50	Potatoes	3.29	30.00
Foodstuffs	197.90	307.40	Meat	45.00	120.00
Carpentry	181.50	318.30	Butter	92.00	240.00
			Milk	50.00	350.00
			Kerosene	14.00	360.00
			Firewood	90.00	150.00
Average wage increase: 169%			Average price increase: 764%		

Of course, Soviet historians tended to draw the blackest picture of life in Siberia under Kolchak (although less so in the 1920s than in later decades, and the afore-cited results were drawn from surveys carried out in Siberia during 1919). But theveracity of their figures is attested to by other evidence. An émigré economist of the 1920s, for example, found similarly astronomical inflation in the price of food at Vladivostok in 1919.[110] Meanwhile, terrible shortages of basic foods at Omsk in 1919 were confirmed by a government commission which could discover in the capital's stores only 18% of the flour, 14% of the sugar and 24% of the salt it considered necessary to feed the population. Interestingly, the same source, George Guins, claimed that there were sufficient supplies of other foodstuffs at Omsk – notably of butter and meat.[111] This is feasible, for Omsk was at the centre of a rich agricultural and dairy-farming region. However, Guins makes no secret of the fact that the situation was much worse in the industrial region of the Urals – there, he noted, no bread was available for much of the time and miners were drinking not tea but an infusion of grass cuttings from their billies.[112] This picture of the hungry Urals was confirmed by Bernard Pares: 'At Ekaterinburg,' he noticed, 'the market place was so empty that even the dogs and pigeons had stopped using it.'[113]

It was, therefore, the need to secure food which more than any other factor was occupying the minds of striking Siberian workers or those who fled the factories for the countryside. 'Workers are literally groaning in helplessness and hunger', declared a branch of the railway workers' union in July 1919, while even the official press – which was usually more concerned with speculation as to when Red Moscow was going to 'die out' – had to concede that 'there exists a category of workers who are struggling to make ends meet on a semi-starvation or simply a starvation diet'.[114] Finally, that workers' stomachs rather than class consciousness were the motive force behind the strike movement was graphically demonstrated by the fact that when men at the Aleksandrov mechanical works occupied their Urals factory in March 1919, their first act was not to proclaim support for the Soviet

110 A.I. Pogrebetskii found that a pood of meat, which had cost 60 kopecks at Vladivostok in 1917 and 1.00 rouble in 1918, cost 1.60 roubles in January 1919, 6.00 roubles in July 1919, and 11.5 roubles in October 1919. The price of butter (per pood) at Vladivostok experienced the following increments: 4.90 roubles (1917), 6.00 roubles (1918), 7.00 roubles (January 1919), 12.00 roubles (July 1919), 40 roubles (October 1919). See Pogrebetskii, A.I. *Denezhnoe obrashchenie i denezhnye znaki Dal'nego Vostoka za period voiny i revoliutsii*. Harbin (1924), p. 129.

111 Guins, Vol. 2, pp. 219–20. Butter remained so plentiful in western Siberia in 1919 that, according to Bernard Pares, it was used to lubricate the wheels of locomotives – see Pares, B. *My Russian Memoirs*. London (1931), p. 540.

112 Guins, Vol. 2, p. 211.

113 Pares, p. 562.

114 Kal'nin, p. 137; *Pravitel'stvennyi vestnik* (Omsk) No. 56, 30.i.1919.

Government or opposition to Kolchak but to sell their factory's stockpiles of coal in order to buy food.[115]

Hard on the heels of hunger, as was to be expected, came disease. Bodies weak from malnutrition were easy prey to waves of the typhus, typhoid fever, flu and scarlet fever which were to reach epidemic proportions in Kolchakia in 1919. Sanitation had never been a strongpoint of the frontier-type society of Siberia; and during the civil war the system broke down altogether. The Chief Surgeon of the American Expeditionary Force made the following assessment: 'A general description of the sanitary situation in Siberia is most readily conceived by the perfectly truthful remark that practically none exists.'[116] Hospitals simply could not cope with the growing number of cases – at Ufa, for example, 859 hospitalised cases of typhus in January 1919 had already filled the available beds, but by March there were 1,134 patients in the city's care.[117] Very soon the hospitals of Siberia became a place to send the dead rather than those seeking a cure. One sick British officer recalled, 'It was not the thought of death which worried me, but the fear of a Russian hospital.'[118] Unhospitalised cases, however, only made the sanitary

115 Taniaev, p. 84.

116 Graves, *America's Siberian Adventure*, p. 140. The sanitary crisis could hardly have been helped by the extremely unhygienic regimen in the camps holding German and other POWs, particularly where (as at, for example Krasnoairsk) they were situated near major towns. For first-hand accounts of life in the Siberian camps see Dwinger, E.E. *The Army Behind the Wire*. London (1930); Markovits, R. *Siberian Garrison*. London (1929); Wild, M. *Secret Service on the Russian Front*. London (1932); Price, H.J. *Boche and Bolshevik: Experiences of an Englishman in the German Army and in Russian Prisons*. London (1919); Kröger, T. *The Forgotten Village: Four Years in Siberia*. London (1920); Schwazer, F. *Soldner im Sibirien: Erlebnisse eines Sudetendeutschen*. Breslau (1932); Stoffa, Major P. *Around the World to Freedom: Being the Escapes and Adventures of Major Paul Stoffa*. London (1933); Stoss, E. *Kriegsgefangen in Siberien, Erlebnisse eine Wiener Landsturmmannes im Weltkrieg*. Vienna (1927); Brändström, E. *Among Prisoners of War in Russia and Siberia*. London (1929); Brun, Captain A.H. *Troublous Times: Experiences in Bolshevik Russia and Turkestan*. London (1931). Studies of the camps include: Montandon, G. *Im Schmelztiegel des fernen Osten: Geschichte der sibirischen Mission des Internationalen Komitees vom Roten Kreuz zu Gunsten der österreichischen und ungarischen Kriegsgefangen März 1919 bis Juni 1921*. Vienna (1923); Scharping, K. *Kulturelle und wirtschaftlichte: Leistungen der deutschen Kriegsgefangenen in Russland 1914–1918*. Berlin: (1939); Volgyes, I. 'Hungarian Prisoners of War in Russia, 1916–1919', *Cahiers du monde russe et soviétique* Vol. 14 (1973), Nos. 1–2, pp. 54–85; Davis, G.H. 'The Life of Prisoners of War in Russia, 1914–1921', in Richardson, S.R. and Pastor, P. (eds.) *Essays on World War I: Origins and Prisoners of War (War and Society in East Central Europe, Vol. 5)*. New York (1983), pp. 163–196.

117 *Vestnik Rossii* (Ufa) No. 14, 5.iv.1919.

118 Horrocks, B.H. *A Full Life*. London (1960), p. 57.

situation worse, as they passed the disease on to others before meeting their own demise. 'The dead contaminated the living and Omsk became a city of the living dead' according to one account; while 'See Omsk and die' was a jest founded upon sad experience among Americans in the region.[119]

That the first step to restoring production in the factories of Siberia and the Urals was to supply workers with food was a basic fact of which the Omsk Government should have been well aware. As early as November 1918 the Chief Engineer of the Urals Mining Region had issued Kolchak with a 'Report Concerning the Catastrophic Situation of Workers and Enterprises' in his region. He stated that 200,000 Urals workers were virtually starving and warned that unless something was done urgently their growing despair would 'inevitably lead to political turmoil and even to sympathy for the Bolsheviks'; 'no sorts of laws or threats' would persuade workers to return to work and to work normally, and there could be no possibility of resuscitating the region's industry, he added, unless the factories were supplied with food.[120] Similarly, in a report of February 1919, the Chief of the Kizelovsk Mining District found that reasons for the drastic fall in production in his mines in recent months 'were many', but averred that 'the greatest of them is still the lack of food'.[121] Finally, and most emphatically, in April 1919 Kolchak's proconsul, the Governor General of the Urals *krai*, Engineer Postnikov, was moved to proffer his resignation as he found it 'impossible to lead industry' in the prevailing conditions: 'There is no food and no provisions in the central and northern Urals', Postnikov complained, as a consequence of which 'almost no workers' could be persuaded to perform necessary work and the region's industry was threatening to come to 'a standstill' in the near future.[122]

Yet, in spite of the graphic picture of hunger in the factories which such reports provided, very little was done by the authorities at Omsk to try and remedy the situation during the crucial months of late 1918 and early 1919 when all attention was focussed on the preparation of the spring offensive. In fact, steps were taken at that time which, both Soviet and White accounts agree, contributed significantly to

119 Gidney, p. 327.

120 Luchebnikov, pp. 191–2.

121 Taniaev, pp. 83–4.

122 Guins, Vol. 2, pp. 183–6.

the *deterioration* of the food supply situation in the rear. In particular, in response to pressure on the government from Trades and Industry organizations, the responsibility for provisioning factories and towns was taken away from the Ministry of Food and Supply at Omsk during the first months of Kolchak's rule and placed instead in the hands of Siberia's rather poorly developed private trading organizations.[123] This was done, no doubt, because of the Whites' general ideological commitment to private enterprise. However, there was almost certainly an added ingredient of prejudice at work: prejudice against the very idea of centralized, public provision which was associated with the Bolsheviks;, and prejudice against the Ministry of Food and Supply itself which, upon its creation during the summer of 1918, had taken over the Soviet Government's *Khleboles* supply network in which co-operative (and often SR-sympathizing) agents had been active. Thus, whilst holding the western democracies up as their model, the Siberian anti-Bolsheviks were too busy paying tribute to the virtues of private enterprise to notice that increased levels of government interference in the economy had made a significant contribution to the war efforts of all combatant nations in the Great War.

It was only during the late spring of 1919 that reports began to appear indicating that the Omsk Government was taking some positive steps to expedite the supply of food to urban Siberia and to the Urals industrial region. The change in attitude was signalled when Kolchak himself addressed a Special Conference of the Trades and Industry representatives of the Urals at Ekaterinburg on May 10th. He placed great emphasis on the importance of keeping workers at their benches and stated that:

> This will not be done by compulsion (except in cases of dire necessity) but by the understanding of mutual interests and solid economic ties. This will require a guarantee to the workers that they will be supplied with the necessities of life and that a fair rate of wages will be fixed.[124]

For once the Supreme Ruler seems to have progressed beyond the realms of cant, as a stream of government actions tried to ameliorate food supply: on May 17th the Railway Transportation Committee of the Ministry of Food and Supply announced

123 Sukin (*Leeds Russian Archive*), pp. 199–200.

124 *Irtysh* (Omsk) No. 20, 1.vi.1919.

that more goods wagons would be made available to supply foodstuffs to the towns; on May 26th the Ministry of Ways and Communications declared that the Council of Ministers was committing 44,000,000 roubles to the Railway Food Supply Section for food purchases (i.e. some 480 roubles per railway worker); and in mid-June a deal was announced whereby the Omsk Government would purchase 49,000,000 poods of sugar from Britain to be made available to railway workers at no more than two roubles per pood.[125] These were quite substantial commitments, but they were too piecemeal and they came too late in the day to have any effect on workers' attitudes to the White régime and too late to save the economy. Within weeks of their announcement Kolchak's major industrial asset, the Urals, would be in Red hands – an event which marked the beginning of the end for his régime.

Even had the Omsk Government been committed at an earlier stage to provide food and other necessities for industrial workers, it has to be said that many more problems would have remained to be overcome. One major obstacle was that the towns of Siberia had become severely overcrowded with several million refugees from central Russia. Omsk itself, for example, had had a population of about 130,000 in 1917; by 1919 estimates as to its population range from 500,000 to a million.[126] The élite among the refugees lived in opulent style – some memoirists talk fondly of duck-shoots, lazy days at the horse races, parties, balls and theatre outings at Omsk, or of river excursions and picnics with ministers; equally, more critical observers of the Omsk scene were dismayed at the fashionably dressed clientele of the capital's Aquarium Gardens and their penchant for squandering 'extravagant sums derived from unknown sources on luxuries and absurdities' while workers starved and diseased soldiers languished in filthy hospital corridors.[127]

125 *Nasha zaria* (Omsk) No. 104, 17.v.1919; *Nasha zaria* (Omsk) No. 114, 31.v.1919; *Zemlia i trud* (Kurgan) No. 136 (303), 27.vi.1919.

126 N.N. 'Zapiski belogvardeitsa', *Arkhiv russkoi revoliutsii* (Berlin), Vol. 10 (1923), p. 90; Rouquérol, J.G.M. *La Guerre des Rouges et des Blancs: L'Aventure de l'Amiral Koltchak.* Paris (1929), p. 15; Rodney, W. 'Siberia in 1919 – a Canadian Banker's Impressions', *Queens Quarterly* (Kingston, Ontario) Vol. 79, No. 3 (Autumn 1972), p. 332.

127 For impressions of the gay life of Omsk see Dubarier, G. 'Omsk Under Kolchak' *The Living Age* (New York), Vol. 322, No. 4179; Prinsep, E.S.M. 'Knox's Mission to Siberia, 1919–1920: the Personal Reminiscences of one of its Members', *Army Quarterly* Vol. 81, No. 1 (October 1960), pp. 60ff; and Arnol'dov, V. *Zhizn' i revoliutsiia. Groza piatogo goda. Belyi Omsk.* Shanghai (1935), p. 202. For a more critical view of Omsk's excesses see Pares, B. 'Report on the Political Conditions in Western Siberia, 20.vi.1919' (*Pares Papers*, Box 41), p. 7.

However, the suggestion of an Omsk Bolshevik that 'with the exception of workers and peasants all groups of the population...are being given cake from the table at which the Siberian counter-revolution is celebrating its orgy' was surely an exaggeration.[128] There was indeed an over-privileged and to some degree debauched élite of White society, but the vast majority of the refugees, just like the Siberian working class, were fighting a losing battle against inanition. Even relatively rich refugees were crowded ten to a room in the limited hotel accommodation offered by Kolchak's capital and thousands more lived in cramped railway wagons which had been shunted onto a network of specially laid lines in the square before the station. As one observer speculated, if these people were occasionally to be seen throwing their money about, then perhaps it was only in desperation, a sense of '*après nous le déluge*': 'all were animated with the one desire', wrote a British witness of Omsk cafe life, 'to find a respite from the anxieties of tomorrow'.[129] Another Briton, at Barnaul, found that:

> It was often pathetic to watch the efforts of the better class to recall the happy and prosperous prewar days, the women clad in all the ancient finery they could muster and the men in dilapidated uniforms, their badges of rank often marked in indelible pencil.[130]

Still others, one witness suggested, frequented the cafes because they had nowhere else to go.[131] But least fortunate of all had to be the many thousands among the poorest of the refugee population who could afford neither accommodation nor the cafes and lived instead in shanty towns surrounding the capital where families would huddle together in holes in the ground with only an improvised tin or canvas roof between themselves and the fierce Siberian elements. It was of these latter, who could survive only by begging, that a Czechoslovak Legionnaire recalled: 'Our dogs

128 *Omskie bol'sheviki v bor'be za vlast Sovetov (1917–1920gg.): sbornik dokumental'nykh materialov*. Omsk (1952), p. 140.

129 Archer, J. 'Social Conditions in Siberia', *The Russian Outlook* (London) Vol. 2, No. 27 (8.xi.1919), pp. 639–40.

130 Hodges, P. *Britmis: A Great Adventure of the War (being an Account of Allied Intervention in Siberia and of an Escape Across the Gobi Desert to Peking)*. London (1931), p. 78.

131 Borodin, N.A. *Idealy i deiatel'nost': sorok let zhizni i raboty riadovago russkago intelligenta*. Berlin–Paris (1930), pp. 201–2.

did not like the refugees. They were quite sufficiently intelligent to notice that their food rapidly deteriorated as a result of the arrival of these newcomers.'[132]

Not all refugees, then, lived in luxury; not all were being 'thrown cake'. But whether they caroused with the élite or begged scraps from the Legionnaires, the millions of refugees who poured into the Siberian towns were always in competition with native workers for scarce food supplies; moreover, having often brought their savings and valuables with them, even homeless refugees might out-bid workers when food was to be found in the markets.

It has to be said that an influx of population into towns on this scale would have taxed the resources of any government (which reminds us that there was a silver lining to the urban depopulation experienced by the Soviet government during the civil war). On the other hand, the Kolchak government did prove to be singularly unable to rise to the challenge. In particular, the rivalry between local and central bodies and the subservience of the government to an agenda being set by the military were features of the political life of White Siberia laden with unhappy consequences in the economic field.

Particularly adversely affected by confused administration of the economy of Kolchakia were the mining and metallurgical concerns of the Urals. During the period of Bolshevik rule in this region, from November 1917 to July 1918, the majority of mine-owners had fled – many leaving Russia altogether – so that in the first months of anti-Bolshevik government, those mines which were working tended to be in the charge of engineers appointed by the local White authority, the Urals *oblast'* Government (of July–October 1918), or even by the Technical Department of the Czechoslovak Legion. These engineers, led by the afore-mentioned S.P. Postnikov, soon formed themselves into a collective administration for the mining districts, known as the Urals Industrial Committee (UIC), and proceeded to run the region's industry to the best of their ability on behalf of the anti-Bolshevik governments. Only two of the major mining concerns of the Urals were taken from the jurisdiction of the Committee and returned to their owners in the pre-Kolchak period and the UIC had some initial successes: by fixing prices on raw materials they prevented speculation by private traders; they closed uneconomic factories to

132 Becvar, *The Lost Legion*, pp. 214–5.

preserve resources; they established arbitration procedures to settle wage disputes; and they did their best to supply factories with food.[133]

As the White hold on the Urals was strengthened, however, as the Kolchak dictatorship was established and as the military successes in the north Urals raised hopes of an imminent victory over the Bolsheviks, former proprietors of the Urals industries began to return to the area and attempted to regain control of their factories. The mine-owners' own collective body, the Congress of Mining Industries of the Urals, refused to submit to the directives of the UIC, berated the engineers for 'interference in the normal work of industry', and, in a letter of November 26th 1918 to the Ministry of Trade and Industry at Omsk, insisted that the UIC should be disbanded.[134] The response of the minister, N.N. Shchukin, was typical of the Kolchak Government's kowtowing to the capitalists: in adherence to the principle of the superiority of private enterprise, he informed the mine-owners, the UIC would be reformed or replaced and he asked for their suggestions.[135]

For several months no action was taken to replace the Committee – in fact, the UIC remained in existence until May 1919. However, it was no longer able to work effectively. Shchukin's announcement had left the Committee's legal standing and powers in limbo, its future unclear; soon afterwards its source of funding in the central government dried up. It seems that the minister's idea was to replace the interim co-ordination of Urals industry by the UIC with the temporary co-ordination of industry from his own department (which, he hoped, would be less offensive to the private owners of the mines and factories). If so, the attempt to establish central control was an abject failure, for Shchukin – although impeccably qualified as an engineer – did not have the experience or touch for economic planning on the grand scale; he had no real ideological commitment to centralization which might have inspired that touch, and he did not have the local agencies with which to implement any central control. In fact, according to one of Shchukin's colleagues, although the Ministry of Trade and Industry was supposed to be overseeing Urals industry, 'in the wider sense (i.e. outside of Omsk) the Ministry of Trade and Industry did not exist'.[136] As a result, industrial policy and supply policy simply stalled during

133 Sukin (*Leeds Russian Archive*), p. 111; Taniaev, pp. 59–62.

134 *ibid.*, pp. 66–7.

135 *ibid.*, p. 67.

136 Sukin (*Leeds Russian Archive*), p. 104.

these crucial months of December 1918 to May 1919. Engineer Postnikov wrote repeatedly to Shchukin for advice and for finance, so as to continue the work of the UIC, but to no avail. In despair at government policy, as we have already seen, Postnikov eventually resigned from his post in April 1919. One of his major complaints was that 'we don't know what work the Ministry of Trade and Industry does in Omsk, but as far as we are concerned it does not exist – not one appeal to it has received a reply'.[137]

Eventually, and once again in the wake of Kolchak's May address to the Trade and Industry congress at Ekaterinburg, a new co-ordinating body (consisting of both private businessmen and government appointees) was established at Ekaterinburg to marshal Urals industry and to supply the factories with food.[138] If, however, that body achieved any tangible results in the few weeks it existed before the Red Army captured the Urals, then the facts remain unrecorded.

Urban overcrowding and poorly co-ordinated government agencies were, therefore, two of the obstacles to be overcome in attempting to develop a working supply policy for the factories and towns of Kolchakia. Perhaps the major obstacle, however, was that into the vacuum left by an over-ambitious Ministry taking upon itself responsibilities which it was unable to meet had stepped the Russian Army. The army had taken full control of the administration of the Urals, and the three reports of government agents in that area cited above as finding the lack of food for workers to be the major cause of industrial discontent, all conclude that the *cause* of food shortages was the maladministration of the factory districts by the military authorities and, in particular, the army's monopolization of the railway. So certain was the army leadership of the impending collapse of the Soviet forces that, according to the UIC:

> The military authorities displayed utter scorn towards the needs of the rear...almost completely disrupting the supply of raw materials, fuel and foodstuffs even to those factories which are working exclusively for the needs of the military.[139]

137 Guins, Vol. 2, pp. 183–6.

138 Sukin (*Leeds Russian Archive*), pp. 116–17.

139 Taniaev, p. 85.

Engineer Postnikov confirmed that bread was not available to workers at Ekaterinburg because 'the military pay no heed to the needs of the civilian population' and because the Chief of Military Communications refused to release wagons to bring grain into the city; in April 1919, Postnikov continued, four hundred wagons loaded with grain were standing, rotting under military guard at Shadrinsk even as Ekaterinburg's workers starved.[140]

And it was not only that the army did not itself supply the factories with food: the military were also preventing more enterprising (or desperate) factory managers from securing their own supplies. The Chief of Kizelovsk Mining District, for example, actually received 500,000 roubles from the Ministry of Trade and Industry with which to purchase supplies in January 1919. However, of the eight wagons of grain which his agents bought, only two managed to avoid requisitioning by the army to arrive safely at the mines. When the Kizelovsk Mining Chief then attempted to make good his losses by sending his own requisitioning party out into the countryside, he found that both his men and his carts were themselves mobilized by the army. The first step to getting industry back on its feet, he concluded in a letter of complaint to Omsk, had to be to prevent the military from commandeering supplies intended for the factories.[141]

It was, then, the failure of the White régime to guarantee and to safeguard the supply of food and fuel to industrial districts which lay at the heart of workers' discontent. This was recognized by government agents at local level and, albeit too late to have an effect on the outcome of the war, the Omsk Government did take some ad hoc steps to rectify the situation in May–June of 1919. As has been demonstrated, there were tremendous obstacles to be overcome: notably the government's unyielding commitment to private enterprise and free trade in a time which demanded a degree of regulation and control; the lofty ambitions and low capabilities of the confused supply apparatus at Omsk; the insensitivity of the army to the needs of the rear; and the severe overcrowding of the Siberian towns. It may well have been that such weighty problems, together with the ever present factor of the Whites' confidence in imminent victory (and its corollary, a belief that there was no need to establish a working administration in Siberia), deterred the Kolchak régime from tackling the supply problem until it was too late. Yet, if the dilemmas

140 Guins, Vol. 2, p. 184.

141 Taniaev, pp. 83–4.

faced by the White government in Siberia were enormous, so too were the resources at hand which might have been employed to improve matters. Kolchak was fighting a war, he had to supply an army of several hundred thousand men and he had to meet the needs of a civilian population in Siberia and the Urals which had swelled from around fifteen million in 1917 to well over twenty million by 1919. But he was also regent over an immensely rich agricultural region. According to Zakupsbyt (Siberia's largest co-operative organization) western Siberia alone had the agricultural capacity to support a population of sixty million people.[142] The means to feed Kolchakia did, therefore, exist. What was to prove the fundamental economic problem for the Supreme Ruler, however, was that between the producers and consumers of foodstuffs in his domain yawned the triplex abyss of industrial weakness, financial confusion and transport paralysis – an abyss which he was powerless to bridge.

PART TWO: THE RURAL SCENE

The agricultural base

There was no question of the severe food shortages experienced in the towns of Kolchakia in 1919 being the result either of a history of poor agricultural performance in the region or of a sudden collapse. In fact, the Whites came to power at the very peak of an unprecedented economic boom east of the Urals. The sown area in Siberia had increased by 122% in the two decades before the revolution. This far exceeded the growth rate of the population and, as a result, Siberia's farmers had been able to make available for sale up to 75% of their annual grain harvest (which was more than twice the proportion of grain marketed by the

142 *The Union of Siberian Creamery and Other Co-operative Associations and the Country Served by this Organization*. Boston (1919), p. 27.

farmers of overpopulated European Russia).[143] Animal husbandry was also very strong. Contemporary data gathered by the Siberian co-operatives, presented below as Table 4.8, illustrate that the number of farm animals in the rich western districts of Siberia dwarfed that of the rest of Russia and could even bear comparison with some of the leading agricultural nations of the rest of the world. But the most spectacular Siberian success of all had been achieved in the field of dairy farming. Thirty-six million poods of Siberian butter had been exported between 1894 and 1912, by which time Tomsk and Tobol′sk *guberniias* could claim to lead world production.[144]

The years of the Great War had proved particularly fruitful, as Siberia's fast-developing network of co-operative organizations had secured lucrative contracts to supply the Imperial Army.[145] It was true that with the advent of the civil war there had ensued something of a crisis – but, with the region isolated from its traditional markets in European Russia and Western Europe and with the railway system overloaded with military traffic, it was initially a crisis of over-production. According to figures released by Kolchak's Ministry of Food and Supply (and

Table 4.8: Livestock ownership (per 100 head of population)

	Horses	Cattle	Sheep/Goats	Pigs
USA	21.5	59.0	50.0	65.0
Denmark	25.1	88.8	18.6	90.0
Russia	26.0	34.0	48.0	10.0
Tobol′sk *gub.*	40.0	48.0	35.0	158.0
Tomsk *gub.*	57.0	67.0	77.0	15.0
Akmolinsk *obl.*	112.0	100.0	330.0	1.0
Semipalatinsk *obl.*	100.0	102.0	209.0	4.0

143 Baikalov, A.V. 'Siberia Since 1894', *Slavonic and Eastern European Review* (London) Vol. 11, No. 32 (1933), pp. 331–2; Mote, V.L. 'The Cheliabinsk Grain Tariff and the Rise of the Siberian Butter Industry', *Slavonic Review* Vol. 35, No. 2 (1976), p. 306; *Zemel′nyi vopros v Sibiri*. Moscow (1919), p. 21.

144 *The Union of Siberian Creamery and Other Co-operative Associations*, p. 43; Mote, p. 308; Serebrennikov, I.I. *Sibirvedenie*. Harbin, 1920, p. 156.

145 On the development of the co-operative movement in Siberia see below pp. 434ff.

confirmed by both co-operative and American military intelligence sources) a better than average harvest in 1918 had produced a large surplus of grain which, when added to the stockpile still unused from 1917, left 117,135,259 poods of marketable grain in western Siberia alone (and over 150,000,000 poods in Siberia as a whole) in January 1919.[146] Once again according to the Ministry of Food and Supply, there remained 110,000,000 poods of grain stockpiled in the Siberian villages even by the summer of 1919.[147]

Accounts by those travellers who ventured into the Siberian countryside in 1919 bear startled witness to the agricultural abundance of the region. Arriving at Semipalatinsk, for example, a Russian officer who had become accustomed to the deprivations of life in Omsk and other towns along the Trans-Siberian Railway zone, marvelled that seemingly every type of foodstuff was available at what seemed to him to be a pittance (he could not recall the last time he had seen an egg, but could buy ten for twenty kopecks at Semipalatinsk); there was enough grain in the storehouses of the Altai to 'flood the Siberian market', confirmed American intelligence sources in March 1919.[148] The picture of abundance was much the same in parts of the Far East. Travelling near Nikol'sk, General Graves was reminded of prosperous Kansas by the endless fields of wheat, while Colonel John Ward also remarked upon the 'hundreds of miles of uncarted corn' along the sides of the railway in that district in October 1918. 'As far as the eye could see,' Ward marvelled, 'to the left and right, one vast sea of derelict corn, uncared for on the land and left to rot in the Siberian winter.'[149] But why rotting, why uncarted and why uncared for, when the Siberian towns and the Russian Army were literally starving?

Initially at least it was not that the Siberian peasants were withholding their crops from Kolchak as a symbol of their political allegiance to the Soviet government. Indeed, with the exception of the Cossack lands of South Russia, Siberia was the

146 *Omskie bol'sheviki*, p. 137; *The Russian Co-operator* (London) Vol. 13, No. 3 (March 1919), p. 41; *USMI*, Vol. 7, No. 89 (week ending 8.ii.1919), p. 551.

147 *Sbornik sibirskogo statisticheskogo upravleniia*. Novosibirsk (1921), Vol. 4, p. 3. – cited in Spirin, *Klassy i partii*, p. 350.

148 Il'in, I.S. 'Omsk, Direktoriia i Kolchak', *Novyi zhurnal* Vol. 73 (1963), pp. 218–9; *USMI*, Vol. 7, No. 94 (week ending 15.iii.1919), p. 684.

149 Ward, *With the 'Die-Hards'*, pp. 66–7.

area of the empire least susceptible to the Bolshevik creed. In Siberia, after all, there had developed a society more prosperous, more individualistic, more moderate and less strife-torn than was the case in European Russia. In 1917 Lenin himself had recognized this, writing that Siberia, as a region of 'well-fed, solid and successful farmers, not at all inclined towards socialism', would under normal circumstances prove stony ground for his party.[150]

The major socio-economic difference between Siberia and European Russia was, of course, that landlordism and serfdom, the seigneurial system, had not been experienced to any significant degree in the Siberian countryside. Neither the Chinese nor the Turkic people to the south had ever threatened the Russian state's hold on its eastern territories in the way that Poland, Sweden or Turkey had menaced Russia in the west, so east of the Urals it had not been necessary to build the lowest tiers of the absolutist hierarchy. Of the 1,200,000,000 desiatins identified as Siberia's land fund before the revolution of 1917, only 7,500,000 desiatins had belonged to private landlords. The remainder belonged vaguely to the state or to the tsar himself (the so-called Cabinet Lands or *zemlia Kabineta ego velichestva*, predominantly in the Altai), but were in the possession of the peasants who paid rental or (following the implementation of the 1899 act) redemption payments. This heritage, together with the fact that the redistributive commune was very rare in Siberia, had given rise to a market-based economy, distinct from the feudal traits still prevalent west of the Urals.[151]

There was, moreover, plenty of land to be farmed in Siberia in comparison to the land-hungry areas of the west. Siberian peasants farmed an average of fifteen desiatins of land and utilized three desiatins of woodland per family unit – three times the averages of European Russia. As a result, the Siberian peasant was generally more prosperous than his European cousins. There were, of course, exceptions. Even the best Soviet historians felt obliged to make much of the point that 9.6% of the population in certain *uezds* owned no land at all,[152] while there

150 Lenin, *PSS*, Vol. 39, pp. 39–41.

151 Lipkina, A.G. *1919 god v Sibiri: bor'ba s kolchakovshchinoi*. Moscow (1962), p. 7. Redivisional forms of communal tenure were confined to the most populous, long-settled and economically developed areas of Western Siberia. Elsewhere infrequent, partial redivisions were the norm. See Channon, J. 'Regional Variation in the Commune: The Case of Siberia', in Bartlett, R. (ed.) *Land Commune and Peasant Community in Russia*. London (1990), pp. 66–85.

152 Gromov, I.V. et al. (eds.) *Partizanskoe dvizhenie v Zapadnoi Sibiri (1918–1920gg.): dokumenty i materialy*. Novosibirsk (1959), p. 4.

was something of a campaign in the mid-1960s to prove that the majority of Siberia's peasants could actually be classified as 'poor'.[153] Such juggling with unverifiable statistics, however, tells us very little. Perhaps more significant is that it was also admitted by historians in the Soviet Union that as many as 18–22% of Siberian peasants could be classified as kulaks, i.e. that they were doing very well indeed out of the pre-revolutionary system.[154] The researches of a western scholar suggest, moreover, that if his Soviet colleagues had been more consistent in categorising peasants, then at least 50% of Siberia's farmers could have been classified as kulaks.[155]

Even less quantifiable, but equally inimical to the spread of Bolshevism east of the Urals, was the widely perceived phenomenon that the Siberian peasant had a different spirit than his European counterpart – a more bourgeois spirit, to complement the region's market-orientated economy; a spirit once again traceable to Siberia's separate economic development within the Russian Empire. The greater degrees of political and economic freedoms east of the Urals, where government institutions were few and landlords virtually unknown, had given Siberian peasants the possibility of creating and increasing their own capital and material well-being through their own exertions. This in turn had fostered feelings of independence, self-reliance and self-respect. It was a proud, hardy, resourceful, frontiersmanlike spirit – one common to all members of Siberian rural society in their shared pioneer battle against the hostile elements and awesome expanses of their country.

This, of course, does not accord with the popularly accepted picture of Siberia as one massive penal colony. But the truth was that the prisons were the exception, not the rule. In fact, the convict system had made its own contribution to the evolution of the independent Siberian spirit. Some observers noted the filtering out of free-

153 Tiukhovkin, V.G. *Sibirskaia derevnia nakanune Oktiabria*. Irkutsk (1966), p. 175; Shornikov, M.M. *Bol'sheviki Sibiri v bor'be za pobedu Oktiabr'skoi revoliutsii*. Omsk (1949), p. 151.

154 Gromov, p. 4.

155 Snow, R.E. *The Bolsheviks in Siberia, 1917–1918*. London, 1977, p. 26. Even some pre-*glasnost'* Soviet scholars came close to admitting that what their historical writing had previously characterized as 'middle peasants' in Siberia were actually more akin to the kulaks of European Russia in terms of their wealth and well-being than they were to the middle peasants of west of the Urals. See Iakimova, T.V. 'Politicheskoe nastroenie Zapadno-Sibirskogo krest'ianstva vesnoi 1918g.', in Korablev Iu.V. and Shishkin, V.I. (eds.) *Iz istorii interventsii i grazhdanskoi voiny v Sibiri i na Dal'nem Vostoke, 1917–1922gg*. Novosibirsk (1985), p. 208; Zhurov, Iu.V. 'Bol'shev-istskie organizatsii i pervye revoliutsionnye preobrazovaniia v sibirskoi derevne (1917–1919gg.)', in *Iz istorii Krasnoiarskoi partiinoi organizatsii*. Krasnoiarsk (1974), pp. 56–7.

thinking and democratic ideas from the colonies of political exiles (who often mixed quite freely with the local populations); while the Siberian commentator, A. Baikalov, reminds us that even those exiles classed as 'criminals' were often only the more independent-minded and resourceful of Russian peasants, branded as trouble-makers by their landlords and subsequently banished.[156]

But whatever the Siberian spirit consisted of and whatever its origin, the sheer number of allusions to its existence indicates that there was something tangibly and proudly 'Siberian' which stood in marked contrast to that which was Russian and to all of that country's simmering resentments, grudges and subservience. One visitor to Siberia in the early years of the century noted a transformation in the behaviour of the populace the very moment that he had crossed the Urals. He found that the people were markedly less down-trodden and servile the further east he travelled, reaching a peak at Irkutsk.[157] But it was perhaps M. Phillips Price who provided the definition best suited to western perceptions: 'Just as the British settler in Canada has become a Canadian,' he wrote, 'the Russian settler in Siberia has become a Siberian.'[158]

The individualistic ethos of the Siberian did not preclude the attraction felt by the rural population towards moderate and democratic forms of socialism, perhaps in recognition of the need for mutual support against the climatic and geographic disadvantages of this isolated region and against the incursions of their colonial masters in St Petersburg. The attraction to socialism was exemplified by the sudden and dramatic flourishing of the co-operative movement in the region in the period 1900 to 1917.[159] The co-operatives were predominantly an SR domain and it was that party which had dominated Siberian politics in that brief period when politics had been allowed to flourish in the Russian Empire. The majority of deputies returned to the State Dumas by the region were SRs (no delegate to the right of the Kadets was ever returned) and in the elections to the Constituent Assembly of 1917,

156 Watrous, S.D. 'Russia's "Land of the Future": Regionalism and the Awakening of Siberia, 1819–1894', University of Washington PhD Thesis (1970), pp. 538–9; Baikalov, A.V. 'Siberia since 1894', *Slavonic and East European Review* Vol. 10 (1932), No. 1, pp. 339–40.

157 Fraser, J.F. *The Real Siberia*. London (1902), p. 196.

158 Phillips Price, M. *Siberia*. London (1912), p. vii.

159 See below, pp. 434ff.

PSR candidates had triumphed in virtually every rural and some urban areas, winning as much as 85% of the votes in some areas.[160]

Clearly, then, Siberia was not a natural breeding ground for the Bolshevik spirit which seized much of European Russia in 1917 and 1918: the region lacked the large concentrations of workers (or, indeed of soldiers) who had supported the October Revolution, and it did not have the mass of impoverished and land-hungry peasants whose impatience for reform had been satisfied by Lenin. As the Soviet leader himself wrote:

> We could not give the peasant in Siberia that which the revolution had given him in Russia. In Siberia the peasants did not receive the landowners' land because there was none there and therefore it was easier for them to believe the White Guards.[161]

It was not a land of complete harmony: there were social tensions and frictions which were to be of use to the Bolsheviks in reconquering Siberia in 1919 to 1920 (notably between workers and factory owners, as we have seen, but also between long-established settlers and the millions of recent immigrants, between peasants and Cossacks and between Russians and natives). Yet it seems safe to conclude, along with one Soviet historian, that 'if the October Revolution had not broken out in the heartland, there would have been no revolution in Siberia for decades'.[162]

Lenin's government was aware of the potential problem posed by Siberia from the very first days of the revolution. Quite simply, in the words of one Soviet commentator, 'the great bulk of the Siberian peasants did not support Soviet

160 Radkey, O.H. *Russia Goes to the Polls: The Election to the All-Russian Constituent Assembly, 1917*. Ithaca (1989), pp. 150–1.

161 Lenin, *PSS*, Vol. 39, p. 299. From monastery and other lands the Soviet Government did manage to scrape together just over five million desiatins of land (90% of it in western Siberia) for redistribution among the peasantry east of the Urals in 1917 and 1918. But this, as Soviet historians admit, was an insignificant amount, giving an increment of only 5.6% to the peasant land holdings in Siberia (compared to the 23.7% increment achieved by the revolution for the peasantry of European Russia as a whole and the 50% increment achieved along the middle Volga). See Goriushkin, L.M. 'Pretvorenie v zhizn dekreta o zemle v Zapadnoi Sibiri v kontse 1917–pervoi polovine 1918g.', in *Krest'ianstvo i sel'skoe khoziastvo Sibiri 1917–1961gg.* Novosibirsk (1965), p. 25; Sharapov, G.V. *Reshenie agrarnogo voprosa v Rossii posle pobedy Oktiabr'skoi revoliutsii*. Moscow (1960), p. 129.

162 Riabikov, V.V. *Irkutsk – stolitsa revoliutsionnoi Sibiri*. Irkutsk (1957), pp. 195–6. See also Dvorianov, N.V. and Dvorianov, V.N. *V tylu Kolchaka*. Moscow (1966), pp. 11–12.

power.'[163] Even those peasants willing to accept with indifference the rise and fall of various governments in Petrograd in 1917 were moved to active resistance to the Bolsheviks when it came to the imposition of the policies of the Soviet government on Siberia itself. In January 1918, for example, Lenin had demanded that 'the most strenuous measures be taken for the movement of grain stockpiles to [St] Peter[sburg] from Siberia'.[164] But because of popular resistance to the fixed grain prices being set by the state (resistance encouraged by the large number of SR-dominated soviets in Siberia which refused to set such prices) only some 10 million poods of grain out of an estimated stockpile of 130 million had actually been sent west by June 1918.[165] Efforts made to mobilize Siberian peasants of the 1917, 1918 and 1919 age groups following an order of May 28th were even less successful: 'Our attempts to mobilize the peasant population came to nothing and those detailed to organize the mobilization returned with no conscripts', recalled V.V. Riabakov.[166]

Peasant opposition to Soviet rule even took the form of armed risings against the Bolshevik authorities in the early months of 1918. During the period of January–April 1918, such risings occurred in the *uezds* of Kamensk, Slavgorod, Biisk and Zmeinogorsk; in May peasant rebellions broke out at Ishimsk *uezd* of Tobolsk *guberniia*, at several other *uezds* of Tomsk and Eniseisk *guberniias* and at Kalashinsk Station near Omsk. The largest rising of all took place at Cheremkhovo, the mining centre west of Irkutsk, where Red Guards and Bolshevik miners had to fight off 12,000 local peasants in early 1918.[167] These revolts were something of a general regional phenomenon, as one Soviet survey concluded: by the spring of 1918, 'there was not real calm in a single Siberian *volost'*', wrote Iu.V. Zhurov.[168]

A second wave of peasant risings coincided with the Czechoslovak revolt in the last week of May 1918 – between May 25th and June 1st risings occurred around Mariinsk, Nizhneudinsk, Novonikolaevsk, Kansk, Petropavlovsk, Tomsk and other

163 Spirin, *Klassy i partii*, p. 247.

164 Lenin, *PSS.*, Vol. 50, p. 28.

165 Zhurov, Iu.V. *Grazhdanskaia voina v Sibirskoe derevne*. Krasnoiarsk (1986), pp. 14–15; *Istoriia Sibiri*, Vol. 4, p. 106.

166 Riabikov, V.V. *Tsentrosibir'*. Moscow (1949), p. 72.

167 Malykhina, K.F. *Krasnaia gvardiia Sibiri v bor'be za vlast' Sovetov (1917–1918gg.)*. Novosibirsk (1959), p. 50.

168 Zhurov, p. 17.

centres. And, as Soviet power crumbled and Siberian Bolsheviks attempted to flee into the countryside to escape the Czechoslovak Legionnaires and White Guards, there were several reported cases of peasants spontaneously capturing the Red fugitives and handing them over to the new authorities.[169]

Such active support of the anti-Bolshevik forces may, however, have been an exception. A Siberian Bolshevik recalled that the response of the majority of peasants to the political battles raging in 1918 was one of studied indifference: 'The Whites are fighting the Reds, but what business is that of ours?' was a phrase he heard over and over again in the villages.[170] Similarly, but from the opposite political corner, a Kadet newspaper of July 1918 reported that 'the attack of the Czechoslovaks on Achinsk has not notably excited the countryside – just as the fall of the Bolsheviks did not'.[171]

Even if access to the archives of the former Soviet Union is ever fully granted to western historians, it will probably be impossible to adjudge whether hostility or indifference to the Soviet administration was the norm in this huge, diverse and isolated region in the spring of 1918. What can be said, however, is that the conclusion of the first wave of Soviet research into the subject in the late 1950s and early 1960s, that most peasants were definitely anti-Soviet, was tempered by the early 1970s to a point where the majority of peasants were said to have been neither anti-Soviet nor pro-SR but simply indifferent to the whole affair. The historians of this latter period (roughly, the Brezhnev era), tended to stress the importance of other factors in the fall of Soviet power in Siberia – principally the Czechoslovak rising, Allied interference and the growth of the SR and White Guard underground.[172] This typically perverse debate among Soviet historians, with their

169 *Gorniaki Sibiri*, p. 136; Guins, *Sibir'*, Vol. 1, pp. 132–3.

170 Gromov, I.V. 'V boiakh za Sovety', in *Za vlast' Sovetov (vospominaniia uchastnikov partizanskoi dvizhenii v tylu Kolchaka)*. Novosibirsk (1947), p. 50.

171 *Svobodnaia Sibir'* (Krasnoiarsk), 11.vii.1918.

172 Zhuravlev, M.N. 'Kommunisticheskaia partiia – organizator razgroma voennoi interventsii i vnutrennoi kontrrevoliutsii v Sibiri', in *Boevye gody*. Novosibirsk (1959), p. 13; Reznichenko, A.N. 'Nachalo grazhdanskoi voiny v Sibiri', in *ibid.*, p. 43; Stishov, M.I. *Bol'shevistskoe podpol'e i partizanskoe dvizhenie v Sibiri v gody grazhdanskoi voiny (1918–1920gg.)*. Moscow (1962), p. 42; Plotnikova, M.E. 'Sovremennaia sovetskaia istoricheskaia literatura o pozitsiakh sibirskogo krest'ianstva v 1918–1919gg.', in *Iz istorii grazhdanskoi voiny i interventsii, 1917–1922gg.* Moscow (1974), pp. 421–2; Zhurov, Iu.V. *Eniseiskoe khrest'ianstvo v gody grazhdanskoi voiny*. Krasnoiarsk (1972), p. 75; Gushin, N.Ia. et al. *Soiuz rabochego klassa i krest'ianstva Sibiri v periode postroeniia sotsializma (1917–1937)*. Novosibirsk (1978), p. 78.

agendas set by the prevailing mood in the Kremlin, reached a point where the chief exponent of one side attempted to prove his point by assigning every *volost′* in Siberia to categories of support for the Soviet régime, indifference to it, or hostility to it (although he failed to explain how one scientifically measures indifference).[173] Such pedantry, however, serves only to cloud the issue. Perhaps the best that can be said is that in terms of its dominant political mood, Siberia should not have been a bad place from which to mount an anti-Bolshevik campaign in 1918; that, at least on the surface of things, there should have been hope for both the Provisional Siberian Government and for Kolchak. Why, even areas such as Kansk and Minusinsk *uezds*, which were later to be the most active centres of *opposition* to the Whites, did not move in defence of the Soviet authorities in May–June of 1918.

Why then, to return to our original question, were the Siberian peasants denying their grain to White authorities even by the autumn of 1918? Why was it that by November of 1918 the Governor General of Eniseisk *guberniia* had to report to the Minister of the Interior at Omsk that 'the entire rural population' was against the government, 'even those layers of the population who had eagerly overthrown Soviet rule and helped strengthen the position of the Provisional Siberian Government'?[174] Why was it that by mid-1919 peasants all across Siberia and the Far East were flocking to join a wave of armed revolts against the Kolchak government – revolts which, remarked one officer, came to resemble the rapid progression of a case of typhus when plotted with red dots on a map at the *stavka*?[175] Why was it that even the more prosperous of the peasants of Kolchakia could be found in the ranks of partisan armies 150,000 strong which had overrun massive swathes of the Siberian rear even before the Red Army was to sweep down from the Urals to join them in ousting Kolchak in the autumn of 1919?

173 Zhurov, *Eniseiskoe khrest′ianstvo*, p. 86.

174 *Partizanskoe dvizhenie v Sibiri. Tom 1 (Prieniseiskii krai)*. Moscow–Leningrad (1925), p. 123.

175 Budberg, A.P. von 'Dnevnik', *Arkhiv russkoi revoliutsii* Vol. 15 (1924), p. 327.

The economic foundations of rural discontent

A major cause of rural discontent in White Siberia was, of course, the brutal and bloody misrule inflicted upon much of Kolchak's domains by local cossack chieftains – the atamans Semenov, Kalmykov, Gamov, Ivanov-Rinov, Annenkov and others – over whom the Supreme Ruler and the Omsk government could exert only nominal control. The panoply of abuses which characterized their barbaric regional tyrannies (infamous to history as the *atamanshchina*, execrated by the Whites' enemies as 'the dictatorship of the whip' and castigated by Kolchak himself as 'Bolshevism of the Right'), has been extensively described and studied elsewhere, and will not be dwelt upon here.[176] It will suffice to note that when pondering upon the question of why it was that so many of Siberia's prosperous peasants had come to welcome Red victory, Guins could only concede that 'they simply could not help but succumb to Bolshevism as a revolutionary ideology while Cossack units were passing through their villages'.[177]

Equally damaging to Kolchak's standing in the villages were the savage punitive detachments sent into those areas resisting the payment of taxes, refusing to institute the mobilizations announced almost weekly by the army, or suspected of harbouring

176 According to one witness to 'the inhuman cruelty, the devilish sadism' of the eastern atamans' inner circle, Semenov would boast that he could not sleep peacefully at night unless he had killed someone that day – see Alioshin, D. *Asian Odyssey*. London (1941), p. 48. If so, he must have enjoyed many nights of uninterrupted slumber, for in a single incident at Adrianovka in January 1920 he had over 1,000 people put to death in a three-day orgy of violence – see Osnos, I. 'Semenov – stavlennik iaponskoi interventsii', *Istoricheskie zapiski* Vol. 1 (1937), pp. 54–63. 'During the first day the victims were slaughtered by the firing of volleys, on the second day by the sword, on the third day by poison and asphyxiation, and the fourth – as a grand finale – by being burned alive', according to one account – see Baerlin, H. *The March of the Seventy Thousand*. London (1926), p. 261. Other similar testimonies to Semenov's crimes were heard by the US Senate Committee on Education and Labour which denied him leave to settle in the USA in 1922 – see US Senate *The Deportation of Grigorie Semenoff*. Washington (1922). On Kalmykov, who was estimated to have butchered 4,200 people during his fourteen-month hold on Khabarovsk, see Artem'ev, I.K. *Epizody revoliutsii na Dal'nem Vostoke*. Tientsin (1939). On Annenkov, whose bandits at Semipalatinsk were distinguished by a skull and crossbones tattoo (complete with the legend 'God is With Us'), see Rylkin, G. *Krovavyi ataman*. Moscow (1927); Pavlovskii, P.I. *Annenkovshchina*. Moscow (1927); and Dubrovskii, K.V. *V tsarstve nagaiki i viselitsy*. Moscow–Leningrad (1929). Smith, C.F. 'Atamanshchina in the Russian Far East', *Russian History*, Vol. 6 (1979), pp. 57–67 and Smith, C.F. 'The Ungernovshchina: How and Why', *Jahrbücher für Geschichte Osteuropas*, Vol. 28 (1980), pp. 590–5, provide a considered overview and further sources.

177 Guins, Vol. 2, p. 307.

partisan bands. Kolchak, Lebedev and other leaders would regularly issue orders to the effect that in carrying out such tasks the army should ensure that only the guilty were punished, that they were punished strictly according to the letter of the law and that 'there should be no infringement on the personal rights' of other, innocent peasants.[178] As revanchist White officers were almost invariably unable to distinguish between Bolshevist rebellion and justifiable grievance, however, that was rarely the case in practice. America's Ambassador Morris, for example, charged that it was precisely the 'utter insecurity of person and property, the orgy of arrests without charges and confiscation without colour of authority', which lay at the root of the peasantry's hatred of the Whites.[179] General Knox agreed, reporting in April 1919:

> In a village near the front yesterday I asked an old peasant, who had had experiences of both sides, which he liked best. He said 'the side that robs least. We lived better under the laws of Nicholas than we live now. They call this liberty, but we call it only robbery.'[180]

In the rear, at Kansk (where partisan activity was rife), General Janin, was told much the same story, reporting of the activities of a punitive detachment under Krasil′nikov that:

> His band steal more than the rebels, who are called Bolsheviks, and the peasants consider that the latter are better disciplined. In one village a Bolshevik who was found guilty of raping a schoolmistress was sentenced to death, but when Krasil′nikov's people arrived they looted the place clean with impunity. In Kansk people are executed without a second thought, where their only crime has been their unwillingness to hand over their money.[181]

After Krasil′nikov had departed another observer passed through Eniseisk *guberniia* and noted:

> The Whites...had burned the country and had killed much of the population. Many of the villages were ploughed up, leaving nothing to indicate that there had once been a

178 *Iz istorii grazhdanskoi voiny*, Vol. 2, pp. 255–7; Luchebnikov, pp. 171–2.

179 *FRUS: 1919 (Russia)*, p. 400.

180 FO 371/4095/61248 'Knox (Omsk) to WO, 8.iv.1919'.

181 Janin, 'Otryvki', p. 123.

> prosperous settlement on the spot. I could understand the rage of the former ruling class, but I could not understand the efficacy of such a method of reconstructing Russia.[182]

And in the Far East, at Imansk, even the White governor had to concede of the local rebel leader, Grishka Khromov, that, in comparison to the White authorities:

> ...the Grishka band were not a burden on the population... On the contrary, the peasants respected him. Grishka became the real leader in the countryside because he gave the countryside that which we did not. He dispensed law and order without any red tape, he dealt with family arguments, set up [police] patrols. To him were drawn all the outraged and repressed.[183]

The total extent of the damage inflicted upon the Siberian countryside by the White army's unfettered repression and requisitioning is probably impossible to quantify. Early Soviet surveys attempted to do so – one talking of 'no less than 20% of the population of the Ekaterinburg district killed or whipped', during White rule; another (often quoted since) claiming with rather dubious precision that across all Siberia 33,000 peasants were executed, 5,685 farmhouses and 19,252 outhouses were burned, and that 28,738 horses and 9,659 head of cattle were stolen, together with 652,707 poods of grain and flour.[184] Whatever the veracity of such figures, however, there seems little doubt that the extent of the killing and requisitioning was very substantial. General Graves, for example, ventured that: 'I am very well on the side of safety when I say that the anti-Bolsheviks killed a hundred people in Eastern Siberia to every one killed by the Bolsheviks.' He was equally certain about the effect of the pillage and mass murder indulged in by the atamans, claiming that to say that there were ten times more committed Bolsheviks in Siberia after its experience of White rule than there had been before it would be a most conservative estimate.[185]

182 Alioshin, p. 57.

183 Andrushkevich, N.A. 'Posledniaia Rossiia', *Beloe delo* No. 4 (1928), p. 134.

184 Bykov, P.M. and Niporskii (eds.) *Rabochaia revoliutsiia na Urale: epizody i fakty*. Ekaterinburg (1921), pp. 76–7; Tumarkin, D. 'Kontr-revoliutsiia v Sibiri', *Sibirskie ogni* (Novonikolaevsk), No. 1 (1922), p. 92; Zhurov, *Enisieiskoe khrest'ianstvo*, pp. 45–6.

185 Graves, pp. 108, 339.

It is really stating the obvious, however, to say that the evils of the *atamanshchina* were responsible for repelling many potential supporters of the anti-Bolshevik cause among Siberia's relatively affluent and contented peasantry and for swelling the ranks of the partisan armies which during 1919 came to embellish the map of White Siberia with large blotches of fiery red. What needs to be established in addition – not least because Kolchak and the Omsk Government, all too well aware of the damage it was inflicting upon the White régime, denounced the Cossack rapine as fervently as Lenin and Trotsky would castigate their own miscreant commanders – is that, even had there been no *atamanshchina*, the economic and financial chaos which was the hallmark of the White government would have determined that its rural constituents evolved into the enemies of Kolchak.

This is an area of research almost entirely absent from émigré historiography of the Whites and one much understated in Soviet works. It was only in the relatively free period of the 1920s that Soviet authors felt at liberty to suggest that the Siberian partisan movement had origins independent of the agitational and organizational work of Bolshevik or pro-Bolshevik agents who roused the peasantry against the White atamans. B. El′tsin, for example, wrote in a pioneering work of 1926 that the partisan movement arose almost exclusively as a result of a 'lack of co-ordination between the state of the agricultural market and the demands of the peasant economy', and noted that the movement was both most violent and most general (encompassing both rich and poor peasants) in areas dependent upon the internal and external market for grain (primarily the Altai and southern Eniseisk *guberniia*).[186] With the creeping development of Stalinist orthodoxy, however, any historical writing which did not stress the allegedly omnipotent powers of the Bolshevik Party came to be castigated as exhibiting 'a vulgar Trotskyist-SR influence' and, as such, continued to be considered by Soviet historians as an essentially impermissible way for researchers to approach the subject. This was still the case during the brief window of liberalization under Khrushchev and remained so for the doyens of Soviet Siberian historiography as they celebrated the 50th anniversary of the victory over Kolchak in 1970. It was encouraging that a survey of the Siberian partisan movement published in 1986 admitted that the economic and financial conditions prevailing in Siberia were 'very serious for the peasantry', but *glasnost′* did not

186 El′tsin, V. 'Krest′ianskoe dvizhenie v Sibiri v periode Kolchaka', *Proletarskaia revoliutsiia* (Moscow–Leningrad), No. 2 (1926), pp. 5–7.

extend beyond this generality and the disarray of the Russian historical profession in recent years has prohibited further study.[187]

The Siberian peasants' financial and economic predicament was, in fact, quite simple to appreciate but was almost impossible for the Kolchak government to do anything about in the prevailing conditions of 1918 to 1919. The farmers were withholding their grain because they had come to realize that there was no point in selling crops to the government or to private traders or in taking their goods to market to sell themselves when all that they might receive in return would be some amount of one or more of the multifarious types of currency then circulating in Siberia – currencies whose only common factor was a tendency towards a colossal loss of purchasing power from one day to the next. Those members of the Kolchak government who cared to enquire into this matter knew that this was the case, as did foreign observers.[188] It was also widely known that many of the region's peasants had already accumulated large (nominal) sums of various paper monies and that there was little hope of their accepting any more in return for their crops unless there was a possibility that the money they acquired could be used for purchasing something desirable or useful.[189] In the words of the British High Commissioner, it was 'less trouble for [the peasants] to produce sufficient food only for their own consumption than to earn money which they cannot spend'.[190] And this is precisely what the peasantry were doing in 1918 and 1919, as the Siberian towns and the Russian Army went hungry.

What in particular the Siberian peasants desired to purchase were manufactured goods and agricultural machinery and tools. The region's relatively prosperous and

187 Shelestov, D.K. 'O nachale povorota sibirsko-trudovogo krest'ianstva v storonu Sovetskoi vlasti', *Istoriia SSSR* (Moscow), No. 1 (1962), p. 123; Sherman, I.L. *Sovetskaia istoriografiia grazhdanskoi voiny v SSSR (1920–1931gg.)*. Khar'kov (1964), pp. 101–3; Plotnikova, M.E and Razgon, I.M. 'Nekotorye itogi i zadachi izucheniia osnovikh problem istorii bor'by s kolchakovshchiny', in Razgon, I.M. and Bozhenko, L.I. (eds.) *K 50-letiiu osvobozhdeniia Sibiri ot kolchakovshchiny: materialy nauchnoi konferentsii*. Tomsk (1970); Zhurov, *Grazhdanskaia voina*, p. 45.

188 Guins, Vol. 2, p. 163; FO 371/4105/1168 'Eliot (Omsk) to FO, 31.xii.1918'.

189 R.N. 'V poiskakh ustoichivogo rubliia (istoricheskie dokumenty kolchakovskogo pravitel'stva)', *Ekonomicheskoe stroitel'stvo* (Moscow), No. 2 (1923), p. 127; FO 371/4095/61248 'Knox (Vladivostok) to WO, 8.iv.1919'. In the Altai alone, American investigators found, peasants held some 10,000,000,000 roubles in savings – see *USMI*, Vol. 7, No. 94 (week ending 15.iii.1919), p. 684.

190 FO 371/3367/1690967 'Eliot (Omsk) to FO, 7.x.1918'.

progressive peasantry had long utilized agricultural machinery to a greater extent than had their cousins in European Russia. Some 60–80% of the peasants of Altai, Tomsk, Eniseisk and Irkutsk *guberniias*, for example, utilized machinery, according to the findings of a 1917 survey,[191] while it has been calculated that by 1911 Western Siberia alone made use of 36,519 reaping machines compared to the 66,381 employed in the whole of European Russia (which was ten times more populous). 100,000 ploughs a year were also being sold in Western Siberia by 1914.[192] Although most basic items (nails, hand tools etc.) had been supplied via the Imperial Land Resettlement Administration, this high degree of utilization of machinery in Siberia was a legacy of the thorough penetration of this frontier territory of the Russian Empire by foreign companies such as Kunst & Albers of Germany (which had a turnover of 150,000,000 roubles per annum by 1913) and, in particular, by the International Harvester Corporation of the USA which was said to have secured a virtual monopoly in its own field through its two hundred retail outlets across the region.[193] Pre-war importers had also been keen to meet the increasing demand for domestic appliances from the prosperous rural communities of Siberia – of Singer Sewing Machines, for example, in 1913 a young American traveller had gained the

Table 4.9: Import of metal tools and agricultural machinery into Western Siberia, 1913–1916 (in poods)

1913	4,339,168
1914	2,319,029
1915	1,364,214
1916	597,554

191 [Tsentralnoe statisticheskoe upravlenie] *Pouezdnye itogi Vserossiiskoi sel'skokhoziastvennoi i pozemel'noi perepisi 1917 goda. Po 57 guberniiam i oblastiam.* Moscow (1923), pp. 148–68.

192 Poppe, N. 'The Economic and Cultural Development of Siberia', in Katkov, G. et al. (eds.) *Russia Enters the Twentieth Century*. London (1971), p. 146; Beable, pp. 147–52.

193 Shornikov, M.M. *Bol'sheviki Sibiri v bor'be za pobedy Oktiabr'skoi revoliutsii.* Moscow (1963), pp. 121–2.

impression that 'there is scarcely a log cottage in the whole of north Asia, be it ever so many days' lonely sledge journey from a town or railroad, which has not one of them'.[194] Table 4.9 (above) reveals, however, that during the war, with Russia's western ports blockaded and Vladivostok entirely given over to the war effort, the supply to Siberia not only of home comforts but also of vital agricultural tools and machinery began to dry up.[195]

The demand for such scarce items during the years of the civil war was, consequently, very high. In April 1919 the official Canadian Economic Commission to Siberia established that $100,000,000 worth of agricultural machinery and tools could be disposed of in Siberia before the end of the year (including 20,000 mowers, 20,000 horse rakes, 12,000 Sief Rake Mowers, 12,000 *lobogreiki* reaping machines, 4,000 binders, 12,000 Emery grinders, 10,000 John Deere ploughs, 150,000 bags of bailer twine and $500,000 worth of spare parts). Also much in demand were smaller items such as scythes, harrows, seed-drills, roofing and fencing materials, candles, tea, sugar, soap etc.[196] Some manufactured items did, of course, filter through to the countryside either through official channels or (more often) through the black market. Because of their scarcity, however, such items could command prices so astronomically inflated as to make the price of food in the towns seem almost reasonable – compare Table 4.10 (below) with Table 4.6 (above, p. 364).[197]

Thus, there was a very strong disincentive for the farmers either to produce or to sell surplus crops. As a result, although the sown area declined by only around 10% across Siberia in 1918 to 1919, it was anticipated that peasants would only put 5% of their crops on the market and would store the rest. Some observers recognized the grave implications of the situation: an anonymous letter to Kolchak of January 1919 predicted that 'if by springtime there is no agricultural machinery in the countryside, your government will not be able to hold on and that will be the end of it'.[198]

194 Wright, R.L. and Digby, B. *Through Siberia: An Empire in the Making*. New York (1913), p. 65.

195 El'tsin, V. (ed.) *Po tu storona Urala (V tsarstve Kolchaka)*. Ufa (1919), p. 30.

196 *Report of the CEC*, pp. 9, 29; *USMI*, Vol. 7, No. 91 (week ending 22.ii.1919), p. 165; *The Union of Siberian Creamery and Other Co-operative Associations*, p. 29.

197 Maslov, P.P. 'Economic Problems in Siberia', *Struggling Russia* (New York) Vol. 1, No. 20 (July 1919), p. 292.

198 Zhurov, *Eniseiskoe khrest'ianstvo*, pp. 34–5; *USMI*, Vol. 7, No. 89 (week ending 8.ii.1919), p. 551; Ioffe, *Kolchakovskaia avantiura*, p. 226. Ironically, substantial stocks of precisely the sorts of wares in demand in Siberia were held at some factories in the Urals, but could not be moved

Table 4.10: Inflation in prices of goods commonly purchased by peasants (1913 = 100)

Item	1918
Roofing iron	2,000
Fencing bars	3,750
Nails	4,000
Carts	2,000
Glass	9,375
Manufactured goods	6,792
Sugar	11,672
Tea	4,000
Kerosene	22,500
Makhorka (poor tobacco)	8,333

The unenviable task of the Supreme Ruler and his government, therefore, was to attempt to re-establish the supply of manufactured goods to the countryside and thereby persuade the Siberian farmers to sell crops in 1919 in the sort of quantities necessary not only to feed the urban population and the soldiers of the Russian Army, but also to finance the importation of the war materials it needed to defeat the Bolsheviks – materials which, as we have seen, the region's own industrial base could not supply and which the Allies could not be expected to supply for free indefinitely. Some efforts were made to meet the demand for machinery. The Ministry of Agriculture, for example, purchased 10,000 pieces of agricultural machinery in the USA for use in Siberia as well as a certain amount of bailer twine.[199] The latter, however, arrived at Vladivostok just ten days before the 1919 harvest began, and anyway the entire effort was never going to be more than a drop in the ocean of what was required.

east because of the military's monopolization of railway traffic. American investigators, for example, found 100,000 clay pipes at one factory and 12,000,000 roubles' worth of nails and tacks at another. See *USMI*, Vol. 7, No. 93 (week ending 8.iii.1919), p. 660.

199 Sukin (*Leeds Russian Archive*), pp. 198–9.

PART THREE: THE ECONOMIC AND FINANCIAL POLICIES OF THE OMSK GOVERNMENT

Ultimately, the truth may have been that for as long as the White régime at Omsk remained the government of Siberia alone, and for as long as it remained a government intent upon waging war, simple geography would prevent it from achieving success no matter what economic policies it pursued. No combatant in a civil war, however, can be expected to resign himself to defeat without a struggle and by a decree of February 18th 1919 Kolchak established a Committee for the Elaboration of Government Economic Policy, charged with 'working out a general plan with the aim of increasing the productive forces of the country'. The Committee first met on March 13th; it was chaired by the Minister of Agriculture and included ministers and department heads of other interested government offices.[200] According to one of its leading members, the Minister of Foreign Affairs I.I. Sukin, however, the work of the Committee 'had no results'. In fact, recalled Sukin, the Kolchak government 'failed to establish a general economic policy in the first months of its activity' and had not even done so by the end of its existence (even though the Ministry of Finance and the Ministry of Trade and Industry were combined under the direction of Ivan Mikhailov from May 1919 onwards in an attempt to further expedite the creation of a co-ordinated policy). This failure Sukin attributed to a tendency on the part of inexperienced ministers like Mikhailov to deal with the economy on a day-to-day basis, with ad hoc and emergency measures, as well as to the dire shortage of trained officials in the ministries in question.[201]

Nevertheless, even if no general economic strategy was formulated by this addition to the plethora of government committees at Omsk in 1919, it is possible to discern the skeleton of what might be called the economic policy of the Kolchak government. It was a policy which was aimed at ameliorating the economic crisis in Siberia by the mounting of a two-pronged attack: firstly through improving the

200 *Velikaia Rossiia* (Ufa) No. 13, 14.iv.1919; *Sobranie uzakonenii i rasporiazhenii pravitel'stva, izdavaemoe pri pravitel'stvuiushchem senate* (Omsk) No. 9, 15.vi.1919.

201 Sukin (*Leeds Russian Archive*), p. 104. The Ministry of Finance itself blamed its difficulties on a shortage of trained staff – see *Obozrenie deiatel'nosti Ministerstva finansov – vtoroi poloviny 1918g.* Omsk (1919), p. 12.

financial standing of the government and stabilizing the currency situation in Siberia; and secondly through a variety of efforts to increase foreign trade and to provide facilities and transportation for that trade.

Government poverty, the Imperial Gold Reserve and the failure of the Mikhailov monetary reform

The first step towards enticing workers back to work, persuading Siberia's farmers to part with their produce and facilitating the import of both the war materials and the manufactured goods it needed was identified by the Omsk government as the reform and resurrection of the financial system of Kolchakia. By 1918 a host of paper currencies were in circulation east of the Urals: thirty types were counted by British agents – including everything from Romanov roubles and Kerensky tokens, through notes produced by the Bolsheviks and Komuch to the (much coveted) label from a particular brand of cigarettes. Also in use was a wide variety of specie of ancient and modern mintage.[202] The confusion this engendered and the competition between these monies was clearly contributing to the paralysis of both foreign and domestic trade and, in order to find a solution to what was officially termed 'the single question of the internal life of Siberia which can in no way be avoided', a remarkable number of esteemed Russian economists were gathered at Omsk under the auspices of the Minister of Finance, Ivan Mikhailov. Among them were A.I. Putilov, V.P. Anichkov, V.I. Novitskii, P.P. Maslov and the former Minister of Finance of the tsarist government, V.N. Kokovtsev.[203]

The major obstacle which faced them in attempting to provide a solution, however, was the sheer poverty of the Omsk government. Although the Bolsheviks had been rapidly driven from Siberia during the summer of 1918, they had managed to take with them the majority of funds and precious metals which had been deposited in local branches of the State Bank: in all 167 poods of gold, 500 poods of silver and 917,000,000 roubles in currency had been removed by the fleeing

202 *DBFP*, p. 708.

203 R.N., p. 127.

soviet authorities.[204] Consequently, as of July 1st 1918, the newly established Provisional Siberian Government could boast of assets in currency of only 230,000,000 roubles.[205] This, of course, was at a time when government expenditure was beginning to rocket as the anti-Bolshevik régime took upon itself the upkeep of the Siberian Army and the railway system and the financial support of the region's industrial organizations and banks, many of which were on the point of collapse.

A number of measures were taken to try and boost the income of the government. From July 27th onwards, for example, a series of large increases were made in indirect taxes on items which the government itself admitted to be 'necessities': tea, tobacco, matches, yeast and vodka were among the goods affected. As a result of these measures it was calculated at the end of 1918 that since 1917 the taxes on tea and vodka had risen by 1,000% and on matches and yeast by 400%.[206] A second tactic involved the establishment of a government monopoly on the sales of sugar, wine and spirits and the hurriedly organized selling off of the 4,704,781 *vedros* of vodka currently held in government warehouses (said to be worth at least 750,000 roubles).[207] However, even according to its own figures (presented above as Table 4.11), in the second half of 1918 government revenue totalled a mere 20% of its expenditure.[208]

Obviously, in the prevailing circumstances of the war it would have been very difficult, if not absolutely impossible, for the Omsk government to balance its budget. Nevertheless, with spirits running high as a result of the military successes in the northern Urals during November and December 1918, considerable optimism

204 FO 371/4105/30740 'Memorandum by the Minister of Finance for the Russian Legation in London, February 1919'. Another government source puts the amount of currency evacuated by the Bolsheviks at 1,011,544,307.95 roubles. See *Obozrenie deiatel'nosti Ministerstva finansov*, pp. 4–5.

205 *Zaria* (Omsk) No. 24, 11.vii.1918. Later estimates put the Provisional Siberian Government's assets at 220,000,000 roubles. See FO 371/4105/30740 'Memorandum by the Minister of Finance'.

206 *Obozrenie deiatel'nosti Ministerstva finansov..*, pp. 23–5; Sokolov, N.G. 'Antinarodnaia sushchnost' nalogovoi politiki v derevne esero-men'shevistskogo pravitel'stva i kolchakovskogo rezhima v Sibiri (1918–1919gg.)', in *Neproletarskie partii i organizatsii natsional'nykh raionov Rossii v Oktiabr'skoi revoliutsii i grazhdanskoi voiny*. Moscow (1980), pp. 265–73.

207 *Zaria* (Omsk) No. 24, 11.vii.1918; *Pravitel'stvennyi vestnik* (Omsk) 6.ii.1919; *USMI*, Vol. 7, No. 95 (week ending 22.iii.1919), pp. 727–8; Voronov, D.N. 'Vinnaia monopoliia v Sibiri v 1919g.', *Vestnik finansov* (Moscow), No. 2 (1925), p. 141.

208 *Obozrenie deiatel'nosti Ministerstva finansov*, p. 37.

Table 4.11: Government revenue and expenditure (in millions of roubles), July–December 1918

	July	Aug.	Sept.	Oct.	Nov.	Dec.	Total
Taxes	0.53	1.03	1.89	3.56	6.68	8.89	22.58
Duties	0.40	0.55	1.53	1.88	1.35	2.26	7.97
Excise	1.87	1.45	3.94	3.86	7.14	7.26	25.52
Vodka	–	1.52	3.11	1.46	11.09	21.99	39.17
Railways	18.44	18.24	19.07	22.58	23.51	24.00	125.84
Customs	4.16	4.16	3.90	12.36	16.62	11.60	52.80
Income	25.40	27.56	32.44	50.51	66.39	76.01	278.31
Expenditure	124.28	156.58	122.88	174.24	156.33	619.74	1354.05
Balance	*−98.88*	*−129.02*	*−90.44*	*−123.73*	*−89.94*	*−543.73*	*−1075.74*

was evident in both public and private statements made by the Minister of Finance: as new territories were captured, as the government became more efficient in collecting taxes, as the populace became more dutiful in paying taxes and as more vodka was sold from 'limitless stocks', income would expand, predicted Mikhailov confidently; by early in the new year, 1919, he hoped it might even begin to approach the level of expenditure, which he forecast would level out at around 567,000,000 roubles per month (including 150,000,000 roubles per month on the army). The Minister's concluding rodomontade was that by the spring of 1919 the government would be self-sufficient with the exception of military expenditure.[209]

The financial future drawn by Mikhailov seemed very rosy. But it was not to be. The spring offensive of the Russian Army was an enormously expensive failure and, as the year wore on, far from extending its control over wider areas within Siberia, the government found itself denied the tax returns and other riches of ever greater swathes of the region by the spread of partisan activity. By July 1919 Mikhailov was being made to eat his words, admitting to an Omsk journalist that since May the government's monthly expenditure had actually topped the billión roubles mark (of which 700,000,000 roubles was swallowed up by the army alone).[210] Meanwhile,

209 *ibid.*, pp. 18, 42; *The Times* (London) 17.xii.1918; *Russkii soldat-grazhdanin vo Frantsii* (Paris) No. 324, 18.xii.1918.

210 Arnol'dov, p. 231.

Table 4.12: Government revenue (in roubles), Jan.–July 1919	
Vodka monopoly and excise	326,000,000
Railways	244,000,000
Customs	98,000,000
Post and Telegraph	59,000,000
Duties	41.000,000
Forestry revenues	19,000,000
Total Income	787,000,000

the official figures presented as Table 4.12 (above) inform us that government income for the entire first half of the year 1919 totalled only 787,000,000 roubles.[211] This was almost a threefold improvement on the previous six months, but could cover less than *one month's expenditure* at the current rates. Thus, far from approaching expenditure in 1919, as Mikhailov had predicted, income had actually fallen in relative terms to cover only about one-eighth of what was being spent. And from July 1919 onwards the situation could only get worse, for it was from that date that Kolchak's chief benefactors, the British and French governments, who had been supplying the Siberian forces with free armaments and other matériel, began to transfer the bulk of their aid to Denikin in South Russia.

Despite the poverty which is evident from his government's accounts, however, Kolchak was actually the custodian of an extremely valuable asset: in his possession was a large proportion of what remained of the Imperial Gold Reserve. This mighty store of treasure had come into the hands of the Supreme Ruler by a curious, roundabout route.

By 1914 Russia had amassed a gold reserve larger than that of any other state and amounting to a sum of 1,695,000,000 roubles.[212] During the World War considerable amounts of this stock had been shipped out of Russia via Vladivostok

211 Sack, A.J. 'The Finances of the All-Russian Government at Omsk', *Struggling Russia* (New York) Vol. 1, No. 30–2 (October 1919), p. 499.

212 In 1914 the gold reserve of the United Kingdom amounted to the equivalent of 800,000,000 gold roubles and that of France to 1,500,000,000 gold roubles. In 1914 the exchange value of the rouble was 1 rouble =2s 2½d = £0.11. In the course of the war it declined by approximately 10%, but all values cited here in relation to the gold reserve are those of 1914.

and Arkhangel′sk in order to service foreign loans and to pay off debts to those Allied states not disposed to grant credit to the Tsar. The Kerensky Government had exported yet more gold during 1917 to pay for its war orders.[213] Despite these expenditures, however, the new Soviet government could lay claim to reserves of 1,101,690,000 roubles in October 1917. Of this reserve, a portion (worth 120,799,000 roubles) was handed over to the Central Powers as an indemnity after Brest-Litovsk; and a further portion was stored in vaults at Moscow and Petrograd.[214] The bulk of the reserve, however, was concentrated at the Volga city of Kazan during the months of March to June 1918. This was intended as a safety measure – in case of further German encroachments from the west and in the light of Allied landings in North Russia during the spring of 1918 – but when the civil war ignited on the Volga and, on July 22nd, the neighbouring city of Simbirsk fell to Czechoslovak troops and forces of the People's Army, plans were hurriedly laid to transfer the gold on barges back up the Volga to Nizhnii Novgorod and thence via the River Oka to Moscow and Kolomna. On August 6th–7th, however, on the very eve of the planned evacuation, Kazan fell to the Komuch forces and little if any of the gold was saved.

The reserve now fell into the hands of Komuch and was temporarily stored at Ufa, where it became another of the many bones of contention between the SR government at Samara and the Provisional Siberian Government. At the Cheliabinsk Conferences of July and August 1918, Mikhailov demanded, on behalf of the Omsk government, that (purely for safety's sake, of course!) the reserve be transferred east to the Siberian capital. Komuch refused; and even the Directory was too suspicious of the intentions of Mikhailov (their own Minister of Finance) to move the gold further east than Cheliabinsk, as the Red Army approached Ufa during the summer of 1918. Nevertheless, by means which remain obscure, but which almost certainly involved the bribery of the units guarding the train on which the reserve was stored,

213 On these shipments of gold see Clarke, W. *The Lost Fortune of the Tsars*. London (1994), pp.176–81.

214 Novitskii, V. 'Russia's Gold Reserve' in *Russian Gold: A Collection of Articles and Newspaper Editorials Regarding the Russian Gold Reserve and Shipments of Soviet Gold*. New York (1928), pp. 11–15; 'The Russian Gold Reserve – What Became of It?', *The Economist* (London) Vol. 50, No. 4 (30.v.1925). Further detail on these transactions and on the fate of the gold reserve in general may be found in Smele, J.D. 'White Gold: The Imperial Russian Gold Reserve in the Anti-Bolshevik East, 1918–? (An Unconcluded Chapter in the History of the Russian Civil War)', *Europe–Asia Studies* Vol. 46 (1994), No. 8, pp. 1317–47.

Table 4.13: Contents and value (in roubles) of the portion of the Imperial Russian Gold Reserve captured from the Bolsheviks at Kazan, August 1918

Gold bullion, Russian and foreign coinage	651,535,834.64
17 packets of gold from laboratories	486,598.00
514 cases of gold and platinum objects	453,811,000.00
Silver ingots	58,497.25
Silver coinage	11,185,830.90
Copper coinage	3,009.18
7 packets of objects from Kursk	270,000.00
Bank notes and Treasury bonds	100,000,000.00

Mikhailov had the gold shipped by rail to Omsk during late September 1918.[215] Thereafter, according to official figures, passed into the hands of the Directory, and ultimately of Kolchak, the amounts of gold and other treasures detailed above as Table 4.13.[216]

215 According to one contemporary account, Mikhailov had the gold moved to Omsk 'on his own initiative...without bothering to ask anyone's permission'. See *The Russian Outlook* (London) Vol. 1, No. 14 (9.viii.1919), p. 332. It appears that the Komuch inspectors who had accompanied the gold train to Cheliabinsk had rather unwisely left the station to find safer storehouses for the treasure; having selected for that purpose some grain elevators and the vaults of the local branch of the State Bank, they returned to find that the gold train had departed for the east without them. Novitskii, pp. 18–19; Gan, A. *Rossia i bol'shevizmom: materialy po istorii revoliutsii i bor'by s bol'shevizm (Chast' pervaia, 1914–1920)*. Shanghai (1921), pp. 256–7. This was quite possibly the largest gold heist in history.

216 *The Russian Outlook* (London) Vol. 1, No. 14 (9.viii.1919), p. 332; 'Les quantités d'or sauvées des mains Bolchévikes', *Union (Bureau de Presse Russe)* (Paris) No. 11, 27.viii.1919. Whether the entire amount of the gold which had been stored by the Bolsheviks at Kazan arrived safely at Omsk is a matter of some debate. Mikhailov himself, in an official report filed as late as December 1919, suggested that some millions might have gone astray during the transfer of the reserve from Kazan via Ufa to Omsk (see *Iz istorii grazhdanskoi voiny v SSSR*, Vol. 4, p. 299). Other White sources maintain, however, that the Bolsheviks managed to evacuate some 100 cases of gold (worth 6,000,000 roubles) before the fall of Kazan (see Sack, pp. 256–7), while Soviet sources claim that no gold was evacuated, that 657 million roubles worth were captured at Kazan and that if only 651 millions arrived at Omsk then 6 million must have been expended by Komuch – see *Revoliutsiia 1917–1919gg. v Samarskoi gubernii: khronika sobytii*. Samara (1929), Vol. 2, p. 162 and Kladt, A.P. and Kondrat'ev, V.A. '"Zolotoi eshelon" (vozvrashchenie zolotogo zaloga RSFSR mart–mai 1920g.)', *Istoricheskii arkhiv* (Moscow) 1961, No. 1, pp. 20–1. Perhaps the most credible explanation, however, is provided by a Czech witness to the capture of Kazan: Jan Kudela argued that although Soviet records captured with the reserve at Kazan and initially

Kolchak, then, was actually in possession of a veritable fortune – and one which, it should not be forgotten, Siberia's many gold, silver and platinum mines were constantly augmenting.[217] Foreign Minister Sukin recalled that in 1919 advice was pouring into his office from around the world to the effect that the Supreme Ruler should 'realize' his assets for the benefit of the entire anti-Bolshevik movement. For the first six months of his rule, however – those crucial six months in which the Siberian White government was established and the Russian Army's offensive was planned and (unsuccessfully) executed – Kolchak adamantly refused to touch the gold reserve. White sources maintain that the Supreme Ruler was 'instinctively' against expending the nation's gold, that he was adopting the principled stance that the Omsk government, as a provisional government, had no mandate to diminish 'the patrimony of the people', and that the reserve had to be maintained intact for the benefit of the future, regenerated Russian state.[218] It must surely have been the case, however, that this principle was intimately connected with the Whites' overbearing self-confidence and a belief that it was simply not *necessary* to make use of the reserve in order to defeat the 'German-Bolsheviks'. For, as we shall see, from May 1919 onwards, when the Russian Army was in retreat and Moscow no longer seemed to be within the grasp of the Russian Army, principles were ignominiously divested of and much of the reserve *was* expended.

publicized by the Komuch commander Colonel V.I. Lebedev indicated that the treasure consisted of gold to the value of 657 million roubles, this figure was incorrect and that only 651,535,834 roubles' worth was, in fact, captured (see Kudela, J. *O russkem zlatem poklade a ceskoslovenskych legiich*. Prague (1922), p. 10). Lebedev himself left a fascinating account of the capture of Kazan – see Lebedev, V.I. *The Russian Democracy*. New York (1919), pp. 21–30 – but is imprecise on the amount of gold in the town.

217 Sukin (*Leeds Russian Archive*), p. 10. The Ministry of Finance recorded receipts of 203 poods of gold and 33 poods of platinum in 1919 – see *Bulletin of the Russian Liberation Committee (Union)* (London) No. 36, 25.x.1919. But a later survey has it that 399 poods of gold were extracted from mines in Western and Eastern Siberia and the Urals in only the first half of that year (compared to 1,268.6 poods extracted in 1918 and 4,056.2 poods extracted in 1914) – see Shmotin, V.P. 'Gold Mining in Russia', *Russkii Dal'nyi Vostok* (Tokyo), No. 1 (October 1920).

218 Sukin (*Leeds Russian Archive*), pp. 10–11; Guins, *Sibir'*, Vol. 2, pp. 118, 585. And, as contemporary analysts pointed out, the treasure may actually have been worth even more than the figures suggest: since the value of the reserve had last been calculated the official price of gold had risen from 4.5 roubles per *zolotnik* (1 *zolotnik* = 0.15 ounces) to 50 roubles per *zolotnik* (while prices of 100–120 roubles per *zolotnik* were common on the black market); thus the 651,535,834.84 roubles of gold bullion held by Kolchak might actually have been worth as much as 16.5 billion roubles to the Whites. See *Bulletin of the Russian Liberation Committee (Union)* (London) No. 27, 25.viii,1919.

For the meantime, however, whatever the rights and wrongs of using the gold reserve, Kolchak was strongly advised by the caucus of economists he had gathered at Omsk that the financial situation in Siberia was far too unstable to consider utilizing the reserve as a guarantee for a new currency issue.[219] Consequently, in a desperate attempt to meet runaway expenditures, as well as to expedite what was becoming a partial currency famine in Siberia as peasants and merchants began to hoard the more respected of the region's bank notes, the successive governments at Omsk had to resort to the printing and circulation of ever increasing amounts of paper tokens.

The Provisional Siberian Government, from the very first days of its existence, tried to satisfy currency hunger by issuing state bonds (in imitation of the Imperial Government's 5% interest-bearing notes), interest loan bonds and various other devices. When its presses' capacity to supply such notes proved insufficient to meet demand, Omsk began to legalize currency substitutes previously issued on the territories of Komuch, the Orenburg Cossack Government, the Urals *oblast'* Government and even the former Soviet authorities of Transbaikal and the Far East. However, as these measures failed even to meet the mushrooming requirements of the Treasury itself, let alone those of the population at large, eventually, under the stewardship of Mikhailov, the Ministry of Finance declared itself to be compelled to adopt the course of issuing its own currency.[220] In December 1918 Mikhailov was still maintaining that the touchstone of his financial policy was one of 'abstinence from introducing new bank notes into circulation'. But he had to admit that for the time being there was simply 'no other way out'.[221] By January 1st 1919, 730,000,000 roubles of the new notes had been issued; and, in total, the Provisional Siberian Government and the Kolchak government together may have put into circulation by the end of 1919 some 15,000,000,000 roubles' worth of what were variously known as the Omsk, Kolchak or Siberian Roubles, 'yellow money' or, familiarly, *sibirki*.[222] As the presses rolled day in and day out at Omsk, in the

219 R.N., pp. 133–4.

220 Pogrebetskii, A.I. 'Currency Difficulties under the Kolchak Government' (*Hoover Institution Archives*), p. 1.

221 *Obozrenie deiatel'nosti Ministerstva finansov*, pp. 32, 44.

222 *ibid.*, pp. 32, 44; *USMI*, Vol. 7, No. 92 (week ending 1.iii.1919), pp. 633–5. On White currency issues see also Nikolaev, R. *Dengi beloi gvardii*. St Petersburg (1993).

words of a contemporary economist, 'the value of the Siberian Rouble inflated and multiplied until it approached the point at which begins complete nullification'.[223]

This dénouement must surely have been foreseen, even by such a ministerial novice as Mikhailov. As the brainchild of a government which was not recognized and had no available gold backing, the *sibirki* could hope at best to replace some other token as the *least* respected of Siberia's multifarious currencies. This was made immediately clear when the major Russian and foreign banks in the Far East announced that they would not accept transactions or deposits in Siberian Roubles, as only the State Bank had the right to issue new currency.[224] Eventually pressure from Omsk and the Allied governments persuaded some of the smaller banks (such as the Bank of Canada and the Bank of Korea) to recognize the *sibirki* in principle, although this did not prevent their Russian branches from ignoring (or at best discounting) the notes in practice.[225] The most important of the region's banks, however, including the Hong Kong and Shanghai Bank, remained unmoved.[226] Mikhailov attempted to bring the banking community round by arguing that the new issue was not of bank notes *per se*, but of 5% interest-bearing Treasury Bonds of low denomination guaranteed by the stock of higher denomination Imperial Treasury Bonds which Kolchak had acquired along with the gold reserve. Therefore, vouched the minister, he was not increasing the national debt by making the issue, but simply replacing one set of bonds by another.[227] But, unsurprisingly, neither the bankers nor the public at large were convinced. Clearly any unrecognized authority issuing paper currency guaranteed only by more paper would have had to enjoy an extraordinary level of public confidence if it was to be successful; in a region where governmental leapfrog had become the norm in 1918, Mikhailov's efforts were foredoomed to failure. Moreover, as the bankers pointed out, the expiry date of the

223 Pogrebetskii, *Denezhnoe obrashchenie i denezhnye znaki*, p. 10.

224 FO 371/3366/173851 'Alston (Vladivostok) to FO, 6.x.1918'; FO 371/3366/213523 'Alston (Vladivostok) to FO, 29.xii.1919'; Pogrebetskii (*Hoover Institution Archives*), p. 5.

225 FO 371/4104/20923 'Alston (Vladivostok) to FO, 4.ii.1919'.

226 This was particularly galling for the Kolchak Government because it was only through the special dispensation of the Ministry of Finance that the Hong Kong and Shanghai Bank had been permitted to open a branch at Vladivostok in 1919. FO 371/4104/177983 'Lampson (Irkutsk) to FO, 5.xii.1919'.

227 FO 371/4104/30740 'Finances of the All-Russian Government at Omsk (Memorandum by Mr Mikhailov for the Russian Delegation in London, February 1919)'.

Imperial Treasury Bonds held at Omsk had been passed and they could consequently be regarded as dishonoured bills.[228]

Quite apart from their rather dubious legality, the *sibirki* issues were frowned upon both by banks and by the general public because of their appalling technical qualities. According to Guins, the government had too few printing presses, too little paper and an insufficient supply of skilled artists and technicians to be able to produce a high quality and standardized issue. As a result, one batch of notes was rarely the same size or colour as the last; the issuing body was sometimes cited as the 'State Treasury Section (*otdel*)' when it should have read 'State Treasury Department (*vedomstvo*)'; and there were even occasions when spelling mistakes appeared on the Omsk notes.[229] The experience of one visitor to the White capital was typical:

> You might calculate on having five or ten per cent of your money returned with the remark that it was counterfeit. But no-one seemed in the least bit perturbed, for the following day the bank would accept these and return others which they now characterized as bad, and so on ad infinitum.

And it comes as no surprise to learn that on one famously embarrassing occasion for the government, the State Bank at Omsk refused to accept a consignment of Siberian Roubles which had arrived hot off the Treasury presses for fear that they were forgeries.[230] All in all, the dirty, easily torn and crudely fashioned bills were not of a standard to inspire confidence in either themselves or the issuing body.

Particular difficulties were experienced in trying to introduce the *sibirki* into the Far East, into the busy commercial centres of Vladivostok and Harbin, where over 50% of government business was transacted and the vast majority of the entire region's trade took place. Here two further obstacles were added to the problems of the legitimacy and technical quality of the new issue. The first was that in the Far East the Kolchak currency faced a particularly tenacious competitor – the Japanese

228 FO 371/4113/166666 'Memorandum Prepared by Mr Novitskii, Assistant Minister of Finance, on the Monetary Reform for Siberia, 17.x.1919'.

229 Guins, Vol. 2, pp. 118, 404–7.

230 Archer, W.J. 'Money Difficulties in Siberia', *The Russian Outlook* (London), Vol. 2 (1919), No. 28, pp. 660–1; Krol', L. *Za tri goda*, pp. 185–6. Because the Siberian notes were neither numbered nor signed they were, indeed, very easy to forge. See FO 371/4113/118927 'Memorandum on the Currency Situation in Harbin, 20.vi.1919, by H.E. Sly'.

yen. Pursuing its aim of securing economic control of Manchuria and the Russian Far East, the Japanese Expeditionary Force was circulating its own yen (known as Headquarters Notes) in Primorskii *krai* and along the Chinese Eastern Railway zone. Japanese merchants, who arrived in the train of their army, received instructions to accept only payments made in yen, while Japanese agents in the area promised railway workers that they would receive goods at low prices if they appealed to their bosses to be paid in yen. According to American intelligence sources, these tactics were successful and even by the autumn of 1918 the yen was threatening to 'rule the Rouble out of the field in Eastern Siberia'.[231]

The second obstacle encountered by the *sibirki* in the Far East was speculation. Taking advantage of the confused financial situation during the civil war and the incessant panicky runs on this or that variety of currency, almost everybody speculated. British Foreign Office and official Russian accounts tend to lay the charge of speculation at the feet of the region's Chinese merchants alone. They, however, were only the most conspicuous transgressors: the truth was that all sections of the population engaged daily in more or less shady currency deals. According to one of their number, for example, all of the officers in the British Mission at Vladivostok bought and sold roubles in the hope of making a killing.[232] The activities of the Chinese, however, who dominated the wholesale and retail trade of the Far East, was undoubtedly the most damaging to the Siberian currency. Chinese traders had taken to only accepting in their shops any variety of rouble for which there happened to be a particular demand at a given time. They would then withdraw the currency from circulation, pushing up its value by adding to its scarcity, in order to sell it later at a premium.[233] The currency they most contemned was generally the one most recently introduced, and in 1918 to 1919 it was the *sibirki* which fell into that category.[234] As a consequence, the purchasing power of the *sibirki* diminished rapidly to the point where even its architect, Mikhailov, had to acknowledge that it was valued and respected 'less than any other

231 Svetachev, *Imperialisticheskaia interventsiia*, p. 137 (n, 104); *USMI*, Vol. 4 (week ending 26.x.1918), p. 70.

232 Savory, R. 'Letter from Vladivostok, 1.vi.1919' (*Savory Papers*, NAM 7603/93/23)

233 FO 371/4113/1666666 'Memorandum by Mr Novitskii'.

234 Savory, R. 'Letter from Vladivostok, 10.vii.1919' (*Savory Papers*, NAM 7603/93/23); Sukin (*Leeds Russian Archive*), p. 95.

kind of monetary note circulating on Russian territory'.[235] An incident reported in the Far Eastern press during July 1919 gives some idea of just how low was the regard in which the *sibirki* were held: when a Russian attempted to pay a Harbin rickshaw-puller with Omsk money which he had only just withdrawn from the bank, the Chinese was so insulted that he not only refused point blank to accept the notes but physically attacked his passenger as a cheat; the police were called...and duly arrested the Russian.[236]

Equally deleterious to the financial well-being of the Kolchak government was the fact that custom and fear had combined to determine that, while the *sibirki* were the least respected, the *most* cherished currencies in Siberia and the Far East were those notes issued by the last recognized Russian governments. Romanov notes were the most treasured (in denominations of 1, 3, 5, 10, and 25 roubles), but had virtually disappeared from circulation to be hoarded by thrifty Russian peasants and Chinese speculators. Next in line were the Kerensky Roubles – the so-called *kerenki* or 'green money' – issued by the Provisional Government of 1917 in denominations of 20 and 40 roubles (in the form of large sheets to be cut up into individual notes by the user). As the smaller denominations of the Romanov notes gradually disappeared in 1917 to 1918, the *kerenki* had become the chief means of everyday trade throughout the region. However, once that the disrespected *sibirki* came to be widely introduced, in accordance with Gresham's Law, the more respected *kerenki* acquired a sort of crumenal kudos and they too began to be withdrawn and hoarded.[237]

As the Omsk notes were predominantly of larger denomination, however, the situation arrived at was not only one in which the central government's currency was discounted against others, but one in which Siberia was left with a crippling shortage of small change for everyday transactions. Shops and restaurants tried to oil the wheels of commerce by offering their own promissory notes and markers as change to their customers – 'no one minded: they were just as good as the rest', recalled an Englishwomen who had produced the notes issued by her father's iron-

235 FO 371/4113/1666666 'Memorandum by Mr Novitskii'.

236 *Peking and Tientsin Times* (Peking) 12.vii.1919. During September 1919, peasants of Tobol'sk *guberniia* even refused to accept Omsk roubles in exchange for goods from the steamer of Kolchak himself, as the Supreme Ruler sailed up the Irtysh towards the front. See Guins, Vol. 2, p. 364.

237 FO 371/4113/111356 'Memorandum on the Currency Situation in Harbin on and about May 22nd 1919, by H.M. Commercial High Commissioner to Siberia, Mr W.J. Hinton'.

mongers' shop at Krasnoiarsk.[238] This, however, gave little respite to the tens of thousands of workers along the Trans-Siberian and Chinese Eastern Railways who were being paid by the government's railway administration in Omsk roubles of large denomination. A group of ten workers, for example, might receive a 5,000 rouble note as their wages. This would cause 'rage against the government and the owners', observers reported, for such was the disregard in which the *sibirki* were held, and such was the premium on notes of small denomination, that the Kolchak currency could command only about 60% of the purchasing power of the 20- and 40-rouble denomination *kerenki* by May 1919 – the point at which workers on the Chinese Eastern Railway went on strike demanding a 40% supplement to their wages when paid in *sibirki* to compensate for the surcharge they had to pay the Chinese for purchases made in that currency.[239]

As if this situation was not bad enough, the Omsk government had also to face the problem that the *kerenki* tokens which were so coveted among the population were a currency over which its Treasury had no control. Firstly, the *kerenki* (like the *sibirki*) were not true bank notes but government tokens and were, consequently, both unnumbered and unsigned. As such they were extremely simple to forge, and often were – untold millions of *kerenki*, indistinguishable from the real thing, poured into Siberia from China and the other limitrophe states of the Far East.[240] Secondly, and even more injurious to the finances of Kolchakia, was that the original plates for producing authentic *kerenki* had been seized by the Bolsheviks in October 1917. Billions of roubles' worth of the notes had been produced in Soviet Russia since that date – so many, in fact, that they threatened to swamp the Siberian financial system if it was ever fully exposed to them. Sufficient *kerenki* had been smuggled across the Urals by Bolshevik agents during late 1918 to cause concern; but what was most worrying was the thought of what would happen if Kolchak's army continued to advance into the Volga region and on into central Russia, as it began to do in March and April of 1919. A British observer noted that the

238 Savory, R. 'Vladivostok, 1919–1920' (*Savory Papers*, NAM 7603/93/26), p. 156; Stanford, D. *Sun and Snow: a Siberian Adventure*. London (1963), p. 111.

239 *Sibirskaia zhizn'* (Tomsk) No. 193, 10.v.1919; FO 371/4113/111356 'Memorandum on the Currency Situation in Harbin on and about May 22nd 1919, by H.M. Commercial Consul to Siberia, Mr W.J. Hinton'; *USMI*, Vol. 7, No. 92 (week ending 1.iii.1919), p. 635 and Vol. 7, No. 93 (week ending 8.iii.1919), p. 662.

240 Greener, F.W 'Paper Money in Siberia', *The Russian Outlook* (London), Vol. 1, No. 10 (12.viii.1919), p. 234.

population of the Volga region held many more *kerenki* per head than did the population of Siberia where the tokens were at a premium. Thus, he reported, 'every advance of the front throws more of this money into Siberian circulation, disorganizing exchange and drawing much needed goods out of Siberia'.[241] The businessmen of Western Siberia were particularly alive to this unwelcome by-product of military success and in March–April of 1919 they besieged the Ministry of Finance at Omsk demanding that something be done before the further influx of *kerenki* should ruin them.[242] And such petitions were not without effect: it was in the light of the mixture of celebration and concern occasioned by the Russian Army's successful commencement of the spring offensive, that in April 1919 Mikhailov decided that something would, indeed, have to be done.[243]

Superficially, a solution seemed simple enough. The flood of Bolshevik-produced currency which was undermining commerce in Western Siberia was the same as that which in the Far East was undermining the value of the *sibirki*. All that needed to be done, therefore, was for the government to declare the troublesome *kerenki* no longer to be legal tender, to call them in to the banks and replace them once and for all with the *sibirki*, as the first step towards making the Omsk currency the sole medium of exchange east of the Urals (and in all of Russia once that the Bolsheviks were defeated). And, on April 18th 1919, that is precisely what the Minister of Finance did. Mikhailov announced that between May 15th and June 15th 1919 all 20- and 40-rouble *kerenki* tokens should be handed in at authorized agencies. In return the depositor would receive a government receipt which could then be presented at branches of the State Bank at any time up to January 1st 1920. Presenters of such receipts would be granted half the face value of their *kerenki* in new Omsk roubles and the other half in the form of a twenty-year interest-bearing Government Bond (realizable after July 1st 1920). Less favourable terms were

241 FO 371/4112/61989 'Robertson (Vladivostok) to FO, 18.iv.1919 (Summary of a Report on the Financial Situation in Siberia by Mr Hinton)'.

242 *Velikaia Rossiia* (Ufa) No. 15, 6.iv.1919.

243 Mel'gunov, S.P. *Tragediia admirala Kolchaka (iz istorii grazhdanskoi voiny na Volge, Urale i v Sibiri)*. Belgrade (1930–1931), Part 3, Vol. 1, p. 251.

offered for *kerenki* surrendered between June 15th and July 15th 1919, whilst after the latter date the tokens would no longer be legal tender.[244]

In a perfect world Mikhailov's currency reform would have queered the pitch of the speculators in the Far East whilst at the same time achieving the government's dual aims in financial policy of unifying the currencies of Siberia and of severing the region from the monetary system of Soviet Russia. Whatever the Arcadian dreams of the authorities at Omsk at the height of Russian Army's military success, however, Kolchak's Siberia was far from being a perfect world. It has to be said that in a sense what ensued was not directly attributable to Mikhailov or to any shortcomings in the details of his reform – in fact, Allied financial experts were united at the time in declaring the withdrawal of the *kerenki* to be 'necessary and wise' for any government intent upon regenerating the Siberian and Russian economies.[245] On the other hand, there were a number of unavoidable corollaries of the reform which the Minister of Finance should have foreseen and should have taken steps to mitigate.

Beyond the Minister of Finance's control was the fate of Kolchak's spring offensive. Had he known on April 18th that within a fortnight the Western Army, the spearhead of the White advance, was to be smashed by the counter-attack of the 5th Red Army, Mikhailov would certainly not have embarked upon such a revolutionary currency reform. Had he even been made aware of the possibility of a slowing of the advance, he might have postponed the introduction of his reform. But, under the influence of the usual misleadingly optimistic reports from the front, on April 18th Mikhailov was still under the impression that, in the words of his decree, 'the hour is at hand when from the mighty blow of the Russian Army, the Soviet government will be shattered like a stone under a hammer'.[246] Thus, a measure which depended for its success upon popular faith in the Kolchak government was introduced at precisely the worst moment possible – on the eve of a series of crushing military defeats and the consequent dashing of hopes of

244 *Vpered* (Omsk) No. 50, 25.iv.1919; *The Russian/Russkii Zhurnal* (London), Vol. 1, No. 34 (5.vi.1919); FO 371/4112/68519 'United States Consul (Omsk) to United States Consul (Vladivostok), 22.iv.1919'.

245 FO 371/4113/118927 'Minutes of the Meeting of the British Chamber of Commerce (Harbin), 12.vi.1919'.

246 *Vpered* (Omsk) No. 50, 25.iv.1919.

international recognition which, together, were finally to subvert any potential popular confidence in the Kolchak régime.[247]

Initially the Minister of Finance put a brave face on things. In April and May he talked to the press of a definite 're-stabilization of the country's finances', of 'an end to the downward course of the rouble in the Far East,' and would boast of the *sibirki* being in use 'from the Urals to the Pacific' and of 'fully favourable results' for his reform.[248] However, although a certain number of *kerenki* were being exchanged in April and May (some 233,059,000 roubles by May 8th) it was only a fraction of the number in circulation; and as the Russian Army retreated and Kolchak's stock fell, fewer people were willing to take the risk of making the exchange, for nobody wanted to be in possession of White currency when the Reds arrived. Meanwhile, in the money markets and in the shops of Siberia and the Far East, the *kerenki* remained far more respected and valued than Mikhailov's ailing *sibirki* – despite the threat of 3,000-rouble fines being levied by local military authorities against traders who refused to accept or who discounted the Omsk money.[249]

Also of major concern to Mikhailov was that immediately following his announcement of the withdrawal of the 20- and 40-rouble *kerenki*, rumours began circulating that the next form of currency to be withdrawn would be the 250- and 1,000-rouble *kerenki* notes. Such canards were deliberately fuelled by Chinese speculators (who, as we have seen, had an interest in augmenting the premium on small notes vis-à-vis the large).[250] As a result the value of the large notes vis-à-vis the small was further discounted, while the value of the rouble as a whole began to plummet because by 1919 the 250- and 1,000-rouble *kerenki* were the only Russian notes exchangeable for foreign currencies and imported goods in the markets of the Far East.[251] Subsequently, the rouble fell to rock bottom against the yen.

247 Pogrebetskii (*Hoover Institution Archives*), p. 4.

248 *Svobodnaia Sibir'* (Krasnoiarsk) No. 93, 4.v.1919; *Eniseiskii vestnik* (Eniseisk) No. 84, 20.v.1919; Arnol'dev, p. 230.

249 *Nasha zaria* (Omsk) No. 104, 17.v.1919; *Report of the CEC*, p. 59; 'Siberian Money', *The Russian Outlook* (London), Vol. 1, No. 14 (9.viii.1919), p. 333.

250 FO 371/4113/111356 'Memorandum...by Mr Hinton'; FO 371/4113/118927 'Jordan (Peking) to FO (Memorandum on the Currency Situation in Harbin on June 12th 1919, by Mr H.E. Sly), 28.vi.1919'.

251 FO 371/4113/118927 'Memorandum...by Mr H.E. Sly, 20.vi.1919'.

Table 4.14: Rate of exchange (roubles for 1.0 yen) at Harbin, 1919

Minimum Rate		Maximun Rate		Monthly Average
31st May	13.0	17th May	18.0	15.5
2nd June	12.5	30th June	18.8	15.6
2nd July	17.0	31st July	38.0	27.5
11th August	35.0	30th August	40.0	37.5
1st September	40.0	29th September	65.0	52.5
3rd October	58.0	31st October	90.0	74.0
15th November	191.0	19th November	180.0	185.5
24th December	120.0	18th December	168.0	144.0

Immediately prior to the Mikhailov reform the rate of exchange of the yen in the Far East had been fixed at 9.90 roubles; its upward spiral thereafter is traced above in Table 4.14.[252]

Various other points were made at the time by critics of the Mikhailov reform, concerning consequences that the Minister of Finance should have foreseen. It was pointed out, for example, that in their current, crude form the *sibirki* were actually even simpler to forge than were the *kerenki*.[253] Businessmen complained that the period of the worst disruption following the reform coincided with the busiest trading period in the Far East, as frozen rivers became open to traffic.[254] Others added that, although it was reasonable enough for the government to end dealings in an unregulated currency which was being produced by their enemies, the

252 *ibid.*, p. 29; Pogrebetskii (*Hoover Institution Archives*), p. 3. Pogrebetskii (a member of the Political Centre – see below, p. 573 and Chapter 6 *passim*) ascribed the sudden improvement in the fortunes of the rouble in December 1919, at the very nadir of the Kolchak administration's fortunes, as reflecting the popular hopes that a new government capable of consolidating Eastern Siberia and Transbaikalia was about to replace the White dictatorship. This was only a temporary phenomenon, however. In general the Siberian rouble continued to decline in value until its annulment by the Zemstvo Government of the Maritime Provinces (it had long since been annulled in Soviet Siberia) on June 5th 1920, by which time the exchange rate was 2,500 roubles = 1 yen. See Pogrebetskii (*Hoover Institution Archives*), pp. 6–7.

253 FO 371/4113/118927 'Memorandum...by Mr H.E. Sly, 20.vi.1919'.

254 'Siberian Money', *The Russian Outlook* (London), Vol. 1, No. 4 (9.viii.1919), p. 333.

corollary was that Kolchak had effectively cut himself off from the populations of Red-held areas both within and without Siberia who had no opportunity to exchange their *kerenki* for *sibirki* and who now were provided with one more economic incentive for supporting the Bolsheviks.[255] Still others voiced the fear, and not without reason, that in declaring Siberia's prime medium of exchange to be invalid, the government might cause the peasantry finally to lose faith in paper money in general – a development which would greatly impede the resurrection of domestic trade and normal economic life.[256]

The major criticism to be made of Mikhailov's reform, however, was that, for all its printing of money, by mid-1919 the Omsk Treasury had simply not produced sufficient notes to fill the vacuum left by the sudden withdrawal of the *kerenki* tokens. There was only one paper mill at work in all Kolchakia (in the Urals) and even though its output was monopolized by the Ministry of Finance, Mikhailov had only been able to supply 1,500,000,000 roubles in *sibirki* by May 1919. There were estimated to be at least 70,000,000,000 roubles of 20- and 40-rouble *kerenki* tokens in circulation in Russia as a whole; what proportion of these were to be found in Siberia is unknown, but it was certain to exceed the 2.1% of that total covered by Mikhailov's *sibirki*.[257] Moreover, the *sibirki* being produced were generally in large denominations (in an attempt to maximize the utility of the region's meagre paper resources) resulting in a further shortage of notes of small denomination for everyday use.

Thus, what had been a currency shortage was soon transformed into a currency famine by the attempt to withdraw the *kerenki*. Immediately, from the vital markets of the Far East, at Harbin and Vladivostok, came reports of a 'chaotic situation',

255 *Ekho* (Vladivostok) No. 38, 16.iv.1919; Krol', L. *Za tri goda*, p. 186.

256 Guins, Vol. 2, p. 162. In Mikhailov's defence it must be said that he was aware of the need for a vigorous propaganda and information programme in the countryside if his reform was to succeed – see his remarks in *Svobodnii krai* (Krasnoiarsk) No. 93 (499), 4.v.1919. But only the feeblest propaganda campaign was actually undertaken and at least one witness attests to the utter confusion which reigned in the villages away from the railway as to what currency was valid and what was not: 'When is all of this going to stop', pleaded one baffled *muzhik* to a White officer. See Fedotoff-White, D. *Survival Through War and Revolution in Russia*. Philadelphia (1939), p. 309.

257 *Report of the CEC*, p. 56.

with all trade 'at a complete standstill'.[258] A number of increasingly desperate measures had to be resorted to in an attempt to alleviate the crisis. Firstly, notes and tokens which had been printed by various local authorities in the Far East had again to be declared legal tender by the Omsk government.[259] Then the State Bank was instructed by the Ministry of Finance to 'view with indulgence' any counterfeit *sibirki* it might identify, 'so long as their technical characteristics...do not deviate too greatly from the authentic ones'.[260] Finally, when a Japanese citizen was apprehended trying to smuggle two million roubles' worth of counterfeit *sibirki* into Vladivostok, the government ordered that his high quality forgeries be put into circulation![261] Such panicky and piecemeal efforts as these, however, could never have filled the vacuum which would have been left by the withdrawal of the *kerenki* tokens.

Mikhailov's currency reform seems, therefore, to have been extremely precipitate and badly planned. On the eve of its implementation, however, he had vehemently denied that he was acting rashly. In response to warnings from business circles and from government colleagues that there would be insufficient *sibirki* available to meet demand, the Minister of Finance announced that a colossal amount of bank notes would shortly be arriving from the USA and that their delivery would more than compensate for the shortfall of notes being produced by the Omsk Treasury. In fact, Mikhailov claimed that his reform was only proceeding at all at that time because of the certain and imminent arrival of the notes from America.[262] At best, however, the minister's claims must be dismissed as short-sighted and over-optimistic; at worst, the whole enterprise was, as one contemporary commentator put

258 FO 371/4113/118927 'Memorandum...by Mr H.E. Sly, 20.vi.1919'; FO 371/4112/68836 'Robertson (Vladivostok) to FO, 29.iv.1919'; *Report of the CEC*, p. 56.

259 Pogrebetskii, *Denezhnoe obrashchenie i denezhnye znaki*, p. 253. By the autumn of 1919 virtually every type of note which had previously been cancelled was put back into circulation by the Ministry of Finance. See Flerov, V.S. 'Iz istorii denezhnogo obrashcheniia v Sibiri perioda inostrannoi interventsii i grazhdanskoi voiny', *Trudy Tomskogo oblastnogo kraevedcheskogo muzeia* (Tomsk), Vol. 6, Part 2 (1963), pp. 13–16.

260 Pogrebetskii (*Hoover Institution Archives*), p. 3.

261 Pogrebetskii, *Denezhnoe obrashchenie i denezhnye znaki*, p. 9; Hodges, B. *Britmis: A Great Adventure of the War*. London (1931), p. 59.

262 Guins, Vol. 2, pp. 118, 162.

it, 'a bungle'.[263] For, in truth, no casual observer, let alone a fully-briefed and responsible government minister, could be forgiven for believing that the arrival of the American notes was at all imminent. The notes had, in fact, been the subject of a prolonged diplomatic wrangle which was far from being resolved in April 1919.

The saga of the American roubles

Early in 1917 the United States National Bank Corporation of New York had been commissioned by the Provisional Government to produce bank notes to the value of 3,900,000,000 roubles in denominations of 25 and 100 roubles. The notes were duly printed, but following the October Revolution they remained in storage in New York. In late 1918 the Russian ambassador to Washington, B.A. Bakhmet′ev, was instructed to press for their release to the Kolchak government; and spirits were raised in cash-hungry Siberia when the ambassador reported that about a third of the notes (1,425,000,000 roubles) were to be shipped across the Pacific during November.[264]

Bakhmet′ev, however, was conveying a false impression to Omsk. President Wilson might have allowed the notes to be shipped across the Pacific, but he had in no way agreed to their release. In December 1918, Acting Secretary of State Polk made it very clear to Omsk that the ambassador had jumped the gun and that the notes were not going to be handed over to Kolchak's representatives at Vladivostok. Rather, the notes were to be held in escrow until all of the Allies had agreed that it was proper that they should be released.[265] The major obstacles to their release, from the American point of view, were: firstly, that the Kolchak government, being unrecognized, was not legally entitled to act in the name of the Russian State Bank which was cited as the issuing body on the notes; and secondly that Washington did not wish to be party to any issue of currency which had 'no legal or actual basis'

263 'Siberian Money', *The Russian Outlook* (London), Vol. 1, No. 14 (9.viii.1919), p. 333.

264 FO 371/3360/078509 'Alston (Vladivostok) to FO, 25.x.1918'; FO 371/3366/210037 'Barclay (Washington) to FO, 21.xii.1919'; FO 371/3366/210051 'Barclay (Washington) to FO, 21.xii.1919'. On Bakhmet′ev's persist efforts to encourage President Wilson to assist the Kolchak government see: Killen, L. 'The Search for a Democratic Russia: Bakhmetev and the United States', *Diplomatic History* Vol. 2 (1978), pp. 237–356.

265 *FRUS: 1918*, Vol. 3, pp. 96–8.

in gold.[266] The pleadings of Omsk, via Bakhmet′ev, continued into the New Year, but to no avail. In fact, to add insult to injury, in January 1919 even those notes which had arrived in Vladivostok were shipped on to Manila for safekeeping, whilst an order was issued by the president forestalling the transfer of more of the notes from New York to San Francisco.[267]

Mikhailov could not honestly have claimed, therefore, that the American notes were going to be available to replace the withdrawn *kerenki* in April 1919. By that time, it was true, a portion of the notes had been returned to Vladivostok from the Philippines and had been placed in Russian hands. But this was only on the condition imposed by Wilson that the notes be surcharged to indicate that they were an issue of the Omsk government and not the Russian State Bank.[268] It had rapidly emerged, however, that it was beyond the means of the White authorities to undertake even this simple process, for they lacked both the staff and the equipment required.[269] There was no indication by April that the president would withdraw his conditions for their release. Mikhailov's claims of preparedness for his currency reform were, therefore, quite without foundation.

What is even *more* astounding is that when eventually the Americans were prevailed upon by Kolchak's British supporters to release the notes (without a surcharge) during the summer of 1919, it was decided at Omsk that they should not be put into circulation because they were of denominations too high to have any beneficial effect upon the small change famine. The whole process of obtaining bank notes to replace the *kerenki* had to begin all over again; and notes in denominations which actually were in demand were eventually ordered, quite separately, from the Chinese Government's Board of Engraving.[270]

It seems, therefore, that the capacity for 'unplanning' which Colonel Lebedev had brought to Kolchak's military strategy had its mirror in Mikhailov's chaotic financial policies. Mikhailov was, after all, a second-rate economist and a newcomer to public

266 FO 371/3366/210037 'Barclay (Washington) to FO, 21.xii.1918'.

267 *FRUS: 1918*, Vol. 3, pp. 98, 101.

268 *FRUS: 1919 (Russia)*, pp. 450, 454–5; FO 371/4104/33254 'Eliot (Omsk) to FO, 27.ii.1919'; Mints, I.I. (ed.) 'Vneshnaia politika kontr-revoliutsionnykh pravitelstv′ vo nachale 1919g. (iz dokumentov parizhnogo posol′stva)', *Krasnyi arkhiv* (Moscow), Vol. 37, 1929, pp. 196–7.

269 *FRUS: 1919 (Russia)*, p. 456; FO 371/4112/83258 'Eliot (Omsk) to FO, 28.v.1919'.

270 FO 371/4112/99150 'Robertson (Vladivostok) to FO, 2.vii.1919'; F0 371/4113/111356 'Memorandum on the Currency Situation in Harbin'.

office, a man who, acording to Sukin, 'even considered *himself* to be an ignoramus in finance', and one who was generally viewed by others as being 'more interested in political intrigue than in finance'.[271] He lacked the experience to deal with the intractable financial problems facing White Siberia, and only made things worse when he tried. Yet, because of his role in bringing Kolchak to power and his personal friendship with the admiral, Mikhailov had been placed in a position of complete control over the economic policy of the Omsk government during the first half of 1919. Even when presented with the catalogue of misfortune which Mikhailov's reform had engendered Kolchak was unwilling to dispense with his services; only in August 1919 would a series of representations from other ministers persuade the admiral to request Mikhailov's resignation.

In conclusion it should be noted that Mikhailov's successor as Minister of Finance, the eminently more qualified banker, L.V. von Goyer, did eventually persuade the United States Government to hand over all of the notes which had been printed in New York, albeit on modified terms. It was agreed by October 1919 that Omsk could deliver Washington of any responsibilities it felt towards the notes through simply purchasing them anew, in a straightforward financial transaction, for private use. To purchase the notes $1,300,000 (or 2,522,000 gold roubles) were to be deposited with the United States Treasury Department before January 1st 1920.[272] This, however, was far too late to have any effect on the ultimate fate of the Kolchak régime or to restore faith in the Kolchak currency. By autumn of 1919 the value of the ill-starred Siberian notes was declining at such a rate that a British officer, who had lost *sibirki* equivalent to £1,000 in card games during the first days of a journey from Omsk to Vladivostok, was able to pay off his debts with a five-pound note upon reaching the Pacific coast a week or two later.[273]

271 Sukin (*Leeds Russian Archive*), p. 23; *USMI*, Vol. 7, No. 92 (week ending 1.iii.1919), p. 633.

272 'L'Unification Monétaire en Sibérie', *Union (Agence Télégraphique Russe)* (Paris) No. 165, 15.ix.1919; *FRUS: 1919 (Russia)*, pp. 421, 457–8.

273 Prinsep, 'Knox's Mission to Siberia', pp. 67–8. Prinsep's recollection that at Vladivostok he found 'people were using money to paper their walls as it was cheaper than wallpaper (even if wallpaper could be found)' sounds hyperbolic, but conveys the spirit of the times.

Expenditure of the Gold Reserve

The Omsk government could only afford to make the afore-mentioned last minute financial arrangement with the Americans because circumstances had prevailed upon Kolchak to abandon his principles with regard to the use of that part of the Imperial Gold Reserve which he had inherited.

Whatever the needs of Siberia in terms of currency reform and so forth, Kolchak's economic advisers had come to realize in early 1919 that their efforts in that direction would come to nought unless the régime could create foreign balances to meet the desperate needs of the military, of industry and of the population in general. Table 4.15 (below) demonstrates, however, that Siberia's balance of trade was deeply in the red in 1919; such a poor level of exports was unable to support the rouble at a steady or effective rate of exchange.[274] Moreover, from a very early stage it had been realized that Allied subvention would be limited and could be curtailed at any time. Imported goods would, therefore, have to be paid for. The problem was, however, that in 1918 the western powers had forbidden the importation of roubles, making it very difficult for Kolchak to effect purchases abroad because his infant government possessed no substantial foreign currency reserve.[275]

The urgent need to boost imports into Siberia was one of the matters discussed by a diplomatic conference held at Omsk in July and August of 1919. The conference had been organized to examine the means by which the Allies could assist Kolchak in the light of the promises made in the notes of May 26th and June 12th and was attended by the senior military and diplomatic representatives of the powers. During its proceedings ministers of the Omsk government took turns to present lists of their most urgent needs, calculations were made and, eventually, a plan proposed by the United States Ambassador to Japan, Mr Morris, was recommended to the Allied governments. Central to Morris's scheme was the proposal that all the Allies should

274 *Biulleten' otdela informatsii pri vedomstve pressa etat-maiora Glavnokommanduiushchago* (Omsk) 16.vii.1919.

275 FO 371/4105/30740 'Memorandum by the Minister of Finance..., February 1919'. That Japan would still accept roubles was of little comfort to Omsk because Tokyo's intent seemed to be to buy up the rouble in the Far East in order to replace it with the yen. See *Report of the CEC*, p. 12 and Rodney 'Siberia in 1919', p. 329.

Table 4.15: Siberia's foreign trade (in roubles), 1919

	Imports	Exports	Balance
January	97,200,000	3,800,000	*−93,400,000*
February	99,200,000	5,300,000	*−93,900,000*
March	128,900,000	17,200,000	*−111,700,000*
April	139,000,000	10,800,000	*−128,200,000*
Total	464,300,000	37,100,000	*−427,200,000*

immediately grant credits to the Kolchak Government to the value of $200,000,000 to enable it to begin purchasing supplies abroad.[276] The prerequisite of extending government credits, however, had to be the *de jure* recognition of the Kolchak government by the powers. Morris and other diplomatic representatives at Omsk, pursuing the logic of the Allies' promise to assist Kolchak to its conclusion, urged this step upon their governments during these months as the only possible salvation of the White cause.[277] But to no avail. As the Russian Army's retreat continued unabated into the summer of 1919, Morris was informed by his Secretary of State that Congress was now more opposed than ever to the recognition of Kolchak and that, consequently, no credit facilities could be expected from the United States Government. The Japanese government, the only other power in a financial and geographical position to be of real assistance to Omsk, took an identical line.[278]

If financial aid from foreign governments was beyond Omsk's reach, however, there remained the hope of obtaining credit from private financial institutions and manufacturing companies around the globe. In fact, it was widely believed in Omsk

276 *FRUS: 1919 (Russia)*, pp. 405–10. On the diplomatic conference see also below, pp. 483ff.

277 *FRUS: 1919 (Russia)*, pp. 408–9; FO 371/4113/118927 'Memorandum...by Mr Sly'. The British High Commissioner in Siberia, Sir Charles Eliot, who believed that the Omsk régime was by then beyond salvation, was a notable dissenter from the other Allied agents' campaign to have Kolchak recognized during the early summer of 1919 (see *DBFP*, p. 454).

278 *FRUS: 1919 (Russia)*, pp. 421–2; *Iaponskaia interventsiia 1918–1922gg. v dokumentakh*. Moscow, 1934, p. 26. A request to the French Government for a loan of 690,000,000 francs of March 1919 had already met with a negative response. See Kim, R.M (ed.) 'Iz arkhiva organizatorov grazhdanskoi voiny i interventsii v Sovetskoi Rossii', *Istoricheskii arkhiv* (Moscow), No. 6 (1961), p. 70. At one point the official press did announce the securing of a $50,000,000 loan from Washington, only to discover that the Americans had extended the credit not to Siberia but to Liberia! See *FRUS: 1918*, Vol. 2, p. 460.

circles that foreign investors and businessmen, alive to the mighty economic potential of Siberia and the Urals, would be falling over each other in vying for the opportunity of getting in on the ground floor.[279] However, Kolchak's poor military showing during the late spring and summer of 1919 and his failure to achieve *de jure* recognition by the Allied governments had a knock-on effect in the private sector. A Ministry of Agriculture delegation to the USA, for example, found that even companies with a long-standing and profitable interest in Siberia (such as International Harvester) refused to extend credit to the unrecognized and clearly floundering régime at Omsk.[280]

With both governmental and private sources of credit unforthcoming, Kolchak's only alternatives were to pay for the goods he needed, cash on the nail, or to provide collateral for loans. Both amounted to the same thing – the use of his only financial resource, that part of the Imperial Gold Reserve which had been captured from the Bolsheviks at Kazan during the summer of 1918: 'At a time when the government finds itself at death's door, it is not only just, it is our duty [to draw upon the reserve]', explained a White economist to the press at Omsk.[281] So it was that, in May 1919, the Supreme Ruler duly set out his stall and had Mikhailov (who was 'cracking jokes like an undertaker at a funeral' according to one source) conduct Allied representatives on a guided tour of the gold reserve.[282] News of the riches at the disposal of the Supreme Ruler then flashed around the world. There were a few minor qualms in western capitals as to whether a Russian admiral whom they did not recognize in his pretensions to governmental authority had the right to dispose of his nation's assets, but these were soon set aside and American, British and French banks were informed that their governments found no technical or legal objections to business being done, on a private basis, with Kolchak.[283] Without pausing to ponder the double standards of governments who would not offer him

279 Sukin (*Leeds Russian Archive*), p. 113.

280 Borodin, *Idealy i deiatel'nosti*, pp. 207–8.

281 Subbotovskii, I. *Soiuzniki i russkie reaktsionery: kratkii obzor (iskliuchitel'no po ofitsial'nym arkhivnym dokumentam Kolchakovskogo pravitel'stva)*. Leningrad (1926), pp. 234–3

282 Janin, 'Otryvki', p. 118.

283 FO 371/4112/62225 'Curzon (FO) to Robertson (Vladivostok), 22.iv.1919'; *FRUS: 1919 (Russia)*, pp. 430, 436.

credit but were only too willing to take a share of Russian gold, Kolchak began transporting bullion from Omsk towards the east in May of 1919.[284]

In total 237,277,000 gold roubles' worth of bullion – over one-third of the gold held at Omsk by the Kolchak government – was despatched by train (usually under the guard of members of the Middlesex Regiment) to the State Bank at Vladivostok, where by the summer of 1919 no less than eighteen foreign banks, eager for a share in Russian business, had established branches. Thereafter the gold was either to be sold on the international market (usually through the medium of the Hong Kong and Shanghai Bank) in exchange for foreign currency, in which case it would be shipped out to Hong Kong or to Shanghai; or it would be transferred to the vaults of banks

Table 4.16: Disposal of that portion of the Imperial Russian Gold Reserve held at Omsk in 1919 (in roubles)

Balance of the Imperial Russian Gold Reserve, October 1917	1,101,690,000
Of which:	
captured from the Bolsheviks, October 1918	651,532,000
transported from Omsk to Vladivostok from May 1919	237,277,000
seized by Semenov at Chita, September 1919[285]	42,251,000
Total arrived at Vladivostok	195,026,000
Of which:	
sold to the French Government, May 1919	2,661,185
sold to the British Government, May 1919	10,898,182
sold to the British and French Governments, July 1919	14,753,114
sold to the Japanese Government, August 1919	13,559,381
sold to the Japanese Government, September 1919	10,550,254
sold to the French Government, September 1919	15,839,381
Total sold	*68,261,497*
deposited against credits opened in Japan	31,680,765
deposited against credits from Anglo-American banks	90,860,437
deposited against credits for arms purchased in the USA	4,224,102
Total utilized as security	*126,765,304*

284 Equally hypocritical was that the Allies were only too eager to accept interest and amortization payments on Imperial Russia's foreign debts from the Kolchak Government which they refused to recognize as the rightful heir to the tsars' fortune. See Sack, p. 18.

285 On the mysterious fate of this portion of the gold reserve, at least part of which can be traced to Japan, see Smele, 'White Gold', pp. 1334–9; and Petrov, S. 'Skol′ko rossiiskogo zolota okazalos′ za granitsei v 1914–1920 godakh? (Doklad)', in Romanovskii, S.K. (ed.) *Diplomaticheskii ezhegodnik*. Moscow (1995), pp. 240–53.

in Yokohama, Osaka, Shanghai, Hong Kong and San Francisco, as security for loans. As Table 4.16 (above) reveals, over 68,261,000 gold roubles' worth of bullion had been sold to the British, French and Japanese governments by September 1919 and 126,765,000 gold roubles' worth had been deposited as security for loans obtained from private companies in the United States, Great Britain, Japan and China (notably from an Anglo-American banking consortium set up for the purpose by Baring Brothers and Kiddler, Peabody & Co.).[286]

The depletion of the gold reserve in this manner, however, could not provide a long-term solution to Kolchak's economic and political plight. The Supreme Ruler might boast to Allied diplomats at Omsk in August 1919 that as long as he held the gold reserve he could 'continue to fight the Bolsheviks for another three years', whether or not he was recognized and subsidized by the powers,[287] but in fact nearly 40% of his gold had already been expended, deposited abroad as collateral or stolen by Cossack bandits by September 1919. At that rate of depletion Kolchak's store of bullion would barely have lasted into 1920. Moreover, although financial experts were agreed that the credits opened by the Omsk government in London, Paris, New York and Tokyo might temporarily boost imports, they were equally sure that by depleting its reserves through the sale of gold the White régime would still further depress the value of the rouble vis-à-vis other currencies, thereby storing up trouble for the not too distant future.[288]

The Northern Sea Route Expedition of 1919

Ultimately, the Siberian economy would not be regenerated and the rouble would not achieve lasting stability on the international market unless the export of Siberian agricultural produce and raw materials, the foundations of the region's wealth, was re-established. This in turn would not be achieved unless producers of such goods (i.e. the peasantry) could be paid with a respected currency for releasing their

286 Novitskii, pp. 15–20; 'The Russian Gold Reserve – What Became of It?' *The Economist* (London) Vol. 100, No. 4,266 (30.v.1925), pp. 1066–7; 'Russia's Gold Reserve – How it has been Dispersed' *Bankers' Magazine* (October 1920).

287 FO 371/4096/119017 'Knox (Omsk) to WO, 17.viii.1919'; *FRUS: 1919 (Russia)*, pp. 214–16.

288 FO 371/4105/1168 'Alston (Vladivostok) to FO, 31.xii.1919'; FO 371/4112/58998 'Robertson (Vladivostok) to FO, 12.iv.1919'; FO 371/4112/61989 'Report...by Mr Hinton'.

produce. Observers were agreed, however, that no currency would be respected, no matter what the financial ploys of the Omsk government, unless its nominal value could be demonstrated as signifying real purchasing power; and for this the commodities in demand among the rural population would have to be provided through an expansion of imports.[289] The key to the resurrection of the region's economy, in other words, was the re-establishment of the foreign trade upon which Siberia had traditionally relied.

There were certainly plenty of goods in Siberian warehouses awaiting export. In February 1919, for example, one co-operative organization estimated that there were 73,861 tons of produce in its stores, ranging from 36,000 tons of butter to 61 tons of feathers and down.[290] The problem was how to initiate trade whilst fighting a major war and with the rouble in such disarray. This was highlighted when, in April 1919, the British government hinted that they might after all permit some limited transactions involving the exchange of roubles for pounds sterling, but only at a rate of between forty and fifty roubles to the pound. As co-operative sources pointed out, such a rate would entail losses for the Siberian producer – of up to thirty roubles per pood for the Siberian wool producer, for example, even before taking account of freight, insurance and other costs.[291] It was hoped in Omsk that such obstacles to trade might gradually become less significant as the standing of the rouble improved. In the meantime, however, a good deal of attention was given to the possibility of circumventing currency difficulties through the direct exchange of goods, i.e. through barter. In particular, high hopes were placed on plans emanating from a number of sources to undertake large-scale barter operations in 1919 involving the import and export of goods to and from the very heart of Siberia – not by rail but by water. This, one of the White's most interesting and little known enterprises, was Kolchak's attempt to utilize the Northern Sea Route to Europe.

As far back as the sixteenth century the native fishermen of Arkhangel′sk had reached the mouth of the Ob in their flat-bottomed boats. For the next three centuries tsarist absolutism, ever wary of foreign penetration of its lands, had made the utilization of the sea route into Asia problematic. However, as Siberia's

289 *FRUS: 1918*, Vol. 3, pp. 73, 149–50; FO 371/4104/1168 'Eliot (Omsk) to FO, 31.xii.1918'.

290 *USMI*, Vol. 7, No. 91 (week ending 22.ii.1919), p. 615.

291 Morozov, K.I. 'The Rouble Exchange and Trade With Siberia', *The Russian Co-operator* (London), Vol. 3, No. 4 (April 1919), pp. 53–4.

economic potential came to be realized towards the end of the nineteenth century, the possibility of conducting regular trade between Europe and Siberia via the Northern Sea Route had been much discussed – particularly since the Norwegian sealers had rediscovered the route into the Kara Sea in the 1860s and the British seafarer, Captain Joseph Wiggins, had voyaged to the mouths of the Ob and Enisei in 1874 to 1875.[292] The advantages of the route were obvious: the mighty rivers Ob and Enisei and their tributaries were navigable for 40,000 km and 25,000 km respectively, and together they served a basin of some 5 million square kilometres, embracing the most productive and populous areas of Siberia's hinterland. The disadvantages, however, were equally striking: the icy Kara Sea was navigable for a mere eight to twelve weeks each year (from August to October) and there was no port at the mouth of either river at which the necessary transshipment of goods from ocean-going vessels to river transports (and vice versa) could be made. An additional problem was that western merchants were generally poorly informed of the requirements of the Siberian people and lacked the organizational and administrative machinery necessary to collect and distribute goods among the scattered settlements of the vast Siberian hinterland.

Consequently, although numerous individual voyages were made, no large-scale commercial ventures incorporating the Northern Sea Route were attempted prior to World War I – particularly as the construction of the Trans-Siberian Railway seemed (at least from the non-Siberian point of view) to obviate the need for a sea and river route.[293] There was, however, an interesting precedent for Kolchak's venture, in that in 1905 (in co-operation with Germany) the Imperial Government had sent into Siberia, via the Kara Sea, goods which the railway had been unable to handle because of its commitment to the war effort in the Far East. Moreover, despite the difficulties it presented, governmental and commercial interest in the Northern Sea Route had not altogether expired – from 1912 to 1916 a network of

292 On Wiggins see Johnson, H. *The Life and Times of Joseph Wiggins*. London (1907).

293 On the pre-revolutionary Russian voyages along the Northern Sea Route see Vostrotin, S.V. 'Severnyi morskoi put'', in *Aziatskaia Rossiia*. St Petersburg (1914), Vol. 2, pp. 561–616; Krypton, C. *The Northern Sea Route: Its Place in Russian Economic History Before 1917* (2 Vols.). New York (1953–1956), which includes an extensive bibliography; Vasil'ev, V.N. 'Severnyi morskoi put': kratkii istoricheskii ocherk', *Sibirskie ogni* (Novonikolaevsk), No. 5 (1924), pp. 190–212; and Pinkhenson, D.M. *Problema Severnogo Morskogo Puti v epokhe kapitalizma. Istoriia otkrytiia i osvoeniia Severnogo Morskogo Puti, tom vtoroi*. Leningrad (1962). Later developments are surveyed in Armstrong, T. *The Northern Sea Route: Soviet Exploitation of the North East Passage*. Cambridge (1952).

radio stations was developed in the western Arctic Ocean and in those same years an Anglo-Norwegian concern, the Siberian Steamship Manufacturing and Trade Co., plied the route with an annual expedition.[294]

Revolution and civil war had put an end to the operations of the Siberian Steamship Co. in 1917,[295] but the leading light of the company, the Norwegian adventurer and capitalist Jonas Lied, remained fascinated by the profits he knew were to be made in Siberian trade. Interviews with both Lenin and Trotsky soon after the October Revolution, however, had convinced him that the Soviet Government would not 'do business'. So, having established his own Northern Sea Route Surveying Co. (or Lied Inc.) in New York, Lied travelled to Omsk in January 1919, and there, through his numerous Siberian contacts (he had been Norwegian consul in Novonikolaevsk before the war), he obtained a personal interview with Kolchak. 'You are bound to need us,' he told the Supreme Ruler, 'trade is the sinews of war and therefore of counter-revolution.' Kolchak was evidently convinced – his imagination was perhaps stirred by memories of his own arctic adventures (in the course of which he had himself journeyed up both the Enisei and the Lena to the Siberian interior) and by his later work at the Admiralty (which had involved the designing of two steel-hulled, ice-breaker survey vessels, 'Taimyr' and 'Vaigach', to facilitate communications along Russia's northern littoral) – and by April the indefatigable Norwegian was back in London with the admiral's commission to explore the possibility that 2,800,000 poods of goods (worth £1,000,000) might be shipped from Britain into Siberia along the Ob in return for

294 Fridtjof Nansen, the Norwegian explorer and statesman, participated in the voyage of 1913 – see Nansen, *Through Siberia, passim.*

295 Although in October 1918 B.A. Vilkitskii (an anti-Bolshevik officer who had continued to work at the Admiralty during the first months of Soviet rule) did use funds and equipment originally assigned to him by none other than Trotsky to undertake an experimental sortie to the mouth of the Enisei on behalf of the Chaikovskii régime at Arkhangel′sk. There Vilkitskii made contact with a steamer carrying 160,000 roubles' worth of supplies which had been sent down-river from Krasnoiarsk in accordance with plans he had made in collaboration with another anti-Bolshevik officer at Petrograd shortly before the latter had fled east to become, in due course, a servant of the Provisional Siberian Government. Vilkitskii thereby set the pattern for what was to occur in 1919 and was, in addition, responsible for establishing the radio station at Dudinka, near the mouth of the Enisei, via which the North Russian régime was to extend its recognition to Kolchak in December 1918. See Vilkitskii, B.A. 'Kogda, komu i kak ia sluzhil pod bol′shevikami', *Russian Émigré Archives* (Fresno, CA) Vol. 5, 1974, pp. 14–29; Shepeleva, T. (ed.) 'Ispol′zovanie interventov Severno-morskogo puti, 1918–1919gg.', *Krasnyi arkhiv* (Moscow), No. 1 (1941), pp. 152–3.

a corresponding consignment of Siberian butter, grain, flax and other produce to be shipped out by the same route.[296]

Nor was Lied the only interested party. In December 1918 the Minister of Marine, Admiral Smirnov, had informed the Council of Ministers that 'the breakdown of railway transportation and the need to find new means of supplying the army illustrates the dire necessity of utilizing the Northern Sea Route'. And, having broadcast its interest, by the end of April 1919 Omsk was reporting that enquiries about the opportunities for trade along the Northern Sea Route that summer had been received from London, Paris, Stockholm and elsewhere.[297] This, of course, was at the apogee of Kolchak's military and diplomatic campaigns – the Russian Army was approaching the Volga and the powers seemed set to recognize him as Supreme Ruler. Clearly, western businessmen were being caught up in the wave of optimism surrounding the White cause and, anticipating the imminent demise of the Bolsheviks, were looking for the first opportunity to establish commercial links with the Kolchak régime at Omsk which might bear rich fruit once the admiral was installed in the Kremlin or the Winter Palace. Britain was particularly drawn to the openings presented by Kolchak's need for trade: *The Times* was moved to re-christen the Kara Sea 'a British route to Siberia', while the Foreign Office urged its agents in Siberia 'to impress upon the Omsk Government that every facility should be accorded to this [Northern Sea Route] expedition in view not only of the present military, political and commercial advantages, but also of the possible future development of trading between Siberia and this country'.[298]

This is not to imply that enthusiasm for the Northern Sea route venture was confined to Europeans keen to exploit Siberia's natural wealth and untapped markets. There was also considerable enthusiasm for the route from within the region. The co-operative movement – which had grown to massive proportions in fulfilling government contracts during World War I only to suffer commensurate

296 *Nash put'* (Chita) No. 133, 13.iv.1919; *The Times* (London) 10.iv.1919; Shepeleva, p. 182. Lied recounts his own remarkable story in *Return to Happiness*. London (1942) and *Siberian Arctic: The Story of the Siberian Company*. London (1960). Other chapters of his extraordinary life included being the intended factotum of an aborted British military intelligence plan to send a motor launch up the Ob to rescue the Romanovs from Tobol'sk – on which see also Summers, A. and Mangold, T. *The File on the Tsar*. London (1976), pp. 255–8 – and working, as a Soviet citizen, on the exploitation of the Northern Sea Route in the 1920s.

297 *Doklad russkago telegrafnogo agentstva* (Omsk) 28.iv.1919; Shepeleva, pp. 154, 156–7.

298 FO 371/4112/89346 'FO to Eliot (Omsk), 17.vi.1919'.

privations as Siberia's trade slumped in 1917 to 1918 – was particularly enthusiastic. Their newspaper *Nasha zaria*, for example, would devote lengthy front page editorials to the 'urgent need' to open up the Kara Sea route and called upon the Kolchak Government to found a Siberian Marine College in order to train captains, engineers and pilots in the special skills necessary to navigate Siberia's broad, icy and poorly charted rivers.[299] And the co-operatives too were looking beyond the current emergency to the future. Being both business-minded and generally sympathetic to Siberian regionalist politics, they regarded the utilization of the Northern Sea Route in 1919 not only as an efficacious means to revive their flagging fortunes but also as a golden opportunity to establish a trade pattern for Siberia on the basis of direct contact with Europe – a move which would prevent Russia from ever again suppressing Siberia's economic potential through the imposition of internal trade barriers (such as the infamous Cheliabinsk Grain Tariff) favouring producers west of the Urals.[300]

In the event, it was chiefly through co-operative channels rather than those of private businessmen that the Northern Sea Route venture of 1919 was pursued. Thus, when by special order of the Supreme Ruler, a Committee for the Utilization of the Northern Sea Route opened its proceedings at Omsk on April 29th 1919, present were not only representatives of those ministries most closely concerned with the enterprise (the Ministries of Marine, Foreign Affairs, Ways and Communications, Agriculture, Trade and Industry and Food and Supply) but also representatives of the Union of Siberian Co-operative Associations (generally referred to by its trading name, Zakupsbyt). The ambitious plans laid down at the Committee's inaugural meeting also reflected the enthusiasm of co-operatives for the Northern Sea Route: a reconnaissance expedition led by one Colonel Kotel′nikov was sent to survey the relevant Siberian rivers during May; meanwhile plans were laid for a new radio station to be established on Novaia Zemlia, for a new port to be constructed at Ust-Eniseisk and for a colossal fleet of river barges to be assembled for the collection and distribution of goods throughout the Ob and Enisei basins. In addition, within days of the Committee's meeting, the Ministry of Finance granted licences to Zakupsbyt for the exportation via the Northern Sea Route of

299 *Nash put′* (Omsk) No. 127, 17.vi.1919.

300 Siberian co-operative leaders expressed such hopes in conversation with Bernard Pares. See Pares, B. 'Siberian Diary' (*Pares Papers*, Box 43), p. 70.

large consignments of agricultural goods: 100,000 roubles' worth of butter, 30,000 roubles of hemp, 20,000 roubles of flax, 20,000 roubles of wool etc.[301]

The high hopes raised in the planning stages of the Northern Sea Route expedition were, however, not to be realized. Military neglect of the needs of the rear and the White authorities' inability to temper their innate hostility to the SR-dominated co-operative movement combined to scupper the 1919 voyage as effectively as any arctic iceberg.

It was hardly an auspicious beginning when the expedition's departure, which had been set for July 20th, had to be postponed for more than a fortnight, thereby cutting into the already limited ice-free period in which traffic was possible via the northern seas. This delay, noted Bernard Pares, was caused by 'general disorganization' and 'the entirely casual attitude' of the military authorities at Omsk. Pares, who was to return to Britain as a passenger on the expedition, was astounded that in spite of the government's sponsorship of the venture, the White military (who, of course, had supreme authority in the Omsk district and in the 'front line' zone to the west of the capital through which the expedition would pass) would assign no stevedores (600 had been requested) but only 196 unfit and disgruntled German POWs as a labour force for the expedition. Moreover, none of the White units detailed to guard the expedition appeared on time and two of the three senior officers assigned to it failed to turn up at all. Most damaging in the long run, however, was that the army could not be persuaded to release sufficient tonnage from the Ob merchant fleet to meet the requirements of the proposed exchange: only one iron barge (of the four ordered) was made available for transshipment, plus a number of wooden lighters which were quite unsuitable for use at sea in high latitudes. The latter were also so dilapidated that several days were lost while they were repaired.[302]

301 *Svobodnaia Sibir'* (Krasnoiarsk) No. 91, 1.vi.1919; *Biulleten' otdela informatsii pri vedomstve pressa etat-maiora Glavnokommanduiushchago* (Omsk), 2.v.1919. The first Chairman of the Northern Sea Route Commission was one General Popov. On June 29th he was replaced, however, by S.V. Vostrotin – a gold mine proprietor, former mayor of Eniseisk, Kadet deputy to the 3rd and 4th State Dumas and a close friend of the ubiquitous Lied. Vostrotin was one of the few men who had actually made the journey along the Northern Sea Route – notably with Nansen and Lied in 1913, although his first trip (on Wiggins's last voyage) had been on his honeymoon in 1894.

302 Pares, B. 'Political Conditions in the Siberian Frontal Zone, ?.viii.1919' (*Pares Papers*, Box 44), p. 14. Pares brought out of Siberia with him on the expedition a trunk containing much of the material upon which this study is based. See also Shepeleva, pp. 174, 179. The army, of course, had its own priorities – notably, fearing a continuation of the Red Army's advance, it was

Table 4.17: Goods (in poods) shipped out of Omsk and Novonikolaevsk by the Northern Sea Route Expedition, August 1919	
Grain	541,692
Butter and Cheese	69,000
Raw materials and fats	29,000
Honey	28,000
Valenki	4,530
Total	672,222

Plans for a contemporaneous expedition along the Enisei to exchange 100,000 poods of grain with a Swedish fleet having been abandoned through lack of time and a shortage of tonnage, it was eventually two modest flotillas (jointly comprising seven steamers and nineteen barges) which embarked upon the 1,600 kilometre journey from central Siberia to the mouth of the Ob. One group left Omsk on August 3rd and a second left Novonikolaevsk on August 8th. On board, according to the figures of the Northern Sea Route Committee, were the goods displayed above in Table 4.17.[303] Of this cargo, only about 100,000 poods were bound for co-operative organizations in Britain in exchange for wares in demand in Siberia. The remainder was intended for the relief of anti-Bolshevik forces in North Russia.[304]

The total amount of goods involved in the exercise was clearly a long way short of the 2,800,000 poods which Kolchak had initially discussed with Lied earlier in 1919; nor did it match the one million pood target later set by the Northern Sea Route Committee. Moreover, an unspecified portion of the expedition's goods are known to have been lost whilst en route to the transshipment point at Nakhodka Bay

engaged in the evacuation of military materials from Tobol'sk to Tomsk via the Ob (see *ibid.*, p. 193). Vostrotin, however, could not excuse the military's entirely negative attitude to the venture and, on July 30th, informed the Ministry of Trade and Industry that, in the light of it, he would refuse to be held responsible for the expedition's fate (*ibid.*, p. 182).

303 Shol'ts, F.A. (ed.) *Severnyi morskoi put' i ego znachenie po vneshnem tovaroobmene Sibiri*. Omsk (1921), p. 60. For a more detailed breakdown of the cargoes see Shepeleva, p. 185.

304 FO 371/4112/11411 'Eliot (Omsk) to FO, 8.viii.1919'.

– an inlet on the eastern shore of the Firth (*guba*) of Ob – because once that the defenceless flotillas had sailed beyond the sphere of the limited protection offered by the civil authorities in central Siberia, military indifference to the fate of the venture soon sharpened into open harassment. The Omsk flotilla was repeatedly waylaid for spurious and time-consuming searches by military authorities in Tobol′sk *guberniia*. Co-operative sources allege that during the course of these raids 'a great quantity of cargo was requisitioned by the army, thrown overboard or simply sunk'. On several occasions, they added, 'it was only by exceptional good favour that the expedition was not fired upon' by the White forces.[305]

Despite these delays the two flotillas were able to rendezvous successfully at the confluence of the Irtysh and the Ob, thence to continue northward to Nakhodka Bay, where they anxiously awaited the arrival of the ships from Europe.

For some months arrangements for the exchange of goods via the Northern Sea Route had been progressing in Britain under the joint auspices of the British Government and the Merchant Trading Company of Liverpool (a subsidiary of the Hudson Bay Company which was keen to take up with Siberian trade where the Siberian Steamship Company had left off). Originally the British War Office had been in favour of utilizing the opportunity offered by the venture to provide Kolchak with a major, six million ton package of supplies.[306] It soon became apparent, however, that it would be impossible to assemble and refit sufficient tonnage in British yards before any fleet would have to embark in order to make use of the ice-free window through the Kara Sea during the summer of 1919. Consequently, the War Office scheme was abandoned in early July.[307] It was proposed instead that a single vessel, the 'Baymingo', chartered from the Merchant Trading Company by Zakupsbyt, should sail from Liverpool carrying some 3,500 tons of merchandise for distribution via the co-operative network in Siberia. She would join eleven British, Russian and Swedish ships which it had been arranged would be despatched from Stockholm and Arkhangel′sk carrying 7,000 tons of British military supplies for the

305 Baikaloff, A.V. 'Siberian Co-operation and the Commercial Exploitation of the Northern Sea Route from Europe to Siberia', *The Russian Co-operator* (London) Vol. 4, No. 6 (June 1920), p. 88.

306 FO 371/4112/93061 'WO to Knox (Omsk), 13.vi.1919'.

307 FO 371/4112/93061 'WO memorandum to FO, 7.vii.1919'; FO 371/4112/110069 'WO memorandum to FO, 31.vii.1919'; Shepeleva, pp. 182, 186.

Russian Army.[308] With the 10,500 ton (651,000 pood) capacity of these vessels alone, therefore, the European fleet would have been hard-pressed to export the 672,222 poods (10,834 tons) of goods said to be on board the Siberian flotillas. This fact was known to the Northern Sea Route Committee before their flotillas had left Omsk and Novonikolaevsk and an urgent request had been made that a Russian cargo ship, the 'Novorossiia' (then at Tilbury) should also be assigned to the expedition. By the time that Vostrotin's message was received in London, however, it was judged to be too late for the 'Novorossiia' to set sail.[309]

When the 'Baymingo' and her escorts began to arrive at Nakhodka Bay on September 1st (four days after the arrival of the Siberian flotillas) it was immediately apparent to the co-operative representatives present that there was little hope either of the agricultural produce they had brought down river being taken out of Siberia or of the manufactured goods and other items on board the 'Baymingo' being brought in.

It was not simply that the sea-going ships had insufficient capacity to handle all of the Siberian goods. Indeed, the unexpected arrival in the first days of September of a second tender ship, the Merchant Trading Company vessel 'Solomon Bodmirovich', should have resolved the dilemma of a shortfall in tonnage. Nor was it only that, having draughts of up to 3.5 fathoms, the 'Baymingo' and the other ships from Europe had to dock 28 km north of Nakhodka Bay (wherein there was clearance of only 3.2 fathoms) entailing a journey of up to three hours even in fine weather (of which there was all too little) – for clearly, given the dearth of sea-going lighters and the absence of port facilities and a trained workforce (of whom 27 unfortunates were to drown on September 7th), even in ideal conditions the exercise would have been fraught with difficulties. Rather, what proved to be the major obstacle to the transshipment of non-military wares was, in the words of a co-operative report, that immediately upon the arrival of the European ships 'the bureaucrat appointed to direct the loading and unloading operation gave orders to the effect that the government cargo should be dealt with first'. As a result of this ruling – which must have been hard for them to stomach given the military's

308 FO 371/4112/26550 'Ministry of Shipping Memorandum, ?.vii.1919'.

309 FO 371/4112/114411 'Eliot (Omsk) to FO, 8.viii.1919'; FO 371/4112/116984 'Ministry of Shipping Memorandum, 16.vi.1919'; Shepeleva, p. 187.

negative attitude to the entire venture – the co-operative representatives at Nakhodka Bay found that their goods could only be moved 'in snatches'.[310]

In fact, by the time that deteriorating weather conditions had forced the premature cessation of the transshipment operation on September 15th and obliged the European fleet to embark upon its return journey a few days later (for fear that they would be trapped at Nakhodka Bay for the winter), some 424,501 poods of the goods from Siberia had not been transshipped. The majority of these goods were subsequently distributed for the relief of the vicinal native and Russian populations of Obdorsk and Berezov; but 76,709 poods of grain, butter and various raw materials were shipped all the way back up river to Novonikolaevsk and 82,000 poods of flour and honey were taken back to Tomsk.[311]

The priority granted during the operations to ordnance and matériel bound for the Russian Army over the manufactures and wares bound for the Siberian population is also evinced by the proportion of those goods which had been successfully transshipped from the European vessels onto the river barges. Table 4.18 (below) details the quantity of items imported according to the calculations of the Northern Sea Route Committee.[312] Even those co-operative goods which were transshipped, however, consisted mainly of equipment for the construction of a saw-mill. This, presumably, was regarded by the authorities as being of greater utility than the remainder of the 'Baymingo's' cargo – consisting chiefly of agricultural machinery

310 Baikaloff, *Siberian Co-operation*, p. 89. It has proven to be be impossible to ascertain either the identity or nationality of this 'bureaucrat' – although it is unlikely that he was the afore-mentioned B.A. Vilkitskii who, although he was commander of the European flotilla, served the co-operatives well both during the 1919 journey (by twice saving the 'Baymingo' and its cargo from the incompetent seamanship of the Norwegian pilot hired by Zakupsbyt) and in the future as a co-operative agent in London (see Vilkitskii, pp. 30–4; Shepeleva, p. 189). Perhaps it was the commander of the ships from Siberia who is here referred to – one Lieutenant Neupokoev. Or it may be of relevance that the senior British diplomat at Arkhangel'sk had counselled the Foreign Office in June that in the matter of the transshipments to take place at Nakhodka Bay 'private interests of co-operatives in civil supplies which will arrive simultaneously [i.e. together with the military supplies being sent from North Russia] are likely to prevail unless British officers accompany the expedition from start to finish'. See FO 371/4112/9417 'Hoare (Arkhangel'sk) to FO, 26.vi.1919'.

311 Shol'ts, pp. 60–1; Shepeleva, p. 197. Goods could not be returned to Omsk because on September 27th the town of Tobol'sk had fallen to the 3rd Red Army, thereby severing the river route to Kolchak's capital.

312 Shol'ts, pp. 60–1. Almost a hundred officers, including three generals, also came into Siberia on board the expedition's ships – see Shepeleva, pp. 192–3.

Table 4.18: Goods (in poods) imported into Siberia from Europe and North Russia via the Northern Sea Route, September 1919

Various goods owned by Siberia Co-operatives		50,063
Military goods		100,000
Goods purchased by the Omsk goverment:	cellulose seeds	6,375 97
Medicine and paper		8,000
Storage batteries		122
Medicinal fish oils		3,521
Total		168,178

and tools intended for distribution among the Siberian peasantry – which was not transshipped and was subsequently returned to Europe.[313]

Soviet sources claim that the military goods imported via the Northern Sea Route consisted of 41,000 uniforms, 41,000 rifles and some 10,000,000 rounds of ammunition.[314] It is unlikely, however, that this matériel could have made any significant contribution to the White war effort, for by the time that the flotillas arrived back in central Siberia in November 1919, the fate of the Russian Army and of the entire counter-revolution east of the Urals had been sealed. The British uniforms and guns may, in fact, have fallen into the hands of the rapidly advancing Red Army even before they could be unpacked.

The Kolchak government and Siberian co-operation

The failure of the Northern Sea Route venture to satisfy the economic needs of the Siberian rear was but one result of a general aura of hostility emanating from the Kolchak régime towards all the operations of the Siberian co-operative movement – hostility manifested in degrees ranging from administrative measures designed to

313 *Siberian Co-operation and the Commercial Exploitation of the Northern Sea Route*. London (1920), p. 5.

314 Spirin, *Razgrom armii Kolchaka*, pp. 180–1.

limit co-operative activity and influence to the arrest, incarceration and even the murder of co-operative agents by the White military. At the root of this hostility lay a triplex political prejudice. Firstly, there was a prejudice against the personnel of the co-operative leadership who, despite their glowing anti-Bolshevik credentials earned in 1918 and despite their rendering of varying degrees of moral and material support to the Russian Army in 1918 and 1919, were tainted in White eyes by their previous history of involvement in SR politics and organizations. Secondly, there existed the Great Russian prejudice of the Omsk régime against the *oblastnik* colouring of the co-operatives' activities in Siberia, which sought, if not autarky, then at least to weaken the centre's stranglehold upon their region's economy. And thirdly, there existed in the corridors of power of Omsk a prejudice against the socialist ethos of co-operation – in particular against the movement's campaign in 1918 and 1919 for greater centralized control over foreign trade. Although this was nothing more than western capitalist states had embraced during World War 1, to the post-revolutionary Russian right – and in particular to a Kolchak régime so closely associated with the Trade and Industry lobby – state control smacked of Bolshevism. Pure and unadulterated 'private initiative' was the nostrum for all Omsk politicians who desired to rise up the government hierarchy, noted Foreign Minister Sukin; while K.N. Nekliutin, the Minister of Food and Supply, opined that 'only in the organization of a private trading apparatus' lay the solution to Siberia's economic ills.[315]

This obdurate commitment to private enterprise on the part of the Omsk régime was, however, extremely debilitating from the point of view of its contribution to the anti-Bolshevik cause, for it flew in the face of Siberian reality. The fact was that private trading companies had never flourished in a colony traditionally run by administrative fiat and that during the war many of those which had gained a foothold had gone out of business. Moreover, the crisis conditions of the civil war demanded a system of uninterrupted buying at the place of production, a widespread organization of permanent agencies and a knowledge of the international market which the private sector could not supply. It could, however, have been supplied by the Siberian co-operative movement, which had grown exponentially in the previous decade; and, but for White prejudice, the co-operatives would have provided Omsk

315 Sukin, (*Leeds Russian Archive*), pp. 108–9; *Russkaia armiia* (Omsk) No. 114, 3.vi.1919.

with the best possible means of economic growth in the Siberian rear during 1918 and 1919.

Kolchak's western allies were certainly aware that the co-operative network provided not only the best means of effecting trade within Siberia, but also a guarantee against undue exploitation of a vulnerable populace. The Canadian Economic Commission to Siberia reported to that effect; both the British and American governments established official trading organizations (the Siberian Supply Company and the War Trade Board of the United States' Russian Bureau Incorporated, respectively) which aimed to by-pass private traders and deal primarily with the co-operatives; and Bernard Pares's ambitious plans for British participation in the post-war reconstruction of Russia were founded upon deals to be struck with Siberian co-operatives during his mission.[316]

Despite such initiatives, however, the Allies would achieve little in this direction. The Canadian Government managed only to set up an exchange of seeds for flax; meanwhile the Siberian Supply Company sent just £280,000 worth of goods into Siberia in 1919 (71.5% of them via co-operative organizations) and had little effect west of Harbin.[317] Washington seemed set to do better, but had hardly even begun to meet the terms of a $25,000,000 deal struck with the Siberian co-operatives in the summer of 1919 when the counter-revolution collapsed in the east.[318] In part, of course, such failures can be attributed to factors on the Allied side – notably, in the case of the Siberian Supply Company, to the western governments' failure to dissuade their own capitalists from attempts to make a killing in Siberia, thereby

316 *Report of the CEC*, pp. 111–12; Murby, R.N. 'The Canadian Economic Commission to Siberia', *Canadian Slavonic Papers* Vol. 11 (1969), No. 3, pp. 377–8; FO 371/3367/153839 'Eliot (Irkutsk) to FO, 28.ix.1919'; *FRUS: 1918*, Vol. 3, pp. 147–50, 165, 169–70; Pares, B. 'Political Conditions in Western Siberia, 20.vi.1919. Appendix "S": Report of a Meeting with Representatives of Zakupsbyt' (*Pares Papers*, Box 41).

317 Murby, pp. 377–8; *DBFP*, pp. 724–5.

318 Ivanov, B.V. *Sibirskaia kooperatsiia v periode Oktiabr'skoi revoliutsii i grazhdanskoi voiny*. Tomsk (1976), pp. 273–7; Prisiazhnyi, A.G. 'Iz istorii sibirskoi kooperatsii perioda revoliutsii i grazhdanskoi voiny', in Bozhenko, R.M. (ed.) *Nekotorye voprosy istorii Sibiri*. Tomsk (1973), Vol. 2, pp. 108–9. For the impressions of a United States Government envoy to the Siberian co-operatives see also Brown, W.A. *The Groping Giant: Revolutionary Russia as seen by an American Democrat*. New Haven (1920).

undermining the official schemes.[319] Ultimately, however, study of the situation within Kolchakia reveals that it was White prejudices which prevented the co-operative movement from realizing its potential service to the anti-Bolshevik cause.

The development of the co-operative movement in Siberia was bound up with dairy farming. The climate and vegetation of western and southern Siberia had contributed to the growth there in the late nineteenth century of herds producing milk with a fat content more than twice the European norm, making it ideal for the production of butter. With the development of the Trans-Siberian Railway around the turn of the century, the export of agricultural goods from Siberia became feasible. Space on trains was limited, however, and this again tended to favour concentration upon the production of goods of a high value/weight ratio, such as butter (of which 132,000 poods were exported in 1899 and 1,944,000 in 1903). It soon transpired, however, that because of the region's isolation and its farmers' commercial inexperience, foreign middlemen – particularly Danes and Dutchmen – were gaining control of the region's butter exports and were extracting considerable profits from it whilst at the same time suppressing the potential sales of Siberian butter in order to protect their own national dairy industries. To combat this tendency the Imperial Government, prompted by Sergei Witte, had channelled funds and expertise into an Organization for the Establishment of Co-operative Creamery Associations in Western Siberia in 1902. Subsequently, under the leadership of A.N. Balakshin, butter-producing co-operatives, which would handle goods from the point of production to the point of sale both at home and abroad, sprang up throughout Siberia; by 1914 their collegiate organ, the Union of Siberian Creamery Associations, could boast of 864 constituent co-operative associations and an annual turnover of some 20,200,000 roubles. The World War seemed likely to put an end to growth because, with the Trans-Siberian Railway monopolized by the army, leaving access only to the limited domestic market, butter prices slumped. In 1915, however, Balakshin saved the day by securing for the Siberian co-operatives a number of lucrative contracts to supply the army with foodstuffs and forage.

319 FO 371/3367/153839. For an analysis of the role of the Siberian Supply Co. see Kolz, A.W.F. 'British Economic Interests in Siberia during the Russian Civil War', *Journal of Modern History*, Vol. 48 (1976), pp. 483–91.

Consequently, by 1918, the number of Creamery Associations had grown to 2,015 with a turnover of some 218,000,000 roubles.[320]

Following the example set by the Union of Creamery Associations, Siberian peasants – often under the guidance of socialist intellectuals – began to combine into other sorts of co-operatives for their mutual benefit. Credit Unions proved very popular, with the Union of Siberian Credit Unions (*Sibkredsoiuz*) boasting 1,230 branches by 1918. Consumer co-operatives also caught the popular imagination – although at first these had tended to be subsumed into the Union of Siberian Creamery Associations. The more radical socialist elements in the movement, however, began to harness the consumer co-operatives' opposition to the increasingly business- and profit-orientated leadership of the Creamery Union and, in August 1916, broke away to form their own All-Siberian Union of Co-operative Associations, known as Zakupsbyt (literally, 'Buy and Sell'). By January 1st 1919 Zakupsbyt had 4,400 constituent associations, with 600,000 members (representing an impressive 42% of the heads of household in Siberia); in 1918 it had had a turnover of 201,507,491 roubles and was estimated to control between a quarter and a third of the entire retail trade of Siberia through its outlets.[321] As its name implies, however, no sooner had Zakupsbyt been established than the scope of its operations was broadened. Not content with supplying goods to its members, Zakupsbyt also undertook to manufacture its own products and to sell both its own products and the products of its members both at home and abroad (with offices established in New York, London and Shanghai during 1917). Some 149 Zakupsbyt enterprises, mostly concerned with the processing of animal and vegetable products (e.g. leather, soap, candles, glue, flour, oils, butter and hemp) or with the maintenance and repair of agricultural goods and machinery were in operation by 1918. Finally, the organization became involved in manufacturing; and by 1918 the Siberian economist N. Oganovskii was estimating that 25% of the region's manufacturing industry was in co-operative hands.[322]

320 Kayden, E.M and Antsiferov, A.N. *The Co-operative Movement in Russia During the War*. New Haven (1929), pp. 381–98; Bubnoff, J.V. *The Co-operative Movement in Russia: Its History, Significance and Development*. Manchester (1917), pp. 77–84.

321 *The Union of Siberian Creamery and Other Co-operative Associations and the Country Served by this Organization*. London (1919), pp. 7, 58; *Sibirskaia kooperatsiia* (Novonikolaevsk) 1919, Nos. 2–3 (February–March), p. 24.

322 Kayden and Antsiferov, pp. 169–93.

But not everything was perfect in the co-operative world. Wartime success had fostered plans and ambitions which had foundered in the confusion of revolution and civil war. In particular, it was noted by contemporary observers that the co-operative unions had tied up major proportions of the liquid assets of their organizations in large-scale purchases of produce (such as furs, hides, butter and fish) which they then found could not be exported and realized upon owing to the transportation deadlock and the currency problems of 1918 to 1919. Consequently, during that period they were short of working capital at the highest level.[323] *Sibkredsoiuz*, for example, expected that in 1919 it would have the resources to supply only 10% of its members' demands.[324] Nevertheless, visitors to Kolchak's Siberia were invariably struck by the industriousness of the co-operatives in comparison to the lethargic performance of the White government and the weakness of private companies. For Bernard Pares 'nothing was more impressive' than the manner in which co-operation had become the very bones of Siberian economic and cultural life, while an American official opined: 'step into the office of one of the co-operatives where forty typewriters are clicking and you can imagine yourself in an office on Broadway'.[325] And, despite the political atmosphere and economic problems of the time, when co-operatives *had* the resources to enter the market, they could invariably offer goods to the needy and hungry Siberian consumer at lower prices than did private firms. At Irkutsk in January 1918, for example, as Table 4.19 (below) indicates, Zakupsbyt was undercutting prices set by private retailers by a considerable margin.[326]

Such a useful service should obviously have been encouraged by an intelligent government. In fact, the entire history of the region's co-operative movement should have alerted Kolchak to the veracity of Zakupsbyt's claim that 'the Siberian co-operatives represent the Siberian population organized so as to form the machinery of a tremendous and solidly built commercial enterprise'.[327] The Supreme Ruler and

323 *Report of the CEC*, pp. 11–12, 59; Rodney, p. 328.

324 Maslov, P.P. 'Economic Problems in Siberia', *Struggling Russia* (New York) Vol. 1, No. 20 (24.vii.1919), p. 294.

325 Pares, B. *My Russian Memoirs*. London (1931), p. 522; Gidney, pp. 259–60.

326 *Izvestiia i trudy Soiuz Sibirskikh kooperativnykh Soiuzov. 'Zakupsbyt'* (Novonikolaevsk) 13.ii.1919, p. 15.

327 *Siberian Co-operation*, p. 5.

Table 4.19: Comparitive prices (in roubles) of goods at co-operative and private outlets at Irkutsk, January 1918

Goods	Co-operative price	Private price
Sheet iron (per pood)	17.00	80.00
Nails (per pood)	43.00	200.00
Scythes (each)	3.50	75.00
Needles (per thousand)	8.00	30.00
Tea brick (per case)	1,000.00	3,800.00
Matches (per case)	175.00	600.00
Overcoats (each)	300.00	900.00
Galoshes (per pair)	25.00	120.00
Salt (per pood)	1.50	15.00
Calico (per *arshin*)	2.85	11.00

his advisers should have been aware that if any organization was capable of salvaging something from the economic mire of Siberia, then the co-operative movement was it.

Apart from their economic contribution to the region, the anti-Bolshevik political credentials of Siberian co-operation might also have been expected to recommend the organizations to Omsk as partners. From the very first post-October days, in fact, Siberian co-operatives had steadfastly opposed Lenin's régime. On November 25th–28th 1917 the 1st All-Siberian Co-operative Congress had convened to resolve not to recognize the Soviet Government and to protest against its armistice with Germany.[328] More concrete measures were taken at a subsequent 2nd All-Siberian Co-operative Congress at Novonikolaevsk on January 6th 1918. Dominated by SRs (75 out of the 88 delegates were affiliated to that party), the 2nd Congress decided that co-operatives should take all possible steps to assist socialist parties in overthrowing Bolshevik power and that, to this end, a fighting fund should be established to which the larger co-operative unions should each pledge 100,000

328 Prisiazhnyi, pp. 98–9.

roubles.[329] And not only finance was offered to the incipient anti-Bolshevik underground – co-operative leaders such as A.V. Sazanov, N.V. Fomin, P.Ia. Mikhailov and B.D. Markov personally entered into anti-Bolshevik cells and their organizations provided cover, in the form of false documents, with which White Guard agents were able to travel through Siberia and purchase weapons and supplies in the run-up to the anti-Bolshevik rising of May–June 1918.[330]

Undoubtedly, then, the co-operatives of Siberia made a very significant contribution to the overthrow of Soviet power in their region. Quite simply, as one participant in the rising recalled, there was nowhere else that the White underground could have looked for funds.[331] And with the co-operatives forming the region's sole surviving network of communication and control in the confusion of the immediate post-coup days of the summer of 1918, the popular jest recalled by one co-operative luminary was probably not far wide of the mark: according to Nils Fomin, in June 1918 'All power in Siberia was transferred to Zakupsbyt.'[332] The ultimate tribute to the contribution made by the co-operatives to the success of the anti-Bolshevik rising came, however, at the 3rd All-Siberian Co-operative Congress of August 28th–September 4th 1918 when Grishin-Almazov himself, the Minister of War of the Provisional Siberian Government, thanked the movement for its 'most fruitful assistance' in the staging of the rising.[333]

This spirit of partnership, however, did not long survive. As anti-Bolshevik politics came increasingly to be dominated by the right at Omsk during the summer and

329 Kas′ian, A.K. 'Antinarodnaia rol′ rukovoditelei kooperatsii Zapadnoi Sibiri v pervom periode sovetskoi vlasti i grazhdanskoi voiny (dek. 1917–no. 1919gg.)', in *Uchenye zapiski Omskogo gosudarstvennogo pedagogicheskogo instituta (Seriia ist. nauka)* (Omsk), Vol. 15 (1962), pp. 54–7; Parfenov, P.S. *Grazhdanskaia voina v Sibiri, 1918–1920*. Moscow (1925), pp. 13–15; Krusser, G.V. *Kolchakovshchina*. Novosibirsk (1927), p. 5. The co-operatives were roused to action when, in a project of December 1917 entitled 'On Consumer Communes', Lenin signalled the Bolsheviks' intention to nationalize co-operative property, so that they should serve the entire rural community and not just their own members. See Lenin, *PSS* Vol. 26, p. 377.

330 Znamenskaia, P.A. *Khrestomatiia po istorii Sibiri*. Novosibirsk (1930), pp. 221–3; Kadeikin, *Sibir′ nepokroennaia*, p. 268.

331 Morozov, K. 'How Siberia was Liberated from the Bolsheviks', *Struggling Russia* (New York) Vol. 1, No. 22 (9.viii.1919).

332 *Sibirskaia kooperatsiia* (Novosibirsk), No. 6 (1918), p. 1.

333 Shikalov, A.S. 'Potrebitel′naia kooperatsiia Sibiri v periode velikoi Oktiabr′skoi revoliutsii i grazhdanskoi voiny (1917–1919gg.)', in *Ocherki istorii potrebitel′noi kooperatsii Sibiri*. Novosibirsk (1965), p. 58.

early autumn of 1918, voices of dissent against the unequivocal support of the White authorities began to be raised within the co-operative movement. Archival sources cited by the two leading Soviet experts on this subject, for example, highlight 'serious differences' between the leadership of the All-Siberian co-operative unions and their local branches which, being at the sharp end of White misrule, soon came to oppose their organizations' support of the PSG and Kolchak and demanded that the co-operatives remain apolitical, purely economic organizations.[334] It was also generally true, however, that producer co-operatives tended to be more inclined to overlook the White malfeasance than were the consumer co-operatives. The Union of Siberian Creamery Associations, for example, supported the PSG in its campaign against the *Sibobduma*, while Zakupsbyt favoured the duma's convocation as a counter to the dominance of Omsk politics by the right.[335]

Subsequent events – the Omsk coup and the massacre of co-operative and SR figures in December – caused the Zakupsbyt leadership again to modify its attitude to the White régime. Its board protested at Kolchak's seizure of power (predicting nothing less than 'the end of civilization' in Russia if such illegal acts were repeated) and local branches called for an end to further co-operative participation in the civil war.[336] Ultimately, however, the Zakupsbyt leadership resolved that 'there can be no absolute apoliticism among co-operatives...but only a real, relative apoliticism – something in the nature of a half-way point between politicism and apoliticism'; in line with this principle it recommended that Zakupsbyt should pursue a 'hostile neutrality' towards the Soviet Government and a 'benevolent neutrality' towards Kolchak.[337] In practice this meant that Zakupsbyt would continue to do business with Kolchak and would support the Russian Army, but would not be used as a propaganda tool for the Omsk Government.

Having won a majority of seats on the permanent Bureau of the All-Siberian Co-operative Congress (*Vsekosovet*) established in September 1918, the producer co-

334 Prisiazhnyi, p. 97; Ivanov, *Sibirskaia kooperatsiia*, pp. 278–84; Ivanov, B.V. 'K legende ob apolitichnosti sibirskoi kooperatsii v periode kolchakovshchiny', in *K 50-letiiu osvobozhdenii Sibiri ot kolchakovshchiny*. Tomsk (1970), p. 52. Other evidence confirms that local co-operative congresses resolved to abstain from all political activity – see the reports from branches at Chita and Novonikolaevsk in *Nasha zaria* (Omsk) No. 127, 17.vi.1919.

335 Berk, S.M. 'The *Coup d'État* of Admiral Kolchak and the Counter-Revolution in Siberia and East Russia, 1917–1918', Columbia University PhD Thesis (1971), pp. 221–9.

336 Zenzinov, *Gosudarstvennyi perevorot*, pp. 153–5.

337 *Sibirskaia kooperatsiia* (Novosibirsk) 1918, Nos. 11–12 (November–December), pp. 50–2.

operatives of Siberia, led by the Union of Siberian Creamery Associations, did not even bother to conceal their support for the Kolchak Government behind notions of 'relative' and 'absolute' apoliticism. *Vsekosovet* transferred its headquarters from Novonikolaevsk to Omsk in October in order to keep in close contact with the White authorities. It then resolved that the co-operatives 'must not interfere in politics', but five of its members subsequently entered into official government bodies while Sazonov fronted the Omsk Bloc and pledged 'irreconcilable' support for Kolchak. Finally, on December 18th 1918, *Vsekosovet* adopted a resolution recognizing the All-Russian Government of Kolchak and pledging itself to support its programme.[338]

The murder of Fomin and his colleagues at Omsk on December 22nd at the hands of the White military forced *Vsekosovet*, like Zakupsbyt, to reconsider its position – and Sazanov even contemplated withdrawing from the Bloc.[339] Nothing came of this review, however, and throughout the spring and summer of 1919, Kolchak could rely upon Sazonov personally and upon *Vsekosovet* and the Union of Siberian Creamery Associations collectively to supply a steady stream of resolutions expressing confidence that his 'wise leadership will guide us to a bright and happy future', offering congratulations upon 'the attention he and the government he leads are paying to the interests of the peasantry' and urging the western powers 'to recognize Admiral Kolchak's Government as a lawful Provisional All-Russian Government, bound to give Russia a National Constituent Assembly, peace, liberty and order'. All of this, of course, was first-grade grist to the mill of Omsk's ongoing propaganda campaign to have Kolchak recognized by the Allies, and hardly a week went by without such resolutions being broadcast to the European capitals via the White press.[340] Just to force the message home Omsk's Ministry of Agriculture even recruited co-operative agents such as N.A. Borodin to undertake lecture tours in Europe on the theme of 'Kolchak as a constitutional dictator'.[341]

338 *Sibirskaia kooperatsiia* (Novosibirsk), Nos. 4–6 (1919), p. 3; *The Russian Co-operator* (London) Vol. 3, No. 3 (March 1919), p. 42; *Vestnik... 'Zakupsbyt'* (Novosibirsk), No. 2–3 (February–March 1919), p. 25.

339 Ivanov, *Sibirskaia kooperatsiia*, pp. 288–9.

340 See, for example, *Bulletin of the Russian Liberation Committee (Union)* (London) No. 14, 24.v.1919; *Struggling Russia* (New York) Vol. 1, Nos. 13–14 (14.vi.1919) and Vol. 1, No. 20 (25.vii.1919), p. 298; *Union (Bureau de Presse Russe)* (Paris) No. 13, 24.ix.1919, p. 14; *The Russian/Russkii zhurnal* (London) Vol. 2, No. 38 (3.vii.1919).

341 *Russkaia zhizn'* (Helsingfors) No. 123, 1.viii.1919.

In addition to such moral support and political credibility as was granted to the Kolchak régime by the co-operatives, account needs also to be taken of the movement's material and financial contributions to the White cause. A variety of separate deals were struck by individual co-operative unions with the authorities at Omsk. Within a matter of days of the Kolchak coup, for example, the Union of Siberian Creamery Associations was contracted to supply footwear and other leather goods to the Russian Army; by November 1919 it had managed to import 500,000 pairs of boots from the USA and, in addition, had spent over 20,000,000 roubles on materials for the Ministry of Supply. *Sibkredsoiuz*, meanwhile, had pledged to supply 180,000,000 roubles' worth of goods to the Russian Army by September 1919. Even Zakupsbyt felt unable to turn down the business opportunities offered by the war and in March 1919 signed contracts with the Ministry of Supply to supply 100,000 pairs of deerskin underboots *(pimy)*, 30,000 sheepskin coats and 2,000 poods of soap (worth a total of 12,900,000 roubles) to the army at the front.[342]

All of this, of course, could be written-off as sound, apolitical business on behalf of the unions' memberships. The same could hardly be said, however, of the financial donations to the Russian Army made by all the major co-operative organizations. The research of Soviet historians has revealed that at the height of the Kolchak offensive during the spring of 1919, the Siberian co-operatives responded to a call by *Vsekosovet* by pledging 5% of their future trading turnover to the Russian Army and by making the immediate monetary donations detailed in Table 4.20 (below).[343] By October 1919, according to government figures, donations from co-operatives to the army were approaching the 200,000,000 roubles mark.[344] Even these figures, however, may well understate the co-operatives' true level of contribution because in 1919 many unions followed the example of the Union of Siberian Creamery Associations in not pressing the Kolchak Government to meet the interest payments due on or to repay entirely the loans White organizations had received from the co-operatives in early 1918.[345]

342 Prisiazhnyi, p. 109; Ivanov, *Sibirskaia kooperatsiia*, p. 259; 'Pour L'Armée', *Union (Agence Télégraphique Russe)* (Paris) No. 162, 9.ix.1919; *Narodnoe delo* (Omsk) No. 198 (May 1919), pp. 25–6.

343 *Trudovaia Sibir'* (Tomsk) No. 27, p. 1, cited in Ivanov, 'K legende', p. 53.

344 *Union (Agence Télégraphique Russe)* (Paris) No. 189, 17.x.1919.

345 Ivanov, *Sibirskaia kooperatsiia*, p. 266.

Table 4.20: Financial contributions (in roubles) to the Russian Army made by Siberian co-operatives, Spring 1919

Tsentrosoiuz	20,000
Sibkredsoiuz	58,000
Union of Siberian Creamery Associations	50,000
The Co-operative Bank	45,000
Zakupsbyt	25,000
Total	198,000

Through their wide-ranging economic and cultural activities and through their consistent moral and financial support of the White movement, therefore, the co-operatives had proven themselves from the very beginning to be worthy partners for Kolchak in the anti-Bolshevik struggle. 'Co-operation in general,' recalled one Omsk minister, 'rendered true assistance to the government.'[346]

At virtually every level, however, and across all Kolchakia, the co-operatives' 'true assistance' to the White cause was repaid by scorn, ingratitude and naked violence towards co-operators on the part of the White government and, in particular, on the part of the Russian Army. Premier Vologodskii might have assured Bernard Pares that the Kolchak Government 'did not equate co-operative activity with Bolshevism, as many say', but all the evidence points to a quite different conclusion – to the veracity of complaints made to Pares a week earlier by co-operative leaders that Siberian and immigrant Russian private traders were set upon regaining the ground they had lost to co-operation in recent years by hook, by crook or, if necessary, by government legislation.[347] For one thing, the co-operatives' suspicion (voiced to Pares) that local Chambers of Commerce were the source of the frequently heard rumours that co-operatives were in alliance with the Bolsheviks was verified by a Soviet historian, who discovered that on November 14th 1918 the All-Russian Congress of Trades and Industry at Omsk had called upon its constituent

346 Sukin (*Leeds Russian Archive*), pp. 109–10.

347 Pares, B. 'Notes of a Meeting with Vologodsky (Omsk, 22.v.1919)' (*Pares Papers*, Box 28); Pares, B. 'Siberian Diary'(*Pares Papers*, Box 43), pp. 81–3.

organizations to assign all possible means for 'the most rigorous and merciless struggle with internal Bolshevism – the co-operatives'; meanwhile, another Soviet expert uncovered evidence that Chambers of Commerce were establishing special sections for the struggle against co-operative socialists (that at Zima, for example, had funds of 800,000 roubles).[348] We can only speculate that this campaign of vilification against the co-operatives was carried to the very top and was impressed upon ministers by representatives of the All-Russian Congress of Trades and Industry within the government, and we can only speculate that the poison probably reached Kolchak's own ear through his personal association with industrialists such as S.G. Feodos′ev; but, nevertheless, the evidence is clear that the manner of government policy and viciousness of military practice towards the co-operative unions of Siberia were matched only by the protectiveness and generosity displayed towards the region's private traders and businessmen – in spite of the fact that events proved the latter both unable and unwilling to contribute resources to the war effort.

At the highest level co-operative representatives were excluded from or under-represented in the policy-making bodies of the government. Soon after the Kolchak coup, for example, N.S. Zefirov, the new Minister of Food and Supply, began to sack co-operative agents within his ministry and chose leading lights of the All-Russian Congress of Trades and Industry to be his deputies.[349] In the New Year the influential Committee on Foreign Trade of the Ministry of Finance was packed with Trades and Industry representatives, while in June 1919 *Vsekosovet* was permitted to send just seven representatives to a Special Conference on Food and Supply organized by the Ministry of Food in comparison to the twenty-five delegates invited from the private sector.[350] It was hardly surprising, therefore, that the Ministry of Finance and the Ministry of Food placed the bulk of their orders with private traders and made railway facilities available to them, while co-operative organizations found it impossible to get their goods either into or out of Siberia.

348 Ivanov, *Sibirskaia kooperatsiia*, p. 209; Parfenov, P.S. *Uroki proshlogo: grazhdanskaia voina v Sibiri (1918, 1919, 1920gg.)*. Harbin (1921), p. 104.

349 Serebrennikov, *Moi vospominaniia*, p. 233.

350 *The Russian Co-operator* (London) Vol. 3, No. 11 (November 1919), pp. 169–70; *Russkaia armiia* (Omsk) No. 114, 3.vi.1919.

Table 4.21: Government loans and subsidies (in roubles) issued to Siberian institutions down to January 10th 1919

Private businesses	109,052,697	*31.0%*
Railway companies	114,093,922	*32.5%*
Private banks	110,000,000	*31.4%*
Zemstvos and municipalities	10,916,600	*03.1%*
Cossack agricultural needs	5,550,000	*01.6%*
Co-operative organizations	1,500,000	*00.3%*
Total	351,113,219	

Nor did the Kolchak Government attempt to ease the cash flow problems being faced by some of the co-operatives through the issuing of loans or subsidies to them. Private enterprises and banks, on the other hand, were showered with government finance from the very beginning of White rule, as is revealed by the official data presented above in Table 4.21.[351]

The co-operatives went out of their way during the spring of 1919 to appear accommodating and to convince the government of their good intentions – apart from the moral and material support already described, for example, *Vsekosovet* urged its constituent organizations to deliver goods to the Siberian population 'fairly and in co-ordination with private industry', while individual unions (including Zakupsbyt) were observed by British agents to be 'cleansing themselves of Bolsheviks and Chernovites' in order to appease Omsk.[352] But it was all to no avail. The amount of support the co-operatives received from the government in the first half of 1919 did rise in relative terms in comparison to the figure for the previous six months, as is clear from Table 4.22 (below). But once the spiralling level of inflation is taken into account the improvement could at best have been only marginal and, indeed, there may actually have been a decline in real terms.[353]

351 *Struggling Russia* (New York) Vol. 1, No. 20 (25.vii.1919), p. 293. (Percentage figures in Tables 4.21 and 4.22 are rounded to the nearest 0.1%.)

352 *The Russian Co-operator* (London) Vol. 3, No. 2 (February 1919), pp. 26–7; Pares, B. 'Report on Political Conditions in Western Siberia, 20.vi.1919' (*Pares Papers*, Box 41), pp. 12–13.

353 *Struggling Russia* (New York) Vol. 1, No. 20 (25.vii.1919), p. 298.

Table 4.22: Government loans and subsidies (in roubles) issued to Siberian institutions, January 11th–June 1st 1919

Private businesses	219,676,483	*36.2%*
Railway companies	150,189,736	*24.8%*
Zemstvos and municipalities	142,813,856	*23.6%*
Cossack agricultural needs	58,944,000	*09.8%*
Co-operative organizations	33,900,000	*05.6%*
Total	605,524,075	

Moreover, even some of the meagre subsidies granted to co-operatives had strings attached to the effect that in order to receive the money the unions had to agree to assist private traders in establishing themselves in areas (geographical and economic) which had previously been a co-operative monopoly.[354] The ultimate insult to the co-operatives came, however, in July 1919 when in the face of the catalogue of contributions which the movement had made to the White cause, Kolchak still saw fit to prohibit the convocation of a planned 4th All-Siberian Co-operative Congress.[355]

It might, of course, be argued that the lack of government patronage to the Siberian co-operative movement could be explained (or even excused) by a recognition in Omsk that the co-operative movement was less in need of support than the ailing private sector. That something more malevolent was at work, however, is evinced by the systematic campaign of violence and intimidation inflicted upon the co-operatives at the hands of the White authorities.

Even before Kolchak came to power Zakupsbyt was complaining to the Directory that 'in the countryside the requisitioning of co-operative goods is occurring on all sides, as well as the arrest of co-operative workers'; while, as instances of military repressions multiplied in the weeks before the coup, co-operative stores in Omsk, Novonikolaevsk and Ufa were raided and boarded-up by the army and, in at least one case, a co-operative newspaper (*Vlast' naroda* of Cheliabinsk) was closed down

354 Ivanov, *Sibirskaia kooperatsiia*, pp. 270–1.

355 Parfenov, *Grazhdanskaia voina*, p. 79.

and its editor (E. Maevskii) murdered by officer organizations.[356] Their confidence boosted by the elevation of Kolchak to the dictatorship, White civil and military authorities stepped up their campaign accordingly. Punitive expeditions against pockets of resistance to government ordinances in the countryside singled out co-operative workers for particularly vicious beatings (often resulting in deaths); unions' shareholders meetings were broken up and banned (or, if permitted, it was insisted upon that military representatives should be present); co-operative libraries were scoured for 'Bolshevik' literature (loosely defined as anything published in 1917 or early 1918); another tactic was the commandeering of co-operative property for military use (as befell, for example, the *Tsentrosoiuz* headquarters at Omsk and the Zakupsbyt centre at Ekaterinburg) – and usually at such short notice that the premises could not be cleared of valuable furniture, typewriters, presses and so on, which the organizations had accrued during their boom period of the war.[357] By February 1919, in fact, *Vsekosovet* had received no less than 177 complaints from sixty separate co-operative unions concerning the requisitioning of co-operative property and the illegal detention of co-operative workers: 'It seems that in every case where an agent of the authorities feels a need for a certain good or product,' wrote one co-operator, 'they appeal not to the "sacred" private sector but to the property of co-operatives and, in particular, Zakupsbyt.'[358] The Kolchak Government even permitted the army to mobilize and send to the front the entire statistical department of one central co-operative organization – even though the Ministry of Finance was at that very time blaming 'the lack of men familiar with accounting techniques' for the government's poor financial performance.[359]

The ideological commitment of the Omsk Government to private enterprise and the advantages it bestowed upon private concerns in terms of government loans,

356 Parfenov, *Uroki*, p. 104; Burevoi, K.S. *Kolchakovshchina*. Moscow (1919), pp. 26–7.

357 Pares, B. 'Siberian Diary' (*Pares Papers* Box 43), p. 34; A.M. *Sibirskaia kooperatsiia v periode voennoi diktatury*. Omsk (1922), pp. 3–23, 29–39; Kas'ian, pp. 61–3, 67–8; Shikalov, pp. 60–5; *The Russian Co-operator* (London) Vol. 3, No. 3 (March 1919), p. 41. One building belonging to the Union of Siberian Creamery Associations at Omsk which was requisitioned by the army later reopened as a private restaurant – see A.M., p. 6.

358 *Vestnik Soveta Vsesibirskikh kooperativnykh S"ezdov* (Novosibirsk), No. 2–3 (1919), p. 25, cited in Ivanov, *Sibirskaia kooperatsiia*, pp. 289–90; A.M., p. 18.

359 *Obozrenie deiatel'nosti Ministerstva finansov*, p. 12; Pares, B. 'Siberian Diary' (*Pares Papers*, Box 43), p. 88.

subsidies and contracts did not pay dividends in terms of the contributions made to the war effort by the Siberian business community. The All-Russian Congress of Trades and Industry at Omsk had, as we have seen, been among the sponsors of moves towards dictatorship in 1918 and it had been strongly supportive of the coup of November 18th. On November 20th, for example, the All-Russian Congress had issued a circular calling upon each and every one of its members 'to render to the new government the most friendly support, to participate in active work to rebuild the economic might of the country and to liquidate the disorganization now within it'.[360] The response from the membership, however, was not encouraging. 'Instead of active support of the government,' recalled Kolchak's first Minister of Food and Supply, Ivan Serebrennikov, 'many Trade and Industry organizations – especially that of Omsk – worried various ministers around the clock to see if it was not possible for them to wriggle out of meeting some contract or whether they might not be paid at such and such a price.'[361] Then, during the New Year, news began to circulate in the Omsk press that government subsidies to private companies were being persistently misused. Mining companies and trading houses in the Urals were using funds supplied by the government to buy up agricultural machinery and manufactured goods from cash-starved co-operatives only to stockpile them and drive up their prices before re-selling them at a massive profit.[362]

On occasion the authorities reacted decisively to such blatant peculation: the Tetiukhinsk silver and lead mines, for example, were actually re-nationalized by Kolchak in 1919 when it was discovered that their proprietors had been illegally exporting silver, lead and zinc which was sorely needed by the Russian Army.[363] The general pattern, however, was exemplified when an Extraordinary Congress of Trades and Industry of the Urals was convened by Kolchak at Ekaterinburg on May 10th 1919. The Supreme Ruler, uncomfortable as ever in his civil capacity, delivered a brief opening address to the Congress before setting off to the front and leaving his secretary, George Guins, to make a keynote speech reminding businessmen of

360 Iakushkin, E. *Kolchakovshchina i interventsiia v Sibiri*. Moscow (1928), p. 28.

361 Serebrennikov, *Moi vospominaniia*, p. 270.

362 Taniaev, *Kolchakovshchina na Urale*, p. 68; Gromov et al., *Partizanskoe dvizhenie*, p. 100.

363 Krushanov, *Grazhdanskaia voina*, Vol. 1, p. 127. Not all the works that might have been re-nationalized were, however: 'Imagine us in England allowing a munitions factory to remain idle throughout the most critical period of the war because its owner had run away without leaving an address', noted a British officer of the situation he had observed in the Urals. 'McCullagh (Omsk) to Knox, 22.vi.1919' (*Pares Papers*, Box 28).

their duty 'to apply all their strength so that industrial activity is carried out above all according to the interests of the Russian state and not because it is profitable'.[364] This, however, made little impression upon an audience which, according to one delegate from the Kadet party, was 'not interested in telling the government what they could do for it in such difficult times, but only in asking what the government could do for them'. 'What man is his own enemy?' was one shouted response from the floor to Guins's call for self-sacrifice in the business community.[365]

Throughout the remainder of the Kolchak Government's existence, in fact, reports indicate that the more conscientious of his ministers and local representatives were engaged in a constant struggle to try and force the private sector to act responsibly, to pay their taxes on time, to pay import duties, and to accept increases in railway freight charges in line with inflation. Counting on the régime's general inability to enforce the law, however, the avoidance of taxes and other responsibilities wherever possible was the norm.[366] Perhaps the most despicable instance of such venality came in July 1919 when Bernard Pares was amongst those shocked to witness the same merchants and capitalists of Ekaterinburg who had for six months been pleading poverty when requested to victual the Siberian Army and their city's hungry workers, breaking open their warehouses and attempting to dispose of hoarded food at knock-down prices before the Urals fell into Bolshevik hands.[367]

Despite such shabby occurrences, for foreign and domestic propaganda purposes the official press attempted to portray Kolchak's relationship with the business community in a good light. The Omsk papers prominently heralded financial contributions made by Trades and Industry Congresses to the Russian Army and to

364 Guins, *Sibir'*, Vol. 2, pp. 190–1.

365 Krol', L. *Za tri goda*, p. 171.

366 Sukin (*Leeds Russian Archive*), p. 103; Menshikov, A. 'Praktika primorskogo zemstva', *Sibirskii arkhiv* (Prague), Vol. 4 (1932), pp. 171–2; Livshits, S.G. *Imperialisticheskaia interventsiia v Sibiri, 1918–1920gg.* Barnaul (1979), pp. 65–7.

367 Pares, B. 'Report on Political Conditions in the Siberian Frontal Zone, ?.viii.1919' (*Pares Papers*, Box 44), p. 13. 'I would boot the whole lot into the arms of the Bolsheviks with the greatest of pleasure', recalled a British officer of the 'fat speculators and their wives' he witnessed monopolizing the railway traffic out of Ekaterinburg, as soldiers and less wealthy citizens were forced to flee on foot. See Hodges, *Britmis*, pp. 86–91.

the relief of refugees.[368] Even official statistics, however, could not mask the bald and damning fact that down to August 1st 1919 Siberian business organizations had donated a mere twelve million roubles to the war effort, compared to the two hundred million which had been proffered by the region's much maligned co-operative organizations.[369]

'The sick man of Siberia': paralysis of the Trans-Siberian Railway under Kolchak

Perhaps no greater condemnation can be made of the Siberian Whites' disservice to their own cause than their refusal to work with the region's co-operative movement. In the end, however, it has to be said that even had the co-operatives been tolerated and even if initiatives such as the Northern Sea Route venture been properly encouraged and efficiently managed, it probably would have been sufficient to preclude any revitalization of Siberian trade in 1918 to 1919 that the always precarious and fragile ribbon of the Trans-Siberian Railway, the single realistic means of transporting the requisite amounts of goods to and from the interior, was in a state approaching complete collapse. Even at its best the line would have been in no way fit to perform the tasks imposed upon it by Kolchak's war efforts on the Volga and in the Urals; but, as White rule took its toll, Siberia's transport artery atrophied under its incompetent and peccant military managers and the corrupt railway administration over which they presided.

With regard to the condition of the Trans-Siberian Railway under the White régime, the findings of the Canadian Economic Commission to Siberia of the spring of 1919 make particularly interesting reading. The Commission concluded that 'the whole success of activities in Siberia, both military and economic, is centred on an improvement to the present means of transportation', i.e. the railway. It was,

368 See, for example, *Nasha gazeta* (Omsk) No. 1, 16.viii.1919 (on the 4,000,000 roubles donated to the army by the Omsk Trades and Industry Congress) and *Bulletin (Agence Télégraphique Russe)* (Omsk) 27.viii.1919 (on the 10,000 roubles donated by businesses for the relief of refugees).

369 *Struggling Russia* (New York) Vol. 2, Nos. 30–2 (25.x.1919), p. 504.

however, profoundly pessimistic anent the likelihood of any improvement being made because it found that the Omsk Government faced one insurmountable physical obstacle. This was that prior to World War I trade had only been conducted through Vladivostok, the eastern terminus of the line, for the inhabitants of regions lying east of Lake Baikal (who constituted only 16% of the population living east of the Urals).

The vast majority of the people of Siberia plus, of course, the entire population of the Urals (the most productive agricultural and industrial portions of Kolchakia) actually lived closer to the ports of the White Sea, the Black Sea and the Baltic than they did to the Pacific; and it had been through those now inaccessible ports that their trade had always been conducted. Omsk, for example, was 3,566 miles from Vladivostok but only 1,868 miles from Petrograd, 2,174 from Riga and 2,522 from Odessa; while Cheliabinsk was a massive 4,064 miles from Vladivostok but only 1,370 miles from Petrograd, 1,676 from Riga and 2,024 from Odessa. Even the town of Achinsk, deep in eastern Siberia, was 2,814 miles from Vladivostok but only 2,620 from Petrograd. The point half-way between Petrograd and Vladivostok – i.e. the point at which, all other factors being equal, trade should have been divided between the eastern and western terminal ports – was somewhere on the line about 100 miles east of Achinsk; out of a total population of Siberia (again excluding the Urals) of around 10,510,200, the Canadian Commission estimated that 7,408,700 (or 70.5%) lived west of that point, or closer to Petrograd than Vladivostok.[370] In these figures was revealed the whole plight of the Kolchak Government.

The only available option was to attempt to convert the Trans-Siberian line from its original role as a means of asserting central control over the eastern marches of the Empire (and beyond) into quite the opposite: a means of servicing and supplying the populations of western and eastern Siberia and the Urals from the Pacific entrepôt of Vladivostok. However, American railway engineers who were working on the line during the civil war found that the Trans-Siberian system was extremely inflexible and resistant to such a conversion. The Americans reported in particular that, because of an over-reliance on supplies of steam coal from the mines of eastern Siberia (chiefly from Cheremkhovo), the Tomsk section of the line (from Novonikolaevsk to Innokent′evskaia) was already severely over-burdened with the

370 *Report of the CEC*, pp. 19–22. On other aspects of the economic problems raised by the segmentation of Russia during the civil war see Nordman, N. *Peace Problems: Russia's Economics*. London (1919), p. 19.

westbound transportation of fuel for the needs of the railway itself. The Trans-Siberian Railway could, therefore, barely handle the traffic norm in peacetime; in any emergency it would not cope. This, in the opinion of the American railroaders, was the pre-eminent cause of delays on the line and, indeed, a major factor contributory to the accumulation at Vladivostok of massive amounts of military supplies sent to Russia by the Allies during World War 1. A subsequent investigation by Soviet researchers confirmed the Americans' impressions, calculating that in 1919 no less than 48.9% of all goods moved on the Tomsk line consisted of coal.[371]

The great stockpiles of military goods and other wares which had accumulated at Vladivostok since the blockade of Russia's main western ports of ingress in 1914 and 1915, were in themselves another barrier to the restoration of Siberia's trade. By the end of 1917 there were over a million tons of materials stored in the port – military supplies and equipment, military vehicles, agricultural implements, food preserves and so on, as well as, in the estimation of a *New York Times* correspondent, '37,000 railway truck wheels, heavy steel rails in such a quantity as to build a third track from the Pacific to Petrograd [and] enough barbed wire to fence Siberia'.[372] Goods overflowed from every warehouse and customs shed to be left rotting and rusting under tarpaulins said to cover every square foot of empty space for miles around the docks. In many cases the ownership of these goods remained uncertain, but even when an owner could be traced the shipping documents for the goods in question were often in the hands of private banks who had no authority to begin sending them into Siberia, let alone to forward anything to Kolchak – at least for as long as he remained unrecognized by the powers. On the other hand, nothing could be removed from Vladivostok by sea because in the

371 Greiner, J.E. 'The American Railway Commission in Siberia and Russia', *Railway Review* Vol. 63, No. 5 (3.viii.1918), pp. 170–2; Johnson, B.O. 'Sidelights on the Russian Railroad Situation', *Railway Age* Vol. 66, No. 17 (25.iv.1919), pp. 1063–4. Merkhalev, L. 'Zheleznye dorogi v Sibiri, 1917–1920gg.', *Trudy Sibirskogo statiticheskogo upravleniia* (Omsk), Vol. 7 (1922), p. 46. On the development of railways in Siberia see Marks, S.G. *The Road to Power: the Trans-Siberian Railway and the Colonization of Asiatic Russia.* New York (1991). On the American railwaymen see also below, n. 431.

372 *Report of the CEC*, p. 8; Ackerman, C.W. *Trailing the Bolsheviks: Twelve Thousand Miles with the Allies in Siberia.* New York (1919), p. 42.

aftermath of the war tonnage was simply not available. It was one gigantic log-jam.[373]

Consequently, it proved extremely difficult for any significant amounts of the supplies so desperately needed in Siberia to be imported through the Far East. Characteristic was the following tale. Footwear was in terribly short supply for the Russian Army and for the Siberian population in general in 1918 and 1919, as the Kolchak Government admitted in an unusually humble and frank appeal for assistance in June of 1919.[374] Yet, at this very time, an enterprising Canadian businessman who had sold his shoe-shop in Calgary and brought his entire stock across the Pacific in an attempt to cash in on the record prices being paid for shoes in Siberia, was being frustrated in his efforts to get his goods off-loaded and stored at Vladivostok until they could be sent up-line. Exasperated, he eventually sold all his shoes (at a loss) to a British businessman who subsequently disposed of the shipment at Shanghai.[375]

With the town and port of Vladivostok in the hands of Kolchak's military governors (General D.L. Horvath until July 1919 and subsequently General S.N. Rozanov) and with the entire Trans-Siberian Railway system subject to military diktat, military supplies alone stood a chance of breaching the effective blockade which the chaos at Vladivostok had imposed upon Kolchakia. The chief British railway engineer in the region, Colonel Jack, found that of the six trains leaving Vladivostok each week in December 1918, three were military trains, one was a passenger train and two were at the disposal of the Japanese (or their puppet atamans in the Far East). A later Soviet survey indicated that the situation may subsequently have worsened: on the Tomsk line in 1919 military journeys outnumbered civilian by a factor of 7:1 (compared to a ratio of 5:1 in 1917); on the Omsk line by 4:1; and on the Trans-Baikal line by 3:1. Of course, the pressure to maximize military traffic was enormous because the White war effort in the Urals was founded almost exclusively on the basis of imported supplies; and, even according to Jack's calculations, with

373 *Report of the CEC*, pp. 8, 19.

374 *Priishim'e* (Petropavlovsk) No. 134 (1656), 26.vi.1919. The British Deputy High Commissioner in Siberia confirmed to the Foreign Office that 'leather, even in the big centres, has ceased to exist'. *DBFP*, p. 340.

375 Wilgress, D. 'From Siberia to Kuibyshev', *International Journal* (Toronto) Vol. 22, No. 3 (Summer 1967), pp. 367–8.

only three military trains a week leaving Vladivostok, it was going to take the Whites two and a half years to transport to the front the 100,000 sets of British uniforms and equipment then arriving at Vladivostok.[376] That said, however, in their dominance of railway traffic, as in so much else, the White military were particularly incogitant in their treatment of the needs of the rear. In late 1918 an American official with first-hand experience of the railway situation opined that:

> most Russian Army officers are indifferent to relief afforded to the civilian population and would be willing to let them starve if supplies intended for civilians could be requisitioned for benefit of the army... It is felt that everything should go to military organization.[377]

Efforts to organize the spring offensive of 1919 hardly moderated this attitude and, despite pleas from the Minister of Ways and Communications to allow more civilian traffic onto the line, the government estimated in May that of the last 1,440 wagons to pass through Manchuli Station (the customs checkpoint on the border of Manchuria and Transbaikalia), only 202 (14.3%) were not carrying military supplies.[378]

This virtual monopolization of the railway by the army had at least two adverse effects upon life in White Siberia and upon the fate of the Kolchak Government. In the first place, it obviously delayed or, at worst, prevented the despatch up-line of any non-military goods which, unlike the Calgary shoes, were off-loaded at Vladivostok – a supply train which the YMCA director in Siberia left loaded with food and medical supplies and ready to roll at Vladivostok in November 1918, for example, only arrived at Omsk some three months later, on February 24th 1919.[379] An additional factor, however, was that until the spring of 1919 no shipment rates for military goods were fixed. At least half of the traffic on the Trans-Siberian line, in other words, provided no revenue for a railway administration which had always had to rely upon government subsidies even in peacetime.[380] And, of course, the

376 FO 371/3365/206326 'Knox (Vladivostok) to WO, 9.xii.1918'; Merkhalev, p. 48.

377 *FRUS: 1918*, Vol. 2, p. 452.

378 *Nasha zaria* (Omsk) No. 117, 4.vi.1919.

379 Gidney, *Witness to a Revolution*, p. 300.

380 FO 371/3365/206326 'Knox (Vladivostok) to WO, 9.xii.1918'; White, J.A. 'The American Role in the Siberian Intervention', *Russian Review*, Vol. 10, No. 1 (January 1951), pp. 26–36.

poverty of the railway administration, thereby deepened, had its own knock-on effects in terms of the underpayment of workers, strikes and the poor maintenance of rolling stock.

Having emerged from the bottleneck of Vladivostok, both military and civilian traffic had to negotiate the many hazards of the Trans-Siberian Railway itself. During the summer and autumn of 1918, the system seems to have coped remarkably well – those travelling into Siberia were apt to register their surprise at services leaving on time (and occasionally even ahead of time) and then at trains keeping to their schedule all the way from Vladivostok to Omsk.[381] As Kolchak's military effort got underway in November–December 1918, however, increasing the demands made upon the system, the situation on the line rapidly deteriorated. 'Railway conditions in Siberia are intolerable', reported an American engineer at the year's end. 'The road had ceased to function for all practical purposes.'[382]

Although the most dramatic, perhaps the least serious threat to the operation of the Trans-Siberian Railway was that posed by attacks launched on the line by the anti-Kolchak partisan forces operating from the Siberian taiga. There were some localized successes for the rebels. In late May and early June of 1919, for example, trains could move only during the day on the Il′insk to Krasnoiarsk section of the Trans-Siberian line because of partisan activity around Taishet.[383] Travellers noted many burnt-out stations and 'scores' of derailed locomotives east of Krasnoiarsk at this time, and one panic-stricken station-master was moved to wire Omsk that:

> The situation is completely catastrophic. The line is defenceless. Every day the track is destroyed, bridges are blown up and the telegraph wire is cut. That which is mended by long and costly effort during the day is destroyed at night by the Reds.[384]

However, a major government offensive against the partisans during June was surprisingly successful and by the end of that month Kolchak's Military Governor of Eniseisk *guberniia*, General Rozanov, was able to report that:

[381] Gidney, pp. 247, 261.

[382] *FRUS: 1918*, Vol. 3, p. 299.

[383] Budberg, Vol. 15, p. 308; Archer, W.J. 'From Vladivostok to Omsk', *The Russian Co-operator*, Vol. 1, No. 23 (11.x.1919), pp. 536–8. Delays could add as much as ten days to the journey from Vladivostok to Omsk.

[384] Iakushkin (1928), pp. 82–3.

> Damage to the railway line and attacks on trains with the aim of disrupting the supply of our Army...have been curtailed on the entire section from Achinsk to Verkhneudinsk inclusive.[385]

But the experience of Eniseisk *guberniia* in May–June of 1919 was the exception which proved the rule: despite the prominence given to partisan activity in Soviet historiography, until the very end of the Kolchak era, the major partisan armies were kept far to the north or south of the Trans-Siberian Railway by the Russian Army's punitive expeditions and by the presence of the Czechoslovak Legion and other Allied contingents (who policed the railway from Omsk to Irkutsk and from Irkutsk to Vladivostok respectively).[386] One western source nevertheless maintains that partisans were responsible for blowing up 800 bridges along the line in 1919.[387] But even if this was so, the damage must have been quite quickly and easily repaired, for traffic was never entirely held up for any length of time by sabotage and records indicate that only one wrecked bridge (at Olovianaia in Manchuria) was damaged beyond repair, thereby necessitating the construction of a pontoon replacement and the moving of trains across the latter in stages.[388] Given the extreme length of the Trans-Siberian Railway and the impossibility of guarding its every forest-lined mile or even the 70 miles of bridge and tunnel along its route, it is in fact surprising that more was not done by the partisans to disrupt Kolchak's supplies. This is especially true when one considers the physical vulnerability of the line which skimping on materials during its hurried construction had engendered – its innumerable small bridges were virtually all made of wood and should have been open to irreparable damage if set afire (in earlier years sparks from passing engines had been observed to do the job themselves!), while the steel rails employed in constructing the line, weighing only 18lbs to the foot, were only two-thirds as resilient as their standard European and American equivalents.[389]

385 *ibid.*, p. 85.

386 See below, n. 435.

387 White, J.A. *The Siberian Intervention*. New York (1950), pp. 292–3. Unfortunately White provides no source for this figure.

388 Sukin (*Leeds Russian Archive*), p. 119.

389 Dmitriev-Mamontov, A.I. and Zdziarskii, A.F. (eds.) *Guide to the Great Siberian Railway (1900)*. Newton Abbot (1971), p. 67; Clarke, F.E. *The Great Siberian Railway – What I Saw on My Journey*. London (1904), p. 133. Carriages could suffer the same fate – see Nansen *Through Siberia*, p. 404.

Far more deleterious to the operation of Kolchak's fragile line of supply along the Trans-Siberian Railway than the attacks of his enemies, the partisans, were the maleficent acts of his supposed subordinates and allies east of Lake Baikal, Ataman Semenov and the Japanese Expeditionary Force.

In January 1919, Colonel Jack of the British Railway Mission reported to his superiors in London that no trains had left Vladivostok for ten days because a dozen echelons had been held up by Semenov in Transbaikalia.[390] And, indeed, when other British agents and observers visited Semenov's domain at that time they discovered no less than 1,200 passenger cars impounded by Semenov at Chita – two hundred were being used to accommodate the renegade ataman's 'Independent Manchurian Army', but the remainder he was leasing out to speculators at inflated rates (an activity said to be netting him some three million roubles per month).[391] Even following his settlement with Kolchak, Semenov did not cease interfering with rail traffic and in February 1919 alone 48 goods trains, including many loaded with military supplies, were held up in Transbaikalia. It was calculated by British and American observers that the ataman was impounding two hundred tons of foodstuffs a day from passing trains. On the basis of Japanese rations, that was sufficient for a force of 60,000 men. By this time, however, Semenov's 'Army' numbered only 3,000–4,000, thus leaving a sizable surplus to be sold to merchants. This activity, plus the profits of a 'super-tax' he illegally imposed on all goods entering Russia through Manchuli, garnered Semenov 20,000 roubles per day. No passing train – not even those of General Knox, Colonel Ward or the United States Ambassador to Japan – could escape a 'custom's inspection' at Manchuli. As Semenov's myrmidons looted private trunks and baggage and their comrades covered the train with frighteningly conspicuous cannon, 'even the locomotive, one felt, stopped breathing from fear', recalled one passenger.[392] Perhaps Semenov's most damaging act, however, was to commandeer sorely needed locomotives. Some he simply used to pull his own armoured trains; the majority, however, were

390 Swettenham, J. *Allied Intervention in Siberia (1918–1919) and the Part Played by Canada.* London (1967), p. 162.

391 *The Times* (London) 31.xii.1918; FO 371/3365/200484 'Knox (Irkutsk) to WO, ?.xii.1918'; FO 371/3365/211255 'Eliot (Omsk) to FO, 23.xii.1918'.

392 Livshits, S.G. 'Verkhovnyi pravitel′ admiral Kolchak i ataman Semenov (k istorii "semenovskogo intsidenta")', in Korablev and Shishkin, *Iz istorii interventsii*, p. 180; *FRUS: 1919 (Russia)*, p. 498; WO 158/740 'Knox (Vladivostok) to General Inagaki, ?.ii.1919'; *USMI*, Vol. 8, No. 106 (week ending 7.vi.1919, p. 1,151; Alioshin, *Asian Odyssey*, p. 18.

cannibalised, their boiler steel used to manufacture armour and makeshift cannon. Ironically, in May 1919 Kolchak's Assistant Minister of Ways and Communications, V.M. Larionov, issued a report condemning Semenov for forcing workers to perform such tasks on the very same day that news reached Omsk of the mendacious Buriat's pledge of 'complete, unconditional recognition of the Russian Government'.[393]

The final act in this particular tragedy for Kolchak came in September 1919 when, in protest at Semenov's general misconduct and illegal interference with railway traffic, the Commander-in-Chief of the American Expeditionary Force, General Graves, refused to permit the despatch up-line from Vladivostok of 14,000 rifles which Kolchak's agents had recently purchased in the USA. Graves announced that he would not permit the removal of the guns until it could be guaranteed that they would reach the Russian Army at the front and would not be purloined at Chita.[394] Thus, as a direct result of Semenov's banditry, as Kolchak's forces struggled in their last major battles with the Red Army, their brand-new Remington rifles lay under American guard on the docks at Vladivostok. Eventually Graves was prevailed upon to release the weapons, but only on condition that they travel under American guard as far west as Irkutsk. And in this manner the rifles got through – although not before Semenov had, predictably, launched an attack on the American trains at Chita on October 24th.[395]

Semenov's iniquitous behaviour was both encouraged and complemented by his paymasters in the Far East, the Japanese Expeditionary Force. As the sympathy of the western Allies for Kolchak became increasingly manifest during the spring of 1919 and as increasing numbers of British, French and American observers poured into Siberia, the Japanese army was eventually forced to moderate its behaviour. In

393 *Nasha zaria* (Omsk) No. 114, 31.v.1919; WO 33/966/1074 'Knox (Omsk) to WO, 4.ii.1919'; WO 33/966/1170 'Knox (Vladivostok) to WO, 19.ii.1919'. By February 1919 Semenov's 'Railway Battalion' had used up half a normal year's supply of boiler steel. Hence the requisitioning of engines; and hence the fact that local workshops could not acquire the steel they needed for repairs – the 1,426 railway workers at Chita were able, consequently, to repair only two locomotives in January and none at all in February. See WO 158/740 'Knox (Vladivostok) to General Inagaki, ?.ii.1919'.

394 *FRUS: 1919 (Russia)*, pp. 514–17, 522; Graves, pp. 257–9; *DBFP*, pp. 573–4.

395 *FRUS: 1919 (Russia)*, p. 540; Graves, *America's Siberian Adventure*, pp. 260–2. By the time that the rifles had reached the front it was too late for them to make a contribution to the White war effort. Over the next decades, however, they were destined to become the principle weaponry of the armies of competing warlords in Manchuria and Sinkiang. See Fleming, P. *News From Tartary*. London (1936), p. 269.

1918, however, they had been less cautious and, in pursuit of their undoubted aim of fostering disorder in the region so as to undermine the authority of Omsk and to open the way for Japanese economic and political domination of the Far East and Manchuria, they had greatly interfered with both military traffic and trade on the railway system.

By November 1918 the Japanese had moved 70,000 troops into the Maritime Provinces, Transbaikalia, Amur and Manchuria, where they seized fishing and timber concessions for Japanese companies. They also impounded the Amur Merchant Fleet – an act which prevented fish and other supplies from being sent to the needy population of Nikol′sk before winter closed the waterways.[396] Two-thirds of the Japanese forces, however, were deployed along the Chinese Eastern Railway and proceeded to raise the Japanese flag above its stations and to eject Russian station-masters and engineers who would not be bribed or cajoled into doing their bidding. No traffic moved on the Chinese Eastern Railway in the autumn of 1918 without Japanese permission – even the train of General Knox, head of Britmis, was held up by Japanese troops.[397] And much of what did move was reported to consist of the goods of Japanese merchants (sometimes disguised as Red Cross supplies). These imports not only took up valuable space on the line, but they did not even contribute to the Russian exchequer because the customs-houses at Vladivostok and on the Korean border through which they had passed had also been seized by the Japanese Army.[398]

The conduct of the Japanese was to become less damaging under Allied pressure in 1919, but another disruption to railway operation Kolchak would never overcome. This was the innate hostility to his régime and to the railway administration of the region's railway workers. Occasionally a resentful or pro-Bolshevik worker would indulge in an individual act of politicized vandalism – a favourite device was to put a handful of sand into the axle-boxes of carriages, thereby causing them to seize up

396 Grigortsevich, S.S. *Amerikanskaia i iaponskaia interventsiia na sovetskom Dal′nem Vostoke i ee razgrom*. Moscow (1957), pp. 33–42; Svetachev, M.I. 'Ekonomicheskoe proniknovenie i sopernichenstvo imperialisticheskikh derzhav na sovetskom Dal′nem Vostoke (1918–1919gg.)', *Uchenye zapiski Moskovskogo gos. ped. instituta, im. V.I. Lenina* (Moscow) Vol. 205 (1964), pp. 96–102; FO 371/3365/21389 'Ledward (Nikol′sk-Ussuriisk) to FO, 14.ix.1918'.

397 Morely, J.W. *Japan's Thrust Into Siberia*. New York (1950), pp. 202–3 and *passim*; *FRUS: 1918*, Vol. 3, pp. 278–9; Ward, pp. 54–8.

398 Savory, R. 'Letter from Vladivostok, 7.vi.1919' (*Savory Papers*, NAM 7603/93/26).

or even to catch fire; sometimes the sabotage was more organized – at the Petropavlovsk yards, recalled one railwayman, 'one team would repair the engines and another would systematically break them'.[399] The general picture, however, was of rumbling discontent at low pay and poor working conditions which would occasionally generate go-slows, stoppages and strikes. Labour relations were in such a catastrophic state on the Trans-Siberian Railway that workshops were left half empty as men fled the service, causing repairs to damaged rolling stock to slow to a snail's pace. Yards which had repaired ten locomotives a month in 1916 were reported to be fixing only three by October 1918.[400] This neglect was particularly damaging in Siberia, where a locomotive in which a fire was not kept stoked for twenty-four hours a day could be immobilized and severely damaged by frost within a matter of minutes. Labour shortages, strikes and deliberate indolence among railway staff (so-called 'Italian strikes') meant that this was precisely what happened on innumerable occasions. The result was that as early as December 1918 a British officer approaching the railway town of Krasnoiarsk in eastern Siberia could observe 'miles' of derelict engines and other pieces of machinery on the sides of the tracks: 'all cast aside as useless', he said, 'there being no place where even minor defects could be repaired'.[401] By the time that winter and the icy Siberian *buran* had taken their toll, travellers in 1919 would note 250 more derelict engines around the town of Cheliabinsk and a further 100 between Cheliabinsk and Ufa.[402]

The available rolling-stock was further depleted by the fact that both the Allied and Russian military had taken to procuring railway waggons and carriages for their personal accommodation. A British officer rather cruelly suggested that 'every little officer who commands a dozen cossacks', thought he had the exclusive right to

399 Savory, R. 'Vladivostok 1919–1920' (*Savory Papers*, NAM 7603/93/23), p. 43; Ashkinadze, D.I. *Zheleznodorozhniki Ishima v bor'be za vlast sovetov (1917–1919gg.)*. Tiumen' (1961), pp. 70–1. Sabotage was not confined to the railway. In February 1919 an American intelligence officer reported that in the previous two months at Omsk alone arsonists had destroyed two large cloth factories, a shoe factory, a tannery, a hat and cap factory and an iron foundry – all of which had been engaged on defence contracts. See *USMI*, Vol. 7, No. 89 (week ending 8.ii.1919), p. 543. See also Naumov, M.V. *Omskie bol'sheviki*. Omsk (1960), pp. 69–70.

400 *FRUS: 1918*, Vol. 3, pp. 283–4; *The Times* (London) 2.xii.1918. Such go-slows also affected other vital works – at a steamship construction company in Vladivostok, for example, only one vessel was repaired during the entire Kolchak period, according to one worker. See Vladimirov, V. 'Profdvizhenie vo Vladivostoke', in *Revoliutsiia na Dal'nem Vostoke*. Moscow–Leningrad (1923), Vol. 1, p. 335.

401 Ward, *With the 'Die-Hards'*, p. 103.

402 *The Times* (London) 24.ii.1919; Gidney, p. 267.

occupy a first-class carriage,[403] but the truth was that Siberia offered no accommodation for soldiers *other* than railway carriages and that even quite senior officers were driven to living in cattle-trucks because their paltry wages would not permit them to compete with the refugee bourgeoisie in the desperately overcrowded Siberian towns. In June of 1919 officers on active service were being paid only just over half the salary of the average Omsk typist (600 and 1,100 roubles respectively).[404] In these circumstances it was hardly surprising that they forsook the hotels and boarding houses for the more modest comforts of the marshalling yards which, particularly at Omsk and Cheliabinsk, became so congested that they formed yet another obstacle to communication and supply.[405]

The net result of these combined crises and pressures on the Trans-Siberian Railway's rolling-stock was assessed by the Assistant Minister of Ways and Communications in a report of May 1919. V.M. Larionov estimated that of the 3,233 passenger wagons in Siberia, only 335 (10.3%) were being put to their proper use on the railway network; 831 were being used to house officers, 749 were being held in reserve by the army, 722 were *hors de combat*, and 525 were at the disposal of the Allied military missions.[406] Meanwhile, of the region's 3,200 locomotives, 1,200 were out of commission; and of its 84,000 goods wagons, 20,000 were in need of repair and somewhere between 7,000 and 25,000 (estimates vary) had been commandeered by the Polish and Czechoslovak Legions.[407] The unexpected and sudden retreat from the Urals in June and July of 1919 made the situation even worse – 600 freight-cars were reported to have been abandoned at Perm and a further 1,000 at Ekaterinburg.[408]

The final, but by no means the least significant impediment to the efficient operation of the Trans-Siberian Railway – and, indeed, to all trade in Kolchakia – was the canker of corruption which had infected both military and civil officialdom from top

403 Ward, p. 7.

404 *The Times* (London) 18.vi.1919.

405 Guins, *Sibir'*, Vol. 2, p. 283; Gidney, *Witness to a Revolution*, pp. 266, 333; Rodney, 'Siberia in 1919', p. 332.

406 *Nasha zaria* (Omsk) No. 114, 31.v.1919.

407 Eikhe, *Oprokinutyi tyl*, p. 123; Sukin (*Leeds Russian Archive*), p. 120; Vitol'dova-Liutik, S. *Na vostok: vospominaniia vremen kolchakovskoi epopei v Sibiri, 1919–1920gg.* Riga (1930), p. 15.

408 FO 371/4097/152139; *FRUS: 1919 (Russia)*, p. 206.

to bottom by 1919. Sanctimonious Little Englanders such as Colonel John Ward were mortally offended by their experience of this fact of Siberian life: 'No Russian officer would dream of doing a straight thing if a crooked one would accomplish his purposes', pontificated the British colonel.[409] More sympathetic observers, however, were aware of the extenuating circumstances which excused at least some part of this Siberian malaise. Bernard Pares, for example, realized that tens of thousands of officers and public servants in White Siberia were so poorly paid and so dreadfully undernourished that mendacity and graft had become their only practical means of survival.[410]

The whole of Siberian society had become accustomed to, if not directly involved in, various improbities: as Acting Minister of War, Baron Budberg put it, in White Siberia 'the criminal had become the general'.[411] But the evil, like so much else in Kolchakia, was centred upon the all-important Trans-Siberian Railway. The trail of interference with imported goods began as they were landed and sorted at the Vladivostok customs-houses, where pilfering was rampant and usually went unpunished, to the dismay of Allied observers in the port.[412] The next obstacle to be faced by goods bound for the Siberian interior was the Chinese Eastern Railway administration. The CER Board (of which Kolchak's Minister of Ways and Communications, L.A. Ustrugov, was a member) was accused by both Russian and foreign engineers of favouring more profitable local traffic in Manchuria at the expense of through trains, thereby adding to the accumulation of goods at Vladivostok and exacerbating the shortages west of Baikal.[413] At a more localized level, British officers accompanying military supply trains on the trip west from Vladivostok were both amazed and shocked to observe how station-masters employed on the CER would invariably supply locomotives too old or weak to pull the trains or would suddenly uncover some mysterious defect with the train in order that one or more carriages had to be detached and left at their station to be 'picked

409 Ward, p. 116.

410 Pares, B. 'Siberian Diary' (*Pares Papers*, Box 43), p. 53.

411 Budberg, Vol. 15, p. 322. The translation provides an appropriate pun!

412 *FRUS: 1919 (Russia)*, pp. 426–7; *DBFP*, p. 708.

413 *Russkii ekonomist* (Vladivostok) 12.ix.1919; *FRUS:1919 (Russia)*, pp. 533–4. The chief American railroad engineer in Siberia maintained that for most of 1919 the CER was handling only 20–25% of the through traffic it was capable of handling. See FO 371/4102/117980 'Minutes of a meeting of the Technical Board of the IARC (Harbin), 22.x.1919'.

up later'. Even as the depleted train was pulling away, labour gangs would appear from a station outhouse to loot the abandoned wagons.[414]

If some pretence of probity was maintained when dealing with the British Army, no such niceties were employed by the railway administration when dealing with the goods of private merchants. Station-masters, their military cohorts and the Cossack bandits of the Far East would all demand their cut from goods in transit. Some sources speak of demands for cash equal to the value of a cargo before it was allowed to pass, others of demands of $40,000 per wagon, yet others of 40,000 roubles. Probably the necessary bribe varied from place to place, but bribery was certainly the rule – as one recalled who was urged by a friend to join the military railway administration at Irkutsk because of the financial rewards to be reaped, 'I cannot remember what puzzled me the most, the figure of $40,000 or the open cynicism with which the whole thing was stated.'[415] Passengers too would find that their ticket alone would rarely suffice to secure passage, and even government ministers found it prudent to bestow a hefty consideration upon railway staff to be sure of a seat on a train.[416]

Once goods had reached central Siberia the raids upon them had only just begun. The Commander-in-Chief of the Siberian Army, for example, made little secret of the fact that as of June 1919 he was ordering supplies from Omsk to feed 250,000 men, even though he had only a maximum of 60,000 men in the field. Such inflation of the muster-rolls was necessary, General Gajda maintained, because, of the supplies despatched to his headquarters at Perm by the Quartermaster General at Omsk or Ekaterinburg, he could only generally count upon receiving 55% of the flour, 65% of the footwear, 35% of the clothing, 54% of the meat, 54% of the forage, 22% of the sugar, 18% of the tobacco and none of the vegetables he had ordered. The remainder mysteriously disappeared en route, subsequently to resurface

414 Savory, R. 'Vladivostok 1919–1920' (*Savory Papers*, NAM 7603/93/26), p. 44. One British supply train which left Omsk with twenty-seven wagons had only six intact by the time that it arrived at Omsk (see Horrocks, *A Full Life*, p. 40); another officer, conversely, found that two trucks – one loaded with caviar and one with tea – had mysteriously attached themselves to his convoy (see WO 106/1320 'Report by Capt. H.C. Peacock on his journey from Vladivostok to Omsk, [n.d]'.

415 Guins, Vol. 2, p. 222; Graves, pp. 242–4; Rouquérol, *La Guerre*, p. 50; Alioshin, p. 55.

416 Ivanov, Vs. N. *V grazhdanskom voine: iz zapisok omskago zhurnalista.* Harbin (1921), p. 35.

on the black market.[417] 'There is a hole somewhere between Omsk and the front,' an official of the Ministry of the Interior once informed General Janin: 'Everything disappears into it.'[418] He might have added that goods would, however, generally reappear – on the black market. Even Red Cross medicines which had been donated free to the Russian Army were apt to vanish from military stores at Ekaterinburg only to rematerialize beneath hefty price tags in the shop windows of the local pharmacies.[419]

Apart from the quest for day-to-day survival, it was, of course, the stark contrasts between regions of plenty and regions of poverty within Kolchakia, and the speculation in commodities engendered by it, which provided the fabric for the all-embracing net of corruption and graft. A merchant who could afford the baksheesh that the journey would demand might still make a massive profit on goods transported up the price gradient from the Far East to the hungry towns of the Siberian interior. For example, a pood of tea which could be sold in Vladivostok in 1919 for 1,480 roubles could command a price of 1,800 roubles at Irkutsk and 2,500 roubles by the time that it reached Novonikolaevsk.[420] This was a situation in which everybody could expect to make a killing by taking advantage of local shortages – in the absence of government regulation and vigilance, noted one Omsk official, 'the entire Trade and Industry class [had] transmuted "freedom of trade" into "freedom to speculate"'.[421] Ordinary citizens also tried to get in on the act – the burghers of Irkutsk, for example, found that the civil war had led to a sudden dearth of domestic servants, as their staff found greater remuneration in spending their lives carrying small parcels of foodstuffs up the line to Omsk than in waiting at table.[422]

The Omsk Government, as the purported champion of order, could not be seen to endorse such behaviour and, within days of assuming power in November 1918, Kolchak had directed his Minister of Justice to frame a new law on speculation. On March 11th 1919, albeit nearly four months later, a law was indeed promulgated

417 Graves, pp. 200–1.

418 Grondijs, L.H. (ed.) *Le Cas Koltchak: contribution à l'histoire de la révolution russe*. Leiden (1939), pp. 235–6.

419 Preston, T. *Before the Curtain*. London (1950), p. 127.

420 *Tri goda bor'by za diktaturu proletariata (1918–1920gg.)*. Omsk (1920), pp. 7–8.

421 *Priishim'e* (Petropavlovsk) No. 134 (1656), 26.vi.1919.

422 Gidney, p. 341.

which prescribed sentences of from one to five years' imprisonment for anyone found guilty of increasing the price of basic necessities beyond reason or of trading without a valid licence.[423] This measure against speculation was supplemented in July by a Ministry of Ways and Communications inquiry into illegal practices on the railway and the reaffirmation that crimes committed on the line were punishable by death under the terms of the prevailing *osadnoe polozhenie*.[424]

However, corruption and speculation were so endemic, so much an everyday part of life in Siberia in 1919, that threats alone were unlikely to eradicate the profiteering. Moreover, the sincerity of the Kolchak régime's indictment of speculators was clearly open to doubt. In March 1919, for example, the co-operative newspaper *Nasha zaria* revealed that the Minister of Food and Supply himself, N.S. Zefirov, had been party to a number of fraudulent deals with an Omsk trading company called *Slon′*. The Ministry of Food and Supply had apparently purchased large quantities of tea from the firm at prices in excess of the market rate and the Minister was accused of sharing in the 60,000,000 roubles *Slon′* had made on the deal. Zefirov was forced to resign from his post and, following a hearing in May, was bailed (for a sum of 100,000 roubles) pending a full investigation. Yet neither Zefirov nor his assistant, Miltonov, who was also implicated in the affair, were ever brought to trial despite repeated assurances from Omsk that they were to appear before a tribunal of the Criminal Investigation Department of the Omsk Governing Senate.[425]

And this was only the most publicized among what *Nasha zaria* termed 'dozens of flagrant abuses' by members of the Kolchak régime. It could be added, for example, that the Ministry of Food and Supply's chief agent in the Urals just happened to be a member of the trading house with which many huge government orders were placed; or that the Minister of Trade and Industry, N.N. Shchukin, resigned in March 1919 following revelations of deals of doubtful probity with the *Voproma* company.[426] Finally, when during the summer of 1919 the Commandant of Omsk railway station was arrested for speculation and for dealing in stolen goods,

423 Guins, Vol. 2, pp. 37–8; *Sobranie uzakonenii i rasporiazhenii pravitel′stva, izdavaemoe pri pravitel′stvuiushchem senate* (Omsk) No. 6, 22.v.1919, pp. 16–17.

424 *Russkaia zhizn′* (Helsingfors) No. 117, 25.viii.1919.

425 *Nasha zaria* (Omsk) No. 114, 31.v.1919; *Velikaia Rossiia* (Ufa) No. 12, 3.iv.1919; *Biulleten′* (Omsk) No. 89, 1.x.1919; *Union (Agence Télégraphique Russe)* (Paris) No. 188, 16.x.1919.

426 Krol′, L. *Za tri goda*, pp. 170–1.

investigations revealed the connivance in his activities of none other than the Chief of Military Supply at the *stavka*, General Kasatkin. A military court subsequently sentenced Kasatkin and seven others to death, but the recollections of Foreign Minister Sukin confirm the long-standing allegation of Soviet historians that, because of his close association with General Lebedev, Kasatkin (and his accomplices) went unpunished.[427] Thus, as Sukin lamented, Kolchak might have declared a 'war on speculation', but it was the 'war on the war on speculation' which ultimately won the day.[428]

The Inter-Allied Railway Agreement

To Kolchak's credit it has to be said that he did recognize the critical importance of the railway for the White movement in Siberia. At the Extraordinary Congress of Trades and Industry at Ekaterinburg on May 10th 1919, he had opined that 'the railway is part of the military organization of the country and it is necessary to pay no less attention to it than to the army'.[429] The Omsk authorities also recognized that it would be beyond their own means to set the railway to rights and, from as early as October 1918 onwards, had been literally pleading with the Allies to take control of the Trans-Siberian and Chinese Eastern railways for the duration of the civil war.[430]

The mechanism for such international control was already in existence, as in May 1917 President Wilson had assigned to the Provisional Government the distinguished engineer John F. Stevens – a veteran of the construction of the Panama Canal and the Great Northern Railway. Stevens had surveyed the Trans-Siberian and other Russian railways and was about to be joined by a 300-strong contingent of American railwaymen (known as the Russian Railway Service Corps and

427 'McCullagh (Omsk) to Pares, 8.viii.1919' (*Pares Papers*, Box 43). Brazenly, there had been little attempt to conceal what was going on: a Dutch correspondent watched as 'every night, on platforms 13 and 14 of Omsk station, soldiers unloaded quantities of luxury goods for ladies – perfume and French underwear'. See Grondijs *La Guerre en Russie et en Sibérie*. Paris (1922), pp. 520–1.

428 Parfenov, *Uroki*, pp. 117–18.

429 *Bulletins of the Russian Liberation Committee (Union)* (London) No. 15, 30.v.1919.

430 *FRUS: 1918*, Vol. 3, p. 274; *FRUS: 1919 (Russia)*, pp. 237–8, 241–2.

commanded by Colonel G. Emerson) when the October Revolution interrupted his work and caused Emerson's men to leave Vladivostok for Japan.[431] Before Stevens and his men could resume their service on behalf of Kolchak, however, a new arrangement had to be made, for not only did the Service Corps' contract to work for the Provisional Government of 1917 not apply to the unrecognized authority at Omsk, but both Japan and certain elements of Russian society needed to be reassured by some form of inter-Allied agreement that Stevens was genuinely working for the benefit of Russia and not merely as an agent for the spreading of American economic influence in Manchuria and Siberia.

Tortuous negotiations among the Allies and between the Allies and Omsk consequently extended over the last quarter of 1918. Proposals and counter-proposals flew back and forth between Omsk, Washington, Tokyo and London, with Japan holding out for a greater say in the running of the Chinese Eastern Railway, with Britain reluctant to pressurize her eastern ally, with the Russian railway administration demanding that they be accorded the ultimate power of veto over any decision arrived at by Allied agents, and with Stevens insisting that his experience of the Russian administration had forced him to the conclusion that nothing less than his personal 'executive supervision' and 'control' would facilitate the running of the Siberian and Far Eastern railway networks.[432] Eventually, however, Japan's isolation induced her to concede ground, while Omsk whipped local opposition into line, and on January 9th 1919 there was signed an 'Agreement Regarding the Inter-Allied Supervision of the Chinese Eastern and Siberian Railway Systems'. This provided for the establishment of a general committee (the Inter-Allied Railway Committee or IARC) of representatives of each Allied power having troops in Siberia (namely Russia, the USA, Japan, China, Great Britain, France, Italy and

431 On the history of the Russian Railway Service Corps see Griener, pp. 170–2; Johnson, pp. 1,063–4; US Department of State, *American Assistance on the Question of the Trans-Siberian Railway* (Russian Series No. 4). Washington (1919); Griener, J.A. 'A Minnesota Railwayman in the Far East, 1917–1918', *Minnesota History* Vol. 38, 1963, pp. 310–25; Johnson, B.O. 'American Railway Engineers in Siberia', *Military Engineer* Vol. 15 (May–June 1923), pp. 187–92; Wright, P. 'The Work of the Russian Railway Service Corps', *Railway Age* (Philadelphia) Vol. 69 (23.vii.1923), pp. 153–6; 'Colonel Emerson's Experiences in Russia', *Railway Age* (Philadelphia) Vol. 68 (14.vi.1919), pp. 1,769–70; Grubbs, C.B. 'American Railroaders in Siberia', *Railway History Bulletin* No. 150 (Spring 1984), pp. 107–14; Estep, R. 'John F. Stevens and the Far Eastern Russian Railways', *Explorers' Journal* Vol. 48 (March 1970), pp. 13–24; St. John, J.D. 'John F. Stevens and American Assistance to Russian and Siberian Railways, 1917–1922', University of Oklahoma PhD Thesis (1970).

432 *FRUS: 1918*, Vol. 3, pp. 281–2, 291–2, 295–6.

Czechoslovakia), which was to have general supervisory powers over all railway affairs. There was to be a Russian Chairman of the IARC (Kolchak's Minister of Ways and Communication, L.A. Ustrugov) and each branch railway would retain its Russian manager. Technical questions and the day-to-day running of the railways, however, were to be the prerogatives of a Technical Board of the IARC, whose agents would have supervisory authority over Russian managers. It had been informally agreed in advance by Japan and the USA that Stevens would chair the Technical Board and it came to be the case that his proposals were almost invariably rubber-stamped by the IARC. In fact, as one historian of the intervention noted, the entire inter-Allied agreement was 'a mere front for the management of the whole railway enterprise' by John Stevens.[433]

Neither the IARC nor its Technical Board convened officially until the early days of March (at Vladivostok and Harbin respectively) and it was not until March 16th that newspapers in the Far East carried the IARC's 'Declaration to the People of Russia' promising to promote the re-establishment of an efficient transport system for the benefit of Russia and not for the profit of any of the Allied powers.[434] Also, it was not until April 1919 that a supplementary agreement paved the way for the creation of another sub-committee of the IARC, the Military Transportation Board (with a Japanese chairman), which was to define the sections of Trans-Siberian and Chinese Eastern Railways to be guarded by each power and to oversee the troop deployments.[435] Stevens, however, had actually resumed his work in January, immediately following the Allied agreement, and with tangible results: the Ministry of Ways and Communication reported a 21% increase in productivity along the lines during February and March 1919 and a 23% increase in freight carried over the same period, while by the spring of 1919 up to five trains a day were sometimes

433 White, *The Siberian Intervention*, p. 148. For the text of the Inter-Allied Railway Agreement see MacMorry, J.V.A. (ed.) *Treaties and Agreements With and Concerning China*. New York (1921), p. 82.

434 *FRUS: 1919 (Russia)*, pp. 256–7; For the Russian text of this declaration see Guins, Vol. 2, pp. 128–32.

435 For full details of the deployment of Allied troops along the Trans-Siberian and Chinese Eastern Railways see Collins, D.N. and Smele, J.D. (eds.) *Kolchak i Sibir': dokumenty i issledovaniia, 1919–1926*. White Plains, NY (1988), Vol. 2, pp. 711–12.

running on the Vladivostok to Irkutsk line and a regular eight-day express passenger service was restored between Omsk and the Pacific coast.[436]

The American engineers involved attributed these successes to the introduction of an American-style despatching circuit from Vladivostok to Omsk (whereby a centralized direction of train movements replaced the Russian station-to-station relay system), as well as to the adoption of improved accounting practices and other technical innovations.[437] The achievement of the IARC (and in particular of its Technical Board) came too late, however, to have more than a marginal effect either upon Kolchak's fortunes at the front or upon the economic situation in Siberia. Moreover, the very formation of the IARC raised a number of further obstacles to the smooth running of the railway system. At a local level, the simple task of communication between the various agencies involved raised the spectre of a modern Tower of Babel. A British officer with first-hand experience of the problems involved left the following picture:

> Russian railway officials, engine drivers and pointsmen; Chinese labour; Japanese sentries; British and American transportation officers trying to co-ordinate the lot and using any foreign language known to them from Hindustani downwards.[438]

And even when the Russian railway officials could understand the instructions of the Technical Board, there was no guarantee that they would carry them out because the Russians stubbornly persisted in wrongly interpreting the Inter-Allied Railway Agreement as granting Stevens's men merely observatory rather than supervisory powers. 'Every time an inspector tried to issue an order,' recalled Sukin, 'our railway administration would reply that to adopt the measure would be contrary to Russian law, service regulations etc.' Such contumacy, he added, was frequently encouraged by the Russian Army commandants at each station when their purely military priorities conflicted with the rather broader purview of the Technical Board.[439]

436 *The Russian/Russkii zhurnal* (London) Vol. 1, No. 4 (17.vii.1919), p. 13; FO 371/4095/76086 'Eliot (Omsk) to FO, 15.v.1919'; Sukin (*Leeds Russian Archive*), pp. 130–1.

437 Johnson, pp. 187–192; Wright, pp. 153–6.

438 Savory, R. 'Vladivostok 1919–1920' (*Savory Papers*, NAM 7603/93/26), p. 45.

439 Sukin (*Leeds Russian Archive*), pp. 130–1.

The question of military interference in railway affairs and the insubordination of Russian officials along the line were at the very head of the agenda of the diplomatic conference convened at Omsk between July 26th and August 20th 1919. In fact, the inaugural session of the conference opened with an examination of the problem of implementing Allied control over the Trans-Siberian and Chinese Eastern Railways and concluded with a declaration by Foreign Minister Sukin that a special decree would be issued by the Kolchak Government suspending all Russian railway bye-laws and regulations for the duration of the war, insisting upon the Russian managers' recognition of the authority of the Technical Board and ordering the military authorities to refrain from interference with railway traffic (whilst reassuring them that military traffic remained the priority).[440] However, Omsk had little more chance of imposing its will upon its local military commanders with regard to this question than it had anent any other; and, of course, there was even less chance of the likes of Semenov agreeing to submit to the dictates of an American engineer than there was of his submission to a Russian authority. Consequently, throughout the remainder of his time in Siberia and the Far East, Stevens never ceased to complain of continued defiance, high-handedness and interference on the part the Russian military and the railway administration.[441]

Quite apart from the difficulties involved in the definition of its remit and authority, the IARC was dogged from the very beginning by fundamental disagreements among the Allies and their local agents which Kolchak was quite powerless to assuage. A major note of discord was the lingering suspicion of American intentions on the part of the Japanese. Much has been written on the subject of Japan's sponsorship and protection of Semenov and of the consequent justice of Washington's suspicion of Tokyo. But note should also be taken of Japan's quite natural baulking at the prospect of an American-dominated railway administration in a region where she had economic and possibly territorial ambitions. Moreover, American activity in the Far East was not as disinterested and charitable as it was claimed to be. President Wilson might insist that he was interested only in maintaining the 'Open Door' in North Asia; but that, of course, was precisely the

440 *Bor'ba za vlast sovetov v Primor'e*. Vladivostok (1955), pp. 199–201; Livshits *Imperialisticheskaia interventsiia*, pp. 178–80.

441 FO 371/4102/117980 'Minutes of a meeting of the Technical Board of the IARC (Harbin), 22.x.1919'.

situation in which the USA, with its powerful trading apparatus, was going to prosper more than smaller nations such as Japan. And it is not even necessary to read between the lines of some of Stevens's reports to understand that he, at least, was very fully aware of the economic and political advantages for his country in 'placing the direction of the operation [of the Trans-Siberian Railway] in American hands'.[442]

This bad blood between the Pacific powers denied Kolchak much of the anticipated fruit of the Inter-Allied Railway Agreement. 'Occasionally', recalled Sukin, 'American–Japanese rivalry paralysed all work' in the IARC.[443] But its most damaging manifestation came when the American commander-in-chief, General Graves, refused to submit to the provision of the Railway Agreement placing the supreme command of Allied troops deployed as sentries along the railways in the hands of the Japanese commander, General Otani. Suspicions of intent in this field stopped only just short of outright hostilities.[444] Moreover, Graves did not even partake of the view that the Inter-Allied Railway Agreement was intended to aid Kolchak and he did not recognize the decision of the Omsk Diplomatic Conference that military traffic was to be given priority on the line. In fact, Graves interpreted the failure of the Railway Agreement not in terms of its failure to assist Kolchak but in terms of its being a failure precisely *because* it had concentrated too much on trying to help Kolchak and the White military. In his view, the value of the agreement was 'absolutely nil' not because it was not bolstering the war effort of the Russian Army but because 'the majority of the people of Siberia enjoyed about the same value from the operation of the railways as did the people of Liberia'.[445] The American commander was sticking rigidly to the letter of President Wilson's aide-mémoire of July 1918 on the aims of the intervention, whereby he was obliged to act so as to assist 'the people of Russia'

442 *FRUS: 1918*, Vol. 3, p. 298. Soviet historians of the Brezhnev era were keen to emphasize the role of American economic imperialism in Siberia through Washington's leading role in the Technical Board and through its control of the Purchasing Committee of the IARC. See, for example, Krushanov, *Grazhdanskaia voina*, Vol. 1, pp. 114–25; and Krushanov, A.I. 'K voprosu o roli Mezhsoiuznogo zhelezno-dorozhnogo komiteta i Tekhnicheskogo soveta v osushchestvlenii imperialisticheskikh planov SShA i Iaponii na Dal′nem Vostoke i v Sibiri, 1918–1919gg.', *Trudy DVF SO AN SSSR* (Seriia ist.) (Vladivostok), Vol. 2 (1965).

443 Sukin (*Leeds Russian Archive*), pp. 133–4.

444 *FRUS: 1919 (Russia)*, pp. 563ff.

445 Graves, pp. 179–80. The Canadian Economic Commission to Siberia shared this view (see *Report of the CEC*, p. 8).

and not any particular government organization. The political situation had, of course, changed somewhat by early 1919 – and was changed fundamentally by America's accession both to the Inter-Allied Railway Agreement and to the Allied notes to Kolchak of May 27th and June 12th – but knowing only the most vicious face of the Kolchak régime, as represented in the Far East by the likes of Semenov and Rozanov, Graves was not inclined to modify his opinion. In fact, the American Commander would not even obey the instruction of the IARC that known Bolsheviks should be prevented from approaching within ten miles of the railway line. Instead he had posters displayed at stations in the zones guarded by American troops provocatively and specifically stating that the railways were being run for the good of *all* Russian citizens, 'irrespective of a person's nationality, religion or politics'.[446]

With such divergent opinions as to what the IARC was supposed to achieve, it has to be doubted whether it could ever have been of great utility to Kolchak. The ultimate impediment to its operation, however, was quite simply a lack of funds. Stevens's Technical Board calculated in March 1919 that the initial financial input required from each power signatory to the Inter-Allied Railway Agreement should be $20,000,000.[447] But there was no way that the war-ravaged Allied nations of Europe would be in a position to contribute even a fraction of that sum within the foreseeable future and, with $100,000,000 already committed to relieving Europe, the American administration too would have been hard pressed to persuade Congress to provide yet more funds for Siberia (particularly while the aims of the intervention remained so ill-defined and open-ended). Thus, by the end of the Kolchak era, the IARC had received just $500,000 from the Chinese Government and $4,000,000 each from Japan and the USA. No other power had contributed a cent and, to the Americans' dismay, the British and the French would not even defray the cost of transporting their own troops on the Siberian railway system as, during the summer of 1919, Kolchakia collapsed and the Allied contingents beat a hasty retreat towards the east.[448]

446 Graves, pp. 186. Graves's conduct so endeared him to the Soviet Government that in the 1930s his memoirs were reprinted in the Soviet Union.

447 *FRUS: 1919 (Russia)*, pp. 257, 263–4.

448 *ibid.*, p. 271.

Chapter 5

White débâcle

July 1st 1919, the first anniversary of the inauguration of the Provisional Siberian Government, was long anticipated as a day of festivities at Omsk. Parades, charity rallies and football matches were among events organized in the capital for the jubilee of White power in Siberia.[1] As the day finally dawned, however, only the most ignorant or intoxicated of revellers could have altogether obscured from their minds feelings of uneasiness engendered by incoming reports of panic and disorder at the front, as the Red Army, having rebuffed Kolchak's spring offensive on the Volga, poured through the Urals passes to debouch onto the West Siberian plain. Indeed, even as the last celebratory cups were being drained towards the evening of the holiday, the devastating news was to reach the capital that Perm, the first jewel in Kolchak's crown, the first trophy of his Siberian Army, had that very day been abandoned to the Reds. It was the beginning of the end for White Siberia.

Kolchak's fragile nerves seem to have cracked altogether under the strain of these military reverses. Interlocutors and supplicants of the Supreme Ruler during July and August invariably talk of his 'appearing to be in a state of extreme nervous tension', looking 'really and truly worn out', and speak of 'gloomy, mistrustful and suspicious moods' alternating with 'uncontrollable fits of anger' as Kolchak snapped pencils or paced manically about his office, railing against everyone from the Allies to the Masons for sabotaging the White cause. The admiral appeared less often in public – and, when he did venture abroad, those who had not seen him for some months were shocked at the marked deterioration in his physical appearance and presence.[2] And, as Kolchak's character broke, White policy became unpredictable

1 Guins, G.K. *Sibir', soiuzniki i Kolchak: povorotnyi moment russkoi istorii, 1918–1920gg. (Vpechatleniia i mysli chlena Omskogo pravitel'stva*. Peking (1921), Vol. 2, p. 239.

2 Baerlin, H. *March of the Seventy Thousand.* London (1926), p. 233; Pepeliaev, V.N. 'Razval kolchakovshchiny', *Krasnyi arkhiv* No. 6 (1928), p. 65; Arnol'dov, V. *Zhizn' i revoliutsiia.* Shanghai (1935), p. 262; Budberg, A.P. von 'Dnevnik', *Arkhiv russkoi revoliutsii* Vol. 15 (1924), p. 255; Enborisov, G.V. *Ot Urala do Kharbina.* Shanghai (1932), p. 77; Rudnev, S.P. *Pri vechernykh ogniakh.* Harbin (1928), p. 286. Some months later, on seeing a photograph of Kolchak (whom he had last met in 1917), Paul Miliukov would remark upon 'wrinkles unknown to me because of their recent origin, bearing witness to a steady, superhuman effort which is far greater than this human frame can bear'. *The New Russia* (London), Vol. 3, p.71.

and subject to violent swings. The ailing Supreme Ruler vacillated during these months between a tentative liberalization of his régime and redoubled authoritarianism: with one hand he would endorse a number of belated initiatives aimed at stanching the economic and political wounds which White rule had inflicted on Siberia and at sealing a rapprochement between his embattled government and elements of Siberian society; yet, with the other, he would undermine the authority of the Council of Ministers and seek refuge in Cossack and military counsel and the tantalizing but fruitless quest for a deal with Japan. Even Guins never knew what to expect from the irascible admiral. Once, he recalled, he invited Kolchak to attend a meeting of the Council of Ministers which was to finalize some economic and political reforms to which the Supreme Ruler had already agreed, but:

> ...he immediately began to shriek, pounding down his fists on his desk and throwing about all of the things on it. He then grabbed a penknife and began to slash furiously at the arm of his chair. From his pained, hysterical yelling it could be gathered that he was venting all the resentment in his disturbed soul. 'Everyone wants to be in command', he said. 'It is not enough for them to be ministers – now they want to be generals! Everything is rotten! Everything must be changed! And so it might be if the enemy was not coming closer with each day that passes!! But what changes can be made now!! Leave me alone in peace. I will forbid any more questions to be asked. I will go today to the Council of Ministers and I WILL ORDER that now AB–SO–LUTE–LY no changes will be permitted!'[3]

The only consistent strand of White policy during the summer and autumn of 1919 was the attempt to rally the necessary forces for a fresh military effort and the concomitant call for a mighty renewed offensive against Bolshevism. Yet both political and military initiatives to this end were of little or no avail. And, in fact, the first anniversary of White power in Siberia was to be the last. Long before the time was due to celebrate a second, scorned by the Siberian people, abandoned by the Allies and lashed by the dual scourge of Red Army and partisan attacks, the Kolchak régime had collapsed: in November 1919, even before the celebration of Kolchak's anniversary as dictator, Omsk itself would be surrendered to the Bolsheviks; by early 1920, the tattered and exhausted vestiges of the Russian Army, dragging scores of thousands of desperate refugees in their wake, would have suffered the longest and most terrible retreat in military history – a 4,000-mile *via dolorosa* from the Urals to the Pacific through the freezing, starving miseries of a

[3] Guins, Vol. 2, pp. 294–5.

Siberian winter, the ravages of pandemic typhus, the frustrations of a paralyzed railway system and the threat of anomie, betrayal and nemesis. It was an ordeal which many, including Kolchak, would not survive.

The dismissal of Gajda and the Cheliabinsk débâcle

Ironically, it was to be at the town of Cheliabinsk – the grain distribution centre on the eastern slopes of the Urals, site of the fateful clash between Czech and Magyar POWs in May 1918 which had sparked off the Czechoslovak revolt and galvanized the anti-Bolshevik movement in the East – that a major strategic blunder was to mark the beginning of the end for the Siberian Whites in the summer of 1919. A series of related events, which culminated on August 2nd in the Red Army's capture of the town and the ignominious surrender of thousands of White soldiers, epitomized the operational shortcomings of the Russian Army and, in the starkest terms, revealed the woeful ineptitude of those at Omsk entrusted with military planning. It was no accident that this débâcle coincided with the zenith of the career of Kolchak's trusted but incompetent confidant, Major-General D.A. Lebedev.

With the fast diminishing Western and Siberian Army Groups retreating and converging upon each other along a contracting Urals front during June–July 1919, the fashioning of a new order at the front – perhaps one for the first time incorporating an authoritative joint command for the armies in the field – seemed to be imperative for Omsk. It was typical of the Kolchak régime, however, that such restructuring could not be achieved without several weeks of backbiting, vituperation and mutual recrimination among senior commanders. First to plunge in the knife was Gajda. In a telegram despatched to the Council of Ministers on May 27th, the wilful but brilliant young Czech general attributed the military reverses of recent weeks to the ineptitude and reactionary politics of both the staff of the Western Army on the flank of his Siberian group and the Omsk *stavka* in his rear. He furthermore insisted that the only solution was for both establishments to be purged and the Chief of Staff, Lebedev, subjected to a court-martial, while he, Gajda, was to be granted overall command of the armies at the front. If these steps were not taken, Gajda threatened, he would resign.[4]

Whatever the veracity of the Czech's allegations, this ultimatum plainly bordered on mutiny and could have warranted instant dismissal – especially when received in conjunction with rumours of a plot being hatched in Gajda's staff to have General Pepeliaev march on Omsk with a couple of divisions to disperse the *stavka*.[5] It was to Kolchak's credit, therefore, that he recognized the Czech to be one of the few White commanders who was genuinely popular amongst his men and perhaps the most skilful and daring of them all on the battlefield. Consequently, rather than the carpeting he might properly have expected, Gajda was summoned to Omsk in order to air his grievances at a meeting on June 7th. By that time the Czech's ire would have been further roused by the fact that on June 2nd Lebedev had engineered the dismissal of his own long-time *bête noire*, the Minister of War, General Stepanov, and had had himself promoted to the post of Acting Minister of War (whilst retaining his role as Chief of Staff).[6] Yet, despite this, a spirit of compromise prevailed at the Kolchak–Gajda talks and the outcome was that the Czech agreed to remain at his post and obey orders, pending the results of an inquiry into the affairs of the *stavka* to be conducted by General Dieterichs.[7]

Dieterichs's report was of a standard to be expected from an officer of his extensive experience. His prime recommendation was that every effort should be made to induce Gajda to remain at his post rather than lose a commander of such proven ability. But he added that Lebedev too should be retained as Minister of War and Chief of Staff, for, whatever his faults, to remove him would be to appear to sanction the indiscipline of Gajda.[8] This balanced counsel Kolchak accepted. Moreover, in an attempt to assuage Gajda's distaste for answering to Lebedev, Kolchak now created a new post of Main Commander-in-Chief of the Eastern Army Group and, on June 20th, promoted Dieterichs to it. In this capacity Dieterichs was

4 *ibid.*, Vol. 2, p. 198; Dotsenko, P. *The Struggle for a Democracy in Siberia*. Stanford (1983), p. 97; Sukin (*Leeds Russian Archive*), p. 250.

5 Kirilov, A.A. 'Sibirskie armii v bor'be za osvobozhdenie', *Vol'naia Sibir'* (Prague), No. 4 (1928), p. 66.

6 *Russkaia armiia* (Omsk), No. 114, 3.vi.1919.

7 Sukin (*Leeds Russian Archive*), p. 251; FO 358/4 'Hodgson (Omsk) to Eliot (Vladivostok), 7.vi.1919'; WO 33/967/2277 'Knox (Omsk) to Britmis (Vladivostok) 8.vi.1919'.

8 Inostrantsev, M.A. 'Pervoe poruchenie admirala Kolchaka', *Beloe delo* Vol. 1 (1926), p. 105.

subordinate only to the Supreme Ruler, and was charged with overseeing the affairs of both Gajda's Siberian Army and the Western Army (the latter now commanded by General K.V. Sakharov, Khanzhin being demoted, shouldering the blame for the failure of the Ufa offensive). In theory only the direction of the minor Southern Army Group would now remain in Lebedev's hands.[9]

Far from appeasing Gajda, however, the promotion of the notoriously reactionary Dieterichs and Sakharov which was involved in the reshuffle was interpreted by the Czech – and, indeed, by British observers – as 'an attempted coup from the right'.[10] Consequently, on June 22nd Gajda refused to recognize Dieterichs as his superior and, once again, tendered his resignation.[11] There are contradictory versions of what then transpired.

According to a statement by Kolchak and the memoirs of Foreign Minister Sukin, the Supreme Ruler refused to accept Gajda's resignation and subsequently journeyed to Ekaterinburg to entreat him to withdraw it and to recognize Dieterichs. When Gajda refused, according to this version, he did not receive his congé, but, retaining the title of Commander-in-Chief of the Siberian Army, was sent on six months' furlough (with full pay) on the condition that he refrain from any political activity and the issuing of statements.[12] Gajda's own accounts, however (on which the reports of British agents appear to be based), portray his final split with Kolchak as acrimonious and premeditated on the Supreme Ruler's part. A Colonel Gusarek, acting on Gajda's instructions, passed a report to the British consul at Ekaterinburg which suggested that prior to meeting with Gajda in the city on July 7th, Kolchak had held a 'secret council' with Generals Dieterichs, Sakharov and Bogdovskii on July 6th 'at which it was decided to remove General Gajda immediately and, if possible, bring him before a Russian tribunal, on the charge of causing the

9 WO 33/967/2326 'Knox (Omsk) to WO, 19.vi.1919'; WO 33/967/2408 'Steveni (Omsk) to WO, 19.vi.1919'.

10 FO 538/4 'Memorandum on the Political Situation at Ekaterinburg by HM Consul, Mr Preston, 25.vi.1919'; WO 33/967/12436 'Blair (Ekaterinburg) to WO, 23.vi.1919'.

11 WO 33/967/2411 'Steveni (Omsk) to WO, 22.vi.1919'.

12 WO 33/967/2466 'Steveni (Omsk) to WO, 26.vi.1919'; Sukin (*Leeds Russian Archive*), pp. 253–4. The official announcement of Gajda's departure stated that he had 'retired due to illness'. See Eikhe, G. Kh. *Oprokinutyi tyl*. Moscow (1966), p. 327.

demoralization of the Russian Army'.[13] The next day, the report continues, in a stormy meeting with Gajda, Kolchak accused the Czech of insubordination and of undermining discipline in the army by his association with known SRs, demanded his immediate resignation and threatened a court-martial. To this Gajda retorted that 'the SRs who are in my army love their Motherland' – more so, he charged, than the band of pro-Japanese and corrupt generals with which Kolchak had immured himself – and welcomed the opportunity of a court-martial if its proceedings could be freely reported in the press 'so that all the world may know what kind of government exists here, what is its orientation and what is the cause of the demoralization of the army and so that others may judge who is guilty and who is right', before storming from the room.[14] Gajda later told Janin that personal insults were also traded at the interview: Kolchak accused the former *Feldscher* of lacking military experience, to which Gajda retorted that 'the Admiral himself cannot really pretend to have such knowledge, having commanded only three boats on the Black Sea'![15]

Whether Gajda and Kolchak parted with regret, as respectful colleagues who had agreed to differ, or as resentful enemies – which, given the affair's dénouement at Vladivostok (see below, pp. 564ff), is perhaps the more likely scenario – the effect was much the same: the Russian Army was deprived of the services of its most able and inspirational commander in the field.

Had General Dieterichs been granted the authority which his new position as Main Commander-in-Chief implied, the cloud cast by the Gajda affair might yet have had

13 FO 371/4097/142512 'Eliot (Omsk) to FO, 17.vii.1919'. An earlier report talks of 'constant intrigue' against Gajda as being 'stirred up' by Lebedev and of staff officers in general only displaying any sort of energy or enthusiasm when engaged in traducing the Czech hero (WO 33/967/2575 'Blair (Ekaterinburg) to Britmis (Vladivostok), 30.vi.1919'). Mention is also made of a 'secret conference' of leading army figures – including Generals Lebedev, Dieterichs, Sakharov and Domontovich – which had resolved to rid White Siberia of Gajda, even if it meant having to unseat Kolchak first (WO 538/4 'Memorandum on the Political Situation at Ekaterinburg by HM Consul, Mr. Preston, 25.vi.1919').

14 FO 371/4097/142512 'Eliot (Omsk) to FO, 17.vii.1919'. The British, of course, were inclined to portray the dismissal of Gajda in the worst light because of fears that it might put an end to the priority previously granted to the northern sector of the front by the Russian Army and scotch plans for a union with the forces at Arkhangel′sk on which the War Office was counting. See, for example, WO 33/967/2411 'Steveni (Omsk) to Britmis, 22.vi.1919'.

15 Janin, [P.T.C.]M. 'Otryvki iz moego sibirskogo dnevnika', in Kornatovskii, N.A. (ed.) *Kolchakovshchina: iz belykh memuarov*. Leningrad (1930), pp. 129–30.

a silver lining. Dieterichs was a commander of great skill – a veteran of the Russo-Japanese War and of campaigns in Turkestan, he had demonstrated his ability to adapt to civil war conditions in leading the Czechoslovak capture of Vladivostok in July 1918. He was also one of the few men willing, when necessary, to present Kolchak with the bitter pills he was famously reluctant to swallow. Whilst advising in June, for example, that Lebedev should be retained as Chief of Staff, Dieterichs had at the same time recommended that a clean broom should be applied to the Augean stables of the *stavka*: 'They have made so many serious mistakes of such an elementary character,' he opined, 'that their repetition might prove catastrophic; and we must thank God that it has not happened already.'[16] Had Dieterichs been empowered to wield the broom, therefore, some good might yet have come of the whole business. After Gajda's departure on July 7th, however, Dieterichs was asked to assume temporary operational command of the Siberian Army. This, as British observers noted, meant that he was unable to devote any time either to ensuring that he kept Kolchak's ear or that, as Main Commander of the army, he remained safely interposed between Lebedev and control of the front. Lebedev, on the other hand, with the thorn of Gajda now removed from his side, immediately reasserted his former malign influence over Kolchak. 'There has been a great change for the worse', noted a British report in the wake of Gajda's dismissal: 'Lebedev now has more influence over the Admiral than anyone else [and] controls everything from Vladivostok to the front.'[17] By cultivating the friendship of Mikhailov and Sukin, added another observer, and by having his 'best friend' Sakharov made Commander of the Western Army, Lebedev had forged 'a combination which is now running the country from both the military and civilian points of view'.[18] The result of this new boost to Lebedev's authority was immediate and catastrophic.

In the opinion of General Dieterichs, the most that the Russian Army could hope for – at least for the next three months – was some form of 'active defence' from entrenched positions to be prepared behind the natural defensive lines of Siberia's south–north flowing rivers (the first of which would be the River Tobol) while the development of Denikin's advance in South Russia relieved the pressure on the Eastern Front. Other senior military figures agreed: both General Andogskii (the

16 Inostrantsev, p. 105.

17 WO 106/1272 'Despatch No. 1 from General Knox at Omsk, 3.viii.1919 (App. A 'Steveni (Omsk) to Knox', 29.vii.1919)'.

18 FO 371/4096/117980 'Eliot (Omsk) to FO, 15.viii.1919'.

former Head of the General Staff Academy who had been promoted to Quartermaster General of the Russian Army on June 30th 1919) and General Knox (still *Chef d'Arrière*) felt that Dieterichs's was the most prudent plan and concurred that there could be 'no thought' of a renewed offensive in the foreseeable future.[19] Reports from the front at this time certainly seem to have attested to the sapience of a plan to win time in which to regroup and concentrate Kolchak's dwindling resources behind a defensive line: observers were painting pictures of a complete breakdown in the discipline of the retreating Russian Army during July–August 1919, and the loss of any will to resist. Russian sources with the Siberian Army, for example, informed Knox:

> As long as the Reds are prepared to advance, the withdrawal of the Siberian Army will continue. The appearance of a party of Reds on a flank is sufficient to cause a further withdrawal. There is no military reason for this – it is simply a case of complete loss of morale. There is no fight left in men or officers.[20]

The collapse was even more complete in the Western Army, whose retreat from the Volga had been the most precipitate. A French officer at Krasnoufimsk recorded that:

> There is complete demoralization. The opposing sides are not even in contact and hardly any firing is heard at the front. The Reds only advance as [the Western Army] retires to loot. Krasnoufimsk is full of drunken Russian officers. One regiment with a strength of four hundred men has a thousand carts loaded with pianos and furniture which the officers have amassed.[21]

Self-mutilation among the demoralized troops was becoming endemic according to General Graves of the American Expeditionary Force who visited the front at this time. Military hospitals were refusing to treat anyone shot in the hand or foot in order to discourage it, but a Dutch observer who visited a hospital train during the retreat estimated that of the patients some 80% had lost their right index finger and

19 WO 33/967/2277 'Knox (Omsk) to WO, 20.vi.1919'; WO 33/967/2725 'Steveni (Omsk) to WO, 14.vii.1919'.

20 WO 33/967/2566 'Knox (Vladivostok) to WO, 10.vii.1919'.

21 WO 33/967/2597 'Blair (Ekaterinburg) to WO, 14.vii.1919'.

only 10% were seriously wounded.[22] Part of the problem was that Kolchak's troops were now retreating into the home districts of many of the mobilized men, who were taking any opportunity to desert – leaving behind them 'divisions' consisting of only 750 men and 'brigades' of 180, and throwing away so much military equipment that their grateful Bolshevik pursuers sent a telegram to General Knox asking him to pass on their regards to the British Government for arming and equipping the Red Army![23]

As the retreat reached Ekaterinburg complete chaos and disorder reigned. Dieterichs issued strict orders to his Siberian Army staff not to leave the city until they had received orders to do so, but could not stop the rot.[24] The British consul and members of the British Railway Mission, who were on the last trains out of the city on July 14th, passed many deserters who complained 'why should we remain at the front when the officers run away first?' and were scandalized to see entire trains 'laden with grand pianos, safes and valuable furniture' being salvaged by fleeing merchants (who had paid the army 40,000–80,000 roubles for the hire of each wagon), while behind them in the Urals 500,000 poods both of copper and cast iron, 1,800,000 poods of pig iron and 300,000 poods of steel rails were left to fall into Bolshevik hands for want of transportation to remove it, along with machinery and entire factories left intact for the want of time having been taken to sabotage them.[25]

However, despite the weight of opinion and evidence to the contrary, Lebedev, now ably seconded by the equally young and only marginally more experienced General Sakharov, was certain that an immediate counter-attack was not only feasible but necessary. 'Lebedev is extremely optimistic and insists that everything now happening at the front is nothing and that within a few weeks the tables will be completely turned', reported a British agent, adding, 'Sakharov keeps telegraphing that the Western Army can begin its offensive any time now.'[26] In fact, Lebedev was adamant that a new offensive must be initiated before the end of

22 *FRUS: 1919 (Russia)*, pp. 212–13; Grondijs, L.H. *La Guerre en Russie et en Sibérie*. Paris (1922), p. 326.

23 *ibid.*, p. 528.

24 WO 106/1272 'Despatch No. 1 from General Knox…(App. A)'.

25 FO 538/4 'Memorandum on Events at Ekaterinburg by HM Consul, Mr Preston, 13–21.viii.1919'; WO 33/967/3035 'Jack (Omsk) to WO, 10.viii.1919'; Preston, p. 137.

26 WO 33/967/2613 'Steveni (Omsk) to WO, 5.vii.1919'.

July. Predicting a loss of morale if an attempt was made to dig in and defend, he talked of a new surge to gain the left bank of the Volga and to unite with Belov's Cossacks for an attack on Tsaritsyn, thereby securing the grain-rich regions of Ufa and Samara and severing Bolshevik communications with Central Asia and the Caspian.[27]

Dieterichs and every other strategist of worth in Siberia opposed Lebedev's pipe dream with every means at their disposal. But still Kolchak sanctioned the plan hatched by his Chief of Staff and Sakharov for a new offensive and, specifically, endorsed their scheme to turn the tide at the front with a complicated manoeuvre at Cheliabinsk. The town itself was a valuable asset, being the centre of a coalmining district, containing important railway repair shops and being situated at the northern terminus of the railway line running south through Troitsk to Kustanai along which was deraigned Belov's Cossack group. Uppermost in Kolchak's mind in arriving at his decision to stand fast at Cheliabinsk, however, was the ongoing diplomatic conference at Omsk where Allied representatives (including the US Ambassador to Japan, Mr Morris) were assessing the Whites' prospects: a clever victory would boost Kolchak's prestige and might yet win recognition for his government. Consequently, Lebedev and Sakharov were allowed to attempt to fool the Reds into believing that the Russian Army was worse off than it actually was by abandoning Cheliabinsk to them without a fight. The plan was that a pincer movement executed by troops to be secretly concentrated to the north (five infantry and one cavalry division under Voitsekhovskii) and south (three infantry divisions and a cavalry brigade under Kappel) of the town would then entrap the entire 5th Red Army.[28] Apparently Lebedev was influenced in his decision-making by the 16,000 reserves in the process of attachment to the Western Army. He was aware that many of them had not even completed their basic training and would be of dubious worth in combat, but, reported a British agent, 'Lebedev considers that their lack of training will not be serious because they will be matched by similar material.' Doubtingly the report concluded: 'We shall see.'[29]

27 WO 33/967/2277 'Knox (Omsk) to WO, 8.vi.1919'. Kolchak, echoing Lebedev, confirmed to Pepeliaev that by attacking he hoped to 'rouse the army...which would soon be lost anyway through demoralization'. Pepeliaev, 'Razval kolchakovshchiny', p. 64.

28 Sakharov, K.V. *Belaia Sibir'*. Munich (1923), pp. 116–21; Sukin (*Leeds Russian Archive*), p. 212.

29 WO 33/967/2613 'Steveni (Omsk) to WO, 5.vii.1919'.

On July 24th–25th elements of the 5th Red Army duly entered a strangely deserted Cheliabinsk, unknowingly giving the signal for Lebedev's planned counter-attack. Predictably, however, the trap failed to shut tight as Kappel's untested corps was brushed aside by the crack Red 26th Division.[30] To the north Voitsekhovskii faired a little better and briefly managed to cut the Cheliabinsk–Ekaterinburg railway line; but his success was short-lived as units of the 3rd Red Army, diverted by Frunze from their attack on Nizhne-Petropavlovsk, cut into his right flank, inspiring Bolshevized elements among the newly mobilized 11th Siberian Division to desert and initiating a general White retreat towards Kurgan and the River Tobol on August 2nd.[31] Behind them, around Cheliabinsk, the Russian Army left 5,000 dead, 15,000 prisoners, 3,500 loaded wagons, 500,000 poods of flour and other provender.[32] Worse still, on August 4th the town of Troitsk had also to be surrendered, ending all hope of re-establishing contact with the Southern Army, which began a lonely retreat into Turkestan. Thereafter the Russian Army was effectively cut in two.[33]

30 The *stavka* ascribed this to simple numerical superiority on the part of their foe, but Knox disagreed: 'As a matter of fact the Bolsheviks' direction of operations is superior to ours,' he conceded, 'and they have some units which fight with conviction, while we have just at the present none.' (WO 106/1272 'Despatch No. 1 from General Knox at Omsk, 3.viii.1919'.) Also of significance was the deficiency of communications on the White side – incredibly no telegraphic link had been established between Sakharov's operational headquarters and the Kappel group. See Sakharov, p. 124. Finally, the fact was that the area in which Lebedev had decided to mount his operations, being a broken terrain of small lakes and woods, was quite unsuitable for the rapid manoeuvering of bodies of troops. See Eikhe, p. 260.

31 Petrov, P.P. *Ot Volgi do Tikhago Okeana*. Riga (1930), pp. 108–10; Sakharov, pp. 120–6; Spirin, L.M. *Razgrom armii Kolchaka*. Moscow (1957), pp. 213–17. According to a Red commander, the Red forces were assisted by 6,000 volunteers from among the workers of Cheliabinsk. See Eikhe, p. 310.

32 *ibid.*, pp. 218–9; Sakharov, p. 126.

33 At this point the Southern Army Group itself split into two. The Urals Cossacks, led by Ataman Tolstov, headed south to Gur′ev at the mouth of the Ural River. With the approach of Red forces, however, 12,000 of them decided to move on to Persia along the eastern shore of the Caspian. Of those who set out through the –30 degree frosts of the fearful Karakum desert, only 3,000 reached Fort Aleksandrovsk and a mere 214 survived to cross the Persian border at Bairam in June 1920. From there they emigrated – chiefly to Constantinople or Australia. See Tolstov, V.S. *Ot krasnykh lap v neizvestnuiu dal′ (pokhod Ural′tsev)*. Constantinople (1921). Meanwhile, after General Belov had failed in an effort to strike north from Atbasar through Kokchetav to re-establish contact with the main body of the Russian Army during October, the Orenburg Cossack elements of the Southern Army, commanded by Ataman Dutov and General Bakich, began a nightmarish odyssey through the desert-steppe region and northern Turkestan during which many thousands died of hunger, cold and endemic typhus, before eventually arriving on the border with Sinkiang in early 1920. There they merged with the Semirech′e Cossack group of Ataman Annenkov, which had been driven out of Sergiopol by Red partisans during January. After squatting on the border

Lebedev's gamble had failed to pay off. The Urals, with their mighty stocks of human and mineral reserves, were to remain in Red hands and the last of Kolchak's Siberian reserves had been expended to no avail. His Red Army opponents were jubilant, for victory had come much more quickly and effortlessly than could have been expected. As recently as May 29th Lenin had telegraphed the Military Revolutionary Committee of the Eastern Front that 'unless we conquer the Urals by winter, I consider disaster to be inevitable for the revolution'.[34] On August 4th, in high summer, soldiers of the 5th Red Army were able to send the following message to Lenin:

> You ordered us to capture the Urals before winter. We have fulfilled your command. Now we are off to Siberia![35]

The Omsk diplomatic conference and the demise of Allied intervention in Siberia

In sanctioning Lebedev's plan to stem the Red tide at Cheliabinsk, Kolchak was undoubtedly alive to the effect a new victory might have upon the concurrent proceedings at Omsk of a conference of the senior Allied diplomats and military

between Lepsinsk and Zaisan for some time, between March and May 1920 most of the 10,000 or so Orenburg Cossack soldiers and refugees who then remained of the 30,000 who had retreated from Orenburg in August, together with 4,000 of Annenkov's men, decided to negotiate a passage across the mountains into China (where they were disarmed and interned at Suidin and other camps by the Chinese authorities). Others remained behind to take advantage of an amnesty offered by the approaching Reds. On these events see Elovskii, I. *Golodnyi pokhod Orenburgskoi armii: iz vospominanii uchastnika pokhoda*. Peking (1921); Zuev, A.V. *Orenburgskie kazaki v bor'be s bol'shevizmom, 1918–1922gg.: ocherki*. Harbin (1937); Serebrennikov, I.I. *Velikii otkhod: razseianie po Azii belykh Russkikh armii* Harbin (1936), pp. 27–40; Dubrovskii, K.V. *V tsarstve nagaiki i viselitsy*. Moscow–Leningrad (1929), pp. 97–100. Dutov was assassinated by one of his own men, reputed to be a Bolshevik agent, in February 1921 – see Markov, J. 'Gibel' atamana Dutova', *Rodimyi krai* (Paris), No. 101 (1972). Annenkov spent three years in Chinese jails and another two in Mongolia before returning to Soviet territory in 1926. He was apprehended at Sverdlovsk and executed in August 1927 after a trial at Semipalatinsk. Some of the evidence of atrocities levelled against him (denounced as fraudulent by most White sources) was published in Pavlovskii, P.I. *Annenkovshchina: po materialam sudebnogo protsessa v Semipalatinske*. Moscow (1928).

34 Meijer, J.M. (ed.) *The Trotsky Papers: 1917–1922*. Vol. 1. The Hague (1964), pp. 482–3.

35 *Istoriia grazhdanskoi voiny v SSSR*. Moscow (1959–1960), Vol. 4, p. 132.

officials accredited to Siberia. The conference had first been mooted in mid-June as a means of determining precisely how the powers could 'further assist' Kolchak in accordance with commitments made in their joint note of June 12th. In the absence of an American High Commissioner or senior general in Siberia, however, Ambassador Morris had to be summoned from Tokyo and General Graves from Vladivostok, thereby delaying the opening of the conference until July 26th.[36] But by that time, of course, the Russian Army's impending loss of the Urals had 'complicated matters', as Sukin euphemized in a note to Sazonov of July 29th, adding that the Russians were now only too well aware that the discussions might now lead to definite plans for the expansion of aid to the Omsk régime 'only in the case of a general improvement of the situation' at the front.[37] When Lebedev's gamble failed to secure such an improvement, Kolchak summoned Knox and, perhaps hoping for sympathy, 'confessed that the futile Cheliabinsk operation had been undertaken to impress the Allies contrary to Dieterichs's wishes'.[38] For the gathering Allied representatives, however, the débâcle at Cheliabinsk was the last straw.

Although the proceedings of the conference were to drag on until August 20th, its key plenary session came on July 29th, just prior to the Cheliabinsk fiasco. At this session Sukin presented requests for the donation of 600,000 full sets of uniform and kit, 400,000 rifles, 500,000,000 rounds of ammunition, 3,000 machine guns and 75,000 cartridge-belts. The Allied plenipotentiaries took note of his desiderata and agreed that the ailing Kolchak government could have no hope of survival, let alone of defeating the Bolsheviks, unless it was first recognized and then immediately resuscitated by just such a massive influx of Allied aid. The minimum requirement they calculated to be a $200,000,000 credit for the purchase of military supplies and commercial products; the provision of additional inspectors and a $20,000,000 credit for the Inter-Allied Railway Committee; the deployment of 40,000 troops to replace the Czechoslovak guard on the Trans-Siberian Railway; and the establishment of Inter-Allied Military and Civilian Supply Committees to supervise the distribution

36 Livshits, S.G. 'Omskoe "diplomaticheskoe" soveshchanie 1919 goda', *Voprosy istorii* (Moscow), No. 6 (1986), p. 178; Volkov, F. *Krakh angliiskoi politiki interventsii i diplomaticheskoi izoliatsii Sovetskogo gosudarstva*. Moscow (1954), pp. 81–2.

37 Kim, P.M. (ed.) 'Iz arkhiva organizatorov grazhdanskoi voiny i interventsii v Sovetskoi Rossii', *Istoricheskii arkhiv* No. 6 (1961), p. 87.

38 WO 33/967/2901 'Knox (Omsk) to WO, 4.viii.1919'.

of imported goods.[39] Having concurred that all this was vitally necessary for Kolchak's survival, however, the delegates disagreed as to whether they should actually recommend to their governments that the lifeline of aid should be extended to him. Ambassador Morris, despite initial scepticism as to the Omsk régime's viability, was apparently willing to believe that Kolchak might be capable of making 'drastic changes in his government' so as to merit such a massive commitment of support.[40] However, both General Knox and General Janin, whose long service in Siberia made their comments all the more dolorous for Kolchak, took quite the opposite point of view. Comments in Janin's diary for July show his increasing frustration with the admiral; while, although as recently as the middle of that month Knox was still urging continued support of Omsk, the Supreme Ruler's decision to ignore his and Dieterichs's advice on strategy in favour of Lebedev's fantastical schemes had finally changed his mind.[41] At the conference, reported Morris, both of the senior Allied officers in Siberia testified that any appeal to Kolchak to put his house in order would be useless 'because in their view he is powerless to act', and made no secret of their opinion that White misadventures in the Urals and continued squabbling in the army command meant that the only solution was for Allied representatives entirely to take over the command of the Russian Army.[42] They recognized that there was little hope of the Russians accepting this, but Knox reported to his superiors in London on August 1st that without 'adequate control' over the 600,000 kits which Sukin had demanded, any further deliveries 'would be like pouring money down a drain'. He added: 'I told [Sukin] that if I were to ask you for this after the scandalous misuse of the 200,000 [uniforms] we had already given, you would telegraph me not to be a "damned fool".'[43]

In fact, irrespective of Knox's contribution to the diplomatic conference – and, indeed, in advance of the receipt of news in the west of the Cheliabinsk affair – the British government was on the point of despatching to Knox, for quite separate

39 *Iz istorii grazhdanskoi voiny v SSSR*. Moscow (1960–1961), Vol. 2. pp. 63–4; WO 33/967/2936 'Knox (Omsk) to WO, 1.viii.1919'; *FRUS: 1919 (Russia)*, pp. 408–10.

40 *ibid.*, pp. 407, 403–4, 409–19. Morris's concern was that if Kolchak's régime was *not* supported something much *less* acceptable to the Allies might come to the fore in Siberia.

41 Janin, pp. 126–8; WO 33 967/4069/2644 'Knox (Omsk) to WO, 14.vii.1919'.

42 *FRUS: 1919 (Russia)*, p. 401.

43 WO 106/1272 'Despatch No. 1 from General Knox at Omsk, 3.viii.1919'; WO 33 967/4069/2899 'Knox (Omsk) to WO, 1.viii.1919'.

reasons, orders deadly to Omsk. On June 27th Churchill's longstanding plans for a joint Anglo-Russian offensive from Arkhangel′sk down the Dvina towards Kotlas (and, hopefully, a rendezvous with Kolchak's Siberian Army), had finally been given the go-ahead by the War Cabinet. After a promising start, however, the Dvina operation soon came to grief as panicky White troops deserted to the Reds, while the river unexpectedly dropped to a depth of 60 cm (its lowest summer level for 50 years) forcing the retirement of the British flotilla which was supporting the ground forces. Coinciding, as this did, with the withdrawal from Glazov of the Siberian Army, the lesson was drawn in London that there would be no Kotlas offensive from either North Russia or Siberia in 1919 and, therefore, no union between the northern and eastern White groups which might facilitate the supply of Kolchak. In the light of this, and under pressure from certain of its members (notably Barnes, Addison and Fisher) to get out of Russia altogether, on July 24th the War Cabinet decided to cut its losses and rationalize its support to the anti-Bolsheviks.[44] Accordingly, on July 29th a reluctant Churchill was instructed to inform the House of Commons that all British troops would be evacuated from North Russia before October 15th 1919,[45] while on August 5th Knox was informed that, in view of the internal difficulties of the Omsk régime, the collapse of the Kotlas offensive and the near exhaustion of surplus stocks in Britain, 'it has been decided that our help

44 Ullman, R.H. *Anglo-Soviet Relations, 1917–1921.* London (1961–1972), Vol. 2, pp. 207–9; Silverlight, M. *The Victors' Dilemma.* London (1970) p. 248–51. On the North Russian operations see Long, J.W. 'Civil War and Intervention in North Russia, 1918–20', Columbia University PhD Thesis (1972); Long, J. 'An Intervention in Russia: The North Russian Expedition, 1918–1919', *Diplomatic History* Vol. 6 (1982), No. 1, pp. 45–68; Rhodes, B.D. *The Anglo-American Winter War with Russia, 1918–1919: A Diplomatic and Military Tragicomedy.* London (1988); Strakhovsky, L.I. *Intervention at Archangel, 1918–1920.* Princeton (1944). First-hand accounts include: Ironside, E. *Archangel 1918–1919.* London (1953), pp. 160–9; Singleton-Gates, G.R. *Bolos and Barishynas: Being an Account of the Doings of the Sadleir-Jackson Brigade, and Altham Flotilla, on the North Dvina during the Summer, 1919.* Aldershot (1920); Altham, E. 'The Dwina Campaign', *Journal of the Royal United Services Institute,* Vol. 68 (1923), pp. 228–53; Neville, Captain J.E.H. *The War Letters of a Light Infantryman.* London (1930); [Anon.] 'Some Naval Work in North Russia', *Naval Review* Vol. 9 (1921), No. 1, pp. 85–155.

45 Gilbert, M. *Winston S. Churchill.* London (1975), Vol. 4, pp. 300–2; Ullman, Vol. 2, pp. 190–4. This was an onerous task for Churchill, who was far from losing faith in the intervention. On July 1st he told Nabokov at a meeting of the 'Russian–British Club' that he would do all in his power to ensure 'decisive results' in 1919 and to maintain the flow of aid to Siberia. See Boiarskii, V.A. (ed.) 'Ob uchastii angliiskikh imperialistov v organizatsii interventsii protiv sovetskoi Rossii', *Istoricheskii arkhiv,* No. 2 (1957), p. 69; *Daily Telegraph* (London), 18.vii.1919. The belligerent Minister of War was also still scouring the Empire for recruits to a volunteer force to be sent to North Russia – see Canada, Dept. of External Affairs *Documents on Canadian External Affairs.* Ottawa (1970), Vol. 3 (1919–1925), pp. 66–7.

should be concentrated on one theatre, the theatre being that of General Denikin'; the second tranche of equipment which had already been promised to Kolchak – including uniforms for 100,000 men and supplies for 125,000 – would now be diverted to South Russia.[46] Behind the logic of this despatch could be discerned a clear message: Denikin was in the early stages of his offensive; the Allies liked a winner; Kolchak now looked very much like a loser.

Meanwhile, across the Atlantic, the Americans too had come to the conclusion that Kolchak was not a good bet. Both Democrat and Republican isolationist opposition to the intervention was becoming increasingly vociferous in the Senate,[47] making it very difficult for the Wilson administration to remain committed to it, even if the President had wanted to (which he did not): news of the Cheliabinsk fiasco was now abroad and as early as August 9th White officials in Washington had been made aware that the State Department had determined that, in the light of his military reverses, whatever the outcome of the diplomatic conference at Omsk no further American aid could be expected. On August 25th Secretary of State Lansing duly informed Morris that although the USA would honour the supply of rifles to which it was already committed, it definitely would not sanction the project discussed by the diplomatic conference on July 29th.[48]

Thus, although they would continue to deal with Kolchak and hope for the best – and although, at the height of the Denikin and Iudenich offensives in October–November 1919, the British and American governments would again toy with the idea of recognizing him as the provisional ruler of Russia[49] – from early August the Allies had effectively written off the Supreme Ruler and his Russian Army in terms of their military significance in the war against Bolshevism. As Knox's telegram of August 1st condemning Kolchak crossed the desk of Lord Curzon, the Foreign Secretary appended a terse but telling minute: 'A lost cause.'[50]

46 WO 33/967/2926 'WO to Britmis (Vladivostok), 5.viii.1919'. On July 16th Knox had already received orders to have the Middlesex and Hampshire Regiments concentrated on Vladivostok, from where they would embark for Britain on September 7th and November 1st respectively. See WO 32/5707 'Report of the Military Mission in Siberia, 10.xii.1919 (App. J)'.

47 See, for example, *Congressional Record*. Washington (1919), Vol. 58, pp. 4816, 4896–901, 5039–40.

48 Kim, 'Iz arkhiva', p. 87; *FRUS: 1919 (Russia)*, p. 421; Ullman, Vol. 2, pp. 246–52.

49 See *ibid.*, p. 447; and Kim, p. 95.

50 Ullman, Vol. 2, p. 207.

During July 1919 one further question of vital importance to Kolchak was resolved by the Allies – again in a manner noxious and fraught with dangers for the White cause. That was the question of when, and how, the Czechoslovak Legion should leave Siberia and what, if any, Allied force was going to replace it as the guardian of the Trans-Siberian Railway. Since the spring Eduard Beneš had been petitioning the Council of Five at Paris to organize a gradual concentration of the Legion on Vladivostok and to provide ships for their repatriation.[51] Consistent pressure exerted on the Czechoslovak government by the Russian Political Conference at Paris and, personally, by Winston Churchill had, however, finally persuaded President Masaryk to endorse a scheme drawn up by the British War Office (and referred to the Supreme War Council by the Council of Five on June 28th). This plan was predicated upon the evacuation of only a *minority* of the Legionnaires via the Far East, while the remainder would fight their way out of Siberia through Kotlas and Vologda for evacuation from Arkhangel'sk.[52] From the Whites' point of view the advantages of this plan were obvious – the troublesome and inactive Legion was to be drawn back into a fighting role which would bolster Kolchak's war effort. From the Czechoslovak point of view it would provide the crowning glory to the new republic's service to the Allied cause and would assuage any fears that their earlier contributions might be forgotten if the Legion left Kolchak to his fate and departed by sea. Churchill hoped that some 30,000 men – two-thirds of the Legion's complement – could be persuaded to join the attack on Kotlas by the promise of evacuation before the end of 1919 if the operation was successful and a delegation under Dr. F.V. Krejci was despatched from Prague to encourage such enlistment.[53]

A drawback to the scheme, as the Americans commented at the time, was that the British government was already committed to the evacuation of North Russia before November and it was most unlikely that any Czechoslovak force could reach

51 *FRUS: 1919 (Russia)*, pp. 280–1.

52 *ibid.*, p. 283–6; *FRUS: PPC*, Vol. 6, pp. 743–5; *Dokumenty ob antinatsional'noi politike Masarika*. Moscow (1955), pp. 63–4; Klevanskii, A.Kh. 'Bor'ba sovetskogo pravitel'stva za normalizatsiiu sovetskogo-chekhoslovatskikh otnoshenii (konets 1918–nachalo 1920gg.)', *Voprosy istorii*, No. 2 (1969), pp. 105–6.

53 WO 33/967/2499 'WO to Knox (Omsk), 2.vii.1919'; *FRUS: 1919 (Russia)*, p. 284. On Krejci's mission see Krejci, F.V. *Poselstvo vlady k csl. vojsku na Sibiri*. Prague (1923); Kvasnicka, J. *Ceskoslovenske legie v Rusku, 1917–1920*. Bratislava (1963), pp. 251–89.

Arkhangel'sk before that time.[54] Even so, it would clearly have been of advantage to the Allies to attempt to have the Legionnaires concentrated at two ports rather than one, as it was already expected that an evacuation via Vladivostok alone might take up to two years to complete. There remained, however, another serious impediment to Churchill's plan: the fact that it was completely at odds with conditions on the ground in Siberia.

From the very beginning Kolchak himself reacted 'coldly' to the scheme, according to Sukin. He did not believe that the miserable Legionnaires could be induced to fight and, even if they could be, he was fearful that the priority they would place on getting out of Siberia might conflict with his own aim of 'saving' Russia.[55] Still, Kolchak was in no position by this time to cavil outright at the Allied plan. In fact, as the Urals slipped from his grasp, he was beginning to clutch at straws. Thus, even though in private he continued to sneer at the Legion as 'those POWs' and to remark that their indiscipline reminded him of nothing so much as the mutinous Russian Army of 1917,[56] he made some effort to persuade the Czechoslovaks to return to the front: senior White spokesmen, such as A.S. Belorussov, were despatched to their barracks to address the men of the Legion; Kolchak himself reviewed Czechoslovak parades and distributed medals and promises of financial rewards (in hard currency payments and pensions) for those who re-enlisted for the fight against the Bolsheviks; and, on July 8th, the Council of Ministers passed a decree granting volunteers generous land rights and commercial concessions in Central Asia, the Far East and on Sakhalin.[57] The Whites' dawning desperation may be deduced from the fact that, according to one account, 'even Cossacks...began to try and strike up friendships with the Czechs on the basis of a shared democratic philosophy'.[58]

As Kolchak suspected, however, the scheme was quite inapposite. Those who had close contact with the Legion, such as its Commander-in-Chief, General Janin,

54 *FRUS: 1919 (Russia)*, pp. 285–6.

55 Sukin (*Leeds Russian Archive*), p. 272; *FRUS: 1919 (Russia)*, pp. 287–8.

56 Grondijs *La Guerre*, p. 527; Grondijs, L.H. *Le Cas Koltchak: contribution à l'histoire de la révolution russe*. Leiden (1939), p. 37.

57 Krol', L. *Za tri goda*. Vladivostok (1921), p. 192; Becvar, G. *The Lost Legion*. London (1939), p. 215; Sukin (*Leeds Russian Archive*), p. 273; Kotomkin, A. *O chekhoslovatskikh legionerakh v Sibiri, 1918–1920gg.: vospominaniia i dokumenty*. Paris (1930), pp. 40–1.

58 Sukin (*Leeds Russian Archive*), p. 271.

were certain that no more than 1,000–2,000 men were ever likely to be induced to fight for Kolchak.[59] Having already witnessed the mutiny of several Czechoslovak regiments near Irkutsk on June 13th, the American Consul, Mr Harris, and IARC supremo Stevens added that far more likely was a contrary scenario, whereby – unless they were evacuated before the onset of cold weather – the mass of the Legion, fed up with fighting other people's battles in such appalling conditions and riddled with Bolshevik propaganda, would reach 'boiling point' and take up arms *against* Kolchak whilst opening negotiations with the Bolsheviks for repatriation via Europe.[60] Kolchak was certainly convinced that such a move was possible; and by the middle of July he was insisting that, if the Czechoslovaks would not go to the front, they should be disarmed and sent to Vladivostok forthwith, before they could cause any further disruption in Siberia. Sukin and Janin agreed that if, as they were sure, the Arkhangel′sk scheme was hopeless, it was 'imperative' that evacuation via the Far East should be got underway as soon as possible and that this be broadcast in order to defuse tension within the Legion.[61]

The Omsk diplomatic conference considered evidence on the Czechoslovak question during its session of July 27th and concurred unanimously with Janin's contention that the Legionnaires 'do not want to go to the front and do not want to continue guarding the railway line' and should, therefore, be evacuated.[62] Moreover, for the first time the corollary of such a withdrawal was spelled out at this session – namely that, with the Legion departed, the Russian Army would not be able to commit sufficient forces to guard the Trans-Siberian Railway; that the Omsk government would, consequently, be unable to survive the winter and might as well be given up for dead unless the Allies sent troops to maintain its lifeline to the Pacific. A minimum of three infantry divisions (36,000 men), one cavalry division (3,000 men) and three artillery batteries would be required to do the job,

59 *FRUS: 1919 (Russia)*, p. 289; WO 33/967/2669 'Steveni (Omsk) to WO. 16.vii.1919'. Also, as Janin pointed out, if the best elements were removed from the body of the Legion to fight at the front, the less loyal men left behind might be even more mutinous. Sukin (*Leeds Russian Archive*), pp. 274–5.

60 *FRUS: 1919 (Russia)*, pp. 281–3.

61 Grondijs, *La Guerre*, p. 527; Grondijs, *Le Cas Koltchak*, p. 37; *FRUS: 1919 (Russia)*, pp. 287–8, 289–90.

62 Livshits, 'Omskoe "diplomaticheskoe" soveshchanie', p. 179.

the conference calculated, and the USA and Japan were duly requested to provide them.[63]

It was a request which the Allied leaders in Paris had been expecting. On July 18th the Council of Heads of Delegations had already decided to ask the governments of Japan and the USA to provide replacements for the Legion.[64] But President Wilson, who had only ever agreed to join the intervention as a means of assisting the Czechoslovaks to get out of Russia, was unlikely to endorse the commitment of new troops now that his aim was being achieved. On August 8th, therefore, he duly announced in Paris that, with 'utmost regret', the United States would be unable to send any further troops to Siberia. None of the western Allies desired that Tokyo alone should garrison the key to communications on the mainland of East Asia, so, at that, discussions turned to the practical question of who was going to foot the bill for the estimated $250–$300 per man it was going to cost to transport the Czechoslovak Legion from Siberia to Bohemia.[65]

The Omsk government kept up a barrage of requests for assistance over the next few weeks. On August 31st, for example, another will-o'-the-wisp scheme for the Legion to fight its way home via South Russia was aired by Vologodskii, while on September 26th Sukin appealed desperately to the Allies to provide troops to guard the railway even if it was only for six months.[66] But to no avail. On September 26th, with the parliament in Prague besieged by families demanding that their sons, fathers and husbands be brought home and with the threat of disorder on the streets as repatriation became a national issue, Beneš instructed Janin to begin moving all Czechoslovak units in Siberia towards Vladivostok – even though no provision whatsoever had been made for their replacement or for maintaining the viability of the Trans-Siberian Railway.[67] Eyes must have been lowered in shame and accusing Russian looks avoided in Paris, London and Washington, for, having agreed that the

63 *ibid.*, pp. 179–80; *FRUS: 1919 (Russia)*, pp. 291–2.

64 *ibid.*, pp. 288–9.

65 *ibid.*, pp. 295–301.

66 Kim, p. 91; Livshits, S.G. *Imperialisticheskaia interventsiia v Sibiri, 1918–1920gg.* Barnaul (1979), pp. 78–9.

67 Bradley, J.F.N. *Allied Intervention in Russia, 1917–1920.* London (1968), pp. 124–5. Beneš's order was given even though by this point the Allied leaders at Paris had only got as far as agreeing in principle that the Czechoslovak Legion should be evacuated before other Allied contingents (and certainly before the repatriation of German, Austrian and Magyar POWs) and had set no date. *FRUS: PPC*, Vol. 8, pp. 307–8, 411–12, 488–9.

Kolchak government they had for so long sponsored stood not the slightest chance of seeing the year out unless the railway was garrisoned, the Allies declined to provide the garrison.

The initial Allied support for the Whites during 1917 and 1918 had been at least partly motivated by the suspicion (apparently confirmed during the spring and summer of 1918 by the collaborationist activities of Ataman Kaledin on the Don and Miliukov in Kiev) that unless they did so the Central Powers would step into the gap and draw post-war Russia into Berlin's orbit. Of course, this prognosis had been difficult to square with the contemporaneous conception of the Bolsheviks as German stooges. Nevertheless, it had been a factor. And, having effectively washed their hands of Kolchak, during the summer of 1919 such concerns were once more to trouble the minds of leaders in London and Paris – not least because hints were being heavily dropped in Omsk that if the western powers were going to withdraw their support, help would have to be sought elsewhere.[68]

As long as Kolchak remained at the head of the anti-Bolshevik movement, however, the Allies' vision of a German–White combination was a bugaboo. As the admiral confided during a farewell interview with Bernard Pares in July 1919, if abandoned by the Allies:

> I am afraid that Russia may come to think of herself as in a position analogous to that of those who lost the war, such as Germany; and then it would be inevitable that she and Germany would draw closer together. But I think that that would be a very bad thing for my country; and the day that it happens, I shall not be there.[69]

In fact, although in desperation certain elements of the Omsk press (notably *Russkoe delo*) and the Kadet leader Zhardetskii began to advocate an agreement with Berlin, Kolchak would have nothing to do with Whites of a pro-German orientation, such as the rogue Western Volunteer Army of the flamboyant Colonel Prince P.M. Bermondt-Avalov and the Army of Western Russia, commanded by the murderous General Rudiger von der Goltz (both of whom were operating in tandem with Freikorps elements in the Baltic theatre during 1919). In fact, Kolchak warned that any force failing to subordinate itself to pro-Allied commanders (in this instance, to

68 *DBFP*, p. 402.

69 Pares, B. *Moscow Admits a Critic*. London (1936), p. 12.

General Iudenich) were to be regarded as 'traitors'.[70] Evidence of the admiral's loyalty to the Allied cause may be further adduced from the fact that, even when approaching the very nadir of his fortunes in October 1919, he would not contemplate accepting alms from Russia's enemy of 1914–1918, asseverating:

> I will never appeal for help to the pro-German counter-revolution and I will never grant anybody the right to do so in my name. In general it is impermissible ever to even raise the question of such help.[71]

If the Siberian Whites would not associate themselves with Germany in 1919, however, they were certainly willing to entertain thoughts of collaboration with Japan – a power whose naked ambitions to disturb the status quo in East Asia were coming to be regarded in London and Washington with hardly less suspicion than had Germany's in Europe. It was obvious that Japanese aid to Omsk would not come cheap and that concessions – economic and perhaps even territorial – would have to be carved from Russian possessions in the Far East. But when faced with the prospect of Allied disengagement during the summer of 1919, there were those in Omsk who thought that no price would be too high to pay. The prominent Kadet, N.V. Ustrialov, for example, mirroring Miliukov's Germanophil gymnastics in the Ukraine, would point out that 'Russia at the moment is not in a position to exploit her natural resources by herself' and might benefit from a partnership with Tokyo; meanwhile General Kornilov's former adjutant, Zavoiko (who was by then calling himself Kurbatov), was active at Omsk, attempting to curry Cossack support for the ceding of territory to Japan in exchange for a more committed intervention.[72] Certain army elements – ideologically and sentimentally attracted to the militaristic nature of Japan at that time – would advocate a full-blown Russo-Japanese alliance for political and economic co-operation in the Far East and, in particular, for combating Bolshevik and German influence in China (opining for good measure that

70 *Istoriia i sovremennost'* (Berlin), 1922, Vol. 1, p. 27, cited in Zimina, V.D. 'Severo-zapadnaia germanofil'skaia i vostochnaia kontrrevoliutsiia: popytki vziamodeistviia i ikh krakh', in Korablev, Iu. V. and Shishkin, V.I. (eds.) *Iz istorii interventsii i grazhdanskoim voiny v Sibiri i na Dal'nem Vostoke, 1917–1922gg.*, p. 159; Guins, Vol. 2, pp. 384–6. On Bermondt-Avalov see: Lenz, W. 'Die Bermondt-Affaire 1919', *Journal of Baltic Studies* Vol. 15 (1984), No. 1, pp. 17–26.

71 *Prizyv* (Berlin), 8.x.1919 (cited in Zimina, p. 160).

72 Ustrialov, N.V. *V bor'be za Rossiiu.* Harbin (1920), p. 42; Ioffe, G.Z. *Velikii Oktiabr' i epilog tsarizma.* Moscow (1987), p. 358.

such a combination should have been Russia's aim at the turn of the century had not the duplicitous Kaiser pushed Nicholas II into the war against Japan).[73]

As hopes for Allied recognition and aid waned during the summer of 1919, therefore, Japan and the 40,000 troops of its Expeditionary Force still stationed in the Russian Far East and in Manchuria exerted a magnetic attraction on the Siberian Whites – and soon an ardent courtship was underway. When a Japanese mission under General Taganaki arrived at Omsk in July, for example, he was approached in private by embarrassing numbers of Russian officers and politicians begging that Japanese forces should be sent to the Urals front.[74] This effort was quickly supplemented through official channels, as Kolchak wired instructions to his embassy in Tokyo that an urgent request was to be made to the Japanese government for two infantry divisions to be moved into Siberia and deployed along the Trans-Siberian Railway from Irkutsk to the Ishim.[75] Much to Kolchak's distress, however, before the end of the month Tokyo notified him that they must turn down his request for troops.[76] According to Sukin, further petitions were made on no less than three occasions over the following months, including one request delivered by a special delegation to Tokyo under General Romanovskii. All met with a polite refusal and the excuse that Japanese public opinion would not accept military involvement west of Baikal.[77] This was despite the fact, according to Sukin, that 'in return' for Japanese military assistance he was offering 'to do everything possible to further the economic expansion of Japan in the Far East'.[78]

Whether Tokyo would ever have agreed, no matter what was on offer, to what amounted to war with Soviet Russia for the sake of Kolchak, is debatable. But there were those at Omsk during the summer and autumn of 1919 who certainly believed that a deal could have been bagged if Sukin had pursued his quarry energetically. Both Guins and General Klerzhe, for example, assert that when in October 1919 a

73 F.B. 'Rossiia, Iaponiia i Kolchak', *Irtysh: golos Sibirskogo Kazach'iago Voiska* (Omsk) No. 29, 30.vii.1919, p. 3.

74 Livshits, *Imperialisticheskaia interventsiia*, p. 75.

75 *ibid.*, p. 76; Piontkovskii, S.A. (ed.) *Grazhdanskaia voina v Rossii (1919–1921gg.): khrestomatiia*. Moscow (1925), pp. 313–4.

76 Livshits (*Imperialisticheskaia interventsiia*, p. 75), has it that the refusal was received on July 30th; American observers cite July 22nd – see *FRUS: 1919 (Russia)*, p. 210.

77 Sukin (*Leeds Russian Archive*), p. 277–85. *FRUS: 1919 (Russia)*, pp. 531–2 mentions a final request being submitted by Kolchak's ambassador at Tokyo on October 1st.

78 WO 33/957/3548 'Britmis (Vladivostok) to WO, 19.ix.1919'.

second Japanese mission under High Commissioner Kato arrived in Omsk, it signalled a change of heart in Tokyo as a result of the realization in Japan that action might have to be taken to reinforce Kolchak in Siberia if the Bolsheviks were not soon to appear on the shores of the Pacific. Both allege, however, that negotiations came to nothing because Sukin did not believe that the Japanese were sincere, while Kato refused to negotiate with the renowned Americanophile Sukin for fear that the 'American Kid' would relate the substance of Japanese demands to Washington. However, even approaches to Kato by other ministers – by the Nipponophile von Goyer, for example – could not persuade Kato to define precisely what rewards Japan would demand for her help. In the light of this possibly sinister prevarication, therefore, Klerzhe's charge that the entire blame for the collapse of the White movement in the East can be laid at Sukin's door seems a little harsh.[79] That is certainly the case if, as one Soviet historian alleged, the desired rewards which Kato would not name included the cession to Japan of both Sakhalin and Kamchatka plus a whole catalogue of railway, fishing, forestry and mining concessions in the Far East on a ninety-nine year lease.[80] Could Sukin or any Russian Foreign Minister have agreed to such terms? And, even if he had, would Britain and the USA have allowed the deal to go ahead?

Panic or reform? The 'ministerial crisis' of August 1919

As the Siberian White movement foundered militarily and diplomatically during the summer of 1919, Kolchak was faced with a choice of potential ways and means to extricate himself from impending catastrophe: either he could carry the principles upon which his régime had been founded to their logical conclusion and court the assistance of the army and the political right, tighten the screws of the military dictatorship, and pour everything into the armed struggle and an attempt to regain the respect of the Allies by stemming the Bolshevik tide; or the harshness of the dictatorship could be tempered, more responsible and representative institutions

79 Klerzhe, G.I. *Revoliutsiia i grazhdanskaia voina: lichnye vospominaniia (Chast' pervaia)*. Mukden (1932), pp. 173–6; Guins, Vol. 2, pp. 383–4.

80 Papin, L.M. *Krakh kolchakovshchiny i obrazovanie Dal'nevostochnoi respubliki*. Moscow (1957), pp. 68–9.

developed and moderate political elements of Siberian society courted and drawn into the government process in an attempt to establish a *union sacrée* of all anti-Bolshevik forces, so as to play upon the Allies' expressed desire to support democratic régimes. In a typically stubborn and obdurately unimaginative manner, however, throughout the summer Kolchak was reluctant to commit himself firmly either one way or the other. Apparently through a fear of appearing weak or inconsistent by bowing to pressure, he informed Ambassador Morris that he 'would not accede, as long as the crisis lasts, to the demands of liberals on the one hand or Cossacks on the other who desire to change the structure of the government'.[81] However, Kolchak was not able to avoid eventually succumbing to powerful elements within Siberia which were hankering for change and, consequently, over the summer of 1919, his increasingly fissiparous régime lurched sometimes to the left and sometimes to the right. Often it seemed to be doing both at once. The quest for an alliance with Japan, for example, connoted that the more militaristic and reactionary option had not been abandoned; as did the Supreme Ruler's graven inclination to rely for political advice on avowed monarchists such as General Dieterichs and General Sakharov. Many other features of Kolchak's rule during the period August–October 1919, however, indicate that – albeit briefly and inconclusively – the advocates of the path of reform and political moderation were gaining the upper hand.

The most palpable indications that moves were afoot to resolve the malaise in political and military affairs surfaced during Kolchak's brief stopover at Omsk in mid-August between lengthy excursions to the front. Although often cited as firm evidence of moderation, however, the significance of this 'ministerial crisis' was not really that clear-cut.

What occurred at this juncture was that, in the light of the Cheliabinsk débâcle, Kolchak was finally prevailed upon to dispense with the services of Lebedev, ending months of the latter's political and military predominance. On August 9th, into Lebedev's place as Chief of Staff and Minister of War was shunted General Dieterichs, who also retained his recent appointment as Main Commander-in-Chief of the Eastern Front. Experienced military observers were heartened to see the demise of the incompetent parvenu Lebedev. At the same time, however, they were

81 *FRUS: 1919 (Russia)*, p. 411.

concerned that one man – even one of Dieterichs's undoubted talents – might be unable to devote sufficient attention to the differing demands of *three* posts.[82] Moreover, apart from being something of a religious fanatic, Dieterichs was of notably reactionary political persuasions and the advice he was to impart to Kolchak as the Supreme Ruler's second-in-command over the coming months was no more welcome to advocates of political moderation than had been Lebedev's. In direct wire conversations with General Riabikov and General Domanovskii during September, for example, Dieterichs would freely opine that 'for Russia there is only one possible form of government – a monarchy'. He also begged to differ from Riabikov's suggestion that it was wrong of the *stavka* to expend so much time and effort in persecuting elements of the army suspected of harbouring leftist sympathies (especially, Riabikov said, citing the example of the Izhevsk-Votkinsk regiments, 'when before us we have a host of examples where it has been precisely the leftist elements who have shown themselves to be our best and staunchest troops'). Moreover, when Riabikov proceeded to assert that 'We must at such a time as this attempt to unite all the political parties and not persecute people because they are our political opponents, for such activity can achieve only our utter downfall', Dieterichs retorted:

> No. That is enough. I don't agree with you. I stick to my opinion and nobody will shake me from it. The stooges of Kerensky and Chernov have had their turn. Such people have no place in our army. In the name of the Russian people, I demand the complete eradication of SR party work.[83]

Hardly more likely than Dieterichs's extremism to boost popular confidence in the régime and to rally disparate opponents of Bolshevism to Kolchak's banner was the outcome of a so-called 'ministerial crisis' played out at Omsk during August. For some time it had been clear that the system of government predicated in the 'Statute on the Provisional Structure of State Power in Russia', Kolchak's November 1918 constitution, had broken down. The admiral took little account of the opinion of his Council of Ministers and, on his increasingly infrequent visits to Omsk, he

82 Budberg, Vol. 15, p. 263; Filat′ev, D.B. *Katastrofa belogo dvizheniia v Sibiri, 1918–1922gg. (vpechatleniia ochevidtsa)*. Paris (1985), p. 80.

83 Mel′gunov, S.P. (ed.) 'Dva generala: k psikhologii grazhdanskoi voiny (razgovor gen. Diderikhsa i Riabikova)', *Golos minuvshago na chuzhoi storone* (Paris), Vol. 14, No. 1 (1926), pp. 195–7.

rarely attended its meetings.[84] Discountenanced by the Supreme Ruler, the cabinet atrophied, allowing itself to become swamped with trivial administrative matters and making little attempt to debate affairs of state or to initiate high policy – on one occasion, recalled a minister, the mandarins of the All-Russian Government at Omsk had spent several days voting on each of the 250 separate articles of a law on the provision of accommodation in the capital.[85]

If the Council as a whole was impotent, however, some individual ministers seemed to be accruing ever more influence – and influence which they would not always utilize for the general good. Particularly damaging to the orderly conduct of government affairs in 1919 had been the empire-building and conspiratorial activities of Omsk's grand vizier, Ivan Mikhailov. Since May (when he had 'winkled out' from their posts Minister of Justice Starynkevich, Minister of Trade and Industry Shchukin and Minister of Education Sapozhnikov), noted Guins, Mikhailov and his henchmen seemed to be running half the government: Mikhailov himself had assumed complete control of the economy by adding the Trade and Industry portfolio to that of Finance, which he already held; while his friend Georgii Tel′berg assumed dominance in legal and administrative affairs by appending to his post of Administrative Secretary to the Council of Ministers both the Ministry of Justice and (during July and August, while the ailing Vologodskii was on leave) the Acting Premiership.[86] And to what effect! These had been the very months which had witnessed Mikhailov's disastrous currency reform and the loss of the Urals. Consequently, by August ministries and public bodies in Omsk were reported to be 'clamouring' alike for the removal of Mikhailov. Sukin too was being singled out for private and public execration, not only for the failure of his foreign policy to secure Allied recognition but as a result of revelations that he had personal financial interests in foreign companies which had been favoured by government contracts.[87]

These charges of incompetence and corruption were put to Mikhailov and Sukin at closed meetings of the Council of Ministers on August 12th (which dragged on into the early hours of the 13th) and 15th. Vologodskii, reclaiming his seat as Premier, also took the opportunity to have Tel′berg accused of using illegal and

84 See above pp. 128–9.

85 Sukin (*Leeds Russian Archive*), pp. 219–20.

86 Guins, Vol. 2, pp. 170–3.

87 Pepeliaev, 'Razval kolchakovshchiny', p. 65.

duplicitous methods during his tenure as Acting Premier by having decided upon important policy questions outwith the Council of Ministers in a so-called 'War Council' together with Mikhailov and Sukin. Meanwhile, Guins lambasted the entire governmental system of the past ten months in which Kolchak and the 'palace camarilla' of the Council of the Supreme Ruler had arbitrarily determined policy in flagrant breach of the November constitution, while Ustrugov and Nekliutin added to the castigation of Sukin by suggesting that he had passed classified information to Allied missions. Numerous resolutions were voted upon in an attempt to resolve this crisis of self-confidence in the government – among them a suggestion that the Council of Ministers should resign en bloc which was rejected for fear that such a move, in conjunction with the reverses at the front, might be interpreted as panic – but all were defeated by a vote of 7:6 or were blocked 6:6 by virtue of the numerical predominance of the Mikhailov group. Eventually, however, on August 15th, the deadlock was broken (precisely how is unclear from the available accounts) and Vologodskii was despatched to the station to meet Kolchak off his train from the front in order to request the Supreme Ruler's assent to the resignation of Mikhailov and Sukin.[88] Faced with such turmoil in the Council of Ministers, Kolchak – albeit with profound reluctance – felt obliged to accept the need for a change of personnel. Having heard Vologodskii's report, on August 16th he signed orders for Guins to replace Tel'berg as Administrative Secretary and, after a few hours' wavering, agreed to accept Mikhailov's resignation. However, he 'resolutely refused' to accept the removal of his confidant Sukin; and this the Council of Ministers accepted, covering its disappointment with the hope that Sazonov might be persuaded to come from Paris to assume full control of his Ministry of Foreign Affairs.[89]

Such was the limited issue of the 'ministerial crisis' of August. Sukin, although disgraced, distrusted and anathematized, retained his post as Head of the Foreign Ministry and Tel'berg retained his major power-base as Minister of Justice. True, Mikhailov's erratic stewardship of economic affairs was now a thing of the past, but the damage had already been done. Moreover, his replacement as Minister of Finance, the former Director of the Shanghai Branch of the Russo-Asiatic Bank, L.V. von Goyer, was hardly a figure to inspire public confidence – his bank having

88 Budberg, Vol. 15, pp. 266, 271; Pepeliaev, pp. 65–6.

89 Budberg, Vol. 15, p. 272; Pepeliaev, pp. 66–7; Guins, Vol. 2, pp. 269–70.

contributed to the collapse of the Omsk Rouble on the Far Eastern markets.[90] But at least the Council of Ministers had flexed its muscles – it had, belatedly, forced upon Kolchak changes in personnel which he certainly would not have made of his own volition and the cabinet would grow in confidence thereafter. Moreover, with its stalwarts Mikhailov and Tel'berg respectively deposed and demoted at a time when Kolchak was more often than not at the front, the chief institutional rival of the Council of Ministers, the Council of the Supreme Ruler, also went into decline and the more important questions of policy came once again to be discussed by the full cabinet. On August 17th, in fact, the Council of Ministers was to rule that the Council of the Supreme Ruler might still convene, but that thenceforth it would have to provide a complete record of its deliberations to the cabinet.[91] On the other hand, as advocates of the pre-August system such as Ivan Sukin noted, this was not necessarily a good thing: the Council of Ministers could deliberate all it wanted, but would it have the ear of Kolchak and would it be party to negotiations with military leaders, as had been, for all its faults, the more informal Council of the Supreme Ruler?[92]

From the point of view of those who wished to see a fundamental change in the way in which anti-Bolshevik Siberia was governed and the development of a central authority more attuned and responsible to Siberian society, the tinkering with personnel in the Council of Ministers meant even less. A regionalist verdict read:

> In our opinion this ministerial crisis is of but little significance. This is a petty domestic squabble... In the place of those who are gone we will find yet more Mikhailovs and Sukins etc. who will not be out of tune with the Omsk ensemble and the ministerial machine will return to its old ways and its old pace until a new internal incident causes a new departure.

Such affairs were meaningful, continued this moderate critic, only when reflecting the clash of large parliamentary blocs or social groups beyond parliament: 'Omsk crises, of course, are nothing of the sort.'[93]

90 Guins, Vol. 2, pp. 170–3.

91 Budberg, Vol. 15, p. 273.

92 Sukin (*Leeds Russian Archive*), p. 221.

93 V.K 'Oblastnoe obozrenie', *Sibirskie zapiski* (Krasnoiarsk), No. 5 (1919), p. 107.

In retrospect, however, this *oblastnik* judgement was a trifle harsh. Despite the ascendency of Lebedev and Mikhailov and the arbitrary nature of the Omsk government in the first half of 1919, voices were being raised within the White establishment calling for a more responsible and systematic form of government. From May onwards, for example, the moderate Kadet editors of the influential Ekaterinburg newspaper *Otechestvennye vedomosti* had been campaigning for the establishment of a new government organ in which senior national statesmen and representatives of Siberian society (to be nominated by the Supreme Ruler) would do preparatory work for government legislation, thereby leaving the Council of Ministers free to devote more time to high policy.[94] Meanwhile the Kadet leader Zhardetskii was working on plans for a more limited and purely advisory body which he called a Technical Services Bureau (sometimes referred to, confusingly, as the Council of the Supreme Ruler), again to consist of prominent public figures nominated by Kolchak.[95] At that time, however, with the Russian Army still clinging to the Urals, Kolchak dismissed all such schemes as 'untimely' or 'inexpedient' and likely to divert attention and resources from the front.[96] Even had he assented though, there would have remained a real problem – where in White Siberia were the statesmanlike figures to be found to fill such an august body? 'One of the calamities of the Omsk government was the insufficiency of men prepared for government work', said Guins; and those who existed were already working at full stretch, filling two or three posts on various ministries and committees – 'I am drowning in a sea of paper and being choked by innumerable meetings and commissions', lamented Budberg.[97]

Of course, had the régime been willing to work with parties or *deiateli* to the left of the Kadets, a larger fund of talent would have been at its disposal. But that is another story. As things were, Zhardetskii rather hoped that senior Russian statesmen could be lured from abroad – he and his party, from the very first days of Kolchak's rule, sent wires to Maklakov in Paris, asking him to recruit 'experienced Russian statesmen' to serve the Supreme Ruler. But who would choose

94 Guins, Vol. 2, pp. 213–4; *Sibirskaia rech'* (Omsk) No. 56, 15.iii.1919 and *Nasha zaria* (Omsk) No. 61, 21.iii.1919.

95 Guins, Vol. 2, pp. 214–5; Arnol'dov, *Zhizn' i revoliutsiia*, pp. 211–12.

96 Rosenberg, W.G. *Liberals in the Russian Revolution: The Constitutional Democratic Party, 1917–1921*. Princeton (1974), pp. 403–4.

97 Guins, Vol. 2, p. 257; Budberg, Vol. 15, p. 288.

to work in Siberia at such a time? Sazonov would persistently find good reasons to remain in Paris rather than decamp to his Ministry of Foreign Affairs at Omsk, while the national Kadet leader, N.I. Astrov, although also importuned by Sukin and others, would repeatedly refuse to come and replace the lame Vologodskii as Premier.[98]

On the other hand, some would-be statesmen did respond. During July and August, for example, there journeyed to Omsk from Paris the former President of the Moscow Stock Exchange, S.N. Tret′iakov. And, concurrently, from South Russia, sailed the quondam Deputy Chairman of the All-Russian Union of Town Councils, Assistant Minister of Trade to the Provisional Government and Deputy Mayor of Moscow, P.A. Buryshkin; the longstanding State Duma representative for Chita, member of the Kadet Central Committee and Assistant Minister of Food to the Provisional Government, N.K. Volkov; and A.A. Cherven-Vodali, a wealthy Bessarabian landowner who had been active in the Union of Town Councils during the war. However, with the possible exception of Tret′iakov, these men were not of the calibre and international reputation which Kolchak needed to improve the backwoods image of his régime. Disappointingly, moreover, after a closer inspection of Omsk, all except Tret′iakov (who was pressed into accepting the post of Minister of Trade in September) refused to associate themselves too closely with the current administration and would not accept ministerial portfolios.[99] It may have been the lamentable working conditions in Kolchak's ministries or the impending defeat (which had not been so clear when they left Europe) which inspired the new arrivals' chariness; it may have been that they valued their reputations and did not relish entanglement in Omsk's scandals and backbiting. Sukin, however, suggests that as all were members of the right-wing, Kadet-dominated underground organization, the National Centre, their reticence had political connotations. The new arrivals were not keen on the idea of a strong executive cabinet, he suggests, for although they supported the development of social organizations to popularize the Kolchak régime, they and their Centre still saw the salvation of the anti-Bolshevik cause in a powerful, charismatic, unipersonal dictatorship, unencumbered by any

98 Sukin (*Leeds Russian Archive*), p. 265; Guins, G.C.[K.] 'Professor and Government Official: Russia, China and California', University of California (Berkeley) Russian Émigré Series (1966), pp. 180–3.

99 Guins, *Sibir′*, Vol. 2, p. 323. Guins later reflected that their arrival was probably too late to make any difference anyway – 'a kind of seasoning offered after the end of the dinner', he mused. See Guins, 'Professor and Government Official', p. 185.

constitutional trappings and enjoying untrammelled executive and legislative authority.[100]

At the opposite extreme of the political spectrum of White Siberia, despite the widespread persecution of socialist organizations perpetrated by the army since November 1918, there remained extant moderate forces of sufficient tenacity and courage to agitate publicly for the summoning of a freely elected and truly democratic assembly with legislative authority and some control over the executive. Zemstvo and co-operative collaborators with the Kolchak government, for example, came increasingly to call for the convening of such a body as it became clear that the dictatorship was failing in the war against Bolshevism. Kolchak himself, however, remained entirely averse to such a move, no matter how ill the fortune of his armed forces: even as the Russian Army was driven from the Urals the Supreme Ruler consistently reiterated his view that constitutional reform could only be considered after military victory was complete.[101]

Moreover, even many of those who might in principle favour the establishment of a representative organ conceded that there were legitimate objections to an attempt to summon one in Siberia in 1919. Guins, for example, posited three obstacles: non-predetermination – Kolchak was only a temporary ruler, with no right to foist law-making bodies upon a future Russia; the fact that the population was weary of elections, raising the possibility that the turnout might be so low as to undermine the legitimacy of any elected assembly; and, finally and most convincingly, the fact that an elected assembly in Siberia could not reasonably legislate on an all-Russian scale on behalf of the All-Russian Government at Omsk (particularly, of course, on such pressing national concerns as the land question, where there existed such peculiar circumstances east of the Urals).[102]

So it came to pass that, as the Russian Army was driven back during the late spring and summer of 1919, prompting calls for changes in the administration, but as were recognized the ideological objections and practical obstacles either to the gathering of a 'star chamber' of the type favoured by Zhardetskii or the summoning of a broader parliamentary organ, reformers within the administration came to invest their hopes in a compromise solution – one associated with an augmentation of the

100 Sukin (*Leeds Russian Archive*), pp. 260–5. On the National Centre and related organizations see above pp. 57ff.

101 *Nadezhda Rossii* (Omsk), 19.viii.1919; *Golos rodiny* (Vladivostok), 7.ix.1919.

102 Guins, *Sibir'*, Vol. 2, pp. 215-6.

powers and a broadening of the membership of one of the most long-standing but, up till then, the most dormant of Omsk's innumerable standing committees.

The State Economic Conference

One of Kolchak's very first acts upon assuming the mantle of dictatorship had been to have his political major-domo, Tel′berg, summon a body of public figures to assist the government in managing the Siberian economy and, specifically, to contribute to the victualling of the army and to the gathering of funds to that end. This was a matter of some urgency in November 1918, for the Czechoslovak supply system, which had served the People's Army and the Siberian Army, was retreating from the front with the Legion, leaving the fledgling Russian Army commissaries in some disarray.[103] A statute drafted by Kolchak's extra-governmental adviser, S.G. Feodos′ev, was hurriedly reviewed by the Council of Ministers – and amended so as to grant greater representation to the co-operatives than Feodos′ev had allowed – before being published on November 22nd. Within days was convened the inaugural meeting of the State Economic Conference (SEC) at Omsk.

Gathered together were heads of the most interested ministries (namely the Ministers of War, Finance, Food, Supply, Trade and Industry, Ways and Communication), the State Comptroller, three representatives of the boards of private and co-operative banks, five representatives of the All-Russian Union of Trade and Industry and three representatives of the Union of Siberian Co-operative Congresses. Taking the chair for the first session, Kolchak informed the SEC that, in addition to feeding the army, it would have access to ministers and might suggest projects for urgently needed financial reforms and measures to increase trade and productivity.[104] With that duty performed, however, Kolchak passed the Chair to Feodos′ev and over the ensuing months, despite its ultra-loyal and closely vetted membership, he allowed the State Economic Conference to languish in relative obscurity, with the broader responsibilities he had promised to confer on it never being legally defined. The conference was never given any useful work to do, was underfunded, and was deplored as a 'talking-shop' by the army (which felt free to

103 Sukin (*Leeds Russian Archive*), pp. 80–1.

104 Guins, *Sibir′*, Vol. 2, pp. 22–3.

ride roughshod over any of its recommendations). Moreover, it was hamstrung in political affairs by a personal vendetta being waged between Feodos′ev and Mikhailov in which the latter, inevitably, came out on top. Subsequent to one particularly nasty public slanging-match during February 1919, the crafty Mikhailov engineered his rival's resignation. The Chairmanship of the SEC was then taken up by George Guins, with whom, despite their differences, Mikhailov was apparently prepared to work. There is no evidence, however, that the SEC influenced, informed or participated in the great debates on economic policy raging in the Kolchak government throughout the spring of 1919; indeed, it is scarcely mentioned in accounts of that period. Its meetings became fewer and attendances dwindled until finally, on May 21st, the atrophied SEC went formally into recess pending a reform of its statute.[105]

Over the following weeks a new statute was drafted by the Council of Ministers. And, as the situation at the front became increasingly alarming at this time and yet Siberian society showed little inclination to help prevent the overthrow of White rule, a new body was summoned with a remit broader than the feeding of the army. The aim now, as one member, Baron Budberg, put it, was that of 'bringing the government closer to the people'. Budberg had perforce to add, however, that 'it is such a pity that all of this was not done four months ago' during the period of military victory and political sanguinity, for then it might have been construed more as a sincere olive branch to Siberian society and less as a panicky last ditch attempt to shore up the crumbling dictatorship with a semblance of popular legitimacy.[106]

Membership of the new SEC was certainly to be much broader, with improved representation for co-operatives (albeit the more conservative of them) and with fewer seats reserved for industrial and banking circles close to the government.[107]

105 *ibid.*, Vol. 2, pp. 120, 150, 218.

106 Budberg, Vol. 14, pp. 294–5.

107 The statute, signed by Kolchak in late May, determined that the new SEC should consist of: i) the Ministers of War, Marine, Trade and Industry, Finance, Food and Supply, Transport, Labour, Agriculture, Internal Affairs and Foreign Affairs and the State Comptroller; ii) the Chief of Staff; iii) 5 representatives to be elected by the All-Russian Union of Trades and Industry; iv) 5 representatives to be elected by the All-Siberian Co-operative Congress (with no less than 3 coming from the relatively conservative Central Co-operative Bureau); v) no more than 20 representatives of zemstvos and municipal dumas (to be selected by the Supreme Ruler from a list of candidates); vi) 2 representatives of the Union of Private Banks; vii) 1 representative of the Moscow Narodnyi Bank;viii) 2 representatives of the Agricultural Society; ix) 2 representatives of the Siberian Engineers' Society; x) 1 representative of the Central Military Industrial Committee; xi) 4 representatives of Cossack Hosts (Siberian, Ural, Orenburg and Transbaikal);

Its powers and responsibilities were also augmented and were more clearly defined: the SEC was now empowered to suggest necessary measures to the government on questions of finance, trade and industry, agriculture, labour, transport and 'all other questions which affect the economic life of the country'; it could discuss the victualling of the army; it could review and express an opinion on the budget; it could summon ministers to appear before it to account for their activities and was promised broad access to government papers and archives; its chairman would have direct access to the Supreme Ruler; finally, and perhaps most significantly of all, under Article 10 of its statute, all government legislation was now to be submitted to the SEC for review (although it had no power of veto and the Council of Ministers could pass laws on to Kolchak for endorsement after a week, whatever the SEC's reservations).[108]

Elements of both left- and right-wing opinion were, however, sceptical that the new State Economic Conference would be any better, or for that matter worse, than the old one. On the one hand the right-wing Kadets of *VOTsK* charged that the whole thing smacked of Kerenskyism, 'pre-parliaments' and the other Socialist Revolutionary baggage of 1917 which would sully the 'purity' (*chistota*) of the dictatorship.[109] On the other hand, for their part, the regionalists, right-SRs and moderate Kadets remaining loyal to Kolchak were generally disappointed that the SEC was not delegated the real legislative authority without which, predicted one critic, 'all its work will consist only of abundant phrasemongering and the wasting of precious paper on endless protocols'.[110]

Procedurally, moreover, moderate socialist elements were particularly incensed that, while organizations such as the Society of Siberian Engineers could nominate their own delegates to the new SEC, Siberian municipalities and zemstvos, for all their purging by the army, were not trusted to do so. Rather, the elected local authorities of Siberia had to present a list of sixty candidates from among whom twenty acceptable to the Supreme Ruler would be admitted to the conference. This was really the ultimate insult so far as many zemstvo men were concerned: a boycott was hurriedly but effectively organized and local government representation

xii) an undetermined number of representatives of the scientific community to be selected by the Supreme Ruler. *Irtysh* (Omsk) No. 20, 1.vi.1919, pp. 3–4.

108 *ibid*, pp. 4–5.

109 Guins, *Sibir'*, Vol. 2, pp. 225–6; *Russkoe delo* (Omsk) No. 3, 8.x.1919.

110 V.K., No. 3, p. 86.

in the SEC was decimated, crippling the organization's legitimacy from the outset, as authorities all across Siberia refused to comply with Kolchak's order of May 4th to nominate candidates.[111] All in all, concluded Guins, who remained Chairman of the SEC, 'the dissatisfied were more numerous than the satisfied...and I knew it would not be easy to safeguard the authority of my establishment'.[112]

That local authorities had so snubbed his new initiative did not deter Kolchak from presenting the official opening of the SEC on June 19th as a grand affair of state and as a symbol of the supposed newfound rapprochement between government and society. The occasion was certainly impressive, as conference delegates and Omsk dignitaries filed into the ceremonial hall of the capital's Judicial Chambers to take their seats (pointedly arrayed in an arc reminiscent of the State Duma at St Petersburg). Before the audience, on a raised dais and flanked by Conference Chairman Guins and Premier Vologodskii, sat the Supreme Ruler; above him hung a huge portrait of the 'Tsar Liberator', Alexander II, whose spirit the diminutive admiral hoped perhaps to silently evoke.[113] In Kolchak's opening remarks, however, a cynical observer might have descried a more basic motive for all this pomp and circumstance. Turning to the area of the hall where the Allied High Commissioners and proconsuls were gathered and acknowledging the debt his régime already owed to the services of Sir Charles Eliot, General Janin, Consul Harris, Bernard Pares and others, he said:

> Our Allies have always been concerned about the policies of the government in relation to the public of the country. Now they witness with their own eyes that as far as the government itself is concerned one of the most pressing problems of the moment is the formation of this conference, where public opinion has the fullest opportunity to voice its criticism and present its own suggestions.[114]

111 *ibid.*, No. 3, p. 88; Mal'tseva, T.V. 'Zemskaia "oppozitsiia" Kolchakovshchinoi', in Korablev and Shishkin, pp. 189–90. Among those authorities supporting the boycott were the zemstvo boards of Primorskii *krai* and Tomsk, Irkutsk, and Enisei *guberniias* and the municipal dumas of Vladivostok and Krasnoiarsk. Other local authorities sent incomplete delegations and only the Altai zemstvo board and the Chita duma supplied a full complement of delegates.

112 Guins, *Sibir'*, Vol. 2, pp. 226, 231.

113 Arnol'dov, pp. 212–5; Budberg, Vol. 15, p. 295.

114 *Nasha zaria* (Omsk) No. 132, 22.vi.1919.

Yet fears that this was to be nothing more than another propaganda exercise to impress western opinion were somewhat allayed by what followed. Although noting the primacy of its role in facilitating the supply of the army at the front, in their addresses to the inaugural meeting of the conference both Kolchak and Guins placed great emphasis on the new and broader powers and responsibilities which the renascent SEC would enjoy. In addition, the Supreme Ruler made an unusual departure from the field of empty generalization in political discourse by specifically requesting that the conference present projects to resolve the questions of wages and industrial relations and the land question. Moreover, although both Guins and Kolchak underlined that in their opinion during times of civil war 'the forms of state structure must be simplified' and averred that 'the calling of a representative assembly with the participation of the entire people is impossible', more than a glimmer of hope for moderate reformers could be detected in passages of the leaders' addresses to the conference by those seeking a commitment of the régime to the path of democratization.

Kolchak, for example, announced that he viewed the State Economic Conference as being a body representative of society, newly endowed with the task of guiding the government in its work. Furthermore, he apologized that 'if hitherto I have allowed myself any delay in this regard, it has not been on principle but from purely practical motives'. And, in his concluding remarks, the admiral seemed to be hinting that in his opinion the SEC was only the first step in broadening the representative nature of his régime: 'ever wider' circles of public figures would be accredited to it, Kolchak pledged, and 'soon the representatives of social organizations will be gathered together for the matters concerning the elections to the National Assembly and autonomous local and regional administrations'.[115] Finally, concluding the ceremony on behalf of the government, Vologodskii then took the stage to assert that 'the government would be far enough removed from practical life if it did not harken to the voice of the people. The government will listen to your voice', the premier promised.[116]

115 *Biulleten'* (Omsk) No. 5, 25.vi.1919; *Priishim'e* (Petropavlovsk) No. 133 (1655), 25.vi.1919; *Nasha zaria* (Omsk) No. 132, 22.vi.1919; Guins, *Sibir'*, Vol. 2, pp. 226–30. Intriguingly, Guins later recalled that the need for a 'substitute representative organ' had been first impressed upon Kolchak by unnamed foreign representatives at Omsk. See Guins, 'Professor and Government Official', p. 195.

116 *The Russian* (London) Vol. 1, No. 41, 24.vii.1919, p. 14.

The response from the floor was muted, but generally respectful. Only a renegade Siberian Cossack delegate struck a sour note by addressing Kolchak as 'Citizen' (*grazhdanin*) Supreme Ruler instead of the customary honorific tribute, 'Your Most High Excellency' (*Vashe Vysokoprevoskhoditel'stvo*).[117] But the implications of Kolchak's words were picked up by some of those present. In a reply from the floor even Anatoli Sazonov, the co-operative leader who had loyally welcomed the coup as doyen of the Omsk Bloc, made it clear that the delegates expected 'the SEC to be only the first stage in the collaboration of the government with society' and expressed the desire that soon 'the conference will be replaced by an organ invested with supreme rights' in order to gain popular approval and legitimacy for the régime.[118]

Taking its cue from the apparent spirit of goodwill pervading its State Opening, over the following weeks the SEC began to extend the scope of its debates into ever wider fields, beyond the question of the economy and supply and into the political arena. Prominent at its meetings – which occasionally even touched upon aspects of military strategy – were a group of delegates attempting to fashion themselves into a 'loyal opposition' to the dictatorship. Led by the right-SRs A.A. Alekseevskii and P.S. Pavbratov, the moderate Kadet delegates from Perm zemstvo, Lev Krol and N.A. Barmuda, and V.A. Vinogradov (a delegate representing the scientific community), according to one of their number 'the opposition were in a majority' within the SEC.[119] Emboldened by Kolchak's apparent willingness to compromise and by widespread concern at the military disasters at Ekaterinburg and Cheliabinsk in July–August, the opposition group went so far as to draw up a quite scathing critique of the White administration which was then signed by nineteen SEC delegates and presented to the Supreme Ruler. In the form of a catalogue of the Omsk misgovernment, their petition read:

> The activity of the central authorities is subordinate to no definite programme. It is haphazard (*sluchaino*) and is frequently subject to hidden, irresponsible influences. In recent times the activities of certain ministries have assumed a character which is

117 Budberg, Vol. 15, p. 295; Arnol'dev, p. 214.

118 *The Russian* (London) Vol. 1, No. 41, 24.vii.1919, p. 14.

119 Krol', L. *Za tri goda*, pp. 179–80.

> contrary to the principles of the strengthening of civil rights and of the law so often advocated by the Supreme Ruler...
>
> The lack of co-ordination between all departments disrupts planned work, while the military authorities interfere in the field of civil administration, breaking the law and infringing upon basic human rights. Corporal punishment is so widespread that the population is beginning to express doubts as to whether the rule of the All-Russian Government is preferable to that of the Bolsheviks.
>
> The army, thanks to the unco-ordinated work of the ministries, remains without clothes and without supplies, while the sick and injured are without assistance. According to the ministries everything is going well, but in reality our armed forces are disintegrating through the inadequacies of supply.

The only certain means of improving the situation, suggested the nineteen oppositionists, was the strict observance of law and order, an end to military control of local government and the rapid summoning of a National Assembly. Until the Assembly could assume sovereign power they demanded the formation of a new Council of Ministers 'on the basis of a democratic programme' and 'the immediate transformation of the SEC into a Council of State – a legal-advisory (*zakonosoveshchatel'nyi*) organ dealing with all questions of legislation and state control, empowered to review all work of the Council of Ministers and to 'exercise control over the activities of the ministries'.[120]

In the weeks following the coup of November 1918 or during the subsequent spring offensive, such a bold indictment of the Omsk régime, no matter how accurate its charges, would certainly have cost its signatories their lives; many, indeed, had been killed for less. By the summer, however, with his army irrefragably 'disintegrating' and with the Allies poised to curtail their support to the Whites, Kolchak knew that he was in no position to scorn any potential source of assistance. His first instinct, upon hearing of the activities of the nineteen, was still to stamp out what he termed the 'encroachment' of the SEC into 'affairs which are not within its domain'; and, choosing his words carefully, he informed Guins that he had decided to 'disperse this Soviet'. His ministers, however, eventually persuaded Kolchak to 'show restraint'.[121] Consequently, when presented with the petition by a delegation of the nineteen oppositionists, Kolchak did not have them imprisoned, as would

120 *ibid.*, p. 182; Guins, *Sibir'*, Vol. 2, pp. 251–3.

121 Pepeliaev, V.N. 'Dnevnik', *Krasnye zori* (1923), No. 5, p. 48; Guins, *Sibir'*, Vol. 2, pp. 250–1. The Russian noun '*sovet*' means only 'council', but even by 1919 had lost the politically neutral connotations of its synonym '*soveshchanie*' (as utilized in '*Gosudarstvennoe ekonomicheskoe soveshchanie*' – the State Economic Conference).

earlier have been the case. Rather, he contented himself with muttering 'My God, so what's new!' Then, with rather uncharacteristic patience, he went on to explain that Belorussov was at that very moment working on a plan for elections to the National Assembly, that he was powerless to end military interference in civilian affairs 'for it is actually impossible to subject these atamans to central control', whilst repeating that 'it is not possible to remove ministers in the absence of suitable replacements – we must make do with what we have'.[122] From a man such as Kolchak this was very humble pie indeed.

On one specific issue, moreover, Kolchak was able to claim that his government was listening to public opinion and was responding to the best of its ability. One of the opposition's concerns was the decline in law and order and the arbitrary nature of military rule in the countryside. In concord with the protests of the SEC delegation, a declaration of the Omsk Bloc's conference of July 15th–17th had charged that 'one of the major factors contributing to the current difficulties at the front is the insufficiently strong and planned introduction of the law and order programme of the Supreme Ruler' – a sentiment reinforced by a Bloc delegation which met Kolchak on July 20th.[123] In response, however, Kolchak could legitimately reply that since May the Minister of Justice had been attempting to rectify matters. Claiming that 'the upholding of the rule of law is now not only a real and vital principle, but the battle order of the day' for the Omsk government, Tel′berg had been encouraging judges to impose their authority, ordering all members of the Public Prosecutor's office to make regular tours not only of *guberniia* centres but also of *uezd* townships and (on July 9th) he had furthermore ordered that they enforce Articles 10 and 11 of the Criminal Code through the visiting of prisons so as to verify the legality of the detention of each and every prisoner and to liberate any interneded without due cause.[124] Meanwhile, Kolchak himself had apparently become aware of the damage that the crimes of the army were doing to the White cause and, in his Order No. 128 of May 10th, had placed the duty of defending peasant property rights squarely upon the army's shoulders, decreeing that:

122 Guins, *Sibir′*, Vol. 2, p. 254.

123 V.K., No. 5, pp. 100–1; Pepeliaev, 'Dnevnik', No. 5, p. 62.

124 *Nasha zaria* (Omsk) No. 104, 17.vi.1919.

> The troops must conduct themselves in such a manner that the people will regard them with esteem and gratitude. It is essential that the troops attend with care to the needs of the peasantry and the whole population and that this attention extends also to their property. There should be no infringement of property rights.[125]

Subsequent events at Ekaterinburg during the retreat from the Urals suggested that this order was being ignored, but Kolchak was clearly concerned and was willing to attempt remedial action. Thus, in direct response to the complaints of the Omsk Bloc and the SEC oppositionists, on July 27th, by Order No. 730 of the Supreme Ruler, there was established a 'Committee for the Defence of Public Order and the Strengthening of Legality in Government', consisting of the Minister of War, the Minister of the Interior and the Minister of Justice.[126] Having recognized that 'the life of the population is regulated in many cases not according to the law but by the innumerable and various binding decrees issued by each local military chief of his own accord and essentially without due consideration' and having confessed that as a result 'the mechanisms to counter illegality do not exist', the government had realized that something had to be done, admitted Tel'berg. The fundamental problem was that under the creeping imposition of military rule across the length and breadth of Siberia, rules laid down in one district were controverted or contradicted in the next, while confusion was compounded by the fact that 'military leaders defending order and civil calm in the districts are not subordinate to the Ministry of Justice'. To remedy this the new Commission on Law and Order would offer 'high-level guidance and supervision over all civil and military leaders operating the emergency measures': it was to be the supreme arbiter of civil *and* military justice.[127] In practice this meant that the Commission could cancel (by telegram) any orders it regarded as illegal which came to the attention of its thrice-weekly meetings – even those promulgated in areas under martial law. Also, any individual citizen could submit a petition to it and was promised a ruling within three days.[128]

125 Guins, *Sibir'*, Vol. 2, p. 191; *Bulletin of the Russian Liberation Committee (Union)* (London) No. 15, 30.v.1919.

126 *Biulleten' otdela informatsii pri vedomstve pressa etat-maiora Glavnokommanduiushchago* (Omsk), 6.viii.1919.

127 Guins, *Sibir'*, Vol. 2, pp. 289–90.

128 Sukin (*Leeds Russian Archive*), p. 183.

That the Committee for the Defence of Public Order, however admirable its motivation, was established too late almost goes without saying. By the summer of 1919 military misrule of the Siberian countryside had long since fanned the embers of peasant economic discontent into open warfare against the White régime, as partisan armies seized control of swathes of territory in northern and southern Siberia before investing the railway zone. Moreover, the panic and desperation engendered in the army by the defeats of the summer and autumn at the front only made matters worse. By October General Dieterichs had to admit that 'instances of illegal and incorrect activity' were still widespread in his army, involving 'violence and cruelty' being inflicted upon entire peasant communities. The general ordered that military leaders punish those involved in such practices and specifically ordered that there should be an end to the burning of villages. But all in all, conceded Sukin, the administration of justice in White Siberia remained 'significantly worse than under the old régime'.[129]

That both reactionaries of Dieterichs's stamp and the moderate socialists of the SEC could agree on the need for the upholding of the law did not, however, mean that the right had accepted the SEC's ambition to be a check upon the dictatorship. In fact, the army, still regarding the SEC as a nest of Kerenskyism, diverted funds intended for the conference into its own coffers and even blocked the attempts of the SEC to involve itself in charity work and the care of refugees. The responsibility for the administration of sanitary units was also deliberately taken out of the SEC's hands by Dieterichs.[130]

Nor did Kolchak's accommodating attitude to the SEC during June and July signify a lasting change of heart. The military disasters of those months seemed to have temporarily subdued his faith in a purely military anti-Bolshevism, but this was a brief interlude. By the end of August Kolchak was again signalling an unwillingness to countenance any institutional check upon his supreme power. This became clear when, under the impression that the admiral's muted receipt of their July petition had been an endorsement of their plans, the SEC opposition proceeded during August to draw up a new Statute for the SEC. Under its provisions, as a Council of State, a transformed SEC would assume all the law-making powers

129 *Biulleten'* (Omsk) No. 107, 19.x.1919; Sukin (*Leeds Russian Archive*), p. 179.

130 Guins, *Sibir'*, Vol. 2, pp. 280–2, 403–4; Budberg, Vol. 15, pp. 292–300, 313–19; Sakharov, *Belaia Sibir'*, pp. 128–9.

previously enjoyed by the Council of Ministers. Moreover, the Supreme Ruler would no longer be able to initiate policy, having the latitude merely to choose between the recommendations of the majority or minority view of the Council of State.[131] Kolchak, however, would not even agree to meet the delegation which came from the SEC bearing these proposals and would not so much as read their project. He had heard of the scheme in advance, and when informed by Guins that an SEC delegation required an audience, he went berserk, 'literally screaming' at the unfortunate Administrative Secretary that 'when our army is being beaten it is interested in fresh underclothes not parliaments!'[132]

This was really the end for the SEC. In protest at what they saw as Kolchak's duplicity, opposition delegates handed in their resignations: several academics returned to Tomsk, V.A. Vinogradov made his way to Vladivostok, while A.N. Alekseevskii and some of his colleagues set off across Siberia on a mission to agitate for a rising of all democratic forces against Kolchak which was to draw them into a network of SR organizations already planning such a move at Irkutsk and in the Far East.[133] With the departure of such figures the SEC became little more than a fiction as a symbol of the unity of government and society. The Omsk Bloc too now fell apart, having of late become critical of the military order. Disillusioned with Kolchak and the White military, Sazonov and others quit the Bloc to join moderate Kadets like Lev Krol in the establishment of an independent political pressure group, the Democratic Union, leaving the Bloc in the hands of a hard core of Kadet National Centre sympathizers who, throughout September and October, were free to renew their campaign for unfettered, pure dictatorship. Now dominant both in the government and in what was left of the government front, rued Guins, 'the Kadets hardened the separation of the government from intelligent and state-minded democratic circles... The government now found itself completely isolated.'[134]

A variety of factors have been or can be suggested as contributing to this new lurch to the right by which Kolchak had alienated both most of the Bloc and his would-be

131 Krol', L., pp. 190–1; Pepeliaev, 'Dnevnik', Vol. 5, pp. 69–70.

132 Guins, *Sibir'*, Vol. 2, p. 292.

133 Krol', L., p. 191; Guins, *Sibir'*, Vol. 2, pp. 332–3.

134 Krol', L., p. 193; Guins, *Sibir'*, Vol. 2, pp. 395–7.

loyal opposition in the SEC. Guins attributed the 'so clear predilection for dictatorship and such intolerance of even moderate socialist parties' which gripped Omsk anew during September and October 1919, to the news then reaching Siberia of Denikin's *éclat* on the Southern Front and Iudenich's success in the North-West which, together, seemed to augur the salvation of the White cause.[135] In the light of these reports Kolchak had less need for an accommodation with socialists or with society for, his representatives in London and Washington informed him, no matter what the standing of his government in Siberia, the Supreme Ruler would be recognized by the powers in advance of a White capture of Moscow or Petrograd to avoid possible embarrassments.[136]

Others, conversely, attributed the renewed rejection of moderation in government policy to internal Siberian factors, noting that the Red Army advance had forced Kolchak to concentrate his attentions on western Siberia and that the dominant political and military force therein was the Siberian Cossack Host. By the autumn local Cossacks were 'the masters of the situation', said Budberg.[137] They were the 'dominant factor in Omsk's political life', confirmed Sukin: as the Siberian Whites sought to galvanize the hitherto rather dormant *voisko* into action, concessions had to be made to the sensibilities of Cossackdom, for 'they were looked upon as our last hope'. Talk in the corridors of power was no longer of progressive land reform or of justice for the Russian peasantry, but of Cossackdom and the prizes the local Host might secure through a redoubled contribution to the White cause. The standing Cossack Conference at Omsk and its Chairman, Colonel Syrobiarskii (said to be an agent of Semenov) 'came to exert an influence on all government and

135 *ibid.*, Vol. 2, p. 395. Since breaking out of the north Caucasus to capture the Don region and Kharkov and then issuing his famous 'Moscow Directive' at the newly captured city of Tsaritsyn on July 3rd 1919, Denikin's AFSR had entered Odessa (August 23rd), Kiev (August 31st) and Voronezh (September 30th) and had also made tenuous contact with the Ural Cossacks at Lake Elton. The AFSR would then proceed to capture Orel (only 340 km south of Moscow) on October 14th before their advance was turned by a Red counter-attack and the disintegration of their rear as a result of the activity of Makhno's anarchist partisans. See Kenez, P. *Civil War in South Russia, 1918–1919: The Defeat of the Whites*. Berkeley (1977), pp. 36–44; Mawdsley, E. *The Russian Civil War*. London (1987), pp. 166–74; Denikin, A.I. *Ocherki russkoi smuty*. Paris–Berlin (1921–1926), Vol. 5, pp. 230–8; Lehovich, D.V. 'Denikin's Offensive', *Russian Review* Vol. 32 (1973), pp. 173–186; Rosenberg, W.G. *A.I. Denikin and the Anti-Bolshevik Movement in South Russia*. Amherst (1961).

136 Kim, p. 95; *FRUS: 1919 (Russia)*, p. 447

137 Budberg, Vol. 15, pp. 295, 307–8.

military affairs', noted Sukin.[138] At one time it requested that Kolchak should disperse the Council of Ministers and form a 'pure' Cossack government; at another it sent a delegation to demand Vologodskii's resignation and the creation of a government 'more resolute and energetic'. All in all, opined Knox, the political activities of the Cossack leadership at this juncture revealed them to be 'the rottenest, most harmful elements in the country'.[139]

Both of these explanations of the swing to the right in Omsk politics have a ring of authenticity to them. We may perhaps speculate in addition, however, that Kolchak's snub to the SEC was yet another instance of the correlation between the Supreme Ruler's willingness to countenance a limited freedom of expression of reformist opinion and the current performance of his army at the front. From June to early August, following the loss of the Urals and the Cheliabinsk fiasco, moderate opinion was tolerated in government forums. It was, however, the briefest *entr'acte*: prior to that, with the Russian Army rampant in Ufa and Perm *guberniias*, there had been little toleration; and subsequent to August, political reform was again discountenanced, as hopes were raised anew for victories at the front when General Dieterichs executed a counter-offensive from the River Ishim. It would be mistaken though to imply that any hard and fast differentiation can be made between moderate and reactionary periods of Kolchak's rule – not least because even as Dieterichs's offensive got under way in September, Kolchak was putting his signature to what elements of the Council of Ministers hoped would be a real step towards a more representative government, a check upon the dictatorship and the crowning glory of Kolchak's governance.

The State Land Assembly

Although he had finally broken with the SEC, Kolchak had not altogether abandoned the notion of summoning a different form of popular assembly to complement and legitimize his rule – one which was not hostage to the party politics of the intelligentsia that was alleged to have befuddled the SEC. In conversation

138 Sukin (*Leeds Russian Archive*), pp. 286–8.

139 Budberg, Vol. 15, p. 292; Dotsenko, *The Struggle for a Democracy*, p. 100; *DBFP*, p. 497.

with Viktor Pepeliaev on August 18th, for example, the admiral had broached the possibility of establishing a peasant conference; then at a Council of Ministers meeting on August 31st, immediately subsequent to his clash with the SEC delegation, he had agreed that at the first sign of success in the offensive planned for September such an assembly would be convened.[140] On September 4th Kolchak departed once more for the front. However, he did return to Omsk on September 14th to take part in the process of framing the statute of a new assembly which one commentator termed 'the last wager of the current government to convince the population of its desire to work for the general good'.[141]

At sessions of the Council of Ministers of September 14th–15th, the constitution and powers of the planned assembly were discussed. It was firmly and unanimously agreed that every effort had to be made to guarantee that the assembly was not hijacked by the intelligentsia and that it did not 'fall foul' of party politics – *partiinost'* was to be 'banished' so as 'to ensure that into the new organ will be drawn true and businesslike representatives of the Siberian populace rather than the upstart (*naezhnyi*) orators who were elected to the *Sibobduma* and the Constituent Assembly'.[142] There had been 'enough pre-parliaments' already, explained the government mouthpiece, *Biulleten'*, again invoking the ghost of the reviled Kerensky; this time it must be guaranteed that the assembly represented the people and did not become 'a mere battlefield for the settling of scores between political parties'.[143]

On September 16th a decree detailing the composition and functions of a new State Land Assembly (*Gosudarstvennoe zemskoe soveshchanie*) was duly signed and published by Kolchak (in the hope of resuscitating the intervention, it was also widely publicized abroad).[144] Recalling his promise at the state opening of the

140 Pepeliaev, 'Razval kolchakovshchiny', p. 68; Guins, *Sibir'*, Vol. 2, pp. 297–9.

141 Budberg, Vol. 15, p. 313.

142 *ibid.*, pp. 312–13; Guins, *Sibir'*, Vol. 2, p. 299. Kolchak might have added 'and the SEC', for he obdurately refused to permit that organ to assume the powers of the new assembly pending its election.

143 *Biulleten'* (Omsk) No. 89, 1.x.1919.

144 Once again the nomenclature was significant – the term '*Gosudarstvennoe zemskoe soveshchanie*' was probably chosen in an attempt to steal the thunder of the SR opposition in the Far East who had just initiated plans for anti-government risings across Siberia in the name of a *Zemskii sobor'* (Congregation of the Lands). See below, pp. 553ff. From Pepeliaev's diary we know that SR strategy had been a subject debated at the Council of Ministers meeting of September 15th. Pepeliaev, 'Razval kolchakovshchiny', p. 71.

SEC to involve broader circles of the population in government affairs when the time was right, the Supreme Ruler announced that that time had now come. Citing early successes in Dieterichs's September offensive and the victories of Denikin in South Russia, Kolchak forecast that 'the joyful moment is approaching when there will be decisive changes in the fortunes of war' and continued:

> Having a firm faith in our final victory in the current struggle, I consider it to be timely to summon the most experienced men of the countryside and to convoke a State Land Assembly for joint activity with my government and with myself and, above all, for assisting in this most difficult time in beginning the fundemental task of the resurrection of Russia.
>
> The State Land Assembly must, moreover, assist the government in effecting the transition from the unavoidably severe military leadership, only natural in a civil war, to a new régime befitting a life of peace and founded upon the vigilant defence of the law, strong guarantees of civil liberty and the safeguarding of person and property.
>
> This ruinous and protracted civil war, which we did not provoke, has consumed all the forces and financial resources of the state. The broad mass of the population, as represented by the peasantry and the Cossacks, has suffered most from the grievous consequences of the war. The legitimate needs of the population remain unavoidably unsatisfied. So the State Land Assembly, consisting of men of the soil, must concern itself with matters affecting the welfare of the population.

In a supplementary instruction to Vologodskii, Kolchak ordered the Premier to furnish him with a statute for the new assembly, defined as 'a consultative organ for the promulgation and elaboration of laws, with the power of questioning ministers and of proffering advice and opinions on the necessity of measures to be adopted pertaining to the administration and legislation of the country'.[145] And, subsequently, a ten-man drafting commission (consisting of five ministers and five loyalist members of the State Economic Conference) was set to work under the chairmanship of Pepeliaev. Acting on the principle that 'universal suffrage atomizes the representatives of separate interests', the commission agreed that alongside elected representatives would have to be admitted representatives of Siberian society and of European Russia nominated by the government.[146]

Some debate then ensued as to whether the State Land Assembly should have direct access to Kolchak or whether it should only operate through the medium of the Council of Ministers (i.e. whether the role of the latter, as defined in the Statute

145 *Biulleten'* (Omsk) No. 76, 18.ix.1919.

146 Guins, *Sibir'*, Vol. 2, p. 329.

of November 18th 1918, should be maintained), but it was eventually accepted that both the Council of Ministers and the Assembly would have to reach consensus before passing draft legislation on to the Supreme Ruler for his approval. Disagreements also arose over the proportion of representatives to be nominated for their seats. Kolchak, for example, pressed for a large, nominated group of churchmen to be co-opted onto the State Land Assembly. And there was some debate on the question of how peasant representatives were to be elected before agreement was reached that 'more authentic peasants' might be found among the *volost'* authorities than in the *uezd* zemstvos, so that elections were to be weighted in favour of the former. No major differences of opinion interrupted the work of Pepeliaev's drafting commission, however, and it has to be said that the projected State Land Assembly would have been a relatively progressive body and a useful one in legitimizing Kolchak's rule, and that – although limited – it was a more realizable plan than any attempt to summon a completely representative assembly in time of war in such a huge region as Siberia. The project also seems to confirm the veracity of Baron Budberg's claim that by September 1919 there were no truly reactionary figures in the Council of Ministers at Omsk – they had either been removed (as was Mikhailov) or they had begun to moderate their opinions (as, it became clear, had Viktor Pepeliaev). What had not changed, however, was the torpid sluggishness and lassitude of Kolchak's ministers and their work. Despite the urgency of the situation, there were only three meetings of Pepeliaev's commission before October 12th and the drafting of the statute was not completed until the end of that month.[147]

And even then it seems that not all questions arising from the matter had been resolved, for although a decree of the Council of Ministers of November 5th laid down that the franchise would be denied to those aged under thirty and to soldiers, and also established the rules of elections at *volost'* and *uezd* levels and in municipalities,[148] it appears that this was not actually published at the time (probably because of the military crisis soon to culminate in the fall of Omsk) but was only made public in the *Pravitel'stvennyi vestnik* of November 16th, after the Council of Ministers had decamped to Irkutsk, at which time it was also finally laid

147 *ibid.*, Vol. 2, pp. 330, 403; Pepeliaev, 'Razval kolchakovshchiny', p. 78.

148 Ioffe, G.Z. *Kolchakovskaia avantiura i ee krakh*. Moscow (1983), p. 231.

down that elections to the assembly were to be completed by January 1st 1920.[149] This schema was later confirmed and elaborated upon when Kolchak's embassy in Washington informed the State Department that the SLA would consist of 50 peasant and Cossack representatives, 23 representatives of the municipalities, 7 representatives of unions and an unspecified number of others representing zemstvos, co-operatives and Orthodox and Old Believer communities.[150] Apparently, however, no decision had as yet been arrived at as to what proportion of the delegates were to be elected and what proportion nominated by the Supreme Ruler (although an earlier report has Kolchak favouring a 2:1 ratio in favour of the former in a conversation with General Knox).[151]

From the sketchy evidence available, therefore, the proposals seem fairly progressive for the time and place of their promulgation. But by November 1919, the question of the fairness of any legislation was really academic. By that time the September counter-offensive had fizzled out and a new retreat, even more panick-stricken than the last, was under way: the Russian Army was on the point of collapse; Omsk was on the point of surrender; peasants were rushing to join anti-government partisans rather than organize elections; and Siberia's zemstvos and co-operatives were not only refusing to co-operate with the envisaged SLA but were actively throwing in their lot with a series of SR-inspired risings all across Siberia. Had the State Land Assembly been tried earlier – even as late as the summer of 1919 – perhaps it would have stood a chance of reconciling Siberia to Kolchak, particularly when account is taken of the glory reflected on him by the achievements of Denikin. But by November, no matter what became of Denikin's advance on Moscow, Kolchak's All-Russian Government had passed the point of no return on a road signposted to oblivion. By November, as one historian has noted, 'even a conference of saints would not have made Kolchak more popular'.[152]

149 *Arkhiv russkoi revoliutsii* (Berlin), Vol. 10, p. 178.

150 *USMI*, Vol. 11, No. 133 (week ending 13.xii.1919), p. 2,444.

151 WO 33/957/3533 'Knox (Omsk) to WO, 18.ix.1919'.

152 Rosenberg, *Liberals*, p. 416.

'The last bet in a losing game': September counter-offensive in the Ishim–Tobol mesopotamia

After their triumph at Cheliabinsk of early August a re-organized Eastern Army Group of Red forces harried Kolchak's battered Russian Army throughout the following month: while the 1st and 4th Red Armies, in a self-contained Turkestan Front under the command of Frunze, turned their attention to pushing the Orenburg and Urals Cossacks back towards the borders of Persia and Chinese Sinkiang, the 3rd and 5th Red Armies drove along the Ekaterinburg–Tiumen–Ishim and Cheliabinsk–Kurgan–Petropavlovsk railways respectively. Tiumen and Kurgan on the River Tobol were abandoned, without resistance, by the fleeing Whites in mid-August and, with Red forces only seventy kilometres from the River Ishim by the end of the month, it appeared that the crossings at Ishim and Petropavlovsk might soon go the same way.[153] If, so the final river barrier before Omsk would be lost and the Red Army would be in command of railheads whence lines converged ominously on Kolchak's capital.

In councils of war at Omsk the question naturally arose, therefore, of whether it was wise for an attempt to be made to turn the Red advance on the Ishim, with the aim of driving the enemy back across the Tobol, in order to secure Omsk; or whether it might be better to evacuate the capital and organize limited holding operations at the front while a strategic defence was prepared further east – on the Ob or even at Baikal. As Director of the Ministry of War, Baron Budberg could countenance only the latter course, arguing to his colleagues that:

> The soldiers do not want to fight on, the majority of officers are incapable of sacrificial deeds, the army is expiring... I fail to understand what sort of offensive there could possibly be with our shattered forces and in the complete absence of technical support. The whole idea is completely stupid, the last bet in a losing game.[154]

Yet, when on August 5th he advised the Council of Ministers that it was imperative that all governmental establishments move east as quickly as possible, the Baron

153 Spirin, *Razgrom armii Kolchaka*, pp. 221–2.

154 Budberg, Vol. 15, pp. 264–5, 275, 280.

found that he was 'stared at as if I had said something improper'.[155] Nor was Kolchak any more receptive to ideas of a tactical withdrawal. In fact, the admiral was now under the sway of Dieterichs, Sakharov and General Andogskii who were all in favour of a counter-offensive. Until this time Andogskii, because of his 'service' with the Bolsheviks, had not been accepted into the Omsk fold. But, having done his penance, he now found his place, drawing the incredibly sanguine conclusion from the Cheliabinsk fiasco that at least the hasty retreat from the Urals demonstrated that the Army could still manoeuvre. Throughout August the former Professor of the Nikolaevskii General Staff Academy spoke repeatedly to the Council of Ministers of the Army's miraculous 'recuperation' (*ozdorovlenie*) and apparently convinced them of it.[156] Meanwhile, on a visit to the front, Kolchak continued to ignore the advice of Budberg and of General Lokhvitskii to the effect that an advance was unthinkable and instead spent hours in meetings to which such pessimists were not even invited. There the admiral was addressed by the young General Sakharov, anxious to assuage the memory of his inglorious contribution to military science at Cheliabinsk with a new adventure. Budberg was exasperated:

> How many times did we see Sakharov's type in the Japanese and German wars. For them such things as the rear, supply, the dependence of the military operations of a massive army on questions of transport and supply do not exist. He has the outlook and horizons of a company commander and for him everything is so simple. He considers it his business only to command and give orders and the rest is for the quartermasters and other riffraff in the rear to worry about.[157]

All things considered, mused Budberg, it would be by far the best thing for the Russian Army if Sakharov was to be captured by the Reds.[158] As a matter of fact he almost was – before Petropavlovsk, on August 23rd – but escaped to persuade Kolchak to ignore the War Ministry's warnings about the state of morale among the troops, about the impossibility of securing food supplies since the loss of the Pri-Ural'sk and Troitsk-Ural'sk Military Districts, and about the deepening fuel shortage since the loss of the Urals. All of these forebodings were soon proven to be accurate. Sakharov, however, dismissed them all as 'highly exaggerated'. The

155 *ibid.*, pp. 258, 261.

156 *ibid.*, pp. 258, 261, 275, 285.

157 *ibid.*, p. 280.

158 *ibid.*, p. 315.

architects of the impending final disaster for the Russian Army derided the prescient Budberg as 'a maniac' or 'a man of the rear, some sort of quartermaster, a grumbler, a critic and a pessimist', and sanguinely continued with their preparations for the counter-attack.[159]

Dieterichs's scheme was for a general push in the centre of the front to be launched around September 1st 1919 from the River Ishim. This was to be co-ordinated with a sudden and decisive blow to the right flank of the oncoming 5th Red Army, which was to be delivered by a large mounted raiding force, thereby cutting off the Reds' retreat to the River Tobol.[160] Given the lack of consideration as to how all of this was actually going to be achieved, however, General Filat′ev was moved to bequeath a new word to the Russian language in an attempt to describe White strategy in this, its final phase: it was, he said, an example of *besplan′e* (unplanning).[161]

The forces at Dieterichs's command with which he hoped to execute the September offensive made not an impressive sight. Visiting the front in mid-August – before it could come to visit him at Omsk – General Knox found that 'the men are slack and listless and there is no sign of the officers taking them in hand... As it retires the Army melts away, men deserting to their villages to convey their families to safety.'[162] On the other hand, the army was at least refashioned during August into a deraignment more befitting the contracting front: in the northern sector

159 *ibid.*, pp. 282, 286.

160 *ibid.*, pp. 131, 265.

161 Filat′ev, *Katastrofa belogo dvizhenie*, p. 93. This strategy was evidently inspired by the spectacular raid behind Red lines on the Southern Front which had been executed during August 1919 by the Don Cossacks of General K.K. Mamontov's 4th Cavalry Corps. But why Dieterichs, who had urged caution in the spring, was now so wrong-headedly optimistic with regard to the chances of a Siberian emulation of Mamontov is a mystery. As an experienced fighting general (distinguishing himself in Macedonia in 1916 to 1917 and in the capture of Vladivostok in the summer of 1918) and a respected administrator (as Chief of Staff to Krýmov and Dukhonin in 1917 and a candidate for the War Ministry itself in September of that year), he should have known better than to underestimate an enemy to such a degree. Perhaps Sukin was right to say that the trauma of war and revolution had 'deeply shaken the balance of his mind'. Sukin (*Leeds Russian Archive*), p. 290. Certainly there was something a little unbalanced in his estimation that the only cause of the Red push on the Eastern Front of May–August 1919 was the desire of Lenin and Trotsky, having 'admitted defeat' in Russia, to flee to India via Turkestan. For examples of this analysis see WO 33/967/2614 'Britmis (Vladivostok) to WO, 13.vii.1919'; WO 33/967/2958 'Knox (Omsk) to WO, 7.viii.1919'.

162 WO 33/967/3007 'Knox (Omsk) to WO, 11.viii.1919'.

the Siberian Army was divided in two to form the 1st Army (under General A.N. Pepeliaev) and, around Ishim, the 2nd Army (under General Lokhvitskii); meanwhile to the south, around Petropavlovsk, the vestiges of the Western Army became the 3rd Army, optimistically dubbed the Moscow Army (under General Sakharov), and an associated Special Steppe Group (which was a sinecure carved out for the disgraced Lebedev).[163]

Reports issued by the *stavka* to Allied missions claimed that the re-organized Russian Army still consisted of some 100,000–130,000 men.[164] However, both the private records of Siberian generals and contemporary Bolshevik estimates place White manpower at a maximum of 50,000–60,000 at the front by August.[165] An additional source of weakness was that the command structure of the army, which had always been very top-heavy, had not been adjusted to accommodate the shrinkage of the Russian Army, while old divisions and regiments had not been disbanded or amalgamated whatever their loss of manpower. Consequently, the former array of staff establishments remained stubbornly *in situ* at army, group, division and brigade level, clogging up the system and ensnaring officers sorely needed at the front. Yet, according to Knox, in terms of the soldiery each 'army' was lucky if it had the numerical strength of a proper division; while, according to Budberg, 'our divisions are, numerically, battalions!' The 3rd Army alone had enough staff officers to service a million men in the opinion of the War Ministry; and on the front as a whole it counted the Staff of the Main Commander-in-Chief, five army staffs (for three armies!), eleven corps staffs and thirty-five divisional and brigade staffs.[166] The division of responsibilities at the commanding heights of the army also remained in disarray, despite the fall of Lebedev. Thus, despite the fact that Budberg was confirmed as Acting Minister of War during August and despite the fact that both Kolchak and Dieterichs expressed their confidence in his ability

163 Sakharov, *Belaia Sibir'*, pp. 127–8; Sukin (*Leeds Russian Archive*), p. 287. Although not completed until August, the reformation of the Russian Army had been ordered by Kolchak on July 14th. See Eikhe, *Oprokinutyi tyl*, p. 310; WO 33/967/2725 'Steveni (Omsk) to WO, 14.vii.1919'.

164 WO 33/957/3487 'Britmis (Vladivostok) to WO, 15.ix.1919'; *FRUS: 1919 (Russia)*, pp. 210, 213.

165 Budberg, Vol. 15, p. 269; Filat'ev, p. 81; Kakurin, N. *Strategicheskii ocherk grazhdanskoi voiny*. Moscow–Leningrad (1926), p. 123; Eikhe, p. 310.

166 WO 33/967/3007 'Knox (Omsk) to WO, 11.viii.1919'; Budberg, Vol. 15, pp. 269–70, 279–80, 291. The 3rd Army alone had sufficient staff to service a million men, according to Budberg (*ibid.*, p. 276).

to administer military affairs, Dieterichs' own Main Staff of the Commander-in-Chief of the Eastern Front usurped more and more of the War Ministry's functions, annexed the control of the Omsk Military District, quite irregularly made appointments which were the prerogative of Budberg when it was known that he would oppose their favoured candidate and, all in all, had very soon established a jealous rivalry between Ministry and *stavka* all too reminiscent of the Stepanov-Lebedev clashes which had bedevilled operations in the spring. When he could stomach no more humiliation Budberg resigned, while General Golovin – who arrived in Omsk on August 26th, supposedly to regularize the administration of the army as a new Chief of Staff – seems to have decided that it was more than his pride or reputation would bear to accept the post and hastily withdrew from Siberia.[167]

Unbridled optimism and a triumphalism which was almost surreal given the circumstances seemed to have gripped Dieterichs and his entourage during the summer just as surely as it had gripped Lebedev and the Staff of the Supreme Commander in the spring. Sakharov was anticipating 'the day when the holy Kremlin will be cleansed of the filthy internationalists' and even years later was certain that, had he been given full support from the rear, by the force of the September offensive, the Red Army 'could have been thrown back across the Urals and then the road to Moscow would have been clear'.[168] Meanwhile Dieterichs, apart from some fanciful ruminations on a return to partisan warfare on the spring 1918 model, did not even pretend to have formulated contingency plans for anything other than the complete triumph of his September offensive.[169]

It was at least recognized, however, while the plans for the offensive were being drawn up in early August, that little could be achieved unless the armies at the front were reinforced and new cohorts of officers deployed. Nor could it be ignored that a Cossack Cavalry Corps, which according to Dieterichs's scheme was to deal the decisive blow to the Red flank, did not as yet exist. Consequently, efforts to meet these requirements occupied military planners throughout August.

167 *ibid.*, Vol. 15, pp. 263–5, 291–2, 300, 313–15, 323–4; Sakharov, pp. 128–9.

168 *ibid.*, pp. 146, 177.

169 Budberg, Vol. 15, pp. 265, 293.

Initially plans were mooted for a general mobilization of the male population (aged between eighteen and forty-three) of Omsk Military District. That idea was set aside, however, when intelligence services voiced fears of an impending anti-government rising in the capital and reported that in adjacent areas peasants were already organizing to make contact with the approaching Red Army.[170] Rather than have weapons fall into the wrong hands, therefore, it was decided to draw exclusively upon bourgeois elements which were likely to be more sympathetic to the régime. This tactic had been assayed before – in a decree of February 3rd 1919, Kolchak had ordered the mobilization of eighteen-to-forty-three-year-olds with education to the fourth grade – but with very disappointing results: despite a poster campaign in the capital and at other centres reminding the intelligentsia that 'when your house is on fire you cannot simply sit in your office and carry on with your work!', by the end of March only 2,300 recruits had come forward from the population of Omsk (by then swollen to a million with the influx of predominantly bourgeois refugees) and only 10,000–12,000 recruits surfaced across all Siberia during the spring instead of the 30,000–40,000 which had been anticipated (despite a renewed plea on April 3rd). The shortfall was generally ascribed to the large proportion of the eligible locals and immigrants who had exempted themselves from military service by securing jobs in government departments at Omsk and elsewhere.[171] But bribery too must have played a part – it was common knowledge, reported a Canadian visitor to Siberia in the spring, that a thousand-rouble gratuity to a recruiting officer was the going rate for an exemption (although it might have to be delivered on more than one occasion to the more 'forgetful' of that breed).[172]

170 FO 538/4 'Memorandum of August 11th 1919 by HM Consul (Ekaterinburg), Mr Preston'; Spirin, *Razgrom armii Kolchaka*, p. 223.

171 Dumova, N.G. *Kadetskaia kontrrevoliutsiia i ee razgrom*. Moscow (1982), p. 223; Eikhe, *Oprokinutyi tyl*, p. 143; WO 32/5707 'Report of the Military Mission..., 15.xii.1919, (App. A, Knox to Kolchak, 29.iii.1919)'. For an example of the recruiting poster see *Pares Papers*, Box 28. Those liable for mobilization might also hide their qualifications: 'It used to be that every local quack and every telegraphist considered himself one of the intelligentsia', noted a White district governor in the Far East. 'But now even the head teacher of a secondary school is inclined to deny his education.' See Andrushkevich, N.A. 'Posledniaia Rossiia', *Beloe delo* No. 4 (1928), p. 136.

172 Rodney, W. 'Siberia in 1919: A Canadian Banker's Impressions', *Queens Quarterly* Vol. 79 (1972), No. 3, p. 333.

Bribery and corruption were endemic in all fields of Siberian life by the summer, but lessons were learned from the earlier levy of the bourgeoisie and when the tactic was again resorted to in August civil servants were no longer exempted – decrees of August 9th and 18th ordered the mobilization of burghers aged eighteen to forty-three with education to secondary level, including employees of government ministries; rural dwellers owning more than fifty desiatins of land or capital in excess of 100,000 roubles were also liable to be called up.[173] But this renewed attempt to stiffen the backbone of the Russian Army by an injection of politically reliable cadres was once again to meet with a weak response from the bourgeoisie. Figures for the August recruitment are hard to come by – perhaps they were never collated in the chaotic conditions of the time – but according to one Soviet account a 25% response was typical for most districts.[174]

With the date set for the counter-offensive fast approaching and with reserves still thin on the ground, panic measures then came to be adopted as, said Guins, shunning the earlier warnings of his intelligence services, 'the Supreme Ruler tried to arm everyone...and mobilized one section of the population after another'. Ultimately, on August 27th, the Council of Ministers decreed that 'every man fit to carry arms must enter the ranks of our glorious army... All those unable to bear arms must enter the ranks of the Red Cross organization or the medical units of the zemstvos.'[175] Once again, no precise figures relating to the result of this new, general mobilization are available. But on September 1st the Ministry of War calculated that the numbers of recruits gathered to date was barely sufficient for one division (although, characteristically, they had already been apportioned among no less than eleven new 'divisions', each with its own staff).[176]

The Russian Army in the field was also still chronically short of officers as it prepared for the counter-offensive. On assuming command in August, Dieterichs had vowed to purge the elephantine *stavka* at Omsk and to send at least 80% of its

173 *Biulleten'* (Omsk) No. 49, 16.viii.1919; *Nadezhda Rossii* (Omsk), 19.viii.1919; *FRUS: 1919 (Russia)*, pp. 410–11; Spirin, *Razgrom armii Kolchaka*, p. 223.

174 *ibid.*, p. 224.

175 Guins, *Sibir'*, Vol. 2, p. 277.

176 Budberg, Vol. 15, pp. 293, 317. By the end of September, according to Knox, 44,000 new recruits had been gathered (WO 32/5707 'Report of the Military Mission in Siberia, 10.xii.1919', p. 15). Few of them, however, could have been trained or deployed before the tide turned for the last time at the front and White resistance came to an end.

complement to the front.[177] Yet little appears to have been done and no sense of urgency was evident, even as the offensive commenced. One witness estimated that there were still some 3,000 staff officers in the capital by September, many of them employed in the most pointless tasks – for example, an artillery battery boasting seventeen officers but not one cannon – as the fate of White Siberia was being decided on the Ishim.[178]

September was also the point at which an earlier scheme to transfer officers from South Russia, where there was a superfluity of their kind, to needy Siberia should have born fruit. General Klerzhe recorded that some senior figures (including Generals D.A. Lebedev, Negaev and Kartsev) did arrive at Omsk. But there is no evidence that they were given work to do. Perhaps, like Klerzhe himself, they were shunned and distrusted by a Siberian military establishment leery of watering down its jealously guarded privileges and hierarchies with a new intake.[179] Or perhaps, like General N. Khrabov, they were shunted into paper-shuffling desk jobs – having arrived at Omsk from the USA on September 16th, Khrabov was made Assistant Head of the Main Artillery Administration, an establishment which as far as the general could tell had the sole function of ensuring that Omsk's image 'conformed to the All-Russian scale' of its pretensions by copying the Petersburg structure to the last jot, for he was never given any useful work to do. In September, keen to see action, Khrabov went on to join an Officers' Regiment then being formed at Omsk, only to discover that, far from being sent to the front, 'the whole thing consisted of a parade of officers in front of the Admiral and the decorating of the author of the idea'.[180] Nor was Khrabov's experience an isolated incident: having journeyed all the way around the world to join a movement which he viewed as 'something akin to a crusade', one young officer was frustrated to find himself delayed for many weeks at Vladivostok during the summer of 1919 without receiving the posting to the front he had requested and eventually joined a Far Eastern unit in despair;[181] another group of officers from South Russia, having narrowly avoided being press-ganged into Semenov's band (and being indicted as 'Bolsheviks' for so doing),

177 FO 538/4 'Memorandum of August 16th 1919 by HM Consul (Ekaterinburg), Mr Preston'.

178 Grondijs, *Le Cas Koltchak*, p. 17.

179 Klerzhe, *Revoliutsiia i grazhdanskaia voina*, pp. 125–45.

180 Khrabov, N. 'Sud'ba i sluchainost'', *Sibirskii arkhiv* (Prague), No. 3 (1930), pp. 126–9.

181 Makovoi, P.P. 'Stanitsy proshlogo', *Russian Émigré Archives* (Fresno, CA), No. 4 (1973), pp. 66–8.

eventually made their own way to Omsk in September only to find that 'for some time we were not attached to any part of the army...and had nothing to do. All day long we walked around town looking in the shop windows.'[182]

The *coup de grâce* of Dieterichs's September offensive, to repeat, was intended to be a raid by a massive Cossack cavalry corps to be launched against the over-extended right flank of the 5th Red Army. As of early August, however, when the 'unplan' was being hatched, the Cossack cavalry simply did not exist. During previous weeks the ataman of the Siberian Cossack *voisko*, Major-General P.P. Ivanov-Rinov (former Commander of the Siberian Army of 1918, but a police officer by training), had been recalled from a posting in the Far East to tour his Cossacks' *stanitsy* (settlements) along the Irtysh valley in order to muster support. On July 28th he had appeared in triumph at Omsk, vowing that his Host would 'rise as a man' to save Siberia and, by express order of Kolchak, was granted priority of access to the capital's dwindling stock of military supplies in order that he might equip his promised divisions.[183] Yet, in spite of the urgency of the situation, it was not until August 5th that the order (No. 494 of the ataman) was given for the mobilization of all Siberian Cossacks aged seventeen to fifty-five years; and it was not until four days later that the call to arms appeared on the front page of the Host's journal.[184]

Much public spectacle surrounded this affair, with a 5th Extraordinary *krug* (council) of the Siberian Cossack Host assembling at Omsk to hail their ataman, to reaffirm his election as their leader and, in the presence of the Supreme Ruler, to swear 'loyalty to our government, our faith, our fathers and our nationality' and to vow to defend Siberia.[185] In return a special mass at Omsk's St Nicholas Cathedral was celebrated on August 10th at which, beneath the standard of Ermak, the Cossacks were blessed by Archbishop Silvester, while Kolchak presented Ivanov-Rinov with a ceremonial sword reputed to have belonged to a saviour of

182 Shebeko, B. 'Russian Civil War (1918–1922) and Emigration', University of California (Berkeley) Russian Émigré Series (1961), pp. 56–8.

183 Guins, *Sibir'*, Vol. 2, p. 258; Budberg, Vol. 15, pp. 333–4; Filat'ev, p. 82.

184 Spirin, *Razgrom armii Kolchaka*, p. 223; *Irtysh: golos Sibirskogo kazach'iago voiska* (Omsk) No. 32, 9.viii.1919.

185 *Nasha gazeta* (Omsk) No. 1, 16.viii.1919; *Rus'* (Omsk) No. 30, 12.viii.1919; *Biulleten' otdela informatsii pri vedomstve pressa etat-maiora Glavnokommanduiushchago* (Omsk), 5.viii.1919.

Christendom from the heathen whom the ataman hoped to emulate – the bane of the Turks at Vienna in 1683, King Jan Sobieski of Poland.[186] Such ceremonials might have been thought a little extravagant had not so much hope and so many resources been invested in Ivanov-Rinov's ability to organize the Cossack Corps and execute the required manoeuvre. Dieterichs himself admitted that 'on the cavalry corps depends the success of the entire operation; on them depends the fate of Russia for many years to come'.[187]

Dismissing the last-minute nature of his commission, Ivanov-Rinov insisted that it could be done. By mid-August he had stockpiled equipment and supplies for a corps of 20,000 men and was promising that that number would be mobilized and ready for action before the planned commencement of the counter-offensive on September 1st.[188] If his promise had been met it would have signified an expansion of the proportion of Cossacks in Kolchak's Russian Army from something well under 5% of the soldiery to over 28% – a ratio which bears comparison with the estimated 32% Cossack-steeled regiments of General Denikin's AFSR.[189]

But given the size of the local host this was a remarkable claim to have made. Of course the Siberian *voisko* was not the only Cossack host in Siberia. However, despite Ivanov-Rinov's boasts to the contrary, there were a number of reasons why a considered review of the situation might have revealed the unlikelihood that the Cossacks of Siberia could make a contribution to the White war effort east of the Urals comparable to their role in South Russia. Imperial Government census figures (see Table 5.1, below) reveal that, compared to South Russia, the Cossack hosts of Siberia were not only much smaller numerically than the pool of fighters upon

186 Graves, W.S. *America's Siberian Adventure*. New York (1931), p. 328; Montandons, G. *Deux ans chez Koltchak et les bolchéviques, 1919–1921*. Paris (1923), pp. 39–40.

187 Budberg, Vol. 15, pp. 293, 309.

188 *ibid.*, Vol. 15, p. 266; Pepeliaev, 'Razval kolchakovshchiny', p. 67; WO 33/967/3120 'Britmis (Vladivostok) to WO, 19.viii.1919'.

189 Ermolin, A.P. *Revoliutsiia i Kazachestvo*. Moscow (1982), p. 157. On the Cossack contribution to the White effort in the south see Karmann, R. *Der Freiheitskampf der Kosaken (Die Weisse Armee in der Russischen Revolution, 1917–1920)*. Puchheim (1985). Also: Kenez, P. 'The Ideology of the Don Cossacks in the Civil War', in Elwood, R.C. (ed.) *Russian and East European History: Selected Papers from the Second World Congress of Soviet and East European Studies*; Efremoff, I.N. *The Cossacks of the Don*. Paris (1919); La Chesnais, P.-G. *The Defence of the Cossacks against Bolshevism*. Paris (1919); Murphy, B. 'The Don Rebellion, March–June 1919', *Revolutionary Russia*, Vol. 6 (1993), No. 2, pp. 315–50; Savchenko, I. *La guerre des Rouges et des Blancs: les insurgés du Kouban*. Paris (1929).

which Denikin was able to draw, but had traditionally been accustomed to sending a far smaller proportion of their menfolk into the army. Moreover, it has also to be taken into account that by August 1919 those elements of the Orenburg and Ural Hosts still loyal to the Whites were completely isolated from Kolchak and were retreating through Turkestan; that the Semirech'e Cossacks (under Ataman Annenkov) were engaged in an independent struggle against Bolshevik and partisan forces around Semipalatinsk and Sergiopol; and that the Zabaikal, Ussuri and Amur Hosts, while nominally subordinate to Omsk, were not only remote from the front but were really the personal janissaries of the renegade atamans Semenov and Kalmykov. Thus, only the Siberian *voisko* remained at Kolchak's disposal. Ivanov-Rinov apparently intended to mobilize more than twice as many men from this small group as had the Tsar at the turn of the century – even though, as the Imperial Government figures reveal, they had little tradition of military organization and, by

Table 5.1: Martial activity of Cossack Hosts in South Russia and Siberia, 1900–1914

Voisko	Mounted Regiments (1914)	Number of Males Under Arms (1900)	% of Cossack Male Population Under Arms (1900)
Denikin's Zone:			
Don	19	70,000	36.0%
Kuban	11	53,100	27.3%
Terek	4	13,000	6.7%
Astrakhan	1	2,300	1.2%
Kolchakia:			
Siberian	3	9,800	5.0%
Zabaikal	4	13,000	6.7%
Amur	1	1,700	0.9%
Ussurii	—	700	0.4%
Semirech'e	1	2,200	1.1%
Orenburg	6	20,000	10.3%
Ural	3	8,800	4.5%

implication, of sacrifice for a cause beyond their local interest, compared to their Don or Kuban counterparts.[190]

In part the contrast between the martial utility of the Siberian Host and that of the Cossacks of the south was a reflection of the physical obstacles to the former's mobilization, which were only to be compounded by the chaos of the civil war. Their settlements did not form a compact unit, but were thinly strung out along a line barely thirty kilometres wide stretching from the marches of Orenburg *guberniia* through Akmolinsk *oblast'* to Omsk and then south for several hundred kilometres up the Irtysh and Bukhtorma Rivers into Semipalatinsk *oblast'*. But there was also an important psychological difference between the Siberian Host and those, for example, of the Don or the Kuban. In fact, Ivanov-Rinov's *voisko* barely qualified as true Cossacks in the accepted sense of the word. They had never been free warriors but consisted, rather, of diverse peasant elements pressed into military service by Alexander II as recently as 1861. They had not the traditions of communal military service of the Don Host and they were, as individuals, up to ten times more likely to be illiterate.

Nor, unlike the Cossacks of south Russia and the north Caucasus, were the Siberian Cossacks particularly wealthy. Average allotments of thirty-five desiatins barely differentiated them from Siberian peasants – but, as their *stanitsy* were on marginal, dry lands ravaged by locusts in summer and swept by freezing winds in winter, they were actually *worse* off than ordinary peasants and had often been quite unable (even in peacetime) to meet the military obligations which their Cossack standing demanded. Their discontent at their service burden was exacerbated by a history of corrupt officials selling off the better of their lands to immigrants, thus breeding a distrust of central authorities.[191] Such a motley host was, therefore, unlikely to have been fearful of the 'unremitting terror' against rich Cossacks promised in Bolshevik orders which the White government had publicized in an attempt to rouse Cossack resistance.[192]

190 Zaitsov, A. *1918 god: ocherki po istorii russkoi grazhdanskoi voiny*. Paris (1934), p. 137. Apart from the Cossack hosts of Siberia listed in Table 5.1, there also existed small *sotni* (squadrons) of Irkutsk and Krasnoiarsk Cossacks, but these groups were numerically and militarily insignificant.

191 Sokol, E.D. 'Siberian Cossacks', *MERSH* Vol. 35, pp. 99–105; Longworth, P. *The Cossacks*. London (1969), pp. 154–5, 258–9, 273. *Grazhdanskaia voina i voennaia interventsiia v SSSR: entsiklopediia*. Moscow (1986), p. 546.

192 Mimeographed copies of this appeal are in *Pares Papers*, Box 47.

Of course there were elements of the Siberian *voisko* who aspired to true Cossackdom. But most of them had long since volunteered for service in the Russian Army. Those who remained in the *stanitsy*, ignoring such incentives as a government promise of July to meet half the cost of every Cossack volunteer's horse, saddle and forage, acted much like Siberian peasants had in the civil war until the recruiting officers or tax collectors of either side arrived, regarding the Red–White struggle as somebody else's business. When Ivanov-Rinov attempted a general levy during August 1919, therefore, he met little positive response. Rather, White intelligence reported, the Cossacks began to organize meetings at which it was said that whether or not troops were sent to the front the Red Army would soon arrive in Western Siberia, so it was far better not to get involved on the White side; while others voiced fears that, in the absence of Cossack menfolk, local Russian peasants would make further incursions into the Host's land and attack their defenceless families.[193]

When the shortfall in Siberian Cossack recruits began to become apparent at Omsk, some additional measures were taken by Kolchak – all members of the Don, Kuban, Terek and Astrakhan Hosts who chanced to reside in Siberia were mobilized, for example.[194] But to no avail. As September 1st, the day of the planned offensive, dawned, Ivanov-Rinov had to admit that only 7,500 Cossacks had been gathered; Bolshevik estimates of the strength of his cavalry corps were even lower, citing figures of 3,000–4,000 men.[195] Nevertheless, despite the Cossacks' unpreparedness, despite the weakness of this keystone of Dieterichs's strategy, the order for the commencement of the counter-offensive was duly issued and, on September 1st, the Volga Corps of the 1st Army went over to the attack. Minister of War Budberg was flabbergasted at the decision to proceed, agonizing to his diary: 'This is so awful that I don't want to believe in the possibility of such monstrous blundering.'[196]

The initial thrust of the counter-attack caught the oncoming Reds by surprise and, as Dieterichs had hoped (and Red commanders later admitted), was able to take

193 *Biulleten'* (Omsk) No. 12, 3.vii.1919; Budberg, Vol. 15, pp. 294, 301.

194 *Union (Agence Télégraphique Russe)* (Paris) No. 163, 10.ix.1919.

195 Filat'ev, p. 82; Budberg, Vol. 15, p. 308; *Grazhdanskaia voina...: entsiklopediia*, p. 547.

196 Budberg, Vol. 15, p. 301.

maximum advantage of the fact that the spearheads of the 5th Red Army had by now steamrollered to a point more than 500 kilometres distant from their Army headquarters at Cheliabinsk.[197] As of September 1st the Russian Army also held a slight but significant numerical superiority – said to be in the order of 3:2 in the central sector where the 1st Army faced the 5th Red Army – due to the withdrawal of Red units in recent weeks as forces were transferred to the Denikin front.[198] Initial developments were less auspicious in the northern sector, where Lokhvitskii's 2nd Army was unable to turn the flank of the 3rd Red Army; Knox reported the White performance here as 'disappointing' against inferior numbers of Reds.[199] Spirits were mightily raised, however, when despite the relative failure of the Cossack mobilization, Ivanov-Rinov emerged victorious from early skirmishes: having by September 7th finished concentrating the men available to him alongside the 7th and 12th Rifle Divisions and the Domazhirov Cavalry Corps around the villages of Iavlennoe, Zverinogolovsk and Nikolaevskoe (all situated south-west of Petropavlovsk), the ataman had led mounted units into the rear of four regiments of the 5th and 35th Divisions of the 5th Red Army near Presnovskaia Station, completely destroying that sector of the Red front by September 9th.[200] The Omsk press was ecstatic at the news of the first Russian Army victories in so many months, trumpeting that 'the hour of our victory draws near... We already live in the glorious days of Russia's renaissance... Bolshevism is dead in Russia. It is already a corpse and is now beginning to decompose.'[201] Meanwhile messages were flashed abroad by the *stavka* claiming 'success on all fronts'.[202] In the excitement of the moment Kolchak even awarded both Ivanov-Rinov and Sakharov

197 Spirin, *Razgrom armii Kolchaka*, p. 228–9; Tukhachevskii, M.N. 'Kurgan–Omsk', in Smirnov, I.N. et al. (eds.) *Bor'ba za Ural i Sibir': vospominaniia i statei uchastnikov bor'by s uchredilovskoi i kolchakovskoi kontrrevoliutsei*. Moscow–Leningrad (1926), pp. 75–8.

198 WO 33/957/3767 'Britmis (Vladivostok) to WO, 7.x.1919'.

199 WO 33/957/3327 'Knox (Omsk) to WO, 2.ix.1919'; WO 33/957/3360 'Knox (Omsk) to WO, 4.ix.1919'.

200 Sakharov, *Belaia Sibir'*, p. 135; Spirin, *Razgrom armii Kolchaka*, pp. 232–4; Eikhe, *Oprokinutyi tyl*, p. 317; WO 33/957/3411 'Knox (Omsk) to WO, 7.ix.1919'.

201 *Biulleten'* (Omsk) No. 67, 9.ix.1919; *Biulleten'* (Omsk) No. 68, 10.ix.1919.

202 *Union (Agence Télégraphique Russe)* (Paris) No. 171, 22.ix.1919.

the Cross of St George, in breach of the established protocol that only the college of Knights of St George itself could confer such honours.[203]

During the following fortnight the 1st, 2nd and 3rd Armies continued to push westwards. But although the press and the public continued to rejoice, informed observers of the operation recognized that tactical victories would signify little in the long run unless Ivanov-Rinov could successfully execute the planned raid on Kurgan in rear of the Reds, so as to cut the railways and bridges and prevent the enemy's orderly retreat across the Tobol.[204] Sukin recalled of mid-September: 'I remember the alarm in Omsk, where we waited from minute to minute for news that the Cossacks had gone onto the attack and were pursuing the enemy.' But... 'We waited a week without hearing anything: the Cossacks stayed put.'[205] Despite being opposed by only one full regiment of the 35th Division of the 5th Red Army and 'battered remnants' of regiments of its 5th Division, Ivanov-Rinov did not attack, reported Knox in horror.[206] Rather, ignoring no less than six direct orders from Dieterichs to commence the Kurgan Raid, Ivanov-Rinov 'rested on his laurels', noted an appalled Budberg:

> Just as I feared – our last trump card, having fallen into the hands of this police sergeant-nonentity and blatant coward, has been lost. After this there is no escape for us.[207]

Dieterichs recalled the miscreant ataman to Omsk, dismissed him on September 19th for dereliction of duty and promoted General Belov to the command of the Cossack Corps.[208] But, as General Filat′ev recalled, the fault was really Dieterichs's own for having entrusted such a vital task to the inexperienced and talentless Ivanov-

203 Budberg, Vol. 15, p. 314; Sukin (*Leeds Russian Archive*), p. 291. In contrast to Denikin and other White leaders, who founded their own decorations and medals, Kolchak (with one or two exceptions) awarded only the established imperial orders. See Kuznetsov, A. *O Beloi armii i ee nagradakh.* Moscow (1991), p. 41.

204 WO 33/957/3513 'Knox (Omsk) to WO, 17.ix.1919'; Sakharov, p. 140.

205 Sukin (*Leeds Russian Archive*), pp. 291–2.

206 WO 33/957/3574 'Knox (Omsk) to WO, 21.ix.1919'. In fact some Cossack units were actually retreating, deserting the front. See Spirin, *Razgrom armii Kolchaka*, p. 234; WO 33/957/3619 'Knox (Omsk) to WO, 25.ix.1919'.

207 Budberg, Vol. 15, p. 314.

208 Pepeliaev, 'Razval kolchakovshchiny', pp. 73–4; Sukin (*Leeds Russian Archive*), p. 292.

Rinov in the first place.[209] It was a promotion made in the face of advice from Minister of War Budberg who, upon hearing of Commander-in-Chief's intention, had gasped:

> What sort of cavalry leader can be made out of this policeman, very competent I'm sure at cutting off ears and administering whippings, but a complete nonentity with regard to military leadership in general and cavalry in particular?[210]

Kolchak agreed that an 'indifferent commander' like Ivanov-Rinov should not have been entrusted with such a task. However, bowing to pressure from the Cossack Conference at Omsk, he was nevertheless obliged to have the ataman reinstated as Commander of the Cossack Corps on September 24th and sent him back to the front to participate in what was left of the offensive.[211]

Reports from the front at this time actually continued to reflect the Whites' temporary success. Along a 300-kilometre front the Russian Army was pushing the Red Army back towards the Tobol at a rate of 40 kilometres a day in some sectors: by September 30th Red units had retired across the river, having surrendered Tobol′sk itself to Pepeliaev's 1st Army.[212] In the process considerable trophies had been captured from the Reds – including 15,000 prisoners, 21 heavy guns and 100 machine guns.[213] Again news of 'success on all fronts' was broadcast to the world by the *stavka*'s press agency,[214] while at Omsk the official press had allowed their joy to transport them into the realms of fantasy: Denikin 'at the gates of Moscow' and the 'fall of Petrograd' to Iudenich, as reported by the government-run *Biulleten′*, strayed only partially from the facts and might be defended as justifiable morale-boosting disinformation; but the same organ's claim of October 5th that the Bolsheviks were suing for peace (on condition that Lenin and others were granted

209 Filat′ev, p. 83.

210 Budberg, Vol. 15, p. 270.

211 *ibid.*, Vol. 15, p. 323; Pepeliaev, 'Razval kolchakovshchiny', p. 76; WO 33/957/3669 'Britmis (Vladivostok) to WO, 30.ix.1919'.

212 Spirin, *Razgrom armii Kolchaka*, pp. 235–6; Guins, *Sibir′*, Vol. 2, pp. 361–3; Sakharov, p. 143; WO 33/977A 'Narrative of Events in Siberia, 1918–1922', pp. 21–2.

213 *FRUS: 1919 (Russia)*, p. 219.

214 *Union (Agence Télégraphique Russe)* (Paris) No. 181, 7.x.1919; No. 183, 9.x.1919; No. 189, 17.x.1919.

safe passage to Argentina) was quite irresponsible.[215] Lulled into a false sense of security by such tales, many families which had been evacuated from Omsk during August began at this time to return to the capital to participate in the promised celebrations of White victory.[216]

Kolchak too was swept along by the renewed wave of optimism, apparently giving credence, in a letter to his wife of this time, to rumours that Iudenich really had captured Petrograd and even confiding to Guins his satisfaction, in retrospect, that the Allies had not recognized the Omsk government in the spring, thereby freeing him from commitments 'offensive to the unity of Russia and injurious to her vital interests' which he might otherwise have been forced to accept.[217] In a secret report to the Council of Ministers, Dieterichs, to his credit, warned against reading too much into the September victories, but he was ignored: 'Optimism ruled', recalled Guins. 'There were few people in Omsk who understood that the end was near.'[218]

What exercised Dieterichs was that his forces' September victories were transparently Pyrrhic. Ivanov-Rinov's fumbling of the Kurgan Raid had scuppered the Commander-in-Chief's strategic plans and any advances made thereafter had consisted of little more than the Russian Army ushering intact Red units back behind the defensive line of the Tobol where they could regroup and summon reinforcements. Moreover, rearguard actions by the retreating Bolshevik forces had meant that the Russian Army had paid a heavy price for their temporary tenancy of the Ishim–Tobol mesopotamia: White infantry units had been depleted by up to half their strength and thousands of officers had been killed or captured.[219] Sakharov, whose 3rd Army had lost 20% of its manpower in the first week of the September offensive and 1,000 officers by the end of the month, had sent increasingly desperate appeals for reinforcements to Dieterichs on September 9th, 15th and 19th. He was promised 30,000 men by the beginning of October but, complained Sakharov bitterly, 'not one promise of the Main Commander-in-Chief of the Eastern Front was

215 *Biulleten'* (Omsk) No. 92, 4.x.1919; No. 93, 5.x.1919; No. 111, 23.x.1919.

216 Guins, *Sibir'*, Vol. 2, p. 378.

217 Kolchak, R.A. 'Admiral Kolchak: ego rod i sem'ia', *Voenno-istoricheskii vestnik* (Paris), No. 16, p. 19; Guins, *Sibir'*, Vol. 2, p. 389.

218 *ibid.*, pp. 304–5.

219 Spirin, *Razgrom armii Kolchaka*, p. 239; Tukhachevskii, 'Kurgan–Omsk', pp. 75–8; WO 33/957/3584 'Knox (Omsk) to WO, 22.ix.1919'.

ever met', no reinforcements arrived and in the meantime he had even to throw his own personal bodyguard into the front line to help Kappel reach the Tobol and had resorted perforce to the mobilization of Red prisoners captured days earlier to fill gaps in the line. However, although he was to blame Dieterichs for failing to provide the men he needed, Sakharov must surely have realized that by insisting throughout August on the feasibility of the September offensive on the basis of a prospective levy of recruits which the War Ministry had insisted could not be found or equipped, he himself would have to accept a share of the blame for its outcome.

And the outcome was clear enough – as the Reds retired towards and across the Tobol, Sakharov noted, 'our ranks were becoming thinner and thinner, whereas theirs with each day were becoming stronger'.[220] Having finally reached the Tobol, Sakharov nevertheless was reported to be conferring with Kolchak on the chances of digging in on the river over winter before launching yet another offensive in the spring. General Filat′ev, however, derided this as 'complete and utter fantasy', pointing out that barely 20,000 reliable men now remained at the Russian Army's disposal and that they would certainly be smashed by any new Red offensive.[221] In the drive to the Tobol the Russian Army had run itself into the ground. As Sukin put it: 'We had no more powder in our powder-flask.'[222]

In the lull before the Red Army's final storming of Kolchak's capital a peculiar, almost comic, episode was played out at Omsk, typifying the desperation and degeneration of the White movement in Siberia by the end of 1919. General Dieterichs, who had been marked out even as a young officer at the General Staff Academy as being prone to bouts of religiosity and mysticism, together with the like-minded General Golytsin, let it be known that both the general and Cossack mobilizations having been such a disappointment, the gaps in the White lines would be filled by the summoning of waves of volunteers committed to 'a holy war'

220 Spirin, *Razgrom armii Kolchaka*, p. 229; Sakharov, p. 136–45. Although they are useful, forthright and entertainingly combative, it would be as well to point out here that General Sakharov's memoirs are highly tendentious and self-exculpatorily selective in their recording of events. For informed critiques see Inostrantsev, M.A. 'General Sacharov als Historiker', *Präger Rundschau* (Prague) Vol. 3 (1933), pp. 191–204; Inostrantsev, M.A. *Istoriia, istina i tendentsiia – po povodu kniga gen.-leit. K.V. Sakharova, 'Belaia Sibir′'*. Prague (1933); and McCullagh, F. '*Belaya Sibir′* by K.V. Sakharov', *Slavonic Review* (London), Vol. 3, No. 9 (March 1925), pp. 720–4.

221 Filat′ev, *Katastrofa belogo dvizheniia*, p. 98.

222 Sukin (*Leeds Russian Archive*), p. 296.

against the Bolshevik antichrist. Thirty thousand of these 'volunteer-crusaders' would be at the front within days, Golytsin promised on September 9th; 'You would have to be either a blind optimist or a cretin to believe that', pronounced Budberg.[223]

The Omsk régime had *ab initio* enjoyed close relations with the Orthodox Church, which abominated Bolshevik materialism and atheism (as well, of course, as objecting to the confiscation of three million hectares of Church lands by the Soviet régime in 1918). As early as 20th November 1918, the Siberian Church Council (of indigenous and refugee clerics) at Tomsk had decreed it to be the duty of all believers to support Kolchak and had then established a new Church Administration for Siberia at Omsk under Archbishop Silvester to liaise with the government. Subsequently no less than five more Archbishops found their way to Omsk; and Silvester's organization was recognized by Kolchak as the All-Russian Provisional High Administration of the Orthodox Church and was granted government subsidies of 32,350 roubles per month. In return Silvester organized parades and services blessing Kolchak's efforts, published tracts on White godliness and Bolshevik apostasy and sent missions abroad to spread the word that Kolchak was fighting the good fight and should be supported (Metropolitan Platon was personally received by President Wilson).[224] All in all, opined *Russkaia armiia*, the Orthodox Church did 'colossal work' for the government.[225] The army was the main beneficiary of the church's efforts. Silvester channelled donations from the eleven Siberian eparchies to the White forces and instructed them to impress upon sceptical Siberian peasants that their divine salvation would be secured by fighting Bolshevism and to sermonize, as a counter to Communist teachings, on the theme

223 Budberg, Vol. 15, p. 305. George Guins for one could see little utility in attempting 'to inspire the population and the troops with the beliefs and institutions of seventeenth-century Muscovy'. See Guins, G. '*The Siberian Intervention*' by J.A. White [Review]', *Russian Review* Vol. 10, No. 2 (April 1951), p. 162. On Dieterichs's predisposition to mysticism see also Mayzel, M. *Generals and Revolutionaries (The Russian General Staff during the Revolution: A Study in the Transformation of a Military Élite)*. Osnabruck (1979), p. 80 n. 1.

224 On the development of the relationship between the Omsk régime and the Church see: Plaksin, R. Ia. *Krakh tserkovnoi kontrrevoliutsii, 1917–1925gg.* Moscow (1968), pp. 96–117; Abrosenko, K.P. *Religiia na sluzhbe kontrrevoliutsii v Sibiri*. Irkutsk (1938), pp. 1–40; Eingorn, I.D. 'Kolchakovshchina i tserkov', in Razgon, I.M. (ed.) *K 50-letiiu osvobozhdeniia Sibiri ot kolchakovshchiny*. Tomsk (1970), pp. 46–50; Flerov, V.S. 'Kontrrevoliutsionnaia rol′ tserkovnikov i sektantov na Dal′nem Vostoke v 1918–1922gg.', *Uchennye zapiski TGU* (Tomsk), No. 37 (1959), pp. 71–133.

225 *Russkaia armiia* (Omsk), 2.v.1919.

that personal wealth did not equate with evil. More practically, no less than 2,000 servants of the Orthodox Church worked in branches of the Special Church Eparchate which Archbishop Ruzetskii ran from offices at the Omsk *stavka*, endeavouring to instil a hatred of Bolshevism into the White soldiery through propaganda work typified by the newspaper *Za Rus' Sviatnuiu* which was distributed from railway wagons near the front.[226] More generally the Church was used as a network for the dissemination of government information and ideas – during the summer of 1919, for example, Silvester ordered all priests to 'do your duty' and 'with a cross at your breast and a rifle in your hand' to lead their parishes against the Bolsheviks.[227]

Once Dieterichs was installed as Main Commander-in-Chief, the line between religious and military duty was increasingly blurred. However, with Dieterichs preoccupied at the front, any further developments had to await the arrival at Omsk of General Golytsin and a Professor V.V. Boldyrev, founder of a shadowy, evangelistical brotherhood of priests, academics and public figures, the Order of Saint Hermogenes (named after the venerable Patriarch who had called upon the Orthodox to rise against the Polish seizure of Moscow in 1611). As early as August 10th 1919 the Order sponsored a 'Holy Cross Day' featuring exhibitions, sermons and speeches aimed at persuading the faithful to enlist in the army.[228] Only when it became clear that the government's own mobilization plans were going awry, however, was Dieterichs allowed to play the religious card to full effect. September 3rd was officially designated a day of prayer at Omsk and Archbishop Silvester addressed a 6,000-strong congregation outside his Cathedral, urging them to found Holy Cross Detachments for which Boldyrev proposed 'the aim of mounting a crusade against Bolshevism' under the rousing slogan of 'Forward for Faith and

226 Abrosenko, p. 40; Eingorn, p. 47; Plaksin, pp. 116–17.

227 *Russkaia armiia* (Omsk), 17.vii.1919.

228 *Russian Outlook* (London) Vol. 1, No. 17, 30.viii.1919. An appeal was made to sympathizers in Britain at this time for as many bibles and religious pictures as possible to be sent to Siberia: 'We gave them material arms to fight for their freedom; why not help them with the spiritual arms to fight for their faith', wrote a member of Britmis. Later he reported that 17,000 copies of the holy book had arrived, courtesy of the Bible Society, but that Russian suspicion of British motives was delaying their distribution. 'McCullagh to Pares, 18.viii.1919', 'McCullagh to Lloyd George, 20.x.1919', 'McCullagh to Pares, 1.xi.1919' (*Pares Papers*, Boxes 28 and 43). McCullagh, a devout Roman Catholic, later anathematized the Soviet régime in *The Bolshevik Persecution of Christanity*. London (1924).

Fatherland.'[229] These were to be armed forces of a new type, with their own special code of honour 'renouncing all acts of callousness, dishonesty, rascality and theft from the population', promised Professor Boldyrev.[230] Not that the worldly needs of the crusaders were to be altogether ignored – the Ministry of War agreed that volunteers to the Holy Cross movement would receive 1,000 roubles upon entering the army and a further 800 roubles after six months' service as well as welfare payments and educational grants to their families, while Kolchak later pledged generous land grants for those who came forward.[231] Meanwhile, in recognition that it might be problematic to organize a holy war from a region which was home to so many non-Christian elements, alongside the Holy Cross detachments Kolchak had the mullahs of a Muslim Conference at Omsk on August 31st declare a *jehad* against Bolshevism and cojointly organize their own believers into Green Banner units.[232]

By September 9th over 5,000 Omsk citizens had enlisted for 'what is sure to be the best part of our army', announced the *stavka*. By the end of the month 20,000 recruits were being claimed.[233] That, however, was certainly a gross exaggeration. According to Budberg, the attendances at Boldyrev's meetings dwindled quickly to nothing and only 200 'crusaders' were forthcoming in the capital. Moreover, far from being saintly heroes and bearers of the volunteer spirit which was to revitalize the Russian Army, they were a motley crew of 'involuntary volunteers', said Budberg, consisting of the hungry and the homeless – desperate refugees who were anticipating regular pay and rations with more relish than noble sacrifices at the front.[234] Both Colonel I.S. Il'in, who led the Holy Cross recruitment in Irkutsk

229 *Report of the Russian Telegraph Agency* (Omsk), 4.xi.1919; *Union (Bureau de Presse Russe)* (Paris) No. 14, 4.x.1919. *Russian Outlook* (London) No. 20, 20.ix.1919, p. 462.

230 *Report of the Russian Telegraph Agency* (Omsk), 1.ix.1919.

231 *Biulleten' otdela informatsii pri vedomstve pressa etat-maiora Glavnokommanduiushchago* (Omsk), 3.ix.1919; Krushanov, A.I. *Grazhdanskaia voina v Sibiri i na Dal'nem Vostoke (1918–1920gg.)*. Vladivostok (1972–1984), Vol. 2, p. 47.

232 *Biulleten'* (Omsk) No. 68, 10.ix.1919; *Biulleten' otdela informatsii pri vedomstve pressa etat-maiora Glavnokommanduiushchago* (Omsk), 4.x.1919; Demidov, V.A. *Oktiabr' i natsional'nyi vopros v Sibiri, 1917–1923gg.* Novosibirsk (1983), p. 176. A small unit of Old Believers was also formed at Omsk – see Eikhe, *Oprokinutyi tyl*, p. 314.

233 *Biulleten'* (Omsk) No. 67, 9.ix.1919; *Biulleten' otdela informatsii pri vedomstve pressa etat-maiora Glavnokommanduiushchago* (Omsk), 4.x.1919; WO 33/957/3616 'Britmis (Vladivostok) to WO, 25.ix.1919'.

234 Budberg, Vol. 15, pp. 290–1, 305, 320.

guberniia, and G.V. Enborisov, who performed that role in the Altai, recalled that the concerts and meetings they held were well enough attended, but that few of the faithful returned the next day to enlist – only 300 souls at Irkutsk and 150 in Semipalatinsk. Still, according to Enborisov some 6,000 volunteers had been enlisted across all Siberia by the end of October.[235] When marshalled into sacerdotal detachments with such names as the 'Jesus Regiment', the 'Regiment of Our Lady' and the 'Regiment of the Banner' they would have made a remarkable impression as they strode out to meet the Red Army beneath ikons and church banners, noted Bernard Pares.[236] These holy hosts were not sufficient to fill the gaping holes in the White front, however. And Il'in had to report that his own volunteers threw down their arms and 'melted away' on their very first engagement with the enemy. Later even Kolchak was to admit that the results of the Holy Cross volunteer movement had been, at best, 'insignificant'.[237]

In contrast to the recruiting difficulties of Kolchak, during a pause in military operations from October 1st to 13th, as the lines faced each other across the Tobol, the Red's Eastern Army Group was reinforced by no fewer than 24,000 new recruits from Cheliabinsk *guberniia*, by units (such as the 35th Rifle Division) which had earlier been withdrawn for despatch to South Russia but which were now returned to the east, and by the deployment of units new to the Eastern Front (such as the 54th Rifle Division, from North Russia). By mid-October the Group was composed of some 65,000 rifles and 9,000 sabres, giving it a 3:1 numerical advantage over the White units waiting across the river. On October 14th orders were given for the Red Army to break out. By the 18th secure Red bridgeheads had been established on the right bank of the Tobol and the Russian Army had begun a retreat which, for those who survived, would only end on the shores of the Pacific Ocean. Tobol'sk was abandoned by the 1st Army on October 22nd, while the 2nd and 3rd Armies fell back on Ishim and Petropavlovsk. Kolchak himself had prophesied that 'at

235 Il'in, I.S. 'Omsk, Direktoriia i Kolchak', *Novyi zhurnal*, Vol. 73 (1963), pp. 224–8; Enborisov, *Ot Urala do Kharbina*, pp. 69–75, 78.

236 Pares, B. *My Russian Memoirs*. London (1931), p. 541.

237 Il'in, Vol. 73, pp. 234; Konstantinov, M.M. (ed.) *Poslednie dni kolchakovshchiny*. Moscow (1926), p. 86. Even after the fall of Omsk, in contrast, Dieterichs was prophesying that 'With cross in hand the Grand Duke Mikhail will stand at the head of the army as it enters the Kremlin.' See Il'in, Vol. 73, p. 233.

Petropavlovsk my fate will be decided'[238]: that crucial town was abandoned without a fight on October 31st; Ishim followed suit, all its bridges intact, on November 4th. Now only 200 km of the West Siberian Plain and the River Irtysh lay between the Red Army and Kolchak's capital.[239]

The fall of Omsk

When, back in August, Kolchak had refused to consider Budberg's advice to evacuate all government establishments from Omsk to Irkutsk on the grounds that such a venture would cause panic in Siberia and a loss of confidence abroad, his decision had been supported by a majority of the Council of Ministers and by General Dieterichs.[240] By early October, however, knowing too well that the gains of September could not be held for long, Dieterichs had changed his mind. Rather than risk the loss of precious time, men and resources in what he forecast would be a futile attempt to defend Kolchak's capital, from the first week of October the Commander-in-Chief began laying plans for the withdrawal of as many men as possible from the front line to be concentrated around Tomsk for rest and rehabilitation; meanwhile nothing more than rearguard actions would be attempted at the front, which would be allowed to creep eastwards through an evacuated Omsk to Novonikolaevsk and the defensive line of the Ob before the onset of winter would put an end to military operations until 1920. Before the spring Dieterichs hoped that a new 'Strategic Reserve' could be built up in the Far East.[241] Later in October

238 Spirin, *Razgrom armii Kolchaka*, p. 227.

239 *ibid.*, pp. 240–51; Tukhachevskii, pp. 78–88; Bol'tin et al. *Tobol'sko–Petropavlovskaia operatsiia (1919g.)*. Moscow (1939); Kakurin, N. *Vosstanie chekhoslovakov i bor'be s Kolchakom*. Moscow–Leningrad (1928), p. 72; Sakharov, pp. 151–2. The commander of the 30th Rifle Division of the 3rd Red Army, S.N. Bogomiagkov, could not recall participating in any serious engagements at all as his unit marched from Tobol'sk to the very outskirts of Omsk. See *V boiakh i pokhodakh*. Sverdlovsk (1959), p. 580.

240 Budberg, Vol. 15, pp. 258, 261; Filat'ev, pp. 79–80. According to American sources an 'Evacuation Committee' had actually been established at Omsk as early as July 11th 1919 – see *FRUS: 1919 (Russia)*, p. 209. If so, very little had been achieved by it before the crisis came in October–November.

241 WO33/957/3779 'Knox (Omsk) to WO, 2.x.1919'; WO 33/957/3780 'Knox (Omsk) to WO, 2.x.1919'; WO 33/957/3855 'Knox (Omsk) to WO, 10.x.1919'; Filat'ev, p. 85.

Dieterichs came to the capital to impress upon Kolchak that, just as Alexander I's abandonment of Moscow to Napoleon in 1812 had proved wise, so too the prestige and continued existence of the White movement in the east depended not upon the symbolic value of Omsk but upon the salvation of a battleworthy army, which only the evacuation of Omsk could secure. His point made, on October 26th Dieterichs returned to the front and began to put his plans into operation: over the following week units of Pepeliaev's 1st Army retired eastwards through Omsk, en route to Tomsk; and on October 29th the order for the evacuation of the capital was issued by the Main Commander of the Eastern Front.[242] But, to Dieterichs's amazement, Kolchak protested against such a move. Perhaps, as Sukin believed, Dieterichs's orders were the result of a misunderstanding of Kolchak's intentions; perhaps, as S.P. Mel′gunov suggested, it signified the preparation of some sort of coup against Kolchak by Dieterichs.[243] Alternatively, it might be conjectured that, as so often in the past, Kolchak had agreed with one policy only to succumb to the blandishments of its opponents and to change his mind over the following days. Certainly some powerful elements in Omsk were averse to implementing Dieterichs's scheme: the leaders of the Siberian Cossacks, for example, charged that the abandonment of the capital, their *voisko*'s own administrative centre, would be 'more than treachery – it would be stupidity'.[244]

Whatever the origin of his decision, on October 30th Kolchak telegraphed Dieterichs to the effect that he was convinced that if Omsk was surrendered it would mean the 'obliteration (*unichtozhenie*) of the White movement in Russia and abroad'. Therefore, said the admiral, he was now taking steps to gather a new force to defend the capital.[245] Over the following days the call to arms went out, yet again, at Omsk: 'The young, the healthy, the strong – to the front!' read one proclamation; 'the surrender of Omsk is impermissible', another. Meanwhile Vologodskii informed the press that the Council of Ministers would remain at Omsk

242 *ibid.*, pp. 91–2; Sukin (*Leeds Russian Archive*), p. 297; WO 33/957/4030 'Knox (Omsk) to WO, 26.x.1919'; WO 33/957/4068 'Knox (Omsk) to WO, 29.x.1919'.

243 Mel′gunov, *Tragediia*, Pt.3, Vol. 2, pp. 38–9; Sukin (*Leeds Russian Archive*), p. 298.

244 El′tsin, V. 'Piataia armiia i sibirskie partizany', in Smirnov et al. *Bor′ba za Ural i Sibir′*, pp. 261–2.

245 Filat′ev, p. 90.

with all essential civil servants and would 'continue to exercise its governmental functions'. According to Sukin, most of the ministers supported this plan.[246]

Kolchak's decision was not an altogether unreasonable one. There was much to be said for the contention, echoed by S.P. Mel′gunov, that the fate of the Russian Army as was had already been decided on the Tobol, that there was no point in Dieterichs attempting to rebuild it on former lines and that Kolchak's only hope of salvation lay in the rallying of social forces around the potent symbol of the defence of the White capital and not in the swapping of capitals.[247] Also, it was at this point far from being certain that Iudenich and Denikin would be unable to capture the European Russian capitals to salvage the White movement. It has to be said however, in the light of what was to transpire in the fortnight thereafter, that had Omsk been evacuated in an orderly manner in late October, many, many lives – if not the Russian Army – would have been saved.

The decision to defend the capital having been taken against the advice of the Main Commander, it came as no surprise when, having been summoned to confer with Kolchak on November 4th, Dieterichs resigned from his post and was pronounced to be at liberty to select his own future occupation and place of residence. (In fact he immediately departed for the Far East.) The following day Kolchak issued orders detailing yet another reshuffling of the army command: into Dieterichs's place as Main Commander-in-Chief of the Eastern Front stepped General Sakharov, former Commander of the 3rd Army; the brave General Kappel, former Commander of the Volga Corps, was made Commander of the 3rd Army; General Voitsekhovskii, an outstanding field commander and one of the heroes of the Czechoslovak Legion's conquest of western Siberia in 1918, now assumed command of the 2nd Army; and Ivanov-Rinov, his sins of September apparently forgiven by Kolchak, was made Deputy to the Main Commander-in-Chief on the recommendation of Sakharov (who had always blamed Dieterichs rather than the ataman for the failure of the Kurgan Raid).[248]

According to Sakharov's memoirs, he was himself of the opinion that Omsk was 'doomed' after the loss of Petropavlovsk and when summoned by Kolchak during

246 *Biulleten′ otdela informatsii pri vedomstve pressa etat-maiora Glavnokommanduiushchago* (Omsk) No. 119, 31.x.1919; Sukin (*Leeds Russian Archive*), p. 299; *Rus′* (Omsk) No. 96, 2.xi.1919; *Union (Agence Télégraphique Russe)* (Paris), 15.xi.1919.

247 Mel′gunov, *Tragediia*, Pt.3, Vol. 2, pp. 38–9.

248 *The Times* (London) 14.xi.1919; *Russkaia zhizn′* (Helsingfors) No. 216, 18.xi.1919.

the night of November 4th–5th to be informed that, as Commander-in-Chief, he must prepare the defence of the capital, he had initially declined to accept the post, only doing so when 'the Admiral insisted'.[249] A variety of other sources, however, have it that the ambitious and reckless Sakharov had actually requested permission to return to Omsk in the first days of November in order to plead with Kolchak that the White capital could *not* be allowed to fall into Red hands. These sources add that Sakharov was present, alongside Ivanov-Rinov, at Kolchak's interview with Dieterichs of November 4th, had willingly pledged to defend the capital and had testified as to the feasibility of mounting a defensive operation on the Irtysh; some also insinuate that Dieterichs's fall was, in fact, the result of a long-standing conspiracy against him mounted by Sakharov and Ivanov-Rinov.[250] Either way, flouting the wisdom common to all armies that 'order plus counter-order equals disorder', under Sakharov's tutelage Dieterichs's plans for an evacuation were thrown hurriedly into reverse, the 1st Army was ordered to return to the front, trains leaving Omsk for the east were halted and the personnel of ministries already evacuated to Novonikolaevsk were instructed to return forthwith to the capital.[251]

Although this sudden reversal of policy gave rise to no little confusion, on November 6th, the day after Sakharov's appointment, General Knox found Kolchak and his new Commander-in-Chief to be 'calm' and confidently predicting that rearguard actions would delay any Red assault on Omsk for 'at least three weeks'. Kolchak was even at this decisive hour to opine that there was little to fear because the Reds' eastward progress signified not a real advance but the flight of Bolshevism from European Russia where Lenin had had to accept that the game was up.[252]

Preparations for the defence of the capital got underway as Sakharov placed General Voitsekhovskii in charge of military operations in the city and Ivanov-Rinov in charge of civilian affairs, ordered (another) general mobilization of adult males in Omsk, pronounced all employees of the Ministry of Ways and Communications and all railway workers to be at the disposal of the Commander-in-Chief and put the

249 Sakharov, pp. 175–81.

250 Guins, *Sibir'*, Vol. 2, pp. 409–10; Filat'ev, pp. 91–2; Sukin (*Leeds Russian Archive*), pp. 300–1; FO 371/4097/151375 'Knox (Omsk) to Britmis (Vladivostok), 4.xi.1919'.

251 Guins, *Sibir'*, Vol. 2, pp. 409–10; Sakharov, pp. 180–1.

252 WO 33/957/4197 'Knox (Omsk) to WO, 6.xi.1919'; *Russkaia zhizn'* (Helsingfors) No. 216, 18.xi.1919.

Ministry of Supply under his own jurisdiction in preparation for the expected siege.[253] Within a few days, however, it became clear that Sakharov's confidence had been misguided. News arrived from the front that entire units were surrendering to the Reds without a fight – among them the 4th and 15th Siberian Divisions.[254] Meanwhile General Pepeliaev informed Sakharov that if he ordered the 1st Army to return to the front it would certainly mutiny; and clear signs of discontent were detected among the 30,000-strong garrison of the capital.[255] Even more worrying was that the River Irtysh, having begun to freeze over as winter set in, suddenly thawed in a warm spell during early November. It was unthinkable to attempt to organize a defensive line along a river across which there was only one bridge and where drift ice now made the laying of a pontoon impractical: such an act, Sakharov knew, would risk the loss of the entire army should the Reds force the Russian Army back to the river within the next few days, as seemed ever more likely. When, unlike the previous year, the Irtysh had not frozen solid by the night of November 10th–11th, Sakharov concluded that all hope was lost and ordered the very evacuation of Omsk he had derided a week earlier, the destruction of military stores and the retreat of all forces to the Tomsk–Taiga railway where, he hoped, another stand could be taken.[256]

Up until this point, according to one of the refugees cowering at Omsk, a sense of disbelief had pervaded the capital, with nobody quite able to bring themselves to accept that the army was beaten and that the Reds were so close.[257] Suddenly, however, a British officer, who was himself to be overtaken by the Red advance, found Omsk transformed into 'a seething mass of terrified people all mad to get

253 Guins, *Sibir'*, Vol. 2, p. 212; Sukin (*Leeds Russian Archive*), p. 301; *Union (Agence Télégraphique Russe)* (Paris) No. 204, 17.xi.1919; WO 33/957/4197 'Knox (Omsk) to WO, 6.xi.1919'.

254 Papin, *Krakh kolchakovshchiny*, p. 61; El'tsin, V. 'Piataia armiia i sibirskie partizany', in Smirnov et al., p. 262. Even Sakharov's own Chief of Staff, General Oberiukhtin, went over to the Reds at this time. See Klerzhe, *Revoliutsiia i grazhdanskaia voina*, p. 146.

255 Sakharov, p. 181; Spirin, *Razgrom armii Kolchaka*, p. 253.

256 *FRUS: 1919 (Russia)*, p. 224; Spirin, p. 253; Sukin (*Leeds Russian Archive*), p. 301; WO 33/957/4224 'Knox (Bolotnaia) to WO, 13.xi.1919'; Sakharov, p. 182.

257 Vitol'dova-Liutik, S. *Na vostok: vospominaniia vremen kolchakovskoi epopei v Sibiri, 1919–1920gg.* Riga (1930), p. 10; *FRUS: 1919 (Russia)*, p. 224. Campaigns for election to the city duma to be held on November 16th were going ahead as normal, according to Ioffe, *Kolchakovskaia avantiura*, p. 232.

away'.[258] Blind panic gripped the city temporarily on November 12th, when rumours started to circulate that Bolshevik forces driving south from Tara were about to cut the railway to the east of the city, and the situation at the railway station became pitiful to behold as thousands of families begged for a space, no matter how small, on any train going east. But by then even those who had secured a berth might find that their trains would not move for days because of the congestion; or, having set off from Omsk, would grind to a halt in the middle of nowhere for lack of fuel, leaving them the choice of staying put and awaiting capture or fleeing on foot or by sledge into the tenebrous Siberian winter.[259]

At least the Allied missions, giving no credence to Sakharov's initial optimism, had escaped on November 7th. So too, on November 10th, had the Council of Ministers – albeit not without some difficulty. Guins suspected that a series of delays to the cabinet's train (involving faulty or misplaced wagons and accidents) were 'not accidental' but the work of military elements antipathetic to the government; he was perhaps too proud to admit that, according to an Omsk journalist, departure was finally secured by the ministers' judicious bribing of a railway official.[260] Certainly in the last days at Omsk there seems to have been a return to the sort of anarchistic military behaviour and the flouting of political authority which had characterized the early weeks of Kolchak's rule. Omsk became 'an army camp', said Guins. Several opposition figures were arrested by the military police at this time and rumours circulated that Mikhailov, Guins and Sukin were all on a death-squad hit list.[261] A general was reported to have shot dead a colleague

258 Horrocks, B.H. *A Full Life*. London (1960), p. 51. An American Red Cross worker noted that among a certain class of the ladies of Omsk and other towns a sudden interest developed at this time in the learning of a few words of English: namely, 'I love you. Kiss me quick. Take me to America.' See Gidney, J.B. (ed.) *Witness to a Revolution: Letters from Russia (1916–1919) by Edward T. Heald*. Kent State University (1972) pp. 347–8. They evidently enjoyed some success, for another source has it that 500 members of the American Expeditionary Force (some 10% of its complement) married Russian women in 1919 – see Marsh, C. 'Glimpses of Siberia, the Russian "Wild East"', *National Geographic*, Vol. 138, No. 6 (1920), pp. 513–36.

259 *The Times* (London) 3.xii.1919. On aspects of the civilian evacuation from Omsk see Vitol'dova-Liutik (1930) and the semi-fictionalized Ilyin, O. *White Road*. New York (1984), *passim*. On the evacuation of Minusinsk and Krasnoiarsk see Stanford, D. *Sun and Snow: a Siberian Adventure*. London (1963).

260 Guins, *Sibir'*, Vol. 2, pp. 408, 413; Ivanov, Vs.N. *V grazhdanskom voine. Iz zapisok omskago zhurnalista*. Harbin (1921), p. 35.

261 Guins, *Sibir'*, Vol. 2, p. 411.

who had refused to accept unreasonable orders.[262] Most disturbingly of all, some 400 political prisoners were massacred at Omsk prison in an orgy of vengeful bloodletting on November 12th, while countless others, many already half dead with typhus, were executed or left to freeze as the trains in which they had been interned were commandeered by the fleeing army.[263]

Like a captain on the bridge of a sinking ship, Kolchak refused to abandon his doomed capital until the last possible moment. Finally, however, during the night of November 13th–14th, the admiral and his entourage slipped out of Omsk station towards the east; attached to the lengthy and imposing five-train convoy of the Supreme Ruler (echelon No. 58) was a train (train 'D') containing what remained of the imperial gold reserve – some 414,254,000 gold roubles' worth of bullion and coinage. Also among the very last to leave were the staffs of General Kappel and General Voitsekhovskii.[264] They were very fortunate indeed to escape capture, for, unbeknownst to them, units of Tukhachevskii's 5th Red Army had undertaken a forced march on Omsk. Covering the 200 km from Petropavlovsk to the Irtysh in just two days, men of the 27th Rifle Division entered Kolchak's capital early on the morning of November 14th to the surprise of those still unable to secure a passage east: at least one senior general, having slept clean through the arrival of the Reds, was later encountered, briefcase in hand, en route to his office at the customary hour of 11.00 a.m., recalled Rifleman N.B. Krasnopuskii.[265] Little more than token resistance was encountered from elements of the White garrison, and by the evening of November 14th all Omsk was in Red hands. Triumphant claims broadcast over the radio by the Red victors to have captured 40,000 prisoners, 1,000 officers, 3

262 Ilyin, p. 71.

263 Naumov, M.B. *Omskie Bol'sheviki v avangarde bor'by protiv belogvardeitsev i interventov*. Omsk (1960), p. 87; Krusser, G.V. *Kolchakovshchina*. Novosibirsk (1927), p. 31; Gromov, I.V. et al. (eds.) *Partizanskoe dvizhenie v Zapadnoi Sibiri (1918–1920gg.): dokumenty i materialy*. Novosibirsk (1959), p. 722. Colonel McCullagh of Britmis, who was trapped at Omsk, verified the massacre. See McCullagh, F. *A Prisoner of the Reds: The Story of a British Officer Captured in Siberia*. London (1921), p. 24. The pattern of killings had already been established by the earlier slaughter of the inhabitants of, for example, Petropavlovsk prison. See Ashkinadze, A.I. *Zheleznodorozhniki Ishima v bor'be za vlast' sovetov (1917–1919gg.)*. Tiumen' (1961), p. 74.

264 Sakharov, p. 182.

265 Andreev, L. (ed.) 'K istorii razgroma vooruzhennykh sil Kolchaka', *Krasnyi arkhiv* (Moscow), No. 6 (1931), pp. 65–80; *Istoricheskii ocherk 27-Omskoi strel'kovoi divizie*. Moscow (1925), pp. 81–4; Berezovskii, N.Iu. and Tarkhanova, N.S. *Omskaia nastupatel'naia operatsiia Krasnoi Armii v 1919g*. Omsk (1989); *V ogne revoliutsii i grazhdanskoi voiny: memuary*. Omsk (1959), p. 193; Spirin, *Razgrom armii Kolchaka*, p. 254.

armoured trains, 3,000 wagons of military supplies and hardware, 40 artillery pieces, 900 machine guns and 5,000,000 rounds of ammunition were sheepishly confirmed to Britmis by Sakharov's staff.[266]

Years later I.I. Serebrennikov asked another former member of the Council of Ministers how it could have been that Omsk was abandoned in such confusion and why such trophies were left for the Reds. The anonymous minister replied:

> We too much believed in our military specialists as a whole. They always assured us that Omsk was in no danger and continued to insist upon this while the Reds advanced to the very gates of the city. We civilians could not disbelieve our military experts.

This was, to say the very least, rather disingenuous – since the summer's débâcle at Cheliabinsk there had been every reason for White 'civilians' to disbelieve their 'military experts'. But it was a fitting epitaph for the anti-Bolshevik government at Omsk, as Serebrennikov recognized, reflecting: 'To what bitterness and disaster was White Russia brought by this military optimism.'[267]

266 *ibid.*, pp. 254-5; Eikhe, *Oprokinutyi tyl*, p. 336; WO 33/957/4360 'Britmis (Vladivostok) to WO, 28.xi.1919'.

267 Serebrennikov, I.I. *Moi vospominaniia*. Tientsin (1937), pp. 262–3.

Chapter 6

White agony

One of the many tens of thousands of refugees fleeing eastwards from Omsk on November 14th 1919 was moved by 'the terrible and at the same time beautiful sight' of fires blazing above parts of the capital to attempt an analogy with the 1812 conflagration of Moscow witnessed by Tolstoy's Natasha in *War and Peace*.[1] And, although actually citing the precedent of the French Government's removal from Paris in 1914, Kolchak too seemed to be evoking the ghosts of Alexander I and Kutuzov when he informed the Allies on November 11th of his decision to evacuate Omsk: predicting the imminent 'awakening of the national spirit in the Russian people', he claimed to 'regard the future with confidence and with complete faith in the ultimate triumph'.[2] Omsk, however, unlike the Moscow of 1812 or the Paris of 1914, had not been reluctantly evacuated according to a plan, but abandoned by an utterly defeated and demoralised army. True, the Supreme Ruler had been saved and was now en route to rejoin his ministers at Irkutsk. But, as the flight began, General Janin was more than entitled to pose the question: 'Will he arrive there as the head of a government?'[3]

If Kolchak really did still believe that the evacuation of Omsk would be temporary, that the White movement in the east was on the eve of a revival and that Russia would yet rally to his flag, then news which was to reach his train over the following days concerning events in the Siberian rear must have finally divested him of such illusions: at Irkutsk on November 13th the leadership of the Czechoslovak Legion announced their decision finally to abandon the White cause; meanwhile, at Vladivostok on November 18th (the anniversary of the Kolchak coup), a rising organized by SRs with the assistance of the envenomed Gajda (and not without some encouragement from Allied representatives in the port) shook Kolchak's hold

1 Vitol'dova-Liutik, S. *Na vostok: vospominaniia vremen kolchakovskoi epopei v Sibiri, 1919–1920gg.* Riga (1930), p. 13.

2 See Smirnov, I.N. et al. (eds.) *Bor'ba za Ural i Sibir': vospominaniia i statei uchastnikov bor'by s uchredilovskoi i kolchakovskoi kontrrevoliutsii.* Moscow–Leningrad (1926), pp. 347–8.

3 Grondijs, L.H. (ed.) *Le Cas Koltchak: contribution à l'histoire de la révolution russe.* Leiden (1939), p. 73.

on the Far East and threatened to sever the White escape route to the Pacific. Together these two heavy blows and their repercussions would ensure that Janin's question was to be answered in the negative.

Renascent SR opposition and the Gajda putsch

Those Siberian Socialists-Revolutionaries who had not entered into some degree of collaboration with the Omsk Government but, rather, had remained hostile to Kolchak, were instructed by their national leadership in May 1919 that, 'independently and not in solidarity with the Bolsheviks', their task was to work diligently for the overthrow of the White dictator. Kolchak's fall, this directive emphasized – evincing the tenacity of the SRs hopes of taking a 'Third Path', neither Red nor White, in the civil war – 'is important for democracy above all because it holds out the possibility for the formation of a front for the Constituent Assembly against the Red Army'.[4] However, so complete was the Siberian SRs' moral and organizational disarray in the aftermath of their disappointments of late 1918, and so extreme was White persecution of their party in the east, that activity was very limited during the first half of 1919. Although to do so is tempting, therefore, one need not necessarily impute entirely sinister motivation to the fact that, as Soviet historians never tired of remarking, the SR opposition remained 'strangely quiet' for as long as Kolchak was victorious and only 'came to life' during the summer of 1919, after the Red Army had decisively smashed the Russian Army and crossed the Urals.[5] Perhaps the Siberian SRs were simply in no state to do anything else.

By the time that the Siberian SRs were ready once again to raise their heads above the parapet of the civil war, however, 1919's demonstration of the durability and dynamism of Soviet power in central Russia had forced them to moderate their programme, at least in the short term. Thus, during the summer of 1919, thoughts

4 Gusev, K.V and Eritsian, Kh.A. *Ot soglashatel'stva k kontrrevoliutsii: ocherki istorii politicheskogo bankrotstva i gibeli partii sotsialistov-revoliutsionerov*. Moscow (1968), p. 43.

5 See, for example, Plotnikova, M.E. 'Kolchak i eserovskaia oppozitsiia', *Voprosy istorii Sibiri* (Tomsk), Vyp. 3, 1967, pp. 178–9; Ioffe, G.Z. *Kolchakovskaia avantiura i ee krakh*. Moscow (1983), p. 235; Spirin, L.M. *Klassy i partii v grazhdanskom voine v Rossii, 1917–1920gg*. Moscow (1968), pp. 365–6.

among the newly reconstituted Siberian Union of SRs and among their sympathizers in White garrisons then being cultivated by a secret Central Bureau of Military Organizations (CBMO), acquired a regionalist hue. Attentions turned to means of removing Kolchak, by force or by persuasion, and of the calling of a Siberian *Zemskii sobor'* ('Congregation of the Lands') in order that, rather than wage war on the Bolsheviks, as the SR Central Committee had prescribed, the region's popular representatives might negotiate a truce with the advancing Red Army prior to the establishment of a separate state authority for Eastern Siberia and the Far East through the election of a Siberian Constituent Assembly. The latter, it was hoped, might form a democratic buffer between the capitalist world and Bolshevism in the east and might facilitate the end of intervention (now regarded with distaste by many SRs since the powers' sponsorship of their party's would-be Nemesis, Kolchak). Eventually, it was calculated, such an entity might develop into the first building-block of a democratic, federal Russia; but, in the short term, continuation of the war against Soviet Russia was ruled out.[6]

Although this brand of non-Bolshevik opposition to Kolchak was to reach maturity with risings in the Far East and at Irkutsk during the autumn and winter of 1919, it had its origin in developments much closer to the centre of White power during the spring and summer of that year. The clash between Gajda and the Omsk authorities during May–June, although rooted in the young Czech's personal ambitions, was symptomatic of discontent among certain strata of the officers of his Siberian Army, particularly NCOs. Imbrued not only with a sense of self-esteem, as a result of their 1918 triumph at Perm, but also with a distinctly democratic and regionalist sensibility, recalled I.I. Sukin, these men cherished the Siberian Army's special

6 For the basic policy documents extant on SR policy in Siberia at this time see FO 371/4097/158330 'Charter Issued by Ivan Iakushev, President of the Siberian Regional Duma (Vladivostok), 5.ix.1919'; 'Declaration of the Central Bureau of Military Organizations (Vladivostok), September 1919', Nikolaevskii Collection (*Hoover Institution*), File 6; 'Proclamation of the Siberian Union of SRs, August 1919', *ibid.*, File 8. The *Zemskii sobor'* was an irregular representative assembly of medieval and early modern Russia, comparable to the medieval parliaments, diets and estates general of the west. By the late sixteenth century it had evolved into a relatively formal consultative assembly with delegates from all the free estates (including Cossacks and 'black' peasants). That of 1613 'elected' the first Romanov Tsar, Michael, but thereafter, as autocracy consolidated its hold on Russia, the power of the *Zemskii sobor'* waned. In the nineteenth century, however, the institution was idealized by the Slavophiles as symbol of the (lost) unity between the Tsar and his people and as an antidote to western liberalism. It was this tradition which was passed on to the SRs via Herzen and Russian Populism.

genesis and role during the Democratic Counter-Revolution of the summer of 1918, proudly continued to display their green and white Siberian cockades and were – among the Whites – remarkably suspicious of non-Siberian concerns and non-Siberian figures, such as Kolchak, whom they held to have hijacked their movement.[7] According to one account, it was only the calming influence of their more phlegmatic commander, General Anatol Pepeliaev, which had forestalled an attempt by the most inveterate of these Siberians to arrest Kolchak during his tour of the front in February 1919.[8] On that occasion Kolchak escaped, but discontent continued to simmer and when the spring offensive foundered with the collapse of the Western Army during May – an event particularly galling, as the Siberian Army was still advancing – it was made manifest in a fiery report to Kolchak by one Captain N.S. Kalashnikov (Head of the Information Section of the Staff of the Siberian Army), a man destined to play a major role in the Supreme Ruler's fate.

Discountenancing Omsk's tendency to concentrate solely on military affairs, Kalashnikov contrarily portrayed the crisis of the régime as a reflection of 'the internal situation' of White Siberia. The government was not popular, he alleged, because of: the 'anti-democratic spirit' of the *stavka* and its antagonism to minority groupings; arbitrary beatings, executions and other 'criminal acts incompatible with the ideas of law and civilization' perpetrated on innocent workers and peasants by renegade military authorities in areas of the rear outwith the control of Omsk; the obvious distaste displayed by Omsk in dealing with local authorities and the co-operatives; the suspiciously slow pace of preparatory work for the elections to the new Constituent Assembly; the inconclusive nature of Omsk's land reform; and the economic disruption caused by the war. The only hope, he averred, was for the government 'categorically to distance itself' from reactionary elements, to honestly elucidate its land policy, to stop employing such confusing terminology as 'National Assembly of a Constituent Character' and to adhere instead to the terminology all democrats had preferred for decades – 'an All-Russian Constituent Assembly' – and immediately to summon a *Zemskii sobor'* of zemstvo and duma figures to act as a provisional legislative organ prior to the convocation of a Siberian Constituent Assembly.[9]

[7] Sukin (*Leeds Russian Archive*), p. 144.

[8] Dotsenko, P. *The Struggle for a Democracy in Siberia*. Stanford (1983), p. 79.

[9] [Kalashnikov, N.S.] 'Itogi vesennogo nastupleniia', *Sibirskii arkhiv* (Prague), Vol. 2 (1929), pp. 81–7.

The advice of this lowly colonel was, not surprisingly, ignored by Kolchak. The programme he advocated, however, was more than a personal view. Rather, it was an articulation of what Kalashnikov's many and close contacts among zemstvo and duma circles of Siberia were thinking. And, despite Kolchak's dismissal of it, the programme did not die, for Kalashnikov's contacts proceeded to endeavour to summon a *Zemskii sobor'* without the government's sanction, in the hope, initially, that the very existence of such a body might 'democratize' the Omsk authorities by osmosis. Thus, at Tomsk, under the auspices of *Sibzemgor*, was founded a Co-ordinating Committee for the Convocation of a *Zemskii sobor'* (*Komitet sodeistviia sozyvu Zemskogo sobora*) or *KssZs*, with branches at Krasnoiarsk, Irkutsk and Vladivostok. Its leading lights, who soon gave up hope of being given a fair hearing by Kolchak and departed for Vladivostok, were mainly right-SRs and lapsed Mensheviks: among them were I.A. Iakushev (former Chairman of the Siberian *oblast'* duma), V.O. Sidorov (Chairman of *Sibzemgor*), and A.A. Krakovetskii (the founder of the Siberian anti-Bolshevik underground in 1918). On their journey to the Far East they made contact with other leading SRs, such as E.E. Kolosov, and were joined by dissident members of the State Economic Conference such as A.N. Alekseevskii.[10]

On September 5th, under the influence of continuing intransigence on the part of the government and the continuing advance of the Red Army, Iakushev was to publish a lengthy *gramota* (charter) of the *KssZs* opposition movement, openly calling for the overthrow of the 'cruel' Kolchak régime and the convocation of a *Zemskii sobor'*.[11] Recognizing that it would be dangerous to attempt to organize elections as long as Kolchak was in power, however, the *KssZs* decided instead that the delegates to the abortive 2nd All-Siberian Congress of Zemstvos and Municipal Dumas (which Kolchak had forbidden to convene at Tomsk in May) should, by early October, make their way to Irkutsk, there to proclaim themselves a Siberian *Zemskii sobor'*. When, however, it transpired that only sixteen *guberniia* and *uezd* zemstvo delegates were able to reach Irkutsk by that date, the meeting was duly

10 Iakushev, I.A. 'Komitet sodeistviia sozyvu Zemskogo sobora', *Sibirskii arkhiv* (Prague), Vol. 2 (1929), pp. 73–80; Mal'tseva, T.V. 'Zemskaia "oppozitsiia" kolchakovshchiny' in Korablev, Iu. V. and Shishkin, V.I. (eds.) *Iz istorii interventsii i grazhdanskoi voiny v Sibiri i na Dal'nem Vostoke, 1917–1922gg.* Novosibirsk (1985), pp. 191–2.

11 FO 371/4097/158330 'Charter issued by Ivan Iakushev..., 5.ix.1919'.

downgraded to a 'Zemstvo-Socialist Conference'.[12] According to a circular of Iakushev's *KssZs* of October 10th, this in turn charged one 'Durov' (the pseudonym of Sidorov) with responsibility for gathering a full zemstvo and duma congress at Irkutsk in November, which was to be supplemented by representatives of Cossack Hosts and of the Siberian native peoples before it might 'declare itself to be the Siberian *Zemskii sobor*''. Meanwhile, continued this circular, the *KssZs* would concentrate its own efforts 'on the creation of the apparatus for a *coup d'état*' to seize power from Kolchak. It was hoped that the coup might coincide with the planned November congress at Irkutsk, which would give 'moral support' to the SR action: 'The congress may announce the coup and will become the source of its authority', postulated the *KssZs* in October.[13]

The organization of a coup, however, let alone the series of co-ordinated coups all across Siberia which it became clear the SRs had in mind, was no simple matter. Initially, neither the *KssZs* nor the Zemstvo-Socialist Conference would countenance collaboration with underground Bolshevik organizations – the Irkutsk meeting specifically rejected a suggestion to that effect, made by P.Ia. Mikhailov and B.D. Markov, as likely to compromise the forces of democracy[14] – yet they knew that their own organization could not count upon any mass rising, least of all in the key urban centres of Krasnoiarsk, Irkutsk and Vladivostok, where the workers remained under Bolshevik influence. It was consequently resolved to attempt to expand influence not over the masses but over discontented elements of White garrisons (particularly among the officers) and to seek the tactical support of the Allies. As Kolosov recalled: 'Above all each of us had the intention to appeal directly to the foreigners for help – to the Czechs, to the French, the British and the Americans, but not to the Russians.'[15]

[12] Mal'tseva, pp. 191–2; Zhurov, Iu.V. *Eniseiskoe krest'ianstvo v gody grazhdanskoi voiny.* Krasnoiarsk (1972), pp. 166–7. The conference elected a standing committee (occasionally referred to as the 'Zemstvo Politburo') of Ia.N. Khodukin (representing Irkutsk), E.E. Kolosov (Krasnoiarsk), I.M. Maiskii (then in Mongolia and consequently deputized by B.A. Kozminskii of Vladivostok). See Kolosov, E.E. *Sibir' pri Kolchake*. Petrograd (1923), p. 28.

[13] *Sibirskii arkhiv* (Prague), Vol. 2 (1929), pp. 91–3.

[14] *ibid.*, pp. 92–3; Mal'tseva, p. 193. Those SRs in favour of supporting the Red Army against Kolchak at this point split to form their own Autonomous Group of Siberian SRs at Novonikolaevsk. See Zhurov, pp. 168–9.

[15] Kolosov, p. 109.

Kolchak's pledge of September to summon a State Land Assembly, although dismissed as political *trompe l'oeil* by the SRs, was a worrying diversion and even before the October conference at Irkutsk intensive propaganda work was being done by the CBMO, now under the personal direction of Kalashnikov and becoming active in all Siberian centres from Omsk to Vladivostok. Interestingly, the Omsk authorities were aware of this activity, but scorned it. On October 7th, for example, Guins issued a statement indicating that 'the government, doubting whether the leaders of this movement can count upon any support from the population, attributes very little importance to this affair. The projected coup will come to nothing.'[16] In its own statement of October 10th, in contrast, the *KssZs* averred that 'in essence the work is already finished' and claimed that in Vladivostok in particular a coup could be successfully launched at any moment.[17]

From the earliest days of the SR conspiracy, Vladivostok was regarded as the prime site for an initial rising which, it was hoped, might then find a response further west and enable the CBMO to engineer the arrest of Kolchak and his staff.[18] In the Pacific port's favour was a tradition of mass discontent with the Kolchak government, as manifested in a huge strike movement of June–August 1919 which had united railwaymen, dockers and factory workers with waiters and cinema usherettes. The strike movement had been bowed but not altogether beaten by successive waves of repression inflicted on the Maritime Provinces by Ataman Dutov, during his special punitive mission of July, and by the ruthless new Governor General of the Far East, Sergei Nikolaevich Rozanov.[19] Moreover, although the local Bolshevik underground was known to have maintained a strong hold over the workers, according to Iakushev, the majority of Vladivostok party members had tacitly agreed that they would not oppose any action launched by the *KssZs* and would refrain from calling for an immediate union of Siberia with Soviet Russia until Kolchak had been toppled.[20]

16 *Union (Agence Télégraphique Russe)* (Paris) No. 185, 13.x.1919.

17 *Sibirskii arkhiv* (Prague), Vol. 2 (1929), pp. 91–3.

18 Solodovnikov, B. *Sibirskie avantiury i General Gaida. Iz zapisok russkago revoliutsionera.* Prague (n.d.), p. 26.

19 Tsiupkhin, S. et al. *Oktiabr'skaia revoliutsiia i grazhdanskaia voina na Dal'nem Vostoke: khronika sobytii (1917–1922gg.).* Moscow–Khabarovsk (1933), pp. 120–31.

20 *Sibirskii arkhiv* (Prague), Vol. 2 (1929), pp. 91–3.

Vladivostok was also favoured as a centre because, despite the repressions inflicted by Ivanov-Rinov earlier in the year (see above, pp. 271ff), and despite the ongoing threatening governance of Rozanov and the proximity of the rapacious Ataman Kalmykov, the presence of many Allied representatives in the port had ensured that it remained the freest city of Kolchakia. As around the clock patrols of a United States militia under Colonel Johnston kept street violence and right-wing intimidation to a minimum, the zemstvo of Primorskii *krai* (under the chairmanship of the SR A.S. Medvedev) operated relatively unhindered, as did the Vladivostok Municipal Duma (under the Menshevik Agapev); all but unashamedly pro-Bolshevik newspapers were published in the town and might, within the bounds of common sense, proffer criticism of the government. This relative haven had acted as a magnet for SRs who had fled White repression and violence in western Siberia – and many more leading party figures, Iakushev and his *KssZs* among them, arrived as 1919 wore on to organize anew around the nucleus of the former Provisional Government of Autonomous Siberia. Petr Derber himself was no longer present – he was by then languishing in Ataman Annenkov's jail at Semipalatinsk – but his quondam 'ministers', among them A.A. Krakovetskii and V.I. Moravskii, retained some influence locally.

The determining factor in the choice of Vladivostok as the first nexus of SR opposition, however, was the belief of *KssZs* that Allied diplomats in the port would support their prospective coup: key figures in the diplomatic community were 'completely in favour' of the action, Iakushev informed his organization in October.[21]

There was some cause for such optimism. The British Consul at Vladivostok, W.E O'Reilly, had been approached by opposition groups as early as July and, by flourishing promises of summoning the popular assembly which Kolchak had fought shy of and the internal reform of which he seemed incapable (whilst maintaining a diplomatic silence with regard to their own planned truce with the Soviet Government), Iakushev and others had inspired the consul to file a series of reports to Whitehall very favourable to *KssZs* over the summer of 1919. Whilst not (as his critics later claimed) positing overt British support for an anti-Kolchak coup, O'Reilly did suggest in his despatches that the strength of the opposition was now

21 *ibid.*, pp. 94–5.

such that Kolchak 'must be forced' to introduce the long-overdue reforms in order to deserve Allied recognition, draw the sting of the opposition movement and quash any possibility of a coup.[22] According to O'Reilly, US Ambassador Morris, who passed through Vladivostok en route back to Japan in September, was not unsympathetic to this point of view; elements of the French mission were also known to be supportive.[23] And even more propitious from the *KssZs* point of view was that important Allied military figures at Vladivostok seemed to have had enough of the ruthless bandits Kolchak routinely chose as his representatives in the Far East. General Graves's distaste for the Whites was by now public knowledge; but an indication that he was not alone in so feeling came when on September 18th (in response to the ferment occasioned by Iakushev's *gramota* of the 5th) Rozanov requested that British officers and their cadets from the Russian Island Officer Training School in the Golden Horn should participate in crushing a prospective rising. To the Whites' annoyance, and the SRs' joy, the local British commander, Colonel Blair, politely demurred. Meanwhile, on September 21st Colonel Johnston of the American Military Mission interposed his militia between Rozanov's forces and the known headquarters of the CBMO at Vladivostok, preventing Rozanov from acting independently to crush the opposition. It must have seemed that the Americans were tacitly encouraging the SRs to continue with their work.[24]

Of course the decisive power in Vladivostok – indeed, in the entire Far East – was Japan, which still had 40,000 troops on the mainland; and the CBMO and *KssZs* well knew that no coup could succeed if Tokyo opposed it. In mid-September, consequently, Iakushev petitioned General Boldyrev – the former Commander-in-Chief of the Siberian Army who, having resigned after Kolchak's investiture, was now resident in Tokyo and known to enjoy the respect of the

22 *DBFP*, pp. 476–7, 541–2, 568, 580–2. From O'Reilly's point of view, Kolchak's decision to summon the State Land Assembly was only made because of pressure being exerted by the opposition (and, in particular, Iakushev's *gramota* of September 5th). This he regarded as a vindication of his own contacts with the opposition. And, *pace* those who accused him of inciting rebellion against Omsk, O'Reilly actually welcomed Kolchak's September 16th initiative and hoped that it might 'dampen down the [SR] movement here so that things move in the way we want'. FO 371/4096/13365 'O'Reilly (Vladivostok) to FO, 22.ix.1919'. Only when Kolchak failed to summon the Assembly would O'Reilly again venture that 'other instruments' than Kolchak might be of more utility to the Allies in the struggle against Bolshevism. *DBFP*, p. 596.

23 *DBFP*, pp. 596–7; Lasies, J. *La tragédie sibérienne: le drame d'Ekaterinenbourg. La fin de l'amiral Koltchak*. Paris (1920), p. 198.

24 *Dal'istpart* (Vladivostok), Vol. 2 (1924), pp. 167–72; Solodovnikov, p. 31; WO 33/975/3531 'Blair (Vladivostok) to Knox (Omsk), 18.ix.1919'.

Japanese military – to request that he should come to Vladivostok to join the opposition movement.[25] Boldyrev refused. But all was not lost. After all, it was known that the Japanese had no great love for Kolchak and that any support they had offered him theretofore had been for purely selfish motives. It might reasonably be supposed, therefore, that they could be induced, on the right terms, to switch their support to the opposition. Hopes were raised on this score on September 26th, when the Japanese representatives at Vladivostok put their names to a joint Allied *démarche* to Rozanov.

This remarkable protest came about in the following manner. Until July 1918 the former Chief of the CER, the venerable General Horvath, had enjoyed wide-ranging authority in the Far East with, as Kolchak's High Plenipotentiary for the region, his own Council of Ministers and a semi-autonomous administration. On July 10th, however, the respected, statesmanlike and diplomatic Horvath was dismissed, *in absentia*, by a meeting of the Council of the Supreme Ruler at Omsk. Pepeliaev and Sukin had charged that Horvath's administration was 'completely inactive'. Both Guins and Sir Charles Eliot, however, suggested that jealousy and the centralizing tendency of the Ministry of the Interior were behind the dismissal and the subsequent incorporation of the Far East into the regular Omsk purview. Whatever the motivation for the dismissal, however, Guins and the British and American representatives in the Far East were united in their opinion that there was 'no excuse' for then replacing Horvath as Governor General and Commander of the Far Eastern Military District with the 'ungovernable and irresponsible' General Rozanov, who arrived with the reputation of 'a bloody and unscrupulous administrator' from service at Krasnoiarsk. There his contribution to the civil war had consisted of hanging ten hostages from telegraph poles along the railway for every government soldier killed during instances of unrest – a policy which had added fuel to a partisan movement unequalled for its anti-government ferocity anywhere in Siberia. Most observers at Vladivostok consequently interpreted Rozanov's arrival as 'a deliberate affront to the Allies'.[26]

25 Boldyrev, V.G. *Direktoriia, Kolchak, interventy: vospominaniia*. Novosibirsk (1925), pp. 241, 547–9.

26 Pepeliaev, V.N. 'Razval kolchakovshchiny (iz dnevnika V.N. Pepeliaeva)', *Krasnyi arkhiv* No. 6 (1928), pp. 56–7; Guins, G.K. *Sibir', soiuzniki i Kolchak: povorotnyi moment russkoi istorii, 1918–1920gg. (Vpechatleniia i mysli chlena Omskogo pravitel'stva)*. Peking (1921), Vol. 2, pp. 247–9; FO 371/4096/66 'Eliot (Omsk) to FO, 11.vii.1919'; WO 106/1273 'Britmis (Vladivostok) to WO, 7.ii.1919'; Graves, p. 217.

The new Vladivostok governor soon embellished his sanguinary reputation. 'Rozanov's administration would have been a disgrace to any government, no matter how desperate', opined one diplomat.[27] Among his first acts was the promotion of Ataman Kalmykov, who for the past year had been terrorizing the inhabitants of Khabarovsk with a régime so base that even the hardened killers of his own band had been known to turn on their chief in revulsion. As Rozanov's official second in command, the ataman was graced with the title of Plenipotentiary for the Maintenance of Law and Order in Khabarovsk and Iman Districts. He immediately demonstrated his interpretation of 'law and order' by detaining and torturing two American marines at Iman and by hanging ten 'Bolsheviks' without trial at Khabarovsk.[28] This, however, apparently recommended Kalmykov to Rozanov, for far from disciplining such iniquities, the governor summoned the ataman and 4,000 of his rapacious minions to Vladivostok to assist in the 'maintenance of order' against the burgeoning opposition movement. As the Cossacks poured into Vladivostok during September, disorder on a scale not before witnessed in the port errupted – at least two more American and two Czech soldiers were killed by Kalmykov's gang and many more were beaten up. Finally, on September 23rd, Kalmykov had his men abduct one of his more legitimate rivals to the atamancy of the Ussurii Cossacks. The kidnapping was committed in broad daylight on Vladivostok's main thoroughfare. The victim was then shot and his body dumped nearby – apparently he had been on his way to present Allied diplomats with evidence of the atrocities already committed by Kalmykov at Khabarovsk.[29]

It was in response to these and other Cossack peccadilloes that an outraged meeting of the Inter-Allied Committee of Diplomatic Representatives at Vladivostok met on September 26th and determined to send a terse ultimatum to Rozanov, squarely blaming Kalmykov for recent disorders in the port and demanding that all troops who had been brought into the town since September 1st should be removed. If this was not done by September 29th, the note read, the Allies would resort to force of arms to ensure compliance. The salient feature of all this from the point of

[27] Preston, T. *Before the Curtain*. London (1950), p. 140.

[28] WO 95/5433 'Britmis (Vladivostok) Monthly War Diary, 2.ix.1919'; Graves, W.S. *America's Siberian Adventure*. New York (1931), pp. 248–50; *DBFP*, p. 568.

[29] *FRUS: 1919 (Russia)*, p. 521; Savory, R. 'Vladivostok 1919–20' (*Savory Papers*, National Army Museum 7603/93/26), pp. 109-13; WO 33/957/3642 'Britmis (Vladivostok) to Knox (Omsk), 27.ix.1919'.

view of Iakushev and the SR opposition, to repeat, was that figuring prominently among the signatories of this unprecedentedly united and severe Allied challenge to the White authorities, was the Chairman of the Diplomatic Committee, General Inagaki of the Japanese Military Mission.[30]

Although, following a stern protest from Kolchak on September 29th, to the effect that Vladivostok was 'a Russian city' and that he regarded the ultimatum as 'an infringement of the sovereign rights of the Russian people',[31] the *démarche* was withdrawn and Kalmykov's troops stayed put, the opposition apparently had little cause to be disheartened. For one thing, despite Kolchak's protest, Rozanov was prevailed upon by the diplomatic corps to confine all Russian troops to barracks, while a report was prepared for despatch to Omsk detailing all the recent misconduct.[32] Moreover, in subsequent weeks representatives of the Japanese military, perhaps fearing that their sponsorships of the likes of Semenov and Kalmykov was about to rebound upon them, actually began making contact with opposition figures and encouraging them in their endeavours: 'Russia needs democratic reforms', pronounced, through gritted teeth, General Oi (the departing Commander-in-Chief of Allied Forces in the Far East) at a press conference, asserting that the Allies would support all forces intent upon such reforms.[33] Meanwhile, in the wake of the Allies' shot across his bows, even Rozanov was to be seen making his surreptitious way to the rebels' headquarters to hint that, in the event of Kolchak's fall, he might declare himself to be the provisional ruler of a Far Eastern state, pending elections to a popular assembly of the type favoured by *KssZs*.[34]

There is no evidence of how much credibility the SR plotters accorded the intriguing offers of Generals Oi or Rozanov, but they would surely have been

30 'Golos Rodiny' (ed.) *Deistviia Iaponii v Priamurskom krae: sbornik offitsial'nykh dokumentov otnosiashchikhsiia k interventsii derzhav v predelakh Priamur'ia*. Vladivostok (1921), p. 21.

31 *ibid.*, p. 22.

32 Guins, Vol. 2, p. 340; Savory, 'Vladivostok, 1919–20' (*Savory Papers*, NAM 7603/9326), p. 113; WO 33/957/3681 'Britmis (Vladivostok) to WO, 1.x.1919'. Apparently the report had some effect, for on October 28th orders were issued summoning Rozanov to Omsk to account for himself – see WO 33/957/4081 'Britmis (Vladivostok) to WO, 30.x.1919'. Because of the deteriorating military situation in Western Siberia, however, the summons was rescinded a few days later – see WO 33/957/4113A 'Britmis (Vladivostok) to WO, 3.xi.1919'.

33 *Golos rodiny* (Vladivostok) 7.xi.1919.

34 Boldyrev, pp. 238, 273; WO 33/957/4163 'Britmis (Vladivostok) to WO, 7.xi.1919'.

unwise to have flattered them with very much: some strange alignments of forces had arisen during the civil war in Siberia, but one combining Rozanov, the Japanese Army and their puppet Kalmykov on one hand with an admixture of SRs and Mensheviks on the other in a struggle for democracy would have been a most unappetizing cocktail. In fact, in the light of the bloody dénouement when the SRs did come out in open rebellion against Kolchak, it might not be going too far to interpret the entire history of this incident as a deliberate provocation on the part of Rozanov and the Japanese (who had, by Rozanov's admission, formed a secret military agreement on September 15th, which envisaged the division of responsibility in the Far East between Semenov and Rozanov in the event of Kolchak's demise):[35] joint approaches to the rebels might, in other words, have been intended to encourage the SRs to reveal their hand too early; while Japanese encouragement of the likes of O'Reilly and Blair might have been intended to sow discord among the Allies and lead to a rift between the Anglo-American interests and Kolchak, facilitating the hiving off of the Far East into Japanese tutelage. O'Reilly himself claimed in October to have ascertained that this indeed was the Japanese game and that, having initiated the idea of the September 26th *démarche*, General Oi had assured Rozanov in advance that nothing would be allowed to come of it.[36] If so, it was a very clever ruse, and an effective one: the note of September 26th damaged Kolchak's reputation and alienated him from the powers whilst plunging Allied staffs into an embarrassing disarray – senior Allied representatives at Omsk poured invective on their juniors at Vladivostok for encouraging the 'mad movement' of the SRs and for listening to 'local tittle-tattle'; and before the end of October both Blair and O'Reilly had been dismissed (the latter despatched, on the first available boat, to the diplomatic backwater of La Paz).[37]

In retrospect, there was little hope of the SRs winning official Allied support in September–October 1919. This was, of course, the time at which, under the influence both of Kolchak's offensive from the Ishim and the advances on the capitals of European Russia being attempted by Denikin and Iudenich, the powers were again considering the recognition of the Supreme Ruler. Yet still the plotters were not disheartened: B. Solodovnikov, a new arrival at the headquarters of the

35 *FRUS: 1919 (Russia)*, pp. 543–4; *DBFP*, p. 640.

36 FO 371/4097/140206 'O'Reilly (Vladivostok) to FO, 8.x.1919'.

37 WO 33/957/3559 'Britmis (Vladivostok) to WO, 20.ix.1919'; Ullman, R.H. *Anglo-Soviet Relations, 1917–1921*. London (1961–1972), Vol. 2, pp. 239–40.

CBMO, was quite astonished that, in the absence of Kalashnikov (who had left Vladivostok to begin organizing at Irkutsk), its local leaders, ensconced in their rooms reading newspapers, were making very little effort to spread propaganda in order to popularize their cause, and had troubled themselves to raise only a paltry subsidy of 152,000 roubles from the co-operatives when it was clear to him that millions were going to be required. Solodovnikov himself tracked down a printing press and began to produce leaflets but, by his own admission, only 30,000 were distributed across the Far East. A note of urgency *was* temporarily injected into the proceedings by the arrival at Vladivostok of the seasoned SR military organizer, Krakovetskii. But, recalled Solodovnikov, the other local leaders of the CBMO (Molotovskii, Kashkadanov and Kozlov) were so certain that Allied (and, in particular, Czechoslovak) troops in Vladivostok would come to their aid when the signal for the coup was given, that they made no secret of regarding preparatory and propaganda work as a waste of time.[38] In part this indolence reflected a misreading of the state of readiness to rebel and the number of sympathetic officers at the front, Solodovnikov thought.[39] Of major significance, however, was that the SR military organization had a curious ace up their sleeves: the co-option into their ranks of the enigmatic Czech leader, Radola Gajda.

Although Baron Budberg had warned Kolchak that, given the uncertain situation in the Far East, it would be wiser to exile Gajda via Mongolia and China after his clash with the admiral of July 1919, the Czech general was permitted to head east for Vladivostok in his own train, leaving Omsk on July 15th.[40] How much Gajda knew at that time of the incipient plot involving his former subordinate Kalashnikov is uncertain. He did vaingloriously record in his memoirs that, as he journeyed east 'often, in many towns, representatives of different political tendencies would visit my train and beg me not to leave Siberia' and claimed that such supplications led him to conclude that 'all Siberia was on my side'.[41] Gajda does not mention, however, that present on his train from Novonikolaevsk to Transbaikalia was

38 Solodovnikov, pp. 35–9.

39 *ibid.*, pp. 26–7.

40 Budberg, A.P. von 'Dnevnik', *Arkhiv russkoi revoliutsii* Vol. 15 (1924), p. 310.

41 Gajda, R. *Moje pameti: Ceskolovenska anabase zret na Urale proti Bolshevikum. Admiral Kolchak.* Prague (1924), p. 189.

Evgenii Kolosov of *KssZs*, who would certainly have apprised the Czech of his colleagues' plans.

The SRs well knew that Gajda was a volatile and egotistical character; they were aware too that he had been intimately associated with the establishment of the Kolchak dictatorship and the suppression of democratic organizations in Siberia in 1918. He was clearly no democrat. Rather, any willingness he might have had to engage in a plot to remove the admiral was inspired by a desire for vengeance against the man who had rewarded his service to anti-Bolshevism with insults and dismissal. Nevertheless, both Kolosov and (in a personal letter to the general) Iakushev expressed the hope that Gajda could be induced to support their action against Kolchak. Aware that the SRs' own credentials, tarnished by the failure to contain the forces of reaction in 1918, were unlikely to win them mass support, their hope was that a figure of Gajda's 'authority in the army' might at least stifle opposition from that sphere or even bring more officers over to their side.[42] Moreover, any doubters as to Gajda's utility to *KssZs* were assured, the Czech would act as 'a diplomatic lightning-conductor' to neutralize any suspicions on the part of the Allies that the movement was associated with the Bolsheviks.[43] Still, not everyone was convinced – and when Gajda's sponsors first presented him to SRs at Irkutsk, many refused outright to have anything to do with a man who less than a year earlier had passed westwards through their town as a conspirator in the Kolchak coup.[44]

Nor, at least according to his own memoirs, was Gajda himself entirely convinced that he should be co-operating with the SR underground. In his account he maintains that until his arrival at Vladivostok he still intended to leave Russia and only resolved to remain and serve the CBMO when, on August 27th, contrary to assurances given before the Czech's departure from Omsk in July, Kolchak published an order through Rozanov stripping Gajda of his cherished rank of

42 Kolosov, pp. 181–3; *Sibirskii arkhiv* (Prague), Vol. 2 (1929), pp. 87–8 (Iakushev to Gajda, 1.ix.1919).

43 Solodovnikov, p. 29.

44 'N', 'Poslednie dni kolchakovshchiny' *Sibirskie ogni* (Novonikolaevsk), No. 2 (1922), pp. 76–7; see also the unattributed editorial comments on a letter from Krakovetski to General Graves of September 20th 1919 published in *Sibirskii arkhiv* (Prague), Vol. 4 (1932), p. 184. For years afterwards embarrassed SRs would maintain that their party *per se* had had 'nothing to do' with Gajda and that the events at Vladivostok were the province of 'a few individuals'. See Rakov, D.F. *V zastenkakh Kolchaka: golos iz Sibiri*. Paris (1920), p. 45; and Gurevich, B. 'Rets. na Krol', L.A. *Za tri goda*', *Letopis' revoliutsii* (Berlin), Vol. 3 (1923), p. 309.

Lieutenant-General in the Russian Army. He then determined to 'obtain satisfaction' for this 'insult', claims Gajda.[45] S.P. Mel′gunov portrays Gajda's account as an excuse dreamed up specifically for his memoirs.[46] If the Czech was being disingenuous, however, he was being so long before the publication of that account, for in the first days of September 1919 Gajda presented himself to the head of Britmis at Vladivostok and vowed, in the words of that officer, that 'although up to date he has never moved a finger against Kolchak, [he] now intends to do all in his power to overthrow him and his government'.[47]

Already, on September 2nd in a letter to Iakushev, Gajda had promised to do everything he could to further the SR cause.[48] Indeed, it had been the very recruitment of Gajda which had inspired Iakushev to issue his inflammatory *gramota* of September 5th elucidating the aims of the movement.[49] Now sure of the Czech's support, the CBMO had established a new headquarters in wagon 119 of Gajda's train at Vladivostok station and, on September 7th, at a meeting between Gajda and all branches of the opposition forces at the city duma buildings, it was agreed to stage a coup to place a triumvirate of SR potentates (Iakushev, Moravskii and Krakovetskii) in power at Vladivostok within the next few days.[50] By the middle of the month British reports were talking of 'the new government' as a fact, at Omsk the Council of Ministers were debating the chances of a coup, while at Vladivostok Rozanov was fretting that, if the SRs moved, the 8,000 Czechoslovak troops in the port would rally to their countryman and hero of 1918, Gajda.[51] Everyone expected an attempt to be made before the end of September. Yet no attempt came. Either because of Rozanov's concentration of Cossacks in the port or because of the SRs' desire to arrange for a series of simultaneous risings under the less auspicious circumstances prevailing further west, a period of phoney war set in.

45 Gajda, p. 197. For the text of Rozanov's order see WO 33/957/372 'Britmis (Vladivostok) to Knox (Omsk), 5.ix.1919'.

46 Mel′gunov, S.P. *Tragediia admirala Kolchaka (iz istorii grazhdanskoi voiny na Volge, Urale i v Sibiri)*. Belgrade (1931–1932), Pt.3, Vol. 2, p. 9.

47 WO 33/957/3486 'Blair (Vladivostok) to Knox (Omsk), 15.ix.1919'.

48 *Sibirskii arkhiv* (Prague), Vol. 2 (1929), p. 88.

49 *ibid.*, p. 76.

50 Solodovnikov, p. 35; Ioffe, *Kolchakovskaia avantiura*, p. 238.

51 WO 33/957/3531 'Britmis (Vladivostok) to Knox (Omsk), 18.ix.1919'; Budberg, Vol. 15, pp. 309–11.

Preparations both for the rising and its suppression continued throughout October under an increasingly tense atmosphere of confrontation, as General Rozanov repeatedly threatened to unleash Kalmykov's Cossacks against the SRs' station stronghold. Meanwhile, however, the rapidly deteriorating position of the Russian Army at the front set a natural date for a new attempt. On November 7th Gajda laconically informed British officials that his organization would 'seize power on or shortly after the date of the fall of Omsk' and confidently predicted that, with White power so clearly expiring in Siberia, 'there will be no military opposition except from the atamans.'[52]

Taking their cue from the news that Omsk had indeed fallen, early on the rainy Monday morning of 17th November, in the vicinity of Vladivostok station, the CBMO began distributing leaflets carrying the inaugural proclamation of the 'Provisional People's Government of Siberia', announcing the nomination of Gajda as Commander-in-Chief of a new People's Army, the overthrow of Kolchak, and the impending opening of armistice negotiations with the Soviet government to put an end to the civil war. Above the pullman HQ of the 'government' was raised the new flag of democratic Siberia – green and white segments as in 1918, but now differenced diagonally by a thin red stripe. Initial reactions were quite favourable: an artillery detachment, brought from Russian Island into Vladivostok by Rozanov to celebrate the anniversary of the formation of Alekseev's Volunteer Army, rallied to the SR cause; the Marine Riflemen of the fortress's garrison marched into the station to assist the rebels; men on the street were seen queueing up to enlist; and, according to British intelligence officers (operating from an apartment directly opposite to the station), 'at least six instances were observed of people jumping and shouting with delight' at news of the coup. At 8.00 a.m. strikes were proclaimed in some factories and by 10.30 a.m. the station and docks area was in the hands of some 2,000 insurgents (although less than half were bearing arms).[53] At this point an elated Iakushev gave an interview to the Russian Telegraph Agency and

52 WO 33/957/3531 'Britmis (Vladivostok) to WO, 7.xi.1919'.

53 Savory, 'Vladivostok, 1919–20' (*Savory Papers*, NAM 7603/93/26), pp. 128–9; *Bor'ba za vlast' Sovetov v Primor'e (1917–1922)*. Vladivostok (1955), pp. 48–51; *Dal'istpart* (Vladivostok) Vol. 2, 1924, p. 149; WO 106/1324 'Events Leading up to the Anti-Government Movement at Vladivostok of 17.xi.1919', pp. 1–3. Soviet sources insist that local Bolsheviks had earlier resolved to support any SR rising by bringing workers out onto the streets. On the day, however, they forecast that the SRs would fail and decided against any such orchestrated action. But their orders were not received and unco-ordinated street demonstrations and strikes occurred. See Papin, M. *Krakh kolchakovshchiny i obrazovanie Dal'nevostochnoi respubliki*. Moscow (1957), p. 81.

predicted that 'this evening we will enter the town'. By early evening, however, far from marching in triumph down the Svetlanskaia, Gajda had formed a rather different impression of how things might turn out: 'I knew that the game was up', he recalled.[54]

What had transpired was that during the afternoon of the 17th, the 8,000 Czechoslovak Legionnaires in and around the port of Vladivostok, contrary to the SRs' fondest hopes, had expressed sympathy for the aims of the movement but had proclaimed a policy of strict neutrality in the developing conflict, in line with a declaration by Allied representatives of 3.00 p.m.[55] Both Soviet and White sources concur that, despite the prominent role of the 'lightning conductor' Gajda in the CBMO and in the new government, the Allied declaration and the Czechoslovak decision were prompted by intelligence passed on from Rozanov to the effect that at least a quarter of the rebel forces consisted of 'the blackest and most hot-headed' Bolshevized elements of the workers.[56]

Even had the workers not come out in sympathy with the coup, however, it has to be doubted whether the Allies would have acted differently. The Czechs at Vladivostok were only interested in leaving Russia and were not at all inclined to throw away their lives and energies in yet another internecine Siberian conflict. The only forces capable of influencing the situation militarily, therefore, were the Japanese. And where Tokyo's sympathies lay was soon revealed when the Japanese command's particular contribution to the professed Allied neutrality was manifested in what was euphemistically termed the 'localizing of hostilities'. This consisted of the throwing of a *cordon sanitaire* around the station, thereby sealing it off completely from potential working class support within the town and hemming in the rebels between the docks to their rear (whence the guns of the White Volunteer Navy were concentrated upon them), the battery of cannon mounted on Kalmykov's armoured train blocking the exit to the station, and the artillery and machine-guns which Rozanov was free to deploy along the town side of the marshalling yards.

54 Mel'gunov, Pt.3, Vol. 2, p. 28; Gajda, p. 214.

55 *DBFP*, pp. 650–1; *FRUS: 1919 (Russia)*, pp. 547–8; Svetachev, M.I. *Imperialisticheskaia interventsiia v Sibiri i na Dal'nem Vostoke (1918–1920gg.)*. Moscow (1983), p. 187.

56 Mel'gunov, Pt.3, Vol. 2, p. 28; Guins, Vol. 2, p. 444; Papin, p. 82.

What ensued was both bloody and predictable.[57] Some half-hearted cease-fire negotiations conducted through the Legion's General Chechek were unilaterally broken off by a Colonel Tomlin on behalf of Rozanov (although the latter claimed not to have sanctioned such a move) and a bombardment of the station began at 2.30 a.m. on the 18th.[58] Throughout the rest of the night shells rained down on the rebel positions, pounding Gajda's putative People's Army into submission. 'Hundreds of them came rushing out of the station and stood on the steps with their hands up, surrendering', one Vladivostok resident recounted: 'Rozanov calmly had the machine-gun aimed at them and shot the whole lot.'[59] 'By 8.00 a.m. on the 18th it was all over except for the occasional shot, a cowering man in a corner or an occasional civilian who was in the way', recalled another observer of the sorry scene.[60]

Most of the rebel leaders, however, escaped serious harm. Gajda, 'presenting a miserable appearance' according to one witness, was taken prisoner after having been shot through the foot and was hastily put aboard a Czechoslovak transport and exiled without trial. (Officially the leniency with which he was treated was 'in respect of his military record';[61] in fact, of course, it was an action taken so as to avoid stirring up trouble among the Legion.) Meanwhile, Iakushev, Krakovetskii and Moravskii, the triumvirate leadership of the 'Provisional People's Government of Siberia', took refuge not with the Siberian people but with US forces and were sheltered from Rozanov's vengeance by General Graves.[62] Others, however, were not so fortunate. In an order posted on November 17th Rozanov had promised

57 There are abundant eye-witness accounts of the crushing of the SR-Gajda rising at Vladivostok: Savory, 'Vladivostok, 1919–20' (*Savory Papers*, NAM 7603/96/26), pp. 130–9; Preston, pp. 140–2; Gajda, pp. 199–216; Solodovnikov, pp. 56–8; Khartling, K.N. *Na strazhe rodiny: sobytiia vo Vladivostoke (konets 1919–nachalo 1920gg.)*. Shanghai (1935); Galton, D. and Keep, J. (eds.) '[J. and D. Findlay's] Letters from Vladivostok, 1918–23', *Slavonic and East European Review* Vol. 45 (1967), pp. 515–18; *FRUS: 1919 (Russia)*, pp. 547–9; *DBFP*, pp. 650–2; WO 106/1324 'Events...at Vladivostok, 17.xi.1919', pp. 3–5.

58 Apparently the bombardment began before Rozanov actually gave the order. See 'Slavianofil' *Cheshskie argonavty v Sibiri*. Tokyo (1921), p. 17.

59 Galton and Keep, p. 518; Preston also witnessed surrendering rebels being shot (see Preston, p. 142). At least 300 of Gajda's men were killed or wounded at the station; Rozanov's casualties totalled 12 killed and 53 wounded. WO 106/1324 'Events...at Vladivostok, 17.xi.1919', p. 6.

60 Savory, 'Vladivostok, 1919–20' (*Savory Papers*, NAM 7603/96/26), p. 139.

61 WO 106/1324 'Events...at Vladivostok, 17.xi.1919', p. 5; *Union (Agence Télégraphique Russe)* (Paris) No. 209, 5.x.ii.1919.

62 Graves, pp. 285–6.

courts-martial for his prisoners. But, of the 1,500 captured, the ringleaders were tossed alive into the waters of the harbour and sniped at, while many of the rank and file were taken to the rear of the station and executed: 'Between 8.00 a.m. and 9.00 a.m. machine gun fire was heard from the station buildings', noted the British intelligence centre across the street. 'It was surmised that wholesale murder was being carried out.'[63] When Allied diplomats protested against the mayhem, Rozanov considerately had his prisoners marched a short distance from the town centre to be discretely bayonetted in a field.[64] The total number of executions will probably never be known: Graves estimated that Rozanov had killed 500–600 in retribution by the end of the year; but a French observer put it at 500 killed on the first day of the round-up. [65]

Whatever the final death-toll, the lesson of the failed putsch at Vladivostok for the opponents of Kolchak was immediately clear. Having witnessed the lethal effect of the Japanese cordon around the harbour, Solodovnikov (promoted, at the eleventh hour, to Chief of Staff of the fictional People's Army) reflected: 'I understood the complete hopelessness of an enterprise such as ours in territory practically occupied by the Japanese.'[66] For the Whites too, however, the Vladivostok affair was of dark significance: it posed the question of whether *they* would be able to retain power for very much longer in areas outwith the Japanese sphere of influence.

White government *réchauffé*: 'The Cabinet of Solidarity'

On the very day that the Gajda putsch was being crushed in Vladivostok (which was, coincidentally, the first anniversary of the Omsk coup) Kolchak's refugee cabinet arrived at Irkutsk, the town designated as the new capital of White Siberia. There the ministers were notified that Omsk had fallen – news which left them

63 Solodovnikov, p. 88; WO 106/1324 'Events...at Vladivostok, 17.xi.1919', p. 5. Among the first batch were twenty cadets from the Russian Island Officer Training School in their British uniforms. Savory, 'Vladivostok, 1919–20' (*Savory Papers*, NAM 7603/96/26), p. 143.

64 *ibid.*, p. 144.

65 Graves, p. 324–5; Lasies, p. 237.

66 Solodovnikov, p. 71.

'destitute' according to one witness.[67] But even without these ill winds blowing from both east and west the ministers' moods would have been black enough. Although Irkutsk, often feted as the 'Paris of Siberia', was the only urban centre east of Omsk with anything like the infrastructure to support even a pretence of government, it had a disturbing reputation for violence and crime.[68] Moreover, although it might conceivably have been construed as a good omen that another prewar nickname of Irkutsk was 'The White City', because none at Omsk had had the forethought to prepare an abri for bad times, during the civil war Irkutsk had been allowed to develop into and remain 'exclusively an SR town'.[69] Despite the restrictive electoral laws introduced by the Kolchak government, both the municipal duma and the Irkutsk *guberniia* zemstvo retained majority socialist contingents (led, respectively, by the Menshevik M.M. Konstantinov and the SR Ia.N. Khodukin) which enjoyed the protection of a Governor General of moderate repute, P.D. Iakovlev. The latter's restraining influence on the army had encouraged many prominent socialists to seek refuge in the town – including the Mensheviks Akhmatov, Anisimov, Tarakanov and Maiskii and the SRs Kudriatsev, Fedorovich, Alekseevskii, Kalashnikov, B. Markov and P.Ia. Mikhailov. Pointedly, not one representative of the Irkutsk political community or of Irkutsk society – not even Governor Iakovlev himself – was at the station to greet the incoming government on November 18th.[70]

Having surveyed the empty scene at the station, it was reportedly only their greater fear of Semenov which prevented the forlorn ministers clambering back into their carriages and heading on to Chita, for the White hold on power at Irkutsk was clearly even more precarious than it was at Vladivostok.[71] The mood of the garrison was tremulous – and here there was no Japanese shield behind which the

67 *DBFP*, p. 657. For an account of the ministers' fretful journey east by a passenger on their train see Rudnev, pp. 289–91.

68 At what they termed 'Irkutsk the unregenerate' pre-war American visitors found that 'in spring a young man's fancy turns to thoughts of blood' – the outcome of which was several hundred murders a year and an atmosphere generally reminiscent of the 'wild west'. See Wright, R.L. and Digby, B. *Through Siberia: An Empire in the Making*. New York (1913), pp. 80–1, 137.

69 Elachich, S.A. 'Obryvki vospominanii' (*Hoover Institution Archives*), p. 102; Krol', L. *Za tri goda: vospominaniia, vpechatleniia i vstrechi*. Vladivostok (1921), p. 198.

70 Guins, Vol. 2, p. 440.

71 Parfenov, P. 'Poslednie dni pravitel'stva Kolchaka', *Sibirskie ogni* (Novosibirsk), No. 5 (1927), p. 95.

government might shelter in the event of a rising. Moreover, the local Czechoslovak Legionnaires, although professing neutrality as had their comrades at Vladivostok, seemed to have come down firmly on the side of the opposition in the ongoing struggle. On November 13th at all railway stations and public places in the region had been posted a swingeing denunciation of the Kolchak régime over the signatures of Boris Pavlu and Dr V. Girsa, the leaders (since September) of the Czechoslovak National Council, which was based at Irkutsk. Complaining that 'under the cover of Czechoslovak arms local Russian military authorities are allowed to commit acts which would horrify the world' and citing 'the razing of villages, the wholesale slaughter of innocent Russian civilians and the execution of representatives of democracy', this pair proclaimed that the Legion would turn a blind eye no longer to the evils of White rule and, pending repatriation, would henceforth oppose disorder 'no matter from which side it comes'.[72]

Some 3,000 km to the west, Kolchak and his retinue were outraged by this insulting 'stab in the back', recalled Admiral Smirnov.[73] And they were more than a little surprised by it – Pavlu had been personally recommended for his post by none other than General Stefanik (a known advocate of maximizing the Legion's pro-White activity in Siberia) and in October had himself appeared keen to enter another round of negotiations aimed at having his men fight their way home through Soviet Russia.[74] But in October, of course, the prospects of White victory in the war and of an easy passage through Russia had seemed bright because of Denikin's victories. By mid-November the outlook had changed drastically for the worse.[75] The White gamble had failed and there was growing clamour in the Legion for immediate repatriation – reliable sources now indicated that, unless the Czechoslovaks were moved out soon via Vladivostok, some two-thirds of their units would certainly begin fraternization with the approaching Reds for whom their

72 Konstantinov, M.M. (ed.) *Poslednie dni kolchakovshchiny*. Moscow (1926), pp. 112–3.

73 Smirnov, M.I. *Admiral Kolchak: kratkii biograficheskii ocherk*. Paris (1930), pp. 54–5. All the more insulting to Kolchak was that he only came to hear of the Czechoslovak declaration through newspaper reports. See *Arkhiv russkoi revoliutsii*, Vol. 10 (1923), pp. 177–8.

74 Guins, Vol. 2, pp. 528–9.

75 Mel'gunov (Part 3, Vol. 2, pp. 48–51) suggests that Pavlu was also under pressure from Masaryk to distance the Legion from Kolchak in order to stave off a socialist challenge to the leadership of the new government in Prague. See also Fink, P. *Biely admiral: profil kolcakovshiny*. Prague (1922), p. 159.

experience of Kolchak's rule had incubated no little sympathy.[76] Moreover, Pavlu's first duty, since Beneš's order of September 26th, was to supervise the safe evacuation of his men; and if Kolchak was incapable of facilitating the move east, he probably regarded it as his legitimate right to look elsewhere. Moreover, any qualms the soldierly Pavlu may have entertained about abandoning Kolchak were probably assuaged by his socialist colleague, Doctor Girsa.

Above all the Czechoslovak leaders would have been aware that the White hold on power in eastern Siberia was precarious and that the SR star was in the ascendent. The action at Vladivostok had failed, but at Irkutsk other elements of the opposition were still concentrating and on November 12th a secret All-Siberian Congress of Zemstvos and Dumas had been convened (as planned by Iakushev's *KssZs* the previous month). At the Congress was formed the Political Centre, consisting of SR and Menshevik members of Irkutsk duma and *guberniia* zemstvo and representatives of the so-called Zemstvo Politburo created by the Zemstvo-Socialist Conference of October. The Centre set itself the specific task of preparing for the overthrow of White rule and the establishment of an independent Siberian authority.[77] If, as seemed possible, the Political Centre was successful in these aims, the Czechoslovak National Council would require their assistance in the evacuation of the Legion. Pavlu and Girsa could simply not afford to allow to continue, therefore, the widespread resentment among Siberia's socialists of the Legion's service with Kolchak – resentment made bluntly manifest as recently as October 28th when the Irkutsk duma board had, by a majority of 23:13, voted not to participate in the first anniversary celebrations of the Czechoslovak Republic and had denounced the Legion as 'the lapdog of international imperialism'.[78] Hence the fact that a representative of Pavlu had been present at the illegal congress of November 12th; hence the memorandum of November 13th; and hence the fact that

76 *FRUS: 1919 (Russia)*, p. 227. The Legionnaires' emotions were poignantly portrayed in cartoons carried by their daily paper at this time: one contrasted a group of shackled Russian convicts in Siberia beneath the date '1880' with a group of Czechoslovak soldiers in shackles marked 'Allies' beneath the date '1920'; a second portrayed haggard Legionnaires, covered in moss and fungus, on the shores of the Pacific reading a newspaper dated '1970'. See Kozhevnikov, S. 'Konets bor'by s Chekho-slovakami', in Smirnov et al. *Bor'ba za Ural i Sibir'*, p. 339.

77 Mal'tseva, p. 192; Papin, pp. 76–7.

78 Janin, 'Otryvki', p. 135; Mel'gunov, Pt.3, Vol. 2, pp. 50–1.

on that same day Pavlu and Girsa expressed to Political Centre member Fedorovich their sympathies with the SRs' intentions.[79]

If Kolchak's ministers had not immediately understood the motivation of the Czechoslovak memorandum, its implications and the implication of their frosty welcome at Irkutsk were clear enough. Even prior to disembarking at Irkutsk, recalled Guins, ministers had been brooding over the question of 'who *does* now support the government?' and had found themselves struggling to come up with a convincing answer. After the events at Vladivostok and rumours about the growth of the CBMO, he added, 'the government was even scared of its own officers'. The conclusion drawn was that an entirely new approach was necessary. An emollient, contrite proclamation was hastily drafted by the Minister of Labour, the lapsed Menshevik Shumilovskii, and was issued at Irkutsk on November 19th, the day after the cabinet's arrival. Reiterating that the government had 'no other aim than the salvation of divided and disrupted Russia', it opined that nothing would be achieved 'without the closest links with broad, progressive circles of society, although their outlook may not always be identical to the government's' and invited such groups to rally around the government's standard. On this tabula rasa Shumilovskii inscribed a new set of slogans for the régime: 'For the land, for the defence of a new law on free labour, for culture, legality, for true democracy and for the Constituent Assembly.'[80] The use of the last term was significant. A year after its banishment from the official lexicon it had been revived; and a year after the massacre of SR members of the 1917 Assembly in western Siberia and the Urals, the Kolchak government was inviting the party back into the anti-Bolshevik political fold.

The possibility of attracting leading SR moderates into a reformed government had actually been broached as early as October 20th – when the Council of Ministers was still resident at Omsk – by Viktor Pepeliaev; and, later, whilst en route to Irkutsk, the Minister of the Interior had specifically mentioned to Guins that he had contacts with regionalist elements in the army (via one Colonel Kononov) who might be able to induce Evgennii Kolosov to join the Council of Ministers and

79 Parfenov, 'Poslednie dni', p. 95; Vendrykh, G.A. *Dekabr'sko–ianvarskie boi 1919–1920gg. v Irkutske*. Irkutsk (1957), p. 16.

80 Guins, Vol. 2, pp. 440–1, 445–6; *The Times* (London) 1.xii,1919.

thereby grant that moribund institution a life-saving veneer of popular legitimacy.[81] When on arrival at the new capital Pepeliaev attempted to put his plan into operation, however, he was to be sorely disappointed. On 19th November, over tea with Kolosov (now Chairman of the Zemstvo Politburo and a member of the Political Centre) and Ia.N. Khodukin (Chairman of Irkutsk *guberniia* zemstvo), on the neutral ground of Governor Iakovlev's office, the minister explained that he and his colleagues had renounced the past and had 'firmly decided to liquidate the military régime and go over to a new civilian administration', and asked for their participation in a new government. This was akin to the prime mover of the Kolchak coup admitting that his actions of a year earlier had been criminally mistaken. Both Kolosov and Khodukin, however, rejected the invitation, saying that in order for Siberian society to trust any new authority, a *réchauffé* cabinet would not suffice. Rather, 'it would be necessary to dispense with all those responsible for the formation of the dictatorship and, above all, to dispense with one man'.

'Who?', enquired Pepeliaev.

'Why, you, Viktor Nikolaevich,' they chorused almost gleefully.[82]

At that rude point the interview was terminated. But later, in a meeting with the Council of Ministers, Iakovlev added that the Irkutsk socialists would accept nothing short of:

> The abdication of the Supreme Ruler and the resignation of his commanding staff; the transfer from military rule to a civilian government – and on a purely Siberian not an All-Russian scale; and, finally, the summoning of a *Zemskii sobor*'.

Many ministers were outraged by these demands. Others, however, among them the neophyte democrat Pepeliaev, continued to hope that this was a maximalist programme and that perhaps some degree of compromise was yet possible.[83]

81 Pepeliaev, p. 80; Guins, Vol. 2, p. 450.

82 'N', 'Poslednie dni kolchakovshchiny', *Sibirskie ogni* (Novosibirsk), No. 2 (1922), p. 78. The index of this journal attributes the authorship of this article to E.E. Kolosov – see *Sibirskie ogni – ukazatel' soderzhaniia, 1922–64*. Novosibirsk (1967), Item 4611. As, however, Kolosov was not in Irkutsk at the time that seems unlikely. Others have named the author as Iakovlev himself – see, for example, Varneck, E. and Fisher, H.H. (eds.) *The Testimony of Admiral Kolchak and Other Siberian Materials*. Stanford (1935), p. 412.

83 'N', pp. 81–2. In conversation with Guins, the possibility of persuading Kolchak to leave Siberia whilst retaining the title 'Supreme Ruler' had already been mooted by Pepeliaev. See Guins, Vol. 2, p. 450.

Although exposed to these socialist pressures at Irkutsk, the ministers were at least now removed from the penumbra of the Supreme Ruler's military coterie and felt free to present Kolchak with the blunt facts of the parlous White position. On November 20th both Guins and Vologodskii despatched telegrams to the train of the Supreme Ruler (which was by now just east of Tatarsk) and, on the following day, the Prime Minister spoke frankly with Kolchak on the direct wire. These urgent communications spoke of the 'very threatening' situation at Irkutsk and demanded, in quite unprecedentedly blunt language, that decisions on reform should be made immediately 'because tomorrow may be too late'. Even the formerly passive premier did not mince his words, warning:

> The authority of the government, and of yourself personally, decline with each day that passes. The infelicitous choice of the higher military commanders who have had pretensions towards exclusive influence over you, who completely ignore the Council of Ministers, cannot but exacerbate this situation.

The solution for these ills, the ministers urged, was for military power to be curtailed and for a new 'Cabinet of Solidarity' to be 'granted the full possibility to be an active authority, operating on the support of broad social circles'.[84]

Both Guins and Vologodskii also specifically recommended in their pleas to Kolchak that Pepeliaev should be promoted to the office of Premier (it having already been agreed on October 31st that Vologodskii should step down). And, in preparation for such a nomination, Pepeliaev himself was busy during these days making a series of notes on the envisaged programme of the Cabinet of Solidarity – drafts which might be interpreted as either surprisingly radical or predictably desperate. Among his plans were the granting of full legislative authority to the Council of Ministers; the abolition of the Council of the Supreme Ruler; the dismissal of 'the inexperienced and tactless hands' at the head of the army and the reinstatement of General Dieterichs as Commander-in-Chief; the accreditation of a permanent representative of the cabinet at the *stavka*; and, perhaps most controversially of all, the court-martialling of General Sakharov for his part in the Omsk débâcle and the prosecution of Mikhailov, Sukin, Nekliutin and von Goyer on various counts of corruption and peculation.[85] In addition, although he

84 Konstantinov, pp. 126–9; Guins, Vol. 2, p. 409.

85 Konstantinov, pp. 131–2.

apparently did not dare commit this thought to paper, Pepeliaev was talking privately of persuading Kolchak to step down as Supreme Ruler and to quit Siberia in order to deflect criticism of the new régime. When taking his turn to petition Kolchak on the direct wire on November 22nd, Pepeliaev was not so bold as to broach such topics in detail. But, in a fairly frank exchange, he did at least induce the admiral to admit that 'the basic cause underlying the unsatisfactory state of internal affairs is the illegal activities of the lower echelons of government, both military and civilian' and, having presented a diluted programme of reform based on the 'union of the healthy forces of society', was instructed to regard himself as the Prime Minister.[86]

As Pepeliaev endeavoured to fashion a Cabinet of Solidarity over the coming days, however, his constringing room for manoeuvre became apparent. It was already known that Irkutsk society was not enamoured of the portly Viktor Nikolaevich himself, yet there had been no-one else with sufficient standing (or nerve) in the government to take on the post of premier. Also, added Guins, it was felt that only one whom Kolchak trusted would be of utility in persuading the Supreme Ruler to sanction a programme of reform and, if possible, in cajoling him to step down in order to win the support of society. On the other hand, it did at least seem possible that the most indolent or corrupt ministries, such as those of Marine and Food and Supply, could be disbanded; and it was an easy enough matter to have Vologodskii, Tel'berg, Sukin and Smirnov removed 'as men too unpopular and too closely connected to the very acme of tyranny, the Supreme Ruler', recalled Guins.[87] But the problem was, who was going to replace them? With the refusal of local socialist elements to compromise themselves by sitting in the cabinet, the tactic resorted to was to call upon the services of the men of alleged 'national standing' recently arrived from Europe and South Russia: into the Cabinet came S.N. Tret'iakov (as Deputy Premier and Acting Minister of Foreign Affairs), P.A. Buryshkin (as Minister of Finance) and A.A. Cherven-Vodali (as head of the Ministry of the Interior). But naturally this move did nothing to enhance the government's reputation among Irkutsk society, because all of the newcomers could be regarded, in Siberian terms, as '*navoznye liudi*' ('dirty interlopers'). In fact, the

86 *ibid.*, pp. 132–4. The promotion of Pepeliaev to the post of Prime Minister was officially announced on November 23rd. See *ibid.*, pp. 135–6.

87 Guins, Vol. 2, pp. 448–50.

Cabinet of Solidarity was more foreign to Siberia than had been the old one.[88] Moreover, far from the democratization of the cabinet, the elevation of the reviled Pepeliaev and the promotion of Tret′iakov, who had been a prominent Kornilovite in 1917, could be (and was) interpreted as a step to the right; while the political demise of the renowned Americanophile Sukin, for all his faults, could be (and was) read as manifesting a pro-Japanese orientation in the new government, with all that that entailed in terms of a possible resort to the summoning of Japanese puppet atamans from Transbaikalia.[89]

In contrite press conferences and in apologetic speeches to a reconvened SEC at Irkutsk, Guins and Tret′iakov assured Siberia that this was not the case and that the reshuffle constituted more than a change of faces at the top: 'The old policy of the government cannot be allowed to continue', they said, pledging that 'abuses of power by the military' would no longer be tolerated and that the 'crimes against the state' of the former Ministers of Food, Supply and Finance would not go unpunished. All in all there would be 'a subordination of the military to the civilian authorities' and 'a rapprochement with the people' for 'new methods of struggle', they vowed. The reliance on purely military solutions would be replaced by a commitment to firm policies concerned with the provision of food to the population, a stable currency and an efficient transport system. Above all they promised 'the convocation at the earliest opportunity of the State Land Assembly'.[90] During the first week of December these promises were formalized. On December 2nd the RTA broadcast a nine-point programme corresponding to the ideas which Guins and Tret′iakov had been espousing.[91] Then, on December 3rd, *Pravitel′stvennyi vestnik* announced that the government had, in addition, decided to exclude from the State Land Assembly all delegates who were to have been nominated by the Supreme Ruler and to replace them by supplementary representatives to be elected by the zemstvos. It was also decreed that the Assembly would meet before the end of the year and that, rather than be a purely advisory body, it would have an enhanced role in the preparation of legislation. Finally, the RTA reported that Viktor Pepeliaev, the

88 *ibid.*, p. 276.

89 Boldyrev, p. 276, 450; *FRUS: 1919 (Russia)*, pp. 227, 450.

90 Guins, Vol. 2, pp. 447–9, 463; *Union (Agence Télégraphique Russe)* (Paris) No. 213, 13.xii.1919; *Arkhiv russkoi revoliutsii* (Berlin), Vol. 10 (1923), p. 180; Krol′, L., pp. 200–2.

91 *Union (Agence Télégraphique Russe)* (Paris) No. 210, 9.xii.1919; Guins, Vol. 2, pp. 458–9.

new premier, was pledged to 'reorganize the entire governmental system on the basis of decentralization'.[92]

Even Guins had later to admit that this volte-face, this sudden rush of populistic fervour and obeisance at the shrine of democracy after a year of political lassitude and military reaction, did not reflect well on the Cabinet of Solidarity. 'The situation arose in which the government might lose power,' he conceded, 'and it reeled like a drunken man.'[93] And the SRs knew that the government was running scared: 'Only on the very day that the revolution was knocking at your door were you panicked into giving assurances that there would be no nominated members of the State Land Assembly', Khodukin was later to remind the ministers.[94] The Political Centre, therefore, saw no reason for compromise: the government's promises and programme were answered by a resolution of the Irkutsk *guberniia* zemstvo, proclaiming bluntly that the Kolchak régime had 'neither the moral nor legal right to summon a Land Assembly' (which should anyway be fully legislatively empowered), while the municipal duma passed a resolution of no confidence in the Cabinet of Solidarity and demanded the creation of 'a homogeneous socialist government based on the zemstvo and duma organs of self-determination and the class organs of the workers and peasants'. Far from evincing a degree of willingness to compromise, as Pepeliaev had hoped, every word the socialists spoke screamed 'down with the government', trembled Guins.[95]

The final insult came on December 8th when ministers attended the inaugural meeting of the State Economic Conference at an Irkutsk theatre so as to unveil the government programme. Their speeches were deliberately directed to the public gallery where the representatives of the Political Centre were gathered. All the desperate impetrations of Guins and Tret'iakov, however, were met with a stony-faced silence until a dissident SEC delegate, A. Emolin of Zakupsbyt, rose and demanded the government's 'open recognition of the need to establish a civil peace on all Russian territories'. When an angry minister queried 'peace with whom, the Bolsheviks?', Emolin replied, to the clamant approval of the gallery, 'Yes, the

92 *Union (Agence Télégraphique Russe)* (Paris) No. 210, 9.xii.1919; Guins, Vol. 2, p. 467; Ioffe, *Kolchakovskaia avantiura*, p. 251.

93 Guins, Vol. 2, p. 463.

94 *Peregovory o sdache vlasti Omskim pravitel'stvom Politicheskomu Tsentru (v prisutsvim Vysokhikh Kommissarov i Vyshchago Kommandovaniia soiuznykh derzhav).* Harbin (1921), pp. 35–6.

95 Guins, Vol. 2, pp. 460–1; Krejci, F.V. *U sibirske armady.* Prague (1923), p. 187; 'N', p. 79.

Bolsheviks!' At that, with heads bowed, the dispairing ministers rose and left the auditorium.[96] Guins for one sensed that the White government had 'played its last card' and began to pack his bags. There were a few more mutterings in the official press over the next fortnight concerning yet more concessions relating to powers to be afforded the State Land Assembly and, on December 25th, appeared a final, apologetic 'Appeal to the Population'. But by that time, as Guins put it, 'it was clear that the game was up west of Baikal and there was only one thing to do – to salvage the vestiges of statehood in the Far East'. Tret′iakov, in fact, was already at Chita, canvassing the opinion of Semenov.[97]

Kolchak resilient

The Political Centre was undoubtedly wise to treat the Cabinet of Solidarity and its promises with circumspection. For whatever the sincerity of Pepeliaev and his colleagues' newfound commitment to democracy and reform, their projects would remain projects until they were ratified by the Supreme Ruler. Every element of the Irkutsk programme, consequently, bore the envoi: 'It is expected that Admiral Kolchak will confirm this decision upon his arrival at Irkutsk.'[98] But Kolchak was not destined to arrive at Irkutsk as Supreme Ruler. And, for as long as he retained his title in transit, the admiral would actually *refuse* the request of the Council of Ministers that he should ratify their new project on the State Land Assembly and would even attempt to forbid the reconvention of the SEC at Irkutsk.[99]

Of course, the developing spirit of resilement and retraction on the train of the Supreme Ruler could not be known during Pepeliaev's attempts at rapprochement with the Irkutsk socialists in late November. But there was already very good reason for the ministers to suspect that the Cabinet of Solidarity was not the path along which Kolchak expected to find the salvation of the White cause. During his afore-

96 *Arkhiv russkoi revoliutsii* (Berlin), Vol. 10 (1923), p. 180; Guins, Vol. 2, p. 463; Krol′, L., pp. 200–2.

97 Guins, Vol. 2, pp. 467, 471; *Union (Agence Télégraphique Russe)* (Paris) No. 216, 27.xii.1919.

98 *Union (Agence Télégraphique Russe)* (Paris) No. 210, 9.xii.1919; *Struggling Russia* (New York) Vol. 1, No. 41, 27.xii.1919, p. 654.

99 Guins, Vol. 2, p. 467; Konstantinov, pp. 133, 144–5.

mentioned direct-wire conversations with Vologodskii and Pepeliaev (of November 21st and 22nd), for example, in almost the same breath in which the Supreme Ruler had deemed the regeneration of the Council of Ministers to be 'absolutely necessary' and had held it to be 'unthinkable that the country could be run' without a Cabinet of Solidarity, he had announced his intention to establish a new advisory council on his own train, a body which he termed the 'Supreme Council'. This was to consist of the Main Commander-in-Chief and his deputy, the Chief of Staff, the Quartermaster General, the Premier and the Ministers of War, the Interior, Foreign Affairs, Ways and Communications, Food and Supply and their deputies.

Kolchak insisted that this new, irregular Star Chamber would be a purely advisory body, concerned only with affairs at the front, and that it would not impinge upon the prerogatives of the Council of Ministers in the manner in which the former Council of the Supreme Ruler had done.[100] That, however, was not the logical conclusion to be drawn from the decree, drafted by Ivanov-Rinov and signed by Kolchak on November 21st, which established the body. According to this document, the remit of the Supreme Council would include 'the elaboration of general instructions (*ukazaniia*) for the governing of the country in order to unite the activities of separate departments and co-ordinate their work with the army'.[101] As Guins commented, just as the Cabinet of Solidarity was trying to find its feet, this decree 'effectively abolished the Council of Ministers, replacing it with a semi-military, semi-civilian body'.[102] In fact, as only the Minister of Ways and Communications and the Deputy Minister of the Interior were actually aboard Kolchak's train at the time, the Supreme Council was more militaristic and less balanced than Guins implied – within days reports were reaching Allied representatives in the Far East and the newspapers of Vladivostok that on Kolchak's new 'Supreme Military Council' the army 'will control everything'.[103]

Such leaks must have damaged Pepeliaev's hopes for parley with the Political Centre. Had certain other aspects of the new premier's direct-wire conversations with Kolchak been made public, however, the Cabinet of Solidarity would have

100 Konstantinov, pp. 128–9, 132, 134.

101 Guins, Vol. 2, p. 457. According to Guins the Supreme Council had issued a number of decrees by November 25th, including a forlorn appeal for volunteers to a new Volunteer Army.

102 *ibid.*, p. 458.

103 Filat'ev, pp. 96–7; WO 33/957/4398 'Britmis (Vladivostok) to WO, 2.xii.1919'; *Ekho* (Vladivostok) 26.xi.1919.

been even more compromised. To Pepeliaev's suggestion that 'a rapprochement with the Czechs' should be a principle of the new régime, Kolchak had rejoined: 'What sort of rapprochement do you mean?' He expressed grave doubts as to whether the Legion would be interested in improving relations and retorted, 'I would rather pose to you the question of a rapprochement with Japan, who alone is in a position to help us with real force.'[104] Of course, back in October, the Kato mission to Omsk had not resulted in a concrete agreement (see above, pp. 494–5). But evidently Kolchak was not yet divested of the illusion that elements of the five Japanese divisions in the Far East under the command of General Suzuki, together with their Semenovite auxiliaries, might yet be induced to march as far west as the Novonikolaevsk–Taiga–Tomsk region so as to staunch the Red advance, thereby facilitating the withdrawal of the Czechoslovak Legion and providing a shield behind which the Whites might eliminate opposition in the rear and prepare a new offensive for 1920. At councils of war hosted by Commander-in-Chief Sakharov in early December this will-o'-the-wisp strategy had been approved by Kolchak (in preference to the equally fantastical alternative of heading south with the remains of the Russian Army to rendezvous with the forces of Dutov and Ataman Annenkov in the Barnaul–Biisk region, before retreating into Sinkiang and Mongolia pending a new struggle in the spring).[105]

In fact, by early December Kolchak seems to have determined that Japan was his only hope. This calculation, indeed, may well have been behind his decision to establish the Supreme Council – a martial edifice more likely to command respect among Tokyo's Expeditionary Force than a Cabinet of Solidarity and its flirting with the socialists. The Supreme Ruler was also at this time receiving misleading reports from his Quartermaster General, General Zankevich, that Japan was now more favourable to the White cause, and that 'two or three divisions might soon reach Baikal'. Consequently, on December 5th, Kolchak had telegraphed Sazonov in Paris to the effect that Russia would have to 'pay for her stupidity' with territory and with her natural resources: 'If Japan agrees to render assistance to Russia then she will

104 Konstantinov, p. 133.

105 Sakharov, K.V. *Belaia Sibir'*. Munich (1923), pp. 192–3. A less ambitious plan, possibly hatched some time later, was mentioned by Tret'iakov to Grondijs – it entailed the Japanese only coming as far west as Cheremkhovo to run the mines and hold the line while the Russian Army was re-organized in the Far East. See Grondijs, *Le Cas Koltchak*, pp. 65–6.

have the right to territorial compensation', the admiral declared, in a mood of evident desperation.[106]

It seems, therefore, that Kolchak had become set on a path quite contrary to the reformist road favoured by the Cabinet of Solidarity at Irkutsk. In fact, the only real concession that ministers were able to wring from the admiral in late November was a pledge not to launch what could only have been a suicidal attack on the Czechoslovak Legion in rebuttal of Pavlu and Girsa's memorandum of November 13th. On November 25th at Irkutsk had been received the text of an order from Kolchak's train – an obloquy which, whilst interpreting the memorandum as 'an attempt at political intrigue and blackmail on the part of its signatories' and not necessarily a reflection of the views of the Legion as a whole, nevertheless employed the most inflammatory and censorious language in deriding 'elements' of the Czechoslovak forces for maintaining links with 'groups indistinguishable from the Bolsheviks' and for a list of alleged 'anti-government' misdemeanours ranging from attempts to interfere in the composition of the government during 1918 to complicity in the Gajda putsch.[107] Kolchak's vitriolic tirade prompted the despatch of a barrage of telegrams from members of the Cabinet on November 26th–27th, on the one hand critical of the peremptory nature of the note (there had been no prior consultation with the government) and on the other warning that such a blunt and tactless challenge to the Czechoslovaks would be 'ruinous' and 'fatal to the whole national cause' because the very elements of Irkutsk society they were endeavouring to win over to the régime were in sympathy with the Legion and agreed with the substance of Pavlu and Girsa's critique of White rule. Having been told that Pepeliaev would otherwise resign as premier – and probably calculating on reflection that his own journey to Irkutsk might otherwise prove problematic – on November 30th, albeit with obvious reluctance, Kolchak agreed to 'suspend' his protest.[108] By that time, however, the damage would have been done. For, being in control of telegraph facilities from Novonikolaevsk to Irkutsk, the Legionnaires would certainly have intercepted and deciphered the offending missive and learned – if they were not already aware – of the Supreme Ruler's true regard for their eighteen-month service in Siberia.

106 Konstantinov, pp. 117–22; Livshits, S.G. *Imperialisticheskaia interventsiia v Sibiri, 1918–1920gg.* Barnaul (1979), p. 82.

107 Konstantinov, pp. 113–15.

108 *ibid.*, pp. 140–4.

The admiral was, of course, incorrigibly undiplomatic and such forbearance was not likely to last – indeed, within a month, as we shall see, he was to deliver the ultimate insult to the Czechoslovaks. In the meantime, however, in an attempt to forestall the broadcast of any more offensive diatribes and in order to have the Supreme Ruler officially endorse the programme of the Cabinet of Solidarity, Pepeliaev decided that he should return west to join Kolchak on his train in order to act as his chaperon. So it was that on December 2nd the premier embarked upon a journey which was to be not only fruitless but, ultimately, fatal.

Although Kolchak had left Omsk only a matter of days after his ministers, his eastward progress had been considerably slower than theirs, encumbered as he was by the trains of his entourage and the gold train as well as by his determination to remain in contact with the vestiges of the 2nd and 3rd Armies (themselves retreating, under the command of Voitsekhovskii and Kappel respectively, alongside the Trans-Siberian Railway and behind the train of Commander-in-Chief Sakharov). Consequently, it was only on the early morning of December 8th, three whole weeks after his departure from his capital, that the Supreme Ruler pulled into Station Taiga – the junction of the Tomsk branch line 900 km east of Omsk and, since early November, the headquarters of the 1st Army (which, it will be recalled, had been retired by Dieterichs before his replacement by Sakharov). At Taiga Kolchak was awaited by Viktor Pepeliaev and his younger brother Anatol, the Commander of the 1st Army. Together the stout and chain-smoking Siberian brothers and the increasingly nervy and emotional Kolchak spent the entire day ensconced in the admiral's wagon-lit before, towards evening, being joined by the newly arrived General Sakharov. When informed by Kolchak that the Pepeliaevs were hinting that the 1st Army might rebel and attempt to arrest the Supreme Ruler, Sakharov – whose animus against Anatol Pepeliaev had already been fully charged by the latter's refusal to participate in the abortive defence of Omsk in November and who was suspicious of the general's regionalist leanings – attempted to have Kolchak relieve the military brother of his command and merge the 1st Army with Voitsekhovskii's group. The Pepeliaevs' rejoinder was that the incompetent anti-hero of the defence of Omsk, Sakharov, should himself be replaced as Commander-in-

Chief by General Dieterichs, who for all his reactionary reputation might, as a seasoned commander, at least rekindle the confidence of the army.[109]

Whether Viktor Pepeliaev had gone west to join his brother in a premeditated attempt to have Kolchak either accept radical changes of government policy or have him removed is open to debate. In his memoirs Guins says that he, personally, doubted it.[110] Transcripts of direct wire conversations between the brothers prior to Viktor Nikolaevich's departure from Irkutsk which were published by Soviet historians later in the 1920s, however, do suggest that they had something of the kind in mind: details were studiously avoided, but their conversations of November 22nd, 24th and 26th were littered with vague allusions to 'that of which we spoke in Omsk' (presumably as Anatol had passed through the capital with his retiring army in October), observations that as nothing had really changed since the summer 'things cannot be delayed any longer', and urgings on the part of Anatol for his brother to come west because 'it is necessary for the affair'.[111]

Nevertheless, in a manner premeditated or not, after their face-off with Kolchak and Sakharov of the 8th, the brothers Pepeliaev were swift to act. On the morning of December 9th General Sakharov awoke to find himself and his staff under arrest and his train surrounded by machine-gun toting chasseurs of General Pepeliaev's personal guard. On being roughly escorted to the Pepeliaevs' train, the Commander-in-Chief was informed that he had 'too much influence' over Kolchak, that his conduct of military affairs would now be investigated and that Dieterichs was being summoned to resume command of the army in the field.[112] Then, some hours later on the 9th, the brothers despatched an extraordinary telegram to Kolchak (who had left Taiga during the night and was by then at Sudzhensk), urging the Supreme

109 Sakharov, pp. 193–5.

110 Guins, Vol. 2, p. 464.

111 Konstantinov, pp. 137–9. Back in August Viktor Pepeliaev had visited his brother at Tiumen after having received a telegram to the effect that Anatol believed the White movement could only be salvaged by 'the immediate convocation of a *Zemskii sobor*'. See Pepeliaev, V.N. 'Dnevnik', *Krasnye zori* (1923) Vol. 5, p. 50; and Pepeliaev, 'Razval kolchakovshchiny', pp. 64–6. Unfortunately an account of their deliberations at that meeting is missing from the published versions of Pepeliaev's diary.

112 Sakharov, pp. 197–9 and 'Sakharov (Taiga) to Kolchak, ?.xii.1919', in Smirnov et al. *Bor'ba za Ural i Sibir'*, pp. 348–50. Rumours at the time had it that Sakharov had been removed because since the loss of Omsk he had been solidly drunk. See Mel'gunov, Pt.3, Vol. 2, p. 79. The first news of the Taiga events to reach the outside world employed the practised euphemism that Sakharov had 'retired for reasons of health'. See *Union (Agence Télégraphique Russe)* (Paris) No. 214, 18.xii.1919.

Ruler to sign an act 'summoning a Siberian *Zemskii sobor'*, in the guise of which the people themselves may take into their hands the reconstruction of Siberia and choose a Siberian government'. Warning the admiral that 'this will not wait' and avowing that 'God and the people will be our judge', the brothers Pepeliaev gave the Supreme Ruler until midnight to sign a draft, which they appended, instructing the Council of Ministers to draw up an electoral law for the *Zemskii sobor'*. There was no indication of what action they – or, by implication, Anatol's 1st Army – might take if the order was not signed; and, in a subsequent conversation of December 9th with Kolchak's aide, General A.A. Mart'ianov, Viktor Pepeliaev denied that the note constituted an 'ultimatum'. It was, he said, 'an attempt to save the Supreme Ruler in spite of himself (*pomimo ego voli*)'.[113] And, at least for the time being, they clearly wanted Kolchak to sign rather than resign – his offer to relinquish supreme power had actually been refused by the brothers on the 8th, according to Sakharov. But an ultimatum, nevertheless, is what it amounted to.

There is no record of a direct response by Kolchak to the brothers' demands, although over the following forty-eight hours he did accept Sakharov's unusual departure from office and he did nominate General Kappel as Commander-in-Chief (having heard that Dieterichs's condition for resuming control was that he, Kolchak, must quit Siberia forthwith).[114] Nor, in the heat of the moment, had Pepeliaev even had Kolchak give written consent to the programme of the Cabinet of Solidarity which had been the ostensible aim of his mission west.[115] But by December 12th Kolchak was not under pressure from the Pepeliaevs to do anything. In fact, on that day Viktor Nikolaevich sent an apologetic message to the admiral (who was by then at Krasnoiarsk) in which he professed that he never had taken nor ever would 'take any action against the person of the bearer of Supreme authority' and had meant only to imply that, in his humble opinion, the government would fall unless a *Zemskii sobor'* was sanctioned.[116]

113 Konstantinov, pp. 146–7.

114 Sakharov, p. 199. Sakharov was subsequently released from incarceration on the evening of December 10th upon the arrival at Taiga of General Kappel. Meanwhile, however, at Irkutsk, at Pepeliaev's bidding the Council of Ministers was preparing a court-martial for him. See Konstantinov, pp. 148–9.

115 Guins, Vol. 2, p. 464.

116 Konstantinov, p. 149.

No attempt has ever been made to explain why Viktor Pepeliaev retreated from the brink of armed confrontation with the man whom he, more than any other individual, had been responsible for elevating to power. Yet, within days of the ultimatum, he was to leave his brother at Taiga and rush east to rejoin Kolchak's entourage at Krasnoiarsk. Perhaps he saw proximity to the Supreme Ruler as the best guarantee of personal safety and of a passage back to Irkutsk. Probably, moreover, he had concluded that western Siberia could not, in reality, be salvaged for the Whites by a *Zemskii sobor′*. For around Pepeliaev's ears, by the second week in December, White Siberia was all too clearly falling apart. And, if anything, his own actions had contributed to the general collapse. As General Filat′ev noted, however honourable were the Pepeliaevs' motives, the very fact that the commander-in-chief could be deposed so irregularly might only have served to demonstrate how weak was the authority of the Supreme Ruler and how disjointed his army.[117] Or, as Guins put it: the arrest of Sakharov 'was an illustration of the general collapse... It gave the signal for the outbreak everywhere of disorder and indiscipline.'[118]

Anomie

Nowhere in Siberia during the first half of December 1919 was 'disorder and indiscipline' more rampant than at Novonikolaevsk, the first important urban centre east of Omsk upon which, in hot pusuit of the Russian Army, elements of the 5th Red Army were bearing down at a rate of 25 km per day. As the Red Juggernaut approached, White intelligence reports from the town began to talk of discipline among soldiers of the town's military cantonment being 'altogether absent', of soldiers refusing to salute their officers, defiantly smoking at their posts and 'throwing away their arms at every opportunity'; meanwhile the local burghers were buying up railway wagons and fleeing east, and the less wealthy citizenry were keeping their heads down and attempting to avoid any excuse for retribution on the part of the Reds by refusing to have any contact with government forces. The workers of Novonikolaevsk were said to be welcoming the Bolshevik approach,

117 Filat′ev, D.B. *Katastrofa belogo dvizheniia v Sibiri, 1918–1922gg.* Paris (1985), p. 108.

118 Guins, Vol. 2, pp. 464–5.

while the peasantry of the district were interested only in seeing an end to the war: 'many care neither one way nor the other how it finishes – with a victory for the Siberian Government or for the Bolsheviks – as long as it finishes', read one report.[119]

Sensing an opportunity in these circumstances to overthrow the White authorities before the Red Army could claim the town for Soviet Russia, on December 6th–7th SR elements of the district zemstvo formed a Committee of Salvation and, in collaboration with a group of discontented officers of the 1st Siberian (Barabinsk) Regiment led by a twenty-six year old Captain Ivakin, attempted to seize the station and arrest General Voitsekhovskii and the staff of his 2nd Army as they passed through Novonikolaevsk. General Sakharov later insinuated that Ivakin was acting on the orders of his Commander-in-Chief, General Pepeliaev.[120] And, given that just three days later and 200 km to the east, the latter was himself to intern the Main Commander-in-Chief, that possibility cannot be totally discounted. Also, as one Soviet historian has pointed out, Ivakin and Pepeliaev had in common a demand for the immediate convocation of a Siberian Assembly.[121] However, as among Ivakin's desiderata was also a call for a truce with Soviet Russia – something which the Pepeliaevs were certainly *not* considering – the more likely scenario is that his action at Novonikolaevsk was the westernmost manifestation of the Political Centre and the associated CBMO, which, as we have seen, having despaired of raising a popular rebellion under the SR flag, had formulated the plan of igniting revolts among discontented elements of the White army from Vladivostok to the front. In this instance, however, the attempt failed, for in close proximity to Novonikolaevsk were retreating Allied contingents, in the shape of some 5,000 members of the Polish Legion, with no interest in having their eastward passage disrupted by mutinies. The Poles liberated Voitsekhovskii, forcibly dispersed the Committee of Salvation and arrested Ivakin (who was subsequently tried and shot alongside thirty-two of his cohorts).[122]

The Poles' unilateral action, however, could not restore the potency of the Russian Army's rearguard. The 2nd and 3rd Armies were now immobilized behind

119 Konstantinov, pp. 64–5.

120 Sakharov, p. 188.

121 Parfenov, 'Poslednie dni', pp. 90–1.

122 Papin, p. 85; Parfenov, P.S. *Bor'ba za Dal'nyi Vostok, 1920–1922gg.* Leningrad (1928), pp. 7–8; Mel'gunov, Pt.3, Vol. 2, pp. 86–8.

a 100 km log-jam of refugee trains stretching east from Chulym to Novonikolaevsk itself, while within the town increasing numbers of men from the 1st Army were deserting to celebrate the imminent arrival of the Reds in a desperate drunken spree which was not quieted even when the garrison commander had all the vodka he could find poured into the Ob (the revellers simply waited downstream for the alcohol to float to the surface of the river and siphoned it off).[123] When the 27th Division of the 5th Red Army reached the town a week later, on December 14th, they claimed to have captured 2,000 officers (including 30 generals), 31,000 troops, 1,000 machine-guns, 2 armoured trains, 190 echelons of military supplies and the last 200 pieces of White artillery.[124] Such figures may well have been exaggerated. But it is incontestable that after the events at Novonikolaevsk the Russian Army simply disintegrated, as White Siberia itself lay prostrated in agony before the Red advance: among the military detritus around the town the Bolsheviks counted 30,000 dead of typhus.[125]

From Novonikolaevsk the Red 30th Division pushed on along the Great Siberian Highway towards the university town of Tomsk where the Novonikolaevsk events were to repeat themselves – this time with a little more success for the SRs, although still falling short of their aim of gaining power in an urban stronghold in advance of the Red Army's arrival. Reports of precisely what happened here are few and sketchy, but it seems that on December 16th–17th at Tomsk and Taiga the 12th and 46th Regiments of the 1st Army, constituting the majority of the troops remaining at General Pepeliaev's disposal, refused to obey orders to evacuate the region. Instead they arrested and shot a number of their officers and announced their intention to sue for peace with the Red Army in the name of an autonomous Siberia.[126] The soldiers may well have been acting in response to the Political

123 Shebeko, B. 'Russian Civil War (1918–1922) and Emigration', University of California (Berkeley) Russian Émigré Series (1961), pp. 66–7.

124 *Istoriia Sibiri*. Leningrad (1968), Vol. 4, p. 131; *Istoriia grazhdanskoi voiny v SSSR*. Moscow (1959–1960), Vol. 4, pp. 350–1; Papin, p. 62; Andreev L. (ed.) 'K istorii razgroma vooruzhennykh sil Kolchaka', *Krasnyi arkhiv* No. 6 (1931), pp. 80–92; *Grazhdanskaia voina i voennaia interventsiia v SSSR: entsiklopediia*. Moscow (1983), pp. 400–1.

125 Stewart, G. *The White Armies of Russia*. New York (1933), p. 300.

126 Gromov, I.V. et al (eds.) *Partizanskoe dvizhenie v Zapadnoi Sibiri (1918–1920gg.): dokumenty i materialy*. Novosibirsk (1959), p. 725; FO 371/4100/210689 'Hodgson (Vladivostok) to FO, 19.i.1920' (Annex No. 1).

Centre-style appeals being distributed amongst them since December 9th by the Tomsk *guberniia* Organization of SRs.[127] Subsequent Soviet accounts, however, asserted that no formal Political Centre body was founded at Tomsk and that when Red Army units entered the town on December 20th they were greeted by a successful workers' rising instigated by a Bolshevik Revolutionary Committee in the name of Soviet power.[128] 30,000 White soldiers of the 1st Army and the Tomsk garrison then surrendered, without a battle, to the 3,000-strong advance guard of the Red Army, according to these sources.[129]

Before the Red's arrival at Tomsk, the last of the elements of the White 2nd and 3rd Armies still loyal to Kolchak had left the district and were defiling slowly eastwards towards the Eniseisk *guberniia* centre of Krasnoiarsk, reaching Achinsk by December 31st. Meanwhile at Krasnoiarsk, however, there had developed a situation in which another SR bid for power upped the ante in a number of respects: at Krasnoiarsk the Political Centre staked its claim not only *before* White forces had passed through and on to the east (rather, the vestiges of the Russian Army were fast approaching the town from the west), but before even the Supreme Ruler *himself* had left the town – Kolchak and his trains were still in the station. Moreover, on this occasion, as a result of the recruitment to their cause of very senior members of the Kolchak administration, at Krasnoiarsk the Political Centre agents were able to pretend to power not for a matter of hours or days, as at Novonikolaevsk or Tomsk, but for two whole weeks.

Kolchak's echelons had arrived at Krasnoiarsk on December 17th and there, shunted ignominiously into a siding, they remained until, having come to an arrangement with a particularly recalcitrant Czech station commandant on December 21st, the Supreme Ruler was allowed to proceed (albeit with a considerably diminished convoy). Little did Kolchak realize, however, that throughout his entire four-day stay at Krasnoiarsk, in a train parked next to his own, the staff of the official newspaper of General Zinevich's 1st Central Siberian Corps (*Na strazhe svobody*) was engaged in the printing and distribution of Political Centre propaganda

127 An example is included in Piontkovskii, S.A. (ed.) *Grazhdanskaia voina v Rossii (1919–1921gg.): khrestomatiia*. Moscow (1925), pp. 338–40.

128 Gromov, p. 725; *Istoriia grazhdanskoi voiny v SSSR*, Vol. 4, p. 351.

129 Eikhe, G.Kh. *Oprokinutyi tyl*. Moscow (1966), p. 340; Spirin, L.M. *Razgrom armii Kolchaka*. Moscow (1957), pp. 260–1.

– notably a 5,000-word leaflet signed by the 'Group of Democratic Organizations of Krasnoiarsk' calling for a truce with the Red Army and the convocation of a Siberian Constituent Assembly. The journalists, among them Mensheviks who had been serving the Russian Army for some time, were now actively engaged in plotting the overthrow of White power in collaboration with a so-called Committee of Salvation in Krasnoiarsk itself (the Committee being composed of SR elements of the *uezd* zemstvo board and the Eniseisk *guberniia* zemstvo board and led by the latter's chairman, G. Sibir'tsev, and the Political Centre agent, E.E. Kolosov).[130] By the time that Kolchak was able to depart, on December 21st, the Committee's influence was so great that only the station remained as a safe area for government forces. The commander of the Garrison, General Markovskii, no longer enjoyed any authority within the town and, on December 23rd, fled east, leaving General Zinevich in charge. The latter, who had just returned from a meeting with the Pepeliaevs at Taiga, decided to recognize the provisional authority within Eniseisk *guberniia* of the Political Centre organizations. He did so, he later explained in a wire to Kolchak's train, to avoid the pointless bloodshed he had witnessed during the earlier risings at Novonikolaevsk and Tomsk. The repentant general also appealed to the Supreme Ruler to step down in favour of a popular assembly and then, after consultation with Kolosov, issued orders for the arrest of Kolchak and his staff and began negotiations for a cease-fire in direct-wire conversations with commissars of the approaching Red Army.[131]

Initially it appeared that Zinevich was going to be successful in arranging some kind of local deal between the oncoming Bolsheviks and the Political Centre. However, the SRs had made the mistake – and not for the first or last time – of freeing all political prisoners in the town. Among them were the local Bolshevik leaders, N. Molchanov and D. Zorin, who proceeded to marshal their own considerable forces in this most industrialized of the Siberian towns and, with elements of the garrison supporting them, were able to seize power in the name of a Revolutionary Committee in a rising against Kolosov and Zinevich of January 3rd–4th 1920. Consequently, the screen Zinevich had planned to erect west of

130 Shidlovskii, G. 'Poslednie dni kolchakovshchiny', *Krasnaia letopis'* (Moscow–Leningrad), No. 1 (1929), p. 218; Zhurov, *Eniseiskoe khrest'ianstvo*, p. 173.

131 Konstantinov, pp. 140ff.

Krasnoiarsk as a guarantee against Red incursions never got off the ground and, on January 8th, Red Army units entered the town.[132]

Developments at Krasnoiarsk were a severe blow to General Kappel, Sakharov's successor as Commander-in-Chief of the Russian Army, who had actually been planning a desperate last stand in that region and had issued orders to that effect – his first as commander – on December 12th. By the end of the month, however, events had made such a scheme unworkable. It was not simply the psychological and logistical damage wrought by the series of anti-government risings of December which was undermining Kappel's plans, however. Nor was it only the tightening Czechoslovak grip on the Trans-Siberian Railway throughout the month – although, as we shall see, that was very damaging to the Whites. Quite simply, Kappel no longer had an army with which to fight: since the panic-stricken evacuation of Omsk, so encumbered by refugees and their own wives and children as to 'resemble more the migration of some nomadic tribe to fresh pastures than the manoeuvres of a regular army', in the words of one officer of the Russian Army, 'we were now a mere rabble pretending to be soldiers'.[133]

Harrowing accounts of the Russian Army's 1,500 km trek from Omsk to Krasnoiarsk through the depths of the Siberian winter are unmatched for their piteous horror, even by the tales of the retreat of the *Grande Armée* from Moscow in 1812 – for at least the French were going home; the Siberian Whites knew not where they were bound. Along a path forty kilometres south of the Trans-Siberian Railway the 3rd Army and its straggling civilian retinue crawled east by horse, sleigh and on foot through the exposed Barabinsk steppe and the roadless, primaeval and wolf-infested Shcheglovsk taiga. In these barren regions settlements – most of them boasting more letters in their names than inhabitants – were often some 100–150 km apart and, even when encountered, had usually been long since stripped bare of food and warm clothing by earlier arrivals. 'It was the graveyard of the 3rd

132 *Nezabyvaemoe. Vospominaniia uchastnikov revoliutsionnykh sobytii v Krasnoiarskom krae (1917–1920gg)*. Krasnoiarsk (1957), p. 100; Shidlovskii, pp. 219–21; *Istoriia Sibiri*, Vol. 4, p. 134. Among the Bolshevik sympathizers was Zinevich's Chief of Staff, Colonel Rozanov – a relative of General S.N. Rozanov. See *Gody ognevnye: sbornik vospominanii uchastnikov bor'by za vlast' sovetov (1918–1920gg.)*. Krasnoiarsk (1926), pp. 373–4. According to Mel'gunov, Zinevich was later executed by the Reds (see Mel'gunov, Pt.3, Vol. 2, p. 90). A Soviet source has it, however, that he was imprisoned but later released (Shidlovskii, p. 221).

133 Fedotoff-White, D. *Survival Through War and Revolution in Russia*. Philadelphia (1939), pp. 235, 263.

Army', recalled one survivor of the terrible Shcheglovsk march some half a century later: 'I can still see those drawn faces and sunken eyes – men moving like the living dead through the taiga.'[134] Meanwhile further north, along the railway and along the Siberian *trakt*, struggled the 2nd Army and the few remaining loyalist units of the 1st. Theirs should have been a more commodious route, but the stream of scores of thousands of refugees also heading along it made it no more passable, particularly after the revolts at Novonikolaevsk and Taiga: 'Crowds of pedestrians and innumerable sleigh trains from the region north of the highway shouldered into our traffic, playing havoc with it', recalled an officer's wife of this path.[135] And, as their progress slowed to a mere ten or twelve kilometres a day, the rearmost echelons were gradually overhauled by the Reds – 180 trains were in Bolshevik hands by December 18th. The northern route lay also through districts more populous and rich in foodstuffs than was the southern. But even when they had stocks, the wary Siberian peasants shunned the passing White convoys for fear of reprisals when the Reds arrived.[136]

Along both routes the common enemies were the cold and typhus. At least half of the refugees were afflicted with the latter scourge by some counts.[137] A British officer was told that 60,000 died of typhus at Novonikolaevsk alone from November 1919 to April 1920 and that the Bolsheviks found 20,000 more corpses between Omsk and the Ob, yet he had seen only one coffin during his traversal of that sector. The ground was frozen too solidly to bury the dead anyway, so cadavers were stacked 'like logs of wood' alongside the stations, where their infected clothes were stolen by passers-by, thus to pass the disease on to others.[138] Stricken soldiers in a hospital train overtook another observer, looking like 'uniformed skeletons':

> They did not walk but crawled around our train, emaciated from hunger and typhus; their fevered brains unable to control their senseless activity; they crawled about eating

134 Shebeko, pp. 72–3.

135 Ilyin, O. *White Road*. New York (1984), p. 89.

136 Grondijs, L.H. *La Guerre en Russie et en Sibérie*. Paris (1922), p. 536.

137 Shebeko, p. 62; Koudrey, V. *Once a Commissar*. London (1938), pp. 223ff; Levinson, A. 'Poezdka iz Peterburga v Sibir′ v ianvare 1920g.', *Arkhiv russkoi revoliutsii* (Berlin), Vol. 3, pp. 190–209.

138 McCullagh, F. *A Prisoner of the Reds: The Story of a British Officer Captured in Siberia*. London (1921), pp. 31, 35.

> snow. Really they were just awaiting the same fate as those whose bodies were already piled high by the side of the tracks.[139]

Others did not wait, but surrendered themselves to an early death, prefaced by a lunatic, intoxicated relief, through imbibing motor fuels.[140]

Cruelly, the typhus would surface mainly when a sufferer was at last able to find shelter in some warm hut or railway carriage. Outside the harsh Siberian frost would usually keep the virus and the lice which carried it dormant.[141] But outside the terrible Siberian blizzard (the *buran*) could also freeze a man or even a horse solid within minutes: quaking evacuees, all too aware that they could be next, passed entire groups of their predecessors, sometimes still in the saddle, but long dead, black-limbed and petrified by the cold.[142] To avoid such a fate, drastic preventative measures had sometimes to be taken to counter incipient frostbite: 'I once saw a soldier sitting on a bank with his shoes off, cutting off his frozen toes with a pair of shears', recalled Boris Shebeko.[143]

One final contribution to the plight of civilian refugees and to the peril of the Russian Army was the fact that, as the White régime disintegrated, peasant partisan armies more or less sympathetic to the Bolshevik cause began appearing – or, rather, reappearing – in the railway zone. As far back as the summer of 1918, the iniquities and cruelties of White rule in the Siberian countryside had been met by militant armed resistance on the part of the region's peasantry. Even in the richest agricultural districts, where the rural population was among the most prosperous of the old Empire and was not naturally inclined towards Bolshevism, White misrule, economic mismanagement and, in particular, attempts at forced mobilizations – especially when the local administration was in the hands of one of Kolchak's recusant Cossack governors – had inspired the Siberian yeomanry to oppose the Omsk régime by force of arms. There were estimated to be some 35,000–40,000

139 Vitol'dova-Liutik, p. 20.

140 McCullagh, pp. 15–16. See also McCullagh, F. 'In Red Ekaterinburg', *Fortnightly Review* No. 108 (1920), pp. 724–37.

141 Shebeko, p. 62; Serebrennikov, I.I. *Velikii otkhod: razseianie po Azii belykh russkikh armii, 1919–1923gg.* Harbin (1936), pp. 12–13.

142 Khudiakov, N. 'Iz perezhitago' *Slovo* (Shanghai) No. 168, cited in Serebrennikov, p. 10.

143 Shebeko, p. 62.

partisan fighters in Siberia by the middle of 1919. Evgennii Kolosov, who made a contemporary study of the phenomenon, constructed a map upon which, on the basis of government reports, he plotted partisan activity: 'There was not a single *uezd* from Semipalatinsk to Irkutsk and beyond into Amur and the Far East across which was not drawn the line of a partisan front', he recorded.[144] The *stavka* had its own map, on which risings were plotted with red dots. According to Budberg, by the middle of 1919 the countenance of White Siberia had come to resemble that of one afflicted with an advanced case of typhus.[145]

The partisan movement had considerable military success against the Whites in 1918 and 1919. Important regional centres such as Slavgorod, Zmeinogorsk and Minusinsk were in rebel hands for some time, while, immediately to both the north and south of the railway zone in eastern Siberia, so-called 'partisan republic' exclaves were hewn from White territory around the *volost'* centres of Taseevo (Kansk *uezd*) and Stepnoi Badzhei (Krasnoiarsk *uezd*), whence some occasionally cripplingly effective raids were launched upon the railway. A concerted government offensive during the late spring and summer of 1919 – an operation which had involved the commitment of some 20,000–30,000 troops – and the declaration of martial law throughout Eniseisk and Irkutsk *guberniias*, eventually succeeded in driving the partisan menace either north into the *taiga* or south towards Uriankhaiskii *krai* (Tuva) and the borders of Mongolia. But although temporarily contained, the partisans were not eradicated – and when the Kolchak régime began to crumble, with their ranks swelled by new recruits to a total of 150,000 across all Siberia, the partisans converged afresh on the Trans-Siberian Railway. There, either independently or in co-ordinated operations with the vanguard of the Red Army, the partisans sniped at the flanks of the fleeing Whites. During November–December 1919 the Altai partisans (the Western Siberian Partisan Army) under E.M. Mamontov and I.V. Gromov captured Slavgorod (November 20th), Kamen (November 28th) and Barnaul (December 10th) and had closed on Kainsk and Novonikolaevsk in time to assist regular Red Army units in establishing Soviet rule. Meanwhile, in Eniseisk *guberniia*, partisans commanded by P.E. Shchetinkin and A.D. Kravchenko had driven north from their summer fastness at Belotsarsk (Kyzyl) to engulf Minusinsk (which had been abandoned by its terrified White garrison) on

144 Kolosov, *Sibir' pri Kolchake*, p. 48.

145 Budberg, Vol. 15, p. 327.

September 13th before closing on Krasnoiarsk and Achinsk in December, and uniting with the 5th Red Army outside the latter town on January 2nd 1920. On that same day a force under V.G. Iakovenko emerged from the *taiga* at Kansk and awaited the arrival of the 5th Red Army, joining it on January 15th. Further east, before December's end much of Irkutsk *guberniia* was in the hands of partisan groups loyal to D.E. Zverev and N.A. Kalandarashvili, who were biding their time, merely harrying the passing refugee traffic, before attempting an assault on the new White capital on the Angara.[146]

When those refugees who had taken the southern route finally began to emerge from the forests near Achinsk, hoping to rejoin the railway traffic, a further cruel blow awaited them – on December 17th a huge explosion at the station, caused by the

146 Over the years an almost absurdly voluminous historiography of the partisan movement in Siberia was developed in the Soviet Union – *vide* the bibliographical collection *Bor'ba za vlast' Sovetov vo Vostochnoi Sibiri*. Irkutsk (1962), which listed no less than 1,434 publications on the subject (compared to only twenty-one on urban working class opposition to the Whites). Most works, however, are at best of marginal interest – being more concerned with substantiating the dubious claims a) that there was an exclusively Bolshevik leadership and motivation among the partisans and b) that the movement was equally hostile to both the democratic counter-revolution and the Whites than with an objective history of the phenomenon. Beginning with the works of A. Abov [A.A. Anson] – 'Neobkhodimo vnesti iasnost', *Sibirskie ogni* (Novosibirsk), No. 10 (1930), pp. 91–4; *O partizanskom dvizhenii v Sibiri*. Novosibirsk (1932) – and the later works of V.D. Vegman – *Vooruzhennye vosstaniia protiv Kolchaka v gorodakh i raionakh Sibiri*. Novosibirsk (1928) and *Povstanicheskoe dvizhenie na Altae*. Novosibirsk (1935) – the Stalinist orthodoxy reached its nadir with the publication of the heavily doctored memoirs of A.D. Kravchenko – *Za vlast' Sovetov*. Moscow (1947) – but had already drawn sufficient ammunition from the publication of unashamedly pro-Bolshevik memoirs in the late 1920s: *vide* Shchetinkin, P.E. *Bor'ba s kolchakovshchinoi*. Novosibirsk (1929); Chuev, G. 'Chernodol'skoe vosstanie', *Sibirskie ogni* (Novosibirsk), Nos. 5–6 (1926), pp. 157–66; Obukhov, N.K. 'Vosstanie minusinskikh khrest'ian v 1918g.', *Sibirskie ogni* (Novosibirsk), No. 6 (1929), pp. 140–51. Few refinements were made to the orthodox approach by the studies of the post-Stalin period, although some are notable (and useful) in that, for the first time in this vast literature, they attempted to present a general, all-Siberian account of events: *vide* Plotnikov, I.F. *V belogvardeiskom tyle*. Sverdlovsk (1978); Zhurov, Iu.V. *Grazhdanskaia voina na Sibirskoi derevne*. Krasnoiarsk (1986). The most complex and rounded approach, therefore, is still to be found in publications of the pre-Stalin era: *vide* El'tsin, V. 'Krest'ianskoe dvizhenie v Sibiri', *Proletarskaia revoliutsiia*, No. 49 (1926), pp. 5–48, No. 50 (1926), pp. 51–82; Kolosov, E.E. 'Krest'ianskoe dvizhenie pri Kolchake', *Byloe*, Vol. 20 (1922), pp. 223–67 and *Sibir' pri Kolchake*, pp. 9–56; Maksakov, V. *Partizanskoe dvizhenie v Sibiri*. Moscow (1926). But they too often had a political axe to grind (usually Trotskyist or SR) and need to be treated with care. Consequently, the first post-*glasnost'* review of the literature was justified in concluding that 'trustworthy information is practically absent' in the polemical Soviet historiography and that 'in sum, today it is not possible on the basis of published materials to present a scientifically authenticated general picture of the partisan movement' – Shishkin, V.I. 'Diskussionnye problemy istorii partizanskogo dvizheniia v Sibiri v Sovetskoi istoriografii 20-x–nachala 30-x godav', in Gushchin, N.Ia. (ed.) *Sotsial'naia aktivnost' trudiashchikhsia sovetskoi sibirskoi derevni*. Novosibirsk (1988), p. 6.

mishandling of naval mines on a munitions train, had entirely blocked the line.[147] Both soldiers and civilians who still had the strength then continued on foot towards Krasnoiarsk, passing miles of stationary trains. They were hoping for refreshment and rest in the town, only to receive news as they approached of Zinevich's desertion to the rebels.[148]

For the vast majority of civilian refugees from the west this was to be the end of the line. Their terrible 1,200 km flight from Omsk had been in vain, for there was no further movement of trains through Krasnoiarsk – except for those of the Polish Legion which negotiated a passage with the rebels – and to plunge once again into the *taiga* was too horrible to contemplate. As for the army, there was no question of attempting to recapture the town from the rebels - many soldiers had already discarded their arms in order to lighten their loads and the last of the artillery had been abandoned at Novonikolaevsk.[149] On December 27th, therefore, Kappel was only too glad to receive orders from Kolchak to the effect that he should retire to the east, with as many men as could be saved, avoiding any towns en route unless they could be taken without a fight.[150] On January 6th the order was duly given and the remaining loyal elements of the Russian Army proceeded to circumnavigate Krasnoiarsk and set off on a new 'ice march'. At least 25,000 soldiers, however, finally deserted the White cause at Krasnoiarsk.[151] Among them were many officers, who attempted to conceal their rank in fear of the fast approaching Reds: 'the streets were so thickly littered with epaulettes as to suggest the idea of fallen leaves in autumn', recalled a witness to these events.[152] Others, too weak to proceed further but terrified of the Bolshevik Nemesis, took another way out: 'there was an epidemic of suicides', recalled N. Khudiakov, citing cases of the desperate

147 Klerzhe, G.I. *Revoliutsiia i grazhdanskaia voina: lichnye vospominaniia (Chast' pervaia)*. Mukden (1932) pp. 180–1, and Prinsep, E.S.N. 'Knox's Mission to Siberia: The Personal Experiences of one of its Members', *Army Quarterly* Vol. 81 (1960), No. 1, p. 67 give eye-witness accounts of this event without providing casualty figures. Ilyin (*White Road*, p. 135) makes the hyperbolic claim that 'thousands were killed'.

148 'Kapitan K.', 'Lednoi pokhod' *Russkoe obozrenie* (Peking), cited in Serebrennikov, *Velikii otkhod*, p. 10.

149 Guins, *Sibir'*, Vol. 2, pp. 549–50; Serebrennikov, *Velikii otkhod*, pp. 13–14.

150 Konstantinov, *Poslednie dni*, p. 91. This was the last message Kolchak was able to transmit to Kappel, as from the beginning of January Zinevich and his subsequent Bolshevik masters at Krasnoiarsk cut communications between the Supreme Ruler and the Commander-in-Chief.

151 Filat'ev, *Katastrofa*, pp. 97, 100–1.

152 McCullagh, p. 22; 'McCullagh Report, December 1919' (*Pares Papers*, Box 41).

throwing themselves under the wheels of the all too infrequently passing trains, or begging their friends to shoot them. He himself witnessed one old colonel, who had been refused a berth on a Polish train, shooting his wife and daughter before committing suicide on a station platform.[153]

Even the most senior staff officers in Kappel's train now realized, in the words of General Klerzhe, that thenceforth it had to be 'every man for himself'. Klerzhe and some companions then proceeded to make their way through Krasnoiarsk, incognito, aboard a Polish echelon. Having passed through the town, they concluded that it might actually have been recaptured, even with the dilapidated force at Kappel's disposal: 'But now nobody was seriously thinking of resurrecting the front,' said Klerzhe: '"To Baikal! To Baikal" was the motto of those terrible days.'[154]

'Drowning men'

The Trans-Siberian Railway was, of course, still in the hands of its Czechoslovak garrison. But this was of cold comfort to the fleeing Whites by December 1919, for by that time the Legionnaires had every reason to be heartily sick of Kolchak, Siberia and the thankless task of policing the line to which the Allies had condemned them. Publications celebrating the first anniversary of the founding of the Czechoslovak Republic burned with a longing to return home to the world of democracy and freedom – and warmth.[155] Yet, despite official protests having been lodged through General Janin by the Legion's commander, General Jan Syrovy, the decision taken by the Allies to evacuate the Czechoslovaks remained at the level of a general principle throughout the autumn of 1919, with no practical steps having been taken towards the repatriation of the units already in the Far East, let alone the 200 echelons of the 1st and 2nd Czechoslovak Divisions deployed along the railway from Irkutsk to Krasnoiarsk and from Krasnoiarsk to Taiga

153 Khudiakov, in Serebrennikov, *Velikii otkhod*, p. 12.

154 Klerzhe, p. 181.

155 See, for example, Kudela, J. *Pervaia godovshchina Chekhoslovatskoi respubliki*. Irkutsk (1919), pp. 20, 27 and *passim*.

respectively.[156] The memorandum of November 13th had already signalled the querulous mood of the Legion as a result of this delay. But far worse was to come. Kolchak's vicious attack on Pavlu and Girsa of November 25th, although not published, was certainly not unknown to the Czechoslovak leaders. Moreover, they were also aware of the impending rising at Irkutsk, of the open rebellions at Novonikolaevsk, Tomsk and Krasnoiarsk, of the disarray of the Russian Army evinced by the arrest of Sakharov at Taiga, and of the imminent descent upon their precious railway link to the coast of the partisan armies swarming through Eniseisk and Irkutsk *guberniias*. White Siberia, never a comfortable billet for the moderate-tempered sons of Bohemia and Moravia, had descended into chaos by the beginning of December 1919 and, venting their frustration, the Legionnaires began to conduct themselves in a manner which could only complete that dissolution and seal the fate of the Supreme Ruler: as a man, and of their own accord, the Czechoslovaks began to move east.

As the White order collapsed, the only way in which the Legion could be sure of getting all its men out of eastern Siberia was to ensure that their own trains remained at the head of the eastbound flood of traffic. And, as the Legionnaires were the effective proprietors of the Trans-Siberian line by December – in control of stations, traffic direction, the supply of fuel and rolling stock and masters of the telegraph system – this they could do without too much difficulty. Thus, as early as November 28th 1919, General Sakharov was angrily complaining to General Syrovy that Czechoslovak units were commandeering all locomotives in the Taiga sector of the line in order to move their own men east and were even uncoupling engines from westbound coal trains, thereby compounding the log-jam of stranded engines west of Tomsk and contributing to the catalogue of refugee deaths.[157]

The anti-government risings and disorders of the first fortnight of December added a final note of urgency to the Legion's efforts to extricate itself from the White mire and to complete its long katabasis. Along the line some regiments (for example the 6th, near Achinsk) now began openly fraternizing with rebel forces and forming local armistices with Red partisans in their efforts to ensure a trouble free passage east.[158] The Legion's command structure seemed to be breaking down,

156 WO 33/957/3781 'Britmis (Vladivostok) to WO, 8.x.1919'.

157 Kotomkin, A. *O chekhoslovatskikh legionerakh v Sibiri, 1918–1920gg. Vospominaniia i dokumenty*. Paris (1930), pp. 85–6; see also *FRUS: 1919 (Russia)*, p. 227.

158 Becvar, G. *The Lost Legion: A Czechoslovakian Epic*. London (1939), pp. 225–32.

anarchy threatened, and on December 12th General Syrovy informed his nominal superior, Janin (who was at Irkutsk), that unless the order was immediately given to begin the evacuation of the Legion, he would be unable to answer for the consequences. Moreover, insisted Syrovy, the order of evacuation must be precisely that which had previously been determined by the Allied command – namely, first the Czechoslovaks; then the Poles and the small contingents of Rumanians, Serbs and Italians; and, finally, the Russians. Recognizing that nothing was going to stop the Czechoslovaks' flight and probably hoping that a semblance of official sanction might enable him to reimpose his authority over the men at a later date, Janin gave Syrovy permission to proceed. Within days the Legion had replaced all Russian station commanders east of the Ob with its own men, bearing specific orders from Syrovy (dated December 15th) to permit no Russian echelons to move in sectors east of Novonikolaevsk until all Czechoslovak traffic was clear. The eastbound (southern) line of the double-tracked Trans-Siberian Railway was to be reserved exclusively for those Czech trains, while the westbound (northern) line was used only for the movement of coal from the Cheremkhovo mines near Irkutsk into the fuel-starved sector from Taiga to Krasnoiarsk.[159]

The effect of all this on the Russian evacuation was devastating: Kolchak and his seven echelons were initially detained at Mariinsk (on December 10th) as local Czechoslovaks commandeered the Supreme Ruler's own locomotives, and then put on a siding at Krasnoiarsk to simmer impotently at the Legion's effrontery for several days. Meanwhile, at Achinsk, Commander-in-Chief Kappel also had his engine impounded.[160] Most tragically of all, some 120 echelons of civilian refugees, including many hospital trains, ground to a halt west of Novonikolaevsk and waited, terrified, without food or fuel, to be overtaken by the Red Army at a rate of 10–20 trains a day.[161] This was too much for some of the Russians to bear. From Kolchak's train Colonel Syroboiarskii telegraphed Janin, fuming about 'treachery unequalled in history'; while General Kappel, at Taiga, dashed off a brusque wire to Syrovy on December 18th demanding either a reversal of his evacuation order or 'satisfaction', in the form of a duel, for the Czech commander's

159 Grondijs, *La Guerre*, pp. 532–3; WO 33/957/4537 'Britmis (Vladivostok) to WO, 22.xii.1919'.

160 Grondijs, *Le Cas Koltchak*, pp. 75–82; Parfenov, 'Poslednie dni', pp. 91–2.

161 WO 33/957/4542 'Britmis (Vladivostok) to WO, 23.xii.1919'.

having slighted the honour of the Supreme Ruler and the Russian Army.[162] Kolchak himself, meanwhile, let fly a vitriolic circular to Allied representatives, inveighing against the Czechoslovak interference with his own progress and demanding that passage should at least be afforded to civilian refugees and to the sick and wounded of the Russian Army.[163]

This bitter invective against Syrovy was redoubled in accounts of this affair over the next half-century: accusations of Syrovy's 'blatant betrayal of the Allies' are embellished by extravagant claims that at least half of the 'damned' Czechoslovak trains which he had given free rein to move east were devoted to the transportation of booty or brothels or both, while 'thousands of Russian men, women and children were condemned to death'.[164] Others, however, who were perhaps better acquainted with Siberian reality during the civil war, whilst decrying Syrovy's decision to block civilian traffic as 'odious', denied that the Legion's trains were particularly lavish – some had, after all, housed 100–150 men and their baggage for nearly two years.[165] Syrovy himself, having promised Kappel that they might cross swords after the last Czech soldier had left Siberia and his duty had been thereby discharged, countered the Russian bluster at the time and justified his decision by claiming that had Kolchak's railway administration done its job in previous months and made contingency plans for the stockpiling of coal on the Taiga–Krasnoiarsk sector, it would not have been necessary for him to deny eastbound traffic access to the up line, thereby facilitating a faster rate of evacuation for all. Moreover, continued the vexed, one-eyed general, far more trains had attempted to depart west from Omsk in November than the system could possibly sustain as far as Irkutsk even without the ongoing complications of the White collapse.[166] In addition, he alleged, with some justification, since the fall of Omsk 'dozens of Russian echelons' conveying Russian Army generals in panic-stricken flight had been forcing their way east, on both lines, disrupting the coal supply and paying scant regard to the effects

162 Kotomkin, pp. 94–8; Skacel, J. *S geralem Syrovym v Sibiri*. Prague (n.d.), pp. 111–19.

163 Grondijs, *Le Cas Koltchak*, pp. 85–6.

164 Nefedrov, N. 'Kak bylo zaversheno pravitel'stvo admirala Kolchaka', *Veche* (Paris), No. 2 (1985), pp. 128–35; Fedulenko, B. 'Rol' byvshchikh soiuznikov Rossii po otnosheniiu k Belomu dvizheniiu' (*Museum of Russian Culture*), pp. 23–4; Mel'gunov, *Tragediia admirala Kolchaka*, Pt.3, Vol. 2, p. 74.

165 Grondijs, *Le Cas Koltchak*, p. 40; Grondijs, *La Guerre*, p. 532.

166 *Ceskoslovensky denik* (Irkutsk) 23.xii.1919; WO 33/957/4542A 'Knox (Irkutsk) to Britmis (Vladivostok), 23.xii.1919'.

their selfishness would have on the removal of civilians and the wounded, breaching the agreed order of evacuation, and making it ever more likely that overtaken Czechoslovaks would be drawn into a rearguard battle with the Reds which he had specific instructions from Prague to avoid at all costs. Finally, and barbedly, Syrovy ventured that Kolchak himself was hardly helping to ease the fuel shortages and congestion on the line by having insisted on travelling in seven trains – why even Tsar Nicholas II had been satisfied with five during World War I, he noted.[167]

Although many commentators on this episode have devoted considerable space to the allocation of guilt vis-à-vis Syrovy and the Russian military (very few of them being charitable to the Czech) it seems a rather pointless exercise. As General Knox reported of the conflicting charges at the time, 'there is probably truth in both versions'.[168] Certainly the most pertinent summation was made by the Dutch war correspondent, L.H. Grondijs. Vis-à-vis the Trans-Siberian Railway, he said:

> The relative positions of the Russians and the Czechoslovaks resembled two drowning men, both scrambling to get onto a plank which could bear the weight of only one man.[169]

In such a situation the issue is resolved not by threats, recrimination or moral justification but by the application of power. It was might, not right, that mattered. And in that game the Legionnaires, with their monopoly of the line from Novonikolaevsk to Irkutsk, seemed to hold all the trumps, as they proceeded in their single-minded evacuation in defiance of Russian bluster and accusation. However, Kolchak and the Whites did have one ace up their sleeve. The problem was that to play it might ultimately prove more dangerous than keeping it hidden.

At some point after leaving Omsk – in all probability following his conference on Sakharov's train during the first week in December at which possible strategies were discussed – Kolchak had already enquired of Ataman Semenov, the cruel master of Transbaikalia, as to whether it was within his power to establish a secure bastion for further White operations in the east by despatching Cossacks to Irkutsk to reinforce

167 Grondijs, *Le Cas Koltchak*, pp. 105–6; Grondijs, *La Guerre*, p. 532.

168 WO 33/957/4542A 'Knox (Irkutsk) to WO, 23.xii.1919'.

169 Grondijs, *La Guerre*, p. 533.

the town's potentially unsound garrison.[170] As December waned, the need to buttress such a refuge became all the more urgent – because the trail of SR risings along the Trans-Siberian Railway threatened to culminate in a seizure of power by the Political Centre at Kolchak's new capital. This was as clear to the ministers already in the town as it was to their eastbound leader and, having been snubbed by the Political Centre, Acting Prime Minister Tret′iakov had visited General Janin on December 15th to ask for Allied assistance in pacifying Irkutsk. The supplicant minister received a curt reply to the effect that the crisis was all of Kolchak's own making and that he, Janin, could do nothing. Then, proudly scorning the Frenchman's suggestion that he throw himself on the charity of the Legion, Tret′iakov too decided to play the Semenov card: he departed for Chita and an interview with the ataman which he described to local Allied representatives as being the 'last hope' of the Whites.[171]

Semenov's response to appeals for assistance from those whose endeavours he had been deliberately and maliciously frustrating for the past eighteen months seemed, initially, to be surprisingly amiable and accommodating. On December 20th, after his meeting with Tret′iakov, he issued an impassioned declaration 'To ALL! All! All!', appealing to Syrovy and the Czechoslovaks, 'in the name of Slav brotherhood and in the name of humanity', to return the requisitioned engines to Kolchak and to speed the passage east of the echelons of sick and wounded trapped by their actions. This fraternal appeal, however, concluded with a threat:

> Brothers! Stop! Think!... If you do not accede to this demand I, with a heavy heart, will apply all the military means at my disposal to force you to do your duty before humanity for the sake of your tormented Sister, Russia.[172]

However, when it came to the committing of troops to Kolchak's service rather than the issuing of sentimental appeals and threats, Semenov was – as always – more reticent. Via his official envoy on Kolchak's train, General Syroboiarskii, the ataman had been intimating that he would not feel able, as was Kolchak's conation, to reinforce Irkutsk unless his own base in Transbaikalia was secure. To this end, he 'requested' a promotion to the rank of Commander-in-Chief of all Forces in the Far

170 Konstantinov, pp. 157–8.

171 *DBFP*, pp. 684–5, 687, 699–700; Parfenov, 'Poslednie dni', p. 92.

172 *Vostochnyi kur′er* (Chita) 20.xii.1919, cited in *ibid.*, p. 93.

East and on the CER zone. At first the admiral declined to issue such an order, citing procedural difficulties in having such a move sanctioned by the Allied commanders in the Far East, a general (and uncharacteristically judicious) reluctance to issue orders of the repercussions of which he could not be certain, and adding for good measure that he could not for the life of him see what bearing Semenov's rank had on his martial ability to secure Irkutsk. Still, on Semenov's instructions, Syroboiarskii continued to press the matter until on December 21st his interview with the Supreme Ruler was curtailed as the admiral bawled, 'This is simply blackmail!'[173]

Within forty-eight hours, however, Kolchak had changed his mind. News that SR risings were erupting in Cheremkhovo, Irkutsk and other points on his route east as well as renewed indignities in the shape of Czechoslovak interference with his train as it crawled east along the sector between Krasnoiarsk and Nizhneudinsk, had apparently convinced him that he should pay Semenov's price. In the end it was a decision which was to cost him his life. On December 23rd, having notified General Oi of his intentions, Orders No. 240 and No. 241 of the Supreme Ruler were issued, promoting Semenov to the rank of Lieutenant-General and uniting under him – one who had insulted Kolchak so often and done more than any other to discredit the White régime both at home and abroad – the command of Zabaikalskaia *oblast′*, Priamurskii *krai* and the Irkutsk Military District. His task was said to be 'the safeguarding of state security and order in the deep rear'.[174]

Semenov's promotion was decreed entirely without reference to the government at Irkutsk. Even the new Minister of War, General Khanzhin, was not informed. This was hardly surprising, as Guins accepted, because by this time the Cabinet of Solidarity at Irkutsk had, to all intents and purposes, ceased to exist – Premier Pepeliaev was on Kolchak's train, his deputy, Tret′iakov, was in Chita and at least half a dozen ministers, having found their presence elsewhere to be urgently required, had also slipped away to the east. Nevertheless, the fact that such an important move had been made without their knowledge could not but further discredit the remaining ministers: 'It placed the government in an extremely illogical and difficult position', said Guins. The Allied High Commissioners gathered at Irkutsk might now disregard the opinions of the Cabinet altogether if they chose to

173 Konstantinov, pp. 158–60; *DBFP*, p. 684.

174 Tinskii, G. *Ataman Semenov: ego zhizn′ i deiatel′nost′*. n.p. (n.d.), pp. 21–2.

do so.[175] More immediately, any lingering thoughts among the Political Centre of reaching a peaceful accommodation with the government evaporated with Kolchak's summoning of Semenov over the cabinet's head; while, at the same time, Czechoslovak fury at Kolchak for having called upon such a notorious bandit to restore order was distilled into Syrovy's one-word reply to Semenov's missive of December 20th: '*Poprobuite*! (Try it!)'.[176]

The simple promotion of Semenov, however, was probably not sufficient in itself to have put the last nail into the coffin of Kolchakia. The measure infuriated both the Legion and the rebels whilst – as Kolchak had himself had known – in no way augmenting Semenov's capacity or desire to secure a White abri at Irkutsk for the Supreme Ruler. Semenov owed the power he enjoyed in 1919 to the employment of terror and to the support of the Japanese, not to the ability to marshal troops for large-scale military operations. In fact, at the absolute maximum, he had no more than 8,000 reliable men at his disposal who, according to a British survey, were unlikely to have prevailed against the mass risings beginning to engulf Irkutsk *guberniia* – to say nothing of the 30,000 envenomed Czechoslovaks still flooding east. Not that Semenov was willing to commit his 8,000. On December 24th he was to issue an order for the transfer to Irkutsk of only a small force under Ataman Skipetrov, consisting of two cavalry regiments, two infantry regiments and three armoured trains.[177] As we shall see, the Skipetrov expedition had a minimum military impact upon events at Irkutsk whilst serving only to confirm in the minds both of the SRs who wanted to grab power in Eastern Siberia and the Legionnaires who wanted to leave the region that the main threat to them was not now the Red Army to the west but the forces of reaction to the east.

There may also, however, have been an additional element to Skipetrov's mission which finally hardened Czechoslovak hearts against Kolchak and ultimately served to bury both the Supreme Ruler and White Siberia. In late December both British and American representatives in the region filed reports that 'Kolchak has sent an insane telegram to Semenov ordering him to blow up important tunnels so as to cut off the Czechoslovak retreat'. This information, which clearly refers to the forty tunnels which carry the Trans-Siberian Railway around the mountainous

175 Guins, *Sibir'*, Vol. 2, pp. 473–4.

176 Parfenov, 'Poslednie dni', p. 93.

177 Vendrykh, *Dekabr'sko–ianvarskie boi*, p. 26; Grondijs, *La Guerre*, p. 534–5.

southern littoral of Lake Baikal, whose destruction would have plugged the Legion's evacuation like a cork in a bottle, was said to have been supplied by Czechoslovak sources at Harbin and Irkutsk (among them the notoriously anti-Kolchak Girsa).[178] In their memoirs, which generally give credence to the reports, members and associates of the French Military Mission place the issuing of this 'suicidal' order by Kolchak on either December 21st or 24th.[179] The text of the order, however, has never been published. If it existed in either Soviet or Czechoslovak archives, it must be assumed, it would have appeared by now. Nor is there any independent verification of the Legionnaires' additional claims that, having waylaid Skipetrov, they found written instructions to destroy the Baikal tunnels on his person and impounded two wagons full of dynamite primed to do the job at Baikal and Sliudianka stations.[180] And the fact that the only White Russian source to refer to the telegram – the memoirs of General Sakharov – cites its provenance as Novonikolaevsk in *early* December serves only to further cloud the issue.[181]

It was in the light of such scant and confusing evidence surrounding the issue of Kolchak's order to blow the tunnels that the pioneer chronicler of the Siberian counter-revolution, Gutman-Gan, refuted the accuracy of the French and Czechoslovak claims, while S.P. Mel′gunov's conclusion was: 'I think that the telegram is one of many myths.'[182] Their conclusions are supported by the memoirs (published recently but actually written in 1930) of General Filat′ev who, serving as Head of Chancery on Kolchak's train, should have been in a position to know of such an order.[183] In the light of all this, it does seem possible that the order was a piece of calumnious propaganda against Kolchak on the part of the Czechoslovaks, broadcast as an excuse for their decision to cut and run. On the other hand, it seems eminently possible that, in one of the fits of rage and frustration to which he was increasingly prone, trapped by the Legion at some godforsaken

178 WO 33/957/4559 'Knox (Vladivostok) to WO, 28.xii.1919'; *DBFP*, p. 743; *FRUS: 1919 (Russia)*, pp. 232, 235.

179 Pages, E. *Campagne de misère. Sibérie 1919*. Paris (1933), p. 172; Grondijs, *La Guerre*, pp. 534–5.

180 For the Czechoslovak claims see WO 106/1276/4 'Diary Report of S.B.O. (Chita), 21–31.i.1920'.

181 Sakharov, *Belaia Sibir′*, p. 186.

182 Gan, A. *Rossiia i bol′shevizmom: materialy po istorii revoliutsii i bor′by s bol′shevizm (chast′ pervaia, 1914–1920gg.)*. Shanghai (1921), p. 174; Mel′gunov, Pt.3, Vol. 2, pp. 85–6.

183 Filat′ev, *Katastrofa*, p. 124.

station in the middle of nowhere, Kolchak *had* dashed off such a thoughtless instruction. Suffice to note that the two western biographers of Kolchak, whose accounts are very sympathetic to the admiral, accept the veracity of the Czechoslovak claims.[184] However, the only hard evidence to support such a view (which, incidentally, neither biographer cites) is a report of December 26th from Irkutsk by the new British High Commissioner to Siberia, Mr Lampson, to the effect that members of the Kolchak government had personally confirmed to Allied representatives in the town that the order to destroy the Baikal tunnels had been issued. The government members are not identified in this report, however; and, given that the cabinet was in only intermittent communication with Kolchak by that time, even their testimony may well have been apocryphal.[185]

Perhaps what is really significant in this episode is that Kolchak's record of traducement of the Legion was so lengthy and his reputation for imbalance and imprudence now so widespread that the climate of opinion had been created in which the Czechoslovaks – be they defamers of Kolchak or faithful interpreters of his orders – could have their claims believed by experienced diplomats and by such close associates of the admiral as General Knox and General Janin. On December 15th Tret'iakov had already told Janin that Kolchak's telegrams should no longer be given credence 'because everyone is now convinced that he has gone mad' ('I had to agree', commented the general).[186] Either rumours or the actual existence of an order to blow the tunnels could only, therefore, have confirmed an impression which was *already* general. Among the body of the Legion, the men who had already been subjected to a year of insults from the Supreme Ruler culminating in the promotion of Semenov, the suggestion that he would now spitefully attempt to cut off their retreat to the sea would probably only have been met by a resigned shrug of the shoulders. In other words, even if Kolchak did not order the destruction of the

184 Fleming, P. *The Fate of Admiral Kolchak*. London (1963), p. 178; Connaughton, R.M. *The Republic of the Ushakovka: Admiral Kolchak and the Allied Intervention in Siberia*. London (1990), pp. 153–4.

185 WO 106/1273/10 'Lampson (Irkutsk) to FO, 27.xii.1919'. On Lampson see: Steeds, D. 'The Ending of a Highly Discreditable Enterprise: Miles Lampson in Siberia, 1919–1920', *International Studies* No. 1 (1981), pp. 1–26.

186 Grondijs, *Le Cas Koltchak*, p. 102. The US Consul at Irkutsk, Mr Harris, agreed: 'It is felt by Allied representatives that Kolchak's mentality is breaking up under the strain of the past two months', he reported on December 28th. *FRUS: 1919 (Russia)*, p. 235.

Baikal tunnels – and the charge must remain not proven – by the very character of his rule he had long since burned his bridges.

The Irkutsk rising and the last days of the Kolchak régime

Whatever was the veracity of reports and rumours about the imminent destruction of the circum-Baikal tunnels, the only lesson that the SR-led opposition to Kolchak at Irkutsk could reasonably draw from the promotion of Semenov was that it was essential to topple the Kolchak régime in the new White capital before the ataman's marauders could arrive from the east with their own peculiar brand of 'order' and before the Supreme Ruler himself could arrive from the west to revive his government's waning authority. Another factor was that sizable partisan forces under the command of the Bolshevik D.E. Zverev were reported to be closing rapidly on the town from their strongholds in the taiga of northern Irkutsk *guberniia*. Should the Political Centre not have the reins of power firmly in its grip before the arrival of this well-armed, pro-Bolshevik force, its own longevity had to be open to doubt.[187] More positive auguries for the SRs could be found, however, in the fact that Irkutsk was clearly ripe for rebellion. A series of attempted crackdowns by the army since November, soaring inflation and a dire food shortage (as a result of the evacuation's overloading of the Trans-Siberian line) having already 'excited the inhabitants to such an extent that trouble is hourly expected', according to one report of mid-December 1919.[188]

Since its formation in November, all non-Bolshevik elements of the opposition had crystallized around the Political Centre and its programme of peace with Soviet Russia, the withdrawal of foreign troops and the establishment of a separate, democratic state in the east – a message which Kalashnikov's CBMO (termed locally the Military-Socialist Union) was spreading amongst the officers and men

[187] On the Zverev and Kalandarashvili partisans see Dvorianov, N.V. and Dvorianov, V.N. *V tylu Kolchaka*. Moscow (1966), pp. 121–97; and Novgorodov, A.I. *Oktiabr'skaia revoliutsiia i grazhdanskaia voina v Iakutii*. Novosibirsk (1969), pp. 184–6.

[188] WO 106/1273/5 'Lampson (Vladivostok) to WO, 15.xii.1919'. American observers had predicted a rising at Irkutsk in favour of the SRs as early as April 1919 – see *FRUS: 1919 (Russia)*, pp. 201–2. On the deteriorating social conditions at Irkutsk see also Guins, *Sibir'*, Vol. 2, pp. 441.

of the Irkutsk garrison with some success.[189] Support for the endeavour, both overt and covert, seems also to have been offered by the Czechoslovaks, who were coming to regard an arrangement with the SRs as the best means of expediting their evacuation. According to one source the Political Centre was supplied with arms by the Legionnaires, while at least one historian has interpreted as deliberate collusion with the Political Centre the decision of the Czech commandant at Nizhneudinsk to delay the eastward progress of Kolchak – he was to remain at the town for two weeks after arriving there on December 24th – until the power struggle at Irkutsk had been decided in the SRs' favour.[190]

Another good omen for the success of a rising at Irkutsk was that the series of risings which the Centre had ignited in western Siberia were now spreading to the east. Kolchak had actually arrived at Nizhneudinsk to find that its garrison had already revolted and seized control of the town, leaving only the station confines in the hands of the Legion. Meanwhile on December 21st–22nd, and once again under the aegis of the Military-Socialist Union, officers and men of the White garrison at Cheremkhovo, the important mining centre just 80 km west of Irkutsk, had arrested local representatives of the government and the district commandant of the Russian Army and had declared an end to the rule of Kolchak in a sector from Tulun to Polovina by Christmas Eve.

As 1919 drew to a close and as White power evaporated, therefore, there were numerous encouraging signs that a Political Centre rising at Irkutsk itself might be successful and that the Czechoslovaks might at least refrain from intervening. However, it was highly significant too that the Cheremkhovo rising also posed the question of whether the Political Centre had either the political ability or the popular support (beyond the sympathies of a war-sick soldiery who would offer support to *any* group promising peace) to go beyond that and consolidate a real hold on power: for, within days, the initiative in the Cheremkhovo Basin had passed from pro-Political Centre officers to rapidly organized workers' militias and the partisan bands emerging from the *taiga* which, on December 28th, recognized the regional authority

189 Shiriamov, A. 'Irkutskoe vosstanie i rasstrel Kolchaka', *Sibirskie ogni* (Novonikolaevsk), No. 4 (1924), p. 123.

190 Bradley, J.F.N. *Civil War in Russia*. London (1975), pp. 108–9; Fleming, pp. 176–7.

of a *Bolshevik* Revolutionary Committee. On that day the disappointed SRs withdrew from Cheremkhovo and returned to Irkutsk.[191]

The Bolsheviks' success at Cheremkhovo was their first challenge to the SR domination of the opposition to Kolchak which had been a feature of the autumn. It was something of a renaissance for the party, for in no other field of its activity had the Kolchak government been so successful as in its near total eradication of Bolshevik organizations from the Siberian towns during 1919. The party had been in a rather weak position to start off with. With only half of the seventy-two Siberian *uezds* hosting even the pretence of a district organization in 1917,[192] and with little goodwill for Communism being won east of the Urals by the harsh food requisitioning policies of early 1918, the Bolsheviks had been in no position to withstand the White terror administered for Kolchak at the end of that year by the army and the police network the Supreme Ruler had inherited from the old régime: 'The situation is murderous – 99% of our comrades have been killed', one Siberian activist reported to Moscow in December 1918.[193] As a result, the 13,620 active members claimed for the spring of 1918 had been culled to just 2,500 by the beginning of 1919.[194] This underground party rump was then thoroughly infiltrated by the White counter-espionage system – as is clear from those of its reports to Omsk published by Soviet historians, which minutely detail the finances, activities, plans and personnel of the fugitive Bolsheviks.[195] Consequently, the ill-advised decision of the party's 1st All-Siberian Underground Conference (Tomsk, November 23rd 1918) to stage a series of risings in the Siberian towns during the early months of 1919 had failed miserably and led to a wave of arrests and executions. The nadir

191 Konstantinov, 164–6; Papin, p. 87; Shiriamov, A. 'Konets kolchakovshchiny', *Bor'ba klassov* (Moscow), Nos. 1–2 (1935), pp. 90–1. Two weeks earlier, on December 8th–10th, an attempt by Bolsheviks and partisans to seize the notorious Aleksandrovsk Central Prison near Irkutsk had been mercilessly crushed by the White garrison, with 274 rebel lives lost. See Dvorianov and Dvorianov, pp. 193–5.

192 Safronov, V.P. *Oktiabr' v Sibiri*. Krasnoiarsk (1962), p. 533.

193 Spirin, L.M. 'O deiatel'nosti Sibirskogo biuro TsK RKP(b) v gody grazhdanskoi voiny', *Voprosy istorii KPSS* (Moscow), No. 2 (1961), pp. 107–8.

194 Logvinov, V.K. *V bor'be s kolchakovshchinoi (ocherki o Krasnoiarskom bol'shevistskom podpol'e i partizanskim dvizhenii v Eniseiskom gubernii, 1918–1920gg.)*. Krasnoiarsk (1980), p. 20; Gromov et al., *Partizanskoe dvizhenie*, p. 135.

195 Smirnov et al., *Bor'ba za Ural i Sibir'*, pp. 232–6, 237–8; *Iz istorii grazhdanskoi voiny v SSSR*. Moscow (1960–1961), Vol. 1, pp. 457–61.

of the Bolsheviks' fortunes was reached when a police spy (one Karpovich) was able to gain admission to a 2nd All-Siberian Underground Conference at Omsk of March 20–21st. On the basis of his leaked information a spate of arrests across the entire region in subsequent weeks decimated what little remained of the party: almost the entire Siberian *oblast'* Committee (*obkom*) was arrested in April and three of its leading members (P.A. Vavilov, M.M. Rabinovich and A.N. Masslenikov) were shot.[196] After that, recalled one of the few Bolshevik leaders to remain at liberty, 'at Irkutsk was the only party committee in eastern Siberia functioning properly'.[197]

Even at Irkutsk, however, infiltration of the party committees led to arrests during September 1919.[198] And it was possibly as a result of the perceived weakness instilled by this that, initially, the Bolshevik *guberniia* Committee was inclined to countenance entering into negotiations with the Political Centre (itself reconsidering the chances of developing support among the working class elements under Bolshevik influence) with the aim of organizing a joint revolt against

196 The most significant risings occurred at Omsk (December 21st 1918), Kansk (December 27th), Bodaibo (January 26th 1919), Eniseisk (February 6th), Tomsk (March 1st), Tiumen (March 13th) and Kolchuginsk (April 7th). There was also a rising at Krasnoiarsk in August 1919. The standard Soviet accounts of these events are Kadeikin, B.A. *Rabochie Sibiri v bor'be za vlast' Sovetov*. Kemerovo (1966); Kadeikin, B.A. *Sibir' nepokroennaia*. Kemerovo (1968); Stishov, M.I. *Bol'shevistskoe podpol'e i partizanskoe dvizhenie v Sibiri v gody grazhdanskom voine (1918–1920gg.)*. Moscow (1962); Plotnikov, I.F. *Bol'shevistskoe podpol'e v Sibiri v periode imperialisticheskoi interventsii i grazhdanskoi voiny*. Sverdlovsk (1966); Plotnikov, I.F. *Revoliutsionnaia bor'ba trudiashchikhsia Urala v tylu interventov i belogvardeitsev (1918–1919gg.)*. Sverdlovsk (1968); Plotnikov, I.F. *V belogvardeitskom tylu*. Sverdlovsk (1978).

197 Shiriamov, A. 'Bor'ba s kolchakovshchinoi', in Konstantinov, *Poslednie dni*, p. 21. The persistent claims of later Soviet historians to the effect that some 200 party organizers bearing millions of roubles were sent from Moscow into Siberia during 1919 to reinforce the local party branches would seem to be a gross exaggeration – see, for example, Spirin, L.M. 'O deiatel'nosti Sibirskogo biuro TsK RKP(b) v gody grazhdanskoi voiny', *Voprosy istorii KPSS* (Moscow), No. 2 (1961), p. 103; Kazakov, A. Ia. 'Rukovodstvo TsK RKP(b) deiatel'nostiu sibirskikh bol'shevikov v tylu belogvardeitsev (1918–1920gg.)', *Voprosy istorii KPSS*, No. 6 (1966), pp. 39–49; Shindin, A.M. 'Sibirskoe biuro TsK RKP(b) – organizator i rukovoditel' partiinogo podpol'ia v tylu belogvardeitsev i interventov', in *Velikii Oktiabr' i sotsialisticheskie preobrazovaniia v Sibiri*. Novosibirsk (1980), pp. 45–54. On the Irkutsk Bolsheviks see also Dvorianov and Dvorianov, pp. 144–7 and Vendrykh, pp. 19–21. Spirin (in his *Klassy i partii*, p. 359) attributed the Irkutsk Bolsheviks' survival to their cultivation of support through the trade unions. Their power would, therefore, have been augmented when the Siberian TUC decamped from Omsk to Irkutsk in November and co-opted two local Bolsheviks onto its committee – see Shemelev, V. *Profsoiuzy Sibiri v bor'be za vlast' Sovetov (1917–1919gg.)*. Novosibirsk (1928), pp. 213–14.

198 Bursak, I.N. 'Konets belogo admirala', in Spirin, L.M. (ed.) *Razgrom Kolchaka: vospominaniia*. Moscow (1969), p. 269; Dvorianov and Dvorianov, pp. 187–8.

Kolchak. On November 13th, however, the day after the foundation of the Centre, a 3rd All-Siberian Bolshevik Conference meeting at Irkutsk elected a new *Obkom*, which decided that although the presence of Czechoslovak and other Allied forces in Irkutsk precluded any separate revolt by the party, in the long run the approach of the Red Army and the partisans meant that the cards were stacked in their favour and against the longevity of any régime which the Political Centre might be able to establish on the basis of its limited support among the intelligentsia and the officers of Kolchak's garrisons. Consequently, it was resolved that, whilst the party would offer whatever tactical support it could to Political Centre attempts to seize power in the town, its fundamental strategic task was 'to deepen and make altogether unbridgeable that abyss' separating the SRs and Mensheviks from the masses, rather than disorientate workers (and possibly incur part of the blame for a failure, as had happened at Vladivostok) through the espousing of democratic slogans or co-operation with the Centre. Subsequently, Bolsheviks who had accepted the Centre's invitations to participate in its meetings withdrew and, in line with the ultra-leftist dictates of the November conference, severed all official contacts with the SRs and set about building their own cells in the Irkutsk garrison.[199]

Despite the severance of relations with the Bolsheviks, the Political Centre proceeded with plans to seize power in Irkutsk throughout December 1919, operating quite openly from the 21st onwards when the events at Cheremkhovo and Nizhneudinsk gave presentiment of success. At the same time, however, having come to hear of Kolchak's swing to the right and of his promotion of Semenov, and having been heartened by the news, reactionary elements among the crumbling White authorities at Irkutsk determined to clamp down on socialist opposition in anticipation of the arrival of assistance and reinforcements from the east. The first clashes occurred on December 22nd, as the army forcibly dispersed a conference of zemstvo and duma representatives at Irkutsk which had broadcast appeals for the convocation of a Siberian Constituent Assembly (even though the majority of delegates also voted in favour of continuing the war against Soviet Russia).[200] Then, on the following day, counter-intelligence units under one Captain

199 Smirnov et al., *Bor'ba za Ural i Sibir'*, pp. 283–4; Shiriamov, 'Bor'ba' in Konstantinov, *Poslednie dni* (1926), pp. 21–3, 26; Shiriamov, 'Konets', pp. 88–90; Papin, *Krakh kolchakovshchiny*, pp. 89–90.

200 *The Times* (London) 1.ii.1920; *Struggling Russia* (New York) Vol. 1, No. 41, 27.xii.1919, p. 658.

Cherepanov swooped on premises around the town and rounded up some 150 prominent oppositionists. Among them were leading Political Centre activists such as V. Ermolaeva and Captain Petrov as well as Boris Markov and Pavel Mikhailov (the latter pair being former members of the Western Siberian Commissariat and architects of the overthrow of Bolshevik power in Siberia during the spring of 1918). The Political Centre initially appealed for their release to the Head of Irkutsk Garrison, General Artem′ev, undertaking not to oppose the government by force of arms if their colleagues were liberated. By the 24th, however, as the arrests continued and as it came to the Centre's attention that, on Semenov's orders, Artem′ev (who had presided over a relatively benign military régime at Irkutsk) had been supplanted by the ferocious General Sychev (former ataman of the Zabaikal Cossacks and not a character with whom deals could be made), the decision was taken by the SRs to move against White power, whatever the unfortunate consequences for their hostage colleagues.[201] At a meeting of the Centre on the evening of the 24th, however, it was agreed that because the recent arrests had so disrupted the organization within the town of Irkutsk proper, it would be unwise to attempt a revolt in the city centre itself. Rather, it was towards the suburbs that the SRs' attention and energies were directed.[202]

At this juncture it is necessary to adumbrate some features of the topography of Irkutsk (see Map 5). The city centre, with its public buildings, hotels and the cathedral, lies on the right bank and within a great curve of the mighty Angara River, some 100 km from its Baikal egress. To the north the town is bounded by the Angara's tributary, the River Ushakovka. And across the Ushakovka in 1919, lay the prison and the working class districts of Znamenskoe (later Martovskoe) and Rabochee. Beyond the Angara from the city centre, and itself defined to the north by another affluent, the River Irkut, lay the industrial suburb of Glaskovo (later Sverdlovsk) which contained the Irkutsk No. 1 Railway Station and, in 1919, the barracks of the 53rd Siberian Regiment of the Russian Army.

It was towards Glaskovo that, on the night of December 24th, the Political Centre decided to direct its appeals for revolt. And for good reason. For one thing the 53rd was a notoriously ill-disciplined troop which, had the government enjoyed any real authority, would have been removed from the environs of Irkutsk weeks earlier,

201 Parfenov, P.S. *Bor′ba za Dal′nyi Vostok, 1920–1922gg.* Leningrad (1928), pp. 21–2.

202 'N', 'Poslednie dni', p. 87.

according to Guins.[203] Moreover, by the 24th the Political Centre knew it could summon the regiment to revolt without fear of interference by the more loyal elements of the garrison in Irkutsk proper or by the die-hard officer detachments being organized there by Sychev, as for some days the Angara had been all but impossible to cross. In 1919 the River Angara, like the Irtysh before it, was to freeze unusually late – with dreadful consequences for the Whites, who must have felt that even nature was turning against them. On the night of December 21st–22nd the pontoon which generally bridged the river from Glaskovo to Irkutsk was swept away by a large floe. Until the river froze solid, consequently, it was only traversable by the four small steamers of the city. Like all other means of communication in eastern Siberia, these were in Czechoslovak hands and three of them remained firmly moored to the western bank of the Angara, out of the reach of Sychev.[204] The Kolchak government and the Irkutsk garrison were, therefore, to all intents and purposes isolated from the outside world – and largely, incidentally, as a result of the fact that the peculiar principles of the construction of the Trans-Siberian Railway had caused it to avoid Irkutsk centre (just as it had skirted the centre of Omsk and had altogether bypassed Tomsk, the traditional Siberian 'capital').

According to one witness, the Political Centre had their plan approved by the Legion before moving.[205] Be that as it may, during the evening of December 24th Kalashnikov and a Commissar detailed to him by the Centre, Colonel Merkhalev, were able (with Czechoslovak connivance) to pass over the Angara to Glaskovo, where, at 10.30 p.m., they convened a meeting at the headquarters of the 53rd Regiment. There an appeal was issued to the effect that 'it is time to dispense with the bloodthirsty government of Kolchak and his Cabinet of Speculators'. Subsequently, the entire 53rd Regiment and the majority of the 1st and 2nd Irkutsk Territorial Brigades and the 38th Zabaikal Infantry rallied to Kalashnikov's proclamation of a new People's Revolutionary Army under his command, and by midnight the station suburb and its environs had fallen into insurgent hands with hardly a shot having been fired. The peregrinatory diplomatic community of the

203 Guins, Vol. 2, p. 477.

204 According to some reports the approach of the ice had been monitored upstream by railwaymen employees of the Ministry of Ways and Communications, but the information was deliberately withheld. WO 106/1276 'Report on the Revolutionary Movement at Irkutsk, of December 24th 1919 to January 6th 1920, 27.ii.1920'.

205 Ivanov, Vs.N. *V grazhdanskom voine: iz zapisok omskago zhurnalista*. Harbin (1921), p. 76.

Allied High Commissioners, together with General Janin, witnessed events from the Glaskovo platforms as, interrupting the High Commissioners' Christmas celebrations on the 25th, rebel units, resplendent in their British uniforms and led in many cases by British-trained NCOs, noisily celebrated their desertion of the Whites and despatched sorties down the line to the outer suburb of Innokent′evskaia and the arsenal at Batereinaia (30 km west of Irkutsk), where more British ordnance fell into their hands and more recruits filed into the rebel ranks 'by the hour'.[206]

Not surprisingly in these circumstances, the night of December 24th–25th was passed in an 'excruciatingly alarming' atmosphere by sleepless government ministers in their rooms at Irkutsk's modest Ritz, the Hotel Moderne, as Guins recalled. With the disturbances having deprived the town of both heat and light for some days, at any moment it was expected that the events at Glaskovo would be echoed by a rebellion of the 3,500-strong force within Irkutsk centre. On the morn of the 25th, however, Sychev was able to report that, at least for the time being, the garrison (consisting predominantly of the 54th Siberian Regiment) remained loyal, as did the junkers of the local military school.[207] Moreover, as Sychev informed the government, a message had already been transmitted to Semenov, via friendly Japanese channels, requesting assistance; and a favourable answer had been received.[208] In the light of these circumstances, Sychev told a council of war at the Moderne, it was possible to commence operations to crush the Political Centre rising. 3" and 6" howitzers were then deployed in the city and a message was passed to the Allied representatives that it was the government's intention to bombard Glaskovo on the morning of the 26th in order to dislodge the rebels. General Janin, however, immediately replied that it was his duty to maintain communications through Irkutsk and, in view of that and the fact that Allied missions were resident in Glaskovo, he could not permit such an action. If Sychev attempted a bombardment, Janin warned, he would have to order Czechoslovak armoured trains to return fire. To defuse the situation a conference of the Allied High Commissioners on the 26th proposed that, at least until all of the Allied troops had

206 FO 371/4099/187294 'Lampson (Harbin) to FO, 17.i.1920: "Daily Précis of Events at Irkutsk (by HM High Commissioner, Mr Lampson, and Acting French High Commissioner, M Maugras)"'; Konstantinov, *Poslednie dni*, pp. 168–9; Vendrykh, *Dekabr′sko–ianvarskie boi*, pp. 34–5; Janin, 'Otryvki', pp. 137–8.

207 Guins, Vol. 2, p. 478.

208 Parfenov, *Bor′ba za Dal′nyi Vostok*, p. 22; 'N', p. 88.

been withdrawn, the stations and the railway from Krasnoiarsk to Myssovaia Station should be declared a neutral zone and that both rebel and government forces should be excluded from it.[209]

On what authority the western diplomatists made such a ruling on Russian territory is unclear. Moreover, by this time, of course, the railway was the only hope of the White régime – not for victory, but for survival. At the Moderne this and Janin's threat were, therefore, unsurprisingly 'interpreted as a decision to liquidate the government of Admiral Kolchak'.[210] And quite properly so – for behind the neutral zone, policed now punctiliously by the Legion, the rebels were free to gather their forces without government harassment while, across the Angara, the government itself remained quarantined. There was nothing the ministers could do, however, other than in a memorandum passed to the High Commissioners by General Vagin (Deputy Minister of War), insist that the neutrality should be observed fairly and vigorously – that is, that the rebels be forcibly expelled from Glaskovo and that the railway officials they had arrested be freed. So far this had not been done. Yet, for their part, the government were expected to accept that any further westward movement of the Skipetrov force would be in breach of the neutrality (and were informed that the Japanese had been requested to forestall the Semenovites' expedition).[211]

As Vagin negotiated with the High Commissioners at Glaskovo, a new political initiative was being essayed by the government (which now, with so many ministers having absented themselves from Irkutsk, was reduced to a triumvirate of Cherven-Vodali, General Khanzhin and the Acting Minister of Communications, V.M. Larionov). The planned bombardment of the rebels having been thwarted, on December 26th Cherven-Vodali responded positively to mediation from Iakovlev and, that evening, he received in his office at the Moderne a delegation of zemstvo and duma leaders (notably Alekseev and Khodukin) with an aim to arranging a cease-fire, the peaceful evacuation of government forces to Transbaikalia, and the

209 FO 371/4099/187294 'Daily Précis'; WO 106/1273 'Britmis (Vladivostok) to WO, 7.ii.1920: "Unrest at Vladivostok"'; WO 106/1276/1 'Report on the Revolutionary Movement at Irkutsk'; Vendrykh, p. 29.

210 Guins, Vol. 2, pp. 478–9.

211 *ibid.*, pp. 481–3; WO 106/1273/15 'Legget (Vladivostok) to FO, 3.i.1920'; WO 106/1273/10 'Legget (Vladivostok) to FO, 29.xii.1919'. The Bolshevik leader Shiriamov thought that but for the Allied declaration of neutrality the rebels would certainly have been crushed. See Shiriamov, 'Bor'ba', in Konstantinov, *Poslednie dni*, p. 26.

transfer of local authority (in Irkutsk *guberniia*) to the Political Centre. According to Soviet commentators this was 'a ruse', a blatant case of playing for time by the Whites.[212] According to Guins, however, it was an honest attempt to arrange the passage of the Russian Army to the east through the tightening Irkutsk occlusion and to ensure that whoever was left in power in the region would not capitulate to the Bolsheviks.[213] Whatever the motivation, however, the talks were doomed to failure, for although the Political Centre was willing to permit White troops to move through Irkutsk (it could not, in truth, have stopped them), it baulked at Cherven-Vodali's demands that Kolchak should be allowed to take the gold reserve with him into Transbaikalia and refused to undertake to continue fighting the Bolsheviks.[214] Moreover – and notwithstanding Cherven-Vodali's promise that he would endeavour to have Kolchak resign and his reaffirmation of the goverment's commitment to a *Zemskii sobor'* – having learned the lesson of 1918, the SRs were rightly suspicious that, while the Political Centre held the ring at the front, the forces of reaction would replenish their strengths in the rear before returning to Irkutsk to swamp them.

In any event, hardly had the negotiations resumed on the morning of the 27th than Cherven-Vodali was obliged to bring them to a close. The leading triumvir had heard from Sychev that Skipetrov – either in conscious breach of the neutrality agreement or, as the British suspected, because the Japanese had deliberately not apprised him of it – had reached Litvinichnogo with his expedition, and that from there the following message had been received: 'We are advancing on Irkutsk and will arrive soon.'[215] As the SRs departed from the Moderne, Sychev ordered 'every effort' to be made by loyal forces to support the approach of Skipetrov.[216]

Even without Cherven-Vodali's termination of the talks, however, it has to be doubted whether the Political Centre was in a position to have its unruly supporters observe a cease-fire. At 3 p.m. on the 27th, before he had come to hear of the imminent arrival of Skipetrov, Governor Iakovlev was informed that, despite his orders forbidding action for the duration of the talks, the commander of his Special

212 Ioffe, G.Z. *Velikii Oktiabr' i epilog tsarizma*. Moscow (1977), pp. 209–10.

213 Guins, Vol. 2, pp. 478–80.

214 *ibid.*, p. 484.

215 Mel'gunov, Pt.3, Vol. 2, p. 103. A message had also been received from Tret'iakov at Chita, informing the ministers that Semenov was vehemently opposed to any deal with the Political Centre. See Guins, Vol. 2, p. 484; Parfenov, *Bor'ba za Dal'nyi Vostok*, p. 24.

216 Vendrykh, p. 30.

Detachment (Captain Reshetin), in the name of the governor, had ordered his men to surround the Hotel Moderne and arrest the government. Reshetin had already concentrated a group of mutineers on Speranskii Square, had seized the telegraph and telephone offices, and seemed likely to capture the State Bank on Amur Street. With Sychev poised to move against the rebels within the town, Iakovlev then decided to inform Reshetin of the approach of Skipetrov before himself resigning and slipping away to Harbin. (In the 1920s Iakovlev would return, voluntarily, to the Soviet Union, where he was executed.)

The governor's motives for such a disclosure are unclear. It was not simply that he was saving the rebels from Skipetrov by forewarning them, for had the news not been leaked it is possible that sufficient of the garrison would have rallied to Reshetin and the Political Centre to foil any attack by the ataman – some junkers from the Officer Training School were joining the crowd on Speranskii Square, for example. As it was, however, Iakovlev's broadcast of the arrival of Skipetrov (whose bloody suppression of disturbances in the town during December 1917 had earned a place in local folklore) unnerved and deterred potential Political Centre recruits within the town, who returned to their barracks. The already committed elements of the Special Detachment and others were then forced to regroup and, at 11.00 p.m., retreated north across the Ushakovka, leaving Sychev to regain control of Irkutsk centre.[217] Throughout the 28th–29th December Political Centre sorties were launched and relaunched across the small river, but were repulsed (with heavy losses to the insurgents) by the superior number of forces and the artillery at Sychev's disposal. The government troops were unable, however, to reach the northern shore to eradicate this second Political Centre front.[218]

With the situation on the Ushakovka front stable during the final days of December, the focus of attention returned to events at Glaskovo and the anticipated arrival of Skipetrov. Already on the 28th, having heard of the ataman's breach of the neutrality agreement and that he had ignored a further Czechoslovak request to halt at Mikhailevo, the rebels had themselves decided to breach the neutral zone and had

217 WO 106/1276 'Report on the Revolutionary Movement at Irkutsk'; Vendrykh, pp. 30–1. Guins (1921), Vol. 2, pp. 484–6 suggests that Iakovlev decided to resign and abandon his earlier hopes of finding common ground with the Political Centre when he realized that the SRs would not be persuaded to continue war against Soviet Russia.

218 Vendrykh, pp. 31–3; 'N', pp. 90–3.

reoccupied the station. From there, when Skipetrov arrived on the outskirts of town on the morning of the 30th and began to shell the rebel positions with his four artillery pieces, Kalashnikov had a surprise in store for him – an unmanned locomotive was sent hurtling down the line with its throttle wedged open. It smashed the ataman's two leading armoured trains (on which his guns were mounted), blocked the track and forced him to continue his advance on foot. Still outgunning and outnumbering the rebels, however, Skipetrov drove forwards and captured Glaskovo by midday, as the People's Revolutionary Army retreated across the Irkut and prepared to abandon Irkutsk and transfer its headquarters west to Innokent′evskaia. At around 3.00 p.m., however, the tide of battle turned, as militia detachments of miners from Cheremkhovo, bearing arms purloined from Batereinaia, together with partisan detachments loyal to Kalandarashvili and Zverev, entered Glaskovo to reinforce Kalashnikov's efforts and to drive Skipetrov back. By nightfall Semenov's expeditionaries were back at Mikhailevo, having suffered 170 casualties and having had any hopes of a new offensive dashed as workers ripped up a section of the line before Irkutsk.[219]

For reasons unknown, only around 150 of Skipetrov's men had taken the opportunity of their brief ascendancy at Glaskovo to seize a steamer ('The Buriat') and cross the Angara to reinforce Sychev's loyalist garrison. Observers who had gathered along the city rivage to await the outcome of the battle opposite noted this and, in the words of one, realized that 'the battle for Irkutsk was decided' by the ataman's retreat and his failure to transfer substantial forces to the town.[220] Consequently, the fear of Cossack punishment no longer deterring them, on December 31st droves of Sychev's men began deserting across the Ushakovka to join the rebel lines. A new attack was then launched from Znamenskoe early on January 1st and soon rebel bridgeheads were established on the left bank of the river, within Irkutsk itself. There were now some 6,000 men in the two groups of the People's Revolutionary Army and, with the Angara set to freeze and expedite a joint operation against the city, the longevity of the Sychev group and of the

219 Vendrykh, pp. 33–5; FO 371/4099/187294 'Précis of Daily Events'; WO 106/1273/20 'Legget (Vladivostok) to FO, 7.i.1920'; WO 106/1276/1 'Report on the Revolutionary Movement at Irkutsk..'; Guins, Vol. 2, pp. 488–9.

220 'N', p. 93. Serebrennikov, I.I. *Moi vospominaniia*. Tientsin (1937), pp. 276–7 provides another eye-witness account of these events.

Kolchak government at the Hotel Moderne seemed calculable in minutes rather than hours as the New Year dawned.[221] As a British military intelligence report put it:

> There was a great depression in the government and staff HQs on the evening of this day [January 1st]. The defeat of Skipetrov's attack, the numerous desertions, the meagre reinforcements sent by Semenov and the announcement that the three Japanese battalions which had arrived at the station during the day had come for purposes only of transporting to Transbaikalia the Allied High Commissioners' echelons, all combined to force the conclusion on the government that their cause was lost and that further bloodshed was useless.[222]

The Triumvirate's first instinct was to seek assistance from the Allied High Commissioners, who were ensconced at Glaskovo No. 1 Station. On the afternoon of January 2nd, therefore, Cherven-Vodali, Khanzhin and Larionov led a delegation to the High Commissioners' trains and, having reasserted that the current cabinet had renounced the former policies of the Kolchak Government as 'entirely wrong', and having pledged that 'with a clear conscience we have already begun to realize a liberalization of policy', went on to request that Allied troops be deployed to keep order in Irkutsk and Glaskovo and that the Allies guarantee the free passage to the east of the Russian Army, Kolchak, all his ministers and the remaining loyalist elements of the Irkutsk garrison as well as the transfer to Transbaikalia of the gold reserve and 90% of the paper currency in the local branch of the State Bank.[223] Having considered these requests in camera, however, the diplomats pronounced that, in strict accordance with the Allies' policy of neutrality and non-interference in Russian internal affairs, they could not undertake to act as arbiters between the rebels and the government. If both sides were willing, the Commissioners were disposed to act as intermediaries, so as to arrange a cease-fire; beyond that, however, everything had to be a matter for direct negotiations between the government and

221 Konstantinov, *Poslednie dni*, pp. 170–1; Vendrykh, pp. 35–6; Shiriamov, 'Irkutskoe vosstanie', p. 127.

222 WO 106/1276 'Report on the Revolutionary Movement at Irkutsk'. One witness estimated that there were between 1,500 and 2,000 Japanese troops in the locality. See Essen, R. *Zwischen der Ostsee und dem Stillen Ozean. Asiatische Probleme und Erinnerungen*. Frankfurt (1935), pp. 280–9. However, they did nothing to aid Skipetrov.

223 *Peregovory o sdache vlasti Omskim pravitel'stvom Politicheskomu Tsentru* (hereafter *Peregovory*), pp. 4–9, 13–14.

the Political Centre.[224] Admittedly the triumvirs' requests had represented a maximum programme, but they must nevertheless have been surprised by the Allies' apparent abandonment of the White cause – to say nothing of the further advice the diplomats offered to the effect that power should be transferred forthwith to the Political Centre because it had 'nothing in common' with Bolshevism.[225]

The High Commissioners' motives in tempering the support offered to the Whites and in facilitating a settlement between the two warring parties at Irkutsk are clear enough – continued strife on the railway, particularly in the bottleneck of Irkutsk and the circum-Baikal defile, would hamper the evacuation of the Czechoslovak Legion and of the Allied missions, as the Bolshevik wave threatened to engulf them from the west; the sooner the clearly predominant Political Centre supplanted the crippled government and put an end to disorder and uncertainty the better, from their point of view. The government's motives in accepting the Allies' invitation to arrange talks with the Political Centre can also be easily discerned – Irkutsk was slipping from their grasp and there was no immediate prospect of rescue either from forces in the west or those in the east (particularly as the ministers were now aware that, following clashes at Baikal Station on January 1st between Czechoslovak forces and Skipetrov in which the former had suffered a significant number of casualties, the Allied High Commissioners had, via Kato, ordered Semenov to clear all his men from the circum-Baikal sector).[226] Their only hope, therefore, was to throw themselves on the clemency of the Allies and to pray that time and concessions could be salvaged from negotiations, so as to expedite the most profitable evacuation from Irkutsk to a new base in the east. Cherven-Vodali and his partners were not in an enviable situation – their posture struck British and French observers as 'abject', their supplications as 'an appeal *misericordiam*'[227] – but they had no obvious alternative.

What is less clear is what the Political Centre hoped to gain from such negotiations. Yet, even though it was already poised to seize power in Irkutsk on January 2nd, when invited that evening by an emissary of Janin to send a delegation

224 *ibid.*, pp. 14–15. Parfenov (*Bor'ba za Dal'nyi Vostok*, p. 27) claims that the Allied declaration was prompted by a warning from the Legion that a new White formation in the Far East, centred on Semenov, would be a further hindrance to the evacuation.

225 Guins, Vol. 2, p. 492.

226 *Peregovory*, pp. 3–4.

227 FO 371/4099/187294 'Précis of Daily Events'.

to Glaskovo so as to arrange a cease-fire, the Centre nevertheless agreed to do so. The SRs portrayed their decision to treat with the Triumvirate as a humanitarian gesture, aimed at minimizing the loss of life.[228] Soviet historians, however, have interpreted the move as calculated to win the goodwill of the Allies and perhaps the kudos of official recognition by the western powers.[229] The latter would certainly have been a welcome boost to the Political Centre's authority and popularity, for as we shall see the organization's control over the developing rising at Irkutsk was more apparent than real.

After a preliminary meeting of the two sides at Glaskovo, at 1.45 a.m. on January 3rd a 24-hour cease-fire was agreed, to commence at noon of that day. This was subsequently extended by twelve hours (to midnight of January 4th–5th). Meanwhile, in protracted sessions of January 3rd and 4th, delegates of the Political Centre and the government engaged in a series of barbed and pointless (although not altogether ill-humoured) exchanges. Initially the two sides remained in separate carriages on the station, with Allied diplomats braving the cold to act as go-betweens. Later they were persuaded to meet face to face across a table in the car of Mr Hodgson, the Acting British High Commissioner. It was always unlikely, however, that an agreement would be reached for, as Guins said, whereas the government was looking for a means of tactical retreat the Centre was seeking its complete capitulation.[230] Thus, the Triumvirate again offered to recognize the local authority of the Political Centre and to have supreme power transferred from Kolchak to Denikin if the admiral, his ministers, his army and the gold reserve were permitted passage to Transbaikalia, and if an undertaking was given that the rebel forces would continue the struggle against the Reds. But they could not truly have hoped for such terms to be accepted. Cherven-Vodali had already informed the Allies that he regarded the Political Centre not as an independent force but as one 'intended only to open the door to Bolshevism'.[231] And, for their part, although they might have been willing to countenance the passage of Kolchak to the east and

228 *Peregovory*, p. 18.

229 Vendrykh, p. 37; Papin, p. 90.

230 Guins, Vol. 2, p. 495.

231 *Peregovory*, pp. 7–8. At least Cherven-Vodali had the forbearance to keep his opinions to himself during sessions with the Political Centre. General Vagin, on the other hand, could not restrain his detestation of the SR negotiants and was overheard by the stenographer to be muttering furiously of 'Bolsheviks!' on more than one occasion. (*ibid.*, pp. 39–40).

to reserve the right only to detain certain unnamed 'criminals', the Centre could not agree to such terms for two reasons: they were wary that the Russian Army would reform in the Far East and then return to Irkutsk ('You want to rally your troops and then march against the people, against democracy', they charged); and they disputed the right of the Kolchak government to dispose either of the gold reserve or of supreme power.

> Denikin does not have the right to pretend to an inheritance which, as of now, for God's sake, does not exist... After all, what is the extent of your empery – why only a few streets around the Hotel Moderne!

mocked Ivanitskii-Vasilenko for the Political Centre.[232]

This, of course, begged the question of why negotiations were attempted with so powerless a government. And, soon, the SRs came to realize, as I.I. Akhmatov charged, that the triumvirs were 'playing for time'.[233] Yet still the Political Centre remained at the table – even when the government's procrastinating tactics were laid bare with their arrival for the talks on the 4th (scheduled for 2.30 p.m.) no less than four hours late; and despite the fact that before this tardy arrival a senior Cossack officer of the Irkutsk garrison interrupted proceedings at Glaskovo with what the stenographer recorded as a 'bombshell', saying that no matter what the outcome of the negotiations his men would no longer agree to fight the Political Centre.[234]

It was anybody's guess how long the shadow-boxing at Glaskovo might have endured but for developments at Irkutsk during the evening of January 4th. As it was, hardly had the proceedings got under way that evening than rumours began to reach the conference that something was amiss across the Angara. Then gunfire was heard from the direction of Irkutsk. Feigning illness, Khanzhin slipped from the room to find out more; he was tailed by Lieutenant Zorkin of the Political Centre. At 10.00 p.m., the latter returned with a report that government units within Irkutsk

232 *ibid.*, pp. 20–50, 52, 54.

233 *ibid.*, pp. 22–3.

234 *ibid.*, p. 47. Guins, Vol. 2, pp. 496–7 claimed that the government delegation was late because of a prolonged meeting of the Council of Ministers, called to decide whether, in Kolchak's absence, the Triumvirate had the legal right to arrange the transfer of power to the Political Centre. On arrival, however, Cherven-Vodali attributed his tardiness to fog on the Angara (*Peregovory*, p. 47). Yet another version has it that the delegation was late because it had been engaged in last-ditch talks with an agent of Semenov at Glaskovo. See Dubarbier, G. *En Sibérie après l'Armistice*. Paris (1924), p. 144.

were breaking the terms of the cease-fire. Soon afterwards General Janin entered the carriage to report 'complete anarchy in the town' with bands of Skipetrov's men on the loose. This, at last, prompted the SRs to act. At 11.25, amidst a flurry of shouted protests and the noise of chairs being knocked over, Zorkin announced that the cease-fire was over and that his commander-in-chief, Kalashnikov, had given orders for the People's Revolutionary Army to move into Irkutsk to restore order. Khodukin then demanded quiet and pronounced:

> I declare the meeting closed. The old government has fallen and, by the will of the people, the Political Centre will fulfil its duty and transfer power to a National Assembly to be called in the near future.[235]

By 1.00 a.m. on January 5th Kalashnikov's forces advancing from Glaskovo met those from Znamenskoe on Speranskii Square. The next morning, at a meeting at its headquarters in the building of the Russo-Asiatic Bank, the Political Centre formally assumed power and issued a 'Manifesto to All the Peoples of Siberia' proclaiming freedom of speech and of assembly and free elections to a Provisional Siberian Council of Popular Administration. It also announced its intention of bringing to an end the war against Soviet Russia as the only means of ending 'the enslavement of the country to foreign imperialist powers'.[236]

So ended fourteen months of White rule in Siberia, with the final configuration of the Kolchak Government, the Cabinet of Solidarity, in such disarray as to make a mockery of its name. Several cabinet members, of course, had long since followed Tret'iakov's example and found pressing business to attend to east of Baikal. Now, as the storm broke in Irkutsk on the night of January 4th–5th 1920, many of those ministers and ex-ministers who remained in the town were arrested by the forces of the Political Centre and imprisoned; among them were the triumvirs Cherven-Vodali and Larionov. Some, such as the more fortunate triumvir Khanzhin, managed to slip

235 *Peregovory*, pp. 60–5.

236 Konstantinov, *Poslednie dni*, pp. 123–5, 172–8; WO 106/1726/3 'Manifesto of the Political Centre at Irkutsk'; Parfenov, *Bor'ba za Dal'nyi Vostok*, pp. 42–5. The Political Centre government consisted of the following 'Heads of Ministries': I.I. Akhmatov (Foreign Affairs and Labour); I.I. Pogrebetskii (Finance); V.O. Sidorov (Interior); G.B Patushinskii (Justice); A.P. Belotserkovets (Ways and Communications); P. Bykhovskii (Agriculture); N.S. Kalashnikov (War); A.Ia. Goncharov (Education); I.I. Galaktionov (Food and Supply); M.M. Konstantinov (Press and Information); K.A. Popov (Central Investigating Commission); L.K. Soldatov (Secretary).

away, if they could beg or buy a berth on an Allied train. Others, however, fled with more haste and less dignity – according to one witness Admiral Smirnov had somehow acquired the garb of a British Tommy, while Sukin fled disguised as an American Red Cross nurse.[237] But they flattered themselves: even at the death

237 Nachbaur, A. *Le Dossier Koltchak: Sibérie, 1918–20.* Peking (1920). Another witness relates that Smirnov's escape was hampered because he insisted on taking two large suitcases with him. Later one of them burst open to reveal stacks of Omsk Roubles. See Il'in, I.S. 'Omsk, Direktoriia i Kolchak', *Novyi zhurnal* Vol. 73 (1963), p. 238. The leading White politicians captured by the insurgents at Irkutsk and elsewhere in Siberia at the end of 1919 were subsequently brought to trial at Omsk in May 1920, charged on a number of counts of incitement to rebellion against Soviet power, attempting to re-establish the old régime, inflicting robbery and mass murder on the population, calling in foreign powers to wage war on the Soviet Republic, transferring Soviet property to foreign governments, the destruction of state and private property, etc. (see *Pravda*, 27.v.1920). Rather surprisingly, given the vehemence with which the prosecution's case was made, only some of the accused were executed (on July 23rd): Cherven-Vodali, Larionov, Shumilovskii, Krasnov, Morozov, Gratsianov and the Kadet leader, Klafton. Another seventeen were given prison terms ranging from 5–10 years to life, from which some were later released and re-admitted to Soviet society (P.I. Preobrazhenskii, for example, returned to work at Perm University in 1923, and did not die until 1944). On the trial see Raivid, N. and Bykov, V. (eds.) *Kolchakovshchina: sbornik.* Ekaterinburg (1924), pp. 146–64; an interesting photograph of the proceedings was published in *Izvestiia TsK KPSS* (Moscow), No. 2 (1991), p. 113. Of those White leaders not brought to trial in 1920, Zhardetskii, who had refused to leave Omsk, was captured by the Bolsheviks and killed. Guins, Smirnov and Petrov made a forlorn attempt to influence events in the east as a 'Conference of Former Ministers' at Harbin in 1920. Petrov then vanished. Smirnov emigrated to Paris. Guins (together with Ivan Serebrennikov and Tel'berg) taught various courses at the Harbin Law School before emigrating in 1941 to the USA, where he pursued a successful career as a lecturer at Berkeley before his death in 1971 (although his magnum opus, *The History of Russia as a Multinational Empire*, remains, to date, unpublished). Vologodskii lived out his days quietly at Harbin; he died in 1925. The Kadets Ustrialov and Kliuchnikov became founders of the *Smena vekh* (Change of Landmarks) movement at Harbin, campaigning for a reconciliation with Moscow. Ustrialov, after working for the Soviets on the CER, returned to Moscow in 1935 to write anti-fascist literature for Moscow's Institute of Transport Engineers; Kliuchnikov returned to the Soviet Union in 1922 to serve Chicherin's *Narkomindel.* Mikhailov also slipped away to Harbin, where he, in contrast, worked for the Japanese intelligence services on the Bureau for the Affairs of Russian Émigrés during the Manchukuo period, before being captured by the Red Army in 1945 in the same operation which netted Semenov (who, following a failed attempt to gain admittance to the USA and Canada in 1922, had also served the Japanese in Manchuria between the wars). Both were flown to Moscow and executed; see Stephen, J.J. *The Russian Fascists.* London (1978), pp. 175, 352–4. Kalmykov, after plundering Khabarovsk, fled into Manchuria in February 1920, where he was arrested on murder charges by the Chinese authorities and shot dead whilst trying to escape from prison. Gajda returned to Prague, where in 1926 he helped found the Czech Fascist Party; he was shot, as a collaborator, in 1948. Horvath became the recognized leader of the émigré community in Peking, where he died in 1937. Of the White military, Krasil'nikov died of typhus at an Irkutsk hospital in January 1920, while his Cossack partner in the Omsk coup of 1918, Volkov, was killed (reputedly by his own men) during the retreat. Lebedev worked for Japan in the Far East before his death in 1928. General Boldyrev served in various White authorities in the Far East down to 1922, when he was captured by the Soviet authorities. He was granted an amnesty in 1926 and subsequently had a distinguished career on the Siberian branch of Gosplan, before dying, a victim of the purges, in 1936. Ivanov-Rinov, rather surprisingly, also returned to the

Kolchak's mandarins remained anonymous, distant figures, having lodged no image of their countenances in the minds of the Siberian populace. As Guins found, when he returned briefly to the Moderne on the 5th (to dismiss the cabinet's bodyguard which his colleagues, in their haste to escape, had forsaken), it was quite possible for a minister to walk freely among the rebel troops celebrating on the streets of Irkutsk without fear of recognition.[238]

The fate of Admiral Kolchak

But what, meanwhile, of Kolchak himself? Surprisingly, given the isolation of the Supreme Ruler's eastbound echelons in the middle of Siberia, it is possible to construct a quite detailed picture of the admiral's progress – not least because of the preservation of the diaries of two of his staff officers, General Zankevich and Lieutenant-Colonel Malinovskii.[239] They record a tortuous journey accompanied by continual strife between Kolchak and the Czechoslovaks from Station Taiga onwards, with the admiral now at the mercy of those whom he had insulted for so long. Tempers frayed first at Mariinsk on December 10th, when a lieutenant of the Legion's Army Transportation Staff insisted that Kolchak's seven trains – like all

Soviet Union and found work in the Red Army. Anatoli Pepeliaev led a White partisan movement in the Far East during 1920–1922, eventually mounting a raid deep into Iakutia, where he was captured by the Red Army in 1923. His death sentence was commuted to ten years' imprisonment when he appealed to his followers to surrender and recognize the Soviet government – see Vishnevskii, E.K. *Artonavty beloi mechty. Opisan'e iakutskago pokhoda Sibirskoi Dobrovol'cheskoi Druzhiny*. Kharbin (1933); and Grachev, G. 'Iakutskii pokhod gen. Pepeliaeva', *Sibirskii arkhiv* (Prague), Vol. 1 (1929), pp. 23–40. He eventually perished, a victim of the purges, in 1938. Dieterichs was prominent in the Japanese-sponsored government in the Maritime Provinces of 1920–1922 and was ultimately to be proclaimed 'Ruler of the Maritime Region' by its zemstvo congress. When the Japanese withdrew from the mainland in October 1922, however, he was forced to retire to Tokyo. Later he lived (initially in some poverty as a bank teller and a cobbler) in Shanghai, where he died in 1937. Sakharov emigrated briefly to the USA (working as a labourer at the California Steel Corporation, San Francisco), before writing his memoirs in Europe and, finally, settling as a farmer in Shanghai, where he died in 1955. Budberg also emigrated to San Francisco, where he died in the 1950s.

238 Guins, Vol. 2, pp. 499–500.

239 Zankevich, M.I. 'Obstoiatel'stva soprovozhdavshie vydachu adm. Kolchaka revoliutsionnomu pravitel'stvu v Irkutske', *Beloe delo* (Berlin), Vol. 2 (1927), pp. 150–6; FO 538/3 'Nash (Chita) to Lampson (Harbin), 31.i.1920: "Diary of Lieutenant-Colonel D.A. Malinovskii"' (cited hereafter as 'Malinovskii Diary'). The latter also appeared as Malinovskii, D.A. 'Kak predali Kolchaka', *Novaia Russkaia zhizn'* (Helsingfors) 26.xi.1920.

non-Czechoslovak transport – should be relegated to the slow line and, before allowing them to proceed, uncoupled an engine from them. Ominously, Zankevich's protests to the Legion's commander, Janin (who was at Irkutsk), elicited no response and, on December 13th, seething with impotent fury, Kolchak finally crawled on towards Krasnoiarsk at the miserable pace of 90 km per diem, sustained only by the hope that things might improve and priority be restored to his trains further east.[240]

That, however, was a vain hope, for Janin had by now tacitly concurred with a report from Syrovy that 'to ensure the Admiral's personal safety and in view of the state of feelings against him among the Czechoslovak troops, it was better that he should take his place in the main stream of traffic'.[241] Consequently, at Krasnoiarsk Kolchak was delayed for several more days (December 17th–21st) while both tracks of the Trans-Siberian were monopolized by trains bearing coal from Cheremkhovo to fuel the Czechoslovak evacuation. According to Malinovskii, renewed appeals to Janin from Krasnoiarsk also 'met with no results' and it was only after 'long conversations' between Kolchak's representatives and the local Czechoslovak railway controller that an agreement was reached covering the Supreme Ruler's further progress. However, the agreement was that only the personal trains of Kolchak and Pepeliaev, together with those carrying the gold reserve, might move east; to the inhabitants of all remaining trains in the admiral's convoy were granted only a 'guarantee of safe passage to the east in turn with the Czechoslovak echelons' which, in the circumstances, was likely to be of meagre comfort to those involved.

Kolchak had departed from Krasnoiarsk just as the Zinevich affair broke and the town fell into rebel hands. He well knew, however, that his escape was not complete and that towns to the east were also being captured by the forces of the Political Centre. On December 25th, at Ilianskaia Station, news reached the Supreme Ruler's train of the events at Cheremkhovo and of the imminent loss of the next major station on his route, Nizhneudinsk. There was no choice, however, but to proceed and on the 27th Kolchak and his entourage steamed cautiously into Nizhneudinsk. The Czech station commander, Major Hasek, ordered that the echelons should be manoeuvred into a siding and had nearby wagons removed to afford a clear view of all comings and goings. The area was then surrounded by machine-gunners of the

240 Grondijs, *Le Cas Koltchak*, pp. 38, 75–82.

241 Janin, M. *Ma mission en Sibérie, 1918–20*. Paris (1933), p. 148.

Legion's 6th Regiment and the guns of the armoured train 'Orlik' were trained on Kolchak's echelon. Hasek informed the Supreme Ruler that all this was being done for his own safety, in accordance with orders from Irkutsk that he should proceed no further east. The major would further have disarmed Kolchak's guard. When the Russians protested to Janin, however, the Czech was told by Janin that although Kolchak should be detained at Nizhneudinsk, in the light of the Allied decision to make the railway a neutral zone, he should not be disarmed. Rather, in the event of a clash between government forces and local insurgents, both sides should be disarmed.[242] In this humiliating posture Kolchak remained, surrounded and almost completely isolated, for the best part of a fortnight. Blinds were kept drawn on his trains and few passengers dared to venture outside, for it was known that rebels now controlled the town and that only the presence of the Legionnaires was preventing them from attacking the train. Intermittent attempts to establish contact with the outside world came to nought. As Malinovskii noted:

> The bearing of the Czechoslovaks towards us was outwardly courteous... They agreed to summon this or that person to the telegraph. But when the conversation had begun it turned out that either communications were cut or that the person wanted had not come to the telegraph. When General Zankevich asked permission to speak with Irkutsk the Czechs answered that General Janin had replied: 'General Janin cannot speak with General Zankevich and General Lokhvitskii [Kolchak's personal representative at Irkutsk] is not to be found at Irkutsk.' All our efforts to speak with the ministers also had no result. The general impression given was that neither the Czechs nor Irkutsk desired to converse with us.[243]

Efforts to contact the Russian Army command, who were still 1,000 km to the west, proved equally fruitless. Even when Hasek could be persuaded to grant access to the telegraph, messages were intercepted by Zinevich at Krasnoiarsk, who informed Malinovskii that he was 'controlled by local organizations and is powerless'.[244]

242 FO 371/538/3 'Malinovskii Diary'; Zankevich, pp. 150–1; Kotomkin, A. (ed.) *O chekhoslovatskikh legionerakh v Sibiri, 1918–1920: vospominaniia i dokumenty*. Paris (1930), p. 89.

243 FO 538/3 'Malinovskii Diary'.

244 FO 538/3 'Malinovskii Diary'. According to a member of Kappel's staff, a line was briefly opened in the opposite direction, from the train of the Commander-in-Chief to Nizhneudinsk. However, the Czechoslovaks informed Kappel that no messages could be passed to Kolchak's train. See Fedotoff-White, *Survival Through War and Revolution*, pp. 280–1.

If – as it clearly did – it suited both the Legion and the Allied High Commissioners to have Kolchak and the gold train waylaid, incommunicado, on a Siberian backwater, and discussions as to their ultimate fate postponed until the political and military battles being waged at Irkutsk had resolved themselves, then it was a respite they were not long afforded. On December 31st Janin received an urgent note from Hasek informing him that all of Nizhneudinsk apart from the station was now in the hands of pro-Bolshevik rebels who had declared the region to be a republic and were threatening to sabotage the railway unless both Kolchak and the gold reserve were surrendered to them. Against the local rebels, Hasek said, he could hold out. However, several thousand partisans were known to be massing north of Nizhneudinsk and if they descended on the town there would be little his 1,300 men would be able to do to safeguard either Kolchak or the gold.[245] The High Commissioners' response was swift and decisive: on January 1st an offer was made to the Kolchak government at Irkutsk to have the gold reserve transported to Vladivostok with an Allied escort and, the Triumvirate's agreement having been secured, that same day Janin issued instructions to the effect that the Czechoslovaks at Nizhneudinsk should place the bullion under close guard 'in the interests of the Russian people'.[246] In respect of the person of Kolchak, the High Commissioners acted equally swiftly and decisively: also on January 1st, they issued Janin with the following directive:

> The Allied High Commissioners declare that all means must be taken to secure, as far as it is humanly possible to do so, the personal safety of Admiral Kolchak.
>
> If Admiral Kolchak finds himself obliged to appeal in this matter for the protection of Allied troops, it is indubitably the duty of such troops to afford him protection and to take any steps necessary to ensure his conveyance to whatever place shall be designated by the Allied governments, bearing in mind the need (should it arise) of negotiating with all the parties concerned.
>
> Should Admiral Kolchak consider that the circumstances are not such as to compel him to seek the protection of Allied troops, it is clearly possible that a situation will arise in which it will be difficult for the Allied troops to decide what action to take. For the matter then becomes a question of Russian internal politics, in which Allied troops cannot be expected to intervene. Even so, however, it will be their duty in such

245 *Peregovory*, p. 9; Grondijs, *Le Cas Koltchak*, pp. 129–31.

246 *ibid.*, p. 137; *Peregovory*, pp. 28–9; FO 371/4099/187294 'Daily Précis of Events at Irkutsk', App. 18.

a situation to make every effort to guarantee the personal safety of Admiral Kolchak by resorting to methods of conciliation.[247]

This was clear enough: if the famously stubborn Kolchak refused to seek assistance, the Allies would still do their best, in a situation over which they had no control, to extricate him from Siberia; but if he asked for help, it would be immediately given.

Peter Fleming was correct to point out that Janin's treatment of this very clear instruction was somewhat 'equivocal'.[248] For rather than forward a full copy of the note to Hasek, he sent a personal interpretation of it, which very firmly stressed the need to observe neutrality in relation to Russian affairs and emphasized that 'We can only intervene *if the Admiral seeks our protection*.'[249] This seemed to understate the third paragraph of the Commissioners' instruction. However, in Janin's defence it has to be said that his first duty was to protect the men under his command, that is the Czechoslovak Legion, not Kolchak.

Besides, the question of the admiral declining to seek sanctuary with the Allies did not arise. He may have been stubborn, but he was not foolish enough to imagine that he could extricate himself, his entourage and the gold train from the perilous situation at Nizhneudinsk without the assistance of Czechoslovak troops. Thus, on January 3rd, responsibility for guarding the gold train was granted to the 1st Battalion of the Legion's 6th Regiment and on the 4th Kolchak despatched a cipher telegram to the High Commissioners intimating that he was resolved to step down as Supreme Ruler in favour of Denikin, vouchsafing that an order to this effect would be signed upon his arrival at Verkhneudinsk and requesting their assistance in conveying him there 'speedily'.[250] Earlier on the 3rd Kolchak had received an appeal from his Council of Ministers 'insisting' that he abdicate in order to smooth the path of the ongoing negotiations with the Political Centre at Glaskovo.[251] We know from Malinovskii's diary, however, that the relevant decision had already been

247 FO 371/4099/187294 'Daily Précis of Events at Irkutsk'; Grondijs, *Le Cas Koltchak*, p. 133.

248 Fleming, pp. 187–9.

249 Grondijs, *Le Cas Koltchak*, p. 133 (my italics).

250 FO 538/3 'Malinovskii Diary'; FO 371/4100/210689 'Report on the Events Connected with the Handing Over to the Political Centre and Execution by the Military Revolutionary Committee of the RSFSR of the Late Admiral Kolchak at Irkutsk, by Captain Shilling (Vladivostok), 26.iii.1920' (Hereafter 'Shilling Report').

251 Konstantinov, *Poslednie dni*, pp. 162–3; Livshits, *Imperialisticheskaia interventsiia*, p. 85.

taken, at an emergency conference held on Kolchak's train during the night of 2nd–3rd January, and that it had been taken in the light of the communication to Kolchak by Hasek of orders from Janin to the effect that, should Kolchak appeal for aid, 'all of the echelons of the Supreme Ruler, under Allied flags, will be escorted to the east, to a safe zone'.[252]

There was, however, a codicil to Janin's instructions – of which, in fairness to the French and Czechoslovak authorities, it has to be emphasized that Kolchak's train was also apprised. This was, as Malinovskii recorded, that 'if for any reason it is not possible to despatch all echelons', only Kolchak and his most senior staff (Malinovskii lists six names) were to be 'saved and escorted to the Far East'.[253] It came not altogether out of the blue, therefore, when early on January 5th at Nizhneudinsk there was duly delivered to Kolchak an order from Janin to the effect that he would be furnished with just one wagon and that only such staff as could be accommodated in it would be taken east by the Legion. This restriction, however, placed Kolchak in a most invidious position, for although many of the original complement of 1,500 fellow travellers with which he had left Omsk in November had since departed, there still remained some sixty officers and 500 men in his convoy. He therefore had Zankevich fire off an indignant message to the High Commissioners:

> The Admiral has asked me to inform you that for moral reasons he cannot abandon his subordinates to the fury of the mob and he is resolved to share their fate, however terrible that may be.[254]

Although this broadside also quite erroneously protested that the restriction on numbers was contrary to earlier promises to convey all Kolchak's companions to the east, its injured inaccuracy may be forgiven, for it has to be admitted that there was something a little brutal and malicious in Janin's delivery of the order. He had, in fact, waited until the High Commissioners had left Irkutsk on January 5th before despatching it and the first that the Allied diplomats knew of the order was when they received Zankevich's protest against it. The most charitable interpretation to put

252 FO 538/3 'Malinovskii Diary'.

253 FO 538/3 'Malinovskii Diary'. Malinovskii mentions 'the Admiral, General Zankevich, Colonel Kakitkin [?] and myself and two others'.

254 Zankevich, pp. 151–2; FO 538/3 'Malinovskii Diary'; Grondijs, *Le Cas Koltchak*, p. 153.

on the incident might be that General Janin was unable to consult with the High Commissioners and, with the situation at Irkutsk and throughout the Irkutsk *guberniia* becoming increasingly perilous for his Czechoslovak charges as the Kolchak government collapsed on the 5th, he had honestly decided that he could do no more for the admiral. Indeed, a garbled telegram from Janin did subsequently arrive at Nizhneudinsk, claiming that 'all that has been possible to do for the Admiral has been done' and declaring that the provision of just one wagon was final.[255] But whether a different decision might have been taken had the High Commissioners remained in Irkutsk for another day, whether General Janin was venting the accumulated spleen of having been ignored and contradicted by Kolchak from the very day of his arrival at Omsk (when, it will be recalled, the Frenchman had been refused the command of the Russian Army which he had expected to receive), and whether Janin was right to suppose that the Czechoslovak Legionnaires could not possibly have been prevailed upon to convey Kolchak's complete suite through Irkutsk to the east, are all matters which must remain in the realm of speculation.

Equally, however, it might be speculated that Admiral Kolchak was not dealing altogether honestly with his reluctant saviours. After all, despite the advice proffered by his Council of Ministers on January 3rd to the effect that he should abdicate *immediately* – advice clearly seconded by the High Commissioners, who had granted the Triumvirate the facility to transmit this message to Nizhneudinsk – in his cipher note of January 4th, as we have seen, Kolchak undertook to put his signature to the necessary documents only once the Allies had conveyed him safely to Transbaikalia. This, especially when considered in conjunction with the fact that on January 4th Kolchak signed a supplementary note granting 'full military and civilian authority in the Far East' to Ataman Semenov,[256] could very well be construed as an attempt to leave the door open to a resumption of power by the admiral if he could get safely through to the east, out of the Czechoslovak zone and into a region dominated by the Japanese on whom – as we know – many on his train were placing their last hopes. Such at least was the conclusion of one officer

255 FO 538/3 'Malinovskii Diary'.

256 FO 371/4098/175782 'Kolchak *ukaze* of January 4th, 1920'.

accompanying Kolchak, while Janin and other French officers claimed later that they had been suspicious in January that this was what the admiral secretly intended.[257]

Janin's mean offer may, therefore, have reflected a suspicion of Kolchak's true intentions. Mean or not, however, the offer was accepted by Kolchak. There was initially some wild talk at a conference on the Supreme Ruler's train of the admiral, his staff and personal bodyguard setting off across country to Mongolia on sledges, with whatever portion of the gold reserve they could manage. General Filat′ev was even issued with orders to equip such a convoy.[258] However, outside the train rumours were rife among Kolchak's guard – whose morale had already been weakened through their subjection to propaganda from the local rebels – that the Allies had abandoned them, and the prospect of a 2,000 km winter trek through the Gobi Desert was not calculated to maintain their loyalty: 'The soldiers at first timidly and then impudently began to pack their belongings and arms and left in groups for the town, having torn off their shoulder straps', recorded Malinovskii. To an enthusiastic reception from the rebel lines outside the station, Kolchak's private band 'went into town playing the "Marseillaise"'. The desertion of his hand-picked escort, recalled Zankevich, was 'a grave moral blow' to the admiral, who 'suddenly went grey over night'.[259]

Their soldiers having deserted, the option was then considered of the officers making the attempt to reach Mongolia alone. Filat′ev was issued with new orders to make the necessary preparations, and the Czechs – who probably reasoned that their own progress might be smoother if unencumbered by Kolchak – proffered maps and intelligence on partisan operations twixt Nizhneudinsk and the Mongolian frontier. For their part, however, although Kolchak himself was apparently still keen on the plan, his staff were coming to the conclusion that their only chance of

257 Filat′ev, *Katastrofa*, p. 111; *Russkoe ekho* (Shanghai) (a conversation between Janin and one Shendrikov), cited in Mel′gunov, Pt.3, Vol. 2, p. 141; Dubarbier, p. 146. Filat′ev (pp. 109–11) also raises the interesting constitutional question of whether Kolchak was in breach of the *Polozhenie* of November 18th 1918, which had not made provision for such a move, but only (under Article 6) for the transfer of the plenitude of state power to the Council of Ministers in the event of the death or incapacity of the Supreme Ruler. However, by January 4th the Council of Ministers was clearly in no position to accept such a transfer, even had it been offered, and it advised Kolchak to step down in favour of Denikin. On November 19th 1919, by order of Kolchak, the latter had already been granted supreme authority over all territory controlled by the AFSR (see Grey and Bouderier, p. 229) and by an order of June 24th 1919 had been named as Deputy Supreme Commander-in-Chief. See *Russkaia zhizn′* (Helsingfors) No. 110, 17.vii.1919.

258 Filat′ev, pp. 119–20.

259 FO 538/3 'Malinovskii Diary'; Zankevich, p. 153.

success in such a venture would be for the admiral to remain behind with the Czechs. One officer dared put this to Kolchak, who asked bitterly: 'Are you deserting me?' 'No, we will go with you if you want', was the obviously forced reply. To break the embarrassing impasse Zankevich tried a more subtle approach and suggested that, while the officers fled, the admiral should avail himself of the opportunity to disguise himself as a soldier and hide on a Czechoslovak train. Kolchak, however, refused: 'No. I do not want to be beholden to those Czechs for my salvation', was his haughty retort – even though, in reality, he was already beholden to the Legion for his safety at Nizhneudinsk and even though, through suffering the indignity of such a move, he would have relieved his companions of their dangerous obligation to remain at his side. Of course, Kolchak did formally release all officers from their duties and told them to act as their consciences dictated. And some, according to the Dutch war correspondent Grondijs, did then make good an escape across Mongolia to China. The majority of his staff deemed, however, that their leader could not honourably be deserted and that all should continue together towards Irkutsk and their shared fate.[260]

On the morning of January 6th, therefore, Kolchak repeated *en clair* to Irkutsk his resolution to abdicate at Verkhneudinsk, while Zankevich informed the High Commissioners that in view of what he euphemistically termed 'local circumstances' it was now 'possible to place in one wagon the admiral and those who accompany him'.[261]

Later that day a second-class passenger car was duly produced by the Czechs. Kolchak and Timireva occupied one coupé while between seventy and a hundred officers and others squeezed into the remaining compartments and the corridor. The dreadful crush was eased when Pepeliaev somehow procured a second coach and the Czechs were prevailed upon to spare a freezer-wagon for the group's luggage. Then, in final preparation for the journey and in line with Janin's instructions to Hasek, the flags of the Allies – Britain, France, Czechoslovakia, the USA and Japan – were affixed to Kolchak's carriages and a picket from the Legion's 6th Regiment, commanded by Major Gustav Becvar, was posted around them. On the following day, January 7th, the carriages were coupled to the train of the 6th Regiment, which

260 Filat'ev, pp. 119–20; Grondijs, *La Guerre*, p. 538.

261 Grondijs, *Le Cas Koltchak*, pp. 155–6.

itself occupied a place behind the twenty-nine wagons of the gold train, and the newly constituted echelon No. 58 set out on the 500 km haul to Irkutsk.[262]

It was a humiliating journey for Kolchak. Before its commencement his retinue had been disarmed and two Czech officers had appeared in his carriage to verify that the admiral was still on board and had not fled. 'The Admiral went out into the corridor and said sharply, "Yes, I am here"', recorded Malinovskii. 'It was evident that it was hard for him to pronounce these words and that the inspection was insulting.' Nor was it a comfortable trip. Apart from the overcrowding, noted Malinovskii, 'we almost never had hot food and there was a time when it was impossible to obtain water for the Admiral to drink'; and only a meagre supply of coal to heat the stoves could be bribed from the Czech guard. Nor could the company have felt particularly secure. They were warned before the journey started not to lean out of the windows of their wagon – not for fear of partisan snipers, but 'because the Czechoslovak soldiers were incensed against the admiral'.[263] Initially, however, it does not seem that Kolchak's suite were overly fretful as to their fate. That the Legion was an unwilling host was obvious, noted Zankevich: 'But we knew that at Irkutsk there were two battalions of Japanese and we firmly believed that they would be charged with escorting the Admiral further.' Wagers were even laid as to whether their ultimate destination would be Harbin or Vladivostok.[264]

As the days passed, however, the situation became increasingly alarming for the Russian passengers. White administration had by now collapsed throughout Irkutsk *guberniia* and angry bands of partisans and workers met the train at every passing station, waving banners and shouting demands that Kolchak and the gold should be handed over. The Czechoslovaks refused, but at Station Zima on January 12th, when the partisans of I.M. Novokshinov threatened to blow up the line and halt their evacuation, they were forced to permit a rebel representative (one Sosedko) onto Kolchak's train. Moreover, Novokshinov was able to telegraph ahead to Cheremkhovo, now firmly in the hands of Zverev's band, and forewarn them of Kolchak's arrival. Knowing of this Becvar ordered evasive action and had the trains steam at speed right through Cheremkhovo on January 13th. At Polovina, however,

262 FO 538/3 'Malinovskii Diary'; Becvar, pp. 240–1.

263 FO 538/3 'Malinovskii Diary'.

264 Zankevich, p. 153.

12 km further east, they were flagged down and warned that the basin's miners were already on strike and that no coal would be supplied to the rest of the Legion's evacuating echelons unless partisans were permitted to join the guard over Kolchak. The Czech commander was forced to relent and several dozen workers and partisans clambered aboard echelon No. 58.[265]

At this point the situation on the train became truly nervewracking. Nobody dared venture outside the carriage, but whenever the train stopped its inhabitants could descry two Red sentries outside of Kolchak's window alongside the customary Czechoslovak picket. 'We are no longer free and only guarded – we are now prisoners', lamented Malinovskii to his journal: 'Our fate is now clear.' Some Czech officers extended a final offer of assistance, suggesting to the Russians that a blind eye would be turned 'if they went for a walk and did not return to the wagon'. And, on the 14th, at Innokent′evskaia, Zankevich took advantage of this merciful offer. He slipped away and attempted to contact Janin by telegraph to alert him to Kolchak's plight; only to be informed, however, that the French commander had left Baikal Station and could not be contacted. Hearing rumours that Janin and Syrovy had already decided that Kolchak should be handed over to the revolutionaries at Irkutsk and that he would be informed of this when he arrived there, Zankevich then made his way into the city to survey the situation. At midday on January 15th his terse report was passed to the Supreme Ruler's train by a sympathetic Czech: 'Irkutsk: situation indefinite but alarming', it read.[266]

Zankevich's warning was only confirmed when echelon No. 58 finally pulled into Irkutsk at 3 p.m. on January 15th and drew to a halt on one of the Glaskovo sidings. From his window Kolchak would have been able to see prominently displayed wall posters heralding the arrival of 'the leader of the treacherous government which has for so long oppressed the people' and urging vigilance to ensure that he did not escape the people's justice.[267] Moreover, about a hundred Political Centre troops were formed up along the platform, their red rosettes and armbands only slightly less alarming than the grenades and machine-guns which they brandished ostentatiously in the direction of the train. In a move apparently

265 Dvorianov and Dvorianov, pp. 215–17; Vendrykh, p. 48; Shemelev, *Profsoiuzy Sibiri*, pp. 218–19.

266 FO 538/3 'Malinovskii Diary'; Zankevich, p. 154.

267 WO 32/5720 'Report of Captain A. Stilling [sic] on the Execution of Admiral Kolchak (Vladivostok), 26.iii.1919', p. 3.

prearranged with the Czechoslovaks, it was this force which mounted a guard around Kolchak's carriage. However, there was not as yet total despair on board, as Malinovskii related:

> Even this circumstance did not permit us to lose all hope, as we and the Admiral trusted overmuch in the honour of the Allies. We trusted Janin too much and his telegram regarding our unhindered passage to the east. We regarded the Allied flags, and were reassured thereby.[268]

And there was always the 1,000-strong contingent of Japanese troops at the station – two battalions of them, on whose trains a permanent head of steam was kept up. And indeed, although neither the Czech guard nor the 'prisoners' themselves actually knew it, on the 15th the Japanese commander *had* gone to Syrovy and requested that Kolchak should be placed in his care.[269] Peering through the gathering darkness at their station surroundings, recorded Malinovskii, the Russians expected at any minute to be transferred to the protection of the Japanese:

> We eagerly gazed at each passing Japanese and impatiently awaited the time when our Japanese friends, who crowded around our wagon, would come up and take us into their safe protection.[270]

But it was not to be. Syrovy turned down the Japanese request, saying that if any attempt was made to remove Kolchak from Irkutsk it was certain that the Cheremkhovo miners and Irkutsk rebels would block the Legion's evacuation. He had not made such a move independently. In fact, he had already been in consultation with his superior, Janin, on the matter of Kolchak's fate – which, it now transpired, *was* to be of surrender to the Irkutsk rebels. Thus, when at 6 p.m. Becvar and his colleague, Major Krasa, having collected orders from the Legion's headquarters, boarded Kolchak's train they had to declare, with evident shame:

268 FO 538/3 'Malinovskii Diary'.

269 WO 32/5720 'Report of Captain Stilling', p. 3; FO 371/4100/210689 (Annex 2) 'Colonel Fukuda (Irkutsk) to Chief of Staff of the Japanese Expeditionary Force, 16.i.1920'; Becvar, *The Lost Legion*, p. 244.

270 FO 538/3 'Malinovskii Diary'.

> We have just come from the staff of the Czechoslovak corps, where, in accordance with the orders of General Janin, we received the order to hand over Admiral Kolchak and all those accompanying him to the forces of the local government.

Stepping from his compartment Kolchak demanded that the message be repeated in his presence and, that having been done, noted Malinovskii, 'with blazing eyes and a bitter smile', he said:

> So, this is the meaning of the guarantee given to me by General Janin... An act of international treachery. Well, I am ready for anything.

With Czech connivance several of Kolchak's staff, Malinovskii amongst them, now took the opportunity to escape, dodging the bullets loosed after them by the Red guards. Kolchak remained on board the train, almost alone, awaiting his fate.[271]

It seems that the Political Centre had formally demanded the surrender of Kolchak earlier on the 15th January and, permission having been secured from Janin (who was by then at Verkhneudinsk), the necessary act of transfer was drawn up and signed at 8.55 p.m. by the Czech representative, Dr Blagosh, at the apartment of the Deputy Chairman of the Political Centre, B. Kozminskii.[272] Precisely one hour later the document was passed to the Czechoslovak command at Glaskovo over the signatures of the Political Centre's M.S. Fel′dman, Nesterov and V.N. Merkhalev. Kolchak, wearing a black fur coat of the *Borchatki* type decorated with admiral's epaulettes and a Cross of St George, Timireva (who refused to be parted from the admiral) and Pepeliaev, were duly presented to the Centre's delegation in the station's 1st class waiting room; a formal receipt was issued and, at approximately 1.30 a.m., under a joint escort of partisans from Polovina and members of the Irkutsk workers' militia, the trio were marched off across the frozen Angara in the direction of the city. The recent shelling in the area had left the thin ice fractured, however, and the going underfoot proved difficult. At one point Kolchak stumbled and his guards feared for a moment that he was attempting to commit suicide; but he had merely sustained a bootful of water and proffered a courteous '*merci*' for the workmen's assistance in emptying it. Eventually, with the exhausted Timireva on the point of collapse, the strange procession reached the far

271 FO 538/3 'Malinovskii Diary'; Zankevich, p. 156; Becvar, pp. 242–3.

272 Parfenov, 'Poslednie dni', p. 111; Grondijs, *Le Cas Koltchak*, p. 50.

bank where, near the Kurbatov baths, a lorry with a cavalry escort awaited the prisoners. From there it could only have taken a few minutes to cross the city to the low, rectangular stone building crouching sinisterly beyond the Ushakovka – Irkutsk prison.[273]

Belying the careful and orderly manner in which the affair was consummated, the Political Centre's decision to demand custody of Kolchak – a rescindment, it should be recalled, of promises given during the Glaskovo negotiations of January 2nd–4th – was actually more a reflection of the SR organization's inability to control events at Irkutsk than it was a sign of its authority. From the very moment of its advent at Irkutsk during the night of January 4th–5th, the Political Centre had been able to exert only the simulacrum of power in the town, and not even that beyond its limits. The putative authority of the SRs was subverted by right-wing terror on the one hand and the developing influence of the Irkutsk Bolsheviks on the other. The consequence of the SR's impuissance was Kolchak's incarceration.

The disturbances at Irkutsk during the evening of January 4th which had interrupted the Triumvirate–Political Centre negotiations were sparked off when the Commander of the Irkutsk garrison, General Sychev, had initiated the peremptory evacuation of the officers, soldiers and junkers still recognizing his authority, together with those elements of the Skipetrov group which had entered the town. This action, which was in direct contravention of the terms of the armistice agreement with Kalashnikov's People's Army, had been inspired (perhaps accidentally) when, during the afternoon of the 4th, prior to departing for that day's session of the talks at Glaskovo, Cherven-Vodali had let slip to Sychev that the Political Centre's authority would have to be recognized by the government. It seems that it was at that point that the general decided to get out while the going was good.[274]

The Political Centre would probably have been only too glad to see the back of the 300 or so White die-hards whom Sychev had concentrated on the Chita Road, ready for evacuation, by the evening of the 4th, and might well have let them go unhindered. However, battle was joined when it became known that Sychev was

273 'Konets Kolchaka – vospominaniia G. Vladimirova', in Vegman, V. (ed.) *Gorniaki Sibiri: revoliutsiia i grazhdanskaia voina (Profsoiuznoe stroitel'stvo, 1917–1927gg. – sbornik statei i vospominaniia)*. Novosibirsk (1927), pp. 158–9.

274 Guins, *Sibir'*, Vol. 2, pp. 496–7; Serebrennikov, *Moi vospominaniia*, p. 279.

disinclined to flee empty-handed. Part of his intended booty was recovered when a joint Czechoslovak–People's Army patrol under a Captain Malyshev interrupted a group of *semenovtsy* in the act of loading 400 poods of gold onto trucks outside the State Bank on Amur Street. However, Sychev himself could not be prevented from abducting thirty men and one woman from among the internees at Irkutsk prison. The hostages, who included thirteen members of the PSR (including the eminent Mikhailov and Markov) and six Bolsheviks, were selected from amongst those arrested at the time of the government's December crackdown on the opposition. With this human booty in tow, the general then made his way eastward out of Irkutsk and along the right bank of the Angara to Mikhailevo. There he crossed over the river to join the waiting trains of the Skipetrov expedition.[275]

Immediately that Sychev's initial breach of the armistice became known at Glaskovo, both sets of negotiators were alive to the possibility of hostage-taking and Cherven-Vodali had freely acceded to the request of the Centre's Ivanitskii-Vasilenko that all political prisoners in Irkutsk should be afforded Czech protection.[276] Then, when it was realized that it was too late to protect the hostages already reaven, on the advice of the High Commissioners a further order – perhaps the last order of the Kolchak government – was signed by Cherven-Vodali, Larionov and General Vagin ordering Sychev to attend to the welfare of the prisoners in his charge.[277] Finally, on January 8th, after incidents around Baikal during which the renegade *semenovtsy* had interrupted telegraphic communications, attacked some American marines and fired on the train of the US Consul, Mr Harris, Janin issued orders for Czechoslovak and American troops to disarm all Semenov's forces in the circum-Baikal region. By January 10th a 200 km stretch of line around the lake, including the vulnerable tunnels, was in Allied hands. The thirty-one hostages, however, were not found and hopes for their survival were not raised when at Mikhailevo and at Sliudianka the Czechs uncovered the cruelly mutilated bodies of eighteen railway officials who had refused to co-operate with Sychev and Skipetrov.[278]

275 WO 106/1276 'Report on the Revolutionary Movement at Irkutsk'; Konstantinov, *Poslednie dni*, pp. 172–3; Il′in, 'Omsk' Vol. 73 (1963), pp. 236–7; 'N', 'Poslednie dni', pp. 90–3.

276 *Peregovory*, p. 63.

277 Grondijs, *La Guerre*, p. 543.

278 *ibid.*, p. 544; Parfenov, *Bor′ba za Dal′nyi Vostok*, p. 47.

On the 13th it was duly confirmed by a joint Political Centre–Czechoslovak investigation that all thirty-one of the hostages abducted from Irkutsk had been murdered on the orders of Skipetrov, and in the most barbaric fashion. The official report related how, having been incarcerated by Skipetrov's henchman Cherepanov in the 3rd-class buffet of the ice-breaker 'Angara', the unfortunates had been shipped out onto the lake from Baikal Station harbour at dawn on January 6th. After a few hours' carousing, Cherepanov then had them summoned one by one up the companion way and through a hatch onto the deck. As they emerged, each prisoner was clubbed and tossed – some dead, some still living – into the frozen lake by the rough hands of a Colonel Sipailo (later to perfect his sanguinary trade as a mainstay of Ungern-Sternberg's bestial tyranny at Urga) and a renegade British mercenary called Grant.[279]

Unfortunately for Kolchak news of the grisly fate of the thirty-one at the hands of those perceived as being the loyal servants of his régime reached Irkutsk before he did. The resulting outcry then predetermined not only that the Political Centre should demand his surrender but that his sickened Czechoslovak custodians should grant it. At Irkutsk Allied representatives found that 'this crime is now quoted freely as a justification for reprisals against Kolchak'. In the words of a British observer in the town, Captain Shilling: 'The news of the murder of the prisoners by Skipetrov...disgusted the Czechoslovaks and, by arousing general indignation amongst the Russians, rendered the task of saving Kolchak more difficult.' After this sadistic debauch, noted Shilling, the Legionnaires were 'prepared to subordinate all other considerations' to their one aim of getting out of Siberia, 'including the execution of the obligations they had accepted' with regard to the conveying of Kolchak to safety.[280]

On the afternoon of January 14th General Syrovy at the Legion's headquarters at Irkutsk spoke on the direct wire with Janin, who was at Verkhneudinsk, informing his commander that, as a result of recent developments, the situation at Irkutsk was approaching crisis point: workers were on strike and, according to Syrovy, were preparing to waylay Kolchak by the seizure of Glaskovo Station. This, he claimed,

279 Smirnov et al., *Bor'ba za Ural i Sibir'*, pp. 268–72; Grondijs, *La Guerre*, pp. 546–7; Parfenov, *Bor'ba za Dal'nyi Vostok*, pp. 47–8. The Newcastle-upon-Tyne-built 'Angara' remains extant on the lake and was once scheduled to be converted into a museum. See Massey Stewart, J. 'Britain's Siberian Connection', in *Siberia: Two Historical Perspectives*. London (1984), p. 10.

280 FO 371/4099/187294 'Daily Précis of Events at Irkutsk'; WO 32/5723 'Despatch of HM Consul at Vladivostok, Relative to the Death of Admiral Kolchak'.

would imperil the Legion and its evacuation and he therefore feared that it would not now be possible to convey Kolchak (then at Innokent′evskaia) beyond Irkutsk. To this Janin replied:

> I have no right to breach the orders I have received or to prescribe an intervention which would place the [Czechoslovak] Army in danger. Do your best to safeguard the name of the Czechoslovaks. I will support you.[281]

Hence Kolchak's reception at Glaskovo: hence his transfer from the asylum of a train flying the flags of the Allied nations to a three-metre by two-metre cell at the Irkutsk prison.

It could have come as no surprise to Şyrovy and Janin that their decision to allow Kolchak to fall into rebel hands elicited a calamitous deluge of protests. Officers in Transbaikalia immediately founded a 'League for Janin's Blood'; while the Allied High Commissioners, who had left Irkutsk on January 5th with the understanding that Janin would expedite the admiral's passage to the east in accordance with their instructions of January 1st, expressed 'astonishment' at his conduct and, in notes of January 22nd and 24th, demanded an explanation from him.[282] Subsequently, in a circular telegram to the High Commissioners and in interviews with the local and western press, Janin and Syrovy attempted to justify their action. Syrovy's case was that:

> According to the orders of our government, our attitude vis-à-vis the Russians had to consist of a strict neutrality with regard to the internal situation. That was the sole means of facilitating the evacuation of our troops from Russia... Thus, we did not have the right to engage, in order to save Kolchak, in any combat which risked the well-being of the entire Army.

Even had he issued an order to convey the Admiral through Irkutsk, Syrovy argued, it would not have been obeyed, for:

> Kolchak had committed a crime against the Czechoslovaks in the order to Ataman Semenov to stop our evacuation to the east by any means available... The

281 Janin, *Ma mission*, p. 158.

282 *The Times* (London) 29.i.1920; FO 371/4099/187295 'Lampson (Harbin) to FO, 28.i.1920', pp. 79–80.

> Czechoslovak Army knew this and considered him their enemy, culpable of imperilling their evacuation which had been decided upon by the Allies.[283]

In a series of lengthy notes to the High Commissioners of January 23rd, 26th and 29th, Janin seconded Syrovy. He described in detail the threatening situation at Irkutsk, caustically confirming that, as the Legion's Commander-in-Chief, he:

> ...could not risk the destruction of the Czechoslovak Army for the sake of the man who, having lost Siberia, had recommended the blowing up of the [Baikal] tunnels in order likewise to bring about the annihilation of that army.

Of course, as has been demonstrated, it remains a moot point as to whether Kolchak *had* actually issued such an order. Still, it may be appropriate to give Janin the benefit of the doubt and accept that he sincerely believed that such an order had been issued. He maintained, moreover, that the surrender of Kolchak to the Political Centre was not actually in breach of the High Commissioners' note of January 1st, because that had only committed the Czechoslovaks to protect Kolchak *if* he abdicated supreme power and put himself in Allied care as a private person. But in his notes of January 4th and 6th, said Janin, Kolchak 'had not submitted his resignation. He said, "I am resolved to submit my resignation at Verkhneudinsk."' As such he remained the putative leader of one of the warring parties in Russia, whom the Legion was under no obligation to protect or convey to the east.[284]

The logic of Janin and Syrovy cannot be faulted. However, their rather blunt and remorseless language – and Janin's in particular – caused considerable rancour among the High Commissioners (who were by then at Harbin). The tone of Janin's notes was 'querulous and offensive', said the British High Commissioner. Rather than content himself with stating that in the circumstances nothing further could have been done by the Legion to rescue Kolchak and leaving the facts to justify themselves, his communiqués were laced with acerbic asides against the Allied diplomats safe in their 'peaceful havens' in the east and their 'heartfelt indignation' that he, Janin, had 'not allowed [Legionnaires] to be killed on Kolchak's behalf' whilst they had refused to send their own men west to escort the admiral. If anyone

283 Grondijs, *Le Cas Koltchak*, pp. 187, 189–90. See also *Ceskoslovensky dennik* (Irkutsk) 29.i.1920; *The Times* (London) 5.ii.1920.

284 FO 371/4099/187295 'Lampson (Harbin) to FO, 28.i.1920', pp. 81–3. See also *Le Matin* (Paris) 16.vii.1919.

was to blame, the petulant general went on to allege, it was the Japanese Military Mission, which had failed to go to Kolchak's aid at Irkutsk.[285] And indeed, although there was something to be said for Janin's critics' rebuttal of this – namely, that if the entire Czechoslovak Legion could not, as Syrovy vouched, save Kolchak, it was unreasonable to expect two Japanese battalions to do so – the Japanese emerged not *altogether* unblemished from this affair. True, as we have seen, Syrovy had forbidden them to even try to act at Irkutsk on the 14th.[286] But still it might not be altogether unreasonable to argue that, as the only Allied contingent in Siberia which was both sizable and reliable, the Japanese should have offered to protect Kolchak at the beginning of January. The suspicion might further be harboured that they only offered to do so on the 14th, when it was obviously too late, in order to cover themselves from criticism for not having tried at all.

However, any merit there may have been in Janin's attempt at self-exculpation was offset by its rudeness (his apologias were conspicuously bereft of apologies); by the fact that, just like the High Commissioners, he too had left Irkutsk (claiming illness) before Kolchak arrived there; and by the fact that he refused to offer even a *hint* of regret for what had occurred. Indeed, his frequent pronouncements over previous weeks – for example, to Cherven-Vodali on January 2nd – to the effect that if Kolchak did not escape it would be 'all his own fault',[287] smacked of *Schadenfreude* and hinted of premeditation. Above all the question arises of why no attempt was made by Janin (or for that matter Syrovy) to forewarn Kolchak of what was awaiting him at Irkutsk. Guilty or not of Kolchak's deliberate and malicious betrayal, in other words, Janin both looked and acted as guilty as hell.

This, generally, has been sufficient for western commentators to conclude that the unrepentant Janin and Syrovy must bear 'direct responsibility' for Kolchak's 'betrayal'; it has been sufficient to fuel speculation that their 'odious deed' at Irkutsk, this 'cold political calculation' typical of the maltreatment of Kolchak since the fall of Omsk, was 'the logical culmination of a long-term plan for [Kolchak's] abandonment and destruction'.[288] Émigré accounts are invariably and furiously

285 FO 371/4099/187295 'Lampson (Harbin) to FO, 28.i.1919'.

286 FO 371/4100/210689 'Hodgson (Vladivostok) to FO, 19.vi.1920'.

287 *Peregovory*, p. 11.

288 Chamberlin, W.H. *The Russian Revolution*. New York (1935), Vol. 2, p. 202; Fleming, pp. 226–9; Grondijs, *Le Cas Koltchak*, p. 48. Curiously it fell to one of Kolchak's staunchest supporters to concede that Janin may have had no choice: 'Every allowance must be made for

censorious of this 'Cain-like affair', with some White partisans raging bitterly against Janin's 'filthy treachery' more than half a century after the event.[289] Whilst basically rehearsing arguments as to whether the Legion was obliged under the High Commissioners' instruction of January 1st to protect Kolchak in the circumstances prevailing after January 6th – which, as Janin maintained, was actually rather debatable – and concentrating on the moral question of whether Janin and Syrovy should have attempted to save the admiral, however, insufficient attention has been paid in existing accounts to two other issues raised by the events at Irkutsk on January 15th 1920. Firstly, the question arises of whether Janin and Syrovy were correct to assert that any attempt to save Kolchak *must* have failed because there was no other way out for the Czechoslovaks other than to surrender him to the Political Centre; and, secondly, an assessment of what Janin thought would become of Kolchak *if he was* surrendered is surely of some relevance.

With regard to the first point, it has only very rarely been maintained that the surrender of Kolchak to the Political Centre was the Legion's 'sole means of salvation', or that, in the words of an anonymous Britmis report, 'a choice had to be made between continuing the evacuation and protecting a Russian from the Russians'.[290] White observers of the Irkutsk scene point out that the military forces of the Political Centre were so weak and unreliable that the Legion could, if it had so desired, have conveyed Kolchak to safety.[291] Also, both Legras and Montandon of the French mission noted that, during their stay in Siberia after February 1920, they never once heard a single Bolshevik claim that the Allies had had no choice but to hand Kolchak over to the Siberian people; and, indeed, the doyen of early Soviet authorities on the subject, P.S. Parfenov (Altaiskii), concluded laconically: 'The

the difficulties of this officer's position', ventured Winston Churchill in *The World Crisis: the Aftermath*. London (1929), p. 249.

289 Fedulenko, B. 'Rol′ byvshikh soiuznikov Rossii po otnosheniiu Belomu dvizheniiu' (*Museum of Russian Culture*), p. 26; Nefedrov, 'Kak byl zaversheno', p. 140; Nefedrov, N. 'Poslednie dni admirala Kolchaka', in *Zheleznyi zanaves – dve velikie provokatsii i dr.*. New York (1978), p. 157.

290 Essen, p. 290; WO 106/1273 'Britmis (Vladivostok) to WO, 7.ii.1920: "Unrest in Irkutsk, November 1919–January 1920"'.

291 Filat′ev, pp. 127–8; Guins, Vol. 2, p. 514. Guins conceded the possibility that Janin was misinformed by Syrovy of the balance of forces at Irkutsk (*ibid.*, p. 568). A Czechoslovak report of January 26th described the Legion's forces as: West of Irkutsk the 2nd and 3rd Divisions on 120 trains, constituting 60% of Czechoslovak forces (i.e. circa 25,000 men); east of Baikal, from Chita to Vladivostok, the 1st Division on 60 trains. See *USMI*, Vol. 12, No. 46 (week ending 13.iii.1920), p. 3,427.

Allies might have saved him. They certainly possessed sufficient armed forces.'[292] Peter Fleming came down on this side too, quoting at length from a summation of the situation at Irkutsk by a British diplomat, Mr Hodgson, to the effect that the Political Centre 'could not be looked upon as a serious menace to so powerful a military organization as the Czechs', who, no matter what the attitude of the local opposition, could easily have kept the railway running and coal flowing from the Cheremkhovo basin on their own. Hodgson also adduced the fact that, even without the use of the railway, many thousands of Russian soldiers and a host of sick and wounded civilians were able to make it past Irkutsk to Transbaikalia on foot.[293]

However, the point was that by January 1920 Janin was the Commander-in-Chief of the Legion in name only and it is therefore quite pointless to speculate as to what the Legion was capable of militarily. It is graphically clear from Janin's despatches of December 1919 that the Legionnaires were now only obeying him when it suited their purpose to do so.[294] Had he not gone along with their desires 'it would have caused a rebellion', said one observer.[295] Indeed, while ruing the fact, the aforementioned Hodgson (in a passage of his report not quoted by Fleming) endorsed an intelligence report enclosed with his note which concluded:

> When he was handed over it was a question of Admiral Kolchak's safety and of the safety of thousands of Czech lives, and I think, taking into consideration the attitude of the Czechs at that time and since at Irkutsk and to the west of that town, *had Janin decided that Kolchak should not be handed over to the Political Centre, the Czechs would have handed him over all the same*, as they were well aware of their own position and their sympathies were undoubtedly with the SRs.[296]

That is to say, the Czechs could have saved Kolchak if they had so desired, but they quite patently did not desire to do so. Such an attempt would have cost them 'thousands of lives' and delayed their railway evacuation. True, they could have

292 Legras, J. 'L'agonie de la Sibérie', *Le Monde Slave* (Paris), No. 2 (1928), p. 88; Montandon, G. *Deux ans chez Koltchak et les bolchéviques, 1919–1921*. Paris (1923), p. 69; Parfenov, *Bor'ba za Dal'nyi Vostok*, p. 49.

293 Fleming, p. 227, quoting FO 371/4100/210689 'Hodgson (Vladivostok) to FO, 19.vi.1919'. Mel'gunov, Pt.3, Vol. 2, pp. 142–6 makes a similar point; as does Skacel, pp. 348–57.

294 Grondijs, *Le Cas Koltchak*, pp. 179ff, 191ff, 201ff, 217ff.

295 Essen, p. 120. This was also the conclusion of American observers. See the letter of Colonel Johnston to H.H. Fischer referred to in Varneck and Fischer, n. 1; and Graves, pp. 300–1.

296 FO 371/4100/210689 (Annex 1) 'Shilling Report', p. 228 (my italics).

walked. But that would have entailed condemning thousands of their number to a thousand-kilometre exodus to the east which, in the depths a Siberian winter, no man could have wished upon his fellows. Really, given their desire to escape from Russia, given the rapid approach of the Red Army and the abuse which had been heaped upon them by Kolchak for the past year, it has surely to be wondered that the Legion did not ditch their unwelcome passenger earlier rather than that they ditched him at all.

With regard to our second point: the wrath of Janin's critics fuelled as it is by Kolchak's ultimate fate at the hands of the Bolsheviks, has denied any rational consideration of the fact that the French general endorsed the Supreme Ruler's surrender not to the supporters of Lenin but to a predominantly SR authority whose representatives the Allied High Commissioners had already received and recognized at Irkutsk as trustworthy and honest negotiators (certainly preferring them to the temporizing and scabrous members of the Kolchak government) and who were known, as a Czech pointed out, to be opposed to the death penalty.[297] Although worthy of attention, however, this observation cannot be used to exonerate Janin for, as one observer at Irkutsk noted, from the day of Kolchak's surrender 'there was not the slightest doubt as to the fate awaiting those arrested'.[298] Significantly, even Janin himself did not attempt to employ such an argument. Even if the Political Centre did not fall and held on to power at Irkutsk, as one observer noted, it was inevitable that the SRs would use both Kolchak and the gold as bargaining chips in winning concessions from Moscow.[299]

That the Political Centre might survive long enough to engage in such horse-trading, however, was not the most likely scenario. The British High Commissioner himself reported, as he and his colleagues hastily departed Irkutsk during the disturbances of January 5th, that the SR authority had no resources to withstand inevitable Bolshevik pressure.[300] The tone of Janin's communiqués of early January clearly reveals that he too was sure that the Political Centre was incapable of holding on to power at Irkutsk and that they would be succeeded forthwith by the

297 Krejci, F.V. *U sibirske armady*. Prague (1923), p. 270.

298 Essen, p. 119.

299 Grondijs, *Le Cas Koltchak*, p. 54.

300 *DBFP*, pp. 760–2.

Bolsheviks.[301] And, indeed, how could Janin or anybody else believe in the longevity of the Centre when the story was in circulation around Irkutsk that, during a celebratory banquet at the apartment of a leading SR on the night of January 5th, a Czech officer had remarked to a Political Centre member: 'So you are now the government. But for how long?'

'We don't know ourselves', came the lacklustre reply.[302]

Towards a Red Siberia

From the beginning the Political Centre enjoyed only the simulacrum of power at Irkutsk. Like its short-lived precursors at Novonikolaevsk, Tomsk and Krasnoiarsk, the Centre seems to have drawn little sustenance from mass support. Rather, it blossomed under the care and attention of local Czechoslovak forces, whom White intelligence sources found to have been devoting their own print shops to flooding the town with anti-Kolchak leaflets detailing the collapse of the Russian Army in order to draw latent SR support out of the woodwork.[303] Furthermore, once in power at Irkutsk, the Political Centre's authority was only extended around the southern shore of Baikal in the wake of the Legion's operations of January 7th–10th aimed at clearing the *semenovtsy* from that sector; and it was on Czechoslovak trains that the Centre's representatives were despatched eastwards to (unsuccessfully) claim power at Verkhneudinsk and Vladivostok.[304] But, for all their nurturing, the Political Centre authorities transparently remained 'the artificial creations of politicians and the Czechoslovak command', as one observer put it.[305] And, just as during the summer of 1918 such chimerical SR governments could provide no barrier to the inroads on power of the military and the right, so in January 1920 they would be unable to withstand the approaching Red juggernaut and its local outriders.

301 See Grondijs, *Le Cas Koltchak*, pp. 207–11.

302 Vendrykh, pp. 40–1.

303 Sychev, E. 'Vosstanie v Irkutske, 23 dek. 1919–5 ianv. 1920' (*Hoover Institution Archives*).

304 Papin, *Krakh kolchakovshchiny*, pp. 99–100; Parfenov, *Bor'ba za Dal'nyi Vostok*, p. 47.

305 Grondijs, *Le Cas Koltchak*, pp. 44–5.

Although, by virtue of its foreign friends, the Political Centre was thrust to the front of the political stage at Irkutsk during the events of December 1919–January 1920, a far more potent and popular authority at Irkutsk was enjoyed by the local Bolshevik organization. The Bolsheviks, as we have seen, had supported the SRs' staging of a coup against Kolchak, whilst refraining from openly associating with groups tainted by the recent débâcle involving Gajda at Vladivostok. Unfortunately, the only evidence available to assess the precise extent of local Bolshevik influence is that cited in the predictably partisan accounts of Soviet historians. However, given the developing course of events at Irkutsk, their conclusions must be afforded some credence. Broadly speaking the accepted line of Soviet historiography was: that from the very beginning 'although formally the Irkutsk rising was led by the Political Centre, the real forces of the rebels were under the leadership of the Irkutsk Committee of the RKP(b)'; that much of the key 53rd Regiment was thoroughly Bolshevized in advance of the rising of December, as was Iakushev's Special Detachment (as evinced by the latter's insistence on the liberation of 400 political prisoners, including some Bolshevik leaders, from the Irkutsk jail on December 29th in defiance of Political Centre orders); that whilst paying lip-service to Kalashnikov's staff of the People's Army, a thousand or more of the Irkutsk rebels were actually controlled by a parallel Bolshevik military organization, the Workers' and Peasants' Militia, with its own staff at Glaskovo under Mironov (who had tailed Kalashnikov across the Angara on the night of the 24th December); and that, as the partisan forces of Kalandarashvili and Zverev entered Irkutsk during the first days of January 1920, the power of Mironov's staff was augmented to the extent that, when on the night of January 4th–5th the White authorities fled, it could have claimed power in the name of the Bolsheviks but refrained from doing so because 'an armed rising with a call for the establishment of Soviet power...would have been premature, for the threat of action by the interventionists still hung over Irkutsk'.[306]

Rather than antagonize the Czechoslovaks, therefore, a 'tactical manoeuvre' was resorted to and the Political Centre was permitted to assume power on January 5th, even though the SR organization was 'pitiful and powerless, having under its command no territory apart from its own meeting hall and no "masses" to represent

306 Papin, pp. 89–90, 97–100; Vendrykh, pp. 41–6; Shiriamov 'Irkutskoe vosstanie', pp. 129–30; Parfenov, *Bor'ba za Dal'nyi Vostok*, pp. 47–52.

other than a few waitresses who served the tea at their meetings'.[307] The Political Centre's stock fell further, it is claimed, when the populace realized that, in the absence of an alternative source of manpower to run its administration, the SRs called upon the services not merely of men compromised by the failure of previous SR initiatives (in the Provisional Siberian Government, the Directory and Gajda's People's Administration) but even the servants of Kolchak. Particular ire was aroused by the fact that Kalashnikov's staff consisted of former officers of the Russian Army, while much damage was done to the Political Centre's reputation by the employment of G.B. Patushinskii (a former member of the Provisional Siberian Government) as Minister of Justice. In Patushinskii's department worked generally reviled judges and prosecutors of the Kolchak era, while even the majority of the White prison administration remained at their posts. Soviet sources also claimed that popular hostility to the Centre was aroused by the fact that any civil servants of the old régime who wished to move to the east were allowed to leave (with two weeks' wages). It was only due to the vigilance of the Bolshevik militia that a clutch of former ministers of Kolchak were arrested at Irkutsk, they maintained, and even asserted that it was only due to pressure from the Bolshevik Committee that the Political Centre demanded the surrender of Kolchak himself in the wake of the murder of the thirty-one hostages.[308]

Such extensive claims may invite a degree of scepticism. It is certain, however, that the Bolsheviks, under a new *gubkom* elected on January 6th, took maximum advantage of the freedoms of assembly and speech proclaimed by the Political Centre to hold mass meetings of workers and soldiers and to broadcast pro-Soviet agitation through a number of new broadsheets from January 7th onwards. And that such activity was effective is demonstrated by the fact that as early as January 10th–12th a Congress of Irkutsk Railwaymen passed a vote of no confidence in the Political Centre, while on January 12th a meeting of the Trades Union Congress of Irkutsk *guberniia* demanded the summoning of a Soviet in the town.[309]

Against such attacks on its authority the Political Centre fought back on January 10th–11th with the organization of elections to its promised provisional democratic authority for the region. The 'Provisional Siberian Council of Popular

307 Shiriamov, 'Bor'ba', p. 19.

308 Papin, pp. 98–9; Vendrykh, p. 44.

309 Konstantinov, *Poslednie dni*, p. 190.

Administration', which was to administer the region until the summoning of a full Siberian Constituent Assembly, was to consist of eight representatives of the Centre itself, six from the zemstvos, three from the city duma and three each from the co-operatives, the peasantry and the labour unions. Soviet sources, however, claimed that the body (which convened on the 12th) was largely ignored – except in a resolution of the *guberniia* Trades Union Congress demanding greater representation for workers. Certainly the Centre seems to have felt that something was lacking in its authority, for on January 12th–13th it once again appealed to the local Bolsheviks to join. The *gubkom*, however, refused.[310]

With authority at Irkutsk clearly slipping from its grasp and with the local Bolshevik organization refusing to offer support, even before the *gubkom*'s refusal the Political Centre had decided that its only chance of survival was to reach an agreement with the central Soviet authorities. Counting on Sovnarkom's current preoccupation with Wrangel and the Poles in the west and on Moscow's ignorance of the true state of affairs at Irkutsk, it had been decided at the Centre's meeting of January 8th to send a delegation to meet the Military Revolutionary Committee of the 5th Red Army (then at Tomsk) – a delegation which, if necessary, could go on to Moscow. On January 11th, having secured a train, communication facilities and a guarantee of free passage to the west from their Czechoslovak friends, the Political Centre plenipotentiaries, V.M. Konogov (an SR) and I.I. Akhmatov (a Menshevik), set off; they were to rendezvous with the leading delegate, E.E. Kolosov at Krasnoiarsk, and, making difficult progress against the eastbound tide of retreating armies and refugees, would eventually reach Tomsk on January 18th. For their delegates' own security the Centre had asked that a Bolshevik join the mission, and were pleased when the party *gubkom* not only (for once) acceded to their request but selected as their representative the rather independently-minded and accessible Aleksandr Krasnoshchekov rather than a hardliner such as A.A. Shiriamov. From the Bolsheviks' point of view, as we shall see, the choice of delegate turned out to be a bad one. The *gubkom* had calculated, however, that it would be in their interest to accredit a delegate (and an amenable one) to the westbound mission, as this was the only means by which a Bolshevik might get through the retreating Russian Army

310 Vendrykh, pp. 45–6; Papin, pp. 50–2.

and the Czechoslovak lines so as to apprise the leadership of the 5th Red Army of the real state of play at Irkutsk.[311]

The dream of Siberian SRs and of the Political Centre was the establishment of a viable buffer state, independent of both the Soviet government and the influence of the capitalist west and Japan, in the Far East. During the Glaskovo negotiations of January 4th, Akhmatov had revealed that the purpose of such an entity would be to act as a model, the first in a chain of democratic units to surround Soviet Russia and, ultimately, to succeed it.[312] When negotiations commenced at Tomsk on January 18th, however, a rather different gloss was put upon the matter. To a Red delegation (consisting of I.N. Smirnov, R.I. Eikhe, T.V. Fal'ko and others) Kolosov dissembled, presenting the notion of a buffer state centred on Irkutsk not as a bridgehead for a new democratic counter-revolution, but as the only means of saving the Soviet Republic from dangerous clashes with the remnants of Kolchak's forces and the interventionists (especially the Japanese) in the Far East. Throughout the first week of January, in messages passed to the approaching Red Army from his base at Krasnoiarsk, Kolosov had already engaged in a programme of disinformation, talking-up the authority and popularity of the Political Centre at Irkutsk and warning Smirnov that, although the Red Army might now be the victor of the civil war, the Bolsheviks should not overestimate their strength and should unite with the forces of democracy against the eastern hydra of reaction and counter-revolution 'which is stronger than you might think'.[313] Since then, of course, his own Political Centre style government at Krasnoiarsk had given way to Bolshevik control. Yet, face to face at Tomsk, Kolosov rather daringly threw down the gauntlet to the Chairman of the 5th Red Army MRC, Ivan Smirnov:

> If Soviet Russia already has sufficient forces for the immediate crushing of the armed might of Japanese reaction and militarism, then there is only one answer to the question – the uninterrupted advance of Soviet forces through Siberia to Irkutsk and beyond. In such a case no buffer state would be necessary.

311 Vendrykh, p. 46; Papin, pp. 101–3; Parfenov, *Bor'ba za Dal'nyi Vostok*, pp. 52–5; Shiriamov, 'Irkutskoe vosstanie', p. 130.

312 *Peregovory*, p. 50. When it became aware of the assumption of power by the Political Centre, the SR Central Committee at Moscow hailed it as 'the first organizational centre of a Federated Russian Democratic Republic'. See Konstantinov, *Poslednie dni*, pp. 187–9.

313 *ibid.*, pp. 180–2.

If, however, he cautioned, the Soviet government could not crush them immediately, the vestiges of reaction in the Far East would look to Japan and would buy her support with gold and with the cession of Kamchatka, Sakhalin and the CER. In the knowledge that, in Moscow, Sovnarkom had already accepted the possible utility of a buffer state in the east because of the renewed threat in the west, Smirnov was swayed by Kolosov's argument. It was agreed that Soviet Russia would help establish the armed forces of an eastern buffer state and that, in return, both Kolchak and the gold reserve would be returned to Moscow. However, although Lenin's plans had previously envisaged an eastern buffer abutting Soviet territory at Chita (or, at worst, Verkhneudinsk), Smirnov accepted the Political Centre's terms of a border *west* of Baikal, along the Oka (crossing the Trans-Siberian Railway at Zima) and the northern Angara, which would have left both Irkutsk and the Cheremkhovo Basin under the SRs' control. Soviet historians of a later era adduced this 'betrayal' by Smirnov and Eikhe as indicative of the 'Trotskyism' for which they would both be purged in the 1930s. More pertinent, however, was the fact that at no point during the negotiations did the delegate of the Irkutsk Bolsheviks, Krasnoshchekov, raise any objection to Kolosov's partial account of the situation at Irkutsk and his exaggeration of SR power in the city – Krasnoshchekov, in fact, seemed rather more interested in having his nomination secured to the post of Special Plenipotentiary of the Soviet Government to the putative buffer state.[314]

Smirnov immediately made contact with Lenin, who signalled his approval of the Tomsk agreement in a telegram of January 21st (with the sole proviso that the Political Centre should be augmented by one or two Soviet representatives who would have access to all meetings).[315] This Kolosov accepted, and his delegation left Tomsk in apparent triumph, having secured the Soviet leader's recognition of the Political Centre's territorial and political integrity. Before he had even reached Krasnoiarsk, however, Kolosov received via the Czechs the alarming news of two events in the east which were to dash SR hopes for a buffer state to be established on their terms: at Irkutsk the Political Centre had already liquidated itself and had voluntarily transferred power to a Bolshevik Revolutionary Committee on January 21st; meanwhile, on January 20th, elements of the retreating White forces were reported to be massing outside Nizhneudinsk and threatening to recapture the town

314 'Protokol ob″edinennogo zasedaniia mirnoi delegatsii Polittsentra s RVS 5-i armii i Sibrevkom ot 18–19 ianv. 1920', *Sibirskie ogni* (Novosibirsk), No. 5 (1927), pp. 140–6.

315 Lenin, *PSS*, Vol. 51, p. 334. The telegram was also signed by Trotsky.

from rebel forces. The two developments were not altogether unconnected. As we have already seen, following a few brief skirmishes west of Krasnoiarsk during the first days of 1920, on January 6th the new Commander-in-Chief of the Russian Army, General Kappel, had ordered all the forces remaining to him to avoid engagement with the Reds and move around the town. Of those who obeyed, some followed General Voitsekhovskii past the southern limits of Krasnoiarsk and then on, along the Siberian High Road towards the east. Kappel himself, however, chose to take other troops on a rather tortuous route to the north. He led his men (predominantly of the Izhevsk-Votkinsk battalions and the Ufa Division of the 2nd Army) up the River Enisei to its confluence with the Kan and then back down that tributary towards Kansk. Kappel's hope was to shake off any Red pursuit, whilst taking advantage of the reputedly well-stocked villages away from the railway zone to replenish his stores, and to use the clear path afforded by the frozen rivers to speed his retreat.[316] However, accounts of this literal 'ice march' recall that the troops' progress was problematic – food was not really more plentiful than it had been before and, despite frosts reaching –50 degrees, the river ice remained stubbornly unsupportive. In fact, the Kan route had to be abandoned, as many men and horses were lost through the unsound ice. Kappel himself was at one point submerged up to his waist in the freezing stream – an ultimately fatal dunking.[317]

The White Commander-in-Chief's manoeuvre did, however, undoubtedly save many of his troops from falling into the hands of Red Army contingents which reached Krasnoiarsk on January 8th. The Reds had been following the retreating Whites at a safe distance. After Krasnoiarsk, however, they accelerated their pace, only to encounter not the Russian Army (Kappel's men having moved aside) but Allied contingents – specifically some Serbs and the weak and demoralised Polish Legion of some 5,000 men, who constituted the rearguard of the Allied evacuation. Frozen-in near Klukvennaia, as the Czechoslovaks pushed ahead, and without fuel or food, it was clear that the Poles were not going to fight. Anticipating mutiny, on January 5th the Commander-in-Chief of the Polish Legion, General Iasinskii-Stakhurek had already appealed to Syrovy to permit trains carrying Polish sick and wounded to move east ahead of their due turn. Syrovy, however, refused and

316 Serebrennikov, *Velikii otkhod*, p. 15; Guins, *Sibir'*, Vol. 2, pp. 549–50. Efimov, A.G. *Izhevtsy i Votkintsy (Bor'ba s bol'shevikami, 1918–22)*. San Francisco (1974), pp. 242–50.

317 Petrov, P.P. *Ot Volgi do Tikhogo okeana*. Riga (1930), pp. 202–9; Shebeko, pp. 77–83; Sakharov, pp. 242–55.

insisted on a strict observance of the agreed order of evacuation – inspiring the Polish commander to curse him as 'a blackguard and a coward' before, on January 8th, coming to an agreement with the approaching Reds for the surrender and repatriation of his men through European Russia.[318]

With the Poles neutralized there now remained only a tiny, straggling Rumanian contingent between the Red Army and the tail of the Czechoslovak Legion. Even that buffer evaporated, however, as the Rumanians, who had been evacuating on foot, attempted to board Czechoslovak trains; they were repulsed and surrendered in disgust to the Red Army (after blowing up a bridge west of Kansk in an attempt to spite their Bohemian tormentors). Now fighting broke out between advance patrols of the Red Army and the Czechoslovaks themselves before, on January 13th, the last of the Legion's echelons passed through Kansk.[319]

Two days later Kappel's bedraggled columns emerged from the taiga at Kansk. An attempt to seize the town from a Bolshevik advance guard which was garrisoning it narrowly failed; but, as yet, there were insufficient Red forces in the district to prevent the Whites from capturing supplies of arms and ammunition and continuing on their eastbound exodus. It was this force which, as Kolosov was informed, went on to defeat a joint Political Centre and partisan force at Uk on January 20th before proceeding to drive the rebel garrison from Nizhneudinsk on the following day. There the utterly exhausted Whites rested until they were joined by Voitsekhovskii's column and other straggling units, bringing the men at Kappel's command up to a reputed 30,000. At a council of war of January 23rd, at the station which had been Kolchak's prison for a fortnight, reports of events at Irkutsk were discussed by the White commanders and plans were set in train for a move against the Political Centre with the aim of liberating the Supreme Ruler, recapturing the gold reserve and, with supplies and reinforcements to be drawn from Semenov's realm in Transbaikalia, establishing a new anti-Bolshevik front west of Irkutsk. The following day (January 24th) a group of the most unfit soldiers set off eastwards across country towards Verkholensk–Barguzin in the hope of crossing the northern reaches of Baikal unopposed. The bulk of the White forces, however, was divided

318 Kotomkin, pp. 92–4; Klerzhe, p. 185. On the Poles see also Baginski, H. *Wojsko Polskie na Wschadzie, 1914–20*. Warsaw (1921); and Dyboski, R. *Siedem lat w Rosji i na Syberji (1915–1921): przy gody i wrazenia*. Warsaw (1922), pp. 105–43.

319 Parfenov, *Bor'ba za Dal'nyi Vostok*, p. 54. It was the bridge destroyed by the Rumanians which delayed the journey of the Political Centre mission to Tomsk.

into two columns (based on the structure of the 2nd and 3rd Armies) under Generals Voitsekhovskii and Sakharov, and set off on paths parallel to the Great Siberian Highway straight into the jaws of the insurgency at Irkutsk.[320]

Inspired by their mission to redeem the White cause and fired by the ordeal they had already survived, the cohesiveness and discipline of the advance was remarkable. Even General Janin was later to pay tribute to the dogged and desperate march of the men who had now redubbed themselves the *kappel'evtsy*. Theirs was, Janin said, 'an unprecedented piece of endurance'.[321] But it was not without its casualties. Although the commissaries of the Czechoslovak rearguard, which was moving in tandem to the White columns, were willing to exchange food for the last of the Whites' personal gold and jewellery, typhus and cold still took their toll. Among the first to succumb was Kappel himself. Since his semi-immersion in the Kan the general had developed frostbite in both legs, which was now complicated by gangrene and a bout of pneumonia. He accepted the ministrations of a doctor from the Legion, but proudly refused the offer of a berth on a warm Czech train; for although he had won early renown for his operations with the Legion during the summer of 1918, he could not forgive them their disloyalty to Kolchak. There was time only on January 25th for him to sign an order passing on the supreme command to Voitsekhovskii before, on January 26th at the village of Utai, General Kappel, the thirty-nine year old veteran, joined the canon of White martyrs. As a mark of respect the Czechoslovaks agreed to convey his body to Chita for burial.[322]

Meanwhile at Irkutsk the Political Centre made but one half-hearted attempt to impose its authority when on January 13th its new Provisional Siberian Council passed a law on military justice and ordered Kalashnikov to disband the Bolshevik-led Workers' and Peasants' Militia. The commander had not the means to do so, however. And, in fact, the outcry against the attempt was to force the Centre to concede to the popular demand that a soviet should be convened before the end of the month. It was hoped that the situation could be temporarily calmed by this

320 Sakharov, pp. 262–3; Guins, Vol. 2, pp. 553–4; Efimov, pp. 251–8.

321 Janin, *Ma mission*, p. 169.

322 Serebrennikov, *Moi vospominaniia*, pp. 26–7; Petrov, p. 220; Sakharov, pp. 265–7. On Kappel's life see Fedorovich, A. *General Kappel'*. Melbourne (1967); and the anonymous, eulogistic *General-leitenant Vladimir Oskarovich Kappel'*. Vladivostok (1922).

concession. Actually, however, the crisis continued to build, as news arrived in the town of the relentless eastward progress of the *kappel'evtsy*. The number of advancing Whites quoted ranged from 5,000 to 35,000. But any figure was sufficient to cause concern, for the Political Centre had only some 3,000 men under arms and seemed either unwilling or unable to initiate any action to defend either the city or its treasures (Kolchak and the gold). Despite reports of the Whites having dealt very harshly with the rebels at Nizhneudinsk, 'not one measure to defend the city had been taken', recalled the Bolshevik leader Shiriamov. Suspicions even began to gain currency in some quarters that there were elements in the Political Centre who were averse to offering resistance to the *kappel'evtsy*, because they still entertained hopes of utilizing White officers as the nucleus of a new anti-Bolshevik army.[323]

Consequently, on January 20th the Bolsheviks summoned a conference of their party *gubkom* and *obkom* at Irkutsk, together with representatives of the Staff of the Workers' and Peasants' Militia and of the Siberian Organization of Left-SRs, at which votes were taken expressing no confidence in the Political Centre's ability to defend Irkutsk from the forces of reaction either to the west or the east, and demanding that a soviet should be convened on January 25th to take over the administration of Irkutsk. Meanwhile a five-man Military Revolutionary Committee would assume provisional authority. The next day this *revkom* (consisting of Shiriamov, as chairman, three other Bolsheviks and a Left-SR) presented their demands at a meeting with the Political Centre. On the advice of their own Commander-in-Chief, Kalashnikov – who had already seen his own authority wither when his men had elected a Bolshevik, I.N. Bursak, as Commandant of Irkutsk on the 17th – that it was now beyond their ability to marshal a loyal force at Irkutsk, the Centre conceded all Bolshevik demands and formally relinquished their claims to power. At 6.00 p.m. on January 25th the Irkutsk Soviet duly gathered at the city's Musical Comedy Theatre (with a Bolshevik/Left-SR majority of 395 of the 543 delegates) to endorse a programme of re-nationalization of mines and factories and increased expenditure on the supply of food to the city, to recognize the executive power of Shiriamov's *revkom* and to support the efforts it was making to forge a new East Siberian Army of the disparate units in Irkutsk. Soon nine regiments of this force were ready, under the command of the partisan chief Zverev, who sent an

323 Shiriamov, 'Irkutskoe vosstanie', p. 132.

advance guard west under a Captain Nestorov to delay the approach of the envenomed *kappel'evtsy*.[324]

This new correlation of political forces at Irkutsk was not unduly disturbing for the Czechoslovak command. Although the Political Centre might have been more politically acceptable to the Legion's soldiery, what General Syrovy above all required was the presence of a *stable* authority in eastern Siberia to grease the wheels of his evacuation. Despite all the Legion's aid, the floundering Political Centre, quite patently, had not been that. At the meeting of *revkom* and the Political Centre of January 21st a plenipotentiary of the Legion's command had, therefore, guaranteed that the new Bolshevik authority would be recognized by his army provided that agreements previously arrived at with the SRs, guaranteeing the Legion's free passage to the east (with its arms) in return for an undertaking to hand back the gold reserve and to refrain from any interference in Russian affairs, were not reneged upon. Shiriamov readily agreed these stipulations, clauses to that effect were duly inserted into the proclamations of *revkom* and soon relations between the two sides were cordial enough for the Czechs to consider selling arms and ammunition to Zverev's Bolshevik army.[325]

Although neither side desired it, however, friction very soon developed between the Bolshevik authority and the Czechoslovaks at Irkutsk. On January 26th *revkom* felt obliged to order the exclusion of all Legionnaires from Irkutsk centre after clashes in which a Czech official had been shot dead by one of Kalandarashvili's irregulars. This brought forth protests from the Legion, which in turn sparked off demonstrations of workers against the intervention.[326] Meanwhile, news arrived from the west that the unofficial, tacit cease-fire which had been operating since Kansk between the 5th Red Army's vanguard (the 30th Rifle Division) and the Czechoslovak rearguard had been breached by the latter's deliberate destruction of the Biriusa bridge near Nizhneudinsk; the Reds had retaliated, capturing four of the Legion's coal trains. The upshot of this skirmish was that Army Commissar Smirnov sent orders to the Irkutsk *revkom* calling upon Shiriamov to attack the

324 Konstantinov, *Poslednie dni*, pp. 192–5; Vendrykh, pp. 49–56; Parfenov, 'Poslednie dni', pp. 116–17; Shiriamov, 'Irkutskoe vosstanie', pp. 131–5. Some Political Centre leaders remained at their posts to assist the new régime – Kalashnikov, Tarakhanova and Galaktionov, for example – while the majority departed for Vladivostok.

325 Shiriamov, 'Irkutskoe vosstanie', p. 134; Konstantinov, *Poslednie dni*, p. 196.

326 Shiriamov, 'Irkutskoe vosstanie', p. 134.

Czechoslovak forces in his sector so as to disrupt the Legion's rear. Given the meagre forces of Zverev's East Siberian Army, however, such an attack would have been suicidal and could have resulted in the Legion making off with both the gold train and Kolchak. On the other hand, for their part, the Legion's commanders at Irkutsk had no desire to allow any minor hiccups to distract from the business of evacuation. Consequently, at a meeting of January 27th between Dr Blagosh of the Czechoslovak National Council and Shiriamov, it was agreed to despatch a joint delegation to meet Smirnov's MRC so as to arrange an official armistice between the Legion and the Red Army. That same day a delegation (consisting of Surnov and Riabikov of *revkom* and a Lieutenant Gub from the Czechoslovak staff) embarked on a journey which, although at times threatening to lapse into farce – they came under fire from both sides on the line, on one occasion found themselves lost in the taiga, on another had to drag a Czech commander from his wife's birthday party to sign a permit – eventually made contact with the 5th Red Army at Tulun on February 2nd and got negotiations underway.[327]

Before the talks at Tulun could reach fruition, however, the fragile Bolshevik–Czechoslovak détente at Irkutsk was severely tested once again. On January 30th at Zima the Nestorov perdues from Irkutsk came into contact with a large advance contingent of *kappel'evtsy*. A five-hour battle commenced on the banks of the Oka, which seemed eventually to be going the Bolsheviks' way until, at 3.00 p.m., the Czechoslovak station garrison (part of the Legion's 3rd Division under Colonel Przhkhal) intervened on the White side and initiated a cannonade of Red positions. Within a few hours, however, Przhkhal received instructions from Syrovy himself to cease firing and to free any prisoners. This he subsequently proceeded to do.[328] He did also, however, permit the White units to move on freely and, according to one source, 'surreptitiously' passed supplies to them.[329]

327 Smirnov, I.N. 'Konets bor'by. Peremirie s chekho-slovakami', in Smirnov et al., *Bor'ba za Ural i Sibir'*, pp. 307–8; Sunov, I. 'Pervaia vstrecha partizana s Krasnoi Armii', in *ibid.*, pp. 320–30.

328 Efimov, pp. 260–9; Sakharov, *Belaia Sibir'*, p. 268; Konstantinov, *Poslednie dni*, pp. 200, 205. According to a Soviet source some of the prisoners were allowed to fall into the hands of the *kappel'evtsy* and were duly executed (Vendrykh, *Dekabr'sko–ianvarskie boi*, p. 56). According to the Czechs themselves, Przhkhal's men were only 'accidentally' drawn into the battle at Zima when a group of Enisei Cossacks, whom the Legion had been sheltering, deliberately provoked the Reds into firing on a Czech train (Kotomkin, pp. 111–12).

329 *ibid.*, p. 113.

By now greatly alarmed at Kappel's progress, early on February 2nd the Irkutsk *revkom* upgraded the state of martial law which had existed in the city since January 29th to a state of siege law and braced itself for the White onslaught. At the same time, however, a last-ditch diplomatic initiative was attempted to avert an attack on Irkutsk, when a *revkom* member, Gornstein, was sent to make contact with a British intelligence officer still resident at Irkutsk, namely Captain Shilling, so as to request that Voitsekhovskii should be prevailed upon by the Allies to avoid the inevitable bloodshed of an assault on Irkutsk. After all, warned Gornstein, if an attack came it would be the simplest of matters for his organization to deny the Whites their prime objective by having Kolchak disposed of; in addition, to enlist Czechoslovak support for his mission, he hinted that in any battle the Baikal tunnels might be the first casualty. On the evening of January 31st Shilling passed the message on to Syrovy and Blagosh. They in turn conveyed it to Voitsekhovskii, who was by then at Innokent′evskaia, just 40 km west of Irkutsk.

Hopes that a clash could be avoided were dashed, however, when the White leader's reply was received at Irkutsk late on February 1st (and passed to *revkom* at 1.00 a.m. on the 2nd). In language framed in the strongest possible terms, Voitsekhovskii agreed to skirt Irkutsk and leave *revkom* in power only on the conditions that: there was no opposition from the Bolsheviks, in either word or deed, to his troops' passage to the east; that all units of the East Siberian Army between Cheremkhovo and Irkutsk removed to a distance at least 100–150 km north of the railway for a period of not less than two days; that 200,000,000 roubles (including 50,000,000 in gold and silver) were provided for the upkeep of the *kappel′evtsy*; that food for 50,000 men and forage for 20,000 horses was deposited at stations around Baikal; that Kolchak and all those detained with him at Irkutsk were surrendered; and that there was no movement of Red troops east of Irkutsk for a full week after the passing of the White army.[330]

One must surely doubt the sagacity of Voitsekhovskii in issuing such an ultimatum to the Irkutsk Bolsheviks, for there was not the remotest possibility that the *revkom* would agree to such terms – apart from anything else, Shiriamov and his colleagues would probably have had to pay with their lives, once the Red Army reached Irkutsk, had they surrendered Kolchak and the gold to the Whites, and so would never have agreed to do so. Indeed, the Irkutsk *revkom* did not even deign

330 WO 33/5520 'Stilling [sic] Report', pp. 4–5, App. C, App. D; Konstantinov, *Poslednie dni*, pp. 201–3.

to reply to Voitsekhovskii's note. Instead, on February 3rd, it issued orders mobilizing all Bolshevik party members in the city and distributed an urgent appeal for volunteers in a leaflet, 'Red Irkutsk in Peril'. According to Soviet accounts some 2,000 new recruits were mustered. Of them the best were sent out a few kilometres beyond the city limits to soak up the first wave of the expected White onslaught, while defences were prepared in the centre: the Angara ice was mined, all the buildings on Naberezhskaia Street were fortified and barricades and berms constructed along the shore; meanwhile the guard on the gold train was redoubled and more tracks destroyed so as to immobilize it. As a last resort, in case it proved impossible to hold the town, caches of weapons and food were concealed in the forests to the north and south.[331]

By such steps alone, however, the *revkom* could not seriously have hoped to have prevailed at Irkutsk in a battle against the Whites. That much was made graphically clear when, on February 4th–5th, the *kappel'evtsy* simply brushed aside the Reds' advance guard and entered the suburbs of Glaskovo. Moreover, the Bolsheviks were menaced by news of an impending advance from the east by the forces of Semenov; and, more immediately, were threatened by the sudden sprouting of posters and leaflets around Irkutsk calling for a rising to save Kolchak from 'the Jews', which seemed to attest to the existence of a White underground movement in the city (despite the arrest of a number of former officers during raids on February 3rd). Finally, Shiriamov had to consider the presence of the Czechoslovaks – they had been firmly excluded from the city centre since January 31st, but it was certainly not beyond the realms of possibility that, if Voitsekhovskii looked like taking Irkutsk, the opportunistic Syrovy might yet order his Legion to rejoin the battle against the Bolsheviks so as to obviate any friction with the Whites over his earlier surrender of Kolchak.[332]

The dilemma of Kolchak's jailer, Shiriamov, at Irkutsk in February 1920 was closely analogous to that of the Romanovs' Bolshevik custodians at Ekaterinburg in July 1918. And the solution found was identical. Initially it was thought possible to conceal the admiral somewhere in the taiga as the Whites passed through Irkutsk *guberniia*.[333] But upon receipt of Voitsekhovskii's ultimatum of February 1st, so

331 Vendrykh, p. 56; Shiriamov, 'Irkutskoe vosstanie', p. 135.

332 *ibid.*, p. 137; Parfenov, *Bor'ba za Dal'nyi Vostok*, p. 64; Efimov, pp. 269–75.

333 Smirnov et al., *Bor'ba za Ural i Sibir'*, p. 201.

as to deny him even a remote chance of recapturing the figurehead of the White cause and so as to demonstrate the futility of an assault on Irkutsk, *revkom* decided that Kolchak would have to be executed.[334] On February 3rd Orders No. 24 and No. 25 of *revkom* restored to the legal code the death penalty which had been renounced by the Political Centre and accorded the Irkutsk Cheka the power to administer it.[335] The following day, Shiriamov recalled, the Chairman of the Irkutsk Cheka, S. Chudnovskii, presented him with a list of no less than eighteen candidates for execution from among the prisoners held at Irkutsk jail. For the moment, though, only the names of Pepeliaev and Kolchak were selected by *revkom*. It was felt, however, that such an irrevocable step could only be taken with the sanction of the nearest representatives of the central authorities of the Soviet Republic and, on February 6th, an official request for permission to execute Kolchak and his last premier was made to the Chairman of the Military Revolutionary Committee of the 5th Red Army, Smirnov.[336] Later on the same day a message from Smirnov was received at Irkutsk to the effect that, even though orders had been received from Lenin that Kolchak should be taken alive to Moscow for trial, if there was the slightest possibility that he might be liberated by the *kappel'evtsy*, the former dictator of Siberia must be shot.[337]

Since January 21st Kolchak had been subjected to a series of interrogation sessions in the office of the Governor of Irkutsk prison. The establishment of an Extraordinary Investigatory Commission had actually been among the very last acts of the Political Centre before its transfer of power to the *revkom*. The commission's composition reflected that provenance – it consisted of a five-man team, including a Chairman, the afore-mentioned Chudnovskii; a Bolshevik lawyer, K.A. Popov (who was to be the sharpest of Kolchak's interlocutors in the coming sessions); as

334 Once again, as in the case of the Romanovs, the belief was later fostered among the Russian diaspora that the order to execute Kolchak came directly from Lenin. See Fel'shtinskii, I. 'Lenin i rasstrel Kolchaka', *Russkaia mysl'* (Paris) No. 3499, 12.i.1984, p. 12. In contrast to the case of the Romanovs, however, *glasnost'* in the writing of Soviet and post-Soviet history has not yet produced any evidence to refute the version of Shiriamov and others, which portrays the execution as a decision initiated by the local Bolshevik leadership.

335 FO 371/4100 'Hodgson (Vladivostok) to FO, 19.vi.1920', App. F, App. G; Konstantinov. *Poslednie dni*, p. 203.

336 Shiriamov, 'Irkutskoe vosstanie', p. 137.

337 Smirnov et al., *Bor'ba za Ural i Sibir'*, pp. 302, 310.

well as two Left-SRs and a Menshevik. Their aim, Popov recalled, 'was to reconstruct through the examination not only the history of the Kolchak régime...but also the biography of Kolchak himself, in order to have a more complete picture of this leader of the counter-revolutionary offensive against the young Soviet Republic'. The second of their objectives was certainly met, as Kolchak traced his career down to November 1918 in a series of monologues of almost encyclopaedic detail. It took eight sessions to extract this information – the last of them on February 4th – and even Popov had to admit that Kolchak was 'frank enough' in his soliloquy.[338] The admiral recounted without compulsion, for example, his contacts with the British and Japanese armed services during 1918, even though such information would have been used against him in the show trial which both he and his interrogators expected; and he did not hesitate, when pressed for an opinion on such subjects as politically sensitive as that of epaulettes, to express views in favour of them – even when he knew that to his captors they were an abhorrent symbol of the old régime.[339] All in all it was a gentle resumé of Kolchak's career down to November 1918 – the otiose pace of the process and the urbane questioning of the SR and Menshevik investigators more resembled an after-dinner chat than a political interrogation throughout these sessions.

However, when the panel reassembled for what was to be its final meeting on February 6th all traces of gentility were gone. Popov (who, but for his confinement to hospital with typhus, would certainly have been among those murdered at Omsk in December 1918) now took the lead in the questioning and attempted to meet what he set as the first aim of the interrogation – the reconstruction of the history of the Kolchak régime – which the commission had thus far ignored. Unfortunately, he failed. He failed because in this final session the questions were hurried and haphazard; Kolchak's replies were correspondingly testy and curt.[340] The problem was that by this time the decision to execute the prisoner had already been taken and, rather than extract a broad account of the history of the Omsk government, the interrogators were anxious to extract from Kolchak specific confessions of its alleged crimes. Probably they were seeking justification for the coming deed. The admiral, however, would admit to no crimes. He did not even – uncharacteristically

338 Popov, K.A. (ed.) *Dopros Kolchaka*. Leningrad (1925), pp. iii–vii.

339 *ibid.*, pp. 3–179.

340 *ibid.*, pp. 180–213.

– lose his temper and, as Popov had grudgingly to concede, he remained 'entirely dignified' throughout his final testimony:

> In this he differed markedly from most of his ministers with whom I had to deal as an investigator in the trial of the Kolchak Government. In the cases of those men there was – with the odd exception – cowardice, a desire to represent themselves as involuntary participants in a dirty business initiated by someone else; even a desire to portray themselves as being opposed to these others. There was none of this in Kolchak's demeanour... He steered clear of the slightest chance of supplying material for the indictment of persons who had already fallen, or might yet fall, into the hands of the Soviet authorities.[341]

Little the wiser, the investigatory commission rose and Kolchak was sent back to his cell.

A cell-mate of Timireva's at the prison later recalled that although Kolchak was visibly upset by his incarceration – he was eating and sleeping very poorly – as a group the prisoners did not live too badly at first and could communicate freely with one another. News of the advance on Irkutsk of the *kappel'evtsy*, however, soon disturbed their well-being. There were constant searches of the cells, an increase in security and no exercise periods after February 4th.[342] When the sound of gunfire was heard from across the river, Kolchak guessed that, for him at least, it was the end: 'They will kill me, naturally', he confided in a note slipped covertly to his mistress.[343] And around 2.00 a.m. on February 7th Chudnovskii and Bursak duly entered the cells. Pepeliaev broke down, sobbing and begging for mercy. Kolchak, however, retained his composure, merely commenting: 'So, there will be no trial.'

'Yes, Admiral, just so – as you and your assistants gunned down thousands of our comrades', spat back the Cheka boss.

Chudnovskii later recalled that he was somewhat surprised to find Kolchak up and dressed in a fur coat and freshly shaved. He surmised that he was expecting to be rescued 'at any moment'.[344] And, in fact, the admiral had been contacted at the

341 *ibid.*, pp. iii–vii.

342 Almazova, G. 'Kolchak i Pepeliaev v tiur'me', *Russkii golos* (Harbin) ?.ii.1920, reproduced in Kotomkin, pp. 114–16.

343 Timireva, A.V. 'Vospominaniia', *Novyi zhurnal* Vol. 159 (1985), p. 228.

344 Bursak, I.N. 'Konets belogo admirala', in Spirin, L.M. (ed.) *Razgrom Kolchaka: vospominaniia*. Moscow (1969), pp. 279–80; *Pravda* (Moscow), 16.i.1935.

prison by representatives of a fugitive officer organization, the British Captain Shilling was informed by a reliable source. However, the admiral had refused their offer of springing him from prison, saying that he 'would rather face whatever was before him than attempt to escape at the expense of the lives of many of his adherents'.[345]

After a wait in the governor's office during which Kolchak was allowed to dictate a final message to his wife ('tell my wife that I bless my son', he said), at 4.00 a.m. the handcuffed admiral and deplumed premier were taken out into the –32 degrees frost and marched from the prison to what Chudnovskii later identified only as 'the appointed place'.[346] Kolchak, having refused a blindfold, stood calm and erect – 'like an Englishman', thought the Chekist; but Pepeliaev had to be dragged into place and slumped, with his eyes closed, before two ragged volleys from the firing squad rang out. Both men died instantly. On the suggestion of one of his militiamen, Chudnovskii then had the bodies thrown through a hole in the ice on the nearby River Ushakovka, close by its confluence with the Angara. Thus, Kolchak's mortal remains were borne northwards towards what had perhaps remained his greatest love, the Arctic Ocean.[347]

345 WO 32/5720 'Stilling Report', p. 5.

346 A prisoner on Kolchak's corridor called Struiskii was later informed by a warder that the execution had taken place at the Znamenskoe graveyard. See Mel′gunov, Pt.3, Vol. 4, p. 175.

347 Chudnovskii, S. 'Rasstrel Kolchaka i Pepeliaeva', originally published in *Sovetskaia Sibir′*, was reproduced in *Poslednaia novosti* (Paris) No. 1477, 17.ii.1935 and, in a slightly different form, in *Pravda* (Moscow) 16.i.1935. Despite Chudnovskii's efforts some fanciful accounts of Kolchak's end have appeared over the years. One has the admiral drawing coolly on a cigarette while the firing squad refuses to shoot him; eventually he has himself to give the order to fire because he desires to be executed by 'men in Russian uniforms' not their Bolshevik commissar. See Bell, J.M. *Sidelights on the Siberian Campaign*. Toronto (1920), p. 126. According to one 2nd Lieutenant Lukin, Kolchak had to be shot by the Chekist Itaev when the firing-squad mutinied. See Fedorovich, A.A. 'Admiral Kolchak', *Edinenie* (Sydney) No. 21, 27.v.1960. Other myths have Kolchak's wife, Sofia, journeying incognito to Irkutsk to recover his body in the summer of 1920 (in fact she remained in exile and lived out her days in London and then Paris), and Timireva committing suicide when she heard the news of the execution (in fact she was released from Irkutsk prison in 1922 and returned to Moscow where, apart from a period of further imprisonment under Stalin – from 1938 to 1946 – she remained until her death in 1975). See Klarov, Iu. 'Fakty svidetel′stvuiut: o nekotorikh mifakh vokrug imeni "verkhovnogo pravitelia" Kolchaka', in Ivanov, B.A. (ed.) *Perepiska na istoricheskie temy. Dialog vedet chitatel′*. Moscow (1989), p. 279. For a fictionalized account of the dramatic events in eastern Siberia of the winter of 1919–1920 which adheres more closely to the facts see Klarov, Iu. *Dopros v Irkutske*. Moscow (1972).

As soon as it was light on February 7th *revkom* had its Order No. 27 posted around Irkutsk, explaining that in order to deter Voitsekhovskii's attack it had been necessary to execute Kolchak and Pepeliaev. Its postscript ran:

> Better the execution of two criminals long deserving of death than that there should be hundreds of innocent victims.[348]

Throughout the remainder of February 7th sporadic fighting continued between Red units and the *kappel'evtsy* in the outskirts of Irkutsk, with the Whites threatening to overwhelm Glaskovo. Meanwhile down the line at Kuitun, however, that same day an agreement was signed between Lieutenant Gub and Smirnov which formalized Soviet terms for the final evacuation of the personnel and property of the Legion in return for the strict observance of neutrality by the Czechoslovaks and their pledge to return the gold reserve intact to the Soviet authorities upon departing Irkutsk.[349] When news of this treaty reached the Legion's headquarters at Irkutsk on February 8th an ultimatum (signed by Blagosh and Colonel Krejci) was duly delivered to Voitsekhovskii, warning him that, so as to preserve the neutrality of the railway zone, any attempt on his part to force an entry to Glaskovo would be repulsed by Czechoslovak arms.[350]

Even before the receipt of this document the White commanders at Innokent'evskaia had received confirmation of the execution of Admiral Kolchak and Pepeliaev. Nevertheless, at a council of war an angry General Sakharov and others were moved to press for an all-out assault on Irkutsk to exact revenge upon the Bolsheviks for the deed. The more sober General Voitsekhovskii, however, overruled them and, during the night of February 8th–9th, the White forces at Glaskovo received orders to disengage.[351]

348 Konstantinov, *Poslednie dni*, pp. 208–9; WO 32/5720 'Stilling [sic] Report' contains an original copy of this document, signed and with the official stamp of the Bolshevik *revkom*.

349 Smirnov et al., *Bor'ba za Ural i Sibir'*, pp. 330–45, 353–63; Steidler, F.V. *Ceskolovenskii hnuti na Rusi*. Prague (1922), p. 107.

350 Parfenov, *Bor'ba za Dal'nyi Vostok*, pp. 66–7.

351 Sakharov, *Belaia Sibir'*, pp. 271–9; Konstantinov, *Poslednie dni*, pp. 212–13; Guins, *Sibir'*, Vol. 2, p. 554.

Throughout the following week columns of the weary and disappointed *kappel'evtsy* passed to the north and south of the city of Irkutsk, thence to struggle on across the surface of Baikal, which the cold had by then twisted into alternating mountains and valleys of ice. By the end of February 1920, almost five months after the commencement of their 'ice march', some 12,000 haggard men, the very skeleton of the dead Kolchak's Russian Army, so very far removed from its triumphs of a year earlier in the Urals, limped into Chita. 'We were practically in shreds and tatters', recalled one survivor of the White agony.[352]

Meanwhile the evacuation of the Czechoslovak Legion from eastern Siberia continued apace. On March 1st 1920, their last contingent left Irkutsk bound for Prague. Precisely one week later, on March 8th, units of the 5th Red Army marched ceremonially through Irkutsk's triumphal arch to unite Siberia west of Baikal under Soviet rule and to reclaim for the Soviet Government what remained of the imperial gold reserve. A special train was prepared later that month to carry the treasure back to Kazan. Along its side was unfurled a banner which read:

'To Dear Vladimir Ilyich, from the city of Irkutsk.'[353]

352 Shebeko 'Russian Civil War', pp. 88–97. See also Efimov, pp. 282–97 and 'Kapitan K.', 'Lednoi pokhod', *Russkoe obozrenie* (Peking) ?.xii.1920, cited in Serebrennikov, *Velikii otkhod*, pp. 19–21. Later in March the *kappel'evtsy* were rejoined by the group led by General Sukin which had parted from Kappel on the Kan to journey on north down the River Enisei and then up the Angara and the Ilim, whence some of their number had marched down the Lena to Ust-Kut and to the north of Lake Baikal, while others marched up the Lena and, via Olkhon Island, across Lake Baikal to Barguzin. See *ibid.*, pp. 20–1.

353 Gak, A.M., Dvorianov, V.N. and Papin, L.M. 'Kak byl spasen zolotoi zapas Rossii', *Istoriia SSSR* (Moscow), No. 1 (1960), p. 142; Livshits, S.G. 'Novoe o "zolotom eshelone"', *Altai* (Barnaul), No. 4 (1969), pp. 75–89; Kladt, A.P. and Kondrat'ev, V.A. '"Zolotoi eshelon": vozvrashchenie zolotogo zapasa RSFSR, mart–mai 1920g.' *Istoricheskii arkhiv* (Moscow), No. 1 (1961), pp. 29–34. In the course of its conveyance to Irkutsk from Nizhneudinsk (i.e. whilst under Czechoslovak guard) between Taishet and Zima, some thirteen cases of gold (valued at 780,000 roubles) went missing after a minor collision involving the gold train (*ibid.*, p. 23). The 'Bureau des Porteurs de Titres Russes' of Paris later claimed to have evidence of the missing gold being exchanged for yen at Harbin by 'Czechoslovak irregulars' in 1920 – see *The Economist* (London) Vol. 100, No. 4,266, 30.v.1925, p. 1,067. Such charges were strenuously denied in Prague – see Kudela, I.F. *O rossiiskom zolotom zapase i chekhoslovatskikh legionakh*. Prague (1924); and Solodovnikov, B. *Nash schet*. Berlin (1922). For a fanciful, fictionalized account of the gold reserve being hidden in mineshafts by the Whites, later to become the object of the Nazis' attentions, see Garfield, B. *Kolchak's Gold*. London (1974).

Conclusion

'History will probably lay the blame for the military failure on Kolchak', asserted General Knox in a final report to the War Office upon his return to Britain from Siberia at the end of 1919.[1] He was not wrong. In 1933, for example, the American clergyman and scholar, George Stewart, chose to conclude his pioneering study of the White armies precisely with the claim that 'the chief cause of failure was Kolchak himself'.[2] If it has demonstrated anything at all, however, our study of the circumstances of the admiral's personal, political and military demise has surely demonstrated that Stewart's summation was altogether too severe and too glib in its exclusive personalization of the White failure in Siberia. In an addendum to his afore-mentioned report, which raises a number of important supplementary points, Knox explained why:

> The entire responsibility for the failure in Siberia must not be attributed to Admiral Kolchak. There were, it is true, traits in his character which ill-fitted him to be Supreme Ruler at such a time. Although he was obstinate, he was deficient in real strength of character and fell easily under the influence of any individual who happened to be continually in his company. He was much too soft hearted and allowed the military machine to be seriously affected by the constant jealousies and bickerings of his subordinates, rather than compel honest, patriotic work by stern measures. He wasted time in attempting to direct military operations, of which he knew nothing, and neglected the civil administration in the rear. Moreover, he was deficient in diplomatic skill, and being of a shy disposition offended the loyalty of the civilian population by rarely appearing in public.
>
> On the other hand, Admiral Kolchak was undoubtedly honest and intensely patriotic. He had power of command and a reputation as a leader of men, gained when in command of the Black Sea Fleet. In politics his ideas were progressive and he was genuinely anxious to improve the conditions of life of the peasants, whom he believed must inevitably become the dominating class in Russia. All Englishmen who came into contact with Admiral Kolchak were impressed by his sincerity and determination; they felt that he was the best man in Siberia, and consequently worthy of support.
>
> If the task proved too big for him, it was not Admiral Kolchak's fault. For success to have been obtained, a Napoleon, at least, would have been required. It must be

1 WO 33/5707 'Report of the Military Mission in Siberia, 10.xii.1919', p. 10.

2 Stewart, G. *The White Armies of Russia: A Chronicle of Counter-Revolution and Allied Intervention*. New York (1933), p. 321.

> remembered that a state of chaos existed through the length and breadth of Siberia, the developed resources of which were inconsiderable at any time. Siberia had no manufactories and Kolchak was unable to supply the needs of the Army or of the civilian population. He was entirely dependent on military stores sent by the Allies, which he received in insufficient quantities and on foreign credits, which he could not obtain at all. Consequently, the Army was ill-equipped, and the people in want of the necessities of life. And that so little could be done to cope with this situation by improvisation and making the best use of such resources as were available, was due to the total absence of even moderately honest and capable officials to undertake the administration of the military forces and of the country. The inevitable result was that, in spite of Admiral Kolchak's personal efforts, the Army gradually lost such fighting value as it had, the civilian population became more and more discontented and disloyal, and, at last, were ready to welcome the Bolsheviks.[3]

The first thing that needs to be said of Knox's commendably balanced assessment of Kolchak's character is that it was, in a sense, a self-indictment. After all, to a greater degree than any other individual it had been Knox who, during the summer of 1918, had paved the path to power of this emotional, easily influenced, undiplomatic admiral who knew nothing of land warfare. The virulently anti-Bolshevik British general had allowed Kolchak's positive qualities of leadership and national reputation to blind him to the man's flaws of character. And he was not the only one to do so. The leaders of the Kadets in Siberia, Viktor Pepeliaev and Zhardetskii, finished the task which Knox had begun and refashioned their organization into the party of Kolchak's *coup d'état,* even though the admiral, to his credit, had specifically forewarned them that 'a dictatorship must have two foundations: a background of military victory and great personal qualities. I have neither the one nor the other.'[4]

To a certain extent, therefore, Knox and others were guilty of a lack of foresight in promoting Kolchak as a candidate for the dictatorship; they surely deserve as much vilification for having thrust the role of 'Supreme Ruler' upon the admiral as he deserves for accepting it. In their own defence, however, both the sponsors of the coup and (modesty permitting) Kolchak himself might properly claim that, during the summer of 1918, no other figure emerged in the east who might more ably have performed the task to which Russian and Allied anti-Bolsheviks had committed themselves, the rallying of forces for a military campaign against Lenin. This,

3 WO 33/977A 'Narrative of Events in Siberia, 1918–1920', p. 25.

4 Pepeliaev, V.N. 'Dnevnik', *Krasnye zori* No. 4 (1923), p. 85.

perhaps, was the real 'tragedy' of Admiral Kolchak and of anti-Bolshevism in general. For all their party's theoretical political support, the Socialists-Revolutionaries did not produce a leader capable of rousing the masses against the Bolsheviks – not even during the summer of 1918, when the chances of success were so much greater than for Kolchak's assault on the more consolidated and better armed Soviet Republic of the following year. Meanwhile, it was adequate testimony to the desperation of conservative forces in Siberia and the Far East during the period of 'democratic counter-revolution' that, before Kolchak's arrival on the scene, they had variously placed their hopes on the lame Vologodskii, the staid, uninspiring tsarist administrator, General Horvath, or the heinous bandit, Semenov. Nor at any later point did a figure emerge in the eastern White camp to provide a potential alternative to Kolchak – who, it will be recalled, was a very sick man by the end of 1918, and might have been only too willing to hand over the reins of power to a Kornilov or an Alekseev. But by the end of 1918 both Kornilov and Alekseev were dead: the volatile Gajda would have been no substitute, nor would the erratic and reactionary General Dieterichs (although both would have been better suited to fill the role of commander-in-chief which Kolchak was unwise enough to delegate, to all intents and purposes, to the criminally incompetent and inexperienced General Lebedev during the key operations of 1919).

The fact that there appeared to be no alternative to Kolchak, however, would not enable him to overcome the lingering impression in some circles that his dictatorship had been foisted upon the anti-Bolshevik movement in the east. In contrast to the rise of General Denikin, the natural heir of Kornilov and Alekseev in South Russia and a key figure in their Volunteer movement from day one of the counter-revolution, Kolchak's assumption of power could be regarded, even by elements within the White ranks in Siberia, as illegitimate, a breach of the tenuous pattern of seniority which had been established during the spring and summer of 1918. It was certainly no coincidence that throughout 1919, quite apart from the opposition to his rule from political moderates and from the revolutionary left, those renegade generals and atamans with whom Kolchak was in constant friction and whose misdeeds were so to besmirch the White banner, were precisely the men who had founded the militarist branch of the counter-revolution in 1918 and who, rightly or wrongly, regarded themselves as deserving of recognition for having driven the Bolsheviks from Siberia: the collective nose of Semenov, Annenkov, Ivanov-Rinov, Rozanov et al. was put badly out of joint by the ascendancy of Admiral Kolchak.

He was to pay the price for having slighted them, however unwittingly. It chafed the White old guard, moreover, that for all the 'power of command' and 'reputation as a leader of men' identified in Kolchak by Knox and his other sponsors, he was, after all, a sailor. Semenov vented his contemporaries' grievance most concisely: 'For us, officers of the land army, an admiral is a sort of civilian', the unruly ataman sniped.[5]

Of course, had Kolchak had the autocratic will to dictate, had his sheer presence commanded the loyalty of his nominal subordinates, these petty jealousies and complaints might have been attenuated. But, as Knox was to rue, Kolchak, for all his nobility, patriotism and sympathetic characteristics, *had not the will to dictate* and *was not* a figure blessed with an innate ability to inspire loyalty. It was in this that the weakness of his régime lay, rather than in the fact that it purported to be a dictatorship: Chernov and Vol′skii, after all, offered democracy, but were looked upon askance by the Russian people when it came to a call to arms; Lenin and Trotsky promised nothing other than a dictatorship – and, during the civil war, they delivered it – as they fashioned a Red Army five million strong. Kolchak promised a provisional dictatorship and claimed to be 'a real dictator'; he issued sharp reprimands and swingeing insults when angered (as, all too often, he allowed himself to become); but *he did not dictate*. The result was recorded with eloquent succinctness in the diary of Baron Budberg:

> In the army decay; at the *stavka* ignorance and incompetence; in the government moral breakdown, squabbles, the intrigues of ambitious egoists...in society at large panic, selfishness, bribery and all sorts of scandalous behaviour.[6]

It all went unchecked by the dictator *manqué* at Omsk. Indeed, it is surely misleading to refer to Kolchak's régime as a 'dictatorship'. Rather, in the words of an early SR account of the civil war in Siberia:

> The dictatorship of Kolchak was only a symbol, shielding the dictatorships of the numerous *uezd, guberniia* and *oblast′* petty dictators, imbued with a deep love of their own power but who were actually displaying epaulettes on their shoulders for the first time and who were often in command of no more than a few dozen men. The only other thing that all these dictators held in common was a belief that the salvation of

5 Grondijs, L.H. *La Guerre en Russie et en Sibérie*. Paris (1922), p. 513.

6 Budberg, A.P. von 'Dnevnik', *Arkhiv russkoi revoliutsii* Vol. 15 (1924), p. 269.

> Russia lay in the whip and only in the whip: the whip in the barracks, the whip in the the villages, the whip against the peasants and, in particular, the whip against the workers, all of whom were considered to be Bolshevik troublemakers.[7]

This insensate, insubordinate disloyalty and splintering of authority within the putatively monolithic White camp in Siberia was characteristic of the behaviour of officers and atamans from the Urals to the Pacific, but was perhaps most graphically and damagingly manifested in the repression of Siberian co-operation and in the murder of members of the Constituent Assembly at Omsk in December 1918. It was a key paradox of the White 'dictatorship'.

A second paradox of Kolchak's rule was that although, as Knox noted, the admiral's patriotic credentials were unimpeachable, the Omsk government and the Russian Army relied, *ab initio*, on foreign alms and foreign arms. It had been the Czechoslovak Legion which had overthrown Soviet rule in Siberia and the Japanese who had completed the task in the Far East. During the summer of 1918 both were encouraged in their anti-Bolshevik activity by politicians and military strategists in London and Paris. By the time that Kolchak had assumed power, however, the international situation had changed irrevocably. On November 11th 1918 the Allies' war against Germany suddenly ended and they immediately began to lose interest in the struggle against Bolshevism which they had begun as an adjunct of that greater struggle. Had the Kaiser been able to hold out into 1919, the Czechoslovak Legion would not have deserted the Urals and the Allies would have been forced to find the means of increasing their supply of the putative new Eastern Front.[8]

As it was, although the initial tranches of arms were duly delivered over the winter of 1918 to 1919, in the wake of the armistice armed intervention on anything like the scale which would have been necessary to crush the Bolsheviks was out of the question. It was not only that Lloyd George, Clemenceau and Wilson had to consider that their peoples, their conscripts and elements of their governments were politically or morally opposed to the intervention; nor was it only that their countries might only afford to maintain a commitment to the intervention at the price of

7 Rakitnikov, N.I. *Sibirskaia reaktsiia i Kolchak*. Moscow (1920), p. 32.

8 Paradoxically, therefore – although the Whites had staked much on their belief that the Bolsheviks, as 'puppets' who had been 'invented by the Germans', would collapse when denied the aid of Berlin – Kolchak's fate was much more closely linked to that of the Kaiser than was Lenin's.

trimming the already threadbare budgets of the postwar 'homes fit for heroes': the fact was that the Allied leaders had more than enough on their plates with the myriad problems associated with the refashioning of the world order at Paris during the first half of 1919, without having to worry about Russia. The only Allied power with both the will and the ability to intervene in Siberia on a substantial scale was Japan. But she did so for reasons that had little or nothing to do with the fight of White against Red and in a manner which was nothing but debilitating to Kolchak's cause. Indeed, the Japanese intervention was not really intended to save Russia from Bolshevism; it was, rather, but one chapter in Japan's struggle *against* Russia for economic and political predominance in East Asia and along the Pacific littoral – a struggle which began with Russia's seizure of Sakhalin in 1852 and continues to this day in the disputed sovereignty of the Kuril Islands.

As we have seen, the manifest reluctance of the Allies, whatever was their political antipathy to Bolshevism, to fund and arm the White cause had profound repercussions in Siberia. Not least it was the desire to win back the respect and support of Paris and London – 'the spectre of recognition', in General Sakharov's memorable phrase – which guided White military strategy in 1919, determining the timing of the Russian Army's precipitate spring offensive, inspiring the costly gamble at Cheliabinsk in August and, at least in part, determining the fateful decision to attempt to defend Omsk rather than allow the Russian Army to retire to the east, intact, to fight another day. It was here – rather than, as has often been fallaciously assumed, in influencing the northerly bias of Kolchak's military strategy – that the hidden hand of Allied policy can be detected. The irony was that it proved to be as injurious to the White cause as any number of Red divisions.

Even had there not existed the very real need to make an impression in Paris, however, it seems unlikely that before making their move in the spring of 1919, Kolchak and his young 'wet-behind-the ears' staff officers would have paused to consider the implications of advancing across the Urals before a trained reserve had been established in Siberia. From the very dawn of the October Revolution officers and others who would eventually have to fight for their very lives with the Soviet régime had fatally underestimated the tenacity and skill of the Bolsheviks: believing that Lenin's régime would last no more than a week or two at most, many had looked upon his seizure of power with 'unconcerned indifference', according to General Knox; others, noted Trotsky with puzzled satisfaction, were so possessed by their hatred for Kerensky and the SRs that they had even helped the Red Guard to defend Petrograd from the toppled premier's abortive attack in November 1917.[9] Even during the summer of 1918, as the Red terror was launched and as anti-Bolsheviks began to flee central Russia to mass in the embryonic White camps of the periphery, few found it within themselves to take the Bolshevik threat more seriously: 'When I left Moscow there was not just a hope but a certainty that [the capital] would soon be in White hands', was the recollection of that time not of a politically uneducated officer but a leading Kadet intellectual. 'I even left things of importance in my flat,' admitted N.A. Borodin, 'counting on returning in the near future.'[10]

Buoyed up by the Siberian Army's victory at Perm, as we have seen, encouraged by Lebedev's hubristic dreams of a 'Russian Constantinople', and finding fertile soil in Omsk's inexperienced but ambitious staff officers, the seed of what a more cautious military thinker, Baron Budberg, termed 'this unhealthy optimism' blossomed in the east at the beginning of 1919 and found form in the Russian Army's headlong spring offensive. On May 2nd, the day that Buguruslan fell to the 5th Red Army's lightning counter-offensive, a day that marked the beginning of the end of Admiral Kolchak's military effort, Budberg inscribed a bitter valedictory to White strategy in his diary:

> The *stavka* had no plan of action. They simply flew towards the Volga and expected the fall of Kazan, Samara and Tsaritsyn. But of what should be done in the case of any other outcome they did not think. And they do not want to think now.[11]

It was to Kolchak's credit that in August, in a moment of contemplation during one of all his too brief sojourns in his capital, he was able to admit the error of his military ways in conversation with an American diplomat. According to Ambassador Morris:

9 Knox, A. *With the Russian Army, 1914–1917: Being Chiefly Extracts from the Diary of a Military Attaché*. London (1921), Vol. 2, pp. 707–11; Trotsky, L.D. *Sochineniia*. Moscow–Leningrad (1925–1927), Vol. 3 (Part 2), p. 100. See also Mel'gunov, S.P. *Kak bol'sheviki zakhvatili vlast': Oktiabr'skoi perevorot 1917g*. Paris (1953), p. 244.

10 Borodin, N.A. *Idealy i deiatel'nost': sorok let zhizni i raboty riadovago russkago intelligenta (1879–1919)*. Berlin–Paris (1930), p. 200.

11 Budberg, Vol. 15 (1924), p. 229.

> He attributed the present collapse to a mistaken estimate of the Bolshevik strength: his government had made its plans on the assumption, which events proved to be false, that the Bolshevik government would not survive an aggressive military campaign this spring; he had therefore concentrated his attention on the military situation to the exclusion of pressing financial and economic problems.[12]

Indeed, it would not be going too far to contend, in the words of another critical pillar of the régime, that 'the Siberian White struggle, in essence, chanced everything on complete [military] success'.[13] The question then arises, however, of whether there was any other choice. The White régime, in terms of its personnel and collective psychology, was orientated towards military solutions. Throughout 1918 and the first half of 1919 even its Kadet supporters, the would-be westernized liberals of Russia, prostrated themselves before the shrine of the generals and Cossack atamans. When the Kadets and their like were disappointed by the Russian Army, when they came to realize that (with some noble exceptions) its officers were not self-sacrificing heroes, but rather, as one observer put it, 'in success corrupt and pleasure-loving, in defeat demoralised and cowardly, in both given over to drunkenness',[14] they changed tack with unseemly haste. The result was the tentative reforms essayed at Omsk during the summer and early autumn of 1919. But by then it was too late. And certainly the chance had long gone by April 1920, when exiled members of the Kadet party gathered at Paris would formally abandon their commitment to non-predetermination and would call for radical land reform, the summoning of popularly elected local governments and the granting of autonomy to the minority nationalities in advance of a military victory and the summoning of a Constituent Assembly.[15] But even had the Kadets been able to persuade the more reactionary elements of the White movement to adopt such a programme when such issues were being debated at Omsk in early 1919 – which has to be open to doubt, for there existed a very entrenched opposition to reform in the highest military and political strata of the movement – would it have made any difference to the outcome to the struggle?

12 *FRUS: 1919 (Russia)*, p. 415.

13 Filat'ev, D.B. *Katastrofa belogo dvizheniia v Sibiri, 1918–1922gg.* Paris (1985), p. 65.

14 *DBFP*, p. 707.

15 *The New Russia* (London), Vol. 2, No. 14 (6.v.1919), p. 29. See also Rosenberg, W.G. *Liberals in the Russian Revolution: The Constitutional Democratic Party, 1917–1921*. Princeton (1974), pp. 442–7.

Clausewitz's dictum that 'war is an extension of politics by other means' has become a cliché. What has sometimes been less generally appreciated, however, is that, in the modern world, both war and politics are extensions of economics and geography. As we have seen, Kolchak's domain was severely disadvantaged on those counts. Ironically, it had been the tool of Imperial Russia's putative economic (and military) conquest of east Asian geography, the Trans-Siberian Railway, which had brought counter-revolution to Siberia, in the shape of the Czechoslovak Legion, refugee officers and democratic and right-wing politicians. Equally ironically, the very fact that the majority of Siberia's peasant populace were relatively wealthy and content in comparison to their impoverished, land-hungry cousins west of the Urals, had been adduced as providing a fertile soil in which to plant the seed of anti-Bolshevism. The experience of 1918 and 1919 was to prove, however, that the hopes placed both in the railway, as a means of facilitating an anti-Bolshevik campaign, and in the peasantry, as a source of food and recruits, were false. Precisely because the Trans-Siberian Railway, the economic lifeline of the region, could no longer service the needs of the rural population, as its new military managers laboured as Sisyphus against the vastness of Siberian geography to transform the track from a conduit of eastbound Russian influence into a means of servicing the Urals front, the trade in grain and dairy products which had been the foundation of the peasants' wealth was wrecked. Their first, instinctive response was to withhold their stocks of food from the Whites, causing hunger and its attendant disorder in the Siberian towns of a régime which had, paradoxically, staked its very claim to legitimacy on the restoration of order; their second, equally injurious to Kolchak, was to withhold their sons from the Russian Army's *levées*. Abstract promises of democratic reform and free elections to a new Constituent Assembly at Moscow were most unlikely to have altered the Siberian peasants' minds, even had these been offered. Their concerns were more material and more local.

Of course, it did not help the Supreme Ruler's cause that White politics were so unappealing. There was no advantage in the fact that his military governors were so cruelly unjust and tyrannical. Nor was it of assistance that many of his closest advisers were men of narrow vision, second- or third-rate scions of the outmoded tsarist system: relics, who had 'learned nothing new and forgotten little that was old', as Budberg put it; 'the same old cabbage soup, but a little thinner', as another pithily quipped.[16] That the Allied intervention did not live up to its initial promise was also a crippling blow. Ultimately, however, the fate of White Siberia was determined by the fact that, at the wrong end of a fragile, 4,000-mile long ribbon of steel, Admiral Kolchak was challenging the Bolshevik hold on central Russia from a front and from a base that was considerably closer to Vienna than it was to Vladivostok.

16 Budberg, Vol. 14 (1924), p. 298; Il'in, I.S. 'Omsk, Direktoriia i Kolchak', *Novyi zhurnal* Vol. 72 (1963), p. 201.

Appendix

The Anti-Bolshevik Governments in Siberia, 1918–1920

PROVISIONAL GOVERNMENT OF AUTONOMOUS SIBERIA	WESTERN SIBERIAN COMMISSARIAT		PROVISIONAL SIBERIAN GOVERNMENT		ALL-RUSSIA[N] PROVISIONA[L] GOVERNMEN[T]	
	P.M. Mikhailov V. Sidorov B.O. Markov M.E. Lindberg		THE COUNCIL OF FIVE P.V. Vologodskii V.M. Krutovskii G.B. Patushinskii I.A. Mikhailov M.B. Shatilov		THE DIRECTORY N.D. Avksent'ev V.M. Zenzinov P.V. Vologodskii V.A. Vinogradov V.G. Boldyrev	
Tomsk 26.i.1918	Tomsk 1.vi.1918		Omsk 1.vii.1918		Omsk 5.xi.1918	
N. Ia. Derber S.A. Kudriatsev G.B. Patushinskii A.A. Krakovetskii A. Petrov E.E. Kolosov I.A. Iakushev E. Zakharov I.I. Serebrennikov V.I. Moravskii P.V. Vologodskii V.M. Krutovskii I.A. Mikhailov M.B. Shatilov N. Zhernakov A. Trutnev I. Tarasov V. Tiber-Petrov G. Neumetulov A.E. Novoselov A.I. Sulim I.S. Iudin S. Maren-Zavinskii L.A. Ustrugov					COUNCIL OF MINIST[ERS]	
			Minister of Foreign Affairs	P.V. Vologodskii	Chairman (Prime Minister)	Vol
			Minister of Native Affairs	M.B. Shatilov	Deputy Chairman	Vin
	Head of Military Affairs	A.N. Grishin-Almazov	Minister of War	A.N. Grishin-Almazov	Ministry of War and Marine	K
	Business Cabinet Chairman: V.V. Sapozhnikov		Minister of the Interior	G.B. Patushinskii	Ministry of the Interior	Gatt
	Head of Justice Department	A.P. Morozov	Minister of Justice	A.P. Morozov	Ministry of Justice	Star
			Minister of Finance	I.A. Mikhailov	Ministry of Finance	Mi
			Administrative Council		State Comptroller	K
	Head of Trade & Industry Dept.	P.P. Gudkov	Ministry of Trade	P.P. Gudkov	Ministry of Trade & Industry	Sh
	Head of Foreign Affairs Department	M.P. Golovachev	Ministry of Foreign Affairs	M.P. Golovachev	Ministry of Foreign Affairs	Kliu
	Head of Agriculture Dept.	N.I. Petrov	Ministry of Agriculture	N.I. Petrov	Ministry of Agriculture	P
			Ministry of Ways & Communications	A.A. Stepanenko	Ministry of Ways & Communications	Us
	Head of Supply Department	N.S. Zefirov	Ministry of Supply	I.I. Serebrennikov	Ministry of'Supply	Sere
			Ministry of Food	N.S. Zefirov	Ministry of Food	Z
	Head of Labour Department	L.I. Shumilovskii	Ministry of Labour	L.I. Shumilovskii	Ministry of Labour	Shu
	Head of Education Department	V.V. Sapozhnikov	Ministry of Education	V.V. Sapozhnikov	Ministry of Education	Sap
	Administrative Seretary	G.K. Guins	Administrative Secretary	G.K. Guins	Administrative Secretary	

ALL-RUSSIAN PROVISIONAL GOVERNMENT

Supreme Ruler and Commander-in-Chief of all Russian Land and Sea Forces

ADMIRAL ALEXANDER VASIL'EVICH KOLCHAK

Omsk 18.xi.1918						Irkutsk 22.xi.1919	
UNCIL OF MINISTERS						COUNCIL OF MINISTERS	
rman Minister)	P.V. Vologodskii	G.G. Tel'berg (Acting, July 1919	P.V. Vologodskii (August 1919)			Chairman (Prime Minister)	V.N. Pepeliaev
istry arine	M.I. Smirnov (Director)					Ministry of Marine	M.I. Smirnov
istry War	V.I. Surin (Acting Minister)	N.A. Stepanov (January 1919)	D.A. Lebedev (June 1919)	M.K. Dieterichs (August 1919)	B.A. Budberg (Sept. 1919)	Ministry of War	M.V. Khanzhin
istry Interior	A.N. Gattenberger	V.N. Pepeliaev (April 1919)				Ministry of the Interior	V.N. Pepeliaev
istry stice	S.S. Starynkevich	G.G. Tel'berg (May 1919)				Ministry of Justice	A.P. Morozov
istry nance	I.A. Mikhailov	L.V. von Goyer (August 1919)				Ministry of Finance	P.A. Buryshkin
ate troller	G.A. Krasnov					State Comptroller	G.A. Krasnov
try of Industry	N.N. Shchukin	I.A. Mikhailov (May 1919)	S.N. Tret'iakov (September 1919)			Ministry of Trade & Industry	M.A. Okoropov
try of Affairs	I.V. Kliuchnikov (Director)	I.I. Sukin (Director, Jan. 1919)				Ministry of Foreign Affairs	S.N. Tret'iakov (Director)
istry culture	N.I. Petrov					Ministry of Agriculture	N.I. Petrov
of Ways unications	L.A. Ustrugov					Ministry of Ways & Communications	L.A. Ustrugov
istry pply	I.I. Serebrennikov	Ministry of Food and Supply (December 1918)	N.S. Zefirov (December 1918)	N.S. Nekliutin (March 1919			
istry ood	N.S. Zefirov						
istry abour	L.I. Shumilovskii	L.I. Shundevskii (March 1919)	L.I. Shumilovskii (May 1919)			Ministry of Labour	L.I. Shumilovskii
istry cation	V.V. Sapozhnikov	P.I. Preobrazhenskii (May 1919)				Ministry of Education	P.I. Preobrazhenskii
istrative etary	G.K. Guins					Administrative Secretary	G.K. Guins

Bibliography

Archival Sources

The Papers of Sir Bernard Pares (Library of the School of Slavonic and East European Studies, University of London).

Boxes 27–28, 41–44, 46–48 and 50 of this collection contain the unsorted materials which Pares gathered during and immediately after his mission to Siberia of January–September 1919, including diverse pamphlets and posters, some of the official publications of the Omsk Government listed separately below, personal correspondence with General Knox and Captain McCullagh of Britmis, and:

— 'Resolutions of the Omsk Bloc' (19.xii.1918; 9.ii.1919).
— Notes on personal interviews with Admiral A.V. Kolchak (21.v.1919), P.V. Vologodskii (22.v.1919), I.A. Mikhailov (n.d.) and G.G. Tel'berg (15.v.1919).
— '3-ia Vostochnaia konferentsiia Partii narodnoi svobody (22.v.1919)'.
— 'Reports to the Foreign Office, Siberia February–September 1919'.
— 'Siberian Diary' (6.i.1919–22.ix.1919).

The boxes also contain incomplete runs of the following Siberian newspapers of 1918 and 1919: *Biulleten'* (Omsk); *Ekho* (Vladivostok); *Eniseiskii vestnik* (Eniseisk); *Irtysh: golos Sibirskogo kazach'iago voiska* (Omsk); *Nash put'* (Ufa); *Nasha gazeta* (Omsk); *Nasha zaria* (Omsk); *Nashe delo* (Irkutsk); *Otechestvo* (Perm'); *Peking and Tientsin Times* (Peking); *Pravitel'stvennyi vestnik* (Omsk); *Priishim'e* (Petropavlovsk); *Rus'* (Omsk); *Russkaia armiia* (Omsk); *Sibirskaia rech'* (Omsk); *Sibirskii strelok* (Perm'); *Sibirskii vestnik* (Omsk); *Svobodnaia Sibir'* (Krasnoiarsk); *Svobodnoe slovo* (Tiumen'); *Svobodnyi krai* (Irkutsk); *Velikaia Rossiia* (Ufa); *Vol'naia Sibir'* (Eniseisk); *Vpered* (Ufa); *Zaria* (Omsk); *Zemlia i trud* (Kurgan).

British Government Papers (Public Records Office, Kew).

Foreign Office, Political Departments (FO 371): Siberia 1918–1919 (3365–3367, 4094–4116).
Foreign Office, Vladivostok Commission (FO 538).
War Office Telegrams (WO 32): Report of Military Mission in Siberia (5707); Events at Irkutsk, December 1919 – February 1920 (5720, 5723).
War Office Telegrams (WO 33): Siberia 1918–1919 (962, 966, 967A, 975); Narrative of Events (977A).
War Office, War of 1914–1918 – War Diaries (WO 95): Operations of the Middlesex and Hampshire Regiments in Siberia, 1918–1919 (5433).
War Office, Directorate of Military Operations and Intelligence 1837–1960 (WO 106): Siberia, 1918–1920 (1215–1342).
War Office, War of 1914–1918 – Correspondence of Military Headquarters (WO 158): Diary of Operations in Siberia, 1919–1921 (737–744, 971–972).

P. Ustrukhov Archive (Hoover Institution Archives, Stanford).

Collection of newspaper articles of 1918–1919 from: *Ekho* (Vladivostok); *Golos Primor'ia* (Vladivostok); *Golos rabochego* (Ufa); *Russkaia armiia* (Omsk); *Sibirskaia rech'* (Omsk); *Zaria* (Omsk).

B.I. Nikolaevskii Collection (Hoover Institution Archives, Stanford), Box 1.

File 1: 'Sibirskaia oblastnaia duma (sentiabr′ 1918–sentiabr′ 1919)'.
File 6: 'Polozhenie vo Vladivostoke' (includes the manifesto of the Central Bureau of Military Organizations, September 1919).
File 8: 'Circular of the Central Bureau of SRs in Siberia, August 1919'.

Manuscripts:

Dotsenko, P. 'The Struggle for the Liberation of Siberia, 1918–1921' (University of California, Berkeley: Russian Émigré Series, Oral History Project), 1960.
Elachich, S.A. 'Obryvki vospominanii' (Hoover Institution Archives).
Fedulenko, V.V. 'Rol′ byvshikh soiuznikov Rossii po otnosheniiu k Belomu dvizheniiu v Sibiri′ (Museum of Russian Culture, San Francisco), 1961.
'Russian Émigré Life in Shanghai' (University of California, Berkeley: Russian Émigré Series, Oral History Project), 1967.
Guins, G.C. 'Professor and Government Official: Russia, China and California' (University of California, Berkeley: Russian Émigré Series, Oral History Project), 1966.
Pogrebetskii, A.I. 'Currency Difficulties under the Kolchak Government' (Hoover Institution Archives).
Shebeko, B. 'Russian Civil War (1918–1922) and Emigration' (University of California, Berkeley: Russian Émigré Series, Oral History Project), 1961.
Sukin, I.I. 'Zapiski I.I. Sukina' (The Leeds Russian Archive, University of Leeds).
Sychev, E. 'Vosstanie v Irkutske, 23.xii.1919–1.i.1920' (Hoover Institution Archives).
Savory, R. 'Vladivostok, 1919–1920' (National Army Museum, London).
'Letters from Vladivostok' (National Army Museum, London).

Official Publications of the Anti-Bolshevik Governments, 1918–1919, and Publications of their Supporters in Siberia, South Russia and Abroad

Andogskii, A.I. *Akademiia general′nago shtaba v 1917–1918gg.* Omsk (1919).
Agelov, E. *Kolchak ili Lenin? K vam soldatu, krest′iane i rabochie!* Rostov-on-Don (1919).
Almazov, E. *Kak pravitel′stvo obezpechivaet voinov i ikh sem′i zemli.* Novonikolaevsk (1919).
Auslander, S.A. *Verkhovnyi pravitel′ admiral Kolchak.* Omsk (1919).
Verkhovnyi pravitel′ na fronte. Omsk (1919).
'B.I. Ch.' *Admiral Kolchak.* Rostov-on-Don (1919).

Bonch-Osmolovskii, A.F. *Komu zemlia dostanetsia.* Omsk (1919).
Gramota Verkhovnogo pravitelia o zemle. Omsk (1919).

Dieterichs, M.K. *Bei zhidov.* Omsk (1919).

Dolgorukov, P.D. *Natsional'naia politika i Partiia narodnoi svobody.* Rostov-on-Don (1919).

Golos Vserossiiskoi vlasti (Vols. 1–2). Helsingfors (1919).

Iurtovskii, N.S. *Sibirskoe zemstvo v pervyi god ego sushchestvovanii.* Omsk (1919).

Lebedev, V.I. 'Bor'ba na Volge', *Russkii soldat-grazhdanin vo Frantsii* (Paris), No. 344 (11.ii.1919); No. 345 (13.ii.1919); No. 346 (15.ii.1919); No. 347 (18.ii.1919).
The Russian Democracy and its Struggle Against the Bolshevik Tyranny. New York (1919).

Milenko, G.L. *Rossiiskoe pravitel'stvo i ego zadachi.* Omsk (1919).

Ministerstvo finansov *Obozrenie deiatel'nosti Ministerstva finansov – vtoroi poloviny 1918g.* Omsk (1919).

Morskoi, N. *Vozhd' i geroi Rossii – kto takoi Kolchak?* (Narodnaia Biblioteka No. 3). Rostov-on-Don (1919).

[Novaia Rossiia] *Komu zemlia.* Omsk (1919).
Chto dali bol'sheviki rabochemu. Novonikolaevsk (1919).
Chto otniali u nas bol'sheviki. Novonikolaevsk (1919).
Rol' ofitsera v dele vospitaniia soldata. Novonikolaevsk (1919).
Sibir' i Moskva. Novonikolaevsk (1919).
Zachem nemtsev bol'sheviki vydumali. Novonikolaevsk (1919).

Novosel'skii, M.P. *Kak razreshit' zemel'nyi vopros v Rossii.* Omsk (1919).

Obshchestvo vozrozhdeniia Rossii *Bulletin Russe* (Lausanne), Nos. 1 (15.ii.1919)–10 (1.vii.1919).
La Russie Démocratique (Paris), (1919).

Ol'gin, I. *Verkhovnyi pravitel' – ad. A.V. Kolchak.* Kharkov (1919).

Pinegin, M.N. (ed.) *Nastol'nyi kalendar na 1919g.* (izd. Ministerstva prosveshcheniia). Tomsk (1918).

The Russian Information Bureau in the United States *Struggling Russia – a Weekly Magazine* (New York), Vols. 1–2 (1919–1920).

The Russian Liberation Committee *Bulletins of the Russian Liberation Committee (Union)* (London), No. 1 (26.ii.1919)–No. 36 (25.x.1919).
Memorandum on the Baltic Provinces Question (Publications of the Russian Liberation Committee No. 6). London (1919).
What Kolchak Wants! Political Programme of Admiral Kolchak's Government. London (1919).

The New Russia: A Weekly Review of Russian Politics (London), Vols. 1–3 (1920).

The Russian Political Conference *Proposal of the Russian Political Conference in Paris to the Peace Conference on the Question of the Nationalities in Russia.* Paris (15.iii.1919).

Russkoe Biuro Pechati *Angliia–Rossii.* Omsk (1919).

Chto spaset Rossiiu. Omsk (1919).

Pravitel'stvennyi vestnik (Omsk), 1918–1919.

Sbornik 'Russkago Biuro Pechati': Edinaia, nedelimaia Rossiia. Tokyo, No. 1 (1919).

Union (Bureau de Presse Russe) (Paris), No. 1 (2.iv.1919)–No. 4 (4.x.1919).

Zverstvo bol'shevikov. Omsk (1919).

Russkoe Telegrafnoe Agentstvo *Declaration of Admiral Kolchak's Government (23.ii.1919).* London (1919).

Union (Agence Télégraphique Russe) (Paris), Nos. 1–220 (1919–1920).

Shepkin, G. *Sibir' i Kolchak.* Novocherkassk (1919).

Soloveichik, A. *Bor'ba za vozrozhdenie Rossii na Vostoke.* Rostov-on-Don (1919).

Vedomstvo pressa etat-maiora Glavnokommanduiushchago *Biulleten' otdela informatsii pri vedomstve pressa etat-maiora Glavnokommanduiushchago.* Omsk (1919).

Vladimirtsev, V. *Kak rabochie i krest'iane vozstali protiv bol'shevikov.* Omsk (1919).

'Vpered' *Admiral A.V. Kolchak.* Omsk (1919).

Vremennoe pravitel'stvo avtomnoi Sibiri *Vestnik Vremennogo pravitel'stva avtomnoi Sibiri.* Vladivostok (1918).

Vremennaia Sibirskaia oblastnaia duma *Stenograficheskii otchet. Sessiia 2-ia, zasedanie 1-e.* Tomsk (1919).

Vremennoe sibirskoe pravitel'stvo *Sobranie uzakonenii i rasporiazhenii Vremennogo sibirskogo pravitel'stva* (Omsk), No. 1 (5.vii.1918)–No. 6 (17.viii.1918).

Vremennoe Vserossiiskoe pravitel'stvo [Direktoriia] *Vestnik Vremennogo vserossiiskogo pravitel'stva* (Omsk), No. 1 (6.x.1918).

Vremennoe vserossiiskoe pravitel'stvo *Sobranie uzakonenii i rasporiazhenii pravitel'stva izdavaemoe pri pravitel'stvu-iushchem senate* (Omsk), No. 1 (April 1919)–No. 10 (June 1919).

Other Contemporary Siberian Periodical Publications and Pamphlet Literature

Golochek, V. *Chekhoslovatskoe voisko v Rossii*. Irkutsk (1919).

Kudela, Ia[J]. *Pervaia godovshchina Chekhoslovatskoi respubliki*. Irkutsk (1919).

Sibirskaia kooperatsiia (Novosibirsk), 1918 (Nos. 10–12), 1919 (Nos. 1–12).

V.K. 'Oblastnoe obozrenie', *Sibirskie zapiski* (Krasnoiarsk), No. 3, pp. 84–93; No. 4, pp. 89–96; No. 5, pp. 96–109.

[Zakupsbyt] *Izvestiia i trudy Soiuza Sibirskikh kooperativnykh Soiuzov 'Zakupsbyt'* (Novonikolaevsk), 12.xii.1918–1.v.1919.

Vestnik 'Zakupsbyt', Soiuz Sibirskikh kooperativnykh Soiuzov. (Novonikolaevsk), 15.v.1919–1.xi.1919.

Other Contemporary European and American Periodical Publications and Pamphlet Literature

D'Avigdor and Windsor, D.C.H. *La Sibérie orientale et le Japan. Etude politique économique. Suive de la Déclaration de Baron Shidehara à la Conférence de Washington sur la politique japonaise en Sibérie*. Paris (1922).

[Baikalov, A.V.] *Siberian Co-operation and the Commercial Exploitation of the Northern Sea Route from Europe to Siberia*. London (1920).

The Japs in Siberia: An Appeal to International Organized Labour. London (1922).

King, J. *Three Bloody Men: Mannerheim 'The Butcher'; Denikin the KCB; Kolchak 'The Bloody One'*. Glasgow (1919).

Partiia sotsialistov-revoliutsionerov *Sovremennyi moment v otsenke Partii sotsialistov-revoliutsionerov*. Paris (1919).

Rosett, J. *Kolchak, Autocrat and Tyrant: The Actual Story of Kolchak and his Methods told by an American Official Recently Returned from Siberia*. n.p. [Canada] (1919).

The Rise of a New Russian Autocracy. London (1919).

The Russian/Russkii zhurnal (London), Vol. 1 (1919).

The Russian Co-operator (London), Vol. 1 (1917)–Vol. 4 (1920).

The Russian Outlook (London), Vol. 1 (1919).

Russkaia zhizn' (Helsingfors).

The Times (London).
The Union of Siberian Creamery and Other Co-operative Associations *The Union of Siberian Creamery and Other Co-operative Associations and the Country Served by this Organization*. Boston (1919).
Yarkov, G.M. *The Union of Siberian Creamery Associations*. London (1919).

Contemporary Periodical Publications and Pamphlet Literature from Soviet Russia

Bovich, A. *Krovavyi opyt: otkrytnoe pis'mo byvshego men'shevika*. Moscow (1919).
Burevoi, K.S. et al. *K prekrasheniiu voiny vnutri demokratii*. Moscow (1919).
Chetyre mesiatsa uchredil'ovshchiny: istoriko-literaturnyi sbornik. Samara (1919).
Izvestiia (Moscow), 1918–1920.
Karzanskii, N. *Chekho-Slovaki v Rossii*. Moscow (1918).
Kolchak, Chekhoslovakiia i Rossiia. Moscow (1921).
Muna, A. *A kto takie Chekho-Slovaki?* Moscow (1918).
Pravda (Moscow), 1918–1920.
Sibiriakov [Vilenskii], V.D. *Chto prinet Kolchak sibirskom rabochim i krest'ianam*. Moscow (1919).
Vilenskii [Sibiriakov], V.D. *Chernaia godina sibirskoi reaktsii (Interventsiia v Sibiri)*. Moscow (1919).
Doloi tsarskikh atamanov! (K sibirskomu kazachestvu). Moscow (1919).
Zemel'nyi vopros v Sibiri. Moscow (1919).

Published Documents

Adamov, E. 'Rol' Anglii v interventsii', *Vestnik Narodnogo komissariata inostrannykh del*. (Moscow), Nos. 6–7 (25.viii.1920), pp. 1–12.
Andreev L. (ed.) 'K istorii razgroma vooruzhennykh sil Kolchaka', *Krasnyi arkhiv* (Moscow), No. 6 (1931), pp. 55–91.
Beaumont, A. *The Heroic Story of the Czechoslovak Legion*. Prague (1919).
Belov, G.A. et al. (eds.) *Direktivy glavnogo komandovaniia Krasnoi armii (1917–1919gg.)*. Moscow (1969).

Bernshtam, M.S. (ed.) *Ural i Prikam'e, noiabr' 1917–ianvar' 1919: dokumenty i materialy*. Paris (1982).

Boiarskii, V.A. (ed.) 'Ob uchastii angliskikh imperialistov v organizatsii interventsii protiv Sovetskoi Rossii', *Istoricheskii arkhiv* (Moscow), No. 2 (1957), pp. 65–84.

Bondarenko, M. (ed.) 'Taseevskii partizanskii raion v 1919g.' *Krasnyi arkhiv* (Moscow), No. 6 (1936).

Bor'ba s kolchakovshchinoi: sbornik dokumentov. Moscow–Leningrad (1926).

Bor'ba s kontrrevoliutsei v Sibiri i na Dal'nem Vostoke. Chita (1922),

Bor'ba za Kazan': sbornik materialov o chekhochredil'skoi interventsii v 1918g. Kazan' (1924).

Bor'ba za Sovetskuiu vlast' na Iuzhnom Urale (1917–1918gg.): sbornik dokumentov i materialov. Cheliabinsk (1957).

Bor'ba za vlast' Sovetov v Irkutskoi gubernii (oktiabr' 1917–iiul' 1918): sbornik dokumentov. Irkutsk (1957).

Bor'ba za vlast' Sovetov v Primor'e (1917–1922gg.): sbornik dokumentov. Vladivostok (1955).

Bor'ba za vlast' Sovetov v Tobol'skoi-iumen'skoi gubernii (1917–1920gg.). Tiumen' (1967).

Bor'ba za vlast' Sovetov v Tomskoi gubernii (1917–1921gg.): sbornik dokumental'nykh materialov. Tomsk (1957).

Bourne, K. and Watt, D.C. (eds.) *British Documents on Foreign Affairs from the Foreign Office Confidential Print. Part 2: From the First to the Second World Wars (Series A: Soviet Union, 1917–1939)*. Fredrick, MD (1984).

Browder, R.P. and Kerensky, A.F. (eds.) *The Russian Provisional Government, 1917* (3 Vols.). Stanford (1961).

[Bullitt, W.C.] *The Bullitt Mission to Russia: Testimony Before the Committee on Foreign Relations of the United States*. New York (1919).

Bunyan, J. (ed.) *Intervention, Communism and Civil War in Russia (April–December 1918)*. New York (1976).

Bunyan, J. and Fisher, H.H. (eds.) *The Bolshevik Revolution, 1917–1918: Documents and Materials*. Stanford (1961).

Bushmanov, Z.I. et al. (eds.) *Iuzhnoe Zaural'e v periode grazhdanskoi voiny (1918–1920gg.): sbornik dokumentov*. Kurgan (1963).

Canada (Dept. of External Affairs) *Documents on Canadian External Relations (Vol. 3: 1919–1925)*. Ottawa (1970).

Canada (Dept. of Trade and Commerce) *Report of the Canadian Economic Commission to Siberia (Supplement to the Weekly Bulletin of the Dept. of Trade and Commerce).* Ottawa (1919).

Chemezov, V.N. et al. (eds.) *Bor'ba za ustanovlenie i uprochenie sovetskoi vlasti v Iakutii: sbornik dokumentov.* Iakutsk (1926).

Coates, W.P. and Coates, Z.K. *Armed Intervention in Russia, 1918–1922.* London (1935).

Collins, D.N. and Smele, J.D. (eds.) *Kolchak i Sibir': dokumenty i issledovaniia, 1919–1926* (2 Vols.). New York (1988).

Cumming, C.K. and Pettit, W.W. (eds.) *Russian–American Relations (March 1917–March 1920).* New York (1920).

Dieterichs, M.K. (ed.) *Ubiistvo tsarskoi sem'i i chlenov doma Romanovykh na Urale* (2 Vols.). Vladivostok (1922).

Direktivy komandovaniia frontov Krasnoi armii (1917–1922gg.): sbornik dokumentov (4 Vols.). Moscow (1971–1978).

Dokumenty i materialy po istorii sovetsko-chekhoslovatskikh otnoshenii (Vol. 1). Moscow (1973).

'Dokumenty istoricheskoi bor'by'. Sbornik dokumentalnykh materialov posviashchennykh bor'be protiv inostrannoi interventsii i vnutrennoi kontrrevoliutsii na territorii Eniseiskoi gubernii (1918–1920gg.). Krasnoiarsk (1959).

Dokumenty ob antinatsional'noi politike Masarika. Moscow (1955).

'Dokumenty o zolote Kolchaka', in Romanovskii, S.K. (ed.) *Diplomaticheskii ezhegodnik.* Moscow (1995), pp. 297–303.

'Dokumenty: Protokoly doprosa adm. Kolchaka Chrezvychainoi sledstvennoi kommisei v Irkutske (21 ianv.–7 fev. 1920)', *Arkhiv russkoi revoliutsii* (Berlin), Vol. 10 (1923), pp. 177–321.

Dokumenty vneshnei politiki SSSR (Vol. 1). Moscow (1957).

Elagin, Vl. (ed.) 'Iz istorii semenovshchiny v 1919g.', *Krasnyi arkhiv* (Moscow), No. 6 (1934), pp. 131–146.

El'tsin, V. (ed.) *Po tu storonu Urala (V tsarstve Kolchaka).* Ufa (1919).

Far Eastern Republic (Special Delegation) *Japanese Intervention in the Russian Far East.* Washington (1922).

Trade and Industries of the Far Eastern Republic. Washington (1922).

Filatieff, Général 'L'Amiral Koltchak et les événements militaires en Sibérie (1918–1919) – documents', *Revue d'histoire de la Guerre Mondiale* (Paris), Vol. 10 (1932), pp. 165–200, 271–303.

Flug, V. 'Otchet o komandirovke iz Dobrovol'cheskoi armii v Sibiri', *Arkhiv russkoi revoliutsii* (Berlin), Vol. 9 (1923), pp. 243–304.

'Frantsiia v bor'be protiv Sovetskoi vlasti (po bumagam Ministerstva inostrannykh del Omskogo pravitel'stva)', *Vestnik Narodnogo komissariata inostrannykh del* (Moscow), No. 8 (15.x.1920), pp. 21–25.

'Golos Rodiny' *Deistviia Iaponii v Priamurskom krae: sbornik ofitsial'nykh dokumentov otnosiashchikhsia k interventsii derzhav v predelakh Priamur'ia.* (Biblioteka Svobodnoi Rossii, No. 15). Vladivostok (1921).

Goriunov, I. (ed.) *Kolchakovshchina: sbornik dokumentov i boevykh vospominanii.* Moscow–Samara (1932).

Grazhdanskaia voina v Orenburzh'e (1917–1919gg.): dokumenty i materialy. Orenburg (1958).

Gromov, I.V. et al. (eds.) *Partizanskoe dvizhenie v Zapadnoi Sibiri (1918–1920gg.): dokumenty i materialy.* Novosibirsk (1959).

Grondijs, L.H. (ed.) *Le Cas Koltchak: contribution à l'histoire de la révolution russe.* Leiden (1939).

Grush, D.V. et al. (eds.) *Dokumenty geroicheskoi bor'by: sbornik dokumental'nykh materialov posviashchennykh bor'be protiv inostrannoi interventsii i vnutrennei kontrrevoliutsii na territorii Eniseiskoi gubernii (1918–1920gg.).* Krasnoiarsk (1959).

Gubel'man, M.I. (ed.) 'Partizanskoe dvizhenie v Primor'e', *Krasnyi arkhiv* (Moscow), No. 3 (1937).

Gukhovskii, A. (ed.) 'Iz istorii iaskogo soveshchaniia', *Krasnyi arkhiv* (Moscow), No. 5 (1926), pp. 105–118.

Hosoya, C. (ed.) 'Japanese Documents on the Siberian Intervention, 1917–1922', *Hitotsubashi Journal of Law and Politics*, Vol. 1 (1960), pp. 30–37.

Inostrannaia voennaia interventsiia i grazhdanskaia voina v Srednei Azii i Kazakhstane (2 Vols.). Alma-Ata (1963).

Ivanov, F.A. *Bor'ba trudiashchikhsia za ustanovlenie Sovetskoi vlasti na Altae (1917–1919gg.): sbornik dokumentov.* Barnaul (1957).

Iz istorii grazhdanskoi voiny v SSSR (3 Vols.). Moscow (1960–1961).

Iziumov, A.F. (ed.) 'Ufimskoe gosudarstvennoe soveshchanie', in *Russkii istoricheskii arkhiv* (Sbornik No. 1). Prague (1929), pp. 57–280.

Kakurin, N. (ed.) *Kak srazhalas' revoliutsiia* (2 Vols.). Moscow–Leningrad (1925–1926).

[Kalashnikov, N.S.] 'Itogi vesennego nastupleniia', *Sibirskii arkhiv* (Prague), No. 2 (1929), pp. 81–87.

Kim, P.M. (ed.) 'Iz arkhiva organizatorov grazhdanskoi voiny i interventsii v Sovetskoi Rossii', *Istoricheskii arkhiv* (Moscow), No. 6 (1961), pp. 58–116.

Kladt, A.P. and Kondrat′ev, V.A. (eds.) '"Zolotoi eshelon" (vozvrashchenie zolotogo zapasa RSFSR mart–mai 1920g.)', *Istoricheskii arkhiv* (Moscow), No. 1 (1961), pp. 20–53.

Konstantinov, M.M. (ed.) 'Omskie sobytiia pri Kolchake (21–23 dek. 1918g.)', *Krasnyi arkhiv* (Moscow), No. 7 (1924), pp. 201–246; No. 8 (1925), pp. 176–192.

Poslednie dni kolchakovshchiny. Moscow (1926).

'Konstitutsiia ufimskoi Direktorii', *Arkhiv russkoi revoliutsii* (Berlin), Vol. 12 (1923), pp. 189–194.

Kostomarov, G.D. (ed.) 'Belofinny v sluzhbe anglo-frantsuzskikh interventov v 1919g.', *Krasnyi arkhiv* (Moscow), No. 1 (1940), pp. 31–67.

Kotomkin, A. (ed.) *O chekhoslovatskikh legionerakh v Sibiri, 1918–1920: vospominaniia i dokumenty*. Paris (1930).

Kuzdeev, R.G. and Iuldashbaev, K. *Oktiabr′skaia sotsialisticheskaia revoliutsiia i rozhdenie sovetskoi Bashkiri*. Ufa (1959).

Lenin, V.I. *Polnoe sobranie sochinenii* (5th ed.). Moscow (1964–1970).

Long, J.W. and Hopkins, C.H. 'T.G. Masaryk and the Strategy of Czechoslovak Independence: An Interview in Russia on 27 June 1917', *Slavonic and East European Review* (London), Vol. 56 (1978), pp. 88–96.

Luchebnikov, P.S. (ed.) *Grazhdanskaia voina na iuzhnom Ural′e (1918–1919gg.): sbornik dokumentov i materialov*. Cheliabinsk (1962).

MacMurray, J.V.A. *Treaties and Agreements With and Concerning China*. New York (1921).

Maksakov, K.V. (ed.) *Partizanskoe dvizhenie v Sibiri. Tom 1: Prieniseiskii krai*. Moscow–Leningrad (1926).

'K istorii interventsii v Sibiri', *Krasnyi arkhiv* (Moscow), No. 28 (1929), pp. 126–165.

Maksakov, K.V. and Turunov, A. (eds.) 'Vremennoe pravitel′stvo avtomnoi Sibiri', *Krasnyi arkhiv* (Moscow), Vol. 4 (1928), pp. 86–138; Vol. 4 (1929), pp. 37–106; Vol. 5 (1929), pp. 31–60.

Manusevich, A. Ia. (ed.) *Internatsionalisty*. Moscow (1987).

Meijer, J.M. (ed.) *The Trotsky Papers, 1917–1922* (2 Vols.). London–The Hague (1964–1973).

Mel′gunov, S.P. (ed.) 'Dva generala (k psikhologii grazhdanskoi voiny): razgovor gen. Diderikhsa i Riabikova', *Golos minuvshago na chuzhoi storone* (Paris), Vol. 14, No. 1 (1926), pp. 189–199.

Mints, I.I. (ed.) 'Vneshnaia politika kontr-revoliutsionnykh pravitel'stv v nachale 1919g.: iz dokumentov Parizhskogo posol'stva', *Krasnyi arkhiv* (Moscow), Vol. 37 (1929), pp. 69–101.
Iaponskaia interventsiia, 1918–1922gg.: v dokumentakh. Moscow (1934).

Miroshchenko, P. (ed.) 'Iz istorii kolchakovshchiny', *Krasnyi arkhiv* (Moscow), Vol. 3 (1928), pp. 225–228.
'Pravitel'stvo Kolchaka i Soedinennye Shtaty', *Vestnik Narodnogo komissariata inostrannykh del* (Moscow), Nos. 9–10 (15.xii.1920), pp. 53–67.

Moulis, E. and Bergonier, E. (eds.) *En morge du conflict mondial: la guerre entre les alliés et la Russie, 1918–1920*. Paris (1937).

Nelidov, N. (ed.) 'Kolchak i Finlandiia', *Krasnyi arkhiv* (Moscow), No. 33 (1929), pp. 83–114.

Nikiforov, P. (ed.) *Istoricheskie dokumenty o deistviakh i zamyslakh mezhdunarodnykh khishchnikov na Dal'nem Vostoke*. Moscow (1923).

Okladnikov, A.P. (ed.) *Vengerskie internatsionalisty v Sibiri i na Dal'nem Vostoke, 1917–1922gg*. Moscow (1980).

Omsk v dni Oktiabria i ustanovlenie Sovetskoi vlasti (1917–1919gg.): sbornik dokumental'nykh materialov. Omsk (1947).

Pavlovskii, P.I. (ed.) *Annenkovshchina (po materialam sudebnogo protsessa v Semipalatinske 25.vii.1927–12.viii.1927)*. Moscow (1928).

Peregovory o sdache vlasti Omskim pravitel'stvom Politicheskomu Tsentru (v prisutsvim Vysokikh Kommissarov i Vyshchago Kommandovaniia soiuznykh derzhav). Gorod Irkutsk (stantsiia). Ianvar' 1920g. Stenograficheskii otchet. Harbin (1921).

Piontkovskii, S.A. (ed.) 'Materialy po istorii kontrrevoliutsii: pis'mo Avksent'eva k eserami iuga Rossii, 31.x.1918', *Proletarskaia revoliutsiia* (Moscow), No. 1 (1921), p. 114–121.
'Materialy po istorii kontrrevoliutsii: pis'ma Sazonova Predsetateliu sov. min. prav. Kolchaka Vologodskomu i Nabokova Kolchaku', *Krasnyi arkhiv* (Moscow), No. 1, 1921, pp. 122–131.
'Kontr-revoliutsiia v Sibiri: doklad podpolkovnika Glukhareva', *Krasnaia letopis'* (Moscow), No. 5 (1923), pp. 356–370.
Grazhdanskaia voina v Rossii (1919–1921gg.): khrestomatiia. Moscow (1925).
'Ufimskoe gosudarstvennoe soveshchanie i Vremennoe sibirskoe pravitel'stvo', *Krasnyi arkhiv* (Moscow), No. 6 (1933), pp. 58–81.

Popov, K.A (ed.) *Dopros Kolchaka*. Leningrad (1925).

'Protokol ob"edinennogo zasedanii mirnoi delegatsii Polittsentra s RVS 5-oi armii i Sibrevkom ot 18–19 ianvaria 1920g.', *Sibirskie ogni* (Novosibirsk), No. 5 (1927), pp. 140–146.

'R.N.' 'V poiskakh ustoichivogo rubliia (istoricheskie dokumenty kolchakovskogo pravitel'stva)', *Ekonomicheskoe stroitel'stvo* (Moscow), No. 2 (1923), pp. 127–136.

Riabikov, V.V. (ed.) *Tsentrosibir'*. Moscow (1949).

Shishkin, V.I. (ed.) 'K istorii kolchakovskogo perevorota (pis'mo A.D. Syromiatnikova)', *Izvestiia sibirskogo otdeleniia Ak. nauk SSSR (seriia istorii, filologii i filosofii)* (Novosibirsk), Vol. 1 (1989), pp. 59–62.

Shepeleva, T. (ed.) 'Ispol'zovanie interventami Severno-morskogo puti', *Krasnyi arkhiv* (Moscow), Vol. 1 (1941), pp. 151–198.

Smirnov, I.N. (ed.) 'Ot kolchakovshchiny k Sovetam: peregovory s Polit-tsentrom v ianvare 1920g.', *Sibirskie ogni* (Novosibirsk), No. 5 (1927), pp. 134–147.

Sovety Tomskoi gubernii (mart 1917–mai 1918gg.): sbornik dokumentov i materialov. Tomsk (1976).

Speranskii, L. (ed.) 'Materialy k istorii interventsii: rol' Iaponii v istorii Sibirskoi atamanshchinoi po materialam arkhiva Narodnogo komissariata inostrannykh del', *Sbornik Narkomindel* (Moscow), Nos. 1–3 (1922).

Sworakowski, W.S. 'A Churchill Letter in Support of the Anti-Bolshevik Forces in Russia in 1919', *Russian Review*, Vol. 28, No. 1 (1954), pp. 77–82.

Taniaev, A. (ed.) *Kolchakovshchina na Urale*. Moscow (1930).

Trotsky, L.D. *Sochineniia*. Moscow–Leningrad (1925–1927).

How the Revolution Armed (5 Vols.). London (1979–1981).

United States (Department of State) *Documents Relating to the Organization and Purposes of the Anti-Bolshevik Forces in Siberia* (Russian Series No. 3). Washington (1919).

American Assistance in the Operation of the Trans-Siberian Railway (Russian Series No. 4). Washington (1919).

Documents Relating to the Foreign Relations of the United States: 1918 (3 Vols.). Washington (1931–1932).

Documents Relating to the Foreign Relations of the United States: 1919 (Russia). Washington (1937).

Documents Relating to the Foreign Relations of the United States: 1919 (The Paris Peace Conference) (13 Vols.). Washington (1939–1940).

United States (Senate) *The Deportation of Grigorie Semenoff: Hearings of the Committee on Education and Labour, United States Senate (67th Congress, 2nd Division, Relative to the Deporting of Undesirable Aliens – April 12th, 13th, 17th, 18th 1922)*. Washington (1922).

United States Military Intelligence, 1917–1927: Weekly Summaries. New York (1978).

'V.M.' (ed.) 'K istorii interventsii v Sibiri', *Krasnyi arkhiv* (Moscow), No. 34 (1929), pp. 126–165.

Varneck, E. and Fisher, H.H. (eds.) *The Testimony of Admiral Kolchak and Other Siberian Materials.* Stanford (1935).

'V bor'be s kontrrevoliutsii': sbornik dokumental'nykh materialov (1918–1922gg.). Omsk (1959).

Vilenskii [Sibiriakov], V. (ed.) *Soiuznicheskaia interventsiia na Dal'nem Vostoke i v Sibiri: doklad Pishona.* Moscow–Leningrad (1924).

18 fevral' 1919g.: materialy i dokumenty po istorii perekhoda Bashkiri na storonu Sovetskoi vlasti. Ufa (1923).

Woodward, E.L. and Butler, R. (eds.) *Documents on British Foreign Policy* (First Series, Vols. 2–3). London (1948–1949).

Zaiontchkovsky, A. et al. (eds.) *Les Alliés contre la Russie avant, pendant et après la guerre mondiale. Faits et documents.* Paris (1926).

Zenzinov, V. (ed.) *Gosudarstvennyi perevorot admirala Kolchaka v Omske 18 noiabria 1918 goda.* Paris (1919).

Za vlast' Sovetov: sbornik dokumentov o bor'be trudiashchikhsia Zabaikal'ia v 1917–1922gg. Chita (1957).

Za vlast' Sovetov: sbornik dokumentov o bor'be za vlast' Sovetov v Eniseiskoi gubernii (mart 1917–iiul' 1918gg.). Krasnoiarsk (1957).

Znamenskaia, P.A. (ed.) *Khrestomatiia po istorii Sibiri.* Novosibirsk (1930).

Zulina, K.N. and Kazakov, B.N. 'O rabote podpol'nykh bol'shevistskikh organizatsii Sibiri (1918–1919gg.), *Istoricheskii arkhiv* (Moscow), No. 2 (1962), pp. 96–111.

Autobiographies and Memoirs, Published Diaries and Letters

Ackerman, C.W. *Trailing the Bolsheviks: 12,000 miles with the Allies in Siberia.* New York (1919).

Akulin, I.G. 'Ural'skoe kazach'e voisko v bor'be s bol'shevizmom', *Beloe delo* (Berlin), No. 2 (1927), pp. 122–147.

Orenburgskoe kazach'e voisko v bor'be s bol'shevikami, 1917–1920gg. Shanghai (1937).

Alekseev, S.A. (ed.) *Nachalo grazhdanskoi voiny.* Moscow (1926).

Grazhdanskaia voina v Sibiri i v severnoi oblasti. Moscow (1927).

Alioshin, D. *Asian Odyssey.* London (1941).

Andrushkevich, N.A. 'Posledniaia Rossiia', *Beloe delo* (Berlin), No. 4 (1928), pp. 108–146.

Argunov, A.A. *Mezhdu dvumia bol'shevizami.* Paris (1919).

'Bez svobody', *Golos minuvshago na chuzhoi storone* (Paris), Vol. 13 (1925), pp. 86–130.
'Omskie dni v 1918g.', *Sibirskii arkhiv* (Prague), Vol. 5 (1935), pp. 191–206.

Arkhangel'skii, V.G. 'Kazan' vo vremia bor'by s bol'shevikami', *Volia Rossii* (Prague), Nos. 8–9 (1928), pp. 260–286.

Arnol'dov, V. *Zhizn' i revoliutsiia. Groza piatogo goda. Belyi Omsk.* Shanghai (1935).

Artem'ev, I.K. *Vospominaniia: epizody revoliutsii na Dal'nem Vostoke.* Tientsin (1939).

Astrov, N. 'Priznanie gen. Denikinym adm. Kolchaka', *Golos minuvshago na chuzhoi storone* (Paris), Vol. 14 (1926), pp. 210–221.

Baerlin, H. *The March of the Seventy Thousand.* London (1926).

Baturin, V. 'Eshelon smerti: vospominaniia rabochego', *Sibirskie ogni* (Novosibirsk), No. 6 (1929).

Becvar, G. *The Lost Legion: A Czechoslovak Epic.* London (1939).

Bell, J.M. *Sidelights on the Siberian Campaign.* Toronto (1920).

Bigelow, P. *Japan and Her Colonies: Being Extracts from a Diary made whilst visiting Formosa, Manchuria, Shantung, Korea and Saghalin in the Year 1921.* London (1923).

Boldyrev, V.G. *Direktoriia, Kolchak, Interventy: vospominaniia.* Novosibirsk (1925).

Borman, A. 'My Meetings with White Generals', *Russian Review*, Vol. 27, No. 2 (1968), pp. 215–224.

Borodin, N.A. *Idealy i deiatel'nost: sorok let zhizni i raboty riadovago russkago intelligenta (1879–1919).* Berlin–Paris (1930).

Brändström, E. *Among Prisoners of War in Russia and Siberia.* London (1929).

Brown, W.A. *The Groping Giant: Revolutionary Russia as Seen by an American Democrat.* New Haven (1920).

von Budberg, Baron A.P. 'Dnevnik', *Arkhiv russkoi revoliutsii* (Berlin), Vol. 12 (1923), pp. 197–290; Vol. 13 (1924), pp. 197–312; Vol. 14 (1924), pp. 225–341; Vol. 15 (1924), pp. 254–345.

Bullard, A. *The Russian Pendulum: Autocracy, Democracy, Bolshevism.* New York (1919).

Bursak, I.N. 'Konets belogo admirala', in Spirin, L.M. (ed.) *Razgrom Kolchaka: vospominaniia.* Moscow (1969), pp. 268–280.

Buxhoeveden, S. *Left Behind: 14 Months in Siberia During the Revolution (December 1917–February 1919).* London (1929).

Buxton, C.R. *In a Russian Village.* London (1922).

Channing, C.G.F. *Siberia's Untouched Treasure, Its Future Role in the World.* New York (1923).

Chaulkin, T.B. 'Siberia in 1918–1919', *Royal Canadian Mounted Police Quarterly* (Ottawa), Vol. 9, No. 2 (October 1941).

Chechek, S. 'Ot Penzy do Urala', *Volia Rossii* (Prague), Nos. 8–9 (1928), pp. 246–265.

Cheremnyi, S.F. 'Omskoe vosstanie', in Spirin, L.M. (ed.) *Razgrom Kolchaka: vospominaniia*. Moscow (1969), pp. 239–255.

Chernov, V.N. *Mes tribulations en Russe soviétique*. Paris (1921).

Pered burei: vospominaniia. New York (1953).

Chernova, O. *New Horizons: Reminiscences of the Russian Revolution*. London (1936).

Chernov-Andreyev, O. *Cold Spring in Russia*. Ann Arbor (1970).

Chudnovskii, S. 'Kak byl rasstrelian Kolchak', *Sibirskaia derevnia* (Novosibirsk), No. 9 (1924), pp. 4–6.

'L'Execution de Koltchak et de Pépéliaev', *Le Monde Slave* (Paris), Vol. 13 (1925), pp. 477–481.

'Kak byl rasstrelian Kolchak', *Poslednie novosti* (Paris), 17.ii.1925.

'Rasstrel Kolchaka i Pepeliaeva', *Pravda* (Moscow), 16.i.1935.

'Konets Kolchaka', in *Gody ognevnye, gody boevye*. Irkutsk (1961), pp. 204–209.

Chuev, T. 'Chernodol'skoe vosstanie', *Sibirskie ogni* (Novosibirsk), Nos. 5–6 (1926), pp. 157–166.

Clingan, G.F. 'Siberian Sideshow', *The Legionary* (Ottawa), Vol. 30, No. 1 (June 1955).

Daurets, N.P. *Semenovskie zastenki: zapiski ochevidtsa*. Harbin (1921).

Denikin, A.I. *Ocherki russkoi smuty* (5 Vols.). Paris–Berlin (1921–1926).

Staraia armiia. Paris (1930).

Dotsenko, P. *The Struggle for a Democracy in Siberia: An Eye-Witness Account of a Contemporary*. Stanford (1983).

Dubarbier, G. *En Sibérie après l'Armistice*. Paris (1924).

Duncan, W.V. 'A Siberian Notebook (The Czechoslovak Campaign Against the Bolsheviks)', *The Yale Review* (Oct. 1919), pp. 54–84.

Dunham, W.E. 'The Canadians in Siberia', *Maclean's* (Toronto), Vol. 32, No. 5 (May 1919).

Dwinger, E.E. *The Army Behind the Wire: A Siberian Diary*. London (1930).

Between White and Red. New York (1932).

Dybowski, R. *Siedem lat w Rosji i na Syberji (1914–1921): przy gody i wrazenia*. Warsaw (1922).

Efimov, A.G. *Izhevtsy i Votkintsy: bor'ba s bol'shevikami, 1918–1922gg*. Concord, CA (1975).

Eikhe, G.Kh. *Forsirovanie reki Beloi chastiami 5-i armii Vostochnogo fronta v iiune 1919g*. Moscow (1928).

Elovskii, I. *Golodnyi pokhod orenburgskoi armii (iz vospominanii uchastnika pokhoda)*. Peking (1921).

El'tsin, V. 'Piataia armiia i sibirskie partizany', in Smirnov, I.N. et al. (eds.) *Bor'ba za Ural i Sibir': vospominaniia i statei uchastnikov bor'by s uchredilovskoi i kolchakovskoi kontrrevoliutsei*. Moscow–Leningrad (1926), pp. 261–280.

[Emerson, G.H.] 'Colonel Emerson's Experiences in Russia', *Railway Age*, Vol. 68 (14.vi.1920), pp. 1769–1770.

Enborisov, G.V. *Ot Urala do Kharbina: pamiatka o perezhitom.* Shanghai (1932).

Essen, R. *Zwischen der Ostsee und dem Stillen Ozean: Asiatische Probleme und Erinnerungen.* Frankfurt (1935).

Ettighoffer, P.C. *Tovarish: The Odyssey of a Siberian Exile.* London (1935).

Farthing, C.H. 'In Siberia, 1918–1919: A Memoir', *Sbornik of the Study Group on the Russian Revolution* (Leeds), Vol. 8 (1982), pp. 93–99.

Fedotoff-White, D. *Survival Through War and Revolution in Russia.* Philadelphia (1939).

Filat′ev, D.B. *Katastrofa belogo dvizheniia v Sibiri, 1918–1922gg. (vpechatleniia ochevidtsa).* Paris (1985).

Filimonov, B.B. *Na putiakh k Uralu (pokhod Stepnykh polkov letom 1918g.).* Shanghai (1934).

Forbath, L. *The New Mongolia (As Related by Joseph Geleta).* London (1936).

Francis, D.R. *Russia from the American Embassy, April 1916–November 1918.* New York (1922).

Galton, G. and Keep, J. (eds.) 'Letters from Vladivostok', *Slavonic and East European Review,* (London), Vol. 45, No. 2 (1967), pp. 497–530.

Gajda, R. *Moje pameti: Ceskoslovenska anabase zret na Ural proti Bolshevikum. Admiral Kolchak.* Prague (1924).

Gendlin, A.S. 'V kolchakovskom zastenke', in Nikitin, I.I. (ed.) *Nezabyvaemye gody: sbornik vospominanii starykh chlenov KPSS.* Yaroslavl′ (1963), pp. 95–101.

Gerasimov, A. *God v kolchakovskom zastenke.* Ekaterinburg (1923).

Gerhardie, W. *Memoirs of a Polyglot.* London (1931).

Gidney, J.B. (ed.) *Witness to a Revolution: Letters from Russia (1916–1919) by Edward T. Heald.* Kent State University (1972).

Gloss, I. 'Chekhoslovaki i Sibirskaia oblastnaia duma', *Vol′naia Sibir′* (Prague), No. 4 (1928), pp. 28–35.

Gody ognevnye: sbornik vospominanii uchastnikov bor′by za vlast′ sovetov (1918–1920gg.). Krasnoiarsk (1926).

Gody ognevye, gody boevye. Sbornik vospominanii. Irkutsk (1961).

Goleevskii, N.N. 'Leto na Volge. 1918g.', *Russian Émigré Archives* (Fresno), Vol. 2 (1973), pp. 1–37.

Gopper, G. *Chetyre katastrofy.* Riga (1933).

Grachev, G. 'Iakutskii pokhod gen. Pepeliaeva', *Sibirskii arkhiv* (Novosibirsk), Vol. 1 (1929), pp. 23–40.

Graves, W.S. *America's Siberian Adventure, 1918–1920.* New York (1931).

Grazhdanskaia voina na Dal′nem Vostoke (1918–1922gg.): vospominaniia veteranov. Moscow (1973).

Griener, J.E. *The Russian Railway Situation and Some Personal Observations.* Baltimore (1918).

'The American Railway Commission in Siberia', *Railway Age,* Vol. 63, No. 5 (1918), pp. 170–172.

Grishin-Almazova 'Kolchak i Pepeliaev v tiurm′e', *Russkii golos* (Harbin), February 1921.

Gromov, I.V. 'Nash tyl', *Sibirskie ogni* (Novosibirsk), No. 4 (1935), pp. 128–134.

'V boiakh za Sovety', in *Za vlast' Sovetov (vospominaniia uchastnikov partizanskoi dvizhenii v tylu Kolchaka*. Novosibirsk (1947).

Grondijs, L.H. *La Guerre en Russie et en Sibérie*. Paris (1922).

Guins [Gins], G.K. *Sibir', soiuzniki i Kolchak: povorotnyi moment russkoi istorii, 1918–1920gg. (Vpechatleniia i mysli chlena Omskogo pravitel'stva)* (2 Vols.). Peking (1921).

Gurevich, V.Ia. *Grazhdanskaia voina na vostoke* (3 Vols.). Berlin (1922).

Hodges, P. *Britmis: A Great Adventure of the War (Being an Account of Allied Intervention in Siberia and of an Escape across the Gobi Desert to Peking)*. London (1931).

Hoover, H. *The Memoirs of Herbert Hoover* (Vol. 1). London (1952).

Horrall, S.W. 'The Force's Siberian Patrol', *Royal Canadian Mounted Police Quarterly* (Ottawa), Vol. 36 (1971), No. 5.

Horrocks, B.H. *A Full Life*. London (1960).

Hunt, F. 'I Capture Vladivostok', in Lyons, E. (ed.) *We Cover the World*. New York (1937), pp. 77–89.

Iakovenko, V.G. *Zapiski partizana*. Moscow (1925).

Iakushev, I.Ia. 'Dal'nevostochnoe samoupravlenie v bor'be za vlast' (1917–1919gg.)', in *Mestnoe samoupravlenie* (Trudy Obshchestva rossiiskikh emigrantov v Chekho-Slovaki). Prague (1926).

'Ocherki oblastnicheskogo dvizheniia v Sibiri', *Vol'naia Sibir'* (Prague), Vol. 4 (1928), pp. 100–113; Vols. 6–7 (1928), pp. 88–103.

'Komitet sodeistviia sozyvu Zemskogo sobora', *Sibirskii arkhiv* (Prague), Vol. 2 (1929), pp. 73–80.

Il'in, I.S. 'Komuch', *Novyi zhurnal* (New York), Vol. 65 (1961), pp. 221–242.

'Omsk, Direktoriia i Kolchak', *Novyi zhurnal* (New York), Vol. 72 (1963), pp. 198–217; Vol. 73 (1963), pp. 216–243.

Il'iukov, N. and Titov, M. *Partizanskoe dvizhenie v Primor'e*. Leningrad (1928).

Inostrantsev, M.A. 'Pervoe poruchenie admirala Kolchaka', *Beloe delo* (Berlin), Vol. 1 (1926), pp. 149–156.

Ivanov, Vs.N. *V grazhdanskom voine: iz zapisok omskago zhurnalista*. Harbin (1921).

Iz proshlogo: pervyi sbornik vospominanii. Kolchakovshchina. Kungur (1922).

Janin, Général [P.T.C.M.] 'Fragments de mon journal sibérien', *Le Monde Slave* (Paris), No. 2 (1924), pp. 221–240; No. 3 (1925), pp. 339–355.

'Le journal sibérien du général Janin', *Le Monde Slave* (Paris), No. 4 (1925), pp. 19–24.

Moje ucast na ceskoslovenskem boji za svobodu. Prague (1928).

'Otryvki iz moego sibirskogo dnevnika', in Kornatovskii, N.A. (ed.) *Kolchakovshchina: iz belykh memuarov* (1930), pp. 103–146.

Ma mission en Sibérie, 1918–20. Paris (1933).

Johnston, B.O. 'American Railway Engineers in Siberia', *Military Engineer*, Vol. 15 (1921), pp. 187–192.

Kazakov, V.G. *Nemye svideteli*. Shanghai (1936).

Kehler, H. *The Red Garden*. London (1922).

Khartling, K.N. *Na strazhe rodiny: sobytiia vo Vladivostoke (konets 1919–nachalo 1920gg.)*. Shanghai (1935).

Khrabov, N. 'Sud′ba ili sluchainost′', *Sibirskii arkhiv* (Prague), Vol. 3 (1930), pp. 121–132.

Kirilov, A.A. 'Sibirskaia armiia v bor′be za osvobozhdenie', *Vol′naia Sibir′* (Prague), No. 4 (1928), pp. 36–68.

Kislitsyn, V.A. *V ogne grazhdanskoi voiny: memuary*. Harbin (1936).

Panteon voinskoi doblesti i chesti. Harbin (1941).

Klante, M. *Von der Wolga zum Amur: Die Tschechische Legion und der Russische Bürgerkrieg*. Berlin (1931).

Klerzhe, G.I. *Revoliutsiia i grazhdanskaia voina: lichnye vospominaniia (chast′ pervaia)*. Mukden (1932).

Klimushkin, P.D. *Chekhoslovatskoe vystuplenie. Tom 1: 'Volzhskoe dvizhenie' i obrazovanie Direktorii*. Prague (1925).

'Pered vol′zhkim vosstaniem', *Volia Rossii* (Prague), Vols. 8–9 (1928), pp. 213–222.

'Bor′ba za demokratiiu na Volge', in *Grazhdanskaia voina na Volge* (Sbornik 1). Prague (1930), pp. 38–102.

Kniazhev, V.V. *Zhizn′ dlia vsekh i smert′ za vsekh: zapiski lichnogo ad″iutanta Verkhovnogo pravitelia admirala A.V. Kolchaka, rotmistra V.V. Kniazheva*. Jordanville, NY (1971).

Knox, A. *With the Russian Army, 1914–1917: Being Chiefly Extracts from the Diary of a Military Attaché* (2 Vols.). London (1921).

Koganitskii, I. 'V chernye dni v Sibiri', *Proletarskaia revoliutsiia* (Moscow), No. 2 (1922), pp. 254–262.

Kohn, H. *Living in a World Revolution: My Encounters with History*. New York (1964).

Kolomeitsev, N.N. 'Russkaia poliarnaia ekspeditsiia, 1900–1903gg.', *Russian Émigré Archives* (Fresno), Vol. 5 (1974), pp. 1–50.

Kolosov, E.E. 'Kak eto bylo? Massovye ubiistva pri Kolchake v dekabre 1918g. v Omske i gibel′ N.V. Fomina', *Byloe* (Petrograd), Vol. 21 (1923), pp. 250–298.

Kornatovskii, N.A. (ed.) *Kolchakovshchina: iz belykh memuarov*. Leningrad (1930).

Kotomkin, A. 'S chekhoslovatskimi legionami ot Volgi do Tikhogo okeana', *Belyi arkhiv* (Paris), Vols. 2–3 (1928), pp. 211–235.

Koudrey, V. *Once a Commissar*. London (1938).

Kozhevnikov, S. 'Konets bor′by s chekho-slovakami', in Smirnov, I.N. et al. (eds.) *Bor′ba za Ural i Sibir′: vospominaniia i statei uchastnikov bor′by s uchredilovskoi i kolchakovskoi kontrrevoliutsei*. Moscow–Leningrad (1926), pp. 336–40.

Kratovchil, J. *Cesta revoluce*. Prague (1928).

Kravchenko, A.D. *Za vlast′ Sovetov*. Moscow (1947).

Krejci, F.V. *Poselstvo vlady k csl. vojsku na Sibiri*. Prague (1923).

U sibirske armady. Prague (1923).

Kröger, T. *The Forgotten Village: Four Years in Siberia*. London (1920).

Krol′, L. *Za tri goda: vospominaniia, vpechatleniia i vstrechi*. Vladivostok (1921).

Krol′, M.A. 'Sibirskoe pravitel′stvo i avgustovskaia sessiia Sibirskoi oblastnoi dumy', *Vol′naia Sibir′* (Prague), No. 4 (1928), pp. 69–82.

Kukushkin, I. *Chernye dni pri beloi vlasti*. Omsk (1921).

Kuznetsov, P.A. (ed.) *Grazhdanskaia voina v Bashkiri: vospominaniia uchastnikov*. Ufa (1932).

Lasies, J. *La Tragédie sibirienne: le drame d'Ekaterinbourg, la fin de l'amiral Koltchak*. Paris (1920).

Lebedev, V.I. 'Ot Petrograda do Kazani: vosstanie na Volge v 1918g. (ot arkhiva V.I. Lebedeva)', *Volia Rossii* (Prague), Vols. 8–9 (1928), pp. 50–197.

Legras, J. 'L'agonie de la Sibérie (1918–1920)', *Le Monde Slave* (1928) No. 2, pp. 161–195.

Levinson, A. 'Poezdka iz Peterburga v Sibir′ v ianvare 1920g.', *Arkhiv russkoi revoliutsii* (Berlin), Vol. 3 (1921), pp. 190–209.

Lied, J. *Return to Happiness*. London (1943).

Prospector in Siberia: The Autobiography of Jonas Lied. Oxford (1945).

Siberian Arctic: the Story of the Siberian Company. London (1960).

Lindberg, I. *Nevedomaia stranitsa (popytka pokusheniia na Kolchaka)*. Chita (1921).

Littauer, V.S. *Russian Hussar*. London (1965).

Lloyd George, D. *Memoirs of the Peace Conference*. New Haven (1939).

Lukomskii, A.S. *Vospominaniia* (2 Vols.). Berlin (1922).

McCullagh, F. 'In Red Ekaterinburg', *Fortnightly Review* No. 108 (1920), pp. 724–737.

A Prisoner of the Reds: The Story of a British Officer Captured in Siberia. London (1921).

Maiskii, I.M. *Demokraticheskaia kontrrevoliutsiia*. Moscow (1923).

Makeev, A.S. *Bog voiny: Baron Ungern (vospominaniia byvshago adiutanta Nachal′nika Aziatskoi konnoi divizii)*. Shanghai (1934).

Makovoi, P.P. 'Stranitsy proshlogo, 1916–1920gg.', *Russian Émigré Archives* (Fresno), Vol. 4 (1973), pp. 1–99.

Malinovich, J.D. *Uspomene iz Sibira 1918–1919 i put okeanom domovinu 1920*. Belgrade (1926).

Mannerheim, K.G. *The Memoirs of Marshal Mannerheim*. London (1953).

Marsh, C. 'Glimpses of Siberia and the Russian "Wild East"', *National Geographic*, Vol. 138, No. 6 (1920), pp. 513–536.

Masaryk, T.G. *The Making of a State: Memoirs and Observations, 1914–1918*. London (1927)

Menshikov, A. 'Praktika primor′skogo zemstva', *Sibirskii arkhiv* (Prague), Vol. 4 (1932), pp. 155–182.

Miakotin, V.A. 'Iz nedalekago proshlogo', *Golos minuvshago na chuzhoi storone* (Paris), Vol. 2 (1923), pp. 178–200.

Molchanov, N. *Oktiabr′ i kolchakovshchina*. Minusinsk (1922).

Molotov, K.M. *Kontrrevoliutsiia v Sibiri i bor′ba za Sovetskuiu vlast′*. Saratov (1921).

Montandon, G. *Deux ans chez Koltchak et les bolchéviques, 1919–1921*. Paris (1923).

'N' 'Poslednie dni kolchakovshchiny', *Sibirskie ogni* (Novosibirsk), No. 2 (1922), pp. 76–95.

'N.N.' 'Zapiski belogvardeitsa', *Arkhiv russkoi revoliutsii* (Berlin), Vol. 10 (1923), pp. 56–113.

Nabokov, K.D. *Ordeal of a Diplomat*. London (1921).

Nesterov, A.G. 'Arest Kolchaka', in *Gody ognevye, gody boevye*. Irkutsk (1961).

'Nezabyvaemoe'. Vospominaniia uchastnikov revoliutsionnykh sobytii v Krasnoiarskom krae, 1917–1920gg. Krasnoiarsk (1957).

Nielson, R.F. 'Combating the Cold in Siberia', *Maclean's* (Toronto), (October 1972).

Nikiforov, P.M. *V gody reaktsii v Irkutskom tiurm′e*. Moscow (1932).
Zapiski prim′era DVR. Moscow (1974).

Nikolaev, S.N. 'Vozniknovenie i organizatsiia Komucha', *Volia Rossii* (Prague), Nos. 8–9 (1928), pp. 233–245.
'Narodnaia armiia v Simbirske', *Volia Rossii* (Prague), Nos. 10–11 (1928).
'Politika Komucha', in *Grazhdanskaia voina na Volge v 1918 (Sbornik 1)*. Prague (1930), pp. 103–164.
'Konets Komucha', *Sovremennye zapiski* (Paris) No. 45 (1931), pp. 333–361; No. 46 (1931), pp. 287–320.

Noskov, K. *The Black Years*. Harbin (n.d.).

Novombergsky, M.A. *My Siberian Life*. London (1956).

O'Connor, Lt.-Colonel Sir F. *On the Frontier and Beyond: A Record of Thirty Years Service*. London (1931).

[O'Higgins, G.] 'Cherez Sibiri k svobode', *Belyi arkhiv* (Paris), Vol. 1 (1926), pp. 158–162.

'Onlooker' 'With the British Mission in Siberia', *National Review* (New York), (May 1920), pp. 386–396.

Papushek, Ia. 'Prichiny Chekhoslovatskogo vstupleniia v 1918g.', *Volia Rossii* (Prague), Nos. 8–9 (1928), pp. 287–350.

Pares, B. *Day by Day with the Russian Army*. London (1915).
My Russian Memoirs. London (1931).
Moscow Admits a Critic. London (1936).
A Wandering Student: The Story of a Purpose. Syracuse (1948).

Pavlov, G. 'Kolchak nastupal', *Sibirskie ogni* (Novosibirsk), No. 6 (1929), pp. 109–116.

[Pepeliaev, V.N.] 'Dnevnik', *Krasnye zori* (Irkutsk), No. 4 (1923), pp. 75–90; No. 5 (1923), pp. 32–50.

'Razval kolchakovshchiny (iz dnevnika V.N. Pepeliaeva)', *Krasnyi arkhiv* (Moscow), No. 6 (1928), pp. 51–80.

Petrov, F. *Past and Present: Reminiscences*. Moscow (1961).

Petrov, P.P. *Ot Volgi do Tikhago okeana*. Riga (1930).

Rokovye gody, 1914–1920. California (1965).

Pichon, Colonel 'Le Coup d'État de l'amiral Koltchak', *Le Monde Slave* (1925) No. 1 pp. 1–26; No. 2, pp. 248–270.

Postyshev, P.P. *Grazhdanskaia voina na vostoke Sibiri*. Moscow (1928).

Preston, T. *Before the Curtain*. London (1950).

Price, H.J. *Boche and Bolshevik: Experiences of an Englishman in the German Army and in Russian Prisons*. London (1919).

Prinsep, E.S.M. 'Knox's Mission to Siberia, 1919–1920: the Personal Experiences of one of its Members', *The Army Quarterly* (London), Vol. 81, No. 1 (1960), pp. 54–69.

Ptashkina, N. *Dnevnik, 1918–1920*. Paris–Berlin (1922).

Quénet, C. 'L'Arrière sibérien', *Le Monde Slave* (1926) No. 8, pp. 161–82; (1926) No. 9, pp. 321–350; (1926), No. 10, pp. 12–39.

Ragozin, T. *Partizany Stepnogo-Badzheia (zapiski uchastnikov)*. Moscow (1926).

Rakov, D.F. *V zastenkakh Kolchaka: golos iz Sibiri*. Paris (1920).

de Robien, L. *Journal d'un Diplomate en Russie, 1917–1918*. Paris (1967).

Rodney, W. 'Siberia in 1919: A Canadian Banker's Impressions', *Queens Quarterly* (Kingston, Ontario), Vol. 79, No. 3 (1972), pp. 324–335.

Ross, E.A. *Russia in Upheaval*. New York (1919).

Rouquérol, J.G.M. *La Guerre des Rouges et des Blancs: l'aventure de l'amiral Koltchak*. Paris (1929).

Rudnev, S.P. *Pri vechernykh ogniakh: vospominaniia*. Harbin (1928).

Rutger, E. *Mezhdu Baltiiskim morem i Tikhim okeanom*. Frankfurt (1925).

Sakharov, K.V. *Belaia Sibir': vnutrennaia voina, 1918–1920gg*. Munich (1923).

Die verratlene Armee. Berlin (1939).

Savich, N. 'Tri vstrechi: adm. Kolchak i gosudarstvennaia duma', *Arkhiv russkoi revoliutsii* (Berlin), Vol. 10 (1923), pp. 168–174.

de Savitsch, E. *In Search of Complications: An Autobiography*. London (1941).

Sayler, O.M. *Russia White or Red*. Boston (1919).

Skacel, J. *S generalem Syrovym v Sibiri*. Prague (1923).

Ceskoslovenska armada v Rusku a Kolcak (protivo-bolsevicky boj v Roce, 1918–1920). Prague (1926).

Schwazer, F. *Soldner im Sibirien: Erlebnisse eines Sudetendeutschen*. Breslau (1932).

Semchevskaia, E. *Ocherki iz sibirskogo ledianogo pokhoda, 1919–1920gg*. Shanghai (1920).

Semenov, G.M. *O sebe: vospominaniia, mysli i vstrechi*. Harbin (1938).

Serebrennikov, I.I. 'Iz istorii Sibirskogo pravitel'stva', *Sibirskii arkhiv* (Prague), Vol. 1 (1929), pp. 5–22.
Moi vospominaniia. Tientsin (1937).

Sergeev, V.L. *Ocherki po istorii belogo dvizheniia na Dal'nem Vostoke*. Harbin (1937).

Shcherebakov, K.F. *V plenu u Kolchaka*. Voronezh (1934).

Shchetinkin, P.E. *Bor'ba s kolchakovshchinoi (ocherk partizanskoi bor'by na Minusinskom fronte)*. Novosibirsk (1929).

Shidlovskii, G. 'Poslednie dni kolchakovshchinoi', *Krasnaia letopis'* (Petrograd), No. 1 (1924), pp. 218–222.

von Shildknecht, E. 'Vstrechi s Kolchakom', *Morskoi zhurnal* (Paris), No. 1 (1958), pp. 87–95.

Shiriamov, A. 'Irkutskoe vosstanie i rasstrel Kolchaka', *Sibirskie ogni* (Novonikolaevsk), No. 4 (1924), pp. 122–139.
'Bor'ba s kolchakovshchinoi', in Konstantinov, M.M. (ed.) *Poslednie dni kolchakovshchiny*. Moscow (1926), pp. 19–42.
'Konets kolchakovshchiny', *Bor'ba klassov* (Moscow), Nos. 1–2 (1935), pp. 86–100.

Smirnov, I.N. 'Konets bor'by: peremirie s chekho-slovatskami', in Smirnov et al. *Bor'ba za Ural i Sibir': vospominaniia i statei uchastnikov bor'by s uchredilovskoi i kolchakovskoi kontrrevoliutsei*. Moscow–Leningrad (1926), pp. 305–317.

Smirnov, I.N. et al. (eds.) *Bor'ba za Ural i Sibir': vospominaniia i statei uchastnikov bor'by s uchredilovskoi i kolchakovskoi kontrrevoliutsei*. Moscow–Leningrad (1926).

Smirnov, M.I. 'Admiral Kolchak vo vremia revoliutsii v Chernomorskom flote', *Istoriia i sovremennost'* (Berlin), No. 4 (1923), pp. 3–28.

Smith, C.H. 'What Happened in Siberia', *Asia*, Vol. 22 (1922), pp. 373–378, 402–403.
'Four Years of Mistakes in Siberia', *Asia*, Vol. 22 (1922), pp. 479–483.
'The Smoke-Screen between Siberia and Washington', *Asia*, Vol. 22 (1922), pp. 639–644.

Soboleff, Major I.S.K. *Cossack at Large*. London (1974).

Sofronov, G.L. *Pravda o revoliutsii i grazhdanskoi voiny*. San Francisco (1983).

Sokolov, K.N. *Pravlenie generala Denikina*. Sofia (1921).

Solodovnikov, B. *Sibirskie avantiury i general Gaida: iz zapisok russkago revoliutsionera*. Prague (n.d.).

Spath, B. *Unter den Fahnen des Prasidenten Koltschak: als Kosak und Matrose unter Koltschaks Fahne in Siberien*. Konstanz (1925).

Spirin, L.M. (ed.) *Razgrom Kolchaka: vospominaniia*. Moscow (1969).

Stanford, D.N. *Sun and Snow: A Siberian Adventure*. London (1963).

Steidler, F.V. *Ceskoslovenske hnuti na Rusi*. Prague (1921).
Nase vystoupeni v Rusku. Prague (1923).

Stepanov, A.P. 'Simbirskaia operatsiia', *Beloe delo* (Berlin), No. 1 (1926), pp. 83–85.

Stoffa, Major P. *Around the World to Freedom: Being the Escapes and Adventures of Major Paul Stoffa*. London (1933).

Stoss, E. *Kriegsgefangen in Siberien, Erlebnisse eine Wiener Landsturmmannes im Weltkrieg*. Vienna (1927).

Strod, I. *Civil War in the Taiga: A Story of Guerrilla Warfare in the Forests of Eastern Siberia*. London (1933).

Sukhomlinov, V.A. *Vospominaniia*. Moscow (1926).

Surnov, I. 'Pervaia vstrecha partizanov s Krasnoi armii', in Smirnov, I.N. et al. (eds.) *Bor′ba za Ural i Sibir′: vospominaniia i statei uchastnikov bor′by s uchredilovskoi i kolchakovskoi kontrrevoliutsei*. Moscow–Leningrad (1926), pp. 122–135.

Sutton, F.A. *One-Arm Sutton*. London (1933).

Timireva [-Kniper], A.V. 'Vospominaniia', *Novyi zhurnal* (New York), Vol. 159 (1985), pp. 196–238.

'Fragmenty vospominanii', *Minuvshee* (Paris), No. 1 (1986), pp. 99–190.

Toll, E.V. *Die Russische Polarfahrt der 'Sarja', 1900–1902*. Berlin (1909).

Tolstov, V.S. *Ot krasnykh lap v neizvestnuiu pal′ (pokhod ural′tsev)*. Constantinople (1921).

Trubetskoi, G.N. *Gody smuty i nadezhdy: 1917–1919gg*. Montreal (1981).

Tukhachevskii, M.N. 'Kurgan–Omsk', Smirnov, I.N. et al. (eds.) *Bor′ba za Ural i Sibir′: vospominaniia i statei uchastnikov bor′by s uchredilovskoi i kolchakovskoi kontrrevoliutsei*. Moscow–Leningrad (1926).

Ustrialov, N. 'Iz proshlogo', *Russkaia zhizn′: al′manakh* (Harbin), No. 3 (Dec. 1922), pp. 39–58.

Utgov, V.L. 'Ufimskoe gosudarstvennoe soveshchanie (iz vospominanii uchastnika)', *Byloe* (Petrograd), No. 16 (1921), pp. 15–42.

V boiakh i pokhodakh. Sverdlovsk (1959).

Vergé, A. *Avec les Tchécoslovaques*. Paris (1926).

Vilkitskii, B.A. 'Kogda, komu i kak ia sluzhil pod bol′shevikami', *Russian Émigré Archives* (Fresno), Vol. 5 (1974), pp. 11–55.

Vining, L.E. *Held by the Bolsheviks: The Diary of a British Officer in Russia, 1919–1920*. London (1924).

Vishnevskii, E.K. *Argtonavty beloi mechty: opisanie iakutskago pokhod Sibirskoi dobrovol′cheskoi druzhiny*. Harbin (1933).

Vishniak, M. 'Iz istorii grazhdanskoi voiny', *Sovremennye zapiski* (Paris), No. 40 (1931), pp. 472–502; No. 41 (1931), pp. 312–346; No. 45 (1931), pp. 306–332.

Vserossiiskoe uchreditel′noe soveshchanie. Paris (1932).

Gody emigratsii, 1919–1969gg. Stanford (1970).

Vitol′dova-Liutik, S. *Na vostok: vospominaniia vremen kolchakovskoi epopei v Sibiri, 1919–1920gg*. Riga (1930).

Vladimirova, V. 'Profdvizhenie vo Vladivostoke', in *Revoliutsiia na Dal'nem Vostoke* (Vol. 1). Moscow–Petrograd (1923), pp. 330–340.

V ogne revoliutsii i grazhdanskoi voiny: vospominaniia. Omsk (1959).

V ogne revoliutsionnykh bity: vospominaniia. Tomsk (1962).

Voinov, N. and Lebedev, I.I. *Ognevnye gody: Krasnaia armiia v Sibiri.* Novosibirsk (1927).

Ward, J. *With the 'Die-Hards' in Siberia.* London (1920).

Welzl, J. *Thirty Years in the Golden North.* London (1932).

Wild, M. *Secret Service on the Russian Front.* London (1932).

Wilgress, D. *Memoirs.* Toronto (1967).

'From Siberia to Kuibyshev', *International Journal* (Toronto), Vol. 22, No. 3 (1967), pp. 364–375.

Williams, A.R. *Through the Russian Revolution.* New York (1921).

Wrangel [Vrangel'], P.N. *Always with Honour.* New York (1957).

Wright, P. 'The Work of the Russian Railway Service Corps'. *Railway Age* Vol. 69 (1923), pp. 153–156.

Xydias, J. *L'Intervention français en Russie, 1918–1919: souvenirs d'un témoin.* Paris (1927).

Yurlova, M. *Cossack Girl.* London (1934).

Zankevich, M.I. 'Obstoiatel'stva soprovozhdavshie vydachu adm. Kolchaka revoliutsionnomu pravitel'stvu v Irkutske', *Beloe delo* (Berlin), Vol. 2 (1927), pp. 148–157.

'Za vlast' Sovetov!' Sbornik vospominaniia uchastnikov grazhdanskoi voiny v Primor'e v 1917–1922gg. Vladivostok (1957).

'Za vlast' Sovetov': Vospominaniia uchastnikov partizanskogo dvizheniia v tylu Kolchaka. Novosibirsk (1947).

Zenzinov, V.M. *Iz zhizni revoliutsionera.* Paris (1919).

Road to Oblivion. London (1932).

Zubashev, E.L. 'Moia komandirovka v Sibiri', *Vol'naia Sibir'* (Prague), No. 1 (1927), pp. 58–65.

Zubov, A.I. '22 dekiabria', in *V ogne revoliutsii i grazhdanskoi voiny: vospominaniia uchastnikov.* Omsk (1959).

Zuev, A.V. *Orenburgskie kazaki v bor'be s bol'shevizmom, 1918–1922gg.: ocherki.* Harbin (1937).

Monographs and Studies

A.M. *Sibirskaia kooperatsiia v periode voennoi diktatury.* Omsk (1922).

Abrosenko, K.P. *Religiia na sluzhbe kontrrevoliutsii v Sibiri.* Irkutsk (1938).

Agalakov, V.T. *Sovety Sibiri, 1917–1918gg.* Novosibirsk (1978).

Agurskii, M. *Ideologiia natsional-bol'shevizma.* Paris (1980).

Aminev, Z.A. *Oktiabr'skaia sotsialisticheskaia revoliutsiia i grazhdanskaia voina v Bashkiri (1917–1919gg.).* Ufa (1966).

Anishev, A. *Ocherki istorii grazhdanskoi voiny, 1917–1920gg.* Leningrad (1925).

Anson, A.A. *O partizanskom dvizhenii v Sibiri.* Novosibirsk (1932).

Ashkinadze, D.I. *Zheleznodorozhniki Ishima v bor'be za vlast' Sovetov, 1917–1919gg.* Tiumen' (1961).

Babikova, E.N. *Dvoevlastie v Sibiri.* Tomsk (1980).

Baginski, H. *Wojsko Polskie na Wschadzie, 1914–1920.* Warsaw (1921).

Balakshin, P. *Final v Kitae: vozniknovenie, razvitie i ischeznovenie Beloi emigratsii na Dal'nem Vostoke* (2 Vols.). San Francisco (1958–1959).

Baranov, A. *Oktiabr' i nachalo grazhdanskoi voiny na Urale.* Sverdlovsk (1928).

Beable, W.H. *Commercial Russia.* London (1918).

Berezkin, A.V. *SShA – aktivnyi organizator i uchastnik voennoi interventsii protiv Sovetskoi Rossii (1918–1920gg.).* Moscow (1949).

Berezovskii, N.Iu. and Tarkhova. N.S. *Omskaia nastupitel'naia operatsia Krasnoi armii v 1919g.* Omsk (1989).

Bochagov, A.K. *Alash-Orda: kratkii istoricheskii ocherk o natsional'no-burzhuaznom ubezhenie v Kazakhstane perioda 1917–1918gg.* Kyzyl-Orda (1927).

Bol'tin, E.A. *Kontrnastuplenie Iuzhnoi gruppy Vostochnogo fronta i razgrom Kolchaka (1919g.).* Moscow (1949).

Bol'tin, E.A. et al. *Tobol'sko–Petropavlovskaia operatsiia (1919g.).* Moscow (1939).

Bolton, G. *Czech Tragedy.* London (1955).

Bradley, J.F.N. *La Légion tchécoslovaque en Russie, 1914–1920.* Paris (1965).
Allied Intervention in Russia, 1917–1920. London (1968).
Civil War in Russia. London (1975).
The Czechoslovak Legion in Russia, 1914–1920. New York (1991).

Brianskii, A.M. *Sel'skoe khoziaistvo Dal'nevostochnoi oblasti v gody revoliutsii (1917–1923gg.).* Khabarovsk (1925).

Brinkley, G.A. *The Volunteer Army and the Allied Intervention in South Russia, 1917–1921: A Study in the Politics and Diplomacy of the Civil War.* Notre Dame, IN (1960).

Brough, R. *White Russian Awards to British and Commonwealth Servicemen during the Allied Intervention in Russia, 1918–1920.* London (1991).

Brovkin, V.N. *Behind the Front Lines of the Civil War: Political Parties and Social Movements in Russia, 1918–1922.* Princeton (1994)

Bubnoff, J.V. *The Co-operative Movement in Russia (Its History, Significance and Character).* Manchester (1917).

Bubnov, V.I. *Ural v gody grazhdanskoi voiny (mai 1918–1920gg.).* Sverdlovsk (1962).

Burevoi, K.S. *Kolchakovshchina.* Moscow (1919).
Raspad, 1918–1922. Moscow (1922).

Bykov, P.M. *Krasnaia armiia v bor'be za Ural.* Sverdlovsk (1928).

Carely, M.J. *Revolution and Intervention: the French Government and the Russian Civil War, 1917–1919.* Montreal–Kingston (1983).

Chamberlin, W.H. *The Russian Revolution* (2 Vols.). New York (1935).

de Chessin, S. *L'Apocalypse russe: La révolution bolchévique, 1918–1921.* Paris (1921).

Channing, C.G.F. *Siberia's Untouched Treasure, Its Future Role in the World.* New York (1923).

Cherkashin, N. *Zvezda Kolchaka: razmyshleniia nad starami fotografami.* Moscow (1993).

Churchill, W.S. *The World Crisis: The Aftermath.* London (1929).

Chursin, G. *Izhevsk v ogne grazhdanskoi voiny: 1917–1918gg.* Izhevsk (1927).

Coleman, F. *Japan Moves North: The Story of the Struggle for Siberia.* London (1918).

Connaughton, R.M. *The Republic of the Ushakovka: Admiral Kolchak and the Allied Intervention in Siberia, 1918–1920.* London (1990).

Curry, R.W. *Woodrow Wilson and Far Eastern Policy, 1913–1921.* New York (1968).

Danchik, I. *Oktiabr' i grazhdanskaia voina v Viatskoi gubernii.* Viatka (1927).

Demidov, V.A. *Oktiabr' i natsional'nyi vopros v Sibiri, 1917–1923gg.* Novosibirsk (1983).

Dobson, C. and Millar, J. *The Day They Almost Bombed Moscow: The Allied War in Russia, 1918–1920.* London (1986).

van Doorn, J. *The Soldier and Social Change.* London (1975).

Drage, C. *General of Fortune: The Story of One-Arm Sutton.* London (1963).

Dragomiretskii, V.S. *Chekhoslovaki v Rossii, 1914–1920.* Paris–Prague (1928).

Dubina, I.D. *Partizanskoe dvizhenie v vostochnoi Sibiri, 1917–1920gg.* Irkutsk (1967).

Dubrovskii, K.V. *V tsarstve nagaiki i viselitsy: sibirskaia kontrrevoliutsiia, 1918–1919gg.* Moscow–Leningrad (1929).

Dumova, N.G. *Kadetskaia kontrrevoliutsiia i ee razgrom.* Moscow (1982).

Dupey, R.E. *Perish by the Sword: The Czechoslovakian Anabasis and our Supporting Campaigns in North Russia and Siberia, 1918–1920.* Harrisburg (1939).

Dvorianov, N.V and Dvorianov, V.N. *V tylu Kolchaka.* Moscow (1966).

Eayers, J. *In Defense of Canada: From the Great War to the Great Depression.* Toronto (1964).

Eikhe, G.Kh. *Takticheskie poucheniia grazhdanskoi voiny.* Moscow (1931).

Ufimskaia avantiura Kolchaka (mart–aprel' 1919g.): pochemu Kolchak ne udalos' prorvat'sia k Volge na soedinenie s Denikinym. Moscow (1960).

Oprokinutyi tyl. Moscow (1966).

Eingorn, I. *Oktiabr'skaia revoliutsiia i pozitsiia tserkovnikov Zapadnoi Sibiri.* Novosibirsk (1969).

Ermolin, A.P. *Revoliutsiia i kazachestvo*. Moscow (1982).

Espe *God v tsarstve Kolchaka (materialy po istorii rabochego dvizheniia v Sibiri s iiunia 1918 do iiunia 1919g.)*. Kazan' (1920).

Faulstich, E.M. *The Siberian Sojourn*. New York (1974).

Faust, W. *Russlands Goldener Boden: Der Sibirische Regionalismus in der Zweiten Halfte des 19. Jahrhunderts*. Cologne (1980).

Fedorov, A. *Permskaia katastrofa i kontrnastuplenie Vostochnogo fronta*. Moscow (1940).

Fedorovich, A. *General Kappel'*. Melbourne (1967).

Fic, V.M. *The Revolutionary War for Independence and the Russian Question: The Czechoslovak Army in Russia, 1914–1918*. New Delhi (1977).

The Bolsheviks and the Czechoslovak Legion: The Origins of their Armed Conflict (March–May 1918). New Delhi (1978).

The Collapse of American Policy in Russia and Siberia, 1918: Wilson's Decision not to Intervene (March–October, 1918). Boulder, CO (1995).

Filimonov, B.B. *Belopovstantsy (Khabarovskoi pokhod zimy 1921–1922gg.)*. Shanghai (1933).

Konets belogo primor'ia. Rockville, MD (1971).

Finer, S.E. *The Men on Horseback: The Role of the Military in Politics*. London (1976).

Fink, P. *Beily admiral: profil kolcakovshiny*. Prague (1922).

Fleming, P. *The Fate of Admiral Kolchak*. London (1963).

Footman, D. *Civil War in Russia*. London (1961).

Forsyth, J. *A History of the Peoples of Siberia: Russia's North Asian Colony, 1581–1990*. Cambridge (1992).

Fowler, W. *British-American Relations, 1917–1918: The Role of Sir William Wiseman*. Princeton (1969).

Gai, G.D. *Pervyi udar po Kolchaku (voenno-istoricheskii ocherk)*. Leningrad (1926).

Gan [Gutman], A. *Rossiia i bol'shevizmom: materialy po istorii revoliutsii i bor'by s bol'shevizm (chast' pervaia, 1914–1920)*. Shanghai (1921).

Gardener, L.C. *Safe for Democracy: The Anglo-American Response to Revolution, 1913–1923*. Oxford (1984).

Garmiza, V.V. *Krushenie eserovskikh pravitel'stv*. Moscow (1970).

General-lietenant Vladimir Oskarovich Kappel'. Vladivostok (1922).

Gilbert, M. *Winston S. Churchill* (Vol. 4). London (1975).

Girchenko, V. *Revoliutsionnaia deiatel'nost' innostrannykh internatsionalistov voennoplennykh v vostochnoi Sibirii*. Verkhneudinsk (1933).

Imperialisticheskaia interventsiia v Buriat-Mongolii (1918–1922gg.). Ulan Ude (1940).

Goldhurst, R. *The Midnight War: The American Intervention in Russia, 1918–1920*. New York (1978).

Golovin, N.N. *Rossiiskaia kontr-revoliutsiia v 1917–1918gg. (Chast' 4: Osvobozhnie Sibiri i obrazovanie 'belogo' voennogo fronta grazhdanskoi voiny).* Paris–Tallinn (1937).

Gordon, A. *The Russian Civil War: A Sketch for History.* London (1937).

Gorky, M. et al. (eds.) *History of the Civil War in Russia* (2 Vols.). Moscow (1937–1947).

Goriushkin, L.M. *Agrarnye otnosheniia v Sibiri perioda imperializma.* Novosibirsk (1976).

Goriushkin, L.M. et al. *Promyshlennost' i rabochie Sibiri v periode kapitalizma.* Novosibirsk (1980).

Graf, H. *The Russian Navy in War and Revolution: From 1914 up to 1918.* Munich (1923).

Grey, M and Bourdier, J. *Les Armées Blanches.* Paris (1968).

Grigortsevich, S.S. *Amerikanskaia i iaponskaia interventsiia na sovetskom Dal'nem Vostoke i ee razgrom.* Moscow (1957).

Griswald, A.W. *The Far Eastern Policy of the United States.* New York (1938).

Gudoshnikov, S.G. *Ocherki po istorii grazhdanskoi voiny v Sibiri.* Irkutsk (1959).

Gusev, K.V. *Partiia eserov: ot melko-burzhuaznogo revoliutsionerizma k kontr-revoliutsii.* Moscow (1975).

Gusev, K.V. and Eritsian, Kh.A. *Ot soglashatel'stva k kontrrevoliutsii: ocherki istorii politicheskogo bankrotstva i gibeli partii sotsialistov-revoliutsionerov.* Moscow (1968).

Gushin, N.Ia. et al. *Soiuz rabochego klassa i krest'ianstva Sibiri v periode postroeniia sotsializma (1917–1937).* Novosibirsk (1978).

Gutman [Gan], A. Ia. *Gibel' Nikolaevska na Amure: stranitsy iz istorii grazhdanskoi voiny na Dal'nem Vostoke.* Berlin (1924).

Haigh, R.H. *Unhappy Landings: British–Soviet Relations, the Russian Civil War and Intervention.* Sheffield (1980).

Hindus, M. *The Cossacks.* Westport, CT (1970).

Hohlfeld, A. *Versailles und die russische Frage 1918–1919.* Hamburg (1940).

Hovi, K. *Cordon Sanitaire or Barrière de l'Est: The Emergence of the New French Eastern European Alliance Policy, 1917–1919.* Turku (1975).

Howard, M. *Soldiers and Governments.* London (1957).

Huntington, S.P. *The Soldier and the State.* Cambridge, MA (1957).

Hurwicz, E. *Geschichte des russischen Bürgerkriegs.* Berlin (1927).

Iadrintsev, N.M. *Sibir' kak koloniia v geograficheskom, etnograficheskom i istoricheskom otnoshenii.* St Petersburg (1882).

Iakushkin, E. *Kolchakovshchina i interventsiia v Sibiri, 1918–1919gg.* Moscow–Leningrad (1928).

Iaroslavtsev, N.N. and Kabatov, A.I. *Cheremkhovskii kamennougol'nyi bassein, 1917–1920gg.* Cheremkhovo (1921).

Ignat′ev, V.P. *Nekotorye fakty i itogi chetyrykh let grazhdanskoi voiny*. Moscow–Petrograd (1922).

Ioffe, G.Z. *Krakh rossiiskoi monarkhicheskoi kontrrevoliutsii*. Moscow (1977).

Velikii Oktiabr′ i epilog tsarizma. Moscow (1977).

Kolchakovskaia avantiura i ee krakh. Moscow (1983).

Beloe delo: General Kornilov. Moscow (1989).

Istoricheskii ocherk 27-Omskoi strel′kovoi divizii. Moscow (1925).

Iurasova, M.K. *Omsk: ocherki po istorii goroda*. Novosibirsk (1965).

Ivanov, B.V. *Sibirskaia kooperatsiia v periode Oktiabr′skoi revoliutsii i grazhdanskoi voiny*. Tomsk (1976).

Ivanov, G. *Taseevskaia respublika, 1918–1920gg*. Krasnoiarsk (1969).

Ivanov, N.Ia. *Kontrrevoliutsiia v Rossii i ee razgrom*. Moscow (1977).

Jackson, R. *At War with the Bolsheviks: The Allied Intervention into Russia, 1917–1920*. London (1972).

James, R.R. *Victor Cazalet: A Portrait*. London (1976).

Janowitz, M. *The Professional Soldier*. Illinois (1960).

The Military and the Political Development of New Nations. Chicago (1964).

Johnson, H. *The Life and Times of Joseph Wiggins*. London (1907).

Kadeikin, V.A. *Rabochie Sibiri v bor′be za vlast′ Sovetov (no. 1917–avg. 1918gg.)*. Kemerovo (1966).

Sibir′ nepokorennaia. Kemerovo (1968).

Kakurin, N. *Strategicheskii ocherk grazhdanskoi voiny*. Moscow–Leningrad (1926).

Vosstanie chekhoslovakov i bor′ba s Kolchakom. Moscow–Leningrad (1928).

Kaputsgovich, I.S. *Prikam′e v ogne grazhdanskoi voiny*. Perm′ (1969).

Karmann, R. *Der Freiheitskampf der Kosaken (Die Weisse Armee in der Russischen Revolution, 1917–1920)*. Puchheim (1985).

Karmashev, V. *Poslednie dni sovetskoi vlasti v Zapadnoi Sibiri v 1918g*. Moscow (1921).

Katkov, G. *The Kornilov Affair*. London (1980).

Katkov, N.F. *Agitatsionno-propagandistskaia rabota bol′shevikov v baisakh i tylu belogvardeitsev v periode 1918–1920gg*. Leningrad (1977).

Katsenelenbaum, Z.S. *Russian Currency and Banking, 1914–1924*. London (1925).

Kavraiskii, V. *Klassovoe rassloenie sibirskoi derevni*. Novosibirsk (1927).

Kawakami, K.K. *Japan's Pacific Policy*. New York (1922).

Kayden, E.M. and Antsiferov, A.N. *The Co-operative Movement in Russia During the War*. New Haven (1929).

Kenez. P. *Civil War in South Russia, 1918: The First Year of the Volunteer Army*. Berkeley (1971).

Civil War in South Russia, 1918–1919: The Defeat of the Whites. Berkeley (1977).

Kennan, G. *Siberia and the Exile System*. London (1891).

Kennan, G.F. *Soviet–American Relations, 1917–1920: Vol. 1, Russia Leaves the War*. London (1956).

Soviet–American Relations, 1917–1920: Vol. 2, The Decision to Intervene. London (1958).

Kennedy, K.H. *Mining Tsar: The Life and Times of Leslie Urquhart*. London (1986).

Kennedey, Captain M.D. *The Estrangement of Britain and Japan, 1917–1935*. Manchester (1969).

Kerensky, A.F. *The Catastrophe*. New York (1927).

Russia and History's Turning Point: The Kerensky Memoirs. New York (1965).

Kettle, M. *Russia and the Allies, 1917–1920: Vol. 1, The Allies and the Russian Collpase, March 1917–March 1918* London (1981).

Russia and the Allies, 1917–1920: Vol. 2, The Road to Intervention, March–November 1918. London (1988).

Russia and the Allies, 1917–1920: Vol. 3, Churchill and the Archangel Fiasco, November 1918–July 1919. London (1992).

Khaptaev, P.T. *Buriatiia v gody grazhdanskoi voiny*. Ulan-Ude (1967).

Khesin, S.S. *Oktiabr'skaia revoliutsiia i flot*. Moscow (1971).

Kholodovskii, V.M. *Finlandiia i Sovetskaia Rossiia, 1918–1920gg*. Moscow (1975).

Khudiakov, A. *Grazhdanskaia voina na Altae*. Barnaul (1952).

Killen, L. *The Russian Bureau: A Case Study in Wilsonian Diplomacy*. Lexington (1984).

Kindall, S.G. *American Soldiers in Siberia*. New York (1945).

Kletkin, I.D. *Bor'ba trudiashchikhsia Omska i oblasti protiv interventov i belogvardeitsev*. Omsk (1959).

Klimenko, V.A. *Bor'ba s kontrrevoliutsiei v Moskve, 1917–1920gg*. Moscow (1978).

Kolmogorov, N.S. *Vosstanie Omskikh rabochykh protiv Kolchaka, 22 dekiabria 1919g*. Omsk (1957).

Kolosov, E.E. *Sibir' pri Kolchake*. Leningrad (1923).

Krasil'nikov, S.A. and Soskin, V.L. *Intelligentsiia Sibiri v periode bor'by za pobedu i utverzhdenie Sovetskoi vlasti*. Novosibirsk (1985).

Krushanov, A.I. *Grazhdanskaia voina v Sibiri i na Dal'nem Vostoke (1918–1920gg.) (Kniga 1: Vooruzhennaia bor'ba rabochikh i krest'ian protiv ob"edinennykh sil interventov i vnutrennei kontrrevoliutsii, aprel' 1918–mart 1919gg.)*. Vladivostok (1972).

Grazhdanskaia voina v Sibiri i na Dal'nem Vostoke (1918–1920gg.) (Kniga 2: aprel' 1918–mart 1920gg.). Vladivostok (1984).

Krusser, G.V. *Kolchakovshchina*. Novosibirsk (1927).

Sibirskie oblastniki (ot 1864g. do epokhi Kolchaka). Novosibirsk (1931).

Krypton, C. *The Northern Sea Route and its Place in Russian Economic History Before 1917*. New York (1953).

Kudela, J. *O rossiiskom zolotom zapase i chekhoslovatskikh legionakh*. Prague (1924).

Kudriatsev, F.A. *Irkutsk. Ocherki po istorii goroda*. Irkutsk (1958).

Kutiakov, I. *Razgrom Ural'skoi beloi kazach'ei armii*. Moscow (1931).

Kuz'min, G.V. *Grazhdanskaia voina i voennaia interventsiia v SSSR*. Moscow (1958).

Razgrom interventov i belogvardeitsev v 1917–1922gg. Moscow (1977).

Kuznetsov, A. *O Beloi armii i ee nagradakh, 1917–1922gg*. Moscow (1991).

Lange, R. *La Bianca Russia*. Florence (1935).

Levin, N.G. *Woodrow Wilson and World Politics*. London (1968).

Lincoln, W.B. *Red Victory: A History of the Russian Civil War*. New York (1989).

Lipkina, A.G. *1919 god v Sibiri: bor'ba s kolchakovshchinoi*. Moscow (1962).

Lisovskii, N.K. *Razgrom Dutovshchiny (1917–1919gg.)*. Moscow (1964).

Livshits, S.G. *Imperialisticheskaia interventsiia v Sibiri, 1918–1920gg*. Barnaul (1979).

Logvinov, B.K. *V bor'be s kolchakovshchinoi*. Krasnoiarsk (1980).

Logvinov, V.K. and Popov, I.M. *A.D. Kravchenko*. Krasnoiarsk (1983).

Longworth, P. *The Cossacks*. London (1969).

Luckett, R. *The White Generals*. Harrow (1971).

Maclaren, R. *Canadians in Russia*. Toronto (1976).

Maddox, R.J. *The Unknown War With Russia*. San Rafael (1977).

Makhov, V. *Potrebitel'naia kooperatsiia Sibiri*. Novonikolaevsk (1923).

Malykhina, K.F. *Krasnaia gvardiia Sibiri v bor'be za vlast' Sovetov (1917–1918gg.)*. Novosibirsk (1959).

Manning, C.A. *The Siberian Fiasco*. New York (1952).

Marguilles, M.S. *Gody interventsii* (3 Vols.). Berlin (1923).

Marks, S.G. *The Road to Power: The Trans-Siberian Railway and the Colonization of Asiatic Russia*. New York (1991).

Martianko, N.I. *Alash-Orda*. Kyzyl-Orda (1929).

Mawdsley, E. *The Russian Civil War*. Boston (1987).

Mayer, A.J. *The Politics and Diplomacy of Peacemaking: Containment and Counter-Revolution at Versailles*. London (1968).

Mayzel, M. *Generals and Revolutionaries (The Russian General Staff During the Revolution: A Study in the Transformation of a Military Élite)*. Osnabruck (1979).

McCuen, J.J. *The Art of Counter-Revolutionary War*. London (1966).

Medek, R. *The Czechoslovak Anabasis across Russia and Siberia*. London (1929).

Medek, R., Vanecek, O. and Holecek (eds.) *Za svobodu: Obrazkova kronika Csl. revoluchniho hnuti na Rusi, 1914–1920* (4 Vols.) Prague (1925–1929).

Medvedev, E.I. *Grazhdanskaia voina v srednem Povol'zhe*. Saratov (1974).

Melchin, A.I. *Amerikanskaia interventsiia na sovetskom Dal'nem Vostoke v 1918–1922gg.*. Moscow (1951).

Mel'gunov, S.P. *Tragediia admirala Kolchaka (iz istorii grazhdanskoi voiny na Volge, Urale i v Sibiri)* (3 Vols.). Belgrade (1930–1931).

Kak bol'sheviki zakhvatili vlast': Oktiabr'skii perevorot 1917g. Paris (1953).

Miliukov, P.N. *Russia Today and Tomorrow*. New York (1922).

Rossiia na perelome: bol'shevistskii period russkoi revoliutsii. Paris (1927).

Millard, T.F. *Democracy and the Eastern Question: The Problem of the Far East as Demonstrated by the Great War, and its Relation to the United States of America*. London (1919).

Miller, F. *The Wild Children of the Urals*. London (1966).

Mints, I.I. *Istoriia Velikogo Oktiabria*. Moscow (1968).

Mirzoev, V.G. *Partizanskoe dvizhenie v Zapadnoi Sibiri (1918–1919gg.)*. Kemerovo (1957).

von Mohrdenschildt, D. *Towards a United States of Russia: Plans and Projects for a Federal Reconstruction of Russia in the Nineteenth Century*. London (1982).

Moore, F.F. *Siberia Today*. New York (1919).

Moore, J.R. et al. *The History of the American Expedition Fighting the Bolsheviks*. Detroit (1920).

Morely, J.W. *Japan's Thrust into Siberia*. New York (1950).

Morse, H.B. and MacNair, H.F. *Far Eastern International Relations*. Cambridge, MA (1931).

Mosina, I.G. *Formirovanie burzhuazii v politicheskuiu silu v Sibiri*. Tomsk (1978).

Moulies, E. and Bergonnier, E. *La Guerre entre les Alliés et la Russie, 1918–20*. Paris (1937).

Mukhachev, B.I. *Stanovlenie sovetskoi vlasti i bor'ba s inostrannoi ekspansiei na Severo-Vostoke SSSR (1917–1920gg.)*. Novosibirsk (1975).

Mukhariamov, M.K. et al. *Grazhdanskaia voina v Povol'zhe, 1918–1920gg.* Kazan' (1976).

Murtazin, M.L. *Bashkiria i Bashkirskie voiska v grazhdanskoi voine*. Ufa (1927).

Nachbaur, A. *Le Dossier Koltchak: Sibérie, 1918–1920*. Peking (1920).

La Vérité sur Koltchak. Peking (1920).

Naida, S.F. *O nekotorykh voprosakh istorii grazhdanskoi voiny v SSSR*. Moscow (1958).

Naumov, M.B. *Omskie bol'sheviki v avangarde bor'by protiv belogvardeitsev i interventov*. Omsk (1960).

Nekrasov, G. *North of Gallipoli: The Black Sea Fleet at War, 1914–1917*. Boulder, CO (1992).

Nenarokov, A.P. *Vostochnyi front 1918*. Moscow (1969).

Nicholson, Colonel G.W.L. *Canadian Expeditionary Force, 1914–1919*. Ottawa (1962).

Nikolaev, R. *Dengi beloi gvardii*. St Petersburg (1993).

Nordman, N. *Peace Problems: Russia's Economics*. London (1919).

Norton, H.K. *The Far Eastern Republic of Siberia*. London (1923).

Novgorodov, A.I. *Oktiabr'skaia revoliutsiia i grazhdanskaia voina v Iakutii*. Novosibirsk (1969).

Nyman, L.-E. *Great Britain and Chinese, Russian and Japanese Interests in Sinkiang, 1918–1934*. London (1977).

Ogorodnikov, T.E. *Udar po Kolchaku vesnoi 1919g*. Moscow (1938).

Okladnikov, A.P. et al. *Rabochii klass Sibiri v periode stroitel'stva sotsializma (1917–1937gg.)*. Novosibirsk (1982).

Krest'ianstvo Sibiri v periode stroitel'stva sotsializma (1917–1937gg.). Novosibirsk (1983).

Osvobozhdenie Sibiri ot Kolchaka. Novosibirsk (1939).

Papin, M. *Krakh kolchakovshchiny i obrazovanie Dal'nevostochnoi respubliki*. Moscow (1957).

Parfenov, P.S. *Uroki proshlogo: grazhdanskaia voina v Sibiri (1918, 1919, 1920gg.)*. Harbin (1921).

Grazhdanskaia voina v Sibiri. Moscow (1924).

Bor'ba za Dal'nyi Vostok, 1920–1922gg. Leningrad (1928).

Parlett, Sir H. *A Brief Account of Diplomatic Events in Manchuria*. London (1925).

Pasvolsky, L. *Russia in the Far East*. New York (1922).

Pavlov Ia.S. *Narodnaia voina v tylu interventov i belogvardeitsev*. Minsk (1983).

Pavlova, I.V. *Krasnaia gvardiia v Sibiri*. Novosibirsk (1983).

Perlmutter, A. *The Military and Politics in Modern Times*. New Haven (1977).

Petrov, S.M. *Razgrom Dutovshchiny*. Cheliabinsk (1940).

Phillips, G.D.R. *Dawn in Siberia – the Mongols of Lake Baikal*. London (1942).

Pipes, R. *The Formation of the Soviet Union: Communism and Nationalism, 1917–1923*. Cambridge, MA (1954).

Russia under the Bolshevik Regime, 1919–1924. London (1994).

Plaksin, U.Iu. *Krakh tserkovnoi kontrrevoliutsii, 1917–1923gg*. Moscow (1968).

Platonov, A.V. *Chernomorskoi flot v revoliutsii 1917g. i admiral Kolchak*. Leningrad (1925).

Plotnikov, I.F. *Bol'shevistskoe podpol'e v Sibiri v periode imperialisticheskoi interventsii i grazhdanskoi voiny*. Sverdlovsk (1966).

Revoliutsionnaia bor'ba trudiashchikhsia Urala v tylu interventov i belogvardeetsev (1918–1919gg.). Sverdlovsk (1968).

Geroicheskoe podpol'e. Moscow (1968).

V belogvardeiskom tylu. Sverdlovsk (1978).

Revoliutsionnaia bor'ba trudiashchikhsia Urala v tylu interventov i belogvardeetsev (1918–1919gg.). Sverdlovsk (1980).

Vo glave revoliutsionnoi bor'by v tylu kolchakovskikh voisk; Sibirskoe (Uralo-Sibirskoe) biuro TsK RKP(b) v 1918–1920gg. Sverdlovsk (1989).

Podshivalov, I. *Grazhdanskaia bor'ba na Urale, 1917–1918gg.: opyt voennogo istoricheskogo issledovaniia.* Moscow (1925).

Pogrebetskii, A.I. *Denezhnoe obrashchenie i denezhnye znaki Dal'nego Vostoka za period voiny i revoliutsii.* Harbin (1924).

Poliakov, Y.A. *The Civil War in Russia: Its Causes and Significance.* Moscow (1981).

Popov, F. *Chekho-slovatskii miatezh i samarskaia uchredil'ka.* Moscow (1932).

Dutovshchina: bor'ba s kazach'ei kontrrevoliutsei v Orenburgskom krae. Moscow–Samara (1934).

Pozner, V. *Bloody Baron: The Story of Ungern-Sternberg.* New York (1938).

Price, M. Philips *Siberia.* London (1932).

Quested, R.K.I. *'Matey Imperialists': The Tsarist Russians in Manchuria, 1895–1917.* Hong Kong (1982).

Ragozin, T. *Partizany Stepnogo Badzhaia.* Moscow (1926).

Raimov, R.M. *Obrazovanie Bashkirskoi ASSR.* Moscow (1952).

Rakitnikov, N.I. *Sibirskaia reaktsiia i Kolchak.* Moscow (1920).

Read, C. *From Tsar to Soviets: The Russian People and Their Revolution, 1917–1921.* London (1996).

Rhodes, B.D. *The Anglo-American Winter War with Russia, 1918–19: A Diplomatic and Military Tragicomedy.* London (1988).

Riabikov, V.V. *Irkutsk – stolitsa revoliutsionnoi Sibiri.* Irkutsk (1959).

von Rimscha, H. *Der russische Bürgerkrieg und die russische Emigration, 1917–1921.* Jena (1924).

Rosenberg, W.G. *Liberals in the Russian Revolution: The Constitutional Democratic Party, 1917–1921.* Princeton (1974).

Roshchevskii, P.I. *Grazhdanskaia voina v Zaural'e.* Sverdlovsk (1966).

Ross, E.A. *The Russian Soviet Republic.* London (1923).

Rozinskii, V.D. *Ocherki po istorii grazhdanskoi voiny, 1917–1922.* Melbourne (1977).

Rupen, R.A. *Mongols of the Twentieth Century.* Bloomington (1964).

Rylkin, G. *Krovavyi ataman.* Moscow (1927).

Safronov, V.P. *Oktiabr' v Sibiri.* Krasnoiarsk (1962).

Sakharov, K.V. *Cheskie legiony v Sibiri.* n.p. (1930).

Sayers, M. and Kahn, A.E. *The Great Conspiracy Against Russia.* New York (1946).

Schild, G.M. *Between Ideology and Realpolitik: Woodrow Wilson and the Russian Revolution, 1917–1921.* London (1995).

Schmid, A.P. *Churchills privater Krieg: Intervention und Konterrevolution im russischen Bürgerkrieg 1918–1920.* Zürich (1974).

Serebrennikov, I.I. *Velikii otkhod: razseianie po Azii belykh russkikh armii, 1919–1923gg.* Harbin (1936).

Serge, V. *Year One of the Russian Revolution.* London (1974).

Sesiunina, M.G. *G.N. Potanin i N.M. Iadrintsev – ideologi sibirskogo oblastnichestva*. Tomsk (1974).

Sharapov, G.V. *Reshenie agrarnogo voprosa v Rossii posle pobedy Oktiabr'skoi revoliutsii*. Moscow (1960).

Shafir, Ia.M. *Belogvardeetsy i krest'ianstvo*. Moscow–Leningrad (1928).

Shelestov, D.K. *Bor'ba za vlast' Sovetov na Altae, 1917–1919gg*. Moscow (1959).

Shelton, B.K. *President Wilson and the Russian Revolution*. Buffalo (1957).

Shemelev, V. *Profsoiuzy Sibiri v bor'be za vlast' Sovetov (1917–1919gg.)*. Novosibirsk (1928).

Shisha, A. *Rol' inostrannogo kapitala v ekonomicheskoi zhizni Sibiri*. Novosibirsk (1922).

Shishkin, S.N. *Grazhdanskaia voina na Dal'nem Vostoke*. Moscow (1957).

Shmeral', B. *Chekhoslovaki i esery*. Moscow (1922).

Shornikov, M.M. *Bol'sheviki Sibiri v bor'be za pobedy Oktiabr'skoi revoliutsii*. Moscow (1963).

Shtein, B.E. *'Russkoi vopros' na parizhskoi mirnoi konferentsii (1919–1920gg.)*. Moscow (1949).

Shukletsov, V.T. *Grazhdanskaia voina na territorii Novosibirskoi oblasti*. Novosibirsk (1970).
Sibiriaki v bor'be za vlast' sovetov. Novosibirsk (1981).

Shol'ts, F.A. *Severnyi morskoi put' i ego znachenie vo vneshnem tovaroobmenie Sibiri*. Omsk (1921).

Silverlight, M. *The Victors' Dilemma: Allied Intervention in the Russian Civil War*. London (1970).

Skaba, A.D. *Parizhskaia mirnaia konferentsiia i inostrannaia interventsiia v strane Sovetov*. Kiev (1971).

'Slavianofil' *Cheskie argonavty v Sibiri*. Tokyo (1921).

Smirnov, M.I. *Admiral Kolchak: kratkii biograficheskii ocherk*. Paris (1930).

Smith, C.F. *Vladivostok under Red and White Rule*. Seattle (1975).

Smith, C.J. *Finland and the Russian Revolution*. Athens, GA (1958).

Snow, R.E. *The Bolsheviks in Siberia, 1917–1918*. London (1977).

Sokol, E.D. *The Revolt of 1916 in Central Asia*. Baltimore (1954).

Sokolsky, G.E. *The Story of the Chinese Eastern Railway*. Shanghai (1929).

Solodiankin, A.G. *Kommunisty Irkutska v bor'be s kolchakovshchiny*. Irkutsk (1960).

Solodovnikov, B. *Nash schet*. Berlin (1922).

Solov'ev, O.F. *Velikii Oktiabr' i ego protivniki: o roli soiuza Antanta i vnutrennoi kontrrevoliutsii v razviake interventsii i grazhdanskoi voiny*. Moscow (1968).

Spahn, M. and Sakharov, K.W. *Die Wahrheit uber die Tschechischen Legionen im Weissen Sibirien*. Berlin (1932).

Spirin, L.M. *Razgrom armii Kolchaka*. Moscow (1957).
Na Kolchaka! Moscow (1962).
Klassy i partii v grazhdanskom voine v Rossii, 1917–1920gg. Moscow (1968).

Krushenie pomeshchichikh i burzhuaznykh partii v Rossii. Moscow (1977).

Stearns, M. *British Relations with Russia from the Armistice to the Signing of the Trade Agreement*. Stanford (1931).

Stepanov, V.V. *Pravda ob atamane Stepanov*. Budapest (1921).

Stephen, J.J. *The Russian Fascists: Tragedy and Farce in Exile, 1925–1945*. London (1978).

Stewart, G. *The White Armies of Russia: A Chronicle of Counter-Revolution and Allied Intervention*. New York (1933).

Stishov, M.I. *Bol'shevistskoe podpol'e i partizanskoe dvizhenie v Sibiri v gody grazhdanskoi voiny (1918–1920gg.)*. Moscow (1962).

Strakhovsky, L.I. *Intervention at Archangel: The Story of Allied Intervention and Russian Counter-Revolution in North Russia, 1918–1920*. Princeton (1944).

Subbotovskii, I. *Soiuzniki i russkie reaktsionery: kratkii obzor (iskliuchitel'no po ofitsial'nym arkhivnym dokumentam Kolchakovskogo pravitel'stva)*. Leningrad (1926).

Summers, A. and Mangold, T. *The File on the Tsar*. London (1976).

Svetachev, M.I. *Imperialisticheskaia interventsiia v Sibiri i na Dal'nem Vostoke (1918–1920gg.)*. Leningrad (1983).

Sviatitskii, N. *Reaktsiia i narodovlastie*. Moscow (1920).

K istorii Vserossiiskogo uchreditel'nogo sobraniia: S''ezd' chlenov uchreditel'nogo sobraniia (sentiabr'–dekabr' 1918g.). Moscow (1921).

Svidine, N. *The Treasure of the White Army*. London (1976).

Swain, G. *The Origins of the Russian Civil War*. London (1995).

Swettenham, J. *Allied Intervention in Russia (1918–1919) and the Part Played by Canada*. London (1967).

Szajkowski, Z. *Kolchak, Jews and the American Intervention in Siberia, 1918–1920*. New York (1977).

Tang, P.S.H. *Russian and Soviet Policy in Manchuria and Outer Mongolia, 1911–1931*. Durham, NC (1959).

Taniaev, A. *Kolchakovshchina na Urale*. Sverdlovsk (1929).

Thomas, J. (ed.) *Illustrierte Geschichte des Bürgerkrieges in Russland 1917–1921*. Berlin (1929).

Thompson, J.M. *Russia, Bolshevism and the Versailles Peace*. Princeton (1966).

Thunig-Nitter, G. *Die Tschechoslowakische Legion in Russland: ihre Geschichte und Bedeutung bei der Entstehung der 1. Tschechoslowakischen Republik*. Wiesbaden (1970).

Tikhomorov, B. *Rabochii klass pod igom belogvardeishchiny, 1918–1920gg.* Moscow–Leningrad (1928).

Tinskii, G. *Ataman Semenov: ego zhizn' i deiatel'nost'*. n.p. (n.d.).

Tipeev, Sh. *Osnovnye etapy v istorii natsional'nogo dvizheniia v sovetskoi Bashkiri*. Ufa (1929).

Tiukovkin, V.G. *Sibirskaia derevnia nakakune Oktiabria*. Irkutsk (1966).

Tompkins, P. *American–Russian Relations in the Far East*. New York (1949).

Treadgold, D.W. *The Great Siberian Migration: Government and Peasant in Resettlement from the Emancipation to the First World War*. Princeton (1957).

Trotsky, L. *Stalin: an Appraisal of the Man and his Influence*. London (1947).

Tupper, H. *To the Great Ocean: Siberia and the Trans-Siberian Railway*. London (1965).

Turakaev, I. *Bashkirskie chasti v grazhdanskom voine*. Ufa (1929).

Ullman, R.H. *Anglo–Soviet Relations, 1917–1921: Vol. 1, Intervention and the War*. Princeton (1961).

Anglo–Soviet Relations, 1917–1921: Vol. 2, Britain and the Russian Civil War. Princeton (1965).

Anglo–Soviet Relations, 1917–1921: Vol. 3, The Anglo–Soviet Accord. Princeton (1972).

Unterberger, B.M. *America's Siberian Expedition, 1918–1920: A Study of National Policy*. Durham, NC (1956).

American Intervention in the Siberian Civil War. Boston (1969).

The United States, Revolutionary Russia and the Rise of Czechoslovakia. Chapel Hill (1989).

Ustrialov, N.V. *V bor'be za Rossiiu: sbornik statei*. Harbin (1920).

Pod znakom revoliutsii. Harbin (1927).

Vegman, V.D. *Vooruzhennye vosstaniia protiv Kolchaka v gorodakh i raionakh Sibiri*. Novosibirsk (1928).

Povstanicheskoe dvizhenie na Altae. Novosibirsk (1935).

Vendrykh, G.A. *Dekabr'sko–ianvarskie boi 1919–1920gg. v Irkutske*. Irkutsk (1957).

Vesely, I. *Chekhi i Slovaki v revoliutsionnoi Rossii*. Moscow (1965).

Vilenskii [Sibiriakov], V.D. *Bor'ba za sovetskuiu Sibir', 1917–1918gg*. Moscow (1926).

Tsarstvo Kolchaka. Moscow (1931)

Vinacke, H.M. *A History of the Far East in Modern Times*. London (1928)

Vladimirova, V.F *Kontrrevoliutsiia v 1917g*. Moscow (1924).

God sluzhby 'sotsialistov' kapitalistami: ocherki po istorii kontrrevoliutsii v 1918g. Moscow–Leningrad (1927).

Vorob'ev, V.F. *Oborona Orenburga. Aprel'–mai 1919g*. Moscow (1938).

Washington, B.T. *The Siberian Intervention*. New York (1950).

Weeks, C.J. *An American Naval Diplomat in Revolutionary Russia: The Life and Times of Vice Admiral Newton A. McCully*. Annapolis (1993).

Welter, G. *La guerre civile en Russie*. Paris (1936)

White, J.A. *The Siberian Intervention*. New York (1950).

White, J.D. *The Russian Revolution, 1917–1921: A Short History*. London (1994).

Wildman, A.K. *The End of the Russian Imperial Army: Vol. 1, The Old Army and the Soldiers' Revolt, March–April 1917*. Princeton (1980).

The End of the Russian Imperial Army: Vol. 2: The Road to Soviet Power and Peace. Princeton (1987).

Zaitsov, A.A. *1918 god: ocherki po istorii russkoi grazhdanskoi voiny*. Paris (1934).

Zhukov, V.A. *Chernomorskoi flot v revoliutsii, 1917–1918gg*. Moscow (1932).

Zhurov, Iu.V. *Eniseiskoe krest'ianstvo v gody grazhdanskoi voiny*. Krasnoiarsk (1972).

Grazhdanskaia voina v Sibirskoi derevne. Krasnoiarsk (1986).

Unpublished Doctoral Theses and Dissertations

Beattie, S. 'Canadian Intervention in Russia, 1918–1919'. McGill University (1957).

Berk, S.M. 'The *Coup d'État* of Admiral Kolchak and the Counter-Revolution in Siberia and East Russia, 1917–1918'. Columbia University (1971).

Bock, B. 'The Origins of the Inter-Allied Intervention in Eastern Asia, 1918–1920'. Stanford University (1940).

Carley, M.J. 'The French Intervention in the Russian Civil War, 1917–1921'. Queen's University (1981).

Channon, J. '"Peasant Revolution" and "Land Reform": Land Redistribution in European Russia, October 1917–1920'. University of Birmingham (1983).

Dacy, D.A. 'The White Russian Movement: A Study of the Failure of the Counter-Revolution, 1917–1921'. University of Texas at Austin (1972).

Drujina, G. 'The History of the North-West Army of General Iudenich'. Stanford University (1950).

Kolz, A.W.F. 'British Foreign Policy and the Kolchak Government (November 1918–February 1920)'. Boston University (1965).

Ingram, A.E. 'The Root Mission to Russia in 1917'. Louisiana State University (1970).

Long, J.W. 'Civil War and Intervention in North Russia, 1918–1920'. Columbia University (1972).

Perrins, M. 'The Russian Military 1904–1917 and its Role in Russian Political Affairs'. London University (1980).

St. John, J.D. 'John F. Stevens: American Assistance to Russian and Siberian Railroads, 1917–1922'. University of Oklahoma (1969).

Stetten, N. 'The National Question and the Russian Civil War, 1917–1921'. University of Chicago (1977).

Thompson, J.M. 'The Russian Problem at the Paris Peace Conference, 1919'. Columbia University (1960).

Watrous, S.D. 'Russia's "Land of the Future": Regionalism and the Awakening of Siberia, 1819–1894'. University of Washington (1970).

Woodward, D.R. 'The West and the Containment of Russia, 1914–1923'. University of Georgia (1964).

Articles

Abov, A. 'Neobkhodimo vnesti iasnost', *Sibirskie ogni* (Novosibirsk), Vol. 10 (1930), pp. 91–94.

Abrams, A. 'United States Intervention Abroad: The First Quarter Century', *American Historical Review*, Vol. 79 (1974), No. 1, pp. 72–102.

Adams, C.E. 'Der Wiederaufstieg der russischen Kriegsmarine in den Jahren 1910–1915', *Marine Rundschau*, Vol. 61 (1964), pp. 12–21.

Agalkov, V.Y. 'Tsentrosibir'', *Voprosy istorii Sibiri* (Tomsk), Vol. 4 (1969), pp. 133–147.

Aksiutin, Iu.V. 'Kolchak i rabochii vopros', in Korablev, Iu.V. and Shishkin, V.I. (eds.) *Iz istorii interventsii i grazhdanskoi voiny v Sibiri i na Dal'nem Vostoke, 1917–1922gg.* Novosibirsk (1985), pp. 184–188.

Akulov, M.P. 'Profsoiuzy Zapadnoi Sibiri v bor'be protiv kontrrevoliutsionnogo esero-menshevistskogo pravitel'stva i kolchakovshchiny za vosstanovlenie Sovetskoi vlasti (mai 1918–noiabr' 1919gg.)', in *Boevye gody*. Novosibirsk (1959), pp. 72–91.

Alekseev, V. 'Bor'ba s Chekho-slovatskim miatezhom v Povol'zhe', *Proletarskaia revoliutsiia* (Moscow), No. 4 (1929), pp. 45–89.

Alekseev, V.K. 'K voprosu o politicheskoi pozitsii sibirskoi maslodel'cheskoi kooperatsii v periode Oktiabr'skoi revoliutsii i grazhdanskoi voiny', in *Partiinye organizatsii Sibiri v sotsialisticheskom stroitel'stve*. Novosibirsk (1973), pp. 24–43.

Allison, A.P. 'Siberian Regionalism in the Revolution and Civil War, 1917–20', *Siberica* (Portland), Vol. 1 (1990), No. 1, pp. 78–97.

Ansonov, A. 'Oktiabr' v Vostochnoi Sibiri', *Sibirskie ogni* (Novosibirsk), No. 4 (1924), pp. 107–121.

Arkhipokhov 'Evakuatsiia Krasnoiarskogo soveta', *Proletarskaia revoliutsiia* (Moscow), No. 2 (1922), pp. 312–315.

Aver'ev, V. 'Agrarnaia politika kolchakovshchiny', *Na agrarnom fronte* (Moscow), No. 6 (1929), Part.1, pp. 24–45.

Babikova, E.N. 'Bor'ba s kontrrevoliutsionnym zemstvom v Tomskoi gubernii (1917–aprel' 1918gg.)', *Voprosy istorii Sibiri* (Tomsk), Vol. 4 (1969), pp. 189–202.

Baikalov, A.V. 'The Conquest and Colonization of Siberia', *Slavonic and East European Review* (London), Vol. 10 (1932), pp. 557–571.

'Siberia since 1894', *Slavonic and East European Review* (London), Vol. 11 (1933), pp. 328–340.

Balaleva, N.M. 'Kontrrevoliutsionnaia deiatel'nost zarubezhnykh khristianskikh missii na Dal'nem Vostoke (1917–1922gg.)', *Dal'nyi Vostok* (Khabarovsk), No. 10 (1970), pp. 139–144.

Barr, W. 'Aleksandr Vasil'evich Kolchak: Arctic Scientist and Explorer', *Polar Record* (Cambridge), Vol. 20 (1981), No. 129, pp. 507–524.

Barrows, D.P. 'Japan as Our Ally in Siberia', *Asia*, Vol. 19 (1919), pp. 927–931.

Belousov, G.M. 'Eserovskoe vooruzhennoe podpol'e v Sibiri', in *Sibirskii istoricheskii sbornik*. Irkutsk (1974), Vol. 2, pp. 129–151.

Berezovskii, F. 'A.E. Novoselov', *Sibirskie ogni* (Novonikolaevsk), No. 2 (1922), pp. 157–158.

de Berg-Poggenpohl, N. 'À propos de l'amiral Koltchak', *Revue de Paris* (Paris), No. 28, Part 3 (15.v.1921), pp. 441–448.

Berk, S.M. 'The Democratic Counter-Revolution: Komuch and the Civil War on the Volga', *Canadian Slavic Studies*, Vol. 7 (1973), No. 7, pp. 443–459.

'The Class Tragedy of Izhevsk: Working Class Opposition to Bolshevism in 1918', *Russian History*, Vol. 2 (1975), No. 2, pp. 176–190.

Bernshtam, M.S. 'Storony v grazhdanskom voine 1917–1922gg.: problematika, metodologiia, statistika', *Vestnik Russkogo khristianskogo dvizheniia* (Paris), No. 128 (1979), pp. 252–357.

Bolotovskaia, K.I. 'Rabota politorganov Piatoi armii sredi soldat kolchakovskoi armii v periode bor'by za osvobozhdenie Sibiri (1919–1920gg.)', in *Voprosy istorii sovetskoi Sibiri*. Novosibirsk (1970), pp. 81–90.

Bonch-Osmolovskii, A. 'Vneshnaia torgovlia Dal'nego Vostoka za vremia voiny i revoliutsii', *Novyi vostok* (Moscow), Vol. 5 (1924), pp. 156–164.

Bradley, J.F.N. 'The Czechoslovak Revolt Against the Bolsheviks', *Soviet Studies* (Glasgow), Vol. 15 (1963–1964), pp. 124–151.

'T.G. Masaryk et la révolution russe', *Études slavs et est-européennes* (Montreal), Vol. 9 (1964), pp. 3–20, 78–99.

'The Allies and Russia in the Light of French Archives', *Soviet Studies* (Glasgow), Vol. 16 (1964–1965).

'The Allies and the Czech Revolt Against the Bolsheviks in 1918', *Slavonic and East European Review* (London), Vol. 43 (1965), pp. 275–292.

'L'intervention française en Sibérie (1918–1919)', *Revue historique* (Paris), Vol. 234 (1965), pp. 375–388.

Brovkin, V. 'Identity, Allegiance and Participation in the Russian Civil War', *European History Quarterly*, Vol. 22 (1992), No. 4, pp. 541–567.

Bushnell, J. 'The Tsarist Officer Corps, 1881–1914: Customs, Duty, Efficiency', *American Historical Review*, Vol. 86 (1981), No. 4, pp. 753–781.

Butenii, N.A. 'Krushenie esero-men'shevistskogo kontrrevoliutsii na Dal'nem Vostoke v 1918g.', in *Voprosy istorii obshchestvenno-politicheskoi zhizni Sibiri perioda Oktiabria i grazhdanskoi voiny*. Tomsk (1982), pp. 103–120.

Carley, M.J. 'The Origins of the French Intervention in the Russian Civil War, January–May 1918: A Reappraisal', *Journal of Modern History*, Vol. 48 (1976), No. 3, pp. 413–439.

'Allied Intervention and the Russian Civil War', *International History Review*, Vol. 11 (1989), No. 4, pp. 689–700.

'From Revolution to Dissolution: The Quai d'Orsay, the Banque Russo-Asiatique and the Chinese Eastern Railway, 1917–1926', *International History Review*, Vol. 12 (1990), No. 4, pp. 221–261.

Castagne, J. 'Le Bolchévisme et l'Islam', *Revue du monde mussulman* (Paris), Vol. 51 (1922), pp. 169–191.

Channon, J. 'White Agrarian Policy: A Research Commentary and Documentary Material', *Sbornik of the Study Group on the Russian Revolution*, Vol. 12 (1986), pp. 108–117.

'Regional Variation in the Commune: The Case of Siberia', in Bartlett, R. (ed.) *Land Commune and Peasant Community in Russia*. London (1990), pp. 66–85.

'Siberia in Revolution and Civil War', in Wood, A. (ed.) *The History of Siberia: From Russian Conquest to Revolution*. London (1991), pp. 158–180.

Chuev, G. 'Chernodol′skoe vosstanie', *Sibirskie ogni* (Novosibirsk), Vols. 5–6 (1926), pp. 157–166.

'Civil War in Russia: A Roundtable Discussion', *Russian Studies in History*, Vol. 32 (1993–1994), No. 4, pp. 73–95.

Collins, D.N. 'Kabinet, Forest and Revolution in the Siberian Altai to May 1918', *Revolutionary Russia*, Vol. 4 (1991), No. 1, pp. 1–27.

Davis, D.E. and Trani, E.P. 'The American YMCA and the Russian Revolution', *Slavonic and East European Review* (London), Vol. 33 (1974), pp. 469–491.

Demidov, V.A. 'Sibirskie oblastniki i burzhuaznye natsionalisty', in *Voprosy istorii sotsial′no-ekonomicheskoi i kul′turnoi zhizni Sibiri*. Novosibirsk (1976).

van Doorn, J. 'Ideology and the Military Mind', in Janowitz, M. (ed.) *On Military Ideology*. Rotterdam (1971).

'The Military and the Crisis of Legitimacy', in Harris-Jenkins, G. and van Doorn, J. (eds.) *The Military and the Problem of Legitimacy*. London (1976).

Efimkin, A. 'Zoloto respubliki', in Romanovskii, S.K. (ed.) *Diplomaticheskii ezhegodnik*. Moscow (1995), pp. 227–240.

Eingorn, I.D. 'Kolchakovshchina i tserkov', in *K 50-letiiu osvobozhdeniia Sibiri ot kolchakovshchiny*. Tomsk (1970), pp. 46–50.

El′tsin, V. 'Krest′ianskoe dvizhenie v Sibiri v periode Kolchaka', *Proletarskaia revoliutsiia* (Moscow), No. 49 (1926), pp. 5–48; No. 50 (1926), pp. 51–82.

Epstein, F.T. 'Studien zur Geschichte der "Russischen Frage" auf der Pariser Friedenskonferenz von 1919', *Jahrbücher für Geschichte Osteuropas*, Vol. 7 (1959), pp. 431–478.

Estep, R. 'John F. Stevens and the Far Eastern Railways, 1917–1923', *Explorer's Journal*, Vol. 48 (1970), pp. 13–24.

Ewing, T.E. 'Russia, China and the Origins of the Mongolian People's Republic, 1918–1921: A Reappraisal', *Slavonic and East European Review* (London), Vol. 58 (1980), No. 3, pp. 399–421.

Faulstitch, E.M. 'The Canadian Expeditionary Force in Siberia, 1918–1919', *The Postal Historical Journal* (Yonkers, NY), (1968).

Fedorovich, A.A. 'Admiral Kolchak', *Edinenie* (Sydney), No. 21 (27.v.1960).

Fedotov, B.F. 'O maloizvestnykh istochnikakh perioda grazhdanskoi voiny i inostrannoi voennoi interventsii v SSSR', *Voprosy istorii* (Moscow), No. 8 (1968), pp. 18–30.

Fel′dman, B.B. 'Sostoianie ural′skoi promyshlennosti v 1920 gody', in Lisovskii, N.K. and Grigor′ev, B.V (eds.) *Grazhdanskaia voina na Urale*. Cheliabinsk (1983).

Fel′shtinskii, Ia. 'Lenin i rasstrel Kolchaka', *Russkaia mysl′* (Paris), No. 3,499 (12.i.1984), p. 11.

Finkel′shtein, N. 'Obzor deiatel′nosti kammenougol′nykh kopei Urala za god (iiul′ 1919–iiul′ 1920gg.)', *Gornoe delo* (Moscow), Vol. 1 (1920), No. 4, pp. 112–116.

Flerov, V.S. 'Kontrrevoliutsionnaia rol′ tserkovnikov i sektantov na Dal′nem Vostoke v 1918–1923gg.', *Uchenye zapiski Tomskogo gosudarstvennogo universiteta* (Tomsk), Vol. 37 (1959), pp. 71–133.

'Iz istorii denezhnogo obrashcheniia v Sibiri v periode inostrannoi interventsii i grazhdanskoi voiny', *Trudy Tomskogo oblastnogo kraevoi muzeia* (Tomsk), Vol. 6 (1963), No. 2, pp. 11–20.

Footman, D. 'The Red Army and the Civil War in the East', *History Today*, Vol. 6 (1956), No. 2, pp. 96–102.

'Siberian Partisans in the Civil War', *St Antony's Papers* (Oxford), Vol. 1 (1956), pp. 25–54.

'Civil War in the Baltic Area: The Northwestern Army', *St Antony's Papers on Soviet Affairs* [Unbound] (1959).

Fry, M.G. Britain, the Allies and the Problem of Russia', *Canadian Journal of History*, Vol. 2 (1967), No. 2, pp. 146–171.

Gakh, A.M. et al. 'Kak byl spasen zolotoi zapas Rossii', *Istoriia SSSR* (Moscow), No. 1 (1960), pp. 137–143.

Garmiza, V.V. 'Bankrotstvo politiki "Tret′ego puti" v revoliutsii (Ufimskoe gosudarstvennoe soveshchanie, 1918g.)', *Istoriia SSSR* (Moscow), No. 6 (1965), pp. 3–25.

'Direktoriia i Kolchak', *Voprosy istorii* (Moscow), No. 10 (1976), pp. 16–32.

'Bankrotstvo eserovskoi sistemy upravleniia i samoupravleniia (Komuch, Sibir′ – 1918g.)', in Mints, I.I. (ed.) *Neproletarskie partii Rossii v 1917g. i v grazhdanskoi voiny*. Moscow (1980), pp. 216–222.

Garthoff, R.L. 'The Military as a Social Force', in Black, C.E. (ed.) *The Transformation of Russian Society*. Cambridge, MA (1960).

Germanov, L. 'Denezhnoe obrashchenie i banki v tsarstve Kolchaka', *Ekonomicheskaia zhizn′* (Moscow), No. 148 (1919), p. 2.

Geronimus, A.I. 'Pomoshch′ SShA Kolchaku', *Istoricheskie zapiski* (Moscow), Vol. 29 (1949), pp. 33–47.

Gibson, J.R. 'The Significance of Siberia to Tsarist Russia', *Canadian Slavonic Papers*, No. 14 (1972), pp. 442–453.

Gilbreath, O. 'The Sick Man of Siberia: The Story of the Trans-Siberian Railway', *Asia*, Vol. 19, No. 6 (1919), pp. 546–552.

Golisheva, L.A. 'Natsional′naia politika pravitel′stva Kolchaka i ee krakh', in *K 50-letiiu osvobozhdeniia Sibiri ot kolchakovshchiny*. Tomsk (1970), pp. 63–67.

Golubtsov, V.S. 'Materialy uralskikh organov VSNKh ob ushcher′be, nanesennom uralskoi promyshlennosti v rezultatakh grazhdanskoi voiny i interventsii', in *Iz istorii zavodov i fabrik Urala: sbornik statei* (Vol. 1). Sverdlovsk (1960).

Goriushkin, L.M. 'Pretvorenie v zhizn′ dekreta o zemle v Zapadnoi Sibiri v kontse 1917–pervoi polovine 1918g.', in *Krest′ianstvo i sel′skoe khoziastvo Sibiri 1917–1961gg.* Novosibirsk (1965).

Graves, S. 'Japanese Aggression in Siberia', *Current History* Vol. 14 (May 1921), pp. 239–245.

Griener, J.A 'A Minnesota Railroadman in the Far East, 1917–18', *Minnesota History*, Vol. 38 (Sept. 1963), pp. 310–325.

Grubbs, C.B. 'American Railroaders in Siberia, 1917–1920', *Railroad History Review*, Vol. 150 (1984), pp. 107–114.

Guins, G.C. 'The Siberian Intervention', *Russian Review*, Vol. 28, No. 4 (1969), pp. 428–440.

'*The Siberian Intervention* by J.A. White [Review]', *Russian Review*, Vol. 10, No. 2 (1951), pp. 161–164.

Gurevich, V.Ia. '*Za tri goda*, L.A. Krol′ [Review]', *Letopis′ revoliutsii* (Berlin–Petrograd–Moscow), Vol. 1 (1923), pp. 308–311.

'Real′naia politika v revoliutsii (kadetskaia taktika)', *Volia Rossii* (Prague), No. 2 (1923), pp. 13–21.

'Real′naia politika v revoliutsii (rol′ i znachenie ufimskoi Direktorii, prichiny neudachy)', *Volia Rossii* (Prague), No. 14 (1923), pp. 17–31.

Gutman-Gan, A. 'Dva vosstaniia', *Beloe delo* (Berlin), Vol. 3 (1927), pp. 173–179.

Hölzle, E. 'Versailles und der russische Osten', *Ostdeutsche Wissenschaft* (Munich), Vol. 5 (1958), pp. 486–503.

Hopkins, K. 'Civil-Military Relations in Developing Countries', *British Journal of Sociology* (London), Vol. 42 (1966), pp. 165–182.

Horall, S.W. 'The Force's Siberian Patrol', *Royal Canadian Mounted Police Quarterly* Vol. 36 (1971), No. 5.

Iakimova, T.V. 'Politicheskoe nastroenie Zapadno-Sibirskogo krest′ianstva vesnoi 1918g.', in Korablev, Iu.V. and Shishkin, V.I. (eds.) *Iz istorii interventsii i grazhdanskoi voiny v Sibiri i na Dal′nem Vostoke, 1917–1922gg.* Novosibirsk (1985), pp. 204–210.

Ioffe, G.Z. 'Pomeshchich′e-burzhuaznaia organizatsiia "Sovet gosudarstvennogo ob″edineniia Rossii", 1918–1920gg.', in Mints, I.I. (ed.) *Neproletarskie partii Rossii v 1917g. i v grazhdanskoi voiny*. Moscow (1980), pp. 223–233.

'Ot kontrrevoliutsii "demokraticheskoi" k burzhuazno-pomeshch-ich'ei diktature (Omskii perevorot)', *Istoriia SSSR* (Moscow), No. 1 (1982), pp. 108–119.

'K voprosu o mezhpartiinykh ob"edineniakh rossiiskoi kontr-revoliutsii', in *Velikii Oktiabr' i neproletarskie partii*. Moscow (1982), pp. 11–21.

'Iz istorii kadetsko-monarkhicheskoi kontrrevoliutsii v Rossii', in Korablev, Iu.V. and Shishkin, V.I. (eds.) *Iz istorii interventsii i grazhdanskoi voiny v Sibiri i na Dal'nem Vostoke, 1917–1922gg.* Novosibirsk (1985), pp. 161–169.

Iorodanskii, I. 'Admiral Kolchak', *Put'* (Helsingfors), 11.ii.1921.

Iuldashbaev, B.Kh. 'Natsional'nyi vopros v Bashkiri na pervom etape sovetskogo natsional'no-gosudarstvennogo stroitel'stva', *Istoricheskie zapiski* (Moscow), Vol. 115 (1989), pp. 46–7.

Ivanov, B.V. 'K legende ob apolitichnosti sibirskoi kooperatsii v periode kolchakovshchiny', in *K 50-letiiu osvobozhdeniia Sibiri ot kolchakovshchiny*. Tomsk (1970), pp. 50–54.

'Antinarodnaia rol' rukovodstva sibirskoi kooperatsii v periode kolchakovshchiny', *Voprosy istorii Sibiri* (Tomsk), Vol. 7 (1973).

'Sibirskaia kooperatsiia posle pobedy sotsialisticheskoi revoliutsii (okt. 1917–mai 1918)', *Voprosy istorii Sibiri* (Tomsk), Vol. 8 (1974), pp. 74–85.

Janowitz, M. 'Armed Forces and Society', in van Doorn, J. *Armed Forces and Society*. The Hague (1968).

Jansen, M. 'L.H. Grondijs and Russia: The Acts and Opinions of a Dutch White Guard', *Revolutionary Russia*, Vol. 7 (1994), No. 1, pp. 20–33.

Johnston, B.O. 'Sidelights on the Russian Railway Situation', *The Railway Age* Vol. 66, No. 17 (25.iv.1919), pp. 1063–1064.

Jones, D.R. 'The Officers and the October Revolution', *Soviet Studies* (Glasgow), Vol. 28 (1970), pp. 207–223.

Kabanov, V.V. 'O "neitral'nosti" kooperatsii v 1917–1920gg.', in *Bankrotstvo melkoburzhuaznykh partii Rossii, 1917–1922gg.* (Vol. 2). Moscow (1977), pp. 98–106.

Kadeikin, B.A. 'Zabastovochnoe dvizhenie sibirskykh rabochikh vo vtoroi polovine 1918g.', in Flerov, V.S. (ed.) *Bor'ba za vlast' sovetov v Sibiri i na Dal'nem Vostoke*. Tomsk (1968), pp. 114–144.

'Antinarodnaia rol' Vremennogo sibirskogo pravitel'stva', *Voprosy istorii Sibiri* (Tomsk), Vol. 4 (1969).

Kakurin, N. 'Rol' derzhavov Antanty v voennoi ekonomike belykh pravitel'stv vo vremia grazhdanskoi voiny v Rossii', in *Kto dolzhnik: sbornik*. Moscow (1926).

Kal'nin, I.A. 'Trud pri belykh (po arkhivam Ministerstva truda byvshego Kolchakovskogo pravitel'stva)', *Sibirskie ogni* (Novosibirsk), No. 3 (1929), pp. 134–142.

Kalvoda, J. 'Czech and Slovak Prisoners of War in Russia during the War and Revolution', *War and Society in East Central Europe* Vol. 5 (1982), pp. 215–218.

'The Origins of the Czechoslovak Army, 1914–1918', *War and Society in East Central Europe*, Vol. 9 (1985), pp. 419–435.

Kamskii 'Belye v Kitae', *Sibirskie ogni* (Novonikolaevsk), Nos. 1–2 (1923), pp. 78–112.

Kas′ian, A.K. 'Antinarodnaia rol′ rukovoditelei kooperatsii Zapadnoi Sibiri v pervom periode Sovetskoi vlasti i grazhdanskoi voiny (dek. 1917–no. 1919)', *Uchenye zapiski Omskogo gos. ped. instituta (Seriia ist. nauk)* (Omsk), Vol. 15 (1962), pp. 51–73.

Katkov, G. 'The Russian Navy and the Revolution, 1905–1921', in Saunders, M.G. (ed.) *The Soviet Navy*. London (1958), pp. 84–92.

Kazakov, A.Ia. 'O vremeni sozdaniia i meste deiatel′nosti Sibirskogo biuro TsK RKP(b)', *Voprosy istorii KPSS* (Moscow), No. 1 (1960).

'Rukovodstvo TsK RKP(b) deiatel′nostiu sibirskikh bol′shevikov v tylu belogvardeitsev (1918–1920gg.)', *Voprosy istorii KPSS* (Moscow), No. 6 (1966), pp. 39–49.

[Kedrov, M.A.] 'S.P. Mel′gunov, *Tragediia admirala Kolchaka* [Review]', *Morskii zhurnal* (Paris), Vol. 34 (1930), pp. 7–10.

Kenez, P. 'The Russian Officer Corps before the Revolution: the Military Mind', *Russian Review*, Vol. 31 (1972), No. 3, pp. 226–237.

'Changes in the Social Composition of the Officer Corps During World War 1', *Russian Review*, Vol. 31 (1972), No. 4, pp. 369–376.

'Autocracy and the Russian Army', *Russian Review*, Vol. 33 (1973), No. 2, pp. 201–206.

'A Profile of the Pre-revolutionary Officer Corps', *California Slavic Studies*, Vol. 7 (1973), pp. 128–145.

'The Ideology of the White Movement', *Soviet Studies* (Glasgow), Vol. 32 (1980), pp. 58–83.

Kennan, G.F. 'The Czechoslovak Legion', *Russian Review*, Vol. 16 (1957), No. 4, pp. 3–16; Vol. 17 (1958), No. 1, pp. 1–28.

'Russia and the Versailles Conference', *American Scholar*, Vol. 30 (1960–1961), pp. 13–42.

Killen, L. 'The Search for a Democratic Russia: Bakhmetev and the United States', *Diplomatic History*, Vol. 2 (1978), pp. 237–356.

Klarov, Iu. 'Fakty svidetel′stvuiut: o nekotorykh mifakh vokrug imeni "Verkhovnogo pravitelia" Kolchaka', in Ivanov, V.A. (ed.) *Perepiska na istoricheskie temy. Dialog vedet chitatel′*. Moscow (1989), pp. 267–280.

Klevanskii, A.Kh. 'Bor′ba sovetskogo pravitel′stva za normalizatsiiu sovetsko-chekhoslovatskikh otnoshenii (konets 1918–nachalo 1920gg.)', *Voprosy istorii* (Moscow), No. 2 (1969).

Knox, A. '"Fragments de mon Journal Sibérien", by General Janin', *Slavonic Review* (London), Vol. 3 (1925), No. 9, p. 724.

Koenker, D. 'Urbanization and Deurbanization in the Russian Revolution and Civil War', *Journal of Modern History*, Vol. 57 (1983), No. 3, pp. 424–450.

Kolchak, A.V. 'Led Karskogo i Sibirskogo morei', *Imperialisticheskaia Akademiia Nauk: Zapiski* (St Petersburg), Series 8, Vol. 26, No. 1 (1909).

'The Arctic Pack and Polynia', in Joerg, W.L. (ed.) *Problems of Polar research*. New York (1928).

Kolchak, R.A. 'Admiral Kolchak: ego rod i sem'ia', *Voenno-istoricheskii vestnik* (Paris), No. 16 (1960), pp. 14–20.

Kolosov, E.E. 'Krest'ianskoe dvizhenie pri Kolchake', *Byloe* (Petrograd), Vol. 20 (1922).

Kolz, A.W.F. 'British Economic Interests in Siberia During the Russian Civil War', *Journal of Modern History*, Vol. 48 (1976), pp. 483–491.

Korzhavin, V.K. 'K voprosu ob "oblastnichestskoi idee" v Sibiri', in *Istoricheskie aspekty ekonomicheskogo, kul'turnogo i sotsial'nogo razvitiia Sibiri*. Novosibirsk (1978).

Kosarev, V. 'Voenno-sotsialisticheskii soiuz', *Sibirskie ogni* (Novosibirsk), No. 1 (1922), pp. 65–70.

Kozlova, S.A. 'Trud i okhrana truda v Sibiri pri Kolchake (po neizdannym materialam Omskogo arkhivnogo biuro)', in *Iz proshlogo*. Omsk (1927), pp. 69–99.

Kriuk, V.A. 'Malye narody Severo-Vostoka v periode grazhdanskoi voiny i interventsii (1918–1922gg.)', in *Tret'ia nauchnaia konferentsiia po istorii, arkheologii i etnografii Dal'nego Vostoka* (Vol. 1). Vladivostok (1962), pp. 53–55.

Krushanov, A.I. 'K voprosu o roli Mezhsoiuznogo zhelezno-dorozhnogo komiteta i Tekhnicheskogo soveta v osushchestvlenii imperilisticheskikh planov SShA i Iaponii na Dal'nem Vostoke i v Sibiri v 1918–1919gg.', *Uchenye zapiski Dal'nevostochnogo gosudarstvennogo universiteta (Seriia obshchestvenno-politicheskikh nauk)* (Vladivostok), Vol. 2 (1958), pp. 69–78.

Kutskii, G.S. 'Iz istorii bor'by rabochego klassa Primor'ia protiv interventov i kolchakovshchinoi (iiul' 1918–ianvar' 1920gg.)', in *Dal'nyi Vostok za 40 let Sovetskoi vlasti*. Komsomol'sk-na-Amure (1958), pp. 215–263.

'Grodekovskii i Zabaikal'skii fronty vesnoi i letom 1918g.', *Trudy Dal'nevostochnogo filiala Sib. otdeleniia AN SSSR (Seriia istoricheskaia)* (Khabarovsk), Vol. 5 (1963), pp. 11–22.

Lasch, C. 'American Intervention in Siberia: A Reinterpretation', *Political Science Quarterly*, Vol. 77 (1962), No. 2, pp. 205–223.

Leont'ev, E. 'Verkhovnyi pravitel' Rossii admiral A.V. Kolchak', *Pod belom krestom* (Buenos Aires), No. 7 (1955), pp. 11–13.

Litvin, A.L. 'Krakh agrarnoi politiki kontrrevoliutsii (1918–1919gg.)', *Uchenye zapiski Kazanskogo gos. ped. instituta (Voprosy istoriografii i istochnikovedeniia)* (Kazan'), Vol. 4 (1969), pp. 168–237.

Livshits, S.G. 'Iz istorii imperialisticheskoi interventsii v Sibiri (1918–1919gg.)', in *Voprosy novoi i noveishei istorii.* Novosibirsk (1966).

'Novoe o "zolotom eshelone"', *Altai* (Barnaul), No. 4 (1969), pp. 75–89.

'K istorii Zapadno-sibirskogo komissariata', *Uchennye zapiski Barnaulsk. gos. ped. instituta* (Barnaul), Vol. 67 (1974).

'Vneshnepoliticheskii kurs Pravitel′stva avtomnoi Sibiri', in *Voprosy istorii novoi i noveishei istorii.* Barnaul (1974).

'Krakh Vremennogo pravitel′stva avtomnoi Sibiri', *Voprosy istorii* (Moscow), No. 8 (1974), pp. 87–99.

'Vremennoe sibirskoe pravitel′stvo', *Voprosy istorii* (Moscow), No. 12 (1979), pp. 98–108.

'Kolchakovskii perevorot', *Voprosy istorii* (Moscow), No. 3 (1982).

'"Verkhovnyi pravitel′" Kolchak i Ataman Semenov (K istorii "semenovskogo intsidenta")', in Korablev, Iu.V. and Shishkin, V.I. (eds.) *Iz istorii interventsii i grazhdanskoi voiny v Sibiri i na Dal′nem Vostoke, 1917–1922gg.* Novosibirsk (1985), pp. 176–184.

'Omskoe "diplomaticheskoe" soveshchanie 1919 goda', *Voprosy istorii* (Moscow), No. 6 (1986), pp. 178–180.

Livshits, S.G. and Beloglovskii, E.S. 'Rol′ strany antanty v ustanovlenii diktatury Kolchaka', *Voprosy istorii, ekonomiki i filosofii* (Cheliabinsk), Vol. 49 (1970).

Lobazov, P.K. 'Iz istorii tserkovnoi kontrrevoliutsii na Dal′nem Vostoke', in *Voprosy istorii Sovetskogo Dal′nego Vostoka* (Vol. 3). Vladivostok (1965), pp. 39–42.

Long, J. 'General Sir Alfred Knox and the Russian Civil War', *Sbornik of the Study Group on the Russian Revolution*, Vol. 9 (1983), pp. 54–64.

Lukin, A. 'Admiral Kolchak', *Poslednie novosti* (Paris), 21.ii.1930.

McCullagh, F. '*Belaia Sibir′*, by K.V. Sakharov', *Slavonic Review* (London), Vol. 3 (1925), No. 9 pp. 720–724.

Machray, R. 'The Situation in the Far East', *Fortnightly Review* No. 107 (1920), pp. 397–407.

Mcneal, R.H. 'The Conference at Jassy – An Early Fiasco of the Anti-Bolshevik Movement', in Curtiss, J.S. (ed.) *Essays in Russian History.* Leiden (1963), pp. 221–235.

Maddox, R. 'Woodrow Wilson, the Russian Embassy and the Siberian Intervention', *Pacific Historical Review*, Vol. 36 (1967), No. 4, pp. 435–448.

Mahon, E.K. 'Kolchak', *National Review* (June 1920), pp. 485–492; *National Review* (July 1920), pp. 682–692.

Malinovskii, D.A. 'Kak predali Kolchaka', *Novaia russkaia zhizn′* (Helsingfors), 26.xi.1920.

Mal′tseva, T.B. 'Tomskoe gubernskoe zemstvo v periode "demokraticheskoi" kontrrevoliutsii (iiun′–noiabr′ 1918g.)', in Bozhenko, L.I. (ed.)

Nekotorye voprosy istorii Sibiri: sbornik statei molodykh uchennykh istoriko-filologicheskogo fakul'teta. Tomsk (1972–1973), Vol. 2, pp. 113–138.

'Zemskaia "oppozitsiia" kolchakovshchiny', in Korablev, Iu.V. and Shishkin, V.I. (eds.) *Iz istorii interventsii i grazhdanskoi voiny v Sibiri i na Dal'nem Vostoke, 1917–1922gg.* Novosibirsk (1985), pp. 188–193.

Markov, J. 'Gibel' atamana Dutova', *Rodimyi krai* (Paris), No. 101 (July 1972).

Massey Stewart, J. 'Britain's Siberian Connection', in *Siberia: Two Historical Perspectives.* London (1984), pp. 1–20.

Mazler, B.S. 'Chekhoslovatskii korpus i Kolchak', in *K 50-letiiu osvobozhdeniia Sibiri ot kolchakovshchiny.* Tomsk (1970), pp. 36–46.

'Chekhoslovatskii korpus, soiuznaia interventsiia i Kolchak', *Baikal,* No. 5 (1970), pp. 141–149.

Merkhalev, L. 'Zheleznye dorogi v Sibiri, 1917–1919gg', *Sbornik Sibirskogo statisticheskogo upravlenie* (Omsk), Vol. 2 (Trudy Sib. stat. upravlenie No. 7), pp. 41–54.

Mikhailova, E. 'Zheleznodorozhniki v bor'be s Kolchakom', *Partiinyi rabotnik zhelezno-dorozhnogo transporta,* No. 9 (1940), pp. 37–40.

'Profsoiuzy i razgrom Kolchaka', *Profsoiuzy SSSR* (Moscow), No. 10 (1940), pp. 61–70.

Mote, V.L. 'The Cheliabinsk Grain Tariff and the Rise of the Siberian Butter Industry', *Slavic Review,* Vol. 35, No. 2 (1976), pp. 304–318.

Mukhachev, B.I. 'Razgrom kontrrevoliutsionnykh sil na severe Dal'nego Vostoka', in *Istoriia, arkheologiia i etnografiia narodov Dal'nego Vostoka.* Vladivostok (1973), Vol. 1, pp. 184–187.

Murby, R.N. 'The Canadian Economic Commission to Siberia', *Canadian Slavonic Papers,* Vol. 11, (1969), No. 3, pp. 374–393.

Naumov, N.I. 'Natsional'nyi vopros vo vneshnei politike kolchakovskogo pravitel'stva', in Razgon, I.M. (ed.) *Voprosy istorii obshchestvenno-politicheskoi zhizni Sibiri perioda Oktiabria i grazhdanskoi voiny.* Tomsk (1982), pp. 121–132.

Nazimok, V.N. 'K istorii tak nazyvaemogo "Vremennogo pravitel'stva avtomnoi Sibiri"', *Trudy Tomskogo gos. universiteta* (Tomsk), Vol. 205 (1969).

Nefedrov, N. 'Poslednie dni admirala Kolchaka', in *Zheleznyi zanaves – dve velikie provokatsi i dr.* New York (1978), pp. 149–161.

'Kak byl zaversheno predatel'stvo admirala Kolchaka', *Veche* (Paris), No. 20 (1985), pp. 127–144.

Newman, H.W. 'Siberia under Kolchak's Dictatorship', *New York Times Current History* (New York), (May 1920), pp. 300–309.

Novitsky, V. 'Russia's Gold Reserve', in *Russian Gold: A Collection of Articles, Newspaper Editorials and Reports and Statistical Data Regarding the Russian Gold Reserve and Shipments of Soviet Gold.* New York (1928), pp. 9–26.

Obukhov, N.K. 'Vosstanie minusinskikh krest′ian v 1918g.', *Sibirskie ogni* (Novosibirsk), No. 6 (1929), pp. 140–151.

Osnos, I. 'Semenov – stavlennik iaponskoi interventsii', *Istoricheskie zapiski* (Moscow), Vol. 1 (1937), pp. 54–63.

Pares, B. '*Dopros Kolchaka*, by K.A. Popov [Review]', *Slavonic and East European Review* (London), Vol. 8 (1929), No. 22, pp. 225–30.

'John Ward', *Slavonic and East European Review* (London), Vol. 13 (1935), No. 39, pp. 680-683.

Parfenov, P.S. 'Sibirskie es-ery i rasstrel slavgorodskikh krest′ian v avguste 1918g. (k protsessu eserov)', *Proletarskaia revoliutsiia* (Moscow), No. 7 (1922), pp. 59–71.

'Peregovory s komandovaniembelykh sibirskikh armei v 1920–1921gg.', *Proletarskaia revoliutsiia* (Moscow), No. 11 (1926), pp. 143–194; No. 12 (1926), pp. 208–233.

'Poslednie dni pravitel′stva Kolchaka', *Sibirskie ogni* (Novosibirsk), No. 5 (1927), pp. 90–117.

Pearce, B. 'Zinovii Sverdlov-Peshkov', *Revolutionary Russia*, Vol. 6 (1993), No. 1, pp. 148–153.

Pelissier, J. 'La reconnaissance du gouvernment de Koltchak et la problème des nationalités en Russie', *Tribune libre des nationalités* (Paris), Vol. 10 (1919), pp. 177–181.

Pereira, N.G.O. 'White Power during the Civil War in Siberia (1918–1920): Dilemmas of Kolchak's "War Anti-Communism"', *Canadian Slavonic Papers*, No. 1 (1987), pp. 2–19.

'The Democratic Counter-Revolution of 1918 in Siberia', *Nationality Papers*, Vol. 16 (1988), No. 1, pp. 71–94.

'Regional Consciousness in Siberia before and after October 1917', *Canadian Slavonic Papers*, No. 1 (1988), pp. 2–21.

'The Partisan Movement in Western Siberia, 1918–20', *Jahrbücher für Geschichte Osteuropas*, Vol. 38 (1990), No. 1, pp. 87–96.

Petrov, P. 'Novoe o gibeli tsentrosibirtsev', *Sibirskie ogni* (Novosibirsk), No. 7 (1964), pp. 163–165.

Petrov, S. 'Skol′ko rossiiskogo zolota okazalos′ za granitsei v 1914–1920 godakh? (Doklad)', in Romanovskii, S.K. (ed.) *Diplomaticheskii ezhegodnik*. Moscow (1995), pp. 240–253.

Pinckney, R. 'The Theory and Practice of Military Government', *Political Studies*, Vol. 21 (1973), No. 2, pp. 152–166.

Pipes, R.E. 'The First Experiment in Soviet National Policy: The Bashkir Republic, 1917–1920', *Russian Review*, Vol. 9 (1950), No. 4, pp. 303–319.

Plotnikova, M.E. 'Rol′ Vremennogo sibirskogo pravitel′stva v podgotovke kolchakovskogo perevorota', *Voprosy istorii Sibiri* (Tomsk), Vol. 167 (1964).

'Kolchak i eserovskaia oppozitsiia', *Voprosy istorii Sibiri* (Tomsk), Vol. 3 (1967), pp. 168–181.

'K istorii eserovskoi kontrrevoliutsii v Sibiri v 1918g.', *Voprosy istorii Sibiri* (Tomsk), Vol. 214 (1969).

Pokrovskii. M.N. 'Kto byl Kolchak', *Pravda* (Moscow), 30.vi.1930.

Poliak, A. 'Deistviia 5-oi Krasnoi armii ot reki Tobola do ozera Baikala', in *Sbornik trudov voenno-nauchnogo obshchestva pri Voennoi akademii* (Vol. 2). Moscow (1922).

Poliakov, Iu.A. and Kiselev, I.N. 'Chislennost′ i natsional′nyi sostav naselenii Rossiia v 1917g.', *Voprosy istorii* (Moscow), No. 6 (1980), pp. 39–49.

'Polozhenie sibirskoi promyshlennosti, 1917–1920gg. (doklad Sibbiuro VSNKh)', *Narodnoe khoziaistvo* (Moscow), No. 3 (1921), pp. 56–75; Nos. 6–7 (1921), pp. 53–76.

Pomerants, V. 'Kak kolchakovskaia pechat′ staralas′ i kak u nee ne vykhodilo (po materialam arkhiva)', *Vlast′ truda* (Moscow), 4.i.1925.

Popova, E.I. 'Missiia Stevensa i proval zheleznodorozhnoi politiki SShA v Rossii i Kitae, 1917–1922gg.', *Istoricheskie zapiski* (Moscow), Vol. 60 (1957), pp. 31–85.

Poppe, N. 'The Economic and Cultural Development of Siberia', in Katkov, G. et al. (eds.) *Russia Enters the Twentieth Century*. London (1971), pp. 140–149.

Prikhod′kov, L.I. 'Reaktsionnaia rol′ russkoi pravoslavnoi tserkvi na Dal′nem Vostoke (1917–1922gg.)', in *Voprosy istorii Sovetskogo Dal′nego Vostoka* (Vol. 3). Vladivostok (1965), pp. 37–39.

Prisiazhnyi, A.G. 'Potrebitel′skaia kooperatsiia Zapadnoi Sibiri v gody kolchakovshchinoi', in *K 50-letiiu osvobozhdeniia Sibiri ot kolchakovshchiny*. Tomsk (1970), pp. 54–58.

'Iz istorii sibirskoi kooperatsii perioda revoliutsii i grazhdanskoi voiny', in Bozhenko, L.I. (ed.) *Nekotorye voprosy istorii Sibiri: sbornik statei molodykh uchennykh istoriko-filologicheskogo fakul′teta*. Tomsk (1972–1973), Vol. 2, pp. 96–112.

Quigley, H.S. 'The Far Eastern Republic: A Product of Intervention', *American Journal of International Law*, Vol. 18 (1924), No. 1, pp. 82–92.

Ray, O.A. 'The Imperial Russian Army Officer', *Political Science Quarterly*, Vol. 76 (1961), No. 4.

Razgon, I.M. and Plotnikova, M.E. 'G.N. Potanin v gody sotsialisticheskoi revoliutsii i grazhdanskoi voiny v Sibiri', *Voprosy istorii Sibiri* (Tomsk), Vol. 158 (1968), pp. 138–153.

Redakova, E.P. 'Provedenie v zhizn′ pervykh agrarnykh zakonov sovetskoi vlasti v Shadrinskom uezde (1918–1920gg.), *Uchenye zapiski Kurganskogo pedagogicheskogo instituta* (Kurgan), No. 4 (1962).

Richard, C.J. 'The Shadow of a Plan: The Rationale behind Wilson's 1918 Siberian Intervention', *Historian*, Vol. 49 (1986), No. 1, pp. 64–84.

Rosenberg, W.G. 'Russian Municipal Duma Elections of 1917: A Preliminary Computation of Returns', *Soviet Studies* (Glasgow), Vol. 21 (1969), pp. 131–163.

Roshchevskii, P.I. 'Komissary Vremennogo pravitel'stva v Sibiri', in *Istoricheskii sbornik Tiumen'skogo gos. ped. instituta* (Vol. 3). Tiumen' (1970), pp. 40–58.

'Russia's Gold Reserve – How it has been Dispersed', *Bankers' Magazine* (Oct.1920), pp. 478–479.

Scheibert, P. 'Saratov – Stadt und Gouvernement in Revolution und Bürgerkrieg (Oktober 1917 bis 1922), in *Russland, Deutschland, Amerika. Festschrift für F.T Epstein zum 80. Geburtstag*. Wiesbaden (1978), pp. 198–211.

Sellen, R.W. 'The British Intervention in Russia, 1917–1920', *Dalhousie Review*, Vol. 40 (1960), pp. 360–371, 520–521.

Serebrennikov, I.I. 'The Siberian Autonomous Movement and its Future', *Pacific Historical Review*, Vol. 3 (1934), pp. 400–415.

Seton-Watson, G.H.N. 'Russia: Army and Autocracy', in Howard, M. (ed.) *Soldiers and Governments*. London (1957).

Shafir, Ia.M. 'Ekonomicheskaia politika belykh', *Narodnoe khoziaistvo* (Moscow), No. 4 (1921), pp. 22–40.

Shapiro, Captain S. 'Allied Intervention in Russia, 1918–1919', *United States Naval Institute Proceedings* Vol. 99 (1973), pp. 52–61.

Shelestov, D.K. 'O nachale povorota sibirsko-trudovogo krest'ianstva v storonu Sovetskoi vlasti', *Istoriia SSSR* (Moscow), No. 1 (1962), pp. 122–135.

Sherower, M.M. 'The Nikolaevsk Massacre', *The Nation*, Vol. 111 (21.viii.1920), pp. 175–177.

Shikalov, A.S. 'Potrebitel'skaia kooperatsiia v periode Oktiabr'skoi revoliutsii i grazhdanskoi voiny (1917–1919gg.)', in *Ocherki istorii potrebitel'skoi kooperatsii Sibiri*. Novosibirsk (1965), pp. 46–80.

Shikanov, L.A. 'K voprosy o khronologicheskikh ramkakh "demokraticheskoi" kontrrevoliutsii v Sibiri', in Korablev, Iu.V. and Shishkin, V.I. (eds.) *Iz istorii interventsii i grazhdanskoi voiny v Sibiri i na Dal'nem Vostoke, 1917–1922gg*. Novosibirsk (1985), pp. 62–67.

Shilovskii, M.V. 'Sibirskoe oblastnichestvo i kontrrevoliutsiia: k probleme vziamootnosheniia', in Korablev, Iu.V. and Shishkin, V.I. (eds.) *Iz istorii interventsii i grazhdanskoi voiny v Sibiri i na Dal'nem Vostoke, 1917–1922gg*. Novosibirsk (1985), pp. 169–175.

Shimkin, M. and Shimkin, M. 'From Golden Horn to Golden Gate: The Flight of the Siberian Russian Flotilla', *California History*, Vol. 64 (1985), No. 4, pp. 290–294

Shindin, A.M. 'Sibirskoe biuro Tsk RKP(b) – organizator i rukovoditel' partiinogo podpol'ia v tylu belogvardeitsev i interventov (dek. 1918–mart 1920gg.)', in *Velikii Oktiabr' i sotsialisticheskie preobrazovaniia v Sibiri*. Novosibirsk (1980), pp. 45–54.

Shishkin, S.N. 'Kontrnastuplenie Krasnoi armii na Vostochnom fronte protiv Kolchaka (aprel'–iiun' 1919g.)', in Naida, S.F. et al. (eds.) *Reshaiushchie pobedy sovetskogo naroda nad interventsii i belogvardeitsam v 1919g. (sbornik statei).* Moscow (1960), pp. 69–120.

Shishkin, V.I. 'Sibirskie esery i kolchakovshchina', in *Bol'sheviki v bor'be s neproletarskimi partiami, gruppami i tendentsiiami.* Moscow (1983), pp. 98–110.

Shlain, B.I. 'Zapadno-Sibirskii uglepromyshlennyi raion v 1914–1919gg.', *Gornoe delo* (Moscow), Vol. 1 (1920), Supplement No. 1, pp. 24–31.

Shmotin, V.P. 'Gold Mining in Russia', *Russkii Dal'nyi Vostok* (Tokyo), No. 1 (October 1920).

Shpilev, G. 'Iz istorii partiinoi raboty v Sibiri pri Kolchake', *Proletarskaia revoliutsiia* (Moscow), No. 1 (1928), pp. 67–85.

Smele, J.D. 'Labour Conditions and the Collapse of the Siberian Economy under Kolchak', *Sbornik of the Study Group on the Russian Revolution*, Vol. 13 (1987), pp. 31–60.

'An Attempt to Utilize the Northern Sea Route to Siberia in 1919', *Sibirica (Report of the British Universities' Siberian Studies Seminar)* (Lancaster), Vol. 4 (1989), pp. 28–39.

'"What Kolchak Wants!": Military versus Polity in White Siberia, 1918–1920', *Revolutionary Russia*, Vol. 4 (1991), No. 1, pp. 51–108.

'White Gold: The Imperial Russian Gold Reserve in the Anti-Bolshevik East, 1918–? (An Unconcluded Chapter in the History of the Russian Civil War)', *Europe–Asia Studies* Vol. 46 (1994), No. 8, pp. 1317–1347.

Smirnov, M.I. 'Admiral Kolchak', *Slavonic and East European Review* (London), Vol. 11 (1933), No. 32, pp. 373–387.

Smith, C.F. 'Atamanshchina in the Russian Far East', *Russian History*, Vol. 1 (1979), No. 1, pp. 57–67.

'The Ungernovshchina: How and Why?', *Jahrbücher für Geschichte Osteuropas*, Vol. 28, (1980), pp. 590–595.

Smith, C.H. 'What Happened in Siberia', *Asia*, Vol. 22 (1922), pp. 373–378, 402–403.

'Four Years of Mistakes in Siberia', *Asia*, Vol. 22 (1922), pp. 479–483.

'The Smoke-Screen between Siberia and Washington', *Asia*, Vol. 22 (1922), pp. 639–644.

Smith, G. 'Canada and the Siberian Intervention', *American Historical Review*, Vol. 64 (1959), No. 4, pp. 866–877.

Smolka, H.P. 'Arctic Siberia: Its History and Development', *Slavonic and East European Review* (London), Vol. 16 (1937), No. 46, pp. 60–70.

Snow, R.E. 'The Russian Revolution of 1917–1918 in Transbaikalia', *Soviet Studies* (Glasgow) Vol. 22 (1971), No. 2, pp. 201–215.

Sofinov, P.G. 'Permskaia katastrofa i likvidatsiia ee posledstvii', *Istoricheskii zapiski* (Moscow), Vol. 30, pp. 31–82.

Sokolov, N.G. 'Antinarodnaia sushchnost′ nalogovoi politiki v derevne esero-men′shevistskogo pravitel′stva i kolchakovskogo rezhima v Sibiri (1918–1919gg.)', in *Neproletarskie partii i organizatsii natsional′-nykh raionov Rossii v Oktiabr′skoi revoliutsii i grazhdanskoi voiny*. Moscow (1980), pp. 265–273.

Spence, R.B. 'White Against Red in Uriankhai: Revolution and Civil War on Russia's Asiatic Frontier, 1918–1921', *Revolutionary Russia*, Vol. 6 (1993), No. 1, pp. 97–120.

Spirin, L.M. 'O deiatel′nosti Sibirskogo biuro TsK RKP(b) v gody grazhdanskoi voiny', *Voprosy istorii KPSS* (Moscow), No. 2 (1961), pp. 97–112.

'Razgrom belogvardeiskikh armii na Urale letom 1919g.', *Istoricheskie zapiski* (Moscow), Vol. 56 (1956), pp. 26–51.

Steeds, D. 'The Ending of a Highly Discreditable Enterprise: Miles Lampson in Siberia, 1919–1920', *International Studies*, Vol. 1 (1981), pp. 1–26.

Svetachev, M.I. 'Ekonomicheskoe proniknovenie i sopernichestvo imperialisticheskikh derzhav na sovetskom Dal′nem Vostoke (1918–1919gg.)', *Uchenye zapiski MGU* (Moscow), Vol. 205 (1964), pp. 96–202.

'Imperialisticheskaia politika "pomoshchi" i ee rol′ v antisovetskoi interventsii v Sibiri v 1918–1919gg.', *Voprosy istorii Dal′nego Vostoka* (Khabarovsk), Vol. 2 (1972).

'Interventsiia i sibirskaia kontrrevoliutsiia (no. 1917–no. 1918gg.)', *Voprosy istorii Dal′nego Vostoka* (Khabarovsk), Vol. 3 (1973).

'Sibir′ i Dal′nyi Vostok v kolonial′nykh planakh Antanty i SShA (no. 1917–no. 1918gg.)', *Istoricheskie zapiski* (Moscow), Vol. 103 (1979), pp. 62–106.

Taniaev, A. 'Vtoraia volna nastupleniia burzhuazno-pomeshchichei reaktsii: perevorot 18 no. 1918g. i burzhuaziia', *Ural-Kommunist* (Sverdlovsk), No. 3 (1929), pp. 33–43.

Timoshkov, I.S. 'Razgrom iuzhnoi armii Kolchaka', *Voenno-istoricheskii zhurnal* (Moscow), No. 3 (1940).

Toupine, A. 'La Tragédie Sibérienne', *Mercure de France* (Paris), 1.ii.1920, pp. 657–683.

Trani, E.P. 'Woodrow Wilson and the Decision to Intervene in Russia: A Reconsideration of the Evidence', *Journal of Modern History*, Vol. 48 (1976), pp. 440–461.

Tromp, H.W. 'The Assessment of the Military Mind', in van Gils, M.R. (ed.) *The Perceived Role of the Military*. Rotterdam (1971).

Tumarkin, D. 'Kontrrevoliutsiia v Sibiri', *Sibirskie ogni* (Novonikolaevsk), No. 1 (1922), pp. 87–99.

Unterberger, B.M. 'President Wilson and the Decision to send American Troops to Siberia', *Pacific Historical Review*, Vol. 24 (1955), pp. 63–74.

'The Russian Revolution and Wilson's Far Eastern Policy', *Russian Review*, Vol. 16 (1957),No. 2, pp. 35–47.
'Woodrow Wilson and the Bolsheviks: The "Acid Test" of Soviet-American Relations', *Diplomatic History*, Vol. 11 (1987), pp. 71–90.
'Woodrow Wilson and the Russian Revolution', in Link. A. (ed.) *Woodrow Wilson and a Revolutionary World, 1913–1921*. Chapel Hill (1982).

Varneck, E. 'Siberian Native Peoples after the February Revolution', *Slavonic and East European Review* (London), Vol. 21 (1943), No. 1, pp. 70–88.

Vasil′ev, V.N. 'Severnyi morskoi put′: kratkii istoricheskii ocherk', *Sibirskie ogni* (Novonikolaevsk), No. 5 (1924), pp. 190–212.

Vegman, V.[D.] 'O zolote kotoroe vyvezli kolchakovtsy iz Sibiri', *Izvestiia VTsIK* (Moscow), 12.iv.1922.
'Poslednie dni Kolchaka', *Rabochii put′* (Omsk), 7.ix.1922.
'Kak i pochemu pala v 1918g. Sovetskaia vlast′ v Tomske', *Sibirskie ogni* (Novonikolaevsk), Nos. 1–2 (1923), pp. 127–147.
'Oblastnicheskie illiuzii rasseiannye revoliutsei (k istorii vozniknovenii Sibirskoi oblastnoi dumy),' *Sibirskie ogni* (Novonikolaevsk), No. 3 (1923), pp. 89–117.
'Sibobduma', *Sibirskie ogni* (Novonikolaevsk), No. 4 (1923), pp. 89–112.
'Oblastnicheskie illiuzii vozrozhdennye kolchakovshchinoi', *Sibirskie ogni* (Novonikolaevsk), Nos. 5–6 (1923), pp. 140–162.
'Sibirskie kontrrevoliutsionnye organizatsii v 1918g.', *Sibirskie ogni* (Novonikolaevsk), No. 1 (1928), pp. 135–146.
'Pervye dni kolchakovshchiny', *Sovetskaia Sibir′*, 30.xi.1928 (also *Krasnoe znamia*, 30.xi.1928).
'Vosstanie omskikh rabochikh protiv kolchakovshchiny', *Sibirskie ogni* (Novosibirsk), No. 1 (1934), pp. 200–207.
'V Sibiri uzhas i smert', *Sibirskie ogni* (Novosibirsk), No. 1 (1935), pp. 46–55.

Vigor, P.H. 'The Military Strategy of the Russian Civil War', *Sbornik of the Study Group on the Russian Revolution*, Vol. 3 (1977), pp. 13–19.

Volkov, F.D. 'Novye dokumenty ob ispol′zovanii plennykh chekhoslovakov dlia interventsii protiv Sovetskoi Rossii', *Voprosy istorii* (Moscow), No. 2 (1971), pp. 103–108.

Vorob′eva, V.Ia. 'Put′ men′shevikov Povol′zhia i Sibiri ot "chistoi demokratii" k kolchakovskoi diktature', *Uchenye zapiski Moskovskogo gos. ped. instituta* (Moscow), Vol. 309 (1969), pp. 339–376.

Voronov, D.N. 'Vinnaia monopoliia v Sibiri v 1919g.', *Vestnik finansov* (Moscow), No. 2 (1925), pp. 140–144.

Watrous, S. 'The Regionalist Conception of Siberia, 1860–1920', in Diment, G. and Slezkine, Y. (eds.) *Between Heaven and Hell: The Myth of Siberia in Russian Culture*. London (1993), pp. 134–151.

Weeks, C.J. and Bayen, J.O. 'James H. Glennon's Mission to Russia, June–July 1917', *The New Review*, Vol. 13 (1976), pp. 14–31.

'Admiral Kolchak's Mission to the United States', *Military Affairs*, Vol. 40 (1976), No. 2), pp. 63–67.

White, J.A. 'The American Role in the Siberian Intervention', *Russian Review*, Vol. 10 (1951), No. 1 (1951).

Williams, A. 'American Intervention in Russia, 1917–1920', in Horrowitz, D. (ed.) *Containment and Revolution: Western Policy Towards Social Revolution, 1917 to Vietnam*. New York (1967).

Williams, R.A. 'The Czech Legion Revisited', *East-Central Europe*, Vol. 6 (1979), No. 1, pp. 20–39.

Williams, W.A. 'American Intervention in Russia, 1917–1920', *Studies on the Left*, Vol. 3 (1963), pp. 24–48; Vol. 4 (1964), pp. 39–57.

Wood, A. 'Sex and Violence in Siberia: Aspects of the Tsarist Exile System', in *Siberia: Two Historical Perspectives*. London (1984), pp. 22–42.

'From Conquest to Revolution: The Historical Dimension', in Wood, A. (ed.) *Siberia: Problems and Prospects for Development*. London (1987).

Woodward, D.R. 'The British Government and the Japanese Intervention in Russia During World War 1', *Journal of Modern History*, Vol. 46 (1974), pp. 663–685.

Yokoi, T. 'Japan's Policy Towards Russia', *Nineteenth Century*, No. 84 (1918), pp. 194–204.

Zhukov, A.F. 'Izhevskii miatezh esero-men'shevikov', *Voprosy istorii* (Moscow), No. 3 (1987), pp. 173–178.

Zhukov, V.A. 'Chernomorskoi flot v revoliutsii 1917g.', *Proletarskaia revoliutsiia* (Moscow), Nos. 8–9 (1927), pp. 143–167.

Zhuravlev, M.N. 'Ekonomicheskaia interventsiia v Sibiri v 1918–1919g.', *Trudy Novosibirskogo instituta inzhenerov vodnogo transporta* (Novosibirsk), No. 51 (1970), pp. 5–28.

Zhurov, Iu.V. 'Organy sel'skoi vlasti i upravleniia Eniseiskoi gubernii v gody grazhdanskoi voiny (iiun' 1918–ianvar' 1920g.)', in *Iz istorii krest'ianstva Vostochnoi Sibiri*. Krasnoiarsk (1966).

'Partizanskoe dvizhenie i revoliutsionnye preobrazovaniia v sibirskoi derevne (1918–1920gg.)', in *Problemy agrarnoi istorii sovetskogo obshchestva*. Moscow (1971).

'Bol'shevistskie organizatsii i pervye revoliutsionnye preobrazovanii v sibirskoi derevne (1917–1919gg.)', in *Iz istorii Krasnoiarskoi partiinoi organizatsii*. Krasnoiarsk (1974).

Zimina, V.D. 'Severo-Zapadnaia germanofil'skaia i vostochnaia kontrrevoliutsiia: popytki vziamodeistviia i ikh krakh', in Korablev, Iu.V. and Shishkin, V.I. (eds.) *Iz istorii interventsii i grazhdanskoi voiny v Sibiri i na Dal'nem Vostoke, 1917–1922gg*. Novosibirsk (1985), pp. 156–161.

Sborniki

Astrov, N.I. et al. (eds.) *Pamiati pogibshikh.* Paris (1929).

Avdeev, N.A. (ed.) *Iz istorii grazhdanskoi voiny i interventsii na Dal'nem Vostoke.* Khabarovsk (1978).

Belaia Rossiia (Al'bom No. 1). New York (1937).

Bozhenko, L.I. (ed.) *Nekotorye voprosy istorii Sibiri: sbornik statei molodykh uchennykh istoriko-filologicheskogo fakul'teta* (2 Vols.). Tomsk (1972–1973).

Iz istorii krest'ianstva Sibiri: sbornik. Tomsk (1978).

Voprosy istorii sovetskoi Sibiri. Tomsk (1980).

Iz istorii obshchestvenno-politicheskoi zhizni Sibiri. Tomsk (1981).

Bubnov, A. et al (eds.) *Grazhdanskaia voina* (3 Vols.). Moscow (1928–1930).

Burzhuaznye i melkoburzhuaznye partii Rossii v Oktiabr'skoi revoliutsii i grazhdanskoi voiny. Moscow (1980).

Bykov, P.M. and Nipporkin, N.G. (eds.) *Rabochaia revoliutsiia na Urale: epizody i fakty.* Ekaterinburg (1921).

[Dal'istpart] *Sbornik materialov po istorii revoliutsionnogo dvizheniia na Dal'nem Vostoke* (3 Vols.). Chita–Vladivostok (1923–1925).

Flerov, V.S. (ed.) *Bor'ba za vlast' Sovetov v Sibiri i na Dal'nem Vostoke.* Tomsk (1968).

Golinkov, D.L. (ed.) *Krushenie antisovetskogo podpol'ia v SSSR (1917–1925gg.)* (2 Vols.). Moscow (1978).

Iarmenko A.N. (ed.) *Revoliutsiia na Dal'nem Vostoke.* Moscow (1923).

[Istpart] *Byloe Sibiri* (2 Vols.). Tomsk (1922–1923).

Byloe Urala (3 Vols.). Ufa (1922–1924).

Revoliutsiia na Dal'nem Vostoke. Moscow (1923).

Sbornik Istparta (No. 1). Novonikolaevsk (1923).

Iz istorii grazhdanskoi voiny i interventsii na Dal'nem Vostoke. Khabarovsk (1978).

Iz istorii grazhdanskoi voiny v SSSR, 1917–1922gg.: sbornik statei. Moscow (1974).

Iz istorii sotsial'no-ekonomicheskoi i politicheskoi zhizni Sibiri. Tomsk (1980).

Korablev, Iu.V. and Shishkin, V.I. (eds.) *Iz istorii interventsii i grazhdanskoi voiny v Sibiri i na Dal'nem Vostoke, 1917–1922gg.* Novosibirsk (1985).

K 50-letiiu osvobozhdeniia Sibiri ot kolchakovshchiny: materialy nauchnoi konferentsii (2 Vols.). Tomsk (1970).

Krushanov, A.I. (ed.) *Imperialisticheskaia interventsiia na Sovetskom Dal'nem Vostoke.* Vladivostok (1988).

Krushanov, A.I. et al. (eds.) *Etikh dnei ne smolknet slava: stat'i, ocherki i materialy o bor'be za vlast' Sovetov v Primor'e v 1917–1922gg.* Vladivostok (1966).

Lukinskii, F.A. et al. (eds.) *Voprosy istorii sotsial'no-ekonomicheskoi i kul'turnoi zhizni Sibiri* (2 Vols.). Novosibirsk (1971).

Meshcheriakov, N.L. (ed.) *Kooperatsiia i sotsializm: sbornik statei*. Moscow (1920).

Mints, I.I. (ed.) *Iz istorii grazhdanskoi voiny i interventsii, 1917–1922gg*. Moscow (1974).

Neproletarskie partii Rossii v 1917g. i v grazhdanskoi voiny. Moscow (1980).

Naida, S.F. et al. (eds.) *Iz istorii bor'by sovetskogo naroda protiv inostrannoi voennoi interventsii i vnutrennoi kontrrevoliutsii v 1918g*. Moscow (1956).

Reshaiushchie pobedy sovetskogo naroda nad interventsii i belogvardeitsam v 1919g.: sbornik statei. Moscow (1960).

Nikiforov, P.M. et al. (eds.) *Bor'ba za vlast Sovetov na Dal'nem Vostoke, 1918–1922gg.: sbornik dal'ne-vostochnogo zemliachestva*. Moscow (1932).

50-let osvobozhdeniia Zabaikalia ot belogvardeitsev i inostrannoi interventov: materialy nauchnoi konferentsii. Chita (1972).

Po rodnomu kraiu: kratkii ocherk DVR i Pribaikal'ia. Verkhneudinsk (1922).

Raivid, N. and Bykov, V. (eds.) *Kolchakovshchina: sbornik*. Ekaterinburg (1924).

Razgon, I.M. (ed.) *Voprosy istorii obshchestvenno-politicheskoi zhizni Sibiri perioda Oktiabria i grazhdanskoi voiny*. Tomsk (1982).

Razgon, I.M. et al. (eds.) *Iz istorii grazhdanskoi voiny v Sibiri: sbornik nauch. dokladov*. Novosibirsk (1973).

Riabtsev, I. (ed.) *Bol'sheviki v bor'be protiv melkoburzhuaznykh partii v Rossii, 1910–1920gg*. Moscow (1969).

Russkaia zhizn: al'manakh. Harbin (1922).

Smyshliaev, V.A. (ed.) *Bor'ba kommunisticheskoi partii protiv neproletarskykh partii, grupp i techenii*. Leningrad (1982).

Vegman, V. (ed.) *Gorniaki Sibiri: revoliutsiia i grazhdanskaia voina (Profsoiuznoe stroitel'stvo, 1917–1927gg. – sbornik statei i vospominaniia)*. Novosibirsk (1927).

Vilenskii, V.D. (ed.) *Tsentrosibirtsy: sbornik pamiaty pogibshikh chlenov Tsentral'no-ispolnitel'nogo komiteta Sibiri 1918g*. Moscow–Leningrad (1927).

Voprosy novoi i noveishei istorii. Barnaul (1974).

Wood, A. (ed.) *The History of Siberia: From Conquest to Revolution*. London (1991).

Zhukovskii, I. and Mokina, Z. (eds.) *Krasnaia golgofa: sbornik posviashchennyi pamiati tovarishchei, pogibshikh za raboche-krest'ianskoe delo*. Blagoveshchensk (1920).

Zolnikov, D.M. et al. (eds.) *Klassy i politichskie partii v Oktiabr'skoi revoliutsii i grazhdanskoi voine v Sibiri*. Novosibirsk (1991).

Chronologies

Meshcheriakov, P.B. *Bor'ba za vlast' Sovetov na Iuzhnom Urale i v Zaural'e (khronika istoriko-revoliutsionnykh sobytii za 1917–1919gg.).* Cheliabinsk (1957).

Maksakov, V.V. and Turunov, A. *Khronika grazhdanskoi voiny v Sibiri.* Moscow–Leningrad (1926).

Razgon, I.M. and Goriushkin, L. (eds.) *Oktiabr' v Sibiri: khronika sobytii.* Novosibirsk (1987).

Revoliutsiia 1917–1918gg. v Samarskoi gubernii: khronika sobytii (2 Vols.). Samara (1929).

Timofeev, I.A. *Khronika bor'by za vlast' Sovetov v Vostochnoi Sibiri.* Irkutsk (1937).

Tsiupkin, S. et al. *Oktiabr'skaia revoliutsiia i grazhdanskaia voina na Dal'nem Vostoke: khronika sobytii (1917–1922gg.).* Moscow–Khabarovsk (1933).

Reference Works

Aziatskaia Rossiia (izdanie Pereselencheskago upravleniia Glavnogo upravleniia zemleustroistva i zemledeliia (3 Vols.). St Petersburg (1914).

Baedeker, K. *Russia with Teheran, Port Arthur and Peking.* Leipzig (1914).

Cheremnykh, S.G. (comp.) *Liudi bol'shevistskogo podpol'ia Urala i Sibiri, 1918–1919gg.* Moscow (1988).

Dmitriev-Mamontov, A.J. and Zdziarski, A.F. *Guide to the Great Siberian Railway (1900).* Newton Abbot (1971).

Grazhdanskaia voina i voennaia interventsiia v SSSR: entsiklopediia. Moscow (1983).

Grazhdanskaia voina v SSSR (2 Vols.). Moscow (1980–1986).

[Geographical Section of Naval Intelligence Division, Naval Staff Admiralty] *A Handbook of Siberia and Arctic Russia* (3 Vols.). London (1918).

Istoriia grazhdanskoi voiny v SSSR (Vols. 3–4). Moscow (1959–1960).

Istoriia Sibiri (Vol. 4). Leningrad (1968).

Jackson, D. and Devlin, R. (eds.) *Dictionary of the Russian Revolution.* London (1989).

Markov, A. *Entsiklopediia belago dvizheniia.* n.p. (n.d.)

de Mowbray, S.A. *Key Facts in Soviet History: Vol. 1, 1917–1941.* London (1990).

Peacock, N. (comp.) *The Russian Year-Book, 1916.* London (1916).

The Russian Almanac, 1919. London (1920).

Preev, Z.N. *The Russian Revolution and Who's Who in Russia.* London (1917).

[Prothero, G.W. (ed.)] *Peace Handbooks, Vol. IX: The Russian Empire*. London (1920).
Shukman, H. (ed.) *The Blackwell Encyclopedia of the Russian Revolution*. Oxford (1988).
Toynbee, A.J. *Survey of International Affairs, 1920–1923*. London (1925).
Sibirskaia sovetskaia entsiklopediia (2 Vols.). Novosibirsk (1929–1932).
Wallace, Sir D.M. (ed.) *The Times Book of Russia: Finance, Commerce, Industries*. London (1916).
Wieczynski, J.L. (ed.) *The Modern Encyclopedia of Russian and Soviet History* (55 Vols.). Virginia (1976–1993).

Bibliographical and Historiographical Works

Arans, D. (ed.) *'How We Lost the Civil War': Bibliography of Russian Émigré Memoirs of the Russian Revolution, 1917–1920* (Russian Bibliography Series, No. 6). Newtonville, MA (1988).
Azovtsev, N.N. and Naumov, V.P. 'Study of the History of the Military Intervention and Civil War in the USSR', *Soviet Studies in History* Vol. 10 (1971–1972), No. 4, pp. 327–360.
Batalov, A.N. 'Ob ispol′zovanii belogvardeiskoi literatury pri issledovanii kolchakovshchiny', in *K 50-letiiu osvobozhdeniia Sibiri ot kolchakovshchiny*. Tomsk (1970), pp. 88–91.
Belov, V. *Belaia pechat′: ee ideologia, rol′, znachenie i deiatel′nost′ (Materialy dlia budushchego istorika)*. Petrograd (1923).
Collins, D.N. (ed.) *Siberia* (World Bibliography Series, No. 127). Oxford (1991).
Burtsev, V. 'The Russian Archives in Prague', *Slavonic and East European Review* (London), Vol. 5 (1926–1927), pp. 687–692.
Deutsche Gesellschaft zum Studium Osteuropas *Die Geschichtswissenschaft in Sowet-Russland, 1917–1927: Bibliographischer Katalog herausgegeben*. Berlin (1928).
Dobranitskii, M. (ed.) *Sistematicheskii ukazatel′ literatury po istorii Russkoi revoliutsii*. Moscow–Leningrad (1926).
Dossick, J.J. (comp.) *Doctoral Research on Russia and the Soviet Union*. New York (1960).
Doctoral Research on Russia and the Soviet Union, 1960–1975. New York (1979).
Dumesnil, A. (comp.) *Bibliothèque de documentation internationale contemporaine et musée de la grande guerre. Catalogue méthodique de fonds russe de la bibliothèque*. Paris (1932).
Egorov, D.N. (ed.) *Bibliografiia Vostoka (Vyp. 1 – Istoriia, 1917–1925)*. Moscow (1928).

Erikson, J. 'Pens versus Swords: A Study of Studying the Civil War', in Abramsky, C. and Williams, B. (eds.) *Essays in Honour of E.H. Carr.*

Florovsky, A. 'The Work of Russian Emigrés in History (1921–1927)' *Slavonic and East European Review* (London), Vol. 7 (1928).

Fomin, S.F. 'Kritika sovremennoi anglo-amerikanskoi burzhuaznoi istoriografii grazhdanskoi voiny i inostrannoi interventsii v SSSR (istochnikovedcheskie aspekty)', in Korablev, Iu.V. and Shishkin, V.I. (eds.) *Iz istorii interventsii i grazhdanskoi voiny v Sibiri i na Dal'nem Vostoke, 1917–1922gg.* Novosibirsk (1985), pp. 68–77.

Foster, L.A. (ed.) *Bibliography of Russian Émigré Literature, 1918–1968* (2 Vols.). London (1970).

'The Revolution and Civil War in Russian Emigre Novels', *Russian Review*, Vol. 31 (1972), No. 2, pp. 153–162.

Fradkina, Z.L. (ed.) *Istoriia SSSR: annotirovannyi perechen' russkikh bibliografii izdannykh do 1965g.* Moscow (1966).

Frame, M. (comp.) *The Russian Revolution, 1905–1921: A Bibliographic Guide to Works in English.* London (1995).

Furmanov, D. 'Kratkii obzor literatury (neperiodicheskoi) o grazhdanskom voine (1918–1920gg.)', *Proletarskaia revoliutsiia* (Moscow), No. 5 (1923), p. 321–341.

Gladkova, T.L. and Ossourguine, T.A. (eds.) *L'Émigration russe: revues et receuils 1920–1928 (Index géneral des articles).* Paris (1988).

Gorodetskii, E.N. (ed.) *Sovetskaia strana v periode grazhdanskoi voiny, 1918–1922gg.: bibliograficheskii ukazatel' dokumental'nykh publikatsii.* Moscow (1961).

Grierson, P. (comp.) *Books on Soviet Russia, 1917–1942: A Bibliography and a Guide to Reading.* London (1943).

Gukhovskii, A. 'Obzor beloi emigratskoi literatury po grazhdanskoi voiny', *Istorik-marksist* (Moscow), Vol. 11 (1929), pp. 266–270.

Gushchin, N.Ia. et al. (eds.) *Istoriografiia Sovetskoi Sibiri (1917–1945gg.).* Moscow (1968).

Hartley, J.M. (comp.) *Guide to Documents and Manuscripts in the United Kingdom Relating to Russia and the Soviet Union.* London (1987).

Iakushev, I. Ia. (ed.) *Materialy dlia sibirskoi bibliografii: grazhdanskaia voina i interventsiia, 1917–1922gg.* Prague (1930).

Inostrantsev, M.A. *Istoriia, istina i tendentsiia – po povodu knigi gen.-leit. K.V. Sakharova 'Belaia Sibir''.* Prague (1933).

'General Sacharoff als Historiker', *Präger Rundschau* (Prague), Vol. 3 (1933), pp. 191–204.

Istoriia Sibiri: tekushchii ukazatel' literatury. Novosibirsk (1966–).

Ivanov, D.D. (ed.) *Narodnoe khoziaistvo SSSR v 1917–1920gg.: bibliograficheskii ukazatel' knizhnoi i zhurnal'noi literatury na russkom iazyke (1917–1963gg.).* Moscow (1967).

Kadeikin, V.A. *Grazhdanskaia voina v Sibiri: istoriografiia sovetskoi Sibiri (1917–1945)*. Novosibirsk (1968).

Keep, J. 'Social Aspects of the Russian Revolutionary Era (1917–1923) in Recent English Language Historiography', *East European Quarterly* Vol. 34 (1990), No. 2, pp. 159–184.

Kenez, P. 'Western Historiography of the Russian Civil War', in Schelbert, L. and Ceh, N. (eds.) *Essays in Russian and East European History: Festschrift in Honor of Edward C. Thaden*. Boulder, CO (1995), pp. 197–215.

Kennan, G.F. 'Soviet Historiography and America's Role in the Intervention', *American Historical Review*, Vol. 65 (1960), No. 2, pp. 302–323.

Kirilova, S.A. 'Rol′ "Sibirskikh ognei" v stanovlenii istoriografii Oktiabr′skoi revoliutsii v Sibiri (20-e i nachalo 30-x godov)', in *Voprosy istorii obshchestvenno-politicheskoi zhizni Sibiri perioda Oktiabr′ i grazhdanskoi voiny*. Tomsk (1982), pp. 188–204.

Kislitskaia, I.A. 'Publikatsiia dokumentov po istorii grazhdanskoi voiny v Sibiri na stranitsakh zhurnalov "Proletarskaia revoliutsiia" i "Krasnyi arkhiv"', in *Klassy i partii v Sibiri nakanune perioda Velikoi Oktiabr′skoi sotsialisticheskoi revoliutsii*. Tomsk (1977).

Kniga i revoliutsiia. Petrograd (1921–1923).

Komarov, N.S. 'Sozdanie i deiatel′nost′ Istparta', *Voprosy istorii KPSS* (Moscow), No. 5 (1958), pp. 153–166.

Kulikova, L.K. and Maslova, A.N. (eds.) *Dal′nyi Vostok v periode Velikoi Oktiabr′skoi sotsialisticheskoi revoliutsii i grazhdankoi voiny – ukazatel′ literatury*. Khabarovsk (1968).

Lachaeva, M. 'Angliiskie spravochniki kak istochnik po istorii inostrannogo kapitala v gornoi promyshlennosti Urala i Sibiri v nachale XX v.', *Vestnik Moskoskogo universiteta (seriia 9: istoriia)*, No. 4 (1976), pp. 71–80.

Lalevich, G. 'Literatura o samarskoi Uchredilke', *Proletarskaia revoliutsiia* (Moscow), Nos. 8–9 (1924), pp. 366–373.

Leadenham, C.A. (comp.) *Guide to the Collections in the Hoover Institution Archives Relating to Imperial Russia, the Russian Revolution and Civil War and the First Emigration*. Stanford (1986).

Lebedeva, A.N. et al. (eds.) *Ukazatel′ bibliograficheskikh posobii po Sibiri i Dal′nemu Vostoku (XIX v.–1968g.)*. Novosibirsk (1975).

Litvin, A.L. 'Memuarnaia literatura o razgrome kolchakovshchiny', in Spirin, L.M. (ed.) *Razgrom Kolchaka: vospominaniia*. Moscow (1969), pp. 281–287.

'Sovetskaia istoriografiia krakha "demokraticheskoi" kontr-revoliutsii v Rossii', *Voprosy istorii* (Moscow), No. 1 (1982), pp. 111–119.

Long, J.W. 'Red Versus White: The Russian Civil War in the Slavic and Baltic Divisions Pamphlet Collection', *Bulletin of Research on the Humanities*, Vol. 87 (1987), Nos. 2–3, pp. 158–171.

Lur′e, F.M. (ed.) *Khraniteli proshlogo: zhurnal 'Byloe'*. Leningrad (1990).

Materialy k ukazateliu literatury o Sibiri na evropeiskikh iazykakh s 1917g. po 1930g. Leningrad (1931).

Matveev, Z.N. 'Bibliografiia po istorii revoliutsii i interventsii na russkom Dal′nem Vostoke', in *Sbornik materialov po istorii revoliutsionnogo dvizheniia na Dal′nem Vostoke* (Vol. 2). Vladivostok (1924), pp. 317–328.

Mehnert, K. *Die Sovet-Union, 1917–1932: Systematische, mit Kommentaren versehne Bibliographie der 1917–1932 in deutscher Sprache ausserhalb der Sovet-Union veröffentlichen 1900 wichtigsten Bücher und Aufsätze über den Bolschewismus und die Sovet-Union.* Königsberg (1933).

Meijer, J. 'The Civil War in Russia: Sources and their Use', *Survey*, Vol. 30 (1959), pp. 71–76.

Naida, S.F. and Naumov, V.P. 'Grazhdanskaia voina i inostrannaia voennaia interventsiia v SSSR', in *Ocherki po istoriografii sovetskogo obshchestva.* Moscow (1965).

Letopis′ geroicheskoi bor′by: Sovetskaia istoriografiia grazhdanskoi voiny i inostrannoi interventsii v SSSR. Moscow (1966).

Naumov, V.G. 'K istoriografii belocheshkogo miatezha v 1918g.', in *Sbornik statei po istorii rabochego klassa i sovetskoi istoriografii.* Moscow (1958).

Letopis′ geroicheskoi bor′by: Sovetskaia istoriografiia grazhdanskoi voiny i inostrannoi interventsii v SSSR. Moscow (1972).

'Vedushchie problemy istoriografii grazhdanskoi voiny', in *Iz istorii grazhdanskoi voiny i interventsii, 1917–1922gg.: sbornik statei.* Moscow (1974).

Neganov, V,F. 'Vospominaniia I.M. Maiskogo "Demokraticheskaia kontrrevoliutsiia" kak istochnik po istorii krakha Komucha', in *Burzhuaznye i melkoburzhuaznye partii Rossii v Oktiabr′skoi revoliutsii i grazhdanskogo voiny.* Moscow (1980).

Nikitin, A.N. 'Memuary 1919 – pervoi poloviny 30-x godov kak istochnik po istorii partizanskoi dvizhenii v Sibiri', in *Klassy i partii Sibiri nakanune i v periode Velikoi Oktiabr′skoi sotsialisticheskoi revoliutsii.* Tomsk (1977), pp. 151–168.

Ossourguine-Bakounine, T. and Volkoff, A (eds.) *L'Émigration Russe en Europe – Catalogue Collectif des Périodiques Russes* (2 Vols.). Paris (1976–1977).

Osteuropäische Bibliographie für das Jahr. 1920–1923. Breslau (1921–1928).

Oulianoff, N. 'In Commemoration of S.P. Melgunov', *Russian Review*, Vol. 17 (1958), No. 3, pp. 193–200.

Pares, B. 'English Books on Soviet Russia', *Slavonic and East European Review* (London), Vol. 10 (1931–1932), pp. 525–546.

Pavlova, I.V. 'Iz istorii izucheniia grazhdanskoi voiny v Sibiri (20–30-e gody)', in Korablev, Iu.V. and Shishkin, V.I. (eds.) *Iz istorii interventsii i grazhdanskoi voiny v Sibiri i na Dal'nem Vostoke, 1917–1922gg.* Novosibirsk (1985), pp. 50–57.

Pereira, N.G.O. 'Soviet Historiography of the Civil War in Siberia', *Revolutionary Russia*, Vol. 4 (1991), No. 1, pp. 28–56.

Plotnikova, M.E. 'Istpartovskie izdaniia o grazhdanskoi voiny v Sibiri', *Voprosy istorii Sibiri* (Tomsk), Vol. 4 (1969), pp. 203–217.

Sovetskaia istoriografiia grazhdanskoi voiny v Sibiri (1918–pervaia polovina 1930-x godov). Tomsk (1974).

'Sovremennaia sovetskaia istoricheskaia literatura o pozitsiakh sibirskogo krest'ianstva v 1918–1919gg.', in *Iz istorii grazhdanskoi voiny i interventsii, 1917–1922gg.* Moscow (1974).

'O problematike sovremennoi sovetskoi istoriografii grazhdanskoi voiny v Sibiri', in Razgon, I.M. (ed.) *Voprosy istorii obshchestvenno-politicheskoi zhizni Sibiri perioda Oktiabria i grazhdanskoi voiny.* Tomsk (1982), pp. 205–215.

'Sovremennaia sovetskaia istoriografiia Bol'shevistskogo podpol'ia i partizanskogo dvizheniia v Sibiri', in Korablev, Iu.V. and Shishkin, V.I. (eds.) *Iz istorii interventsii i grazhdanskoi voiny v Sibiri i na Dal'nem Vostoke, 1917–1922gg.* Novosibirsk (1985), pp. 41–49.

Plotnikova, M.E and Razgon, I.M. 'Nekotorye itogi i zadachi izucheniia osnovikh problem istorii bor'by s kolchakovshchiny', in Razgon, I.M. and Bozhenko, L.I. (eds.) *K 50-letiiu osvobozhdeniia Sibiri ot kolchakovshchiny: materialy nauchnoi konferentsii.* Tomsk (1970).

Plotnikova, M.E. and Shishkin, V.I. 'Krest'ianstvo Sibiri v gody grazhdanskoi voiny i interventsii', in *Istoriografiia krest'ianstva sovetskoi Sibiri.* Novosibirsk (1976).

Postnikov, S.P. (ed.) *Bibliografiia russkoi revoliutsii i grazhdanskoi voiny, 1917–1921 (iz kataloga biblioteki Russkogo Zagranichnogo Istoricheskogo Arkhiva).* Prague (1938).

Potanova, N.K. et al. (eds.) *Bor'ba za vlast' Sovetov v Vostochnoi Sibiri, 1917–1922gg.: bibliograficheskii ukazatel'.* Irkutsk (1962).

Poznanskii, V.S. 'Voprosy istorii grazhdanskoi voiny v "Sibirskoi Sovetskoi Entsiklopedii"', *Voprosy istorii Sibiri* (Tomsk), Vol. 190 (1967), pp. 193–201.

Reikhberg, G.E. and Shurygin, A.P. *Burzhuaznaia istoriografiia Oktiabria i grazhdanskoi voiny v Sibiri.* Novosibirsk (1981).

Semenova, N.M. 'Sibirskaia periodicheskaia pechat' o rabochem dvizhenii v periode "demokraticheskoi" kontrrevoliutsii', in Bozhenko, L.I. (ed.)

Nekotorye voprosy istorii Sibiri: sbornik statei molodykh uchennykh istoriko-filologicheskogo fakul'teta. Tomsk (1972–1973), Vol. 2, pp. 65–78.

'Periodicheskaia pechat' Sibiri kak istochnik po istorii professional'nogo dvizheniia Tomskoi gubernii v periode "demokraticheskoi" kontrrevoliutsii', in Bozhenko, L.I. (ed.) *Nekotorye voprosy istorii Sibiri: sbornik statei molodykh uchennykh istoriko-filologicheskogo fakul'teta*. Tomsk (1972–1973), Vol. 2, pp. 79–95.

Sherman, I.A. *Sovetskaia istoriografiia grazhdanskoi voiny v SSSR(1920–1931gg.)*. Kharkov (1964).

Shelestov, D.K. 'Sovetskaia istoriografiia grazhdanskoi voiny i voennoi interventsii v SSSR', *Voprosy istorii* (Moscow), No. 2 (1964), pp. 22–48.

'Noveishaia istoriografiia grazhdanskoi voiny v SSSR', *Voprosy istorii* (Moscow), No. 11 (1968), pp. 152–62.

'On the Study of the Historiography of the Civil War in the USSR', *Studies in Soviet History*, Vol. 8 (1969–1970), No. 1, pp. 3–30.

Shishkin, V.I. 'Sovremennaia sovetskaia istoriografiia inostrannoi interventsii i grazhdanskoi voiny v Sibiri', in Korablev, Iu.V. and Shishkin, V.I. (eds.) *Iz istorii interventsii i grazhdanskoi voiny v Sibiri i na Dal'nem Vostoke, 1917–1922gg*. Novosibirsk (1985), pp. 20–40.

Pervye istoriki Oktiabr'skoi revoliutsii i grazhdanskoi voiny v Sibiri. Novosibirsk (1988).

'Diskussionnye problemy istorii partizanskogo dvizheniia v Sibiri v Sovetskoi istoriografii 20-x–nachala 30-x godov', in Gushchin, N. Ia. (ed.) *Sotsial'naia aktivnost' trudiashchikhsia sovetskoi sibirskoi derevni*. Novosibirsk (1988), pp. 6–29.

Shukletsov, V.T. 'Obzor istochnikov i literatury po istorii revoliutsii i grazhdanskoi voiny v Zapadnoi Sibiri', in *Voprosy istoriografii partiinykh organizatsii Sibiri*. Novosibirsk (1974).

Sibirskie ogni – ukazatel' soderzhaniia (1922–1964gg.). Novosibirsk (1967).

Sidorenko, S.A. 'Sborniki dokumentov po istorii bor'by za vlast' Sovetov v Sibiri', *Voprosy istorii* (Moscow), No. 5 (1959), pp. 176–187.

Smele, J.D. (comp.) *The Russian Revolution and Civil War: An Annotated Bibliography of Works in Western European Languages*. London (1999) [forthcoming].

Sokolova, B.P. and Zhdanova, M.L. (eds.) *Sibir' v periode Velikoi Oktiabr'skoi sotsialisticheskoi revoliutsii, inostrannoi interventsii i grazhdanskoi voiny (mart 1917–1920gg.): bibliograficheskii ukazatel'*. Novosibirsk (1973).

Späth, M. *Bibliography of Articles on East European and Russian History (Selected from English Language Periodicals, 1850–1938)*. Berlin (1981).

Stishov, M.I. 'Obzor literatury i istochnikov po istorii Sibiri perioda grazhdanskoi voiny', in Stishov, M.I. (ed.) *Bol'shevistskoe* *podpol'e i partizanskoe dvizhenie v Sibiri v gody grazhdanskoi voiny*. Moscow (1962).

Tematicheskii ukazatel' literatury po grazhdanskoi voine. Leningrad (1929).

Thompson, J.M. 'Allied-American Intervention in Russia, 1918–1921', in Black, C.E. (ed.) *Rewriting Russian History: Soviet Interpretations of Russia's Past*. London (1957), pp. 334–400.

Turunov, A. and Vegman, V. (eds.) *Revoliutsiia i grazhdanskaia voina v Sibiri: ukazatel' knig i zhurnal'nykh statei*. Novosibirsk (1928).

Ural v periode Velikoi Oktiabr'skoi revoliutsii, inostrannoi interventsii i grazhdanskoi voiny, 1917–1919gg.: ukazatel' literatury (2 Vols.). Sverdlovsk (1965–1969).

Vas'kovskii, O.A. 'Deiatel'nost' Ural'skogo (Sverdlovskogo) istparta po razrabote istorii grazhdanskoi voiny', in *Iz istorii partiinykh organizatsii Urala: sbornik statei*. Sverdlovsk (1966).

'Sovetskaia istoriografiia istorii grazhdanskoi voiny na Urale', in *Voprosy sovetskoi istoriografii Urala*. Sverdlovsk (1967).

Istoriografiia i sotsial'no-politicheskie problemy istorii grazhdanskoi voiny na Urale. Sverdlovsk (1981).

Victoroff-Toporoff, V. *Rossica et Sovietica. Bibliographie des ouvrages parus en français de 1917 à 1930 inclus relatifs à la Russie et à l'U.R.S.S.* Saint-Cloud (1931).

Vitkind, N.Ia. *Materialy k bibliografii istorii grazhdanskoi voiny na Sovetskom Vostoke*. Moscow (1934).

'Volia Rossii' – sistematicheskii katalog statei, pomeshchennykh v 'Vole Rossii' za 1922–1926gg. Prague (1926).

Zhuchkova. L.A. et al. (eds.) *Ural – annotirovannyi ukazatel' literatury*. Sverdlovsk (1963).

Ural v periode Velikoi Oktiabr'skoi sotsialisticheskoi revoliutsii, inostrannoi voennoi interventsii i grazhdanskoi voiny (mart 1917–avgust 1919gg.): ukazatel' literatury za 1957–1962gg. Sverdlovsk (1965).

Zverev, R.Ia. *'Krasnyi arkhiv' – istoricheskii zhurnal, 1922–1941: annotirovannyi ukazatel' soderzhaniia*. Moscow (1960).

Travel Writings

Borodin, G. *Soviet and Tsarist Siberia*. London (1943).

Clarke, F.E. *The Great Siberian Railway: What I Saw on my Journey*. London (1904).

Deutsch, L. *Sixteen Years in Siberia: 1884–1900*. London (1903).

Fleming, P. *News From Tartary: A Journey from Peking to Kashmir*. London (1936).

Fraser, J.F. *The Real Siberia (Together with an Account of a Dash Through Manchuria).* London (1902).

Gerrard, W. *Greater Russia: The Continental Empire of the Old World.* London (1903).

Haviland, M. 'A Bird Lover in the Taiga', *National Review*, No. 391 (1915).
'Wild Geese', *National Review*, No. 393 (1915).

Howard, B.D. *Life with Transsiberian Savages.* London (1893).

Jefferson, R.L. *Roughing it in Siberia.* London (1897).

Nansen, F. *Through Siberia: The Land of the Future.* London (1914).

Price, J.M. *From the Arctic Ocean to the Yellow Sea: Narrative of a Journey, 1890–1891.* London (1892).

Seebohm, H. *Siberia in Asia: A Visit to the Valley of the Yenesay in East Siberia.* London (1882).

Shoemaker, M.M. *The Great Siberian Railway from St Petersburg to Pekin.* New York (1903).

Simpson, Sir G. *Side-Lights on Siberia: Some Account of the Great Siberian Railroad, the Prisons and Exile System.* Edinburgh (1898).

Stadling, J. *Through Siberia.* London (1901).

Swayne, H. *Through the Highlands of Siberia.* London (1904).

Taft, M.L. *Strange Siberia: Along the Trans-Siberian Railway.* New York (1911).

Turner, S. *Siberia: A Record of Travel, Climbing and Exploration.* London (1905).

Wenyon, C. *Across Siberia on the Great Post Road.* London (1896).

de Windt, H. *The New Siberia.* London (1896).
From Paris to New York by Land. London (1903)

Wright, R.L. and Digby, B. *Through Siberia: An Empire in the Making.* New York (1913).

Fiction

Anov, N. *Interventsiia v Omske.* Alma-Ata (1978).

Anson, A.A. (ed.) *Kolchakovshchina: sbornik rasskazov.* Novosibirsk (1935).

Dorokhov, P.N. *Kolchakovshchina: khronika.* Moscow–Leningrad (1924).

Fox, R. *Storming Heaven.* London (1928).

Furmanov, D.A. *Chapayev.* London (1935).

Garfield, B. *Kolchak's Gold.* London (1974).

Ilyin, O. *Dawn of the Eighth Day.* New York (1951).
White Road. New York (1984).

Klarov, Iu. *Dopros v Irkutske.* Moscow (1972).

Kotomkin, N.E. *Za Rossiiu.* Paris (1927).

Maksimov, V. *Zaglianut' v bezdnu.* Paris–New York (1986).

Markovits, R. *Siberian Garrison.* London (1929).

Matveyev, V. *Commissar of the Gold Express: An Episode of the Civil War.* London (1933).

Pages, E. *Campagne de Misère: Sibérie 1919.* Paris (1933).

Vetulgin, A. *Avantiuristy grazhdanskoi voiny.* Paris (1921).

Index

Printed in Great Britain
by Amazon

71771515R00447